Chapter 12 Time Line and Map of West Africa
  Lesson 1 Physical Geography Map of West Africa
        Climate Map of West Africa
        Landlocked vs. Coastline Graphic Organizer
        Offshore Drilling Lecture Slide
        Wet vs. Dry Seasons Image
        West Africa Resources Map
        Comparing Rivers Chart
  Lesson 2 First Trading Kingdoms Map
        Freetown, Sierra Leone Image
        Empires in West Africa Lecture Slide
        Slavery in West Africa Map
        Mansa Musa Image
        Drag-And-Drop Game: Trade in West Africa
        Imperialism and Independence in West Africa Map
  Lesson 3 Population Map of West Africa
        Pidgin and Creole Language Lecture Slide
        Challenges in West Africa Graphic Organizer
        Infrastructure Lecture Slide
        Ethnic Groups in West Africa Chart
        Contrasting Settlements Images

Chapter 13 Time Line and Map of Southern Africa
  Lesson 1 Africa's Size Infographic
        Physical Geography of Southern Africa Map
        Resources Map of Southern Africa
        Namibia Plateaus
        Drag-And-Drop Game: Landforms and Waterways of
          Southern Africa
        Tropic of Cancer and Tropic of Capricorn Lecture Slide
        Making Diamonds into Jewelry Chart
        Climate Map of Southern Africa
        Hydroelectric Power Image
        Wildlife Preserves in Southern Africa
  Lesson 2 Colonization and Independence of Southern Africa Map
        Early History of Southern Africa
        History of Apartheid
  Lesson 3 Population Map of Southern Africa
        Markets in Southern Africa Image
        Progress in South Africa Map
        360° View: Johannesburg, South Africa
        Life in the City Graphic Organizer
        Challenges in Southern Africa Graphic Organizer
        Population Pyramid Chart of Southern Africa
        Urban vs. Traditional Life Image
        Health Issues in Southern Africa Chart
        Ethnic and Cultural Groups of Southern Africa Chart
        Religions and Languages of Southern Africa Chart

Unit 4
    Oceania, Australia, New Zealand, and Antarctica Video Montage
    Drag-and-Drop Physical Geography Game of Oceania, Australia,
      New Zealand, and Antarctica
    Interactive Maps of Oceania, Australia, New Zealand, and Antarctica

Chapter 14 Time Line and Map of Australia and New Zealand
  Lesson 1 Physical Geography Map of Australia and New Zealand
        Landforms and Waterways of New Zealand Graphic Organizer
        Climate Map of Australia and New Zealand
        Problems with Kangaroos Lecture Slide
  Lesson 2 Dingoes Interactive Photo
        Tikanga Lecture Slide
        Maori Culture Interactive Photo
        Comparing Aborigines and Maori Graphic Organizer
        Australian Gold Rush Time Line
  Lesson 3 Comparing Football Around the World Lecture Slide
        Population Map of Australia and New Zealand
        Chart of Australian and New Zealand Universities
        Resources Map of Australia and New Zealand
        Australia's Economy Chart
        Population Pyramid Charts of Australia and New Zealand

Chapter 15 Time Line and Map of Oceania
  Lesson 1 Physical Geography Map of Oceania
        Lagoons Image
        Climate Map of Oceania
        Tropics Lecture Slide
        Comparing Rainfall: Oceania and the United States Chart
        Resources Map of Oceania
  Lesson 2 Colonizing Oceania Interactive Photo
        Oceania in World War II Map
        Population of Papua, New Guinea Chart
        Population of Oceania Map
        Pidgin Language Lecture Slide
  Lesson 3 Roads and Accessible Resources Map of New Guinea
        Scarce Resources in Oceania Graphic Organizer
        Resources Map of Oceania
        Economy of Oceania Graphic Organizer
        MIRAB Economies Lecture Slide
        Human Migration in Oceania Cause and Effect Chart

Chapter 16 Time Line and Map of Antarctica
  Lesson 1 Hot Springs Image
        Comparing Continent Sizes Chart
        Physical Geography of Antarctica Map
        Icebergs Interactive Photo
        Climate Map of Antarctica
        Resources of Antarctica Map
  Lesson 2 Antarctica Explored Animated Map
        Research Stations
        Antarctic Food Chain Graphic Organizer

Worksheets

These printable worksheets are available for every lesson, chapter, or unit.
- Guided Reading Activities
- Physical Geography Activity
- Cultural Geography Activity
- Chapter Summaries (available in English and Spanish)
- Reading Essential and Study Guide Workbook and Answer Key

These printable assessment worksheets are available for every unit or chapter and can be edited on eAssessment.
- What Do You Know? Background Knowledge Assessment
- Vocabulary Builder Academic and Content Vocabulary Assessment
- Physical Location GeoQuiz
- Political Location GeoQuiz
- City Location GeoQuiz

These printable worksheets are for point-of-use instruction.

Unit 1
Environmental Case Study: Maintaining Fresh Water Sources
Geolab Activity: Desalinating Water

Chapter 1
Lesson 1 Geography Skills Activity: Understanding Lines on a Map
Lesson 2 Technology Skills Activity: Using Geospatial Technology

Chapter 2
Lesson 1 Geography and History Activity: Participating in the Global Warming Debate
Geography Skills Activity: Reading a Thematic Map of Wind and Ocean Currents

Chapter 3
Lesson 1 Writing Skills Activity: Investigating Population Movement
Lesson 2 Critical Thinking Skills Activity: Comparing and Contrasting Changes in Government Through History
Lesson 3 Geography and Economics Activity: Understanding both the Pros and Cons of Free Market Trade

Unit 2
Environmental Case Study: Making Policy
GeoLab Activity: Using Natural Dyes to Create Indian Textiles

Chapter 4
Lesson 1 Geography and History Activity: Analyzing the Effect Mt. Fuji has on Japanese Culture
Lesson 2 Writing Skills Activity: Creating Haiku
Lesson 3 Technology Skills Activity: Citing Internet Sources on Japan's 2011 Earthquake

Chapter 5
Lesson 1 Geography and Economics Activity: Understanding the Relationship Between Aid and Recovery to Those Affected by Natural Disasters
Lesson 2 Reading Skills Activity: Researching First Person Stories About the Vietnam War
Geography Skills Activity: Understanding Time Lines Relating to the War in Vietnam and Cambodia

Chapter 6
Lesson 3 Critical Thinking Skills Activity: Weighing the Pros and Cons of Working in Indian Call Centers

Chapter 7
Lesson 1 Technology Skills Activity: Analyzing Data on a Spreadsheet
Lesson 2 Geography Skills Activity: Learning How to Read and Use Time Zones

Chapter 8
Lesson 2 Technology Skills Activity: Using Visuals to Learn More About the Kurds
Lesson 3 Geography and Economics Activity: Learning About Oil Reserves and Production

Unit 3
Environmental Case Study: Improving Global Health
GeoLab Activity: Making a Glacier
Critical Thinking Skills Activity: Analyzing UN Peacekeeping Missions

Chapter 9
Lesson 1 Technology Skills Activity: Comparing and Contrasting the Suez
        Canal with Another Man-Made Waterway
Lesson 3 Reading Skills Activity: Learning About the Human and Physical
        Geography of Cairo, Egypt

Chapter 10
Lesson 2 Geography and Economics Activity: Understanding the Impact of
        Trade on East Africa's Ancient Kingdoms

Chapter 11
Lesson 1 Geography Skills Activity: Using a Map of Resources in Central
        Africa
Lesson 2 Reading Skills Activity: Learning How the Agricultural Revolution
        Changed the Region
Lesson 3 Writing Skills Activity: Balancing Economic Growth with
        Environmental Concerns

Chapter 12
Lesson 2 Geography and History Activity: Learning how the Bantu People
        Influenced the Region
        Critical Thinking Skills Activity: Understanding the Early History of
        the Slave Trade

Chapter 13
Lesson 3 Geography and Economics Activity: Discussing Population
        Technology Skills Activity: Collaborating Online

Unit 4
Environmental Case Study: Considering Climate Change
Writing Skills Activity: Presenting Views on Global Warming

Chapter 14
Lesson 1 Geography Skills Activity: Reading a Climate Map
Lesson 2 Reading Skills Activity: Learning About New Zealand's Maori
        People

Chapter 15
Lesson 1 Geography and History Activity: Learning Why Oceania is Divided
        Into Three Regions
        Technology Skills Activity: Creating a PowerPoint Presentation

Chapter 16
Lesson 1 Technology Skills Activity: Creating a Multi-Media Presentation
        Critical Thinking Skills: Drawing Conclusions about Exploring in
        Antarctica
Lesson 2 Geography and Economics Activity: Analyzing the Antarctic Treaty

Hands-On Chapter Projects and Digital Hands-On Projects

Developed in partnership with EdTechTeacher, these chapter projects can be used with or without the use of technology in an individual or collaborative setting.

Chapter 1 Create Map from School to Home
Create Digital Travel Brochure

Chapter 2 Build Large Wall Map of the Earth
Design Physical Features Map of the Earth Using Online
Map-Making Program

Chapter 3 Assemble Present-Day Time Capsule
Create Family Scrapbook Using Online Ancestry Resources

Chapter 4 Compose Magazine Article with Imagery
Create and Record Virtual Speaking Avatars

Chapter 5 Organize Illustrated Time Lines of Southeast Asian Countries
Produce Online Presentation Using Collaborative Writing Platform

Chapter 6 Prepare and Perform Simulated News Broadcast
Produce Video Documentary Using Online Resources

Chapter 7 Craft and Assemble Quilt Squares into Large Quilt
Compose and Record Audio Travel Journal Script

Chapter 8 Design Illustrated Encyclopedia Pages
Produce Short Video Documentary Using Web-Based Video
Creation Site

Chapter 9 Create Maps with Plastic Overlays
Conduct and Document Virtual Archeological Dig

Chapter 10 Construct 3-D Model of East Africa
Write Quizzes Using Online Quiz, Poll, or Survey Creation Tool

Chapter 11 Create Thematic Maps Using Colors or Graphics
Build Topical Infographics using Online Resources

Chapter 12 Design and Illustrate Flag for West African Country
Produce Video Newscast Using Web-Based Movie Program

Chapter 13 Design Board Game
Create and Add QR Codes to Outline Map

Chapter 14 Engage in Class Debate on Controversial Topic
Generate Online Interest in Conservation

Chapter 15 Design "Choose Your Own Adventure" Book
Build Interactive Infographics

Chapter 16 Assemble Illustrated Graphic Organizer
Create Online Interactive Map of Antarctica

Environmental Case Studies Unit Projects

These case studies develop student awareness of major global issues.
Every project can be extended with ePals®, which allows your students to collaborate with schools around the world.

Unit 1 Maintenance of Fresh Water Sources

Unit 2 Policy-making

Unit 3 Global Health

Unit 4 Climate Change

HOW TO USE THE TEACHER EDITION

TO THE TEACHER Welcome to the McGraw-Hill **netw⊛rks** Teacher Edition—a new approach to the Teacher Edition based on the principles of *Understanding By Design*.

Planning the Unit

Understanding By Design®
All Networks programs have been created using the approach developed by Jay McTighe, coauthor of *Understanding By Design*.

- The main goal is to focus on the desired results before planning each unit's instruction.
- The Unit Planner lists the Enduring Understandings and the Essential Questions that students will learn and use as they study the chapters in the unit.
- Identifying the Predictable Misunderstandings will help you anticipate misconceptions students might have as they read the chapters.
- Information in the Unit Planners is expanded upon in the Chapter Planners.

Differentiated Instruction
Activities are designed to meet the needs of:

BL Beyond Level

AL Approaching Level

ELL English Language Learners

In addition, activities are designed to address a range of *learning styles*.

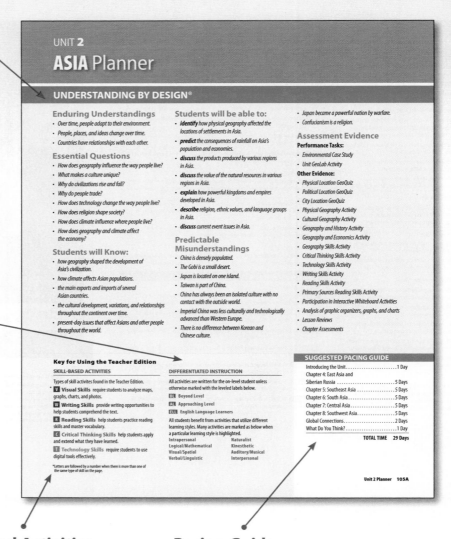

UNIT **2**

ASIA Planner

UNDERSTANDING BY DESIGN®

Enduring Understandings
- Over time, people adapt to their environment.
- People, places, and ideas change over time.
- Countries have relationships with each other.

Essential Questions
- How does geography influence the way people live?
- What makes a culture unique?
- Why do civilizations rise and fall?
- Why do people trade?
- How does technology change the way people live?
- How does religion shape society?
- How does climate influence where people live?
- How does geography and climate affect the economy?

Students will Know:
- how geography shaped the development of Asia's civilization.
- how climate affects Asian populations.
- the main exports and imports of several Asian countries.
- the cultural development, variations, and relationships throughout the continent over time.
- present-day issues that affect Asians and other people throughout the world.

Students will be able to:
- **identify** how physical geography affected the locations of settlements in Asia.
- **predict** the consequences of rainfall on Asia's population and economies.
- **discuss** the products produced by various regions in Asia.
- **discuss** the value of the natural resources in various regions in Asia.
- **explain** how powerful kingdoms and empires developed in Asia.
- **describe** religion, ethnic values, and language groups in Asia.
- **discuss** current event issues in Asia.

Predictable Misunderstandings
- China is densely populated.
- The Gobi is a small desert.
- Japan is located on one island.
- Taiwan is part of China.
- China has always been an isolated culture with no contact with the outside world.
- Imperial China was less culturally and technologically advanced than Western Europe.
- There is no difference between Korean and Chinese culture.

- Japan became a powerful nation by warfare.
- Confucianism is a religion.

Assessment Evidence
Performance Tasks:
- Environmental Case Study
- Unit GeoLab Activity

Other Evidence:
- Physical Location GeoQuiz
- Political Location GeoQuiz
- City Location GeoQuiz
- Physical Geography Activity
- Cultural Geography Activity
- Geography and History Activity
- Geography and Economics Activity
- Geography Skills Activity
- Critical Thinking Skills Activity
- Technology Skills Activity
- Writing Skills Activity
- Reading Skills Activity
- Primary Sources Reading Skills Activity
- Participation in Interactive Whiteboard Activities
- Analysis of graphic organizers, graphs, and charts
- Lesson Reviews
- Chapter Assessments

Key for Using the Teacher Edition

SKILL-BASED ACTIVITIES

Types of skill activites found in the Teacher Edition.
V Visual Skills require students to analyze maps, graphs, charts, and photos.
W Writing Skills provide writing opportunities to help students comprehend the text.
R Reading Skills help students practice reading skills and master vocabulary.
C Critical Thinking Skills help students apply and extend what they have learned.
T Technology Skills require students to use digital tools effectively.

*Letters are followed by a number when there is more than one of the same type of skill on the page.

DIFFERENTIATED INSTRUCTION

All activities are written for the on-level student unless otherwise marked with the leveled labels below.
BL Beyond Level
AL Approaching Level
ELL English Language Learners

All students benefit from activities that utilize different learning styles. Many activities are marked as below when a particular learning style is highlighted.
Intrapersonal   Naturalist
Logical/Mathematical   Kinesthetic
Visual/Spatial   Auditory/Musical
Verbal/Linguistic   Interpersonal

SUGGESTED PACING GUIDE

Introducing the Unit.......................1 Day
Chapter 4: East Asia and
Siberian Russia ....5 Days
Chapter 5: Southeast Asia ....5 Days
Chapter 6: South Asia ....5 Days
Chapter 7: Central Asia ....5 Days
Chapter 8: Southwest Asia................5 Days
Global Connections.......................2 Days
What Do You Think? ....1 Day

TOTAL TIME 29 Days

Unit 2 Planner 105A

Skill-Based Activities
Print-based and digital activities throughout the unit are designed to teach a range of skills, including:

C Critical Thinking Skills

V Visual Skills

R Reading Skills

T Technology Skills

W Writing Skills

Pacing Guide
Suggestions are provided on how to pace the unit's content based on your state's curriculum and number of school days.

Planning the Unit (continued)

Unit Opener Planner

The Unit Opener Planner provides a menu of the print and digital resources available to teach the Unit Opener. These activities are organized by skill type, level, and learning style.

Introduce the Unit

Every unit has activities that introduce students to the region. The activities may include discussion questions or brief cooperative learning activities to help students make connections to the unit content.

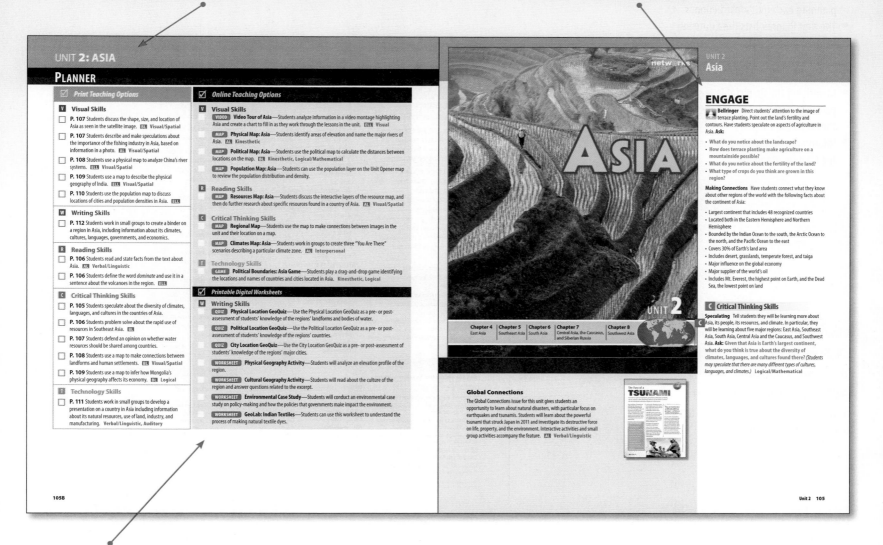

Online Teaching Activities

Digital assets and activities are cited here throughout the Teacher Edition to help you teach unit, chapter, and lesson content.

Teaching activities are provided for every digital asset in the Teacher Edition.

Digital assets include:

- interactive maps
- photos
- animations
- slide shows
- whiteboard activities
- lesson videos
- worksheets

Planning the Chapter

Understanding By Design®

Like the Unit Planner, the Chapter Planner focuses on *Understanding By Design®* principles, including learning expectations, student misconceptions, and assessment options.

Standards

Each Chapter Planner identifies the National Geography Standards that are covered in the chapter.

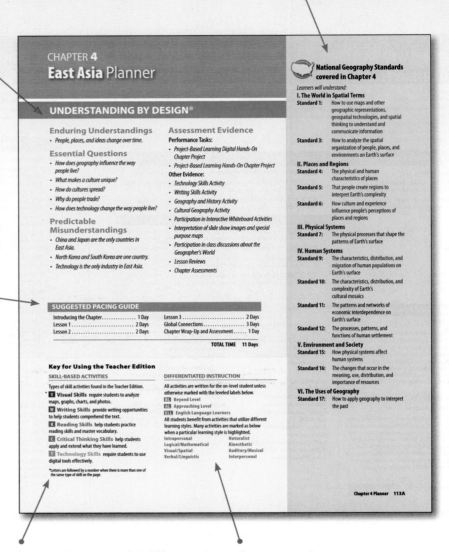

CHAPTER 4
East Asia Planner

UNDERSTANDING BY DESIGN®

Enduring Understandings
- People, places, and ideas change over time.

Essential Questions
- How does geography influence the way people live?
- What makes a culture unique?
- How do cultures spread?
- Why do people trade?
- How does technology change the way people live?

Predictable Misunderstandings
- China and Japan are the only countries in East Asia.
- North Korea and South Korea are one country.
- Technology is the only industry in East Asia.

Assessment Evidence
Performance Tasks:
- Project-Based Learning Digital Hands-On Chapter Project
- Project-Based Learning Hands-On Chapter Project

Other Evidence:
- Technology Skills Activity
- Writing Skills Activity
- Geography and History Activity
- Cultural Geography Activity
- Participation in Interactive Whiteboard Activities
- Interpretation of slide show images and special purpose maps
- Participation in class discussions about the Geographer's World
- Lesson Reviews
- Chapter Assessments

SUGGESTED PACING GUIDE

Introducing the Chapter	1 Day	Lesson 3	2 Days
Lesson 1	2 Days	Global Connections	3 Days
Lesson 2	2 Days	Chapter Wrap-Up and Assessment	1 Day

TOTAL TIME 11 Days

Key for Using the Teacher Edition

SKILL-BASED ACTIVITIES

Types of skill activities found in the Teacher Edition.
V Visual Skills require students to analyze maps, graphs, charts, and photos.
W Writing Skills provide writing opportunities to help students comprehend the text.
R Reading Skills help students practice reading skills and master vocabulary.
C Critical Thinking Skills help students apply and extend what they have learned.
T Technology Skills require students to use digital tools effectively.

Letters are followed by a number when there is more than one of the same type of skill on the page.

DIFFERENTIATED INSTRUCTION

All activities are written for the on-level student unless otherwise marked with the leveled labels below.
BL Beyond Level
AL Approaching Level
ELL English Language Learners
All students benefit from activities that utilize different learning styles. Many activities are marked as below when a particular learning style is highlighted.
Intrapersonal   Naturalist
Logical/Mathematical   Kinesthetic
Visual/Spatial   Auditory/Musical
Verbal/Linguistic   Interpersonal

National Geography Standards covered in Chapter 4

Learners will understand:
I. The World in Spatial Terms
Standard 1: How to use maps and other geographic representations, geospatial technologies, and spatial thinking to understand and communicate information
Standard 3: How to analyze the spatial organization of people, places, and environments on Earth's surface

II. Places and Regions
Standard 4: The physical and human characteristics of places
Standard 5: That people create regions to interpret Earth's complexity
Standard 6: How culture and experience influence people's perceptions of places and regions

III. Physical Systems
Standard 7: The physical processes that shape the patterns of Earth's surface

IV. Human Systems
Standard 9: The characteristics, distribution, and migration of human populations on Earth's surface
Standard 10: The characteristics, distribution, and complexity of Earth's cultural mosaics
Standard 11: The patterns and networks of economic interdependence on Earth's surface
Standard 12: The processes, patterns, and functions of human settlement

V. Environment and Society
Standard 15: How physical systems affect human systems
Standard 16: The changes that occur in the meaning, use, distribution, and importance of resources

VI. The Uses of Geography
Standard 17: How to apply geography to interpret the past

Chapter 4 Planner 113A

Pacing Guide

Time management suggestions for teaching the chapter are provided.

Skills-Based Activities and Differentiated Instruction

Print-based and digital activities throughout the chapter and lessons are designed to teach a range of skills, including:

C **Critical Thinking Skills**

V **Visual Skills**

R **Reading Skills**

T **Technology Skills**

W **Writing Skills**

Planning the Chapter (continued)

Planners

The Chapter Opener and Lesson Planners provide a snapshot of the resources available to enhance and extend learning. The activities are organized by skill type, level, and learning style.

Student Objectives

Using *Understanding By Design®* as the framework, the planners outline the content and skills that students will be expected to know.

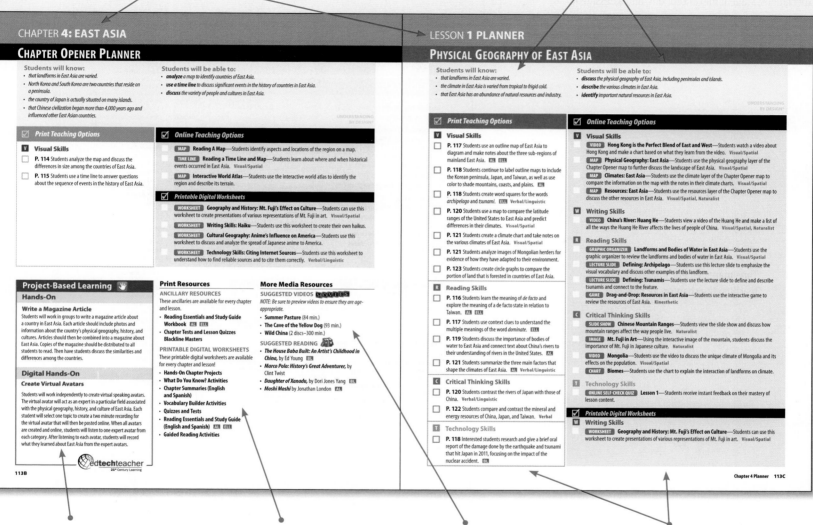

Project-Based Learning

Cumulative projects bring the subject to life for the student and help you assess your students' level of understanding. The program includes Hands-On Projects, as well as Digital Hands-On Projects.

Print Resources

Every chapter includes printable worksheets, including tests, quizzes, and materials to build vocabulary and improve reading comprehension.

Make It Relevant

Enrich and extend the content with videos and books.

Print and Digital Options

Each planner has two columns listing print-based activities and online digital options, including printable digital worksheets.

Don't forget! You can customize all your Lesson Plans online.

Using the Wraparound Resources and Activities

STUDENT EDITION PAGES AND WRAPAROUND ACTIVITIES

The entire Student Edition appears in the Teacher Edition. Activities and recommended resources appear in the side and bottom margins of the Teacher Edition, at point of use.

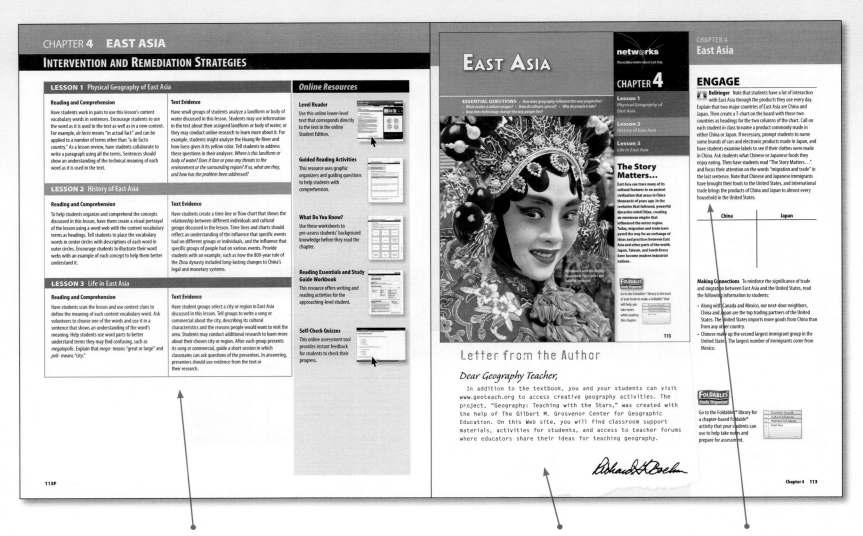

Intervention and Remediation
Each Chapter Planner concludes with intervention and remediation strategies for every lesson, as well as Online Resources that can be used to help students understand the content.

Author Letter
Each chapter begins with the author's perspective about key concepts found in the chapter.

Introduce the Chapter
Each chapter begins with activities to engage students' interest in the chapter's content.

Using the Wraparound Resources and Activities (continued)

Step Into the Place/Step Into the Time
These two pages of the Chapter Opener are designed to help students locate the region in the world that they will learn about, along with important historical events that took place in that region.

The Teacher Edition contains activities and discussion questions for these features.

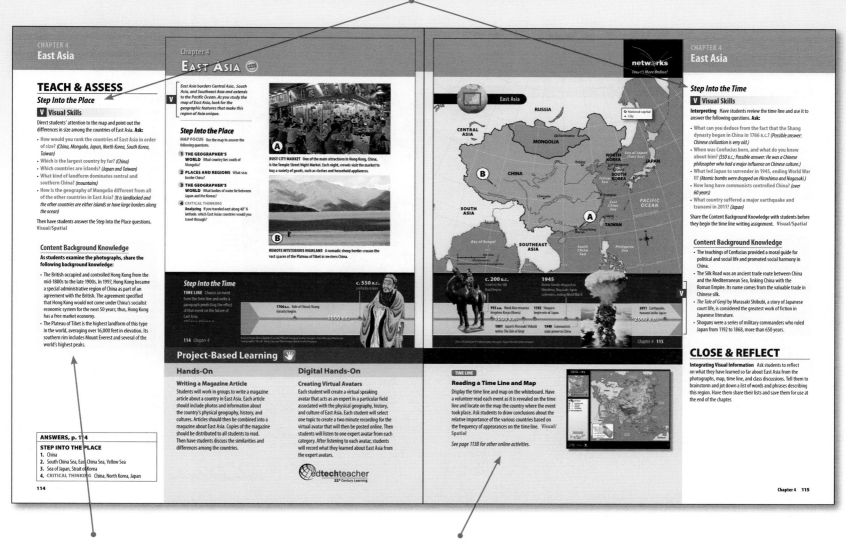

Print-Based Activities
Activities in the margins correspond to the text in the Student Edition. These activities are coded to indicate their level and the learning style they support.

Online Digital Activities
Online digital activities for the lesson appear at the bottom of each page. The gray icon indicates the type of activity available in the online Teacher Center. Activities include interactive whiteboard activities, animations, videos, interactive maps, images, and worksheets. Activities can be projected or used on your classroom whiteboard. Worksheets can be edited and printed, or assigned online, depending on student access to technology.

ENGAGE

Every lesson begins with an Engage activity designed to motivate students and focus their attention on the lesson topic.

Guiding Questions

Guiding Questions in the Student Edition point out key knowledge that students need to acquire to be able to answer the chapter's Essential Questions.

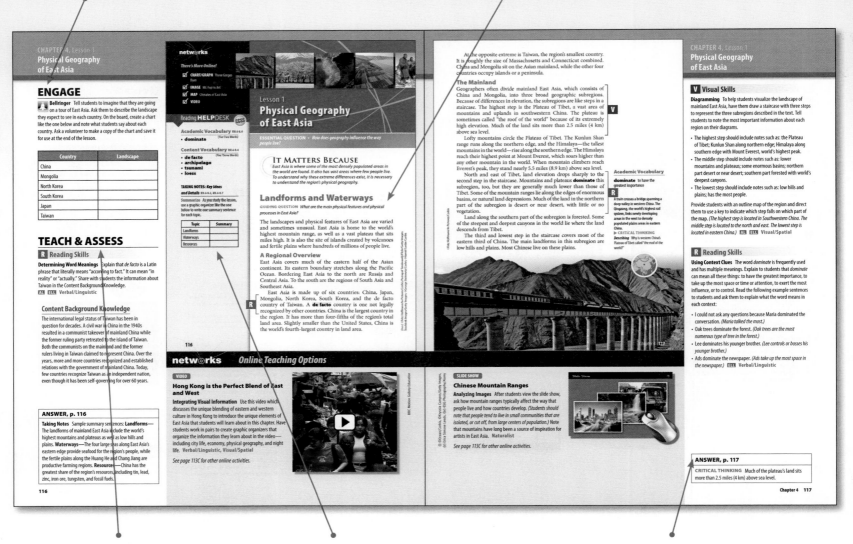

TEACH & ASSESS

Teach & Assess is the core of the lesson. It contains activities, lecture notes, background information, and discussion questions to teach the lesson.

Reading Help Desk

- Academic Vocabulary
- Content Vocabulary
- Note-Taking Activity and Graphic Organizer

Answers

Answers to questions and activities in the Student Edition appear in the bottom corner of the Teacher Edition pages.

Using the Wraparound Resources and Activities (continued)

Brackets
Brackets on the Student Edition page correspond to teaching strategies and activities in the Teacher Edition. As you teach the lesson, the brackets show you where to use these activities and strategies.

Reading Progress Check
A Reading Progress Check appears at the end of each topic in the Student Edition to help gauge student reading comprehension.

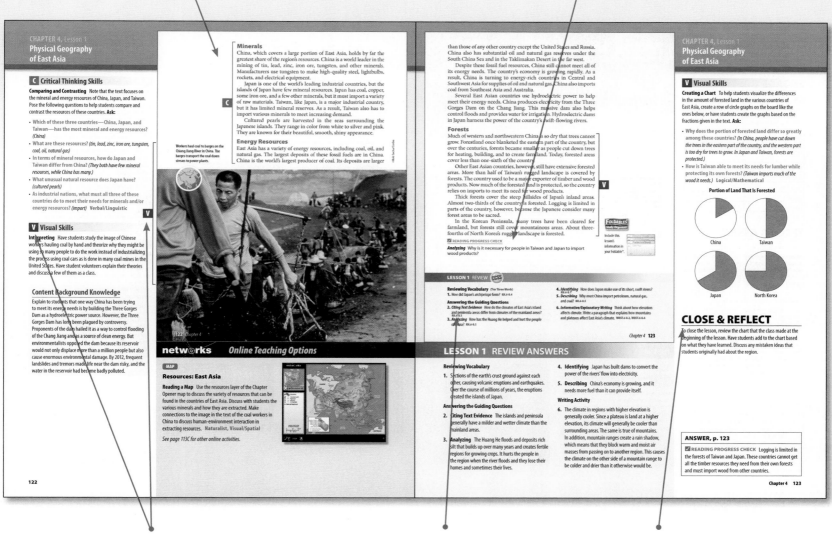

Letters
The letters on the reduced Student Edition page identify the type of activity. See the key on the first planning page of each chapter to learn about the different types of activities.

Common Core State Standards
Questions and activities throughout the Student Edition are correlated to the Reading Standards for Literacy in History/ Social Studies 6-8 (RH.6-8) and the Writing Standards for Literacy in History/ Social Studies 6-8 (WH.6-8).

CLOSE & REFLECT
Each lesson ends with activities designed to help students link the content to the lesson's Guiding Questions and the chapter's Essential Questions.

Don't forget! You can customize all your Lesson Plans online.

Special Features

Global Connections

Global Connections are provided for each unit. Each Global Connections feature focuses on an event or a topic that affects the world community.

The online Global Connections includes numerous interactive digital assets to enrich your teaching. Digital assets include:

- animations
- photos
- maps, charts, and diagrams
- videos
- worksheets
- whiteboard activities

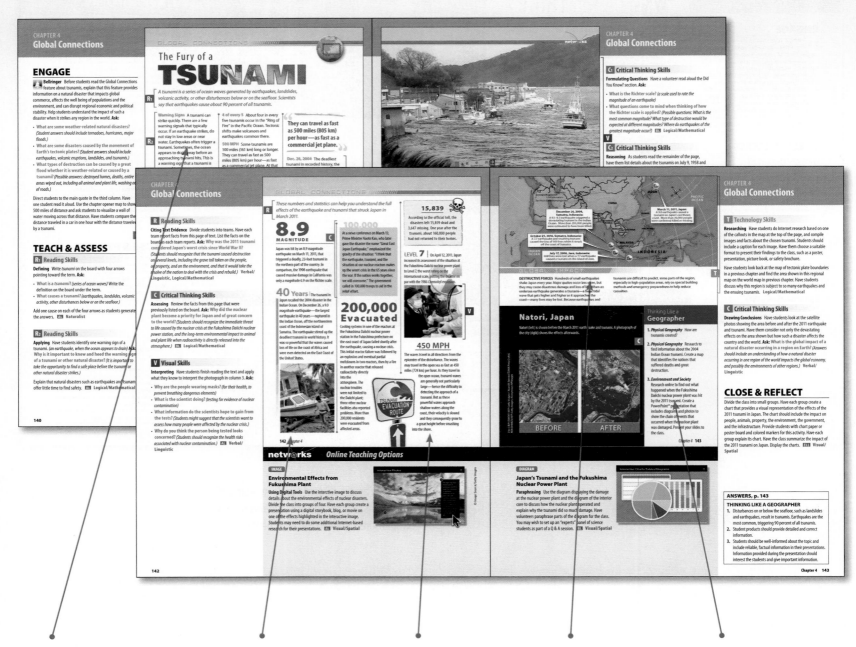

Background information is provided to help students understand the event or topic.

Dynamic photos enrich the study of the content.

Fun and interesting statistics and facts are listed in a magazine-like format.

Maps, graphs, charts, and diagrams are engaging and student-friendly.

Questions assess students' understanding of the information in the feature.

Special Features (continued)

What Do You Think?

Each unit includes a What Do You Think? feature. Students are asked to analyze different points of view on current world issues and events.

Background information is provided to help students understand why there are opposing viewpoints about the issue or event.

Two primary sources present opposing points of view.

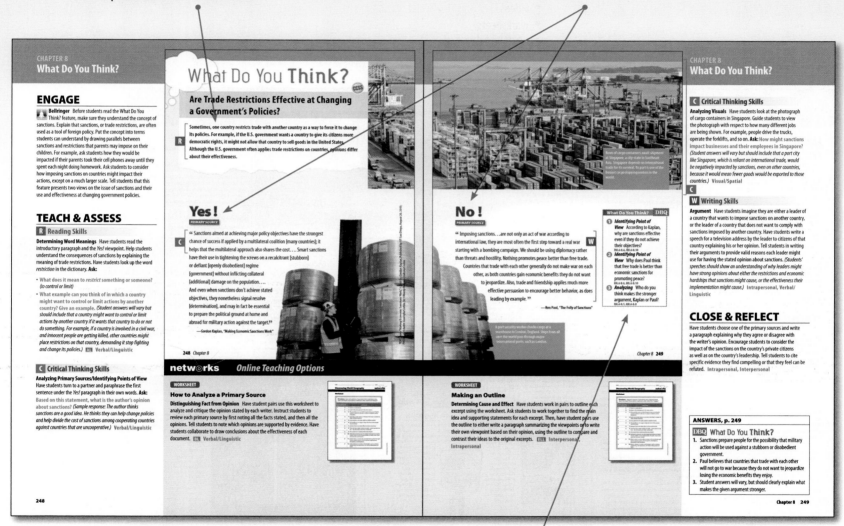

Questions assess students' understanding of both points of view and ask students to make comparisons between the arguments.

Activities and Assessment

Chapter Assessment

Each chapter ends with a chapter assessment that includes the following:

- Foldables® Writing Activity
- 21st Century Skills Activity
- Thinking Like a Geographer Activity
- Geography Activity
- Review the Guiding Questions
  Standardized Test Practice
- Document-Based Questions and Writing
  Activities

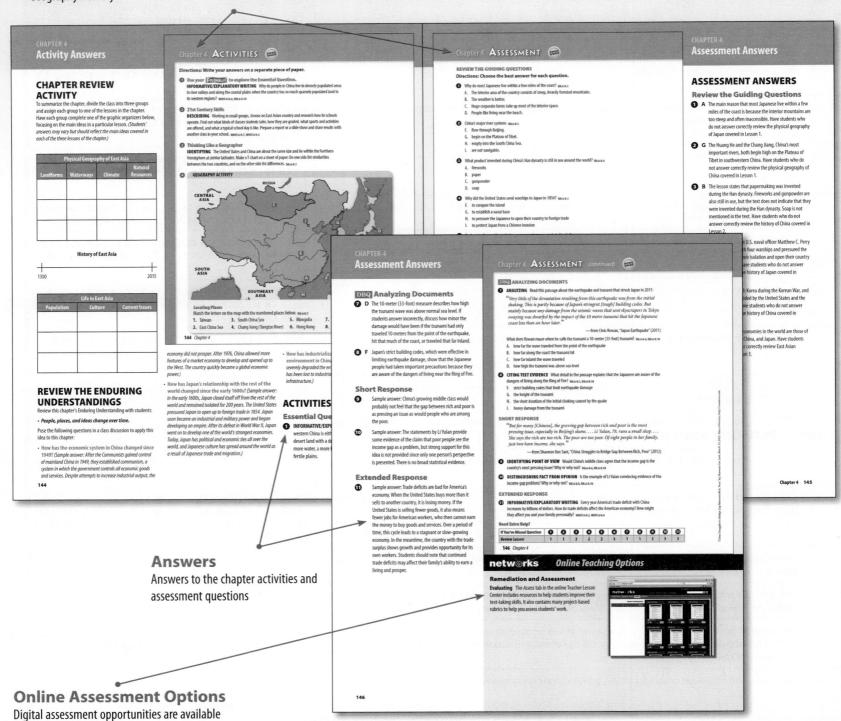

Answers

Answers to the chapter activities and
assessment questions

Online Assessment Options

Digital assessment opportunities are available
for every chapter.

The revised National Council for the Social Studies Standards continue to be focused on ten themes, like the original standards. They represent a way of categorizing knowledge about the human experience, and they constitute the organizing strands that should thread through a social studies program.

Theme and Learning Expectation	Student Edition Chapter/Lesson
1. CULTURE	
1. "Culture" refers to the socially transmitted behaviors, beliefs, values, traditions, institutions, and ways of living together for a group of people	**Ch 3** L2; **Ch 4** L3; **Ch 5** L2, L3; **Ch 6** L2, L3; **Ch 7** L3; **Ch 8** L3; **Ch 9** L3; **Ch 10** L3; **Ch 11** L3; **Ch 12** L3; **Ch 13** L3; **Ch 14** L2, L3; **Ch 15** L2, L3
2. Concepts such as beliefs, values, mores, institutions, cohesion, diversity, accommodation, adaption, assimilation, and dissonance	**Ch 3** L2; **Ch 4** L2, L3; **Ch 5** L2, L3; **Ch 6** L2, L3; **Ch 7** L3; **Ch 8** L3; **Ch 9** L3; **Ch 10** L3; **Ch 11** L2; **Ch 12** L2, L3; **Ch 13** L3; **Ch 14** L2, L3; **Ch 15** L2, L3
3. How culture influences the ways in which human groups solve the problems of daily living	**Ch 3** L2; **Ch 4** L3; **Ch 5** L2, L3; **Ch 6** L2; **Ch 7** L3; **Ch 8** L3; **Ch 9** L3; **Ch 10** L3; **Ch 11** L3; **Ch 12** L3; **Ch 13** L3; **Ch 14** L3; **Ch 15** L2, L3
4. That the beliefs, values, and behaviors of a culture form an integrated system that helps shape the activities and ways of life that define a culture	**Ch 3** L2; **Ch 4** L3; **Ch 5** L3; **Ch 6** L3; **Ch 7** L3; **Ch 8** L3; **Ch 9** L3; **Ch 10** L3; **Ch 11** L3; **Ch 12** L3; **Ch 13** L3; **Ch 14** L3; **Ch 15** L3
5. How individuals learn the elements of their culture through interactions with others, and how individuals learn of other cultures through communication and study	**Ch 1** L1; **Ch 3** L2, GC; **Ch 4** L3; **Ch 6** L3; **Ch 7** L3; **Ch 8** L3; **Ch 9** L3; **Ch 10** L3; **Ch 11** L3; **Ch 12** L3; **Ch 13** L3; **Ch 14** L3; **Ch 15** L3
6. That culture may change in response to changing needs, concerns, social, political, and geographic conditions	**Ch 3** L1, L2, GC; **Ch 4** L3; **Ch 6** L3; **Ch 7** L2, L3; **Ch 8** L3; **Ch 9** L2, L3; **Ch 10** L3; **Ch 11** L2, L3; **Ch 12** L2, L3; **Ch 13** L2, L3; **Ch 14** L2, L3; **Ch 15** L3
7. How people from different cultures develop different values and ways of interpreting experience	**Ch 3** L2; **Ch 4** L2, L3; **Ch 6** L2, L3; **Ch 7** L2, L3; **Ch 8** L3; **Ch 9** L3; **Ch 10** L3; **Ch 11** L3; **Ch 12** L2, L3; **Ch 13** L2, L3; **Ch 14** L3; **Ch 15** L2, L3
8. That language, behaviors, and beliefs of different cultures can both contribute to and pose barriers to cross-cultural understanding	**Ch 3** L1, L2; **Ch 4** L2, L3; **Ch 5** L2; **Ch 6** L2, l3; **Ch 7** L2, L3; **Ch 8** L2, L3; **Ch 9** L3; **Ch 10** L3; **Ch 11** L3; **Ch 12** L3; **Ch 13** L2, L3; **Ch 14** L2, L3; **Ch 15** L2, L3
2. TIME, CONTINUITY, AND CHANGE	
1. The study of the past provides a representation of the history of communities, nations, and the world	**Ch 4** L2; **Ch 5** L2; **Ch 6** L2; **Ch 7** L2; **Ch 8** L2; **Ch 9** L2; **Ch 10** L2; **Ch 11** L2; **Ch 12** L2; **Ch 13** L2; **Ch 14** L2; **Ch 15** L2
2. Concepts such as: chronology, causality, change, conflict, complexity, multiple perspectives, primary and secondary sources, and cause and effect	**Ch 1** CO, WDYT; **Ch 4** CO, L2, L3; **Ch 5** CO, L2, L3; **Ch 6** CO, L2, L3; **Ch 7** CO, L2; **Ch 8** CO, L2, WDYT; **Ch 9** CO, L2; **Ch 10** CO, L2; **Ch 11** CO, L2, WDYT; **Ch 12** CO, L2; **Ch 13** CO, L2; **Ch 14** CO, L2; **Ch 15** CO, L2; **Ch 16** CO, L1
3. That learning about the past requires the interpretation of sources, and that using varied sources provides the potential for a more balanced interpretive record of the past	**Ch 8** WDYT; **Ch 11** WDYT
4. That historical interpretations of the same event may differ on the basis of such factors as conflicting evidence from varied sources, national or cultural perspectives, and the point of view of the researcher	**Ch 1** WDYT; **Ch 8** WDYT; **Ch 11** WDYT
5. Key historical periods and patterns of change within and across cultures (e.g., the rise and fall of ancient civilizations, the development of technology, the rise of modern nation-states, and the establishment and breakdown of colonial systems)	**Ch 4** L2; **Ch 5** L2; **Ch 6** L2; **Ch 7** L2; **Ch 8** L2; **Ch 9** L2; **Ch 10** L2; **Ch 11** L2; **Ch 12** L2; **Ch 13** L2; **Ch 14** L2; **Ch 15** L2
6. The origins and influences of social, cultural, political, and economic systems	**Ch 3** L3, GC; **Ch 4** L2, L3; **Ch 5** L2, L3; **Ch 6** L2, L3; **Ch 7** L2, L3; **Ch 8** L2, L3; **Ch 9** L2, L3; **Ch 10** L2, L3; **Ch 11** L2, L3; **Ch 12** L2, L3; **Ch 13** L2, L3; **Ch 14** L2, L3; **Ch 15** L2

Note: CO=Chapter Opener; WDYT=What Do You Think?; GC=Global Connections

Theme and Learning Expectation	Student Edition Chapter/Lesson
7. The contributions of key persons, groups, and events from the past and their influence on the present	**Ch 4** L2; **Ch 5** L2; **Ch 6** L2; **Ch 7** L2; **Ch 8** L2; **Ch 9** L2; **Ch 10** L2; **Ch 11** L2; **Ch 12** L2; **Ch 13** L2; **Ch 14** L2; **Ch 15** L2; **Ch 16** L1
8. The history of democratic ideals and principles, and how they are represented in documents, artifacts and symbols	**Ch 3** L2; **Ch 14** L3; **Ch 15** L2
9. The influences of social, geographic, economic, and cultural factors on the history of local areas, states, nations, and the world	**Ch 3** L2, L3, GC; **Ch 4** L2; **Ch 5** L2; **Ch 6** L2; **Ch 7** L2; **Ch 8** L2; **Ch 9** L2; **Ch 10** L2; **Ch 11** L2; **Ch 12** L2; **Ch 13** L2; **Ch 14** L2; **Ch 15** L2; **Ch 16** L2

3. PEOPLE, PLACES, AND ENVIRONMENTS

1. The theme of people, places, and environments involves the study of the relationships between human populations in different locations and geographic phenomena such as climate, vegetation, and natural resources	**Ch 1** L1; **Ch 2** L1; **Ch 3** L3; **Ch 4** L1, L3; **Ch 5** L1; **Ch 6** L1, L3; **Ch 7** L1, L; **Ch 8** L1, L3; **Ch 9** L1, L3; **Ch 10** L1, L3; **Ch 11** L1, L2, L3; **Ch 12** L1; **Ch 13** L1; **Ch 14** L1, L2, GC; **Ch 15** L1, L2; **Ch 16** L2
2. Concepts such as: location, region, place, migration, as well as human and physical systems	**Ch 1** L1; **Ch 2** L1, L2; **Ch 3** L1, L2; **Ch 4** L1; **Ch 5** L1, L2; **Ch 6** L1, L2, L3; **Ch 7** L1, L2, L3; **Ch 8** L2; **Ch 9** L3; **Ch 10** L2, L3, GC; **Ch 11** L2, L3; **Ch 12** L1; **Ch 13** L3; **Ch 14** L1, L2, L3; **Ch 15** L3; **Ch 16** L1
3. Past and present changes in physical systems, such as seasons, climate, and weather, and the water cycle, in both national and global contexts	**Ch 1** L2; **Ch 2** L1, L3; **Ch 3** L1; **Ch 6** L3; **Ch 8** L3; **Ch 9** L1; **Ch 10** L1; **Ch 11** L2; **Ch 12** L1; **Ch 14** L1; **Ch 15** L3; **Ch 16** L2
4. The roles of different kinds of population centers in a region or nation	**Ch 4** L3; **Ch 5** L3; **Ch 6** L3; **Ch 7** L3; **Ch 8** L3; **Ch 9** L3; **Ch 10** L3; **Ch 11** L3; **Ch 12** L3; **Ch 13** L3; **Ch 14** L3; **Ch 15** L3; **Ch 16** L2
5. The concept of regions identifies links between people in different locations according to specific criteria (e.g., physical, economic, social, cultural, or religious)	**Ch 1** L1; **Ch 3** L2; **Ch 4** L2, L3; **Ch 5** L2; **Ch 6** L1, L3; **Ch 7** L1, L3; **Ch 8** L2, L3; **Ch 9** L3; **Ch 10** L3; **Ch 11** L3; **Ch 12** L3; **Ch 13** L3; **Ch 14** L1, L2, L3; **Ch 15** L1, L2, L3
6. Patterns of demographic and political change, and cultural diffusion in the past and present (e.g., changing national boundaries, migration, and settlement, and the diffusion of and changes in customs and ideas)	**Ch 3** L1; L2; **Ch 4** L3; **Ch 5** L2, L3; **Ch 6** L3; **Ch 7** L2, L3; **Ch 8** L2, L3; **Ch 9** L3; **Ch 10** L2, L3, GC; **Ch 11** L2, L3; **Ch 12** L2, L3; **Ch 13** L2, L3; **Ch 14** L2, L3; **Ch 15** L2, L3
7. Human modifications of the environment	**Ch 1** L1; **Ch 2** L1, L2; **Ch 3** L1, L3; **Ch 5** L3; **Ch 7** L2, L3; **Ch 8** L3; **Ch 9** L1, L3; **Ch 11** L1; **Ch 12** L1, L2; **Ch 14** L2, L3, GC; **Ch 15** L2, L3
8. Factors that contribute to cooperation and conflict among peoples of the nation and world, including language, religion, and political beliefs	**Ch 3** L2, L3; **Ch 4** L3; **Ch 5** L2, L3; **Ch 6** L3; **Ch 7** L2, L3; **Ch 8** L2; **Ch 9** L2, L3; **Ch 10** L3, GC; **Ch 11** WDYT; **Ch 12** L2, L3; **Ch 13** L2, L3; **Ch 14** L2, L3; **Ch 15** L2, L3; **Ch 16** L2
9. The use of a variety of maps, globes, graphic representations, and geospatial technologies to help investigate the relationships among people, places, and environments	**Ch 1** CO, L2, WDYT; **Ch 2** CO; **Ch 3** CO; **Ch 4** CO, L2, L3; **Ch 5** CO, L2; **Ch 6** CO; **Ch 7** CO, L1, L2, L3; **Ch 8** CO, L2, L3; **Ch 9** CO, L2; **Ch 10** CO, L1, L2, GC; **Ch 11** CO, L2; **Ch 12** CO, L1, L2; **Ch 13** CO, L3; **Ch 14** CO, GC; **Ch 15** CO; **Ch 16** CO

4. INDIVIDUAL DEVELOPMENT AND IDENTITY

1. The study of individual development and identity helps us know that individuals change physically, cognitively, and emotionally over time	**Ch 3** L2, GC; **Ch 11**, L3; **Ch 9** L3; **Ch 14** L3
2. Concepts such as: development, change, personality, learning, individual, family, groups, motivation, and perception	**Ch 3** L2; **Ch 4** L3; **Ch 5** L3; **Ch 6** L3; **Ch 7** L3; **Ch 8** L3; **Ch 9** L3; **Ch 10** L3; **Ch 11** L3; **Ch 12** L3; **Ch 13** L3; **Ch 14** L3; **Ch 15** L3
3. How factors such as physical endowment, interests, capabilities, learning, motivation, personality, perception, and beliefs influence individual development and identity	**Ch 3** L2; **Ch 5** L3; **Ch 6** L3; **Ch 9** L3; **Ch 10** L3; **Ch 11** L3; **Ch 12** L3; **Ch 14** L2, L3
4. How personal, social, cultural, and environmental factors contribute to the development and the growth of personal identity	**Ch 3** L2; **Ch 5** L3; **Ch 6** L3; **Ch 9** L3; **Ch 10** L3; **Ch 11** L3; **Ch 12** L3; **Ch 13** L2, L3; **Ch 14** L3; **Ch 15** L3
5. That individuals' choices influence identity and development	**Ch 3** L1, L2 GC; **Ch 4** L3; **Ch 5** L3; **Ch 6** L3; **Ch 7** L3; **Ch 8** L3; **Ch 9** L3; **Ch 10** L3; **Ch 11** L3; **Ch 12** L3; **Ch 13** L3; **Ch 14** L3; **Ch 15** L2, L3

	Theme and Learning Expectation	Student Edition Chapter/Lesson
6.	That perceptions are interpretations of information about individuals and events, and can be influenced by bias and stereotypes	**Ch 5** L2; **Ch 6** L2; **Ch 8** L2; **Ch 9** L2; **Ch 10** L2; **Ch 11** L2; **Ch 12** L2; **Ch 13** L2, L3; **Ch 14** L2; **Ch 15** L2

5. INDIVIDUALS, GROUPS, AND INSTITUTIONS

	Theme and Learning Expectation	Student Edition Chapter/Lesson
1.	This theme helps us know how individuals are members of groups and institutions, and influence and shape those groups and institutions	**Ch 1** L1; **Ch 3** L2, GC; **Ch 4** L2, L3; **Ch 5** L2, L3; **Ch 6** L3; **Ch 7** L2, L3; **Ch 8** L2; **Ch 9** L3; **Ch 10** L2; **Ch 11** L3; **Ch 12** L3; **Ch 13** L3; **Ch 14** L2, L3; **Ch 15** L2, L3
2.	Concepts such as: mores, norms, status, role, socialization, ethnocentrism, cultural diffusion, competition, cooperation, conflict, race, ethnicity, and gender	**Ch 3** L1, L2; **Ch 4** L3; **Ch 5** L3; **Ch 6** L3; **Ch 7** L3; **Ch 8** L3, WDYT; **Ch 9** L3; **Ch 10** L3, GC; **Ch 11** L3, WDYT; **Ch 12** L3; **Ch 13** L3; **Ch 14** L3; **Ch 15** L3; **Ch 16**, L2
3.	Institutions are created to respond to changing individual and group needs	**Ch 3** L2, L3; **Ch 5** L3; **Ch 11** WDYT; **Ch 13** L2
4.	That ways in which young people are socialized include similarities as well as differences across cultures	**Ch 3** L2, GC; **Ch 4** L3; **Ch 6** L3; **Ch 7** L3; **Ch 9** L3; **Ch 12** L3; **Ch 13** L2, L3; **Ch 14** L3
5.	That groups and institutions change over time	**Ch 3** L2, L3, GC; **Ch 4** L3; **Ch 6** L2, L3; **Ch 7** L2, L3; **Ch 9** L2, L3; **Ch 11** L2; **Ch 12** L2; **Ch 13** L2, L3; **Ch 14** L3; **Ch 15** L3
6.	That cultural diffusion occurs when groups migrate	**Ch 3** L2, GC; **Ch 5** L3; **Ch 11** L3; **Ch 7** L3; **Ch 8** L3; **Ch 9** L3; **Ch 10** L3, GC; **Ch 11** L3; **Ch 12** L2, L3; **Ch 14** L1, L2, L3; **Ch 15** L2, L3
7.	That institutions may promote or undermine social conformity	**Ch 3** L1, L2; **Ch 5** L3; **Ch 11** WDYT; **Ch 13** L2
8.	That when two or more groups with differing norms and beliefs interact, accommodation or conflict may result	**Ch 3** L2; **Ch 4** L3; **Ch 5** L3; **Ch 6** L2, L3; **Ch 7** L2, L3; **Ch 8** WDYT; **Ch 9** L2, L3; **Ch 10** L2, L3, GC; **Ch 11** L2, L3, WDYT; **Ch 12** L2, L3; **Ch 13** L2, L3; **Ch 14** L3; **Ch 15** L2, L3; **Ch 16** L2
9.	That groups and institutions influence culture in a variety of ways	**Ch 3** L2, GC; **Ch 4** L2, L3; **Ch 5** L2, L3; **Ch 6** L3; **Ch 7** L3; **Ch 8** L3; **Ch 9** L2, L3; **Ch 10** L3; **Ch 11** L2; **Ch 12** L3; **Ch 13** L2, L3; **Ch 14** L2, L3; **Ch 15** L3

6. POWER, AUTHORITY, AND GOVERNANCE

	Theme and Learning Expectation	Student Edition Chapter/Lesson
1.	Rights are guaranteed in the U.S. Constitution, the supreme law of the land	**Ch 3** L2
2.	Fundamental ideas that are the foundation of American constitutional democracy (including those of the U.S. Constitution, popular sovereignty, the rule of law, separation of powers, checks and balances, minority rights, the separation of church and state, and Federalism)	**Ch 3** L2
3.	Fundamental values of constitutional democracy (e.g., the common good, liberty, justice, equality, and individual dignity)	**Ch 3** L2; **Ch 5** L2; **Ch 9** L3; **Ch 13** L3; **Ch 14** L2, L3; **Ch 15** L2
4.	The ideologies and structures of political systems that differ from those of the United States	**Ch 3** L2; **Ch 4** L2, L3; **Ch 5** L2, L3; **Ch 6** L3; **Ch 7** L3; **Ch 9** L3; **Ch 10** L2; **Ch 13** L2; **Ch 14** L2, L3; **Ch 15** L2
5.	The ways in which governments meet the needs and wants of citizens, manage conflict, and establish order and security	**Ch 3** L2; **Ch 4** L3; **Ch 7** L2, L3; **Ch 9** L2, L3; **Ch 10** L2, L3; **Ch 11** L3; **Ch 12** L3; **Ch 13** L2, L3; **Ch 14** L2, L3; **Ch 15** L3

7. PRODUCTION, DISTRIBUTION, AND CONSUMPTION

	Theme and Learning Expectation	Student Edition Chapter/Lesson
1.	Individuals, government, and society experience scarcity because human wants and needs exceed what can be produced from available resources	**Ch 3** L3; **Ch 4** L2; **Ch 5** L3; **Ch 9** L3; **Ch 10** L2; **Ch 11** L3; **Ch 12** L3; **Ch 13** L3; **Ch 15** L3
2.	How choices involve trading off the expected value of one opportunity gained against the expected value of the best alternative	**Ch 3** L3
3.	The economic choices that people make have both present and future consequences	**Ch 3** L3; **Ch 4** L3; **Ch 5** L3; **Ch 6** L3; **Ch 7** L3; **Ch 8** L3; **Ch 9** L3; **Ch 10** L2, L3; **Ch 11** L3; **Ch 12** L3; **Ch 13** L3; **Ch 14** L3; **Ch 15** L3
4.	Economic incentives affect people's behavior and may be regulated by rules or laws	**Ch 3** L3; **Ch 4** L3; **Ch 5** L3; **Ch 8** WDYT; **Ch 12** L3; **Ch 13** L3; **Ch 15** L2
5.	That banks and other financial institutions channel funds from savers to borrowers and investors	**Ch 5** L3; **Ch 9** L3; **Ch 12** L3; **Ch 13** L3; **Ch 15** L3

Theme and Learning Expectation	Student Edition Chapter/Lesson
6. The economic gains that result from specialization and exchange as well as the trade-offs	**Ch 3** L3; **Ch 4** L3; **Ch 5** L3; **Ch 10** L3; **Ch 12** L3; **Ch 13** L2; **Ch 14** L3; **Ch 15** L3
7. How markets bring buyers and sellers together to exchange goods and services	**Ch 3** L3; **Ch 4** L3; **Ch 5** L3; **Ch 12** L3; **Ch 13** L2, L3; **Ch 14** L3
8. How goods and services are allocated in a market economy through the influence of prices on decisions about production and consumption	**Ch 3** L3; **Ch 4** L3
9. How the overall levels of income, employment, and prices are determined by the interaction of households, firms, and the government	**Ch 3** L2, L3; **Ch 4** L3; **Ch 5** L3; **Ch 9** L3; **Ch 12** L3; **Ch 14** L3; **Ch 15** L3

8. SCIENCE, TECHNOLOGY, AND SOCIETY

1. Science is a result of empirical study of the natural world, and technology is the application of knowledge to accomplish tasks	**Ch 1** L2, WDYT; **Ch 5** L2; **Ch 14** L2; **Ch 15** L2; **Ch 16** L2
2. Society often turns to science and technology to solve problems	**Ch 1** L2, WDYT; **Ch 5** L2; **Ch 7** L2, L3; **Ch 9** L1; **Ch 14** L1, GC; **Ch 15** L2; **Ch 16** L2
3. Our lives today are media and technology dependent	**Ch 1** WDYT; **Ch 3** GC; **Ch 14** L3; **Ch 15** L2; **Ch 16** L2
4. Science and technology have had both positive and negative impacts upon individuals, societies, and the environment in the past and present	**Ch 1** WDYT; **Ch 2** L1; **Ch 3** L3; **Ch 4** L3, GC; **Ch 5** L2; **Ch 7** L3; **Ch 9** L1; **Ch 10** L1; **Ch 11** L2; **Ch 12** L2; **Ch 14** L1, L3, GC; **Ch 15** L2; **Ch 16** L2
5. Science and technology have changed peoples' perceptions of the social and natural world, as well as their relationship to the land, economy and trade, their concept of security, and their major daily activities	**Ch 1** L2, WDYT; **Ch 3** L1, L3, GC; **Ch 5** L2, L3; **Ch 12** L2; **Ch 13** L3; **Ch 14** L3; **Ch 15** L3; **Ch 16** L2
6. Values, beliefs, and attitudes that have been influenced by new scientific and technological knowledge (e.g., invention of the printing press, conceptions of the universe, applications of atomic energy, and genetic discoveries)	**Ch 1** WDYT; **Ch 3** GC; **Ch 15** L2; **Ch 16** L2
7. How media are created and received depends upon cultural contexts	**Ch 1** WDYT; **Ch 3** GC; **Ch 8** L18; **Ch 14** L3
8. Science and technology sometimes create ethical issues that test our standards and values	**Ch 1** L WDYT; **Ch 3** GC; **Ch 5** L3; **Ch 8** WDYT; **Ch 14** L1, GC
9. The need for laws and policies to govern scientific and technological applications	**Ch 4** L3; **Ch 5** L3; **Ch 6** L3; **Ch 7** L3; **Ch 14** L2, L3; **Ch 15** L3; **Ch 16** L2
10. That there are gaps in access to science and technology around the world	**Ch 5** L3; **Ch 9** L3; **Ch 10** L3; **Ch 11** L3; **Ch 12** L3; **Ch 14** L3

9. GLOBAL CONNECTIONS

1. Global connections have existed in the past and increased rapidly in current times	**Ch 1** WDYT; **Ch 3** L1, L2, GC; **Ch 4** L2, L3, GC; **Ch 5** L3; **Ch 6** L3; **Ch 7** L3; **Ch 8** WDYT; **Ch 9** L2; **Ch 11** L2, WDYT; **Ch 12** L2; **Ch 14** L3, GC; **Ch 15** L2, L3; **Ch 16** L2
2. Global factors such as cultural, economic, and political connections are changing the places in which people live (e.g., through trade, migration, increased travel, and communication)	**Ch 3** L1, GC; **Ch 4** L3; **Ch 5** L3; **Ch 6** L3; **Ch 7** L2; **Ch 8** WDYT; **Ch 9** L2, L3; **Ch 10** L2, L3, GC; **Ch 11** L2, L3, WDYT; **Ch 12** L3; **Ch 13** L3; **Ch 14** L3; **Ch 15** L3
3. Spatial relationships that relate to ongoing global issues (e.g., pollution, poverty, disease, and conflict) affect the health and well-being of Earth and its inhabitants	**Ch 1** L1; **Ch 2** L1, L3; **Ch 3** L1; **Ch 4** L3, GC; **Ch 5** L3; **Ch 6** L3; **Ch 7** L3; **Ch 8** WDYT; **Ch 9** L3; **Ch 10** L3, GC; **Ch 11** WDYT; **Ch 12** L3; **Ch 13** L3; **Ch 15** L3
4. Global problems and possibilities are not generally caused or developed by any one nation	**Ch 4** L3; **Ch 5** L2, L3; **Ch 6** L2; **Ch 8** WDYT; **Ch 11** WDYT; **Ch 13** L2; **Ch 15** L2
5. Global connections may make cultures more alike or increase their sense of distinctiveness	**Ch 3** L2, GC; **Ch 9** L2, L3; **Ch 10** GC; **Ch 11** WDYT; **Ch 14** L2, L3
6. Universal human rights cut across cultures but are not necessarily understood in the same way in all cultures	**Ch 3** L2; **Ch 4** L3; **Ch 9** L3; **Ch 11** L2; **Ch 13** L2; **Ch 14** L3; **Ch 15** L3

Theme and Learning Expectation	Student Edition Chapter/Lesson
10. CIVIC IDEALS AND PRACTICES	
1. The theme of civic ideals and practices helps us to learn about and know how to work for the betterment of society	**Ch 3** L2; **Ch 9** L2; **Ch 12** L3; **Ch 13** L2; **Ch 14** L3; **Ch 16** L2
2. Concepts and ideals such as: individual dignity, liberty, justice, equality, individual rights, responsibility, majority and minority rights, and civil dissent	**Ch 3** L2; **Ch 5** L2, L3; **Ch 6** L2, L3; **Ch 7** L2, L3; **Ch 9** L2, L3; **Ch 13** L2; **Ch 14** L3; **Ch 15** L3
3. Key practices involving the rights and responsibilities of citizenship and the exercise of citizenship (e.g., respecting the rule of law and due process, voting, serving on a jury, researching issues, making informed judgments, expressing views on issues, and collaborating with others to take civic action)	**Ch 3** L2; **Ch 9** L3; **Ch 13** L2; **Ch 14** L2, L3
4. The common good, and the rule of law	**Ch 3** L2; **Ch 4** L3; **Ch 5** L2; **Ch 9** L2, L3; **Ch 10** L2; **Ch 11** L3, WDYT; **Ch 12** L2, L3; **Ch 13** L2; **Ch 14** L2, L3; **Ch 15** L3
5. Key documents and excerpts from key sources that define and support democratic ideals and practices (e.g., the U.S. Declaration of Independence, the U.S. Constitution, the Gettysburg Address, the Letter from Birmingham Jail; and international documents such as the Declaration of the Rights of Man, and the Universal Declaration of the Rights of Children)	**Ch 3** L2; **Ch 16** L2
6. The origins and function of major institutions and practices developed to support democratic ideals and practices	**Ch 3** L2; **Ch 9** L3; **Ch 11** WDYT; **Ch 12** L3; **Ch 13** L2; **Ch 14** L2, L3
7. Key past and present issues involving democratic ideals and practices, as well as the perspectives of various stakeholders in proposing possible solutions to these issues;	**Ch 3** L2; **Ch 5** L2, L3; **Ch 7** L2, L3; **Ch 8** WDYT; **Ch 9** L2, L3; **Ch 12** L3; **Ch 13** L2, L3; **Ch 14** L2, L3; **Ch 15** L3
8. The importance of becoming informed in order to make positive civic contributions	**Ch 1** WDYT; **Ch 4** L3; **Ch 8** WDYT; **Ch 11** WDYT; **Ch 13** L2; **Ch 14** L3

Correlation of *Discovering World Geography: Eastern Hemisphere* to the National Geography Standards

The second edition of *Geography For Life,* as in the first edition, ensures that the National Geography Standards continue to challenge students and address the most important and enduring ideas in geography. The second edition of *Geography For Life* also incorporates new ideas about geography, the learning process, and additional skills that transcend disciplinary boundaries.

The goal of the National Geography Standards is to help students become geographically informed through knowledge and mastery of factual knowledge, mental maps and geographic tools, and ways of thinking.

The Six Essential Elements and Related National Geography Standards	Student Edition Chapter/Lesson
Essential Element: The World in Spatial Terms	
Geography Standard 1 **How to use maps and other geographic representations, geospatial technologies, and spatial thinking to understand and communicate information** The geographically informed person must use maps and other geographic representations, geospatial technologies, and spatial thinking to acquire, understand, and communicate information.	**Ch 1** CO, L1, L2, WDYT; **Ch 2** CO; **Ch 3** CO, GC; **Ch 4** CO, L2, L3, GC; **Ch 5** CO, L2; **Ch 6** CO, L1, L2; **Ch 7** CO, L1, L2, L3; **Ch 8** CO, L2, L3; **Ch 9** CO, L2; **Ch 10** CO, GC; **Ch 11** CO, L2; **Ch 12** CO, L1, L2; **Ch 13** CO, L3; **Ch 14** CO, GC; **Ch 15** CO, L1; **Ch 16** CO
Geography Standard 2 **How to use mental maps to organize information about people, places, and environments in a spatial context** A geographically informed person must mentally organize spatial information about people, places, and environments and must be able to call upon and use this information in appropriate contexts.	**Ch 1** CO, L1, L2, WDYT, ACT; **Ch 2** CO, L1, ACT; **Ch 3** CO, GC; **Ch 4** CO, L1, L2, L3, GC, ACT; **Ch 5** CO, L1, L2, ACT; **Ch 6** CO, L1, L2, ACT; **Ch 7** CO, L1, L2, L3, ACT; **Ch 8** CO, L2, L3, ACT; **Ch 9** CO, L2, ACT; **Ch 10** CO, L1, L2, GC, ACT; **Ch 11** CO, L1, L2, ACT; **Ch 12** CO, L1, L2, ACT; **Ch 13** CO, L3, ACT; **Ch 14** CO, L1, GC, ACT; **Ch 15** CO, ACT; **Ch 16** CO, L1, ACT
Geography Standard 3 **How to analyze the spatial organization of people, places, and environments on Earth's surface** The geographically informed person must understand that physical and human phenomena are distributed across Earth's surface and see meaning in their arrangements across space.	**Ch 1** CO, L1, L2, WDYT; **Ch 2** CO, L2, L3; **Ch 3** CO, L1, L2; **Ch 4** CO, L1, L3; **Ch 5** CO, L1; **Ch 6** CO, L1, L2; **Ch 7** CO, L1, L2, L3; **Ch 8** CO, L1, L3; **Ch 9** CO, L1, L2; **Ch 10** CO, L1, L2, GC; **Ch 11** CO, L1, L2; **Ch 12** CO, L1, L2; **Ch 13** CO, L1, L3; **Ch 14** CO, L1, GC; **Ch 15** CO, L1, L2; **Ch 16** CO, L1
Essential Element: Places and Regions	
Geography Standard 4 **The physical and human characteristics of places** The geographically informed person must understand the genesis, evolution, and meaning of places. Places are locations having distinctive features that give them meaning and character that differs from other locations.	**Ch 1** L1, WDYT; **Ch 2** L1, L2, L3; **Ch 3** L1, L2; **Ch 4** L1, L3; **Ch 5** L1, L3; **Ch 6** L1, L2, L3; **Ch 7** L1, L2, L3; **Ch 8** L1, L3; **Ch 9** L1, L3; **Ch 10** L1, L3; **Ch 11** L1, L3; **Ch 12** L1, L3; **Ch 13** L1, L3; **Ch 14** L1, L3; **Ch 15** L1, L3; **Ch 16** L1
Geography Standard 5 **That people create regions to interpret Earth's complexity** The geographically informed person must understand the origins and functions of regions. Regions are human creations used to manage and interpret the complexity of Earth's surface. They help us understand and organize the arrangements of people, places, and environments.	**Ch 1** L1; **Ch 3**, L1, L2; **Ch 4** CO, L1, L2; **Ch 5** CO, L1; **Ch 6** CO, L1, L2; **Ch 7** CO, L1, L2; **Ch 8** CO, L1, L2; **Ch 9** CO, L1, L2; **Ch 10** CO, L1, L2; **Ch 11** CO, L1; **Ch 12** CO, L1; **Ch 13** CO, L1, L3; **Ch 14** CO, L1; **Ch 15** CO, L1

Note: CO=Chapter Opener; WDYT=What Do You Think?; GC=Global Connections; ACT=Chapter Activities

The Six Essential Elements and Related National Geography Standards	Student Edition Chapter/Lesson
Geography Standard 6 **How culture and experience influence people's perceptions of places and regions** The geographically informed person must understand that our own culture and life experiences shape the way we perceive places and regions. Perceptions are the basis for understanding a place's location, extent, characteristics, and significance. Throughout our lives, culture and experience shape our worldviews, which in turn influence our perceptions of places and regions.	**Ch 1** L1; **Ch 3** L2; **Ch 4** L3; **Ch 5** L3; **Ch 6** L3; **Ch 7** L3; **Ch 8** L2, L3; **Ch 9** L2, L3; **Ch 10** L3; **Ch 11** L2; **Ch 12** L2, L3; **Ch 13** L2, L3; **Ch 14** L1, L2, L3; **Ch 15** L2, L3
Essential Element: Physical Systems	
Geography Standard 7 **The physical processes that shape the patterns of Earth's surface** The geographically informed person must understand that physical systems create, maintain, and modify the features that constitute Earth's surface. The physical environment provides the essential background for all human activity on Earth.	**Ch 2** L1, L2, L3; **Ch 4** L1, GC; **Ch 5** L1; **Ch 6** L1; **Ch 7** L1; **Ch 8** L1; **Ch 9** L1; **Ch 10** L1; **Ch 11** L1; **Ch 12** L1; **Ch 13** L1; **Ch 14** L1; **Ch 15** L1; **Ch 16** L1
Geography Standard 8 **The characteristics and spatial distribution of ecosystems and biomes on Earth's surface** The geographically informed person must understand that Earth's surface is home to multiple biophysical communities. All elements of the environment, including the human, are part of many different but nested ecosystems that comprise different biomes.	**Ch 1** L1; **Ch 2** L1, L3; **Ch 4** L1; **Ch 5** L1; **Ch 6** L1; **Ch 7** L1; **Ch 8** L1; **Ch 9** L1; **Ch 10** L1; **Ch 11** L1; **Ch 12** L1; **Ch 13** L1; **Ch 14** L1, GC; **Ch 15** L1; **Ch 16** L1
Essential Element: Human Systems	
Geography Standard 9 **The characteristics, distribution, and migration of human populations on Earth's surface** The geographically informed person must understand that the growth, spatial distribution, and movements of people on Earth's surface are driving forces behind not only human events but also physical events. Human population is a dynamic force in reshaping the planet.	**Ch 1** L1; **Ch 3** L1, L2; **Ch 4** L2; **Ch 5** L3; **Ch 6** L3; **Ch 7** L2, L3; **Ch 8** L2; **Ch 9** L3; **Ch 10** L2, L3, GC; **Ch 11** L2, L3; **Ch 12** L2, L3; **Ch 13** L3; **Ch 14** L1, L2, L3
Geography Standard 10 **The characteristics, distribution, and complexity of Earth's cultural mosaics** The geographically informed person must understand that culture is an intricate and complex idea. As the learned behavior of people, culture shapes each group's way of life and its own view of itself and other groups.	**Ch 3** L1, L2, GC; **Ch 4** L2, L3; **Ch 5** L2, L3; **Ch 6** L2, L3; **Ch 7** L2, L3; **Ch 8** L2, L3; **Ch 9** L2, L3; **Ch 10** L2, L3; **Ch 11** L3; **Ch 12** L2, L3; **Ch 13** L2, L3; **Ch 14** L1, L2, L3
Geography Standard 11 **The patterns and networks of economic interdependence on Earth's surface** The geographically informed person must understand the spatial organization of the economic, transportation, and communication systems that support networks of trade in raw materials, manufactured goods, capital (human and monetary), ideas, and services.	**Ch 1** L1; **Ch 3** L3; **Ch 4** L3; **Ch 5** L3; **Ch 6** L3; **Ch 7** L3; **Ch 8** L3, WDYT; **Ch 11** L2; **Ch 12** L2; **Ch 13** L3; **Ch 14** L3
Geography Standard 12 **The processes, patterns, and functions of human settlement** The geographically informed person must understand the varying forms of human settlements in terms of their size, composition, location, arrangement, organization, function, and history.	**Ch 1** L1; **Ch 3** L1, L2; **Ch 4** L2, L3; **Ch 5** L2, L3; **Ch 6** L2, L3; **Ch 7** L2, L3; **Ch 8** L2, L3; **Ch 9** L3; **Ch 10** L2, L3, GC; **Ch 11** L3; **Ch 12** L3; **Ch 13** L2, L3; **Ch 14** L2, L3; **Ch 16** L2

The Six Essential Elements and Related National Geography Standards	Student Edition Chapter/Lesson
Geography Standard 13 **How the forces of cooperation and conflict among people influence the division and control of Earth's surface** The geographically informed person must understand how and why different groups of people have divided, organized, and unified areas of Earth's surface. Competing for control of areas of Earth's surface, large and small, is a universal trait among societies and has resulted in both productive cooperation and destructive conflict between groups.	**Ch 3** L1, L3; **Ch 4** L2, L3; **Ch 5** L2; **Ch 6** L2, L3; **Ch 7** L2, L3; **Ch 8** L2, L3; **Ch 9** L2, L3; **Ch 10** L2, L3, GC; **Ch 11** L2, L3, WDYT; **Ch 12** L2, L3; **Ch 13** L2, L3; **Ch 14** L2, L3; **Ch 16** L2
Essential Element: Environment and Society	
Geography Standard 14 **How human actions modify the physical environment** The geographically informed person must understand the human imprint on the physical environment. Many of the important issues facing modern society are the result of human modifications of the physical environment. Some of these modifications are intended and positive; others unintended and negative. These changes have political, economic, and social implications at all scales, from global to local.	**Ch 1** L1; **Ch 2** L1, L2; **Ch 3** L1, L3; **Ch 4** L1, L2, L3, GC; **Ch 5** L3; **Ch 6** L2, L3; **Ch 7** L1, L2; **Ch 8** L3; **Ch 9** L1, L2; **Ch 10** L3; **Ch 11** L1; **Ch 12** L1; **Ch 13** L1; **Ch 14** L2, L3, GC
Geography Standard 15 **How physical systems affect human systems** The geographically informed person must understand how humans are able to live in various physical settings and the role the physical features of those settings play in shaping human activity.	**Ch 2** L1; **Ch 4** L1, L3, GC; **Ch 5** L3; **Ch 6** L1, L3; **Ch 7** L1, L3; **Ch 8** L3; **Ch 9** L1, L2, L3; **Ch 10** L1; **Ch 11** L1, L3; **Ch 12** L1; **Ch 13** L1; **Ch 14** L3; **Ch 16** L2
Geography Standard 16 **The changes that occur in the meaning, use, distribution, and importance of resources** The geographically informed person must understand that a "resource" is a cultural concept. A resource is any physical material constituting part of Earth that people need and value. The uses and values of resources change from culture to culture and from time to time.	**Ch 1** L1; **Ch 3** L3; **Ch 4** L2, L3; **Ch 5** L3; **Ch 6** L3; **Ch 7** L3; **Ch 8** L3; **Ch 9** L3; **Ch 10** L1; **Ch 11** L2, L3; **Ch 12** L2; **Ch 13** L2, L3; **Ch 14** L1, L3
Essential Element: The Uses of Geography	
Geography Standard 17 **How to apply geography to interpret the past** The geographically informed person must understand the importance of bringing spatial and ecological perspectives of geography to bear on the events of history, and vice versa, and the value of learning about the geographies of the past.	**Ch 1** L1; **Ch 4** L2; **Ch 5** L2; **Ch 6** L2; **Ch 7** L2; **Ch 8** L2; **Ch 9** L2; **Ch 10** L2; **Ch 11** L2; **Ch 12** L2; **Ch 13** L2; **Ch 14** L2; **Ch 15** L2
Geography Standard 18 **How to apply geography to interpret the present and plan for the future** The geographically informed person must understand that the study of geography is critical to understanding the world, now and in the future, and is not simply an exercise for its own sake. Geography is valuable for comprehending current events and planning for the future in geographically-appropriate and sustainable ways.	**Ch 1** L2; **Ch 3** L1, L2, L3; **Ch 4** L3; **Ch 5** L3; **Ch 6** L3; **Ch 7** L3; **Ch 8** L3; **Ch 9** L3; **Ch 10** L3; **Ch 11** L3; **Ch 12** L3; **Ch 13** L3; **Ch 14** L3; **Ch 15** L3; **Ch 16,** L2

Common Core State Standards for English-Language Arts and Literacy in History/Social Studies, Science, and Technical Subjects

The following pages contain correlation charts to the Common Core State Standards. The first chart contains the College and Career Readiness (CCR) Anchor Standards for Reading. The chart that follows the CCR Anchor Standards for Reading chart identifies specifically what students should understand and be able to do by the end of grades 6–8. The CCR and grade-specific standards are necessary complements—the former providing broad standards, the latter providing additional specificity—that together define the skills and understandings that all students must demonstrate.

College and Career Readiness Anchor Standards for Reading

KEY IDEAS AND DETAILS

1. Read closely to determine what the text says explicitly and to make logical inferences from it; cite specific textual evidence when writing or speaking to support conclusions drawn from the text.	**Student Edition:** *Lesson Review: Answering the Guiding Questions, Analyzing* 25, 33, 51, 65, 81, 89, 123, 131, 139, 155, 163, 169, 181, 205, 211, 219, 247, 271, 287, 301, 333, 339, 345, 367, 373, 393, 401, 455, 479, 485; *Describing* 51, 58, 139, 317, 322, 333, 339, 345, 387; *Citing Text Evidence* 57, 123, 231, 239, 467; *Identifying* 65, 123, 155, 193, 231, 359, 387 *Reading Progress Check: Analyzing* 27; *Drawing Conclusions* 139 *What Do You Think? DBQ: Citing Text Evidence* 35; *Identifying* 38; *Analyzing* 249, 487 *Chapter Assessment: Short Response, Analyzing* 38, 68, 172, 222, 252, 324, 404, 446, 470; *Question 9* 104 *Reading HELP Desk: Taking Notes, Key Ideas and Details, Identify* 52; *Describe* 124; *Organize Information* 132; *Identifying* 150; *Describing* 156; *Categorizing* 206 *Chapter Assessment: Review the Guiding Questions* 67, 103, 145, 171, 221, 251, 288, 323, 349, 375, 403, 469 *Chapter Assessment: DBQ Analyzing Documents, Identifying* 68, 172, 222, 376; *Citing Text Evidence* 146, 324; *Analyzing* 172, 196, 222, 252, 290, 324, 404, 446; *Analyzing Information* 350; *Determining Word Meanings* 376 *Global Connections: Thinking Like a Geographer, Environment and Society* 93 *Reading Progress Check* 120, 121, 123, 128, 129, 131, 133, 137, 139, 152, 153, 155, 159, 161, 163, 165, 167, 169, 177, 179, 181, 185, 187, 191, 193, 201, 204, 205, 210, 211, 215, 217, 219, 229, 230, 231, 235, 239, 241, 245, 247, 267, 270, 271, 275, 276, 279, 283, 285, 287, 297, 299, 301, 304, 307, 309, 313, 315, 317, 330, 332, 333, 335, 338, 339, 343, 344, 345, 356, 358, 359, 362, 363, 365, 367, 370, 372, 373, 383, 385, 387, 389, 391, 393, 397, 399, 401, 421, 422, 423, 427, 431, 435, 437, 439, 453, 454, 455, 458, 461, 465, 467, 477, 479, 481, 485 *Chapter Activities: Thinking Like a Geographer, Identifying* 144; *Analyzing* 348, 468 *Chapter Activities: Use Your Foldables® to Explore the Essential Question, Analyzing* 312 *What Do You Think? DBQ: Analyzing* 347 **Teacher Edition:** **ENGAGE: T** 15, 69, 325, 351, 413; **B** 39, 116, 173, 223, 377; **CAC** 147 **TEACH & ASSESS: R₁** 2, 106, 204, 206, 254, 273, 305, 306, 307; **C** 6, 10, 11, 18, 19, 29, 32, 42, 43, 50, 72, 73, 76, 83, 109, 130, 143, 149, 150, 151, 156, 159, 164, 167, 182, 202, 203, 211, 212, 218, 219, 232, 234, 240, 243, 245, 255, 264, 266, 269, 270, 272, 273, 276, 277, 280, 281, 285, 300, 301, 306, 315, 317, 321, 327, 344, 358, 359, 360, 363, 367, 372, 384, 405, 419, 428, 443, 451, 457, 462, 467, 481, 485, 486, 487; **O** 13, 61, 74, 82, 115, 134, 186, 190, 208, 228, 244, 248, 454; **R** 21, 26, 30, 31, 57, 79, 86, 92, 94, 128, 137, 142, 167, 168, 179, 203, 205, 207, 208, 212, 239, 267, 268, 269, 275, 278, 284, 287, 295, 297, 302, 309, 310, 313, 315, 316, 318, 320, 333, 360, 363, 385, 396, 406, 439, 452, 453, 459, 465, 478, 481; **R₂** 29, 140, 216, 254, 274, 440; **C₁** 85, 141, 283, 286, 298, 303, 311, 319, 366, 380; **V** 115, 129, 139, 148, 157, 159, 162, 181, 190, 191, 229, 233, 235, 236, 238, 242, 247, 264, 275, 285, 302, 304, 318, 417, 418, 426, 437, 450; **V₁** 121, 134, 153, 169, 184, 227, 383, 475; **C₂** 141, 168, 215, 319, 338, 434; **V₂** 153, 169, 227, 342, 386; **W** 215; **T** 344, 367 **CLOSE & REFLECT: S** 17; **FQ** 149; **HS** 163; **MI** 199; **TC** 247; **DC** 401, 461; **O** 431
2. Determine central ideas or themes of a text and analyze their development; summarize the key supporting details and ideas.	**Student Edition:** *Reading HELP Desk: Taking Notes, Key Ideas and Details, Identifying* 18, 294, 301; *Describing* 26, 188; *Summarize* 42, 272, 280, 380, 394, 416, 432, 456, 474; *Determining Central Ideas* 57, 65, 480; *Organize* 82, 94, 334, 354, 450; *Summarizing* 116, 200, 212, 310; *Organizing* 176; *Identify* 226; *Determining the Main Idea* 240; *Find the Main Idea* 324, 340; *Describe* 360; *Compare and Contrast* 368 *Reading Progress Check: Determining Central Ideas* 24, 54, 131, 133, 169, 208, 239, 275, 279, 299, 309, 335, 338, 362, 367, 370, 393, 397, 423, 431, 477, 485; *Describing* 81, 87; *Identifying Central Issues* 333; *Summarizing* 467 *Lesson Review: Answering the Guiding Questions, Identifying* 25, 81, 101, 205, 219, 239, 247, 309, 317, 367, 373, 393, 423, 431, 439, 455, 461, 467, 479, 485; *Describing* 33, 231, 373; *Determining Central Ideas* 89, 101, 139, 163, 169, 181, 187, 211, 239, 271, 279, 287, 317, 339, 345, 359, 367, 393, 401, 431, 455, 479 *What Do You Think? DBQ: Describing* 35; *Identifying* 35 *Chapter Assessment: Review the Guiding Questions* 37, 67, 103 *Chapter Assessment: DBQ Analyzing Documents, Citing Text Evidence* 38, 252; *Analyzing* 68; *Identifying* 104, 196; *Determining Central Ideas* 446, 470 *Chapter Assessment: Short Response, Citing Text Evidence* 38; *Identifying* 104; *Determining Central Ideas* 290, 324, 350, 376, 404, 470; *Describing* 290 *Critical Thinking, Determining Central Ideas* 95, 246, 283, 303, 314, 425, 435 *Chapter Activities: Thinking Like a Geographer, Determining Central Ideas* 102, 374; *Integrating Visual Information* 194; *Sequencing Events* 220; *Identifying* 250 *Chapter Assessment: Answering the Guiding Questions* 171, 195, 221, 251, 289, 323, 349, 375, 403, 445, 469 *Chapter Activities: 21st Century Skills, Determining Central Ideas* 468

Codes used for the Teacher Edition pages are the initial caps of the activities.

College and Career Readiness Anchor Standards for Reading

Teacher Edition:

TEACH & ASSESS: **R** 8, 22, 48, 51, 56, 72, 77, 90, 119, 121, 127, 129, 131, 152, 154, 157, 164, 165, 178, 185, 193, 200, 217, 229, 240, 255, 281, 298, 311, 339, 343, 362, 382, 388, 393, 398, 399, 401, 422, 426, 429, 461, 467, 474, 476, 479; **W** 14; **O** 18, 42, 53, 111, 120, 125, 143, 216, 230, 249, 269, 307, 315, 357, 416, 456, 460, 487; **C** 44, 64, 101, 106, 111, 122, 126, 132, 138, 142, 161, 177, 180, 183, 186, 192, 210, 226, 233, 245, 247, 275, 284, 299, 320, 343, 345, 355, 358, 387, 390, 391, 394, 396, 398, 400, 407, 408, 409, 411, 425, 438, 442, 459, 460, 463, 482; **V₁** 53, 244, 317, 483; **V** 62, 73, 234, 241, 331, 332, 438; **C₂** 85, 205, 207, 267, 286, 311, 312, 316, 319, 441; **C₁** 92, 160, 168, 207, 209, 215, 267, 316, 339, 430; **V₂** 133, 342; **T** 161, 166, 230, 231, 237, 244, 333, 337, 421, 434, 457, 460; **R₂** 204, 279, 307, 381; **R₁** 272, 274, 300, 437 CLOSE & REFLECT: **SI** 14; **TC** 51, 65, 487; **A** 71; **S** 112, 225, 327, 345, 353, 359, 415, 467, 473; **D** 143; **ICI** 387, 439

---

3. Analyze how and why individuals, events, or ideas develop and interact over the course of a text.

Student Edition:

Step Into the Place 16, 40, 70, 114, 146, 176, 200, 238, 272, 332, 364, 394, 440, 464, 490, 514, 540, 578, 608, 642, 668, 694, 730, 764, 788
Step Into the Time 16, 40, 70, 114, 146, 176, 200, 238, 272, 332, 364, 394, 440, 464, 490, 514, 540, 578, 608, 642, 668, 694, 730, 764, 788
Critical Thinking: Human–Environment Interaction 23;
Thinking Like a Geographer 29, 134, 158, 167, 187, 208, 253, 288, 309, 343, 371, 374, 380, 412, 436, 507, 529, 544, 683, 699, 801
Reading HELP Desk: Taking Notes, Key Ideas and Details, Identify 52; *Determining Cause and Effect* 72, 740, 778
Human Actions 57
Effects of Migration 79; *Western Colonization* 475–477
Causes and Effects of Urbanization 80–81; *Crowded Cities/Favelas* 257–258; *Urban Growth and Change* 714
Lesson Review: Answering the Guiding Questions, Identifying 81; *Argument Writing* 603
Global Connections: Social Media in a Social World 90–93; *Global Impact* 93, 225, 267, 389, 459, 637, 759; *NAFTA and Its Effects* 222–225; *Rain Forest Resources* 264–267; *Aging of Europe's Population* 386–389; *The Fury of a Tsunami* 456–459; *Sudan: Refugees and Displacement* 634–637; *Unfriendly Invaders* 756–759
Settling the Land 128–131
Challenges Facing the Region 166–169, 219; *Canada's Challenges* 194–195; *Challenges* 217–218; *Connections and Challenges* 262–263; *Challenges and Change* 284–285; *Ongoing Issues* 290–291; *Ongoing Issues* 315–317; *Change and Conflict* 346–349; *Current Challenges* 356–357; *Issues in Northern and Southern Europe* 384–385; *Conflict and Communism* 405–407; *The Regions in the Modern Era* 407–409; *Issues in Eastern Europe and Western Russia* 416–417; *Current Issues in East* 453–455; *Issues in Southeast Asia* 483–485; *Issues in South Asia* 508–509; *Relationships and Challenges* 533–535; *Issues in Southwest Asia* 561–563; *Society in North Africa* 599–601; *North Africa's Future* 601–603; *Challenges* 631–633; *Regional Issues* 661; *Challenges Facing the Regions* 688–689; *Health Issues* 715–716; *Current Issues* 754–755; *Issues Facing the Region* 781–783

Teacher Edition:

ENGAGE: **B** 222, 264, 318, 366, 378, 386, 456, 662, 756; **T** 729 TEACH & ASSESS: **V** 4, 5, 7, 9, 11, 13, 17, 177, 195, 232, 266, 514, 636, 668, 684; **O** 8, 17, 50, 72, 76, 77, 88, 107, 136, 161, 168, 212, 213, 214, 231, 241, 250, 262, 289, 351, 368, 375, 399, 408, 423, 427, 443, 453, 454, 457, 458, 469, 481, 483, 495, 508, 530, 546, 550, 551, 553, 557, 558, 559, 561, 562, 565, 583, 584, 585, 615, 620, 622, 624, 626, 627, 628, 629, 634, 635, 636, 637, 646, 647, 648, 653, 654, 658, 663, 674, 676, 677, 678, 681, 684, 686, 688, 707, 711, 712, 715, 746, 748, 773, 782, 792, 799; **C** 23, 34, 78, 99, 235, 236, 266, 427, 478, 575, 755; **V₂** 50, 201, 758; **W** 168, 195, 239, 587; **R** 168, 264, 340; **C₂** 223, 635, 654, 757; **T** 242, 246, 249; **R₂** 346, 756; **C₁** 349, 757 CLOSE & REFLECT: **TC** 279; **D** 459, 637; **HS** 759; **S** 783

CRAFT AND STRUCTURE

4. Interpret words and phrases as they are used in a text, including determining technical, connotative, and figurative meanings, and analyze how specific word choices shape meaning or tone.

Student Edition:

Reading HELP Desk: Academic Vocabulary 18, 26, 42, 52, 58, 72, 82, 94, 116, 124, 132, 150, 156, 164, 176, 182, 188, 200, 206, 212, 226, 232, 240, 264, 272, 280, 294, 302, 310, 328, 334, 340, 354, 360, 368, 380, 388, 394, 416, 424, 432, 450, 456, 462, 474, 480
Reading HELP Desk, Content Vocabulary 18, 26, 42, 52, 58, 72, 82, 94, 116, 124, 132, 150, 156, 164, 176, 182, 188, 200, 206, 212, 226, 232, 240, 264, 272, 280, 294, 302, 310, 328, 334, 340, 354, 360, 368, 380, 388, 394, 416, 424, 432, 450, 456, 462, 474, 480
Critical Thinking: Determining Word Meanings 25, 80, 89; *Describing* 83, 87, 97, 233
Lesson Review: Reviewing Vocabulary 25, 33, 51, 57, 65, 81, 89, 101, 123, 131, 139, 155, 163, 169, 181, 187, 193, 205, 211, 219, 231, 239, 247, 271, 279, 287, 301, 309, 317, 333, 339, 345, 359, 367, 373, 387, 393, 401, 423, 431, 439, 455, 461, 467, 479, 485
Lesson Review: Answering the Guiding Questions, Determining Word Meanings 25, 51, 65, 81, 169, 193, 247, 461; *Identifying* 33; *Describing* 247
Chapter Assessment: Review the Guiding Questions 37, 67, 103, 145, 171, 195, 221, 289, 323, 349, 375, 403, 445, 469
Reading Progress Check, Identifying 46; *Determining Word Meanings* 60, 75, 344
Chapter Assessment: Short Response, Determining Word Meanings 68, 222, 252, 446
Chapter Assessment: DBQ Analyzing Documents, Determining Word Meanings 104; *Analyzing* 146; *Identifying* 470
Reading HELP Desk: Taking Notes, Key Ideas and Details, Organizing 206
Chapter Activities: Use Your Foldables® to Explore the Essential Question, Informative/Explanatory 468

Teacher Edition:

ENGAGE: **B** 18, 34, 113, 240, 248, 440; **T** 197, 351 TEACH & ASSESS: **R₂** 2, 106, 206, 213, 272, 273, 300, 306, 436, 437; **C₁** 3, 141, 205, 312, 338; **C** 8, 30, 50, 64, 227, 254, 313, 329, 340, 358, 367; **R** 18, 23, 26, 32, 33, 44, 45, 46, 54, 64, 74, 82, 87, 95, 96, 99, 116, 117, 124, 150, 154, 161, 166, 183, 198, 201, 209, 210, 228, 229, 230, 232, 233, 235, 237, 238, 245, 246, 248, 266, 280, 294, 301, 311, 312, 326, 329, 331, 335, 336, 338, 341, 355, 359, 364, 368, 369, 371, 407, 414, 416, 417, 419, 424, 435, 450, 451, 454, 456, 464, 475; **O** 19, 21, 24, 27, 32, 59, 79, 95, 96, 100, 108, 128, 141, 234, 419; **R₁** 29, 140, 151, 216, 265, 279, 346, 381, 436, 440; **V** 50, 59, 62, 176, 191, 285, 337, 417, 458; **V₂** 118; **V₁** 133; **T** 138, 202, 314, 460; **W** 268; **C₂** 303, 314, 430

Codes used for the Teacher Edition pages are the initial caps of the activities.

College and Career Readiness Anchor Standards for Reading

5. Analyze the structure of texts, including how specific sentences, paragraphs, and larger portions of the text (e.g., a section, chapter, scene, or stanza) relate to each other and the whole.

Student Edition:
Lesson Review: Answering the Guiding Questions, Describing 51, 57, 123, 131, 155, 163, 187, 211, 219, 239, 271, 287, 301, 309, 359, 367, 387, 401, 439, 455, 467, 479, 485; *Identifying* 57
Reading HELP Desk: Taking Notes, Key Ideas and Details, Determining Cause and Effect 72, 424, 462; *Sequence* 182, 232, 388
Chapter Assessment: Review the Guiding Questions 171, 289, 403
Chapter Assessment: Short Response, Describing 290
Step Into the Time: Time Line 326
What Do You Think? DBQ: Analyzing 487

Teacher Edition:
PROJECT-BASED LEARNING: H 471B **ENGAGE: B** 52, 113, 261, 480, 486 **TEACH & ASSESS: C** 9, 27, 49, 55, 78, 95, 97, 99, 120, 122, 130, 137, 152, 189, 212, 218, 219, 232, 235, 239, 240, 268, 310, 334, 335, 343, 353, 356, 364, 373, 385, 395, 412, 425, 427, 431, 439, 452, 455, 477; **R** 30, 136, 276, 317, 330, 334, 484; **O** 50, 72, 135, 153, 165, 167, 177, 184, 192, 210, 217, 229, 234, 249, 277, 286, 321, 341, 371, 390, 391, 394, 397, 417, 419, 420, 429, 433, 453, 465, 474, 476; **V** 96, 157, 158, 234, 238, 278, 301, 341, 366, 392, 428, 429, 456, 457, 478, 479; **C₂** 107, 141, 160, 339, 366, 397; **V₂** 169; **T** 202, 453; **C₁** 281, 319, 434, 441; **V₁** 389; **H** 472 **CLOSE & REFLECT: HS** 163

6. Assess how point of view or purpose shapes the content and style of a text.

Student Edition:
Step Into the Time: Identifying Point of View 70
Reading Progress Check: Identifying Point of View 86, 276, 285, 372, 435
Lesson Review: Answering the Guiding Questions, Identifying Point of View 89, 101, 247, 279, 287
Chapter Assessment: Short Response, Identifying Point of View 172, 350, 376
What Do You Think? 248–249, 346–347, 486–487
What Do You Think? DBQ: Identifying Point of View 249, 347, 487
Chapter Assessment: DBQ Analyzing Documents, Citing Text Evidence 290; *Identifying Point of View* 350

Teacher Edition:
PROJECT-BASED LEARNING: H 413B **ENGAGE: B** 486 **TEACH & ASSESS: O** 29, 347, 438, 486; **C** 34, 35, 248, 486, 487; **T** 162, 246, 270, 284, 308, 367, 465; **T₁** 243; **T₂** 283; **H** 414 **CLOSE & REFLECT: CAC** 347; **TC** 487

INTEGRATION OF KNOWLEDGE AND IDEAS

7. Integrate and evaluate content presented in diverse formats and media, including visually and quantitatively, as well as in words.

Student Edition:
Map Skills 5, 7, 9, 11, 13, 47, 108, 109, 110, 111, 112, 127, 130, 160, 179, 186, 207, 213, 214, 235, 237, 242, 256, 257, 258, 259, 260, 273, 277, 299, 304, 321, 338, 362, 365, 395, 400, 408, 409, 410, 411, 412, 418, 443
Foldables® Study Organizer 15, 39, 69, 123, 147, 173, 197, 223, 261, 291, 325, 351, 377, 413, 447, 471
Step Into the Place: Map Focus 16, 40, 70, 124, 148, 174, 198, 224, 262, 292, 326, 352, 378, 414, 448, 472
Reading HELP Desk: Taking Notes, Key Ideas and Details, Identifying 18, 150, 164, 294; *Describing* 26, 58, 156, 188; *Summarize* 42, 272, 280, 380, 394, 416, 432, 456, 474; *Identify* 52, 226; *Determining Cause and Effect* 72, 424, 462; *Organize* 82, 94, 334, 354, 450; *Summarizing* 116, 201, 212, 310; *Describe* 124, 360; *Organize Information* 132, 264; *Organizing* 176, 302; *Sequence* 182, 232, 388; *Determining the Main Idea* 240; *Find the Main Idea* 328, 340; *Compare and Contrast* 368
Critical Thinking: The Geographer's World 21; *Integrating Visual Information* 27, 305; *Describing* 28, 30; *Analyzing Primary Sources* 59, 88, 122, 159, 167, 184, 189, 217, 230, 241, 331, 358, 451, 459, 460
Chart Skills 24, 84
Lesson Review: Answering the Guiding Questions, Analyzing 25; *Integrating Visual Information* 279
Chapter Activities: 21st Century Skills, Integrating Visual Information 36, 66, 102
Chapter Activities: Thinking Like a Geographer, Integrating Visual Information 36, 194, 288; *Identifying* 170; *Listing* 488
Chapter Activities: Geography Activity, Reading Maps 36; *Locating Places* 66, 144, 170, 194, 220, 250, 288, 322, 348, 374, 402, 444, 468, 488
Diagram Skills 43, 45, 64, 98, 203, 453, 483
Graph Skills 48, 73, 99, 126, 139, 443
Infographic 50, 60, 95, 122, 189, 230, 274, 331, 358
Visual Vocabulary 119, 178, 202, 216
Step Into the Time: Time Line 352

Codes used for the Teacher Edition pages are the initial caps of the activities.

College and Career Readiness Anchor Standards for Reading

Teacher Edition:
ENGAGE: **B** 1, 26, 105, 116, 176, 223, 226, 261, 394, 416, 447; **T** 471 TEACH & ASSESS: **V** 2, 3, 4, 5, 7, 8, 9, 10, 11, 13, 16, 17, 19, 25, 26, 29, 30, 40, 41, 43, 44, 45, 46, 47, 48, 49, 50, 52, 54, 58, 59, 60, 62, 63, 64, 70, 71, 73, 74, 75, 76, 79, 83, 88, 91, 93, 95, 97, 98, 99, 100, 108, 109, 110, 111, 112, 114, 115, 117, 120, 123, 127, 129, 136, 141, 142, 148, 149, 158, 159, 162, 163, 165, 175, 177, 179, 180, 183, 185, 186, 187, 189, 198, 199, 200, 201, 202, 214, 216, 224, 225, 229, 235, 242, 255, 256, 257, 258, 259, 260, 262, 263, 265, 270, 273, 284, 292, 293, 296, 303, 304, 305, 318, 319, 320, 321, 326, 327, 328, 330, 332, 336, 343, 347, 352, 353, 354, 357, 361, 362, 363, 364, 365, 368, 372, 378, 379, 384, 392, 395, 397, 398, 406, 407, 408, 409, 410, 411, 412, 414, 415, 417, 421, 432, 433, 438, 441, 449, 450, 454, 458, 459, 463, 464, 465, 466, 472, 473, 474, 476, 477, 478, 483; **O** 2, 4, 5, 6, 7, 8, 9, 10, 12, 13, 17, 18, 20, 21, 22, 24, 27, 28, 29, 31, 34, 41, 42, 43, 45, 46, 47, 48, 49, 50, 52, 53, 54, 55, 56, 58, 59, 60, 63, 64, 71, 72, 73, 74, 75, 76, 77, 78, 82, 83, 84, 85, 87, 90, 91, 92, 94, 95, 97, 98, 99, 106, 108, 110, 112, 116, 117, 119, 120, 124, 125, 126, 127, 128, 129, 130, 132, 133, 134, 135, 136, 137, 138, 140, 141, 142, 143, 147, 149, 150, 151, 152, 153, 154, 156, 157, 158, 159, 160, 161, 162, 164, 165, 166, 167, 168, 175, 176, 177, 178, 179, 180, 182, 183, 184, 185, 186, 188, 189, 190, 191, 192, 199, 200, 201, 202, 203, 204, 206, 207, 208, 209, 210, 212, 213, 214, 215, 216, 217, 218, 225, 226, 227, 228, 229, 230, 232, 233, 234, 235, 236, 237, 238, 240, 241, 242, 243, 244, 245, 246, 249, 254, 256, 257, 258, 259, 260, 263, 264, 265, 266, 267, 268, 269, 270, 272, 273, 274, 275, 276, 278, 280, 281, 282, 283, 284, 285, 286, 293, 294, 295, 296, 297, 298, 299, 300, 302, 303, 304, 305, 306, 307, 308, 310, 311, 313, 314, 315, 316, 318, 319, 320, 321, 327, 328, 329, 330, 331, 332, 334, 335, 336, 337, 338, 340, 341, 342, 343, 344, 347, 353, 354, 355, 356, 357, 358, 360, 361, 362, 363, 364, 365, 366, 368, 369, 370, 371, 372, 379, 380, 381, 382, 383, 384, 385, 386, 388, 389, 390, 392, 394, 395, 396, 397, 398, 399, 400, 406, 408, 409, 410, 411, 412, 415, 416, 417, 418, 419, 420, 421, 422, 424, 425, 426, 427, 428, 429, 430, 432, 433, 434, 435, 436, 437, 440, 441, 442, 443, 450, 451, 452, 453, 454, 456, 457, 458, 459, 460, 462, 463, 464, 465, 466, 473, 474, 475, 476, 477, 478, 480, 481, 482, 483, 484; **C** 4, 12, 24, 47, 72, 90, 108, 110, 112, 128, 143, 154, 188, 232, 249, 256, 258, 263, 265, 326, 340, 410, 411, 420, 426, 443, 454, 457; **V₁** 6, 12, 22, 28, 107, 118, 125, 134, 174, 217, 294, 342, 383, 386, 391, 442, 448, 449; **V₂** 6, 12, 22, 28, 53, 107, 125, 133, 134, 153, 174, 184, 227, 342, 383, 386, 389, 391, 442, 448, 475; **T** 14, 20, 32, 33, 52, 89, 167, 218, 304, 370, 406, 487; **R** 58, 84, 176, 187, 295, 472; **C₂** 61, 380; **C₁** 91, 338; **R₂** 151, 254; **T₁** 243; **W** 341, 429
CLOSE & REFLECT: **MC** 33; **IVI** 115; **HS** 155; **RR** 231; **TC** 247; **S** 327, 353, 415

8. Delineate and evaluate the argument and specific claims in a text, including the validity of the reasoning as well as the relevance and sufficiency of the evidence.

Student Edition:
What Do You Think? 34–35, 248–249, 346–347, 486–487
What Do You Think? DBQ: Citing Text Evidence 35; *Describing* 35; *Analyzing* 487; *Identifying Point of View* 487
Global Connections 90–93, 140–143, 318–321, 440–443
Lesson Review: Answering the Guiding Questions, Argument Writing 155, 439
Critical Thinking: Analyzing 249, 347, 487

Teacher Edition:
PROJECT-BASED LEARNING: **H** 413B ENGAGE: **B** 486 TEACH & ASSESS: **C** 7, 34, 35, 248, 307, 486, 487; **T** 89, 100, 162, 246, 270, 284, 308, 337, 367, 465; **C₁** 107; **O** 248, 346, 412, 438, 486; **T₂** 283; **C₂** 283; **R₂** 346; **H** 414 CLOSE & REFLECT: **HS** 249; **CAC** 347; **TC** 487

9. Analyze how two or more texts address similar themes or topics in order to build knowledge or to compare the approaches the authors take.

Student Edition:
Chapter Activities: 21st Century Skills, Evaluating 220

Teacher Edition:
PROJECT-BASED LEARNING: **H** 413B ENGAGE: **B** 346, 486 TEACH & ASSESS: **C** 248; **O** 248, 346, 412, 486; **W** 231, 244; **T** 162, 246, 258, 270, 305, 308, 337, 367, 427, 431, 465, 487; **T₂** 283; **R₂** 346 CLOSE & REFLECT: **CAC** 347; **TC** 487

RANGE OF READING AND LEVEL OF TEXT COMPLEXITY

10. Read and comprehend complex literary and informational texts independently and proficiently.

Student Edition:
Thinking Like a Geographer 29, 120, 191, 213, 228, 367, 383, 485
Think Again 31, 78, 96, 125, 155, 239, 269, 301, 331, 396
What Do You Think? 34–35, 248–249, 346–347, 486–487
Chapter Assessment: Exploring the Essential Question, Informative/Explanatory Writing 36
Chapter Assessment: DBQ Analyzing Documents 38, 68, 104, 146, 172, 196, 222, 252, 290, 324, 350, 376, 404, 446, 470
Chapter Assessment: Short Response, Analyzing 38, 68, 104, 146, 172, 196, 222, 252, 290, 324, 350, 376, 404, 446, 470
Global Connections 90–93, 140–143, 318–321, 440–443
Infographic 122, 189, 230, 274, 331, 358
Chapter Activities: 21st Century Skills, Evaluating 220

Teacher Edition:
TEACH & ASSESS: **W** 244; **T** 367

Codes used for the Teacher Edition pages are the initial caps of the activities.

Reading Standards for Literacy in History/Social Studies 6–8

KEY IDEAS AND DETAILS

RH.6-8.1. Cite specific textual evidence to support analysis of primary and secondary sources.

Lesson Review: Answering the Guiding Questions, Analyzing 25, 33, 51, 65, 81, 89, 123, 131, 139, 155, 163, 169, 181, 205, 211, 219, 247, 271, 287, 301, 333, 339, 345, 367, 373, 393, 401, 455, 479, 485; *Describing* 51, 58, 139, 317, 322, 333, 339, 345, 387; *Citing Text Evidence* 57, 123, 231, 239, 467; *Identifying* 65, 123, 155, 193, 231, 359, 387
What Do You Think? DBQ: Citing Text Evidence 35; *Identifying* 38, *Analyzing* 249, 347, 487
Chapter Assessment: Short Response, Analyzing 38, 68, 172, 222, 252, 324, 404, 446, 470; *Question 9* 104
Reading HELP Desk: Taking Notes, Key Ideas and Details, Identify 52; *Describe* 124; *Organize Information* 132; *Identifying* 150; *Describing* 156; *Categorizing* 206
Chapter Assessment: Review the Guiding Questions 67, 103, 145, 171, 221, 251, 288, 323, 349, 375, 403, 469
Chapter Assessment: DBQ Analyzing Documents, Identifying 68, 172, 222, 376; *Citing Text Evidence* 146, 324; *Analyzing* 172, 196, 222, 252, 290, 324, 404, 446; *Analyzing Information* 350; *Determining Word Meanings* 376
Chapter Activities: Thinking Like a Geographer, Identifying 144; *Analyzing* 348, 468

RH.6-8.2. Determine the central ideas or information of a primary or secondary source; provide an accurate summary of the source distinct from prior knowledge or opinions.

Reading HELP Desk: Taking Notes, Key Ideas and Details, Identifying 18, 294, 301; *Describing* 26, 188; *Summarize* 42, 272, 280, 380, 394, 416, 432, 456, 474; *Determining Central Ideas* 57, 65, 480; *Organize* 82, 94, 334, 354, 450; *Organizing* 176; *Summarizing* 116, 200, 212, 310; *Identify* 226; *Determining the Main Idea* 240; *Find the Main Idea* 324, 340; *Describe* 360; *Compare and Contrast* 368
Lesson Review: Answering the Guiding Questions, Identifying 25, 81, 101, 205, 219, 239, 247, 309, 317, 367, 373, 393, 423, 431, 439, 455, 461, 467, 479, 485; *Describing* 33, 231, 373; *Determining Central Ideas* 89, 101, 139, 163, 169, 181, 187, 211, 239, 271, 279, 287, 317, 339, 345, 359, 367, 393, 401, 431, 455, 479
What Do You Think? DBQ: Describing 35; *Identifying* 35
Chapter Assessment: Review the Guiding Questions 37, 67, 103
Chapter Assessment: DBQ Analyzing Documents, Citing Text Evidence 38, 252; *Analyzing* 68; *Identifying* 104, 196; *Determining Central Ideas* 446, 470
Chapter Assessment: Short Response, Citing Text Evidence 38; *Identifying* 104; *Determining Central Ideas* 290, 324, 350, 376, 404, 470; *Describing* 290
Chapter Activities: Thinking Like a Geographer, Determining Central Ideas 102, 374; *Integrating Visual Information* 194; *Sequencing Events* 220; *Identifying* 250
Chapter Assessment: Answering the Guiding Questions 171, 195, 221, 251, 289, 323, 349, 375, 403, 445, 469
Chapter Activities: 21st Century Skills, Determining Central Ideas 468

RH.6-8.3. Identify key steps in a text's description of a process related to history/social studies (e.g., how a bill becomes law, how interest rates are raised or lowered).

Lesson Review: Reviewing Vocabulary 309

CRAFT AND STRUCTURE

RH.6-8.4. Determine the meaning of words and phrases as they are used in a text, including vocabulary specific to domains related to history/social studies.

Reading HELP Desk: Academic Vocabulary 18, 26, 42, 52, 58, 72, 82, 94, 116, 124, 132, 150, 156, 164, 176, 182, 188, 200, 206, 212, 226, 232, 240, 264, 272, 280, 294, 302, 310, 328, 334, 340, 354, 360, 368, 380, 388, 394, 416, 424, 432, 450, 456, 462, 474, 480
Reading HELP Desk: Content Vocabulary 18, 26, 42, 52, 58, 72, 82, 94, 116, 124, 132, 150, 156, 164, 176, 182, 188, 200, 206, 212, 226, 232, 240, 264, 272, 280, 294, 302, 310, 328, 334, 340, 354, 360, 368, 380, 388, 394, 416, 424, 432, 450, 456, 462, 474, 480
Lesson Review: Reviewing Vocabulary 25, 33, 51, 57, 65, 81, 89, 101, 123, 131, 139, 155, 163, 169, 181, 187, 193, 205, 211, 219, 231, 239, 247, 271, 279, 287, 301, 309, 317, 333, 339, 345, 359, 367, 373, 387, 393, 401, 423, 431, 439, 455, 461, 467, 479, 485
Lesson Review: Answering the Guiding Questions, Determining Word Meanings 25, 51, 65, 81, 169, 193, 247, 461; *Identifying* 33; *Describing* 247
Chapter Assessment: Review the Guiding Questions 37, 67, 103, 145, 171, 195, 221, 289, 323, 349, 375, 403, 445, 469
Chapter Assessment: Short Response, Determining Word Meanings 68, 222, 252, 446
Chapter Assessment: DBQ Analyzing Documents, Determining Word Meanings 104; *Analyzing* 146; *Identifying* 470
Reading HELP Desk: Taking Notes, Key Ideas and Details, Organizing 206
Chapter Activities: Use Your Foldables® to Explore the Essential Question, Informative/Explanatory 468

RH.6-8.5. Describe how a text presents information (e.g., sequentially, comparatively, causally).

Lesson Review: Answering the Guiding Questions, Describing 51, 57, 123, 131, 155, 163, 187, 211, 219, 239, 271, 287, 301, 309, 359, 367, 387, 401, 439, 455, 467, 479, 485; *Identifying* 57
Reading HELP Desk: Taking Notes, Key Ideas and Details, Determining Cause and Effect 72, 424, 462; *Sequence* 182, 232, 388
Chapter Assessment: Review the Guiding Questions 171, 289, 403
Chapter Assessment: Short Response, Describing 290
Step Into the Time: Time Line 326
What Do You Think? DBQ: Analyzing 487

Reading Standards for Literacy in History/Social Studies 6–8

RH.6-8.6. Identify aspects of a text that reveal an author's point of view or purpose (e.g., loaded language, inclusion or avoidance of particular facts).	*Step Into the Time: Identifying Point of View 70* *Lesson Review: Answering the Guiding Questions, Identifying Point of View 89, 101, 247, 279, 287* *Chapter Assessment: Short Response, Identifying Point of View 172, 350, 376* *What Do You Think? DBQ: Identifying Point of View 249, 347, 487* *Chapter Assessment: DBQ Analyzing Documents, Citing Text Evidence 290; Identifying Point of View 350*

INTEGRATION OF KNOWLEDGE AND IDEAS

RH.6-8.7. Integrate visual information (e.g., in charts, graphs, photographs, videos, or maps) with other information in print and digital texts.	*Reading HELP Desk: Taking Notes, Key Ideas and Details, Identifying 18, 150, 164, 294; Describing 26, 58, 156, 188; Summarize 42, 272, 280, 380, 394, 416, 432, 456, 474; Identify 52, 226; Determining Cause and Effect 72, 424, 462; Organize 82, 94, 334, 354, 450; Summarizing 116, 201, 212, 310; Describe 124, 360; Organizing 176, 302; Organize Information 132, 264; Sequence 182, 232, 388; Determining the Main Idea 240; Find the Main Idea 328, 340; Compare and Contrast 368* *Lesson Review: Answering the Guiding Questions, Analyzing 25; Integrating Visual Information 279* *Chapter Activities: 21st Century Skills, Integrating Visual Information 36, 102* *Chapter Activities: Thinking Like a Geographer, Integrating Visual Information 36, 194, 288; Identifying 170; Listing 488* *Chapter Activities: Geography Activity, Reading Maps 36; Locating Places 66, 144, 170, 194, 220, 250, 288, 322, 348, 374, 402, 444, 468, 488* *Step Into the Time: Time Line 352*
RH.6-8.8. Distinguish among fact, opinion, and reasoned judgment in a text.	*Chapter Activities: 21st Century Skills, Integrating Visual Information 36* *Lesson Review: Answering the Guiding Questions, Distinguishing Fact From Opinion 57, 461* *Chapter Assessment: Short Response, Distinguishing Fact from Opinion 146* *Reading HELP Desk: Taking Notes, Key Ideas and Details, Identifying 164* *What Do You Think? DBQ: Identifying Point of View 249; Analyzing 249; Distinguishing Fact from Opinion 347*
RH.6-8.9. Analyze the relationship between a primary and secondary source on the same topic.	*Chapter Activities: 21st Century Skills, Evaluating 220*

RANGE OF READING AND LEVEL OF TEXT COMPLEXITY

RH.6-8.10. By the end of grade 8, read and comprehend history/social studies texts in the grades 6–8 text complexity band independently and proficiently.	*Chapter Assessment: DBQ Analyzing Documents, Citing Text Evidence 38, 146, 252, 290, 324; Identifying 38, 68, 104, 172, 196, 376, 470; Analyzing 68, 146, 172, 196, 252, 290, 324, 394, 446; Determining Word Meanings 104, 376; Analyzing Information 350; Identifying Point of View 350; Determining Central Ideas 446, 470* *Chapter Assessment: Short Response, Analyzing 38, 68, 172, 196, 222, 252, 404, 446, 470; Determining Word Meanings 68, 252, 446; Identifying 104; Question 9 104; Identifying Point of View 146, 172, 350; Citing Text Evidence 196; Distinguishing Fact from Opinion 146; Describing 290; Determining Central Ideas 290, 324, 350, 404, 470* *Chapter Activities: 21st Century Skills, Evaluating 220* *What Do You Think? DBQ: Analyzing 487*

Common Core State Standards for English-Language Arts and Literacy in History/Social Studies, Science, and Technical Subjects

The following pages contain correlation charts to the Common Core State Standards. The first chart contains the College and Career Readiness (CCR) Anchor Standards for Writing. The chart that follows the CCR Anchor Standards for Writing chart identifies specifically what students should understand and be able to do by the end of grades 6–8. The CCR and grade-specific standards are necessary complements—the former providing broad standards, the latter providing additional specificity—that together define the skills and understandings that all students must demonstrate.

College and Career Readiness Anchor Standards for Writing	
TEXT TYPES AND PURPOSES	
1. Write arguments to support claims in an analysis of substantive topics or texts using valid reasoning and relevant and sufficient evidence.	**Student Edition:** *Global Connections: Thinking Like a Geographer, Human Geography* 93 *Lesson Review: Answering the Guiding Questions, Argument Writing* 131, 139, 155, 169, 287, 333, 367, 393, 401, 439, 467 *Chapter Assessment: Extended Response, Argument Writing* 378 *Chapter Activities: Thinking Like a Geographer, Determining Central Ideas* 402 **Teacher Edition:** **TEACH & ASSESS: C** 23, 259; **W** 31, 55, 93, 98, 155, 208, 219, 231, 238, 249, 271, 275, 276, 297, 306, 332, 335, 341, 345, 347, 356, 362, 435, 463; **O** 35, 93, 300, 487; **V** 209 **CLOSE & REFLECT: TC** 35; **HS** 249; **CAC** 347
2. Write informative/explanatory texts to examine and convey complex ideas and information clearly and accurately through the effective selection, organization, and analysis of content.	**Student Edition:** *Step Into the Time: Describing* 16; *Drawing Evidence* 40; *Time Line* 114, 148, 174, 198, 224, 262, 292, 326, 414, 448, 472 *Lesson Review: Answering the Guiding Questions, Informative/Explanatory Writing* 25, 33, 51, 57, 81, 89, 101, 123, 163, 181, 193, 205, 239, 271, 279, 301, 317, 339, 345, 359, 423, 455, 479; *Analyzing* 89; *Argument Writing* 211 *Chapter Activities: Exploring the Essential Question, Informative/Explanatory Writing* 36, 102 *Chapter Activities: 21st Century Skills, Integrating Visual Information* 36, 66; *Describing* 144; *Analyzing* 170, 194; *Determining Central Ideas* 468 *Chapter Assessment: Extended Response, Informative/Explanatory Writing* 38, 68, 104, 146, 172, 196, 222, 252, 290, 324, 404, 446, 470; *Analyzing* 350 *Chapter Activities: Use Your Foldables® to Explore the Essential Question, Informative/Explanatory* 66; *Informative/Explanatory Writing* 144, 250, 288, 322, 348, 374, 402, 444, 468, 488; *Analyzing* 170, 194, 220 *Chapter Activities: Thinking Like a Geographer, Describing* 66; *Determining Central Ideas* 102 *Chapter Activities: Geography Activity, Identifying* 102 *Global Connections: Thinking Like a Geographer, Environment and Society* 443 **Teacher Edition:** **PROJECT-BASED LEARNING: DH** 15B, 39B, 147B, 197B, 223B, 261B, 325B, 351B, 413B, 447B; **H** 113B, 173B, 223B, 377B **ENGAGE: B** 58, 380 **TEACH & ASSESS: O** 10, 19, 54, 80, 83, 100, 125, 166, 191, 202, 203, 209, 230, 237, 245, 269, 274, 277, 281, 282, 295, 298, 303, 305, 306, 312, 313, 329, 337, 342, 357, 361, 369, 389, 419, 428, 429, 432, 435, 438, 451, 456, 458; **V** 10, 73, 384; **W₁** 14; **DH** 16, 40, 148, 198, 224, 262, 326, 352, 414, 448; **T** 20, 132, 143, 152, 158, 161, 162, 166, 192, 202, 230, 231, 237, 243, 244, 246, 315, 333, 337, 367, 373, 434, 457; **W** 44, 48, 57, 60, 79, 112, 126, 129, 152, 166, 181, 187, 199, 204, 215, 225, 234, 241, 244, 282, 283, 293, 296, 299, 317, 327, 353, 370, 381, 383, 393, 399, 412, 415, 420, 425, 443, 449, 453, 460, 465, 473, 477, 483, 485; **H** 114, 174, 224, 378; **V₂** 342; **C** 364; **R₂** 381 **CLOSE & REFLECT: A** 71; **S** 112, 359; **RS** 181; **E** 219, 279, 367; **D** 393
3. Write narratives to develop real or imagined experiences or events using effective technique, well-chosen details and well-structured event sequences.	**Student Edition:** *Lesson Review: Answering the Guiding Questions, Narrative Writing* 65, 187, 219, 231, 247, 309, 373, 387, 431, 461, 485 *Step Into the Time: Identifying Point of View* 70 *Global Connections: Thinking Like a Geographer, Human Geography* 321 **Teacher Edition:** **PROJECT-BASED LEARNING: DH** 69B; **H** 173B **TEACH & ASSESS: W₂** 14; **W** 62, 86, 157, 158, 165, 230, 260, 268, 313, 423, 429, 433, 466, 481; **DH** 70; **V** 71; **T** 85; **H** 174

Codes used for the Teacher Edition pages are the initial caps of the activities.

College and Career Readiness Anchor Standards for Writing

PRODUCTION AND DISTRIBUTION OF WRITING

4. Produce clear and coherent writing in which the development, organization, and style are appropriate to task, purpose, and audience.

Student Edition:
Step Into the Time: Describing 16; *Drawing Evidence* 40; *Identifying Point of View* 70; *Time Line* 148, 174, 198, 224, 262, 292, 326, 414, 448, 472
Lesson Review: Answering the Guiding Questions, Informative/Explanatory Writing 33, 51, 57, 81, 101, 123, 163, 181, 193, 271, 279, 301, 317, 345, 359, 455, 470; *Narrative Writing* 65, 187, 219, 231, 247, 309, 373, 387, 431, 461, 485; *Analyzing* 89; *Argument Writing* 131, 139, 155, 169, 211, 287, 367, 393, 401, 439, 467
Chapter Activities: Exploring the Essential Question, Informative/Explanatory Writing 36
Chapter Activities: 21st Century Skills, Integrating Visual Information 36, 322; *Determining Central Ideas* 468
Chapter Assessment: Extended Response, Informative/Explanatory Writing 38, 68, 104, 146, 222, 252, 290, 446; *Analyzing* 350; *Argument Writing* 378
Global Connections: Thinking Like a Geographer, Human Geography 93, 321
Chapter Activities: Geography Activity, Identifying 102
Chapter Activities: Use Your Foldables® to Explore the Essential Question, Informative/Explanatory Writing 194, 220, 239, 288, 348, 444, 468, 488

Teacher Edition:
PROJECT-BASED LEARNING: **DH** 15B, 197B, 223B, 261B, 325B, 447B; **H** 113B, 173B, 223B ENGAGE: **B** 58; TEACH & ASSESS: **V** 10; **W₂** 14; **DH** 16, 198, 224, 262, 326; **C** 23; **W** 48, 55, 57, 62, 79, 86, 93, 98, 126, 129, 152, 155, 157, 158, 166, 181, 187, 204, 208, 215, 219, 230, 231, 234, 238, 244, 249, 260, 268, 271, 275, 276, 282, 283, 296, 297, 313, 315, 317, 327, 332, 335, 341, 345, 347, 353, 356, 362, 370, 381, 383, 399, 412, 415, 420, 423, 425, 429, 433, 435, 443, 453, 460, 463, 466, 477, 481, 485; **O** 100, 202, 203, 237, 277, 306, 337, 342, 451, 458; **H** 114, 174, 224; **T** 132, 158, 166, 192, 202, 230, 237, 244, 246, 337, 367, 373, 393, 448, 487; **T₁** 243 CLOSE & REFLECT: **A** 71; **HS** 249; **CAC** 347; **E** 367

5. Develop and strengthen writing as needed by planning, revising, editing, rewriting, or trying a new approach.

Student Edition:
Chapter Activities: 21st Century Skills, Integrating Visual Information 322; *Peer Review* 488

Teacher Edition:
PROJECT-BASED LEARNING: **DH** 15B, 197B; **H** 197B, 447B ENGAGE: **B** 173, 199, 294 TEACH & ASSESS: **O** 3, 107; **DH** 16, 198; **W** 31, 44, 57, 62, 79, 86, 157, 165, 199, 204, 208, 230, 282, 285, 293, 296, 370, 429, 433, 435, 443, 449; **V** 71, 438; **H** 198, 448, 472; **T** 387 CLOSE & REFLECT: **IVI** 115; **TC** 193; **HS** 443

6. Use technology, including the Internet, to produce and publish writing and to interact and collaborate with others.

Student Edition:
Chapter Activities: 21st Century Skills, Integrating Visual Information 66, 250, 288, 444; *Describing* 144, 402; *Identifying* 348; *Determining Central Ideas* 468
Global Connections: Thinking Like a Geographer, Environment and Society 143
Chapter Assessment: Extended Response, Informative/Explanatory Writing 172, 324
Chapter Activities: Use Your Foldables® to Explore the Essential Question, Informative/Explanatory Writing 374

Teacher Edition:
PROJECT-BASED LEARNING: **DH** 15B, 39B, 69B, 113B, 147B, 173B, 197B, 223B, 261B, 291B, 325B, 351B, 377B, 413B, 447B, 471B; **H** 147B, 223B, 261B, 325B, 377B, 413B ENGAGE: **B** 291 TEACH & ASSESS: **O** 12, 26, 35, 56, 71, 80, 86, 90, 91, 93, 111, 128, 130, 142, 153, 154, 168, 178, 180, 185, 209, 236, 258, 260, 274, 319, 320, 321, 347, 366, 385, 411, 412, 418, 435, 440, 443, 477, 483; **DH** 16, 40, 70, 114, 148, 174, 198, 224, 262, 292, 326, 352, 378, 414, 448, 472; **T** 20, 23, 32, 33, 46, 49, 52, 54, 59, 65, 74, 75, 80, 83, 84, 86, 96, 100, 101, 111, 118, 127, 135, 143, 152, 158, 159, 161, 162, 163, 166, 167, 178, 184, 192, 201, 202, 210, 211, 213, 217, 218, 227, 228, 229, 230, 231, 236, 237, 244, 246, 258, 266, 270, 274, 277, 281, 286, 296, 298, 300, 304, 305, 308, 311, 314, 315, 337, 344, 351, 357, 358, 367, 373, 382, 384, 387, 392, 396, 406, 421, 427, 431, 434, 435, 438, 451, 455, 457, 460, 465, 472, 476, 478, 480, 482, 487; **C** 50, 299; **W** 86, 112, 152, 155, 187, 215, 219, 231, 299, 317, 332, 335, 345, 347, 362, 370, 381, 383, 393, 399, 412, 420, 423, 425, 433, 443, 463, 477, 483, 485; **H** 148, 224, 262, 326, 378, 414; **V₂** 153; **V** 157, 209, 238, 244, 264, 366; **T₁** 243, 283; **T₂** 243, 283; **R** 294; **C₂** 303 CLOSE & REFLECT: **TC** 51, 131; **D** 93, 321; **M** 260; **FQ** 301; **HS** 443

Codes used for the Teacher Edition pages are the initial caps of the activities.

College and Career Readiness Anchor Standards for Writing

RESEARCH TO BUILD AND PRESENT KNOWLEDGE

7. Conduct short as well as more sustained research projects based on focused questions, demonstrating understanding of the subject under investigation.	**Student Edition:** *Chapter Activities: 21st Century Skills, Integrating Visual Information 36, 66, 250, 322, 374, 444; Describing 144, 402; Analyzing 170, 194; Determining Central Ideas 468* *Chapter Assessment: Extended Response, Informative/Explanatory Writing 38, 68, 104, 172, 290, 324, 404; Argument Writing 376* *Step Into the Time: Identifying Point of View 70* *Chapter Activities: Thinking Like a Geographer, Determining Central Ideas 102; Identifying 322* *Global Connections: Thinking Like a Geographer, Physical Geography 143; The Uses of Geography 443; Environment and Society 443* *Chapter Activities: Use Your Foldables® to Explore the Essential Question, Informative/Explanatory Writing 374* **Teacher Edition:** **PROJECT-BASED LEARNING: DH** 69B, 147B, 173B, 223B, 261B, 325B, 351B, 413B, 447B, 471B; **H** 147B, 223B, 261B, 413B **ENGAGE: B** 291 **TEACH & ASSESS: T** 20, 23, 33, 49, 52, 54, 59, 65, 74, 75, 80, 83, 84, 85, 86, 96, 101, 111, 118, 127, 135, 152, 158, 159, 161, 162, 166, 167, 184, 192, 201, 202, 210, 211, 213, 217, 227, 228, 231, 236, 237, 244, 246, 266, 281, 286, 296, 298, 299, 304, 305, 315, 333, 337, 344, 351, 358, 367, 373, 387, 392, 396, 406, 421, 427, 431, 434, 435, 438, 457, 472, 478, 482; **C** 23; **O** 35, 71, 80, 86, 90, 111, 168, 209, 274, 319, 320, 385, 411, 412, 440; **V** 54, 209; **W** 60, 98, 129, 152, 155, 181, 187, 204, 215, 219, 230, 231, 238, 241, 317, 332, 335, 345, 347, 362, 370, 381, 383, 393, 399, 412, 420, 423, 425, 443, 455, 463, 473, 477, 483, 485; **DH** 70, 148, 174, 224, 262, 326, 352, 414, 448, 472; **R** 81; **H** 148, 224, 262, 414; **T₂** 243, 283 **CLOSE & REFLECT: TC** 51; **D** 93, 321; **M** 260; **HS** 443
8. Gather relevant information from multiple print and digital sources, assess the credibility and accuracy of each source, and integrate the information while avoiding plagiarism.	**Student Edition:** *Chapter Activities: 21st Century Skills, Integrating Visual Information 36, 66, 374, 444; Analyzing 170, 194; Evaluating 220; Identifying 348; Describing 402; Determining Central Ideas 468* *Chapter Assessment: Extended Response, Informative/Explanatory Writing 38, 68, 104, 172, 290, 324, 404; Argument Writing 376* *Step Into the Time: Identifying Point of View 70* *Chapter Activities: Exploring the Essential Question, Informative/Explanatory Writing 102* *Chapter Activities: Thinking Like a Geographer, Determining Central Ideas 102* *Global Connections: Thinking Like a Geographer, Physical Geography 143; The Uses of Geography 443; Environment and Society 443* *Chapter Activities: Use Your Foldables® to Explore the Essential Question, Informative/Explanatory Writing 250, 374* **Teacher Edition:** **PROJECT-BASED LEARNING: DH** 69B, 147B, 173B, 223B, 261B, 325B, 351B, 377B, 413B, 447B, 471B; **H** 147B, 223B, 261B, 377B, 413B **ENGAGE: B** 291 **TEACH & ASSESS: O** 3, 30, 35, 71, 80, 111, 128, 130, 142, 153, 154, 168, 178, 180, 185, 209, 236, 260, 274, 319, 320, 321, 347, 366, 385, 411, 412, 418, 420, 435, 440, 443, 477, 483; **T** 20, 23, 32, 33, 46, 52, 54, 59, 65, 74, 75, 80, 83, 84, 85, 86, 90, 96, 101, 111, 118, 127, 135, 143, 152, 158, 159, 161, 162, 163, 166, 167, 178, 184, 192, 201, 202, 210, 211, 213, 217, 218, 227, 228, 229, 230, 231, 236, 237, 244, 246, 258, 266, 270, 274, 277, 281, 286, 295, 296, 298, 300, 304, 305, 308, 311, 314, 315, 333, 337, 344, 351, 357, 358, 367, 373, 382, 384, 387, 392, 396, 406, 421, 427, 431, 434, 435, 438, 451, 455, 457, 460, 465, 472, 478, 480, 482; **C** 23, 299, 387; **V** 54, 94, 157, 212, 238, 264, 366, 436; **W** 60, 86, 98, 129, 152, 155, 187, 204, 215, 219, 230, 231, 238, 241, 299, 317, 332, 335, 345, 347, 362, 370, 381, 383, 393, 399, 412, 423, 425, 433, 443, 463, 473, 477, 481, 483, 485; **DH** 70, 148, 174, 224, 262, 326, 352, 378, 414, 448, 472; **R** 81; **H** 148, 181, 224, 262, 378, 414; **V₂** 153; **T₂** 243, 283; **T₁** 283; **C₂** 303 **CLOSE & REFLECT: D** 93, 321; **TC** 131; **FQ** 205, 301, 455; **M** 260; **HS** 443
9. Draw evidence from literary or informational texts to support analysis, reflection, and research.	**Student Edition:** *Chapter Assessment: Extended Response, Informative/Explanatory Writing 38; Informative/Explanatory 324* *Chapter Activities: 21st Century Skills, Integrating Visual Information 66; Describing 402; Determining Central Ideas 468* *Step Into the Time: Identifying Point of View 70* *Chapter Activities: Thinking Like a Geographer, Determining Central Ideas 102* *Chapter Assessment: Short Response, Informative/Explanatory Writing 172* *Lesson Review: Answering the Guiding Questions, Narrative Writing 231, 431, 485; Argument Writing 333; Informative/Explanatory Writing 423, 479; Citing Text Evidence 467* *Chapter Assessment: Thinking Like a Geographer, Identifying 250, 444; Analyzing 348* *Reading HELP Desk: Taking Notes, Key Ideas and Details, Organize Information 264* *What Do You Think? DBQ: Identifying Point of View 487* **Teacher Edition:** **PROJECT-BASED LEARNING: DH** 147B, 223B, 261B, 325B, 351B, 413B, 447B, 471B; **H** 147B, 223B, 377B **TEACH & ASSESS: T** 20, 23, 33, 46, 49, 52, 54, 59, 65, 96, 143, 152, 157, 158, 159, 161, 162, 166, 192, 201, 202, 213, 217, 230, 237, 246, 296, 315, 333, 337, 357, 367, 373, 387, 427, 434, 451, 455, 457, 460; **C** 23; **V** 54, 94, 117, 157, 274, 384; **W** 98, 129, 152, 155, 158, 165, 181, 187, 204, 215, 219, 231, 238, 241, 299, 317, 332, 335, 345, 347, 362, 370, 381, 383, 393, 399, 412, 420, 421, 423, 425, 443, 463, 477, 483, 485; **DH** 148, 224, 262, 326, 352, 414, 448, 472; **H** 148, 224, 378; **O** 168, 411; **C₂** 380 **CLOSE & REFLECT: TC** 35; **A** 71; **M** 260; **D** 321; **O** 431

Codes used for the Teacher Edition pages are the initial caps of the activities.

College and Career Readiness Anchor Standards for Writing

10. Write routinely over extended time frames (time for research, reflection, and revision) and shorter time frames (a single sitting or a day or two) for a range of tasks, purposes, and audiences.

Student Edition:

Foldables® Study Organizer 15, 39, 69, 123, 147, 173, 197, 223, 261, 291, 325, 351, 377, 413, 447, 471

Step Into the Time: Describing 16; *Drawing Evidence* 40; *Identifying Point of View* 70; *Time Line* 114, 148, 174, 198, 224, 262, 292, 326, 378, 414, 448, 472

Reading HELP Desk: Taking Notes, Key Ideas and Details 18, 26, 42, 52, 58, 72, 82, 94, 116, 124, 132, 150, 156, 164, 176, 182, 188, 200, 206, 212, 226, 232, 240, 264, 272, 280, 294, 302, 310, 328, 334, 340, 354, 360, 368, 380, 388, 394, 416, 424, 432, 450, 456, 462, 474, 480

Lesson Review: Answering the Guiding Questions, Informative/Explanatory Writing 25, 33, 51, 57, 81, 89, 101, 123, 163, 181, 193, 205, 239, 271, 279, 301, 317, 339, 345, 359, 423, 455, 479; *Narrative Writing* 65, 187, 219, 231, 247, 309, 373, 387, 431, 461, 485; *Analyzing* 89; *Argument Writing* 131, 139, 155, 169, 211, 287, 333, 367, 393, 401, 439, 467

Chapter Activities: Exploring the Essential Question, Informative/Explanatory Writing 36

Chapter Activities: 21st Century Skills, Integrating Visual Information 36, 66, 250, 288, 322, 444; *Describing* 144; *Analyzing* 194; *Identifying* 348; *Determining Central Ideas* 468; *Peer Review* 488

Chapter Assessment: Extended Response, Informative/Explanatory Writing 38, 68, 104, 146, 172, 196, 222, 252, 290, 324, 404, 446, 470; *Analyzing* 350; *Argument Writing* 376

Chapter Activities: Use Your Foldables® to Explore the Essential Question, Informative/Explanatory 66, 144, 170, 194, 220, 250, 288, 348, 374, 402, 444, 468, 488; *Analyzing* 170

Chapter Activities: Thinking Like a Geographer, Describing 66; *Determining Central Ideas* 102, 374, 402; *Identifying* 144, 250, 322; *Integrating Visual Information* 194, 288, 444; *Sequencing Events* 220; *Analyzing* 348; *Listing* 488

Global Connections: Thinking Like a Geographer, Human Geography 93, 321; *Environment and Society* 143, 443; *The Uses of Geography* 443

Chapter Activities: Geography Activity, Identifying 102

Teacher Edition:

PROJECT-BASED LEARNING: DH 15B, 39B, 69B, 147B, 197B, 223B, 261B, 291B, 325B, 351B, 377B, 413B, 447B, 471B; **H** 113B, 147B, 173B, 223B, 261B, 377B, 447B, 471B **ENGAGE: B** 58, 116, 124, 132, 173, 176, 182, 188, 272, 294, 377, 380, 388, 394, 480 **TEACH & ASSESS: C** 5, 23, 25, 77, 98, 259, 287, 356, 364, 411, 452, 458; **O** 10, 12, 19, 26, 42, 44, 46, 54, 62, 74, 80, 83, 88, 93, 100, 106, 125, 142, 166, 168, 177, 189, 190, 191, 202, 203, 204, 218, 230, 237, 244, 245, 246, 249, 260, 265, 268, 269, 272, 274, 277, 281, 282, 285, 294, 295, 296, 297, 300, 303, 305, 306, 312, 313, 314, 315, 321, 329, 336, 337, 342, 343, 355, 357, 358, 360, 361, 368, 369, 382, 384, 388, 389, 390, 391, 394, 395, 399, 400, 411, 417, 419, 420, 422, 424, 427, 428, 429, 432, 435, 437, 438, 441, 450, 451, 456, 458, 460, 462, 465, 480; **V** 10, 71, 73, 162, 163, 165, 166, 181, 190, 213, 229, 233, 242, 244, 285, 319, 332, 337, 341, 366, 384, 415, 417, 418, 437, 438, 450, 478; **W₁** 14; **W₂** 14; **DH** 16, 40, 70, 148, 198, 224, 262, 292, 326, 352, 378, 414, 448, 472; **T** 20, 23, 83, 96, 100, 132, 143, 152, 158, 159, 161, 162, 192, 201, 202, 217, 230, 231, 237, 244, 246, 266, 295, 296, 299, 315, 333, 337, 357, 367, 373, 387, 392, 421, 427, 434, 455, 457, 460, 465; **T₁** 21, 243; **R** 23, 54, 478; **W** 24, 31, 44, 48, 55, 57, 60, 62, 79, 86, 93, 98, 112, 126, 129, 135, 152, 155, 157, 158, 165, 166, 181, 187, 199, 204, 208, 215, 219, 225, 230, 231, 234, 238, 241, 244, 249, 268, 271, 275, 276, 282, 285, 293, 296, 297, 306, 313, 317, 327, 332, 335, 341, 345, 347, 353, 356, 362, 370, 381, 383, 393, 399, 412, 415, 420, 423, 425, 429, 433, 435, 443, 449, 453, 460, 463, 466, 473, 477, 481, 483, 485; **C₁** 107, 168, 319, 338; **H** 114, 148, 174, 224, 262, 378, 448, 472; **V₁** 121, 134, 169, 184, 383, 389, 475; **V₂** 153, 342, 364, 365, 386; **C₂** 215; **R₂** 381 **CLOSE & REFLECT: SI** 14; **S** 17, 112, 287, 345, 359, 415, 473; **MC** 25, 89; **TC** 35, 51, 123, 193, 247, 293; **A** 71; **D** 93, 321, 393; **W** 143; **FQ** 149, 175, 205, 263, 379, 449; **HS** 155, 163, 249; **RS** 181; **E** 219; **RR** 231; **M** 260; **E** 279, 367; **CAC** 347; **ICI** 387, 439; **O** 431; **DC** 461; **DS** 479

Codes used for the Teacher Edition pages are the initial caps of the activities.

Writing Standards for Literacy in History/Social Studies 6–8

TEXT TYPES AND PURPOSES

WHST.6-8.1 Write arguments focused on discipline-specific content.	*Lesson Review: Answering the Guiding Questions, Argument Writing* 131, 139, 155, 169, 287, 333, 367, 393, 401, 439, 467 *Chapter Assessment: Extended Response, Argument Writing* 378 *Chapter Activities: Thinking Like a Geographer, Determining Central Ideas* 402
WHST.6-8.2 Write informative/explanatory texts, including the narration of historical events, scientific procedures/experiments, or technical processes.	*Step Into the Time: Describing* 16; *Drawing Evidence* 40; *Time Line* 114, 148, 174, 198, 224, 262, 292, 326, 414, 448, 472 *Lesson Review: Answering the Guiding Questions, Informative/Explanatory Writing* 25, 33, 51, 57, 81, 89, 101, 123, 163, 181, 193, 205, 239, 271, 279, 301, 317, 339, 345, 359, 423, 455, 479; *Argument Writing* 211 *Chapter Activities: Exploring the Essential Question, Informative/Explanatory Writing* 36, 102 *Chapter Activities: Use Your Foldables® to Explore the Essential Question, Informative/Explanatory* 66; *Informative/Explanatory Writing* 144, 250, 288, 322, 348, 374, 402, 444, 468, 488; *Analyzing* 170, 194, 220 *Chapter Activities: Thinking Like a Geographer, Describing* 66 *Chapter Assessment: Extended Response, Informative/Explanatory Writing* 68, 104, 146, 196, 222, 252, 290, 404, 446, 470; *Analyzing* 350 *Chapter Activities: Geography Activity, Identifying* 102
WHST.6-8.3 (See note; not applicable as a separate requirement)	**Note:** Students' narrative skills continue to grow in these grades. The Standards require that students be able to incorporate narrative elements effectively into arguments and informative/explanatory texts. In history/social studies, students must be able to incorporate narrative accounts into their analyses of individuals or events of historical import. In science and technical subjects, students must be able to write precise enough descriptions of the step-by-step procedures they use in their investigations or technical work that others can replicate them and (possibly) reach the same results.

PRODUCTION AND DISTRIBUTION OF WRITING

WHST.6-8.4 Produce clear and coherent writing in which the development, organization, and style are appropriate to task, purpose, and audience.	*Step Into the Time: Describing* 16; *Drawing Evidence* 40; *Identifying Point of View* 70; *Time Line* 148, 174, 198, 224, 262, 292, 414, 448, 472 *Lesson Review: Answering the Guiding Questions, Informative/Explanatory Writing* 33, 51, 57, 81, 101, 123, 163, 181, 193, 271, 279, 301, 317, 345, 359, 455, 470; *Narrative Writing* 65, 187, 219, 231, 247, 309, 373, 387, 431, 461, 485; *Analyzing* 89; *Argument Writing* 139, 155, 169, 211, 287, 367, 393, 401, 439, 467 *Chapter Activities: Exploring the Essential Question, Informative/Explanatory Writing* 36 *Chapter Activities: Geography Activity, Identifying* 102 *Chapter Assessment: Extended Response, Informative/Explanatory Writing* 146, 222, 252, 446; *Analyzing* 350; *Argument Writing* 378 *Chapter Activities: Use Your Foldables® to Explore the Essential Question, Informative/Explanatory Writing* 194, 220, 239, 288, 348, 444, 488 *Chapter Activities: Thinking Like a Geographer, Determining Central Ideas* 402
WHST.6-8.5 With some guidance and support from peers and adults, develop and strengthen writing as needed by planning, revising, editing, rewriting, or trying a new approach, focusing on how well purpose and audience have been addressed.	*Chapter Activities: 21st Century Skills, Integrating Visual Information* 322; *Peer Review* 488
WHST.6-8.6 Use technology, including the Internet, to produce and publish writing and present the relationships between information and ideas clearly and efficiently.	*Chapter Activities: 21st Century Skills, Integrating Visual Information* 66, 250, 288, 444; *Describing* 144; *Identifying* 348 *Chapter Assessment: Extended Response, Informative/Explanatory Writing* 172, 324 *Chapter Activities: Use Your Foldables® to Explore the Essential Question, Informative/Explanatory Writing* 374

Writing Standards for Literacy in History/Social Studies 6–8

RESEARCH TO BUILD AND PRESENT KNOWLEDGE

WHST.6-8.7 Conduct short research projects to answer a question (including a self-generated question), drawing on several sources and generating additional related, focused questions that allow for multiple avenues of exploration.	*Chapter Assessment: Extended Response, Informative/Explanatory Writing* 68, 290, 324, 404 *Chapter Activities: 21st Century Skills, Describing* 144; *Analyzing* 170, 194; *Integrating Visual Information* 250, 322, 374, 444 *Chapter Activities: Thinking Like a Geographer, Identifying* 322
WHST.6-8.8 Gather relevant information from multiple print and digital sources, using search terms effectively; assess the credibility and accuracy of each source; and quote or paraphrase the data and conclusions of others while avoiding plagiarism and following a standard format for citation.	*Chapter Assessment: Extended Response, Informative/Explanatory Writing* 38, 104 *Chapter Activities: 21st Century Skills, Integrating Visual Information* 66, 374; *Analyzing* 170, 194; *Identifying* 348; *Describing* 402 *Chapter Activities: Exploring the Essential Question, Informative/Explanatory Writing* 102 *Chapter Activities: Use Your Foldables® to Explore the Essential Question, Informative/Explanatory Writing* 250
WHST.6-8.9 Draw evidence from informational texts to support analysis reflection, and research.	*Chapter Assessment: Extended Response, Informative/Explanatory Writing* 38 *Chapter Assessment: Short Response, Informative/Explanatory Writing* 172 *Lesson Review: Answering the Guiding Questions, Narrative Writing* 231, 431, 485; *Argument Writing* 333; *Informative/Explanatory Writing* 423, 479; *Citing Text Evidence* 467 *Chapter Assessment: Thinking Like a Geographer, Identifying* 250, 444; *Analyzing* 348 *Reading HELP Desk: Taking Notes, Key Ideas and Details, Organize Information* 264 *Chapter Activities: 21st Century Skills, Describing* 402; *Determining Central Ideas* 468 *What Do You Think? DBQ: Identifying Point of View* 487

RANGE OF WRITING

WHST.6-8.10 Write routinely over extended time frames (time for reflection and revision) and shorter time frames (a single sitting or a day or two) for a range of discipline-specific tasks, purposes, and audiences.	*Lesson Review: Answering the Guiding Questions, Informative/Explanatory Writing* 25, 205, 339, 89; *Narrative Writing* 65, 187, 219, 248, 309, 373, 387, 461; *Argument Writing* 131 *Chapter Activities: Thinking Like a Geographer, Describing* 66; *Determining Central Ideas* 102, 374; *Sequencing Events* 220; *Integrating Visual Information* 288, 444; *Identifying* 322; *Listing* 488 *Step Into the Time: Time Line* 114, 378 *Chapter Activities: Use Your Foldables® to Explore the Essential Question, Informative/Explanatory* 144, 170, 402 *Chapter Assessment: Extended Response, Informative/Explanatory Writing* 196 *Chapter Activities: 21st Century Skills, Integrating Visual Information* 288; *Peer Review* 488

USING FOLDABLES® IN THE CLASSROOM

by Rhonda Meyer Vivian, Ph.D., and Nancy F. Wisker, M.A.

Graphic Organizers

Current research shows that graphic organizers are powerful teaching and learning tools. Most of us are familiar with common graphic organizers such as diagrams, maps, outlines, and charts, all of which are two-dimensional. Foldables® are three-dimensional, interactive graphic organizers that were created more than 30 years ago by educator Dinah Zike.

Graphic organizers are visual representations combining line, shape, space, and symbols to convey facts and concepts or to organize information. Graphic organizers, when designed and used appropriately:

- Speed up communication
- Help organize information
- Are easy-to-understand
- Show complex relationships
- Clarify concepts with few words
- Convey ideas and understanding
- Assess comprehension

Graphic organizers help students organize information in a visual manner. This is a profound concept, especially as the number of non-native English-speaking students increases. A student is able to use graphic organizers to clarify concepts or to convey ideas and understandings with fewer words.

Graphic organizers also make complex relationships or concepts easier to understand, particularly for visual learners. Foldables take that process to the next level, most notably, for tactile/kinesthetic learners.

When to Use Graphic Organizers

Graphic organizers may be used at any point during instruction, but just as with any other instructional strategy, they are most successful when they are built into the instructional plan, rather than presented as an "extra" activity.

Graphic organizers may work better than outline notes in helping students discover or understand relationships between concepts. Foldables help teach students how to take notes by visually and kinesthetically chunking information into sections.

Foldables may be used as an alternative form of assessment in the classroom. Because the Foldable has readily identifiable sections, a teacher can quickly see gaps in student knowledge.

Reading, Writing, and Social Studies

Graphic organizers have been shown to be highly effective in literacy development. In numerous studies, graphic organizers help improve the development of literacy skills—including oral, written, and comprehension.

Graphic organizers have been found to help students organize information from expository social studies texts and comprehend content area reading. They also help students develop critical thinking skills and help transfer these skills to new situations and content areas.

Students With Special Needs

Graphic organizers may help English language learners improve higher-order thinking skills.

Because of their visual organization, graphic organizers seem to be quite beneficial for use with learning disabled students. They appear to help students understand content area material, to organize information, and to retain and recall content.

Conclusions

Graphic organizers may lead to improved student performance, whether measured by classroom-based observation, textbook assessments, or standardized assessments, when compared with more traditional forms of instruction.

When students construct their own graphic organizers, as they do with Foldables, they are active participants in their learning.

Our goal as educators is to help students glean important information and understand key concepts and to be able to relate these concepts or apply them to real-world situations. Graphic organizers help support and develop students' note-taking skills, summarizing skills, reading comprehension, and vocabulary development, which leads to better understanding and application of social studies content.

Foldables® are found in every chapter of *Discovering World Geography* so that students can take notes and organize the chapter information.

Dinah Zike is an award-winning author, educator, educational consultant, and inventor, known internationally for graphic organizers known as Foldables®. Based outside of San Antonio, Texas, Zike is a frequent keynote speaker and conducts seminars for over 50,000 teachers and parents annually.

Rhonda Meyer Vivian, Ph.D., is CEO of Dinah-Might Adventures, LP, and Nancy F. Wisker, M.A., is Director of Math and Science for Dinah-Might Adventures, L.P.

btw
McGraw-Hill's Current Events Web Site

The *btw* current events Web site was created specifically for students. It provides up-to-date coverage of important national and world news, along with contests, polls, and activities.

Each news story has activities and questions to extend the content and provide skills practice, including:

- Tips on how to use *btw* articles in your social studies classroom
- Ideas for using social media and other technology resources
- 21st Century Skill options

Use *btw* as a bellringer activity, to activate critical thinking, or to engage students in high-interest projects.

Engaging, student-friendly content guides readers through the major events that affect our nation and our world. *Top Stories* examine everything from unrest in Libya to the newest shows on television.

You Decide asks students to take a stand after they analyze different points of view on issues around the United States and the world.

Election Central takes a closer look at upcoming elections with information about party platforms, candidates, and important issues.

Real people *Profiles* provide first-person accounts of events, such as what it is like to be a soldier in Iraq or to testify in front of Congress.

Be an Active Citizen! helps students learn more about the government, courts, and economy to help them become informed citizens.

Visit the *btw* Current Events Web site at **blog.glencoe.com**.

UNDERSTANDING BY DESIGN®
by Jay McTighe

Understanding by Design® (UbD®) offers a planning framework to guide curriculum, assessment, and instruction. Its two key ideas are contained in the title: 1) focus on teaching and assessing for understanding and transfer, and 2) design curriculum "backward" from those ends. UbD is based on seven key tenets:

1. UbD is a way of thinking purposefully about curricular planning, not a rigid program or prescriptive recipe.

2. A primary goal of UbD is developing and deepening student understanding: the ability to make meaning of learning via "big ideas" and transfer learning.

3. Understanding is revealed when students autonomously make sense of and transfer their learning through authentic performance. Six facets of understanding—the capacity to explain, interpret, apply, shift perspective, empathize, and self assess—serve as indicators of understanding.

4. Effective curriculum is planned "backward" from long-term desired results though a three-stage design process (Desired Results, Evidence, Learning Plan). This process helps to avoid the twin problems of "textbook coverage" and "activity-oriented" teaching in which no clear priorities and purposes are apparent.

5. Teachers are coaches of understanding, not mere purveyors of content or activity. They focus on ensuring learning, not just teaching (and assuming that what was taught was learned); they always aim and check for successful meaning making and transfer by the learner.

6. Regular reviews of units and curriculum against design standards enhance curricular quality and effectiveness.

7. UbD reflects a continuous improvement approach to achievement. The results of our designs —student performance—inform needed adjustments in curriculum as well as instruction.

Three Stages of Backward Design

In UbD, we propose a 3-stage "backward design" process for curriculum planning. The concept of planning "backward" from desired results is not new. In 1949 Ralph Tyler described this approach as an effective process for focusing instruction. More recently, Stephen Covey, in the best selling book, *Seven Habits of Highly Effective People*, reports that effective people in various fields are goal-oriented and plan with the end in mind. Although not a new idea, we have found that the deliberate use of backward design for planning curriculum units and courses results in more clearly defined goals, more appropriate assessments, more tightly aligned lessons, and more purposeful teaching.

Backward planning asks educators to consider the following three stages:

Stage 1 – Identify Desired Results

What should students know, understand, and be able to do? What content is worthy of understanding? What "enduring" understandings are desired? What essential questions will be explored?

In the first stage of backward design we consider our goals, examine established Content Standards (national, state, province, district), and review curriculum expectations. Since there is typically more "content" than can reasonably be addressed within the available time, teachers must make choices. This first stage in the design process calls for setting priorities.

More specifically, Stage 1 of UbD asks teachers to identify the "big ideas" that we want students to come to understand, and then to identify or craft companion essential questions. Big ideas reflect transferable concepts, principles and processes that are key to understanding the topic or subject. Essential questions present open-ended, thought-provoking inquiries that are explored over time.

More specific knowledge and skill objectives, linked to the targeted Content Standards and Understandings, are also identified in Stage 1. An important point in UbD is to recognize that factual knowledge and skills are not taught for their own sake, but as a means to larger ends. Ultimately, teaching should equip learners to be able to use or transfer their learning; i.e., meaningful performance with content. This is the "end" we always want to keep in mind.

Stage 2 – Determine Acceptable Evidence

How will we know if students have achieved the desired results? What will we accept as evidence of student understanding and proficiency? How will we evaluate student performance?

Backward design encourages teachers and curriculum planners to first "think like an assessor" before designing specific units and lessons. The assessment evidence we need reflects the desired results identified in Stage 1. Thus, we consider in advance the assessment evidence needed to document and validate that the targeted learning has been achieved. Doing so invariably sharpens and focuses teaching.

In Stage 2, we distinguish between two broad types of assessment—Performance Tasks and Other Evidence. The performance tasks ask students to apply their learning to a new and authentic situation as means of assessing their understanding. In UbD, we have identified six facets of understanding for assessment purposes[1]. When someone truly understands, they:

- Can **explain** concepts, principles and processes; i.e., put it in their own words, teach it to others, justify their answers, show their reasoning.

- Can **interpret**; i.e., make sense of data, text, and experience through images, analogies, stories, and models.

- Can apply; i.e., effectively use and adapt what they know in new and complex contexts.

- Demonstrate **perspective**; i.e., can see the big picture and recognize different points of view.

- Display **empathy**; i.e., perceive sensitively and "walk in someone else's shoes."

- Have **self-knowledge**; i.e., show metacognition, use productive habits of mind, and reflect on the meaning of their learning and experience.

These six facets do not present a theory of how people come to understand something. Instead, the facets are intended to serve as indicators of how understanding is revealed, and thus provide guidance as to the kinds of assessments we need to determine the extent of student understanding. Here are two notes regarding assessing understanding through the facets:

1) All six facets of understanding need not be used all of the time in assessment. In social studies, Empathy and Perspective may be added when appropriate.

2) Performance Tasks based on one or more facets are not intended for use in daily lessons. Rather, these tasks should be seen as culminating performances for a unit of study.

In addition to Performance Tasks, Stage 2 includes Other Evidence, such as traditional quizzes, tests, observations, and work samples to round out the assessment picture to

Examples of Essential Questions in Social Studies	
Understandings or Big Ideas	**Essential Questions**
History involves interpretation, and different people may interpret the same events differently.	*Whose "story" is this? How do we know what <u>really</u> happened in the past?*
The geography, climate, and natural resources of a region influence the culture, economy, and lifestyle of its inhabitants.	*How does <u>where</u> we live influence <u>how</u> we live?*
History often repeats itself. Recognizing the patterns of the past can help us better understand the present and prepare for the future.	*Why study the past? What does the past have to do with today?*
Governments can change based on the changing needs of their people, the society, and the world.	*What makes an effective government? Why do/should governments change?*

[1] Wiggins, G. and McTighe, J. and (1998, 2005). *Understanding By Design*. Alexandria, VA: The Association for Supervision and Curriculum Development.

UNDERSTANDING BY DESIGN®
(continued)

determine what students know and can do. A key idea in backward design has to do with alignment. In other words, are we assessing everything that we are trying to achieve (in Stage 1) or only those things that are easiest to test and grade? Is anything important slipping through the cracks because it is not being assessed? Checking the alignment between Stages 1 and 2 helps insure that *all* important goals are appropriately assessed.

Stage 3 – Plan Learning Experiences and Instruction

How will we support learners in coming to an understanding of important ideas and processes? How will we prepare them to autonomously transfer their learning? What enabling knowledge and skills will students need in order to perform effectively and achieve desired results? What activities, sequence, and resources are best suited to accomplish our goals?

In Stage 3 of backward design, teachers now plan the most appropriate learning activities to help students acquire important knowledge and skills, come to understand important ideas and processes, and transfer their learning in meaningful ways. When developing a plan for learning, we propose that teachers consider a set of instructional principles, embedded in the acronym W.H.E.R.E.T.O. These design elements provide the armature or blueprint for instructional planning in Stage 3 in support of our goals of understanding and transfer.

Each of the W.H.E.R.E.T.O. elements is presented in the form of questions to consider.

W = *How will I help learners know –
What they will be learning?
Why this is worth learning?
What evidence will show their
learning? How will their
performance be evaluated?*

Learners of all ages are more likely to put forth effort and meet with success when they understand the learning goals and see them as meaningful and personally relevant. The "W" in W.H.E.R.E.T.O. reminds teachers to clearly communicate the goals and help students see their relevance. In addition, learners need to know the concomitant performance expectations and assessments through which they will demonstrate their learning so that they have clear learning targets and the basis for monitoring their progress toward them.

H = *How will I hook and engage
the learners?*

There is wisdom in the old adage: "Before you try to teach them, you've got to get their attention." The best teachers have always recognized the value of "hooking" learners through introductory activities that "itch" the mind and engage the heart in the learning process, and we encourage teachers to deliberately plan ways of hooking their learners to the topics they teach. Examples of effective hooks include provocative essential questions, counter-intuitive phenomena, controversial issues, authentic problems and challenges, emotional encounters, and humor. One must be mindful, of course, of not just coming up with interesting introductory activities that have no carry-over value. The intent is to match the hook with the content and

BananaStock/PictureQuest

the experiences of the learners—by design—as a means of drawing them into a productive learning experience.

E = *How will I equip students to master identified standards and succeed with the transfer performances? What learning experiences will help develop and deepen understanding of important ideas?*

Understanding cannot be simply transferred like a load of freight from one mind to another. Coming to understand requires active intellectual engagement on the part of the learner. Therefore, instead of merely covering the content, effective educators "uncover" the most enduring ideas and processes in ways that engage students in constructing meaning for themselves. To this end, teachers select an appropriate balance of constructivist learning experiences, structured activities, and direct instruction for helping students acquire the desired knowledge, skill, and understanding. While there is certainly a place for direct instruction and modeling, teaching for understanding asks teachers to engage learners in making meaning through active inquiry.

R = *How will I encourage the learners to rethink previous learning? How will I encourage on-going revision and refinement?*

Few learners develop a complete understanding of abstract ideas on the first encounter. Indeed, the phrase "coming to understand" is suggestive of a process. Over time, learners develop and deepen their understanding by thinking and re-thinking, by examining ideas from a different point of view, from examining underlying assumptions, by receiving feedback and revising. Just as the quality of

writing benefits from the iterative process of drafting and revising, so to do understandings become more mature. The "R" in W.H.E.R.E.T.O. encourages teachers to explicitly include such opportunities.

E = *How will I promote students' self-evaluation and reflection?*

Capable and independent learners are distinguished by their capacity to set goals, self-assess their progress, and adjust as needed. Yet, one of the most frequently overlooked aspects of the instructional process involves helping students to develop the metacognitive skills of self-evaluation, self-regulation, and reflection. The second "E" of WHERETO reminds teachers to build in time and expectations for students to regularly self-assess, reflect on the meaning of their learning, and set goals for future performance.

T = *How will I tailor the learning experiences to the nature of the learners I serve? How might I differentiate instruction to respond to the varied needs of students?*

"One size fits all teaching" is rarely optimal. Learners differ significantly in terms of their prior knowledge and skill levels, their interests, talents, and preferred ways of learning. Accordingly, the most effective teachers get to know their students and tailor their teaching and learning experiences to connect to them. A variety of strategies may be employed to differentiate *content* (e.g., how subject matter is presented), *process* (e.g., how students work), and *product* (e.g., how learners demonstrate their learning). The logic of backward design offers a cautionary note here: the Content Standards and Understandings should *not* be differentiated (except for students with Individualized Education Plans—I.E.P.s).

In other words, differentiate means keeping the end in mind for all.

O = *How will I organize the learning experiences for maximum engagement and effectiveness? What sequence will be optimal given the understanding and transfer goals?*

When the primary educational goals involve helping students acquire basic knowledge and skills, teachers may be comfortable "covering" the content by telling and modeling.

However, when we include understanding and transfer as desired results, educators are encouraged to give careful attention to how the content is organized and sequenced. Just as effective story tellers and filmmakers often don't begin in the "beginning," teachers can consider alternatives to sequential content coverage. For example, methods such as the Case Method, Problem or Project-Based Learning, and Socratic Seminars immerse students in challenging situations, even before they may have acquired all of the "basics." They actively engage students in trying to make meaning and apply their learning in demanding circumstances without single "correct" answers.

Conclusion

Many teachers who are introduced to the backward design process have observed that while the process makes sense in theory, it often feels awkward in use. This is to be expected since the principles and practices of UbD often challenge conventional planning and teaching habits. However, with some practice, educators find that backward design becomes not only more comfortable, but a way of thinking. The resources found in this program support teaching and assessing for understanding and transfer.

WHY TEACH WITH TECHNOLOGY?

by Tom Daccord and Justin Reich, EdTechTeacher

✔ **Technology is transforming the practice of historians and should transform history classrooms as well.** While printed documents, books, maps, and artwork constitute the bulk of the historical record before 1900, the history of the last century is also captured in sound and video recording and in Web sites and other Internet resources. Today's students need to learn how to analyze and build arguments using these multimedia records as well as traditional primary sources.

✔ **So many of the sources that helped historians and history teachers fall in love with the discipline are now available online.** In recent decades, universities, libraries, archives, and other institutions have scanned and uploaded many vast treasure troves of historical sources. The Internet-connected classroom increasingly has access to the world's historical record, giving students a chance to develop critical thinking skills as well as learning historical narratives.

✔ **Whoever is doing most of the talking or most of the typing is doing most of the learning, and the more people listening the better.** Technology allows us to transfer the responsibility for learning from teachers to students, and to put students in the driver's seat of their own learning. Students who are actively engaged in creating and presenting their understandings of history are learning more than students passively listening. Technology also allows students to publish their work to broader audiences of peers, parents, and even the entire Internet-connected world. Students find the opportunities challenging, exciting, and engaging.

✔ **The more ways students have to engage with content, the more likely they are to remember and understand that content.** The Internet can provide students and teachers with access to text documents, images, sounds and songs, video, simulations, and games. The more different ways students engage with historical content, the more likely they are to make meaning of that material.

✔ **Students live in a technology-rich world, and classrooms should prepare students for that world.** When students spend most of their waking hours connected to a worldwide, online network of people, resources, and opportunities, they experience dissonance and disappointment in entering a "powered-down" school. Many students will leave school to go on to workplaces completely transformed by technology, and teachers have a responsibility to prepare students for these environments.

Integrating Technology Effectively

Ben Shneiderman, in his book *Leonardo's Laptop,* lays out a four-part framework for teaching with technology: Collect-Relate-Create-Donate. This framework is a helpful blueprint for designing projects and learning experiences with technology.

Collect Students should begin a project by collecting the resources necessary to produce a meaningful presentation of their understanding. In some cases, students might collect these resources through textbook reading and teacher lecture, but students should also collect resources from

---

edtechteacher
21st Century Learning

For More Information

Visit the EdTechTeacher Web sites for more links, tutorials, and other resources.

Teaching With Technology

In addition to the many other online resources in this program, EdTech Teacher has created digital project-based learning activities for every chapter. These can be used independently or with the print chapter-based hands-on activities. These cumulative projects bring geography to life and reveal student understanding through performance assessment. The digital hands-on projects integrate technology with instruction. Students use software and the Internet to create projects that are fun and challenging.

online collections, school library Web sites, and online searches.

Relate Technology greatly facilitates the process of students working together socially. The ability to collaborate is essential to the workplace and civic sphere of the future. In creating technology projects, students should have the chance to work together, or at least comment on each other's work, using blogs, wikis, podcasts, and other collaborative publishing tools.

Create Using multimedia publishing tools, students should have the opportunity to design presentations and performances of their historical understanding. They should make historical arguments in linear text, as well as through images, audio and video recordings, and multimedia presentations.

Donate Finally, students should create work not just for their teachers, but for broader audiences. Students who have a chance to share their work with their peers, their families, their community, and the Internet-connected world find that opportunity rewarding. Today's students experience very few barriers to expression in their networked lives, and they crave these opportunities in schools.

Learn More about Teaching Geography with Technology

EdTechTeacher has several Web sites designed to help social studies and geography teachers learn more about teaching with technology. The Best of History Web Sites (www.besthistorysites.net) is the Internet's authoritative directory of social studies-related resources, Web sites, games, simulations, lesson plans, and activities. Teaching History with Technology (www.thwt.org) has a series of white papers, tutorials, and guides for enriching teaching strategies (lecturing, discussion, presentations, assessments, and so forth) with educational technology. EdTechTeacher (www.edtechteacher.org) has additional teaching resources and information about learning opportunities such as free webinars and other professional development workshops.

Tom Daccord and Justin Reich are co-Directors of EdTechTeacher. Together they authored Best Ideas for Teaching With Technology: A Practical Guide for Teachers by Teachers.

Guidelines for Successful Technology Projects

1) **Plan for problems.** Things can go wrong when working with technology, and learning how to deal with these challenges is essential for students, and for their teachers. As you start using technology in the classroom, try to have an extra teacher, aide, student-teacher, or IT staff member in the room with you to help troubleshoot problems. When things do go wrong, stay calm, and ask your students to help you resolve challenges and make the most of class time. Always have a back up, "pencil and paper" activity prepared in case there are problems with computers or networks. Over time, teachers who practice teaching with technology experience fewer and fewer of these problems, but they can be very challenging the first time you experience them!

2) **Practice from multiple perspectives.** Whenever you develop a technology project, try to do everything that students will do from a student's perspective. If you create a blog or wiki with a teacher account, create a student account to test the technology.

3) **Adapt to your local technology resources, but don't let those resources keep you from using technology.** Some schools have excellent and ample technology resources—labs and laptop carts—that make completing technology projects straightforward. Other schools have fewer resources, but virtually every student can get access to a networked computer in school, at the library or at home, especially if you give them a few nights to do so. Many technology activities are described as if you could complete them in a few class periods, but if resources are limited, you might consider spreading the activity out over a few days or weeks to give students the chance to get online.

4) **Plan with a partner.** Going it alone can be scary. If possible, have another teacher in your department or on your team, design and pilot technology projects with you to help solve the challenges that crop up whenever trying out new pedagogies.

5) **It's harder, then it gets easier.** Learning new teaching strategies is always hard. With technology, however, once you get past the initial learning curve there are all sorts of ways technology can make teaching more efficient and simultaneously make learning more meaningful for students.

BACKGROUND KNOWLEDGE:
THE KEY TO UNDERSTANDING
by Doug Fisher, Ph.D., and Nancy Frey, Ph.D.

Mention background knowledge and most middle school educators will tell you that it is an essential component of history and social studies learning. They will discuss the importance of activating it in their students and building it when there are gaps. Yet most will also confess to being unsure of how to accomplish this in a systematic way beyond asking some questions about prior experiences. As for the gaps, how can anyone find the time to build it when there is so much new information to be covered?

The answer is to integrate background knowledge activation, building, and assessment into the heart of the lesson, not just as bookends to new learning. The reasons for this are pretty striking. Background knowledge directly influences a learner's ability to understand new information and act upon it (RAND Reading Study Group, 2002). In addition, background knowledge is demonstrated through the use of academic vocabulary and academic language, an important measure of content learning (Cromley & Azevedo, 2007). Finally, students with strong background knowledge about a topic process text better, especially in their ability to monitor and correct comprehension difficulties (Cakir, 2008).

Cultivating Background Knowledge

The key to understanding new information is to link it to what is already known. A feature of initial learning is that we aren't very good at doing so. Our efforts to focus on what is unfa-

miliar temporarily blind us to what we already know. It is helpful to have well-placed reminders about what is already known, because it assists us in marshalling the familiar in order to understand the new.

When we ask questions of students about prior experiences, or invite them to engage in a quickwrite about a previously taught topic, we are activating their background knowledge. More importantly, we are providing the signposts they need to direct them to the most salient information they will need to learn the new material. For example, a study of Ancient Rome doesn't merely begin with the legendary founding of a great city by two boys raised by wolves. It also requires knowledge of the influence of ancient Greek civilization on Rome's governance, military, art, and culture. It is easy, however, for students to temporarily forget everything they have learned about Greece in their effort to assimilate new information. Well-placed questions, writing opportunities, and graphic organizers can remind them of what they have previously learned.

Another means for cultivating background knowledge is to assess what students know (or think they know) about a topic. This shouldn't be a quiz of isolated facts, but instead should focus on the anticipated misconceptions that a learner is likely to hold about a new topic. For instance, it is easy for students to confuse what they have learned about Greek mythology when learning about Roman gods

and goddesses. Those terms (gods and goddesses) alone suggest that for Romans this was at the heart of their religious beliefs. But Roman mythology differs from Greek mythology. For Greeks, mythology formed the heart of religion. For Romans, the gods and goddesses made for good stories, but weren't necessarily worshipped. Posing questions that are designed to surface misconceptions such as this help to rectify incorrect perceptions before they are ingrained.

Assessing Background Knowledge

Despite the efforts of caring educators, families, and communities, students come to us with gaps in their background knowledge. This can be due to a variety of causes, including frequent moves, second language acquisition, lack of experience with a topic, or difficulty with the content itself. Students at the middle school level face the additional well-documented challenges of transitioning from elementary school, where one teacher made connections for them to background knowledge, to a middle school schedule with many teachers and content areas. These changes require them to make more of their own connections across subjects.

In addition, a middle school schedule leaves us with less time across the day to get to know our students and the background knowledge they possess. It is useful to have formative assessment embedded into lessons in order to gauge where gaps might exist.

Activities that draw on core background knowledge necessary for deep understanding of new information provide these opportunities. Lessons that invite students to construct graphic organizers using both new knowledge and background knowledge give us such a window. A well-placed question invites students to consider what they already know.

If and when students have difficulty with activities like this, the teacher can pause to supply missing background knowledge. This may be done through direct explanation, by drawing their attention to features in the text, and even to returning to a previous chapter to revisit information. These need not be seen as delays, but rather as time well spent to solidify foundational knowledge.

Building Background Knowledge

Effective middle school educators take a proactive stance to building background knowledge by creating opportunities to do so. They conduct read alouds and shared readings of text and provide visual information to build students' mental image banks. Texts and images related to necessary background knowledge are especially useful in history and social studies, where students are required to understand and use primary source documents. A challenge is that many of these are hard for students to make sense of on their own, as they often use archaic language and represent ideas that are not contemporary to adoles-

cent lives. Texts and images carefully selected with middle school students in mind can build their background knowledge of the people and times being studied, and help them more fully appreciate the influences one culture has upon another. For example, illustrations of Greek and Roman architecture invite comparison. Maps of the ancient world highlight why empires fought over land.

Student background knowledge is also built through deeper understanding of the academic vocabulary and language that lies at the heart of history and social studies. By using a think aloud technique, teachers build

their students' background knowledge about the derivation of the term, as well as the way they approach an unfamiliar word. This ensures that students will recall the term more precisely while also equipping them with a problem-solving strategy to apply to other new words.

Conclusion

McGraw-Hill **networks** learning system offers middle school educators the tools needed to activate, assess, and build student background knowledge by infusing approaches like this into the lesson design. The habit of mind of drawing on what one already knows and seeking information to fill in knowledge gaps begins with educators like you who show students how this is done.

Doug Fisher, Ph.D., and Nancy Frey, Ph.D., are professors in the School of Teacher Education at San Diego State University.

Cakir, O. (2008). The effect of textual differences on children's processing strategies. *Reading Improvement, 45*(2), 69-83.

Cromley, J. G., & Azevedo, R. (2007). Testing and refining the direct and inferential mediation model of reading comprehension. *Journal of Educational Psychology, 99*(2), 311-325.

RAND *Reading Study Group. (2002). Reading for understanding: Toward an R&D program in reading comprehension.* Office of Educational Research and Improvement. Santa Monica, CA: RAND.

COLLEGE AND CAREER READINESS

Why Is College & Career Readiness Crucial?

- Only 70% of American students receive a high school diploma.
- Of that 70% of high school graduates, 53% of those who make it to college require remedial help.
- Over 90% of new jobs that will be available to students in the 21st century will require some postsecondary education.
- Most employers today cannot compete successfully without a workforce that has solid academic skills.
- The average difference in salary between someone with a high school degree and someone with postsecondary credentials can be $1 million over their lifetimes.

What Is College & Career Readiness?

Students are college and career ready when they have the level of preparation needed to academically, socially, and cognitively complete a postsecondary course of study without remediation. Students are prepared when they can enter the workforce at a level at which they are in line for promotion and career enhancement.

The ultimate goal of the college and career readiness initiative is to maintain America's competitive edge in the global economy of today. The workforce of the 21st century is an increasingly global, knowledge-based economy that demands the ability to:

- Think critically
- Solve problems
- Create and innovate
- Communicate
- Collaborate
- Learn new skills
- Use ICT (information and communications technology)

Explain College & Career Readiness to Students

One of the first steps you should take is to provide students with a framework that will help them see the relevancy of what they do in school. The three principal elements of College and Career Readiness (CCR) are:

- an understanding of core academic skills and the ability to apply them in educational and employment settings
- familiarity with skills valued by a broad range of employers such as communication, critical thinking, and responsibility
- mastery of the technologies and skill sets associated with a career pathway

Once students have been exposed to these elements, it is critical for them to see how they relate to their own plans for continuing education and career choice. Mention that CCR is more than just a personal issue, and it affects the country and our quality of life.

Most students—as well as many adults—consider work to be an obligation that they must perform in order to have money. Earning a salary is, of course, a central benefit of working, but so is the sense of satisfaction that comes from doing a job well. Moreover, every job contributes to the quality of life in our communities and our nation. Being prepared to pursue an education or get a job after high school is the hallmark of a good citizen.

Recognize That All Careers Are Important

Without question, the greatest challenge faced by educators, parents, and the public is recognizing that all jobs are important. When you discuss careers, be generous with your reflections and encourage your students to do the same. Be sure to mention the enormous variety of opportunities available to them in diverse fields.

Mark Scott/Getty Images

The more that students can recognize the rich possibilities of whatever career they pursue, the more likely they will be to enjoy success and personal satisfaction.

Students typically have a relatively narrow perspective on the careers and jobs available to them. As part of the discussion of careers, broaden this perspective by reviewing some opportunities that your students might not be aware of. An interesting place to start is in the high profile industries of sports and entertainment.

Many students dream of being celebrities and have no idea about how unlikely this is. What they don't realize is that for every professional athlete, singer, or movie star, there are a hundred or more fascinating careers including sports trainers, writers, administrative assistants, drivers, and a seemingly endless list of other jobs. Not surprisingly, students usually respond positively when they learn that just in case they are not the next superstar in sports or entertainment, there are other opportunities that will allow them to achieve their dream in a slightly different way.

Students can explore careers in many ways; one way is by reviewing the 16 career clusters. Career clusters are groups of similar occupations and industries. They were developed by the U.S. Department of Education as a way to organize career planning. Students can visit the Career Center at http://ccr.mcgraw-hill.com/ to begin their explorations.

Make It Clear That There Are Various Paths To Success

A surprisingly small percentage of adults reach their careers through a direct and well-planned strategy. Familiarizing students with the various paths to success provides them with a realistic view of what life is like after high school and college. It may also give them an anchor in their own lives in the future when they find that they are wandering, which most of them will inevitably do.

Divergence from a direct path to a career is almost inevitable, and in many cases, is a desirable and enriching experience. Helping students to recognize this will make their future challenges seem less intimidating.

Have students investigate and discuss the career paths of people they know personally and by reputation, including celebrities. This discussion will promote engagement while showing the twists and turns that usually lead to success. Be sure to include some common but less-known paths, like the college benefits associated with military service or the arrangements nurses might make with a hospital to exchange tuition payments for a commitment of several years.

College & Career READINESS

Make College & Career Readiness a regular part of interactive classroom discussions.

Unlike many other school subjects, a critical aspect of College & Career Readiness is its focus is on the future of each student, not the content of a course. Perhaps the best way to have students recognize this is to be sure that the time you spend discussing students' future pathways is truly interactive, with at least as much commentary from students as there is from you or other adult participants.

Because students are more willing to participate in discussions that have personal meaning to them, consider using these questions as starting points. These are "self-mentoring" questions that will help students clarify their thinking.

- What is something you really want to do in the next 10 years?
- How do you plan to get there?
- What is your back-up plan?
- What is something that you have done that made you proud?
- In which postsecondary courses do you think you would do best? Why do you think this?
- Imagine that you are going into the military. This choice involves activities that are hard physically and mentally. How would you handle these challenges?
- When you can't make up your mind about something important, what do you do?

Have students explore college & career readiness on their own at http://ccr.mcgraw-hill.com/

MEETING THE DIVERSE NEEDS OF OUR STUDENTS

by Douglas Fisher, Ph.D.

Today's classroom contains students from a variety of backgrounds with a variety of learning styles, strengths, and challenges. As teachers we are facing the challenge of helping students reach their educational potential. With careful planning, you can address the needs of all students in the social studies classroom. The basis for this planning is universal access. When classrooms are planned with universal access in mind, fewer students require specific accommodations.

What Is a Universal Access Design for Learning?

Universal design was first conceived in architectural studies when business people, engineers, and architects began making considerations for physical access to buildings. The idea was to plan the environment in advance to ensure that everyone had access.

As a result, the environment would not have to be changed later for people with physical disabilities, people pushing strollers, workers who had injuries, or others for whom the environment would be difficult to negotiate. The Center for Universal Design at www.design. ncsu.edu/cud defines Universal Design as:

The design of products and environments to be usable by all people, to the greatest extent possible, without the need for adaptation or specialized design.

Universal Design and Access in Education

Researchers, teachers, and parents in education have expanded the development of built-in adaptations and inclusive accommodations from architectural space to the educational experience, especially in the area of curriculum.

In 1998, the National Center to Improve the Tools of Educators (NCITE), with the partnership of the Center for Applied Special Technology (CAST), proposed an expanded definition of universal design focused on education: *In terms of learning, universal design means the design of instructional materials and activities that allows the learning goals to be achievable by individuals with wide dif-ferences in their abilities to see, hear, speak, move, read, write, understand English, attend, organize, engage, and remember.*

How Does Universal Design Work in Education?

Universal design and access, as they apply to education and schooling, suggest the following:

✔ **Inclusive Classroom Participation**
Curriculum should be designed with all students and their needs in mind. The McGraw-Hill social studies print and online texts and materials were designed with a wide range of students in mind. For example, understanding that English learners and students who struggle with reading would be using this text, vocabulary is specifically taught and reinforced. Similarly, the teacher-support materials provide multiple instructional points to be used depending on the needs of the students in the class. Further, the text is written such that essential questions and guiding questions are identified for all learners.

✔ **Maximum Text Readability**
In universally designed classrooms that provide access for all students, texts use direct language, clear noun-verb agreements, and clear construct-based wording. In addition to these factors, the McGraw-Hill social

studies texts use embedded definitions for difficult terms, provide for specific instruction in reading skills, use a number of visual representations, and include note-taking guides.

✔ Adaptable and Accommodating

The content in this textbook can be easily translated, read aloud, or otherwise changed to meet the needs of students in the classroom. The lesson and end-of-chapter activities and assessments provide students with multiple ways of demonstrating their content knowledge while also ensuring that they have practice with thinking in terms of multiple-choice questions. Critical thinking and analysis skills are also practiced.

How Is Differentiated Instruction the Key to Universal Access?

To differentiate instruction, teachers must acknowledge student differences in background knowledge and current reading, writing, and English language skills. They must also consider student learning styles and preferences, interests, and needs, and react accordingly. There are a number of general guidelines for differentiating instruction in the classroom to reach all students, including:

✔ Link Assessment With Instruction

Assessments should occur before, during, and after instruction to ensure that the curriculum is aligned with what students do and do not know. Using assessments in this way allows you to plan instruction for whole groups, small groups, and individual students. Backward planning, where you establish the assessment before you begin instruction, is also important.

✔ Clarify Key Concepts and Generalizations

Students need to know what is essential and how this information can be used in their future learning. In addition, students need to develop a sense of the big ideas—ideas that transcend time and place.

✔ Emphasize Critical and Creative Thinking

The content, process, and products used or assigned in the classroom should require that students think about what they are learning. While some students may require support, additional motivation, varied tasks, materials, or equipment, the overall focus on critical and creative thinking allows for all students to participate in the lesson.

✔ Include Teacher- and Student-Selected Tasks

A differentiated classroom includes both teacher- and student-selected activities and tasks. At some points in the lesson or day, the teacher must provide instruction and assign learning activities. In other parts of the lesson, students should be provided choices in how they engage with the content. This balance increases motivation, engagement, and learning.

How Do I Support Individual Students?

The vast majority of students will thrive in a classroom based on universal access and differentiated instruction. However, wise teachers recognize that no single option will work for all students and that there may be students who require unique systems of support to be successful.

Classroom Activity

Display a map of imperialism in Africa around 1914. Discuss with students the map's general information and have them list each country under the European power that controlled it.

To differentiate this activity:

- Have students imagine they are living in the early 1900s. Have them write a letter to a British newspaper about colonial rule in Africa.
- Have students record the number of African countries under European rule. Have them take the data and create a bar graph that shows which European powers were the most active colonizers at the time.
- Have students compose a song or poem about European rule in Africa, from an African's point of view.
- Have students choose a country of modern Africa to research. Have them write a three-page paper discussing how that country was affected by colonialism and how it has changed since the days of European rule.

professional
development

MEETING THE DIVERSE NEEDS OF OUR STUDENTS
(continued)

Tips For Instruction

The following tips for instruction can support your efforts to help all students reach their maximum potential.

✔ Survey students to discover their individual differences. Use interest inventories of their unique talents so you can encourage contributions in the classroom.

✔ Be a model for respecting others. Adolescents crave social acceptance. The student with learning differences is especially sensitive to correction and criticism, particularly when it comes from a teacher. Your behavior will set the tone for how students treat one another.

✔ Expand opportunities for success. Provide a variety of instructional activities that reinforce skills and concepts.

✔ Establish measurable objectives and decide how you can best help students who meet them.

✔ Celebrate successes and make note of and praise "work in progress."

✔ Keep it simple. Point out problem areas if doing so can help a student effect change. Avoid over-

whelming students with too many goals at one time.

✔ Assign cooperative group projects that challenge all students to contribute to solving a problem or creating a product.

How Do I Reach Students With Learning Disabilities?

✔ Provide support and structure. Clearly specify rules, assignments, and responsibilities.

✔ Practice skills frequently. Use games and drills to help maintain student interest.

✔ Incorporate many modalities into the learning process. Provide opportunities to say, hear, write, read, and act out important concepts and information.

✔ Link new skills and concepts to those already mastered.

✔ If possible, allow students to record answers on audio.

✔ Allow extra time to complete assessments and assignments.

✔ Let students demonstrate proficiency with alternative presentations, including oral reports, role plays, art projects, and musical presentations.

✔ Provide outlines, notes, or recordings of lecture material.

✔ Pair students with peer helpers, and provide class time for pair interaction.

How Do I Reach Students With Behavioral Challenges?

✔ Provide a structured environment with clear-cut schedules, rules,

seat assignments, and safety procedures.

✔ Reinforce appropriate behavior and model it for students.

✔ Cue distracted students back to the task through verbal signals and teacher proximity.

✔ Set goals that can be achieved in the short term. Work for long-term improvement in the big areas.

How Do I Reach Students With Physical Challenges?

✔ Openly discuss with the student any uncertainties you have about when to offer aid.

✔ Ask parents or therapists and students what special devices or procedures are needed and whether any special safety precautions need to be taken.

✔ Welcome students with physical challenges into all activities, including field trips, special events, and projects.

✔ Provide information to assist class members and adults in their understanding of support needed.

How Do I Reach Students with Visual Impairments?

✔ Facilitate independence. Modify assignments as needed.

✔ Teach classmates how and when to serve as visual guides.

✔ Limit unnecessary noise in the classroom if it distracts the student with visual impairments.

✔ Provide tactile models whenever possible.

✔ Foster a spirit of inclusion. Describe people and events as they occur in the classroom. Remind classmates that the student with visual impairments cannot interpret gestures and other forms of nonverbal communication.

✔ Provide recorded lectures and reading assignments for use outside the classroom.

✔ Team the student with a sighted peer for written work.

How Do I Reach Students With Hearing Impairments?

✔ Seat students where they can see your lip movements easily and where they can avoid any visual distractions.

✔ Avoid standing with your back to the window or light source.

✔ Use an overhead projector so you can maintain eye contact while writing information for students.

✔ Seat students where they can see speakers.

✔ Write all assignments on the board, or hand out written instructions.

✔ If the student has a manual interpreter, allow both student and interpreter to select the most favorable seating arrangements.

✔ Teach students to look directly at each other when they speak.

How Do I Reach English Learners?

✔ Remember, students' ability to speak English does not reflect their academic abilities.

✔ Try to incorporate the students' cultural experience into your instruction. The help of a bilingual aide may be effective.

✔ Avoid any references in your instruction that could be construed as cultural stereotypes.

✔ Preteach important vocabulary and concepts.

✔ Encourage students to preview text before they begin reading, noting headings.

✔ Remind students not to ignore graphic organizers, photographs, and maps since there is much information in these visuals.

✔ Use memorabilia and photographs whenever possible to build background knowledge and understanding. An example of this would be coins in a foreign currency or a raw cotton ball to reinforce its importance in history.

How Do I Reach Gifted Students?

✔ Make arrangements for students to take selected subjects early and to work on independent projects.

✔ Ask "what if" questions to develop high-level thinking skills. Establish an environment safe for risk taking in your classroom.

✔ Emphasize concepts, theories, ideas, relationships, and generalizations about the content.

✔ Promote interest in the past by inviting students to make connections to the present.

✔ Let students express themselves in alternate ways such as creative writing, acting, debates, simulations, drawing, or music.

✔ Provide students with a catalog of helpful resources, listing such things as agencies that provide free and inexpensive materials, appropriate community services and programs, and community experts who might be called upon to speak to your students.

✔ Assign extension projects that allow students to solve real-life problems related to their communities.

Classroom Activity

Students respond eagerly to a subject when they can relate it to their own experiences. With the growing number of students who come from other world regions, explaining geography through a global theme (such as volcanoes) can give them a worldwide as well as a regional perspective. To develop this awareness, display a large world map. Have students use the library or the Internet to research the latitude and longitude of 15 major volcanoes around the world. Ask them to mark these locations on the map and answer the following questions:

- What patterns do you see in volcanic activity?
- What causes volcanic activity?
- Where in the world are volcanoes most active?

As a follow-up, suggest students use the Internet to find legends about the origins of some of the world's volcanoes. Encourage students to share what they find with the class.

ACADEMIC VOCABULARY

How Can I Help My Students Learn Academic Vocabulary?

What Is Academic English?

Academic English is the language used in academics, business, and courts of law. It is the type of English used in textbooks, and contains linguistic features associated with academic disciplines like social studies. Proficiency in reading and using academic English is especially related to long-term success in all parts of life.

By reinforcing academic English, teachers can help learners to access authentic, academic texts—not simplified texts that dummy down the content. In this way, they can provide information that will help build their students' background knowledge rapidly.

What Is Academic Vocabulary?

Academic vocabulary is based on academic English. By the time children have completed elementary school, they must have acquired the knowledge needed to understand academic vocabulary. How many words should they acquire to be able to access their texts? A basic 2,000-word vocabulary of high-frequency words makes up 87% of the vocabulary of academic texts. Eight hundred other academic words comprise an additional 8% of the words. Three percent of the remaining words are technical words. The remaining 2% are low-frequency words. There may be as many as 123,000 low-frequency words in academic texts.

Why Should Students Learn Academic Vocabulary?

English learners who have a basic 2,000-word vocabulary are ready to acquire most general words found in their texts.

Knowledge of academic words and general words can significantly boost a student's comprehension level of academic texts. Students who learn and practice these words before they graduate from high school are more likely to master academic material with increased

BananaStock/PictureQuest

confidence and speed. They waste less time and effort in guessing words or consulting dictionaries than those who only know the basic 2,000 words that characterize general conversation.

How Do I Include Academic Vocabulary and Academic English in My Teaching?

Teachers can provide students with academic vocabulary and help students understand the academic English of their text.

To develop academic English, learners must have already acquired basic proficiency in everyday English.

Academic English should be taught within contexts that make sense. In terms of instruction, teaching academic English includes providing students with access to core curriculum—in this case social studies.

Academic English arises in part from social practices in which academic English is used. The acquisition of academic vocabulary and grammar is necessary to advance the development of academic English.

Tips for Teaching Academic Vocabulary

✔ **Expose Students to Academic Vocabulary** You do not need to call attention to words students are learning because they will acquire them subconsciously.

✔ **Do Not Correct Students' Mistakes When Using the Vocabulary Words** All vocabulary understanding and spelling errors will disappear once the student reads more.

✔ **Help Students Decode the Words Themselves** Once they learn the alphabet, they should be able to decode words. Decoding each word they don't recognize will help them more than trying to focus on sentence structure. Once they can recognize the words, they can read "authentic" texts.

✔ **Do Not Ignore the English Learner in This Process** They can learn academic vocabulary before they are completely fluent in oral English.

✔ **Helping Students Build Academic Vocabulary Leads to Broader Learning** Students who have mastered the basic academic vocabulary are ready to acquire words from the rest of the groups. To help determine which words are in the 2,000-word basic group, refer to *West's General Service List of English Words,* 1953. The list is designed to serve as a guide for teachers and as a checklist and goal list for students.

Guidelines for Teaching Academic Vocabulary

1. Direct and planned instruction
2. Models—that have increasingly difficult language
3. Attention to form—pointing out linguistic features of words

Classroom Activity

Writing About Modern America

Give students a brief writing assignment. Ask them to write a short essay about one of the topics listed below in the left column. Have students use as many of the academic vocabulary words in the right column as they can in their essay. When completed, ask student volunteers to share their writing. Note what academic vocabulary words they use.

Topic	Academic Vocabulary
The challenges of reducing poverty in America	sufficient minimum medical income
Recent technological advances	innovate technology media potential data transmit

ePals GlobalCommunity
Where learners connect™

Stockbyte/Punchstock

ePals®, a global community of more than one million K-12 classrooms in 200 countries and territories, provides teachers with the opportunity to facilitate safe, authentic, and dynamic exchanges with other classrooms. McGraw-Hill Education, The Smithsonian Institution, International Baccalaureate, and leading educators around the globe have partnered with ePals® to help make learning dynamic for students, improve academic achievement, and meet multiple Common Core standards.

What Is Global Collaboration?

Global collaboration leverages the power of social media to connect classrooms around the world for real-life lessons and projects in virtual study groups, in and out of school. Students can safely work together on ePals® using familiar social media tools to collaborate on research, discussions, and multimedia projects. By connecting with peers in other parts of the world, students can discover people, places, and cultures far beyond the classroom.

Why Collaboration Is Crucial

Research shows that collaborative learning has a positive effect on student achievement. Collaborative, project-based experiences inspire students with real-world problems and bring lessons to life with dynamic, participatory learning. Students

are more motivated and try harder because they're communicating with a real person, for a real purpose. ePals®collaboration benefits students and educators in a variety of ways:

- Facilitates classroom-led delivery of Common Core-aligned, project-based learning experiences, including Writing 6 and Writing 7

- Demonstrates student knowledge by publishing written projects to share ideas and receive feedback from an international audience

- Develops core academic, college and career skills such as critical thinking, problem solving, communication and global awareness

Connect Globally

On ePals®, teachers can browse hundreds of thousands of classroom profiles and projects by location, age range, language, and subject matter, to find collaboration partners. Classrooms then partner in virtual project workspaces for digital collaboration around tailored projects, activities, and content. Each project workspace enables roundtable classroom collaboration and includes a suite of safe social media tools (private to that workspace and controlled by the teacher), including blogs, wikis, forums, and media galleries. ePals® also provides safe student email accounts for one-on-one student exchanges.

ePals® is specifically designed for safe K-12 communication and collaboration, compliant with the Children's Online Privacy Protection Act (COPPA), Family Educational Rights and Privacy Act (FERPA) and Children's Internet Protection Act (CIPA). A team of ePals® educators moderates all classroom profiles and projects to maintain a robust education community safe for K-12 students.

Tips for Collaborating Globally on ePals®

Pair Students With Global Peers: Pair students within a project workspace with peers from other countries to accomplish specific goals, such as completing joint-inquiry projects.

Host Online Discussions: Host dynamic discussions between students by posting forum topics for students to build on one another's ideas and learn to express their own thoughts clearly and persuasively.

Share Student Work: Have students publish their work and ideas to the project group using media galleries and encourage peer review.

Create Collaborative Content: Use wikis to have student groups author joint content, such as digital presentations and multimedia research reports.

To get started, visit ePals® at <u>www.epals.com/learningcenter</u>

REFERENCE ATLAS

Reference Atlas Maps	RA1
World: Political	RA2
World: Physical	RA4
North America: Political	RA6
North America: Physical	RA7
United States: Political	RA8
United States: Physical	RA10
Canada: Physical/Political	RA12
Middle America: Physical/Political	RA14
South America: Political	RA16
South America: Physical	RA17
Europe: Political	RA18
Europe: Physical	RA20
Africa: Political	RA22
Africa: Physical	RA23
Middle East: Physical/Political	RA24
Asia: Political	RA26
Asia: Physical	RA28
Oceania: Physical/Political	RA30
World Time Zones	RA32
Polar Regions	RA34
A World of Extremes	RA35
Geographic Dictionary	RA36

ATLAS KEY

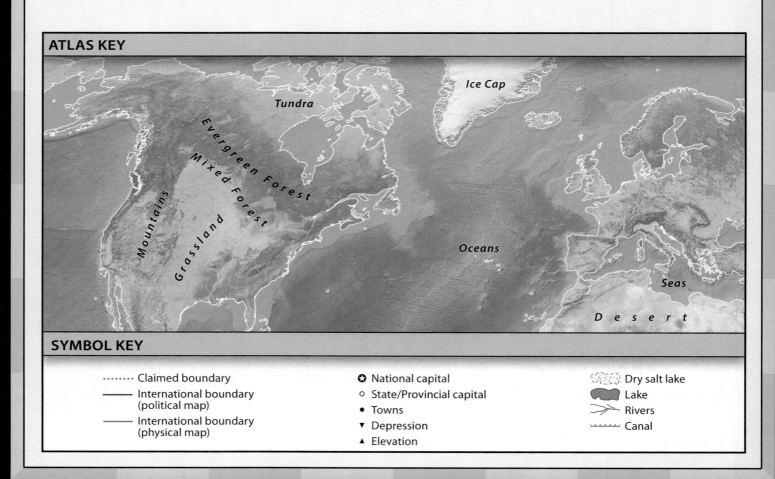

SYMBOL KEY

.... Claimed boundary

——— International boundary (political map)

——— International boundary (physical map)

✪ National capital

○ State/Provincial capital

• Towns

▼ Depression

▲ Elevation

Dry salt lake

Lake

Rivers

Canal

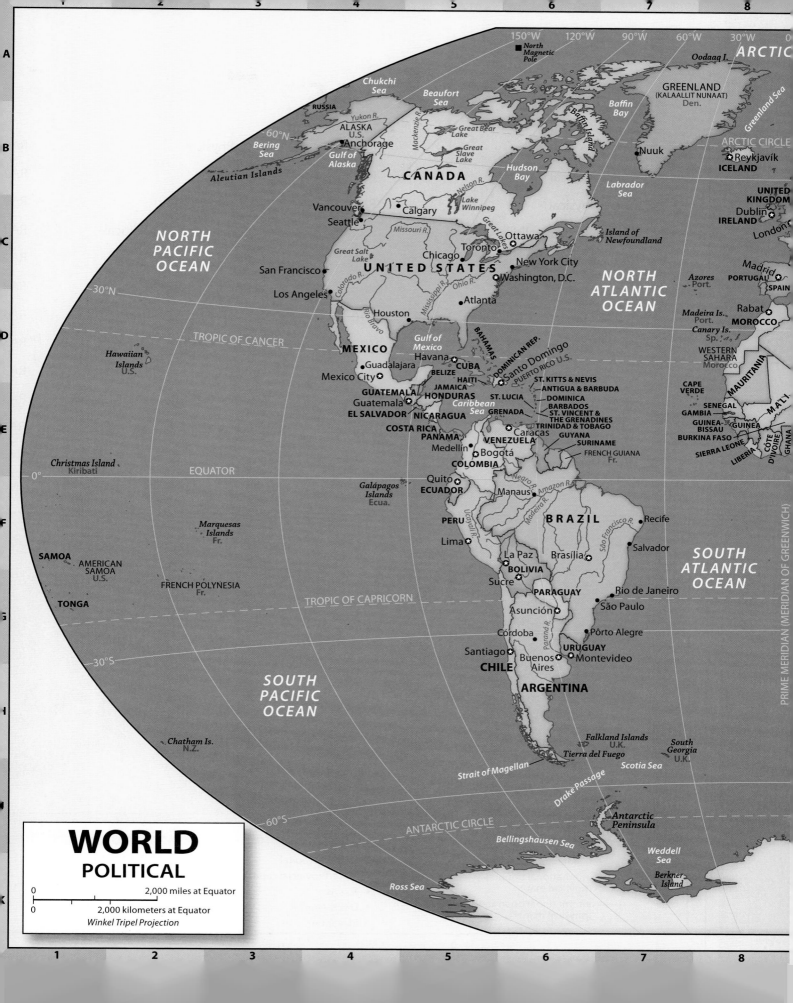

WORLD
POLITICAL

0   2,000 miles at Equator

0   2,000 kilometers at Equator

Winkel Tripel Projection

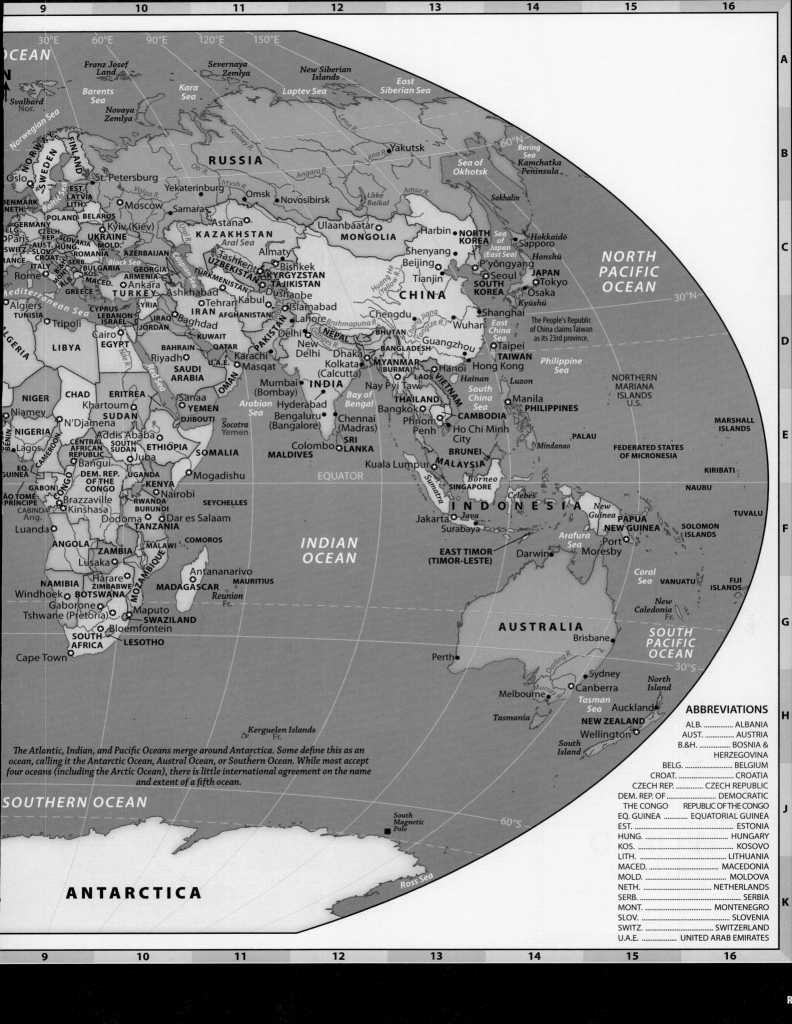

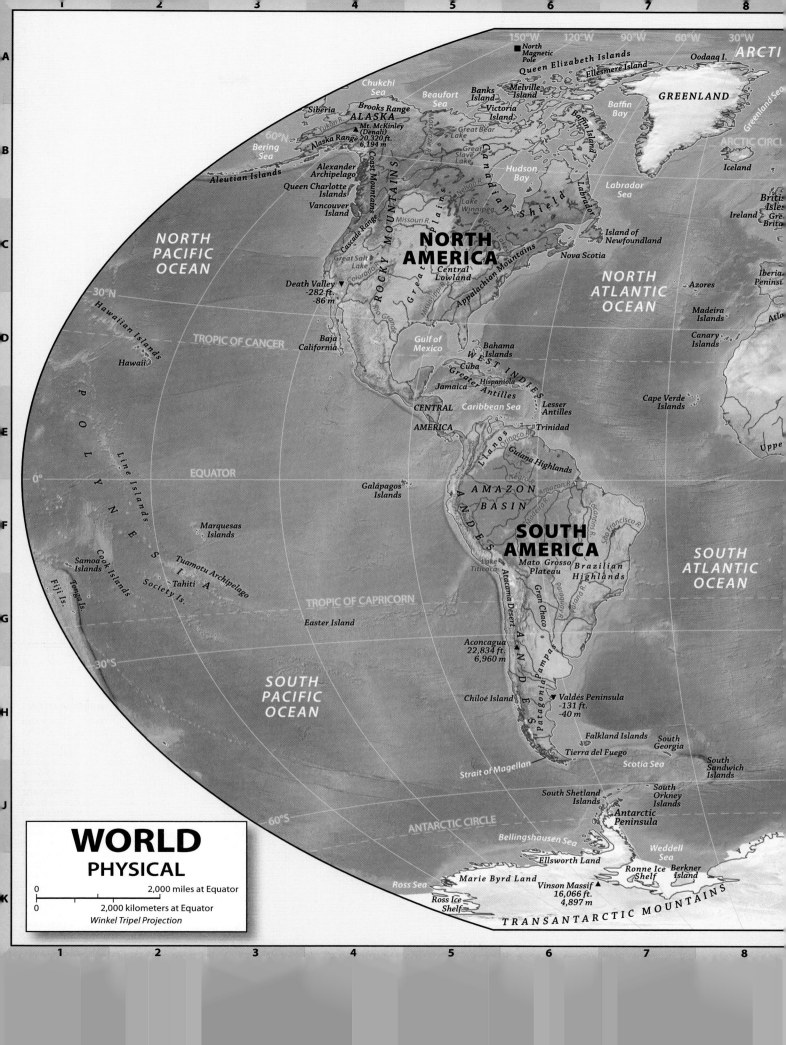

WORLD
PHYSICAL

0 ——————— 2,000 miles at Equator
0 ——————— 2,000 kilometers at Equator
Winkel Tripel Projection

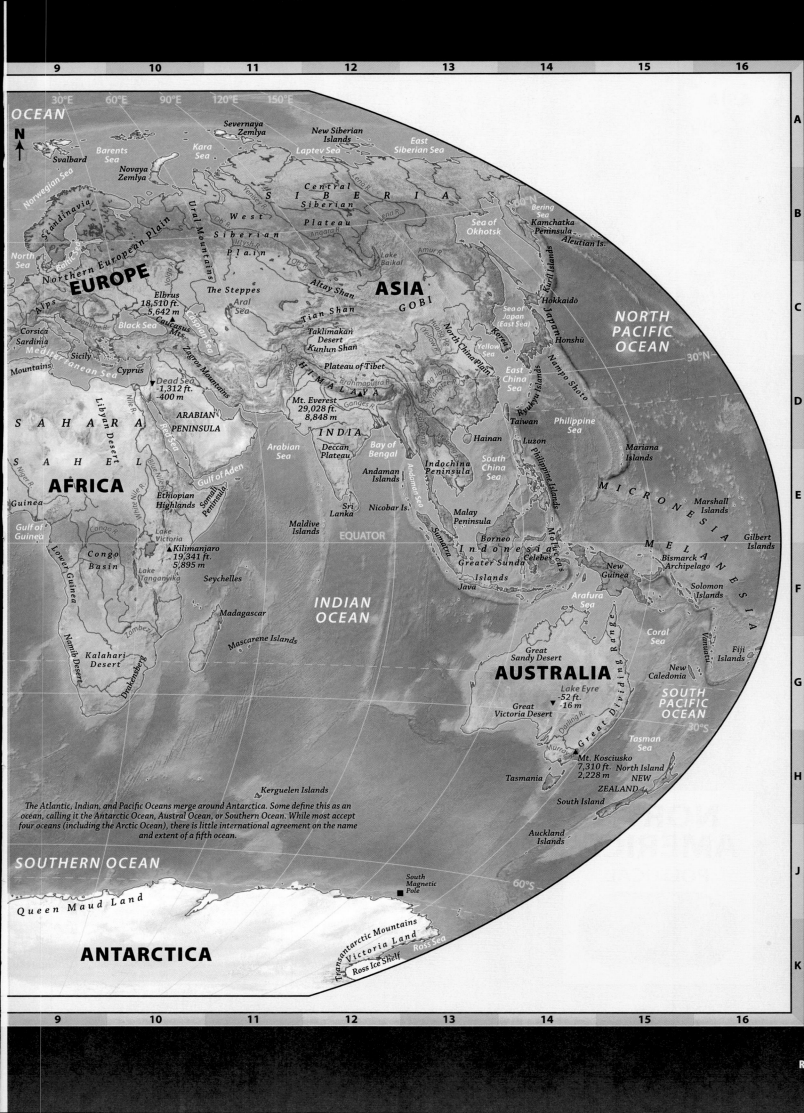

30°E   60°E   90°E   120°E   150°E

OCEAN

N

A

ARCTIC OCEAN

Svalbard

Norwegian Sea

Barents Sea

Novaya Zemlya

Kara Sea

Severnaya Zemlya

New Siberian Islands

Laptev Sea

East Siberian Sea

B

Scandinavia

North Sea

Baltic Sea

Ural Mountains

Yenisei R.

West Siberian Plain

Ob R.

Irtysh R.

Ob R.

Central Siberian Plateau

S I B E R I A

Lena R.

Angara R.

Amur R.

Lake Baikal

60°N

Bering Sea

Kamchatka Peninsula

Aleutian Is.

C

EUROPE

Alps

Northern European Plain

Volga R.

Danube R.

Elbrus 18,510 ft. 5,642 m

Caucasus Mts.

Black Sea

Caspian Sea

The Steppes

Aral Sea

Altay Shan

Tian Shan

ASIA

GOBI

Sea of Okhotsk

Kuril Islands

Hokkaidō

Sea of Japan (East Sea)

Honshū

NORTH PACIFIC OCEAN

Corsica

Sardinia

Sicily

Mediterranean Sea

Cyprus

Zagros Mountains

Dead Sea -1,312 ft. -400 m

Taklimakan Desert

Kunlun Shan

Plateau of Tibet

H I M A L A Y A

Mt. Everest 29,028 ft. 8,848 m

Ganges R.

Indus R.

Brahmaputra R.

Huang He (Yellow)

North China Plain

Chang Jiang

Yangtze R.

Korea

Yellow Sea

East China Sea

Ryukyu Islands

Taiwan

Nampo Shoto

30°N

D

Mountains

S A H A R A

Libyan Desert

Nile R.

Red Sea

ARABIAN PENINSULA

Arabian Sea

INDIA

Deccan Plateau

Bay of Bengal

Andaman Islands

Mekong R.

Indochina Peninsula

Hainan

South China Sea

Luzon

Philippine Sea

Philippine Islands

Mariana Islands

E

S A H E L

Guinea

Gulf of Guinea

AFRICA

White Nile R.

Blue Nile R.

Ethiopian Highlands

Somali Peninsula

Gulf of Aden

Maldive Islands

Sri Lanka

Nicobar Is.

Andaman Sea

Malay Peninsula

Borneo

Celebes

Moluccas

New Guinea

M I C R O N E S I A

Marshall Islands

Gilbert Islands

M E L A N E S I A

Niger R.

Congo R.

Lower Guinea

Congo Basin

Lake Victoria

Kilimanjaro 19,341 ft. 5,895 m

Lake Tanganyika

Seychelles

EQUATOR

Sumatra

I n d o n e s i a

Greater Sunda Islands

Java

Bismarck Archipelago

Solomon Islands

F

Namib Desert

Zambezi R.

Madagascar

Mascarene Islands

INDIAN OCEAN

Arafura Sea

Coral Sea

Vanuatu

Fiji Islands

G

Kalahari Desert

Drakensberg

Great Sandy Desert

AUSTRALIA

Great Dividing Range

Lake Eyre -52 ft. -16 m

Great Victoria Desert

New Caledonia

SOUTH PACIFIC OCEAN

30°S

Murray R.

Darling R.

Mt. Kosciusko 7,310 ft. 2,228 m

Tasman Sea

North Island

NEW ZEALAND

H

Kerguelen Islands

Tasmania

South Island

The Atlantic, Indian, and Pacific Oceans merge around Antarctica. Some define this as an ocean, calling it the Antarctic Ocean, Austral Ocean, or Southern Ocean. While most accept four oceans (including the Arctic Ocean), there is little international agreement on the name and extent of a fifth ocean.

Auckland Islands

SOUTHERN OCEAN

60°S

J

Queen Maud Land

South Magnetic Pole

Transantarctic Mountains

Victoria Land

Ross Sea

ANTARCTICA

Ross Ice Shelf

K

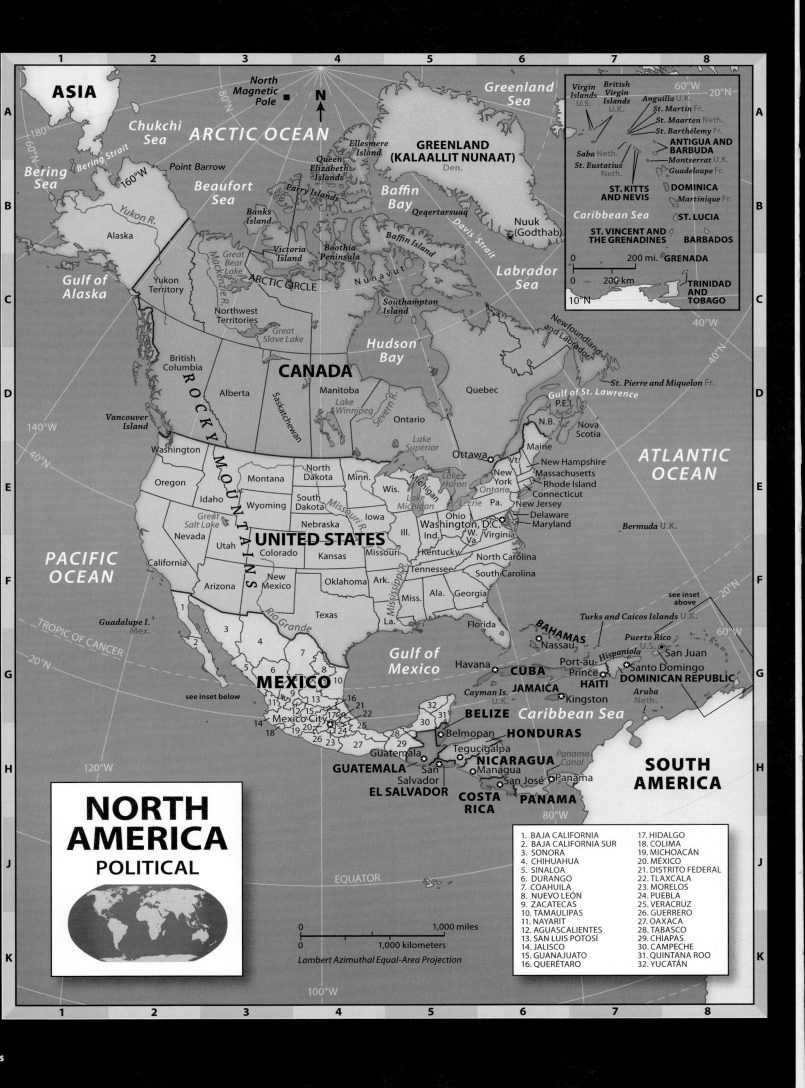

NORTH AMERICA
POLITICAL

Lambert Azimuthal Equal-Area Projection

1. BAJA CALIFORNIA	17. HIDALGO
2. BAJA CALIFORNIA SUR	18. COLIMA
3. SONORA	19. MICHOACÁN
4. CHIHUAHUA	20. MÉXICO
5. SINALOA	21. DISTRITO FEDERAL
6. DURANGO	22. TLAXCALA
7. COAHUILA	23. MORELOS
8. NUEVO LEÓN	24. PUEBLA
9. ZACATECAS	25. VERACRUZ
10. TAMAULIPAS	26. GUERRERO
11. NAYARIT	27. OAXACA
12. AGUASCALIENTES	28. TABASCO
13. SAN LUIS POTOSÍ	29. CHIAPAS
14. JALISCO	30. CAMPECHE
15. GUANAJUATO	31. QUINTANA ROO
16. QUERÉTARO	32. YUCATÁN

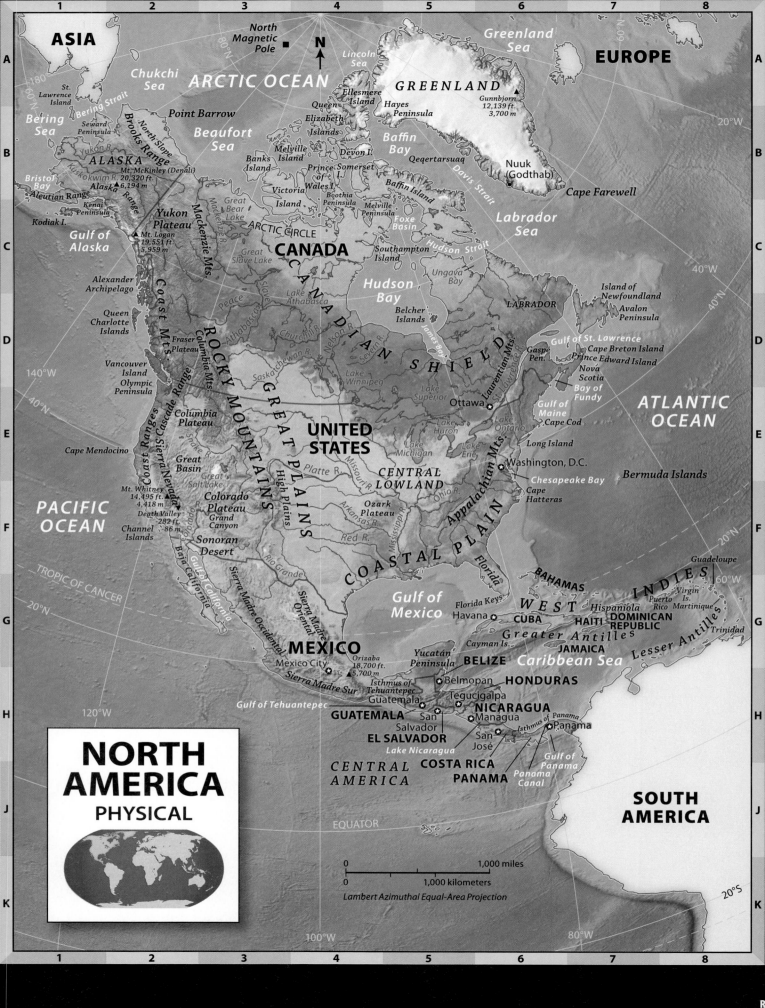

NORTH AMERICA
PHYSICAL

ASIA

EUROPE

North Magnetic Pole ■

N

Chukchi Sea

ARCTIC OCEAN

Greenland Sea

Lincoln Sea

GREENLAND

Point Barrow

Beaufort Sea

Ellesmere Island

Queen Elizabeth Islands

Hayes Peninsula

Gunnbjorn 12,139 ft. 3,700 m

St. Lawrence Island

Bering Strait

North Slope

Brooks Range

Melville Island

Banks Island

Devon I.

Somerset I.

Baffin Bay

Qeqertarsuaq

Nuuk (Godthab)

Bering Sea

Seward Peninsula

Yukon R.

ALASKA

Mt. McKinley (Denali) 20,320 ft. 6,194 m

Prince of Wales I.

Boothia Peninsula

Baffin Island

Davis Strait

Cape Farewell

Bristol Bay

Kuskokwim R.

Alaska Range

Victoria Island

Melville Peninsula

Aleutian Range

Kenai Peninsula

Yukon Plateau

Mackenzie Mts.

Great Bear Lake

Foxe Basin

Labrador Sea

Kodiak I.

Gulf of Alaska

Mt. Logan 19,551 ft. 5,959 m

ARCTIC CIRCLE

Great Slave Lake

Hudson Strait

Island of Newfoundland

Alexander Archipelago

Coast Mts.

CANADA

Southampton Island

Ungava Bay

Avalon Peninsula

Queen Charlotte Islands

Fraser Plateau

Columbia Mts.

Peace R.

Athabasca R.

Slave R.

Lake Athabasca

CANADIAN SHIELD

Hudson Bay

Belcher Islands

James Bay

LABRADOR

Gulf of St. Lawrence

Cape Breton Island

Prince Edward Island

Vancouver Island

Olympic Peninsula

Cascade Range

ROCKY MOUNTAINS

Churchill R.

Nelson R.

Saskatchewan R.

Lake Winnipeg

Laurentian Mts.

St. Lawrence R.

Gaspé Pen.

Nova Scotia

Bay of Fundy

Cape Mendocino

Coast Ranges

Sierra Nevada

Columbia Plateau

Snake R.

Severn R.

Lake Superior

Lake Huron

Ottawa

Lake Ontario

Gulf of Maine

Cape Cod

ATLANTIC OCEAN

GREAT PLAINS

Great Basin

UNITED STATES

Platte R.

Missouri R.

Lake Michigan

Lake Erie

Appalachian Mts.

Long Island

Washington, D.C.

PACIFIC OCEAN

Mt. Whitney 14,495 ft. 4,418 m

Great Salt Lake

Colorado Plateau

High Plains

CENTRAL LOWLAND

Ozark Plateau

Ohio R.

Chesapeake Bay

Cape Hatteras

Bermuda Islands

Death Valley 282 ft. –86 m

Channel Islands

Grand Canyon

Arkansas R.

Mississippi R.

Sonoran Desert

Baja California

Rio Grande

Red R.

COASTAL PLAIN

Florida

Sierra Madre Occidental

Gulf of Mexico

Florida Keys

BAHAMAS

WEST INDIES

Guadeloupe

TROPIC OF CANCER

20°N

Sierra Madre Oriental

Havana

CUBA

Greater Antilles

Hispaniola

HAITI

Puerto Rico

Virgin Is.

Martinique

MEXICO

Orizaba 18,700 ft. 5,700 m

Yucatán Peninsula

BELIZE

DOMINICAN REPUBLIC

Lesser Antilles

Mexico City

JAMAICA

Trinidad

Sierra Madre Sur

Isthmus of Tehuantepec

Belmopan

Caribbean Sea

Cayman Is.

HONDURAS

Gulf of Tehuantepec

Guatemala

Tegucigalpa

GUATEMALA

San Salvador

NICARAGUA

Managua

Isthmus of Panama

Panama

EL SALVADOR

San José

Gulf of Panama

Lake Nicaragua

COSTA RICA

PANAMA

Panama Canal

CENTRAL AMERICA

EQUATOR

SOUTH AMERICA

20°S

1,000 miles

1,000 kilometers

Lambert Azimuthal Equal-Area Projection

UNITED STATES
POLITICAL

RUSSIA

ARCTIC

Bering Sea

St. Lawrence Island

Bering Strait

Point Barrow

Seward Peninsula

Norton Sound

Brooks Range

Beaufort Sea

Nunivak Island

ALASKA

Yukon R.

Fairbanks

ARCTIC CIRCLE

Alaska Range

Bristol Bay

Alaska Peninsula

Anchorage

Kodiak I.

Gulf of Alaska

Alexander Archipelago

Juneau

Tacoma Seattle
Olympia
WASH. Spokane
MONTANA

Portland
Helena
Salem
Butte Billings
Eugene
OREGON IDAHO
Boise

Cascade Range

Snake R.

ROCKY

Great Salt Lake

WYOMING

Reno
Salt Lake City

Sacramento Carson City
San Francisco
Sierra Nevada
NEVADA UTAH

Las Vegas

CALIFORNIA

Los Angeles
ARIZONA
Santa Fe
San Diego
Phoenix Albuquerque
NEW MEXICO
Tucson

El Paso

PACIFIC OCEAN

Honolulu

HAWAII

Hilo

TROPIC OF CANCER

0   500 miles
0   500 kilometers
Lambert Azimuthal Equal-Area Projection

40°N
170°E
50°N
180°
170°W
70°N
60°N
160°W
150°W

170°E

180°

30°N

170°W

20°N

160°W

10°N

150°W
140°W
130°W
120°W
110°W

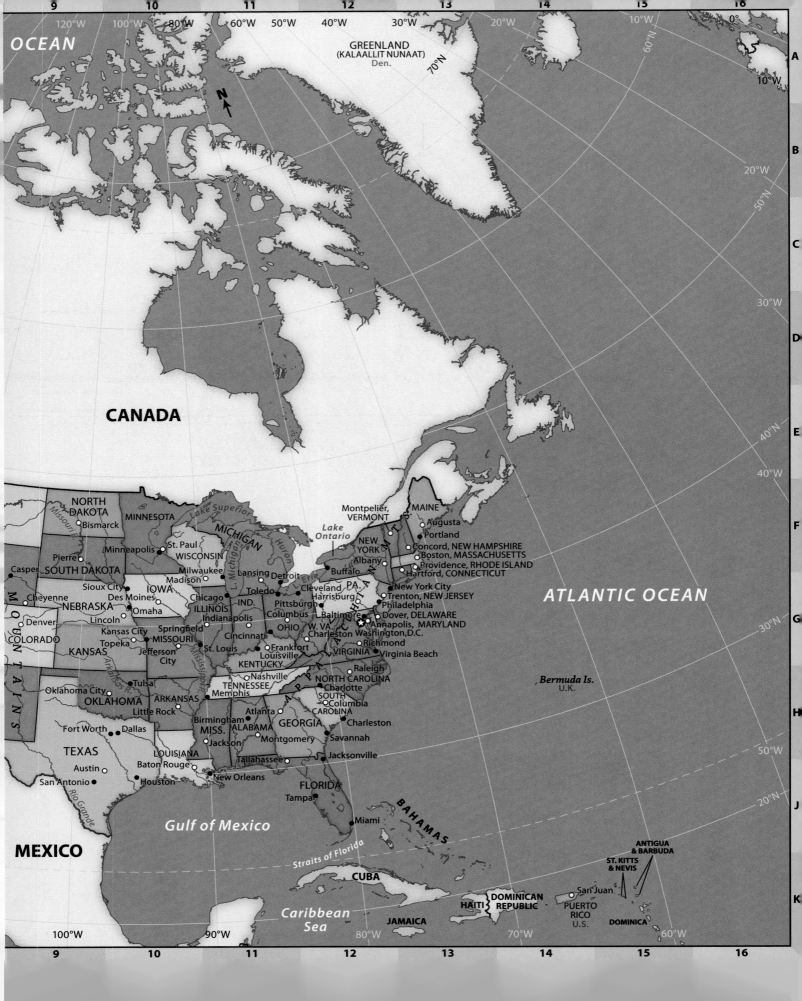

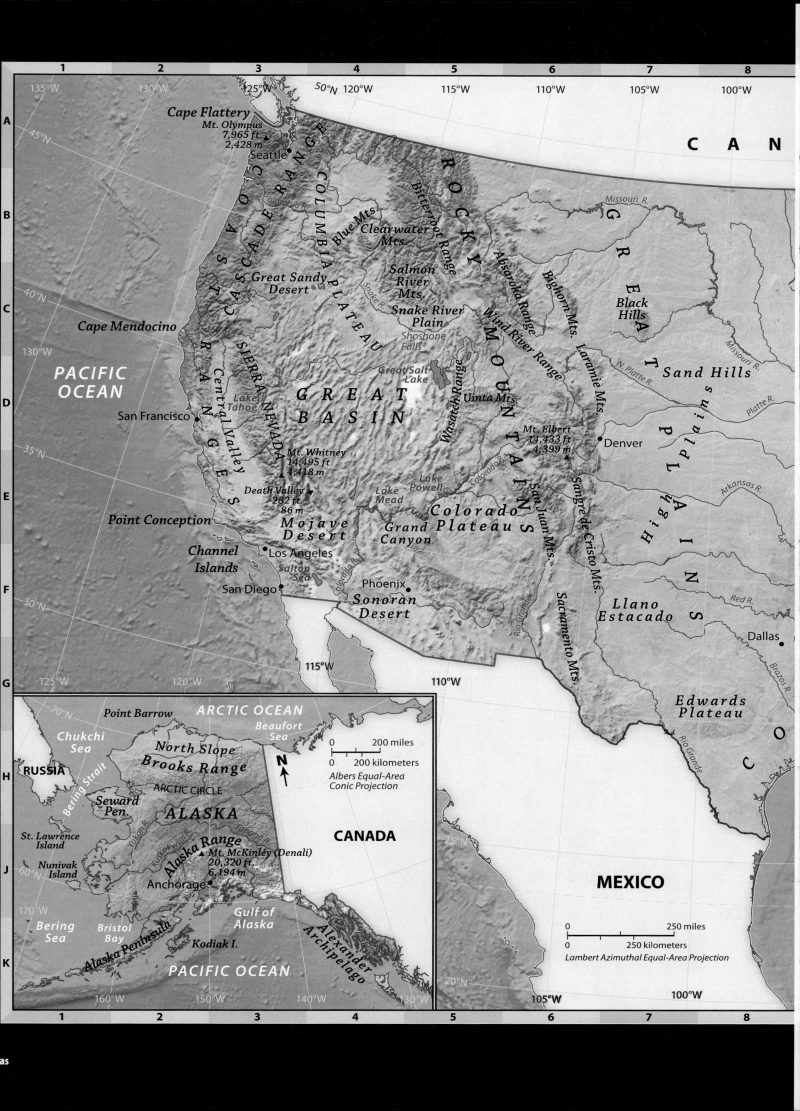

Main map labels:

A B C D E F G H J K
1 2 3 4 5 6 7 8

135°W 130°W 125°W 50°N 120°W 115°W 110°W 105°W 100°W
45°N
40°N
35°N
30°N

C A N ...

Cape Flattery
Mt. Olympus
7,965 ft.
2,428 m
Seattle

CASCADE RANGE
COLUMBIA PLATEAU
Columbia R.
Blue Mts.
Clearwater Mts.
Bitterroot Range
ROCKY
Great Sandy Desert
Salmon River Mts.
Absaroka Range
Bighorn Mts.
G R E A T
Cape Mendocino
Snake River Plain
Snake R.
Wind River Range
Laramie Mts.
Black Hills
Shoshone Falls
Missouri R.
Sand Hills
PACIFIC OCEAN
130°W
SIERRA NEVADA
Great Salt Lake
Wasatch Range
Uinta Mts.
Missouri R.
N. Platte R.
G R E A T   B A S I N
Lake Tahoe
Central Valley
M O U N T A I N S
Mt. Elbert
14,433 ft
4,399 m
Denver
Platte R.
P L A I N S
San Francisco
Mt. Whitney
14,495 ft
4,418 m
Lake Powell
Colorado R.
San Juan Mts.
Sangre de Cristo Mts.
Arkansas R.
Death Valley
282 ft
-86 m
Lake Mead
C o l o r a d o   P l a t e a u
Point Conception
M o j a v e   D e s e r t
Grand Canyon
H i g h   P l a i n s
Channel Islands
Los Angeles
Salton Sea
Colorado R.
Sacramento Mts.
Rio Grande
Llano Estacado
Red R.
San Diego
Phoenix
S o n o r a n   D e s e r t
Dallas
115°W
110°W
Edwards Plateau
Rio Grande
C O
Brazos R.
MEXICO
25°N
20°N

Alaska inset map:

70°N
Point Barrow
ARCTIC OCEAN
Beaufort Sea
Chukchi Sea
North Slope
Brooks Range
0   200 miles
0   200 kilometers
N
Albers Equal-Area Conic Projection
RUSSIA
Bering Strait
ARCTIC CIRCLE
Seward Pen.
A L A S K A
CANADA
St. Lawrence Island
Yukon R.
Kuskokwim R.
Tanana R.
Alaska Range
Mt. McKinley (Denali)
20,320 ft.
6,194 m
Anchorage
Nunivak Island
60°N
170°W
160°W
150°W
140°W
130°W
Bering Sea
Bristol Bay
Gulf of Alaska
Alexander Archipelago
Alaska Peninsula
Kodiak I.
PACIFIC OCEAN

0   250 miles
0   250 kilometers
Lambert Azimuthal Equal-Area Projection
105°W
100°W

las

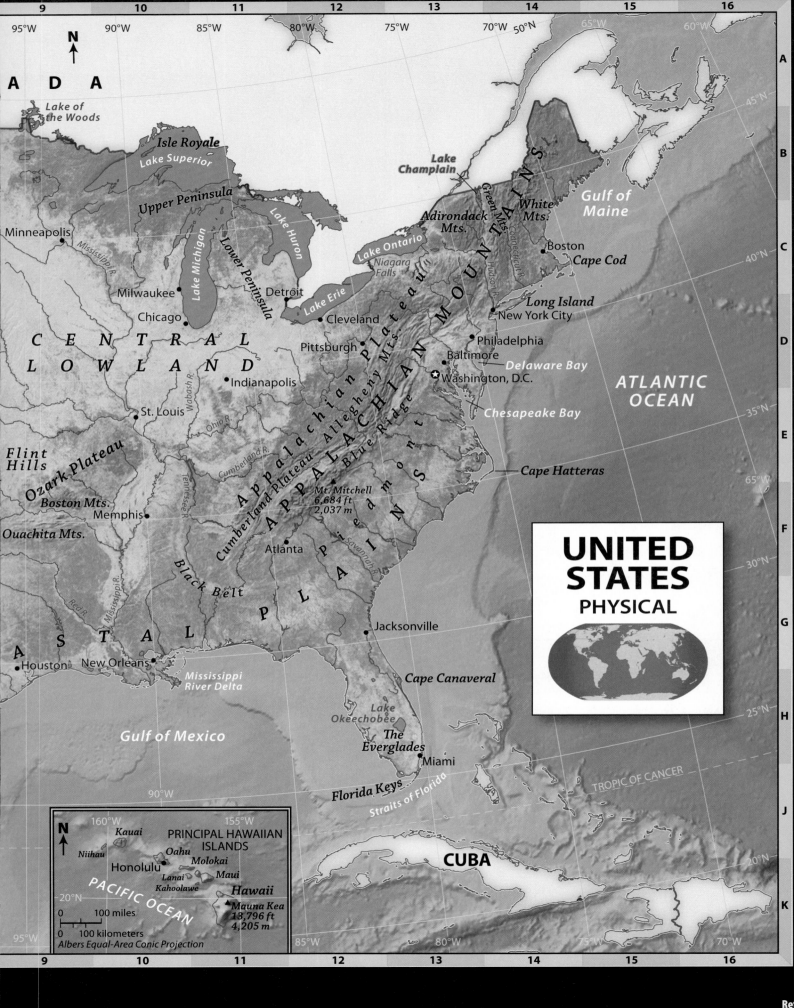

UNITED STATES
STATES
PHYSICAL

Lake of the Woods

Isle Royale
Lake Superior

Upper Peninsula

Minneapolis

Lake Michigan

Lower Peninsula

Lake Huron

Milwaukee

Chicago

Detroit

Mississippi R.

C E N T R A L

L O W L A N D

Wabash R.

Indianapolis

St. Louis

Ohio R.

Cleveland

Pittsburgh

Lake Erie

Lake Ontario

Niagara Falls

Appalachian Plateau

Allegheny Mts.

Lake Champlain

Green Mts.

Adirondack Mts.

White Mts.

Gulf of Maine

Connecticut R.

Boston

Cape Cod

Hudson R.

Long Island

New York City

Philadelphia

Baltimore

Washington, D.C.

Delaware Bay

Chesapeake Bay

ATLANTIC OCEAN

A P P A L A C H I A N   M O U N T A I N S

Cumberland Plateau

Blue Ridge

Cumberland R.

Tennessee R.

Flint Hills

Ozark Plateau

Boston Mts.

Memphis

Ouachita Mts.

P i e d m o n t

Mt. Mitchell
6,684 ft
2,037 m

Atlanta

Savannah R.

Cape Hatteras

A S T A L   P L A I N S

Black Belt

Mississippi R.

Red R.

Houston

New Orleans

Mississippi River Delta

Gulf of Mexico

Jacksonville

Cape Canaveral

Lake Okeechobee

The Everglades

Miami

Florida Keys

Straits of Florida

TROPIC OF CANCER

CUBA

N

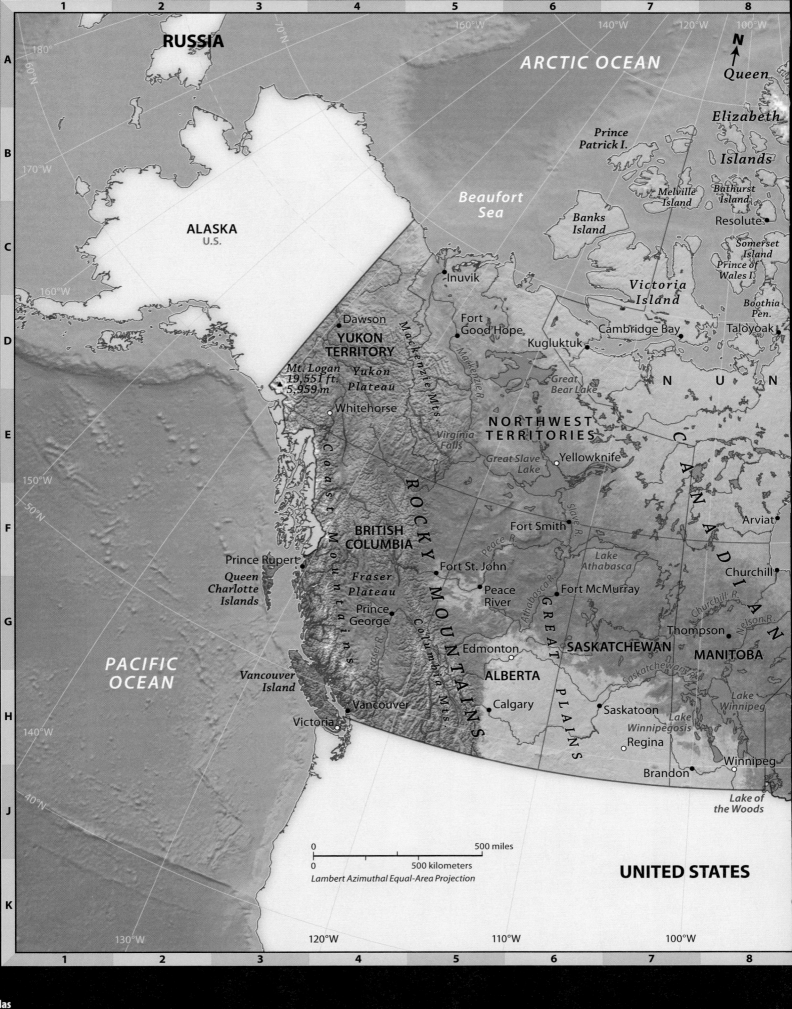

CANADA
PHYSICAL / POLITICAL

Ellesmere Island

Devon Island

GREENLAND
(KALAALLIT NUNAAT)
Den.

ICELAND

Baffin Bay

Arctic Bay

Baffin Island

Igloolik

Davis Strait

Melville Peninsula

Foxe Basin

N U N A V U T

Repulse Bay

Iqaluit

Southampton Island

Hudson Strait

Labrador Sea

Chesterfield Inlet

Ungava Bay

Hudson Bay

Kuujjuaq

Nain

NEWFOUNDLAND AND LABRADOR

Cartwright

Belcher Islands

Schefferville

Happy Valley-Goose Bay

Churchill Falls

Island of Newfoundland

Fort Severn

Kuujjuarapik

Smallwood Reservoir

St. John's

Labrador City

Avalon Peninsula

James Bay

Q U E B E C

Manicouagan Reservoir

Anticosti I.

St.-Pierre & Miquelon
Fr.

S H I E L D

Sept-Îles

Gulf of St. Lawrence

Lake Nipigon

O N T A R I O

Gaspé Pen.

PRINCE EDWARD ISLAND

Sydney

Cape Breton I.

Chicoutimi

ATLANTIC OCEAN

Thunder Bay

Timmins

Rouyn-Noranda

Quebec

NEW BRUNSWICK

Charlottetown

NOVA SCOTIA

Lake Superior

Sudbury

North Bay

Montreal

St. Lawrence R.

Fredericton

Saint John

Halifax

Ottawa

Lake Michigan

Lake Huron

Toronto

L. Ontario

Bay of Fundy

London

Niagara Falls

Lake Erie

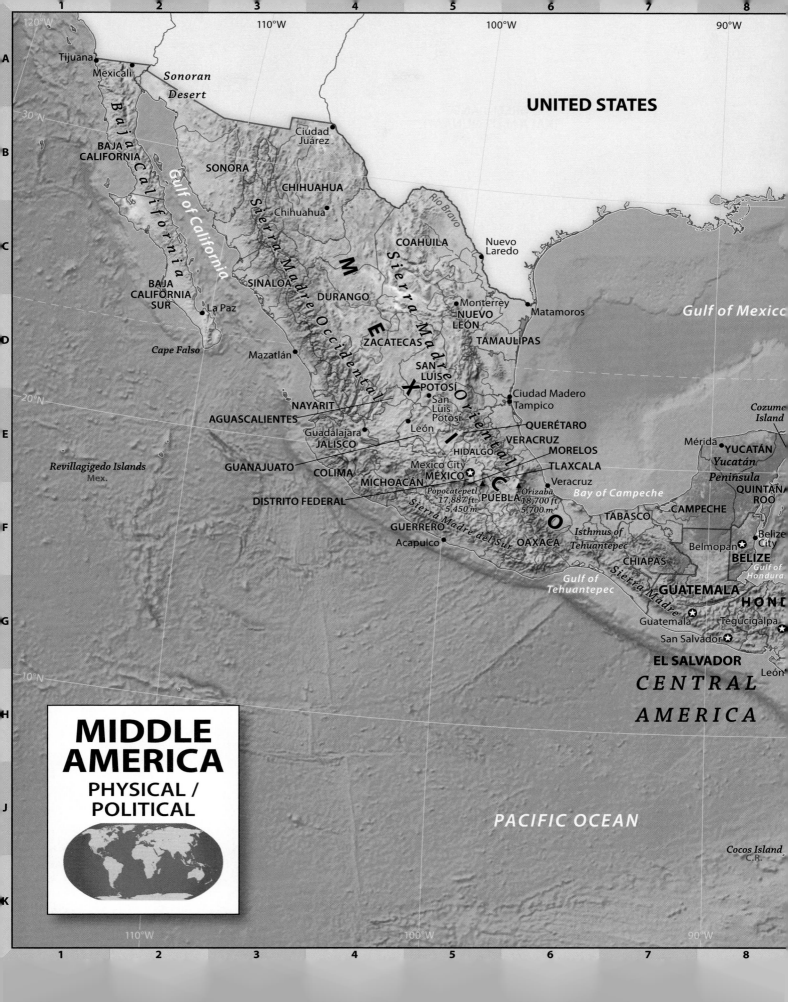

MIDDLE AMERICA
PHYSICAL / POLITICAL

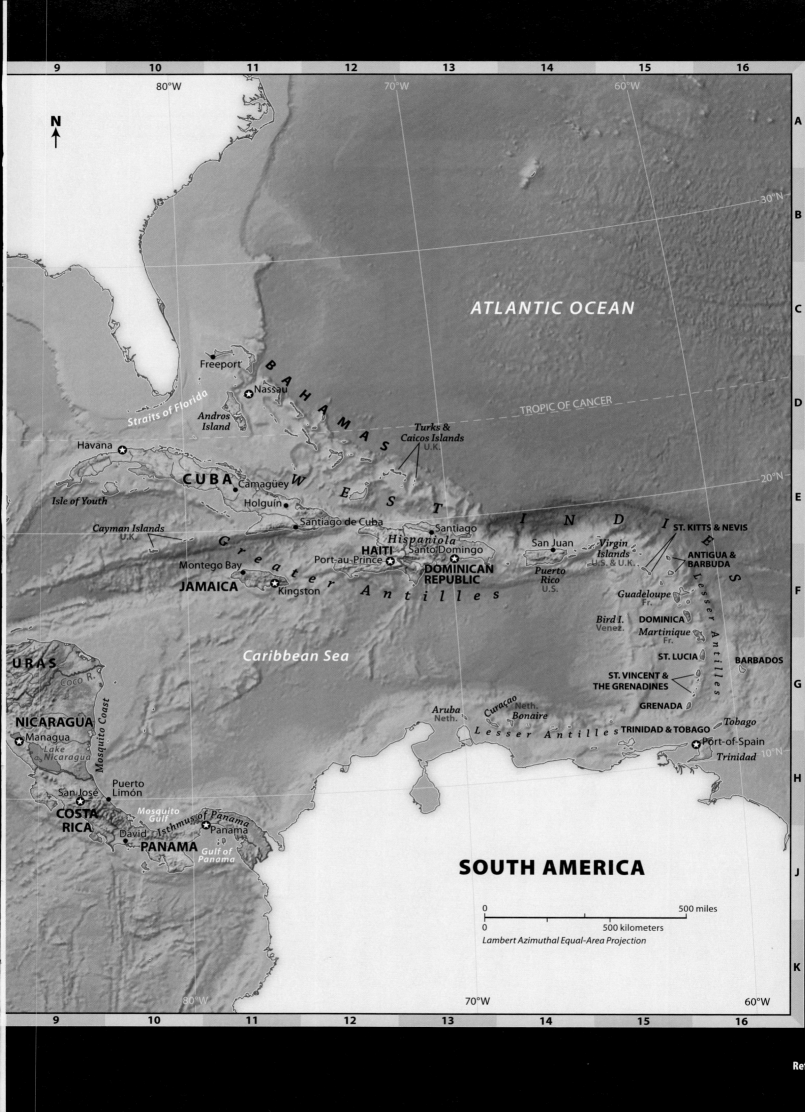

80°W   70°W   60°W

N

A

30°N   B

ATLANTIC OCEAN   C

Freeport

B A H A M A S

Nassau

Straits of Florida   *Andros Island*   Turks &
Caicos Islands
U.K.   TROPIC OF CANCER   D

Havana   20°N   E

CUBA   Camagüey   *W*

Isle of Youth   Holguín   *E*   *S*   *T*

Santiago de Cuba   Santiago   *I*   *N*   *D*   *I*   **ST. KITTS & NEVIS**

Cayman Islands
U.K.   *Hispaniola*   San Juan   *Virgin Islands*
U.S. & U.K.   **ANTIGUA &
BARBUDA**   *E*

G r e a t e r   **HAITI**   Santo Domingo   *Puerto Rico*
U.S.   *S*

Montego Bay   Port-au-Prince   **DOMINICAN REPUBLIC**   *Guadeloupe*
Fr.   F

JAMAICA   Kingston   *A n t i l l e s*   *Bird I.*
Venez.   **DOMINICA**
Martinique
Fr.   *Lesser Antilles*

Caribbean Sea   **ST. LUCIA**   **BARBADOS**   G

**ST. VINCENT &
THE GRENADINES**

U R A S   *Coco R.*   **GRENADA**

Aruba
Neth.   *Curaçao*   Neth.
Bonaire   *Tobago*

NICARAGUA   *Mosquito Coast*   *L e s s e r A n t i l l e s*   **TRINIDAD & TOBAGO**

Managua   *Lake Nicaragua*   Port-of-Spain   10°N   *Trinidad*   H

San José   Puerto Limón

Mosquito Gulf   *Isthmus of Panama*

COSTA RICA   David   Panamá

PANAMA   *Gulf of Panama*   J

SOUTH AMERICA

0   500 miles
0   500 kilometers
Lambert Azimuthal Equal-Area Projection   K

Re

Caribbean Sea

VENEZUELA
Caracas

GUYANA
SURINAME
Georgetown
Paramaribo
Cayenne
FRENCH GUIANA

Lake Maracaibo
Orinoco R.
LLANOS
Angel Falls
Total drop
3,212 ft. 979 m

Bogotá

GUIANA HIGHLANDS

COLOMBIA

Boundary claimed
by Suriname

Marajó Island

Malpelo I.

Quito
ECUADOR

A N D E S

Río Negro

Amazon R.

EQUATOR

A M A Z O N

PERU

Marañón R.

Amazon R.

B A S I N

S e l v a s

Tapajós R.
Xingu R.
Araguaia R.
Tocantins R.
São Francisco R.

Purus R.
Madeira R.
Ucayali R.

BRAZIL

Lima

Machu Picchu

Lake Titicaca

La Paz

BOLIVIA

MATO GROSSO PLATEAU

B R A Z I L I A N

Brasília

Altiplano

Sucre

Salar de Uyuni

H I G H L A N D S

20°S

TROPIC OF CAPRICORN

C H A C O

Paraguay R.

Paraná R.

PARAGUAY

G R A N

San Ambrosio I.

San Félix I.

Iguazú Falls

Asunción

A N D E S

Paraná R.

Uruguay R.

ATLANTIC OCEAN

CHILE

Aconcagua
22,834 ft.
6,960 m

Juan Fernández Is.

Santiago

Buenos Aires

URUGUAY

Montevideo

P A M P A S

Río de la Plata

ARGENTINA

Olorado R.

Negro R.

P A T A G O N I A

Chiloé Island

Valdés Peninsula
-131 ft.
-40 m

Gulf of San Jorge

Taitao Peninsula

PACIFIC OCEAN

Wellington I.

Falkland Islands (Islas Malvinas)

Stanley

Tierra del Fuego

Strait of Magellan

Cape Horn

South Georgia Island

SOUTH AMERICA
PHYSICAL

0   1,000 miles
0   1,000 kilometers
Lambert Azimuthal Equal-Area Projection

A commonly accepted division between Asia and Europe—here marked by a gray line—is formed by the Ural Mountains, Ural River, Caspian Sea, Caucasus Mountains, and the Black Sea with its outlets, the Bosporus and the Dardanelles.

Europe/Asia boundary

ASIA

RUSSIA

KAZAKHSTAN

URAL MOUNTAINS

Barents Sea

Tobseda
Pechora
Murmansk
Ivalo
Kirovsk
Kiruna
Kola Peninsula
Umba
White Sea
Kem'
Arkhangel'sk
Severodvinsk
Kemi
Luleå
Umeå
Oulu
Northern Dvina R.
Syktyvkar
Perm
FINLAND
Lake Onega
Vaasa
Kuopio
Lake Ladoga
Kirov
Ufa
Pori
Tampere
Turku
Helsinki
St. Petersburg
Kazan'
Tallinn
Novgorod
Yaroslavl'
ESTONIA
Nizhniy Novgorod
Orenburg
LATVIA
Tver'
Moscow
Samara
Riga
Daugavpils
Penza
Oral
LITHUANIA
Smolensk
Ryazan'
Saratov
Ural R.
Vilnius
Vitsyebsk
Kaunas
Minsk
Bryansk
Volga R.
Kaliningrad
BELARUS
Homyel'
Kursk
Warsaw
Chernihiv
Volgograd
Vistula R.
Sumy
Don R.
Lviv
Kyiv (Kiev)
Kharkiv
Astrakhan
Vinnytsya
Poltava
UKRAINE
Donets'k
Dnieper R.
Dniester R.
Dnipropetrovs'k
Rostov
Carpathian Mts.
MOLDOVA
Sea of Azov
Stavropol'
Caspian Sea
Chişinău
Odessa
Kerch
Caucasus Mountains
Grozny
ROMANIA
Crimea
Simferopol'
GEORGIA
AZERBAIJAN
Belgrade
Bucharest
Sevastopol'
Yalta
Baku
SERBIA
Constanţa
Balkan Mts.
Varna
Black Sea
KOSOVO
Prishtina
Bosporus
BULGARIA
Sofia
MACEDONIA
Skopje
İstanbul
T U R K E Y
Thessaloniki
Sea of Marmara
GREECE
Dardanelles
Aegean Sea
Athens
Peloponnese
Rhodes
ASIA
Iraklíon
Nicosia
Crete Greece
CYPRUS

Sea
Sea

0 ____ 400 miles
0 ____ 400 kilometers
Lambert Azimuthal Equal-Area Projection

EUROPE
PHYSICAL

N

ARCTIC CIRCLE

Norwegian Sea

ICELAND
Reykjavík

Faeroe Islands

Shetland Islands

NORWAY
Oslo
SWEDEN
Stockholm

Gotland

Orkney Islands

Outer Hebrides

Highlands
British Isles

Edinburgh

Skagerrak
Kattegat

Jutland
Zealand

DENMARK
Copenhagen

Belfast

North Sea

UNITED KINGDOM

IRELAND
Dublin

Irish Sea

Baltic

Celtic Sea

Great Britain

Cardiff

Thames R.
London

NETHERLANDS
Amsterdam

Berlin

N O R T H

POLAND

ATLANTIC OCEAN

Land's End

English Channel

Brussels
BELGIUM

Elbe R.

Rhine R.

GERMANY

Prague
CZECH REPUBLIC

Brittany

Seine R.
Paris

Luxembourg
LUXEMBOURG

Danube R.

Bratislava
SLOVAKI

Loire R.

FRANCE

LIECHTENSTEIN
Vienna
Vaduz
AUSTRIA
Budapest
HUNGAR

Bay of Biscay

Cantabrian Mountains

Bern
SWITZERLAND

Massif Central

Mont Blanc
15,771 ft.
4,807 m

A L P S

Drava R.

SLOVENIA
Ljubljana
Zagreb
CROATIA

Po R.

Rhône

Pyrenees

Andorra la Vella
ANDORRA

MONACO

Riviera

SAN MARINO

Adriatic Sea

BOSNIA & HERZEGOVINA
Sarajevo

I B E R I A N

Douro R.

Ebro R.

Madrid

Corsica

ITALY

MONTENEGRO
Podgorica

Lisbon
PORTUGAL

Tagus R.

SPAIN

P E N I N S U L A

Rome

Tiranë
ALBANIA

Cape St. Vincent

VATICAN CITY
(within Rome)

Baetic Mountains

Balearic Islands

Sardinia

M e d i t e r r a n e a n

Tyrrhenian Sea

Ionia
Sea

Strait of Gibraltar
GIBRALTAR

Sicily
Etna
10,902 ft.
3,323 m

MALTA
Valletta

AFRICA

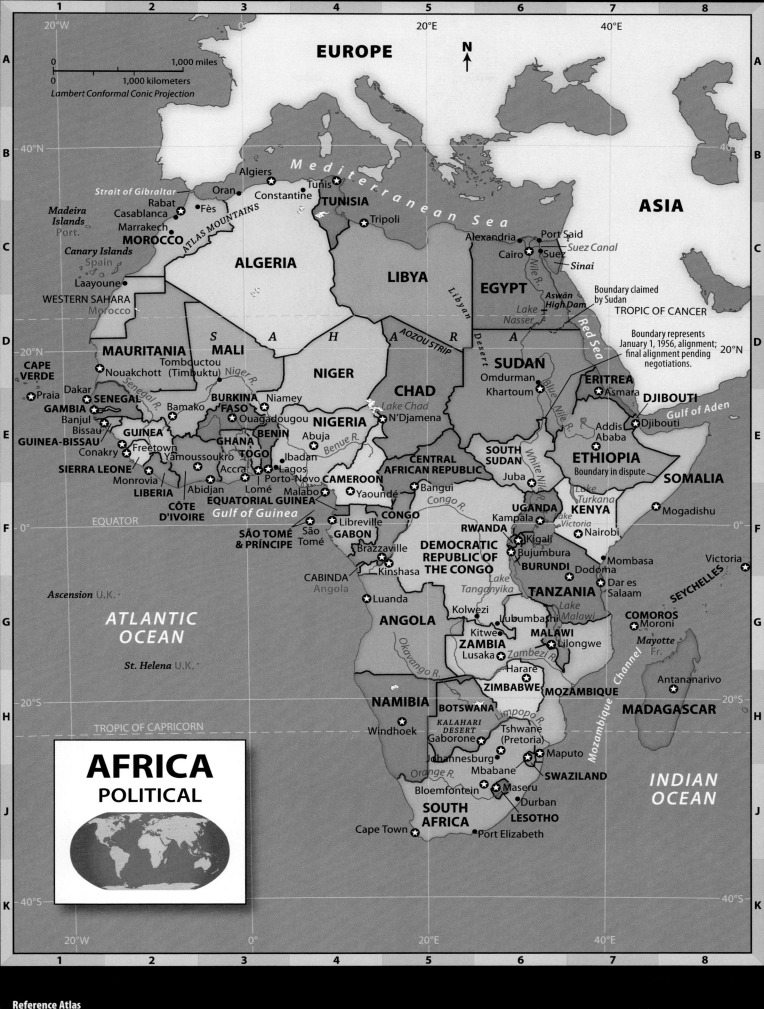

AFRICA
POLITICAL

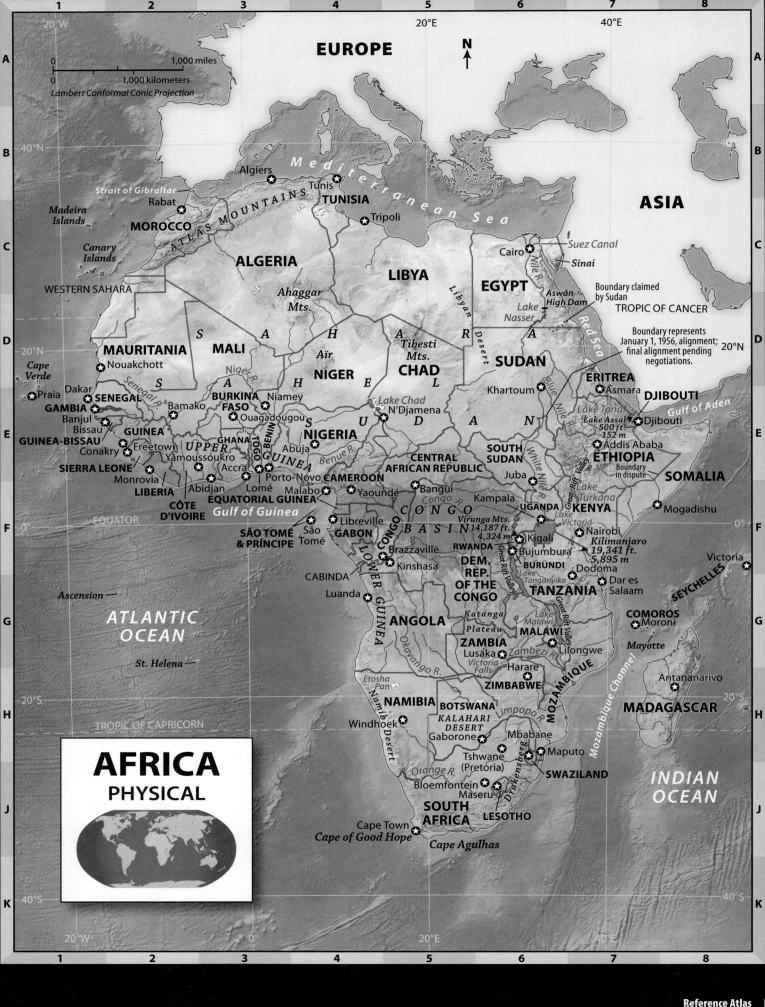

AFRICA
PHYSICAL

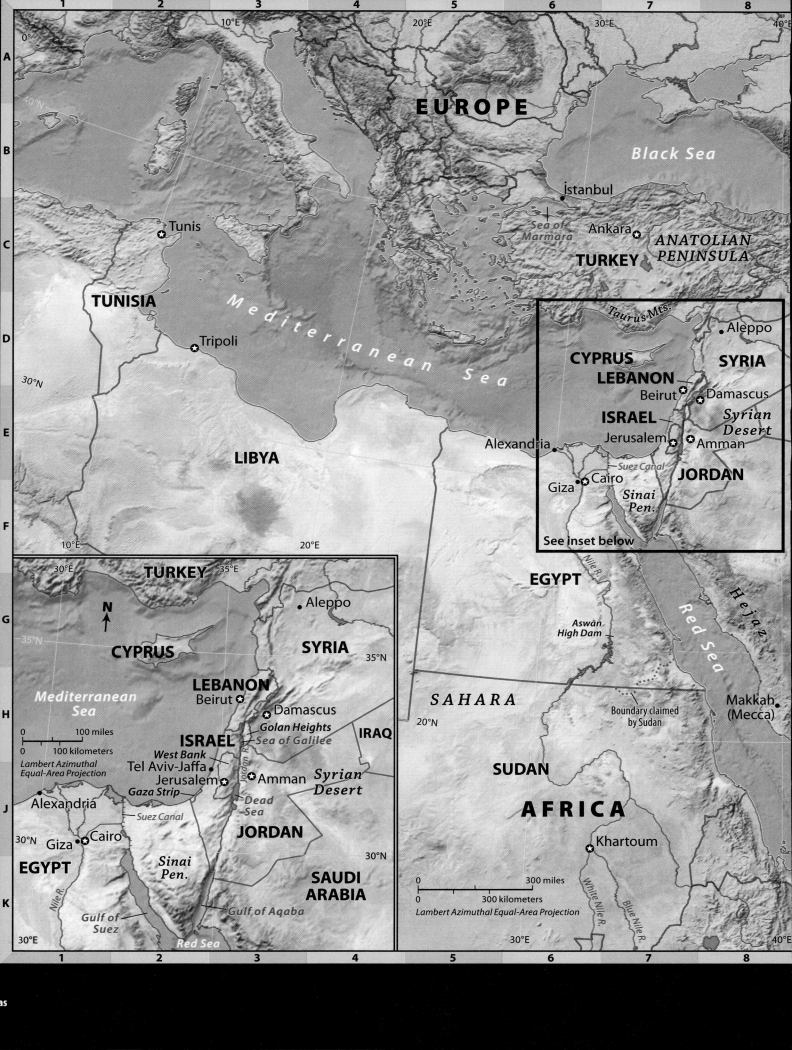

Main map labels:

EUROPE

Black Sea

İstanbul

Sea of Marmara

Ankara · ANATOLIAN PENINSULA

TURKEY

Tunis

TUNISIA

Mediterranean Sea

Tripoli

30°N

LIBYA

Taurus Mts.

CYPRUS
LEBANON
Beirut

Aleppo
SYRIA
Damascus
Syrian Desert

ISRAEL
Jerusalem · Amman

Alexandria
Suez Canal
JORDAN

Giza · Cairo
Sinai Pen.

See inset below

EGYPT

SAHARA

20°N

Nile R.

Aswān High Dam

Red Sea

Hejaz

Boundary claimed by Sudan

Makkah (Mecca)

SUDAN

AFRICA

Khartoum

White Nile R.

Blue Nile R.

Inset map labels:

30°E TURKEY 35°E

N

CYPRUS

Mediterranean Sea

35°N

Aleppo

SYRIA 35°N

LEBANON
Beirut

Damascus
Golan Heights
Sea of Galilee

ISRAEL
West Bank
Tel Aviv-Jaffa
Jerusalem · Amman
Gaza Strip

IRAQ

Jordan R.

Syrian Desert

Dead Sea

0   100 miles
0   100 kilometers
Lambert Azimuthal Equal-Area Projection

Alexandria

Suez Canal

30°N Giza · Cairo

EGYPT

Nile R.

Sinai Pen.

JORDAN

30°N

SAUDI ARABIA

Gulf of Aqaba

Gulf of Suez

Red Sea

30°E

0   300 miles
0   300 kilometers
Lambert Azimuthal Equal-Area Projection

30°E   40°E

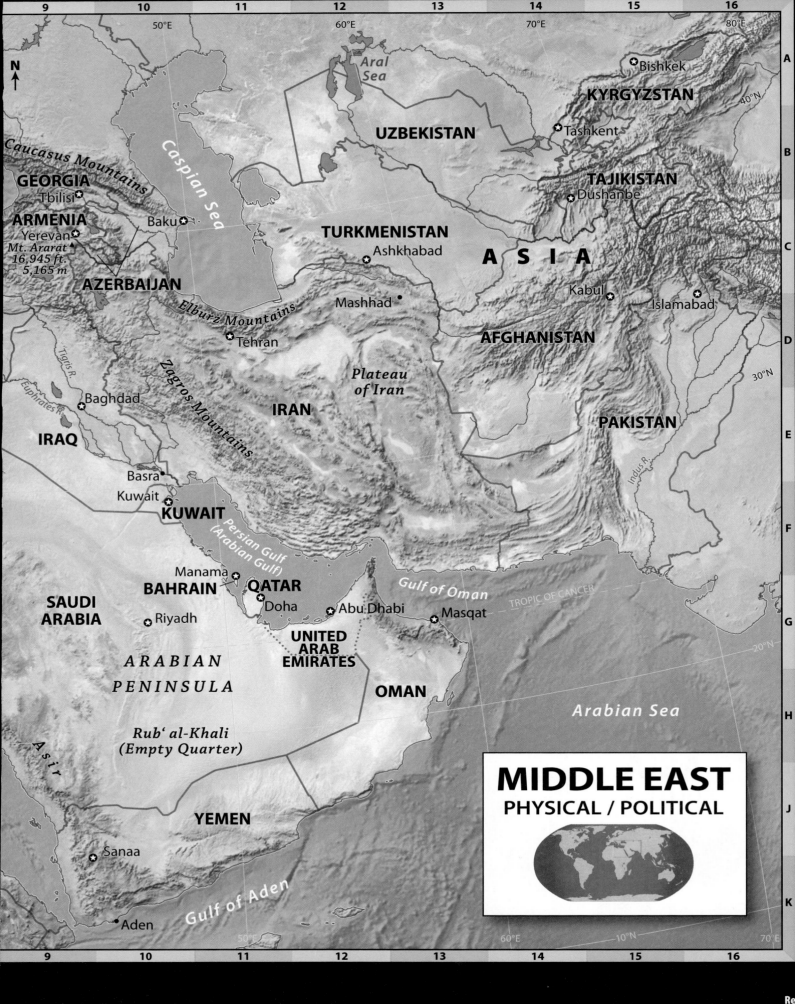

MIDDLE EAST
PHYSICAL / POLITICAL

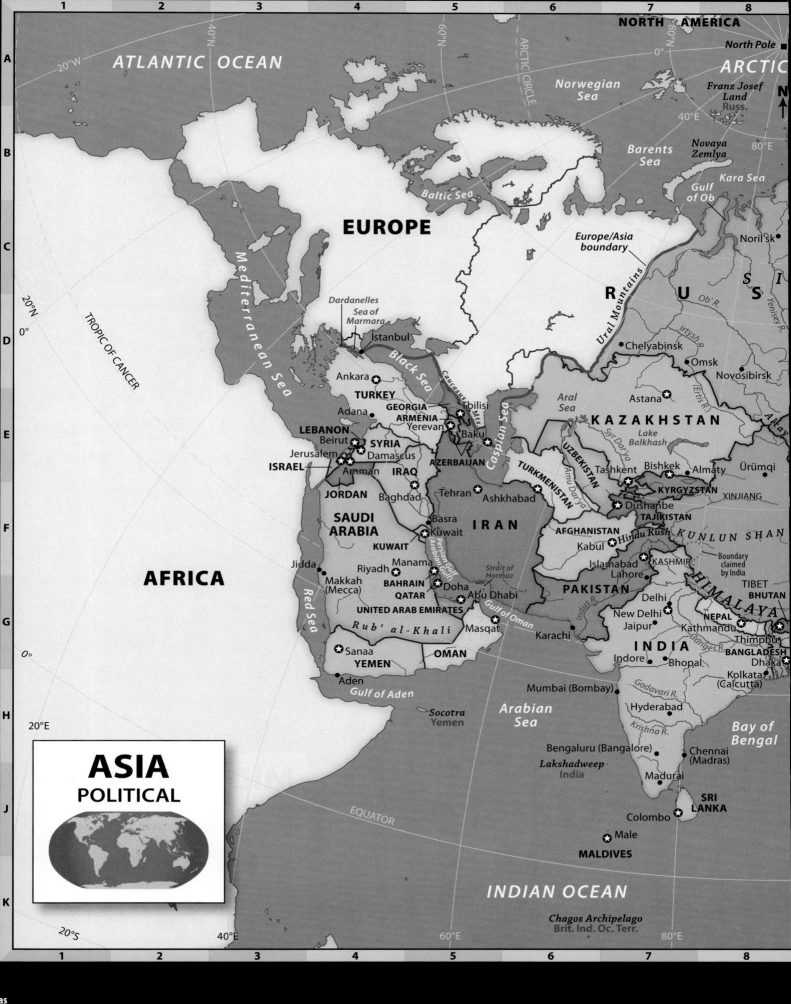

ASIA
POLITICAL

NORTH AMERICA

North Pole

ARCTIC

ATLANTIC OCEAN

Norwegian Sea

Franz Josef Land Russ.

Barents Sea

Novaya Zemlya

Baltic Sea

EUROPE

Gulf of Ob

Kara Sea

Noril'sk

Europe/Asia boundary

R
U
S
S
I

Ural Mountains

Ob' R.

Irtysh R.

Chelyabinsk

Omsk

Novosibirsk

Mediterranean Sea

Dardanelles *Sea of Marmara*

İstanbul

Black Sea

Caucasus Mts.

Ankara

TURKEY

Adana

GEORGIA Tbilisi

ARMENIA Yerevan

Baku

Aral Sea

Astana

KAZAKHSTAN

Lake Balkhash

Yenisey R.

(Ertis R.)

LEBANON
Beirut

Jerusalem
ISRAEL
Amman

SYRIA Damascus

IRAQ

AZERBAIJAN

Caspian Sea

TURKMENISTAN

UZBEKISTAN

Syr Darya

Tashkent

Bishkek

Almaty

Ürümqi

KYRGYZSTAN

XINJIANG

JORDAN

Baghdad

Tehran

Ashkhabad

Amu Darya

Dushanbe

TAJIKISTAN

SAUDI ARABIA

Basra
Kuwait

IRAN

AFGHANISTAN

Kabul *Hindu Kush*

KUNLUN SHAN

AFRICA

Jidda

Makkah (Mecca)

Riyadh

Manama

BAHRAIN
QATAR

Doha

Abu Dhabi

Persian Gulf (Arabian Gulf)

Strait of Hormuz

Islamabad

Lahore

KASHMIR

Boundary claimed by India

HIMALAYA

TIBET

BHUTAN

KUWAIT

UNITED ARAB EMIRATES

Red Sea

Rub' al-Khali

Masqat

OMAN

Gulf of Oman

Karachi

PAKISTAN

Indus R.

Delhi

New Delhi

Jaipur

NEPAL

Kathmandu

Thimphu

BANGLADESH

Dhaka

Sanaa

YEMEN

Aden

Gulf of Aden

Socotra Yemen

Arabian Sea

Indore

Bhopal

INDIA

Godavari R.

Kolkata (Calcutta)

Mumbai (Bombay)

Hyderabad

Krishna R.

Bay of Bengal

Bengaluru (Bangalore)

Lakshadweep India

Chennai (Madras)

Madurai

EQUATOR

SRI LANKA

Colombo

Male

MALDIVES

INDIAN OCEAN

Chagos Archipelago Brit. Ind. Oc. Terr.

TROPIC OF CANCER

20°W

20°N

0°

0°

20°E

20°S

40°E

60°E

80°E

40°N

60°N

80°N

0°

40°E

80°E

20°N

N

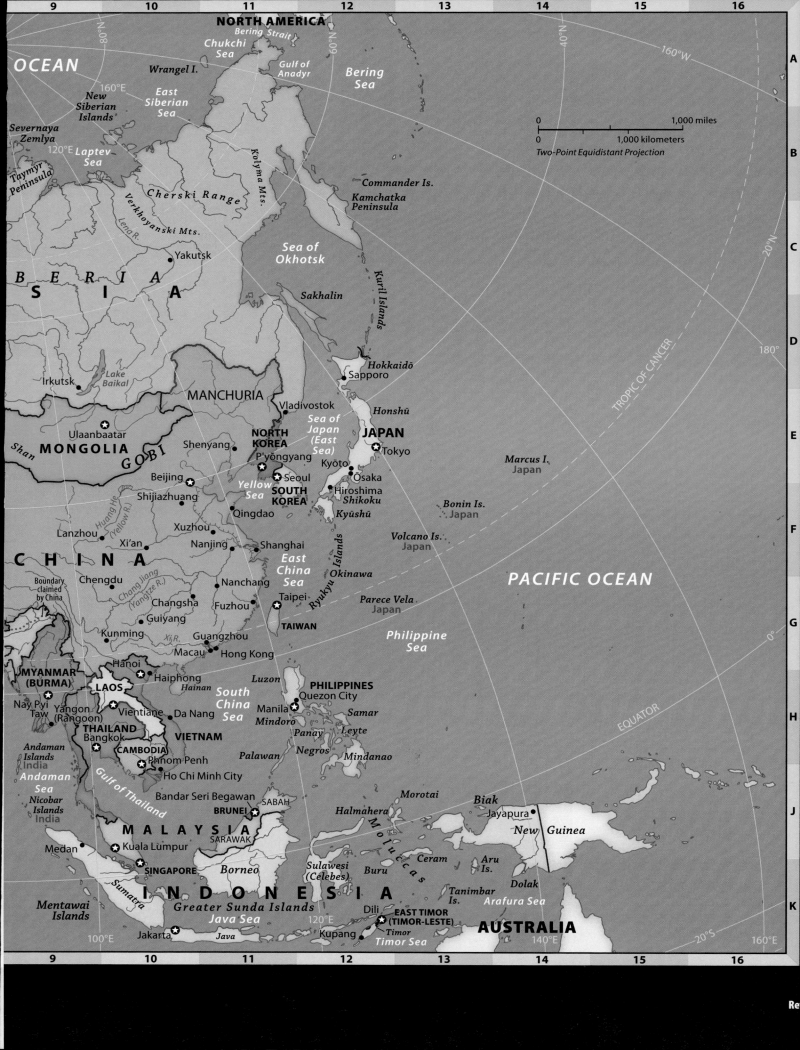

ASIA
PHYSICAL

NORTH AMERICA

North Pole ■

ARCTIC

N

ATLANTIC OCEAN

20°W

40°N

60°N

ARCTIC CIRCLE

0°

40°E

Norwegian Sea

Franz Josef Land

80°E

Barents Sea

Novaya Zemlya

Gulf of Ob

Kara Sea

EUROPE

Baltic Sea

Yenisey R.

Europe/Asia boundary

R   **U**   **S**   **S**   **I**

WEST SIBERIAN PLAIN

Ob' R.

Mediterranean Sea

Dardanelles

Sea of Marmara

Aegean Sea

Black Sea

Caucasus Mts.

Caspian Depression

Ural R.

Ural Mountains

Irtysh R.

Ob' R.

Ertis R.

20°N

TROPIC OF CANCER

Ankara

TURKEY

ANATOLIA

GEORGIA

Tbilisi

ARMENIA

Yerevan

Baku

Astana

THE STEPPES

Aral Sea

K A Z A K H S T A N

Lake Balkhash

Altay

0°

LEBANON

Beirut

SYRIA

Damascus

Syrian Desert

Jerusalem

ISRAEL

Amman

AZERBAIJAN

Caspian Sea

TURKMENISTAN

UZBEKISTAN

Tashkent

Bishkek

KYRGYZSTAN

Syr Darya

TIAN SHAN

Tigris R.

IRAQ

Baghdad

Mesopotamia

Euphrates R.

Zagros Mountains

Elburz Mts.

Tehran

Ashkhabad

Amu Darya

IRAN

AFGHANISTAN

Kabul

Hindu Kush

Dushanbe

TAJIKISTAN

TAKLIMAKAN DESERT

Kunlun Shan

JORDAN

Dead Sea −1,312 ft. −400 m

Sinai

SAUDI ARABIA

Kuwait

KUWAIT

BAHRAIN

Riyadh

QATAR

ARABIAN PENINSULA

Persian Gulf

Arabian Gulf

Strait of Hormuz

Abu Dhabi

Islamabad

KASHMIR

PLATEAU OF TIBET

HIMALAYA

BHUTAN

NEPAL

Kathmandu

Thimphu

AFRICA

Red Sea

Rub' al-Khali

UNITED ARAB EMIRATES

Masqat

Gulf of Oman

PAKISTAN

Thar Desert

New Delhi

Mt. Everest 29,028 ft. 8,848 m

Ganges R.

Dhaka

BANGLADESH

20°E

Sanaa

YEMEN

OMAN

Gulf of Aden

Socotra

Arabian Sea

Indus R.

Narmada R.

I N D I A

DECCAN PLATEAU

Western Ghats

Eastern Ghats

Godavari R.

Krishna R.

0°

Laccadive Sea

Lakshadweep

SRI LANKA

Colombo

Bay of Bengal

EQUATOR

Maldive Islands

Male

MALDIVES

INDIAN OCEAN

20°S

20°E

40°E

60°E

80°E

Chagos Archipelago

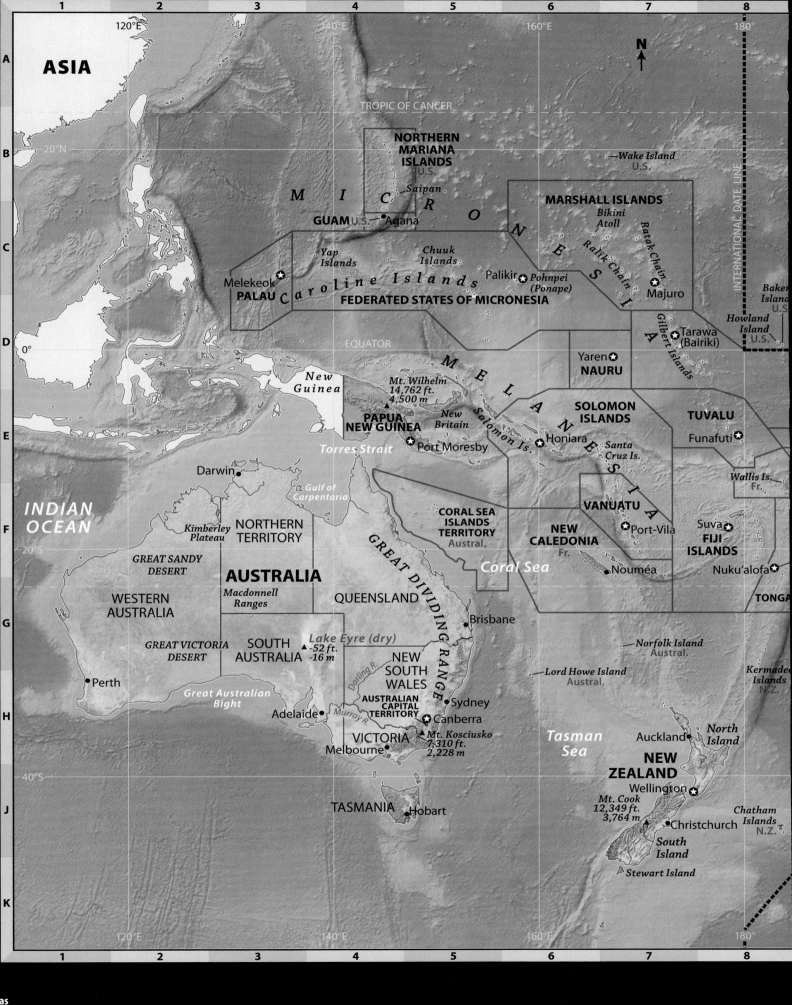

ASIA

TROPIC OF CANCER

20°N

**NORTHERN
MARIANA
ISLANDS**
U.S.

M I C R O N E S I A

Saipan

Wake Island
U.S.

MARSHALL ISLANDS

*Bikini
Atoll*

GUAM
U.S. Agana

*Yap
Islands*

*Chuuk
Islands*

Caroline Islands

Palikir Pohnpei
(Ponape)

Ralik Chain

Ratak Chain

Majuro

INTERNATIONAL DATE LINE

*Baker
Island*
U.S.

Melekeok

PALAU

FEDERATED STATES OF MICRONESIA

EQUATOR

*Howland
Island* U.S.

0°

*New
Guinea*

Mt. Wilhelm
14,762 ft.
4,500 m

M E L A N E S I A

Yaren
NAURU

*Gilbert
Islands*

Tarawa
(Bairiki)

**PAPUA
NEW GUINEA**

*New
Britain*

Solomon Is.

**SOLOMON
ISLANDS**

Honiara

*Santa
Cruz Is.*

TUVALU

Funafuti

Torres Strait

Port Moresby

Solomon Is.

*Wallis Is.
Fr.*

Darwin

*Gulf of
Carpentaria*

**CORAL SEA
ISLANDS
TERRITORY**
Austral.

VANUATU

Port-Vila

Suva

**FIJI
ISLANDS**

**INDIAN
OCEAN**

20°S

*Kimberley
Plateau*

**NORTHERN
TERRITORY**

**NEW
CALEDONIA**
Fr.

Coral Sea

Nouméa

Nuku'alofa

*GREAT SANDY
DESERT*

AUSTRALIA

*Macdonnell
Ranges*

G R E A T   D I V I D I N G   R A N G E

TONGA

**WESTERN
AUSTRALIA**

*GREAT VICTORIA
DESERT*

**SOUTH
AUSTRALIA**

Lake Eyre (dry)
-52 ft.
-16 m

QUEENSLAND

Brisbane

Norfolk Island
Austral.

Lord Howe Island
Austral.

*Kermadec
Islands*
N.Z.

**NEW
SOUTH
WALES**

Perth

*Great Australian
Bight*

Adelaide

Darling R.

Murray R.

**AUSTRALIAN
CAPITAL
TERRITORY**

Sydney

Canberra

Auckland

*North
Island*

*Tasman
Sea*

**NEW
ZEALAND**

40°S

VICTORIA

Melbourne

▲ Mt. Kosciusko
7,310 ft.
2,228 m

Wellington

TASMANIA

Hobart

Mt. Cook
12,349 ft.
3,764 m

Christchurch

*Chatham
Islands
N.Z.*

*South
Island*

Stewart Island

120°E

140°E

160°E

180°

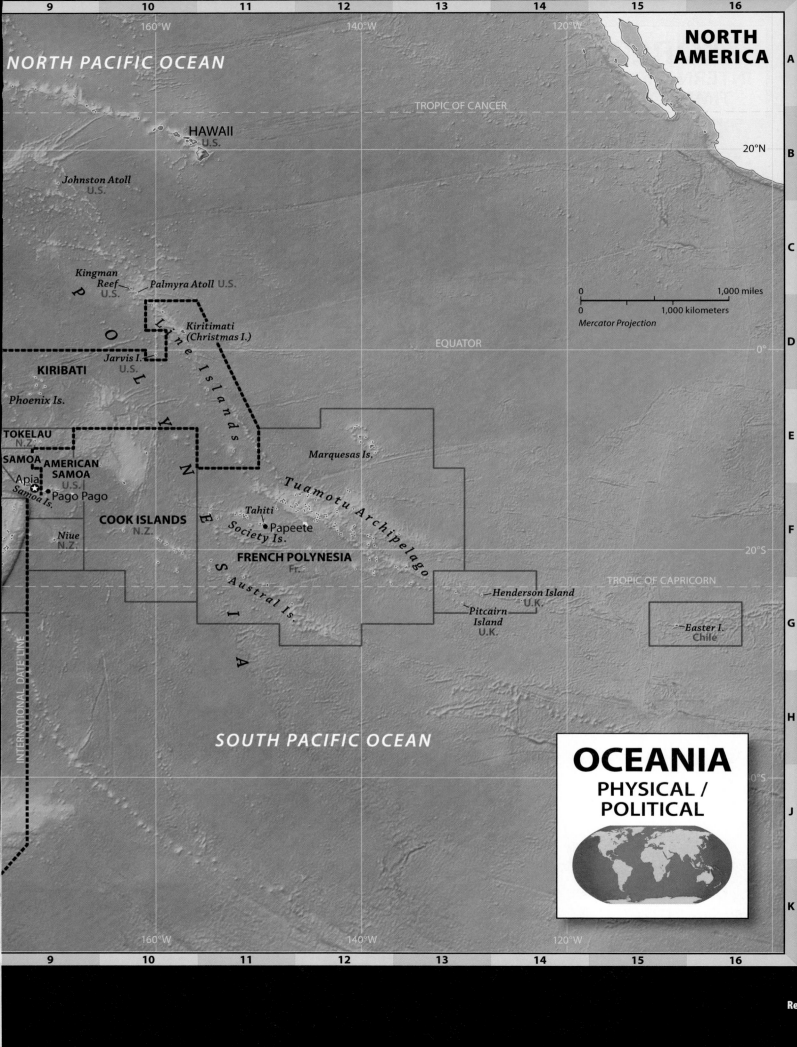

NORTH PACIFIC OCEAN

NORTH AMERICA

TROPIC OF CANCER

HAWAII
U.S.

20°N

Johnston Atoll
U.S.

*Kingman
Reef*
U.S.   *Palmyra Atoll* U.S.

P
O
L
Y

Line Islands

*Kiritimati
(Christmas I.)*

EQUATOR

0°

Jarvis I.
U.S.

KIRIBATI

Phoenix Is.

TOKELAU
N.Z.

E

SAMOA   AMERICAN
SAMOA
Apia   U.S.
Samoa Is. Pago Pago

Marquesas Is.

Tuamotu Archipelago

N
E

COOK ISLANDS
N.Z.

Tahiti
Papeete
Society Is.

Niue
N.Z.

FRENCH POLYNESIA
Fr.

20°S

S
I

Austral Is.

TROPIC OF CAPRICORN

Henderson Island
U.K.

A

*Pitcairn
Island*
U.K.

Easter I.
Chile

G

SOUTH PACIFIC OCEAN

INTERNATIONAL DATE LINE

OCEANIA
PHYSICAL /
POLITICAL

160°W   140°W   120°W

0   1,000 miles
0   1,000 kilometers
Mercator Projection

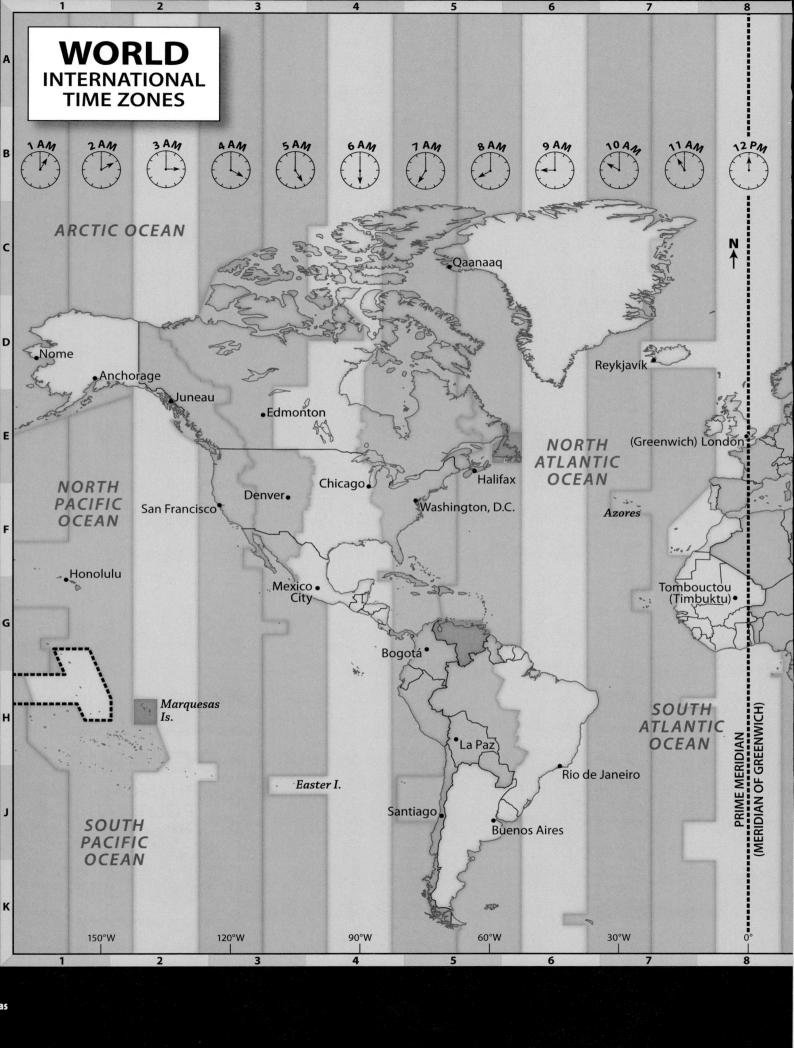

WORLD
INTERNATIONAL TIME ZONES

1 AM 2 AM 3 AM 4 AM 5 AM 6 AM 7 AM 8 AM 9 AM 10 AM 11 AM 12 PM

ARCTIC OCEAN

N

Qaanaaq

Nome

Anchorage

Juneau

Reykjavík

Edmonton

NORTH ATLANTIC OCEAN

(Greenwich) London

NORTH PACIFIC OCEAN

Chicago

Halifax

Denver

Washington, D.C.

San Francisco

Azores

Honolulu

Mexico City

Tombouctou (Timbuktu)

Marquesas Is.

Bogotá

SOUTH ATLANTIC OCEAN

La Paz

Easter I.

Rio de Janeiro

Santiago

Buenos Aires

SOUTH PACIFIC OCEAN

PRIME MERIDIAN
(MERIDIAN OF GREENWICH)

150°W   120°W   90°W   60°W   30°W   0°

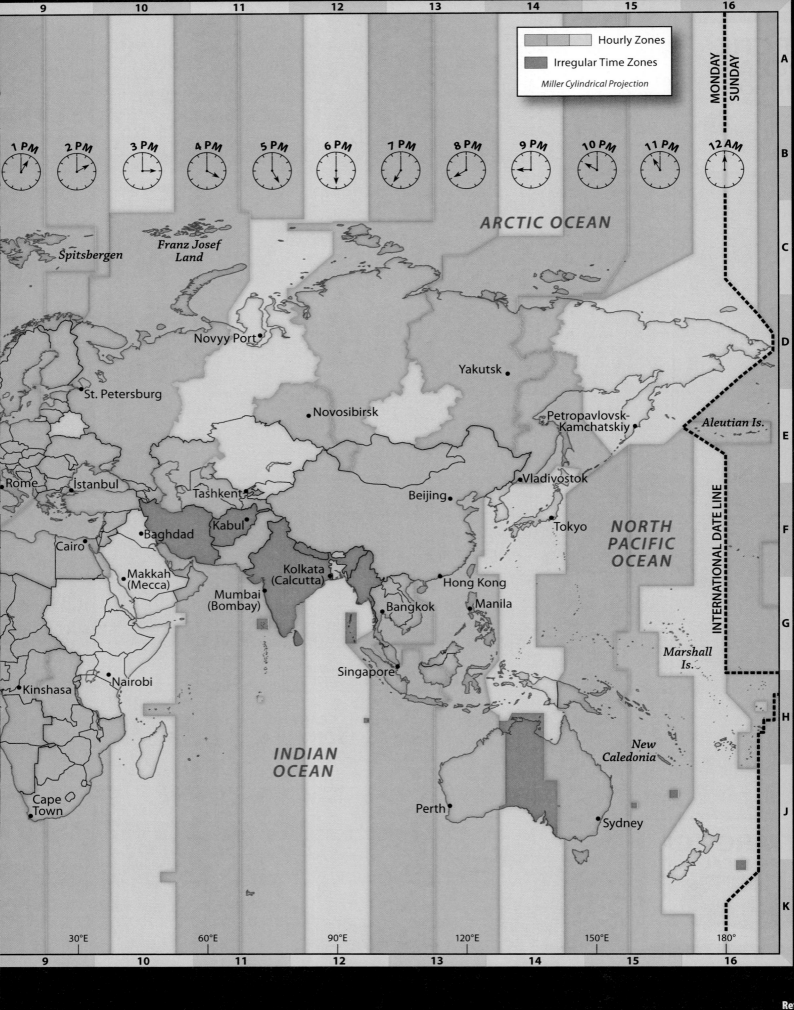

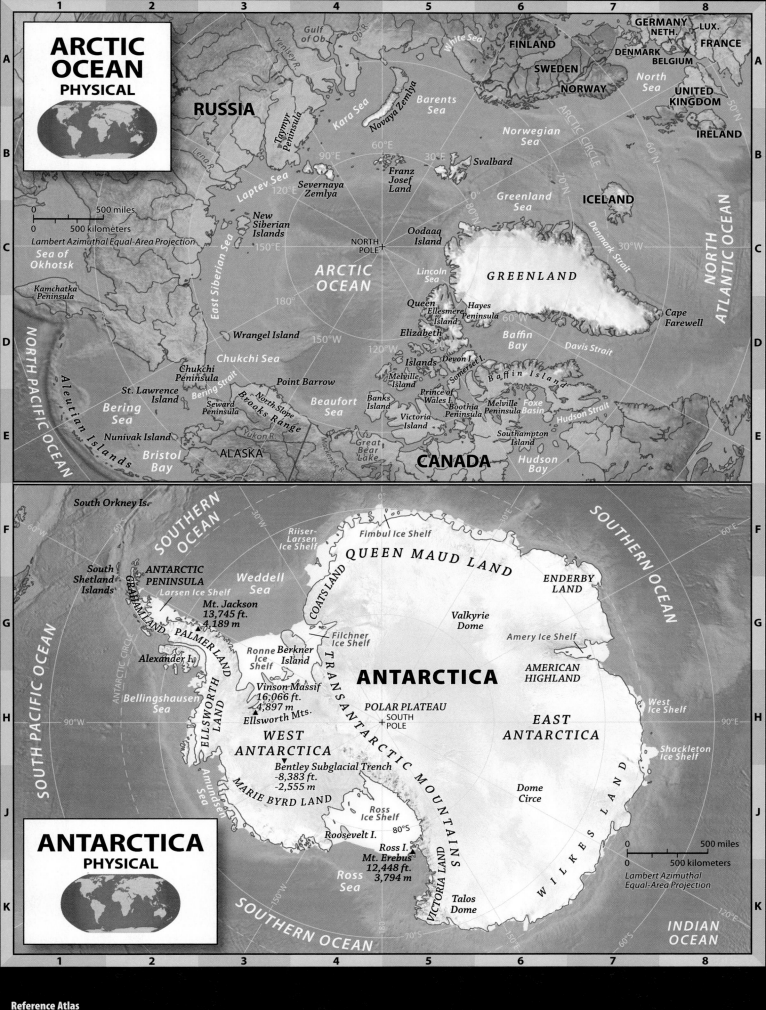

ARCTIC OCEAN
PHYSICAL

0 500 miles
0 500 kilometers
Lambert Azimuthal Equal-Area Projection

RUSSIA

Gulf of Ob
Yenisey R.
Ob R.
Taymyr Peninsula
Kara Sea
Novaya Zemlya
White Sea
Barents Sea
FINLAND
SWEDEN
NORWAY
GERMANY
NETH.
DENMARK
BELGIUM
LUX.
FRANCE
North Sea
UNITED KINGDOM
IRELAND

Lena R.
Laptev Sea
Severnaya Zemlya
Franz Josef Land
Svalbard
Norwegian Sea
ICELAND

Sea of Okhotsk
New Siberian Islands
NORTH POLE
Oodaaq Island
Greenland Sea
ARCTIC CIRCLE

Kamchatka Peninsula
East Siberian Sea
ARCTIC OCEAN
Lincoln Sea
GREENLAND
Denmark Strait

Wrangel Island
Chukchi Sea
Queen
Ellesmere Island
Hayes Peninsula
Cape Farewell
NORTH ATLANTIC OCEAN

NORTH PACIFIC OCEAN
Chukchi Peninsula
Point Barrow
Elizabeth
Islands
Devon I.
Baffin Bay
Davis Strait

St. Lawrence Island
Bering Strait
North Slope
Brooks Range
Beaufort Sea
Melville Island
Somerset I.
Baffin Island

Aleutian Islands
Seward Peninsula
Banks Island
Prince of Wales I.
Melville Peninsula
Foxe Basin
Hudson Strait

Bering Sea
Nunivak Island
Yukon R.
Victoria Island
Boothia Peninsula
Southampton Island

Bristol Bay
Mackenzie R.
ALASKA
Great Bear Lake
CANADA
Hudson Bay

ANTARCTICA
PHYSICAL

0 500 miles
0 500 kilometers
Lambert Azimuthal Equal-Area Projection

South Orkney Is.
SOUTHERN OCEAN
Riiser-Larsen Ice Shelf
Fimbul Ice Shelf
SOUTHERN OCEAN

South Shetland Islands
ANTARCTIC PENINSULA
Weddell Sea
QUEEN MAUD LAND
ENDERBY LAND

GRAHAM LAND
Larsen Ice Shelf
COATS LAND
Valkyrie Dome
Amery Ice Shelf

PALMER LAND
Mt. Jackson
13,745 ft.
4,189 m
Filchner Ice Shelf

Alexander I.
Ronne Ice Shelf
Berkner Island
TRANSANTARCTIC MOUNTAINS
ANTARCTICA
AMERICAN HIGHLAND

SOUTH PACIFIC OCEAN
ANTARCTIC CIRCLE
ELLSWORTH LAND
Vinson Massif
16,066 ft.
4,897 m
Ellsworth Mts.
EAST ANTARCTICA
West Ice Shelf

Bellingshausen Sea
POLAR PLATEAU
SOUTH POLE
Shackleton Ice Shelf

WEST ANTARCTICA
Bentley Subglacial Trench
-8,383 ft.
-2,555 m
Dome Circe

Amundsen Sea
MARIE BYRD LAND
Ross Ice Shelf
WILKES LAND

Roosevelt I.
80°S
0 500 miles
0 500 kilometers
Lambert Azimuthal Equal-Area Projection

Ross Sea
Ross I.
Mt. Erebus
12,448 ft.
3,794 m
VICTORIA LAND

SOUTHERN OCEAN
Talos Dome
INDIAN OCEAN

A WORLD OF EXTREMES

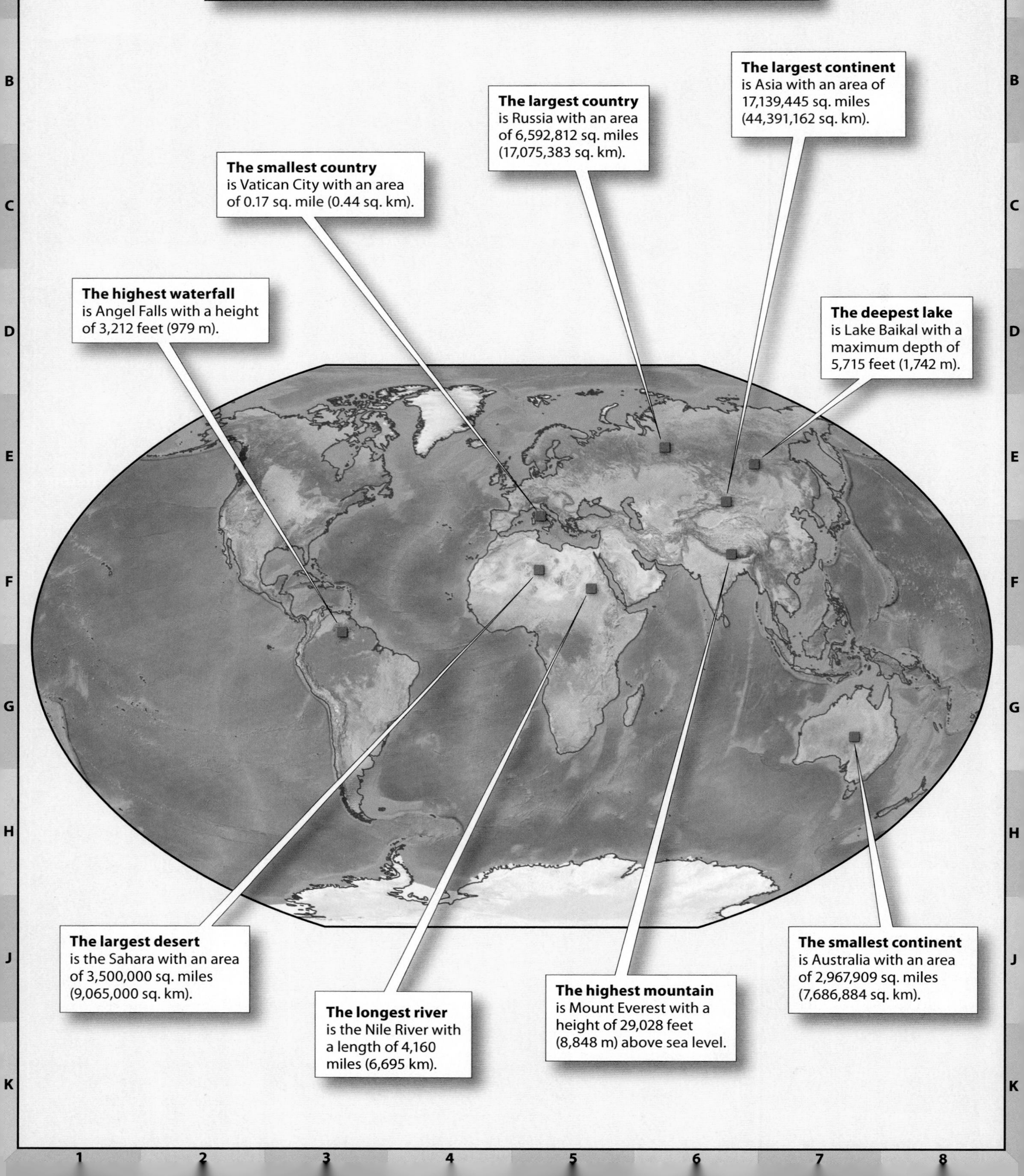

The largest continent
is Asia with an area of
17,139,445 sq. miles
(44,391,162 sq. km).

The largest country
is Russia with an area
of 6,592,812 sq. miles
(17,075,383 sq. km).

The smallest country
is Vatican City with an area
of 0.17 sq. mile (0.44 sq. km).

The deepest lake
is Lake Baikal with a
maximum depth of
5,715 feet (1,742 m).

The highest waterfall
is Angel Falls with a height
of 3,212 feet (979 m).

The largest desert
is the Sahara with an area
of 3,500,000 sq. miles
(9,065,000 sq. km).

The longest river
is the Nile River with
a length of 4,160
miles (6,695 km).

The highest mountain
is Mount Everest with a
height of 29,028 feet
(8,848 m) above sea level.

The smallest continent
is Australia with an area
of 2,967,909 sq. miles
(7,686,884 sq. km).

Archipelago

Gulf

ean

Reservoir

Volcano

Isthmus

Plateau

Canyon

Highlands

Cliff

Cape

Bay

Harbor

Reef

Island

Channel

Peninsula

archipelago a group of islands

basin area of land drained by a given river and its branches; area of land surrounded by lands of higher elevations

bay part of a large body of water that extends into a shoreline, generally smaller than a gulf

canyon deep and narrow valley with steep walls

cape point of land that extends into a river, lake, or ocean

channel wide strait or waterway between two landmasses that lie close to each other; deep part of a river or other waterway

cliff steep, high wall of rock, earth, or ice

continent one of the seven large landmasses on the Earth

delta flat, low-lying land built up from soil carried downstream by a river and deposited at its mouth

divide stretch of high land that separates river systems

downstream direction in which a river or stream flows from its source to its mouth

escarpment steep cliff or slope between a higher and

glacier large, thick body of slowly moving ice

gulf part of a large body of water that extends into a shoreline, generally larger and more deeply indented than a bay

harbor a sheltered place along a shoreline where ships can anchor safely

highland elevated land area such as a hill, mountain, or plateau

hill elevated land with sloping sides and rounded summit; generally smaller than a mountain

island land area, smaller than a continent, completely surrounded by water

isthmus narrow stretch of land connecting two larger land areas

lake a sizable inland body of water

lowland land, usually level, at a low elevation

mesa broad, flat-topped landform with steep sides; smaller than a plateau

mountain land with steep sides that rises sharply (1,000 feet or more) from surrounding land; generally larger

Labels on image: Mountain Peak, Desert, Oasis, Basin, Mountain Range, Sound, Source of River, Glacier, Valley, Tributary, Hills, Strait, Upstream, Lake, Downstream, River, Mouth of River, Escarpment, Lowland, Plain, Delta, Seacoast

mountain peak pointed top of a mountain

mountain range a series of connected mountains

mouth (of a river) place where a stream or river flows into a larger body of water

oasis small area in a desert where water and vegetation are found

ocean one of the four major bodies of salt water that surround the continents

ocean current stream of either cold or warm water that moves in a definite direction through an ocean

peninsula body of land jutting into a lake or ocean, surrounded on three sides by water

physical feature characteristic of a place occurring naturally, such as a landform, body of water, climate pattern, or resource

plain area of level land, usually at low elevation and often covered with grasses

plateau area of flat or rolling land at a high elevation, about 300 to 3,000 feet (90 to 900 m) high

river large natural stream of water that runs through the land

sea large body of water completely or partly surrounded by land

seacoast land lying next to a sea or an ocean

sound broad inland body of water, often between a coastline and one or more islands off the coast

source (of a river) place where a river or stream begins, often in highlands

strait narrow stretch of water joining two larger bodies of water

tributary small river or stream that flows into a large river or stream; a branch of the river

upstream direction opposite the flow of a river; toward the source of a river or stream

valley area of low land usually between hills or mountains

volcano mountain or hill created as liquid rock and ash erupt from inside the Earth

SCAVENGER HUNT

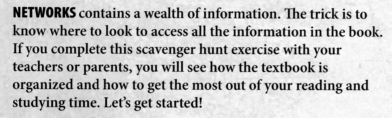

NETWORKS contains a wealth of information. The trick is to know where to look to access all the information in the book. If you complete this scavenger hunt exercise with your teachers or parents, you will see how the textbook is organized and how to get the most out of your reading and studying time. Let's get started!

1 **How many lessons are in Chapter 2?**
Chapter 2 has three lessons.

2 **What does Unit 1 cover?**
Unit 1 covers the world.

3 **Where can you find the Essential Questions for each lesson?**
The Essential Questions are located at the beginning of each lesson, after the lesson title.

4 **In what three places can you find information on a Foldable?**
Foldables are found on the chapter opener, before each lesson review, and on the chapter activities page.

5 **How can you identify content vocabulary and academic vocabulary in the narrative?**
Content vocabulary terms are bold and highlighted yellow. Academic terms are bold.

6 **Where do you find graphic organizers in your textbook?**
Graphic organizers are at the beginning of each lesson in the Reading Helpdesk.

7 **You want to quickly find a map in the book about the world. Where do you look?**
The Reference Atlas section is easy to find in the front of your book and contains world and regional maps.

8 **Where would you find the latitude and longitude for Dublin, Ireland?** You can find latitude and longitude as well as important geographic features and country capitals in the Gazetteer.

9 **If you needed to know the Spanish term for *earthquake*, where would you look?**
The English-Spanish glossary contains the Spanish terms and definitions for the content and academic vocabulary.

10 **Where can you find a list of all the charts in a unit?**
The Diagrams, Charts, and Graphs section in the front of your book lists the title and page number of every diagram, chart, and graph in each unit.

(t) Image Source/Punchstock; (c) ScotStock/Alamy; (b) Ingram Publishing/Alamy

Our World: The Eastern Hemisphere Planner

UNDERSTANDING BY DESIGN®

Enduring Understandings

- *People, places, and ideas change over time.*
- *Over time, people adapt to their environment.*
- *Countries have relationships with each other.*

Essential Questions

- *How does geography influence the way people live?*
- *How do people adapt to their environment?*
- *What makes a culture unique?*
- *Why do people make economic choices?*

Students will know:

- *the five themes of geography (location, place, region, human-environment interaction, movement) and the six essential elements.*
- *of the parts, styles, and purposes of a world map and use it to identify places.*
- *the geography, climate, resources, political boundaries, and population of the continents.*
- *the aspects of life that occur on Earth happen because of Earth's position to the sun, its axis, its rotation, and its revolution.*
- *Earth has a variety of climates that help to sustain its wide variety of species.*
- *what a culture is, what makes up cultural regions, and how and why cultures change.*
- *different forms of government and the definition of globalization.*

Students will be able to:

- *use a **world map** to identify physical features, political boundaries, population density, economic resources, and climate.*
- *identify and apply a geographer's tools including globes, maps, and geospatial technologies.*
- *describe Earth's six major climate zones and explain what factors determine the climate of an area.*
- *describe the physical characteristics of places including landforms and bodies of water.*
- *describe the physical processes that shape the patterns of Earth's surface including weathering and erosion.*
- *explain human characteristics and how culture and experience influence people's perceptions of places and regions.*

Predictable Misunderstandings

- *Geography is just the names of states and their capitals.*
- *Lines of latitude and longitude actually appear on Earth.*
- *Geography is static and unchanging, serving merely as a backdrop to people's activities.*
- *Earth is a solid planet.*
- *The planets in the solar system are all like Earth.*
- *Humans have very little effect on the environment.*
- *The ocean floor is flat.*
- *Families around the world are organized like those found in the student's local community.*
- *All countries have governments like that found in the United States.*
- *The customs students enjoy originated in the United States.*

Assessment Evidence

Performance Tasks:

- *Unit GeoLab Activity*
- *Environmental Case Study*

Other Evidence:

- *Physical Location GeoQuiz*
- *Political Location GeoQuiz*
- *City Location GeoQuiz*
- *Physical Geography Activity*
- *Cultural Geography Activity*
- *Geography and History Activity*
- *Geography and Economics Activity*
- *Geography Skills Activity*
- *Critical Thinking Skills Activity*
- *Participation in Interactive Whiteboard Activities*
- *Contribution to small-group activities*
- *Interpretation of slide show images and special purpose maps*
- *Participation in class discussions about the world*
- *Analysis of graphic organizers, graphs, and charts*
- *Lesson Reviews*
- *Chapter Assessments*

Key for Using the Teacher Edition

SKILL-BASED ACTIVITIES

Types of skill activites found in the Teacher Edition.

* **V** **Visual Skills** require students to analyze maps, graphs, charts, and photos.

W **Writing Skills** provide writing opportunities to help students comprehend the text.

R **Reading Skills** help students practice reading skills and master vocabulary.

C **Critical Thinking Skills** help students apply and extend what they have learned.

T **Technology Skills** require students to use digital tools effectively.

*Letters are followed by a number when there is more than one of the same type of skill on the page.

DIFFERENTIATED INSTRUCTION

All activities are written for the on-level student unless otherwise marked with the leveled labels below.

BL **Beyond Level**

AL **Approaching Level**

ELL **English Language Learners**

All students benefit from activities that utilize different learning styles. Many activities are marked as below when a particular learning style is highlighted.

Intrapersonal	Naturalist
Logical/Mathematical	Kinesthetic
Visual/Spatial	Auditory/Musical
Verbal/Linguistic	Interpersonal

SUGGESTED PACING GUIDE

Introducing the Unit	3 Days
Chapter 1	6 Days
Chapter 2	8 Days
Chapter 3	8 Days
Global Connections	3 Days
What Do You Think?	3 Days
TOTAL TIME	**31 Days**

PLANNER

☑ *Print Teaching Options*

V Visual Skills

☐ **P. 2** Students use photo, text, and prior knowledge of the oceans to identify and catergorize sea plants and animals.

☐ **P. 3** Students interpret an image of a desert and infer why a camel is a good means of transportation in a desert.

☐ **P. 6** Students contrast a political and physical map of the world, and then answer questions on the political map.

☐ **P. 9** Students compare a physical map to a population density map of the world to answer questions.

☐ **P. 11** Students analyze maps to recognize the relationship between natural resources and physical landforms. **ELL**

☐ **P. 12** Students use maps to recognize the relationship of climate to physical features and population density. **BL**

W Writing Skills

☐ **P. 14** Students use a photo to write a narrative.

☐ **P. 14** Students summarize what they have learned about the five types of maps.

R Reading Skills

☐ **P. 2** Students define what it means to study geography.

☐ **P. 2** Students categorize natural resources as renewable or nonrenewable.

☐ **P. 8** Students use a physical map and a polulation map to identify how physical features affect population. **BL**

C Critical Thinking Skills

☐ **P. 3** Students create a list and speculate on how landforms influence how people relate to the environment. **BL**

☐ **P. 4** Students compare and contrast North America and South America on a physical map of the world. **BL**

☐ **P. 5** Students transfer knowledge to write questions and answers about a physical map of the world.

☐ **P. 7** Students make inferences about countries on a political map of the world.

☐ **P. 10** Students use an economic map to draw conclusions about how natural resources affect countries.

☐ **P. 13** Students hypothesize to make connections between the Earth's shape and its climate zones. **AL**

T Technology Skills

☐ **P. 14** Student groups create maps and presentations using the unit maps and online research.

☑ *Online Teaching Options*

V Visual Skills

☐ **MAP** **The World: Physical Map**—Students use a physical map to identify and mark physical features. **AL** Kinesthetic

☐ **MAP** **The World: Population Density Map**—Students use a population map to discuss the impact of high population density. **BL** Visual/Spatial

☐ **MAP** **Regional Map**—Students use the regional map to connect the images from the text to their location on the map.

☐ **MAP** **The World: Political Map**—Students can use a political map to review the political boundaries of the world.

W Writing Skills

☐ **MAP** **The World: Economic Map**—Students use a resources map to write a paragraph to explain why coastal cities are built. Verbal/Linguistic

☐ **MAP** **The World: Climate Map**—Students use a climate map to write about climate and vegetation regions. **BL** Visual/Spatial

C Critical Thinking Skills

☐ **VIDEO** **A World Tour**—Students watch a video montage and then create charts. Visual

☐ **SLIDE SHOW** **How to Read a Map**—Students use the slide show to identify locations on maps. Visual/Spatial

☐ **CHART** **Precipitation and Temperature Chart**—Students use the chart to study the factors that impact where people live. Verbal/Linguistic

T Technology Skills

☐ **GAME** **The Physical World Game**—Students use a physical map game to drag and drop names of continents and major bodies of water. **AL** Kinesthetic

☐ **GAME** **The Political World Game**—Students use a political map game to drag and drop names of cities and countries. Kinesthetic

☑ *Printable Digital Worksheets*

W Writing Skills

☐ **WORKSHEET** **Environmental Case Study: Maintenance of Fresh Water Sources**—Students will use the worksheet to review and discuss the significance of Earth as a water planet.

☐ **WORKSHEET** **GeoLab: Desalinization of Water**—Students use the worksheet to understand the process of desalinization.

☐ **WORKSHEET** **Physical Geography Activity**—Students will analyze an elevation profile of the ocean.

☐ **WORKSHEET** **Cultural Geography Activity**—Students will read about the term *culture* and answer questions about the excerpt.

☐ **QUIZ** **Physical Location GeoQuiz**—Use the Physical Location GeoQuiz as a pre- or post-assessment of students' knowledge of the world's landforms and bodies of water.

☐ **QUIZ** **Political Location GeoQuiz**—Use the Political Location GeoQuiz as a pre- or post-assessment of students' knowledge of the world's countries.

☐ **QUIZ** **City Location GeoQuiz**—Use the City Location GeoQuiz as a pre- or post-assessment of students' knowledge of the world's major cities.

OUR WORLD: THE EASTERN HEMISPHERE

McGraw-Hill
networks

UNIT 1

Chapter 1
Earth's Land, People, and Environments

Chapter 2
The Physical World

Chapter 3
The Human World

Harry Kikstra/Flickr/Getty Images

Global Connections

Discussing The Global Connections issue of this unit is *Rain Forest Resources*. This feature gives students an opportunity to learn about rain forest resources, its people, and its global economic and environmental importance. Students will investigate the challenges faced by rain forest regions, including pressures on the regions for farming and exploitation of its natural resources. Students also will investigate the pressures placed on indigenous rain forest populations.

ENGAGE

Bellringer Share with students that the image is of a mountain climber. Ask students to analyze the details in the photo. **Ask:**

- What protective gear does the mountain climber wear? What is the purpose of the gear? *(insulated clothes, hood, gloves, goggles, oxygen mask; to protect against the extreme cold and thin atmosphere at high altitudes)*
- What type of dangers do you think mountain climbers face? *(extreme wind and temperatures, powerful snow storms, lack of shelter, loss of equipment, reduced oxygen, must carry all provisions, confusion, cracks in the ice)* **Visual/Spatial**

Making Connections Read the following information to students.

The Himalayas, or Nepali Himalaya, are the highest mountains in the world. This great mountain system forms a barrier between the Plateau of Tibet to the north and the alluvial plains to the south in Asia.

- The Himalayas include the highest mountains in the world.
- There are 110 mountain peaks included in the Himalayas.
- Many of the mountain peaks rise to elevations of 24,000 feet (7,300 meters).
- Mount Everest is the most prominent mountain in the world, with an elevation of 29,035 feet (8,850 meters).
- In 1999 an American expedition implanted a GPS device on the highest rock on Mount Everest to assess the current elevation of the mountain peak. The device shows that Mount Everest is actually rising. It rises about 1/3 of an inch each year (from 3 to 6 millimeters) and moves to the northeast about 3 inches each year.
- The first successful climb, often called summit or ascent, of Mount Everest took place in 1953 by the team of Sir Edmund Hillary of New Zealand and Tenzing Norgay of Nepal.
- Those who scale the mountain face many dangers, including extremely cold temperatures, severe weather conditions, an atmosphere low in oxygen, and the ever-present danger of avalanches.
- Mount Everest is known for its extremely cold temperatures which average −33°F but can drop to −76°F in January. In July the average temperature is −2°F.
- Early May is the best time to climb Mount Everest, though in September of 1988, Stacey Allison from Portland, Oregon made the first ascent by an American woman.

Tell students they will be learning more about mountains and other aspects of the world's regions and resources.

TEACH & ASSESS

R1

R1 Reading Skills

Naming Have a volunteer read these pages aloud. **Ask:**

- **What do you learn about when you study geography?** *(Earth's land, water, plants, and animals)*
- **Why do some people call Earth "the water planet"?** *(Water covers almost 70 percent of Earth's surface.)* **AL Verbal/Linguistic**

V Visual Skills

Identifying Have students discuss what they observe in the image of the boat on the water and refer them again to the paragraph, "Bodies of Water." **Ask:**

- **What are the five oceans?** *(Pacific, Atlantic, Indian, Southern, Arctic)*
- **What can be said about the water that makes up the five oceans?** *(It is a continuous body of water that encircles Earth.)*

Have students share what they think undersea explorers might find as they investigate the oceans. Have students categorize items as either sea animals or underwater plants. Create a two-column chart on the board as students generate answers. **Visual/Spatial**

R2 Reading Skills

Categorizing Write *Natural Resources* on the board, and have a volunteer read the paragraph, "Natural Resources." **Ask: What are natural resources?** *(products from Earth that people use to meet their needs)* Write *renewable* and *nonrenewable* under *Natural Resources.* Ask students to define these resources. To clear up any misconceptions, explain that renewable resources are ones that can be replenished after being used, such as trees used for building houses. Nonrenewable resources are resources that once used are gone forever or for a long period of time. **Ask:**

- **What are some examples of renewable resources?** *(plants, water, sun)*
- **What are some examples of nonrenewable resources?** *(oil, coal, natural gas)* **Naturalist**

EXPLORE the WORLD

Geography is the study of Earth and all of its variety. When you study geography, you learn about the planet's land, water, plants, and animals. Some people call Earth "the water planet." Do you know why? Water—in the form of streams, rivers, lakes, seas, and oceans—covers nearly 70 percent of Earth's surface.

V

1 BODIES OF WATER A long, narrow wooden boat on Vietnam's Mekong River is steered by oars. Almost all of Earth's water consists of a continuous body of water that circles the planet. This body of water makes up five oceans: the Pacific, the Atlantic, the Indian, the Southern, and the Arctic.

R2

2 NATURAL RESOURCES Natural resources are products of Earth that people use to meet their needs. Natural resources include land, minerals, plants, fish, and animals such as these sheep in southern Australia.

2 Unit 1

networks *Online Teaching Options*

VIDEO

A World Tour

Creating Charts Display the video montage of images from the unit as an introduction to this lesson. Divide the class into four groups. Assign a region to each group (forest, river valley, open prairie, ocean coast area). Have each group discuss the sights and sounds of the video, and how the region they have been assigned might influence how people living there relate to their environment. Create a group chart of the information generated by the students. Keep the chart to refine with the class during the unit's study. **Visual/Spatial, Auditory/Musical**

Comstock Images/Jupiterimages

3 LANDFORMS Landforms are features of the land, such as the great deserts of Egypt. Landforms influence where people live and how they relate to their environment.

C₁

C₂

FAST **FACT**

Earth's longest mountain range is underwater.

Unit 1 3

C₁ Critical Thinking Skills

Speculating Have students read the paragraph, "Landforms," and describe what they see in the large image corresponding to it. As a class, create a list of all the landforms students can think of. Discuss familiar landforms students have in their community. **Ask:**

- **How might landforms influence where people live?** *(Students might say that people live near water and food sources.)*
- **How do landforms influence how people relate to their environment?** *(Students might note that the environment determines the types of shelters people have and the types of food they eat.)* **BL** **Verbal/Linguistic**

V

V Visual Skills

Interpreting Direct students' attention to the image of the desert, the pyramids, and the boy on the camel. Have students share what they know about the desert, pyramids, and camels. **Ask:**

- **Where do you think this picture was taken? How do you know?** *(in Egypt, because Egypt is known for its desert climate and its pyramids)*
- **Why is a camel a good means of transportation in a desert?** *(Possible answers: Camels store water in their bodies and can travel with much less water than an animal such as a horse. Also camels' feet are better adapted to travel on sand.)* **Logical/Mathematical**

C₂ Critical Thinking Skills

Making Connections Read aloud the Fast Fact information. Remind students that landforms can be found both above and below the ocean. Explain that islands, such as the islands of Japan, are actually the tops of underwater mountains that rise above the surface of the ocean and provide living space for plants and animals above the water. **Ask: What benefits do landforms below the ocean's surface serve?** *(Possible answer: habitat for fish and other marine animals and plants)* **AL**

WORKSHEET

Environmental Case Study

Evaluating The case study for this unit is about maintenance of fresh water sources. This topic will help them understand the significance of Earth as a water planet. Divide the students into groups and distribute the case study worksheets. Allow students in-class time for planning. Have groups share their findings with the class. **Verbal/Linguistic**

V Visual Skills

Reading a Map Point out to students that this is a physical map, and have students work in pairs to analyze the features of a physical map. Then discuss the map as a group, noting the difference between landforms and bodies of water, types of labeling, and use of color. Identify lines of longitude and latitude for students. Note that lines of latitude run horizontally and are parallel to each other while lines of longitude run vertically and show the curve of Earth. Point out the map key. **Ask:**

- **What does the map key show?** *(the elevation of the world's landforms)*
- **What do the changes in color signify about those landforms?** *(They indicate elevation changes.)*
- **What do you notice about the elevation of the world's landforms?** *(Students might answer that there are regions of high mountains and lower elevations in all parts of the world.)*

Have students identify regions on the map, then **ask:**

- **What are the names of the continents?** *(North America, South America, Asia, Africa, Australia, Europe, Antarctica)*
- **What are the names of the world's large bodies of water?** *(North and South Atlantic Ocean, North and South Pacific Ocean, Indian Ocean, Arctic Ocean)* **AL ELL Visual/ Spatial**

C Critical Thinking Skills

Compare and Contrast Have students compare and contrast North America and South America. **Ask:**

- **What physical features are similar in both North America and South America?** *(mountain ranges in western regions, lower elevations in central parts)*
- **How do the sizes of North America and South America compare?** *(Students might note that North America seems wider and larger than South America.)*
- **What is the same about North and South America?** *(both have mountains, rivers, low lying regions, coastal areas)*
- **What is different about North and South America?** *(Equator runs through South America making it more tropical; mountains in South America are narrower, but taller)* **BL**

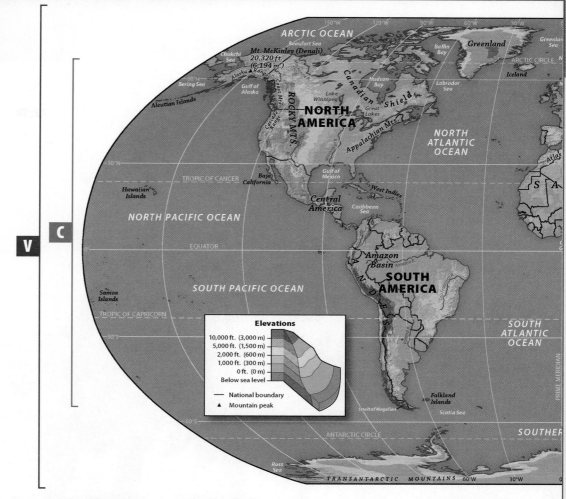

OUR WORLD

4 *Unit 1*

netw⊛rks *Online Teaching Options*

MAP

The World: Physical Map

Identifying Display the interactive Physical Map of the World on the whiteboard. As a class, discuss the various physical features. Then have volunteers use whiteboard tools to put an X on the mountain ranges, a circle around the seas, and a star on the continents. **AL Kinesthetic**

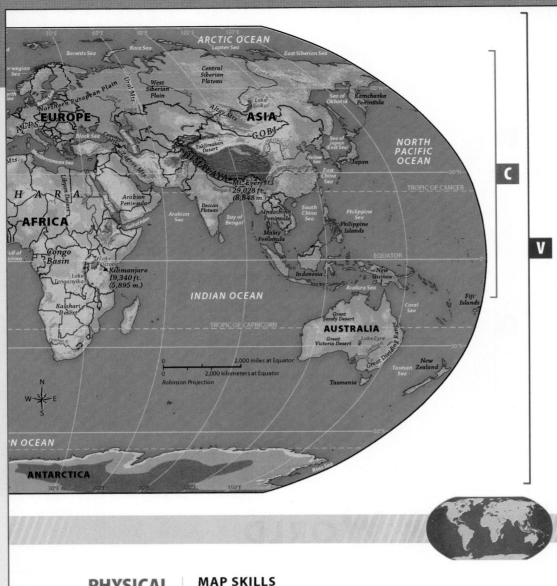

PHYSICAL

MAP SKILLS

1. **THE GEOGRAPHER'S WORLD** What part of Asia has the highest elevation?

2. **THE GEOGRAPHER'S WORLD** What body of water is located west of Australia?

3. **PLACES AND REGIONS** How would you describe Southern Africa?

Unit 1 **5**

V Visual Skills

Reading a Map Continue to have students analyze the features found on the map. Explain that the world is divided into the Northern Hemisphere and Southern Hemisphere along the Equator, and into the Eastern Hemisphere and Western Hemisphere along the Prime Meridian and the International Date Line. Have a volunteer identify and point out the Equator and the Prime Meridian. **Ask:**

- **In which continent are the highest elevations found in the Eastern Hemisphere?** *(Asia)*
- **On which continents are elevations below 1,000 feet found?** *(all continents)*
- **What do you notice about the distribution of land above and below the Equator?** *(There is more land above the Equator.)*
- **Why is Australia defined as a continent?** *(It is a large, disconnected landmass.)*
- **Which regions of the world do you think have the hottest climates?** *(near the Equator)*
- **Which regions of the world do you think are the coldest?** *(high mountain ranges, Arctic, Antarctic)* **AL** **Visual/Spatial**

C Critical Thinking Skills

Transferring Knowledge Write the following questions on the board. Have students write out the questions and answers with a partner. Then as a class, discuss the answers. **Ask:**

- **What physical features of Europe and Africa are different?** *(Africa is larger, has more areas of higher elevations)*
- **Which continent contains the largest land mass with the highest elevations?** *(Asia)*
- **Which direction would you travel to get from Japan to the United States in the least amount of time?** *(East)*
- **How might a ship travel from the Mediterranean Sea to the Indian Ocean?** *(Students may answer around Africa or through the Suez Canal.)*

If needed, explain that today the Suez Canal exists that allows ships to travel between the two bodies of water. **Logical/Mathematical**

The Physical World Game

Identifying Display the Physical Map of the World on the interactive whiteboard. Have volunteers identify continents and major bodies of water on the map. Once a student has dragged and dropped the correct location name, have the student ask a question or tell a fact about the location. **AL** **Kinesthetic**

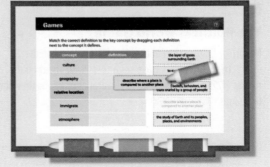

ANSWERS, p. 5

MAP SKILLS

1. Himalayan ranges
2. Indian Ocean
3. It has a low elevation and includes the Kalahari Desert.

V1 Visual Skills

Contrasting Explain to students that this is a political map. It shows the divisions between countries and identifies them by name. **Ask: What is the difference between a political map and a physical map?** (*A political map shows human-made features like national boundaries, national capitals, and cities. A physical map focuses on natural landforms and water features like rivers, mountains, and deserts.*) **AL**

V2 Visual Skills

Identifying Allow students to work in pairs as they refer to the previous physical map and the political map of North America. Allow time for students to locate the United States, Mexico, and Canada. **Ask:**

- **What bodies of water surround these three countries?** (*North Atlantic Ocean, North Pacific Ocean, Gulf of Mexico, Arctic Ocean*)
- **Which country has the largest landmass?** (*Canada*)
- **How can northern Canada be described?** (*northern Canada is made up of a series of islands*)
- **What physical feature separates part of Canada from the United States?** (*a series of large lakes*)

Then have the partners analyze and discuss South America. **Ask:**

- **Which country has the largest landmass in South America?** (*Brazil*)
- **What do you notice about the area where North America and South America meet?** (*There are several small countries, some of which are island countries.*)
- **What is the capital city of Guyana?** (*Georgetown*)

Explain that navigation between the North Atlantic Ocean and the North Pacific Ocean was once very difficult, however, today a large canal exists in Panama that allows ships to travel between the two oceans.

C Critical Thinking Skills

Drawing Conclusions Ask: How can landforms both facilitate trade between countries and impede it? (*Landforms like mountain ranges make it very difficult to travel from one region to another, while water routes facilitate trade.*) **ELL** **Logical/Mathematical**

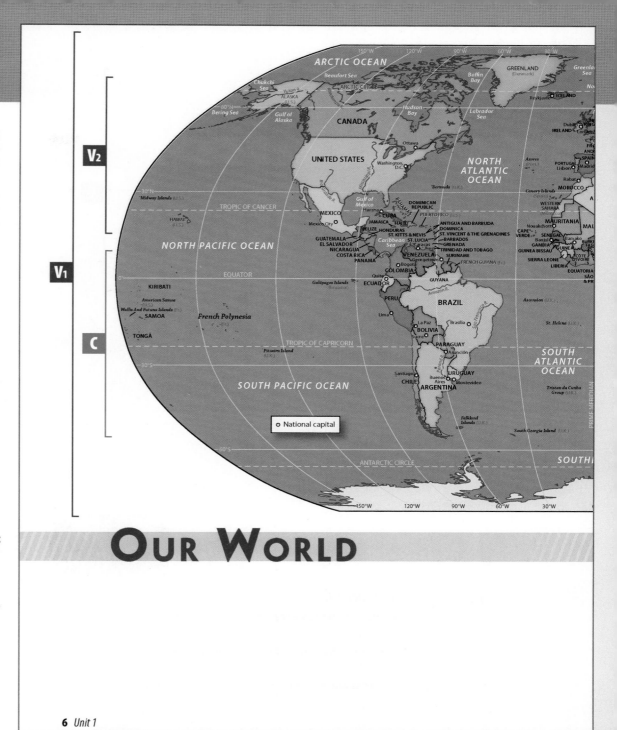

OUR WORLD

6 *Unit 1*

netw⊙rks   *Online Teaching Options*

GAME

The Political World Game

Naming Display the Political Map of the World on the interactive whiteboard. Have volunteers drag and drop the names of cities and countries to the proper places as they play the game. **Kinesthetic**

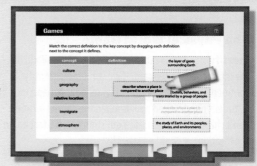

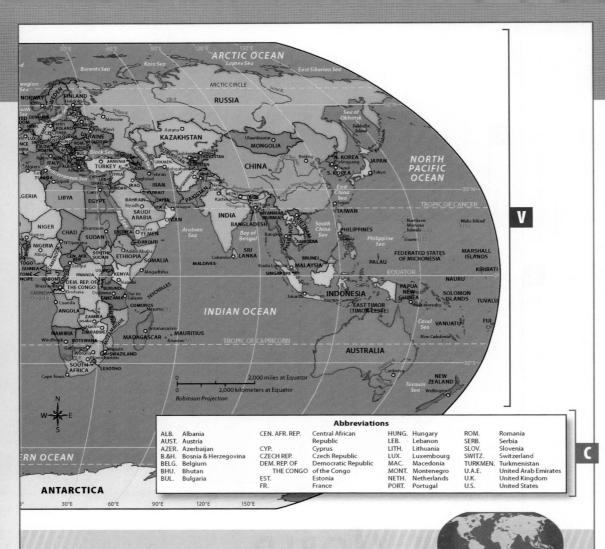

ARCTIC OCEAN

RUSSIA

KAZAKHSTAN

MONGOLIA

CHINA

N. KOREA
S. KOREA
JAPAN

NORTH
PACIFIC
OCEAN

TROPIC OF CANCER

INDIA

MYANMAR
BURMA

TAIWAN

PHILIPPINES

FEDERATED STATES
OF MICRONESIA

MARSHALL
ISLANDS

EQUATOR

NAURU

KIRIBATI

INDIAN OCEAN

INDONESIA

PAPUA
NEW
GUINEA

SOLOMON
ISLANDS

TUVALU

EAST TIMOR
(TIMOR-LESTE)

VANUATU

FIJI

TROPIC OF CAPRICORN

AUSTRALIA

NEW
ZEALAND

2,000 miles at Equator

2,000 kilometers at Equator

Robinson Projection

ANTARCTICA

30°E   60°E   90°E   120°E   150°E

Abbreviations

ALB.	Albania	CEN. AFR. REP.	Central African	HUNG.	Hungary	ROM.	Romania
AUST.	Austria		Republic	LEB.	Lebanon	SERB.	Serbia
AZER.	Azerbaijan	CYP.	Cyprus	LITH.	Lithuania	SLOV.	Slovenia
B.&H.	Bosnia & Herzegovina	CZECH REP.	Czech Republic	LUX.	Luxembourg	SWITZ.	Switzerland
BELG.	Belgium	DEM. REP. OF	Democratic Republic	MAC.	Macedonia	TURKMEN.	Turkmenistan
BHU.	Bhutan	THE CONGO	of the Congo	MONT.	Montenegro	U.A.E.	United Arab Emirates
BUL.	Bulgaria	EST.	Estonia	NETH.	Netherlands	U.K.	United Kingdom
		FR.	France	PORT.	Portugal	U.S.	United States

POLITICAL

MAP SKILLS

1 **PLACES AND REGIONS** How would you describe the region north of Australia?

2 **THE GEOGRAPHER'S WORLD** Which country is located west of Egypt?

3 **PLACES AND REGIONS** What is the capital of Mongolia?

Unit 1 **7**

Physical Geography Activity

Evaluating Use the Physical Geography Activity worksheet to analyze the elevation profile of the ocean. Have students compare their analyses. **Intrapersonal**

V Visual Skills

Reading a Map Have students compare the number of political boundaries in the Eastern Hemisphere with that of the Western Hemisphere. Explain that, though physical regions remain the same, political boundaries change through armed conflict and civil uprisings. The names of countries may be different from maps representing different time periods as new governments take over a region, at times dissolving one country and forming others. Direct students' attention to the countries of the Eastern Hemisphere. **Ask:**

- **How does use of color help you read this map?** *(easy to compare the size and shape of the different countries)*
- **How does the key help you read this map?** *(provides the names of different countries)*
- **Why are there so many different countries among the continents of the Eastern Hemisphere?** *(Students may speculate that wars resulted in the formation of different countries.)*
- **What can be said about the different countries?** *(have different governments, languages, traditions)*
- **What might the people who live in the same physical region but in different countries share?** *(similar ways to use the land)*
- **What would you expect to happen between countries that share a physical region?** *(trade, possibly conflict for territorial gain)* **BL** **Visual/Spatial**

C Critical Thinking Skills

Reasoning Focus students' attention to the Abbreviation Key at the bottom of the map. Discuss and pronounce a few of the countries. **Ask:**

- **How might size affect the political power of a country?** *(Possible answer: the larger the country the more room for people to live there making it powerful)*
- **Which country in Asia might hold a great deal of power in the region?** *(China or Russia)* **Logical/ Mathematical**

ANSWERS, p. 7

MAP SKILLS

1. It consists of numerous island countries.
2. Libya
3. Ulaanbaatar

R Reading Skills

Recognizing Relationships Explain that population density is the number of people living in a region. Show a rock and a sponge. Explain that the density of the rock is greater than the density of the sponge, just as the population density of North America's East Coast is greater than the population density of the continent's Northwest region. **Ask:**

- **What is shown on this map?** *(The population density of different countries and regions of the world.)*
- **What can you interpret about the land's physical features and population density on a map?** *(That there is a relationship between the population density and the ability of the land to support the population.)* **BL**

V Visual Skills

Interpreting Have students study the population density map focusing on the Western Hemisphere. **Ask:**

- **Where is the greatest population density in North America?** *(East Coast of the United States and central Mexico)*
- **Where is the greatest population density in South America?** *(along the coastlines)*
- **Why do you think the population density diminishes in the far northern region of North America and the far southern region of South America?** *(Cold environments make it difficult for human habitation.)*
- **Why do you think large cities are found on or near coastal areas?** *(access to trade and ability of the land to support higher population densities because there is a supply of water)*
- **What physical feature do you think has the greatest influence on the growth of a region's population density?** *(Students might speculate that a region's abundance of natural resources may be the most influential physical feature.)* **Visual/Spatial**

C Critical Thinking Skills

Drawing Conclusions Have students discuss the landforms in the local area and which landforms most people tend to live near. **Ask:** Which landforms limit population? *(landforms such as mountain ranges and deserts)* **Logical/Mathematical**

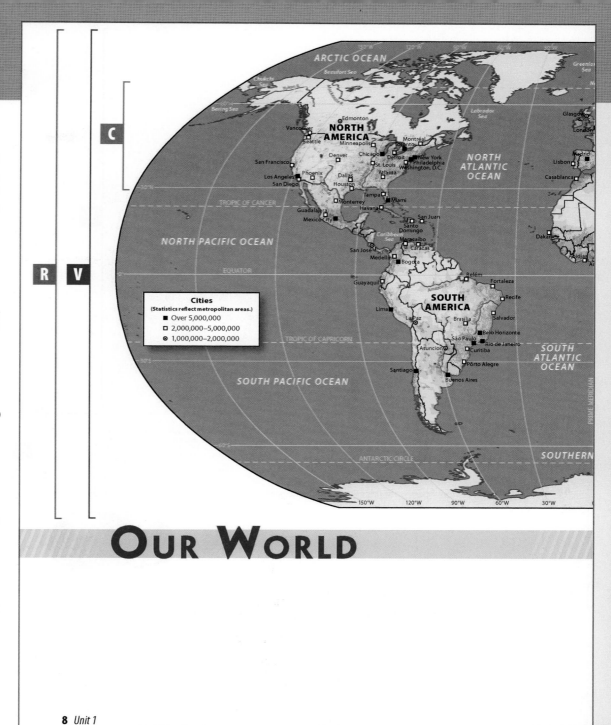

OUR WORLD

networks — *Online Teaching Options*

MAP

The World: Population Density Map

Speculating Use the interactive Population Density Map of the World to highlight regions of greatest population density. Have students make a list of countries with the highest population densities. Have students discuss how high population density impacts a region's natural resources and speculate on possible problems that could be caused by high population density. **BL** **Visual/Spatial**

POPULATION DENSITY

POPULATION	
Per sq. mi.	Per sq. km
1,250 and over	500 and over
250–1,249	100–499
63–249	25–99
25–62	10–24
2.5–24	1–9
Less than 2.5	Less than 1

0   2,000 miles at Equator
0   2,000 kilometers at Equator
Robinson Projection

MAP SKILLS

1 **PLACES AND REGIONS** What parts of Asia are the most densely populated?

2 **PLACES AND REGIONS** Which part of Africa has the lowest population density?

3 **ENVIRONMENT AND SOCIETY** In general, what population pattern do you see in northern Africa?

Unit 1 **9**

SLIDE SHOW

How-To: Read a Map

Synthesizing View the How-To slide show about reading maps. To help students synthesize the information on maps play "10 questions". Have each student write down a location. Ask for a student volunteer. Have the class take turns asking 10 "yes" or "no" questions to determine the volunteer's location. Have the student who guesses the location be the next volunteer. **Visual/Spatial**

Slide Show

V Visual Skills

Reading a Map Have students compare the physical map with the population map on this spread. Discuss the physical features that create barriers to population expansion, including mountain ranges, deserts, and oceans. **Ask:**

- **What regional aspects of population density do you see?** *(Possible answers: concentrated population in Europe and parts of Asia near water, and lower populations in the interior of the continents)*

- **Where are the highest population densities found in Asia?** *(India and Southeast Asia)*

- **What can be said about the population density of Europe?** *(fairly evenly spread throughout Europe)*

- **What do you notice about the population density of Africa?** *(High population densities occur both along coastal regions and in parts of the interior of the continent.)*

- **What physical feature of the continent allows for greater population density in the interior of Africa?** *(rivers that allow for navigation and trade)* **Visual/Spatial**

C Critical Thinking Skills

Determining Cause and Effect Have students consider the pressures on governments to meet the needs of a country's population when the population density exceeds the country's level of natural resources required to support the people. Explain to students that natural resources include such things as fresh water, rich soil to grow food, or trees to build houses. Stress that there are many resources that are necessary to sustain life. There are also natural resources that are not vital to sustaining life, such as gold, diamonds, or other minerals. **Ask:**

- **What problems might countries with high population densities experience if they do not have enough natural resources in their country?** *(lack of proper housing, poverty, or starvation)*

- **Which country in Asia might be experiencing such difficulties?** *(Students might speculate that India or China could be experiencing difficulties meeting the needs of the people because the populations in those countries are very high.)* **Logical/Mathematical**

ANSWERS, p. 9

MAP SKILLS

1. northern part of South Asia, East Asia along the Pacific, and islands of Southeast Asia.
2. the upper northern part, where the Sahara is located
3. Northern Africa is less densely populated.

Unit 1 **9**

V Visual Skills

Recognizing Relationships Help students recognize the relationship between natural resources and the physical characteristics of a region. Have students analyze both the physical and economic maps. Draw students' attention to the mountain regions along the western regions of North America and South America. **Ask: What resources are found along these two mountain regions?** *(coal, uranium, copper, gold, silver, petroleum)*

Then allow time for students to work in teams and analyze the economic map. Have them read the map keys and discuss the location of natural resources and land use. **Ask:**

- **What types of resources does the map key highlight?** *(natural resources of metals, minerals, and fossil fuels)*
- **Why do you think these resources are considered "natural"?** *(Students' answers may vary but students should reason that these resources are naturally part of Earth.)*
- **What types of resources are found in the central regions of North America?** *(petroleum, lead, coal)*
- **What types of resources are near the Amazon River?** *(bauxite, manganese, iron ore)*
- **Which resource is shown by a red symbol on the map key?** *(uranium)*
- **What types of things does the map key of land use focus on?** *(farming, fishing, livestock and herding, foresting, and manufacturing and trade)*
- **Notice the location of manufacturing and trade areas in North America. Why are these areas located where they are?** *(Possible answer: all of manufacturing and trade areas are located around large cities)*
- **What type of land use covers most of the northern region of South America?** *(forests, this area is almost all tropical rain forest area)* **ELL** **Visual/Spatial**

C Critical Thinking Skills

Drawing Conclusions Have students consider the importance of natural resources to the economic viability of a country. **Ask:**

- **What do countries need to do if they lack natural resources, such as a lack of sufficient oil to serve transportation?** *(purchase resources from other countries)*
- **How might a country's natural resources affect its economy?** *(Students may suggest that countries that have a wealth of natural resources are able to bring money into the country by selling its natural resources to other countries that lack them.)* **Logical/Mathematical**

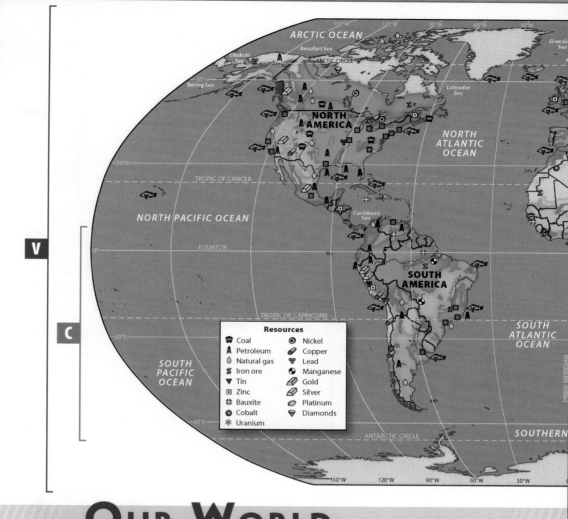

Resources

🐚	Coal	⊗	Nickel
A	Petroleum	▱	Copper
◊	Natural gas	♙	Lead
✗	Iron ore	♤	Manganese
▼	Tin	◲	Gold
⊡	Zinc	⊘	Silver
⠿	Bauxite	⊘	Platinum
◉	Cobalt	▽	Diamonds
✳	Uranium		

OUR WORLD

netw⊙rks *Online Teaching Options*

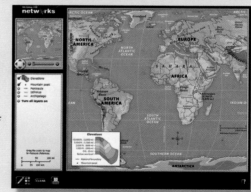

MAP

The World: Economic Map

Explaining Display the interactive Economic Map of the World on the whiteboard. As a class, review the regions and the location of resources. Have students write a paragraph explaining why coastal cities were built in certain places. *(Answers will vary but should demonstrate an understanding of the resources coastal areas provide.)* **Verbal/Linguistic**

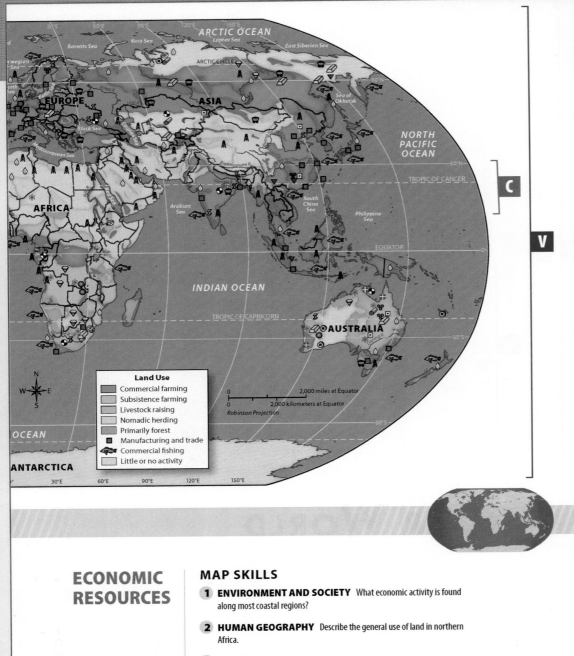

Land Use

- Commercial farming
- Subsistence farming
- Livestock raising
- Nomadic herding
- Primarily forest
- Manufacturing and trade
- Commercial fishing
- Little or no activity

0   2,000 miles at Equator
0   2,000 kilometers at Equator
Robinson Projection

ECONOMIC RESOURCES

MAP SKILLS

1 **ENVIRONMENT AND SOCIETY** What economic activity is found along most coastal regions?

2 **HUMAN GEOGRAPHY** Describe the general use of land in northern Africa.

3 **PLACES AND REGIONS** Which area produces the most oil—Australia or Southwest Asia?

V   Visual Skills

Reading a Map   Direct students' attention to the land use map key. Help them understand the relationship between land use and availability of natural resources. **Ask:**

- **What is the purpose of the land use map key?** *(shows how the land is used by different countries)*
- **What type of land use does dark green shading show?** *(commercial farming)*
- **What type of land use does yellow shading show?** *(nomadic herding)*
- **Where type of land use occurs in the central region of Australia?** *(livestock raising)*
- **What type of land use is shown for a large part of the northern region of Africa?** *(little or no activity)*
- **What would explain this type of land use in northern Africa?** *(desert)*
- **What type of land occurs in Southeast Asia?** *(primarily forest)*
- **What explains the difference in land use in North Africa from that in Southeast Asia?** *(Students should recognize that the two regions have very different climates and thus different land uses.)*   **Visual/Spatial**

C   Critical Thinking Skills

Hypothesizing   Point to the northern region of Africa. Explain that all around this area is the Sahara Desert. **Ask:**

- **What explains the band of commercial farming in the desert of North Africa?** *(The Nile River flows through the desert, so this provides water to the area, which is needed for farming.)*
- **What natural resource is also found in this area and why is this a good place for oil fields?** *(Students should answer that oil is found there and may speculate that not very many people live in the desert so oil fields will not affect living conditions in the area.)* **AL**   **Logical/Mathematical**

Cultural Geography Activity

Evaluating   Use the Cultural Geography Activity worksheet as a pre- or post-assessment of students' knowledge of culture.   **Intrapersonal**

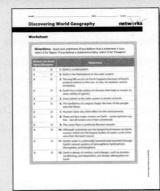

ANSWERS, p. 11

MAP SKILLS

1. commercial fishing
2. nomadic herding
3. Southwest Asia

V1 Visual Skills

Visualizing **Ask:** What type of map is this? *(a map showing the world's climates)* Explain that maps highlighting the world's climates have a direct relationship to both physical and population density maps. Ask students to visualize a desert environment where little plant or animal life exists because of the lack of rainfall and high daytime temperatures. **Ask:**

- **What relationship is there between the physical features of a desert and low population density?** *(Few people live in the desert because the land cannot support the population.)*
- **What might governments do to increase the ability of a desert region to support a larger population density?** *(improve the land, supply water to the area)* **BL**

V2 Visual Skills

Reading a Map Direct students' attention to the map key. **Ask:**

- **What do the colors on the key indicate?** *(different climates found throughout the world)*
- **Which colors indicate a tropical climate?** *(light and dark pink)*
- **Which color indicates a Mediterranean climate?** *(orange)*
- **Which color indicates a tundra?** *(dark purple)*
- **Where is the tropical climate region located in South America?** *(across the northern half of the continent)*
- **Where is the desert climate region located in Africa?** *(across the top third of the continent)*
- **What do you notice about climates as you read the map moving north and moving south of the Equator?** *(They get colder and drier.)*
- **Which climate region is located mostly in the north central region of the United States?** *(humid continental)*
- **What can you say about the country of Greenland from reading this map?** *(It is a region of extreme cold.)* **Visual/Spatial**

C Critical Thinking Skills

Formulating Questions **Ask:** What two questions could be answered from reading this climate map? *(Students may suggest such questions as, "Where is it really cold in the world?" or "Why are climates along the Equator consistently hotter than those farther north or south?")* **Logical/Mathematical**

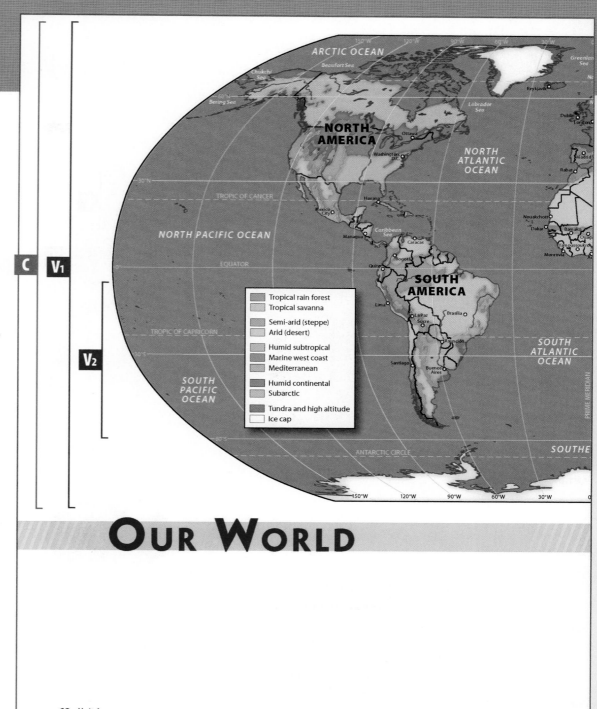

OUR WORLD

12 *Unit 1*

netw⚙rks *Online Teaching Options*

MAP

The World: Climate Map

Comparing In pairs, have students compare the climate and vegetation regions as they study the interactive Climate Map of the World. Have partners write down four comparisons that they have noted. Then as a class, have students share and discuss their comparisons. **BL** **Visual/Spatial**

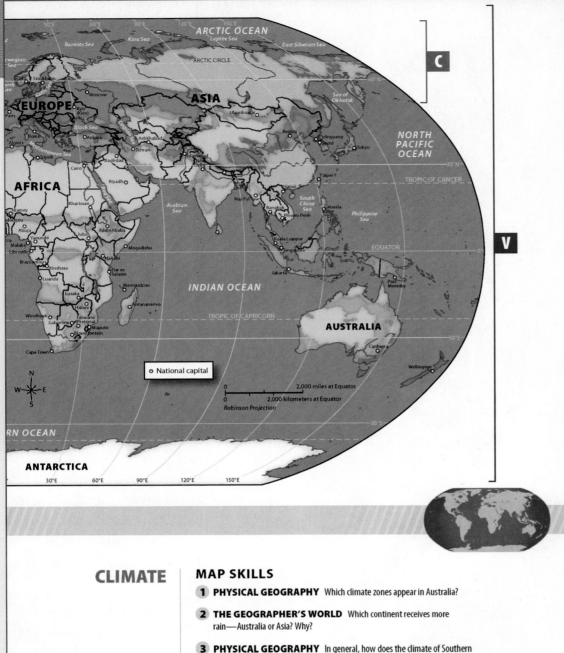

CLIMATE

MAP SKILLS

1. **PHYSICAL GEOGRAPHY** Which climate zones appear in Australia?

2. **THE GEOGRAPHER'S WORLD** Which continent receives more rain—Australia or Asia? Why?

3. **PHYSICAL GEOGRAPHY** In general, how does the climate of Southern Africa compare with the climate of North Africa?

Unit 1 **13**

V Visual Skills

Reading a Map Help students recognize that climates are regionalized. **Ask:**

- **What regional aspects to climate do you see?** *(Climate areas are located over large areas.)*
- **What can you state about climate regions and latitude?** *(Students should note that, in general, similar climate zones occur at specific lines of latitude.)*
- **What type of climate covers most of Europe?** *(marine west coast)*
- **What type of climate covers most of the continent of Australia?** *(arid and desert)*
- **What is the difference between the climate that covers most of Russia and India's climate?** *(While Russia experiences, for the most part, a subarctic climate, most of India experiences a tropical savanna climate.)*
- **With the exception of the Middle East region, what can be said about the climates of countries surrounding the Indian Ocean?** *(mostly tropical climates)*
- **What is the same about the climates of Australia and South Africa?** *(They both experience arid climates.)* **Visual/Spatial**

C Critical Thinking Skills

Recognizing Relationships Have students consider the impact of the shape of Earth on its climate zones. **Ask:**

- **Why would areas to the far north and far south of the Equator experience colder climates?** *(Areas to the far north and far south do not receive as much direct sunlight.)*
- **Look back at the economic map of resources and this map. India has a tropical savanna climate. How do you think its climate affects its land use practices?** *(Students might answer that because India has a humid, hot climate, it is able to use its land for agricultural purposes.)* **AL Logical/Mathematical**

CHART

Precipitation and Temperature Chart

Drawing Conclusions Have students use the Climate Map and interactive chart to study the world climates and levels of precipitation and temperature. Guide a class discussion to help students draw conclusions about how levels of precipitation and temperature impact where people live. **Verbal/Linguistic**

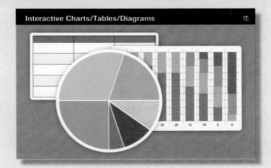

Interactive Charts/Tables/Diagrams

ANSWERS, p. 13

MAP SKILLS

1. Tropical savanna, Semi-arid, Arid, Humid subtropical, Marine west coast
2. Asia; Australia has primarily an arid climate.
3. Both include arid and desert climates.

T Technology Skills

Using Visual Aids Organize students into six groups. Provide an outline map of each continent (do not assign Antarctica), to each of the six groups of students. Explain that each group will research additional cities and countries on their continent and label them on their maps. Start by having students transfer the cities shown on the political map to their maps. Have students use the political map, as well as other maps and atlases, to locate additional cities for their continent. Next, have them use other maps to identify and label the physical features and natural resources found on the continents. Make sure that students create a key that will represent the population, natural resources, and physical features for their maps.

Allow class time for groups to research other aspects that are unique to their continent. Groups should prepare index cards that list 5 to 7 facts about their continent that they have **T** learned from their research.

After students have had time to finish, have groups present information about their continent maps. Presentations should include showing and discussing cities and countries on the maps, as well as explaining the researched facts about why their continent is unique.

W Writing Skills

Narrative Have students use the photo to help them visualize what it would be like to see Earth from space. Ask students to imagine that they are astronauts traveling in space. Then write a short story about being an astronaut and looking down at this image of Earth.

CLOSE & REFLECT

Summarizing Information Have students reflect on the types of maps they have studied and what they have learned about the maps. Then have students write three sentences that summarize what they learned.

14 Unit 1

netw⊙rks *Online Teaching Options*

MAP

Regional Map

Making Connections Display the interactive regional map to students. Select some of the images that are connected to the map and place them in context of the map and the textbook. Guide a discussion helping students to identify the content of the images and then to make a connection between the image and the map location. **Visual/Spatial**

CHAPTER 1

Earth's Land, People, and Environments Planner

UNDERSTANDING BY DESIGN®

Enduring Understandings

- *People, places, and ideas change over time.*

Essential Questions

- *How does geography influence the way people live?*

Predictable Misunderstandings

- *Geography is just the names of states and their capitals.*
- *Lines of latitude and longitude actually appear on Earth.*
- *Geography is static and unchanging, serving merely as a backdrop to people's activities.*

Assessment Evidence

Performance Tasks:

- *Project-Based Learning Digital Hands-On Chapter Project*
- *Project-Based Learning Hands-On Chapter Project*

Other Evidence:

- *Geography Skills Activity*
- *Technology Skills Activity*
- *Participation in Project-Based Learning Activities*
- *Participation in Interactive Whiteboard Map Activities*
- *Contribution to small-group activities*
- *Interpretation of slide show images and special purpose maps*
- *Participation in completing the Six Essential Elements Digital Chart*
- *Participation in class discussions about the Geographer's World*
- *Lesson Reviews*
- *Chapter Assessments*

National Geography Standards covered in Chapter 1

Learners will understand:

I. The World in Spatial Terms

Standard 1: How to use maps and other geographic representations, geospatial technologies, and spatial thinking to understand and communicate information

II. Places and Regions

Standard 4: The physical and human characteristics of places

Standard 5: That people create regions to interpret Earth's complexity

IV. Human Systems

Standard 9: The characteristics, distribution, and migration of human populations on Earth's surface

V. Environment and Society

Standard 14: How human actions modify the physical environment

SUGGESTED PACING GUIDE

Introducing the Chapter	1 Day	What Do You Think?	3 Days
Lesson 1	2 Days	Chapter Wrap-Up and Assessment	1 Day
Lesson 2	2 Days		

TOTAL TIME 9 Days

Key for Using the Teacher Edition

SKILL-BASED ACTIVITIES

Types of skill activities found in the Teacher Edition.

- **V** **Visual Skills** require students to analyze maps, graphs, charts, and photos.
- **W** **Writing Skills** provide writing opportunities to help students comprehend the text.
- **R** **Reading Skills** help students practice reading skills and master vocabulary.
- **C** **Critical Thinking Skills** help students apply and extend what they have learned.
- **T** **Technology Skills** require students to use digital tools effectively.

*Letters are followed by a number when there is more than one of the same type of skill on the page.

DIFFERENTIATED INSTRUCTION

All activities are written for the on-level student unless otherwise marked with the leveled labels below.

- **BL** Beyond Level
- **AL** Approaching Level
- **ELL** English Language Learners

All students benefit from activities that utilize different learning styles. Many activities are marked as below when a particular learning style is highlighted.

Intrapersonal	Naturalist
Logical/Mathematical	Kinesthetic
Visual/Spatial	Auditory/Musical
Verbal/Linguistic	Interpersonal

CHAPTER OPENER PLANNER

Students will know:
- *the parts, styles, and purposes of a world map.*

Students will be able to:
- ***identify** the seven continents using a world map.*
- ***use a time line** to discuss significant events in history that significantly changed people's view of the world.*

UNDERSTANDING
BY DESIGN®

☑ *Print Teaching Options*

V Visual Skills

☐ **P. 16** Students learn about the American cartographer John Paul Goode and use a Goode map of the world to identify the seven continents and other world features.

☐ **P. 17** Students use a time line to answer questions about the sequence of events in the development of knowledge of the world and world maps.

☑ *Online Teaching Options*

☐ **MAP Reading a Map**—Students identify aspects and locations of the region on a map.

☐ **TIME LINE Reading a Time Line and Map**—Students use the time line and map to learn about where historical events occurred in the world. **AL Visual/Spatial**

☐ **MAP Interactive World Atlas**—Students use the interactive world atlas to identify the region and describe its terrain.

☑ *Printable Digital Worksheets*

☐ **WORKSHEET Geography Skills: Understanding the Lines on a Map**—Students use the geography skills worksheet to practice and apply the skills of using latitude and longitude lines on a map.

☐ **WORKSHEET Technology Skills: Geospatial Technologies**—Students use the worksheet to investigate the latest forms of geospatial technologies.

Project-Based Learning

Hands-On

Create Maps

Students will create a mental map that shows the route they travel from their homes to their school. Students will then illustrate this map on paper. Maps should include elements such as a compass rose and key. Then in groups, students will analyze the maps to identify the five themes of geography that appear on the map. Students will present their maps to the class, along with identifying where the five themes of geography appear on them.

Digital Hands-On

Create Online Interactive Maps

Students will create digital travel brochures after analyzing locations around the world using an online interactive mapping site. Students should include information about the location and physical features of the location. Travel brochures can be shared with other students so they can make suggestions about including additional geographic information.

Print Resources

ANCILLARY RESOURCES

These ancillaries are available for every chapter and lesson.

- **Reading Essentials and Study Guide Workbook AL ELL**
- **Chapter Tests and Lesson Quizzes Blackline Masters**

PRINTABLE DIGITAL WORKSHEETS

These printable digital worksheets are available for every chapter and lesson.

- **Hands-On Chapter Projects**
- **What Do You Know? Activities**
- **Chapter Summaries (English and Spanish)**
- **Vocabulary Builder Activities**
- **Quizzes and Tests**
- **Reading Essentials and Study Guide (English and Spanish) AL ELL**
- **Guided Reading Activities**

More Media Resources

SUGGESTED VIDEOS

NOTE: Be sure to preview any clips to ensure they are age-appropriate.

- **Inside Planet Earth** (120 min.)
- **Six Degrees Could Change the World** (50 min.)
- **Raging Planet** (8 episodes-387 min.)

SUGGESTED READING

- ***National Geographic Student Atlas of the World,*** by The National Geographic Society **BL**
- ***The Coast Mappers,*** by Taylor Morrison
- ***Follow That Map! A First Book of Mapping Skills,*** by Scot Ritchie **AL**

How Geographers Think

Students will know:
- the five themes of geography (location, place, region, human-environment interaction, movement).
- meanings of and how to calculate relative and absolute locations.
- meanings of important terms: latitude, longitude, Equator, Prime Meridian, landscape, environment, landform, climate, resource.
- the six essential elements.

Students will be able to:
- *explain* why geographers study more than a place's location and dimensions.
- *identify* examples of human systems.
- *describe* the physical and human characteristics of a community.

UNDERSTANDING BY DESIGN®

☑ *Print Teaching Options*

V Visual Skills

☐ **P. 19** Students describe physical features of a landscape.

☐ **P. 22** Students identify human and physical features and compose an advertisement for their community. **ELL**

☐ **P. 22** Students use lines of latitude and longitude to identify absolute location.

☐ **P. 25** Students discuss how visuals such as graphs, charts, diagrams, and photographs convey information. **ELL**

W Writing Skills

☐ **P. 24** Students write informative paragraphs about the benefits and disadvantages of forms of technology used for communication. **AL ELL**

R Reading Skills

☐ **P. 18** Students develop a geography vocabulary list of words, meanings, and drawings in their notebooks. **ELL**

☐ **P. 20** Students make connections between their experiences and the way geography is organized. **AL**

☐ **P. 21** Students calculate relative locations.

☐ **P. 22** Students paraphrase to explain why geographers study regions. **AL ELL**

☐ **P. 23** Students apply knowledge of key features of the environment to the local area. **AL ELL**

C Critical Thinking Skills

☐ **P. 18** Students draw conclusions about how physical features on Earth have changed over time. **BL**

☐ **P. 19** Students use knowledge of human and physical features to make inferences.

☐ **P. 20** Students make connections between their experiences and human and physical features of the world.

☐ **P. 23** Students identify problems that human activities have caused in the environment. **AL**

☐ **P. 24** Students use chart skills to compare and contrast.

T Technology Skills

☐ **P. 20** Students research how a place has changed over time and how the changes have impacted the place.

☑ *Online Teaching Options*

V Visual Skills

☐ **IMAGE** **360° View: Times Square**—Student use a 360° image of Times Square, New York, to understand the idea of location. **Visual/Spatial**

☐ **SLIDE SHOW** **The Ninth Ward in New Orleans**—Students interpret the slide show images of New Orleans taken before and after Hurricane Katrina struck the city to describe how a place changes over time. **Visual/Spatial**

☐ **VIDEO** **Corals and Oceans**—Students watch a video about the physical geography of the world. They identify the main ideas about the geography of the world portrayed in the video and discuss them with a partner. **AL Verbal/Linguistic, Interpersonal**

R Reading Skills

☐ **GAME** **Drag-and-Drop: Vocabulary Game**—Students use the game to build their knowledge of content and academic vocabulary words used in Lesson 1. **Verbal, Kinesthetic**

☐ **CHART** **Chart of Six Essential Elements**—Students use a chart to apply and reinforce their knowledge of the six essential elements of geography that they learned in the lesson. **Verbal/Linguistic, Interpersonal**

C Critical Thinking Skills

☐ **ANIMATION** **Disney World in Orlando, Florida**—Students use the animation to identify the physical and human features and describe the relative location of a place. **Visual/Spatial**

☐ **SLIDE SHOW** **How People Are Affected by Geography**—Students use the slide show to discuss how human structures can adversely affect the environment. **BL Visual, Interpersonal**

T Technology Skills

☐ **ANIMATION** **Animated Globe**—Students use the animated globe to explain geographic terms. **AL Verbal/Linguistic**

☐ **ANIMATION** **Regions of Earth**—Students use the animation to further discuss geographic terms and the concept of a region.

☐ **ONLINE SELF-CHECK QUIZ** **Lesson 1**—Students receive instant feedback on their mastery of lesson content.

☑ *Printable Digital Worksheets*

W Writing Skills

☐ **WORKSHEET** **Geography Skills: Understanding the Lines on a Map**—Students use the geography skills worksheet to practice and apply the skills of using latitude and longitude lines on a map.

GEOGRAPHERS AND THEIR TOOLS

Students will know:
- *why geographers study regions.*
- *the parts, styles, and purposes of different kinds of maps.*

Students will be able to:
- ***identify*** *differences in general-purpose maps and thematic maps.*
- ***analyze*** *how geospatial technologies could help a business.*
- ***draw a map*** *of a place, including the relevant map features.*

UNDERSTANDING
BY DESIGN®

☑ *Print Teaching Options*

V Visual Skills

☐ **P. 26** Students create a mental map and sketch it, and then describe the relative location of things on the map.

☐ **P. 28** Students identify the parts of a map and types of information they convey. ELL

☐ **P. 29** Students use math and map skills to compute distances on a map.

☐ **P. 30** Students analyze a historical map and connect it to the history of the time it was made.

W Writing Skills

☐ **P. 31** Students work in groups to identify the pros and cons of GPS apps that allow parents to track their children. Then they write persuasive paragraphs.

R Reading Skills

☐ **P. 26** Students paraphrase to explain why a globe is the most accurate way to show places on Earth. AL ELL

☐ **P. 29** Students define the multiple meanings of the word *scale*.

☐ **P. 29** Students explain different purposes of maps.

☐ **P. 30** Students apply the map skills they are learning to explain elevation.

☐ **P. 32** Students use context clues to find meaning of unknown words. ELL

☐ **P. 33** Students identify the limits of geospatial technologies in the study of geography. AL

C Critical Thinking Skills

☐ **P. 27** Students compare and contrast maps and globes, recording their work in a Venn diagram.

☐ **P. 29** Students analyze map projections.

☐ **P. 30** Students make connections and apply map skills to give examples of thematic maps.

☐ **P. 32** Students make inferences about the information gathered by a geographic information system.

T Technology Skills

☐ **P. 33** Students use technology to access NASA weather satellite images and evaluate the importance of the information.

☑ *Online Teaching Options*

V Visual Skills

☐ **ANIMATION** **Elements of a Globe**—Students use the animated globe to explain geographic terms related to maps. AL **Visual/Spatial**

☐ **SLIDE SHOW** **Special Purpose Maps**—Students use the slide show of various special purpose maps to discuss the kinds of information the maps convey. **Visual/Spatial**

☐ **SLIDE SHOW** **Mapmaking Over Time**—Students use the slide show to discover how mapmaking has changed over time. **Visual/Spatial**

W Writing Skills

☐ **VIDEO** **Mapping the World: Google Maps**—Students watch a video and formulate questions about the tools of geography. **Verbal/Linguistic, Interpersonal**

R Reading Skills

☐ **GRAPHIC ORGANIZER** **Organizing: Forms of Technology**—Students use the interactive graphic organizer to review and organize what they have learned about the forms of geospatial technology. **Verbal/Linguistic**

C Critical Thinking Skills

☐ **GAME** **Map Legends**—Students use a matching game to build their understanding of how the physical features in an area correspond to symbols of those features on a map. **Visual/Spatial, Naturalist**

T Technology Skills

☐ **ONLINE SELF-CHECK QUIZ** **Lesson 2**—Students receive instant feedback on their mastery of lesson content.

☑ *Printable Digital Worksheets*

W Writing Skills

☐ **WORKSHEET** **Technology Skills: Geospatial Technologies**—Students use the worksheet to investigate the latest forms of geospatial technologies. **Interpersonal**

LESSON 1 How Geographers Think

Reading and Comprehension

Help students understand content vocabulary terms that may be confusing. For example, students may have trouble distinguishing between relative location and absolute location.

Tell students to use flashcards to write six different locations, some relative and some absolute. Have students take turns quizzing each other about which locations are relative and which are absolute.

Then have students make flashcards for other content vocabulary from the lesson to quiz their partners. For example, for the term *latitude,* students might say "I run east to west, but I measure distance north to south."

Text Evidence

Organize students into five groups, and assign one of the five themes of geography to each group. Have students review the lesson and create a pictorial summary of their assigned theme. Students may use images that they found online, magazine photographs, or create their own pictures to convey the theme's meaning. For example, students might create a map to show a certain region. To express human-environment interaction, students might draw people driving along roads, and so on.

LESSON 2 Geographers and Their Tools

Reading and Comprehension

Help students visualize concepts from this lesson by mapping an imaginary trip around the world. Students should work with a partner to plan their journey. Tell students to write a paragraph describing their trip. Have pairs use at least three content vocabulary terms in their paragraphs to demonstrate knowledge of the vocabulary words' meaning as used in the text. For example, students may describe how they used a GPS to help them plan a route from one place to another, or how reading a map's elevation helped them determine how to cross a certain mountain range.

Text Evidence

Organize students into small groups. Tell students they will act as contestants on a television game show called "Tools of the Trade." Students should designate one member of their group to act as host, or two who will then take turns, and ask the contestants a series of questions about geographer's tools.

Tell hosts they may ask multiple-choice or fill-in-the-blank questions. Tell contestants they may refer to the text to find evidence to support their answers. You may wish to use a timer and set a time limit for students to answer each question. For every correct answer, a group gets five points. The team with the most points wins the game.

Online Resources

Leveled Reader

Use this online lower-level text that corresponds directly to the text in the online Student Edition.

Guided Reading Activities

This resource uses graphic organizers and guiding questions to help students with comprehension.

What Do You Know?

Use these worksheets to pre-assess students' background knowledge before they study the chapter.

Reading Essentials and Study Guide Workbook

This resource offers writing and reading activities for the approaching-level student.

Self-Check Quizzes

This online assessment tool provides instant feedback for students to check their progress.

How Do I Incorporate the
Common Core State Standards
in My Lessons?

The Common Core State Standards (CCSS), are national standards focused on ensuring that students master language arts skills by the time they complete high school. In grades 6 through 12, the standards require that some of this skill development and skill practice be part of other subjects, such as social studies.

Step 1 Familiarize Yourself with the Standards.

- The Common Core Solutions Web site, **http://www.commoncoresolutions.com**, has several free training modules on the CCSS.

- The Common Core State Standards Toolbox Web site, **http://www.mhecommoncoretoolbox.com**, has articles and tips from other teachers and professionals that you can refer to throughout the year.

Step 2 Incorporate the Standards into Your Lessons.

- Common core activities are clearly marked in the McGraw-Hill print teacher and student editions and online teacher lesson plans to help you incorporate the standards into your lessons.

- Activities are correlated to the Common Core State Standards.

Step 3 Use Resources in the Online Resource Library to Promote Student Skill Mastery.

Slide Shows that help students learn how to:
- Identify main ideas
- Understand cause and effect
- Compare and contrast
- Draw conclusions
- Analyze visuals, documents, videos

Writing and Analyzing Templates to help students:
- Write drafts
- Evaluate writing samples
- Write persuasive text
- Create expository text
- Compose narrative

EARTH'S LAND, PEOPLE, AND ENVIRONMENTS

ESSENTIAL QUESTION · *How does geography influence the way people live?*

Prisma/SuperStock

A geographer drills for an ice sample.

netw✺rks

There's More Online about Earth's Land, People, and Environments.

CHAPTER 1

Lesson 1
How Geographers Think

Lesson 2
Geographers and Their Tools

The Story Matters...

Since ancient times, people have drawn maps to show their known world. As people explored, they came into contact with different places and people, which expanded their understanding of the world. Today, what we know about the world continues to grow as geographers study the world's environments with the latest technology. More importantly, by understanding the connections between humans and the environment, geographers can find solutions to significant problems.

FOLDABLES
Study Organizer

Go to the Foldables® library in the back of your book to make a Foldable® that will help you take notes while reading this chapter.

15

ENGAGE

Think-Pair-Share Have students brainstorm in groups why people make maps, and then share ideas with the class. Students might cite that people want to share with others how to reach a specific destination or where locations are relative to each other. Then have students read "The Story Matters..." about geographers' use of maps.

Discuss with the class what it means to understand the connections between humans and the environment. **Ask: What significant problems might a geographer find solutions for?** *(Possible answers: Where should a store be located in a city? How does drought affect a region's food production?)*

Tell students in this chapter they will learn about how geographers think and how they use maps and globes.

Making Connections Share the following information with students. Maps are used for communication. Here are some facts about maps:

- The oldest maps were made in Babylon on clay tablets around 2300 B.C.
- By 350 B.C., geographers accepted the idea of Earth being a sphere.
- In 1492, Martin Behaim, a German cartographer, made the first globe. It still exists today.
- Until the use of aerial photography after World War I, much of the world was not shown accurately on maps.

To get students thinking about how maps are used and the types of information they show, have them use their Reference Atlas map of the United States in the front of their Student Editions to determine which city is farther west—Reno, Nevada, or Los Angeles, California. *(Reno, Nevada)*

FOLDABLES
Study Organizer

Go to the Foldables® library for a cumulative chapter-based Foldable® activity that your students can use to help take notes and prepare for assessment.

Letter from the Author

Dear Geography Teacher,

The geographer's world is a mosaic of people, places, and environments, all viewed from a spatial perspective. Geographers have an interest in where people settle and why, along with learning about their various cultures. People move constantly and often settle in places for a variety of reasons. Each place has unique characteristics, both physical (climate, vegetation) and cultural (religion, ethnic origins, occupations, and so on). Geographers try to make sense out of our dynamic, changing world.

Richard H. Boehm

TEACH & ASSESS

Step Into the Place

V **Visual Skills**

Reading a Map Explain to students that this map presents the entire world on one map and accurately shows the sizes and shapes of the landmasses. Have students compare the sizes and shapes of the continents on this world map to those on the world maps in the Unit 1 Opener.

Next have students identify the seven continents on this map and locate the Equator. Discuss which continents are located primarily north of the Equator and which are located primarily south of the Equator.

Have students speculate why this world map would have been made like this. Discuss how students might make a sphere from the map if they could cut it out. Read the Content Background Knowledge below to students to explain how this type of world map developed and why it is useful.

Then have students use the map to answer the Step Into the Place questions. **Visual/Spatial**

Content Background Knowledge

John Paul Goode (1862–1932) was an American geographer, cartographer, and teacher whose career goal was to make geography an enjoyable and easy-to-understand subject for his students. In 1916 he developed a world map that showed landmasses in proper proportions by "interrupting" the oceans on the map.

Some people describe Goode's map as looking like flattened orange peels. Goode also developed an atlas for students, creating many maps and putting them together in one book. The atlas was first published in 1923. It is still used today and is updated every few years using the latest mapping technology.

ANSWERS, p. 16

STEP INTO THE PLACE

1. North and South America, Europe, Asia, Africa, Australia, Antarctica
2. Pacific, Atlantic, Indian, Southern and Arctic Oceans
3. rivers
4. **CRITICAL THINKING** Possible answer: The map shows the continents, oceans, and Equator.

Chapter 1 EARTH'S LAND, PEOPLE, AND ENVIRONMENTS

Geography is the study of Earth in all of its variety. When you study geography, you learn about the physical features and the living things—humans, plants, and animals—that inhabit Earth.

Step Into the Place

MAP FOCUS Use the map to answer the following questions.

1 **THE GEOGRAPHER'S WORLD** What are the names of the large landmasses on the map?

2 **THE GEOGRAPHER'S WORLD** What are the names of the large bodies of water on the map?

3 **THE GEOGRAPHER'S WORLD** What do you think the blue lines are that appear within the landmasses?

4 **CRITICAL THINKING** **Analyzing** How is this world map similar to other maps you have seen?

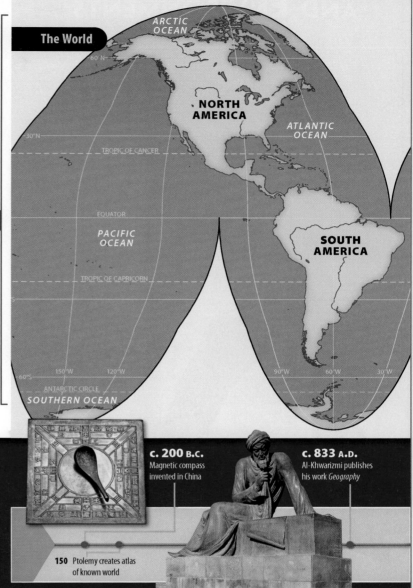

The World

Step Into the Time

DESCRIBING Choose an event from the time line and write a paragraph describing how it might have changed how people understood or viewed the world in which they lived.
WHST.6-8.2, WHST.6-8.4

c. 200 B.C. Magnetic compass invented in China

c. 833 A.D. Al-Khwarizmi publishes his work *Geography*

150 Ptolemy creates atlas of known world

16 *Chapter 1*

(l) Hans-Joachim Schneider/Alamy; (r) Egmont Strigl/age fotostock

---

Project-Based Learning ✋

Hands-On

Creating a Mental Map

Students will create a detailed mental map of home to school, including essential parts of a map. In groups, students will analyze the maps to understand the five themes of geography based on their communities. Students will present their maps and their analysis to the class using any visuals decided upon in their groups.

Digital Hands-On

Creating a Travel Brochure

Students will create digital travel brochures after analyzing given locations around the world using an online interactive mapping site. Students will use coordinates, location, place and other geographic features as well as information from geographic Web sites and the textbook. Travel brochures will be collaboratively shared for students to comment and add other geographic information.

edtechteacher
21st Century Learning

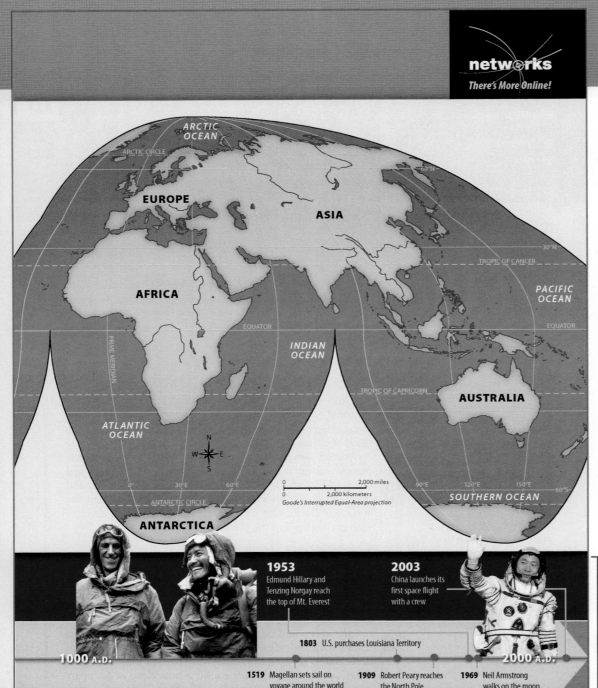

1953
Edmund Hillary and Tenzing Norgay reach the top of Mt. Everest

2003
China launches its first space flight with a crew

1803 U.S. purchases Louisiana Territory

1000 A.D.

2000 A.D.

1519 Magellan sets sail on voyage around the world

1909 Robert Peary reaches the North Pole

1969 Neil Armstrong walks on the moon

(l) ©HO/Reuters/Corbis; (r) AFP/Getty Images

Chapter 1 **17**

Step Into the Time

V Visual Skills

Reading a Time Line Remind students that time lines help to sequence events visually in time. Discuss the elements of a time line, such as the title, start and end dates, event markers on the line, and labels for each date. Ask students to share their ideas on other ways time lines can be used. *(to sequence directions and processes)*

Have students review the time line and as a class discuss its major points of interest. **Ask:**

- **What period of time is shown on the time line?** *(from 200 B.C. to 2000)*
- **Ptolemy lived in Alexandria, Egypt. Which continents were most likely not in his atlas of the known world?** *(North and South America, Australia, Antarctica)*
- **Magellan's fleet was the first to sail around the world. When did they set sail?** *(1519)*
- **Did Edmund Hillary reach the top of Mt. Everest before or after Neil Armstrong walked on the moon?** *(before)*
- **Why do you think it took longer for people to reach the top of Mt. Everest than it took to reach the North Pole?** *(Students' answers will vary, but they should recognize the extreme cold of both places and the lack of oxygen at the top of the world's tallest mountain as a likely reason why it took longer to reach.)*

Ask students to identify historical events that they know of and tell where they could be added to the time line. *(Students' answers will vary but should include accurate event placement.)*
Visual/Spatial, Verbal/Linguistic

V

CLOSE & REFLECT

Summarizing Have students write one or two sentences to summarize what they learned in the Chapter Opener. Collect and read the summaries to review the information with students. Tell students that they will learn more about geographers and maps as they study this chapter. **AL**

TIME LINE

Reading a Time Line and Map

Identifying Display the time line and map on the whiteboard. Have volunteers read each event as it is revealed on the time line. Ask students to identify where in the world the event took place and find its location on the map. **AL Visual/Spatial**

See page 15B for other online activities.

ENGAGE

Bellringer Before students begin the lesson, ask them to define the term *geography*. Then read the Essential Question aloud and have students discuss geographical and environmental features in their area that may or may not affect the way people live or where they choose to live. **Ask: What geographical features would be important to you in choosing a new place to live?** Have students explain why these features would be necessary or appealing. *(Student answers will vary but should include mention of specific physical features, such as oceans, mountains, and rivers, or human features, such as cities, states, and human-made attractions.)*

TEACH & ASSESS

R Reading Skills

Determining Word Meanings Explain to students that important academic and content vocabulary words will appear in boldface type throughout a lesson. The meanings of these terms will be given in the text. Have students begin a vocabulary list in their notebooks by writing the word *geography* at the top of a blank piece of paper. As a class, discuss what is included in the study of *geography*. Have students write their own definitions to explain the word. Encourage them to include drawings if desired. Remind students to add words to their lists as they encounter new vocabulary. **ELL** **Verbal/ Linguistic**

C Critical Thinking Skills

Drawing Conclusions Physical features are landforms and bodies of water that occur naturally on Earth. Have students give examples of physical features that they know. **Ask: What might scientists conclude after measuring the height, width, and depth of a glacier and determining its distance from other landforms?** *(Student answers may vary but should demonstrate an understanding of natural processes, such as erosion that cause changes in landforms.)* **BL** **Naturalist**

ANSWER, p. 18

Taking Notes location, place, region, human-environment interaction, movement

---

---

networks

There's More Online!

☑ **CHART/GRAPH** Six Essential Elements of Geography

☑ **IMAGES** Places Change Over Time

☑ **ANIMATION** Regions of Earth

☑ **VIDEO**

Reading HELPDESK ⓒⓒⓢⓢ

Academic Vocabulary RH.6-8.4
(Tier Two Words)
- dynamic
- component

Content Vocabulary RH.6-8.4
(Tier Three Words)
- geography
- spatial
- landscape
- relative location
- absolute location
- latitude
- Equator
- longitude
- Prime Meridian
- region
- environment
- landform
- climate
- resource

TAKING NOTES: *Key Ideas and Details* RH.6-8.2, RH.6-8.7

Identifying As you read the lesson, list the five themes of geography on a graphic organizer like the one below.

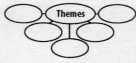

Themes

18

Lesson 1
How Geographers Think

ESSENTIAL QUESTION · *How does geography influence the way people live?*

IT MATTERS BECAUSE
Thinking like a geographer helps you understand how the world works and appreciate the world's remarkable beauty and complexity.

Thinking Spatially

GUIDING QUESTION *What does it mean to think like a geographer?*

Our understanding of the world is based on a combination of information from many sources. Biology is the study of how living things survive and relate to one another. History is the study of events that occur over time and how those events are connected. **Geography** is the study of Earth and its peoples, places, and environments. Geographers look at people and the world in which they live mainly in terms of space and place. They study such topics as where people live on the surface of Earth, why they live there, and how they interact with each other and the physical environment.

Geographers Think Spatially
Geography, then, emphasizes the spatial aspects of the world. **Spatial** refers to Earth's features in terms of their locations, their shapes, and their relationships to one another.

Physical features such as mountains and lakes can be located on a map. These features can be measured in terms of height, width, and depth. Distances and directions to other features can be determined. The human world also has spatial dimensions. Geographers study the size and shape of cities, states, and countries. They consider how close or far apart

(l to r) ©Kent Kolbersteen/National Geographic Society/Corbis; Aerial Archives/Alamy; TOPIC PHOTO AGENCY IN/age fotostock; TOPIC PHOTO AGENCY IN/age fotostock

---

networks   *Online Teaching Options*

VIDEO

Coral and Oceans

Finding the Main Idea Use the video to introduce the lesson about geography and life both above and below the oceans. After viewing, have students think about the main ideas that were presented, and then turn to a partner to share these main ideas. Then have volunteers share what they discussed with the class. Discuss with students how coral reef systems and the extreme depths of the ocean are both examples of unique geography in our world. **AL** **Verbal/Linguistic, Interpersonal**

See page 15C for other online activities.

BBC Motion Gallery Education

these human features are to one another. Geographers also think about the relationships between human features and physical features.

But thinking spatially is more than just the study of the location or size of things. It means looking at the characteristics of Earth's features. Geographers ask what mountains in different locations are made of. They examine what kinds of fish live in different lakes. They study the layout of cities and think about how easy or difficult it is for people to move around in them.

The Perspective of Place

Locations on Earth are made up of different combinations of physical and human characteristics. Physical features such as climate, landforms, and vegetation combine with human features such as population, economic activity, and land use. These combinations create what geographers call places.

Places are locations on Earth that have distinctive characteristics that make them meaningful to people. The places where we live, work, and go to school are important to us. Our home is an important place. Even small places such as our bedroom or a classroom often have a unique and special meaning. In the same way, larger locations, such as our hometown, our country, or even Earth, are places that have meaning for people.

One way that geographers learn about places is by studying landscapes. **Landscapes** are portions of Earth's surface that can be viewed at one time and from one location. They can be as small as the view from the front porch of your home, or they can be as large as the view from a tall building that includes the city and surrounding countryside.

The geography theme of *place* describes all of the characteristics that give an area its own special quality. The Taj Mahal was built by an Indian ruler in the 1600s. The white marble dome and the slender towers reflect the Islamic influence at the time.

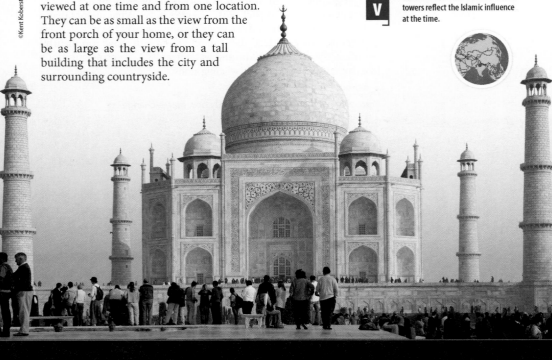

©Kent Kobersteen/National Geographic Society/Corbis

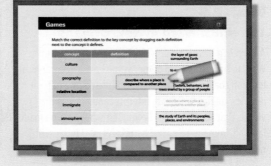

GAME

Drag-and-Drop: Vocabulary Game

Reviewing Display the drag-and-drop game on the whiteboard. Have volunteers read each of the vocabulary words. Play the game as a class activity. Then have students choose three to five vocabulary words and use them in a paragraph. **Verbal/Linguistic, Kinesthetic**

See page 15C for other online activities.

C Critical Thinking Skills

Making Inferences Explain to students that the relationships between human features and physical features are part of the spatial aspects of the world that are studied by geographers. Students need to think about the issues and relationships such as these that are presented in the text and use what they already know about the world to make inferences about what they are reading. **Ask:**

- **How would farming on the side of a mountain be different from farming on flat land?** *(Student answers may vary but should discuss the differences in terrain and how those differences would affect the types of crops planted and the equipment used.)*
- **How would fishing in a lake or river be different from fishing in the ocean?** *(Student answers may vary but should discuss the differences in size and currents of the bodies of water that would require different types of boats and fishing techniques to catch the different kinds of fish that live in the different bodies of water.)*

Have students discuss the relationships of the people and the land and water in your area. **Visual/Spatial**

V Visual Skills

Visualizing The landscape surrounding the school is a small portion of Earth that can be viewed. Have students work with a partner to use their five senses to describe the landscape they can view from the classroom window or out the front door of the building. Have partners share their descriptions. **AL** **Visual/Spatial, Naturalist**

Analyzing Images Discuss how landscape paintings also show a small portion of Earth that the artist viewed. Have students who are ready for more of a challenge work with a partner to research art books in the library that show landscapes. Have partners write a description of one of the landscapes and share their description and the painting with the class. **BL** **Visual/Spatial, Verbal/Linguistic**

How Geographers Think

C Critical Thinking Skills

Making Connections Have students make connections between their experiences and their understanding of the world. **Ask: What physical or human features have you experienced that help you understand the world?** *(Student answers may vary but encourage them to tell of experiences that are different from those mentioned in the text, such as experiencing a tornado or flood, body surfing in the ocean, or going to a national park.)* **Verbal/Linguistic**

T Technology Skills

Researching on the Internet and Using Visual Aids Have students think about why places change over time. These changes may be the result of natural processes, natural disasters, or human-made changes. Have students complete the following activity for homework.

Have students choose a place that has changed over time, such as your community, a big city, a forest, a glacier, or a reservoir. Direct them to find pictures on the Internet of what the place looked like in the past and then later after it changed. Then have them write a paragraph to go with the pictures describing the changes, explaining the cause, and identifying the impact the changes had on the place. **Visual/Spatial, Logical/Mathematical**

R Reading Skills

Making Connections Large topics are often difficult and mind-boggling to understand. However, organizing the material into smaller sections makes comprehension easier. Explain that textbooks and other reading material use headings, sections of text, and other elements to help organize material and make it easier to understand. **Ask: When has understanding parts of a subject helped you understand the whole concept?** *(Student answers may vary, but should include relevant details about a large topic and its parts.)* **AL Interpersonal**

Whether we visit a landscape or we look at photographs of the landscape, we can tell much about the people who live there. Geographers look at landscapes and try to explain their unique combinations of physical and human features. As you study geography, notice the great variety in the world's landscapes.

The Perspective of Experience

C Geography is not something you learn about only in school or just from books. Geography is something you experience every day.

We all live in the world. The seasons change. Birds chirp and car horns honk. We walk on sidewalks and in forests. People ride in cars along streets and highways. We shop in malls and grocery stores. We fly in airplanes to distant places. By surfing the Internet or watching TV, we learn about people and events in our neighborhood, our country, and the world.

This is all geography. By learning about geography in school, we can better appreciate and understand this world in which we live.

Academic Vocabulary

dynamic always changing

A Changing World

T Earth is **dynamic**, or always changing. Rivers shift course. Volcanoes suddenly erupt, forming mountains or collapsing the peaks of mountains. The pounding surf removes sand from beaches.

The things that people make change, too. Farmers shift from growing one crop to another. Cities grow larger. Nations expand into new areas.

Geographers, then, study how places change over time. They try to understand what impact those changes have. What factors made a city grow? What effect did a growing city have on the people who live there? What effect did the city's growth have on nearby communities and on the land and water near it? Answering questions like these is part of the field of geography.

☑ READING PROGRESS CHECK

Describing Why do geographers study how places change?

Geography Themes

GUIDING QUESTION *How can you make sense of a subject as large as Earth and its people?*

R To help study geography, geographers organize information about the world into five themes. These themes help them view and understand Earth.

Location

Location is where something is found on Earth. There are two types of location. **Relative location** describes where a place is compared to another place. This approach often uses the cardinal directions—north, south, east, and west. A school might be on the east side of

20 *Chapter 1*

SLIDE SHOW

The Ninth Ward in New Orleans

Analyzing Images Show the slide show of the Ninth Ward in New Orleans to demonstrate how a geographical location changes over time and is affected by a natural disaster. Guide students to interpret and analyze the visuals that show the area before Hurricane Katrina made landfall, immediately after Katrina hit, and today with its overgrowth of plants. **Visual/Spatial**

See page 15C for other online activities.

Slide Show

(l) ©Ocean/Corbis, ©Kryssia Campos/Getty Images, (tr) Erica Simone Leeds, (br) ©JG Photography/Alamy

---

ANSWER, p. 20

☑ READING PROGRESS CHECK Because Earth is always changing and people move and change, too. Why things change and the impact of change is part of geography.

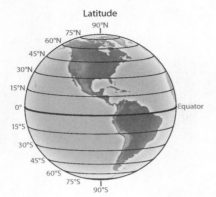

Latitude

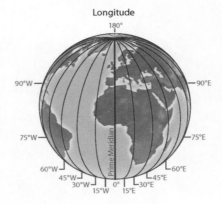

Longitude

town. Relative location can also tell us about the characteristics of a place. For example, knowing that New Orleans is near the mouth of the Mississippi River helps us understand why the city became an important trading port.

Absolute location is the exact location of something. An address like 123 Main Street is an absolute location. Geographers identify the absolute location of places using a system of imaginary lines called latitude and longitude. Those lines form a grid for locating a place precisely.

Lines of **latitude** run east to west, but they measure distance on Earth in a north-to-south direction. One of these lines, the **Equator**, circles the middle of Earth. This line is equally distant from the North Pole and the South Pole. Other lines of latitude between the Equator and the North and South Poles are assigned a number from 1° to 90°. The higher the number, the farther the line is from the Equator. The Equator is 0° latitude. The North Pole is at 90° north latitude (90° N), and the South Pole is at 90° south latitude (90° S).

Lines of **longitude** run from north to south, but they measure distance on Earth in an east-to-west direction. They go from the North Pole to the South Pole. These lines are also called *meridians*. The **Prime Meridian** is the starting point for measuring longitude. It runs through Greenwich, England, and has the value of 0° longitude. There are 180 lines of longitude to the east of the Prime Meridian and 180 lines to the west. They meet at the meridian 180°, which is the International Date Line.

Geographers use latitude and longitude to locate anything on Earth. In stating absolute location, geographers always list latitude first. For example, the absolute location of Washington, D.C., is 38° N, 77° W.

Lines of latitude circle Earth parallel to the Equator and measure the distance north or south of the Equator in degrees. Lines of longitude circle Earth from the North Pole to the South Pole. These lines measure distances east or west of the Prime Meridian.

▶ **CRITICAL THINKING**
The Geographer's World At what degree of latitude is the Equator located?

R

Identifying and Calculating Explain to students that geographers use relative location and absolute location to tell where something, such as a place or a region, is found on Earth. After students read the section about location, ask them the following questions:

- **What terms are used to describe the relative location of a place?** *(the cardinal directions—north, south, east, and west—and its relationship to another place)*
- **How do geographers identify the absolute location of a place?** *(They use a system of imaginary lines called latitude and longitude.)*
- **Which way do lines of latitude run?** *(east to west)*
- **Which location is nearer to the Equator: a city at 25°N latitude or a city at 55°S latitude?** *(A city at 25°N latitude is nearer the Equator.)*
- **Which way do lines of longitude run?** *(north to south)*
- **Which location is nearer to the Prime Meridian: a city at 60°W longitude or a city at 90°E longitude?** *(A city at 60°W longitude is nearer the Prime Meridian.)*
- **What is the relative location of Washington, D.C., in relationship to the location of the Equator and the Prime Meridian?** *(It is located north of the Equator and west of the Prime Meridian.)*
- **What is the relative location of Sydney, Australia in relationship to the location of the Equator and the Prime Meridian?** *(It is located south of the Equator and east of the Prime Meridian.)* **Verbal/Linguistic, Visual/Spatial**

Content Background Knowledge

The International Date Line is an imaginary line that spans north to south across the Pacific Ocean. It is on the opposite side of Earth from the Prime Meridian. It is used to separate two consecutive calendar days. If you travel east across the line, you lose one calendar day, or 24 hours. If you travel west across the line, you gain a calendar day, or 24 hours.

ANIMATION

Animated Globe

Defining with Visuals Display the animated globe on the whiteboard. Use the globe to explain visually the geographic terms related to location: *relative location, absolute location, latitude, longitude, Equator, and Prime Meridian.* **AL Verbal/Linguistic**

See page 15C for other online activities.

ANSWER, p. 21

CRITICAL THINKING The Equator is at zero degrees latitude.

V1 Visual Skills

Integrating Visual Information Physical and/or human features help define a place. Have students work in a small group to identify physical and/or human features of their community. Challenge them to compose an advertising jingle that promotes these features of their community. **ELL**
Visual/Spatial, Auditory/Musical

R Reading Skills

Paraphrasing Have students reread the last paragraph in the section titled, "Region." Ask them to paraphrase, or use their own words, to explain why geographers study regions. Explain why students need to practice paraphrasing content: when they write reports and research papers they will need to paraphrase their sources. *(Geographers study regions to find out what physical and human characteristics they have. They can use these characteristics to find out how regions are the same or different.)*
ELL AL Verbal/Linguistic

V2 Visual Skills

Integrating Visual Information Read the Content Background Knowledge below to students. Then have them identify the lines of latitude and longitude on the photo of Disney World and use them to answer the following question.
Ask: What is the absolute location of Cinderella's Castle?
(It lies between latitude 28°25'8" N and 28°25'12" N and at longitude 81°34'52" W.) **Visual/Spatial**

Content Background Knowledge

To pinpoint the area between latitude and longitude lines more precisely, locations are given in degrees/minutes/seconds. To read the latitude 38°53'55" N, say "38 degrees, 53 minutes, 55 seconds North."

Have students who have used GPS devices to identify the absolute location of a place describe to the rest of the class how this is done.

Disney World, located in Orlando, Florida, attracts millions of visitors every year.
▶ **CRITICAL THINKING**
Human Geography What effect do you think Disney World has on the surrounding communities? **V1**

Place

Another theme of geography is place. The features that help define a place can be physical or human.

Why is Denver called the "Mile High City"? Its location one mile above sea level gives it a special character. Why does New Orleans have the nickname "the Crescent City"? It is built on a crescent-shaped bend along the Mississippi River. That location has had a major impact on the city's growth and how its people live.

Region

Although places are unique, two or more places can share characteristics. Places that are close to one another and share some characteristics belong to the same **region**. For example, Hong Kong and Macau are located in southeastern China. They have some features in common, such as nearness to the ocean. Both cities also have mostly warm temperatures throughout the year.

In the case of those two cities, the region is defined using physical characteristics. Human characteristics can also define regions. For instance, the countries of North Africa are part of the same region. One reason is that most of the people living in these countries follow the same religion—Islam.

R Geographers study regions so they can identify the broad patterns of larger areas. They can compare and contrast the features in one region with those in another. They also examine the special features that make each place in a region distinct from the others.

22 Chapter 1

---

networks *Online Teaching Options*

ANIMATION

Disney World in Orlando, Florida

Identifying Physical Features Display the animated photo of Disney World in Orlando, Florida. Guide students in identifying the physical and human features that define the place. At the bird's-eye level, have students describe the place in terms of its relative location. **Visual/Spatial**

See page 15C for other online activities.

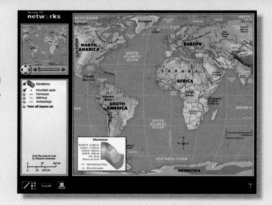

ANSWER, p. 22

CRITICAL THINKING Possible answers: provides employment; causes more traffic; increases business for hotels, motels, and restaurants; increases tax revenue

Human-Environment Interaction

People and the environment interact. That is, they affect each other. The physical characteristics of a place affect how people live. Flat, rich, well-watered soil is good for farming. Mountains full of coal can be mined. The environment can present all kinds of hazards, such as floods, droughts, earthquakes, and volcanic eruptions. **T**

People affect the environment, too. They blast tunnels through mountains to build roadways and drain swamps to make farmland. Although these actions can improve life, they can also harm the environment. Exhaust from cars on the roadways can pollute the air, and turning swamps into farms destroys natural ecosystems. **C**

The **environment** is the natural surroundings of a place. It includes several key features. One is **landforms**, or the shape and nature of the land. Hills, mountains, and valleys are types of landforms. The environment also includes the presence or absence of a body of water. Cities located on coastlines, like Cape Town, South Africa, have different characteristics than inland cities, like Johannesburg, South Africa.

Weather and climate also play a role in how people interact with their environment. The average weather in a place over a long period of time is called its **climate**. The climate in Norlisk, Russia, is marked by long, cold, wet winters and short, mild summers. Jakarta's climate in Indonesia is warm year-round. People in Norlisk interact with their environment differently than the people in Jakarta do. **R**

Another **component**, or part, of the environment is **resources**. These are materials that can be used to produce crops or other products. Forests are a resource because the trees can be used to build homes and furniture. Oil is a resource because it can be used as a source of energy.

Movement

Geographers also look at how people, products, ideas, and information move from one place to another. People have many reasons for moving. Some move because they find a better job.

Academic Vocabulary

component part

Climate affects people in many ways. (Below left) Hot, humid weather during a summer day in Seoul, South Korea, makes it possible for children to swim in nearby streams. (Right) The people must also be prepared to deal with bitterly cold winter days.

T Technology Skills

Researching on the Internet Have students think about and make a list of what environmental hazards affect the state they live in. Then have small groups each take one of the hazards, such as floods, and research the history of it in their state over the past 50 years. Encourage them to include dates and statistics along with any images available, and to report their findings to the class. **Visual/Spatial, Logical/Mathematical**

C Critical Thinking Skills

Identifying Problems Explain to students that people affect the environment. Have students share what human actions they think could harm the environment. *(Students' answers will vary but might include oil spills, spraying chemicals on lawns, polluting air and water, cutting and/or burning forests.)*

Then have small groups take two sides of an environmental issue on how human actions change the environment for better or for worse, such as draining a marsh or a swamp for farm land or for building houses.

Have one group research the benefits of the environmental issue, such as marshes and swamps help prevent flooding and they support a large biodiversity of life. Have the other group defend the environmental change by explaining the benefits of the change for humans such as providing jobs and usable land.

Have the two sides present their information, and then encourage the two groups to come to some sort of compromise on the issue, explaining that compromise is often needed in these situations. **BL Naturalist, Verbal/Linguistic**

R Reading Skills

Applying After reading about the key features that make up the environment, have volunteers identify each feature as you list it on the whiteboard. *(landforms, climate, resources)* Then have small groups of three to four students brainstorm a list of environmental features for the local area (nearby landforms, local climate, and regional natural resources). Bring the class together to share their lists. Encourage students to write the lists and definitions of the features in their notebooks for future reference. **ELL AL**

SLIDE SHOW

How People Are Affected by Geography

Determining Cause and Effect Show the slide show about how people are affected by geography. Discuss why people may choose to build structures within the natural environment. Continue by discussing how human structures can adversely affect the environment and how technology can be both helpful and dangerous during times of climate changes. Have students reflect about their community and how the local geography and human-made structures affect people. **BL Visual/Spatial, Interpersonal**

See page 15C for other online activities.

Slide Show

C Critical Thinking Skills

Reading Charts Using the chart of the Six Essential Elements, read aloud each element of the study of geography and its definition. After discussing each element with students, ask them the following questions:

- **Comparing** Which theme of geography is the essential element Environment and Society similar to? *(Human-environment interaction)*
- **Giving Examples** What is an example of a region of the United States? What makes that area a region? *(Possible answers: Rocky Mountain states have similar physical geography; the corn/soybean/hog belt of the Midwest is a region based on similar farming practices.)*
- **Evaluating** How might a map help you understand the world in spatial terms? *(Possible answer: A map can show where landforms are located and help you compute distances between places.)* **Verbal/Linguistic**

W Writing Skills

Informative/Explanatory Explain to students that the movement of people, products, ideas, and information is an important theme in geography. Have volunteers share reasons why people move within a town, to a different town or region, or even to another country.

Then discuss the movement of products. Have students check product tags on personal items, such as backpacks, shirts, and shoes to determine where items were made. Have students write a list of 10 items that they use frequently and where each was made. **ELL** **AL**

As an alternative exercise, survey the class to determine how many students have cell phones and computers. Have students discuss their ease at using these forms of technology for communication. Have students write a paragraph to answer these questions: **What communication system do you use most frequently? What are its benefits and disadvantages?** *(Students' answers will vary but may include mention of social networking sites. Their paragraphs should include relevant reasons for using the communication system.)* **BL** **Interpersonal**

ANSWERS, p. 24

CRITICAL THINKING The study of volcanoes, ocean currents, and climate is part of Physical Systems.

✓ READING PROGRESS CHECK People change the environment by building roads and constructing buildings. Draining ponds for farmland or polluting the air with factories also changes the environment. Farmers may choose to live in a location because of fertile soil, or people may avoid an area due to hazards.

CHART SKILLS >

THE SIX ESSENTIAL ELEMENTS

Element	Definition
The World in Spatial Terms	Geography studies the location and spatial relationships among people, places, and environments. Maps reveal the complex spatial interactions.
Places and Regions	The identities of individuals and people are rooted in places and regions. Distinctive combinations of human and physical characteristics define places and regions.
Physical Systems	Physical processes, like wind and ocean currents, plate tectonics, and the water cycle, shape Earth's surface and change ecosystems.
Human Systems	Human systems are things like language, religion, and ways of life. They also include how groups of people govern themselves and how they make and trade products and ideas.
Environment and Society	Geography studies how the environment of a place helps shape people's lives. Geography also looks at how people affect the environment in positive and negative ways.
The Uses of Geography	Understanding geography and knowing how to use its tools and technologies helps people make good decisions about the world and prepares people for rewarding careers.

Being aware of the six essential elements will help you sort out what you are learning about geography.
▶ **CRITICAL THINKING**
Identifying The study of volcanoes, ocean currents, and climate is part of which essential element?

Sometimes, people are forced to move because of war, famine, or religious or racial prejudice. Movement by large numbers of people can have important effects. People may face shortages of housing and other services. If new arrivals to an area cannot find jobs, poverty levels can rise.

In our interconnected world, a vast number of products move from place to place. Apples from Washington State move to supermarkets in Texas. Clothes produced in Thailand end up in American stores. Oil from Saudi Arabia powers cars and trucks across the United States. All this movement relies on transportation systems that use ships, railroads, airplanes, and trucks.

Ideas can move at an even faster pace than people and products. Communications systems, such as telephone, television, radio, and the Internet, carry ideas and information all around Earth. Remote villagers on the island of Borneo watch American television shows and learn about life in the United States. Political protestors in Egypt use text messaging and social networking sites to coordinate their activities. The geography of movement affects us all.

The Six Essential Elements

The five themes are one way of thinking about geography. Geographers also divide the study of geography into six essential elements. Elements are the topics that make up a subject. Calling them *essential* means they are necessary to understanding geography.

✓ READING PROGRESS CHECK
Determining Central Ideas How do people and the environment interact?

---

netw⊚rks *Online Teaching Options*

CHART

Chart of Six Essential Elements

Defining To reinforce understanding, display the interactive chart of the Six Essential Elements on the whiteboard and discuss its contents. You may wish to display the chart with empty cells and have the class work together to add the information. **Verbal/Linguistic, Interpersonal**

See page 15C for other online activities.

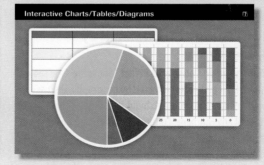

Interactive Charts/Tables/Diagrams

Building Geography Skills

GUIDING QUESTION *How will studying geography help you develop skills for everyday life?*

Many Web sites offer maps and directions to find a location. Have you ever used a Web browser to map a location? If you followed that map to your destination, you were using a geography skill.

Interpreting Visuals

Maps are one tool geographers use to picture the world. They use other visual images, as well. These other visuals include graphs, charts, diagrams, and photographs.

Graphs are visual displays of numerical information. Three of the most commonly used graphs are bar graphs, circle graphs, and line graphs. They can help you compare and analyze information. Charts display information in columns and rows. Diagrams are drawings that use pictures to represent something in the world or an abstract idea. A diagram might show the steps in a process or the parts that make up something.

Critical Thinking

Geographers ask analytical questions. For example, geographers might want to know why earthquakes are more likely in some places than in others. That question looks at causes. They might ask, How does climate affect the ways people live? Such questions examine effects.

Geographers might ask how the characteristics of a place have changed over time. That is a question of analysis. Or they could ask why people in different nations use their resources differently. That question calls on them to compare and contrast.

Learning how to ask—and answer—questions like these will help sharpen your mind. In addition to understanding geography better, you will also be able to use these skills in other subjects.

☑ **READING PROGRESS CHECK**

Determining Word Meanings What is an analytical question?

FOLDABLES Study Organizer — *Geographer's View / Geographer's Tools*

Include this lesson's information in your Foldable®.

LESSON 1 REVIEW (CCSS)

Reviewing Vocabulary (Tier Three Words)
1. Compare and contrast a *landscape* and a photograph. RH.6-8.4

Answering the Guiding Questions
2. *Analyzing* To understand the geography of an island, what would a geographer have to consider? RH.6-8.1
3. *Determining Word Meanings* Explain the difference between place and location. RH.6-8.4

4. *Identifying* Give one example of a way Earth is dynamic and one example of how people make a change. RH.6-8.2
5. *Analyzing* Would a chart, a diagram, or a graph be the best way to show a population comparison for three different years? RH.6-8.7
6. *Informative/Explanatory Writing* Describe the relative location of your school. WHST.6-8.2, WHST.6-8.10

Chapter 1 **25**

LESSON 1 REVIEW ANSWERS

Reviewing Vocabulary

1. A landscape is the view from a single location, such as a window in an office building. A photograph might not include as wide a view, or it can focus on one specific feature, such as a tree.

Answering the Guiding Questions

2. **Analyzing** In addition to physical features of an island, a geographer would have to consider where and why the people live on the island, as well as how they interact with each other.

3. **Determining Word Meanings** Location describes a physical point on Earth, whether in relation to another place or in absolute terms, such as an address. Places, such as a home or a classroom, have distinctive characteristics.

4. **Identifying** Dynamic: a tsunami strikes; Human: building a new road

5. **Analyzing** A graph is usually used for numerical information. One bar could be used to show the population for each year.

6. **Informative/Explanatory Writing** Student answers should refer to landmarks surrounding your school.

V Visual Skills

Interpreting Display samples of various kinds of visuals: graphs *(line, bar, circle)*, charts, diagrams, and photographs, or have students find and display examples of each of these from their textbooks. Discuss how visuals show information more clearly, easily, and concisely than can be said in the words of a text. **ELL** Visual/Spatial

C Critical Thinking Skills

Formulating Questions Have students formulate questions about what they want to learn about in geography this year. Make a class list of six questions that the majority of students have in common, and have a small group of volunteers make a poster of these questions for the class to refer to throughout the year. **ELL AL** Verbal/Linguistic

Content Background Knowledge

A career in geography involves work that focuses on location. Many jobs are related to map making, such as photogrammetrists who use photography from aerial photographs to measure distances between objects. Another example are surveyors who measure land and map boundaries.

Knowledge of geography may also lead to careers in urban planning, real estate development, tourism, forestry, or climatology. Social science geographers may work for the federal government and study foreign policy.

CLOSE & REFLECT

Making Connections To close this lesson, have students think about what geography is and what geographers do. Ask students to write a paragraph about how geography is visible in their own lives; for example, how it affects the way they get to and from school.

ANSWER, p. 25

☑ **READING PROGRESS CHECK** Analytical questions look at causes.

ENGAGE

🔔 **Bellringer** Before students begin this lesson, **ask:** When have you used a map? How did it help you? *(Students' answers may vary but should discuss the use of various types of maps, how students have used them, and whether they helped.)* Display several kinds of maps, such as a road map; a map for an amusement park, museum, or subway; a political map of the world; an economic or resource map; a climate map; and a topographic map. Have students work in small groups to study one of the maps. Then ask each group to explain to the class what information is provided on their map and how someone might use it.

TEACH & ASSESS

V Visual Skills

Creating Visuals Have students close their eyes and picture a room from their home in their mind. Then have them roughly sketch their mental map on paper. Working with a partner, have students use their maps to orally describe the relative locations of objects in their rooms. Tell partners to ask each other questions about where things are located. **Visual/Spatial, Verbal/Linguistic**

R Reading Skills

Paraphrasing Display a globe. **Ask: Why are globes the most accurate way to show places on Earth?** Tell students to use their own words to answer the question. *(Sample answer: Like Earth, a globe is shaped like a sphere or ball; the shapes of land and bodies of water are correct on globes; distances and directions between places are more correct than those on flat maps.)* **ELL AL Verbal/Linguistic**

Remind students to add academic and content vocabulary words to their vocabulary lists. Tell students to write their own definitions and to include drawings if desired. This activity can be done as students encounter the words during class or completed as homework. **ELL AL**

ANSWER, p. 26

Taking Notes Key: explains symbols, colors, and lines; **scale bar:** tells how a measured space on a map corresponds to actual distances on Earth; **compass rose:** shows direction

---

networks

There's More Online!

☑ **SLIDE SHOW** History of Mapmaking

☑ **ANIMATION** Elements of a Globe

☑ **VIDEO**

Reading HELPDESK CCSS

Academic Vocabulary RH.6-8.4
(Tier Two Words)
- **sphere**
- **convert**
- **distort**

Content Vocabulary RH.6-8.4
(Tier Three Words)
- **hemisphere**
- **key**
- **scale bar**
- **compass rose**
- **map projection**
- **scale**
- **elevation**
- **relief**
- **thematic map**
- **technology**
- **remote sensing**

TAKING NOTES: *Key Ideas and Details* RH.6-8.2, RH.6-8.7

Describing As you read the lesson, identify three parts of a map on a graphic organizer. Then, explain what each part shows.

Parts of a Map

26

Lesson 2
Geographers and Their Tools

ESSENTIAL QUESTION · *How does geography influence the way people live?*

IT MATTERS BECAUSE
The tools of geography help you understand the world.

Visual Representations

GUIDING QUESTION *What is the difference between globes and maps?*

V If you close your eyes, you can probably see your neighborhood in your mind. When you do, you are using a mental map. You are forming a picture of the buildings and other places and where each is located in relation to the others.

Making and using maps is a big part of geography. Of course, geographers make maps that have many parts. Their maps are more detailed than your mental map. Still, paper maps are essentially the same as your mental map. Both are a way to picture the world and show where things are located.

Globes

R The most accurate way to show places on Earth is with a globe. Globes are the most accurate because globes, like Earth, are **spheres**; that is, they are shaped like a ball. As a result, globes represent the correct shapes of land and bodies of water. They show distances and directions between places more correctly than flat images of Earth can.

The Equator and the Prime Meridian each divide Earth in half. Each half of Earth is called a **hemisphere**. The Equator divides Earth into two sections called the Northern and Southern Hemispheres. The Prime Meridian, together with the International Date Line, splits Earth into the Eastern and Western Hemispheres. Everything west of the Prime Meridian for 180 degrees is in the Western Hemisphere.

(l to r) Lana Sundman/Alamy; Antenna Audio - Inc./Getty Images; Kathy Collins/Getty Images; spacephotos.com/age fotostock; Chris Wallace/Alamy

---

networks   *Online Teaching Options*

VIDEO

Mapping the World: Google Maps

Writing Questions Use the video to introduce the innovative technology being used for mapping. Ask students if they understand the steps used to map the world with technology. Discuss with students if they have ever used Google Earth, Google Maps, or any other mapping technology. Have students write three questions they have with regard to the video, not placing their names on the questions. Collect the questions and answer a few aloud in class. Then redistribute them and have other students answer the questions. Encourage students to experiment with this technology in their spare time. **Verbal/ Linguistic, Interpersonal**

See page 15D for other online activities.

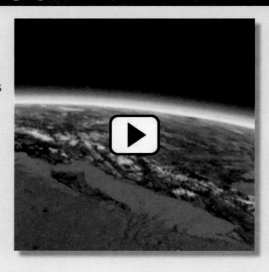

BBC Motion Gallery Education

Maps

Maps are not round like globes. Instead, maps are flat representations of the round Earth. They might be sketched on a piece of paper, printed in a book, or displayed on a computer screen. Wherever they appear, maps are always flat.

Maps **convert**, or change, a round space into a flat space. As a result, maps **distort** physical reality, or show it incorrectly. This is why maps are not as accurate as globes are, especially maps that show large areas or the whole world.

Despite this distortion problem, maps have several advantages over globes. Globes have to show the whole planet. Maps, though, can show only a part of it, such as one country, one city, or one mountain range. As a result, they can provide more detail than globes can. Think how large a globe would have to be to show the streets of a city. You could certainly never carry such a globe around with you. Maps make more sense if you want to study a small area. They can focus on just that area, and they are easy to store and carry.

Maps tend to show more kinds of information than globes. Globes generally show major physical and political features, such as landmasses, bodies of water, the countries of the world, and the largest cities. They cannot show much else without becoming too difficult to read or too large. However, some maps show these same features. But maps can also be specialized. One map might illustrate a large mountain range. Another might display the results of an election. Yet another could show the locations of all the schools in a city.

☑ READING PROGRESS CHECK

Analyzing Why are globes sometimes more accurate than maps?

Academic Vocabulary

sphere a round shape like a ball

convert to change from one thing to another

distort to present in a manner that is misleading

A set of imaginary lines divides Earth into hemispheres.
▶ CRITICAL THINKING
The Geographer's World What line divides Earth into Eastern and Western Hemispheres?

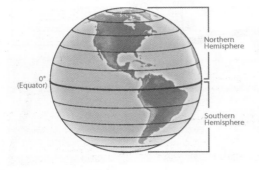
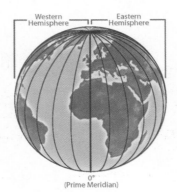

C Critical Thinking Skills

Comparing and Contrasting After students read the section titled, "Maps," **ask: How are maps and globes alike and different?** Have students record their ideas in a Venn diagram and then discuss as a class. *(Like a globe, some maps show the whole world, and both globes and maps can show major physical and political features. However, unlike globes, maps distort physical reality and are not as accurate as globes. Maps can show just parts of the world, whereas globes must always show the whole world. Maps can show more details than globes can and can be easily stored and carried. Maps show more kinds of information than globes and can be specialized.)* **Verbal/Linguistic, Visual/Spatial**

Maps   Globes

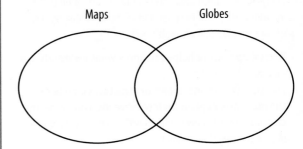

Content Background Knowledge

Prime Meridian In the 1600s, the determination of longitude was critical to the navigation of ships on the ocean. In 1675 the British established the Royal Observatory at Greenwich to study and create fixed degrees of longitude. Thus the Prime Meridian was set there at Greenwich.

The British and Americans used the resulting system of longitude throughout the 1700s and 1800s. During this time, more and more countries adopted the system of longitude that had been created by the British. When an international conference was held in 1884, enough countries were using this system that it became the established system for the world.

ANIMATION

Elements of a Globe

Understanding Visuals Display the animated globe on the whiteboard. Use the globe to visually explain the geographic terms related to maps: *hemispheres, key, scale,* and *compass rose*. Then use the animation to show different map projections. **AL Visual/Spatial**

See page 15D for other online activities.

ANSWERS, p. 27

☑ READING PROGRESS CHECK Globes are more accurate than world maps in the same scale because globes show the correct sizes of the landmasses, whereas maps distort physical reality, or show it incorrectly, because they are flat.

CRITICAL THINKING The Prime Meridian

Maps

V1 **Visual Skills**

Identifying After students read the section titled "Parts of a Map," display a physical map of the world or the United States, and have students identify the map's elements or features, such as map title, key, scale bar, compass rose, insets, and latitude and longitude lines. Discuss the importance of each map feature, and have students give an example of how they might use each feature to find their way on the map.
ELL **Visual/Spatial**

V2 **Visual Skills**

Reading a Map Remind students that maps use tools to visually convey information. Direct students' attention to the maps at the bottom of the page and ask them to identify the parts of each map that are visible. **Ask:**

- **What map feature helps you know what information is on a map?** *(map title)*
- **Identify two streets, areas, or structures on one of the maps and explain their relative location using the compass rose.** *(Student answers will vary but should include the use of cardinal directions.)*
- **What kinds of information are provided in the key for these maps?** *(Student answers should include specific details relative to each map.)*
- **How would you use the map of the Canyon Area?** *(Student answers may vary but should include finding hiking trails, scenic overlooks, or their way back to the parking lot.)*
- **Why does the map of the Canyon Area include the You Are Here label?** *(Student answers may vary but should include the understanding that people could be unfamiliar with the area shown on the map and not know where they are in relationship to the trails.)*
- **How would you use the map of the National Mall?** *(Student answers should include finding the various museums they would want to visit in Washington, D.C.)* **Visual/Spatial, Verbal/Linguistic**

Maps

GUIDING QUESTION *How do maps work?*

Maps are available in many different locations. You can see them in a subway station. Subway maps indicate the routes each train takes. In a textbook, a map might show new areas that were added to the United States at different times. At a company's Web site, a map can locate all its stores in a city. The map of a state park would tell visitors what activities they can enjoy in each area of the park. Each of these maps is different from the others, but they have some traits in common.

Parts of a Map

Maps have several important elements, or features. These features are the tools that convey information.

The map title tells what area the map will cover. It also identifies what kind of information the map presents about that area. The **key** unlocks the meaning of the map by explaining the symbols, colors, and lines. The **scale bar** is an important part of the map. It tells how a measured space on the map corresponds to actual distances on Earth. For example, by using the scale bar, you can determine how many miles in the real world each inch on the map represents. The **compass rose** shows direction. This map feature points out north, south, east, and west. Some maps include insets that show more detail for smaller areas, such as cities on a state map. Many maps show latitude and longitude lines to help you locate places.

Map Projections

To convert the round Earth to a flat map, geographers use **map projections**. A map projection distorts some aspects of Earth in order to represent other aspects as accurately as possible on a flat

Many different kinds of maps are available because maps are useful for showing a wide range of information.
▶ **CRITICAL THINKING**
Describing What is the difference between a large-scale and a small-scale map?

28 Chapter 1

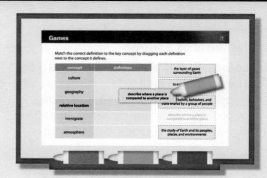

GAME

Mapping the Earth

Identifying Display the game on the whiteboard. Have students match the descriptions of the physical features in an area with their corresponding map symbols. As students correctly identify each symbol, drag it to the correct description. **Visual/Spatial, Naturalist**

See page 15D for other online activities.

ANSWER, p. 28

CRITICAL THINKING A large-scale map shows details of a small area; a small-scale map shows a large area in less detail, as on a road map.

map. Some projections show the correct size of areas in relation to one another. Other map projections emphasize making the shapes of areas as accurate as possible.

Some projections break apart the world's oceans. By doing so, these maps show land areas more accurately. They clearly do not show the oceans accurately, though.

Mapmakers, known as cartographers, choose which projection to use based on the purpose of the map. Each projection distorts some parts of the globe more or less than other parts. Finally, mapmakers think about what part of Earth they are looking at and how large an area they want to cover.

Map Scale

Scale is another important feature of maps. As you learned, the scale bar relates distances on the map to actual distances on Earth. The scale bar is based on the scale at which the map is drawn. **Scale** is the relationship between distances on the map and on Earth.

Maps are either *large scale* or *small scale*. A large-scale map focuses on a smaller area. An inch on the map might correspond to 10 miles (16 km) on the ground. A small-scale map shows a relatively larger area. An inch on a small-scale map might be the same as 1,000 miles (1,609 km).

Each type of scale has benefits and drawbacks. Which scale to use depends on the map's purpose. Do you want to map your school and the streets and buildings near it? Then you need a large-scale map to show this small area in great detail. Do you want to show the entire United States? In that case, you need a small-scale map that shows the larger area but with less detail.

Types of Maps

The two types of maps are general purpose and thematic. The type depends on what kind of information is drawn on the map. General-purpose maps show a wide range of information about an area. They generally show both the human-made features of an area and its natural features.

Political maps are one common type of general-purpose map that shows human-made features. They show the boundaries of countries or of divisions within them, like the states of the United States. They also show the locations and names of cities.

Physical maps display natural features such as mountains and valleys, rivers, and lakes. They picture the location, size, and shape of these features. Many physical maps show **elevation**, or how much above or below sea level a feature is. Maps often use colors to present this information. A key on the map explains what height above or below sea level each color represents.

Physical maps usually show **relief**, or the difference between the elevation of one feature and the elevation of another feature near it.

Chapter 1 **29**

Thinking Like a Geographer

Relief

Relief is the height of a landform compared to other nearby landforms. If a mountain 10,000 feet (3,048 m) high rises above a flat area at sea level, the relief of the mountain equals its elevation: 10,000 feet. If the 10,000-foot-high mountain is in a highland region that is 4,000 feet (1,219 m) above sea level, its relief is *less than* its elevation— only 6,000 feet (1,829 m). The difference in height between it and the land around it is much less than its absolute height. *What would be the relief of a mountain 7,500 feet (2,286 m) high compared to its highest foothill, at 3,000 feet (914 m) high?*

SLIDE SHOW

Special Purpose Maps

Analyzing Images Show the slide show of various types of special purpose maps, such as museum, trail, building emergency exits, celestial, and treasure maps. Discuss the purpose and the kinds of information that are drawn on each map. Have students identify any map that is a projection and have them talk about which parts are distorted. **Visual/Spatial**

See page 15D for other online activities.

Slide Show

C Critical Thinking Skills

Assessing Ask: How does knowing that map projections are always distorted help you choose maps to use? *(Possible answer: You would choose a map based on your purpose for study and use one that projects the area you are interested in as accurately, with the least amount of distortion, as possible.)* **Verbal/Linguistic**

R1 Reading Skills

Defining Ask students to define the word *scale* in geographic terms. Then, discuss with them that the word *scale* has mulitple meanings. Have students use a dictionary to define and draw the different meanings of the word *scale*. **Verbal/Linguistic**

V Visual Skills

Interpreting Display a political map of the world. Have students find the scale bar and identify the relationship between distances on the map and on Earth. Choose two cities on the map and have several volunteers use rulers or yardsticks and their multiplication skills to compute the distance between the locations in both miles and kilometers. Possible city combinations include the following:

- Bern, Switzerland and Vienna, Austria
- New Delhi and Bengaluru, India
- Paris, France and Berlin, Germany
- Cairo, Egypt and Baghdad, Iraq **Visual/Spatial, Logical/Mathematical**

R2 Reading Skills

Explaining Ask: Why wouldn't a map show both country boundaries and land elevations? *(General-purpose maps show either human-made features of an area or its natural features, but not both. Boundaries are human-made features and are shown on political maps. Elevation is a natural feature and is shown on physical maps. Both political maps and physical maps are general-purpose maps.)* **Verbal/Linguistic, Logical/Mathematical**

ANSWER, p. 29

THINKING LIKE A GEOGRAPHER The relief would be 4,500 feet (1,372 m).

Geographers and Their Tools

V Visual Skills

Analyzing Maps Compare and contrast the two maps of the Eastern Hemisphere shown at the top of the page. Invite students to infer when each of the maps was made, and have them explain their reasoning. **Ask: Why do you think only parts of Asia and Australia are shown on the historical map?** *(Possible answer: Explorers had not yet explored all of Asia and Australia when the map was made, and the cartographers could not draw what they did not know was there. The cartographers even wrote "Parts as yet Undiscovered" to acknowledge that the map was incomplete.)* **Verbal/ Linguistic, Visual/Spatial**

R Reading Skills

Applying Discuss the difference between elevation and relief and how they are shown on physical maps. Encourage students to consider why it is important to show relief on a map. **Ask:**

- **What kind of map shows differences in elevation?** *(a physical map)* **Why would it have been important to show elevation on a historical map for people traveling in wagon trains or trade caravans?** *(to know what mountain ranges they had to cross and to plan for that kind of travel)*
- **What width of colors on a physical map would be used for an area with mountains?** *(narrow)* **For an area with flat plains?** *(wide)*

Have students explain why the width of colors varies. *(It shows the relief.)* **Verbal/Linguistic, Visual/Spatial**

C Critical Thinking Skills

Giving Examples Discuss thematic maps that most students will know such as road maps, maps of a local mall or amusement park, or a map of the school. **Ask: What kinds of thematic maps are you familiar with or have used?** *(Student answers will vary but should demonstrate an understanding of what a thematic map is.)* **Interpersonal**

ANSWERS, p. 30

CRITICAL THINKING The historical map is based primarily on speculation or guesswork and on unsophisticated tools. The contemporary map shows greater knowledge and understanding of geography, greater accuracy (as in the shape of continents), and more detail.

☑ **READING PROGRESS CHECK** General-purpose maps show physical or political characteristics of an area. Thematic maps show more specialized information, such as resources or road networks.

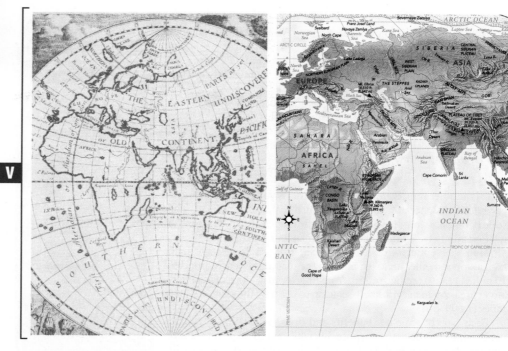

Cartography is the science of making maps. As knowledge of Earth grew, maps became increasingly accurate.
▶ **CRITICAL THINKING**
The Geographer's World Describe two ways in which the historical map differs from the present-day map.

Elevation is an absolute number, but relief is relative. It depends on other landforms that are nearby. The width of the colors on a physical map usually shows the relief. Colors that are narrow show steep places, and colors that are wide show gently sloping land.

Thematic maps show more specialized information. A thematic map might indicate the kinds of plants that grow in different areas. That kind of map is a vegetation map. Another could show where farming, ranching, or mining takes place. That kind of map is called a land-use map. Road maps show people how to travel from one place to another by car. Just about any physical or human feature can be displayed on a thematic map.

☑ **READING PROGRESS CHECK**

Describing What is the difference between thematic and general purpose maps?

Geospatial Technologies

GUIDING QUESTION *How do geographers use geospatial technologies?*

GPS devices and maps are available in many cars and cell phones. These electronic maps are an example of geospatial technologies. **Technology** is any way that scientific discoveries are applied to

---

networks *Online Teaching Options*

WORKSHEET

Geospatial Technologies

Examining Have students investigate the latest forms of geospatial technologies. Have them note their findings on the worksheet. Have students who have used these technologies share their experiences with a partner or with the class. **Interpersonal**

See page 15D for other online activities.

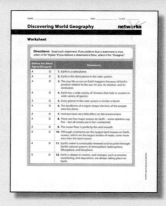

practical use. Geospatial technologies can help us think spatially. They provide practical information about the locations of physical and human features.

Global Positioning System

GPS devices work with a network called the Global Positioning System (GPS). This network was built by the U.S. government. Parts of it can be used only by the U.S. armed forces. Parts of it, though, can be used by ordinary people all over the world. The GPS has three elements.

The first element of this network is a set of more than 30 satellites that orbit Earth constantly. The U.S. government launched the satellites into space and maintains them. The satellites send out radio signals. Almost any spot on Earth can be reached by signals from at least four satellites at all times.

The second part of the network is the control system. Workers around the world track the satellites to make sure they are working properly and are on course. The workers reset the clocks on the satellites when needed.

The third part of the GPS system consists of GPS devices on Earth. These devices receive the signals sent by the satellites. By combining the signals from different satellites, a device calculates its location on Earth in terms of latitude and longitude. The more satellite signals the device receives at any time, the more accurately it can determine its location. Because satellites have accurate clocks, the GPS device also displays the correct time.

W GPS is used in many ways. It is used to track the exact location and course of airplanes. That information helps ensure the safety of flights. Farmers use it to help them work their fields. Businesses use it to guide truck drivers. Cell phone companies use GPS to provide services. And of course, GPS in cars helps guide us to our destinations.

Geographic Information Systems

R Another important geospatial technology is known as a geographic information system (GIS). These systems consist of computer hardware and software that gather, store, and analyze geographic information. The information is then shown on a computer screen. Sometimes it is displayed as maps. Sometimes the information is shown in other ways. Companies and governments around the world use this new tool.

A GIS is a powerful tool because it links data about all kinds of physical and human features with the locations of those features. Because computers can store and process so much data, the GIS can be accurate and detailed.

People select what features they want to study using the GIS. Then they can combine different features on the same map and analyze the patterns.

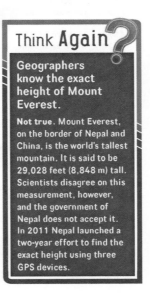

Think Again?

Geographers know the exact height of Mount Everest.

Not true. Mount Everest, on the border of Nepal and China, is the world's tallest mountain. It is said to be 29,028 feet (8,848 m) tall. Scientists disagree on this measurement, however, and the government of Nepal does not accept it. In 2011 Nepal launched a two-year effort to find the exact height using three GPS devices.

W Writing Skills

Argument Explain to students that today parents can download a phone app that uses GPS in real time to keep track of their children through the location of their children's phones. Parents say that they use the app to protect their children. However, children complain that parents are spying on them and that it is an invasion of their privacy.

Have students work together in small groups to brainstorm the pros and cons to these locater apps. Then have students write a persuasive paragraph to answer this prompt: **Should parents use GPS locater apps to keep track of their children?** *(Students' paragraphs need to include a claim either for or against parents using GPS locater apps and at least three ideas or forms of evidence to support the claim.)* **Interpersonal, Logical/ Mathematical**

R Reading Skills

Explaining To make sure students can explain and apply what they are reading about, **ask:** Why is a geographic information system (GIS) an important tool? *(The system links data about all kinds of physical and human features with the locations of those features on Earth. People who use the system can combine different features on the same map and analyze the patterns.)* **Verbal/Linguistic**

Content Background Knowledge

Geocaching is an activity in which people go on treasure hunts without the use of a treasure map looking for objects that other people have concealed. The people who conceal the "treasure," which is generally a weather-proof box containing a log book and small objects, use a GPS device to post the GPS coordinates on a Web site. Those who seek the "treasure" use their own GPS device and the posted GPS coordinates to find the hidden object. People can hide whatever they choose to hide.

SLIDE SHOW

Mapmaking Over Time

Analyzing Visuals Show the slide show of how mapmaking has changed over time. Have students identify the various tools used to make maps (for example, pen and ink with scribe, printmaking, film/ aerial photography) and discuss how mapmaking has become more accurate. **Visual/Spatial**

See page 15D for other online activities.

Slide Show

Geographers and Their Tools

C Critical Thinking Skills

Making Inferences After students read about geographic information systems, **ask: What kinds of questions could be answered with the following information gathered through GIS?**

• Geologists use GIS to make a map of areas in a state most likely to suffer damage from earthquakes. *(Possible answers: How should building codes change to insure the least amount of damage during a quake? Is this a good area to build a specific kind of structure, such as an amusement park?)*

• Meteorologists use GIS to study the paths of hurricanes. *(Possible answers: Where might a hurricane occur? How might a hurricane travel? Do people need to evacuate the area?)*

• Police use GIS to map the specific kinds of crimes in each area of a large city. *(Possible answers: Which areas of the city need more police coverage? Which city areas show an increased gang presence? Have crimes increased around schools?)* **Verbal/Linguistic**

R Reading Skills

Using Context Clues Have students use context clues to find the meaning of *remote sensing.* *("getting information from far away")* **Ask: How does the definition of remote sensing help you understand how satellites are used?** *(Satellites circle the globe in space, which is "far away," collect information about what is happening on Earth, and send the information back to Earth.)* **ELL**

T Technology Skills

Researching the Internet Have students work in small groups to search the Internet for satellite images of their state, community, and neighborhoods. Explain that the cameras on some satellites are so powerful that they can zero in on small areas such as a neighborhood. Have students discuss ways these satellite images could be used. **Visual/Spatial**

ANSWER, p. 32

CRITICAL THINKING Geographers need to know exactly where places are located on Earth so they can provide information to anyone who needs it. Exact locations are important when predicting storm paths and dispatching emergency equipment, and a matter of convenience and safety for travelers.

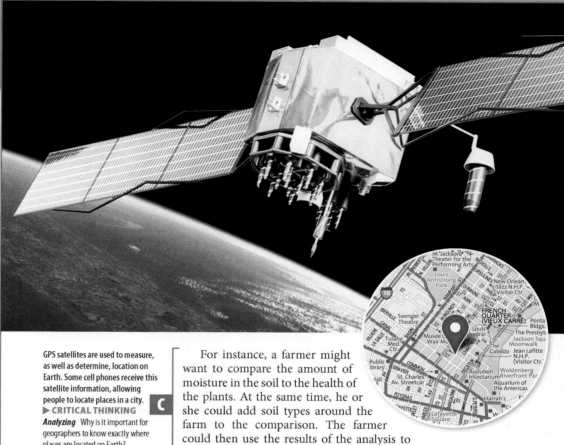

GPS satellites are used to measure, as well as determine, location on Earth. Some cell phones receive this satellite information, allowing people to locate places in a city.
▶ CRITICAL THINKING
Analyzing Why is it important for geographers to know exactly where places are located on Earth?

For instance, a farmer might want to compare the amount of moisture in the soil to the health of the plants. At the same time, he or she could add soil types around the farm to the comparison. The farmer could then use the results of the analysis to answer all kinds of questions. What plants should I plant in different locations? How much irrigation water should I use? How can I drive the tractor most efficiently?

Satellites and Sensors

Since the 1970s, satellites have gathered data about Earth's surface. They do so using remote sensing. **Remote sensing** simply means getting information from far away. Most early satellite sensors were used to gather information about the weather. Weather satellites help save lives during disasters by providing warnings about approaching storms. Before satellites, tropical storms were often missed because they could not be tracked over open water.

Satellites gather information in different ways. They may use powerful cameras to take pictures of the land. They can also pick up other kinds of information, such as the amount of moisture in the soil, the amount of heat the soil holds, or the types of vegetation that

(t) spacephotos.com/age fotostock; (inset) Antenna Audio - Inc./Getty Images

---

net**w**orks   *Online Teaching Options*

Organizing: Forms of Technology

Reviewing Display the interactive graphic organizer on the whiteboard and guide students to organize the forms of technology discussed in this chapter: GPS, GIS, Satellites, Sensors. **Verbal/Linguistic**

See page 15D for other online activities.

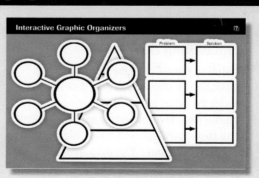

Interactive Graphic Organizers

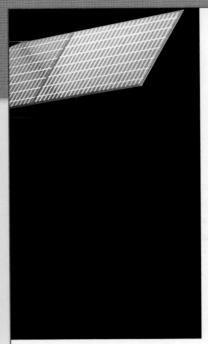

are present. In the early 2000s, scientists used satellites and GIS technology to help conserve the plants and animals that lived in the Amazon rain forest. Using the technology, scientists can compare data gathered from the ground to data taken from satellite pictures. Land use planners use this information to help local people make good decisions about how to use the land. These activities help prevent the rain forest from being destroyed.

T

Some satellites gather information regularly on every spot in the world. That way, scientists can compare the information from one year to another. They look for changes in the shape of the land or in its makeup, spot problems, and take steps to fix them.

Limits of Geospatial Technology

Geospatial technologies allow access to a wealth of information about the features and objects in the world and where those features and objects are located. This information can be helpful for identifying and navigating. By itself, however, the information does not answer questions about why features are located where they are. These questions lie at the heart of understanding our world. The answers are crucial for making decisions about this world in which we live.

R

It is important to go beyond the information provided by geospatial technologies. We must build understanding of people, places, and environments and the connections among them.

FOLDABLES
Study Organizer

Geographer's View
Geographer's Tools

Include this lesson's information in your Foldable®.

☑ **READING PROGRESS CHECK**

Identifying What are the three elements of the Global Positioning System?

LESSON 2 REVIEW **CCSS**

Reviewing Vocabulary (Tier Three Words)

1. How has *remote sensing* changed the way some farmers manage their fields? **RH.6-8.4**

Answering the Guiding Questions

2. *Analyzing* Do you use a mental map or a paper map more often? Explain. **RH.6-8.1**

3. *Identifying* Give examples of three types of thematic maps. **RH.6-8.4**

4. *Identifying* If a museum map shows the location of each exhibit, is it a large-scale or a small-scale map? Explain. **RH.6-8.4**

5. *Describing* Describe the three main features of a map. **RH.6-8.2**

6. *Informative/Explanatory Writing* What tools could you use for a long trip to a national park? Explain. **WHST.6-8.2, WHST.6-8.4**

Chapter 1 **33**

T **Technology Skills**

Analyzing Data Explain to students that NASA is an excellent source for their Internet research work on various geography projects they will do this year. Have students work in small groups to access NASA weather satellite images. Tell them to choose two images and discuss the data and information the images provide and evaluate the importance of the information. Have groups share the images and their analyses with the rest of the class. **Visual/Spatial, Verbal/Linguistic**

R **Reading Skills**

Identifying Have students identify the kinds of information that geospatial technologies can and cannot provide. *(They can tell us about physical features and where they are located, but cannot tell us why they are located where they are.)* **Ask:** Why is it important for people to go beyond the information provided by geospatial technologies in their study of geography? *(Students' answers will vary but should include that people need to understand how people interact with places and how they affect the environment, which geospatial technologies cannot tell us.)* **AL**

Content Background Knowledge

Movement of the Continents The theory of plate tectonics, which students will study in future chapters, was proven with the use of geospatial technologies. These technologies are so precise that they show the continents drifting apart in very small amounts, such as one or two centimeters, over a span of one or more years.

CLOSE & REFLECT

Making Connections To close this lesson, have students think about the different kinds of maps they have used and how the maps helped them find the information they required.

For homework, have students look for maps in their homes that they or their caregivers use. Ask students to discuss what types of maps they found the next day in class.

LESSON 2 REVIEW ANSWERS

Reviewing Vocabulary

1. Remote sensing can show moisture levels and temperatures of soil, allowing farmers to make better decisions about what and when to plant.

Answering the Guiding Questions

2. Analyzing Students will probably say they more often use a mental map, because they envision where they are going; they only need a paper map when they do not know where they are going.

3. Identifying Possible answers: road map, map of resources, map of historical sites

4. Identifying large-scale, because it shows details of the area

5. Describing The key shows the meaning of the symbols, colors, and lines; the scale bar shows the relationship between distance on the map and the real distances; and the compass rose shows directions.

6. Informative/Explanatory Writing GPS, a road map, a map of the park, and a mental map could all be useful. Students should explain the purpose of each tool.

ANSWER, p. 33

☑ **READING PROGRESS CHECK** a network of over 30 satellites, the control system that tracks the satellites, and GPS devices on Earth which receive signals from the satellites

ENGAGE

Bellringer Before students read the What Do You Think? feature, make sure they understand the concepts of globalization and indigenous culture. *Globalization* refers to the linkage of the economies of countries around the world through international trade, communication, and travel, while an *indigenous culture* is the traditional way of life of a group of native people. Discuss the effects of colonization on indigenous cultures in North America: it wiped out some cultures and caused many others to decline. Explain that some of these same effects of colonization occurred in the eastern hemisphere as well. Ask students to imagine how globalization might have similar effects as colonization, and tell them that this feature presents two views on the conflict between globalization and indigenous cultures. Then have students read the introductory paragraph and the *Yes!* viewpoint.

TEACH & ASSESS

C Critical Thinking Skills

Analyzing Primary Sources Pose the following questions to help students analyze the *Yes!* viewpoint. **Ask:**

- **What is the source of the *Yes!* viewpoint?** *(International Forum on Globalization)*
- **Does this source regard globalization's effect on indigenous cultures as positive or negative?** *(negative)*
- **According to this source, how is globalization a threat to indigenous cultures?** *(Global corporations want natural resources on native lands. Dams, mines, pipelines, roads, energy developments, and military intrusions all threaten native lands.)*
- **According to this source, can native communities count on support from national governments?** *(No, the source says national governments do not consult native communities when making decisions on international trade and investments.)*
- **According to this source, why should native communities be saved?** *(to preserve their vast indigenous knowledge and rich culture as well as the natural world and a simpler way of life)*
- **Do you find this argument that globalization is a serious threat to native peoples convincing? Why or why not?** *(Some students may agree with the argument, noting that historically native peoples have often lost out to more powerful groups. Other students may disagree with the argument, noting that indigenous groups have gained legal rights to their lands.)* **Logical/Mathematical, Verbal/Linguistic**

What Do You **Think?** CCSS

Is Globalization Destroying Indigenous Cultures?

Globalization makes it easier for people, goods, and information to travel across borders. Customers have more choices when they shop. Costs of goods are sometimes lower. However, not everyone welcomes these changes. Resistance is particularly strong among indigenous peoples. They see the expansion of trade and outside influences as a threat to their way of life. Is globalization deadly for indigenous cultures?

Yes !

PRIMARY SOURCE

C " Globalization . . . is a multi-pronged attack on the very foundation of [indigenous people's] existence and livelihoods. . . . Indigenous people throughout the world . . . occupy the last pristine [pure and undeveloped] places on earth, where resources are still abundant [plentiful]: forests, minerals, water, and genetic diversity. All are ferociously sought by global corporations, trying to push traditional societies off their lands. . . . Traditional sovereignty [control] over hunting and gathering rights has been thrown into question as national governments bind themselves to new global economic treaties. . . . Big dams, mines, pipelines, roads, energy developments, military intrusions all threaten native lands. . . . National governments making decisions on export development strategies or international trade and investment rules do not consult native communities. . . . The reality remains that without rapid action, these native communities may be wiped out, taking with them vast indigenous knowledge, rich culture and traditions, and any hope of preserving the natural world, and a simpler . . . way of life for future generations. "

—International Forum on Globalization (IFG), a research and educational organization

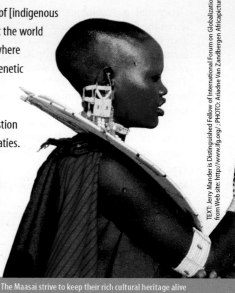

The Maasai strive to keep their rich cultural heritage alive by passing along their traditions from one generation to the next. In this ceremony, Maasai women decorate their faces with a red mixture. They wear flat, round necklaces, which are made up of rows of beads.

TEXT: Jerry Mander is Distinguished Fellow of International Forum on Globalization. This quote is from Web site: http://www.ifg.org/ ; PHOTO: Ariadne Van Zandbergen Africapictures.net/Newscom

34 Chapter 1

---

netw❖rks *Online Teaching Options*

WORKSHEET

How to Analyze a Visual

Analyzing Visuals Divide the class into small groups and have each group follow the steps in the How to Analyze a Visual worksheet using the two photographs in this feature. Allow the groups to share their analyses with the class. **ELL Visual/Spatial**

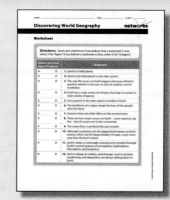

TEXT from "CULTURAL LIBERTY IN TODAY'S DIVERSE WORLD" 2004 United Nations Development Programme. http://hdr.undp.org/en/media/HDR_2004_Chinese.pdf

The Maasai at one time ranged throughout much of Kenya and Tanzania. Much of their land has been taken over for farms, ranches, and parks.

No !
PRIMARY SOURCE

" Indigenous people have struggled for centuries to maintain their identity and way of life against the tide of foreign economic investment and the new settlers that often come with it. ... But indigenous groups are increasingly assertive. Globalization has made it easier for indigenous people to organize, raise funds and network with other groups around the world, with greater political reach and impact than before. The United Nations declared 1995–2004 the International Decade for the World's Indigenous People, and in 2000 the Permanent Forum on Indigenous Issues was created. ... Many states have laws that explicitly recognize indigenous people's rights over their resources. ... Respecting cultural identity [is] possible as long as decisions are made democratically—by states, by companies, by international institutions and by indigenous people. "

—Report by the United Nations Development Programme (UNDP)

Chapter 1 **35**

What Do You Think? DBQ

❶ *Citing Text Evidence*
According to the IFG, why are indigenous people at risk?
RH.6-8.1

❷ *Describing* According to the United Nations report, how has globalization given indigenous people more power? **RH.6-8.2**

Critical Thinking

❸ *Identifying* One effect of globalization is that more tourists are visiting remote places such as wildlife areas in Africa. How do you think indigenous people feel about the growth of tourism in their communities? **RH.6-8.2**

C

C Critical Thinking Skills

Analyzing Primary Sources Use the following questions to help students analyze the *No!* viewpoint. **Ask:**

- **What is the source of the *No!* viewpoint?** *(the United Nations Development Programme)*
- **Would you expect this source to be knowledgeable on this issue?** *(yes)*
- **Does this source regard globalization's effect on indigenous cultures as positive or negative?** *(positive)*
- **What benefit of globalization does the source cite?** *(Globalization makes it easier for indigenous people to organize, raise funds, and network with other groups around the world.)*
- **According to this source, what protection do indigenous groups have from encroachment by foreign investors and settlers?** *(Many states have laws recognizing indigenous people's rights over their resources. Respecting cultural identity is possible as long as decisions are made democratically by states, companies, international institutions, and indigenous people.)*
- **Do all these groups—states, companies, international institutions, and indigenous people—usually make decisions democratically?** *(No, companies do not typically make decisions democratically.)*
- **Do you find this argument convincing? Why or why not?** *(Some students may agree, citing the power of the Internet as an organizing tool to gain worldwide support. Other students may disagree, noting that indigenous groups tend to have little political power while companies tend to have a lot of power.)* **Logical/Mathematical, Verbal/Linguistic**

CLOSE & REFLECT

To close this lesson, have students write a paragraph presenting their own view on this issue. Tell them to support their opinion with facts, and to give reasons for their view. Allow time for volunteers to share their paragraphs with the class. Remind students to be considerate of opposing viewpoints. **Intrapersonal, Interpersonal**

WORKSHEET

Writing Skills: Supporting Opinion with Facts

Argument Have students use the Writing Skills worksheet for this feature to practice researching and writing convincing arguments supported with clear reasons for both sides of a debatable issue. **BL Verbal/Linguistic**

ANSWERS, p. 35

DBQ What Do You **Think?**

1. Indigenous people live on lands with valuable natural resources that international corporations want to exploit.
2. Globalization has made it easier for indigenous people to organize, raise funds, network, and gain political recognition of their rights.
3. Possible answers: Some indigenous people might resent tourists and the environmental damage caused by building hotels, roads, and other infrastructure to support the tourist industry; they might worry about increased commercialization and the loss of traditional values. Others might appreciate the jobs created and the chance to educate others about their cultures.

CHAPTER REVIEW ACTIVITY

Have students create a two-column chart like the one below. In the first column, have them list and define each of the five themes of geography. In the second column, have them give a physical example of each of the five themes of geography and tell whether a map or a globe would be better to use to show where the example is located. *(In the first column students should list the five themes—location, place, region, human-environment interaction, and movement—and provide definitions similar to those given below. In the second column, students' answers will vary but they should give an appropriate example for each of the five themes. Most examples will be better illustrated on a map than on a globe.)*

Five Themes of Geography	
Definition	**Example**
1. **location** – "where something is found on Earth"	
2. **place** – "the physical or human features that make a place unique"	
3. **region** – "places that are close to one another and share some characteristics"	
4. **human-environment interaction** – "how people and the natural surroundings of a place interact"	
5. **movement** – "how people, products, ideas, and information move from one place to another"	

REVIEW THE ENDURING UNDERSTANDINGS

Review this chapter's Enduring Understandings with students:

• ***People, places, and ideas change over time.***

Now pose the following questions in a class discussion to apply the Enduring Understandings to this chapter:

• **What physical features of our area would have encouraged people to settle in this place?** *(Answers will vary but should demonstrate an understanding of the area and how its geography affected settlement.)*

Directions: Write your answers on a separate piece of paper.

❶ **Exploring the Essential Question**
INFORMATIVE/EXPLANATORY WRITING Read the children's fable "The City Mouse and the Country Mouse." Write a synopsis of the story showing the differences between an urban and a country lifestyle. WHST.6-8.2, WHST.6-8.4

❷ **21st Century Skills**
INTEGRATING VISUAL INFORMATION Interview someone who has lived in your community for a number of years to find out how the community has changed in size and appearance. Create a scrapbook of your findings, including text and photos or drawings. RH.6-8.7, RH.6-8.8

❸ **Thinking Like a Geographer**
INTEGRATING VISUAL INFORMATION Locate your city or town on a globe. Find your lines of latitude and longitude. Next, locate the place in the Eastern Hemisphere with the same lines of latitude and longitude. Do the same for the Southern Hemisphere. Name the sites in the other two hemispheres. RH.6-8.7

❹ **GEOGRAPHY ACTIVITY**

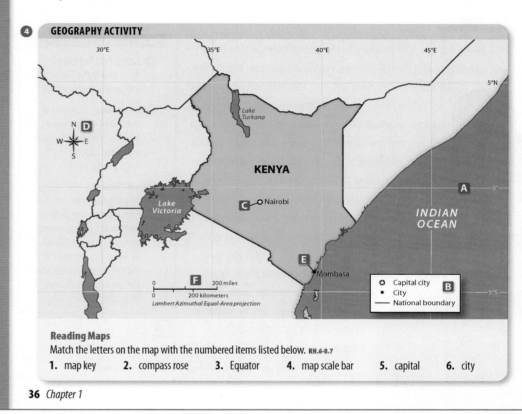

Reading Maps
Match the letters on the map with the numbered items listed below. RH.6-8.7
1. map key   2. compass rose   3. Equator   4. map scale bar   5. capital   6. city

• **Have these physical features changed? If so, how, and what keeps people in this place today?** *(Answers will vary but should acknowledge known changes in the area and changes in the community, such as loss or gain of industry or farming or new building developments.)*

• **If you were to move, where would you choose to go? What physical or human features would draw you to a new place?** *(Answers will vary but students should have a clear understanding of physical and human features and should give a clear description of those features and why they would be attractive.)*

ACTIVITIES ANSWERS

Exploring the Essential Questions

❶ **INFORMATIVE/EXPLANATORY WRITING** Students should discuss how interactions with the environment influence lifestyle, focusing on the differences between rural and urban living conditions.

21st Century Skills

❷ **INTEGRATING VISUAL INFORMATION** Students should interview someone who has lived in your community for a number of years and use the information they gather to make a scrapbook in which they show and describe how the community has changed in size and appearance.

REVIEW THE GUIDING QUESTIONS

Directions: Choose the best answer for each question.

1 The best way to represent abstract ideas is usually on a RH.6-8.4
- A. map.
- B. chart.
- C. diagram.
- D. graph.

2 Each hemisphere on Earth is equal to RH.6-8.4
- F. one-fourth of the planet.
- G. one-half of the planet.
- H. one continent plus one ocean.
- I. one pole and its surrounding land.

3 Because maps are flat representations of a sphere, they RH.6-8.2
- A. do not show as much detail as a globe.
- B. do not use a scale.
- C. must be very large.
- D. distort physical reality.

4 To understand the symbols on a map, you can use the RH.6-8.4
- F. scale bar.
- G. compass rose.
- H. title.
- I. key.

5 West of the river and north of the fire station describes RH.6-8.4
- A. relative location.
- B. absolute location.
- C. longitude.
- D. latitude.

6 Places that are close to one another and have some of the same characteristics are in the same RH.6-8.4
- F. landform.
- G. region.
- H. component.
- I. zone.

Thinking Like a Geographer

3 **INTEGRATING VISUAL INFORMATION** Lines of latitude and longitude should be accurate for students' location and for locations in other hemispheres.

Geography Activity

4 **READING MAPS**

1. B
2. D
3. A
4. F
5. C
6. E

ASSESSMENT ANSWERS

Review the Guiding Questions

1 **C** The best way to represent abstract ideas is usually on a diagram. Diagrams are drawings that use text and pictures to represent abstract ideas. Graphs are visual displays of numerical information and can help one to compare information. Charts display information in columns and rows. Have students who answer incorrectly look back to Lesson 1.

2 **G** Each hemisphere on Earth is equal to one-half of the planet. The Equator divides Earth into the Northern and Southern Hemispheres, and the Prime Meridian and International Date Line divide Earth into the Eastern and Western Hemispheres. Have students who answer incorrectly look back at the beginning of Lesson 2 for an explanation of hemisphere.

3 **D** Because maps are flat representations of a sphere, they distort physical reality. Have students who answer incorrectly look back at the second page of Lesson 2 for an explanation of how maps distort physical reality and are not as accurate as globes.

4 **I** To understand the symbols on a map, you can use the map key. A key unlocks the meaning of the map by explaining the symbols, colors, and lines. Have students who answer incorrectly look back at Lesson 2 for an explanation of map keys.

5 **A** West of the river and north of the fire station describes relative location. Absolute location is the exact location of something and often uses lines of latitude and longitude to locate the place precisely. Have students who answer incorrectly look back at Lesson 1 for explanations of relative and absolute locations.

6 **G** Places that are close to one another and have some of the same characteristics are in the same region. Have students who answer incorrectly look back at Lesson 1 for an explanation of region.

DBQ Analyzing Documents

7 C One common way of dividing Earth into geographic realms is by continent. A realm is an area that has special human (cultural) and physical (environmental) characteristics. Since a realm is an area, answers A, B, and D cannot be correct. Have students who answer incorrectly, reread the passage carefully to understand their error.

8 G An example of a cultural characteristic of a realm is people's actions and attitudes. Explain to students who answer incorrectly that culture has to do with humans and not physical features such as the direction of a river, cloud formations, or the terrain of land. Have students who answer incorrectly look back at Lesson 1 to review the information given in the text about culture.

Short Response

9 Assessing the results of a disaster such as a hurricane, tornado, wildfire, flood, or earthquake helps response teams to better prepare for another, similar event in the future. By being better prepared, teams can speed relief to disaster victims and minimize the impact of the disaster.

10 Relief workers help victims of disasters by providing water, food, shelter, medicines, and other basic items.

Extended Response

11 Possible answer: One base in Antarctica is McMurdo Station. Researchers, including geologists, go there mostly during Antarctica's summer months to do experiments with the ice core to research global warming. Challenges include extreme cold and barren conditions. People must bring all their own supplies, and minimal medical care is available to the researchers.

Chapter 1 **ASSESSMENT** (continued)

DBQ ANALYZING DOCUMENTS

7 CITING TEXT EVIDENCE In the excerpt below, two geographers summarize the content of their geography book.

"In this book we. . . investigate the world's great geographic realms [areas]. We will find that each of these realms possesses a special combination of cultural . . . and environmental properties [characteristics]."

—from H.J. de Blij and Peter O. Muller, *Geography*

What is one common way of dividing Earth into geographic realms? RH.6-8.2, RH.6-8.10

A. by weather patterns

B. by distance to an ocean

C. by continent

D. by crops grown in an area

8 IDENTIFYING Which of the following is an example of a cultural characteristic of a realm? RH.6-8.2, RH.6-8.10

F. the direction a river flows

G. people's actions and attitudes

H. the most common cloud formations of an area

I. the terrain of the land

SHORT RESPONSE

"Hurricanes, wildfires, floods, earthquakes, and other natural events affect the Nation's economy, . . . property, and lives. . . . The USGS gathers and disseminates [gives out] real-time hazard data to relief workers, conducts long-term monitoring and forecasting to help minimize the impacts of future events, and evaluates conditions in the aftermath of disasters."

—from United States Geological Service, *The National Map—Hazards and Disasters*

9 ANALYZING What is the benefit of evaluating conditions after a disaster occurs? RH.6-8.1, RH.6-8.10

10 CITING TEXT EVIDENCE What is the primary focus of relief workers? RH.6-8.2

EXTENDED RESPONSE

Write your answer on a separate piece of paper.

11 INFORMATIVE/EXPLANATORY WRITING Large parts of Antarctica remain relatively unexplored. Research one of the bases that has been set up there. Write an essay explaining who uses the base and why. Also, describe some of the challenges researchers and scientists face in Antarctica and how they handle them. WHST.6-8.8, WHST.6-8.9

Need Extra Help?

If You've Missed Question	1	2	3	4	5	6	7	8	9	10	11
Review Lesson	1	2	2	2	1	1	1	1	1	1	1

GEOGRAPHY: REALMS, REGIONS, AND CONCEPTS, Twelfth Edition, by H.J. de Blij and Peter O. Muller. Copyright ©2006 by H.J. de Blij and Peter O. Muller. Published by John Wiley & Sons, Inc.; From "THE NATIONAL MAP—HAZARDS AND DISASTERS," National Geospatial Program Office, Fact Sheet 2009-3010. U.S. Geological Survey, Department of the Interior/USGS. The USGS home page is http://www.usgs.gov.

---

netw✪rks *Online Teaching Options*

Evaluation and Assessment

Assessing Use eAssessment to create your own tests from hundreds of available questions. eAssessment helps you design assessments that meet the needs of different types of learners.

The Physical World Planner

National Geography Standards covered in Chapter 2

Learners will understand:

I. The World in Spatial Terms

Standard 1: How to use maps and other geographic representations, geospatial technologies, and spatial thinking to understand and communicate information

Standard 3: How to analyze the spatial organization of people, places, and environments on Earth's surface

II. Places and Regions

Standard 4: The physical and human characteristics of places

III. Physical Systems

Standard 7: The physical processes that shape the patterns of Earth's surface

Standard 8: The characteristics and spatial distribution of ecosystems and biomes on Earth's surface

IV. Human Systems

Standard 9: The characteristics, distribution, and migration of human populations on Earth's surface

Standard 12: The processes, patterns, and functions of human settlement

V. Environment and Society

Standard 14: How human actions modify the physical environment

Standard 15: How physical systems affect human systems

VI. The Uses of Geography

Standard 17: How to apply geography to interpret the past

Standard 18: How to apply geography to interpret the present and plan for the future

UNDERSTANDING BY DESIGN®

Enduring Understandings

- *People, places, and ideas change over time.*

Essential Questions

- *How does geography influence the way people live?*

Predictable Misunderstandings

- *Earth is a solid planet.*
- *The planets in the solar system are all like Earth.*
- *Humans have very little effect on the environment.*
- *The ocean floor is flat.*

Assessment Evidence

Performance Tasks:

- *Project-Based Learning Digital Hands-On Chapter Project*
- *Project-Based Learning Hands-On Chapter Project*

Other Evidence:

- *Geography Skills Activity*
- *GeoLab Activity*
- *Geography and History Activity*
- *Participation in Project-Based Learning Activities*
- *Participation in Interactive Whiteboard Activities*
- *Contribution to small-group activities*
- *Interpretation of slide show images and special purpose maps*
- *Participation in class discussions about physical geography topics*
- *Lesson Reviews*
- *Chapter Assessments*

SUGGESTED PACING GUIDE

Introducing the Chapter............... 1 Day	Lesson 3 .... 2 Days	
Lesson 1 ....2 Days	Chapter Wrap-Up and Assessment...... 1 Day	
Lesson 2 ....2 Days		

TOTAL TIME   8 Days

Key for Using the Teacher Edition

SKILL-BASED ACTIVITIES

Types of skill activities found in the Teacher Edition.

* **V Visual Skills** require students to analyze maps, graphs, charts, and photos.

W Writing Skills provide writing opportunities to help students comprehend the text.

R Reading Skills help students practice reading skills and master vocabulary.

C Critical Thinking Skills help students apply and extend what they have learned.

T Technology Skills require students to use digital tools effectively.

DIFFERENTIATED INSTRUCTION

All activities are written for the on-level student unless otherwise marked with the leveled labels below.

BL Beyond Level
AL Approaching Level
ELL English Language Learners

All students benefit from activities that utilize different learning styles. Many activities are marked as below when a particular learning style is highlighted.

Intrapersonal	Naturalist
Logical/Mathematical	Kinesthetic
Visual/Spatial	Auditory/Musical
Verbal/Linguistic	Interpersonal

*Letters are followed by a number when there is more than one of the same type of skill on the page.

CHAPTER OPENER PLANNER

Students will know:
- *Earth is a planet in the solar system.*
- *Earth undergoes constant change and movement.*

Students will be able to:
- *identify places with volcanoes and earthquakes and how these relate to plate tectonics using a map.*
- *analyze a time line to discuss devastating volcanic eruptions and earthquakes that have occurred through history.*

UNDERSTANDING
BY DESIGN®

☑ *Print Teaching Options*

V **Visual Skills**

☐ **P. 40** Students learn about Earth's tectonic plates and use a map to identify plate boundaries and the occurrence of earthquakes and volcanoes along plate boundaries. **AL**

☐ **P. 41** Students use a time line along with the map to answer questions about significant natural disasters in the history of the world. **AL**

☑ *Online Teaching Options*

☐ **MAP** **Reading a Map**—Students identify aspects and locations of the region on a map.

☐ **TIME LINE** **Reading a Time Line and Map**—Students use a time line and a map to learn about where historical events occurred in the world. **Visual/Spatial**

☐ **MAP** **Interactive World Atlas**—Students use the interactive world atlas to identify the region and describe its terrain.

☑ *Printable Digital Worksheets*

☐ **WORKSHEET** **Geography Skills: Reading a Thematic Map**—Students use the worksheet to practice and apply the skills of reading a thematic map on wind currents.

☐ **WORKSHEET** **GeoLab: Desalinization of Water**—Students use the worksheet to analyze how much easily accessible water is on the planet.

☐ **WORKSHEET** **Geography and History: Global Warming Debate**—Students can use the worksheet to review main ideas and key concepts of the global warming debate.

Project-Based Learning

Hands-On

Create Maps

Students will work in groups to create large wall maps of the Earth and symbols that represent Earth's physical forces: volcanoes, hurricanes, cyclones, earthquakes, tsunamis, droughts, and tornadoes. Have students ask fact-based questions about these forces and where they have taken place in the past or recently. Once a student answers the question correctly, he or she can post the cut-out symbol where this event occurred on the map.

Digital Hands-On

Create Online Interactive Maps

Students will work in pairs and use an online map-making program to create a map that shows different physical features of Earth and the absolute locations of the physical features with an embedded photo or video about them. Students may also write short descriptions about the physical features and embed them in the map. Once completed, students will present their maps to the class and then post them on a class Web site or wiki.

Print Resources

ANCILLARY RESOURCES

These ancillaries are available for every chapter and lesson

- **Reading Essentials and Study Guide Workbook** **AL** **ELL**
- **Chapter Tests and Lesson Quizzes Blackline Masters**

PRINTABLE DIGITAL WORKSHEETS

These printable digital worksheets are available for every chapter and lesson.

- **Hands-On Chapter Projects**
- **What Do You Know? Activities**
- **Chapter Summaries (English and Spanish)**
- **Vocabulary Builder Activities**
- **Quizzes and Tests**
- **Reading Essentials and Study Guide (English and Spanish)** **AL** **ELL**
- **Guided Reading Activities**

More Media Resources

SUGGESTED VIDEOS

NOTE: Be sure to preview any clips to ensure they are age-appropriate.

- **Twister** (113 min.)
- **Faces of Earth** (180 min.)
- **Violent Earth** (52 min.)

SUGGESTED READING

- ***One Well: The Story of Water on Earth,*** by Rochelle Strauss **AL**
- ***Forces of Nature,*** by Catherine O'Neill Grace
- ***A Child's Introduction to the World: Geography, Cultures, and People—From the Grand Canyon to the Great Wall of China,*** by Heather Alexander
- ***Paths to Peace: People Who Changed the World,*** by Jane Brekin Zalben **BL**

THE EARTH-SUN RELATIONSHIP

Students will know:
- *Earth is a planet in the solar system.*
- *the aspects of life that occur on Earth happen because of Earth's position to the sun, its axis, its rotation, and its revolution.*
- *Earth is made up of layers.*
- *Earth has a variety of climates that help to sustain its wide variety of species.*

Students will be able to:
- ***identify*** the parts of the solar system.
- ***describe*** how Earth's orbit causes the seasons.
- ***explain*** what factors determine the climate of an area.
- ***describe*** Earth's six major climate zones.

UNDERSTANDING BY DESIGN®

☑ Print Teaching Options

V Visual Skills

- ☐ **P. 42** Students draw a map of the solar system. `AL` `ELL`
- ☐ **P. 43** Students simulate Earth's layers and composition.
- ☐ **P. 44** Students draw symbols for four physical systems. `AL` `ELL`
- ☐ **P. 45** Students simulate the tilted Earth as it orbits.
- ☐ **P. 46** Students use a world map to explain climate zones.
- ☐ **P. 47** Students analyze a wind patterns map. `AL`

W Writing Skills

- ☐ **P. 44** Students write a paragraph describing how a drop of water moves through Earth's four physical systems.
- ☐ **P. 48** Students distinguish weather from climate.

R Reading Skills

- ☐ **P. 44** Students use context clues to find meaning. `ELL`
- ☐ **P. 45** Students use word parts to find meaning. `AL` `ELL`
- ☐ **P. 48** Students summarize text on ocean currents.
- ☐ **P. 51** Students summarize information about how human activities affect weather and climate. `BL`

C Critical Thinking Skills

- ☐ **P. 42** Students recognize the relationship of the sun to Earth and its importance as the source of all energy. `BL`
- ☐ **P. 43** Students draw conclusions about Earth's layers.
- ☐ **P. 44** Students synthesize Earth's four physical systems and explain how they are interdependent.
- ☐ **P. 49** Students apply their understanding of the rain shadow effect to the Essential Question. `AL`
- ☐ **P. 50** Students distinguish climate zones and biomes. `BL`

T Technology Skills

- ☐ **P. 46** Students make predictions about the climate and use the Internet to check their predictions.
- ☐ **P. 47** Students use calculators to apply information about elevation and climate to a specific situation.

☑ Online Teaching Options

V Visual Skills

- `ANIMATION` **Earth's Daily Rotation**—Students dramatize the daily rotation of Earth after watching the animation. `AL` `ELL` **Kinesthetic**
- `DIAGRAM` **The Solar System**—Students analyze Earth's position in the solar system.
- `ANIMATION` **Earth's Layers**—Students label their drawings of Earth's layers after watching the animation. **Verbal/Linguistic**
- `MAP` **World Climates**—Students describe the climate of the local region. **Verbal/Linguistic**
- `MAP` **Wind and Currents**—Students use map to study effects of ocean currents on climate.

R Reading Skills

- `CHART` **Temperature and Precipitation Affect Biomes**—Students use the chart to discuss how climate and elevation affects the environment. **Interpersonal**
- `CHART` **Climate Zones**—Students identify their climate zone and the zones of familiar places.
- `GAME` **Drag-and-Drop: Earth's Physical Systems**—Students can use the game to review.
- `GAME` **Drag-and-Drop: Climate Terms**—Students can use the game to review the lesson.

C Critical Thinking Skills

- `VIDEO` **How Mountains Form**—Students watch a video about planet Earth and analyze the images and main ideas. **Interpersonal**
- `ANIMATION` **Seasons on Earth**—After watching the animation, students name the season for different countries in different hemispheres at different times of the year. **Visual/Spatial**
- `SLIDE SHOW` **Effects of Climate Change**—Students use the slide show to determine causes and effects and possible solutions. **Verbal/Linguistic**

T Technology Skills

- `DIAGRAM` **Rain Shadow**—After viewing the diagram, students apply the information to various areas of the United States. **Logical/Mathematical**
- `MAP` **Types of Climate**—Students use an animated map to review the various climate types.
- `ONLINE SELF-CHECK QUIZ` **Lesson 1**—Students receive instant feedback on their mastery of lesson content.

☑ Printable Digital Worksheets

W Writing Skills

- `WORKSHEET` **Geography and History: The Global Warming Debate**—Students can use the worksheet to review main ideas and key concepts of the global warming debate.

FORCES SHAPING EARTH

Students will know:
- Earth is made up of layers.
- Earth undergoes constant change and movement.

Students will be able to:
- **describe** the evidence that tells scientists that Earth's core is solid.
- **analyze** how the Ring of Fire got its name.
- **identify** evidence that plants cause weathering and erosion.
- **cite text evidence** of how human actions change Earth.

UNDERSTANDING BY DESIGN®

☑ *Print Teaching Options*

V **Visual Skills**

- ☐ **P. 52** Students use a world map to speculate on how the continents may have once fit together.

- ☐ **P. 53** Students create a chart to summarize information on plate movements.

- ☐ **P. 53** Students explain the effects of a force below Earth's surface using photographs.

- ☐ **P. 54** Students analyze a map showing the Ring of Fire and make connections to its effects on states in the United States and on other countries. **BL**

W **Writing Skills**

- ☐ **P. 55** Students note the eroded landforms in this country's national parks and write an argument for creating additional national parks. **BL**

- ☐ **P. 57** Students write a description of how the state's landscape has been altered by people and how much of it remains in a natural state.

R **Reading Skills**

- ☐ **P. 54** Students create vocabulary cards for content vocabulary words. **AL**

- ☐ **P. 56** Students determine central ideas about the effect of water and ice on landforms. **BL**

- ☐ **P. 57** Students list ways humans have changed the environment on Earth.

C **Critical Thinking Skills**

- ☐ **P. 55** Students compare and contrast the related processes of weathering and erosion.

T **Technology Skills**

- ☐ **P. 52** Students use the Internet to conduct research on the classification of continents.

☑ *Online Teaching Options*

V **Visual Skills**

- **VIDEO** **Water Eroding Mountains**—Students watch a video about the forces that shape Earth's surface and analyze the images and main ideas. **Interpersonal**

- **VIDEOS** **Earth's Forces: Old Faithful and Icelandic Volcano**—Students watch the videos about how landforms shape the life of people in the region, and analyze how landforms in the local region affect people. **Verbal/Linguistic**

- **MAP** **Risk of Earthquakes in the United States**—Students analyze the map to discuss the risk of earthquakes to the United States.

C **Critical Thinking Skills**

- **SLIDE SHOW** **Architecture for Earthquakes**—Students use the slide show to interpret how people have adapted to living with natural disasters. **Verbal/Linguistic**

- **VIDEO** **Erosion in Bryce Canyon**—Students watch a video about erosion and integrate what they learned in the video to landforms that have been eroded in their state or region. **Visual**

- **SLIDE SHOW** **Human Impact on Earth**—Students use the slide show to interpret how people have affected Earth's surface by building canals, dams, levees, roads, and cities. **Naturalist**

T **Technology Skills**

- **ONLINE SELF-CHECK QUIZ** **Lesson 2**—Students receive instant feedback on their mastery of lesson content.

EARTH'S LAND AND WATER

Students will know:
- the land of Earth has a wide variety of features.
- the ocean floor of Earth has a wide variety of features.

Students will be able to:
- *give examples* of landforms in their state.
- *describe* how the ocean floor is similar to the surface of dry land.
- *identify* bodies of water as either freshwater or salt water.
- *explain* the water cycle in their own words.

UNDERSTANDING
BY DESIGN®

☑ *Print Teaching Options*

V Visual Skills

☐ **P. 58** Students draw a landscape with landforms. **ELL**

☐ **P. 59** Students use a physical map to identify landforms and bodies of water.

☐ **P. 60** Students use a diagram of freshwater and saltwater facts to answer questions and draw conclusions.

☐ **P. 62** Students create word webs to summarize information on bodies of water. **AL ELL**

☐ **P. 63** Students make a flow chart of the water cycle. **ELL**

☐ **P. 64** Students analyze a diagram of the water cycle. **AL**

W Writing Skills

☐ **P. 60** Students conduct research and write an informative report on life in the deepest, darkest places in the ocean.

☐ **P. 62** Students write a narrative about people's use of water and what is happening in one of two photos.

R Reading Skills

☐ **P. 58** Students use a map to identify elevation. **AL**

☐ **P. 64** Students use context clues to determine meanings of academic vocabulary. **BL**

C Critical Thinking Skills

☐ **P. 60** Students make connections to prior experiences to discuss coastlines and continental shelves.

☐ **P. 61** Students identify problems with the amount of liquid freshwater that is safe for people to drink. **AL**

☐ **P. 61** Students make connections to a girl pumping water from a well and identify where their water comes from.

☐ **P. 63** Students connect the changes of state of water to the preparation of a meal.

☐ **P. 64** Students synthesize what they have learned about the water cycle to make a flow chart. **AL ELL**

T Technology Skills

☐ **P. 59** Students conduct Internet research to determine if Central America belongs to North or South America. **BL**

☐ **P. 65** Students choose a problem with Earth's water to research and present to the class.

☑ *Online Teaching Options*

V Visual Skills

☐ **VIDEOS** **Changing World—Wild Weather**—Students use the video to create a graphic organizer to analyze the content of the video. **Visual/Spatial**

☐ **MAP** **Physical Geography of Earth**—Using the map, students identify and describe landforms and waterways of Earth. **BL** **Visual/Spatial**

☐ **IMAGE** **Ocean Floor**—Students use the interactive image to describe and discuss the geography of the ocean floor and compare that to land.

☐ **GRAPHIC ORGANIZER** **Water: Recreation vs. Livelihood**—Using the graphic organizer, students identify the ways water is used for recreation and for making a living. **Naturalist**

☐ **MAP** **Population of Earth**—Students use this map to discuss the distribution, density, and location of population on Earth. **Visual/Spatial**

W Writing Skills

☐ **IMAGE** **Garbage**—Using the interactive image, students write a paragraph that discusses the weekly collection of garbage in their household and how much could be reused or recycled.

R Reading Skills

☐ **LECTURE SLIDE** **Desalinization Process**—Using the lecture slide, review the content of this process with students for understanding.

C Critical Thinking Skills

☐ **INFOGRAPHIC** **Fresh and Salt Water in the World**—Students use the infographic to identify the amount of fresh and salt water readily available. **BL** **Visual/Spatial**

T Technology Skills

☐ **ANIMATION** **How the Water Cycle Works**—Using the animation, students analyze how water sources are replenished and how water moves around the planet. **Visual, Naturalist**

☐ **ONLINE SELF-CHECK QUIZ** **Lesson 3**—Students receive instant feedback on their mastery of lesson content.

☑ *Printable Digital Worksheets*

W Writing Skills

☐ **WORKSHEET** **GeoLab: Desalinization of Water**—Students use the worksheet to analyze how much easily accessible water is on the planet. **Logical/Mathematical**

☐ **WORKSHEET** **Geography Skills: Reading a Thematic Map**—Students use the worksheet to practice and apply the skills of reading a thematic map on wind currents.

INTERVENTION AND REMEDIATION STRATEGIES

LESSON 1   The Earth-Sun Relationship

Reading and Comprehension

Organize students into small groups. Assign four different content vocabulary words to each group. Have students in each group work together to write a paragraph, using the four terms they have been assigned.

After groups have completed their paragraphs, ask a volunteer from each group to read the paragraph. Provide guidance as needed, ensuring that students have used each term correctly.

Text Evidence

Have students review the lesson and use the headings and subheadings to create an outline of the lesson. Have students write key words and phrases in their notebooks to remind them about important content under each heading and subheading. Then have students quiz a partner, using the words and phrases from their notebook.

LESSON 2   Forces Shaping Earth

Reading and Comprehension

To ensure comprehension of the internal and external forces explained in this lesson, have students take turns acting as the teacher. Assign a key concept, place, or vocabulary word from the lesson for students to explain to the rest of the class.

Have students make a brief presentation to "teach" the topic or term to the rest of the class. Tell students they may use the board to draw diagrams or charts to better explain their assigned concept.

Text Evidence

Organize students into small groups. Tell students they will research a real-life event from one of the following categories: slow change, sudden change, natural force, or human action. Either assign or have students choose the event, ensuring that each group has a different event. Have groups present a summary of their findings to the class, citing textual evidence that supports their research.

LESSON 3   Earth's Land and Water

Reading and Comprehension

Organize students into small groups. Have groups outline key facts and processes related to one of the following topics: surface features on land, the ocean floor, types of water, and the water cycle.

To ensure comprehension of the topics, conduct a question/answer session in which students from each group answer questions about their topic.

Text Evidence

Have students create clues for a "Jeopardy" style game. Have a group of "contestants" provide the correct "question" for each clue. For example, one group might write the clue "a long, narrow cut in the ground that is more than 35,000 feet steep in some places," while the other group writes the question/answer ("What is the Mariana Trench?"). Have groups take turns playing the game.

Online Resources

Level Reader

Use this online lower-level text that corresponds directly to the text in the online Student Edition.

Guided Reading Activities

This resource uses graphic organizers and guiding questions to help students with comprehension.

What Do You Know?

Use these worksheets to pre-assess students' background knowledge before they study the chapter.

Reading Essentials and Study Guide Workbook

This resource offers writing and reading activities for the approaching-level student.

Self-Check Quizzes

This online assessment tool provides instant feedback for students to check their progress.

THE PHYSICAL WORLD

ESSENTIAL QUESTION · *How does geography influence the way people live?*

Carsten Peter/National Geographic/Getty Images

A geologist prepares to enter the crater of Ambrim Island volcano.

Lesson 1
The Earth-Sun Relationship

Lesson 2
Forces Shaping Earth

Lesson 3
Earth's Land and Water

The Story Matters...

Earth is part of a larger physical system called the solar system. Earth's position in the solar system makes life on our planet possible. The planet Earth has air, land, and water that make it suitable for plant, animal, and human life. Major natural forces inside and outside of our planet shape its surface. Some of these forces can occur suddenly and violently, causing disasters that dramatically affect life on Earth.

FOLDABLES
Study Organizer

Go to the Foldables® library in the back of your book to make a Foldable® that will help you take notes while reading this chapter.

39

ENGAGE

 Bellringer Setting a time limit of 30 seconds, ask students to think about and jot down major natural forces on Earth that affect their lives. Students might name such forces as gravity, solar radiation, earthquakes, and volcanic eruptions. Call on volunteers to share their lists. Then have students read "The Story Matters..." and identify the natural forces that are implied in the last sentence (*volcanic eruptions and earthquakes*). Tell students that they will be learning more about the natural forces that shape Earth's geography and influence how people live on the planet.

Making Connections Read the following information to students to help them appreciate the uniqueness of Earth's environment within the solar system.

- Earth is the only planet in the solar system known to sustain life. It is the third planet from the sun, after Mercury and Venus. The fourth planet is Mars. These four planets are called terrestrial (or land) planets because they have rocky, rather than gaseous, surfaces. The atmospheres of the four planets differ greatly, however.
- Mercury, the planet closest to the sun, has very little atmosphere and extreme temperatures. The side of Mercury that faces the sun gets scorched, while the side away from the sun freezes.
- Venus has a thick, toxic atmosphere, consisting mostly of carbon dioxide plus some poisonous gases. Temperatures on Venus are hot enough to melt lead.
- Earth's atmosphere consists mostly of nitrogen and oxygen. Unique among the planets, Earth contains an abundance of liquid water—and comparatively moderate temperatures.
- Mars has a very thin atmosphere of carbon dioxide. The planet has polar ice caps, but its thin atmosphere and cold temperatures keep the water from becoming liquid. Mars may have had liquid water in the past, as evidenced by signs of ancient floods on its surface.

FOLDABLES
Study Organizer

Go to the Foldables® library for a chapter-based Foldable® activity that your students can use to help take notes and prepare for assessment.

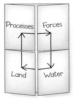

Letter from the Author

Dear Geography Teacher,

The first step in understanding Earth's physical geography is to have a firm understanding of the effects of the Earth-sun relationship. Be sure your students recognize how revolution and rotation affect our climate, wind and ocean currents, length of days, and seasons. In addition, knowledge about physical geography includes an understanding of *insolation*, or how much of the sun's heat and energy reach various parts of the world in the Tropics, mid-latitudes, and polar regions.

Richard H Boehm

TEACH & ASSESS

Step Into the Place

V Visual Skills

Reading a Map Explain to students that the top layer, or crust, of Earth consists of huge, moving slabs of rock called *tectonic plates*. Over millions of years, the movement of these plates has helped shape the surface of Earth.

These tectonic plates sit on the next layer of Earth, the mantle, which is a layer of hot rock that can be moved, shaped, and melted. This melted rock in the mantle layer can flow to the surface of Earth through cracks in the tectonic plate boundaries. When it flows out through a volcano, this melted rock is called lava. The movement of the mantle and the tectonic plates also can cause earthquakes.

As the map shows, these earthquakes and volcanic eruptions often occur near the boundaries between tectonic plates. These processes will be described more fully in Lesson 2; however, invite students who have had any experiences with earthquakes or volcanic eruptions, such as visiting Hawaii's continually erupting volcanoes, to share their experiences with the class.

Have students examine the map and identify the seven continents. **Ask:**

- **What is the symbol on the map for earthquakes?** *(yellow circle)*
- **Which two states in the United States have had the most earthquakes?** *(Alaska and California)*
- **What is the symbol on the map for volcanoes?** *(red triangle)*
- **Where are most of Earth's tectonic plate boundaries located?** *(most boundaries are in the oceans and near the edges of continents)*

Then have students answer the Step into the Place questions.
AL Visual/Spatial

ANSWERS, p. 40

STEP INTO THE PLACE

1. near plate boundaries around the Pacific Ocean
2. South America
3. Asia's east coast; because there are tectonic plate boundaries along Asia's east coast and Australia does not have land near the tectonic boundaries
4. **CRITICAL THINKING** Pacific Ocean

The surface of Earth has changed greatly over time. Some changes come from internal forces associated with plate tectonics.

Step Into the Place

MAP FOCUS Use the map to answer the following questions.

1 **PHYSICAL GEOGRAPHY**
Where are most of the world's volcanoes located?

2 **PHYSICAL GEOGRAPHY**
Are earthquakes more common in Africa or South America?

3 **PHYSICAL GEOGRAPHY**
Where do you think an earthquake is more likely to occur—along Australia's southern coast or Asia's east coast? Why? **V**

4 **CRITICAL THINKING**
Integrating Visual Information Are volcanoes and earthquakes more common in the Atlantic Ocean or the Pacific Ocean?

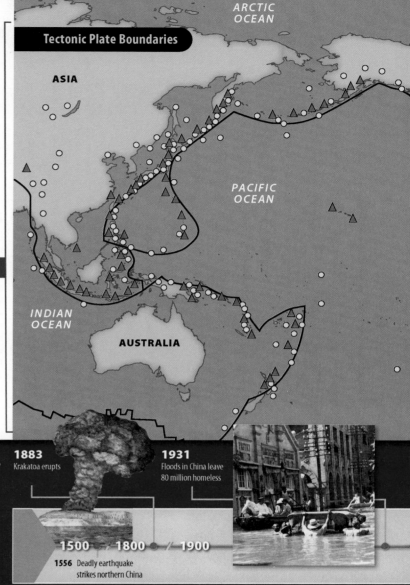

Tectonic Plate Boundaries

ARCTIC OCEAN

ASIA

PACIFIC OCEAN

INDIAN OCEAN

AUSTRALIA

Step Into the Time

DRAWING EVIDENCE Choose one event from the time line and use it to explain how the natural forces that shape the physical geography of a particular place can have a worldwide impact.
WHST.6-8.2, WHST.6-8.4

1883 Krakatoa erupts

1931 Floods in China leave 80 million homeless

1500   1800   1900

1556 Deadly earthquake strikes northern China

Project-Based Learning ✋

Hands-On

Making a Map of Forces

Students will work in groups to create large wall maps of Earth. Then students will use construction paper to create symbols that represent Earth's physical forces: volcanoes, hurricanes, cyclones, earthquakes, tsunamis, droughts, and tornadoes. Have students ask fact-based questions about these forces and where they have taken place in the past or recently. Once a student answers the question correctly, he or she can post the cut-out symbol where this event occurred on the map.

Digital Hands-On

Making a Physical Features Map

Pairs will use an online map-making program to create a map of different physical features of Earth that includes the absolute locations of the features and an embedded photo, video, or description of them. Pairs will present their maps to the class and then post them on a class Web site or wiki.

edtechteacher
21st Century Learning

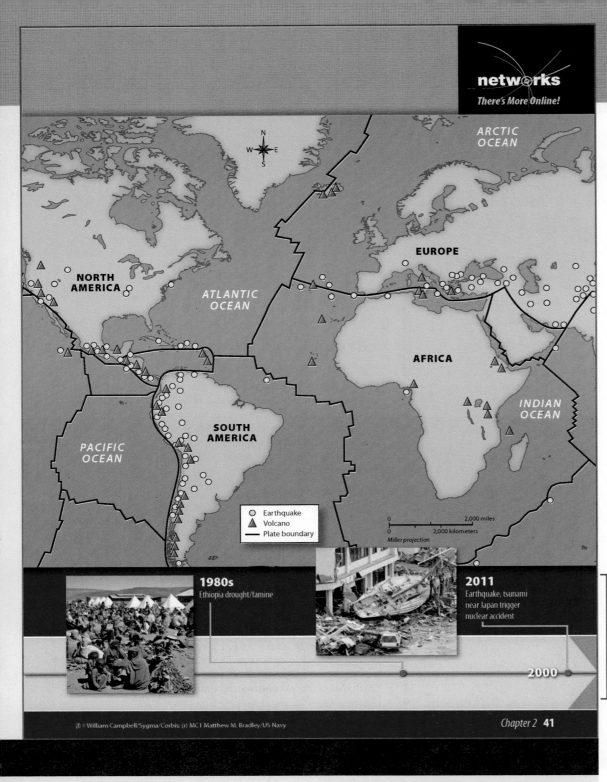

NORTH AMERICA

ARCTIC OCEAN

ATLANTIC OCEAN

EUROPE

AFRICA

SOUTH AMERICA

PACIFIC OCEAN

INDIAN OCEAN

○ Earthquake
△ Volcano
— Plate boundary

2,000 miles
2,000 kilometers
Miller projection

1980s
Ethiopia drought/famine

2011
Earthquake, tsunami near Japan trigger nuclear accident

2000

(l) © William Campbell/Sygma/Corbis; (r) MC1 Matthew M. Bradley/US Navy

Chapter 2 **41**

Step Into the Time

V **Visual Skills**

Integrating Visual Information Use the following questions to guide students in a discussion of the map and the events in the time line. **Ask:**

- **How might the earthquake and tsunami in Japan be related to plate tectonics?** *(Japan is located near a plate boundary where earthquakes occur.)*
- **Why is it not surprising that major earthquakes have occurred in China and Japan?** *(These two countries are near particularly active plate boundaries where many earthquakes and volcanic eruptions occur.)*
- **Consider the events shown for 1931 and the 1980s. What can you infer about the balance of nature?** *(Possible responses: People can be harmed by either too much or too little water—we need a balance. Natural forces can affect us in many different ways all around the globe.)* **AL** **Visual/ Spatial**

Content Background Knowledge

- Earth's crust has seven major plates which are subdivided into smaller plates.
- These plates are in continual motion, moving from 10 to 130 millimeters in a year.
- At their boundaries, the crustal plates either collide or pull apart.
- Plate tectonics explains why most earthquakes, volcanoes, and mountain ranges are located in narrow zones. These zones coincide with plate boundaries.

V

CLOSE & REFLECT

Predicting Consequences Have students find your community's location on the map and predict the likelihood of earthquakes and/or volcanic eruptions in your area. Discuss the kinds of natural forces that most affect your area and how students can stay safe during natural disasters.

TIME LINE

Reading a Time Line and Map

Analyzing Visuals Display the time line and map on the whiteboard. Have volunteers read each event as it is revealed on the time line. Ask students to identify where in the world the event took place and find its location on the map. **Visual/Spatial**

See page 39B for other online activities.

ENGAGE

Bellringer Introduce the lesson by having students skim the lesson headings in their book to preview the lesson content, which focuses on how Earth functions in the solar system, its structure, and its seasons and climates. Help students relate this content to the Essential Question: *How does geography influence the way people live?* Note that seasonal and climatic differences around the world greatly affect people's outdoor time and activities.

Have students suggest outdoor jobs that are impacted by the seasons in your area. Make a list of these on the board. Then make another list of recreational outdoor activites that are impacted by the seasons.

TEACH & ASSESS

V Visual Skills

Drawing Help students develop a map of Earth's place in the solar system by asking them to draw a map of the solar system, labeling the sun and Earth. Note that Earth is the third planet from the sun. Call on a volunteer to share and explain his or her drawing. **AL ELL** Visual/Spatial

C Critical Thinking Skills

Recognizing Relationships Emphasize the importance of the sun as the source of *all* the energy that plants and animals need to survive. Have students use what they already know about how plants and animals interact to consider the importance of the Sun. **Ask:**

- How does the sun provide energy for plants? *(Plants absorb sunlight and convert it into food, from which they get energy. Students may simply say that the Sun enables plants to perform photosynthesis, which gives them energy.)*
- How does the sun provide energy for animals, including human beings? *(Animals depend on plants and other animals for food, from which they get energy. Since plants get their energy from the sun, animals that eat plants or other animals get their energy indirectly from the sun.)*
  BL Naturalist

ANSWERS, p. 42

Taking Notes Answers could include: **Hydrosphere**—all bodies of water; **Lithosphere**—Earth's crust, including land beneath oceans; **Atmosphere**—layer of gases above Earth's surface; **Biosphere**—all living organisms on or near Earth's surface.

---

networks

There's More Online!

☑ **CHART** Climate Zones

☑ **ANIMATION** Earth's Daily Rotation

☑ **IMAGES** Seasons on Earth

☑ **MAP** Rain Shadow

☑ **SLIDE SHOW** Effects of Climate Change

☑ **VIDEO**

Reading **HELP**DESK **CCSS**

Academic Vocabulary RH.6-8.4

- **accurate** *(Tier Two Words)*

Content Vocabulary RH.6-8.4

(Tier Three Words)
- **orbit**
- **axis**
- **revolution**
- **atmosphere**
- **solstice**
- **equinox**
- **climate**
- **precipitation**
- **rain shadow**

TAKING NOTES: *Key Ideas and Details* RH.6-8.2, RH.6-8.7

Summarize As you read, complete a graphic organizer about Earth's physical system.

Element	Description
Hydrosphere	
Lithosphere	
Atmosphere	
Biosphere	

42

Lesson 1
The Earth-Sun Relationship

ESSENTIAL QUESTION · *How does geography influence the way people live?*

IT MATTERS BECAUSE
The processes that change Earth can act slowly or quickly with great fury.

Earth's Structure

GUIDING QUESTION *What is the structure of Earth?*

Earth is one of eight major planets that follow their own paths around the sun. The sun is just one of hundreds of millions of stars in our galaxy. Because the sun is so large, its gravity causes the planets to constantly **orbit**, or move around, it. The sun is the center of the solar system in which we live. Earth is a member of the solar system—planets and the other bodies that revolve around our sun.

Earth and the Sun

Life on Earth could not exist without heat and light from the sun. Earth's orbit holds it close enough to the sun—about 93 million miles (150 million km)—to receive a constant supply of light and heat energy. The sun, in fact, is the source of all energy on Earth. Every plant and animal on the planet needs the sun's energy to survive. Without the sun, Earth would be a cold, dark, lifeless rock floating in space.

As Earth orbits the sun, it rotates, or spins, on its axis. The **axis** is an imaginary line that runs through Earth's center from the North Pole to the South Pole. Earth completes one rotation every 24 hours. As Earth rotates, different areas are in sunlight and in darkness. The part facing toward the sun experiences daylight, while the part facing away has night. Earth makes one **revolution**, or complete trip around the sun,

(l to r) NASA/NOAA; Martin Pudd/Stone/Getty Images; Ariadne Van Zandbergen/Lonely Planet Images/Getty Images; Scott Warren/Aurora/Getty Images

---

networks *Online Teaching Options*

VIDEO

How Mountains Form

Analyzing Images Use this video to introduce the idea that Earth is made up of layers and plates and that those plates are constantly moving, changing the physical geography of Earth. After watching the video, have pairs of students analyze the main ideas and write three questions they have about the content. Collect the questions and discuss them as a class. **Interpersonal**

See page 39C for other online activities.

BBC Motion Gallery Education

in 365¼ days. This is what we define as one year. Every four years, the extra fourths of a day are combined and added to the calendar as February 29th. A year that contains one of these extra days is called a leap year.

Inside Earth

Thousands of miles beneath your feet, Earth's heat has turned metal into liquid. You do not feel these forces, but what lies inside affects what lies on top. Mountains, deserts, and other landscapes were formed over time by forces acting below Earth's surface—and those forces are still changing the landscape.

If you cut an onion in half, you will see that it is made up of many layers. Earth is also made up of layers. Earth's layers are made up of many different materials.

Layers of Earth

The inside of Earth is made up of three layers: the core, the mantle, and the crust. The center of Earth—the core—is divided into a solid inner core and an outer core of melted, liquid metal. Surrounding the outer core is a thick layer of hot, dense rock called the mantle. Scientists calculate that the mantle is about 1,800 miles (2,897 km) thick. The mantle also has two parts. When volcanoes erupt, the glowing-hot lava that flows from the mouth of the volcano is magma from Earth's outer mantle. Magma is melted rock. The inner mantle is solid, like the inner core. The outer layer is the crust, a rocky shell that forms the surface of Earth. The crust is thin, ranging from about 2 miles (3.2 km) thick under oceans to about 75 miles (121 km) thick under mountains.

C

DIAGRAM SKILLS ›

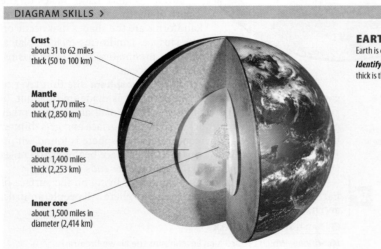

Crust
about 31 to 62 miles thick (50 to 100 km)

Mantle
about 1,770 miles thick (2,850 km)

Outer core
about 1,400 miles thick (2,253 km)

Inner core
about 1,500 miles in diameter (2,414 km)

EARTH
Earth is composed of several layers.

Identifying About how many miles thick is the crust under oceans?

V

C Critical Thinking Skills

Drawing Conclusions Note that Earth's outer core consists of melted rock and that the mantle also contains magma, or melted rock. **Ask:**

- **What can you deduce about the temperature below Earth's crust?** *(It is very hot—hot enough to melt rock.)*
- **What happens to magma after it erupts on Earth's surface?** *(It cools and solidifies.)*
- **How does the new rock that cools on Earth's surface affect Earth's crust?** *(It can build new islands in the ocean such as the Hawaiian Islands or build the height of the volcano it erupted from.)*
- **What can you deduce about the temperature on Earth's surface as compared to the temperature deep within Earth?** *(It is much cooler on Earth's surface than it is deep within Earth.)* **Logical/Mathematical**

V Visual Skills

Simulating Have students think about how they could build a scaled model of Earth's layers using the diagram shown on the page. Students should consider what types of building materials they could use, such as those that would enable them to show the cross-section or materials that could be taken apart to show the inner layers. Students might use some type of clay that could harden and then cut into it. Have students then tell what ratio they would use to relate their model to the actual layers of Earth and how large each layer would be based on that ratio. **Visual/Spatial, Logical/Mathematical**

Content Background Knowledge

Since Earth's interior cannot be observed directly, much of the information about its structure comes from analyzing earthquake waves, from laboratory experiments on rocks and minerals, from studies of Earth's movement within the solar system, and from studies of gravity, magnetic fields, and heat flow. Scientists are continually adding to and refining their knowledge of Earth's structure as new technologies make new data available.

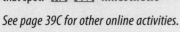

Earth's Daily Rotation

Making Connections After students view the animation, ask a pair of volunteers to dramatize the daily rotation of Earth, using two balls or other round objects to represent the sun and Earth. Mark a large dot on "Earth," and have students identify when it is day and when it is night at that spot. **AL ELL Kinesthetic**

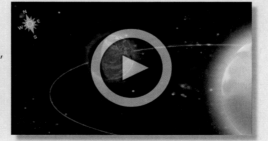

See page 39C for other online activities.

ANSWER, p. 43

Identifying 2 miles (3.2 km)

The Earth-Sun Relationship

R Reading Skills

Using Context Clues Have students read the sentence in which the vocabulary word *accurate* appears, as well as the sentences before and after it. **Ask:**

- Based on the way the word is used, what does *accurate* mean? *(realistic, correct)*
- Can you use the word in another sentence? *(Sample answer: My watch does not keep accurate time.)* **ELL** Verbal/ Linguistic

V Visual Skills

Drawing Have students draw symbols to represent the four physical systems. For example, students might draw a drop of water for hydrosphere, a wavy line for atmosphere, a rock for lithosphere, and a leaf for biosphere. Have volunteers share their symbols and explain why each symbol is appropriate for the physical system it represents. **AL ELL** Visual/Spatial

C Critical Thinking Skills

Synthesizing Explain that the four physical systems are useful concepts for studying and thinking about Earth, but that these four systems are interdependent, not separate. Give students a few minutes to jot down all the interconnections they can think of. Students might note, for example, that the atmosphere contains water vapor, soil contains water, people breathe in air from the atmosphere, and so on. While this activity is appropriate for all levels of students, you might expect advanced students to generate more examples. **Logical/ Mathematical**

W Writing Skills

Informative/Explanatory Have students write a paragraph in which they trace a drop of water as it moves through the hydrosphere, atmosphere, lithosphere, and biosphere. Have students who are struggling work together to draw a diagram that shows the movement of the drop of water through the four physical systems, and then write their paragraphs based on their drawing. Have pairs of students exchange their paragraphs and check the movement described against the diagram they have drawn. Encourage partners to make positive comments about each other's writing and to make constructive criticism if revision is needed. **Verbal/Linguistic, Visual/Spatial**

ANSWERS, p. 44

CRITICAL THINKING Possible response: People and many animals live on land and need water to survive.
☑ **READING PROGRESS CHECK** atmosphere

Academic Vocabulary

accurate correct

R

The deepest hole ever drilled into Earth is about 8 miles (13 km) deep. That is still within Earth's crust. The farthest any human has traveled down into Earth's crust is about 2.5 miles (4 km). Still, scientists have developed an **accurate** picture of the layers in Earth's structure. One important way that scientists do this is by studying vibrations from deep within Earth. The vibrations are caused by earthquakes and explosions underground. From their observations, scientists have learned what materials are inside Earth and estimated the thickness and temperature of Earth's layers.

Earth's Physical Systems

There are powerful processes that operate below Earth's surface. Processes are also at work in the physical systems on the surface of Earth. Earth's physical systems consist of four major subsystems: the hydrosphere, the lithosphere, the atmosphere, and the biosphere.

V

C

About 70 percent of the earth's surface is water. The hydrosphere is the subsystem that consists of Earth's water. Water is found in many places: oceans, seas, lakes, ponds, rivers, groundwater, and ice.

Only about 30 percent of Earth's surface is land. Land makes up the part of Earth called the lithosphere. Landforms are the shapes that occur on Earth's surface. Landforms include plains, hills, plateaus, mountains, and ocean basins, the land beneath the ocean.

The air we breathe is part of the **atmosphere**, the thin layer of gases that envelop Earth. The atmosphere is made up of about 78 percent nitrogen, 21 percent oxygen, and small amounts of other gases. The atmosphere is thickest at Earth's surface and gets thinner higher up. Ninety-eight percent of the atmosphere is found within 16 miles (26 km) of Earth's surface. Outer space begins at 100 miles (161 km) above Earth, where the atmosphere ends.

W

The biosphere is made up of all that is living on the surface of Earth, close to the surface, or in the atmosphere. All people, animals, and plants live in the biosphere.

☑ **READING PROGRESS CHECK**

Identifying Which of Earth's layers contains the air we breathe?

Earth's surface is a complex mix of landforms and water systems.
▶ **CRITICAL THINKING**
Analyzing How do Earth's landforms and water systems help support life on our planet?

NASA/NOAA

44 Chapter 2

---

net**w**◉**rks** *Online Teaching Options*

Earth's Layers

Writing Captions After students view the animation, have them add new information they learned to their own drawings of Earth's layers. They might include this information in the form of a caption for each labeled layer of Earth. **Verbal/Linguistic**

See page 39C for other online activities.

Earth's Seasons

GUIDING QUESTION *How does Earth's orbit around the sun cause the seasons?*

Produce such as lettuce, grapes, and apples cannot grow when the weather is cold and icy. Yet grocery stores across America sell these ripe, colorful fruits all year, even in the middle of winter. Where is it warm enough to grow fruit in January? To find the answer, we start with the tilt of Earth.

Earth is tilted 23.5 degrees on its axis. If you look at a globe that is attached to a stand, you will see what the tilt looks like. Because of the tilt, not all places on Earth receive the same amount of direct sunlight at the same time.

As Earth orbits the sun, it stays in its tilted position. This means that one-half of the planet is always tilted toward the sun, while the other half is tilted away. As a result, Earth's Northern and Southern Hemispheres experience seasons at different times.

On about June 21, the North Pole is tilted toward the sun. The Northern Hemisphere is receiving the direct rays of the sun. The sun appears directly overhead at the line of latitude called the Tropic of Cancer. This day is the summer **solstice**, or beginning of summer, in the Northern Hemisphere. It is the day of the year that has the most hours of sunlight during Earth's 24-hour rotation.

Six months later—about December 22—the North Pole is tilted away from the sun. The sun's direct rays strike the line of latitude known as the Tropic of Capricorn. This is the winter solstice—when winter occurs in the Northern Hemisphere and summer begins in the Southern Hemisphere. The days are short in the Northern Hemisphere but long in the Southern Hemisphere.

R

DIAGRAM SKILLS >

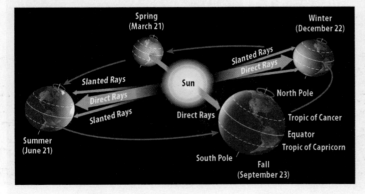

Spring (March 21)

Winter (December 22)

Slanted Rays

Direct Rays

Slanted Rays

Sun

Direct Rays

North Pole

Slanted Rays

Direct Rays

Tropic of Cancer

Summer (June 21)

Equator

Tropic of Capricorn

South Pole

Fall (September 23)

SEASONS
The tilt of Earth as it revolves around the sun causes the seasons to change.

▶ **CRITICAL THINKING**
Analyzing When does the Southern Hemisphere receive direct rays from the sun?

Chapter 2 **45**

R Reading Skills

Determining Word Meanings Explain to the students that the *solstices* and the *equinoxes* mark the beginnings of the seasons. The longest day of the year is the summer solstice, when summer begins. The shortest day of the year is the winter solstice, when winter begins. During a solstice, the sun is at its greatest distance from the celestial equator.

The equinoxes mark the beginning of spring and fall, when day and night are of equal length. During an equinox, the sun is directly above the celestial equator. You might point out the dates of the solstices and equinoxes on a calendar.

Finally, point out that the Latin root *sol-* in the word *solstice* means "sun," while the root *equi-* comes from a Latin word meaning "equal." **AL** **ELL** **Verbal/Linguistic**

V Visual Skills

Simulating Have students demonstrate the tilted position of Earth as it orbits the sun using a globe and a large ball to represent the sun. Have one student hold the sun, and another student hold the globe tilted at about a 25° angle. Then tell the student holding the sun to stay still while the student holding the globe revolves around the sun making sure that the tilt of the globe remains the same throughout the orbit. Encourage students to use the diagram at the bottom of the page as a guide to the simulation. **Ask:**

- **During summer, how is the Northern Hemisphere tilted?** *(toward the sun)*
- **What season is it in the Southern Hemisphere then? Why?** *(winter, because the Southern Hemisphere is tilted away from the sun)*
- **During winter, how is the Northern Hemisphere tilted?** *(away from the sun)*
- **What season is it in the Southern Hemisphere then? Why?** *(summer, because the Southern Hemisphere is tilted toward the sun)* **Kinesthetic**

V

ANIMATION

Seasons on Earth

Applying Information Have students view the animation showing why the seasons differ in the Northern and Southern hemispheres. Then quiz students by naming a few countries in both hemispheres and on different continents, asking what season it is in each location. **Visual/Spatial**

See page 39C for other online activities.

ANSWER, p. 45

CRITICAL THINKING about December 22

Defining The difference between the content vocabulary words *weather* and *climate* is discussed later in this section of the student textbook, but you might explain to students here that the word *climate* refers to the average weather in a particular area over a long period of time. For example, the weather in both Minneapolis, MN and Houston, TX might be cool and rainy on a particular day, but the two cities have very different climates. Houston is generally warm or hot all year round, while Minneapolis has long, cold winters and warm summers. **AL** **ELL** **Verbal/Linguistic**

V Visual Skills

Integrating Visual Information Use a world map or globe to show students the location of the tropics. Emphasize that the tropics receive direct sunlight year-round and so are always hot. Explain how *latitude*—distance north or south of the Equator—affects climate. In general, as you move farther north or south of the tropics, the climate becomes progressively cooler.

To check students' understanding of how latitude affects climate, point to various locations on a world map or globe and ask students to predict features of the area's climate based on its latitude. Have students record their predictions and use them for the following activity. **Visual/Spatial**

T Technology Skills

Researching on the Internet Direct students to use the Internet to check their predictions about the climate of different areas based on latitude. Call on volunteers to share what their predictions were and what they discovered from their research. Have students speculate on why some of their predictions might have been inaccurate. Some students may be aware that elevation, proximity to the ocean, and other factors also influence climate. **Logical/Mathematical**

ANSWERS, p. 46

☑ **READING PROGRESS CHECK** During the solstices, the amount of sunlight varies depending on which hemisphere is tilted toward the sun. During the equinoxes, the amount of daylight and nighttime is equal in both hemispheres.

CRITICAL THINKING Low-latitude areas have a hotter climate because they receive more direct sunlight than high-latitude areas.

Midway between the two solstices, about September 23 and March 21, the sun's rays are directly overhead at the Equator. These are **equinoxes**, when day and night in both hemispheres are of equal length—12 hours of daylight and 12 hours of nighttime everywhere on Earth.

☑ **READING PROGRESS CHECK**

Identifying What is the difference between the solstices and the equinoxes?

R Elements Affecting Climate

GUIDING QUESTION *How do elevation, wind and ocean currents, weather, and landforms influence climate?*

V During the entire year, the sun's direct rays strike the low latitudes near the Equator. This area, known as the Tropics, lies mainly between the Tropic of Cancer and the Tropic of Capricorn. The Tropics circle the globe like a belt. If you lived in the Tropics, you would experience hot, sunny weather most of the year because of the direct sunlight. Outside the Tropics, the sun is never directly overhead. Even when these high-latitude areas are tilted toward the sun, the sun's rays hit Earth indirectly at a slant. This means that no direct sunlight shines on the high-latitude regions around the North and South Poles for as much as six months each year. Thus, the climate in these regions is always cool or cold.

Water swirls down the street of a small town in India after heavy rains.
▶ **CRITICAL THINKING**
Analyzing Why is the climate in low-latitude areas different from the climate in high-latitude areas?

Martin Pudd/Stone/Getty Images

46 – Chapter 2

networks *Online Teaching Options*

MAP

World Climates

Reading a Map Display the climate layer of the Chapter Opener map to introduce students briefly to the variety of climates around the world. Have students write a few sentences describing the climate of the region in which you live or a place they have visited. **Verbal/Linguistic**

See page 39C for other online activities.

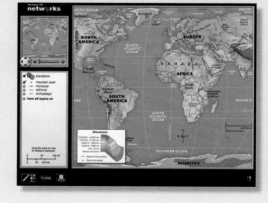

Wind Patterns

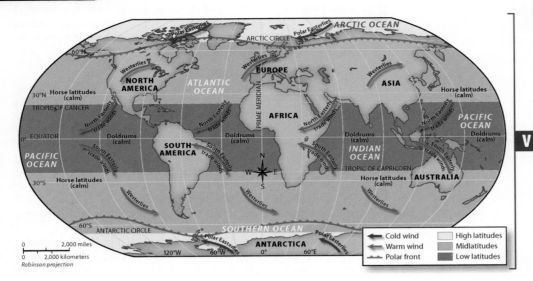

2,000 miles
2,000 kilometers
Robinson projection

Cold wind
Warm wind
Polar front

High latitudes
Midlatitudes
Low latitudes

Elevation and Climate

At all latitudes, elevation influences climate. This is because Earth's atmosphere thins as altitude increases. Thinner air retains less heat. As elevation increases, temperatures decrease by about 3.5°F (1.9°C) for every 1,000 feet (305 m). For example, if the temperature averages 70°F (21.1°C) at sea level, the average temperature at 5,000 feet (1,524 m) is only 53°F (11.7°C). A high elevation will be colder than lower elevations at the same latitude.

Wind and Ocean Currents

In addition to latitude and elevation, the movement of air and water helps create Earth's climates. Moving air and water help circulate the sun's heat around the globe.

Movements of air are called winds. Winds are the result of changes in air pressure caused by uneven heating of Earth's surface. Winds follow prevailing, or typical, patterns. Warmer, low-pressure air rises higher into the atmosphere. Winds are created as air is drawn across the surface of Earth toward the low-pressure areas. The Equator is constantly warmed by the sun, so warm air masses tend to form near the Equator. This warm, low-pressure air rises, and then cooler, high-pressure air rushes in under the warm air, causing wind. This helps balance Earth's temperature.

Chapter 2 **47**

MAP SKILLS

1 **PHYSICAL GEOGRAPHY** In what general direction does the wind pattern sometimes blow over Asia?

2 **PHYSICAL GEOGRAPHY** What air currents flow over the low latitudes?

CHART

Temperature and Precipitation Affect Biomes

Analyzing Use the chart of biomes in relation to climate and temperature to discuss how climate affects the environment of various areas based on elevation. Invite students who have lived or visited other regions of the world to discuss how that region fits into the chart.
Interpersonal

See page 39C for other online activities.

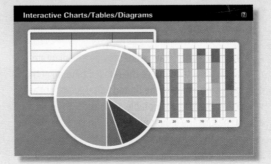

Interactive Charts/Tables/Diagrams

V Visual Skills

Reading Maps Have students examine the wind patterns map and study the legend, noting that warm and cold winds are indicated by different colors. Explain that winds are named for the direction *from* which they blow, so the westerlies, for instance, blow from west to east. The map shows the *prevailing*, or most dominant, winds. **Ask:**

- **Where do warm winds originate?** *(in the low latitudes and midlatitudes)*
- **Where do cold winds originate?** *(near the poles)*
- **How do the prevailing winds over North America, Europe, and Asia differ from those over South America, Africa, and Australia?** *(The prevailing winds over North America, Europe, and Asia are westerlies, while those over South America, Africa, and Australia are easterlies.)* **AL** **Visual/ Spatial**

T Technology Skills

Using Digital Tools Have students use calculators to apply the information about elevation and climate to the following:

A climber is at 5,500 feet, where the temperature is 55°F. She climbs to 9,500 feet. The temperature decreases 3.5° for every 1,000 feet of ascent. What is the temperature at this altitude? *(She ascends 4,000 feet. With the temperature decreasing 3.5°F for every 1,000 feet, the temperature would be 3.5°F x 4, or 14°F, less. 55°F − 14°F = 41°F. The answer is 41°F.)* **Logical/ Mathematical**

C Critical Thinking Skills

Transferring Knowledge Draw students' attention to the poles on the map and note that cold air currents flow generally away from the poles, while the warm westerlies flow generally toward the poles. Emphasize that the effect of these wind patterns is to circulate the sun's heat. Then help students connect the information about warm air rising to their own experience. **Ask: In a two-story home, which floor tends to be warmer? Why?** *(the upper floor; because warm air rises)*

Students might logically raise the question: **If warm air rises, why is it cooler at higher elevations?** Challenge students to find the answer to this puzzle on the Internet. *(At higher elevations, the air is thin. So warm, rising air expands in these low-pressure conditions. As air expands, it cools. In addition, at high altitudes, more heat escapes into space.)* **Logical/ Mathematical**

ANSWERS, p. 47

MAP SKILLS
1. from southwest to northeast
2. northeasterly trade winds and southeasterly trade winds

R Reading Skills

Summarizing Use the following questions to help students summarize the information in the text about ocean currents.
Ask:

• **What pattern occurs in ocean currents?** *(Warm water moves away from the Equator to higher latitudes, and cold water moves from the poles toward the Equator.)*

• **What is the effect of this pattern?** *(It helps to balance the temperature of the planet.)*

• **How is this pattern like that of wind currents?** *(Both help to circulate heat and balance the planet's temperature.)* **Verbal/Linguistic**

W Writing Skills

Making Connections Emphasize that temperature and precipitation are two major components of both weather and climate. Have students demonstrate their understanding of the difference between weather and climate by writing a paragraph describing the weather in your area today and another describing the climate of your area. Call on volunteers to read their paragraphs aloud.

V Visual Skills

Reading a Diagram Assess students' understanding of the Rain Shadow diagram by discussing the Critical Thinking questions as well as the following ones. **Ask:**

• **Which side of the mountain receives a lot of rainfall?** *(the side facing the ocean)*

• **Which side of the mountain receives little rainfall?** *(the side facing away from the ocean)*

• **How does the vegetation on the two sides of the mountain reflect the amount of rainfall received?** *(The plentiful rainfall on the ocean side generally results in forests, while the lack of rainfall on the other side can produce a desert.)* **Visual/Spatial**

R Just as winds move in patterns, cold and warm streams of water, known as currents, circulate through the oceans. Warm water moves away from the Equator, transferring heat energy from the equatorial region to higher latitudes. Cold water from the polar regions moves toward the Equator, also helping to balance the temperature of the planet.

Weather and Climate

Weather is the state of the atmosphere at a given time, such as during a week, a day, or an afternoon. Weather refers to conditions such as hot or cold, wet or dry, calm or stormy, or cloudy or clear. Weather is what you can observe any time by going outside or looking out a window. **Climate** is the average weather conditions in a region or an area over a longer period. One useful measure for comparing climates is the average daily temperature. This is the average of the highest and lowest temperatures that occur in a 24-hour period. In addition to the average temperature, climate includes typical wind conditions and rainfall or snowfall that occur in an area year after year.

Rainfall and snowfall are types of precipitation. **Precipitation** is water deposited on the earth in the form of rain, snow, hail, sleet, or mist. Measuring the amount of precipitation in an area for one day provides data about the area's weather. Measuring the amount of precipitation for one full year provides data about the area's climate.

Landforms

It might seem strange to think that landforms such as mountains can affect weather and climate, but landforms and landmasses change the strength, speed, and direction of wind and ocean

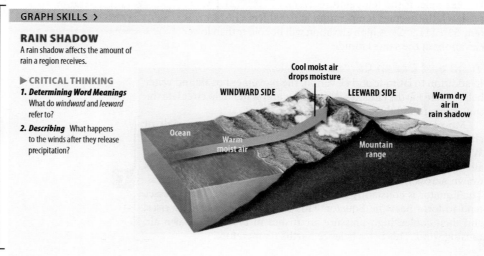

GRAPH SKILLS ›

RAIN SHADOW
A rain shadow affects the amount of rain a region receives.

▶ **CRITICAL THINKING**
1. *Determining Word Meanings* What do *windward* and *leeward* refer to?

2. *Describing* What happens to the winds after they release precipitation?

Cool moist air drops moisture
WINDWARD SIDE   LEEWARD SIDE
Warm dry air in rain shadow
Ocean   Warm moist air   Mountain range

48 *Chapter 2*

---

net**w**rks   *Online Teaching Options*

DIAGRAM

Rain Shadow

Analyzing Visuals Have students view the diagram of a rain shadow to reinforce their understanding of this concept. Using a map of the United States, point out areas where rain shadows are notable, such as the dry areas east of the Cascade Mountains in Washington and Oregon and east of the Coast Ranges in California. Challenge students to explain how rain shadow is a fitting name for this effect. *(Just as an object casts a shadow by blocking sunlight, a mountain casts a rain shadow by blocking rain.)* **Logical/Mathematical**

See page 39C for other online activities.

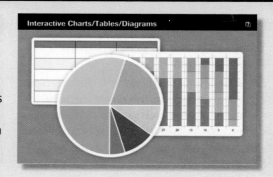

Interactive Charts/Tables/Diagrams

ANSWERS, p. 48

DIAGRAM SKILLS

CRITICAL THINKING

1. *Windward* is the direction from which the wind blows; *leeward* is the direction toward which the wind blows.

2. They become warmer and drier.

currents. Wind and ocean currents carry heat and precipitation, which shape weather and climate. The sun warms the land and the surface of the world's oceans at different rates, causing differences in air pressure. As winds blow inland from the oceans, they carry moist air with them. As the land rises in elevation, the atmosphere cools. When masses of moist air approach mountains, the air rises and cools, causing rain to fall on the side of the mountain facing the ocean. The other side of the mountain receives little rain because of the rain shadow effect. A **rain shadow** is a region of reduced rainfall on one side of a high mountain; the rain shadow occurs on the side of the mountain facing away from the ocean.

The climate in a zone affects how people live and work.
▶ **CRITICAL THINKING**
Identifying Point of View In which climate zone would people be more likely to live: polar or humid temperate? Why?

☑ **READING PROGRESS CHECK**

Identifying What measures are used to compare climates in different areas?

A Variety of Climate Zones

GUIDING QUESTION *What are the characteristics of Earth's climate zones?*

Why do so many people visit Florida and California? These places have cold or stormy weather at times, but their climates are generally warm, sunny, and mild. People in these states can enjoy activities outdoors all year long.

The Zones
In 1900 German scientist Wladimir Köppen invented a system that divides Earth into five basic climate zones. Climate zones are regions of Earth classified by temperature, precipitation, and distance from the Equator. Köppen used names and capital letters to label the climate zones as follows: Tropical (A); Desert (B); Humid Temperate (C); Cold Temperate (D); and Polar (E). Years later, a sixth climate zone was added: High Mountain (F).

Chapter 2 **49**

C Critical Thinking Skills

Reasoning Suggest that students apply the Essential Question: *How does geography influence the way people live?*, to extend their understanding of the rain shadow effect. **Ask:**

- On which side of a mountain would a person most need a raincoat? *(the side facing the ocean)*
- On which side of a mountain might logging be an important industry? *(the side facing the ocean)*
- On which side of a mountain might farmers need to rely on irrigation? *(the side facing away from the ocean)*
- On which side of a mountain would landslides more likely be a problem? *(the side facing the ocean)*
- On which side of a mountain would snow skiing more likely be better? *(the side facing the ocean)* **AL** **Logical/ Mathematical**

V Visual Skills

Transferring Knowledge After students read the information about climate zones, call on volunteers to apply the information to the photographs at the top of the page. **Ask:**

- In what climate zone are the people with the camel? How do you know? *(Desert; because the land is sandy, which means it is dry)*
- In what climate zone are the people with the buckets? How do you know? *(Cold Temperate; because it is snowing and the map shows the region is not far enough north to be polar)* **Visual/Spatial**

T Technology Skills

Researching on the Internet Have students use the Internet to research the climate of a place they would like to visit in the Eastern Hemisphere. Have them find the climate zone of the place and the average temperature and precipitation at the time of year they would most likely go. **Logical/ Mathematical**

CHART

Climate Zones

Identifying After students view the chart on climate zones, have them identify the climate zone in which they live. Then name some other familiar places and ask students to identify the climate zones. **Visual/Spatial**

See page 39C for other online activities.

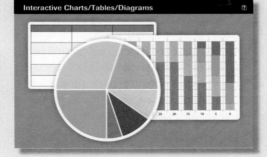
Interactive Charts/Tables/Diagrams

ANSWERS, p. 49

CRITICAL THINKING humid temperate, because food can be grown in that climate
☑ **READING PROGRESS CHECK** average daily temperature, wind conditions, and rainfall or snowfall year after year

V Visual Skills

Creating Charts Pair students and have them create a three-column chart of the six climate zones (tropical, desert, humid temperate, cold temperate, polar, and high mountain) with these three headings: *Climate Zone, Characteristics, Examples.* Students can use the text to list the six climate zones in the first column and their characteristics in the second column. Under Examples in the third column, they should identify three places within each climate zone.

Climate Zones	Characteristics	Examples

Call on volunteers to share the names of places that have each type of climate and identify a factor that influences the climate in the place, such as latitude or elevation. **AL**
ELL Visual/Spatial, Interpersonal

C Critical Thinking Skills

Giving Examples To help students understand the relationship between climate zones and biomes, emphasize that the plants and animals within a certain climate zone form a biome.

Write the biomes listed in the text on the board: *rain forest, desert, grassland, tundra.* Discuss major features of the climate of each biome, and call on volunteers to name some plants or animals that live in each. If students are unable to give examples, direct them to check on the Internet. **BL**
Naturalist

V Each climate zone also can be divided into smaller subzones, but the areas within each zone have many similarities. Tropical areas are hot and rainy and often have dense forests. Desert areas are always dry, but they can be cold or hot, depending on their latitude. Humid temperate areas experience all types of weather with changing seasons. Cold temperate climates have a short summer season but are generally cold and windy. Polar climates are very cold, with ice and snow covering the ground most of the year. High mountain climates are found only at the tops of high mountain ranges such as the Rockies, the Alps, and the Himalaya. High mountain climates have variable conditions because the atmosphere cools with increasing elevation. Some of the highest mountaintops are cold and windy and stay white with snow all year.

Different types of plants grow best in different climates, so each climate zone has its own unique types of vegetation and animal life. **C** These unique combinations form ecosystems of plants and animals that are adapted to environments within the climate zone. A biome is a type of large ecosystem with similar life-forms and climates. Earth's biomes include rain forest, desert, grassland, and tundra. All life is adapted to survive in its native climate zone and biome.

A bull moose stands alert on a tundra field in Alaska. Animals that live in that environment have unique adaptations that help them survive.

©Kennan Ward/Corbis

networks   *Online Teaching Options*

SLIDE SHOW

Effects of Climate Change

Determining Cause and Effect Use the slide show to reinforce students' understanding of global warming and its effects. Encourage students to create a graphic organizer on global warming, identifying its causes, effects, and possible solutions. **Verbal/Linguistic**

See page 39C for other online activities.

Slide Show

(l) ©Ocean/Corbis, ©Kryssia Campos/Getty Images, (tr) ©Erica Simone Leeds, (br) ©JG Photography/Alamy

Changes to Climate

Many scientists believe climates are changing around the world. If this is true, the world could experience new weather patterns. These changes might mean more extreme weather in some places and milder weather in others. Human activities can affect weather and climate. For example, people have cut down millions of square miles of forests in Asia and Africa. As a result, there are fewer trees available to trap and release moisture into the air. This creates a drier climate in the region.

Metal, asphalt, brick, and concrete surfaces in cities absorb a huge amount of heat from the sun. An enormous mass of warmer air builds up in and around the city, affecting local weather.

In recent years, scientists have become aware of a problem called global warming. Global warming is an increase in the average temperature of Earth's atmosphere. Many scientists believe that a buildup of chemical pollution is contributing to the increasing temperature of Earth's atmosphere.

If the temperature of the atmosphere continues to rise, all of Earth's climates could be affected. Changes in climate might alter many natural ecosystems. Another consequence of climate change is that the survival of some plant and animal species will be threatened. It is also likely to be expensive and difficult for humans to adapt to these changes.

✔ **READING PROGRESS CHECK**

Identifying Which climate zone experiences all types of weather with changing seasons?

cold   cool   warm   hot

A thermal image shows heat escaping from the roofs of buildings.
▶ **CRITICAL THINKING**
Analyzing How is it possible for larger cities to change local weather?

R

FOLDABLES
Study Organizer

Include this lesson's information in your Foldable®.

Cultura Science/Joseph Giacomin/Oxford Scientific/Getty Images

---

LESSON 1 REVIEW **CCSS**

Reviewing Vocabulary (Tier Three Words)
1. Explain the difference between the *revolution* and the rotation of Earth. RH.6-8.4

Answering the Guiding Questions
2. ***Describing*** Compare the layers of Earth to the layers of an orange. RH.6-8.1
3. ***Analyzing*** When South Africa is experiencing summer, what season is Central Asia having? RH.6-8.1

4. ***Determining Word Meanings*** Which side of a mountain experiences the rain shadow effect? RH.6-8.4
5. ***Describing*** What is the climate like in a large city like Hong Kong compared with the surrounding area? RH.6-8.5
6. ***Informative/Explanatory Writing*** Describe the climate of your area and the factors that contribute to it. WHST.6-8.2, WHST.6-8.4

Chapter 2 **51**

R **Reading Skills**

Summarizing Discuss with students the changes to climate that scientists say are occurring. Point out that the text gives three examples of how human activities have affected weather and climate. Use the following questions to help students summarize this information. **Ask:**

- **What is the effect of cutting down rain forests in Central and South America?** *(Fewer trees release moisture into the air, causing the region's climate to become drier.)*
- **What effect do metal, asphalt, and concrete surfaces in cities have on weather?** *(These surfaces absorb heat, making the air in and around cities warmer.)*
- **How do chemical pollutants in the air affect the global climate?** *(They contribute to an increase in the average temperature of Earth's atmosphere.)*
- **What is the overall effect of these human activities on climate?** *(They cause the climate to become hotter and drier.)*
- **What do you think people should do considering the effect of these human activities on climate?** *(Students' answers will vary, but should include suggestions such as planting more trees, reducing chemical pollutants, and reducing asphalt surfaces.)* **BL** **Verbal/Linguistic**

CLOSE & REFLECT

To close the lesson, remind students of Earth's uniqueness in the solar system. Have students summarize the physical features of Earth that make life possible on this planet, and compare these features to the other three rocky planets in the solar system.

Have students write a list of steps each of them could take throughout this school year to help preserve the planet. Encourage students to do research as necessary to create their lists. Then have small groups share their lists and exchange their ideas. Have the groups present the best ideas in a class discussion and make a class list that can be posted for future reference.

LESSON 1 REVIEW ANSWERS

Reviewing Vocabulary

1. *Rotation* is the turning of Earth on its axis. *Revolution* is when Earth circles the sun.

Answering the Guiding Questions

2. **Describing** The outer, bright-colored layer of an orange is like Earth's crust. The next layer is the white part of the orange's skin, and it is like Earth's magma and mantle. Below that is the juicy center of the orange, which is like Earth's core.

3. **Analyzing** Central Asia would be having their winter.

4. **Determining Word Meanings** The side of the mountain that is not facing the ocean experiences the rain shadow effect.

5. **Describing** Hong Kong may be warmer than the surrounding area because cities have asphalt and concrete that absorb the sun's heat and have fewer trees that would cool the air and release moisture.

6. **Informative/Explanatory Writing** Answers will vary but should mention proximity to water and mountains, and geographic location relative to the Equator.

ANSWERS, p. 51

CRITICAL THINKING Heat from the sun is absorbed by building materials, which then heats the air in and around cities.
✔ **READING PROGRESS CHECK** humid temperate

ENGAGE

Bellringer Read the "It Matters Because" statement and have students preview the lesson by reading headings and boldface vocabulary words and looking at the photographs. Discuss the topics covered in the lesson: the forces that shape Earth's surface, such as plate movements, erosion, and weathering. Have students predict what caused each of the events shown in the photographs.

TEACH & ASSESS

V Visual Skills

Visualizing Emphasize to students that Earth's surface has changed dramatically over time, but that much of the change has occurred very slowly over many millions of years. Share with students the information in the Content Background Knowledge box below. Then have students look at a world map and speculate on how the continents might have once fit together. **Visual/Spatial**

T Technology Skills

Researching on the Internet Have students identify the seven continents on a world map. Call on a volunteer to read aloud the definition of a continent. **Ask: Based on this definition, do you have any questions or doubts about the classification of seven continents?** *(Students might logically question why Europe and Asia are considered separate continents. Some people even question whether North and South America should be considered separate continents.)*

Suggest that interested students conduct Internet research on the classification of continents and report back to the class. **Logical/Mathematical**

Content Background Knowledge

According to the theory of continental drift, today's continents are separate fragments of one supercontinent called *Pangaea,* which began to break apart about 225 million years ago. The word *Pangaea* means "all lands" in Greek. The theory of plate tectonics explains how the continents broke apart and moved into their present locations.

ANSWER, p. 52

Taking Notes weathering, various types of erosion, buildup and movement, human activity

---

netw⊙rks

There's More Online!

☑ **MAP** Risk of Earthquakes in the United States

☑ **SLIDE SHOW** Human Impact on Earth

☑ **VIDEO**

Reading HELPDESK CCSS

Academic Vocabulary RH.6-8.4
(Tier Two Words)
- intense

Content Vocabulary RH.6-8.4
(Tier Three Words)
- **continent**
- **tectonic plate**
- **fault**
- **earthquake**
- **Ring of Fire**
- **tsunami**
- **weathering**
- **erosion**
- **glacier**

TAKING NOTES: *Key Ideas and Details* RH.6-8.1, RH.6-8.7

Identify As you read, use a graphic organizer like this one to describe the external forces that have shaped Earth.

External Forces
_____
_____
_____
_____

52

Lesson 2
Forces Shaping Earth

ESSENTIAL QUESTION · *How does geography influence the way people live?*

IT MATTERS BECAUSE
Internal and external forces change Earth, the setting for human life.

Constant Movement

GUIDING QUESTION *How was the surface of Earth formed?*

V Since the formation of Earth, its surface has been moving continually. Landmasses have shifted and moved over time. Landforms have been created and destroyed. The way Earth looks from space has changed many times because of the movement of continents.

Earth's Surface

A **continent** is a large, continuous mass of land. Continents are part of Earth's crust. Earth has seven continents: Asia, Africa, North America, South America, Europe, Antarctica, and Australia. The region around the North Pole is not a continent because it is made of a huge mass of dense ice, not land. Greenland might seem as big as a continent, but it is classified as the world's largest island. Each of the seven continents has features that make it unique. Some of the most interesting features on the continents are landforms.

T Even though you usually cannot feel it, the land beneath you is moving. This is because Earth's crust is not a solid sheet of rock. Earth's surface is like many massive puzzle pieces pushed close together and floating on a sea of boiling rock. The movement of these pieces is one of the major forces that create Earth's land features. Old mountains are worn down, while new mountains grow taller. Even the continents move.

(l to r) ©Royalty-Free/Corbis; ©AREF SANDI/epa/Corbis; TED ALJIBE/AFP/Getty Images; ©Radius Images/Corbis; TPG/Getty Images News/Getty Images

---

netw⊙rks *Online Teaching Options*

VIDEO

Water Eroding Mountains

Describing Use the video to introduce the lesson topic: the forces that shape Earth's surface, such as plate movements, erosion, and weathering. Have students share what they learned from this video about the internal and external forces of Earth, and tell if anything surprised them. **Interpersonal**

See page 39D for other online activities.

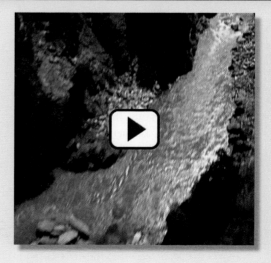

BBC Motion Gallery Education

Plate Movements

Earth's rigid crust is made up of 16 enormous pieces called **tectonic plates**. These plates vary in size and shape. They also vary in the amount they move over the more flexible layer of the mantle below them. Heat from deep within the planet causes plates to move. This movement happens so slowly that humans do not feel it. But some of Earth's plates move as much as a few inches each year. This might not seem like much, but over millions of years, it causes the plates to move thousands of miles.

Movement of surface plates changes Earth's surface features very slowly. It takes millions of years for plates to move enough to create landforms. Some land features form when plates are crushed together. At times, forces within Earth push the edge of one plate up over the edge of a plate beside it. This dramatic movement can create mountains, volcanoes, and deep trenches in the ocean floor.

At other times, plates are crushed together in a way that causes the edges of both plates to crumble and break. This event can form jagged mountain ranges. If plates on the ocean floor move apart, the space between them widens into a giant crack in Earth's crust. Magma rises through the crack and forms new crust as it hardens and cools. If enough cooled magma builds up that it reaches the surface of the ocean, an island will begin to form.

A path leads visitors to the Hakone Hot Springs (left) near Mount Hakone in Japan. Powerful forces within the earth heat groundwater, creating hot springs. Those forces also cause an eruption from Mount Lokon volcano (right) in Indonesia.

▶ CRITICAL THINKING
Describing What can happen if tectonic plates are pushed together?

VIDEOS

Earth's Forces: Old Faithful and Icelandic Volcano

Analyzing Use these videos to begin a discussion about how different landforms shape the life of people in a region. Have students identify the major landforms in your region and analyze how they affect the lives of the people in the region. **Verbal/Linguistic**

See page 39D for other online activities.

V1 Visual Skills

Creating Charts Help students summarize the information about plate movements by creating a two-column chart with these headings: *Type of Plate Movement* and *Landforms Created*. Suggest that students complete their charts as they read the text. Students' charts should look similar to the one below.

Type of Plate Movement	Landforms Created
Edge of one plate pushes up over another	Mountains, volcanoes, ocean trenches
Plates crush together, causing edges of both plates to crumble and break	Jagged mountain ranges
Plates on ocean floor move apart	New crust, islands

Visual/Spatial

V2 Visual Skills

Analyzing Images Explain that the two photographs at the bottom of the page show the effects of a force below Earth's surface. **Ask:**

• **What force is reflected in these two photographs?** *(heat within Earth)*

• **What does this heat produce?** *(hot springs, volcano)* **Verbal/Linguistic, Visual/Spatial**

Content Background Knowledge

The water in hot springs around the world is generally heated in one of two ways. It can be heated by geothermal heat when groundwater seeps deep enough within Earth's crust to come in contact with hot rocks. The rising temperature of the water then brings it to the surface quickly enough to remain hot. People can often bathe in this kind of hot spring as the water is not too hot. However, the water in hot springs can also be heated by volcanic activity. The water in these hot springs can reach the boiling point, and people can be seriously hurt or even killed by entering these hot springs.

ANSWER, p. 53

CRITICAL THINKING Landforms, such as mountains and volcanoes, are created.

R Reading Skills

Defining and Illustrating Clarify the definition of *fault* for students: a break in Earth's crust that results when two plates grind against each other. Have students create vocabulary cards for these content vocabulary words on this page: *fault, earthquake, Ring of Fire,* and *tsunami.* On one side of each card, students should define the word, and on the other side, create an illustration of the word. Have students write a caption for their illustration that uses the word correctly in a sentence. **AL**
ELL Verbal/Linguistic, Visual/Spatial

V Visual Skills

Analyzing a Map Refer students to the Chapter Opener map about tectonic plates and explain that the Ring of Fire borders the continents of Asia, North America, and South America. Have students locate the Ring of Fire, and call on volunteers to identify some countries located near it, such as Japan, China, and the United States. Have students analyze the map and find examples of volcanoes and earthquakes that are not on plate boundaries. Encourage interested students to make predictions why a few earthquakes and volcanoes occur far from plate boundaries and to research some of these events and report back to the class. **Visual/Spatial**

T Technology Skills

Transferring Knowledge Assign students a particular island or island group to research from those located along the western Ring of Fire. Possible island groups: Japan, the Philippines, Micronesia, Hawaii, Indonesia, and New Zealand. Then have students work in groups to research how those specific islands have been affected by their location near the boundary of the Pacific Plate. For example, students may cite specific volcanic eruptions, earthquakes, or tsunamis. Ask if any students have any personal experience with earthquakes or volcanic eruptions, and have them share their experiences with the class. Have groups present their findings to the class.
BL Naturalist

ANSWERS, p. 54

CRITICAL THINKING Earthquakes occur along fault lines. A fault is created when rocks along a crack in the Earth's crust have been moved.
✔ **READING PROGRESS CHECK** millions of years

People attempt to cross a collapsed bridge after a powerful earthquake in the Philippines.
▶ **CRITICAL THINKING**
Describing What is the relationship between a fault and an earthquake?

Academic Vocabulary

intense great or strong

Sudden Changes

Change to Earth's surface also can happen quickly. Events such as earthquakes and volcanoes can destroy entire areas within minutes. Earthquakes and volcanoes are caused by plate movement. When two plates grind against each other, faults form. A **fault** results when the rocks on one side or both sides of a crack in Earth's crust have been moved by forces within Earth. **Earthquakes** are caused by plate movement along fault lines. Earthquakes also can be caused by the force of erupting volcanoes.

Various plates lie at the bottom of the Pacific Ocean. These include the huge Pacific Plate along with several smaller plates. Over time, the edges of these plates were forced under the edges of the plates surrounding the Pacific Ocean. This plate movement created a long, narrow band of volcanoes called the **Ring of Fire**. The Ring of Fire stretches for more than 24,000 miles (38,624 km) around the Pacific Ocean.

The **intense** vibrations caused by earthquakes and erupting volcanoes can transfer energy to Earth's surface. When this energy travels through ocean waters, it can cause enormous waves to form on the water's surface. A **tsunami** is a giant ocean wave caused by volcanic eruptions or movement of the earth under the ocean floor. Tsunamis have caused terrible flooding and damage to coastal areas. The forces of these mighty waves can level entire coastlines.

✔ **READING PROGRESS CHECK**

Determining Central Ideas How long does it take for moving plates to create landforms?

Other Forces at Work

GUIDING QUESTION How can wind, water, and human actions change Earth's surface?

What happens when the tide comes in and washes over a sand castle on the beach? The water breaks down the sand castle. Similar changes take place on a larger scale across Earth's lithosphere. These changes happen much slower—over hundreds, thousands, or even millions of years.

54 Chapter 2

---

netw⊕rks *Online Teaching Options*

SLIDE SHOW

Architecture for Earthquakes

Analyzing Visuals Use the slide show to spark a discussion of how human beings have adapted to living with natural disasters, not only earthquakes but also floods, tornadoes, and hurricanes. For example, besides designing buildings to withstand natural disasters, people have developed emergency warning systems and emergency response procedures. They have also built levees and used sandbagging to hold back floodwaters. Have students write a paragraph about one of these examples that they may have experienced in their lives. **Verbal/Linguistic**

See page 39D for other online activities.

Slide Show

Weathering

Some landforms are created when materials such as rocks and soil build up on Earth's surface. Other landforms take shape as rocks and soil break down and wear away over time. **Weathering** is a process by which Earth's surface is worn away by forces such as wind, rain, chemicals, and the movement of ice and flowing water. Even plants can cause weathering. Plant roots and small seeds can grow into tiny cracks in rock, gradually splitting the rock apart as the roots expand.

You may have seen the effects of weathering on an old building or statue. The edges become chipped and worn, and features such as raised lettering are smoothed down. Landforms such as mountains are affected by weathering, too. The Appalachian Mountains in the eastern United States have become rounded and crumbled after millions of years of weathering by natural forces.

Erosion

Erosion is a process that works with weathering to change the surface features of Earth. **Erosion** is a process by which weathered bits of rock are moved elsewhere by water, wind, or ice. Rain and moving water can erode even the hardest stone over time. When material is broken down by weathering, it can easily be carried away by the action of erosion. For example, the Grand Canyon was formed by weathering and erosion caused by flowing water and blowing winds. Water flowed over the region for millions of years, weakening the surface of the rock. The moving water carried away tiny bits of rock. Over time, weathering and erosion carved a deep canyon into the rock. Erosion by wind and chemicals caused the Grand Canyon to widen until it became the amazing landform we see today.

Weathering and erosion cause different materials to break down at different speeds. Soft, porous rocks, such as sandstone and limestone, wear away faster than dense rocks like granite. The spectacular rock formations in Utah's Bryce Canyon were formed as different types of minerals within the rocks were worn away by erosion, some more quickly than others. The result is landforms with jagged, rough surfaces and unusual shapes.

C

W

©Radius Images/Corbis

Wind erosion created these unusual rock formations in Algeria.
Identifying What are the greatest factors that cause erosion?

Chapter 2 **55**

C Critical Thinking Skills

Comparing and Contrasting Stress that weathering and erosion are related processes and that they occur together. Use the following questions to help students identify the similarities and differences between the two processes. **Ask:**

- **What causes weathering?** *(wind, rain, chemicals, and the movement of ice and water)*
- **What causes erosion?** *(wind, moving water and ice)*
- **What is the difference between weathering and erosion?** *(Weathering is the wearing away of material, while erosion is the movement of that material.)*
- **How are weathering and erosion alike?** *(They have some of the same causes, such as wind and moving water and ice, and both of them change landforms. They work together.)*

Students may wonder how ice can move. Point out that glaciers are large masses of ice that move very slowly down slopes, pulled by gravity. They are responsible for much eroded landscape. **Verbal/Linguistic**

Making Connections Point out to students that examples of erosion are all around them in the outdoors. For instance, the banks of every stream show the effects of erosion, which often exposes the roots of trees. Challenge students to think of ways to present a simple demonstration of erosion. For example, a student might suggest building a mound of dirt or sand and pouring or running water from a hose down one side. If possible, allow students to set up an erosion demonstration.

W Writing Skills

Argument Note that all of the eroded landforms mentioned as examples in the student text are sites of national parks—the Appalachian Mountains (Great Smoky Mountains National Park), Grand Canyon (Grand Canyon National Park), and Bryce Canyon (Bryce Canyon National Park). Have interested students write a few paragraphs focusing on the importance of national parks in preserving scenic wonders and arguing for the creation of additional national parks in the United States or in a country in the Eastern Hemisphere. **BL** **Verbal/Linguistic**

Comstock Images/Jupiterimages

VIDEO

Erosion in Bryce Canyon

Integrating Visual Information Use the video of Bryce Canyon to discuss erosion as a force that reshapes Earth. Have students integrate what they learned to their lives by naming some landforms in your state or region that have been shaped by erosion. **Visual/Spatial**

See page 39D for other online activities.

ANSWER, p. 55

Identifying water, wind, and ice

Forces Shaping Earth

R Reading Skills

Determining Central Ideas Point out that the first paragraph on this page focuses on landforms built up by the action of water—either ocean waves and currents or river water. To help students identify the key points, provide them with the following sentence starters and have them complete the sentences:

- Ocean waves and currents deposit sand to build up *(beaches and islands.)*
- Rivers deposit soil where they empty into oceans to build up *(coastal plains and wetland ecosystems).*

Explain the term *wetland ecosystem.* An ecosystem includes all the plants and animals that live in a particular environment. A wetland is an area with wet soil, such as a marsh or swamp.

BL Verbal/Linguistic

Content Background Knowledge

Share with students the following information about glaciers:

- Glaciers are often referred to as rivers of ice that flow downhill. They are found in mountains on all the continents except Australia.
- Glacial ice is very heavy, and as it slowly moves downhill, it grinds away rock and soil, creating valleys and lakes. Ancient glaciers created the Great Lakes.
- Glacier National Park in northern Montana was named the country's tenth national park in 1910. The park borders Waterton Lakes National Park in Canada. The two became the world's first International Peace Park in 1932.
- The rapid melting of glaciers today is one of the many pieces of evidence supporting the theory of global warming. Since 1850, the glaciers in the Alps of Europe have decreased in volume by about one-half.
- Some of the glaciers in the Karakoram mountains, located in Asia, are getting larger. Scientists are unsure of why this is happening, especially as so many glaciers are shrinking worldwide.

Water is released from the massive Three Gorges Dam in China.
▶ **CRITICAL THINKING**
Analyzing What are the dangers when humans change the natural course of land and waterways?

R

Changing Landforms

The buildup of materials creates landforms such as beaches, islands, and plains. Ocean waves pound coastal rocks into smaller and smaller pieces until they are tiny grains of sand. Over time, waves and ocean currents deposit sand along coastlines, forming sandy beaches. Sand and other materials carried by ocean currents build up on mounds of volcanic rock in the ocean, forming islands. Rivers deposit soil where they empty into larger bodies of water, creating coastal plains and wetland ecosystems.

Entire valleys and plains can be formed by the incredible force and weight of large masses of ice and snow. These masses are often classified by size as glaciers, polar ice caps, or ice sheets. A **glacier**, the smallest of the ice masses, moves slowly over time, sometimes spreading outward over the surface of the land. Although glaciers are usually thought of as existing during the Ice Age, glaciers can still be found on Earth today.

Ice caps are high-altitude ice masses. Ice sheets, extending more than 20,000 square miles (51,800 sq. km), are the largest ice masses. Ice sheets cover most of Greenland and Antarctica.

TPG/Getty Images News/Getty Images

networks   *Online Teaching Options*

SLIDE SHOW

Human Impact on Earth

Discussing Use the slide show as an introduction into a discussion of the many ways that people affect Earth's surface, such as by building canals, dams, levees, roads, and cities. Have students use the Internet to find more examples of how humans impact geography. **Naturalist**

See page 39D for other online activities.

Slide Show

(l) ©Ocean/Corbis, ©Kryssia Campos/Getty Images, (tr) Erica Simone Leeds, (br) ©IG Photography/Alamy

ANSWER, p. 56

CRITICAL THINKING
Such actions can cause landslides and erosion.

Human Actions

Natural forces have the awesome power to change the surface of Earth. Human actions, however, have also changed Earth in many ways. Activities such as coal mining have leveled entire mountains. Humans use explosives such as dynamite to blast tunnels through mountain ranges when building highways and railroads. Canals dug by humans change the natural course of waterways.

Humans have cut down so many millions of acres of forests that deadly landslides and terrible erosion occur on the deforested lands. When the tree roots are no longer there to hold the soil, wind and water can carry the soil away. This can result in a loss of nutrient rich topsoil. Rain forests and trees also help support the water cycle and help replace the oxygen in the atmosphere.

Pollution caused by humans can change Earth, as well. When people burn gasoline and other fossil fuels, toxic chemicals are released into the air. These chemicals settle onto the surfaces of mountains, buildings, oceans, rivers, grasslands, and forests. The chemicals may poison waterways, kill plants and animals, and cause erosion. The buildings in many cities show signs of being worn down by chemical erosion.

Studies show that humans have changed the environment of Earth faster and more broadly in the last 50 years than at any time in history. One major reason is that the demand for food and natural resources is greater than ever, and the demand continues to grow.

Changes to Earth's surface caused by natural weathering and erosion happen slowly. They create different kinds of landforms that make our planet unique. Erosion and other changes caused by humans, however, can damage Earth's surface quickly. Their effects threaten our safety and survival. We need to protect our environment to ensure that the quality of life improves for future generations.

 READING PROGRESS CHECK

Describing How does water erosion form valleys and canyons?

FOLDABLES
Study Organizer

Include this lesson's information in your Foldable®.

LESSON 2 REVIEW

Reviewing Vocabulary (Tier Three Words)
1. How are *faults* and *earthquakes* related? RH.6-8.4

Answering the Guiding Questions
2. *Citing Text Evidence* Give three examples of forces that can lead to weathering. RH.6-8.1

3. *Describing* Describe one way that new islands can form. RH.6-8.5

4. *Determining Central Ideas* Why are Earth's plates in constant motion? RH.6-8.2

5. *Identifying* Place the following types of ice masses in order from smallest to largest: ice cap, ice sheet, glacier. RH.6-8.5

6. *Describing* What are some effects that might result from the development of manufacturing in China? RH.6-8.5

7. *Distinguishing Fact From Opinion* Is the following statement a fact or an opinion? Explain. RH.6-8.8

Humans need to stop engaging in activities that lead to pollution so we can all enjoy a cleaner world.

8. *Informative/Explanatory Writing* Explain the difference between weathering and erosion, and give an example of each that you have seen personally. WHST.6-8.2, RH.6-8.4

Chapter 2 **57**

LESSON 2 REVIEW ANSWERS

Reviewing Vocabulary

1. *Faults* are cracks in Earth's crust. *Earthquakes* are often caused by plates moving along fault lines.

Answering the Guiding Questions

2. Citing Text Evidence Possible answers: wind, rain, chemicals, movement of ice, flowing water, growth of plants

3. Describing If plates move apart on the ocean floor, magma might rise through the crack and harden at Earth's surface. Volcanoes can erupt, sending magma to the surface, where it hardens.

4. Determining Central Ideas The plates are floating on a layer of molten rock.

5. Identifying glacier, ice cap, ice sheet

6. Describing Possible answer: Pollution will result from the burning of fossil fuels to run the machinery. This can add to acid rain, which can damage buildings and plants/trees.

7. Distinguishing Fact from Opinion The statement is an opinion because it does not present a factual statement, such as a measurement.

8. Informative/Explanatory Writing Weathering is a gradual wearing away of a surface due to wind, rain, or other elements. An example would be an old gravestone where the name is barely visible. Erosion occurs when weathered bits are moved by wind, water, or ice. An example would be when a sand dune is blown across the beach over time.

R **Reading Skills**

Listing As they read, have students make a list of the ways human beings have changed the environment on Earth. Then have students form small groups, and challenge the groups to add as many items to the list as they can. You might make the activity a contest to see which group develops the longest list within two minutes.

After the small groups have completed and shared their lists, have them classify each of the changes in their list as a positive or a negative change for Earth's environment. Make sure groups include examples of both positive and negative changes made by humans. **Verbal/Linguistic, Interpersonal**

W **Writing Skills**

Informative/Explanatory Have students view a road map of your state and use it, along with their personal knowledge, to identify areas where streams and landscapes have been changed by people, for example by building dams and creating reservoirs or by building canals.

Direct students to write a paragraph in which they describe how the state's landscape has been altered by people and estimate about how much of it remains in a relatively natural state. If students are struggling, allow pairs to share their ideas or personal knowledge to help those who are struggling. Have pairs then exchange their paragraphs and give constructive criticism to their partner. **Verbal/Linguistic**

CLOSE & REFLECT

Have students reflect on the ways that the land is built up and weathered away naturally on Earth. Have students give examples in the local area of the ways the land has been changed, and identify if those changes occurred naturally or if some of the changes were made by people.

ANSWER, p. 57

 READING PROGRESS CHECK Water wears away rock and moves soil.

ENGAGE

Bellringer Note that many people take the landscape in which they live for granted, but each kind of landscape has its own appeal. Encourage students to identify what is special about the landscape of their home region. Challenge students to write descriptions, draw a local landscape, or bring in photographs they have taken of the local landscape to share with their classmates what makes the local landscape special.

TEACH & ASSESS

R Reading Skills

Applying Have students use a physical map to identify the elevation range within their home state. **Ask:**

- **Is the elevation range narrow or wide?** *(Students' answers should reflect the geography in their state.)*
- **Would you characterize the state as generally flat, hilly, mountainous, or varied?** *(Students' answers should reflect the geography in their state.)*
- **How does the flat, hilly, mountainous, or varied landscape affect the use of the land by farmers, miners, or other workers?** *(Students' answers should reflect the use of the land in their state.)*
- **What relationship, if any, do you see between landscape and population centers?** *(Students' answers should reflect the situation in their state.)* **AL** **Verbal/Linguistic**

V Visual Skills

Diagramming Have students draw a diagram showing a landscape with a plateau, plain, and valley, and label each landform. Explain that students should make their diagrams large enough to add helpful notes to their diagrams as they read. Then encourage students also to diagram and label other landforms that they read about in this lesson. **ELL** **Visual/Spatial**

ANSWER, p. 58

Taking Notes Sample answer: **Plateau:** an area of flat land that rises above the surrounding land; **Plain:** flat or gently rolling land; **Ocean:** a large body of salt water; **Gulf:** a large area of ocean water partially surrounded by land

---

netw☉rks

There's More Online!

☑ **IMAGE** The Ocean Floor
☑ **ANIMATION** How the Water Cycle Works
☑ **VIDEO**

Reading **HELP**DESK **CCSS**

Academic Vocabulary RH.6-8.4

- **transform** *(Tier Two Words)*

Content Vocabulary RH.6-8.4
(Tier Three Words)

- **plateau**
- **plain**
- **isthmus**
- **continental shelf**
- **trench**
- **desalinization**
- **groundwater**
- **delta**
- **water cycle**
- **evaporation**
- **condensation**
- **acid rain**

TAKING NOTES: *Key Ideas and Details* RH.6-8.1, RH.6-8.7

Describing Using a chart like this one, describe two kinds of landforms and two bodies of water.

Lesson 3
Earth's Land and Water

ESSENTIAL QUESTION · *How does geography influence the way people live?*

IT MATTERS BECAUSE
Earth's landforms and bodies of water influence our ways of life.

Various Landforms

GUIDING QUESTION *What kinds of landforms cover Earth's surface?*

What is the land like near an ocean? Are unique landforms located in deserts or on mountains? Have you ever wondered how different kinds of landforms were created? The surface of Earth is covered with landforms and bodies of water. Our planet is filled with variety on land and under water.

Surface Features on Land

When scientists study landforms, they find it useful to group them by characteristics. One characteristic that is often used is elevation.

R Elevation describes how far above sea level a landform or a location is. Low-lying areas, such as ocean coasts and deep valleys, may be just a few feet above sea level. Mountains and highland areas can be thousands of feet above sea level. Even flat areas of land can have high elevations, especially when they are located far inland from ocean shores.

V Plateaus and plains are flat, but a **plateau** rises above the surrounding land. A steep cliff often forms at least one side of a plateau. **Plains** can be flat or have a gentle roll. They can be found along coastlines or far inland. Some plains are home to grazing animals, such as horses and antelope. Farmers and ranchers use plains areas to raise crops and livestock. A valley is a lowland area between two higher sides. Some valleys are small, level places surrounded by hills or mountains. Other

(l to r) ©Roman Konopka/First Light/Corbis; ©Nick Ledger/JAI/Corbis; ©Jochen Schlenker/Robert Harding World Imagery/Corbis

---

netw☉rks *Online Teaching Options*

VIDEO

Changing World—Wild Weather

Analyzing Videos Have students view the video about extreme forms of weather and use a graphic organizer to analyze the forms of weather shown in the video. Then have students share what they learned from the video about landforms and their relationship to weather.
Visual/Spatial

See page 39E for other online activities.

BBC Motion Gallery Education

valleys are huge expanses of land with highlands or mountain ranges on either side. Because they are often supplied with water runoff and topsoil from the higher lands around them, many valleys have rich soil and are used for farming and grazing livestock.

Another way to classify some landforms is to describe them in relation to bodies of water. Some types of landforms are surrounded by water. Continents are the largest of all landmasses. Most continents are bordered by land and water. Only Australia and Antarctica are completely surrounded by water. Islands are landmasses that are surrounded by water, but they are much smaller than continents.

A peninsula is a long, narrow area that extends into a river, a lake, or an ocean. Peninsulas at one end are connected to a larger landmass. An **isthmus** is a narrow strip of land connecting two larger land areas. One well-known isthmus is the Central American country of Panama. Panama connects two massive continents: North America and South America. Because it is the narrowest place in the Americas, the Isthmus of Panama is the location of the Panama Canal, a human-made canal connecting the Atlantic and Pacific oceans.

T

The Ocean Floor

The ocean floor is also covered by different landforms. The ocean floor, like the ground we walk on, is part of Earth's crust. In many ways, the ocean floor and land are similar. If you could see an ocean without its water, you would see a huge expanse of plains, valleys, mountains, hills, and plateaus. Some of the landforms were shaped by the same forces that created the features we see on land.

This map reveals ridges that are underwater mountain chains.

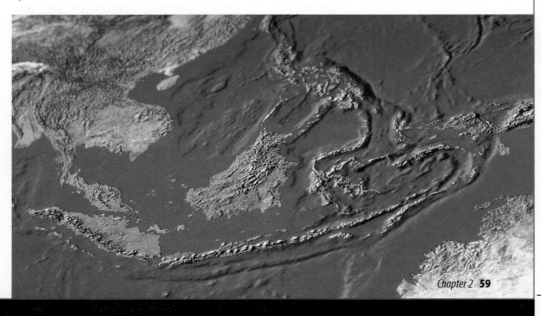

©Roman Konopka/First Light/Corbis

T Technology Skills

Researching on the Internet Students might wonder to what continent Central America belongs. Suggest that interested students conduct Internet research to find out and report back to the class. *(North America)* **BL** **Logical/Mathematical**

V Visual Skills

Reading a Physical Map Have students use the physical map image to review the definitions of all the landforms and bodies of water they have read about. Have them point out the underwater ridges that can be seen in the map and relate these to landforms on land.

Suggest that they also use the image to speculate on the definitions of any unfamiliar terms. Then direct them to the glossary to confirm or refine their definitions. Have them make vocabulary cards or add to the vocabulary lists in their notebooks as needed to keep track of all the new terms they are learning. **Visual/Spatial, Verbal/Linguistic**

V

Content Background Knowledge

Mapping the Ocean Floor The ocean covers roughly two-thirds of Earth's surface. Before the 1800s, little was known about the ocean floor. Most people thought of it as being like a bowl, with a smooth surface. Yet even in the 1500s, a few sailors had discovered that different spots in the open ocean varied in depth, based on soundings with hand lines.

In the 1800s, deep-sea line soundings indicated that the central Atlantic Ocean had underwater mountains. In the early 1900s, echo-soundings further revealed the ruggedness of the ocean floor. Exploration of the ocean floor by many countries in the 1950s led to the discovery of an immense mountain chain that winds almost around the globe and rivals any mountain range on land.

MAP

Physical Geography of Earth

Reading a Map Have students view the physical geography layer of the Chapter Opener map and identify an example of a continent, an island, a peninsula, and an isthmus. Call on volunteers to describe the characteristics of each landform. **BL** **Visual/Spatial**

See page 39E for other online activities.

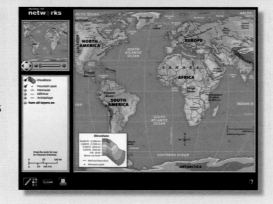

Earth's Land and Water

V Visual Skills

Analyzing an Infographic Have students use the infographic about salt water and freshwater at the top of the page to answer the following questions. **Ask:**

- What percentage of Earth's surface is water? *(about 70 percent)*
- What percentage of the water is salt water? *(about 97 percent)*
- What percentage is freshwater? *(about 3 percent)*
- Even though Earth is largely covered by water, what can you conclude about the amount of water readily available for humans to drink? *(Only a tiny percentage of all the water on Earth is readily available for drinking.)* **Logical/Mathematical**

C Critical Thinking Skills

Making Connections Ask students if they have had any experience with continental shelves. They should realize that the land along a shoreline is a continental shelf, and so if they have ever waded into the ocean, they have been walking on a continental shelf.

Discuss the variety of coastlines along the eastern United States, from the rocky coastlines of Maine in the north to the sandy shores of Florida in the south. Elicit descriptions of the animal life found along continental shelves, such as crabs, sea stars, and mussels. **Naturalist**

W Writing Skills

Informative/Explanatory Tell students that even at the deepest, darkest places in the ocean, scientists have found amazing specimens of sea life. Suggest that interested students research the life found in the ocean depths and write a short report. Allow students to present their reports orally and encourage them to include pictures/photographs in their presentations. **Verbal/Linguistic**

INFOGRAPHIC

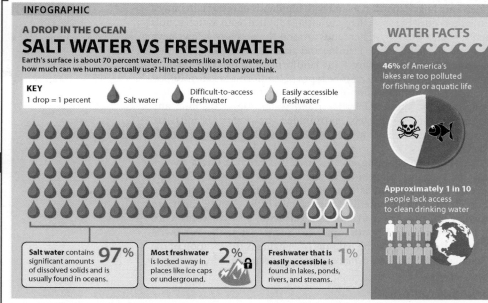

A DROP IN THE OCEAN

SALT WATER VS FRESHWATER

Earth's surface is about 70 percent water. That seems like a lot of water, but how much can we humans actually use? Hint: probably less than you think.

KEY
1 drop = 1 percent — Salt water — Difficult-to-access freshwater — Easily accessible freshwater

Salt water contains significant amounts of dissolved solids and is usually found in oceans. **97%**

Most freshwater is locked away in places like ice caps or underground. **2%**

Freshwater that is easily accessible is found in lakes, ponds, rivers, and streams. **1%**

WATER FACTS

46% of America's lakes are too polluted for fishing or aquatic life

Approximately 1 in 10 people lack access to clean drinking water

The surface of Earth is made up of water and land. Oceans, lakes, rivers, and other bodies of water make up a large part of Earth.

▶ **CRITICAL THINKING**
Analyzing Why is it important to keep freshwater sources clean and easily accessible?

One type of ocean landform is the continental shelf. A **continental shelf** is an underwater plain that borders a continent. Continental shelves usually end at cliffs or downward slopes to the ocean floor.

When divers explore oceans, they sometimes find enormous underwater cliffs that drop off into total darkness. These cliffs extend downward for hundreds or even thousands of feet. The water below is so deep it is beyond the reach of the sun's light. The deepest location on Earth is the Mariana Trench in the Pacific Ocean. A **trench** is a long, narrow, steep-sided cut in the ground or on the ocean floor. At its deepest point, the Mariana Trench is more than 35,000 feet (10,668 m) below the ocean surface.

Other landforms on the ocean floor include volcanoes and mountains. When underwater volcanoes erupt, islands can form because layers of lava build up until they reach the ocean's surface. Mountains on the ocean floor can be as tall as Mount Everest. Undersea mountains can also form ranges. The Mid-Atlantic Ridge, the longest underwater mountain range, is longer than any mountain range on land.

☑ **READING PROGRESS CHECK**

Determining Word Meanings What aboveground landform is a continental shelf similar to?

---

netw✺rks *Online Teaching Options*

INFOGRAPHIC

Fresh and Salt Water in the World

Analyzing Visuals Have students view this infographic, focusing on major bodies of water. Call on volunteers to identify the oceans and major lakes and rivers and determine if they are freshwater or salt water. Then have students compare the size of these bodies of water. **BL** **Visual/Spatial**

See page 39E for other online activities.

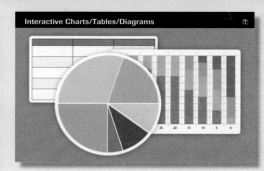

Interactive Charts/Tables/Diagrams

ANSWERS, p. 60

CRITICAL THINKING because there is so little of it compared to the rest of the Earth's water.
☑ **READING PROGRESS CHECK** A plain

Locating Water

GUIDING QUESTION *What types of water are found on Earth's surface?*

Different forms of water are available all around you. Water in each of the three states of matter—solid, liquid, and gas—can be found all over the world. Glaciers, polar ice caps, and ice sheets are large masses of water in solid form. Rivers, lakes, and oceans contain water in liquid form. The atmosphere contains water vapor, which is water in the form of a gas.

Two Kinds of Water

Water at Earth's surface can be freshwater or salt water. Salt water is water that contains a large percentage of salt and other dissolved minerals. About 97 percent of the planet's water is salt water. Salt water makes up the world's oceans and also a few lakes and seas, such as the Great Salt Lake and the Dead Sea.

Salt water supports a huge variety of plant and animal life, such as whales, many kinds of fish, and other sea creatures. Because of its high concentration of minerals, humans and most animals cannot drink salt water. Humans have developed a way to remove minerals from salt water. **Desalinization** is a process that separates most of the dissolved chemical elements to produce water that is safe to drink. People who live in dry regions of the world use desalinization to process seawater into drinking water. But this process is expensive.

Freshwater makes up the remaining 3 percent of the water on Earth. Most freshwater stays frozen in the ice caps of the Arctic and Antarctic. Only about 1 percent of all water on Earth is the liquid freshwater that humans and other living organisms use. Liquid freshwater is found in lakes, rivers, ponds, swamps, and marshes, and in the rocks and soil underground.

The water contained inside Earth's crust is called **groundwater**. Groundwater is an important source of drinking water, and it is used to irrigate crops. Groundwater often gathers in aquifers. These are underground layers of rock through which water flows. When humans dig wells down into rocks and soil, groundwater flows from the surrounding area and fills the well. Groundwater also flows naturally into rivers, lakes, and oceans.

Bodies of Water

You are probably familiar with some of the different kinds of bodies of water. Some bodies of water contain salt water, and others hold freshwater. The world's largest bodies of water are its five vast, salt water oceans.

Finnbarr Webster/Alamy

A young girl from Gambia in West Africa pumps water from a well.
▶ **CRITICAL THINKING**
Describing How does groundwater flow inside Earth's crust?

Chapter 2 **61**

C1 Critical Thinking Skills

Identifying Problems Emphasize that of all the water on Earth, only 1 percent is liquid freshwater, which is what people and other living organisms require. **Ask:**

- **Is all the liquid freshwater on Earth drinkable?** *(No)*
- **Why not?** *(Some of it is polluted with chemicals and waste materials.)*

Note that people in many regions on Earth struggle to find enough drinkable freshwater. **Ask: What are some of the effects of a limited supply of drinking water on a people?** *(Sample answers: It affects the health of the people in the region. Also, when people must spend a great deal of energy getting water, they have less time for other activities, such as going to school or work.)* **AL** **Logical/Mathematical**

C2 Critical Thinking Skills

Making Connections Draw students' attention to the girl pumping water from a well. **Ask:**

- **What do you think the girl will do with the water?** *(Sample answer: Bring it to her home to use for drinking and cooking.)*
- **Where does the water you use at home and at school come from?** *(Students may have well water or they may have water that is provided by a public utility. If the water is provided by a local utility company, have students find out the source of the water supply.)* **Visual/Spatial**

Content Background Knowledge

Desalinization The major users of desalinated water are in the Middle East and North Africa, which are arid regions. In 2002 there were about 12,500 desalination plants in 120 countries. The technology for desalination is not new, and it mimics the water cycle in nature. Water is heated, causing it to evaporate, leaving the salt behind. The water vapor is then cooled so that it condenses and again becomes liquid separate from the salt.

WORKSHEET

Desalinization of Water

Interpreting Have students use the Geolab worksheet about desalinization to analyze how much easily accessible drinking water is actually on the planet.
Logical/Mathematical

See page 39E for other online activities.

ANSWER, p. 61

CRITICAL THINKING Groundwater gathers in underground layers of rock called aquifers, and then flows into wells dug by humans.

Earth's Land and Water

V Visual Skills

Creating Word Webs Suggest that students create word webs to take notes and then summarize the information about bodies of water. Provide students with the sample word web for *ocean* below, and then have them make their own word webs for *bay, gulf,* and *river.*

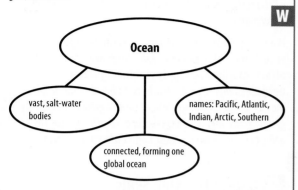

W

Ocean

vast, salt-water bodies

names: Pacific, Atlantic, Indian, Arctic, Southern

connected, forming one global ocean

AL **ELL** Visual/Spatial

W Writing Skills

Narrative Suggest that students choose one of the two photographs and write a brief fictional narrative about the people and action depicted. Encourage students to use their imaginations to develop a plot, while focusing on the people's use of water.

Have them create a simple sequence of events for their plot using a flow chart or an outline of sentences that list the events in order. Then have them use their flow chart or outline to write their narrative. Remind them also to include descriptive words that appeal to the senses of their readers.

You might pair or group students for the benefit of those who struggle with writing. Encourage groups to brainstorm several ideas so not all narratives from the group are the same. Have pairs exchange their narratives and provide positive comments and constructive criticism for any revisions that are needed. **Verbal/Linguistic, Interpersonal**

Humans use bodies of water for recreational activities (top). Bodies of water also help people earn a living like these women collecting seaweed to sell (bottom).

▶ **CRITICAL THINKING**
Describing Describe three ways water affects the lives of people who live near it.

V

From largest to smallest, the oceans are the Pacific, Atlantic, Indian, Southern, and Arctic. The Pacific Ocean covers more area than all of Earth's land combined. The Southern Ocean surrounds the continent of Antarctica. Although it is convenient to name the different oceans, it is important to remember that these bodies of water are connected and form one global ocean. Things that happen in one part of the ocean can affect the ocean all around the world.

When oceans meet landmasses, unique land features and bodies of water form. A coastal area where ocean waters are partially surrounded by land is called a bay. Bays are protected from rough ocean waves by the surrounding land, making them useful for docking ships, fishing, and boating. Larger areas of ocean waters partially surrounded by landmasses are called gulfs. The Gulf of Mexico is an example of ocean waters surrounded by continents and islands. Gulfs have many of the features of oceans, but they are smaller and they are affected by the landmasses around them.

Bodies of water such as lakes, rivers, streams, and ponds usually hold freshwater. Freshwater contains some dissolved minerals, but only a small percentage. The fish, plants, and other life-forms that live in freshwater cannot live in salty ocean water.

Freshwater rivers are found all over the world. Rivers begin at a source where water feeds into them. Some rivers begin where two other rivers meet; their waters flow together to form a larger river. Other rivers are fed by sources such as lakes, natural springs, and melting snow flowing down from higher ground.

A river's end point is called the mouth of the river. Rivers end where they empty into other bodies of water. A river can empty into a lake, another river, or an ocean. A **delta** is an area where sand, silt, clay, or gravel is deposited at the mouth of a river. Some deltas flow onto land, enriching the soil with the nutrients they deposit. River deltas can be huge areas with their own ecosystems.

Bodies of water of all kinds affect the lives of people who live near them. Water provides food, work, transportation, and recreation

62 *Chapter 2*

---

net**w**●**rks**   *Online Teaching Options*

GRAPHIC ORGANIZER

Water: Recreation vs. Livelihood

Listing Encourage students to think about all the ways that water is used for recreation and for making a living. Set a time limit for completing the graphic organizer—maybe 5 minutes—and have students share their ideas to form a class list. *(Sample answers: **Recreation**—swimming, canoeing, kayaking, water skiing, fishing, diving, sailing, boating, scuba diving; **Livelihood**—fishing, mining, oil drilling, shipping, research, tourism, transportation)*
Naturalist

See page 39E for other online activities.

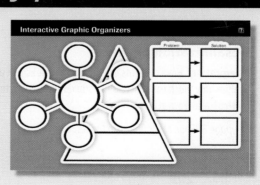

Interactive Graphic Organizers

ANSWER, p. 62

CRITICAL THINKING Possible answers: Water provides food, work, transportation, and recreation.

to people in many parts of the world. People get food by fishing in rivers, lakes, and oceans. The ocean floor is mined for minerals and drilled for oil. All types of waters have been used for transportation for thousands of years. People also use water for sports and recreation, such as swimming, sailing, fishing, and scuba diving. Water is vital to human culture and survival.

☑ **READING PROGRESS CHECK**

Describing How is water important in your life?

Recycling the Water Supply

GUIDING QUESTION *What is the water cycle?*

Water is necessary for all living things. Humans and other mammals, birds, reptiles, insects, fish, green plants, fungi, and bacteria must have water to survive. Water is essential for all life on Earth. To provide for the trillions of living organisms that use water every day, the planet needs a constant supply of fresh, clean water. Fortunately, water is recycled and renewed continually through Earth's natural systems of atmosphere, hydrosphere, lithosphere, and biosphere.

A Cycle of Balance

When it rains, puddles of water form on the ground. Have you noticed that after a day or two, puddles dry up and vanish? Where does the water go? It might seem as if water disappears and then new water is created, but this is not true. Water is not made or destroyed; it only changes form. When a puddle dries up, the liquid water has turned into gas vapor that we cannot see. In time, the vapor will become liquid again, and perhaps it will fill another puddle someday.

C

Scientists believe the total amount of water on Earth has not changed since our planet formed billions of years ago. How can this be true? It is possible because the same water is being recycled. At all times, water is moving over, under, and across Earth's surface and changing form as it is recycled. Earth's water-recycling system is called the **water cycle**. The water cycle keeps Earth's water supply in balance.

Water Changes Form

The sun's energy warms the surface of Earth, including the surface of oceans and lakes. Heat energy from the sun causes liquid water on Earth's surface to change into water vapor in a process called **evaporation**. Evaporation is happening all around us, at all times. Water in oceans, lakes, rivers, and swimming pools is constantly evaporating into the air. Even small amounts of water—in the soil, in the leaves of plants, and in the breath we exhale—evaporate to become part of the atmosphere.

V

C Critical Thinking Skills

Making Connections Note the multitude of experiences that everyone has with water in its various states and with water changing states. Suggest that students think about the ways in which water changes state during the process of preparing a meal. For example, when water is boiled to cook rice, much of the water changes into water vapor. When ice is put into a glass of tea, it begins to melt. Ask students for other examples of water changing state. **Verbal/Linguistic**

V Visual Skills

Creating a Flow Chart Suggest that, as they read, students make a flow chart of the water cycle. If some students have difficulty identifying and paraphrasing the stages in the water cycle, provide them with the following labels:

- Liquid water in ocean, lake, or river
- Liquid water changes to water vapor in air
- Water vapor rises and forms clouds
- Water vapor condenses and forms liquid or solid water
- Liquid or solid water falls as rain, hail, or snow
- Liquid water enters ocean, lake, river, or ground

ELL **Visual/Spatial**

Content Background Knowledge

Special Properties of Water Tell students that water has many properties that make it an especially valuable substance. Share with students the following information:

- Unique among natural substances, water occurs in all three states (liquid, solid, and gas) at the normal temperatures on Earth.
- With most substances, the solid form is more dense than the liquid form. But solid water, or ice, is less dense than liquid water, which explains why ice floats.
- More substances dissolve in water than in any other liquid. So, unless it has been purified, water normally contains various chemicals and minerals.

MAP

Population of Earth

Identifying Display the population layer of the Chapter Opener map to the students. Have students discuss where populations are largest and how that relates to access to water. **Visual/Spatial**

See page 39E for other online activities.

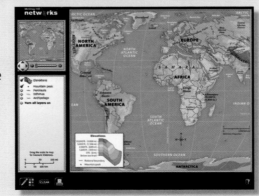

ANSWER, p. 63

☑ **READING PROGRESS CHECK** Accept all responses that demonstrate students' understanding of the lesson content regarding the uses and importance of water to human survival and culture. Sample response: Drinking water is important to my health; water provides food to my family in the form of fish, crabs, lobster, and oysters; water provides recreation for my family when we go canoeing and swimming in a local river.

R **Reading Skills**

Using Context Clues Have students read the sentence in which the academic vocabulary word *transforms* appears. Tell students to use the idea of the entire sentence to help them determine the meaning of the word *transforms*. Have students explain how they determined that *transforms* means "changes." **BL** Verbal/Linguistic

C **Critical Thinking Skills**

Synthesizing Ask students if they can think of three separate words that summarize the water cycle. *(evaporation, condensation, precipitation)* Have students draw a simple flow chart of the water cycle containing those three words, such as the following:

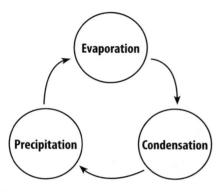

AL **ELL** Visual/Spatial

V **Visual Skills**

Analyzing a Diagram Draw students' attention to the diagram of the water cycle. Call on a volunteer to describe the process shown. **Ask:**

- Is it possible that the water you drank this morning was previously in Canada? *(yes)*
- Is it possible that the same water will be in Europe in the future? *(yes)*

Challenge students to use the diagram to make up a story about the movement of their drinking water through specific places. Call on a volunteer to share such a story. **AL** Visual/Spatial, Verbal/Linguistic

Air that contains water vapor is less dense than dry air. This means that moist air tends to rise. As water evaporates, tiny droplets of water vapor rise into the atmosphere. Water vapor gathers into clouds of varying shapes and sizes. Sometimes clouds continue to build until they are saturated with water vapor and can hold no more. A process called **condensation** occurs, in which water vapor **transforms** into a denser liquid or a solid state. **R**

Condensation causes water to fall back to Earth's surface as rain, hail, or snow. Hail and snow either build up and stay solid or melt into liquid water. Snow stays solid when it falls in cold climates or on frozen mountaintops. When snow melts, it flows into rivers and lakes or melts directly into the ground.

Liquid rainwater returns water to rivers, lakes, and oceans. Rainwater also soaks into the ground, supplying moisture to plants and refilling underground water supplies to wells and natural springs. Much of the rainwater that soaks into the ground filters through soil and rocks and trickles back into rivers, lakes, and oceans. In this way, water taken from Earth's surface during evaporation returns in the form of precipitation. This cycle repeats all over the world, recycling the water every living organism needs to survive. **C**

Academic Vocabulary

transform to change

DIAGRAM SKILLS >

V

Water is constantly moving—from the oceans to the air to the ground and finally back to the oceans. The water cycle is the name given to this regular movement of water.

▶ **CRITICAL THINKING**
Analyzing How does the water on land evaporate?

network *Online Teaching Options*

ANIMATION

How the Water Cycle Works

Have students use the animation of the water cycle to analyze how water sources are replenished and how water moves around the planet. **Visual/Spatial, Naturalist**

See page 39E for other online activities.

ANSWER, p. 64

CRITICAL THINKING The sun evaporates water from the surface of land and turns it into water vapor.

(l) ©Jochen Schlenker/Robert Harding World Imagery/Corbis
(r) ©Alan Abraham/Corbis

Human actions have damaged the world's water supply. Waste from factories and runoff from toxic chemicals used on lawns and farm fields has polluted rivers, lakes, oceans, and groundwater. Chemicals such as pesticides and fertilizers seep into wells that hold drinking water, sometimes poisoning the water and causing diseases.

The fossil fuels we burn release poisonous gases into the atmosphere. These gases combine with water vapor in the air to create toxic acids. These acids then fall to Earth as a deadly mixture called **acid rain**. Acid rain damages the environment in several ways. It pollutes the water humans and animals drink. The acids damage trees and other plants. As acid rain flows over the land and into waterways, it may kill plant and animal life in bodies of water. This upsets the balance of the ecosystem.

Some human activities pollute our lakes and rivers.
▶ **CRITICAL THINKING**
Describing How does acid rain affect animal and plant life?

 T

 FOLDABLES
Study Organizer

Include this lesson's information in your Foldable®.

LESSON 3 REVIEW (CCSS)

Reviewing Vocabulary (Tier Three Words)

1. Why do people who live in extremely dry regions sometimes use the process of *desalinization*? RH.6-8.4

Answering the Guiding Questions

2. ***Determining Word Meanings*** How are plateaus and plains similar and different? RH.6-8.4

3. ***Analyzing*** Why do farmers in some locations want to farm near deltas? RH.6-8.1

4. ***Identifying*** How does driving a car contribute to acid rain? RH.6-8.1

5. ***Determining Central Ideas*** How do underwater features form and change? RH.6-8.2

6. ***Narrative Writing*** Imagine that you are a drop of water. Describe your day as you transform from one state to each of the others. WHST.6-8.4, WHST.6-8.10

Chapter 2 **65**

LESSON 3 REVIEW ANSWERS

Reviewing Vocabulary

1. Desalinization is a process that separates salt and other minerals from salt water so it is safe to drink. People who live in extremely dry regions use this process when there is no freshwater to drink.

Answering the Guiding Questions

2. **Determining Word Meanings** Both are flat surfaces of land, but plateaus are higher than the surrounding land and plains are not.

3. **Analyzing** If a delta flows onto land, it will add a layer of nutrient-rich soil.

4. **Identifying** Burning fossil fuels to run a vehicle pollutes the air. The pollution mixes with water vapor and falls as acid rain.

5. **Determining Central Ideas** Volcanoes can erupt underwater, changing the landscape around them.

6. **Narrative Writing** Student writing will vary but should accurately describe a water drop as it changes state.

T **Technology Skills**

Researching on the Internet/Making Presentations Direct students to conduct Internet research either on the Great Pacific Garbage Patch, a huge mass of litter in the Pacific Ocean, or on the effects of acid rain in a specific location. Have students cite the sources for their research and evaluate the reliability of the content of their sources by making a list of their sources and giving each source a reliability score. This list should be turned in after the presentation.

Discuss the difference between paraphrasing content and giving the source credit and plagiarizing, i.e. copying the content of a source and not giving the source credit. Have students practice paraphrasing if needed. Explain that citing sources applies to photographs and images as well as text. Students should list the source of each image they include in their presentation.

Students might work alone or in small groups to prepare presentations on their subject for the class. If students work in small groups, have the groups assign roles so that every member of the group is involved in the presentation. **Visual/Spatial**

CLOSE & REFLECT

To close the lesson, remind students that they have learned about some of the amazing natural forces and processes that shape our planet. Encourage students to name these natural forces as a quick review. Then have other students name some ways that people have shaped our planet as well.

Place students in pairs. Have each student tell his or her partner one action he or she could take to lessen the negative impact that humans have on Earth. Then come back together and have each member of the pair talk about what their partner's idea is and how easy or difficult it would be to incorporate into the daily life of a student.

ANSWER, p. 65

CRITICAL THINKING Acid rain pollutes drinking water, damages trees and plants, and kills plant and animal life.

CHAPTER REVIEW ACTIVITY

Note that this chapter covered a great deal of information about Earth's structure, forces, and natural processes. Have students create and complete a two-column chart like the one shown below. Then use the chart to lead a review of the chapter's main ideas. *(Students' charts should include the following:* ***Earth's rotation on its axis****—causes day and night;* ***Earth's revolution around the sun****—takes 365 ¼ days, or one year;* ***Cause of seasons****—Earth orbits sun in tilted position, and Northern and Southern Hemispheres receive direct rays of sun at different times;* ***Earth's layers****—inner core of solid metal, outer core of liquid metal, mantle of liquid and solid rock, crust of solid rock;* ***Earth's physical systems****—atmosphere, lithosphere, hydrosphere, biosphere;* ***Factors that influence climate****—latitude, elevation, temperature, precipitation, wind and ocean currents, landforms;* ***Forces that shape Earth's surface****—plate movements, earthquakes, volcanic eruptions, weathering, erosion, ocean waves and currents, glaciers, human actions;* ***Landforms****—plateau, plain, valley, continent, isthmus, continental shelf, trench, volcano, mountain, delta;* ***Water cycle****—Water evaporates, condenses, and precipitates in a recurring cycle.)*

Chapter 2 Main Ideas	Key Details
Earth's rotation on its axis	
Earth's revolution around sun	
Cause of seasons	
Earth's layers	
Earth's physical systems	
Factors that influence climate	
Forces that shape Earth's surface	
Landforms	
Water cycle	

REVIEW THE ENDURING UNDERSTANDINGS

Review this chapter's Enduring Understanding with students:

• *People, places, and ideas change over time.*

Now pose the following questions in a class discussion to apply these understandings to this chapter:

• **How has Earth's surface changed over time?** *(Answers may include the following facts: the continents have moved, mountains have been built up and eroded, glaciers have carved valleys, and wind and water erosion has created a wide variety of landforms.)*

Directions: Write your answers on a separate piece of paper.

❶ Use your **FOLDABLES** to explore the Essential Question.
INFORMATIVE/EXPLANATORY WRITING Select two of the following regions: Asia, Africa, Oceania, Australia, Antarctica. Describe three unique landforms that can be seen in each region. Include photos. WHST.6-8.2, WHST.6-8.4

❷ **21st Century Skills**
INTEGRATING VISUAL INFORMATION With a partner, research the water cycle. Create a slide show presentation illustrating why the water you drink today might have been consumed by a dinosaur millions of years ago. WHST.6-8.6, WHST.6-8.8

❸ **Thinking Like a Geographer**
DESCRIBING Select one volcano that has erupted in Asia. Write an essay explaining the immediate and long-term changes that resulted from this volcano. WHST.6-8.2, WHST.6-8.10

❹ **GEOGRAPHY ACTIVITY**

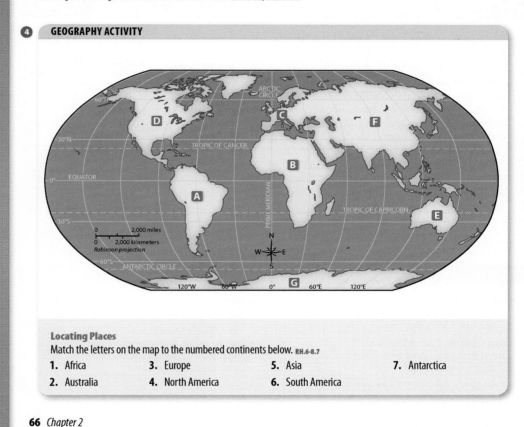

Locating Places
Match the letters on the map to the numbered continents below. RH.6-8.7

1. Africa 3. Europe 5. Asia 7. Antarctica
2. Australia 4. North America 6. South America

• **How have people changed Earth's surface?** *(Answers may include the following facts: people have leveled land to build cities and roads; have built dams and canals; have polluted oceans, streams, and lakes; have cut down trees and removed other vegetation to create farms and ranches; have littered and polluted the land, oceans, rivers, and lakes with a variety of waste materials.)*

• **In what regions is water a limited resource, and what are people doing to meet their needs for water?** *(Water is a limited resource in the American Southwest, the Middle East, North Africa, and other desert regions of the world. In some parts of the world, people are desalinating saltwater and digging ever-deeper wells to meet their needs for water.)*

ACTIVITIES ANSWERS

Exploring the Essential Questions

❶ **INFORMATIVE/EXPLANATORY WRITING** Answers will vary, but students should write a clear description and include photos of three landforms for two of the following places: Asia, Africa, Oceania, Australia, Antarctica.

21st Century Skills

❷ **INTEGRATING VISUAL INFORMATION** Student presentations should clearly show that water is not created or destroyed as it cycles from one state to another.

REVIEW THE GUIDING QUESTIONS

Directions: Choose the best answer for each question.

1 The center of Earth is called its RH.6-8.4

   A. mantle.

   B. core.

   C. magma.

   D. crust.

2 An example of a biome is RH.6-8.4

   F. a rain forest.

   G. cold temperate.

   H. northerly.

   I. climate.

3 Earth's tectonic plates RH.6-8.1

   A. all move in the same direction.

   B. all move at the same speed.

   C. vary in size and shape.

   D. are about the same size and shape.

4 Antarctica is mostly covered by RH.6-8.2

   F. ice caps.

   G. glaciers.

   H. thick grasses.

   I. ice sheets.

5 When water has disappeared from a puddle on a sunny day, we say that it has RH.6-8.4

   A. evaporated.

   B. condensed.

   C. precipitated.

   D. cycled.

6 A long, narrow, steep-sided cut in the ground or on the ocean floor is called RH.6-8.4

   F. a ravine.

   G. a trench.

   H. a continental shelf.

   I. an isthmus.

Chapter 2 **67**

ASSESSMENT ANSWERS

Review the Guiding Questions

1 **B** The center of Earth is called its core. The surface of Earth is called the crust, and magma is melted rock in the layer of Earth under the crust, called the mantle. Have students who answer incorrectly review the four layers of Earth covered in Lesson 1 of the chapter.

2 **F** An example of a biome is a rain forest. Climate is the average weather conditions in a region or an area over a long period of time. Cold temperate is one of the five basic climate zones on Earth. Northerly is an adjective that describes winds or something similar. Have students who answer incorrectly review Lesson 1 of the chapter.

3 **C** Earth's tectonic plates vary in size and shape. Have students who answer D review the map of the tectonic plate boundaries in the chapter opener to see the wide variety of shapes and sizes of the plates. Have students who answer A or B review the part of Lesson 2 about plate movement.

4 **I** Antarctica is mostly covered by ice sheets. Have students who answer F or G review the section of Lesson 2 called Buildup and Movement. Have students who answer H find Antarctica on a world map and identify what is found at the top and bottom of the world.

5 **A** When water has disappeared from a puddle on a sunny day, it has evaporated. Have students who answer incorrectly review the water cycle of Earth covered in Lesson 3 of the chapter.

6 **G** A long, narrow, steep-sided cut in the ground or on the ocean floor is called a trench. Have students who answer incorrectly review the Earth's surface covered in Lesson 2 of the chapter.

Thinking Like a Geographer

3 **DESCRIBING** Essays should address land formations that changed as a result of the volcanic eruption in Asia and the long- and short-term effects the eruption had on humans, plants, and animals.

Geography Activity

4 **LOCATING PLACES**

   1. B

   2. E

   3. C

   4. D

   5. F

   6. A

   7. G

DBQ Analyzing Documents

7 C The characteristics that the author would have taken into consideration are that Jupiter and Saturn are both gas giants that are a great distance from the sun. With a careful reading of the passage, students should understand that the author does not talk about the presence of moons, rings, or water for any of the planets.

8 G The author would consider the size of Mars to classify the planet. With a careful reading of the passage, students should understand that the author focuses on size and distance from the sun of the planets and does not talk about the temperature, presence of water, or ability to support life for any of the planets.

Short Response

9 Twain was probably referring to earthquake waves or aftershocks when he describes "violent joggling up and down." It could have been a result of the building that he was in being damaged and rocked around by the earthquake.

10 It seems like this was the first time he had experienced an earthquake, or one that was severe, because he used words like *terrific shock, joggling up and down,* and *heavy, grinding noise.* He does not seem comfortable with what he is describing.

Extended Response

11 Student letters should show adequate research to understand the gravity of the situation and the damage and destruction earthquakes and volcanic eruptions can cause. Students should offer creative and realistic suggestions to help aid the people of the Pacific Ring of Fire. Letters should also be polite and respectful, properly formatted, and grammatically correct.

DBQ ANALYZING DOCUMENTS

7 ANALYZING In this paragraph, a science writer describes the two types of planets in our solar system.

> "The planets can be divided quite easily into two categories—the inner planets, which are small and rocky, and the gas giants that circle through the outer reaches of the solar system. Within each class, the planets bear a striking resemblance to each other, but the two classes themselves are very different."
>
> —from James S. Trefil, *Space, Time, Infinity*

What characteristic do Jupiter and Saturn share that the author would have taken into consideration? RH.6-8.2, RH.6-8.10

A. presence of moons
B. presence of rings
C. their distance from the sun
D. lack of water

8 IDENTIFYING Which feature of Mars would the author consider to classify the planet? RH.6-8.1, RH.6-8.10

F. temperature
G. size
H. inability to support life
I. lack of water

SHORT RESPONSE

> "There was a great rattle and jar. . . . [Then] there came a really terrific shock; the ground seemed to roll under me in waves, interrupted by a violent joggling up and down, and there was a heavy grinding noise as of brick houses rubbing together."
>
> —from Mark Twain, *Roughing It*

9 DETERMINING WORD MEANINGS What do you think Twain meant by "violent joggling up and down"? RH.6-8.4, RH.6-8.10

10 ANALYZING Based on Twain's description, do you think this was something he had experienced before? Explain. RH.6-8.1, RH.6-8.10

EXTENDED RESPONSE

11 INFORMATIVE/EXPLANATORY WRITING The Pacific Ring of Fire is filled with more than 400 volcanoes, and it is the location of about 90 percent of the world's earthquakes. What have researchers and scientists done to help safeguard the residents of this vast area of the eastern coast of the Eastern Hemisphere? What precautions do the residents have in place in case of disaster? Research these questions and write a letter to the head of a government there, making further suggestions and recommendations. WHST.6-8.2, WHST.6-8.7

Need Extra Help?

If You've Missed Question	❶	❷	❸	❹	❺	❻	❼	❽	❾	❿	⓫
Review Lesson	1	1	2	2	3	3	1	1	2	2	2

---

networks *Online Teaching Options*

Remediation and Assessment

Evaluating The *Assess* tab in the online Teacher Lesson Center includes resources to help students improve their test-taking skills. It also contains many project-based rubrics to help you assess students' work.

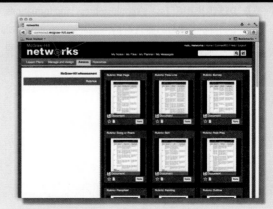

National Geography Standards covered in Chapter 3

Learners will understand:

I. The World in Spatial Terms

Standard 3: How to analyze the spatial organization of people, places, and environments on Earth's surface

II. Places and Regions

Standard 4: The physical and human characteristics of places

Standard 6: How culture and experience influence people's perceptions of places and regions

IV. Human Systems

Standard 9: The characteristics, distribution, and migration of human populations on Earth's surface

Standard 10: The characteristics, distribution, and complexity of Earth's cultural mosaics

Standard 11: The patterns and networks of economic interdependence on Earth's surface

Standard 12: The processes, patterns, and functions of human settlement

Standard 13: How the forces of cooperation and conflict among people influence the division and control of Earth's surface

V. Environment and Society

Standard 14: How human actions modify the physical environment

Standard 15: How physical systems affect human systems

VI. The Uses of Geography

Standard 17: How to apply geography to interpret the past

Standard 18: How to apply geography to interpret the present and plan for the future

---

UNDERSTANDING BY DESIGN®

Enduring Understandings

- *Over time, people adapt to their environment.*
- *People, places, and ideas change over time.*
- *Countries have relationships with each other.*

Essential Questions

- *How do people adapt to their environment?*
- *What makes a culture unique?*
- *Why do people make economic choices?*

Predictable Misunderstandings

- *Families around the world are organized like those found in the student's local community.*
- *All countries have governments like that found in the United States.*
- *The customs students enjoy originated in the United States.*

Assessment Evidence

Performance Tasks:

- *Project-Based Learning Digital Hands-On Chapter Project*
- *Project-Based Learning Hands-On Chapter Project*

Other Evidence:

- *Writing Skills Activity*
- *Critical Thinking Skills Activity*
- *Geography and Economics Activity*
- *Participation in Project-Based Learning Activities*
- *Participation in Interactive Whiteboard Activities*
- *Contribution to small-group activities*
- *Interpretation of slide show images and special purpose maps*
- *Participation in class discussions about human geography topics*
- *Lesson Reviews*
- *Chapter Assessments*

SUGGESTED PACING GUIDE

Introducing the Chapter	1 Day	
Lesson 1	2 Days	
Lesson 2	2 Days	
Lesson 3	2 Days	
Global Connections	3 Days	
Chapter Wrap-Up and Assessment	1 Day	

TOTAL TIME   11 Days

Key for Using the Teacher Edition

SKILL-BASED ACTIVITIES

Types of skill activities found in the Teacher Edition.

- **V Visual Skills** require students to analyze maps, graphs, charts, and photos.
- **W Writing Skills** provide writing opportunities to help students comprehend the text.
- **R Reading Skills** help students practice reading skills and master vocabulary.
- **C Critical Thinking Skills** help students apply and extend what they have learned.
- **T Technology Skills** require students to use digital tools effectively.

DIFFERENTIATED INSTRUCTION

All activities are written for the on-level student unless otherwise marked with the leveled labels below.

BL Beyond Level
AL Approaching Level
ELL English Language Learners

All students benefit from activities that utilize different learning styles. Many activities are marked as below when a particular learning style is highlighted.

Intrapersonal	Naturalist
Logical/Mathematical	Kinesthetic
Visual/Spatial	Auditory/Musical
Verbal/Linguistic	Interpersonal

*Letters are followed by a number when there is more than one of the same type of skill on the page.

CHAPTER OPENER PLANNER

Students will know:
- *that population growth varies around the world.*
- *what a culture is.*

Students will be able to:
- *identify* places on Earth that use the most electricity using a map.
- *analyze* a time line to discuss development of cultures and immigration movements.

UNDERSTANDING
BY DESIGN®

☑ *Print Teaching Options*

V **Visual Skills**

☐ **P. 70** Students study a world thematic map to learn about people's use of electricity throughout the world.

☐ **P. 71** Students use a time line along with the map to answer questions about cultures and immigration.

☑ *Online Teaching Options*

☐ **MAP** **Reading a Map**—Students identify aspects and locations of the region on a map.

☐ **TIME LINE** **Reading a Time Line and Map**—Students use a time line and a map to learn about where historical events occurred in the world. **Visual/Spatial**

☐ **MAP** **Interactive World Atlas**—Students use the interactive world atlas to identify the region and describe its terrain.

☑ *Printable Digital Worksheets*

☐ **WORKSHEET** **Critical Thinking Skills: Investigating Different Forms of Government**—Students use the worksheet to investigate how countries have changed their form of government.

☐ **WORKSHEET** **Geography and Economics: Pros and Cons of Free Market Trade**—Using the worksheet, students review the arguments for and against trading in a free market.

☐ **WORKSHEET** **Writing Skills: Investigating Population Movement**—Students use the worksheet to investigate current global population movement. **Verbal/Linguistic**

Project-Based Learning

Hands-On

Create Time Capsules

Students will work in groups to create time capsules that include cultural, economic, and political objects from their present-day communities. Students in each group must justify their choices for including each object. Completed time capsules should accurately reflect what life is like in the students' community today.

Digital Hands-On

Create Digital Scrapbooks

Students will create digital scrapbooks of their family history. Students should research and include information about their ancestral backgrounds using online census information, ancestry web sites, and personal interviews from family members. The digital scrapbooks might also include family photos that students have uploaded. When scrapbooks are complete, have each student share his or hers with the class.

Print Resources

ANCILLARY RESOURCES

These ancillaries are available for every chapter and lesson.

- **Reading Essentials and Study Guide Workbook** **AL** **ELL**
- **Chapter Tests and Lesson Quizzes Blackline Masters**

PRINTABLE DIGITAL WORKSHEETS

These printable digital worksheets are available for every chapter and lesson.

- **Hands-On Chapter Projects**
- **What Do You Know? Activities**
- **Chapter Summaries (English and Spanish)**
- **Vocabulary Builder Activities**
- **Quizzes and Tests**
- **Reading Essentials and Study Guide (English and Spanish)** **AL** **ELL**
- **Guided Reading Activities**

More Media Resources

SUGGESTED VIDEOS

NOTE: Be sure to preview any clips to ensure they are age-appropriate.

- **History of the World in Two Hours** (120 min.)
- **Human Planet** (3 discs-480 min.)
- **Earth Keepers** (83 min.)

SUGGESTED READING

- *A Life Like Mine: How Children Live Around the World,* by UNICEF
- *What the World Eats,* by Faith D'Aluisio
- *A School Like Mine: A Unique Celebration of Schools Around the World,* by UNICEF **AL**
- *Green Cities,* by Ronald D. Lankford, Jr.

EARTH'S POPULATION

Students will know:
- *about birthrates and death rates.*
- *that population growth varies around the world.*
- *reasons why people move.*

Students will be able to:
- **describe** *three factors that have contributed to Earth's constantly rising population.*
- **determine** *why more people live in some parts of the world than in others.*
- **list** *causes and effects of human migration.*

UNDERSTANDING
BY DESIGN®

☑ *Print Teaching Options*

V Visual Skills

☐ **P. 73** Students summarize a population pyramid.

☐ **P. 74** Students analyze slash and burn agriculture.

☐ **P. 76** Students compare urban and rural places.

☐ **P. 79** Students interpret a photo of refugees. **BL** **ELL**

☐ **P. 80** Students create a collage of images of a city. **ELL**

W Writing Skills

☐ **P. 79** Students write a paragraph describing how moving could affect a family's culture. **ELL**

R Reading Skills

☐ **P. 72** Students identify the main idea. **AL** **ELL**

☐ **P. 77** Students paraphrase information. **AL** **ELL**

☐ **P. 78** Students identify causes of immigration. **AL** **ELL**

☐ **P. 79** Students cite text evidence of the positive effects of the movement of people.

☐ **P. 81** Students map largest cities and megalopolises. **ELL**

C Critical Thinking Skills

☐ **P. 72** Students analyze information about birthrate and death rate and their impact on population growth. **BL**

☐ **P. 73** Students make connections between access to health care and education and population growth.

☐ **P. 76** Students infer why some people immigrate.

☐ **P. 78** Students determine causes and effects of population distribution and immigration rates. **BL**

☐ **P. 80** Students hypothesize about why plant life does better in rural settings than urban settings.

T Technology Skills

☐ **P. 74** Students research an alternative energy source and make an oral presentation with visual aids.

☐ **P. 75** Students research, draw, and label a diagram of how solar panels work.

☐ **P. 80** Students research and plot the top five largest cities on a world map. **AL** **ELL**

☑ *Online Teaching Options*

V Visual Skills

☐ **VIDEO** **Social Media Impact**—Students watch a video about the impact of social media on the spread of information and human geography. **AL** Visual/Spatial

☐ **SLIDE SHOW** **Places Around the World**—Students interpret the images and discuss the variety of places in the world. **AL** Visual/Spatial

R Reading Skills

☐ **SLIDE SHOW** **Population Challenges**—Students list the challenges that the world faces as the population climbs. **BL** Verbal/Linguistic

☐ **GRAPHIC ORGANIZER** **Why Do People Move?**—Students use the graphic organizer to discuss the meanings of *emigrate* and *immigrate* and analyze why people move. **ELL** Verbal/Linguistic

☐ **LECTURE SLIDE** **Immigration Definitions**—Students review the lecture slide for understanding of concepts and definitions. **AL** **ELL**

☐ **LECTURE SLIDE** **Urbanization**—Students review concepts and definitions. **AL** **ELL**

C Critical Thinking Skills

☐ **CHART** **Understanding Population Pyramids**—Students analyze a population pyramid and draw conclusions about the data. **BL** Verbal/Linguistic

☐ **CHART** **Population Pyramids**—Students use the population pyramids of various countries to further explain distribution of population by age and gender.

☐ **MAP** **Landforms, Waterways, and Population**—Using the physical layer of the world map, students discuss how landforms and waterways affect human settlement. **AL**

☐ **VIDEO** **Migration**—After watching the video, students discuss the purpose of refugee camps and why people are forced to leave their country. **ELL** Visual/Spatial

☐ **MAP** **Population Density**—Using the physical and population layers, students relate population density to physical features. **AL** Verbal/Linguistic

☐ **IMAGE** **Refugee Camps**—Students use the photo to review facts about refugee camps.

T Technology Skills

☐ **ONLINE SELF-CHECK QUIZ** **Lesson 1**—Students receive instant feedback on their mastery of lesson content.

☑ *Printable Digital Worksheets*

W Writing Skills

☐ **WORKSHEET** **Writing Skills: Investigating Population Movement**—Students use the worksheet to investigate current global population movement. Verbal/Linguistic

THE WORLD'S CULTURES

Students will know:
- what a culture is.
- what makes up cultural regions.
- how and why cultures change.
- different forms of government.

Students will be able to:
- **analyze** how clothing, behaviors, language, foods, and music give clues about culture.
- **explain** how government affects people's way of life.
- **give examples** of how cultures change over time.
- **write an essay** explaining their cultural traditions.

UNDERSTANDING
BY DESIGN®

☑ *Print Teaching Options*

V Visual Skills

☐ **P. 82** Students draw a map of a country that is important to their culture. AL ELL

☐ **P. 83** Students examine photographs for clues about culture. ELL

☐ **P. 88** Students use an image of a port to discuss globalization and its effect on culture.

W Writing Skills

☐ **P. 86** Students write a narrative describing how people living in the colonies felt about Britain and the emergence of a new culture at the time of the signing of the Declaration of Independence.

R Reading Skills

☐ **P. 82** Students examine meanings of *culture*. AL ELL

☐ **P. 84** Students read a chart of major world religions.

☐ **P. 86** Students note cultural regions in their state. ELL

☐ **P. 87** Students use word parts to find meaning. AL ELL

C Critical Thinking Skills

☐ **P. 83** Students chart roles of ethnic groups. AL ELL

☐ **P. 85** Students give examples of sports played in international competitions and how they influence culture.

☐ **P. 87** Students make connections between types of government and human rights.

☐ **P. 88** Students suggest solutions for the challenges some cultural groups face when they immigrate.

T Technology Skills

☐ **P. 86** Students use the Internet to research two countries and the top products they produce.

☐ **P. 86** Students use presentation software to add images and music to the narrative that they write.

☐ **P. 89** Students research and analyze news features online and evaluate how they affect culture. AL

☑ *Online Teaching Options*

V Visual Skills

☐ **MAP** **World Cultural Regions**—Students consider how cultural regions cover different parts of the world. BL Visual/Spatial

☐ **VIDEO** **World's Best Ancient Sites: North America**—Students watch a video about traditional cultures and consider how the cultures might be affected by changes such as a new government coming to power or climate change. BL Visual/Spatial

☐ **SLIDE SHOW** **Cultural Changes**—Students use the slide show to explain why cultures change and how emigration and immigration affect culture. ELL

R Reading Skills

☐ **GRAPHIC ORGANIZER** **Elements of Culture**—Students complete a graphic organizer about the elements of culture and choose one element and write a paragraph about its importance to culture. AL Verbal/Linguistic

☐ **LECTURE SLIDE** **Globalization**—Students use the lecture slide to review concepts from the lesson.

☐ **LECTURE SLIDE** **Different Languages**—Using this lecture slide, students review the various languages and pronunciations from around the world.

☐ **LECTURE SLIDE** **Comparing Governments**—Students use the lecture slide to review concepts in the lesson.

C Critical Thinking Skills

☐ **CHART** **Major World Religions**—Students use the chart to consider the similarities and differences of the world's religions and their influence on the culture of a region. ELL Visual/Spatial

☐ **CHART** **Types of Government**—Students use the chart to compare and contrast different forms of government, and then choose two of them and make a Venn diagram of their similarities and differences. AL Visual/Spatial

T Technology Skills

☐ **ONLINE SELF-CHECK QUIZ** **Lesson 2**—Students receive instant feedback on their mastery of lesson content.

☑ *Printable Digital Worksheets*

W Writing Skills

☐ **WORKSHEET** **Critical Thinking Skills: Investigating Different Forms of Government**—Students use the worksheet to investigate how countries have changed their form of government.

ECONOMIES OF THE WORLD

Students will know:
- different forms of government.
- the definition of globalization.

Students will be able to:
- **describe** resources they use to get what they want and need.
- **identify** the kinds of economic systems used in the world today.
- **determine** how the world's economies interact and affect one another.
- **explain** the benefits of one economic system and write a persuasive paragraph about why the system is better than others.

UNDERSTANDING BY DESIGN®

☑ Print Teaching Options

V Visual Skills

☐ **P. 94** Students sketch resources of wants and needs. **ELL**

☐ **P. 95** Students evaluate basic problems of economics.

☐ **P. 97** Students relate the factors of production with different economic systems.

☐ **P. 98** Students evaluate the factors of production.

☐ **P. 99** Students analyze a graph about GDP. **BL**

☐ **P. 100** Pairs of students collaborate and use an image to recognize the advantages and disadvantages of trade. **BL**

W Writing Skills

☐ **P. 98** Teams debate whether developing countries should be integrated into the world market.

R Reading Skills

☐ **P. 94** Students discuss wants and needs of countries. **AL**

☐ **P. 95** Students use context clues to find meanings. **ELL**

☐ **P. 96** Students apply opportunity costs to their lives. **ELL**

☐ **P. 99** Students use word parts to define words. **ELL**

C Critical Thinking Skills

☐ **P. 95** Students compare and contrast renewable and nonrenewable resources. **AL**

☐ **P. 97** Students draw a diagram of the three different sectors of economic activities. **AL** **ELL**

☐ **P. 98** Students describe the factors of production.

☐ **P. 99** Students make and check predictions about causes and effects of different economies interacting. **BL**

☐ **P. 101** Students synthesize economic information. **AL**

T Technology Skills

☐ **P. 96** Students conduct Internet research to find out which type of economic system is most successful. **BL**

☐ **P. 100** Students evaluate the web site of the World Trade Organization.

☑ Online Teaching Options

V Visual Skills

☐ **VIDEO** **Emerging Markets in India Bring Westerners and Trade**—After watching the video, students share surprising information about developing markets in the economy. **AL**

☐ **IMAGE** **Types of Economic Activities and Sectors**—Students use the interactive image to review the difference between the economic sectors. **BL** Verbal/Linguistic

☐ **DIAGRAM** **Factors of Production**—Using the diagram, students review the factors of production and review the concepts behind this economic term. **ELL** Visual/Spatial

R Reading Skills

☐ **GRAPHIC ORGANIZER** **Pros and Cons of Trade**—Students use an interactive graphic organizer about why countries trade and the advantages and disadvantages as discussed in the text.

☐ **CHART** **Economic Questions**—Students review the three basic economic questions. Verbal

☐ **GAME** **Bartering and Trade**—Teams provide definitions of terms related to trade. **AL**

☐ **GAME** **Drag-and-Drop: Wants and Needs**—Students review terms from the lesson.

☐ **LECTURE SLIDE** **Renewable Resources**—Students use the lecture slide to enrich understanding of lesson content.

☐ **LECTURE SLIDE** **Economic Terms**—Students use slide to review concepts and definitions.

☐ **GAME** **Drag-and-Drop: Imports and Exports**—Students play a drag-and-drop game to review concepts of trade and how goods pass from one region to another. Kinesthetic

C Critical Thinking Skills

☐ **GAME** **Drag-and-Drop: Economic Systems**—Teams of students sort a list of details about economic systems, needs, and wants. **AL** Interpersonal, Kinesthetic

☐ **GRAPHS** **GDP Around the World**—Using the slide show, students compare and contrast the GDP per capita of the six countries shown. **AL** Verbal/Linguistic

☐ **CHART** **Opportunity Cost**—Using the chart, students can review, define, and illustrate with examples the concept of this economic term.

T Technology Skills

☐ **ONLINE SELF-CHECK QUIZ** **Lesson 3**—Students receive instant feedback on their mastery of lesson content.

☑ Printable Digital Worksheets

W Writing Skills

☐ **WORKSHEET** **Geography and Economics: Pros and Cons of Free Market Trade**—Using the worksheet, students review the arguments for and against trading in a free market.

INTERVENTION AND REMEDIATION STRATEGIES

LESSON 1 Earth's Population

Reading and Comprehension

Have students identify cause-and-effect relationships as they read by looking for signal words. Remind students that words and phrases such as *because, since, as a result, due to, therefore, thus, consequently, so, resulted in, cause,* or *effect* all indicate cause or effect.

Have student pairs practice using these words to explain a concept or central idea in this lesson.

Text Evidence

Have students work in small groups to research population changes in different parts of the world. Tell students to present an analysis of their findings, including charts or graphs to show the impact of the change.

After groups have presented their reports, discuss some of the causes and effects of population change.

LESSON 2 The World's Cultures

Reading and Comprehension

Have students skim the lesson to look for unfamiliar or confusing words. Tell students to write down what they think the word might mean based on context clues in the text. Then have students look up each word in the dictionary to find its definition. Have students count how many correct definitions they wrote based on context clues.

Text Evidence

Have students work in pairs to research facts about different cultures. Assign each set of partners a different country. Explain that their analysis should answer the following questions about the people within that country: *What language do people speak? How do they dress? What do they eat? What religions do people practice? What is the country's form of government?* Have students present their findings to the class.

LESSON 3 Economies of the World

Reading and Comprehension

Have students play a guessing game in which one person gives clues about a content vocabulary term, and the other student tries to guess it. Have pairs compete against other pairs to see who knows or can define the most terms correctly in a certain amount of time. Be sure to explain that the students giving the clues should not use the actual vocabulary term in their clue.

Text Evidence

Students may have trouble grasping the different economic systems discussed in this lesson. Organize students into groups and assign each group one type of economic system: traditional economy, market economy, command economy, and mixed economy. Have students in each group work together to summarize how their assigned economic system works. Encourage students to use content vocabulary terms in their summaries.

Online Resources

Level Reader

Use this online lower-level text that corresponds directly to the text in the online Student Edition.

Guided Reading Activities

This resource uses graphic organizers and guiding questions to help students with comprehension.

What Do You Know?

Use these worksheets to pre-assess students' background knowledge before they study the chapter.

Reading Essentials and Study Guide Workbook

This resource offers writing and reading activities for the approaching-level student.

Self-Check Quizzes

This online assessment tool provides instant feedback for students to check their progress.

THE HUMAN WORLD

ESSENTIAL QUESTIONS · *How do people adapt to their environment?*
· *What makes a culture unique?* · *Why do people make economic choices?*

Aurora Photos/Alamy

**Young girl from the town
of Dori in Burkina Faso**

net*w***rks**
There's More Online about
The Human World.

CHAPTER 3

Lesson 1
Earth's Population

Lesson 2
The World's Cultures

Lesson 3
Economies of the World

The Story Matters...

As part of our study of geography, we study culture, which is the way of life of people who share similar beliefs and customs. A particular culture can be understood by looking at the languages the people speak, what beliefs they hold, and what smaller groups form as parts of their society.

FOLDABLES
Study Organizer

Go to the Foldables® library in the back of your book to make a Foldable® that will help you take notes while reading this chapter.

Adaptations | Cultural Views | Basic Needs

69

ENGAGE

Think-Pair-Share Read the Essential Questions and have students brainstorm reasons why we study the different cultures of the people of the world. Have pairs of students share their ideas. Students might say that each culture is different and that learning about other cultures helps us to better understand them. Then have students read "The Story Matters..." about how we can learn about cultures by studying peoples' languages, beliefs, and customs.

Discuss why it is helpful to understand the connections between humans and culture. **Ask: What attributes make a culture unique from all the other cultures of the world?** *(Possible answers: language, clothes, food, traditions, religion, beliefs, etc.)*

Tell students that they will learn about how cultures are similar and different and how people adapt to their environment.

Making Connections Read the following information to students in order for them to make connections to the content of the chapter.

Languages and customs are important to a culture. Cultures are diverse. Here are some facts about cultures and the languages that are spoken throughout the world:

- There is no set number of cultures in the world.
- English is spoken in 104 countries of the world including the United States.
- Chinese and Chinese dialects are spoken by more human beings than any other language.
- Arabic is the official language in 26 countries on two continents, Africa and Asia.
- Both India and Japan have one official language for each country, and that language is not an official language anywhere else in the world.

FOLDABLES
Study Organizer

Go to the Foldables® library for a cumulative chapter-based Foldable® activity that your students can use to help take notes and prepare for assessment.

Adaptations | Cultural Views | Basic Needs

Letter from the Author

Dear Geography Teacher,

In 2012, the United Nations (UN) hosted the Conference on Sustainable Development. The conference addressed critical issues: jobs, energy, cities, food, water, oceans, and disasters. The UN defined sustainability as development that meets the present needs without compromising future generations' needs. Stabilizing population growth was seen as paramount to achieving progress on all of the issues. Discuss how different cultures might feel about the conference "issues" and "sustainability."

Richard G. Boehm

TEACH & ASSESS

Step Into the Place

V Visual Skills

Reading a Map Explain to students that this map presents the entire world on one map and shows electricity usage by the peoples of the world. Have students identify the regions on each continent where the most and least amount of electricity is used, and have students identify the cities of the world that make the brightest points of light on the map. Discuss how this thematic map would most likely have looked 100 years ago, 50 years ago, and 10 years ago.

Then have students use the map to answer the Step Into the Place questions. **Visual/Spatial**

Content Background Knowledge

People emigrate and immigrate for a variety of reasons. Jobs, families, education, climate, political factors, and natural disasters are some of the factors that push and pull people to and from places. The heaviest immigration worldwide took place from the early 1800s through the Great Depression in the 1930s. During this time period, about 60 million people moved to a new land. Most of the immigrants came from Europe and more than half of these people settled in the United States. Many came to the United States because of the lure of better farm land or the hope of finding a better job.

In 2010, the United States was the top country in the world to receive immigrants. The Russian Federation, Germany, Saudi Arabia, and Canada followed. However, the United States received more than three times as many immigrants as the next country, the Russian Federation. Today many professional people still emigrate for better job opportunities.

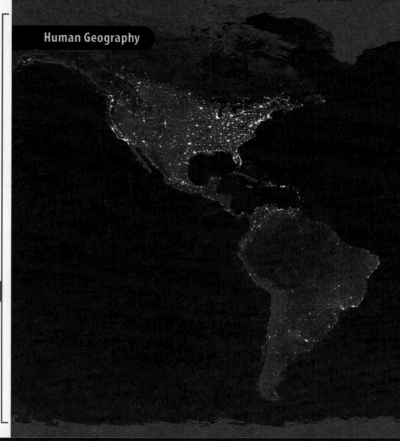

Human Geography

This image shows the world at night. Although the world's population is increasing, people still live on only a small part of Earth's surface. Some people live in highly urbanized areas, such as large cities. Others, however, live in areas where they may not have access to electricity or even running water.

Step Into the Place

MAP FOCUS Use the image to answer the following questions.

1 HUMAN GEOGRAPHY What do you think the brightly lit areas on the map represent?

2 HUMAN GEOGRAPHY Why might some areas be brighter than others? **V**

3 ENVIRONMENT AND SOCIETY Are the lights evenly distributed across the land?

4 CRITICAL THINKING ANALYZING Do you think the darker areas have fewer people than brightly lit areas? Why or why not?

Step Into the Time

IDENTIFYING POINT OF VIEW Research one event from the time line. Write a journal entry describing the daily life of the time.
RH.6-8.6, WHST.6-8.4

c. 4500–4000 B.C. Sumer civilization develops

c. 3500 B.C. Egypt builds trade network with West Asia

70 Chapter 3

(bkgd) Data courtesy Marc Imhoff of NASA GSFC and Christopher Elvidge of NOAA NGDC. Image by Craig Mayhew and Robert Simmon, NASA GSFC; (bl to br) Dorling Kindersley/Getty Images; ©Werner Forman/Corbis

---

Project-Based Learning ✋

Hands-On

Making a Time Capsule
Students will work in groups to create time capsules that include cultural, economic, and political objects from their present-day communities. Students in each group must justify their choices for including each object. Completed time capsules should accurately reflect what life is like in the students' community today.

Digital Hands-On

Making a Digital Scrapbook
Students will create digital scrapbooks of their family history. Students should research and include information about their ancestral backgrounds using online census information, ancestry Web sites, and personal interviews from family members. The digital scrapbooks might also include family photos that students have uploaded. When scrapbooks are complete, have each student share his or hers with the class.

ANSWERS, p. 70

STEP INTO THE PLACE

1. high populations using a large amount of electricity
2. because more electricity is being used
3. no; Eastern North America and Europe are brightest.
4. **CRITICAL THINKING** The darker areas have fewer lights because the regions or countries are not as developed or as populated as the brightly lit areas.

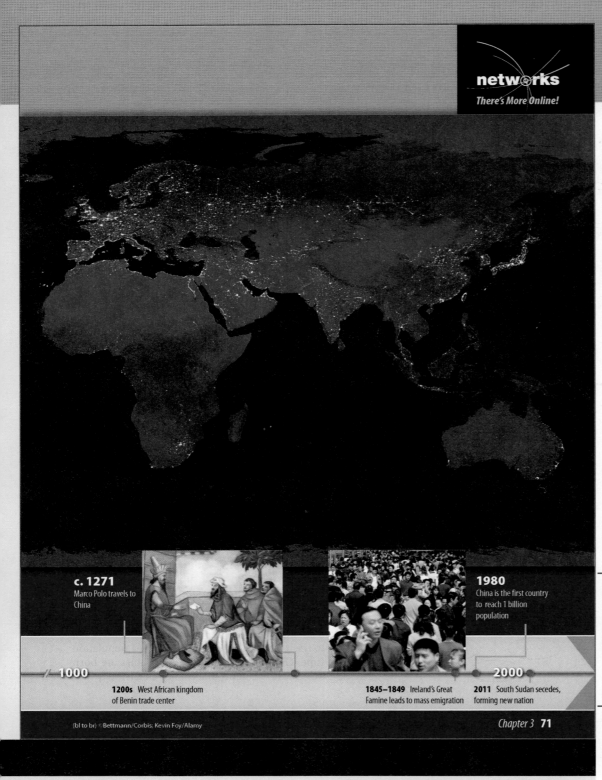

c. 1271
Marco Polo travels to China

1980
China is the first country to reach 1 billion population

1000

1200s West African kingdom of Benin trade center

1845–1849 Ireland's Great Famine leads to mass emigration

2011 South Sudan secedes, forming new nation

2000

(bl to br) ©Bettmann/Corbis; Kevin Foy/Alamy

Chapter 3 71

Step Into the Time

V Visual Skills

Reading a Time Line Remind students that time lines help to show visually the order in which events took place. Discuss the elements of a time line, including the start and end dates, event markers on the line, and labels at each marker. Ask students to share their ideas on how parallel time lines can be used. *(They can be used to compare events that took place in two different countries, regions, or hemispheres.)*

Have students review the time line and as a class, discuss its major points of interest. **Ask:**

- **Which event on the time line shows the greatest length of time?** *(Sumer civilization develops)*
- **Did Ireland's Great Famine occur before or after China's population reached one billion?** *(before)*
- **What abbreviation is used on the time line when the exact year is unknown, and what does it stand for?** *(c.; circa)*
- **Why are events listed from left to right on some time lines?** *(Students might say that time lines are easy to read as events flow from left to right, much like the way people read.)*

Ask students to list some historical events that could be added to the time line. *(Student answers will vary but should include accurate event placement.)*

Before writing their journal entries, have students brainstorm ideas about how events on the time line changed how people understood or viewed the world in which they lived. Have them share their paragraphs with the class. **Verbal/Linguistic**

V

CLOSE & REFLECT

Applying Have students write a paragraph to explain how what they learned in the Chapter Opener helps them to better understand different cultures in their daily lives. Invite students to share their paragraphs with the class. Tell them that they will learn more about world cultures as they study this chapter.

TIME LINE

Reading a Time Line and Map

Analyzing Maps Display the time line and map on the interactive whiteboard. Have students choose an event from the time line and identify where in the world the event took place by finding it on the map. Ask students to research the event further and to share what they learned about the event with the class. **Visual/Spatial**

See page 69B for other online activities.

ENGAGE

Bellringer Before students begin the lesson, ask them what they know about population. Then read the Essential Question aloud and have students discuss how the environment of their area affects the way people live or influences how many people choose to live there. **Ask: In what ways do you need to adapt to the environment in your area?** Have them explain why these adaptations would be necessary. *(Student answers will vary but should include mention of how specific environmental factors such as climate or living in a rural or urban area affects the way they live.)*

TEACH & ASSESS

R Reading Skills

Determining Central Ideas Explain that finding the main idea of a paragraph will help them to better understand the content and give each paragraph meaning and purpose. Point out that the main idea is often stated in the first few sentences of a paragraph. As a class, locate the main idea of the paragraph. *(Many factors cause populations to increase.)* Encourage them to work with a partner to find the main idea of the next paragraph. Explain that finding the main idea of each paragraph and writing main ideas in their notebook is an excellent way to keep notes on their reading. **AL ELL** **Verbal/Linguistic**

C Critical Thinking Skills

Analyzing Information Population growth is determined by death rate and birthrate. **Ask: What kind of graph could be used to show data on the death rate and birthrate in a decade and what would it look like?** *(A line graph could be used. The line showing the death rate could be decreasing while the line showing the birthrate could be increasing.)* **BL** **Visual/Spatial**

ANSWER, p. 72

Taking Notes Responses will vary but should demonstrate an understanding of the main causes and effects of population growth and migration. Sample notes: **Causes of population growth:** Relationships between birth and death rates, people living longer and healthier lives; **Effects:** Growing human populations, crowding, damage to the environment, emigration and migration, urbanization. **Causes of migration:** War, poverty, lack of opportunities, human rights issues, family issues; **Effects:** Cultures are blended and enriched, cities grow and urbanization endangers natural areas; resources are used quickly, environments are polluted.

---

netw⊙rks

There's More Online!

☑ **CHART/GRAPH** Understanding Population

☑ **MAP** Landforms, Waterways, and Population

☑ **SLIDE SHOW** Places around the World

☑ **VIDEO**

Reading **HELP**DESK (CCSS)

Academic Vocabulary RH.6-8.4
(Tier Two Words)
- **mature**

Content Vocabulary RH.6-8.4
(Tier Three Words)
- **death rate**
- **birthrate**
- **doubling time**
- **population distribution**
- **population density**
- **urban**
- **rural**
- **emigrate**
- **immigrate**
- **refugee**
- **urbanization**
- **megalopolis**

TAKING NOTES: Key Ideas and Details RH.6-8.5, RH.6-8.7

Determine Cause and Effect
As you read, use a graphic organizer like this one to take notes about the causes of population growth and migration.

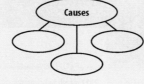
Causes

72

Lesson 1
Earth's Population

ESSENTIAL QUESTION · *How do people adapt to their environment?*

IT MATTERS BECAUSE
Billions of people share Earth. They have many different ways of life.

A Growing Population

GUIDING QUESTION *What factors contribute to Earth's constantly rising population?*

How fast has the world's population grown? In 1800 about 860 million people lived in the world. During the next 100 years, the population doubled to nearly 1.7 billion. By 2012, the total passed 7 billion.

What Causes Population Growth?

How has Earth's population become so large? What has caused our population to grow so quickly? Many factors cause populations to increase. One major cause of population growth is a falling death rate. The death rate is the number of deaths compared to the total number of individuals in a population at a given time. On average, about 154,080 people die every day worldwide. The **death rate** has decreased for many reasons. Better health care, more food, and cleaner water have helped more people—young and old—live longer, healthier lives.

Another major cause of population growth is the global birthrate. The **birthrate** is the number of babies born compared to the total number of individuals in a population at a given time. On average, about 215,120 babies are born each day worldwide. In time, the babies born today will

(l to r) MIXA/Getty Images; Lissa Harrison; ©George Hammerstein/Corbis; Carlos Spottorno/Getty Images News/Getty Images; Leung Cho Pan/Flickr/Getty Images

---

netw⊙rks *Online Teaching Options*

▶ **VIDEO**

Social Media Impact

Determining Cause and Effect Use the video about the impact of social media to discuss how technology is making the world a smaller place. Have students point out parts of the video they find interesting. Discuss with students various social media tools that they use that can bring people closer together. Ask students if these changes are positive or negative for human interaction. Highlight current events, protests, and Internet activism impacted by social media. **AL** **Visual/Spatial**

See page 69C for other online activities.

BBC Motion Gallery Education

mature and have children and grandchildren of their own. This is how more and more people join the human population with each passing day.

However, during the past 60 years, the world's human birthrate has been decreasing slowly, although the global birthrate is still higher than the global death rate. This means that at any given time, such as a day or a year, more births than deaths occur. This results in population growth.

Growth Rates

In some countries, a high number of births has combined with a low death rate to greatly increase population growth. As a result, **doubling time**, or the number of years it takes a population to double in size based on its current growth rate, is relatively short. In some parts of Asia and Africa, for example, the doubling time is 25 years or less. In contrast, the average doubling time of countries with slow growth rates, such as Canada, can be more than 75 years.

Despite the fact that the global population is growing, the rate of growth is gradually slowing. The United Nations Department of Economic and Social Affairs predicts that the world's population will peak at 9 billion by the year 2050. After that, the population will begin to decrease. This means that for the next few decades, Earth's population will continue to grow. In time, however, this growth trend is expected to stop.

C

Academic Vocabulary

mature fully grown and developed as an adult; also refers to older adults

GRAPH SKILLS >

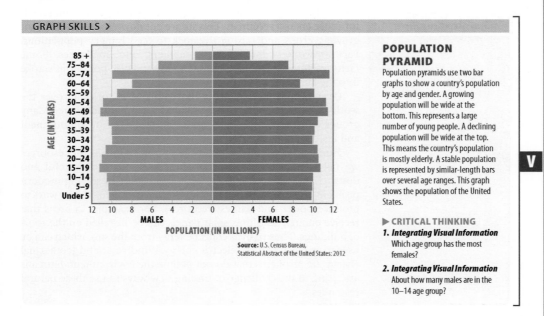

MALES **FEMALES**
POPULATION (IN MILLIONS)

Source: U.S. Census Bureau,
Statistical Abstract of the United States: 2012

POPULATION PYRAMID
Population pyramids use two bar graphs to show a country's population by age and gender. A growing population will be wide at the bottom. This represents a large number of young people. A declining population will be wide at the top. This means the country's population is mostly elderly. A stable population is represented by similar-length bars over several age ranges. This graph shows the population of the United States.

▶ **CRITICAL THINKING**

1. *Integrating Visual Information* Which age group has the most females?

2. *Integrating Visual Information* About how many males are in the 10–14 age group?

V

Chapter 3 **73**

CHART

Understanding Population Pyramids

Analyzing Charts Display the population pyramid chart on the interactive whiteboard. Have volunteers click on the pyramid to reveal different population trends. Then ask students to analyze the chart, comparing gender and age, and draw conclusions about the data. **BL** Verbal/Linguistic

See page 69C for other online activities.

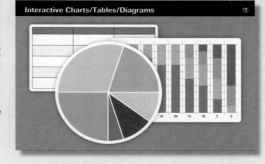
Interactive Charts/Tables/Diagrams

C Critical Thinking Skills

Making Connections Discuss with students the strong relationship between a short doubling time of population growth in certain countries and those countries that do not have adequate access to health care and education. **Ask:**

Why do countries in parts of Asia and Africa have short doubling times compared to those in Europe and North America? *(Student answers may vary but should explain how women who live in some countries in Asia and Africa do not have the education or the access to health care as women in Europe and North America do, and that lack of education and health care often lead to higher birth rates. This contributes to a high population growth and short doubling time.)* **Verbal/Linguistic**

V Visual Skills

Reading a Graph Explain to students that a graph can show a lot of data in a visual way. When reading a graph, it is important to read all of the labels to become familiar with the data. It is also important to understand what is being measured and the amounts of measurement. To read a population pyramid, look at the data on both sides of the graph. Explain that sometimes lower or abbreviated numbers are used so that the amounts fit or are shown more clearly on a graph. **Ask:**

- **What amount is the population being measured in?** *(millions)*
- **What does the label 60–64 stand for?** *(the age group of people who are 60 to 64 years old)*
- **According to the graph, what is the population of males under the age of 5?** *(10 million)*
- **Considering that there are nearly equal amounts of males and females at the bottom and in the middle of the chart, what do you think accounts for the unequal amounts at the top?** *(Women live longer than men.)*

Have students work individually to write a summary of the data that the graph illustrates. Encourage students to consider the data that shows the highest and lowest values, as well as values that are the same for both females and males or are the same in specific age groups. **Visual/Spatial**

ANSWERS, p. 73

CRITICAL THINKING
1. 65–74
2. about 10 million

Earth's Population

V Visual Skills

Analyzing Images Have students look at the picture of the cut trees that are being burned. Discuss how farmers clear land for agriculture by cutting and burning forests. Have students analyze the effects of slash-and-burn agriculture on population and the environment. **Ask:**

- **How does slash-and-burn agriculture hurt the environment?** *(Student answers may vary but should explain how it destroys the homes of animals and pollutes the atmosphere.)*
- **Why do some people use slash-and-burn agriculture even though it harms the environment?** *(Student answers may vary but should include that because of population growth and limited land for growing crops, some people have resorted to clearing forested land for cultivation.)* **Verbal/Linguistic**

T Technology Skills

Making Presentations Have a volunteer read aloud the first two paragraphs under, "Environmental Effects." **Ask: What has happened over time to Earth's atmosphere?** *(Thousands of factories have polluted the Earth's atmosphere with chemical waste.)*

As a class, discuss other factors that have harmed the environment and how and why these factors have come about. After the discussion, pair up students. Have each pair choose a topic on one of the alternative energy resources from the third paragraph of, "Environmental Effects," or other alternative energy resources that students may know about.

Provide an opportunity for students to research their topic using the Internet and to prepare an oral presentation. Suggest that they use visual aids, such as photos and graphs, to make their presentations more interesting. Then have students share their presentations with the class. **Verbal/Linguistic, Visual/Spatial, Interpersonal**

Farmers in many parts of the world clear land by cutting and burning forests.
▶ **CRITICAL THINKING**
Analyzing What is the purpose of slash-and-burn agriculture?

Population Challenges

When human populations grow, the places people inhabit can become crowded. In many parts of the world, cities, towns, and villages have grown and expanded beyond a comfortable capacity.

When the population of an already-crowded area continues to grow, serious problems can arise. For example, diseases spread quickly in crowded environments. Sometimes there is not enough work for everyone, and many households live in ongoing poverty. Where many people share tight living spaces, crime can be a serious problem and pollution can increase.

Environmental Effects

On a global scale, rapid population growth can have a harmful effect on the environment. Each year, more people are sharing the same amount of space. People demand fuel for their cars and power for their homes. Miners drill and dig into the earth in a constant search for more energy resources. Forests are cut down to make farms for growing crops and raising livestock to feed hungry populations. Factory workers build cars, computers, and appliances. Some factories dump chemicals into waterways and vent poisonous smoke into the air.

Over time, and with many thousands of factories all over the world, chemical wastes have polluted Earth's atmosphere. Many groups and individuals are working to clean up the environment and restore polluted areas.

Humans have many methods of finding and using the resources we need for survival. Some of these methods are wasteful and destructive. However, humans are also creative in solving modern problems. People in all parts of the world have invented new ways to produce power and harvest resources. For example, in areas that receive enough sunshine, solar panels can be installed on the roofs of buildings. These panels collect energy from the sun, which can be used to produce heat and electric energy. Wind, solar, and geothermal energy are resources that do not pollute the environment. Humans are rising to the challenge of finding new ways to use these natural resources.

JAMES P. BLAIR/National Geographic Stock

74 Chapter 3

---

networks   *Online Teaching Options*

SLIDE SHOW

Population Challenges

Drawing Conclusions Show the lecture slide show on population challenges. Have students make a list of the challenges that the world faces as the population climbs. Then ask them to write a statement that explains what they think is the greatest challenge caused by population growth. **BL Verbal/Linguistic**

See page 69C for other online activities.

Slide Show

(l) ©Ocean/Corbis, ©Kryssia Campos/Getty Images, (tr) Erica Simone Leeds, (br) ©JG Photography/Alamy

---

ANSWER, p. 74

CRITICAL THINKING to clear land to grow crops and raise livestock

Population Growth Rates

Human populations grow at different rates in different areas of the world for many reasons. Often, the number of children each family will have is influenced by the family's culture and religion. In some cultures, families are encouraged to have as many children as they can. Although birthrates have fallen greatly in many parts of Asia, Africa, and South America in recent decades, the rates are still higher than in industrialized nations.

In locations with the largest and fastest-growing populations, the need for resources, jobs, health care, and education is great. When millions of people living in a small area need food, water, and housing, there is sometimes not enough for everyone. People in many parts of the world go hungry or die of starvation. Water supplies in crowded cities are often polluted with wastes that can cause diseases. Some areas do not have enough land resources and materials for people to build safe, sturdy homes.

Children in areas affected by extreme poverty often do not receive an education. In areas with job shortages, people are forced to live on low incomes. People living in poverty often live in crowded neighborhoods called *slums*. Slums surround many of the world's cities. These places are often dirty and unsafe. Governments and organizations such as the United Nations are working to make these areas safer, healthier places to live. Because populations grow at different rates, some areas experience more severe problems.

R

✓ **READING PROGRESS CHECK**

Determining Word Meanings What is the difference between the birthrate and the death rate?

Solar panels collect energy from the sun. **T**

SLIDE SHOW

Places Around the World

Interpreting Show the slide show on the different types of places in the world. Point out how places can include buildings, streets, or malls, and can be inside or outside places. Discuss how varied places are around the world and within a specific geographic location. Ask students to describe a type of place that is familiar to them. **AL** **Visual/Spatial**

See page 69C for other online activities.

Slide Show

R Reading Skills

Using Context Clues Explain to students that they can look at words around or near a word that is unfamiliar to them to help them understand its meaning. Have students read the last two paragraphs of this page. **Ask:**

- **What words help you to understand the meaning of** *sturdy*? (not enough resources, build, and safe)
- **What words help you to understand the meaning of** *slums*? (poverty, crowded neighborhoods)
- **What other words are unfamiliar to you?** (Possible answer: starvation)
- **What context clues help you to understand their meaning?** (Possible answer: hungry and die) **Verbal/Linguistic, Intrapersonal**

T Technology Skills

Diagramming Have students work in small groups to find out how solar panels work using classroom or library print or digital resources. Ask them to draw and label a diagram on a poster or using computer software. **Ask:** Besides not polluting the environment, why is solar energy an ideal alternative resource? (Student answers may vary but should include that solar energy is an inexhaustible resource that will not run out.) **Visual/Spatial, Interpersonal**

V

V Visual Skills

Analyzing Images Have student pairs review the image in the textbook. Encourage them to discuss the image and make notes about the size of the structures and how closely they are placed next to each other. **Ask:**

- **Why do you think the buildings are placed so closely together?** (Students' answers should suggest that the buildings are placed closely together so they could fit more buildings in one area.)
- **How does the buildings being placed closely together relate to the population of the area?** (Students' answers should suggest that the area is highly populated and therefore, more housing is needed.)

Be sure students make the connection between the population density of the region and the creation of places like slums. **Visual/Spatial**

ANSWER, p. 75

✓ **READING PROGRESS CHECK** Death rate is the number of deaths compared to the number of individuals in a population at a given time. Birthrate is the number of babies born compared to the total number of individuals in a population at a given time.

Earth's Population

V | Visual Skills

Analyzing Visuals Have students study the images on these pages and then draw a Venn diagram. Ask them to label one oval "urban," the other "rural," and the middle "both." Explain that they should fill in their diagrams with examples of how urban and rural places are similar and different by comparing the two images. **Ask: What kind of place do you live in, urban or rural? How do you know?** *(Student answers will vary but should include an explanation such as an urban area has more people, streets, and buildings, while a rural area has less population and often has more open and undeveloped land.)* **Visual/Spatial, Intrapersonal**

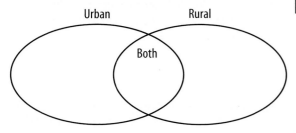

Urban   Rural

Both

C | Critical Thinking Skills

Making Inferences Explain that some people migrate to different places to live, while others remain in the same place for a long time. **Ask: Why do you think that some people move frequently while others never move or stay in the same area?** *(Student answers will vary but could include that people often stay in the same area to be close to family, while others move frequently because of economic factors.)* **Verbal/Linguistic**

Content Background Knowledge

Coastal areas are often the most populated areas around the world. Climate, resources, and economic opportunities are two important factors that affect human settlement and population density and distribution. In 2010, more than half of the world's population lived in urban areas, which marked a milestone in population distribution. Before then, more people lived in rural areas worldwide.

Some cities, like Seoul, South Korea, have a high population density.
▶ **CRITICAL THINKING**
Analyzing How is population density calculated?

Where People Live

GUIDING QUESTION *Why do more people live in some parts of the world than in others?*

Some families live in the same town or on the same land for generations. Other people move frequently from place to place.

Population Distribution

Population growth rates vary among Earth's regions. The **population distribution**, or the geographic pattern of where people live on Earth, is uneven as well. One reason people live in a certain place is work. During the industrial age, for example, people moved to places that had important resources such as coal or iron ore to make and operate machinery. People gather in other places because these areas hold religious significance or because they are government or transportation centers.

Population Density

One way to look at population is by measuring **population density**—the average number of people living within a square mile or a square kilometer. To say that an area is *densely populated* means the area has a large number of people living within it.

Keep in mind that a country's population density is the average for the entire country. Population is not distributed evenly throughout a country. As a result, some areas are more densely populated than their country's average indicates. In Egypt, for example, the population is concentrated along the Nile River; in China, along its eastern seaboard; and in Mexico, on the Central Plateau.

MIXA/Getty Images

---

net**w**orks | *Online Teaching Options*

MAP

Population Density

Determining Cause and Effect Display the interactive Chapter Opener map on the whiteboard. Use the physical and population layers of the map to show areas of high population density around the world and where populations tend to develop. **AL Verbal/Linguistic**

See page 69C for other online activities.

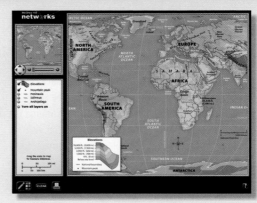

ANSWER, p. 76

CRITICAL THINKING by dividing the total number of people living in an area by the total land area

Anna Creek Station, located in a rural region in south-central Australia, is the world's largest working cattle station.

Where People Are Located

Urban areas are densely populated. **Rural** areas, in contrast, are sparsely populated. People inhabit only a small part of Earth. Remember that land covers about 30 percent of Earth's surface, and half of this land is not useful to humans. This means that only about 15 percent of Earth's surface is inhabitable. Large cities have dense populations, while deserts, oceans, and mountaintops are uninhabited.

C

The main reason people settle in some areas and not in others is the need for resources. People live where their basic needs can be met. People need shelter, food, water, and a way to earn a living. Some people live in cities, which have many places to live and work. Other people make their homes on open grasslands where they build their own shelters, grow their own food, and raise livestock.

R

☑ **READING PROGRESS CHECK**

Identifying Give one example of an urban area and one example of a rural area.

Changes in Population

GUIDING QUESTION *What are the causes and effects of human migration?*

The populations of different areas change as people move from one area to another. When many people leave an area, that area's population decreases. When large numbers of people move into a city, a state, or a country, the population of that area increases. Moving from one place to another is called *migration*.

Medford Taylor/National Geographic/Getty Images

Chapter 3 **77**

MAP

Landforms, Waterways, and Population

Determining Cause and Effect Display the interactive Chapter Opener map on the whiteboard. Use the physical layer of the map to discuss how landforms and waterways affect human settlement and how they may have caused population growth in some areas and not in others.

AL Verbal/Linguistic

See page 69C for other online activities.

See page 69C for other online activities.

C Critical Thinking Skills

Comparing and Contrasting Have students work in small groups to create a two-column graphic organizer that identifies rural and urban places throughout the world.

Rural Places	Urban Places

Students should list real location examples for both rural and urban places on different continents, using their background knowledge and travel experiences as much as possible. Invite students to share their graphic organizers with the class. If time allows, compile each group's information into a class graphic organizer. **ELL** Verbal/Linguistic

R Reading Skills

Paraphrasing Have students reread the last paragraph in the section, "Where People Are Located." Ask them to paraphrase, or use their own words, to explain why people settle in some areas of the world and not in others. *(Possible answer: People move to areas where they can find resources to meet their basic needs.)*

Then discuss other reasons why people settle in some areas of the world and not in others. *(They also move to more favorable climates to escape cold weather for example or to regions that offer better opportunities for education and jobs.)*

Making Connections Ask students if they have ever been to one of the most populous cities in the United States (New York, NY; Los Angeles, CA; Chicago, IL; or Houston, TX). Have them describe what it was like to be in such a large city. Have them describe what they saw, heard, tasted, and so on. Then do the same for anyone who has been to a rural area. **ELL** **AL** Interpersonal

---

ANSWER, p. 77

☑ **READING PROGRESS CHECK** Responses will vary but should demonstrate an understanding that urban areas are cities and rural areas are country or wilderness areas. Sample response: Chicago is an urban area, and horse farms in Kentucky are rural areas.

Earth's Population

R Reading Skills

Applying After students have read about the key causes of the migration of people throughout the world, invite volunteers to identify each cause as you list it on the whiteboard. *(push factors such as war or violence force people to leave their homeland and pull factors such as family, education, and economic opportunities encourage people to move to regions with better opportunities)*

Then have small groups brainstorm a list of causes of migration for their area. Remind them to include the natural resources of the area, the climate, opportunities for education, and job opportunites for adults. Bring the class together to share their lists. **ELL** **AL** **Interpersonal**

C Critical Thinking Skills

Determining Cause and Effect Explain to students that push and pull factors affect population growth, distribution, and density. They also affect immigration rates. **Ask: How do push and pull factors affect immigration and population?** *(Student answers will vary but should demonstrate an understanding of how immigration will most likely increase where people are pulled and population will also increase in those locations. Where there are push factors, immigration will decrease as well as the population.)* **BL** **Verbal/Linguistic**

Content Background Knowledge

According to the UN High Commissioner for Refugees, the number of refugees worldwide decreased from 15.9 million in 2000 to 15.4 million in 2010. Yet the total number of international migrants rose from 150 million in 2000 to 214 million in 2010. Nearly half of those migrants are female. The countries with the fewest number of migrants include South Africa, Slovakia, Turkey, Japan, Nigeria, Romania, India, and Indonesia. Invite students to discuss why they think these countries would have the fewest number of migrants.

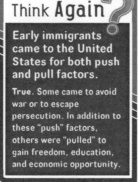

Think Again?

Early immigrants came to the United States for both push and pull factors.

True. Some came to avoid war or to escape persecution. In addition to these "push" factors, others were "pulled" to gain freedom, education, and economic opportunity.

People in rural areas often obtain food in outdoor markets such as this Laotian market.
▶ **CRITICAL THINKING**
Analyzing What is the main reason people choose to settle in one area and not in another?

Migration is one of the main causes of population shifts in our world today. What causes people to leave their homelands and migrate to different parts of the world?

Causes of Migration

To **emigrate** means "to leave one's home to live in another place." Emigration can happen within the same nation, such as when people move from a village to a city inside the same country. Often, emigration happens when people move from one nation to another. For example, millions of people have emigrated from countries in Europe, Asia, and Africa to start new lives in the United States. The term *immigrate* is closely related to *emigrate*, but it does not mean the same thing. To **immigrate** means "to enter and live in a new country."

The reasons for leaving one area and going to another are called push-pull factors. *Push* factors drive people from an area. For example, when a war breaks out in a country or a region, people emigrate from that place to escape danger. People who flee a country because of violence, war, or persecution are called **refugees**. Sometimes people emigrate from an area after a natural disaster such as a flood, an earthquake, or a tsunami has destroyed their homes and land. If the economy of a place becomes so weak that little or no work is available, people emigrate to seek new opportunities.

---

netw⊙rks *Online Teaching Options*

VIDEO

Migration

Interpreting Use the video to discuss what factors would cause people to leave their homes or countries to live in refugee camps, which often have problems and offer very limited opportunites. Be sure to clarify for students the difference between forced migration and other forms of movement. Discuss some of the push-pull factors that affect all people who move from place to place.
ELL **Visual/Spatial**

See page 69C for other online activities.

ANSWER, p. 78

CRITICAL THINKING They tend to live where basic needs—food, shelter, water, jobs— can be met.

Pull factors attract people to an area. Some people move to new places to be with friends or family members. Many young people move to cities or countries to attend universities or other schools. Some relocate in search of better jobs. Families sometimes move to places where their children will be able to attend good schools.

Effects of Migration

The movement of people to and from different parts of the world can affect the land, resources, culture, and economy of an area. Some of these effects are positive, but others can be harmful.

One positive effect of migration is cultural blending. As people from diverse cultures migrate to the same place and live close together, their cultures become mixed and blended. This blending creates new, unique cultures and ways of life. Artwork and music created in diverse urban areas is often an interesting mixture of styles and rhythms from around the world. Food, clothing styles, and languages spoken in urban areas change when people migrate into that area and bring new influences.

Some families and cultural groups work to preserve their original culture. These people want to keep their cultural traditions alive so they can be passed down to future generations. For example, the traditional Chinese New Year is an important celebration for many Chinese American families. Chinese Americans can be part of a blended American culture but still enjoy traditional Chinese foods, music, and arts, and celebrate Chinese holidays. It is possible to adapt to a local culture yet maintain strong ties to a home culture.

R

W

Some people migrate by choice. Others, such as the Libyan refugees shown here, are forced to flee to another country to live.
▶ **CRITICAL THINKING**
Citing Text Evidence What are examples of "pull" causes of migration?

V

Chapter 3 **79**

Carlos Spottorno/Getty Images News/Getty Images

Why Do People Move?

Determining Word Meanings Discuss with students the difference between *emigrate* and *immigrate*. Guide students to interpret their different meanings by pointing out the difference in the prefixes *e* and *im*. Use an interactive graphic organizer to list reasons why people choose to move from or to a place. **ELL** Verbal/Linguistic

See page 69C for other online activities.

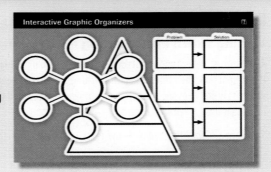

Interactive Graphic Organizers

R Reading Skills

Citing Text Evidence Discuss with students how migration can have beneficial effects for the immigrants as well as the country to which people are moving. **Ask:** What does the text explain is a positive effect of the movement of people? *(cultural blending)* Verbal/Linguistic

W Writing Skills

Informative/Explanatory Explain to students that the migration of people, whether internal, national, or international, affects culture. Have students brainstorm ways in which migration affects culture. Ask them to consider language, customs, and traditions.

Invite students to share if they have moved with their families and how many times. Record the data, including how many students have not moved, on the whiteboard.

Have students write a paragraph to answer these questions:

- **How has moving or not moving affected your family traditions?**
- **How has meeting new people who have moved to your area affected your family traditions and celebrations?**
  (Student answers will vary but should demonstrate understanding of the blending of cultures and adoption of cultural aspects through migration.) **ELL** Interpersonal

V Visual Skills

Interpreting Explain that refugees are often moved from one refugee camp to another as new refugees arrive at a camp that is already full of people escaping violence, war, or persecution. **Ask:** Do you think the refugees in this photograph are coming or going? What details help you to make this interpretation? *(Student answers will vary but should include logical thinking such as people are sitting on their suitcases and appear to be waiting; therefore, they are probably arriving in the camp rather than leaving the camp.)* **ELL** **BL** Logical/Mathematical, Visual/Spatial

ANSWER, p. 79

CRITICAL THINKING friends, family, good schools, better jobs, better standard of living

Earth's Population

V Visual Skills

Creating Visuals Discuss with students that urbanization refers to the growth of cities. Cities often include a large population, businesses, and different forms of transportation, all of which contribute to a stress on natural resources and an increase of pollution.

Also discuss that many cities are located near waterways or bodies of water partly because of the need for water to drink, wash, and cook, and partly because water used to be an important means of transportation. Have students create a visual of an urban area, using pictures from magazines, the Internet, or freehand drawings. **ELL** Visual/Spatial

T Technology Skills

Researching on the Internet Have students work with a partner and use the Internet to research the top five urban areas in the world. Then have them plot the five cities on a world map and consider their location to water and other natural resources. **Ask:** What generalizations can you make about the locations of the largest urban areas in the world? (Sample answer: They are located near bodies of water but are not all on the same continent.) **ELL** **AL** Logical/Mathematical, Visual/Spatial

C Critical Thinking Skills

Hypothesizing Explain to students that pollution caused from urbanization can have a very harmful effect on the environment. Trees and plants generally do not thrive naturally in urban areas. However, urban areas need the benefits of trees to produce oxygen and to clean pollutants from the air. Many large cities include large parks or forest preserves to address this need for the benefits we gain from trees.

Take students outside to make observations of the vegetation in your area. **Ask:** Why do you think trees and plants grow better in rural areas than urban areas? How might pollution affect their growth? (Sample answer: Pollution makes the air and water dirty, and plants need clean air and water to grow.) **Kinesthetic, Naturalist**

Nearly half the world's people live in urban areas. Many live in large cities such as Hong Kong.
▶ **CRITICAL THINKING**
Determining Word Meanings What is urbanization?

Causes and Effects of Urbanization

V Another effect of migration is the growth of urban areas. **Urbanization** happens when cities grow larger and spread into surrounding areas. Migration is a primary reason that urbanization occurs.

People move to cities for many reasons. The most common reason is to find jobs. Transportation and trade centers draw people primarily by creating new opportunities for business. As the businesses grow and people move into an area, the need for services also grows. Workers fill positions in medical services, education, entertainment, housing, and food sectors.

T As more people migrate to cities, urban areas become increasingly crowded. When populations within urban areas increase, cities grow and expand. Farmland is bought by developers to build homes, apartment buildings, factories, offices, schools, and stores to provide **C** for the growing number of people. The loss of farmland means that food must be grown farther from cities, resulting in additional shipping and related pollution.

Urbanization is happening in cities all over the world. In some places, cities have grown so vast that they have reached the outer edges of other cities. The result is massive clusters of urban areas that continue for miles. A huge city or cluster of cities with an extremely large population is called a **megalopolis**. These huge cities are growing larger every day, and they face the challenges that come with population growth and urbanization.

Delhi, one of India's largest cities, is a megalopolis. Its sprawling land area takes in a section called the Old City, which dates from the

Leung Cho Pan/Flickr/Getty Images

80 *Chapter 3*

netw⊕rks   *Online Teaching Options*

WORKSHEET

Writing Skills: Investigating Population Movement

Examining Have students investigate current global population movement. Have them note their findings on the Writing Skills worksheet. Then have students write an essay or create a class presentation based on their investigations. **Verbal/Linguistic**

See page 69C for other online activities.

ANSWER, p. 80

CRITICAL THINKING movement to the cities; growth of urban areas

mid-1600s. It also encompasses New Delhi, the modern capital city built by British colonial rulers in the early 1900s.

The largest megalopolis in the Americas is Mexico City. Because of its size and influence, Mexico City is a primate city, an urban area that dominates the economy and political affairs of its country. Primate cities include Cairo, Egypt, in Africa; Amman, Jordan, in Asia; and Paris, France, in Europe.

R

Examples of Urbanization

Urbanization takes place around the world, but for different reasons and at different rates.

Africa south of the Sahara, for example, is one of the least urbanized regions of the world. The region's urban areas, however, are growing so rapidly that Africa has a high rate of urbanization. Many Africans leave rural villages in order to find better job opportunities, health care, and public services in urban areas. At the same time, population growth has caused cities to spread into the countryside.

Europe is highly urbanized. Beginning in the late 1700s, the Industrial Revolution transformed Europe from a rural, agricultural society to an urban, industrial society. The growth of industries and cities began first in western Europe. Later, after World War II, the process spread to eastern Europe.

✔ **READING PROGRESS CHECK**

Describing In your own words, briefly summarize the main reasons people emigrate from their homelands.

FOLDABLES Study Organizer

Include this lesson's information in your Foldable®.

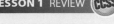

R Reading Skills

Labeling Have students use the world maps they created earlier in the lesson with the five largest urban areas. Ask them now to research five to ten megalopolises around the world and then label them on their maps. Encourage them to use different colors to distinguish the areas on the map and to create a key for their map explaining the use of the colors they chose.
ELL Visual/Spatial

Content Background Knowledge

The term *megalopolis* was coined in 1961 by a French geographer Jean Gottmann after spending two decades in an area of the United States that stretches from New Hampshire to Washington, D.C. In his study, he argued that as population growth increased in the cities in this region, people moved to smaller nearby areas that grew into large suburbs and "merged" with other metropolitan regions in the area.

Have students study this area using a map of the eastern United States. Tell students to use the map scale to figure out the distances between the major cities in this area. Then have students compare these distances with the distances between large cities in the Midwest, South, and western United States.

CLOSE & REFLECT

Making Connections To close this lesson, have students think about how population movement and growth affects cultures. Then have a class discussion about population movement and growth in your area, and how it has affected the cultures in your area.

Finally encourage students to make predictions about how population movement and growth will affect the area in which they live in the next ten years.

LESSON 1 REVIEW

Reviewing Vocabulary (Tier Three Words)
1. Why might people *immigrate* to a new country? **RH.6-8.4**

Answering the Guiding Questions
2. *Analyzing* If parts of Asia and Africa see a doubling of their population every 25 years, how do their birthrate and death rate correlate? **RH.6-8.1**

3. *Identifying* What factors might explain why western China is less densely populated than eastern China? **RH.6-8.2**

4. *Determining Word Meanings* Explain the difference between push and pull factors as they pertain to human migration. **RH.6-8.4**

5. *Informative/Explanatory Writing* Imagine that a war has broken out in your homeland and you have decided to leave. Select a country in Asia, Australia, or Africa as your "home" and describe in a three-paragraph essay what features you will seek in a specific new location. **WHST.6-8.2, WHST.6-8.4**

Chapter 3 **81**

LESSON 1 REVIEW ANSWERS

Reviewing Vocabulary

1. People might prefer to live in a country where the standard of living is higher or where the education system is better.

Answering the Guiding Questions

2. **Analyzing** The birthrate must be significantly higher than the death rate for the population to grow that quickly.

3. **Identifying** The western part has much harsher living conditions and lacks a good transportation system. It is also farther from the coast, so it is more difficult to move goods from western China.

4. **Determining Word Meanings** Push factors make people leave an area, such as war or famine. Pull factors encourage people to settle in an area, such as favorable climate or better job opportunities.

5. **Informative/Explanatory Writing** Essays should address a way to earn an income, lifestyle, climate, and general living conditions as factors in selecting a new home.

ANSWER, p. 81

✔ **READING PROGRESS CHECK** Students should briefly summarize reasons for emigration. Answers should mention emigrating to be near friends and family, emigrating for education or work opportunities, emigrating to escape the dangers of war, the effects of disasters, or threats to rights and freedoms, emigrating away from areas with weak economies to seek better employment.

ENGAGE

Bellringer Before students begin this lesson, **ask:**
What kinds of food do you and your family eat that are traditional to your family? Display several pictures of different ethnic foods or invite students to bring in a food or recipe that is unique or special to their family to share with the class. Invite students to read the recipes for unique ingredients or sample the food to get a taste of cuisines that might be unfamiliar to them. Ask students to share when they prepare these foods and how the foods represent their culture.

TEACH & ASSESS

R Reading Skills

Specifying Explain that a person's culture can relate to his or her traditions, customs, heritage, beliefs, or even language. A person may follow aspects of more than one culture, especially if he or she has moved from one country to another. **Ask: Why is the term *culture* used to refer to the set of beliefs, behaviors, and traits shared by a group of people when it is not specific to any one culture?** *(Sample answer: Culture is used as a more general term that encompasses a person or group's specific traditions and beliefs from others. It is a way to group those similarities. To be more specific, one would refer to a person's cultural group.)* **ELL** **Verbal/Linguistic**

Reinforcing Vocabulary Remind students to add academic and content vocabulary words to their vocabulary lists in their notebooks. Tell students to write their own definitions and to include drawings if desired. **ELL** **AL**

V Visual Skills

Creating Visuals Using a globe as a model, have students work individually to sketch a map of a country that is important to their culture, such as a home country or a country from which relatives emigrated in the past. Working with a partner, have students use their maps as a starting point for a discussion on elements of their culture. Have partners ask each other questions about special food, clothing, music, or art that is unique to their culture. **ELL** **AL** **Interpersonal**

ANSWER, p. 82

Taking Notes Sample responses: There are many different forms of government. Governments differ in how their leaders are chosen, who makes the rules, and how much freedom people have, and control governments have over their lives. Three of the world's most common forms of government are democracy, monarchy, and dictatorship. Some governments limit or restrict human rights.

---

networks

There's More Online!

☑ **MAP** Population Map
☑ **IMAGE** Cultural Change
☑ **VIDEO**

Reading **HELP**DESK **CCSS**

Academic Vocabulary RH.6-8.4
(Tier Two Words)
• **behalf**

Content Vocabulary RH.6-8.4
(Tier Three Words)
• **culture**
• **ethnic group**
• **dialect**
• **cultural region**
• **democracy**
• **representative democracy**
• **monarchy**
• **dictatorship**
• **human rights**
• **globalization**

TAKING NOTES: *Key Ideas and Details* RH.6-8.2, RH.6-8.7

Organize On a graphic organizer like this one, take notes about the different forms of government.

Form of Government

82

Lesson 2
The World's Cultures

ESSENTIAL QUESTION · *What makes a culture unique?*

IT MATTERS BECAUSE
Culture shapes the way people live and how they view the world.

What Is Culture?

GUIDING QUESTION *How is culture part of your life?*

What are some of your favorite foods? Do you like pizza, rice and beans, pasta, *samosas*, or corn on the cob? Have you ever thought about the people and cultures that invented the foods you enjoy eating? Millions of Americans eat foods created, grown, or developed by people of different cultures.

Culture is the set of beliefs, behaviors, and traits shared by a group of people. The term *culture* can also refer to the people of a certain culture. For example, saying "the Hindu culture" can mean the Hindu cultural traditions, the people who follow these traditions, or both.

You might be part of more than one culture. If your family has strong ties to a culture, such as that of a religion or a nation, you might follow this cultural tradition at home. You also might be part of a more mainstream American culture while at school and with friends.

If your family emigrated from Somalia to the United States, for example, you might speak the Somali language, wear traditional Somali clothing, and eat Somali foods. Your family might celebrate holidays observed in Somalia as well as American holidays, such as Thanksgiving and Independence Day. When you are with your friends, you might speak English, listen to American music, and watch American sports.

(l to r) Greg Balfour Evans/Alamy; Jose Luis Pelaez Inc/Blend Images/Getty Images; ©PoodlesRock/Corbis; Ian Gavan/Getty Images Entertainment/Getty Images; PAUL J. RICHARDS/AFP/Getty Images

---

networks *Online Teaching Options*

VIDEO

World's Best Ancient Sites: North America

Drawing Conclusions Use the video about traditional cultures in North America to introduce different cultural elements. Ask students to make a list of the ways the different groups described in the video adapt to their environment and the new ways they are continuing to adapt. Then have students describe how these cultural elements might be affected by elements such as changing governments or climate change. **BL** **Visual/Spatial**

See page 69D for other online activities.

BBC Motion Gallery Education

Ethnic Groups

We can look at members of a culture in terms of age, gender, or ethnic group. An **ethnic group** is a group of people with a common racial, national, tribal, religious, or cultural background. Members of the same Native American nation are an example of people of the same ethnic group. Other examples include the Maori of New Zealand and the Han Chinese. Large countries such as China can be home to hundreds of different ethnic groups. Some ethnic groups in a country are minority groups—people whose race or ethnic origin is different from that of the majority group. The largest ethnic minority groups in the United States are Hispanic Americans and African Americans.

Members of a culture might have special roles or positions as part of their cultural traditions. In some cultures, women are expected to care for and educate children. Most cultures expect men to earn money to support their families or to provide in other ways, such as by hunting and farming. Many cultures respect the elderly and value their wisdom. The leaders of older, traditional cultures are often elderly men or women who have leadership experience. Most cultures have clearly defined roles for their members. From an early age, young people learn what their culture expects of them. It is possible, too, to be part of more than one culture.

C

Cities often have communities within them that share a distinct and common culture, language, and customs.

▶ **CRITICAL THINKING**
Describing What is an ethnic group?

Language

Language serves as a powerful form of communication. Through language, people communicate information and experience and pass on cultural beliefs and traditions. Thousands of different languages are spoken in the world. Some languages have become world languages, or languages that are commonly spoken in many different parts of the world.

Some languages are spoken differently in different regions or by different ethnic groups. A **dialect** is a regional variety of a language with unique features, such as vocabulary, grammar, or pronunciation. People who speak the same language can sometimes understand other dialects, but at times, the pronunciation, or accent, of a dialect can be nearly impossible for others to understand.

T

Greg Balfour Evans/Alamy

C Critical Thinking Skills

Categorizing Read the section on different ethnic groups aloud to the class. **Ask: How are roles that are defined in ethnic groups similar and different?** *(In some cultures, women care for the children and help to educate them. Most cultures expect men to earn money. In most cultures, elderly men and women are respected by young and old.)*

V Record students' ideas on a chart with the headings "Men," "Women," and "Elderly." **ELL** **AL** **Verbal/Linguistic**

Men	Women	Elderly

V Visual Skills

Analyzing Images Remind students that images can reveal a lot about the elements of a culture. **Ask: What does this photograph reveal about the culture of this urban area?** *(Student answers will vary but students may infer that the architecture and sculptures indicate a culture that appreciates design; the traditional dancers may indicate a society that honors ancestral heritage; the Fish & Chips wagon indicates a society with British lifestyles and tastes.)* **ELL** **Visual/Spatial**

T Technology Skills

Researching Have students work in groups and spend some time on the Internet finding other places in the world where cultural centers have developed, such as Chinatown in San Francisco or Little Italy in New York City. Students could also choose to research the cultural influences that shape a city such as the Cuban influence in Miami, Florida, or the French influence in New Orleans.

Have the groups create poster presentations with visuals to discuss their chosen city. Then have those groups present their information to the rest of the class. Display the posters in class as you continue to teach this chapter.

Elements of Culture

Making Connections Display the interactive graphic organizer of elements of culture on the whiteboard. Work with students to complete the chart with all of the elements (language, religion, ethnicity, customs, art, and government). Then have students choose one element and write a paragraph about its importance to a culture. **AL** **Verbal/Linguistic**

See page 69D for other online activities.

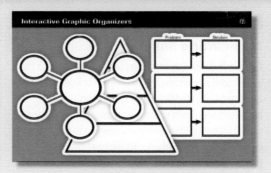

Interactive Graphic Organizers

ANSWER, p. 83

CRITICAL THINKING a group of people with a common racial, national, tribal, religious, or cultural background

The World's Cultures

R Reading Skills

Analyzing Charts Review the chart of major world religions with students. Then ask them the following questions:

- **What do Christianity, Judaism, and Islam share in common?** *(They are all based on the belief in one God.)*
- **How are all of the religions similar?** *(They all share the belief in either one God, one leader such as Buddha, or one eternal spirit such as Brahman.)*
- **How do you think the artwork and music from some cultures are influenced by religion?** *(Student answers may include that the artwork and music depict religious themes, beliefs, leaders, or followers.)* **Verbal/Linguistic**

T Technology Skills

Research Have pairs or small groups of students choose one of the world religions to learn more about by researching it on the Internet. Or you may want to assign a religion to groups to ensure that all religions are covered when class presentations are made.

Make sure students use reliable sources for their research and have them include a list of their sources with their notes. Then have the pairs or groups prepare and give a presentation to the class about the religion they researched. Explain that students should keep the information in their presentation positive and factual, explaining the beliefs of the religion, its history, and the areas in the world where it is predominately followed. **Verbal/Linguistic**

Content Background Knowledge

In some countries, a high percentage of people attend weekly religious services, but it varies widely and regionally. In a study conducted by the Pew Research Center in 2010, ninety-three percent of Jordan's population attended weekly services. The next highest attendance was 65 percent in Indonesia. In the United States the report showed that 35 percent of Americans attend weekly services. Only 4 percent of people living in Japan and Sweden attend religious services.

CHART SKILLS >

MAJOR WORLD RELIGIONS

Religion	Major Leader	Beliefs
Buddhism	Siddhārtha Gautama, the Buddha	Suffering comes from attachment to earthly things, which are not lasting. People become free by following the Eightfold Path, rules of right thought and conduct. People who follow the Path achieve nirvana—a state of endless peace and joy.
Christianity	Jesus Christ	The one God is Father, Son, and Holy Spirit. God the Son became human as Jesus Christ. Jesus died and rose again to bring God's forgiving love to sinful humanity. Those who trust in Jesus and follow his teachings of love for God and neighbor receive eternal life with God.
Hinduism	No one founder	One eternal spirit, Brahman, is represented as many deities. Every living thing has a soul that passes through many successive lives. Each soul's condition in a specific life is based on how the previous life was lived. When a soul reaches purity, it finally joins permanently with Brahman.
Islam	Muhammad	The one God sent a series of prophets, including the final prophet Muhammad, to teach humanity. Islam's laws are based on the Quran, the holy book, and the Sunnah, examples from Muhammad's life. Believers practice the five pillars—belief, prayer, charity, fasting, and pilgrimage—to go to an eternal paradise.
Judaism	Abraham	The one God made an agreement through Abraham and later Moses with the people of Israel. God would bless them, and they would follow God's laws, applying God's will in all parts of their lives. The main laws and practices of Judaism are stated in the Torah, the first five books of the Hebrew Bible.
Sikhism	Guru Nanak	The one God made truth known through 10 successive gurus, or teachers. God's will is that people should live honestly, work hard, and treat others fairly. The Sikh community, or Khalsa, bases its decisions on the principles of a sacred text, the Guru Granth Sahib.

Religion

T Religion has a major influence on how people of a culture see the world. Religious beliefs are powerful. Some individuals see their religion as merely a tradition to follow during special occasions or holidays. Others view religion as the foundation and most important part of their life. Religious practices vary widely. Many cultures base their way of life on the spiritual teachings and laws of holy books. Religion is a central part of many of the world's cultures. Throughout history, religious stories and symbols have influenced painting, architecture, and music.

Customs

Customs are also an important outward display of culture. In many traditional cultures, a woman is not permitted to touch a man other than her husband, even for a handshake. In modern European cultures, polite greetings include kissing on the cheeks. People of many cultures bow to others as a sign of greeting, respect, and

---

netw◉rks *Online Teaching Options*

CHART

Major World Religions

Comparing and Contrasting Display the chart on the whiteboard and discuss the different religions listed on the chart. Have students point out the similarities between them *(most of them are monotheistic)*. Discuss with students how religion can become a major influence on how people see and interact with the world. **ELL Visual/Spatial**

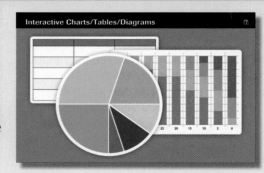
Interactive Charts/Tables/Diagrams

See page 69D for other online activities.

goodwill. The world's many cultures have countless fascinating customs. Some are used only formally, and others are viewed as good manners and respectful, professional behavior.

History

History shapes how we view the world. We often celebrate holidays to honor the heroes and heroines who brought about successes. Stories about heroes reveal the personal characteristics that people think are important. Groups also remember the dark periods of history when they met with disaster or defeat. These experiences too influence how groups of people see themselves. Cultural holidays mark important events and enable people to celebrate their heritage.

The Arts and Sports

Dance, music, visual arts, and literature are important elements of culture. Nearly all cultures have unique art forms that celebrate their history and enrich people's lives. Some art forms, such as singing and dancing, are serious parts of religious ceremonies or other cultural events. Aboriginal people of the Pacific Islands have songs, dances, and chants that are vital parts of their cultural traditions. Art can be forms of personal expression or worship, entertainment, or even ways of retelling and preserving a culture's history.

In sports, as in many other aspects of culture, activities are adopted, modified, and shared. Many sports that we play today originated with different culture groups in the past. Athletes in ancient Japan, China, Greece, and Rome played a game similar to soccer. Scholars believe that the Maya of Mexico and Central America developed "ballgame," the first organized team sport. Playing on a 40- to 50-foot long (12-m to 15-m) recessed court, the athletes' goal was to kick a rubber ball through a goal.

Government

Government is another element of culture. Despite differences, governments around the world share certain features. They maintain order within an area and provide protection from outside dangers. Governments also provide services to citizens. Such services typically include education and transportation infrastructure. Different cultures have different ways of distributing power and making rules.

Jose Luis Pelaez Inc/Blend Images/Getty Images

Soccer is one of the most popular international sports.

Identifying Which culture first played the game of soccer?

C1 Critical Thinking Skills

Making Connections Invite a volunteer to read the paragraph under, "History." **Ask:**

- **In the United States, what holidays are celebrated that honor heroes or heroines?** *(Possible answers may include:* ***Memorial Day:*** *where military men and women who died in service to the United States are honored;* ***Veteran's Day:*** *where former and current military men and women are honored;* ***Presidents' Day:*** *where past United States presidents are honored;* ***Martin Luther King, Jr. Day:*** *to honor his efforts to bring about equal rights to all people in the United States.)*
- **What types of celebrations usually take place on these holidays?** *(parades, memorials, speeches, ceremonies, performances, concerts, or festivals)* **Verbal/Linguistic**

W Writing Skills

Narrative Have students research more about Aboriginal songs, dances, or chants and write a paragraph about what they learn. Encourage students to use descriptive words that give the reader a vivid picture of their writing.

You may want to allow students who struggle with their writing to enhance their descriptions with drawings, or to perform a song or dance for the class. **Auditory/Musical, Visual/Spatial**

C2 Critical Thinking Skills

Giving Examples Sports can bring together cultures, especially when they are played in international competitions. Some sports have been introduced or influenced by other cultures and other countries. **Ask:**

- **What other sports besides soccer are played in countries around the world?** *(Possible answer: basketball, golf, ice hockey, baseball, tennis, cycling, skiing)*
- **Have you played any of these sports?** *(Students' answers will vary.)* **ELL** **Verbal/Linguistic, Intrapersonal**

Chapter 3 **85**

MAP

World Cultural Regions

Analyzing Maps Display the world cultural regions layer of the Chapter Opener map on the whiteboard. Review with students the various cultural regions. Discuss how some cultural regions cover one country, multiple countries, one continent, or more than one continent. Then ask students to make connections between the locations of similar cultural regions. **BL** **Visual/Spatial**

See page 69D for other online activities.

ANSWER, p. 85

Identifying Many different groups from various times and areas played a game similar to soccer. The game cannot be traced back to any one group, however.

T Technology Skills

T Technology Skills

Using and Citing Information Have students work in pairs and guide them to recent economic data by country on the Internet, which can often be accessed by going to a country's government website. Ask them to choose two countries to research and locate the top products or goods that those countries produce. Instruct students to write down the sources they use. As a class, create a world product map or chart in which the data that the students gathered is shown, and have students cite their sources. **Logical/Mathematical, Interpersonal**

R Reading Skills

Discussing Discuss with students the different ethnic groups in your area and how they have influenced traditions, businesses, sports, and other activities in your community. Then relate your area to the state in which you live. **Ask: What cultural regions are in our state or local region?** *(Student answers will vary but should demonstrate understanding of a cultural region.)* **ELL Verbal/Linguistic**

W Writing Skills

Narrative Tell students that the signing of the Declaration of Independence is an important event in our nation's history. The signers took a big risk as they declared their independence from Great Britain. They became Americans and formed a new nation, the United States. Ask students to write a short narrative based on this time period in which they describe how people living in the colonies felt about the emergence of a new culture.

Suggest that students use presentation software in which they can add images and music to their narratives, and then show the final product to the class. Have students who are watching the presentations evaluate them based on event sequence, descriptive details, narrative technique, and transition words. **Auditory/Musical, Visual/Spatial**

ANSWERS, p. 86

✓ **READING PROGRESS CHECK** Accept all reasonable responses that demonstrate an understanding of the basic elements of culture.

CRITICAL THINKING The United States is a representative democracy. Citizens elect officials to make and carry out laws and policies on their behalf.

Economy

T Economies control the use of natural resources and define how goods are produced and distributed to meet human needs. Some cultures have their own type of economy, but most follow the economy of the country or area where they live. This allows people of different cultures living in an area to trade and conduct other types of business with one another. For example, many people in Benin, West Africa, sell goods in open-air markets. Some people bring items to the markets to trade for the goods they need, but others pay for goods using paper money and coins.

Cultural Regions

R A **cultural region** is a geographic area in which people have certain traits in common. People in a cultural region often live close to one another to share resources, for social reasons, and to keep their cultures and communities strong. Cultural regions can be large or relatively small. For example, one of the world's largest cultural areas stretches across northern Africa and Southwest Asia. This cultural region is home to millions of people of the Islamic, or Muslim, culture. A much smaller cultural region is Spanish Harlem in New York City. This cultural region is home to a large and growing Hispanic culture.

✓ **READING PROGRESS CHECK**

Identifying Point of View What cultural traditions do you practice? Make a list of the beliefs, behaviors, languages, foods, art, music, clothing, and other elements of culture that are part of your daily life.

On July 4, 1776, the Second Continental Congress approved the Declaration of Independence, establishing the United States as an independent country.
▶ **CRITICAL THINKING**
Describing What form of government does the United States have? How does that form of government work?

Government

GUIDING QUESTION *How does government affect way of life?*

All nations need some type of formal leadership. What differs among countries is how leaders are chosen, who makes the rules, how much freedom people have, and how much control governments have over people's lives. Many different kinds of government systems operate in the world today. Three of the most common are democracy, monarchy, and dictatorship.

Democracy

In a democracy, the people hold the power. Citizens of a nation make the decisions themselves. A **democracy** is a system of government that is run by the people. In

©PoodlesRock/Corbis

---

networks   *Online Teaching Options*

WORKSHEET

Critical Thinking Skills: Investigating Different Forms of Government

Examining Have students investigate different forms of government such as democracy, monarchy, and dictatorship. Then have them note their findings on the Critical Thinking Skills worksheet. Encourage students to research on the Internet the founding principles behind the idea of a democratic society and government. **BL Verbal/Linguistic**

See page 69D for other online activities.

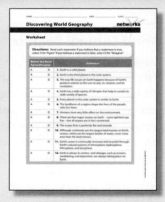

democratic systems of government, people are free to propose laws and policies. Citizens then vote to decide which laws and policies will be set in place. When people run the government, their rights and freedoms are protected.

In some democracies, the people elect leaders to make and carry out laws. A **representative democracy** is a form of democracy in which citizens elect government officials to represent the people; the government representatives make and carry out laws and policies on **behalf** of the people. The United States is an example of a representative democracy.

The queen is the symbolic head of the United Kingdom, but elected leaders hold the power to rule.

Monarchy

A **monarchy** is ruled by a king or a queen. In a monarchy, power and leadership are usually passed down from older to younger generations through heredity. The ruler of a monarchy, called a *monarch*, is usually a king, a queen, a prince, or a princess. In the past, monarchs had absolute power, or complete and unlimited power to rule the people. Today, most monarchs only represent, or stand for, a country's traditions and values, while elected officials run the government. The United Kingdom is an example of a monarchy.

Academic Vocabulary

behalf in the interest of; in support of; in defense of

Dictatorship

A **dictatorship** is a form of government in which one person has absolute power to rule and control the government, the people, and the economy. People who live under a dictatorship often have few rights. With absolute power, a dictator can make laws with no concern for how just, fair, or practical the laws are. North Korea is an example of a dictatorship.

Some dictators abuse their power for personal gain. One negative consequence of abuse of power is lack of personal freedoms and human rights for the general public. **Human rights** are the rights that belong to all individuals. Those rights are the same for every human in every culture. Some basic human rights are the right to life, liberty, security, privacy, freedom from slavery, and fair treatment before the law, as well as the right to marry and have children.

☑ **READING PROGRESS CHECK**

Describing In your own words, describe the system of government that is used in the United States.

Ian Gavan/Getty Images Entertainment/Getty Images

Chapter 3 **87**

CHART

Types of Government

Analyze Charts Display the chart on types of government on the whiteboard. Discuss the similarities and differences among different forms of government, including democracy, monarchy, and dictatorship. Have students work with a partner to complete a Venn diagram on two forms of government. **AL** Visual/Spatial

See page 69D for other online activities.

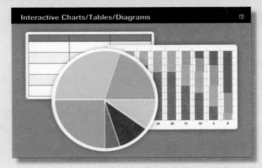

Interactive Charts/Tables/Diagrams

R Reading Skills

Determining Word Meanings Explain that by examining Greek and Latin word meanings, students can break down some words to better understand their meaning. In the Greek language, *demos* means "the people" and *kratia* means "power or rule." **Ask: How does understanding these Greek word meanings help you to determine what democracy means?** *(Sample answer: democracy means "power or rule by the people")* **ELL** **AL** Verbal/Linguistic

C Critical Thinking Skills

Making Connections After reading about different kinds of government, **ask: What kind of government affects people more negatively than the others?** *(dictatorship)* **What connection can you make between this form of government and countries in which human rights may not be promoted and protected?** *(They are closely connected but not always connected. Very often those who live under a dictator have few rights and have few ways to gain more rights and freedom.)*

Have students model the different types of governments they have learned about in this section. Divide the class into four groups, with each group representing one of the three forms of government and the fourth group acting as the citizens. Take turns having each group model the behavior and decision-making that is characteristic of that form of government toward its citizens. **Interpersonal, Kinesthetic**

Content Background Knowledge

Ancient Greece was the birthplace of democracy, but the democratic form of government that the ancient Greeks practiced was different than the kind we use today. The ancient Greeks practiced direct democracy, in which citizens voted directly, not through representatives. In the United States and other countries with democratic forms of government, indirect democracy is practiced, which means that citizens vote to elect representatives who represent them.

ANSWER, p. 87

☑ **READING PROGRESS CHECK** Sample answer: The United States has a representative democracy, in which the people elect others to represent them in government decisions.

V Visual Skills

Analyzing Visuals Have students look at the image of the port in Malaysia and discuss the concept of globalization and its effect on culture in pairs. Next discuss how the port in the photo can influence both what is brought into and what leaves the country. **Ask: In what ways does free trade impact your daily life?** *(Students' answers will vary but should demonstrate understanding of how goods are shipped from all around the world and that they use many of these goods on a daily basis.)* **Intrapersonal, Visual/Spatial**

C Critical Thinking Skills

Suggesting a Solution Explain that when people relocate and bring their cultural traditions with them, they may have to adapt to a new physical environment. Have students consider how people can face these challenges, which may also affect their ability to practice elements of their culture. **Ask: What is a specific challenge of moving to a new region, and how would you solve it?** *(Students' answers will vary but should demonstrate an understanding of how people adapt their cultural traditions to a new region and new environment.)* Have students work in pairs to answer the question. Then have students share their ideas with the class. **Naturalist**

Content Background Knowledge

The United Nations (UN), formed in 1945 shortly after World War II ended, originally had fifty-one member countries. The organization formed for many purposes, including maintaining peace and security through the world, supporting the self-determination of people, solving global, social, cultural, humanitarian, and economic crises, and protecting human rights. Today, with nearly 200 member countries, the UN protects human rights through nearly 80 treaties and declarations and has aided about 30 countries in their quest to hold democratic elections.

Cargo containers are stockpiled and ready to be loaded onto ships in the port of Johor, Malaysia. International trade is the exchange of goods and services between countries. When people trade, they not only trade goods, they also trade customs and ideas.

Cultural Shifts

GUIDING QUESTION *How do cultures change over time?*

Cultures change over time for many reasons. When people relocate, they bring their cultural traditions with them. The traditions often influence or blend with the cultures of the places where they settle. Over time, as people of many cultures move to a location, the culture of that location takes on elements of all the cultures within it. Cities, such as London and New York, are examples of areas that have richly diverse cultures.

Cultural Change

Change can also occur as a result of trade, travel, war, and exchange of ideas. Trade brings people to new areas to sell and barter goods. Whenever people travel, they bring their language, customs, and ideas with them. They also bring elements of foreign cultures back with them when they return home. Throughout history, traders and explorers have brought home new foods, clothing, jewelry, and other goods. Some of these, such as gold, chocolate, gunpowder, and silk, became popular all over the world. Trade in these items changed the course of history.

©Justin Guariglia/Corbis

88 *Chapter 3*

netw⚡rks *Online Teaching Options*

IMAGE

Cultural Change

Determining Cause and Effect Show the image on why cultures change. Explain how some cultures can change over time while some remain the same. Discuss with students how migration, emigration, and immigration affect cultures. In small groups, have students write a list of these effects on cultures and share their findings with the class. **ELL**

See page 69D for other online activities.

NASA/NOAA/SPL/Science Photo Library/Getty Images

T

Culture also can change as a result of technology. The telegraph, telephones, and e-mail have made communication increasingly faster and easier. Television and the Internet have given people in all parts of the world easy access to information and new ideas. Elements of culture such as language, clothing styles, customs, and behaviors spread quickly as people discover them by watching television and using the Internet.

Global Culture

Today's world is becoming more culturally blended every day. As cultures combine, new cultural elements and traditions are born. The spread of culture and ideas has caused our world to become globalized. **Globalization** is the process by which nations, cultures, and economies become integrated, or mixed. Globalization has had the positive effect of making people more understanding and accepting of other cultures. In addition, it has helped spread ideas and innovations. Technology has made communication faster and easier. Travel also has become faster and easier, allowing more people to visit more places in less time. This is resulting in cultural blending on a wider scale than ever before.

The process of cultural blending through globalization is not always smooth and easy. Sometimes it produces tension and conflict as people from different cultures come into contact with one another. Some people do not want their culture to change, or they want to control the amount of change. Sometimes the changes come too fast, and cultures can be damaged or destroyed.

Just as no one element defines a culture, no one culture can define the world. All cultures have value and add to the human experience. As the world becomes more globalized, people must continue to respect other ways of life. We have much to learn, and much to gain, from the many cultures that make our world a fascinating place.

PAUL J. RICHARDS/AFP/Getty Images

✓ **READING PROGRESS CHECK**

Determining Word Meanings What is globalization?

Widespread use of technology, such as cell phones, allows us to share information with a larger audience.

▶ **CRITICAL THINKING**

Analyzing How does technology help spread new ideas?

FOLDABLES
Study Organizer

Include this lesson's information in your Foldable®.

LESSON 2 REVIEW ⓒⒸⓈⓈ

Reviewing Vocabulary (Tier Three Words)
1. Which *human rights* do you think are the hardest to safeguard? Why? RH.6-8.4

Answering the Guiding Questions
2. *Determining Central Ideas* Explain how a language becomes a world language, and predict whether any languages from Asia or Africa are likely to soon become a world language. RH.6-8.2
3. *Identifying Point of View* Why might a dictator want to be in power? RH.6-8.6

4. *Analyzing* Consider countries that are not yet developed. Write an essay explaining whether their cultures change more quickly or slowly than a culture of a developed country and explain your reasoning. RH.6-8.1, WHST.6-8.4
5. *Informative/Explanatory Writing* Think about the various cultures that you belong to. Write a short essay describing these cultures and your place in them. WHST.6-8.2, WHST.6-8.10

Chapter 3 **89**

LESSON 2 REVIEW ANSWERS

Reviewing Vocabulary

1. Answers will vary, but students should give consideration to basic human rights such as liberty, freedom, and fair treatment before the law in giving their answer.

Answering the Guiding Questions

2. **Determining Central Ideas** A language becomes a world language if a lot of people see a reason to be able to communicate using that language and if it is widely taught. Chinese might become a world language because they now produce and export so many goods around the world, but most Chinese and other cultures already teach English, which is a world language. Japanese is also a possibility because people are intrigued with that culture.

3. **Identifying Point of View** Some dictators want to be in power for personal gain. Others might think they know the best way to rule a country or what is best for everyone.

4. **Analyzing** Students should note that cultures in countries that are not developed will not change as fast because ideas will not be spread as quickly. The people do not have access to as many different ideas, products, or opportunities to try new things and adopt them.

5. **Informative/Explanatory Writing** Students' essays will vary but should illustrate their various roles in the world.

CHAPTER 3, Lesson 2
The World's Cultures

T Technology Skills

Analyzing Have students think about how their lives would be different in regard to technology if they had grown up 40 years ago. If need be discuss the technologies today that were not available or just beginning at that time including personal computers, remote controls on TVs, recorders for TVs, digital cameras, cell phones, the Internet, and so on. **AL** Verbal/Linguistic

Analyzing News Media Have students work in small groups to access national or international news features online. Ask them to find a news feature that might affect cultural change and evaluate the importance of the information, ideas, or images that are broadcast. Ask groups to consider if there is any form of bias in the news feature.

Then have groups present their findings and evaluations of the news features to the class. Invite discussion of the news features between groups to see if others would have evaluated the features differently. **BL** Visual/Spatial

CLOSE & REFLECT

Making Connections To close this lesson, discuss how today's world is becoming more culturally blended and the positive results that have come about because of globalization.

Then have students think about how cultures change and how they affect the way people live. Have them offer ways their life has changed by the introduction of new cultures in your area, such as ethnic restaurants, new foods available in grocery stores, and new classmates in school.

Ask them to predict a change to various cultures in the United States within their life times. Invite students to write down their predictions and share them with the class for further discussion.

You may want to keep their predictions to review at the end of the school year to see if students have changed their points of view throughout the school year and would want to make changes to their predictions.

ANSWERS, p. 89

CRITICAL THINKING Technology allows people in all parts of the world easy access to information and the quick spread of ideas.

✓ **READING PROGRESS CHECK** Globalization is the process by which nations, cultures, and economies become integrated, or mixed.

ENGAGE

Bellringer Before students read the Global Connections feature on rain forest resources, explain that all of the Global Connections features in their textbook provide information and facts on global issues. In this case it is focused on the importance of the world's rain forests. Have students share what they know about rain forests. Then, **ask:**

- **Where are rain forests found?** *(in areas where the climate is warm and receives a great deal of rain, including the Amazon Basin in South America, the Congo Basin in Africa, and the Indonesian Archipelago in Southeast Asia)*
- **Why do you think rain forests are called the "Lungs of the Planet"?** *(Answers should include an understanding that all people and animals need a large contribution of oxygen for survival.)* Direct students to the quote on this page. Have a student read it aloud and explain what is meant by "deforestation." Help students recognize that as the rain forests are deforested, the ability of the world's rain forests to act as the "planet's lungs" diminishes, as well.

TEACH & ASSESS

C1 Critical Thinking Skills

Evaluating Have students discuss where the world's rain forests are located and use the images in the textbook to discuss apsects of life for indigenous people who lived in rain forest regions before deforestation began to take place. **Ask:** How do you think indigenous people lived in the rain forests before contact with the outside world? *(Answers will vary but students should recognize that the rain forests satisfied indigenous peoples' needs for food, shelter, and medicine, allowing them to survive in isolation.)* **AL** Logical/Mathematical

R Reading Skills

Determine Central Ideas Have students recognize the cause of deforestation. **Ask:**

- **Why is the deforestation of the world's rain forests occurring?** *(cutting for livestock grazing, agriculture, wood and mining of the land's minerals)*
- **What is the environmental impact of deforestation?** *(reduction in the world's biological diversity)*
- **What efforts are being made to preserve the world's rain forests?** *(plant trees on deforested land, companies operate in ways to minimize damage to rain forests)* **Verbal/Linguistic**

Rain Forest Resources

Many medicines that we use today come from plants found in rain forests. From these plants, we derive medicines to treat or cure diabetes, heart conditions, glaucoma, and many other illnesses and physical problems.

C1 **Largest Rain Forests** The world's largest rain forests are located in the Amazon Basin in South America, the Congo Basin in Africa, and the Indonesian Archipelago in Southeast Asia. The Amazon rain forest makes up more than half of Earth's remaining rain forest.

C2 **The Planet's Lungs** Rain forests are often called the "lungs of the planet" for their contribution in producing oxygen, which all animals need for survival. Rain forests also provide a home for many people, animals, and plants. They are also an important source of medicine and foods.

The People of the Congo Since ancient times, hunter-gatherers have lived in the Congo Basin Rain Forest. The groups, including the Mbuti, Baka, and Aka, are diverse; all have separate languages, religions, and customs.

> **Every year, less and less of the rain forest remains. Human activity is the main cause of this deforestation.** **R**

Deforestation Every year, less and less of the rain forest remains. Human activity is the main cause of this deforestation. Humans cut rain forests for grazing land, agriculture, wood, and the land's minerals. Deforestation harms the native people who rely on the rain forest. The loss of rain forests also has an extreme impact on the environment because the rich biological diversity of the rain forest is lost as the trees are cut down.

C3 **Preserving Rain Forests** More and more people realize that keeping the rain forests intact is critical. Groups plant trees on deforested land in the hope that forests will eventually recover. More companies are operating in ways that minimize damage to rain forests.

More Research Thirty years ago, very little research on the medicines of the rain forest was being done. Today, many drug companies and several branches of the U.S. government, including the National Cancer Institute, are taking part in research projects to find medicines and cures for viruses, infections, cancer, and AIDS.

This unique plant is common in the rain forest of Malaysia. In the Malay language, the plant is called *Jangkang*, which means "stilt roots."

---

net**⊙**rks *Online Teaching Options*

SLIDE SHOW

Medical Treatments from the Rain Forest

Analyzing Images Display the slide show of plants and the uses of plants for medical needs to help students understand the importance of rain forest plants. In teams have students choose one or two plants from the slide show presentation to research where the plants are found and how they are used for medicinal purposes. Teams should provide drawings or diagrams to explain what they learned. Then have volunteers create a display with the visuals. **AL** **ELL** Visual/Spatial, Interpersonal

Slide Show

THERE'S MORE ONLINE

HEAR why the rain forest is important • *SEE* rain forest reduction • *WATCH* plants become drugs

Chapter 3 91

Rain Forest Biome

Simulating Share the infographic with the class. Ask students to explain the rain forest biome. Have students research images and create a visual "snapshot" of the rain forest from the rain forest floor through the canopy to show the variety of animals and plants that inhabit the rain forest. Students who enjoy technology may wish to create an interactive presentation to visually build their "snapshot." Have students share their work. **BL** **Verbal/Linguistic**

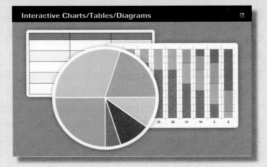

Interactive Charts/Tables/Diagrams

C₂ Critical Thinking Skills

Analyzing Visuals Direct attention to the picture of the boy in the center column. **Ask:**

• **Why is it important to respect the traditions and culture of indigenous people?** *(Answers will vary, but students should recognize that different does not mean wrong and that indigenous people have great knowledge to share about the rain forest environment.)*

• **What might the indigenous people be able to teach the world about the rain forests?** *(They could teach the world about plants in the rain forest that are of medicinal value.)* **Verbal/Linguistic**

V

C₃ Critical Thinking Skills

Speculating Help students become aware of why rain forest environments are limited. **Ask:**

• **Most rain forest environments are found near the Equator. Why is this?** *(little variation in climate yearlong)*

• **How might continued deforestation of the world's rain forests impact the indigenous people who live there?** *(Answers will vary but students should recognize that further destruction of the environment that indigenous people depend on may threaten their ability to survive in the rain forest.)* **Visual/Spatial**

V Visual Skills

Integrating Visual Information Have students analyze the full page image. **Ask:**

• **How is the rain forest environment a safe environment for indigenous people?** *(Indigenous people understand the plants and animals of the rain forest, know which plants are safe and which are not, and how to use the rain forest for shelter and for play.)*

• **How is the tree in the photograph different from the trees you are familiar with?** *(Possible answer: This tree has roots growing from the sides of the trunk high above the ground, which is different from the trees in our area .)* **Visual/Spatial**

R Reading Skills

Citing Text Evidence Create a chart on the board with three headings: *Value for Animals, Value for Medicine,* and *Value for Agriculture.* Have the class identify individual statistics on the page and determine in which category the statistic belongs. Review the information in the chart. **Ask: What does the evidence say about the value of the world's rain forests?** *(Students should recognize and provide specific examples from the text to articulate that rain forests benefit the world in a variety of ways.)* **Logical/Mathematical**

C1 Critical Thinking Skills

Identifying Problems Add a fourth column to the chart on the board. Label the column *Problems.* Have students quantify the ongoing deforestation. **Ask: What has happened to the rain forests in recent times?** *(In 1950 rain forests covered 14 percent of Earth's land, today 7 percent; 32 million acres lost yearly; at current rate rain forests will disappear in 40 years.)* **Logical/Mathematical**

C2 Critical Thinking Skills

Analyzing Review the information about the amount of forest that has been cleared. **Ask:**

- **How does use of the rain forest threaten its survival?** *(Continued deforestation for agriculture and mineral extraction reduces the total acreage of the rain forest and leaves it difficult for the region to recover.)*
- **How does use of the rain forest threaten the survival of those living there?** *(Accept all answers. Students should recognize that without the plants, animals that depend on the rain forest for food and shelter will perish.)*

Content Background Knowledge

Scientists are working with an indigenous group in the rain forest to develop medicines from the slime of a poisonous tree frog. The group has been using the slime as a remedy for illness and pain for centuries. The slime contains compounds with anesthetic and tranquilizing properties. Scientists hope to isolate these compounds and then reproduce them using modern technology in genetics.

Today's scientists are realizing that the traditional knowledge of these indigenous groups in the rain forest is an extremely valuable resource, because they know the many plants and animals of the rain forest much better than anyone else.

R *These numbers and statistics can help you learn about the resources of the rain forest.*

1.4 Billion Acres

The Amazon rain forest covers 1.4 billion acres (5,665,599 sq km). If the rain forest were a nation, it would be the world's thirteenth-largest country.

OVER SEVEN PERCENT

Tropical rain forests make up about 7 percent of the world's total landmass. But found within the rain forest are half of all known varieties of plants.

40 Years

In 1950 rain forests covered about 14 percent of Earth's land. Rain forests cover about 7 percent today. Scientists estimate that, at the present rate, all rain forests could disappear from Earth within 40 years.

80%

About 80 percent of the diets of developed nations of the world originated in tropical rain forests. Included are such fruits as oranges and bananas; corn, potatoes, and other vegetables; and nuts and spices.

120

Today, 120 prescription drugs sold worldwide are derived from rain forest plants. About 65 percent of all cancer-fighting medicines also come from rain forest plants. An anticancer drug derived from a special kind of periwinkle plant has greatly increased the survival rate for children with leukemia.

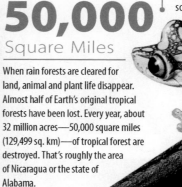

50,000 Square Miles

When rain forests are cleared for land, animal and plant life disappear. Almost half of Earth's original tropical forests have been lost. Every year, about 32 million acres—50,000 square miles (129,499 sq. km)—of tropical forest are destroyed. That's roughly the area of Nicaragua or the state of Alabama.

800,000 POPULATION

An Iban shaman, or healer, in traditional dress along a river side. For centuries, Iban people who lived in the rain forests of Malaysia relied on shamans to cure their ills. Today shamans still play an important role for some of the 800,000 Iban people.

ONE PERCENT

Although ingredients for many medicines come from rain forest plants, less than 1 percent of plants growing in rain forests have been tested by scientists for medicinal purposes.

networks *Online Teaching Options*

ANIMATION

Costs and Benefits of Human Activity in the Rain Forest

Interpreting Use this animation to help students weigh the costs and benefits of using the rain forest, from medical treatment to loss of species, indigenous cultures, habitat, and future medical cures. As a group, have students create a wall-size costs and benefits chart that includes visual images. **ELL Kinesthetic, Interpersonal**

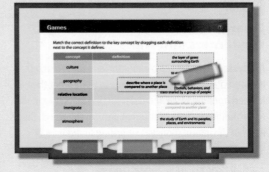

(t) Martin Puddy/Asia Images/Getty Images; (c) A.T. White/The Image Bank/Getty Images; (bl) John Stanmeyer/VII/Corbis; (bc) Bruce Farnsworth/Alamy; (br) Frederic Soltan/Corbis

GLOBAL IMPACT

THE WORLD'S RAIN FORESTS Rain forests are located in a belt around Earth near the Equator. Abundant rain, relatively constant temperatures, and strong sunlight year-round are ideal conditions for the plants and animals of the rain forest.

Rain forests cover only a small part of Earth's surface. The Amazon Basin in South America is the world's largest rain forest area.

Rain Forest Research

Laboratories provide a research base for scientists to conduct environmental research. This laboratory in Mumbai attracts forest scientists from around the world.

Thinking Like a
Geographer

1. **Environment and Society** Why do you think scientists only know about a small fraction of potential medicines from the rain forest?

2. **Environment and Society** How do you think native doctors in the Amazon rain forest discovered medical uses for plants?

3. **Human Geography** Write your government representatives and encourage them to support plans that help save rain forests. State at least three reasons why it is important to save rain forests.

Chapter 3 **93**

GAME

Rain Forest Facts

Collaborating Play this game as a class to allow students to use what they have learned about the rain forest. Afterwards, have the class design an advertising campaign to save the world's rain forests. Group students to make use of technology to create different parts of the advertising campaign. **ELL** **Visual/ Spatial, Verbal/Linguistic**

V Visual Skills

Interpreting Visual Information Discuss with students how the map at the top of the page showing the areas of rain forest left in the world relates to the photograph of the scientist working in a laboratory. First have a volunteer apply the map key to interpret and explain the map. Then have other volunteers apply what they have learned in the previous pages to both the map and photograph. **Ask: Why is the rain forest an important resource for scientists?** *(The scientists want to explore the plants and animals of the rain forest to develop medicines to help humans. The scientists want to work with the indigenous people who understand the plants and animals of the rain forest, and who already use some plants and animals for medicines for the tribe.)* **Visual/Spatial**

W Writing Skills

Arguing As students prepare to write the letter for question #3 in Thinking Like a Geographer, discuss with them the proper format and structure appropriate for writing a letter. Explain that students should state their opinions in the paragraph clearly and support them with convincing facts. **Verbal/ Linguistic**

CLOSE & REFLECT

Divide the class into small groups. Have each group search the Internet for private and governmental efforts to save the rain forests. Provide sticky notes for each group. Have students write on a sticky note information on the efforts of a private or government group that is working to save a part of the rain forest. Students should attach their notes to a large world map. Have each group lead a discussion to evaluate efforts to save the world's rain forests.

ANSWERS, p. 93

Thinking Like a Geographer

1. Because travel in the rain forest is challenging, scientists have not explored the region completely. Scientists may also distrust native medical practitioners, preferring to use chemistry and other laboratory-based methods of finding new medicines.

2. Much of the knowledge develops through trial and error. A plant may have been ingested by accident but be found to be beneficial. Some trials come about because of a plant's appearance, for example, resemblance to an organ or a disease condition like a rash.

3. Student responses may include: Rain forests provide food and shelter for the indigenous people, medicine, biodiversity, and oxygen for the planet.

ENGAGE

Bellringer Before students begin this lesson, have volunteers explain a time when they have wanted something but could not get it because there were none left of the item in their house or in the local stores. Discuss popular items in limited supply or display photos of a number of items that students would be interested in having, but there are limited supplies of the items. Ask students what solutions they can think of to satisfy their wants as well as others' wants when supplies are limited. List their ideas and discuss possible outcomes of each.

TEACH & ASSESS

V Visual Skills

Drawing Have students make sketches of resources that help to provide us with wants and needs. Suggest that they use their text as a guide but also to include additional resources. Remind students to label their sketches as resources that supply *wants* or *needs*. Invite students to share their drawings in small groups or with the class. **ELL** **Visual/Spatial**

R Reading Skills

Applying Discuss with students how countries have wants and needs, too. **Ask: What questions do you think countries must consider when determining what their wants and needs are and how they will fulfill them?** Tell students to use their own words to answer the question. *(Possible answer: Countries must examine their resources and decide what they will need to acquire through trade.)* **Logical/Mathematical**

Reinforcing Vocabulary Remind students to add academic and content vocabulary words to the vocabulary lists in their notebooks. Tell students to write their own definitions and to include drawings if desired. **ELL** **AL**

ANSWER, p. 94

Taking Notes Sample notes: **1. Traditional economy:** resources are distributed mainly through families; farming, herding, and hunter-gatherer; developing, mainly agricultural societies often have traditional economies. **2. Market economy (capitalism):** most means of production are privately owned; production is guided and income is distributed through sales and demand for products and resources. **3. Command economy:** means of production are publicly owned and production and distribution are controlled by a central governing authority (Communism). **4. Mixed economy:** Parts of the economy may be privately owned and parts may be owned by the government or other authority.

---

networks

There's More Online!

☑ **CHART/GRAPH** Economic Questions

☑ **GAME** Bartering and Trade

☑ **VIDEO**

Reading HELPDESK (CCSS)

Academic Vocabulary RH.6-8.4
(Tier Two Words)
- **currency**

Content Vocabulary RH.6-8.4
(Tier Three Words)
- **renewable resource**
- **nonrenewable resource**
- **economic system**
- **traditional economy**
- **market economy**
- **command economy**
- **mixed economy**
- **gross domestic product**
- **standard of living**
- **productivity**
- **export**
- **import**
- **free trade**
- **sustainability**

TAKING NOTES: Key Ideas and Details RH.6-8.2, RH.6-8.7

Organize As you read, summarize the key ideas about each economic system.

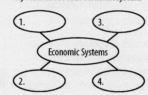

1.

2.

3.

Economic Systems

4.

Lesson 3
Economies of the World

ESSENTIAL QUESTION • *Why do people make economic choices?*

IT MATTERS BECAUSE
People strive to meet their basic needs and their desire for a better life.

Resources

GUIDING QUESTION *How do people get the things they want and need?*

All human beings have wants and needs. How do you get the things you want and the things you need? To obtain these items, people use resources. Resources are the supplies that are used to meet our wants and needs. Some types of resources, such as water, soil, plants, and animals, come from the earth. These are called natural resources.

Other resources are supplied by humans. Human resources include the labor, skills, and talents people contribute. Countries also have wants and needs. Like individuals, nations must use resources to meet their needs.

Wants and Resources

What would happen if 14 students each wanted a glass of lemonade from a pitcher that contained only 12 glasses of lemonade? What if more students wanted a glass of lemonade? No matter how many people want lemonade, the pitcher still contains just 12 glasses. It does not hold enough for everyone to have a full glass. This is an example of a limited supply and unlimited demand. This situation is not uncommon. It happens to individuals and also to countries. You probably can think of many personal examples, as well as current and historical examples, of limited supply and unlimited demand.

(l to r) © Ton Koene/ZUMA Press/Corbis; S. Solum/PhotoLink/Getty Images; Walter Hodges/Photodisc/Getty Images; Jens Kuhfs/Photographer's Choice/Getty Images

---

networks   *Online Teaching Options*

VIDEO

Emerging Markets in India Bring Westerners and Trade

Analyzing Use the video about the emerging markets in India with students. Ask students to share what they learned from the video about developing markets and the opportunities for jobs in different parts of the world. Discuss if any of the information was surprising to them. **AL** **Visual/Spatial**

See page 69E for other online activities.

BBC Motion Gallery Education

One type of resource everyone needs is energy. Energy is the power to do work. Energy resources are the supplies that provide the power to do work. Many types of energy resources exist in our world. Energy resources can be renewable or nonrenewable. **Renewable resources** are resources that can be totally replaced or are always available naturally. They can be regenerated and replenished. Examples of renewable resources include water, trees, and energy from the wind and the sun.

In contrast are nonrenewable resources. **Nonrenewable resources** can not be totally replaced. Once nonrenewable resources are consumed, they are gone. Examples of nonrenewable resources include the fossil fuels oil, coal, and natural gas. These fuels received their name because they formed millions of years ago. Because of our increasing need for energy, supplies of nonrenewable resources are shrinking.

Making Choices

If the people of all nations have unlimited wants but face limited resources, what must happen? We must make choices. Do we continue to use nonrenewable resources? If so, at what rate should we be using them? Should we switch to renewable resources?

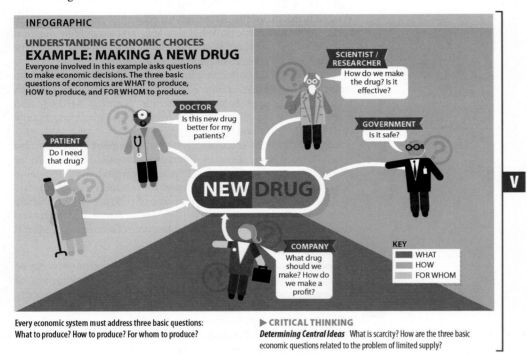

INFOGRAPHIC

UNDERSTANDING ECONOMIC CHOICES
EXAMPLE: MAKING A NEW DRUG
Everyone involved in this example asks questions to make economic decisions. The three basic questions of economics are WHAT to produce, HOW to produce, and FOR WHOM to produce.

SCIENTIST / RESEARCHER
How do we make the drug? Is it effective?

DOCTOR
Is this new drug better for my patients?

GOVERNMENT
Is it safe?

PATIENT
Do I need that drug?

NEW DRUG

COMPANY
What drug should we make? How do we make a profit?

KEY
WHAT
HOW
FOR WHOM

Every economic system must address three basic questions: What to produce? How to produce? For whom to produce?

▶ CRITICAL THINKING
Determining Central Ideas What is scarcity? How are the three basic economic questions related to the problem of limited supply?

Chapter 3 **95**

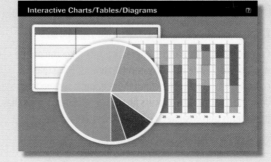

See page 69E for other online activities

Economic Questions

Analyze Charts Display the interactive chart on the whiteboard. Review the three basic economic questions and then invite students to fill in the chart, from top to bottom, with the correct answers: unlimited wants, limited resources, scarcity, and choices. **Verbal/ Linguistic**

Interactive Charts/Tables/Diagrams

R Reading Skills

Using Context Clues Point out to students that by looking at familiar words around or near an unfamiliar word, they can often determine the meaning of the unknown word without having to look the word up in the glossary or dictionary.
Ask: What words help you to infer the meanings of *regenerated* **and** *replenished* **in the first paragraph?**
(Sample answer: The definition of renewable resources in the previous sentence tells me that they are resources that can be totally replaced. Resources that can be totally replaced can be used over and over, so regenerated and replenished might mean "formed or created again" and "to supply or fill fully.")
ELL Verbal/Linguistic

C Critical Thinking Skills

Comparing and Contrasting After students read about renewable and nonrenewable resources, **ask: How are renewable and nonrenewable resources alike and different?** Record students' responses in a Venn diagram.
(Sample answers: Alike: They are both kinds of resources. Different: Renewable resources can be totally replaced or are always available naturally. Nonrenewable resources cannot be replaced.)
AL Visual/Spatial

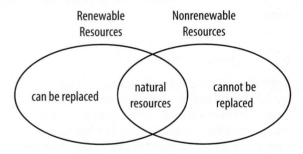

Renewable Resources   Nonrenewable Resources

can be replaced   natural resources   cannot be replaced

V Visual Skills

Interpreting Review the infographic with students. **Ask: What are the three basic questions of economic systems according to this graphic?** *(What to produce? How to produce? For whom to produce?)* **How does the infographic illustrate the three basic questions?** *(by dividing the infographic into three sections, through color and the key, by the questions asked by the people illustrated)* **Visual/Spatial**

ANSWER, p. 95

CRITICAL THINKING Scarcity is the limited supply of an item compared to the unlimited wants of the item. The basic economic questions are questions all societies must ask when dealing with scarcity and efficiently allocating their resources.

R Reading Skills

Applying Review with students the meaning of opportunity cost and how it works in their everyday lives. For example, ask students to suppose they earned $15 doing chores and wanted to spend some of the money. They have enough money to download a music album, but not enough to buy the music and go to the movies with friends. They decide to go to the movies with their friends in hopes that they will earn more money later. **Ask:**

- **What is the opportunity cost?** *(downloading a music album)*
- **What other choice could you have made?** *(Sample answer: I could have downloaded the music album and skipped the movie.)* **ELL** **Logical/Mathematical**

V Visual Skills

Comparing and Contrasting Have students choose two of the different economic systems discussed in the text. Have them draw a Venn diagram to compare and contrast the two systems based on the information in the text and their prior knowledge. **Ask: How are the two economic systems you chose alike? How are they different?** *(Students should be able to verbalize their answers as well as list them in their diagrams.)* **Visual/Spatial**

T Technology Skills

Evaluating Ask students to work with a partner to do research online to find out which type of economic system has had the most successful results. Remind them to use reliable sources and list their sources along with their findings in their notes. **Ask: Were you surprised by your findings? Why or why not?** *(Sample answer: Yes, I was surprised because I thought a market economy was the most successful. Students should also include facts and reasons why the economic system is successful.)* **BL** **Verbal/Linguistic**

ANSWER, p. 96

✓**READING PROGRESS CHECK** Possible answer: Renewable and nonrenewable resources are alike in that they both meet wants and needs. They are different in that renewable resources can be replenished, but once nonrenewable resources are used up, they are gone.

Think Again?

No countries today rely on a command economic system.

Not true. Some countries still have planned economies, including Cuba, Saudi Arabia, Iran, and North Korea. These nations have an economic system in which supply and prices are regulated by the government, not by the market.

We must weigh the opportunity cost, or the value of what we must give up to acquire something else, of using renewable resources versus nonrenewable resources. We must take into account these and many more considerations as we make choices now and in the future. **R**

✓ **READING PROGRESS CHECK**

Describing How are renewable and nonrenewable resources alike, and how are they different?

Economic Resources

GUIDING QUESTION *What kinds of economic systems are used in our world today?*

Economic resources are another important resource. Economic resources include the goods and services a society provides and how they are produced, distributed, and used. How a society decides on the ownership and distribution of its economic resources is its **economic system**. Do you ever stop to think about the goods and services you use in a single day? How do these goods and services become available to you?

Different Economic Systems

We can break down the discussion on economic systems into three basic economic questions: *What should be produced? How should it be produced? How should what is produced be distributed?* Different nations have different answers to these questions.

One type of economic system is the traditional economy. In a **traditional economy**, resources are distributed mainly through families. Traditional economies include farming, herding, and hunter-gatherer societies. Developing societies, which are mainly agricultural, often have traditional economies.

Another type of economic system is a **market economy**, also referred to as capitalism. In market economies, the means of production are privately owned. Production is guided and income is distributed through sales and demand for products and resources. **V**

In a **command economy**, the means of production are publicly owned. Production and distribution are controlled by a central governing authority. Communism is one type of command economy.

What Is a Mixed Economy?

A **mixed economy** is just that—mixed. Parts of the economy may be privately owned, and parts may be owned by the government or another authority. The United States has a mixed market economy. Another economic system is socialism. In socialist societies, property and the distribution of goods and income are controlled by the community. How do individuals get the goods or services they need under each of these economic systems? **T**

---

networks   *Online Teaching Options*

GAME

Drag-and-Drop: Economic Systems

Categorizing Display the interactive sorting game on the whiteboard. Divide the class into two teams. Have teams complete the activity matching the economic system to its description. As a class, discuss how each economic system has its benefits and weaknesses. **AL** **Interpersonal**

See page 69E for other online activities.

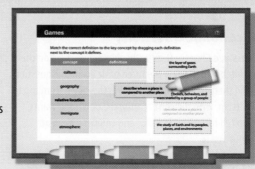

Parts of the Economy

We can break down the economy into parts. In economics, *land* is a factor of production that includes natural resources. Another factor of production is *labor*, which refers to all paid workers within a system. The other factor is *capital*, the human-made resources used to produce other goods. An *industry* is a branch of a business. For example, the *agriculture industry* grows crops and raises livestock. *Service industries* provide services rather than goods. Banking, retail, food service, transportation, and communications are examples of service industries.

Types of Economic Activities

Another way to view the parts of the economy is by the type of economic activity. Economists use the terms *primary sector*, *secondary sector*, and *tertiary sector* to group these activities. The primary sector includes activities that produce raw materials and basic goods. These activities include mining, fishing, agriculture, and logging.

The secondary sector makes finished goods. This sector includes home and building construction, food processing, and aerospace manufacturing. The tertiary sector of the economy is the service industry. Service sectors include sales, restaurants, banking, information technology, and health care.

Buyers and sellers come together in an outdoor market in Kunduz, Afghanistan.

▶ **CRITICAL THINKING**
Describing Is the seller involved in a primary, a secondary, or a tertiary economic activity?

©Ton Koene/ZUMA Press/Corbis

Chapter 3 **97**

V Visual Skills

Integrating Visual Information Have students examine the photograph of the man selling food to a consumer at a market. Discuss the factors of production that were needed. Then ask students to use this information and integrate it with what they already know about different economic systems. **Ask:** **How might globalization affect markets such as this one as well as more traditional economic systems?** *(Students' answers may vary but should demonstrate an understanding that globalization may help the seller to distribute his product beyond the market and to other countries. It may cause more traditional economies to incorporate aspects of market economies.)* **Verbal/ Linguistic, Logical/Mathematical**

C Critical Thinking Skills

Labeling After you read the section on types of economic activities, have students draw a diagram to show the three different sectors of economic activities and label each section of the diagram accurately. **Ask: Why do you think the sectors were divided in this way? What logic was used to determine the structure?** *(Sample answer: Raw materials are at the most basic level, which is primary, because they are pure and have not been modified. Building and manufacturing are in the secondary sector because they require raw materials but use machines and other equipment to produce something out of the raw materials. Services are in the tertiary sector because they may require both raw materials and manufactured materials to provide a service.)* **ELL** **AL** **Visual/Spatial**

Content Background Knowledge

Transportation and communication are not factors of production, but they help to link the factors together. They provide the means for the factors of production to reach the producers, as well as the consumers. Technology, on the other hand, is part of capital, one of the factors of production that includes the tools and equipment needed for production.

NASA/NOAA/SPL/Science Photo Library/Getty Images

IMAGE

Types of Economic Activities and Sectors

Identifying Use the interactive photo to review the information about the different economic sectors. Have students provide descriptions of each sector and then address which sector is being shown in the image. Ask students which sector is thriving in our current economy. **BL** **Verbal/Linguistic**

See page 69E for other online activities.

Interactive Photos

ANSWER, p. 97

CRITICAL THINKING Sales is a service. Services are part of the tertiary sector of the economy.

Economies of the World

V Visual Skills

Analyzing Charts Review the diagram at the top of the page with students. Explain that this is a graphic organizer that displays relationships between items, similar to cause and effect charts. **Ask:** Why do you think the factors of production must begin with natural resources? *(Possible answer: Natural resources or raw materials must be first because without them products could not be produced. Machines and then labor need to be supplied with raw materials or natural resources in order to produce a product for consumers. After a product is produced, it needs to be brought to market in order to reach consumers. Entrepreneurs are the factor of production that supply this need.)* **Visual/Spatial**

C Critical Thinking Skills

Describing After reviewing the factors of production graphic with the class, have students work in small groups to write lyrics for a song with a familiar tune of their choosing that will help them describe the factors of production. Invite groups to perform their songs for the class. **Interpersonal, Auditory/Musical**

W Writing Skills

Argument Explain that today different groups argue about whether developing countries should be integrated into the global market and about what impact globalization will have on them. Divide the class into two teams to debate this issue. Provide an opportunity for students to gather research on their topic to answer this prompt: **Should developing countries be brought into the global market?** Allow each side to present their argument and then ask students to write a multi-paragraph essay in which they write their argument, support their claim with evidence, acknowledge the opposing argument, and organize their writing logically and clearly. *(Students' essays should include coverage of all of these points and be accurate. They should demonstrate understanding of a developing country and globalization.)* **Interpersonal, Verbal/Linguistic**

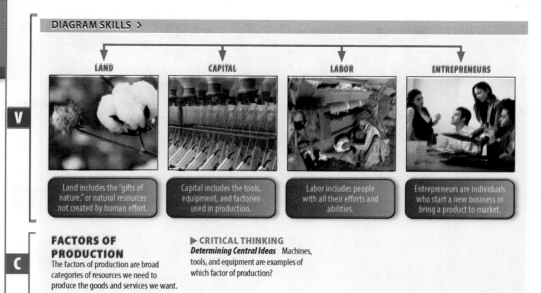

DIAGRAM SKILLS >

LAND — Land includes the "gifts of nature," or natural resources not created by human effort.

CAPITAL — Capital includes the tools, equipment, and factories used in production.

LABOR — Labor includes people with all their efforts and abilities.

ENTREPRENEURS — Entrepreneurs are individuals who start a new business or bring a product to market.

FACTORS OF PRODUCTION
The factors of production are broad categories of resources we need to produce the goods and services we want.

▶ **CRITICAL THINKING**
Determining Central Ideas Machines, tools, and equipment are examples of which factor of production?

Economic Performance

Economic performance measures how well an economy meets the needs of society. Economic performance can be determined by several factors that measure economic success. The **gross domestic product (GDP)** is the total dollar value of all final goods and services produced in a country during a single year. The **standard of living** is the level at which a person, a group, or a nation lives as measured by the extent to which it meets its needs. These needs include food, shelter, clothing, education, and health care. Per capita income is the total national income divided by the number of people in the nation.

When referring to economics, **productivity** is a measurement of what is produced and what is required to produce it. Sustainable growth is the growth rate a business can maintain without having to borrow money. The employment rate is the percentage of the labor force that is employed. These factors help determine a nation's economic strength and performance.

Types of National Economies

National economies also can be classified by types. Developed countries are industrialized countries. Developing countries are less industrialized, agricultural countries that are working to become more advanced economically. Developing countries often have weak economies, and most of their population lives in poverty. Newly industrialized countries (NICs) are in the process of becoming developed and economically secure. Their economies are growing

(l to r) S. Solum/PhotoLink/Getty Images; yang yu/Alamy; Ajit Solanki/AP Images; Rubberball/Getty Images

---

net**works** *Online Teaching Options*

DIAGRAM

Factors of Production

Interpreting Show the diagram about factors of production on the whiteboard and review each factor with students to check for understanding. Then ask students to work in pairs or groups to provide examples of land, capital, labor, and entrepreneurs to bring another product from natural resources to the consumer.
ELL Visual/Spatial

See page 69E for other online activities.

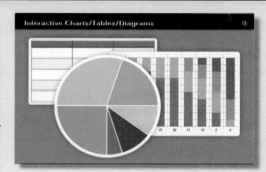

Interactive Charts/Tables/Diagrams

ANSWER, p. 98

CRITICAL THINKING capital

and struggling to become fully developed, but they still face many economic and social challenges.

☑ READING PROGRESS CHECK

Describing How is standard of living a sign of economic performance?

A World Economy

GUIDING QUESTION *How do the world's economies interact and affect one another?*

C

You have read about different economic systems and different types of economies. All the world's nations can be classified into the different economic categories. All nations must find ways to interact with one another. Look at the labels in your clothes or on other products you buy. How many different country names can you find? How and why do we get goods from far across the world?

Trade

Trade is the business of buying, selling, or bartering. When you buy something at the store, you are trading money for a product. On a much bigger scale, nations trade with each other. Countries have different resources. Resources can include raw materials, such as iron ore. Labor also might be cheaper in another country where workers earn lower wages. As a result, goods can be produced in some countries more easily or efficiently than in other countries.

Trade can benefit countries. One country can **export**, or send to another country, a product that it is able to produce. Another country **imports**, or buys that product from the exporting country.

R

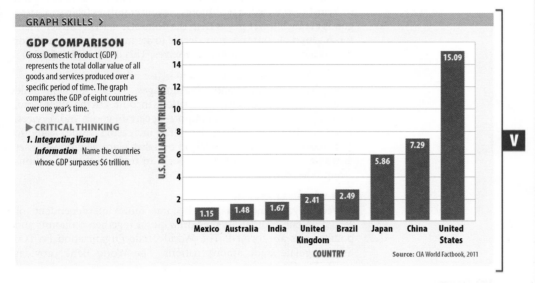

GRAPH SKILLS >

GDP COMPARISON

Gross Domestic Product (GDP) represents the total dollar value of all goods and services produced over a specific period of time. The graph compares the GDP of eight countries over one year's time.

▶ CRITICAL THINKING

1. *Integrating Visual Information* Name the countries whose GDP surpasses $6 trillion.

U.S. DOLLARS (IN TRILLIONS)

| Mexico | Australia | India | United Kingdom | Brazil | Japan | China | United States |
| 1.15 | 1.48 | 1.67 | 2.41 | 2.49 | 5.86 | 7.29 | 15.09 |

COUNTRY

Source: CIA World Factbook, 2011

V

Chapter 3 **99**

C Critical Thinking Skills

Determining Cause and Effect Have students stop reading and work with a partner to predict what the causes and effects are of different countries' economies interacting. Have pairs write their predictions down. Point out to students that there are often multiple effects or even multiple causes to consider in such complex situations.

After students make their predictions, have them read the rest of the section and check their predictions for accuracy. Suggest that they make any necessary changes to their predictions. Explain that making predictions helps readers make connections to what they are reading, and that by checking their predictions as they read, they are more actively engaged in the reading which will help them remember the text and do better on exams. **BL** Verbal/Linguistic

R Reading Skills

Defining Discuss the definitions of *export* and *import* and explain that the prefix *ex* means "out of" or "from" and the prefix *im* can mean "in" or "not." Place students into small groups and have them think of other words with the prefixes *ex* and *im*. Come back together, and as a class make a list of all of the words that students came up with. Then ask them to look up and write down the definitions in their vocabulary lists in their notebooks or to make sketches to illustrate the meanings of the words. **ELL** Verbal/Linguistic

V Visual Skills

Analyze Graphs Review the GDP Comparison graph with students. **Ask:** What generalizations can you make from the data on this chart about GDP and geographic location? *(Possible answer: There is a wide range of GDP in the Eastern Hemisphere, with China leading the way with the highest GDP of the eastern countries listed on the graph.)* **BL** Logical/Mathematical

---

GRAPHS

GDP Around the World

Comparing and Contrasting Show the graph presentation of GDP around the world to students, and discuss the GDP per capita in the six countries shown. Have students compare and contrast the data in small groups, and then explain the economic effects of a high GDP or low GDP orally. **AL** Verbal/Linguistic

See page 69E for other online activities.

Interactive Charts/Tables/Diagrams

ANSWERS, p. 99

☑ **READING PROGRESS CHECK** Standard of living reveals how well and to what extent the needs and wants of the people of a society are being met.

CRITICAL THINKING China and the United States

V Visual Skills

Collaborating Pair students and ask them to discuss how these images reinforce the advantages and disadvantages of trade. **Ask:**

• **How do countries with large shipping ports have**  **advantages in global trade over countries without them?** *(Possible answer: They may have more trading partners and are able to import and export more goods than countries with fewer or smaller ports.)*

• **What effects does shipping have on the environment? What risks are involved?** *(Possible answer: Some ships have accidents and petroleum or other harmful substances can leak into the ocean, killing sea life and causing pollution.)*

• **How do quotas and tariffs affect global trade?** *(Possible answer: They can limit global trade but also protect countries that are importing the goods. With high tariffs, consumers from the importing country may decide to buy a locally produced product over a foreign product.)* **BL** **Verbal/Linguistic**

T Technology Skills

Evaluating a Web Site Discuss the role of the World Trade Organization (WTO) with students. Have students work in pairs or small groups to evaluate the WTO's web site. Ask them to each write an evaluation based on this prompt: **Does the WTO clearly state its mission and goals related to regulating trade?** *(Sample answer: Yes, it has a section about its mission and goals and lists information about trade negotiations, implementation and monitoring, dispute settlement, and making trade more effective for developing countries.)* Discuss students' evaluations and ask them how they would improve upon the web site. **Interpersonal, Verbal/Linguistic**

Content Background Knowledge

Globalization has changed the way that the World Trade Organization, the World Bank, and the International Monetary Fund work—they now work in cooperation with each other through agreements and within a framework. This greater effort to work together is an attempt to bring about greater policymaking for the global economy.

International trade involves preparing cargo for shipping (left) and transporting goods (right).
▶ **CRITICAL THINKING**
Describing What are the advantages of trade?

The country that imported the product can in turn export its products to another country. In global trade, extra fees are often added to the cost of importing products by a country's government. The extra money is a type of tax called a tariff. Governments often create tariffs to persuade their people to buy products made in their own country.

Sometimes a quota, a limit on the amount of one particular good that can be imported, is set. Quotas prevent countries from exporting goods at much lower prices than the domestic market can sell them for. A group of countries may decide to set minimal or no tariffs or quotas when trading among themselves. This is called **free trade**.

Advantages and Disadvantages of Trade

Trade has advantages and disadvantages. Trade can help build economic growth and increase a nation's income. On the other hand, jobs might be lost because of importing certain goods and services. With its benefits and its barriers, increasing trade leads to globalization. Economic globalization takes place when businesses move past national markets and begin to trade with other nations around the world.

Economic Organizations

T In recent years, nations have become more interdependent, or reliant on one another. As they draw closer together, economic and political ties are formed. The World Trade Organization (WTO) helps regulate trade among nations. The World Bank provides

(l) Walter Hodges/Photodisc/Getty Images; (r) Jens Kuhfs/Photographer's Choice/Getty Images

---

networks *Online Teaching Options*

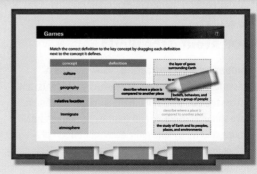

GAME

Bartering and Trade

Informative/Explanatory Display the game about trade on the whiteboard. Have volunteers read each definition and drag and drop the correct term in order to complete it. Play the game as a class activity or in small groups. Then have each student write a paragraph using these terms to explain trade and its impact on countries and people around the world. **AL** **Interpersonal, Kinesthetic**

See page 69E for other online activities.

ANSWER, p. 100

CRITICAL THINKING Answers should include that trade helps build economic growth and increase income.

100

financing, advice, and research to developing nations to help them grow their economies. The International Monetary Fund (IMF) is a group that monitors economic development. The IMF also lends money to nations in need and provides training and technical help. One well-known policy and organization that promotes global trade is the North American Free Trade Agreement (NAFTA). NAFTA encourages free trade among the United States, Canada, and Mexico.

The European Union (EU) is a group of European countries that operate under one economic unit and one **currency**, or type of money—the euro. The Mercado Camon del Sur (formerly called MERCOSUR) is a group of South American countries that promote free trade, economic development, and globalization. The Mercado Camon del Sur helps countries make better use of their resources while preserving the environment.

The Association of Southeast Asian Nations (ASEAN) is a group of countries in Southeast Asia that promote economic, cultural, and political development. The Dominican Republic–Central America Free Trade Agreement (CAFTA-DR) is an agreement among the United States, five developing Central American countries, and the Dominican Republic. The agreement promotes free trade.

Whether a nation produces its own goods or trades, one basic principle must be considered: sustainability. The principle of **sustainability** is central to the discussion of resources. When a country focuses on sustainability, it works to create conditions where all the natural resources for meeting the needs of society are available.

What can countries do to ensure sustainability now and into the future? What can you do to plan for your future and the future of your community? Just as every nation is part of a global system, you are part of your community. The choices you make affect you and those around you. What can you do now to plan for a bright economic future?

Academic Vocabulary

currency paper money and coins in circulation

FOLDABLES
Study Organizer

Include this lesson's information in your Foldable®.

☑ **READING PROGRESS CHECK**

Analyzing What are some possible disadvantages of trade?

LESSON 3 REVIEW ᴄᴄss

Reviewing Vocabulary (Tier Three Words)
1. Provide an example of a *renewable resource* and a *nonrenewable resource.* RH.6-8.4

Answering the Guiding Questions
2. ***Identifying*** Think of two examples of limited supply and unlimited demand. RH.6-8.2

3. ***Identifying Point of View*** Why might a government want to control certain parts of a mixed economy? RH.6-8.6
4. ***Determining Central Ideas*** Why is global trade necessary? RH.6-8.2
5. ***Informative/Explanatory Writing*** Write a short essay that addresses how people in developing versus developed countries likely affect sustainability. WHST.6-8.2, WHST.6-8.4

Chapter 3 **101**

LESSON 3 REVIEW ANSWERS

Reviewing Vocabulary

1. Renewable resources include trees, wind, solar energy, water. Nonrenewable resources include oil, natural gas, coal, and minerals such as gold and diamonds.

Answering the Guiding Questions

2. **Identifying** Answers will vary, but students should demonstrate an understanding of the concept that there is not enough of some things for everyone who wants them to actually have them.

3. **Identifying Point of View** The government might want to step in and force companies to produce certain items that companies do not really want to make because of lack of demand or inability to make

a profit. One example would be a medication for a rare disease.

4. **Determining Central Ideas** Not all countries have all resources, so they have to trade to get them. Some countries can also produce certain items cheaper than other countries can.

5. **Informative/Explanatory Writing** Essays will vary but students should point out that people in developed countries generally use a much greater amount of resources because they have more money to purchase items and services. Those in developing countries do not have the means to consume as many resources.

ANSWER, p. 101

☑ **READING PROGRESS CHECK** As more countries trade, there will be more opportunities for developing countries to export their goods. This could lead to the loss of jobs in countries that are importing those goods if workers there produce the same kinds of goods.

CHAPTER REVIEW ACTIVITY

Have students create a graphic organizer like the one below with boxes on the left for causes and boxes on the right for effects. Ask them to write "population growth," "movement of people," and "change in government or economy" in the cause boxes. Then lead a discussion that allows students to identify the effects of these causes. (*possible effects of population growth: urbanization, poverty, migration, population density;* *effects of movement of people: cultural changes, population distribution, urbanization; effects of change in government or economy: migration, globalization, cultural changes, poverty*)

Population growth	→	
Movement of people	→	
Change in government or economy	→	

REVIEW THE ENDURING UNDERSTANDINGS

Review the Enduring Understandings with students:

- *Over time, people adapt to their environment.*
- *People, places, and ideas change over time.*
- *Countries have relationships with each other.*

Now pose the following questions in a class discussion to apply these to this chapter.

- **How have people adapted to their environment?** *(They find resources in their environment to meet their needs, move to places where their needs can be met, or acquire what they need through trade.)*

- **How have migration, population growth, and changes to a country's government or economy affected cultures?** *(Some cultures have changed as a result of migration, population growth, and political and economic changes. Many cultures try to preserve elements of their cultures even when affected by these factors.)*

- **How has globalization brought countries together and strengthened economic and cultural ties?** *(Globalization has enabled countries to have more economic advantages, which has helped to support their populations. It has benefitted some developing countries and strengthened their economies.)*

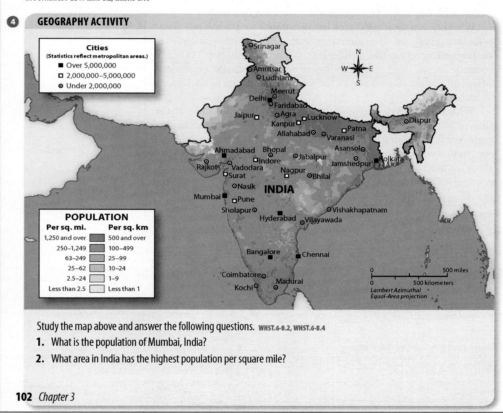

Chapter 3 ACTIVITIES CCSS

Directions: Write your answers on a separate piece of paper.

❶ **Exploring the Essential Question**
INFORMATIVE/EXPLANATORY WRITING Select a geographical region in Africa. Conduct research about the culture of the area. Write a letter to a student there explaining how your culture differs from his or hers. WHST.6-8.2, WHST.6-8.8

❷ **21st Century Skills**
INTEGRATING VISUAL INFORMATION Examine at least 25 items in your home, including your closet. Look at the labels to see where they were made. Make a graph that shows the number of items that were made in China, India, and Japan. RH.6-8.7

❸ **Thinking Like a Geographer**
DETERMINING CENTRAL IDEAS Look up the gross domestic product of 10 countries in Asia and Africa. List them in order from greatest to least GDP. Include a paragraph exploring the success of the country with the largest GDP and another paragraph that explores the struggles for the country with the smallest GDP. RH.6-8.2, WHST.6-8.10

❹ **GEOGRAPHY ACTIVITY**

Study the map above and answer the following questions. WHST.6-8.2, WHST.6-8.4
1. What is the population of Mumbai, India?
2. What area in India has the highest population per square mile?

ACTIVITIES ANSWERS

Exploring the Essential Question

❶ **INFORMATIVE/EXPLANATORY WRITING** Letters will vary depending on the region selected; however, letters should reflect that students have conducted careful research using reliable resources on the culture of a geographical region in Africa.

21st Century Skills

❷ **INTEGRATING VISUAL INFORMATION** Graphs will vary but should include at least 25 typical items in a student's household and where they were made. Graphs will probably show a large number of items made in China.

REVIEW THE GUIDING QUESTIONS

Directions: Choose the best answer for each question.

1 Push and pull factors refer to RH.6-8.4

   A. rural and urban areas.

   B. the reasons people leave or go to an area.

   C. the increase and decrease in birthrate and death rate.

   D. changing forms of government.

2 A dialect is RH.6-8.4

   F. an ethnic group.

   G. a religious group.

   H. harmful to the culture group.

   I. a regional variety of language.

3 Under a dictatorship, RH.6-8.2, RH.6-8.4

   A. the people have few rights.

   B. human rights are of central importance.

   C. people are all treated equally.

   D. power is passed on through heredity.

4 Why do governments create tariffs? RH.6-8.2

   F. to encourage free trade among nations

   G. to achieve a level of sustainability

   H. to prevent countries from exporting goods at lower prices

   I. to persuade their people to buy products made in their own country

5 If the economic performance of a country is improving, then RH.6-8.1

   A. its standard of living is dropping.

   B. its standard of living is improving.

   C. its gross domestic product is down.

   D. its per capita income is shrinking.

Chapter 3 **103**

Thinking Like a Geographer

3 **DETERMINING CENTRAL IDEAS** Answers will vary depending upon which countries students select but they should include the gross domestic product of 10 countries in Asia and Africa in order from greatest to least GDP. They should also include a paragraph exploring the success of the country with the largest GDP and another paragraph that explores the struggles for the country with the smallest GDP.

Geography Activity

4 **IDENTIFYING**

   1. over 5,000,000

   2. the northeast border

ASSESSMENT ANSWERS

Review the Guiding Questions

1 **B** Push and pull factors refer to the reasons people leave or go to an area. Have students who answer incorrectly review Lesson 1, which covers the distinction between rural and urban areas, population movement, the reasons people move, and causes of population growth, and have them review Lesson 2, which covers forms of government.

2 **I** A dialect is a regional variety of language. Have students who answer incorrectly review Lesson 2, which covers elements of culture including language, religion, ethnic groups, and changes to cultures in a region.

3 **A** Under a dictatorship, the people have few rights. Have students who answer incorrectly review Lesson 2, which covers the following three forms of government—democracy, monarchy, and dictatorship—and how the people under each government are treated.

4 **I** Students can become easily confused when learning about tariffs, quotas, and free trade. Students might need to review Lesson 3 to answer this question. Tariffs are created by countries in order to protect its industries. Products with tariffs are more expensive than those products made in the country, so people are more likely to buy the products made at home than those made abroad. Thus, I is the correct answer.

5 **B** If the economic performance of a country is improving, then its standard of living is improving. Make sure students understand that these two generally go hand in hand. Have students who answer incorrectly review Lesson 3, which covers how the different economic systems affect the countries of the world and their people.

DBQ Analyzing Documents

6 G When the author says "booming economy," he means the economy of India is growing rapidly. The author attributes the rapid growth partly to the population growth of India and the large number of working-age youth.

7 C From the text, you can tell that the increase in India's population is largely the result of an increase in the birthrate. The author discusses the population growth of India and the large number of working-age youth. Students who answer incorrectly should reread the passage carefully to see that it makes no mention of improvements in heath care, the death rate, or immigration.

Short Response

8 New schools could be better insulated, have better windows, and use less energy than an older school. The latest energy-saving technology could be used to help the environment.

9 Building new schools takes a great deal of money, which many places do not have. It also takes time, and several buildings could not be built all at one time. So, it would take a long time and a lot of money to make this type of change.

Extended Response

10 Students' essays should discuss problems associated with large population growth such as a shortage of natural resources including electricity, the pollution that will result from so many people using resources, and the stresses of living in crowded conditions. Student responses regarding the government's role to curb population growth will vary, as will their opinions on whether and how to curb the growth.

Chapter 3 **ASSESSMENT** *(continued)* **CCSS**

DBQ ANALYZING DOCUMENTS

6 DETERMINING WORD MEANINGS A news story reports on India's population growth.

> "*India…will surpass China to become the world's most populous country in less than two decades. The population growth will mean a nation full of working-age youth, which economists say could allow the already booming economy to maintain momentum.*"

—from Anjana Pasricha, "India Challenged to Provide Jobs, Education to Young Population," October 2011

What does the author mean by "booming economy"? RH.6-8.4, RH.6-8.10

F. The economy will explode and shrink.
G. The economy is growing rapidly.
H. The economy will change forms.
I. The economy will stay at its current level.

7 IDENTIFYING From the text, you can tell that the increase in India's population is largely the result of RH.6-8.2, RH.6-8.10

A. improvements in health care.
B. a significant decline in the death rate.
C. an increase in the birthrate.
D. immigration.

SHORT RESPONSE

> "*A school that is . . . easy for students, teachers, [and] parents . . .to reach on foot or by bicycle helps reduce the air pollution from automobile use, protecting children's health. Building schools . . . in the neighborhoods they serve minimizes the amount of paved surface . . ., which can help protect water quality by reducing polluted runoff.*"

—from Environmental Protection Agency, "Smart Growth and Schools"

8 IDENTIFYING In what other ways might building new schools help the environment? RH.6-8.2, RH.6-8.10

9 ANALYZING What might be a problem with building new schools in neighborhood locations? RH.6-8.1, RH.6-8.10

EXTENDED RESPONSE

10 INFORMATIVE/EXPLANATORY WRITING Although the increase in India's population will provide India with workers for decades, it will also place stresses on the environment and the people who live there. Research and discuss in an essay what stresses this might include, and also address what the government of India might be able to do to help with the problems that are surely coming. Also consider what steps the people of India should or should not take to curb their population growth. Include a future population projection for about a decade from now. WHST.6-8.2, WHST.6-8.8

Need Extra Help?

If You've Missed Question	❶	❷	❸	❹	❺	❻	❼	❽	❾	❿
Review Lesson	1	2	2	3	3	3	1	1	1	1

"India Challenged to Provide Jobs, Education to Young Population," by Anjana Pasricha, October 31, 2011, *Voice of America*, http://voanews.com; "Smart Growth and Schools," The United States Environmental Protection Agency official Web site. http://www.epa.gov/dced/schools.htm

---

net**w**rks *Online Teaching Options*

Practicing 21st Century Skills

Practicing Your students can practice important 21st Century skills such as geography, reading, writing, and critical thinking by using resources found in the Skills Builder tab of the online Student Learning Center. Resources include templates, handbooks, and slide shows. These same resources are also available in the Resource Library of the Teacher Lesson Center.

UNDERSTANDING BY DESIGN®

Enduring Understandings

- Over time, people adapt to their environment.
- People, places, and ideas change over time.
- Countries have relationships with each other.

Essential Questions

- How does geography influence the way people live?
- What makes a culture unique?
- Why do civilizations rise and fall?
- Why do people trade?
- How does technology change the way people live?
- How does religion shape society?
- How does climate influence where people live?
- How do geography and climate affect the economy?

Students will Know:

- how geography shaped the development of Asia's civilization.
- how climate affects Asian populations.
- the main exports and imports of several Asian countries.
- the cultural development, variations, and relationships throughout the continent over time.
- present-day issues that affect Asians and other people throughout the world.

Students will be able to:

- **identify** how physical geography affected the locations of settlements in Asia.
- **predict** the consequences of rainfall on Asia's population and economies.
- **discuss** the products produced by various regions in Asia.
- **discuss** the value of the natural resources in various regions in Asia.
- **explain** how powerful kingdoms and empires developed in Asia.
- **describe** religion, ethnic values, and language groups in Asia.
- **discuss** current event issues in Asia.

Predictable Misunderstandings

- China is densely populated.
- The Gobi is a small desert.
- Japan is located on one island.
- Taiwan is part of China.
- China has always been an isolated culture with no contact with the outside world.
- Imperial China was less culturally and technologically advanced than Western Europe.
- There is no difference between Korean and Chinese culture.
- Japan became a powerful nation by warfare.
- Confucianism is a religion.

Assessment Evidence

Performance Tasks:

- Environmental Case Study
- Unit GeoLab Activity

Other Evidence:

- Physical Location GeoQuiz
- Political Location GeoQuiz
- City Location GeoQuiz
- Physical Geography Activity
- Cultural Geography Activity
- Geography and History Activity
- Geography and Economics Activity
- Geography Skills Activity
- Critical Thinking Skills Activity
- Technology Skills Activity
- Writing Skills Activity
- Reading Skills Activity
- Primary Sources Reading Skills Activity
- Participation in Interactive Whiteboard Activities
- Analysis of graphic organizers, graphs, and charts
- Lesson Reviews
- Chapter Assessments

Key for Using the Teacher Edition

SKILL-BASED ACTIVITIES

Types of skill activites found in the Teacher Edition.

* **V** **Visual Skills** require students to analyze maps, graphs, charts, and photos.

W **Writing Skills** provide writing opportunities to help students comprehend the text.

R **Reading Skills** help students practice reading skills and master vocabulary.

C **Critical Thinking Skills** help students apply and extend what they have learned.

T **Technology Skills** require students to use digital tools effectively.

*Letters are followed by a number when there is more than one of the same type of skill on the page.

DIFFERENTIATED INSTRUCTION

All activities are written for the on-level student unless otherwise marked with the leveled labels below.

BL Beyond Level

AL Approaching Level

ELL English Language Learners

All students benefit from activities that utilize different learning styles. Many activities are marked as below when a particular learning style is highlighted.

Intrapersonal	Naturalist
Logical/Mathematical	Kinesthetic
Visual/Spatial	Auditory/Musical
Verbal/Linguistic	Interpersonal

SUGGESTED PACING GUIDE

Introducing the Unit . . . . 1 Day

Chapter 4: East Asia and
Siberian Russia . . . . 5 Days

Chapter 5: Southeast Asia . . . . 5 Days

Chapter 6: South Asia . . . . 5 Days

Chapter 7: Central Asia . . . . 5 Days

Chapter 8: Southwest Asia . . . . 5 Days

Global Connections . . . . 2 Days

What Do You Think? . . . . 1 Day

TOTAL TIME   29 Days

PLANNER

☑ Print Teaching Options

V Visual Skills

☐ **P. 107** Students discuss the shape, size, and location of Asia as seen in the satellite image. **BL** Visual/Spatial

☐ **P. 107** Students describe and make speculations about the importance of the fishing industry in Asia, based on information in a photo. **AL** Visual/Spatial

☐ **P. 108** Students use a physical map to analyze China's river systems. **ELL** Visual/Spatial

☐ **P. 109** Students use a map to describe the physical geography of India. **ELL** Visual/Spatial

☐ **P. 110** Students use the population map to discuss locations of cities and population densities in Asia. **ELL**

W Writing Skills

☐ **P. 112** Students work in small groups to create a binder on a region in Asia, including information about its climates, cultures, languages, governments, and economics.

R Reading Skills

☐ **P. 106** Students read and state facts from the text about Asia. **AL** Verbal/Linguistic

☐ **P. 106** Students define the word *dominate* and use it in a sentence about the volcanoes in the region. **ELL**

C Critical Thinking Skills

☐ **P. 105** Students speculate about the diversity of climates, languages, and cultures in the countries of Asia.

☐ **P. 106** Students problem solve about the rapid use of resources in Southeast Asia. **BL**

☐ **P. 107** Students defend an opinion on whether water resources should be shared among countries.

☐ **P. 108** Students use a map to make connections between landforms and human settlements. **BL** Visual/Spatial

☐ **P. 109** Students use a map to infer how Mongolia's physical geography affects its economy. **BL** Logical

T Technology Skills

☐ **P. 111** Students work in small groups to develop a presentation on a country in Asia including information about its natural resources, use of land, industry, and manufacturing. Verbal/Linguistic, Auditory

☑ Online Teaching Options

V Visual Skills

☐ **VIDEO** **Video Tour of Asia**—Students analyze information in a video montage highlighting Asia and create a chart to fill in as they work through the lessons in the unit. **ELL** Visual

☐ **MAP** **Physical Map: Asia**—Students identify areas of elevation and name the major rivers of Asia. **AL** Kinesthetic

☐ **MAP** **Political Map: Asia**—Students use the political map to calculate the distances between locations on the map. **BL** Kinesthetic, Logical/Mathematical

☐ **MAP** **Population Map: Asia**—Students can use the population layer on the Unit Opener map to review the population distribution and density.

R Reading Skills

☐ **MAP** **Resources Map: Asia**—Students discuss the interactive layers of the resource map, and then do further research about specific resources found in a country of Asia. **AL** Visual/Spatial

C Critical Thinking Skills

☐ **MAP** **Regional Map**—Students use the map to make connections between images in the unit and their location on a map.

☐ **MAP** **Climates Map: Asia**—Students work in groups to create three "You Are There" scenarios describing a particular climate zone. **AL** Interpersonal

T Technology Skills

☐ **GAME** **Political Boundaries: Asia Game**—Students play a drag-and-drop game identifying the locations and names of countries and cities located in Asia. Kinesthetic, Logical

☑ Printable Digital Worksheets

W Writing Skills

☐ **QUIZ** **Physical Location GeoQuiz**—Use the Physical Location GeoQuiz as a pre- or post-assessment of students' knowledge of the regions' landforms and bodies of water.

☐ **QUIZ** **Political Location GeoQuiz**—Use the Political Location GeoQuiz as a pre- or post-assessment of students' knowledge of the regions' countries.

☐ **QUIZ** **City Location GeoQuiz**—Use the City Location GeoQuiz as a pre- or post-assessment of students' knowledge of the regions' major cities.

☐ **WORKSHEET** **Physical Geography Activity**—Students will analyze an elevation profile of the region.

☐ **WORKSHEET** **Cultural Geography Activity**—Students will read about the culture of the region and answer questions related to the excerpt.

☐ **WORKSHEET** **Environmental Case Study**—Students will conduct an environmental case study on policy-making and how the policies that governments make impact the environment.

☐ **WORKSHEET** **GeoLab: Indian Textiles**—Students can use this worksheet to understand the process of making natural textile dyes.

ASIA

UNIT **2**

Chapter 4	Chapter 5	Chapter 6	Chapter 7	Chapter 8
East Asia	Southeast Asia	South Asia	Central Asia, the Caucasus, and Siberian Russia	Southwest Asia

‹ Keren Su/Corbis

ENGAGE

Bellringer Direct students' attention to the image of terrace planting. Point out the land's fertility and contours. Have students speculate on aspects of agriculture in Asia. **Ask:**

- What do you notice about the landscape?
- How does terrace planting make agriculture on a mountainside possible?
- What do you notice about the fertility of the land?
- What type of crops do you think are grown in this region?

Making Connections Have students connect what they know about other regions of the world with the following facts about the continent of Asia:

- Largest continent that includes 48 recognized countries
- Located both in the Eastern Hemisphere and Northern Hemisphere
- Bounded by the Indian Ocean to the south, the Arctic Ocean to the north, and the Pacific Ocean to the east
- Covers 30% of Earth's land area
- Includes desert, grasslands, temperate forest, and taiga
- Major influence on the global economy
- Major supplier of the world's oil
- Includes Mt. Everest, the highest point on Earth, and the Dead Sea, the lowest point on land

C Critical Thinking Skills

Speculating Tell students they will be learning more about Asia, its people, its resources, and climate. In particular, they will be learning about five major regions: East Asia, Southeast Asia, South Asia, Central Asia and the Caucasus, and Southwest Asia. **Ask: Given that Asia is Earth's largest continent, what do you think is true about the diversity of climates, languages, and cultures found there?** *(Students may speculate that there are many different types of cultures, languages, and climates.)* **Logical/Mathematical**

Global Connections

The Global Connections issue for this unit gives students an opportunity to learn about natural disasters, with particular focus on earthquakes and tsunamis. Students will learn about the powerful tsunami that struck Japan in 2011 and investigate its destructive force on life, property, and the environment. Interactive activities and small group activities accompany the feature. **AL Verbal/Linguistic**

TEACH & ASSESS

R1 Reading Skills

Stating Read the opening sentence out loud. **Ask:** What do you think makes Asia the largest continent, its land mass or its population? *(Students answers should reflect that both are correct.)* Continue to read the rest of the introductory section out loud to students and have them state facts about Asia based on content in the text. **Ask:**

- What bodies of water border Asia to the west and to the east? *(Mediterranean Sea to the west and the Pacific Ocean to the east)*
- How much of the world's population call Asia home? *(about 60 percent)*
- How much of the land supports Asia's population? *(about 33% or one-third of the land)*
- What is a monsoon? *(winds that bring cool, dry weather in the winter and heavy rainfall and floods in the summer)* **AL Verbal/Linguistic**

C Critical Thinking Skills

Problem Solving Explain that some Southeast Asian countries are using their resources more quickly so they can expand their manufacturing industries. **Ask:** What can countries do to slow their use of resources without seriously affecting their industrialization in a negative way? *(Students answers might suggest finding new ways to manufacture or aggressively pursuing alternative forms of energy.)* **BL**

R2 Reading Skills

Defining Have a student volunteer read the paragraph, "Landforms," out loud. Then have students look up the meaning of the word *dominate* in a dictionary and write it down. Have students use the word in a sentence about the number of volcanoes in Indonesia. Then explain that a volcanologist is a scientist that studies volcanoes and have them write a paragraph about why a volcanologist would like to work in Indonesia. **ELL Verbal/Linguistic**

EXPLORE the CONTINENT

R1 ASIA

is the largest continent on Earth. It extends from the Mediterranean Sea in the west to the Pacific Ocean in the east. Asia is home to about 60 percent of the world's population. Yet, at least two-thirds of the land area is too cold or too dry to support a large population. Winds called monsoons affect climate in much of Asia. They bring cool, dry weather in winter and heavy rainfall and floods in summer.

① NATURAL RESOURCES Asia's numerous resources include petroleum, copper, rice, and fish. Growing populations and industries in cities such as Shanghai, China, demand more and more resources. Asian countries are quickly trying to meet this need.

② LANDFORMS Asia's landforms are varied. Mountain ranges, plateaus, and plains dominate western and central areas. Hundreds of islands dot coastlines in the east. Plate movements formed many of these islands. The island country of Indonesia has about 130 active volcanoes, more than any other country on Earth. **R2**

106 *Unit 2*

networks *Online Teaching Options*

Fresh photos from all over the world/Getty Images

VIDEO TOUR

Video Tour of Asia

Analyzing Images The video tour is a montage of the unit's videos and includes text and audio commentary, and familiarizes students with the sounds of the region. Use the video tour of Asia to introduce the unit. Prior to the video tour, ask students to generate ten questions they have about the physical and human characteristics of Asia. Chart student questions leaving room for answers. Have students write answers to the questions on the chart as they work through the unit. **ELL Visual/Spatial**

③ BODIES OF WATER Water is plentiful in eastern and southern Asia, where many people depend on it for a living. In Sri Lanka, fishers use baitless hooks to snare mackerel and herring. In parts of western Asia, however, water is scarce. The lack of water is a major issue for countries in these areas.

FAST FACT

Asia comprises 30 percent of the world's land area.

WORKSHEET

Environmental Case Study

Evaluating The Environmental Case Study worksheet for this unit is about policy-making. This topic will help students understand how the policies governments make impact the environment. Divide the students into groups and distribute the case study, allowing some in-class time for planning. Have groups share findings with the class. **Logical/Mathematical**

V1 Visual Skills

Interpreting Direct attention to the satellite image and discuss the shape and size of Asia. Explain that both the Arctic Circle and the Equator cross the continent. **Ask: From the satellite image, what can you tell about the climates of Asia?** *(They vary from dry desert climates to tropical climates.)*

Point out that Asia has land area in the Northern, Southern, and Eastern hemispheres. **Ask: What other information about Asia can you learn from the satellite image?** *(Student answers should note mountainous regions, differences in ocean depth, and dark forested areas.)* **BL** Visual/Spatial

V2 Visual Skills

Describing Direct student attention to the large photo and have them read, "Bodies of Water." Allow for comments or questions about the photo. **Ask:**

• **What are the men doing?** *(fishing for mackerel and herring)*
• **What would be the consequences for the people of the region if fish became less plentiful or if a tsunami hit the region?** *(hunger, loss of life; people would probably need to move, disruption of regional economy)* **AL**

C1 Critical Thinking Skills

Defending Tell students that, as on most continents, different parts of Asia have varying amounts of rainfall. Some countries receive abundant amounts of rain, whereas others receive little. **Ask: Do you believe countries and regions should share their supplies of water? Decide how you feel about this issue and list arguments for or against countries' sharing water supplies.** *(Students' lists might include arguments in favor such as in sharing water supplies as compassion for neighboring countries that may be suffering from drought or water shortages, and so forth; the list against sharing water may include a government's duty to its own citizens above others, the difficulty of administering a program of sharing water, and so on.)*

Have students share their lists with the class. As a class, determine what opinions seemed to be the most common. **Verbal/Linguistic, Interpersonal**

C2 Critical Thinking Skills

Contrasting Have students read the Fast Fact and locate the United States outline placed on Asia. Guide students to contrast the size and shape of Asia with the United States. **Ask:**

• **How does the size of the United States contrast with the size of Asia?** *(The size of the United States is much smaller, approximately one-fifth the size.)*
• **How much of the world's land area does Asia include?** *(30 percent)* **Visual/Spatial**

V Visual Skills

Reading a Map Have students locate the area where China's largest river systems begin. Have the students trace the route of each river, paying particular attention to the color changes on the map as the river flows toward the sea. **Ask:**

- **What do the changes in color signify about those landforms?** *(They indicate elevation changes. In most cases, elevation decreases as the rivers flow toward the coast.)*

- **Where does each river end?** *(The Chang Jiang empties into the East China Sea; the Huang He spills into the Yellow Sea.)*

As students trace each river's route, have them also use the political map to list the cities along that route. **Ask:**

- **Why do cities develop along river systems?** *(Rivers provide water resources for large numbers of people and cheap transportation.)*

- **What generalization can be made about how these rivers affect the Chinese economy?** *(These river systems provide productive farmland, large amounts of water required for manufacturing processes, and an inexpensive transportation network to move finished products to seaports for export to other nations.)* **ELL** Visual/Spatial

C Critical Thinking Skills

Making Connections Have students focus on the elevations shown on the physical map. **Ask:**

- **What range of elevation is found in the Taklimakan Desert?** *(2000 ft to 5000 ft, or 600 m to 1500 m)*
- **What is the elevation of Mount Everest?** *(29,035 ft, or 8,850 m)*

Guide the discussion to elevations of various landforms. **Ask: In looking at the landforms found in Asia, where would you expect most settlement to take place?** *(Students should recognize that river valleys provide water and fertile land for settlement, whereas high mountain ranges, desert regions, and the upper latitudes create barriers to settlement.)*

Remind students that nearly 80% of the world's population lives near the water. **Ask: Why might countries in the far southern regions of Asia have an economic advantage over countries found within its interior?** *(Their coastlines are more suitable for agriculture and commerce.)* **BL** Visual/Spatial, Logical/Mathematical

---

ANSWER, p. 108

MAP SKILLS

1. The Plateau of Tibet (Plateau Xizang) is the highest elevation in Asia.
2. The Arctic Ocean borders northern Russia.
3. Southeast Asia consists of a peninsula extending from the Asian mainland into the South China Sea and the Indian Ocean and of thousands of islands.

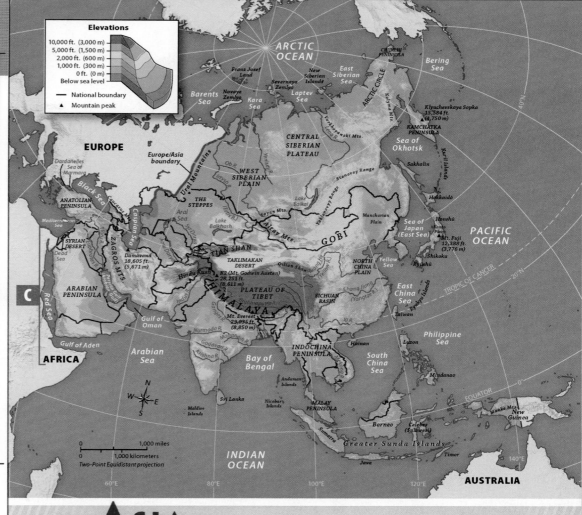

ASIA

PHYSICAL

MAP SKILLS

1 **PHYSICAL GEOGRAPHY** What part of Asia has the highest elevation?

2 **THE GEOGRAPHER'S WORLD** Which ocean borders the Central Siberian Plateau?

3 **PLACES AND REGIONS** How would you describe the region of Southeast Asia?

108 Unit 2

netw⊙rks *Online Teaching Options*

MAP

Asia: Physical Map

Display the interactive Physical Map of Asia on the whiteboard. As a class, have students identify areas of elevation and the various physical regions on the map. Discuss the landforms that create natural barriers to migration and invasion. Then with a partner, have students name the major bodies of water, and identify the source of several rivers following each identified river's flow to a sea or gulf. Also have pairs identify the peninsulas and island chains of Asia. **AL** Kinesthetic

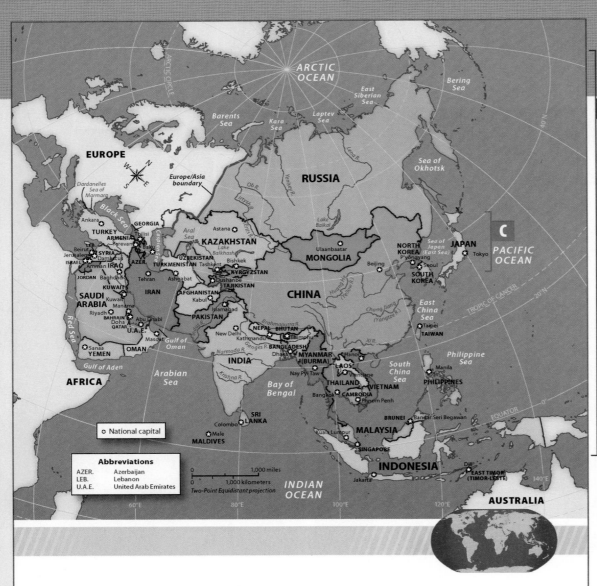

EUROPE

ARCTIC OCEAN

RUSSIA

POLITICAL

MAP SKILLS

1 PLACES AND REGIONS Which country in the region is the largest?

2 THE GEOGRAPHER'S WORLD Which country is located between China and Russia?

3 THE GEOGRAPHER'S WORLD What body of water lies between Kazakhstan and Iran?

GAME

Political Boundaries: Asia Game

Identifying As a class, play the drag-and-drop game to identify country and city names on the map. Then have volunteers use the whiteboard tools to draw a line from one location to another and calculate the following distances: from Sri Lanka to Tokyo, Japan *(about 4172 miles or 6714 km)*; from Astana, Kazakhstan to Seoul, Korea *(about 2827 miles or 4550 km)*; from the capital of Mongolia to the capital of Yemen *(about 4183 miles or 6,730 km)*

BL **Kinesthetic, Logical/Mathematical**

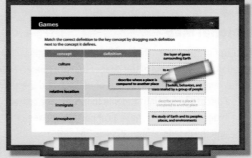

V

V Visual Skills

Analyzing a Map Direct students' attention to the political and physical maps of Asia and have them locate India. Have students describe the physical geography of India. **Ask:**

• **What landforms might have served as natural defenses for the country?** *(Himalaya Mountains)* Then have students examine the political map of India.

• **What political features are noted on the map?** *(capital—New Delhi; major rivers—Ganges, Krishna)*

• **Locate the Persian Gulf on the physical map. What other name is it known by?** *(Arabian Gulf)* Ask students to use the political map to locate the national capitals located on the Persian Gulf. *(Kuwait, Kuwait; Manama, Bahrain; Doha, Qatar; Abu Dhabi, United Arab Emirates; Muscat, Oman)*

Then ask students to examine the Arabian Peninsula. Have them write a list of the physical and political features of the region. *(Students answers will vary and may include peninsula, desert, Saudi Arabia, Kuwait, Yemen, Oman, United Arab Emirates, Bahrain, Qatar, Abu Dhabi, Persian Gulf, Gulf of Aden, Arabian Sea, Gulf of Oman)* **ELL**

C Critical Thinking Skills

Making Inferences Have students locate Mongolia on the political map. Although Mongolia borders China and is the second largest country in East Asia, its economy differs drastically from China's. As a class, have students list the clues the map gives that might suggest geography has an effect on a nation's economy. *(Mongolia is a landlocked nation and has no major river systems that flow to the sea. Its latitude would indicate that the weather is too cold to support more than subsistence farming, which would rule out agricultural exports. It has no large cities, making it unattractive to manufacturers who need large numbers of workers in one place.)*

Direct student attention to Southeast Asia. **Ask:**

• **Which country in this region is landlocked?** *(Laos)*

• **What difficulties do landlocked countries, such as Laos, have?** *(lack of ports for commerce, military defense vulnerabilities)*

• **Why is it important for island countries like the Philippines to maintain strong economic ties with other countries?** *(Students might consider the military vulnerability of island countries as well as their lack of land area and natural resources to provide adequately for human needs.)*
BL **Logical/Mathematical, Verbal/Linguistic**

ANSWER, p. 109

MAP SKILLS

1. China is the largest country in the region.
2. The country of Mongolia is located between China and Russia.
3. The Caspian Sea borders both Kazakhstan and Iran.

V Visual Skills

Integrating Visual Information Review the population map key and use the colors to assist with understanding population density. **Ask:**

- In which regions are high population densities found in Asia? *(in regions where there is ready access to water and other natural resources that can be used to satisfy human needs)*
- In which regions are low population densities found in Asia? *(high latitudes, mountain regions, desert regions)* **ELL**

V

C Critical Thinking Skills

Analyzing Visuals Direct students' attention to the cities map key. Have students answer and discuss the following questions either as a whole class or with partners. **Ask:**

- What do you notice about the location of cities that exceed 5 million people? *(They are all near a water source, such as a river, gulf, bay, or sea.)*
- What is true about the population densities of the island nations of Japan and the Philippines? *(They both have high population densities.)*
- What type of challenges do island nations with high population densities face? *(Possible answers: sufficient food supplies and other natural resources, such as water, to meet the needs of the population, adequate housing, limited land area for population expansion)*
- Why would regions of low population density shown on the map be an expected outcome? *(too cold and/or dry for the region to meet human needs)*
- What statement can be made about the population density of the Arabian Peninsula? *(pockets of high population density along the Red Sea and Gulf of Aden; relatively low population density throughout the remainder of the region)*
- What might explain the high population of cities found deep in the interior of the continent, such as Ürümqi? *(available natural resources, such as minerals, that can be used for economic stability and growth in the region)* **Visual/Spatial, Logical/Mathematical**

ASIA

POPULATION DENSITY

MAP SKILLS

1 **THE GEOGRAPHER'S WORLD** What parts of Asia are the most densely populated?

2 **THE GEOGRAPHER'S WORLD** Which part of the region has the lowest population density?

3 **THE GEOGRAPHER'S WORLD** In general, what population pattern do you see in Southwest Asia?

110 Unit 2

---

netw⊙rks   *Online Teaching Options*

MAP

Regional Map

Making Connections Display the interactive regional map to students. Select some of the images that are connected to the map and place them in context of the map and the unit. Guide a discussion helping students to identify the content of the images and then to make a connection between the image and the map location. **Visual/Spatial**

Land Use

- ☐ Commercial farming
- ☐ Subsistence farming
- ☐ Livestock raising
- ☐ Nomadic herding
- ☐ Primarily forest
- ■ Manufacturing and trade
- 🐟 Commercial fishing
- ☐ Little or no activity

Resources

- ⛏ Coal
- 🛢 Petroleum
- ◊ Natural gas
- ✕ Iron ore
- ⊡ Tin
- ⊡ Zinc
- ⁑ Bauxite
- ◉ Cobalt
- ✳ Uranium
- ⊗ Nickel
- ✿ Copper
- ✦ Lead
- ⬠ Manganese
- ◎ Gold
- ⊘ Silver
- ⊘ Platinum
- ▽ Diamonds

ECONOMIC RESOURCES

MAP SKILLS

1. **PLACES AND REGIONS** What mineral resources can be found around the Persian Gulf?

2. **HUMAN GEOGRAPHY** What economic activity takes place in the South China Sea?

3. **THE GEOGRAPHER'S WORLD** In what part of Russia are gold and silver deposits found?

Unit 2 **111**

Resources Map: Asia

Recognizing Relationships Display the interactive resource map and allow students time to review and discuss the region as each layer is revealed. Ask students to choose one of the countries and further research the natural resources found in the country using the Internet. Then have students create a graph that includes the resources and the current market value of the resources. **AL** **Visual/Spatial**

V Visual Skills

Reading a Map Review the Economic Resources map key and discuss the availability of resources across Asia and the types of land use. **Ask:**

- **Why type of land use occurs in desert regions?** (*nomadic herding*)
- **Where does most commercial fishing occur, and why might this be surprising?** (*Near the island nations; this might be surprising because there are many oceans and seas around Asia, yet commercial fishing is mainly located around the islands and the southern coasts.*)
- **What do you notice about the amount of manufacturing that occurs in Asia?** (*Students should recognize that manufacturing and trade are abundant.*) **Visual/Spatial**

V T Technology Skills

Analyzing Data In small groups, have students research the land use and resources of Indonesia, Kuwait, Myanmar, Thailand, Malaysia, Turkey, Syria, Vietnam, or Georgia on the Internet. Groups should use their research to create a presentation answering the following questions:

- **What are the main uses of the land?**
- **Which resources are found there?**
- **How does the natural resource or land use help support the nation's economy?**
- **How do countries protect from overuse of resources?**

Have groups include visual aids in their presentations. **Verbal/Linguistic, Auditory**

C Critical Thinking Skills

Recognizing Relationships Help students understand the global economic interdependence of countries. **Ask: How do natural resources available for use in Asia impact the global economy?** (*Countries that do not have needed resources must purchase them from other countries, creating an economic interdependence.*)

Have students examine the Persian Gulf and identify the natural resources located in the area. **Ask: Why is the Persian Gulf important to the world's economy?** (*The Persian Gulf has a large supply of oil important to all of the world's countries and the gulf is used as passage to export the oil all over the world.*)

Further explain that approximately 30 percent of the world's oil supplies and 85 percent of the oil used in Asia passes through this narrow channel. **BL** **Logical/Mathematical**

ANSWERS, p. 111

MAP SKILLS

1. oil, petroleum
2. commercial fishing
3. southern and eastern Russia

V Visual Skills

Reading a Map Review the map key noting the different climate groups. **Ask:**

- **Where are tropical rainforests found in Asia?** (*southern regions, Indonesia and Malaysia*)
- **What climate extremes are found in Asia?** (*tundra in the high latitudes to rainforests in the low latitudes*)
- **What type of climate dominates the central region of Asia?** (*semi-arid and arid*)
- **What types of climate are experienced by the western portion of Turkey?** (*Mediterranean and marine west coast*)
- **What stark climate contrast is found in China?** (*from tundra and subarctic to humid subtropical*)
- **What landform is associated with the tundra found in the south central regions of Asia?** (*mountains and high plateaus*) **ELL** Visual/Spatial

C Critical Thinking Skills

Reasoning Encourage students to consider the physical and resources maps. **Ask: What is the relationship between elevation, climate, available resources, and land use?** (*Students should reflect on how elevation impacts a region's climate just as the type of available resources and climate determine land use.*) **Logical/Mathematical**

W Writing Skills

Informative/Explanatory Divide the class into groups of five to seven students and assign each group a region in Asia. Have each group create a binder of information about the region. Allow students to be creative in their binder organization and design and how to present their information, such as an oral presentation, through a set of images or graphs, or a combination of several ways based on student strengths. Have students present their binders and create a classroom display with them. **Verbal/Linguistic**

CLOSE & REFLECT

Summarizing Have students reflect on what they have learned so far about Asia and then write a paragraph summarizing what they recall about the geography and political boundaries of Asia.

ANSWERS, p. 112

MAP SKILLS

1. mostly tropical wet
2. Beijing, because it is located in a humid continental zone while Ulaanbaatar is located in a tundra/dry, steppe zone
3. Coastal: tropical savanna; Ganges River: semi-arid

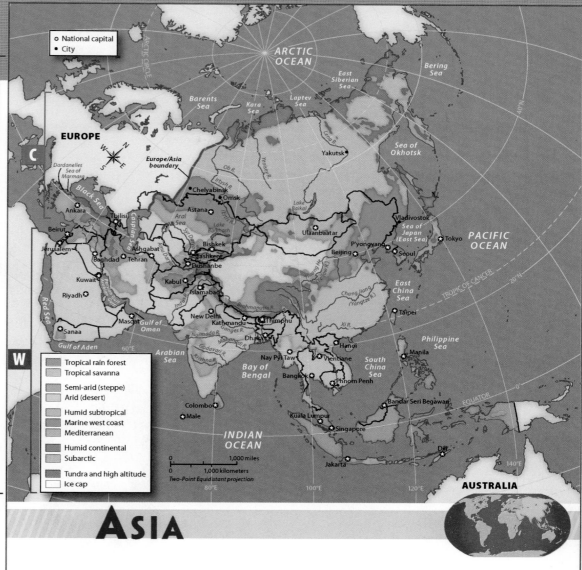

ASIA

CLIMATE

MAP SKILLS

1. **PHYSICAL GEOGRAPHY** How would you describe the climate zones found along the Equator?

2. **PLACES AND REGIONS** Which city do you think receives more rain each year—Beijing or Ulaanbaatar? Why?

3. **PHYSICAL GEOGRAPHY** In general, how does the climate of India's coastal areas differ from the climate of the Ganges River area?

112 Unit 2

networks *Online Teaching Options*

MAP

Asia: Climates Map

Describing Have students use the interactive climate map to discuss the precipitation and temperatures of Asia as a post assessment. Then have students form small groups. Have each group create three "You Are There" scenarios describing a particular regional land use. Each student group should present its scenarios to the class. Have other groups identify the climate in which the scenario could occur in a game-like format. Award game points to each group for correct identification. **AL** Interpersonal

CHAPTER 4
East Asia Planner

National Geography Standards covered in Chapter 4

Learners will understand:

UNDERSTANDING BY DESIGN®

Enduring Understandings

- *People, places, and ideas change over time.*

Essential Questions

- *How does geography influence the way people live?*
- *What makes a culture unique?*
- *How do cultures spread?*
- *Why do people trade?*
- *How does technology change the way people live?*

Predictable Misunderstandings

- *China and Japan are the only countries in East Asia.*
- *North Korea and South Korea are one country.*
- *Technology is the only industry in East Asia.*

Assessment Evidence

Performance Tasks:

- *Project-Based Learning Digital Hands-On Chapter Project*
- *Project-Based Learning Hands-On Chapter Project*

Other Evidence:

- *Technology Skills Activity*
- *Writing Skills Activity*
- *Geography and History Activity*
- *Cultural Geography Activity*
- *Participation in Interactive Whiteboard Activities*
- *Interpretation of slide show images and special purpose maps*
- *Participation in class discussions about the Geographer's World*
- *Lesson Reviews*
- *Chapter Assessments*

I. The World in Spatial Terms

Standard 1: How to use maps and other geographic representations, geospatial technologies, and spatial thinking to understand and communicate information

Standard 3: How to analyze the spatial organization of people, places, and environments on Earth's surface

II. Places and Regions

Standard 4: The physical and human characteristics of places

Standard 5: That people create regions to interpret Earth's complexity

Standard 6: How culture and experience influence people's perceptions of places and regions

III. Physical Systems

Standard 7: The physical processes that shape the patterns of Earth's surface

IV. Human Systems

Standard 9: The characteristics, distribution, and migration of human populations on Earth's surface

Standard 10: The characteristics, distribution, and complexity of Earth's cultural mosaics

Standard 11: The patterns and networks of economic interdependence on Earth's surface

Standard 12: The processes, patterns, and functions of human settlement

V. Environment and Society

Standard 15: How physical systems affect human systems

Standard 16: The changes that occur in the meaning, use, distribution, and importance of resources

VI. The Uses of Geography

Standard 17: How to apply geography to interpret the past

SUGGESTED PACING GUIDE

Introducing the Chapter............... 1 Day	Lesson 3 .... 2 Days
Lesson 1 .... 2 Days	Global Connections.................. 3 Days
Lesson 2 .... 2 Days	Chapter Wrap-Up and Assessment...... 1 Day

TOTAL TIME   11 Days

Key for Using the Teacher Edition

SKILL-BASED ACTIVITIES

Types of skill activities found in the Teacher Edition.

* **V** **Visual Skills** require students to analyze maps, graphs, charts, and photos.

W **Writing Skills** provide writing opportunities to help students comprehend the text.

R **Reading Skills** help students practice reading skills and master vocabulary.

C **Critical Thinking Skills** help students apply and extend what they have learned.

T **Technology Skills** require students to use digital tools effectively.

*Letters are followed by a number when there is more than one of the same type of skill on the page.

DIFFERENTIATED INSTRUCTION

All activities are written for the on-level student unless otherwise marked with the leveled labels below.

BL **Beyond Level**
AL **Approaching Level**
ELL **English Language Learners**

All students benefit from activities that utilize different learning styles. Many activities are marked as below when a particular learning style is highlighted.

Intrapersonal	Naturalist
Logical/Mathematical	Kinesthetic
Visual/Spatial	Auditory/Musical
Verbal/Linguistic	Interpersonal

CHAPTER OPENER PLANNER

Students will know:
- *that landforms in East Asia are varied.*
- *North Korea and South Korea are two countries that reside on a peninsula.*
- *the country of Japan is actually situated on many islands.*
- *that Chinese civilization began more than 4,000 years ago and influenced other East Asian countries.*

Students will be able to:
- *analyze a map to identify countries of East Asia.*
- *use a time line to discuss significant events in the history of countries in East Asia.*
- *discuss the variety of people and cultures in East Asia.*

UNDERSTANDING
BY DESIGN®

☑ *Print Teaching Options*

V **Visual Skills**

☐ **P. 114** Students analyze the map and discuss the differences in size among the countries of East Asia.

☐ **P. 115** Students use a time line to answer questions about the sequence of events in the history of East Asia.

☑ *Online Teaching Options*

☐ **MAP** **Reading A Map**—Students identify aspects and locations of the region on a map.

☐ **TIME LINE** **Reading a Time Line and Map**—Students learn about where and when historical events occurred in East Asia. **Visual/Spatial**

☐ **MAP** **Interactive World Atlas**—Students use the interactive world atlas to identify the region and describe its terrain.

☑ *Printable Digital Worksheets*

☐ **WORKSHEET** **Geography and History: Mt. Fuji's Effect on Culture**—Students can use this worksheet to create presentations of various representations of Mt. Fuji in art. **Visual/Spatial**

☐ **WORKSHEET** **Writing Skills: Haiku**—Students use this worksheet to create their own haikus.

☐ **WORKSHEET** **Cultural Geography: Anime's Influence on America**—Students use this worksheet to discuss and analyze the spread of Japanese anime to America.

☐ **WORKSHEET** **Technology Skills: Citing Internet Sources**—Students use this worksheet to understand how to find reliable sources and to cite them correctly. **Verbal/Linguistic**

Project-Based Learning

Hands-On

Write a Magazine Article

Students will work in groups to write a magazine article about a country in East Asia. Each article should include photos and information about the country's physical geography, history, and cultures. Articles should then be combined into a magazine about East Asia. Copies of the magazine should be distributed to all students to read. Then have students discuss the similarities and differences among the countries.

Digital Hands-On

Create Virtual Avatars

Students will work independently to create virtual speaking avatars. The virtual avatar will act as an expert in a particular field associated with the physical geography, history, and culture of East Asia. Each student will select one topic to create a two minute recording for the virtual avatar that will then be posted online. When all avatars are created and online, students will listen to one expert avatar from each category. After listening to each avatar, students will record what they learned about East Asia from the expert avatars.

edtechteacher
21st Century Learning

Print Resources

ANCILLARY RESOURCES

These ancillaries are available for every chapter and lesson.
- **Reading Essentials and Study Guide Workbook** AL ELL
- **Chapter Tests and Lesson Quizzes Blackline Masters**

PRINTABLE DIGITAL WORKSHEETS

These printable digital worksheets are available for every chapter and lesson!
- **Hands-On Chapter Projects**
- **What Do You Know? Activities**
- **Chapter Summaries (English and Spanish)**
- **Vocabulary Builder Activities**
- **Quizzes and Tests**
- **Reading Essentials and Study Guide (English and Spanish)** AL ELL
- **Guided Reading Activities**

More Media Resources

SUGGESTED VIDEOS

NOTE: Be sure to preview videos to ensure they are age-appropriate.
- **Summer Pasture** (84 min.)
- **The Cave of the Yellow Dog** (93 min.)
- **Wild China** (2 discs–300 min.)

SUGGESTED READING 📚

- ***The House Baba Built: An Artist's Childhood in China,*** by Ed Young BL
- ***Marco Polo: History's Great Adventurer,*** by Clint Twist
- ***Daughter of Xanadu,*** by Dori Jones Yang BL
- ***Moshi Moshi*** by Jonathan London AL

PHYSICAL GEOGRAPHY OF EAST ASIA

Students will know:
- that landforms in East Asia are varied.
- the climate in East Asia is varied from tropical to frigid cold.
- that East Asia has an abundance of natural resources and industry.

Students will be able to:
- **discuss** the physical geography of East Asia, including peninsulas and islands.
- **describe** the various climates in East Asia.
- **identify** important natural resources in East Asia.

UNDERSTANDING BY DESIGN®

☑ Print Teaching Options

V Visual Skills

☐ **P. 117** Students use an outline map of East Asia to diagram and make notes about the three sub-regions of mainland East Asia. **AL ELL**

☐ **P. 118** Students continue to label outline maps to include the Korean peninsula, Japan, and Taiwan, as well as use color to shade mountains, coasts, and plains. **AL**

☐ **P. 118** Students create word squares for the words *archipelago* and *tsunami*. **ELL Verbal/Linguistic**

☐ **P. 120** Students use a map to compare the latitude ranges of the United States to East Asia and predict differences in their climates. **Visual/Spatial**

☐ **P. 121** Students create a climate chart and take notes on the various climates of East Asia. **Visual/Spatial**

☐ **P. 121** Students analyze images of Mongolian herders for evidence of how they have adapted to their environment.

☐ **P. 123** Students create circle graphs to compare the portion of land that is forested in countries of East Asia.

R Reading Skills

☐ **P. 116** Students learn the meaning of *de facto* and explore the meaning of a de facto state in relation to Taiwan. **AL ELL**

☐ **P. 117** Students use context clues to understand the multiple meanings of the word *dominate*. **ELL**

☐ **P. 119** Students discuss the importance of bodies of water to East Asia and connect text about China's rivers to their understanding of rivers in the United States. **AL**

☐ **P. 121** Students summarize the three main factors that shape the climates of East Asia. **AL Verbal/Linguistic**

C Critical Thinking Skills

☐ **P. 120** Students contrast the rivers of Japan with those of China. **Verbal/Linguistic**

☐ **P. 122** Students compare and contrast the mineral and energy resources of China, Japan, and Taiwan. **Verbal**

T Technology Skills

☐ **P. 118** Interested students research and give a brief oral report of the damage done by the earthquake and tsunami that hit Japan in 2011, focusing on the impact of the nuclear accident. **BL**

☑ Online Teaching Options

V Visual Skills

☐ **VIDEO Hong Kong is the Perfect Blend of East and West**—Students watch a video about Hong Kong and make a chart based on what they learn from the video. **Visual/Spatial**

☐ **MAP Physical Geography: East Asia**—Students use the physical geography layer of the Chapter Opener map to further discuss the landscape of East Asia. **Visual/Spatial**

☐ **MAP Climates: East Asia**—Students use the climate layer of the Chapter Opener map to compare the information on the map with the notes in their climate charts. **Visual/Spatial**

☐ **MAP Resources: East Asia**—Students use the resources layer of the Chapter Opener map to discuss the other resources in East Asia. **Visual/Spatial, Naturalist**

W Writing Skills

☐ **VIDEO China's River: Huang He**—Students view a video of the Huang He and make a list of all the ways the Huang He River affects the lives of people of China. **Visual/Spatial, Naturalist**

R Reading Skills

☐ **GRAPHIC ORGANIZER Landforms and Bodies of Water in East Asia**—Students use the graphic organizer to review the landforms and bodies of water in East Asia. **Visual/Spatial**

☐ **LECTURE SLIDE Defining: Archipelago**—Students use this lecture slide to emphasize the visual vocabulary and discuss other examples of this landform.

☐ **LECTURE SLIDE Defining: Tsunamis**—Students use the lecture slide to define and describe tsunamis and connect to the feature.

☐ **GAME Drag-and-Drop: Resources in East Asia**—Students use the interactive game to review the resources of East Asia. **Kinesthetic**

C Critical Thinking Skills

☐ **SLIDE SHOW Chinese Mountain Ranges**—Students view the slide show and discuss how mountain ranges affect the way people live. **Naturalist**

☐ **IMAGE Mt. Fuji in Art**—Using the interactive image of the mountain, students discuss the importance of Mt. Fuji in Japanese culture. **Naturalist**

☐ **VIDEO Mongolia**—Students use the video to discuss the unique climate of Mongolia and its effects on the population. **Visual/Spatial**

☐ **CHART Biomes**—Students use the chart to explain the interaction of landforms on climate.

T Technology Skills

☐ **ONLINE SELF-CHECK QUIZ Lesson 1**—Students receive instant feedback on their mastery of lesson content.

☑ Printable Digital Worksheets

W Writing Skills

☐ **WORKSHEET Geography and History: Mt. Fuji's Effect on Culture**—Students can use this worksheet to create presentations of various representations of Mt. Fuji in art. **Visual/Spatial**

HISTORY OF EAST ASIA

Students will know:
- North Korea and South Korea are two countries that reside on a peninsula.
- that Chinese civilization began more than 4,000 years ago and influenced other East Asian countries.

Students will be able to:
- **describe** early China and its dynasties.
- **explain** spheres of influence and the rise of Japan.
- **describe** modern East Asia.
- **discuss** the creation of North and South Korea and the differences between them.

UNDERSTANDING
BY DESIGN®

☑ *Print Teaching Options*

V Visual Skills

☐ **P. 125** Students create a cluster diagram of the main ideas about the Zhou dynasty. **Visual/Spatial**

☐ **P. 125** Students analyze the photograph of the Great Wall to understand its design, location, and purpose.

☐ **P. 127** Students study the map of the Silk Road to understand its importance and geographic scope. **AL**

☐ **P. 129** Students interpret the differences between Japanese and American cultures based on an image.

W Writing Skills

☐ **P. 126** Students write one-page reports on the beliefs of Confucianism, Daoism, or Buddhism and follow with a class discussion comparing and contrasting them. **BL**

☐ **P. 129** Students write a report about how Mao Zedong was able to establish communist control of China. **BL**

R Reading Skills

☐ **P. 124** Students complete a definition tree for each vocabulary word they encounter and share their sentences with the class. **ELL**

☐ **P. 127** Students summarize the history of Korea and the early history of Japan. **Verbal/Linguistic**

☐ **P. 128** Students discuss China's objections to Japanese and European spheres of influence in the late 1800s.

☐ **P. 129** Students summarize the main ideas about Japanese history beginning in 1542. **Verbal/Linguistic**

☐ **P. 131** Students identify main ideas about development of North Korea, South Korea, and Japan after World War II.

C Critical Thinking Skills

☐ **P. 126** Students discuss main ideas and the significant developments and inventions of the Han dynasty. **AL**

☐ **P. 128** Students use the image of samurai to make a comparison to knights in Europe. **Verbal/Linguistic**

☐ **P. 130** Students compare and contrast the history of China and Taiwan. **Logical/Mathematical**

T Technology Skills

☐ **P. 127** Students use the Internet to research the Silk Road and report their findings to the class. **BL**

☑ *Online Teaching Options*

V Visual Skills

☐ **MAP** **The Silk Road and Trade**—Students use the map to discuss the importance of the Silk Road for trade and the exchange of ideas and inventions. **Logical/Mathematical**

W Writing Skills

☐ **VIDEO** **World's Wonders—The Great Wall of China**—Students watch a video about the history of the Great Wall of China and write three aspects they are interested in learning about the history of the countries of East Asia. **Visual/Spatial**

☐ **IMAGE** **China's Great Wall**—Students write a paragraph summarizing facts about the construction of the Great Wall of China. **Interpersonal**

☐ **IMAGE** **Samurai**—Using the interactive image, students discuss feudalism, the samurai, and the shogunate of Japan. Then students are encouraged to use the Internet to do further research.

R Reading Skills

☐ **GAME** **Drag-and-Drop: Chinese Dynasties**—Students take turns playing the game to review and discuss the dynasties of China. **Kinesthetic**

☐ **LECTURE SLIDE** **History of Korea**—Students can use this lecture slide show to review the history of Korea.

☐ **LECTURE SLIDE** **Defining: Sphere of Influence**—Students use the lecture slide to define this concept for understanding.

☐ **LECTURE SLIDE** **Types of Government**—Students can use this lecture slide to review the content for understanding.

C Critical Thinking Skills

☐ **MAP** **The Korean War**—Using the map, students discuss the Korean War and the demilitarized zone. **Logical/Mathematical**

☐ **MAP** **Japan and the West**—Using the map, students discuss Japan's evolving relations with the West and speculate about their economic success despite size and lack of natural resources.

☐ **CHART** **Governments in East Asia**—Students use the flowchart on the rise of communism to discuss the time period and its impact and summarize the governments in the region today.

T Technology Skills

☐ **ONLINE SELF-CHECK QUIZ** **Lesson 2**—Students receive instant feedback on their mastery of lesson content.

☑ *Printable Digital Worksheets*

W Writing Skills

☐ **WORKSHEET** **Writing Skills: Haiku**—Students use this worksheet to create their own haikus.

LIFE IN EAST ASIA

Students will know:
- *that most of the people in China live in the eastern portion that has low hills and plains.*
- *that within each country of East Asia, the population tends to be ethnically similar.*

Students will be able to:
- *describe* population patterns in East Asia.
- *identify* languages spoken in East Asia.
- *describe* various religions, daily life, and the arts in East Asia.
- *examine* current economic and environmental issues in East Asia.

UNDERSTANDING
BY DESIGN®

☑ *Print Teaching Options*

V Visual Skills

- ☐ **P. 133** Students create word squares for each vocabulary word they encounter and share their examples. **AL** **ELL**
- ☐ **P. 133** Students analyze the photograph to understand how people of East Asia live. **Visual/Spatial**
- ☐ **P. 134** Students create a three-column chart identifying the dominant ethnic group and language of each country of East Asia and contrast these with the United States. **AL**
- ☐ **P. 134** Students compare Western and Chinese cultural influences found in the photograph. **Visual/Spatial**
- ☐ **P. 136** Students analyze the photograph of fans lining up for an animation exhibition. **Visual/Spatial**
- ☐ **P. 139** Students complete a concept web of political issues in East Asia. **Visual/Spatial**

R Reading Skills

- ☐ **P. 136** Students compare their culture with East Asian culture.
- ☐ **P. 137** Students identify popular pastimes, sports, and holidays in East Asia. **AL**

C Critical Thinking Skills

- ☐ **P. 132** Students use a population map of East Asia to ask questions about population patterns in East Asia. **AL**
- ☐ **P. 137** Students compare and contrast the economies and environmental problems of the United States, China, and Japan. **Verbal/Linguistic**
- ☐ **P. 138** Students discuss the challenges of population growth in East Asia and debate possible solutions.

T Technology Skills

- ☐ **P. 135** Small groups research and prepare a short visual and oral class presentation on an East Asian art form.
- ☐ **P. 138** Students use a calculator to determine the amount of trade deficit or surplus in four hypothetical cases. **Logical/Mathematical**

☑ *Online Teaching Options*

V Visual Skills

- ☐ **IMAGE** **Personal Buddhist Shrines**—Based on the interactive image, students learn about the uses of personal shrines and compare the use of shrines in Buddhism with another religion.
- ☐ **SLIDE SHOW** **Influence of Japanese Anime**—Students identify stylistic features of anime and discuss its influence on Western animation. **Visual/Spatial**
- ☐ **MAP** **Population: East Asia**—Students can use the population layer of the Chapter Opener map to further discuss the population distribution and density of the region. **Visual/Spatial**
- ☐ **SLIDE SHOW** **Writing in East Asia**—Students can use the slide show to analyze the different types of calligraphy in East Asia.
- ☐ **IMAGE** **Baseball in Japan**—Students can use the interactive image of baseball in Japan to discuss the influence of western culture and the popularity of baseball in the country.

W Writing Skills

- ☐ **VIDEO** **China Pollution**—Students watch a video about the increase of pollution in China and research whether China's government has policies on pollution. **Verbal/Linguistic**
- ☐ **VIDEO** **Pollution in China**—After watching the video, students will compare how pollution is defined in China and the United States. **Interpersonal**

C Critical Thinking Skills

- ☐ **GRAPHIC ORGANIZER** **Population Pyramids of East Asia**—Students look at population pyramids and discuss how government policies changed the distribution of people across age and gender groups. **Logical/Mathematical**
- ☐ **CHART** **Religion in East Asia**—Students analyze the chart showing the religions of East Asia to answer questions. **Visual/Spatial**
- ☐ **CHART** **Comparing U.S. and East Asia Resources**—Students use the comparison chart to discuss resources used and traded between the United States and East Asia. **Verbal/Linguistic**
- ☐ **VIDEOS** **City Life in East Asia**—Students can reinforce the idea of urban population density with the videos of city life in East Asia.

T Technology Skills

- ☐ **MAP** **Population Concerns in East Asia**—Students can analyze the heat map/population bubble to examine the impact of population on a region.
- ☐ **ONLINE SELF-CHECK QUIZ** **Lesson 3**—Students receive instant feedback on their mastery of lesson content.

☑ *Printable Digital Worksheets*

W Writing Skills

- ☐ **WORKSHEET** **Cultural Geography: Anime's Influence on America**—Students use this worksheet to discuss and analyze the spread of Japanese anime to America.
- ☐ **WORKSHEET** **Technology Skills: Citing Internet Sources**—Students use this worksheet to understand how to find reliable sources and to cite them correctly.

INTERVENTION AND REMEDIATION STRATEGIES

LESSON 1   Physical Geography of East Asia

Reading and Comprehension

Have students work in pairs to use this lesson's content vocabulary words in sentences. Encourage students to use the word as it is used in the text as well as in a new context. For example, *de facto* means "in actual fact" and can be applied to a number of terms other than "a de facto country." As a lesson review, have students collaborate to write a paragraph using all the terms. Sentences should show an understanding of the technical meaning of each word as it is used in the text.

Text Evidence

Have small groups of students analyze a landform or body of water discussed in this lesson. Students may use information in the text about their assigned landform or body of water, or they may conduct online research to learn more about it. For example, students might analyze the Huang He River and how loess gives it its yellow color. Tell students to address these questions in their analyses: *Where is this landform or body of water? Does it face or pose any threats to the environment or the surrounding region? If so, what are they, and how has the problem been addressed?*

LESSON 2   History of East Asia

Reading and Comprehension

To help students organize and comprehend the concepts discussed in this lesson, have them create a visual portrayal of the lesson using a word web with the content vocabulary terms as headings. Tell students to place the vocabulary words in center circles with descriptions of each word in outer circles. Encourage students to illustrate their word webs with an example of each concept to help them better understand it.

Text Evidence

Have students create a time line or flow chart that shows the relationship between different individuals and cultural groups discussed in the lesson. Time lines and charts should reflect an understanding of the influence that specific events had on different groups or individuals, and the influence that specific groups of people had on various events. Provide students with an example, such as how the 800-year rule of the Zhou dynasty included long-lasting changes to China's legal and monetary systems.

LESSON 3   Life in East Asia

Reading and Comprehension

Have students scan the lesson and use context clues to define the meaning of each content vocabulary word. Ask volunteers to choose one of the words and use it in a sentence that shows an understanding of the word's meaning. Help students use word parts to better understand terms they may find confusing, such as *megalopolis*. Explain that *mega-* means "great or large" and *poli-* means "city."

Text Evidence

Have student groups select a city or region in East Asia discussed in this lesson. Tell groups to write a song or commercial about the city, describing its cultural characteristics and the reasons people would want to visit the area. Students may conduct additional research to learn more about their chosen city or region. After each group presents its song or commercial, guide a short session in which classmates can ask questions of the presenters. In answering, presenters should use evidence from the text or their research.

Online Resources

Level Reader

Use this online lower-level text that corresponds directly to the text in the online Student Edition.

Guided Reading Activities

This resource uses graphic organizers and guiding questions to help students with comprehension.

What Do You Know?

Use these worksheets to pre-assess students' background knowledge before they read the chapter.

Reading Essentials and Study Guide Workbook

This resource offers writing and reading activities for the approaching-level student.

Self-Check Quizzes

This online assessment tool provides instant feedback for students to check their progress.

EAST ASIA

There's More Online about East Asia.

CHAPTER 4

Lesson 1
Physical Geography of East Asia

Lesson 2
History of East Asia

Lesson 3
Life in East Asia

The Story Matters...

East Asia can trace many of its cultural features to an ancient civilization that arose in China thousands of years ago. In the centuries that followed, powerful dynasties ruled China, creating an enormous empire that influenced the entire region. Today, migration and trade have paved the way for an exchange of ideas and practices between East Asia and other parts of the world. Japan, Taiwan, and South Korea have become modern industrial nations.

Performers with the Beijing Opera wear facial paint and colorful costumes.

FOLDABLES®
Study Organizer

Go to the Foldables® library in the back of your book to make a Foldable® that will help you take notes while reading this chapter.

| Economic Growth |
| Cultural Influences |
| Mainland and Islands |
| East Asia |

113

ENGAGE

 Bellringer Note that students have a lot of interaction with East Asia through the products they use every day. Explain that two major countries of East Asia are China and Japan. Then create a T-chart on the board with those two countries as headings for the two columns of the chart. Call on each student in class to name a product commonly made in either China or Japan. If necessary, prompt students to name some brands of cars and electronic products made in Japan, and have students examine labels to see if their clothes were made in China. Ask students what Chinese or Japanese foods they enjoy eating. Then have students read "The Story Matters..." and focus their attention on the words "migration and trade" in the last sentence. Note that Chinese and Japanese immigrants have brought their foods to the United States, and international trade brings the products of China and Japan to almost every household in the United States.

China	Japan

Making Connections To reinforce the significance of trade and migration between East Asia and the United States, read the following information to students:

- Along with Canada and Mexico, our next-door neighbors, China and Japan are the top trading partners of the United States. The United States imports more goods from China than from any other country.
- Chinese make up the second largest immigrant group in the United States. The largest number of immigrants come from Mexico.

Letter from the Author

Dear Geography Teacher,

In addition to the textbook, you and your students can visit www.geoteach.org to access creative geography activities. The project, "Geography: Teaching with the Stars," was created with the help of The Gilbert M. Grosvenor Center for Geographic Education. On this Web site, you will find classroom support materials, activities for students, and access to teacher forums where educators share their ideas for teaching geography.

FOLDABLES®
Study Organizer

Go to the Foldables® library for a chapter-based Foldable® activity that your students can use to help take notes and prepare for assessment.

| Economic Growth |
| Cultural Influences |
| Mainland and Islands |
| East Asia |

TEACH & ASSESS

Step Into the Place

V Visual Skills

Direct students' attention to the map and point out the differences in size among the countries of East Asia. **Ask:**

- **How would you rank the countries of East Asia in order of size?** *(China, Mongolia, Japan, North Korea, South Korea, Taiwan)*
- **Which is the largest country by far?** *(China)*
- **Which countries are islands?** *(Japan and Taiwan)*
- **What kind of landform dominates central and southern China?** *(mountains)*
- **How is the geography of Mongolia different from all of the other countries in East Asia?** *(It is landlocked and the other countries are either islands or have large borders along the ocean)*

Then have students answer the Step Into the Place questions.
Visual/Spatial

Content Background Knowledge

As students examine the photographs, share the following background knowledge:

- The British occupied and controlled Hong Kong from the mid-1800s to the late 1900s. In 1997, Hong Kong became a special administrative region of China as part of an agreement with the British. The agreement specified that Hong Kong would not come under China's socialist economic system for the next 50 years; thus, Hong Kong has a free market economy.
- The Plateau of Tibet is the highest landform of this type in the world, averaging over 16,000 feet in elevation. Its southern rim includes Mount Everest and several of the world's highest peaks.

ANSWERS, p. 114

STEP INTO THE PLACE

1. China
2. South China Sea, East China Sea, Yellow Sea
3. Sea of Japan, Strait of Korea
4. **CRITICAL THINKING** China, North Korea, Japan

Chapter 4

EAST ASIA (CCSS)

V East Asia borders Central Asia, South Asia, and Southeast Asia and extends to the Pacific Ocean. As you study the map of East Asia, look for the geographic features that make this region of Asia unique.

Step Into the Place

MAP FOCUS Use the map to answer the following questions.

1. **THE GEOGRAPHER'S WORLD** What country lies south of Mongolia?

2. **PLACES AND REGIONS** What seas border China?

3. **THE GEOGRAPHER'S WORLD** What bodies of water lie between Japan and the Koreas?

4. **CRITICAL THINKING**
   Analyzing If you traveled east along 40° N latitude, which East Asian countries would you travel through?

BUSY CITY MARKET One of the main attractions in Hong Kong, China, is the Temple Street Night Market. Each night, crowds visit the market to buy a variety of goods, such as clothes and household appliances.

REMOTE MYSTERIOUS HIGHLAND A nomadic sheep herder crosses the vast spaces of the Plateau of Tibet in western China.

Step Into the Time

TIME LINE Choose an event from the time line and write a paragraph predicting the effect of that event on the future of East Asia.
WHST.6-8.2, WHST.6-8.10

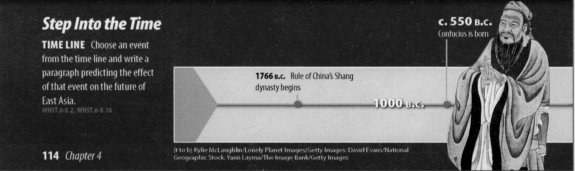

c. 550 B.C. Confucius is born

1766 B.C. Rule of China's Shang dynasty begins

1000 B.C.

114 Chapter 4

(t to b) Kylie McLaughlin/Lonely Planet Images/Getty Images; David Evans/National Geographic Stock; Yann Layma/The Image Bank/Getty Images

---

Project-Based Learning

Hands-On

Writing a Magazine Article
Students will work in groups to write a magazine article about a country in East Asia. Each article should include photos and information about the country's physical geography, history, and cultures. Articles should then be combined into a magazine about East Asia. Copies of the magazine should be distributed to all students to read. Then have students discuss the similarities and differences among the countries.

Digital Hands-On

Creating Virtual Avatars
Each student will create a virtual speaking avatar that acts as an expert in a particular field associated with the physical geography, history, and culture of East Asia. Each student will select one topic to create a two minute recording for the virtual avatar that will then be posted online. Then students will listen to one expert avatar from each category. After listening to each avatar, students will record what they learned about East Asia from the expert avatars.

East Asia

RUSSIA

CENTRAL ASIA

MONGOLIA
•Ulaanbaatar

NORTH KOREA
Sea of Japan (East Sea)
JAPAN
Beijing ☉
P'yŏngyang ☉
Seoul ☉
Tokyo ☉
SOUTH KOREA
Hiroshima
Yellow Sea

CHINA

Huang He (Yellow R.)

Chengdu
Chang Jiang (Yangtze R.)
Brahmaputra R.

Shanghai •

East China Sea
PACIFIC OCEAN

SOUTH ASIA

Taipei ☉
TROPIC OF CANCER
TAIWAN

Bay of Bengal

SOUTHEAST ASIA

Hong Kong
Macao

South China Sea
Philippine Sea

☉ National capital
• City

0   500 miles
0 500 kilometers
Lambert Azimuthal Equal-Area projection

c. 200 B.C.
Travel on the Silk Road begins

1945
Atomic bombs dropped on Hiroshima, Nagasaki; Japan surrenders, ending World War II

935 A.D. Wank Kon renames kingdom Koryo (Korea)

1192 Shoguns begin rule of Japan

1000 A.D.

2011 Earthquake, tsunami strike Japan

2000 A.D.

1001 Japan's Murasaki Shibubi writes *The Tale of Genji*

1949 Communists seize power in China

(l to r) Fotosearch Value/Getty Images; SuperStock/Getty Images

Chapter 4 **115**

Reading a Time Line and Map

Display the time line and map on the whiteboard. Have a volunteer read each event as it is revealed on the time line and locate on the map the country where the event took place. Ask students to draw conclusions about the relative importance of the various countries based on the frequency of appearances on the time line. **Visual/ Spatial**

See page 113B for other online activities.

Step Into the Time

V Visual Skills

Interpreting Have students review the time line and use it to answer the following questions. **Ask:**

- **What can you deduce from the fact that the Shang dynasty began in China in 1766 B.C.?** *(Possible answer: Chinese civilization is very old.)*
- **When was Confucius born, and what do you know about him?** *(550 B.C.; Possible answer: He was a Chinese philosopher who had a major influence on Chinese culture.)*
- **What led Japan to surrender in 1945, ending World War II?** *(Atomic bombs were dropped on Hiroshima and Nagasaki.)*
- **How long have communists controlled China?** *(over 60 years)*
- **What country suffered a major earthquake and tsunami in 2011?** *(Japan)*

Share the Content Background Knowledge with students before they begin the time line writing assignment. **Visual/Spatial**

Content Background Knowledge

- The teachings of Confucius provided a moral guide for political and social life and promoted social harmony in China.
- The Silk Road was an ancient trade route between China and the Mediterranean Sea, linking China with the Roman Empire. Its name comes from the valuable trade in Chinese silk.
- *The Tale of Genji* by Murasaki Shibubi, a story of Japanese court life, is considered the greatest work of fiction in Japanese literature.
- Shoguns were a series of military commanders who ruled Japan from 1192 to 1868, more than 650 years.

CLOSE & REFLECT

Integrating Visual Information Ask students to reflect on what they have learned so far about East Asia from the photographs, map, time line, and class discussions. Tell them to brainstorm and jot down a list of words and phrases describing this region. Have them share their lists and save them for use at the end of the chapter.

ENGAGE

🔔 **Bellringer** Tell students to imagine that they are going on a tour of East Asia. Ask them to describe the landscape they expect to see in each country. On the board, create a chart like the one below and note what students say about each country. Ask a volunteer to make a copy of the chart and save it for use at the end of the lesson.

Country	Landscape
China	
Mongolia	
North Korea	
South Korea	
Japan	
Taiwan	

TEACH & ASSESS

R Reading Skills

Determining Word Meanings Explain that *de facto* is a Latin phrase that literally means "according to fact." It can mean "in reality" or "actually." Share with students the information about Taiwan in the Content Background Knowledge.

AL **ELL** Verbal/Linguistic

Content Background Knowledge

The international legal status of Taiwan has been in question for decades. A civil war in China in the 1940s resulted in a communist takeover of mainland China while the former ruling party retreated to the island of Taiwan. Both the communists on the mainland and the former rulers living in Taiwan claimed to represent China. Over the years, more and more countries recognized and established relations with the government of mainland China. Today, few countries recognize Taiwan as an independent nation, even though it has been self-governing for over 60 years.

ANSWER, p. 116

Taking Notes Sample summary sentences: **Landforms**— The landforms of mainland East Asia include the world's highest mountains and plateaus as well as low hills and plains. **Waterways**—The four large seas along East Asia's eastern edge provide seafood for the region's people, while the fertile plains along the Huang He and Chang Jiang are productive farming regions. **Resources**—China has the greatest share of the region's resources, including tin, lead, zinc, iron ore, tungsten, and fossil fuels.

---

netw⊚rks

There's More Online!

☑ **IMAGE** Mt. Fuji in Art
☑ **MAP** Climates of East Asia
☑ **VIDEO**

Reading **HELP**DESK CCSS

Academic Vocabulary RH.6-8.4
(Tier Two Words)
• **dominate**

Content Vocabulary RH.6-8.4
(Tier Three Words)
• **de facto**
• **archipelago**
• **tsunami**
• **loess**

TAKING NOTES: *Key Ideas and Details* RH.6-8.2, RH.6-8.7

Summarize As you study the lesson, use a graphic organizer like the one below to write one summary sentence for each topic.

Topic	Summary
Landforms	
Waterways	
Resources	

Lesson 1

Physical Geography of East Asia

ESSENTIAL QUESTION · *How does geography influence the way people live?*

IT MATTERS BECAUSE

East Asia is where some of the most densely populated areas in the world are found. It also has vast areas where few people live. To understand why these extreme differences exist, it is necessary to understand the region's physical geography.

Landforms and Waterways

GUIDING QUESTION *What are the main physical features and physical processes in East Asia?*

The landscapes and physical features of East Asia are varied and sometimes unusual. East Asia is home to the world's highest mountain range, as well as a vast plateau that sits miles high. It is also the site of islands created by volcanoes and fertile plains where hundreds of millions of people live.

A Regional Overview

East Asia covers much of the eastern half of the Asian continent. Its eastern boundary stretches along the Pacific Ocean. Bordering East Asia to the north are Russia and Central Asia. To the south are the regions of South Asia and Southeast Asia.

R East Asia is made up of six countries: China, Japan, Mongolia, North Korea, South Korea, and the de facto country of Taiwan. A **de facto** country is one not legally recognized by other countries. China is the largest country in the region. It has more than four-fifths of the region's total land area. Slightly smaller than the United States, China is the world's fourth-largest country in land area.

(l to r) ©Fritz Hoffmann/In Pictures/Corbis; Peerapat Tandavanitj/Flickr/Getty Images; Stocktrek Images/Getty Images; ©George Steinmetz/Corbis; ©Hamid Sardar/Corbis

---

netw⊚rks *Online Teaching Options*

VIDEO

Hong Kong is the Perfect Blend of East and West

Integrating Visual Information Use this video which discusses the unique blending of eastern and western culture in Hong Kong to introduce the unique elements of East Asia that students will learn about in this chapter. Have students work in pairs to create graphic organizers that organize the information they learn about in the video— including city life, economy, physical geography, and night life. **Verbal/Linguistic, Visual/Spatial**

See page 113C for other online activities.

BBC Motion Gallery Education

At the opposite extreme is Taiwan, the region's smallest country. It is roughly the size of Massachusetts and Connecticut combined. China and Mongolia sit on the Asian mainland, while the other four countries occupy islands or a peninsula.

The Mainland

Geographers often divide mainland East Asia, which consists of China and Mongolia, into three broad geographic subregions. Because of differences in elevation, the subregions are like steps in a staircase. The highest step is the Plateau of Tibet, a vast area of mountains and uplands in southwestern China. The plateau is sometimes called "the roof of the world" because of its extremely high elevation. Much of the land sits more than 2.5 miles (4 km) above sea level.

Lofty mountains circle the Plateau of Tibet. The Kunlun Shan range runs along the northern edge, and the Himalaya—the tallest mountains in the world—rise along the southern edge. The Himalaya reach their highest point at Mount Everest, which soars higher than any other mountain in the world. When mountain climbers reach Everest's peak, they stand nearly 5.5 miles (8.9 km) above sea level.

North and east of Tibet, land elevation drops sharply to the second step in the staircase. Mountains and plateaus **dominate** this subregion, too, but they are generally much lower than those of Tibet. Some of the mountain ranges lie along the edges of enormous basins, or natural land depressions. Much of the land in the northern part of the subregion is desert or near desert, with little or no vegetation.

Land along the southern part of the subregion is forested. Some of the steepest and deepest canyons in the world lie where the land descends from Tibet.

The third and lowest step in the staircase covers most of the eastern third of China. The main landforms in this subregion are low hills and plains. Most Chinese live on these plains.

©Fritz Hoffmann/In Pictures/Corbis

Chapter 4 **117**

Academic Vocabulary

dominate to have the greatest importance

A train crosses a bridge spanning a deep valley in western China. The Qingzang, the world's highest rail system, links newly developing areas in the west to densely populated plains areas in eastern China.

► **CRITICAL THINKING**
Describing Why is western China's Plateau of Tibet called "the roof of the world?"

SLIDE SHOW

Chinese Mountain Ranges

Analyzing Images After students view the slide show, ask how mountain ranges typically affect the way that people live and how countries develop. *(Students should note that people tend to live in small communities that are isolated, or cut off, from large centers of population.)* Note that mountains have long been a source of inspiration for artists in East Asia. **Naturalist**

See page 113C for other online activities.

Slide Show

V Visual Skills

Diagramming To help students visualize the landscape of mainland East Asia, have them draw a staircase with three steps to represent the three subregions described in the text. Tell students to note the most important information about each region on their diagrams.

- The highest step should include notes such as: the Plateau of Tibet; Kunlun Shan along northern edge; Himalaya along southern edge with Mount Everest, world's highest peak.
- The middle step should include notes such as: lower mountains and plateaus; some enormous basins; northern part desert or near desert; southern part forested with world's deepest canyons.
- The lowest step should include notes such as: low hills and plains; has the most people.

Provide students with an outline map of the region and direct them to use a key to indicate which step falls on which part of the map. *(The highest step is located in Southwestern China. The middle step is located to the north and east. The lowest step is located in eastern China.)* **AL** **ELL** Visual/Spatial

R Reading Skills

Using Context Clues The word *dominate* is frequently used and has multiple meanings. Explain to students that *dominate* can mean all these things: to have the greatest importance, to take up the most space or time or attention, to exert the most influence, or to control. Read the following example sentences to students and ask them to explain what the word means in each context:

- I could not ask any questions because Maria dominated the conversation. *(Maria talked the most.)*
- Oak trees dominate the forest. *(Oak trees are the most numerous type of tree in the forest.)*
- Lee dominates his younger brother. *(Lee controls or bosses his younger brother.)*
- Ads dominate the newspaper. *(Ads take up the most space in the newspaper.)* **ELL** Verbal/Linguistic

ANSWER, p. 117

CRITICAL THINKING Much of the plateau's land sits more than 2.5 miles (4 km) above sea level.

V1 Visual Skills

Diagramming Direct students to continue to label their outline maps of East Asia as they read about the Korean Peninsula, Japan, and Taiwan. Suggest that students use a brown pencil to shade mountainous areas of the peninsula and islands and a green pencil to shade plains and coastal areas. Students should also label the Korean Peninsula, North Korea, South Korea, the Yellow Sea, the Sea of Japan, Japan, Honshu, Mount Fuji, and Taiwan. *(Students should shade the following areas brown: most of the Korean Peninsula except for the coastline in the south and west, most of Japan, and the central part of Taiwan. Students should shade the following areas green: the southern and western part of the Korean Peninsula, isolated spots in Japan, and the western part of Taiwan.)* **AL** **Visual/Spatial**

V2 Visual Skills

Creating Word Squares Have students create word squares like the ones below for the vocabulary words *archipelago* and *tsunami*. Pronounce these words for students and have them repeat the pronunciations. Note that the *t* in *tsunami* is silent. *(Sample answers: **Archipelago**—a chain of islands; The archipelago stretched for thousands of miles in the Pacific Ocean; a drawing of a chain of islands; Japan. **Tsunami**—a huge ocean wave produced by an earthquake; The tsunami destroyed all the roads and bridges along the coast; a drawing of a wave; very powerful and damaging)* **ELL** **Visual/Spatial**

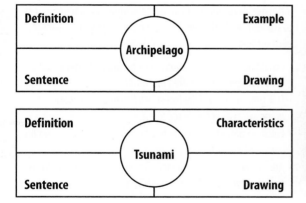

Definition	Example
Archipelago	
Sentence	Drawing

Definition	Characteristics
Tsunami	
Sentence	Drawing

T Technology Skills

Researching on the Internet Direct interested students to research the damage done by the powerful earthquake and tsunamis that hit Japan in 2011, focusing on the nuclear accident that resulted. Ask a student to give a brief oral report to the class. **BL** **Verbal/Linguistic**

ANSWER, p. 118

CRITICAL THINKING Three-fourths of the land consists of forested mountains; the rest of the landscape includes small, isolated plains.

A Peninsula and Many Islands

V1 In addition to the mainland, East Asia includes a large peninsula and, running parallel to the eastern coast, a long string of islands. The Korean Peninsula is a thumb of land that juts southward from the mainland between the Yellow Sea and the Sea of Japan (East Sea). It is home to two countries: North Korea and South Korea. The peninsula is mountainous, especially in the northeast. In the south and west, broad plains stretch between the mountains and the coast.

V2 Along the eastern edge of the Sea of Japan, an arc of islands stretches for roughly 1,500 miles (2,414 km). The islands—four large ones and thousands of much smaller ones—form the **archipelago** (ahr kuh PEH luh goh) of Japan. An archipelago is a group or chain of islands.

The islands of Japan are part of the Ring of Fire, which nearly encircles the Pacific Ocean. In this area, huge sections of Earth's crust grind against each other and cause earthquakes and volcanic eruptions. The islands of Japan were formed by volcanic eruptions millions of years ago.

Forested mountains cover nearly three-fourths of the land on the islands. Plains are generally small and isolated. On Honshū, Japan's largest island, a beautiful, cone-shaped volcano called Mount Fujiyama or Mount Fuji rises about 12,400 feet (3,780 m) above the Kanto plain. Snow-covered Mount Fuji is a well-known symbol of Japan. Although it has not erupted in nearly 300 years, scientists believe it could.

Japan is one of the most earthquake-prone countries in the world. More than 1,000 small earthquakes shake the country every year. Major quakes occur less often, but they can cause tremendous damage and loss of life. When an earthquake occurs below or close to the ocean, it can trigger a **tsunami** (soo NAH mee). This is a huge wave that gets higher as it approaches the coast. Tsunamis can wipe **T** out coastal cities and towns. In 2011 the most powerful earthquake in Japan's history produced massive tsunamis that devastated areas along the northeastern coast.

Hundreds of miles southwest of Japan's main islands lies another large island, Taiwan. Like Japan, Taiwan was formed as a result of volcanic activity. Mountains form a rugged spine that stretches the length of this sweet-potato-shaped

Mount Fuji, on Japan's Honshū island, soars above blooming cherry trees. Each spring, people come to the five lakes around Mount Fuji to view the cherry blossoms with the beautiful mountain in the distance.
▶ **CRITICAL THINKING**
Describing What physical features make up the islands of Japan?

Peerapat Tandavanitj/Flickr/Getty Images

---

netw⊙rks *Online Teaching Options*

IMAGE

Mt. Fuji in Art

Integrating Visual Information Use the interactive image of Mt. Fuji to discuss the importance of this mountain in Japanese culture. Explain that the Japanese people, who traditionally view nature as holy, have long revered Mt. Fuji as a sacred peak. Discuss with students that it has been a source of inspiration for many works of art, including paintings and literature. **Naturalist**

See page 113C for other online activities.

© Image Source/Getty Images

island. The spine is actually the edge of a huge, tilting block of Earth's crust. The western face of the block slopes much more gradually than the steep eastern face. Broad plains spread across the western part of the island.

Bodies of Water

Bodies of water in East Asia provide food for its people, give them a place to live, move their goods, and power factories to light homes. Fish and other seafood caught in the seas and ocean make up an important part of the diet of many East Asians.

Four large seas sit along East Asia's eastern edge. The largest is the South China Sea. It is partly enclosed by Taiwan, southeastern China, and islands of Southeast Asia. Because the South China Sea lies between important ports in the Pacific and Indian oceans, it has some of the busiest shipping lanes in the world.

The East China Sea lies between China and Japan's Ryukyu Islands, a long archipelago extending southwestward toward Taiwan. In the north, this sea meets the Yellow Sea, which is shaped by the Korean Peninsula and the northeastern coast of China. Farther north, Japan, the Korean Peninsula, and the Asian mainland together are shaped like a corral that almost entirely encircles the Sea of Japan (East Sea).

Rivers in China

The water of East Asia's two most important rivers, the Huang He (Yellow River) and the Chang Jiang (Yangtze River), flow across China. Both of these rivers begin high on the Plateau of Tibet in southwestern China and flow down the eastern slope of the plateau. The Huang He flows by twists and turns to the Yellow Sea far to the east. Along the way, it picks up a tremendous amount of yellow-brown silt called **loess** (LEHS). This silt gives the river and the sea their name and color.

In eastern China, silt deposited by floods over millions of years has created a broad, fertile plain called the North China Plain. This is one of China's most productive farming areas. Throughout history, however, floods have regularly destroyed homes and crops and have drowned many people. For this reason, the Huang He is sometimes called "China's sorrow."

Like the Huang He, the Chang Jiang begins on the Plateau of Tibet. From its headwaters, it flows about 3,450 miles (5,552 km) to its mouth at the port city of Shanghai on the East China Sea. It is the longest river in Asia and the third longest in the world. Only the Nile and the Amazon are longer.

The Chang Jiang is China's principal waterway. It also provides water for a fertile farming region where more than two-thirds of the country's rice is grown. Nearly one-third of China's people live in the river's basin.

R

Stocktrek Images/Getty Images

Visual Vocabulary

Peninsula A peninsula is an area of land that juts into a lake or an ocean and is surrounded on three sides by water. The term comes from the Latin words *paene*, meaning "almost," and *insula*, meaning "island."

R Reading Skills

Determining Central Ideas Pose the following questions to help students focus on the main ideas about the seas and rivers of East Asia. As you discuss each body of water, point out its location on a classroom map. **Ask:**

- **Why are the seas of East Asia important in the people's lives?** *(They provide food, power, and transportation.)*
- **Of the four seas along the eastern edge of mainland East Asia, which is the largest and how is it distinctive?** *(South China Sea; It has some of the busiest shipping lanes in the world.)*
- **What are the three other seas?** *(East China Sea; Yellow Sea; Sea of Japan or East Sea)*
- **What are the two most important rivers in East Asia?** *(Huang He or Yellow River, and Chang Jiang or Yangtze River)*
- **How did the Huang He get its name?** *(It gets its name from the yellow-brown silt, called loess, that it carries.)*
- **Why is the silt of the Huang He valuable?** *(It has been deposited by floods over millions of years to create the broad, fertile North China Plain, one of China's most productive farming areas.)*
- **Why is the Chang Jiang an important river?** *(It is the longest river in Asia, it is China's principal waterway, it irrigates a fertile farming region where most of China's rice is grown, and nearly one-third of China's people live in its basin.)* **AL** **Verbal/Linguistic**

Making Connections Help students connect to the information about China's rivers by noting that the Missouri and Mississippi rivers, the two longest rivers in the United States, also cause significant flooding and yet have created fertile floodplains that provide productive farmland. Point out these rivers on a map of the United States. Have students consider the importance of these rivers to the people who live nearby as well as on the country as a whole. Ask students to identify any rivers in your region that similarly provide both benefits and drawbacks. **Naturalist**

GRAPHIC ORGANIZER

Landforms and Bodies of Water in East Asia

Organizing Use this interactive graphic organizer to review with students the various landforms and bodies of water in East Asia that are covered in the text. Have students use the Chapter Opener map that shows the physical geography of East Asia if they need a visual representation of the information. **Visual/Spatial**

See page 113C for other online activities.

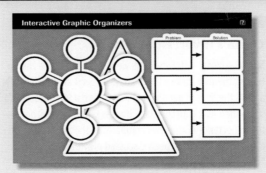

Interactive Graphic Organizers

Problem   Solution

The Huang He flows peacefully past irrigated farmland in eastern China on its way to the Yellow Sea.
▶ **CRITICAL THINKING**
Describing Why is the Huang He sometimes called "China's sorrow?"

C

C Critical Thinking Skills

Contrasting To help students contrast the rivers of Japan with those of China, **ask:** How do Japan's major rivers differ from those of China? *(Japan's rivers are short and steep, while China's are long and not as steep for much of their length.)* **Verbal/Linguistic**

V Visual Skills

Reading Maps and Interpreting Have students refer to a map of East Asia and one of the United States to answer the following questions. **Ask:**

- **What is the latitude range of East Asia?** *(The region extends from about 22°N to about 55°N.)*
- **What is the latitude range of the lower 48 states of the United States?** *(about 25°N to about 50°N)*
- **How does the latitude range of East Asia compare with that of most of the United States?** *(It is roughly the same.)*
- **Based on latitude ranges, how would you expect the climates of the two regions to compare?** *(The climates should be roughly the same.)* **Visual/Spatial, Logical/Mathematical**

Content Background Knowledge

Since rice is the main food source for so much of the world's population, the population explosion places great strains on the production of rice. Scientists, including those working with the International Rice Research Institute (IRRI), have been trying to address this problem in many different ways. Recent scientific breakthroughs include:

- increasing overall production. Scientists have bred rice that has a shorter growth cycle, which means that farmers can grow two or three crops of rice instead of just one each year.
- decreasing risks of disease or pests. Newer varieties of rice have shorter stalks that enable them to handle the weight of powdered pesticides. These newer varieties are also more disease resistant.
- developing nutrient-rich rice, known as Golden Rice. This rice is still under development, but it is hoped that it will provide vitamin A, reducing blindness and death that results from vitamin A deficiency.

Rivers in Japan and Korea

Japan's major rivers are relatively short, steep, and swift. They flow down from the mountains in the interior of the islands to low plains along the coast. Most of the rivers, including the two longest, the Shinano and the Tone, generate hydroelectric power.

The main rivers of the Korean Peninsula flow from inland mountains westward toward the Yellow Sea. The Han River flows through South Korea's capital, Seoul. North Korea's longest river, the Yalu (or Amnok), forms the country's border with China.

☑ **READING PROGRESS CHECK**

Identifying What are some ways the people of East Asia depend on rivers?

Climate

GUIDING QUESTION What are the main factors that affect climate in different parts of East Asia?

A traveler to East Asia would encounter a great range of climates, from hot and rainy to cold and dry. This is partly due to the area's vast size and partly because of its range of elevation.

Climate Factors

East Asia spans a tremendous distance north to south. The region's southernmost lands lie within Earth's hot tropical zone, while the northernmost lands sit closer to the frigid North Pole than to the Equator. Much of the climate variation results from these differences in latitude.

Another important factor is land elevation. Higher areas are generally colder than lower areas. Two areas at the same latitude can have very different climates if one area is much higher than the other. This situation is found in many parts of East Asia.

V

Thinking Like a Geographer

Rice as a Staple Food

Rice is the main source of food for over half the world's people. Most East Asians depend on it as a staple food. Rice is such an important part of Asian cultures that the word for *rice* in some languages is the same as the word for *food*. What foods are considered staples of the American diet?

©George Steinmetz/Corbis

120 Chapter 4

net works *Online Teaching Options*

VIDEO

China's River: Huang He

Summarizing After students view the video of the Huang He, ask them to make a list of all the ways that the Huang He affects the lives of people in China. Call on a few students to share their lists with the class. Discuss with students how the importance of this river compares to the importance of other rivers that have been discussed previously. **Visual/Spatial, Naturalist**

See page 113C for other online activities.

Fresh photos from all over the world/Getty Images

Air masses also play a major role in shaping East Asia's climate zones. A cold, dry, polar air mass spreads southward from northern Asia during the colder months of the year. A warm, moist, tropical air mass spreads northward and eastward from the Pacific Ocean during the warmer months.

R

Climates in the East
Southeastern China stays hot and rainy through much of the year. Vegetation is lush, and conditions are ideal for growing grain, especially rice. Farther north in eastern China, more seasonal variation occurs. Summers are hot and rainy, but winters are cold and fairly dry. China's capital, Beijing, lies in this part of the country. In the summer, temperatures in Beijing often soar above 90°F (32°C). In the winter, icy winds from the northwest whip through the city, and temperatures can drop below 0°F (−18°C).

V1

Being surrounded or nearly surrounded by water affects the climates of East Asia's island and peninsula countries: Taiwan, Japan, and North and South Korea. These countries are generally wetter and experience milder temperatures than mainland areas at the same latitudes.

Climates in the North, Northwest, and Southwest
Across north-central and northwestern China and neighboring Mongolia, the climate ranges from semiarid (somewhat dry) to arid (very dry). Winters are bitterly cold. This sparsely populated area includes the vast, rocky Gobi Desert and the sandy Taklimakan Desert. It also has great expanses of treeless grasslands.

The Plateau of Tibet in southwestern China also has a dry climate. This is mainly because the towering Himalaya block moist air flowing northward from the Indian Ocean. Because the plateau sits at such a high elevation, the weather is cold and windy throughout the year.

☑ **READING PROGRESS CHECK**

Identifying How do the Himalaya affect the climate of the Plateau of Tibet?

Natural Resources

GUIDING QUESTION *What mineral resources are most abundant in East Asia?*

East Asia is rich in minerals, forests, and other natural resources. But the resources are not evenly distributed.

The nomadic Tsaatan herd reindeer and hunt for gold in mountainous areas of northern Mongolia.
▶ **CRITICAL THINKING**
Describing What is the climate like in Mongolia?

©Hamid Sardar/Corbis

Chapter 4 **121**

MAP

Climates: East Asia

Reading a Map Use the climate layer of the Chapter Opener map to discuss with students the varying climate zones of East Asia. Have students compare the information on the map with the notes in their climate charts. Make connections to other climate zones mentioned in previous chapters. **Visual/Spatial**

See page 113C for other online activities.

R Reading Skills

Summarizing Pose the following questions to focus students' attention on the key factors shaping the climates of East Asia.
Ask:

- **What are the three main factors that shape the climates of East Asia?** *(answers may include latitude, elevation, air masses, proximity to the coast)*
- **How does latitude affect climate?** *(Lands closer to the tropics are hotter than lands closer to the North Pole.)*
- **How does elevation affect climate?** *(Lands higher in elevation are colder than lands lower in elevation.)*
- **How do air masses affect climate?** *(Polar air masses bring cold weather, while tropical air masses bring warm weather.)*
AL Verbal/Linguistic

V1 Visual Skills

Creating Charts Suggest that students create a climate chart to take notes on the various climates of East Asia. Provide students with the chart headings below and advise them to list only major ideas in each section. (**Eastern China:** *Hot and rainy in southeastern China, more seasonal variety in north;* **Island and peninsula countries:** *wetter and milder temperatures than mainland areas at same latitude;* **Northern China, Mongolia:** *from semiarid to arid with bitterly cold winters;* **Plateau of Tibet:** *dry, cold, windy)* **Visual/Spatial**

Subregion of East Asia	Climate
Eastern China	
Island and peninsula countries	
Northern China, Mongolia	
Plateau of Tibet	

V2

V2 Visual Skills

Analyzing Images Direct students' attention to the photograph and ask them to cite evidence that these Mongolian herders are adapted to their environment. *(They are wearing clothes made from animal furs and leather; they are aided by a dog; they have reindeer with them; they are heavily clothed to survive the cold; and they are wearing boots and using walking sticks to trudge through the snow.)* **Visual/Spatial**

ANSWERS, p. 121

CRITICAL THINKING The climate in Mongolia ranges from semiarid to arid with bitterly cold winters.
☑ READING PROGRESS CHECK The Himalaya block warm, moist air coming from the Indian Ocean, so the climate on the Plateau of Tibet is cold and dry.

C Critical Thinking Skills

Comparing and Contrasting Note that the text focuses on the mineral and energy resources of China, Japan, and Taiwan. Pose the following questions to help students compare and contrast the resources of these countries. **Ask:**

- **Which of these three countries—China, Japan, and Taiwan—has the most mineral and energy resources?** *(China)*
- **What are these resources?** *(tin, lead, zinc, iron ore, tungsten, coal, oil, natural gas)*
- **In terms of mineral resources, how do Japan and Taiwan differ from China?** *(They both have few mineral resources, while China has many.)*
- **What unusual natural resource does Japan have?** *(cultured pearls)*
- **As industrial nations, what must all three of these countries do to meet their needs for minerals and/or energy resources?** *(import)* **Verbal/Linguistic**

V Visual Skills

Interpreting Have students study the image of Chinese workers hauling coal by hand and theorize why they might be using so many people to do the work instead of industrializing the process using coal cars as is done in many coal mines in the United States. Have student volunteers explain their theories and discuss a few of them as a class.

Content Background Knowledge

Explain to students that one way China has been trying to meet its energy needs is by building the Three Gorges Dam as a hydroelectric power source. However, the Three Gorges Dam has long been plagued by controversy. Proponents of the dam hailed it as a way to control flooding of the Chang Jiang and as a source of clean energy. But environmentalists opposed the dam because its reservoir would not only displace more than a million people but also cause enormous environmental damage. By 2012, frequent landslides and tremors made life near the dam risky, and the water in the reservoir had become badly polluted.

Minerals

China, which covers a large portion of East Asia, holds by far the greatest share of the region's resources. China is a world leader in the mining of tin, lead, zinc, iron ore, tungsten, and other minerals. Manufacturers use tungsten to make high-quality steel, lightbulbs, rockets, and electrical equipment.

Japan is one of the world's leading industrial countries, but the islands of Japan have few mineral resources. Japan has coal, copper, some iron ore, and a few other minerals, but it must import a variety of raw materials. Taiwan, like Japan, is a major industrial country, but it has limited mineral reserves. As a result, Taiwan also has to import various minerals to meet increasing demand.

Cultured pearls are harvested in the seas surrounding the Japanese islands. They range in color from white to silver and pink. They are known for their beautiful, smooth, shiny appearance.

Energy Resources

East Asia has a variety of energy resources, including coal, oil, and natural gas. The largest deposits of these fossil fuels are in China. China is the world's largest producer of coal. Its deposits are larger

Workers haul coal to barges on the Chang Jiang River in China. The barges transport the coal down stream to power plants.

122 Chapter 4

netw⊙rks *Online Teaching Options*

MAP

Resources: East Asia

Reading a Map Use the resources layer of the Chapter Opener map to discuss the variety of resources that can be found in the countries of East Asia. Discuss with students the various minerals and how they are extracted. Make connections to the image in the text of the coal workers in China to discuss human-environment interaction in extracting resources. **Naturalist, Visual/Spatial**

See page 113C for other online activities.

than those of any other country except the United States and Russia. China also has substantial oil and natural gas reserves under the South China Sea and in the Taklimakan Desert in the far west.

Despite these fossil fuel resources, China still cannot meet all of its energy needs. The country's economy is growing rapidly. As a result, China is turning to energy-rich countries in Central and Southwest Asia for supplies of oil and natural gas. China also imports coal from Southeast Asia and Australia.

Several East Asian countries use hydroelectric power to help meet their energy needs. China produces electricity from the Three Gorges Dam on the Chang Jiang. This massive dam also helps control floods and provides water for irrigation. Hydroelectric dams in Japan harness the power of the country's swift-flowing rivers.

Forests

Much of western and northwestern China is so dry that trees cannot grow. Forestland once blanketed the eastern part of the country, but over the centuries, forests became smaller as people cut down trees for heating, building, and to create farmland. Today, forested areas cover less than one-sixth of the country.

Other East Asian countries, however, still have extensive forested areas. More than half of Taiwan's rugged landscape is covered by forests. The country used to be a major exporter of timber and wood products. Now much of the forested land is protected, so the country relies on imports to meet its need for wood products.

Thick forests cover the steep hillsides of Japan's inland areas. Almost two-thirds of the country is forested. Logging is limited in parts of the country, however, because the Japanese consider many forest areas to be sacred.

In the Korean Peninsula, many trees have been cleared for farmland, but forests still cover mountainous areas. About three-fourths of North Korea's rugged landscape is forested.

 V

☑ **READING PROGRESS CHECK**

Analyzing Why is it necessary for people in Taiwan and Japan to import wood products?

FOLDABLES
Study Organizer

Include this lesson's information in your Foldable®.

V **Visual Skills**

Creating a Chart To help students visualize the differences in the amount of forested land in the various countries of East Asia, create a row of circle graphs on the board like the ones below, or have students create the graphs based on the fractions given in the text. **Ask:**

- **Why does the portion of forested land differ so greatly among these countries?** *(In China, people have cut down the trees in the eastern part of the country, and the western part is too dry for trees to grow. In Japan and Taiwan, forests are protected.)*
- **How is Taiwan able to meet its needs for lumber while protecting its own forests?** *(Taiwan imports much of the wood it needs.)* **Logical/Mathematical**

Portion of Land That Is Forested

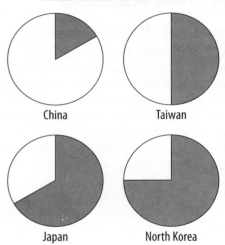

China   Taiwan

Japan   North Korea

LESSON 1 REVIEW (CCSS)

Reviewing Vocabulary (Tier Three Words)
1. How did Japan's *archipelago* form? RH.6-8.4

Answering the Guiding Questions
2. *Citing Text Evidence* How do the climates of East Asia's island and peninsula areas differ from climates of the mainland areas? RH.6-8.1
3. *Analyzing* How has the Huang He helped and hurt the people of China? RH.6-8.1

4. *Identifying* How does Japan make use of its short, swift rivers? RH.6-8.1
5. *Describing* Why must China import petroleum, natural gas, and coal? RH.6-8.5
6. *Informative/Explanatory Writing* Think about how elevation affects climate. Write a paragraph that explains how mountains and plateaus affect East Asia's climate. WHST.6-8.2, WHST.6-8.4

LESSON 1 REVIEW ANSWERS

Reviewing Vocabulary

1. Sections of the earth's crust ground against each other, causing volcanic eruptions and earthquakes. Over the course of millions of years, the eruptions created the islands of Japan.

Answering the Guiding Questions

2. **Citing Text Evidence** The islands and peninsula generally have a milder and wetter climate than the mainland areas.

3. **Analyzing** The Huang He floods and deposits rich silt that builds up over many years and creates fertile regions for growing crops. It hurts the people in the region when the river floods and they lose their homes and sometimes their lives.

4. **Identifying** Japan has built dams to convert the power of the rivers' flow into electricity.

5. **Describing** China's economy is growing, and it needs more fuel than it can provide itself.

Writing Activity

6. The climate in regions with higher elevation is generally cooler. Since a plateau is land at a higher elevation, its climate will generally be cooler than surrounding areas. The same is true of mountains. In addition, mountain ranges create a rain shadow, which means that they block warm and moist air masses from passing on to another region. This causes the climate on the other side of a mountain range to be colder and drier than it otherwise would be.

CLOSE & REFLECT

To close the lesson, review the chart that the class made at the beginning of the lesson. Have students add to the chart based on what they have learned. Discuss any mistaken ideas that students originally had about the region.

ANSWER, p. 123

☑ **READING PROGRESS CHECK** Logging is limited in the forests of Taiwan and Japan. These countries cannot get all the timber resources they need from their own forests and must import wood from other countries.

ENGAGE

Bellringer To introduce the lesson, divide the class into small groups. Give each group five minutes to formulate three questions about the history of the countries of East Asia. After five minutes, have the groups share their questions. Tell the groups to save their questions, and direct them to look for answers to the questions as they study this lesson.

Then have students preview the lesson by looking at the visuals and skimming the captions, headings, and guiding questions. Encourage students to write additional questions or make changes to their questions based on their initial preview of the lesson.

TEACH & ASSESS

R Reading Skills

Defining and Expressing Have students complete a definition tree like the one below for each vocabulary word they encounter, beginning with the word *dynasty*. As students share the sentences they generate, clarify the meaning of the words and correct any misconceptions they may have about the use of each word. *(Sample answer: a line of rulers from a single family; The country was at peace during the entire reign of that dynasty.)*

ELL Visual/Spatial, Verbal/Linguistic

| dynasty | Definition: |
| | Sentence: |

Making Connections Explain that the dynasties of China and other Asian countries were similar to the lines of kings and queens who ruled the countries of Europe. Dynasties formerly ruled Egypt and other countries of Africa as well.

ANSWER, p. 124

Taking Notes Sample answers: **China**—During the Han Dynasty (202 B.C. to A.D. 220), China experienced unity, stability, territorial expansion, and a flourishing of the arts and sciences. The Communists won power in China in 1949. **Japan**—In the 1100s, Japan came under the rule of shoguns. In 1854, the United States pressured Japan to open their country to foreign trade. **Korea**—At the end of the 1300s, the Choson dynasty came to power. Korea was divided into two countries after the end of World War II.

---

networks

There's More Online!

☑ **IMAGES** China's Great Wall
☑ **MAP** The Silk Road and Trade
☑ **VIDEO**

Reading HELPDESK (CCSS)

Academic Vocabulary RH.6-8.1
(Tier Two Words)
- **intertwine**

Content Vocabulary RH.6-8.4
(Tier Three Words)
- **dynasty**
- **shogun**
- **samurai**
- **sphere of influence**
- **communism**

TAKING NOTES: Key Ideas and Details RH.6-8.7, RH.6-8.1

Describe Use a chart like the one below to describe two key events in the histories of China, Japan, and Korea.

	Key Events
China	1.
	2.
Japan	1.
	2.
Korea	1.
	2.

Lesson 2

History of East Asia

ESSENTIAL QUESTIONS · *What makes a culture unique?* · *How do cultures spread?*

IT MATTERS BECAUSE

East Asia has a long, rich, and fascinating history. Learning about the events, innovations, and ideas that shaped the region will give you a better understanding and appreciation of its countries, cultures, and peoples.

Early East Asia

GUIDING QUESTION *What important inventions from East Asia spread across the rest of the world?*

China's civilization is more than 4,000 years old. Throughout its history, Chinese civilization influenced the development of other East Asian countries.

Early China

R For many centuries until the early 1900s, rulers known as emperors or empresses governed China. A **dynasty**, or line of rulers from a single family, would hold power until it was overthrown. Then a new leader would start a new dynasty. Under the dynasties, China built a highly developed culture and conquered neighboring lands.

As their civilization developed, the Chinese tried to keep out foreign invaders. In many ways, this was easy. On most of China's borders, natural barriers such as seas, mountains, and deserts already provided protection. Still, invaders threatened from the north. To defend this area, the Chinese began building the Great Wall of China about 2,200 years ago. Over the centuries, the wall was continually rebuilt and lengthened. In time, it snaked more than 4,000 miles (6,437 km) from the Yellow Sea in the east to the deserts of the west. It remains in place today.

124

---

networks *Online Teaching Options*

VIDEO

World's Wonders—The Great Wall of China

Integrating Visual Information Use this video about the construction and history of the Great Wall of China to generate interest in the history of East Asia. Have students write down three aspects they are interested in learning about with regard to the history of this region. If the video answered any of the questions they had about the history of the countries of East Asia, then encourage them to do research to strengthen their knowledge. Write a list of some of these aspects on the board to refer to as you move through the lesson. **Visual/Spatial**

See page 113D for other online activities.

China's Dynasties

The Shang was the first dynasty to leave written records. From the writings, we learned that the Shang took power about 1600 B.C. in the North China Plain. Like all succeeding dynasties, the Shang faced rebellions by local lords, attacks by Central Asian nomads, and natural disasters such as floods. When the government was stable, it could defend its people against some of these problems. Eventually, however, the dynasty weakened and fell.

After the Shang, the Zhou dynasty ruled for about 800 years, beginning around 1045 B.C. Under Zhou rule, Chinese culture spread, trade grew, and the Chinese began making iron tools.

After the Zhou, powerful dynasties expanded China's territory. In the 200s B.C., the Han united all of China and started building the Great Wall that exists today. Under the Han and Tang dynasties, traders and missionaries spread Chinese culture to all of East Asia.

In the early 1400s, under the Ming dynasty, the naval explorer Zheng He reached as far as the coast of East Africa. The last dynasty of China, the Qing, ruled from the mid-1600s to the early 1900s.

Achievements and Ideas

China underwent many changes during the Zhou dynasty. During this period, laws were recorded for the first time, the first coins were created, and farmers began to use plows pulled by oxen. It was also an age of great thinkers. One of these thinkers was a man named Confucius. He thought people should be morally good and loyal to their families. He also believed that a ruler should lead his people as though he were the head of a family.

Another of the thinkers was Laozi, who founded an important belief system called Daoism. Laozi thought that people should live in harmony with nature.

Think Again

The Great Wall of China is a single, continuous wall.

Not true. The Great Wall, which runs for about 5,500 miles (8,851 km) across northern China, is actually made up of many different walls. Some of the walls run parallel to each other. The best-preserved sections of wall were constructed of bricks and stones during the Ming dynasty (1368–1644). Some walls are made of dirt, gravel, stone, and wood. Long stretches of wall have been destroyed by erosion or buried by blowing sand.

To build the Great Wall, Chinese rulers used teams of workers that included border guards, peasant farmers, and prison convicts.

▶ CRITICAL THINKING
Describing Why was the Great Wall built?

©Image Source/Corbis

V1 Visual Skills

Creating a Cluster Diagram Tell students that they do not need to memorize all the dynasties of China. Instead, they should focus on the Zhou and Han dynasties, whose achievements are detailed. Have students create a cluster diagram of the main ideas about the Zhou dynasty. *(Students' diagrams should include these facts: 1045 to 221 B.C.; Chinese culture spread, trade grew, began making iron tools, laws recorded for first time, first coins created, oxen-pulled plows used, Confucianism and Daoism introduced)* **Visual/Spatial**

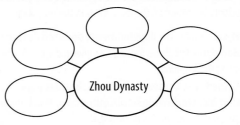

Zhou Dynasty

V2 Visual Skills

Analyzing Images Direct students to examine the photograph at the bottom of the page, focusing on the design and location of the Great Wall. Point out that motor vehicles did not exist at the time the Great Wall was built and that the Great Wall provided defense against invaders traveling on horseback. **Ask:**

• **From examining the photograph, what kinds of difficulties do you think construction of the wall presented?** *(Sample answers: transporting materials up mountains, feeding and sheltering workers, clearing land, severe weather, lack of machinery)*

• **Why do you think the workers who built the Great Wall were border guards, peasant farmers, and prison convicts?** *(Sample answer: They were nearby and could be ordered to do the work without being paid.)*

• **What would have been some advantages and disadvantages of the wall's height?** (***Advantage:*** *It provided a way for guards to look out and see any approaching invaders or attackers.* ***Disadvantage:*** *It would be difficult for workers and soldiers to get onto the wall in a specific location because they would need to enter at a location where there were stairs.)* **Visual/Spatial**

IMAGE

China's Great Wall

Summarizing Display the interactive image of the Great Wall to students, noting that it was built to keep out invaders. Lead a class discussion about the reasons the Great Wall was built and how its construction was completed over time. Have students write a paragraph summarizing the discussion, using support facts from the text. **Interpersonal**

See page 113D for other online activities.

Interactive Photos

© Image Source/Getty Images

ANSWER, p. 125

CRITICAL THINKING The Great Wall was built to protect China from northern invaders.

W Writing Skills

Informative/Explanatory Assign students to write one-page reports on the beliefs of Confucianism, Daoism, or Buddhism. Allow time for student volunteers to read aloud a report on each belief system. Then have a class discussion comparing and contrasting the three belief systems. **BL** **Verbal/Linguistic**

C Critical Thinking Skills

Finding the Main Idea Use the following questions to focus students' attention on the main ideas in the text. **Ask:**

• **What significant developments occurred during the Han dynasty?** *(Papermaking was invented; trade flourished along the Silk Road.)*
• **Name three Chinese inventions, besides papermaking, that had worldwide significance.** *(woodblock printing, gunpowder, and magnetic compass)*
• **Why was woodblock printing important?** *(Large numbers of books could be printed quickly, allowing for ideas to spread more rapidly.)* **AL** **Verbal/Linguistic**

Content Background Knowledge

The inventions of papermaking, printing, gunpowder, and the magnetic compass are called the Four Great Inventions in China because of their historical importance.

• Modern papermaking is still based on the ancient Chinese technology. With paper, the Chinese developed a material that was ideal for writing on, light, easy to store and carry, inexpensive, and possible to mass-produce.
• Before the invention of printing, information and stories were either passed on orally or written and copied by hand. It was slow and expensive to produce handwritten manuscripts.
• The invention of gunpowder changed the nature of warfare, leading to the development of cannons and other weapons.
• The development of the magnetic compass came about after the Chinese discovered magnetite, a mineral that attracts iron and always points north when a piece is suspended. Before the magnetic compass became available, sailors had to navigate by using the North Star, the moon, and the sun. The magnetic compass made ocean navigation more reliable and safer, which led to more exploration.

CHART SKILLS >

DYNASTIES OF CHINA

Dynasty	Time Span
Xia	2200–1700 B.C.
Shang	1766–1080 B.C.
Zhou	1045–221 B.C.
Qin	221–206 B.C.
Han	206 B.C.–A.D. 221
Sui	A.D. 581–618
Tang	A.D. 618–907
Song	A.D. 960–1279
Yuan (Mongol)	1279–1368
Ming	1368–1644
Qing	1644–1911

For centuries, rulers of various dynasties used their power to expand and unite China.

Identifying Which dynasties lasted 500 years or more?

Later, another important belief system called Buddhism was introduced to China from India. Confucianism, Daoism, and Buddhism have been major influences on China and the rest of East Asia for many centuries.

The Han dynasty (202 B.C.–A.D. 220) had such an impact that many of China's people today call themselves the People of Han. With Han rule came unity and stability. The arts and sciences flourished. Papermaking was invented, and government officials began using paper for keeping records. Han rulers encouraged trade along the Silk Road. This was a caravan route that stretched 4,000 miles (6,437 km) between China and Southwest Asia, and then extended into Europe and South Asia. The Chinese sent goods such as silk, tea, spices, paper, and fine porcelain (POHR•suh•luhn) as far west as ports along the Mediterranean Sea in exchange for wool, gold, and silver.

The Han dynasty was followed by several centuries of decline and disunity as individual states fought to gain power. When China was eventually reunified, the stage was set for a long period of stability and cultural advancement under the Tang dynasty (A.D. 618–907) and Song dynasty (A.D. 960–1279).

During the Tang dynasty, probably in the A.D. 800s, a new type of printing emerged. The Chinese developed a way to use blocks of wood and clay to print characters on paper. This invention, known as woodblock printing, made it possible to print large numbers of books quickly, which allowed ideas to spread more rapidly. Another important invention was gunpowder, which was used in explosives and fireworks. The Chinese also invented the magnetic compass, which helped sailors find their direction at sea.

Early Korea and Japan

Korea was first populated thousands of years ago by people who migrated from northern Asia. By the first century A.D., the peninsula was divided among three rival kingdoms. Six centuries later, one of these kingdoms—the Silla—conquered the other two and unified the peninsula. After enduring for three centuries, the Silla kingdom was succeeded in A.D. 935 by the Koryo.

---

netw⊙rks *Online Teaching Options*

GAME

Drag-and-Drop: Chinese Dynasties

Making Connections Display the drag-and-drop game about the various Chinese dynasties. In a class discussion, use the game to review and discuss the various dynasties of China, having student volunteers make suggestions on the correct answers to fill in the game. Then, have a student volunteer drag the appropriate response to its corresponding topic. Encourage them to record their answers for review. **Kinesthetic**

See page 113D for other online activities.

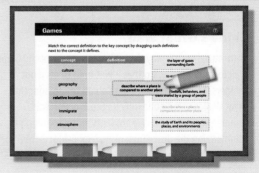

ANSWER, p. 126

Identifying Xia, Shang, Zhou

In the 1200s, the Mongols, a people from the steppes of Central Asia, had conquered North China, parts of Asia, and the northern half of the Korean peninsula. The vast territory became part of the Mongol's Yuan dynasty. At the end of the 1300s, the Mongols were driven out of Korea and a new Korean dynasty called the Choson came to power. It would stay in power until modern times.

Korea went through religious changes during this period. Buddhism had spread from India to China to Korea in the A.D. 300s and became popular during the Koryo dynasty. Later, during the Chosun dynasty, Confucianism became Korea's dominant religion. Chinese characters came to be used for Korean writing. Korean artists and writers were inspired by the art and literature of China. Korean rulers also adopted Confucianism as a basis for government. In some periods, China provided Korea with military protection. In other periods, Koreans lived in fear of Chinese invasion.

R

The history of Japan is **intertwined** with that of its neighbors to the west. The Japanese islands were settled by people from Korea and China. By A.D. 500, the clans and tribal kingdoms of Japan had close ties to Korea. Eventually, the ties extended to China, beginning a flow of ideas and culture that transformed Japan. Japanese people began using the Chinese calendar and the Chinese system of writing.

Academic Vocabulary

intertwine to twist or twine together

MAP SKILLS

1 **THE GEOGRAPHER'S WORLD** What was the Silk Road?

2 **PLACES AND REGIONS** Which areas of the world were linked by the Silk Road?

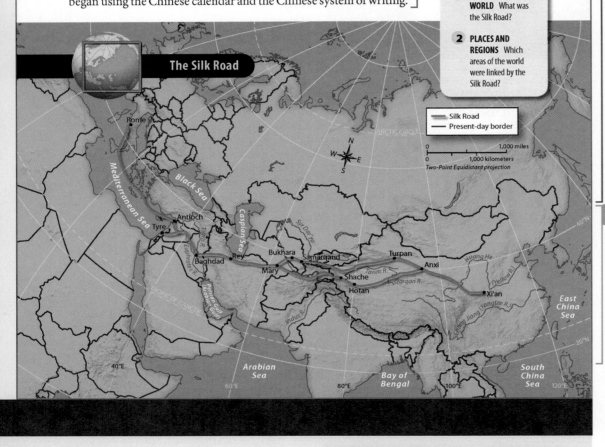

The Silk Road

- Silk Road
- Present-day border

Two-Point Equidistant projection

1,000 miles
1,000 kilometers

MAP

The Silk Road and Trade

Analyzing Maps Use the map of the Silk Road to discuss the importance of this trade route to both China and Europe. Explain that the trade route provided for exchanges of ideas and inventions as well as goods. Ask students to identify ideas and inventions of the Chinese that might have passed along this route. Discuss how these ideas and inventions impact their daily lives.
Logical/Mathematical

See page 113D for other online activities.

V **Visual Skills**

Reading a Map Direct students' attention to the map of the Silk Road. Have students use the map to answer the following questions. **Ask:**

- **What two cities formed the endpoints of the Silk Road?** *(Xi'an, China and Rome, Italy)*
- **What part of China did the Silk Road cross?** *(It began in east central China and headed across northwestern China.)*
- **What two continents did the Silk Road connect?** *(Asia and Europe)* **AL** **Visual/Spatial**

V

T **Technology Skills**

Researching on the Internet Have interested students research the Silk Road on the Internet. Tell students to find answers to the following questions with their research:

- **What kind of terrain did the Silk Road cross?**
- **Through which countries did the Silk Road pass?**
- **What dangers did travelers on the Silk Road face?**
- **How long did journeys on the Silk Road last?**
- **What remains of the Silk Road today?**

Ask students to report their findings to the class. **BL** **Verbal/Linguistic**

T

R **Reading Skills**

Summarizing Use the following questions to help students summarize the history of Korea and the early history of Japan. **Ask:**

- **Who first inhabited Korea?** *(people who migrated from northern Asia)*
- **What dynasty ruled Korea from the end of the 1300s until modern times?** *(the Choson)*
- **How has China influenced Korea?** *(Buddhism spread from China, Chinese characters were used for Korean writing, China's art and literature inspired Korean artists and writers, Korean rulers adopted Confucianism, China provided military protection at times and threatened invasion at other times.)*
- **Who first settled the Japanese islands?** *(people from Korea and China)*
- **What religion spread from Korea to Japan?** *(Buddhism)* **Verbal/Linguistic**

ANSWERS, p. 127

MAP SKILLS

1. a network of trade routes across Asia and Europe
2. East Asia, South Asia, Central Asia, Southwest Asia, Mediterranean Europe

C Critical Thinking Skills

Comparing Draw students' attention to the image of samurai and encourage students to make a comparison to knights in Europe. **Ask: How were the samurai similar to knights?** *(They both wore armor and used swords as weapons.)*

R Reading Skills

Identifying Problems Help students understand why the Chinese strongly resented the Japanese and European spheres of influence in their country. Point out that the Chinese had developed their own civilization for centuries with little input from the West. When Japan and the major European countries established spheres of influence in China in the late 1800s, they were basically carving up the country to boost their own economies. **Ask: Why would the Chinese object to foreign spheres of influence in their country?** *(It conflicted with the Chinese desire and right to control their own economy.)* **Verbal/ Linguistic**

Content Background Knowledge

- Shintoism has no God, no scriptures, and no commandments, nor do followers preach that it is the only true religion. It focuses on devotion to spiritual beings called *kami*, who are worshipped through rituals performed at shrines or at home. Each community has its own local shrine, which is a sacred place where kami live. A shrine may be a temple or a mountain or a grove of trees. Because the religion focuses on the land of Japan, there is no emphasis on spreading the religion outside of Japan.

- During the Middle Ages (A.D. 400s to 1400s), feudalism developed independently in both Japan and Europe. In both the European and the Japanese feudal systems, nobles owned the land, which was farmed by peasants in exchange for military protection. The military class consisted of warriors called samurai in Japan and knights in Europe. Both samurai and knights wore protective armor, rode horses, and wielded swords.

ANSWERS, p. 128

✔ **READING PROGRESS CHECK** Buddhism spread from China to Korea and then to Japan. The Japanese adopted the Chinese calendar, system of writing, technologies, and governmental organization. They also studied Chinese literature, philosophy, art, and science.

CRITICAL THINKING Emperors lost power to landowning families under a feudal system in which high nobles gave land to lesser nobles in return for their loyalty and military service. A military leader called the shogun eventually ruled in the emperor's name with the support of these ranks of warrior nobles.

A Japanese folding screen, produced during the 1700s, displays a battle scene.
▶ **CRITICAL THINKING**
Citing Text Evidence How was early Japan ruled?

C

In addition, the Japanese adopted Chinese technology and Buddhism spread to the islands from Korea and mixed with Shinto, a Japanese religion. Shinto, or "Sacred Way," stressed that all parts of nature—humans, animals, plants, and rivers—have spirits.

Japan was ruled by emperors, but over time, they lost power. Eventually landowning families set up a feudal system. Under the system, high nobles gave land to lesser nobles in return for their loyalty and military service. At the bottom of the social ladder, peasants farmed nobles' estates in exchange for protection. By the 1100s, armies of local nobles had begun fighting for control of Japan. Minamoto Yoritomo (mee•nah•moh•toh yho•ree•toh•moh) became Japan's first **shogun**, or military leader. Landowning warriors, who were called **samurai**, (SA•muh•RY) supported the shogun. Although the emperor kept his title, the shoguns held the real power.

✔ **READING PROGRESS CHECK**

Describing What are some ways in which China influenced Japan?

Change in East Asia

GUIDING QUESTION *How did increased contact with the West influence the region?*

Throughout much of its history, East Asia was mostly isolated from the rest of the world. High mountains, harsh deserts, and vast distances limited the flow of ideas and goods between the region and other parts of Eurasia. From the 1500s onward, however, increasing trade brought East Asian countries into greater contact with other cultures, especially Europe.

Spheres of Influence

R

By the early 1800s, internal problems had weakened China. Meanwhile, European countries were growing more powerful and making stronger claims. By the 1890s, European governments and Japan had claimed large areas of China as spheres of influence. A **sphere of influence** is an area of a country where a single foreign power has been granted exclusive trading rights.

The foreign intrusion in their country made many Chinese people angry. Their anger fueled a revolution in 1911, and the new government could not control the country. By 1927, a military leader named Chiang Kai-shek had formed the Nationalist government.

Roger Viollet/Getty Images

---

netw⦿rks *Online Teaching Options*

IMAGE

The Samurai

Analyzing Images Display the interactive image to students. Engage students in a class discussion in the role of the Samurai in feudal Japan. Be sure to highlight the shogunate and the role of the Samurai in relation to the shogun. Encourage students to conduct research on the aspects unique to the Samurai, such as the code of honor, known as Bushido, or the *Hagakure*. **Visual/Spatial**

See page 113D for other online activities.

© Image Source/Getty Images

Two Chinas

Meanwhile, Chiang's rival, Mao Zedong (MOW dzuh•DUNG), gained support from Chinese farmers. Mao believed in **communism**, a system in which the government controls all economic goods and services. After years of civil war, the Communists won power in 1949. They set up the People's Republic of China on the Chinese mainland. The Nationalists fled to the island of Taiwan. There, they set up a government called the Republic of China.

W

Rise of Japan

Around 1542, a Portuguese ship heading to China was blown off its course and landed in Japan. The traders on the ship became the first Europeans to visit Japan. Soon, more traders began arriving, along with Christian missionaries. By the early 1600s, Japan's rulers had begun to fear that European powers were planning a military conquest of the islands. They decided to isolate Japan by forcing all foreigners to leave, banning European books, and blocking nearly all relations with the outside world.

R

Japan's isolation lasted for roughly two centuries. In 1854 U.S. naval officer Matthew C. Perry sailed to Japan with four warships. He pressured the Japanese to end their isolation and open their country to foreign trade. Not long afterward, rebel samurai forced the shoguns to return full power to the emperor.

Recognizing that European countries were far more advanced and powerful, Japan set out to transform itself by learning everything it could about the West. The country soon became an industrial and military power, and it began developing an empire.

By 1940, Japanese forces had gained control of Taiwan, Korea, parts of mainland Asia, and some Pacific islands. This expansion was one factor that led Japan to fight the United States and its allies in World War II.

☑ READING PROGRESS CHECK

Analyzing How was Korea affected by Japanese expansion?

Modern East Asia

GUIDING QUESTION *What conflicts divided East Asian countries?*

After World War II, East Asia saw substantial changes in its governments and economies. Some of the region's countries developed into important economic powers.

©Bettmann/Corbis

U.S. naval officer Matthew Perry met representatives of the Japanese shogun at the port of Yokohama.
▶ **CRITICAL THINKING**
Describing How did Perry's visit change Japan?

V

Chapter 4 **129**

History of East Asia

C Critical Thinking Skills

Comparing and Contrasting Have students compare and contrast the history of China and Taiwan by answering the following questions. **Ask:**

- How would you describe the political relationship between Taiwan and mainland China in the 1960s and 1970s? *(Taiwan wanted China to treat their leaders as equals, but China would not negotiate with Taiwan.)*
- How did the government and economy of Taiwan differ from that of China by 1970? *(Taiwan had instituted democratic reform and developed a prosperous economy based on capitalism. China's government was stagnant and not democratic, and its economy was based on communism.)*
- How did the economy of China become more like that of Taiwan after the death of Mao in 1976? *(China developed more features of a market economy by allowing people to own businesses and freely sell products and services.)* **Logical/Mathematical**

Content Background Knowledge

As you discuss the rule of Mao Zedong in China, share with students the following information:

Communist leaders closed China off to the outside world from 1958 to 1970 while Mao carried out his disastrous programs. The Great Leap Forward caused immense suffering in China. The famine was so severe that an estimated 30 million people died between 1958 and 1961, either from starvation or malnutrition-related diseases. Those three years are known as the "three bitter years" in China.

Some historians consider Mao's Cultural Revolution an even greater disaster because it turned the Chinese people against one another. Launched in 1966, the Cultural Revolution resulted in fewer deaths—one and a half million—but brought many cities to the brink of chaos as gangs of students and thugs killed people and destroyed almost 500,000 temples and much of the country's cultural treasures. The army had to be called to restore order.

Korean War, 1950–1953

CHINA

UN maximum advancement (November 24, 1950)

Chinese intervention (November 1950)

Yalu R.
Chosan

NORTH KOREA
Wŏnsan
P'yŏngyang

Sea of Japan (East Sea)

Armistice line (July 27, 1953)

Kaesŏng P'anmunjŏm
Inch'ŏn
Seoul

North Korean/ Chinese maximum advancement (January 25, 1951)

Landing of UN forces (September 15, 1950)

SOUTH KOREA

Yellow Sea

North Korean maximum advancement (September 15, 1950)

Pusan

0   100 miles
0   100 kilometers
Lambert Azimuthal Equal-Area projection

← North Korean advances
← United Nations advances

MAP SKILLS

1 THE GEOGRAPHER'S WORLD When and where did the North Koreans make their maximum advance?

2 HUMAN GEOGRAPHY What is the armistice line?

Modern China

After 1949, China became "two Chinas"— one was mainland China ruled by the Communists, and the other was the Nationalist government on the island of Taiwan. In the 1950s, the Communist mainland government took control of businesses and industry. It also took land and created state-owned farms.

In the late 1950s, Mao Zedong introduced the Great Leap Forward. This program's goal was to increase China's industrial output. Many peasants left the fields and began working in factories. Cities grew rapidly. The program failed, however. Poor planning, natural disasters, and a drop in food production led to widespread famine.

During China's Cultural Revolution in the late 1960s, intellectuals such as doctors and teachers were ordered to work on farms. Students also were taken from school and sent to the countryside to work. In this way, Mao hoped to get rid of any cultural elements that did not support his idea of communism.

Taiwan, on the other hand, pursued a goal of "one China"— two parts of one nation moving toward reunification. Taiwan wanted the mainland Communist government to negotiate with Taiwan as an equal, but Communist leaders said no.

At first, the Taiwanese government limited the freedom of its people. By 1970, however, Taiwan's leaders had instituted democratic reform and developed an economy based on capitalism. Prosperity transformed the island into an economic powerhouse.

By comparison, China's Communist government was stagnant. After Mao's death in 1976, though, Chinese leaders started to open China to the West. Economic reforms helped China become a rising global power. Chinese leaders gradually allowed a market economy to develop alongside the communist economy by letting people own businesses and sell products and services freely.

A Divided Korea

After World War II ended, Korea was divided into two countries: South Korea and North Korea. South Korea was supported by the United States, and Communist North Korea had strong ties to China

---

networks Online Teaching Options

MAP

The Korean War

Analyzing Maps Display this map and introduce the history of Korea and their interactions with other countries of East Asia. Discuss with students the events that led to the start of the Korean War, how the war progressed, and the end result of that war. Highlight the demilitarized zone, or DMZ. Discuss the current relationship between North and South Korea. Encourage students to research current events taking place in either country. **Logical/Mathematical**

See page 113D for other online activities.

ANSWERS, p. 130

MAP SKILLS
1. On September 15, 1950, the North Koreans made their farthest advance in the war—to southeastern South Korea, north of Pusan.
2. The armistice line is the boundary separating North Korea and South Korea. Both sides accepted the boundary when the fighting stopped in 1953.

and to the Soviet Union, a powerful communist country that stretched across northern Europe and Asia.

Both Koreas claimed the entire peninsula. In 1950 North Korea invaded South Korea. United Nations forces and the United States rushed to support South Korea, and China helped North Korea. The Korean War ended in 1953 without a peace treaty or a victory for either side. A buffer zone, called the demilitarized zone, was established to separate the two countries.

Stark differences developed between the two Koreas after the war. Over several decades, South Korea followed the path of capitalism and the country's economy began to grow rapidly. In contrast, North Korea's economy, which is strictly controlled by its Communist government, has struggled. North Koreans face many hardships because most resources go to the military.

Modern Japan

After being defeated by the United States and its allies in World War II, Japan was stripped of its overseas territories and military might. The country adopted a democratic constitution, and women and workers gained more rights. During the Korean War, the United States needed Japanese factories to provide supplies for its war effort. Japanese shipbuilders, manufacturers, and electronics industries benefited from giving this assistance.

The Japanese government worked closely with businesses to plan the country's economic growth. Both invested in research and development of electronics products for the home. A highly skilled workforce and the latest technology helped Japan develop its industries. Within a few decades, the Japanese were leading producers of ships, cars, cameras, and computers. By the 1990s, world demand for Japanese-made goods had turned it into a global economic power. Despite some economic ups and downs in the 2000s, Japan's economy remains one of the world's strongest. Based on gross national product, Japan ranks third in the world, trailing only the United States and China.

Include this lesson's information in your Foldable®.

☑ **READING PROGRESS CHECK**

Determining Central Ideas What led to the growth of China's economy beginning in the 1970s?

LESSON 2 REVIEW (CCSS)

Reviewing Vocabulary (Tier Three Words)
1. How can a new *dynasty* form? **RH.6-8.4**

Answering the Guiding Questions
2. *Describing* How did Buddhism spread across East Asia? **RH.6-8.5**
3. *Identifying* Who ruled during the Yuan dynasty? **RH.6-8.5**

4. *Determining Central Ideas* Why did Europeans want access to China and Japan? **RH.6-8.1**
5. *Analyzing* What led to the creation of "two Chinas"? **RH.6-8.1**
6. *Argument Writing* Write a one-page essay explaining which early Chinese invention had the greatest effect on the rest of the world and why. **WHST.6-8.1, RH.6-8.10**

Chapter 4 **131**

LESSON 2 REVIEW ANSWERS

Reviewing Vocabulary

1. An old dynasty must be overthrown.

Answering the Guiding Questions

2. **Describing** Buddhism spread from China to Korea and then into Japan.

3. **Identifying** the Mongols

4. **Determining Central Ideas** Europeans wanted silk, porcelain, and other goods as well as increased trade.

5. **Analyzing** After the Chinese revolution, two leaders formed different governments, the Nationalist and the Communist. The Communists took over mainland China. The Nationalists set up a government in Taiwan.

Writing Activity

6. **Argument Writing** Student answers (papermaking, woodblock printing, the magnetic compass, or gunpowder) should be supported with reasons.

R **Reading Skills**

Determining Central Ideas Note that World War II ended in 1945 and the Korean War started in 1950, just 5 years later. Pose the following questions to help students identify the main ideas about the development of North Korea, South Korea, and Japan after World War II. **Ask:**

- **Who supported North Korea in the Korean War?** (China)
- **Who supported South Korea in the Korean War?** (United Nations forces and the United States)
- **How long did the war last and how did it end?** (It lasted 3 years. It ended without a peace treaty or victory for either side and with a demilitarized zone separating the two countries.)
- **How do the governments and economies of the two countries differ?** (South Korea is democratic and has a rapidly growing economy. North Korea is communist and has a struggling economy.)
- **What happened to Japan after it was defeated in World War II?** (It lost its overseas territories and military might. It adopted a democratic constitution and gave women and workers more rights.)
- **How did Japan become a global economic power?** (Its industries benefited from supplying the United States' war effort during the Korean War. Its government and businesses cooperated, and both invested in research and development of electronics products. With a highly skilled workforce and the latest technology, Japan developed its industries and became a leading producer of ships, cars, cameras, and computers.) **Verbal/Linguistic**

CLOSE & REFLECT

To close the lesson, review the questions that groups of students generated at the beginning of the lesson. Discuss answers to the questions. Then assign any unanswered questions to individuals to answer by conducting Internet research.

ANSWER, p. 131

☑ **READING PROGRESS CHECK** China's leaders introduced reforms that allowed more features of a market economy to develop alongside the communist economy.

Life in East Asia

ENGAGE

🔔 **Bellringer** Remind students that East Asia consists of the countries of China, Mongolia, North Korea, South Korea, Japan, and Taiwan. Give students five minutes to write one geographic fact about each country and speculate on how this fact might affect people's lives. Call on volunteers to share some of their ideas. Tell students to save their writing to see if any of their speculations are confirmed as they read this lesson.

TEACH & ASSESS

C Critical Thinking Skills

Formulating Questions Have students consider the different geographic features of places that are densely populated and the features of those places that are sparsely populated. Have students formulate questions about why this is so. *(Possible questions: Do people move away from areas where the climate is less hospitable? Do people live longer in places with a better climate? Are there ways to use land better so that the areas that are more sparsely populated can be more livable?)* **AL** Verbal/Linguistic

T Technology Skills

Making Presentations In 2012, the world's population was about 7 billion. There are many different estimates for future population growth, but there is general agreement that the world's population is growing at an explosive rate. In 2012, the United Nations predicted that the population would reach 8 billion in 2025 and 9 billion in 2043. There are numerous scientific breakthroughs, including vaccines, medicines, surgical advances, better nutrition, increased farm productivity, and other factors that contribute to this growth. Have students choose a specific scientific breakthrough from the list below and give a short presentation to the class.

- Choose a vaccine, such as polio, smallpox, tuberculosis, measles, or rhoda virus. Learn about its discovery/invention. Tell when it was first used and how it has helped people.
- Research Louis Pasteur and germ theory. Tell about how things are different today as a result of what we know about germs, bacteria, and viruses.
- Find out about different projects that help provide clean water to people in developing countries. **Verbal/Linguistic**

ANSWER, p. 132

Taking Notes Sample answers: The river valleys, basins, deltas, and coastal plains of East Asia are among the most densely populated places in the world. In each Asian country, people tend to be ethnically similar. East Asian cultures place a high value on education. Industrialization has resulted in more women entering the workforce.

---

networks

There's More Online!

- ☑ **IMAGE** Baseball in Japan
- ☑ **ANIMATION** Population Pyramid of East Asia
- ☑ **SLIDE SHOW** Influence of Japanese Anime
- ☑ **VIDEO**

Reading **HELP**DESK

Academic Vocabulary RH.6-8.4

- **structure** *(Tier Two Words)*

Content Vocabulary RH.6-8.4
(Tier Three Words)
- **urbanization**
- **megalopolis**
- **trade deficit**
- **trade surplus**

TAKING NOTES: *Key Ideas and Details* RH.6-8.7, RH.6-8.1

Organize Information As you read the lesson, use a diagram like the one below to record four key facts about the people of East Asia.

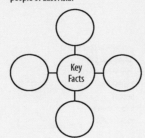

Key Facts

Lesson 3
Life in East Asia

ESSENTIAL QUESTIONS • *Why do people trade?* • *How does technology change the way people live?*

IT MATTERS BECAUSE

East Asia is one of the largest population centers on Earth. China alone holds about one-fifth of the world's people. The powerful economies of the East Asian countries affect global trade and manufacturing.

The People

GUIDING QUESTIONS *Which areas in East Asia have the highest population densities?*

Most people in East Asia live crowded together in river valleys, basins, and deltas, or on coastal plains. These lands and climates are favorable to agriculture and industry and are among the most densely populated places on Earth. In contrast, vast areas in the west and northwest are sparsely populated.

Population Patterns

Throughout much of history, China has had a large population. Two thousand years ago, the number of inhabitants had already reached an astonishing 59 million. Even today, only about two dozen countries have this many people.

For many centuries, China's population growth was slowed by epidemics, famines, warfare, and other factors. After the 1300s, however, growth began to increase steadily, and in the middle of the 1900s, it became explosive. Because the uncontrolled growth was causing many problems, the government enacted a policy in 1979 that required families to have no more than one child. This "one-child" policy helped to slow China's growth. China's 2010 Census showed a population of 1.37 billion people on the mainland and in

132

(l to r) ©George Hammerstein/Corbis; Christian Goupi/age fotostock; Yueliang Yao/Kallum/age fotostock; Philippe Lopez/AFP/Getty Images; Jay Freis/The Image Bank/Getty Images

---

networks *Online Teaching Options*

VIDEO

China Pollution

Comparing and Contrasting Use this video about increased pollution in China and its adverse effects on people and communities. Have students compare and contrast the way pollution is regarded in China and the way it is viewed in the United States. Then, discuss with students any differences in government policies that protect the environment from industrial pollution in China and the United States. Encourage students to research whether China has an agency like the EPA. **Verbal/Linguistic**

See page 113E for other online activities.

BBC Motion Gallery Education

Taiwan and Hong Kong. Far more densely populated in the east than in the west and northwest, China has an average population density of about 140 persons per square mile (54 per sq. km). In contrast, its northern neighbor, Mongolia, has a population density of less than 4 persons per square mile (1.6 persons per sq. km).

Population growth in some other parts of East Asia slowed at the end of the 1900s. Japan's low birthrate means that the average age of its population is increasing. Nearly one-quarter of the population is age 65 or older. Since the mid-1990s, Japan has encouraged more births by providing programs such as child care. Soon the country could face a shortage of workers. A shortage might encourage leaders to allow more foreign workers into the country.

Where People Live

V₁

Throughout China's history, most of its people lived off the land as farmers. Economic reforms in the late 1970s, however, caused a surge of **urbanization**. Millions of peasants left their farms and moved to booming cities in eastern China. Nearly half of the country's people now live in cities. Shanghai has about 11 million people, making it the largest city in China. Just over 7 million people live in Beijing, the capital. Hong Kong, which China regained from Britain in 1997, has more than 5 million people. Dozens of other Chinese cities have populations greater than 1 million.

In other East Asian countries, urbanization began earlier and is farther advanced than in China. In Japan, two-thirds of the people live in cities. The cities of Tokyo, Osaka, Nagoya, and Yokohama form a **megalopolis**, or supersized urban area, along the coast. Greater Tokyo, Japan's capital and its largest city, is home to about 32 million people.

As South Korea industrialized, more people moved to cities. Now, 83 percent of South Koreans live in urban areas. The country's capital city, Seoul, has more than 10 million people. Across East Asia, the standard of living for people in cities is generally higher than that of people in rural areas.

✓ **READING PROGRESS CHECK**

Determining Central Ideas How can a country's growth rate influence its economy?

Because of the lack of building space, Hong Kong's urban skyline is dominated by many high-rise office and apartment buildings. As a result, Hong Kong is described as "one of the most vertical places on Earth."

▶ **CRITICAL THINKING**
Describing What major change has affected East Asia's cities in recent decades?

©George Hammerstein/Corbis

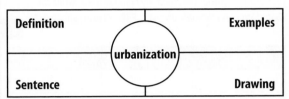

Chapter 4 133

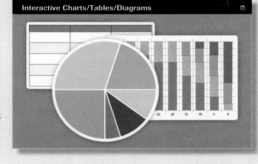
Interactive Charts/Tables/Diagrams

V₁ ### Visual Skills

Creating Visuals Direct students to create a word square like the one below for each vocabulary word they encounter, beginning with the word *urbanization*. Have students share their sentences and examples. *(Sample answer for urbanization: the growth of cities as a result of migration; rapid urbanization can place a strain on city services such as trash collection; the growth of Hong Kong and Shanghai; a picture of a city with suburbs)* **ELL**
AL Visual/Spatial, Verbal/Linguistic

Definition		Examples
	urbanization	
Sentence		Drawing

V₂

V₂ ### Visual Skills

Integrating Visual Information Point out that the photograph at the bottom of the page reinforces the main idea of the section "Where People Live." **Ask:**

- **What main idea does this photograph reinforce?** *(Most of the people of East Asia live in cities.)*
- **What do the high-rise buildings in the photograph remind you of?** *(Students might mention beehives.)*
- **Would you like to live in a city like this? Why or why not?** *(Student responses will vary but should be supported by reasons.)* **Visual/Spatial, Intrapersonal**

Making Connections In 2011 the following cities in the United States had over 1 million people:

- New York City: 8.2 million
- Los Angeles: 3.8 million
- Chicago: 2.7 million
- Houston: 2.1 million
- Philadelphia: 1.5 million
- Phoenix: 1.4 million
- San Antonio: 1.3 million
- San Diego: 1.3 million
- Dallas: 1.2 million

Have students think how life would differ in a city of 11 million compared to a city of less than 1 million. Students should list how transportation, shopping, school, and work would differ.

ANSWERS, p. 133

CRITICAL THINKING urbanization, the growth of cities as a result of the migration of people from the countryside to urban areas

✓ **READING PROGRESS CHECK** A rising growth rate may help a country's economy by increasing the number of young people of working age. It may hurt a country's economy if the population becomes larger than the economy can support.

V1 Visual Skills

Creating Charts Suggest that students create a three-column chart identifying the dominant ethnic group and language of each country of East Asia. (**Japan:** *Japanese, Japanese;* **North Korea and South Korea:** *Korean, Korean;* Mongolia: Mongolian, Khalkha Mongolian; **China:** Han, Mandarin Chinese; **Taiwan:** Taiwanese; Mandarin Chinese and Taiwanese) After students complete their charts, **ask: How do the countries of East Asia differ from the United States in ethnic makeup?** (East Asian countries are ethnically homogeneous, while the United States is ethnically diverse.) **AL** **Visual/Spatial**

Country	Ethnic Group	Language
Japan		
North Korea		
South Korea		
Mongolia		
China		
Taiwan		

V2 Visual Skills

Analyzing Images Direct students' attention to the photograph at the bottom of the page. **Ask:**

- **What evidence of Western culture do you see in this photograph?** *(The people are wearing Western-style clothing.)*
- **What evidence of Chinese culture do you see in the photograph?** *(the ornately decorated shrine, Chinese language symbols)* **Visual/Spatial**

Content Background Knowledge

The minority ethnic groups in China collectively represent about 8 percent of the population. With a population of about 1.3 billion, this is more than 100 million people. Some of China's ethnic groups have their own language, while others mainly speak Chinese. There are differences in religion as well, with some following Islam, Buddhism, and Confucianism.

The Uighurs and Tibetans do not recognize communist China's rule; and there have been many clashes as a result. The Uighur are Muslims and the Tibetans practice a form of Buddhism that has a spiritual leader known as the Dalai Lama. The Dalai Lama has not lived in Tibet since 1959, when he fled the country. Unlike the Uighurs and Tibetans, the Zhuang are accepting of Communist rule.

ANSWER, p. 134

CRITICAL THINKING When the Communists took power, they limited religious practice. More recently, the government has relaxed antireligion policies.

Culture in East Asia

GUIDING QUESTION *What are some of the cultural differences among East Asian countries?*

The people of East Asia have a rich cultural heritage. Traditions, beliefs, art, literature, and other elements that make up their heritage have been shaped by contributions from many different groups. The rise of a global culture has also brought change.

Ethnic and Language Groups

In each East Asian country, people tend to be ethnically similar. In Japan, about 99 percent of the population is ethnic Japanese and speaks the Japanese language. Nearly all the people in North and South Korea are ethnic Koreans who speak the Korean language. About 95 percent of Mongolia's people are ethnic Mongolian, and almost all of them speak the Khalkha Mongolian language.

In China, the Han ethnic group makes up about 92 percent of the population. The other 8 percent belong to more than 50 different ethnic groups. The official language in China is Mandarin Chinese, but many dialects are spoken. In Taiwan, Mandarin Chinese is the official language. Most of the people of Taiwan are Taiwanese, and many also speak the Taiwanese, or Min, language. The official languages of Hong Kong are Cantonese and English.

V1

Worshipers often leave flowers and light candles at street-corner religious shrines in Macau. The territory was under Portuguese rule until becoming part of China in 1999.
▶ **CRITICAL THINKING**
Describing What role does China's government play in setting religious policy?

netw⊙rks *Online Teaching Options*

IMAGE

Personal Buddhist Shrines

Integrating Visual Information Display the interactive image and have students read the text that describes the uses of personal shrines and the reasons for them in Buddhism. Note that shrines are found in many religions, including Christianity, Islam, and Hinduism. Have students compare the use of shrines in Buddhism with their use in another religion. **Verbal/Linguistic**

See page 113E for other online activities.

Interactive Photos

Religion and the Arts

The people of East Asia have many religions and belief systems. Many Chinese practice a mix of Buddhism, Daoism, and Confucianism. The Communist government that took over in 1949 believed that religion had no place in a communist country, so it began limiting religious practice. In recent decades, however, antireligious policies have been relaxed somewhat.

Buddhism has a large following in Korea and Japan, although North Korea's government also limits religious practice. In Japan, many people combine Buddhism with Shinto, the country's traditional religion. In South Korea, Christianity has a strong presence.

A number of art forms have long been popular in East Asia. In China, Korea, and Japan, many artists have painted the rugged landscapes of their countries. Their works reflect a reverence for nature that is part of Daoism and Shinto. Ceramics and pottery have been important parts of East Asian art since ancient—even prehistoric—times. Craftspeople in East Asia are also skilled at weaving, carving, and lacquerwork.

Calligraphy, the art of turning the written word into beautiful, expressive images, is considered one of the highest forms of art in China and Japan. Chinese characters are visually interesting and complex, so they lend themselves well to calligraphy. It is common for East Asians to display works of calligraphers in their homes.

East Asians also have strong literary and theatrical traditions. Japanese poets often write haiku, brief poems that follow a specific **structure**. Japan is famous for its traditional forms of theater. Today, Japan is also known for anime, a type of animation. Comic books and cartoons using this style have become popular all over the world. Jingxi, known to English-speakers as Peking opera, is a popular type of musical theater in China. In Jingxi performances, actors and actresses wear colorful costumes, sing in high-pitched voices, and use gestures, postures, and steps to reveal the attitudes of their characters.

Along with art and literature, East Asians have developed new forms of expression. South Korean "K-pop" is a popular type of music that young people in Japan and other East Asian countries enjoy. It has its roots in dance and electronic music from the West. Communication technology, the Internet, and travel increase the reach of new art forms. At the same time, different countries adopt and change them in unique ways.

For centuries, East Asian artisans have used lacquer, a clear or colored wood finish, to protect and add luster to jewelry boxes, furniture, and other art objects.

Yueliang Yao/Kallum/age fotostock

T

Academic Vocabulary

structure organization

T **Technology Skills**

Making Presentations Divide students into small groups and assign each group one of the East Asian art forms listed below. Have students research the subject on the Internet and prepare a short visual and oral presentation for the class. Tell students to include examples of the art, information about its history, the typical audience, as well as other details they find interesting. Allow one class period for the groups to present their work.

- Japanese landscape woodblock prints
- Chinese calligraphy
- Japanese anime and manga styles
- Japanese pop music or "J-pop"
- Jingxi, or Peking opera
- South Korean "K-pop" **Visual/Spatial, Auditory/Musical**

Content Background Knowledge

The main religion in Mongolia is Buddhism. About 50 percent of Mongolians are Buddhist, and about 40 percent do not practice any religion. In the 1930s, Mongolia's communist government closed Buddhist monasteries in a campaign against religion. Since a new constitution in 1992 guaranteed freedom of religion, Buddhism has made a comeback in the country.

CHART

Religion in East Asia

Analyzing Charts On the whiteboard, display the chart that shows the religions of East Asia. Discuss the similarities and differences in the religions of the region. Ask students questions about the chart to help with understanding such as: **What religion do all the nations have in common? Is there anything you find surprising about the chart? Why is it surprising to you?**

See page 113E for other online activities.

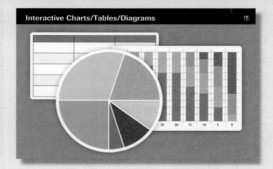

Interactive Charts/Tables/Diagrams

R Reading Skills

Making Connections Have students compare different aspects of American culture with the cultures of East Asia.

- A nuclear family consists of parents and their children. An extended family extends beyond the nuclear family and includes grandparents and other relatives. Several generations of a family sharing a home in rural China or Japan is an example of an extended family. East Asians typically maintain close relations with extended family members. Ask students if they think extended family relationships are important in the United States.

- Students may be aware that high school students in East Asia score higher than American students on international tests in math and science. As explanation, experts point to the fact that high schools in East Asia focus on preparing students for college entrance exams. Just as American educators have been placing more emphasis on standardized tests and common standards especially in math and science, some East Asian countries are looking in the opposite direction. They want to find out how to promote creativity and critical thinking, strengths they see in American students. **Verbal/ Linguistic, Interpersonal**

V Visual Skills

Analyzing Images As students examine the photograph at the bottom of the page, use the following questions to help them verbalize the visual information the picture contains. **Ask:**

- To what age group do the fans in the photograph appear to belong? *(middle-school age group)*
- What style of clothing are the people wearing? *(casual, Western-style clothing)*
- Which of the three backdrops appears the most Asian in style? *(the middle one; The characters are wearing Asian-style costumes or clothing)*
- What mix of cultural elements do you see in this photograph? *(a mix of Asian and Western cultural elements)*
- Why do you think anime appeals to young Asians? *(Answers may vary, but students may respond that young people like stories with adventure, excitement, and strong characters.)* **Visual/Spatial**

Daily Life

Traditionally, the family is the center of social life in East Asia. In rural areas of East Asia, for example, different generations of one family may share the same home. In crowded cities, tall apartment buildings provide housing for many families. As more people have moved into urban areas, some traditional attitudes have begun to change. For example, many women in the region now work outside the home.

East Asian cultures place a high value on education. Teachers are greatly respected, and children are expected to work hard. At a young age, children begin taking important exams that can determine whether they will get into top colleges.

Rice and noodles are staples in the diets of most East Asians, but otherwise cuisine varies widely across the region. For example, China's Sichuan (or Szechuan) Province is known for its bold, spicy dishes. Cantonese cuisine from the Guangdong Province is generally milder, with a careful balance of flavors. In Japan, meals are often built around seafood and soybean-based foods such as tofu. In Mongolia, where many people raise livestock, the cuisine features meat and dairy products.

People in East Asia enjoy many different pastimes, some traditional and some modern. Millions of people young and old practice martial arts such as tai chi (TY CHEE) and tae kwon do (TY KWAHN DOH), both of which originated in the region centuries ago. Baseball, introduced from North America, is widely

Billboards of anime characters form a backdrop to young fans lining up to attend an exhibition of animation, comics, toys, and games in Hong Kong.

Identifying What other new forms of expression have recently developed in East Asia?

Phillipe Lopez/AFP/Getty Images

136 *Chapter 4*

netw⊙rks *Online Teaching Options*

Influence of Japanese Anime

Analyzing Images After you display the slide show about anime in Japan, discuss the influence of this Japanese art form on the West. Ask students to identify some of the stylistic features of anime, such as exaggerated facial expressions and versions of characters that have been used in Western animation. Have students name some Western animated films that show the influence of anime. Have students who like anime volunteer information on particular shows and films they enjoy. **Visual/Spatial**

(l) ©Ocean/Corbis, ©Knyssia Campos/Getty Images, (tr) Erica Simone Leeds, (bl) ©JG Photography/Alamy

See page 113E for other online activities.

ANSWER, p. 136

Identifying new forms of music, such as "K-pop," with roots in dance and electronic music from the West

popular in Japan, Taiwan, and South Korea. Many children play on Little League baseball teams, and Japan has its own major baseball leagues. Basketball, also imported from America, has become one of the top sports in China.

Holidays are also important in East Asia. The biggest holiday of the year in China is Spring Festival, also known as Chinese New Year. It is celebrated with dances, fireworks, traditional foods, and religious ceremonies to honor ancestors. In Japan, people observe New Year's Day by visiting temples and shrines. South Korea's most popular holiday is the Harvest Moon Festival, which is something like Thanksgiving Day in the United States. During this festival, South Koreans celebrate the fall harvest and hold special ceremonies in honor of their ancestors.

☑ READING PROGRESS CHECK

Analyzing Why is religious activity limited in China?

Current Issues in East Asia

GUIDING QUESTION *How do East Asian economies affect economies around the world?*

In the last half-century, rapid economic growth has transformed East Asia. China and Japan now have larger economies than any other country in the world except the United States. With this growth, however, have come problems, including environmental damage.

Economies and Environments

In China, factories, coal-burning power plants, and the growing numbers of cars and trucks have led to dramatic increases in air pollution. Factory waste, sewage, and farm chemicals have poisoned water. Rapidly growing urban areas have eaten up valuable farmland. Many cities face a constant shortage of water.

Japan has similar issues. Polluted air from power plants has produced acid rain and other problems. But as a more developed country with a longer history of industrialization, Japan has engaged in stronger environmental protection efforts. In addition, Japan faces a constant threat of earthquakes.

Members of a Little League team in Tokyo, Japan, prepare for a baseball game. In 2012 a Japanese team won the Little League World Series Championship held in South Williamsport, Pennsylvania.

Identifying What other American sport has become popular in East Asia?

Jay Freis/The Image Bank/Getty Images

Chapter 4 **137**

R Reading Skills

Identifying Have students identify popular pastimes, sports, and holidays in East Asia by answering the following questions. **Ask:**

- **What pastimes are popular in East Asia?** *(the martial arts of tai chi, tae kwon do, baseball, and basketball)*
- **What holidays are important in East Asia?** *(Spring Festival in China, New Year's Day in Japan, Harvest Moon Festival in South Korea)* **AL Verbal/Linguistic**

C Critical Thinking Skills

Comparing Pose the following questions to prompt students to compare and contrast the economies and environmental problems of the United States, China, and Japan. **Ask:**

- **What are the three largest economies of the world?** *(United States, China, Japan)*
- **What environmental problems do these three countries share?** *(air pollution, water pollution, urbanization replacing farmland, water shortages)*
- **Which of these three countries has made the weakest environmental protection efforts?** *(China)* **Verbal/Linguistic**

Content Background Knowledge

Every country that has become a major industrial power has also greatly damaged the environment. China is no different. However, China's speedy rise to becoming a world economic power has resulted in monumental environmental degradation. Almost 500 million people do not have safe drinking water, and the air is unsafe to breathe for 99 percent of the country's urban population. A large part of the problem stems from China's heavy reliance on coal-powered plants to provide energy for the country's industries and growing cities. Coal is the dirtiest source of energy. China's air pollution affects other places, some far away. Much of the particulate pollution in Los Angeles comes from China. And of course, China's air pollution contributes to the problem of global warming, which affects all of the planet. Many Chinese leaders have been reluctant to address environmental problems because doing so would raise the costs of producing Chinese goods.

VIDEO

Pollution in China

Evaluating After showing the video on pollution in China, ask students to evaluate this statement: **Americans and Europeans are partly responsible for China's environmental problems because they have created the demand for the country's cheap products.** Have students write a paragraph explaining whether or not they agree with that statement and have them share their opinions with a neighbor.

Interpersonal, Logical/Mathematical

See page 113E for other online activities.

ANSWERS, p. 137

Identifying basketball

☑ **READING PROGRESS CHECK** The Chinese government that took over in 1949 believed that religion had no place in a Communist country, so it began limiting religious practice.

T Technology Skills

Using Digital Tools To reinforce the meaning of *trade deficit* and *trade surplus*, have students use a calculator to determine the amount of the deficit or surplus in each of the following hypothetical cases:

- Japan exports $544 million worth of goods to country A and imports $639 million worth of goods. *($95 million trade deficit)*
- China exports $333 billion worth of goods to country B and imports $191 billion worth of goods. *($142 billion trade surplus)*
- Taiwan exports $672 million worth of goods to country C and imports $599 million worth of goods. *($73 million trade surplus)*
- Mongolia exports $850 million worth of goods to country D and imports $902 million worth of goods. *($52 million trade deficit)* **Logical/Mathematical**

C Critical Thinking Skills

Identifying Central Issues Tell students that China and Japan are not the only nations with an aging population. This is a challenge facing many industrialized nations. Have students discuss the effects of an aging population.

- Begin by having students consider different age groups within a population. *(babies, school-aged children, college students, people of working age, retired people)*
- Have students consider different pressures on the workforce when the population ages, helping them to see that the workforce needs to produce enough goods and services to meet the needs of the entire population, including all of those who are not part of the workforce.
- Have students list the different types of programs that are provided by taxes paid to the government. Point out that it is the workers who provide taxes to support such services. **Logical/Mathematical**

A boy runs across a rubbish-covered beach in Hainan, a tropical island in the South China Sea. Hainan, a part of China, has seen its economy grow rapidly in recent years.
▶ CRITICAL THINKING
Determining Central Ideas What have been the effects of rapid economic growth in East Asia?

In 2011 the strongest earthquake ever recorded in Japan killed thousands of people and damaged several nuclear power plants. It also disrupted trade and manufacturing around the world.

Trade

Many of the goods manufactured in East Asia are shipped to the United States and Europe. China's exports to the United States include electronic goods, toys and games, clothing, and shoes. From the United States, China imports soybeans, cotton, automobiles, and many other goods. Trade between the two countries, however, is not balanced. In 2010 the U.S. trade deficit with China rose to more than $273 billion. The **trade deficit** means the United States imports more goods from China than it sells to China. A **trade surplus** occurs when a country exports more products than it imports.

Challenges Facing East Asia

Japan and China are dealing with the challenges of population growth. Ever-growing populations put a strain on limited resources and services. In 1979 China began a policy that allowed each family to have no more than one child. The policy did slow population growth. However, with fewer children and better living standards, the percentage of elderly has grown substantially. Economic growth and productivity depend on a labor force of young adult workers. To increase the population of young people, some Chinese are demanding that the government change or repeal the law that penalizes families that have more than one child.

STR/AFP/Getty Images

netw⦿rks *Online Teaching Options*

Comparing Resources of the United States and East Asia

Comparing and Constrasting Use the comparison chart to discuss the resources used and traded between the United States and East Asia. Have students identify resources they use and where these come from. Then have them identify resources developed in their state and decide if any of these are traded with East Asia. **Verbal/Linguistic**

See page 113E for other online activities.

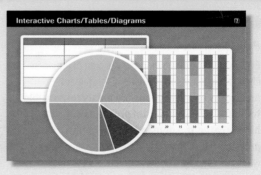

Interactive Charts/Tables/Diagrams

ANSWER, p. 138

CRITICAL THINKING Rapid economic growth has led to urbanization and higher standards of living; however, factory waste, urban sprawl, release of chemicals, and improper disposal of waste have poisoned air and water and destroyed valuable land.

U.S. TRADE DEFICIT WITH CHINA, 2001–2011

DEFICIT (BILLIONS OF DOLLARS)

YEAR

Source: U.S. Department of Commerce; U.S. International Trade Commission (ITC)

The United States depends on imports from China. Except for the 2009 recession, the U.S. trade deficit with Chinas has risen dramatically.

► **CRITICAL THINKING**

1. ***Integrating Visual Information*** In what years since 2001 has the United States had a trade surplus with China?

2. ***Identifying*** In what years was the trade deficit greater than $280 billion?

Political differences in East Asia are another challenge. Japan is in dispute with Russia over a long chain of islands known as the Kuril Islands, which lie north of Japan. Russia claims the entire archipelago, but Japan claims the southernmost islands. North Korea's efforts to develop nuclear weapons have drawn harsh criticism from several countries.

Both China and North Korea face questions about human rights in their countries, and China continues to receive international pressure for its views on Tibet and Taiwan. China's economic boom has drawn many people out of poverty, but the country faces a growing income gap between people in its cities and the countryside.

✔ **READING PROGRESS CHECK**

Drawing Conclusions How might an earthquake in Japan affect the economies of other parts of the world?

Include this lesson's information in your Foldable®.

LESSON 3 REVIEW

Reviewing Vocabulary (Tier Three Words)
1. What parts of Japan make up its *megalopolis*? RH.6-8.4

Answering the Guiding Questions

2. ***Describing*** How is Japan trying to compensate for the rise in the average age of its people? RH.6-8.1

3. ***Determining Central Ideas*** Today, many East Asian families are becoming scattered as people move to cities. Also, more women now work outside the home. How might these changes affect the structure and role of the family? RH.6-8.2

4. ***Analyzing*** In recent decades, hobbies and sports have become more important in the lives of people in China and other East Asian countries. What is the connection between this change and economic growth? RH.6-8.1

5. ***Determining Central Ideas*** What are some of the negative results of economic growth in East Asia? RH.6-8.2

6. ***Argument Writing*** Would you rather live in urban or rural areas in East Asia? Write a paragraph explaining your answer. WHST.6-8.1, WHST.6-8.4

Chapter 4 **139**

LESSON 3 REVIEW ANSWERS

Reviewing Vocabulary

1. The cities of Tokyo, Osaka, Nagoya, and Yokohama make up the megalopolis.

Answering the Guiding Questions

2. **Describing** Japan is encouraging people to have children to lower the average age of its population.

3. **Determining Central Ideas** Families might play a less important role than in the past. Mothers and fathers might both be seen as heads of the family.

4. **Analyzing** A better standard of living means that people have more time and money to pursue leisure activities.

5. **Determining Central Ideas** Negative outcomes include environmental problems, such as air and water pollution.

Writing Activity

6. **Argument Writing** Students' answers will vary but should be supported with logical reasons for preferring urban or rural life. Accept all reasonable answers.

V Visual Skills

Creating a Concept Web As you discuss the political issues in East Asia, create a concept web on the board similar to the one below. Call on students to complete the web. Regarding China's views on Tibet and Taiwan, explain that China claims both areas while both areas have declared their independence. *(Students should fill in the outer circles with notes like these: Russia and Japan dispute ownership of southernmost Kuril Islands. Countries oppose North Korea's nuclear weapons program. Human rights abuses common in China and North Korea. China opposes independence of Tibet and Taiwan. Income gap growing between rural and urban residents in China.)* **Visual/Spatial**

Political Issues in East Asia

Content Background Knowledge

The Universal Declaration of Human Rights, a document created by the United Nations, outlines human rights that should be protected for all people. These rights address treating people as equal under the law, providing fair trials, and allowing people the freedom to move within their country (and out of it). The Declaration of Human Rights addresses slavery, torture, the ability to own property, freedom of religion, and more.

CLOSE & REFLECT

To close the lesson, ask students to look again at the writing they did at the beginning of this lesson in which they speculated on how geography might affect people's lives in the various countries of East Asia. Call on volunteers to share their speculations, and discuss whether the speculations were confirmed in this lesson.

ANSWERS, p. 139

GRAPH SKILLS

CRITICAL THINKING

1. none

2. 2011

✔ **READING PROGRESS CHECK** Manufacturing might be interrupted, which would affect exports to other countries.

ENGAGE

Bellringer Before students read the Global Connections feature about tsunamis, explain that this feature provides information on a natural disaster that impacts global commerce, affects the well being of populations and the environment, and can disrupt regional economic and political stability. Help students understand the impact of such a disaster when it strikes any region in the world. **Ask:**

- **What are some weather-related natural disasters?** *(Student answers should include tornadoes, hurricanes, major floods.)*
- **What are some disasters caused by the movement of Earth's tectonic plates?** *(Student answers should include earthquakes, volcanic eruptions, landslides, and tsunamis.)*
- **What types of destruction can be caused by a great flood whether it is weather-related or caused by a tsunami?** *(Possible answers: destroyed homes, deaths, entire areas wiped out, including all animal and plant life, washing out of roads.)*

Direct students to the main quote in the third column. Have one student read it aloud. Use the chapter opener map to show 500 miles of distance and ask students to visualize a wall of water moving across that distance. Have students compare the distance traveled in a car in one hour with the distance traveled by a tsunami.

C1

TEACH & ASSESS

R1 Reading Skills

Defining Write *tsunami* on the board with four arrows pointing toward the term. **Ask:**

- **What is a *tsunami*?** *(series of ocean waves)* Write the definition on the board under the term.
- **What causes a tsunami?** *(earthquakes, landslides, volcanic activity, other disturbances below or on the seafloor.)*

Add one cause on each of the four arrows as students generate the answers. **AL** **Naturalist**

R2 Reading Skills

Applying Have students identify one warning sign of a tsunami. *(an earthquake, when the ocean appears to drain)* **Ask:** **Why is it important to know and heed the warning signs of a tsunami or other natural disaster?** *(It is important to take the opportunity to find a safe place before the tsunami or other natural disaster strikes.)*

Explain that natural disasters such as earthquakes and tsunamis offer little time to find safety. **AL** **Logical/Mathematical**

The Fury of a
TSUNAMI

R1 *A tsunami is a series of ocean waves generated by earthquakes, landslides, volcanic activity, or other disturbances below or on the seafloor. Scientists say that earthquakes cause about 90 percent of all tsunamis.*

R2 **Warning Signs** A tsunami can strike quickly. There are a few warning signals that typically occur. If an earthquake strikes, do not stay in low areas or near water. Earthquakes often trigger a tsunami. Sometimes, the ocean appears to drain away before an approaching tsunami hits. This is a warning sign that a tsunami is approaching.

4 of every 5 About four in every five tsunamis occur in the "Ring of Fire" in the Pacific Ocean. Tectonic shifts make volcanoes and earthquakes common there.

500 MPH Some tsunamis are 100 miles (161 km) long or longer. They can travel as fast as 500 miles (805 km) per hour—as fast as a commercial jet plane. At that speed, they can cross the Pacific Ocean in less than a day.

Read about two significant tsunamis in recent times:

July 9, 1958 The largest recorded tsunami in modern times luckily struck the isolated region around Lituya Bay, Alaska. Waves rose 1,700 feet (518 m). That is taller than the Empire State Building.

> **They can travel as fast as 500 miles (805 km) per hour—as fast as a commercial jet plane.**

Dec. 26, 2004 The deadliest tsunami in recorded history, the Indian Ocean tsunami killed an estimated 230,000 people. The tsunami swept through a wide area, including Indonesia, India, Madagascar, and Ethiopia. Many people died in the weeks after the tsunami hit because of lack of water and medical treatment.

C2

Did You Know ?

The Richter scale is used to rate the magnitude—or amount of energy released—of an earthquake. Most earthquakes that occur today rate less than 3 on the Richter scale and do not produce much damage. On average, at least one earthquake with a magnitude of 8.0 occurs each year.

Waters flood the city of Miyako shortly after the March 2011 earthquake struck northern Japan. ▶

(t) ©Comstock/JupiterImages; (b) ©US Navy/ZUMA/Corbis; (r) JIJI PRESS/AFP/Getty Images

---

netw⊚rks *Online Teaching Options*

SLIDE SHOW

Search and Rescue

Integrating Visual Information Use the slide show about search and rescue operations to discuss the Red Cross response to natural disasters. Discuss with students other events where Red Cross has provided disaster assistance. Consider inviting a local Red Cross volunteer to your class by contacting the local Red Cross chapter to discuss how Red Cross responds to both local and national disasters.

ELL **Interpersonal**

Slide Show

(l) ©Ocean/Corbis, ©Kryssia Campos/Getty Images, (tr) Erica Simone Leeds, (br) ©IG Photography/Alamy

THERE'S MORE ONLINE

HEAR stories from tsunami survivors • **SEE** before and after images • **WATCH** an animation of a tsunami

Chapter 4 **141**

C₁ Critical Thinking Skills

Formulating Questions Have a volunteer read aloud the Did You Know? section. **Ask:**

• What is the Richter scale? *(a scale used to rate the magnitude of an earthquake)*

• What questions come to mind when thinking of how the Richter scale is applied? *(Possible questions: What is the most common magnitude? What type of destruction would be expected at different magnitudes? Where do earthquakes of the greatest magnitude occur?)* **BL** Logical/Mathematical

V

C₂ Critical Thinking Skills

Reasoning As students read the remainder of the page, have them list details about the tsunamis on July 9, 1958 and December 26, 2004. **Ask:**

• Which tsunami was more destructive? *(2004—killed an estimated 230,000 people)*

• What regions of the world were affected by the two tsunamis? *(1958—Alaska, 2004—Indonesia, India, Madagascar, Ethiopia)*

• How does the information about the two tsunamis help you understand this type of natural disaster? *(Students may explain that tsunamis are highly destructive, very powerful events that can cause many deaths if they hit populated areas.)* **AL** Verbal/Linguistic

V Visual Skills

Interpreting Allow time for students to analyze the full page photograph. Some students may be able to identify that this photo was taken during the tsunami in Japan in 2011. **Ask:**

• What word would you use to describe what is shown in the photo? *(Answers will vary but could include horrific, catastrophic, disastrous, ruinous, terrible, unbelievable.)*

• How might this event have changed the life of the individuals who lived here? *(Students might suggest that they lost their homes and all that they owned; lost their jobs or businesses, and possibly lost family members. Students may comment that people may have had to rebuild whole towns and villages.)* Visual/Spatial

ANIMATION

How Tsunamis Form

Visualizing Use the animation of how tsunamis form to discuss what a wave pattern looks like. Divide students into small groups and have them illustrate what they learned from the animation. Have students listen to stories from tsunami survivors and view the before and after images. As a class, discuss the impact of a tsunami on life and property. **AL** Visual/Spatial, Naturalist

R Reading Skills

Citing Text Evidence Divide students into teams. Have each team report facts from this page of text. List the facts on the board as each team reports. **Ask: Why was the 2011 tsunami considered Japan's worst crisis since World War II?** *(Students should recognize that the tsunami caused destruction on several levels, including the grave toll taken on the people, on property, and on the environment, and that it would take the resolve of the nation to deal with the crisis and rebuild.)* **Verbal/ Linguistic, Logical/Mathematical**

C Critical Thinking Skills

Assessing Review the facts from this page. **Ask: Why did the nuclear plant become a priority for Japan and of great concern to the world?** *(Students should recognize the immediate threat to life caused by the nuclear crisis at the Fukushima Daiichi nuclear power station, and the long-term environmental impact to animal and plant life when radioactivity is directly released into the atmosphere.)* **BL** **Logical/ Mathematical**

V Visual Skills

Interpreting Have students finish reading the text and apply what they know to interpret the photograph in column 3. **Ask:**

- **Why are the people wearing masks?** *(for their health, to prevent breathing dangerous elements)*
- **What is the scientist doing?** *(testing for evidence of nuclear contamination)*
- **What information do the scientists hope to gain from the tests?** *(Students might suggest that the scientists want to assess how many people were affected by the nuclear crisis.)*
- **Why do you think the person being tested looks concerned?** *(Students should recognize the health risks associated with nuclear contamination.)* **AL** **Verbal/ Linguistic**

R *These numbers and statistics can help you understand the full effects of the earthquake and tsunami that struck Japan in March 2011.*

8.9
MAGNITUDE

C

Japan was hit by an 8.9 magnitude earthquake on March 11, 2011, that triggered a deadly, 23-foot tsunami in the northern part of the country. In comparison, the 1998 earthquake that caused massive damage in California was only a magnitude 6.9 on the Richter scale.

40 Years | The tsunami in

Japan recalled the 2004 disaster in the Indian Ocean. On December 26, a 9.0 magnitude earthquake—the largest earthquake in 40 years—ruptured in the Indian Ocean, off the northwestern coast of the Indonesian island of Sumatra. The earthquake stirred up the deadliest tsunami in world history. It was so powerful that the waves caused loss of life on the coast of Africa and were even detected on the East Coast of the United States.

142 *Chapter 4*

100,000

At a news conference on March 13, Prime Minister Naoto Kan, who later gave the disaster the name "Great East Japan Earthquake," emphasized the gravity of the situation: "I think that the earthquake, tsunami, and the situation at our nuclear reactors makes up the worst crisis in the 65 years since the war. If the nation works together, we will overcome." The government called in 100,000 troops to aid in the relief effort.

200,000
Evacuated

Cooling systems in one of the reactors at the Fukushima Daiichi nuclear power station in the Fukushima prefecture on the east coast of Japan failed shortly after the earthquake, causing a nuclear crisis. This initial reactor failure was followed by an explosion and eventual partial meltdowns in two reactors, then by a fire in another reactor that released radioactivity directly into the atmosphere. The nuclear troubles were not limited to the Daiichi plant; three other nuclear facilities also reported problems. More than 200,000 residents were evacuated from affected areas.

15,839

According to the official toll, the disasters left 15,839 dead and 3,647 missing. One year after the tsunami, about 160,000 people had not returned to their homes.

LEVEL 7 | On April 12, 2011, Japan

increased its assessment of the situation at the Fukushima Daiichi nuclear power plant to Level 7, the worst rating on the international scale, putting the disaster on par with the 1986 Chernobyl explosion.

V

450 MPH

The waves travel in all directions from the epicenter of the disturbance. The waves may travel in the open sea as fast as 450 miles (724 km) per hour. As they travel in the open ocean, tsunami waves are generally not particularly large—hence the difficulty in detecting the approach of a tsunami. But as these powerful waves approach shallow waters along the coast, their velocity is slowed and they consequently grow to a great height before smashing into the shore.

---

netw⊙rks   *Online Teaching Options*

IMAGE

Environmental Effects from Fukushima Plant

Using Digital Tools Use the interactive image to discuss details about the environmental effects of nuclear disasters. Divide the class into groups of four. Have each group create a presentation using a digital storybook, blog, or movie on one of the effects highlighted in the interactive image. Students may need to do some additional Internet-based research for their presentations. **AL** **Visual/Spatial**

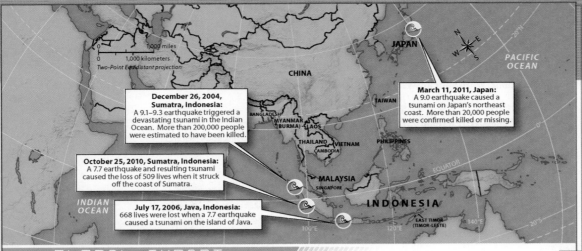

December 26, 2004, Sumatra, Indonesia:
A 9.1–9.3 earthquake triggered a devastating tsunami in the Indian Ocean. More than 200,000 people were estimated to have been killed.

March 11, 2011, Japan:
A 9.0 earthquake caused a tsunami on Japan's northeast coast. More than 20,000 people were confirmed killed or missing.

October 25, 2010, Sumatra, Indonesia:
A 7.7 earthquake and resulting tsunami caused the loss of 509 lives when it struck off the coast of Sumatra.

July 17, 2006, Java, Indonesia:
668 lives were lost when a 7.7 earthquake caused a tsunami on the island of Java.

GLOBAL IMPACT

DESTRUCTIVE FORCES Hundreds of small earthquakes shake Japan every year. Major quakes occur less often, but they may cause disastrous damage and loss of life. When an undersea earthquake generates a tsunami—a huge tidal wave that gets higher and higher as it approaches the coast—many lives may be lost. Because earthquakes and tsunamis are difficult to predict, some parts of the region, especially in high-population areas, rely on special building methods and emergency preparedness to help reduce casualties.

Natori, Japan

Natori (left) is shown before the March 2011 earthquake and tsunami. A photograph of the city (right) shows the effects afterwards.

BEFORE   AFTER

(l to r) BAY ISMOYO/AFP/Getty Images; © Ruaridh Stewart/ZUMA Press/Corbis; KEN SHIMIZU/AFP/Getty Images; Anonymous/AP Images

Thinking Like a Geographer

1. *Physical Geography* How are tsunamis created?

2. *Physical Geography* Research to find information about the 2004 Indian Ocean tsunami. Create a map that identifies the nations that suffered deaths and great destruction.

3. *Environment and Society* Research online to find out what happened when the Fukushima Daiichi nuclear power plant was hit by the 2011 tsunami. Create a PowerPoint® presentation that includes diagrams and photos to show the chain of events that occurred when the nuclear plant was damaged. Present your slides to the class.

Chapter 4 **143**

DIAGRAM

Japan's Tsunami and the Fukushima Nuclear Power Plant

Paraphrasing Use the diagram displaying the damage at the nuclear power plant and the diagram of the interior core to discuss how the nuclear plant operated and explain why the tsunami did so much damage. Have volunteers paraphrase parts of the diagram for the class. You may wish to set up an "experts" panel of science students as part of a Q & A session. **BL** Visual/Spatial

Interactive Charts/Tables/Diagrams

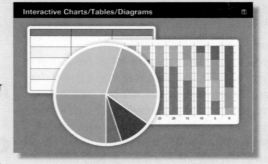

T Technology Skills

Researching Have students do Internet research based on one of the callouts in the map at the top of the page, and compile images and facts about the chosen tsunami. Students should include a caption for each image. Have them choose a suitable format to present their findings to the class, such as a poster, presentation, picture book, or safety brochure.

Have students look back at the map of tectonic plate boundaries in a previous chapter and find the area shown in this regional map on the world map in previous chapter. Have students discuss why this region is subject to so many earthquakes and the ensuing tsunamis. **Logical/Mathematical**

C Critical Thinking Skills

Drawing Conclusions Have students look at the satellite photos showing the area before and after the 2011 earthquake and tsunami. Have them consider not only the devastating effects on the area shown but how such a disaster affects the country and the world. **Ask:** What is the global impact of a natural disaster occurring in a region on Earth? *(Answers should include an understanding of how a natural disaster occurring in one region of the world impacts the global economy, and possibly the environments of other regions.)* **Verbal/Linguistic**

CLOSE & REFLECT

Divide the class into small groups. Have each group create a chart that provides a visual representation of the effects of the 2011 tsunami in Japan. The chart should include the impact on people, animals, property, the environment, the government, and the infrastructure. Provide students with chart paper or poster board and colored markers for this activity. Have each group explain its chart. Have the class summarize the impact of the 2011 tsunami on Japan. Display the charts. **ELL** Visual/Spatial

---

ANSWERS, p. 143

THINKING LIKE A GEOGRAPHER

1. Disturbances on or below the seafloor, such as landslides and earthquakes, result in tsunamis. Earthquakes are the most common, triggering 90 percent of all tsunamis.

2. Student products should provide detailed and correct information.

3. Students should be well-informed about the topic and include reliable, factual information in their presentations. Information provided during the presentation should interest the students and give important information.

CHAPTER REVIEW ACTIVITY

To summarize the chapter, divide the class into three groups and assign each group to one of the lessons in the chapter. Have each group complete one of the graphic organizers below, focusing on the main ideas in a particular lesson. *(Students' answers may vary but should reflect the main ideas covered in each of the three lessons of the chapter.)*

Physical Geography of East Asia			
Landforms	Waterways	Climate	Natural Resources

History of East Asia

1300 — 2015

Life in East Asia		
Population	Culture	Current Issues

REVIEW THE ENDURING UNDERSTANDINGS

Review this chapter's Enduring Understanding with students:

- *People, places, and ideas change over time.*

Pose the following questions in a class discussion to apply this idea to this chapter:

- **How has the economic system in China changed since 1949?** *(Sample answer: After the Communists gained control of mainland China in 1949, they established communism, a system in which the government controls all economic goods and services. Despite attempts to increase industrial output, the*

economy did not prosper. After 1976, China allowed more features of a market economy to develop and opened up to the West. The country quickly became a global economic power.)

- **How has Japan's relationship with the rest of the world changed since the early 1600s?** *(Sample answer: In the early 1600s, Japan closed itself off from the rest of the world and remained isolated for 200 years. The United States pressured Japan to open up to foreign trade in 1854. Japan soon became an industrial and military power and began developing an empire. After its defeat in World War II, Japan went on to develop one of the world's strongest economies. Today, Japan has political and economic ties all over the world, and Japanese culture has spread around the world as a result of Japanese trade and migration.)*

- **How has industrialization changed the environment in China?** *(Air and water pollution have severely degraded the environment, and much farm land has been lost to industrialization and the building of infrastructure.)*

ACTIVITIES ANSWERS

Essential Question

1 **INFORMATIVE/EXPLANATORY WRITING** Much of western China is either mountainous, desert, or near desert land with a dry, cold climate. Eastern China has more water, a more hospitable climate, and fertile plains.

Chapter 4 ACTIVITIES

Directions: Write your answers on a separate piece of paper.

1 Use your **FOLDABLES** to explore the Essential Question.
INFORMATIVE/EXPLANATORY WRITING Why do people in China live in densely populated areas in river valleys and along the coastal plains when the country has so much sparsely populated land in its western regions? WHST.6-8.2, WH.6-8.10

2 **21st Century Skills**
DESCRIBING Working in small groups, choose an East Asian country and research how its schools operate. Find out what kinds of classes students take, how they are graded, what sports and activities are offered, and what a typical school day is like. Prepare a report or a slide show and share results with another class in your school. WHST.6-8.7, WHST.6-8.6

3 **Thinking Like a Geographer**
IDENTIFYING The United States and China are about the same size and lie within the Northern Hemisphere at similar latitudes. Make a T-chart on a sheet of paper. On one side list similarities between the two countries, and on the other side list differences. RH.6-8.1

4 **GEOGRAPHY ACTIVITY**

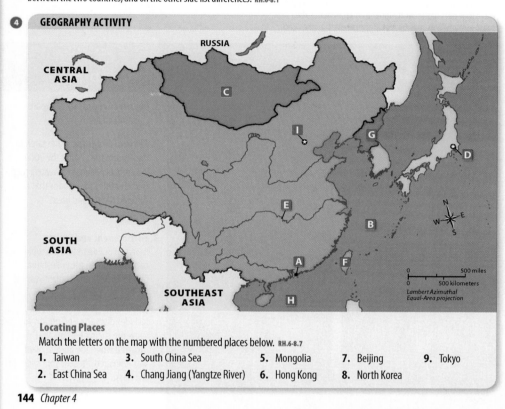

Locating Places
Match the letters on the map with the numbered places below. RH.6-8.7

1. Taiwan
2. East China Sea
3. South China Sea
4. Chang Jiang (Yangtze River)
5. Mongolia
6. Hong Kong
7. Beijing
8. North Korea
9. Tokyo

REVIEW THE GUIDING QUESTIONS

Directions: Choose the best answer for each question.

1 Why do most Japanese live within a few miles of the coast? RH.6-8.1
   A. The interior area of the country consists of steep, heavily forested mountains.
   B. The weather is better.
   C. Huge corporate farms take up most of the interior space.
   D. People like living near the beach.

2 China's major river systems RH.6-8.1
   F. flow through Beijing.
   G. begin on the Plateau of Tibet.
   H. empty into the South China Sea.
   I. are not navigable.

3 What product invented during China's Han dynasty is still in use around the world? RH.6-8.4
   A. fireworks
   B. paper
   C. gunpowder
   D. soap

4 Why did the United States send warships to Japan in 1854? RH.6-8.1
   F. to conquer the island
   G. to establish a naval base
   H. to pressure the Japanese to open their country to foreign trade
   I. to protect Japan from a Chinese invasion

5 During the Korean War, which country sent its troops to help North Korea and fight against American and United Nations forces? RH.6-8.1
   A. Taiwan
   B. Japan
   C. China
   D. South Korea

6 Which two East Asian countries have the largest economies? RH.6-8.1
   F. China and North Korea
   G. China and Taiwan
   H. China and Japan
   I. China and South Korea

Chapter 4 **145**

21st Century Skills

2 DESCRIBING After groups present their slide shows, lead a class discussion using the following questions: Which aspects of East Asian education would you like to see incorporated into American schools? Why?

Thinking Like a Geographer

3 IDENTIFYING Students might list such similarities as large size, range of climates, plentiful natural resources, strong economy, and educated workforce. They might list such differences as system of government; voting rights, freedoms of the press and of speech; standard of living; and language.

Geography Activity

4 LOCATING PLACES

1. F
2. B
3. H
4. E
5. C
6. A
7. I
8. G
9. D

ASSESSMENT ANSWERS
Review the Guiding Questions

1 A The main reason that most Japanese live within a few miles of the coast is because the interior mountains are too steep and often inaccessible. Have students who do not answer correctly review the physical geography of Japan covered in Lesson 1.

2 G The Huang He and the Chang Jiang, China's most important rivers, both begin high on the Plateau of Tibet in southwestern China. Have students who do not answer correctly review the physical geography of China covered in Lesson 1.

3 B The lesson states that papermaking was invented during the Han dynasty. Fireworks and gunpowder are also still in use, but the text does not indicate that they were invented during the Han dynasty. Soap is not mentioned in the text. Have students who do not answer correctly review the history of China covered in Lesson 2.

4 H The text states that U.S. naval officer Matthew C. Perry sailed to Japan with four warships and pressured the Japanese to end their isolation and open their country to foreign trade. Have students who do not answer correctly review the history of Japan covered in Lesson 2.

5 C China helped North Korea during the Korean War, and South Korea was aided by the United States and the United Nations. Have students who do not answer correctly review the history of China covered in Lesson 2.

6 H The three largest economies in the world are those of the United States, China, and Japan. Have students who do not answer correctly review East Asian economies in Lesson 3.

DBQ Analyzing Documents

7 **D** The 10-meter (33-foot) measure describes how high the tsunami wave was above normal sea level. If students answer incorrectly, discuss how minor the damage would have been if the tsunami had only traveled 10 meters from the point of the earthquake, hit that much of the coast, or traveled that far inland.

8 **F** Japan's strict building codes, which were effective in limiting earthquake damage, show that the Japanese people had taken important precautions because they are aware of the dangers of living near the Ring of Fire.

Short Response

9 Sample answer: China's growing middle class would probably not feel that the gap between rich and poor is as pressing an issue as would people who are among the poor.

10 Sample answer: The statements by Li Yulan provide some evidence of the claim that poor people see the income gap as a problem, but strong support for this idea is not provided since only one person's perspective is presented. There is no broad statistical evidence.

Extended Response

11 Sample answer: Trade deficits are bad for America's economy. When the United States buys more than it sells to another country, it is losing money. If the United States is selling fewer goods, it also means fewer jobs for American workers, who then cannot earn the money to buy goods and services. Over a period of time, this cycle leads to a stagnant or slow-growing economy. In the meantime, the country with the trade surplus shows growth and provides opportunity for its own workers. Students should note that continued trade deficits may affect their family's ability to earn a living and prosper.

Chapter 4 **ASSESSMENT** *(continued)*

DBQ ANALYZING DOCUMENTS

7 **ANALYZING** Read this passage about the earthquake and tsunami that struck Japan in 2011:

"*Very little of the devastation resulting from this earthquake was from the initial shaking. This is partly because of Japan's stringent [tough] building codes. But mainly because any damage from the seismic waves that sent skyscrapers in Tokyo swaying was dwarfed by the impact of the 10 metre tsunami that hit the Japanese coast less than an hour later.*"

—from Chris Rowan, "Japan Earthquake" (2011)

What does Rowan mean when he calls the tsunami a 10-meter (33-foot) tsunami? RH.6-8.4, RH.6-8.10

A. how far the wave traveled from the point of the earthquake

B. how far along the coast the tsunami hit

C. how far inland the wave traveled

D. how high the tsunami was above sea level

8 **CITING TEXT EVIDENCE** What detail in the passage explains that the Japanese are aware of the dangers of living along the Ring of Fire? RH.6-8.1, RH.6-8.10

F. strict building codes that limit earthquake damage

G. the height of the tsunami

H. the short duration of the initial shaking caused by the quake

I. heavy damage from the tsunami

SHORT RESPONSE

"*But for many [Chinese], the growing gap between rich and poor is the most pressing issue, especially in Beijing's slums. . . . Li Yulan, 78, runs a small shop. . . . She says the rich are too rich. The poor are too poor. Of eight people in her family, just two have income, she says.*"

—from Shannon Van Sant, "China Struggles to Bridge Gap Between Rich, Poor" (2012)

9 **IDENTIFYING POINT OF VIEW** Would China's middle class agree that the income gap is the country's most pressing issue? Why or why not? RH.6-8.6, RH.6-8.10

10 **DISTINGUISHING FACT FROM OPINION** Is the example of Li Yulan convincing evidence of the income gap problem? Why or why not? RH.6-8.8, RH.6-8.10

EXTENDED RESPONSE

11 **INFORMATIVE/EXPLANATORY WRITING** Every year America's trade deficit with China increases by billions of dollars. How do trade deficits affect the American economy? How might they affect you and your family personally? WHST.6-8.2, WHST.6-8.4

Need Extra Help?

If You've Missed Question	❶	❷	❸	❹	❺	❻	❼	❽	❾	❿	⓫
Review Lesson	1	1	2	2	2	3	1	1	3	3	3

"China Struggles to Bridge Gap Between Rich, Poor," by Shannon Van Sant, March 13, 2012. Voice of America, http://voanews.com

---

netw⊙rks   *Online Teaching Options*

Remediation and Assessment

Evaluating The *Assess* tab in the online Teacher Lesson Center includes resources to help students improve their test-taking skills. It also contains many project-based rubrics to help you assess students' work.

CHAPTER 5
Southeast Asia Planner

National Geography Standards covered in Chapter 5

Learners will understand:

I. The World in Spatial Terms

Standard 1: How to use maps and other geographic representations, geospatial technologies, and spatial thinking to understand and communicate information

Standard 3: How to analyze the spatial organization of people, places, and environments on Earth's surface

II. Places and Regions

Standard 4: The physical and human characteristics of places

Standard 5: That people create regions to interpret Earth's complexity

Standard 6: How culture and experience influence people's perceptions of places and regions

IV. Human Systems

Standard 9: The characteristics, distribution, and migration of human populations on Earth's surface

Standard 10: The characteristics, distribution, and complexity of Earth's cultural mosaics

Standard 11: The patterns and networks of economic interdependence on Earth's surface

Standard 12: The processes, patterns, and functions of human settlement

Standard 13: How the forces of cooperation and conflict among people influence the division and control of Earth's surface

V. Environment and Society

Standard 14: How human actions modify the physical environment

Standard 15: How physical systems affect human systems

VI. The Uses of Geography

Standard 17: How to apply geography to interpret the past

Standard 18: How to apply geography to interpret the present and plan for the future

UNDERSTANDING BY DESIGN®

Enduring Understandings

- *People, places, and ideas change over time.*

Essential Questions

- *How does geography influence the way people live?*
- *What makes a culture unique?*
- *Why does conflict develop?*

Predictable Misunderstandings

- *The islands in Southeast Asia make up one country.*
- *The people of Southeast Asia live mostly in rural areas.*
- *Southeast Asia has always been an island chain.*
- *The people of Southeast Asia speak the same language and have the same culture.*

Assessment Evidence

Performance Tasks:

- *Project-Based Learning Digital Hands-On Chapter Project*
- *Project-Based Learning Print Hands-On Chapter Project*

Other Evidence:

- *Geography Skills Activity*
- *Reading Skills Activity*
- *Geography and Economics Activity*
- *Participation in Interactive Whiteboard Activities*
- *Contribution to small-group activities*
- *Interpretation of slide show images and special purpose maps*
- *Participation in class discussions about cultural and economic topics*
- *Lesson Reviews*
- *Chapter Assessments*

SUGGESTED PACING GUIDE

Introducing the Chapter............... 1 Day	Lesson 3 .... 2 Days
Lesson 1 .... 2 Days	Chapter Wrap-Up and Assessment...... 1 Day
Lesson 2 .... 2 Days	

TOTAL TIME   8 Days

Key for Using the Teacher Edition

SKILL-BASED ACTIVITIES

Types of skill activities found in the Teacher Edition.

* **V Visual Skills** require students to analyze maps, graphs, charts, and photos.

W Writing Skills provide writing opportunities to help students comprehend the text.

R Reading Skills help students practice reading skills and master vocabulary.

C Critical Thinking Skills help students apply and extend what they have learned.

T Technology Skills require students to use digital tools effectively.

*Letters are followed by a number when there is more than one of the same type of skill on the page.

DIFFERENTIATED INSTRUCTION

All activities are written for the on-level student unless otherwise marked with the leveled labels below.

BL Beyond Level
AL Approaching Level
ELL English Language Learners

All students benefit from activities that utilize different learning styles. Many activities are marked as below when a particular learning style is highlighted.

Intrapersonal	Naturalist
Logical/Mathematical	Kinesthetic
Visual/Spatial	Auditory/Musical
Verbal/Linguistic	Interpersonal

CHAPTER OPENER PLANNER

Students will know:

- that many of the countries of Southeast Asia are situated on islands.
- that the region is mostly marked by seas and oceans.
- that Chinese, Indians, and Europeans have at times colonized and influenced the region.

Students will be able to:

- **analyze** a world map to identify countries of Southeast Asia
- **use** a time line to discuss various events in the history of Southeast Asia

UNDERSTANDING
BY DESIGN®

☑ *Print Teaching Options*

V Visual Skills

☐ **P. 148** Students use the map to reinforce map skills and answer questions. **AL** **ELL** Visual/Spatial

☐ **P. 149** Students review the time line and discuss its major points of interest. **BL**

C Critical Thinking Skills

☐ **P. 149** Students infer what challenges Singapore faced when it became an independent country. **BL**

☑ *Online Teaching Options*

☐ **MAP** **Reading a Map**—Students identify aspects and locations of the region on a map.

☐ **TIME LINE** **Reading a Time Line and Map**—Students learn about where and when historical events in Southeast Asia took place. Visual/Spatial

☐ **MAP** **Interactive World Atlas**—Students use the interactive world atlas to identify the region and describe its terrain.

☑ *Printable Digital Worksheets*

☐ **WORKSHEET** **Geography and Economics: Recovering from a Natural Disaster**—Students use this worksheet to write essays about the recovery after the devastation of a natural disaster.

☐ **WORKSHEET** **Reading Skills: The Vietnam War**—Students can use this worksheet to analyze primary sources from soldiers in the Vietnam War.

☐ **WORKSHEET** **Geography Skills: Understanding Time Lines**—Students can use this worksheet to understand more about Vietnam and Cambodian history.

Project-Based Learning

Hands-On

Create Illustrated Time Lines

Students will work in groups to create illustrated time lines of a country in Southeast Asia. Time lines should list facts about the country's history and include current events. Time lines might contain photos from the Internet that reflect events in the country's history. Each group will present their time lines to the class. Display completed time lines in a hallway or other public area in the school.

Digital Hands-On

Create a Collaborative Digital Presentation

Students will work in groups to prepare web-based notes on a collaborative, online writing platform about the countries of Southeast Asia. Students will take notes about the region's governments, history, and cultures. Each group should then create a collaborative digital presentation that includes photos with captions and videos. Students will share their project with each group, and groups will then leave audio or text comments on each other's presentation.

21st Century Learning

Print Resources

ANCILLARY RESOURCES

These ancillaries are available for every chapter and lesson.

- **Reading Essentials and Study Guide Workbook** **AL** **ELL**
- **Chapter Tests and Lesson Quizzes Blackline Masters**

PRINTABLE DIGITAL WORKSHEETS

These printable digital worksheets are available for every chapter and lesson!

- **Hands-On Chapter Projects**
- **What Do You Know? Activities**
- **Chapter Summaries (English and Spanish)**
- **Vocabulary Builder Activities**
- **Quizzes and Tests**
- **Reading Essentials and Study Guide (English and Spanish)** **AL** **ELL**
- **Guided Reading Activities**

More Media Resources

SUGGESTED VIDEOS

NOTE: Be sure to preview videos to ensure they are age-appropriate.

- **Raise the Bamboo Curtain: Vietnam, Cambodia and Burma (Myanmar)** (100 min.)
- **Remembering Vietnam: The Wall at 25** (60 min.)
- **Globe Trekker—Indonesia** (2 discs – 180 min.)

SUGGESTED READING 📚

- ***Thailand (Countries of the World),*** by Kristen Thoennes
- ***Vietnam: The Bloodbath at Hamburger Hill, 24/7: Goes to War,*** by John DiConsiglio **BL**
- ***Cracker! The Best Dog in Vietnam,*** by Cynthia Kadohata **AL**

PHYSICAL GEOGRAPHY OF SOUTHEAST ASIA

Students will know:

- *that many of the countries in Southeast Asia are situated on islands.*
- *that the region is mostly marked by seas and oceans.*
- *that Southeast Asia's climate is generally hot and humid.*
- *that for many centuries, the sea levels were lower and the mainland extended out to many of the areas that are now islands.*
- *that the region has been populated for over 40,000 years.*

Students will be able to:

- ***identify*** the different landforms and bodies of water in Southeast Asia, including peninsulas and islands.
- ***identify*** natural resources found in the region.
- ***describe*** climate, vegetation, and wildlife in the region.

UNDERSTANDING
BY DESIGN®

☑ *Print Teaching Options*

V Visual Skills

☐ **P. 151** Pairs estimate and calculate the miles of coastline the islands of Southeast Asia include. **Mathematical**

☐ **P. 153** Pairs create flash cards to quiz each other in the game "What's That Water?" **Visual/Spatial**

☐ **P. 153** Pairs create a chart of important rivers in the region. **Visual/Spatial**

☐ **P. 155** Student groups use information about climate zones to arrange themselves as a map of Southeast Asia.

W Writing Skills

☐ **P. 152** Students write a news report of a tsunami.

☐ **P. 155** Students write for or against designating some of Southeast Asia's rain forests as protected land. **BL**

R Reading Skills

☐ **P. 151** Students review the meaning of *archipelago* and locate the Malay Archipelago on a map. **AL**

☐ **P. 151** Students listen to the pronunciation of the names of islands in Southeast Asia. **ELL Auditory**

☐ **P. 152** Students summarize text about Indonesia's active volcanoes and its deadliest earthquake in 2004. **AL**

☐ **P. 154** Students identify comparative and superlative words and use the words to show comparison.

C Critical Thinking Skills

☐ **P. 150** Students discuss different advantages to living in mainland and island communities of Southeast Asia. **BL**

☐ **P. 151** Students analyze the aerial photograph and discuss natural disasters along the Ring of Fire.

☐ **P. 152** Students explain to a partner the cause and effect of pressure in Earth's tectonic plates. **BL**

☐ **P. 154** Students create a flow chart of the sequence of events in the harvesting process of latex in Indonesia. **BL**

T Technology Skills

☐ **P. 152** Students work in small groups to research and answer questions on natural resource production, scarcity and impact in the region and present their reports using a software presentation program. **BL Naturalist**

☑ *Online Teaching Options*

V Visual Skills

☐ **VIDEO Around the World—Borneo**—Students watch the video about Borneo and work in pairs to discuss one or two key facts they found interesting or surprising. **AL Visual/Spatial**

☐ **MAP Malaysia/Indonesian Islands**—Students use the map and aerial photograph to help them visualize the regions in Malaysia and the Indonesian Islands. **ELL Visual/Spatial**

☐ **MAP Physical Geography: Southeast Asia**—Students use the physical layer of the Chapter Opener map to discuss the various landforms in this region. **Visual/Spatial**

☐ **MAP Volcanoes in Southeast Asia**—Students use the map to discuss the density of volcanoes and statistics of volcanoes in Southeast Asia. **AL Verbal/Linguistic**

☐ **SLIDE SHOW Wildlife of Southeast Asia**—Students act as a safari tour guide to describe characteristics of a plant or animal of Southeast Asia in the slide show. **AL Kinesthetic**

W Writing Skills

☐ **GRAPHIC ORGANIZER Landforms in Southeast Asia**—Students use the interactive graphic organizer about landforms in this region to review the content.

☐ **GRAPHIC ORGANIZER Seas and Rivers of Southeast Asia**—Students use the interactive graphic organizer to discuss the seas and rivers.

R Reading Skills

☐ **GAME Drag-and-Drop: Mainland or Island Country in Southeast Asia**—Students use the game to discuss the difference between the mainland countries and the island countries.

☐ **GAME Drag-and-Drop: Geographic Terms for Southeast Asia**—Students use the game of definitions to review the geographic terms of the region. **Kinesthetic**

C Critical Thinking Skills

☐ **MAP Volcanic Islands**—Students use the map to compare the volcanoes of Southeast Asia to the other locations in the region made up of volcanic islands.

☐ **IMAGE Indonesian Tsunami**—Students use the interactive image of the destruction in Indonesia post-tsunami to discuss the causes of a tsunami and the effects of the damage. **BL**

☐ **MAP Tectonic Plates**—Students can use this map to review the layout of the tectonic plates and their role in earthquakes, volcanoes, and tsunamis.

T Technology Skills

☐ **ANIMATION How a Tsunami Forms**—Students can use this animation to review how tsunamis form and the force with which they hit land.

☐ **ONLINE SELF-CHECK QUIZ Lesson 1**—Students receive instant feedback on their mastery of lesson content

☑ *Printable Digital Worksheets*

W Writing Skills

☐ **WORKSHEET Geography and Economics: Recovering from a Natural Disaster**—Students use this worksheet to write essays about the recovery after the devastation of a natural disaster.

HISTORY OF SOUTHEAST ASIA

Students will know:
- that the region has been populated for over 40,000 years.
- that Chinese, Indian, and Europeans have at different times colonized and influenced the region.

Students will be able to:
- **describe** the early history of Southeast Asia including kingdoms and empires.
- **discuss** western colonization of Southeast Asia.
- **explain** how countries of Southeast Asia gained their independence.
- **discuss** modern Southeast Asia governments and economies.

UNDERSTANDING
BY DESIGN®

☑ *Print Teaching Options*

V Visual Skills

☐ **P. 157** Small groups create time lines showing when trading societies emerged in Southeast Asia. **BL**

☐ **P. 158** Students compare and contrast images.

☐ **P. 162** Pairs create a flow chart or time line of key events.

☐ **P. 163** Students create a Venn diagram comparing and contrasting the conflicts in Vietnam and Cambodia.

W Writing Skills

☐ **P. 157** Students write a story about a person or people who belonged to one of the trading societies in the text.

☐ **P. 158** Students write a narrative that reflects the way people lived 600–1000 years ago. **Verbal/Linguistic**

R Reading Skills

☐ **P. 157** Students determine central ideas concerning the impact China and India have had on Southeast Asia. **AL**

☐ **P. 161** Students work with a partner to infer the meaning of the term *absolute monarchy*. **AL ELL**

C Critical Thinking Skills

☐ **P. 156** Students infer how its proximity to China and India has impacted Southeast Asia. **AL**

☐ **P. 159** Students discuss how Malaccan rulers took advantage of location to develop a trading empire.

☐ **P. 160** Students infer why the Netherlands became involved with the spice trade. **AL**

☐ **P. 162** Students hypothesize the reasons why the United States ended involvement in the Vietnam War.

T Technology Skills

☐ **P. 159** Students form five trading groups to research and present their trade at an Agricultural Fair. **ELL**

☐ **P. 161** Student groups research a crop or trade item and present a summary of their findings to the class.

☐ **P. 162** Students review the struggle for democracy in Southeast Asia and research Cambodian elections. **BL**

☐ **P. 163** Student groups "produce" a talk show titled "Southeast Asia Today" in which a host interviews historians and economists about the current economy.

☑ *Online Teaching Options*

V Visual Skills

☐ **VIDEO Around the World—Malaysia**—Students watch the video about Malaysia and surmise why Southeast Asia is known as the "Crossroads of the World." **BL Interpersonal**

☐ **MAP Trade in Southeast Asia**—Students can use the map showing trade routes and discuss why this region is called the "Crossroads of the World."

☐ **MAP Islam**—Students use the map on the spread of Islam to discuss how religion spread through trade.

☐ **MAP The Spice Islands**—Students use the map to discuss the Spice Islands and the impact spices had on the region and the current space they occupy in a grocery store. **ELL Visual**

☐ **MAP Resources: Southeast Asia**—Students can use the resources layer in the Chapter Opener map to discuss the other resources of the region.

☐ **VIDEO Vietnam War Memorial**—After watching the video about the Vietnam War Memorial, students discuss the lasting effects of the war on the region. **AL Interpersonal**

W Writing Skills

☐ **GRAPHIC ORGANIZER Southeast Asia Colonization**—Students use the interactive graphic organizer to review the colonies of Southeast Asia under European rule.

☐ **GRAPHIC ORGANIZER Independence in Southeast Asia**—Students can use the interactive graphic organizer to review how nations gained their independence.

C Critical Thinking Skills

☐ **VIDEO Angkor Wat**—Students watch the video about Angkor Wat and discuss the relevance of the religious monument. **AL Interpersonal, Intrapersonal**

☐ **MAP Early Civilizations of Southeast Asia**—Students can use the map with locations of early civilizations to discuss the growth of empires and settlements near water.

☐ **IMAGE Islam in Southeast Asia**—Students use the photo of the mosque to discuss the development of Islam and the importance of religious structures in Southeast Asia. **BL**

☐ **MAP History of Southeast Asian Civilizations**—Students analyze the significance and impact of colonialism in different countries in the region. **AL Interpersonal**

☐ **VIDEO Modern Buddhist Monks**—Students compare and contrast the daily lives of today's Buddhist monks in different regions of Southeast Asia. **BL Verbal/Linguistic**

T Technology Skills

☐ **ONLINE SELF-CHECK QUIZ Lesson 2**—Students receive instant feedback on their mastery of lesson content.

☑ *Printable Digital Worksheets*

W Writing Skills

☐ **WORKSHEET Primary Sources: The Vietnam War**—Students can use this worksheet to analyze primary sources (first-hand accounts or letters) from soldiers in the Vietnam War.

☐ **WORKSHEET Geography Skills: Understanding Time Lines**—Students can use this worksheet to understand more about Vietnam and Cambodian history.

LIFE IN SOUTHEAST ASIA

Students will know:
- *that there are many ethnicities and languages in the region.*
- *that most people in Southeast Asia live in rural areas today, though industry is helping cities to grow.*

Students will be able to:
- *describe population patterns in Southeast Asia.*
- *describe people and cultures in the region.*
- *explore religion, the arts, and daily life in the region.*
- *examine economic issues due to rapid economic growth in the region.*
- *explore economic, environmental, and political challenges in the region.*

UNDERSTANDING
BY DESIGN®

☑ *Print Teaching Options*

V Visual Skills

☐ **P. 165** Student pairs create a Venn diagram comparing and contrasting two photographs. **AL** **ELL**

☐ **P. 169** Pairs create a two-column chart about economic and environmental challenges in Southeast Asia.

☐ **P. 169** Student pairs create a time line of the sequence of events of political challenges. **Visual/Spatial**

W Writing Skills

☐ **P. 165** Students write an essay about living in a primate city such as Manila or a megalopolis like Jakarta. **BL**

☐ **P. 166** Students describe life either in a rural or urban community in Southeast Asia. **AL** **Verbal/Linguistic**

R Reading Skills

☐ **P. 164** Students paraphrase "Population Profile."

☐ **P. 165** Students identify meaning from base words. **AL**

☐ **P. 166** Students identify the word parts of *indigenous* to understand its meaning. **ELL** **Verbal/Linguistic**

☐ **P. 167** Students act out a sport played in Southeast Asia to compare to those played in the United States. **AL** **ELL**

☐ **P. 168** Pairs list crops and indicate where they are grown.

C Critical Thinking Skills

☐ **P. 164** Student pairs analyze and present data on the population imbalance in Java. **Logical/Mathematical**

☐ **P. 167** Students draw conclusions about obstacles facing East Timor in building new schools based on its history.

☐ **P. 168** Students conduct online research about an assigned livelihood or industry and host a Southeast Asian Job Fair in which they "recruit" job seekers.

☐ **P. 168** Students infer why the small country of Singapore has grown to become a major industrial center.

T Technology Skills

☐ **P. 166** Groups research a "Culture Capsule" for an ethnic group as if addressing a team of archaeologists. **BL**

☐ **P. 167** Students use the Internet to research literacy and employment rates in an assigned region of Southeast Asia.

☑ *Online Teaching Options*

V Visual Skills

☐ **MAP** **Population: Southeast Asia**—Students can use the population layer on the Chapter Opener map to discuss the population density of this region. **Visual/Spatial**

☐ **MAP** **Resources: Southeast Asia**—Students can use the resources layer on the Chapter Opener map to discuss the resources of this region. **Visual/Spatial**

☐ **LECTURE SLIDE** **Rice Farming**—Students can use the lecture slide and videos about rice farming to discuss this aspect of life in Southeast Asia. **Visual/Spatial**

W Writing Skills

☐ **VIDEO** **Thai Economy is Booming**—Students watch the video about Thailand's growing economy and write a paragraph about one aspect of the economy that they found interesting. **BL** **Verbal/Linguistic**

☐ **IMAGE** **Minority Groups in Southeast Asia**—Students use the interactive photograph of the minority groups in Southeast Asia to discuss and write a paragraph on the various minorities living in Southeast Asia. **AL** **Interpersonal, Intrapersonal**

☐ **IMAGE** **Ecotourism**—Students write a paragraph arguing for or against the development of ecotourism in Southeast Asia. **BL** **Naturalist**

R Reading Skills

☐ **GRAPHIC ORGANIZER** **Religion in Southeast Asia**—Students can use the interactive graphic organizer to discuss the religions of the region. **Verbal/Linguistic**

☐ **GRAPHIC ORGANIZER** **Challenges in Southeast Asia**—Students can use the graphic organizer to discuss economic, environmental, and political challenges. **Verbal/Linguistic**

C Critical Thinking Skills

☐ **MAP** **Urban Southeast Asia**—Students use the interactive map to discuss the cause-effect relationship between urbanization and issues that plague modern-day cities. **BL** **Logical**

☐ **GRAPHIC ORGANIZER** **Challenges in Southeast Asia**—Students use a graphic organizer to list the economic, environmental, and political challenges facing Southeast Asia. **Logical/ Mathematical, Visual/Spatial, Verbal/Linguistic**

T Technology Skills

☐ **ONLINE SELF-CHECK QUIZ** **Lesson 3**—Students receive instant feedback on their mastery of lesson content.

INTERVENTION AND REMEDIATION STRATEGIES

LESSON 1 Physical Geography of Southeast Asia

Reading and Comprehension

Remind students that Southeast Asia can be described as a puzzle, as some of its countries have different parts that fit together to make one region. Have students analyze physical features noted in this lesson and work in pairs to create a Southeast Asia jigsaw puzzle. Tell students to refer to the chapter opener map as well as images in this lesson. Have students cut out the unlabeled pieces of their puzzle and challenge other groups to fit the pieces together.

Text Evidence

Organize students into five groups and assign them one of the following topics: landforms, resources, bodies of water, climate, and plants and animals. Have students select aspects of their topic covered in the text or conduct online research to learn more about it. Ask groups to come up with at least two questions about their topic to answer in a short report. For example, students might ask: *How different are the temperatures at the top of Puncak Jaya and in Southeast Asia's tropical regions?* Then have groups present their analyses to the class.

LESSON 2 History of Southeast Asia

Reading and Comprehension

Have students skim the lesson to look for unfamiliar or confusing words or phrases. Clarify the meaning of phrases such as "It also made the region prey for foreign powers. . . ." (page 156, paragraph 1). Tell students to look up the words using a print or online dictionary to define the words. Have student pairs play the dictionary game in which one student reads either a real or made up definition, and partners guess which is the real definition.

Text Evidence

Organize students into four groups and assign them the following topics: trading societies, agricultural societies, Islamic states, and European traders. Have each group create posters to describe their topic. Posters should depict facts about the topic based on evidence in the text, or from additional research, and should answer the following questions: *Where did this group live, or migrate to? What was their way of life? How did they dress? What did they eat?* Have groups present their findings to the class.

LESSON 3 Life in Southeast Asia

Reading and Comprehension

To ensure comprehension of the issues and challenges discussed in this lesson, have students create visual flash cards for each content vocabulary term. Have student pairs quiz each other using a picture on one side and the definition of the term on the other. Then have students write sentences using each term. Ask volunteers to read their sentences and explain how the term relates to lesson content.

Text Evidence

Have student groups work together to summarize one of the challenges discussed in this lesson such as issues relating to the consequences of economic growth. Have students in each group summarize the problems related to their topic and how or if the problems are being solved. For example, students may discuss the gap between rich and poor, or how urbanization has led to overcrowding and water shortages. Encourage students to use content vocabulary terms in their summaries.

Online Resources

Level Reader

Use this online lower-level text that corresponds directly to the text in the online Student Edition.

Guided Reading Activities

This resource uses graphic organizers and guiding questions to help students with comprehension.

What Do You Know?

Use these worksheets to pre-assess students' background knowledge before they read the chapter.

Reading Essentials and Study Guide Workbook

This resource offers writing and reading activities for the approaching-level student.

Self-Check Quizzes

This online assessment tool provides instant feedback for students to check their progress.

SOUTHEAST ASIA

ESSENTIAL QUESTIONS • *How does geography influence the way people live?*
• *What makes a culture unique?* • *Why does conflict develop?*

©ADRESS LATIF/X90022/Reuters/Corbis

Royal guard at the Grand Palace in Bangkok, Thailand

networks

There's More Online about Southeast Asia.

CHAPTER 5

Lesson 1
Physical Geography of Southeast Asia

Lesson 2
History of Southeast Asia

Lesson 3
Life in Southeast Asia

The Story Matters...

Southeast Asia is made up of a mainland and hundreds of islands. The mainland has several mountain ranges, coastal plains, and major rivers. The islands also have varied landforms, but their rivers are short and steep. Shaped by tectonic plate movements, these islands have many active volcanoes. Today, plate movements cause dangerous earthquakes, sometimes generating tsunamis. Recovering from such natural disasters presents many challenges to the people of the region.

FOLDABLES
Study Organizer

Go to the Foldables® library in the back of your book to make a Foldable® that will help you take notes while reading this chapter.

147

ENGAGE

Bellringer Point to a political map of Southeast Asia, noting the location of the region in relation to the Equator. Have students locate each country and have them consider how life in the region is affected by its geographic location. Call on volunteers to infer what characteristics these regions might share due to their location. *(Sample response: the countries may have a hot and humid climate due to their proximity to the Equator.)* Then call on other volunteers to list features that are unique to certain countries shown on the map. *(Examples: Laos is surrounded by land, or landlocked; Indonesia is made up of several large islands; the Philippines are made up of several smaller islands.)*

Making Connections Have students read "The Story Matters..." and have them recall what they have learned about tectonic plates. *(Plates are layers of the Earth's crust that shift or collide and create seismic activity such as earthquakes and volcanoes.)* Explain that many of Southeast Asia's islands are located in a region known as the Ring of Fire due to its volcanic activity. **Ask: How do you think this location affects people who live on Southeast Asia's islands?** *(Students may conclude that people in this region face frequent earthquakes and volcanic eruptions, and may have to relocate or rebuild their homes due to damage caused by these natural disasters.)*

Ask students to think about what life would be like in a region with hundreds of islands. Begin with the issue of transportation and have students describe what they think this would be like and how it might affect daily life. *(Students should consider transportation of people and goods, noting that the main way to transport goods from one island to another would be by ship. While some items would be relatively easy to ship and might not be expensive, other items , like cars and heavy machinery would be very costly, leading to less availability or much higher prices.)* Guide students in a discussion that considers how one aspect of life impacts others. For example, if people do not routinely travel among the islands then they may become more isolated.

Tell students that they will learn more about the unique features and cultures of countries in Southeast Asia in this chapter.

FOLDABLES
Study Organizer

Go to the Foldables® library for a cumulative chapter-based Foldable® activity that your students can use to help take notes and prepare for assessment.

Letter from the Author

Dear Geography Teacher,

In this chapter, students will learn how precarious life is in Southeast Asia. Southeast Asia is located in the Ring of Fire. Most of the people in Southeast Asia live in concentrated areas on the coastal lowlands. The lowlands support agriculture and contain large urban areas. The lowlands are also vulnerable to flooding and storm surges from typhoons and tsunamis. In December 2004, an earthquake occurred off of Indonesia launching a tsunami that killed more than 225,000 people.

TEACH & ASSESS

Step Into the Place

V Visual Skills

Reading a Map Have students read the introductory paragraph and look at the map. Explain that this map shows the countries of Southeast Asia. Have students use the map to answer the following questions as well as the Step Into the Place questions. **Ask:**

- **What countries are located on the Indochina Peninsula?** *(northern Myanmar (Burma), northern Thailand, Cambodia, Laos, and Vietnam)*
- **What countries are located on the Malay Peninsula?** *(southeastern Myanmar (Burma), southern Thailand, West Malaysia, and Singapore)*
- **How are the two peninsulas different?** *(The Indochina Peninsula is much larger and wider.)*
- **What do most of the capital cities have in common in this region?** *(Almost all of them are either on the coast or very close to the coast.)* **AL ELL Visual/Spatial**

Content Background Knowledge

- The country of Myanmar officially changed its name from Burma in 1989. The region—rich in natural resources such as jade, gold, and timber—has endured years of ethnic conflict, displacing thousands of villagers who have fled to nearby China.
- With its hundreds of islands and coastline, Southeast Asia is home to some of the world's most beautiful beaches, such as Bali, Indonesia, and Langkawi, Malaysia.
- The island community of Phuket, Thailand, was settled as early as the 1st century B.C., and has become a major seaside resort that draws many tourists every year. Its large harbor serves as the commercial center of Thailand, which specializes in both exports and imports with Malaysia, Singapore, and Myanmar. The city airport has regular flights to Bangkok, making it easily accessible to both tourists and business travelers.

ANSWERS, p. 148

STEP INTO THE PLACE

1. Phnom Penh
2. the Philippines
3. west
4. **CRITICAL THINKING** A landlocked country is entirely surrounded by land. Laos is a landlocked country.

> **V** Two peninsulas form Southeast Asia's mainland—the Indochina and the Malay Peninsulas. Like the mainland, most of the region's islands are mountainous.

Step Into the Place

MAP FOCUS Use the map to answer the following questions.

1 **THE GEOGRAPHER'S WORLD**
What is the capital of Cambodia?

2 **THE GEOGRAPHER'S WORLD**
In what country is the city of Manila located?

3 **THE GEOGRAPHER'S WORLD**
In which direction would you travel to go from Hanoi to Mandalay?

4 **CRITICAL THINKING**
Describing What does it mean to say a country is "landlocked"? Does Southeast Asia have any landlocked countries?

A **URBAN SKYLINE** Skyscrapers dominate Jakarta, the capital and leading economic center of Indonesia. With more than 11 million people, Jakarta has the largest population of any city in Southeast Asia.

B **FLOATING MARKET** Fruit and vegetable dealers sell their wares from boats on Inya Lake in Myanmar (Burma). The artificial lake was created in the 1880s to provide water to Yangon (Rangoon), the capital.

Step Into the Time

TIME LINE Choose an event from the time line and write a paragraph predicting the social, political, or economic causes and effects of that event.
WRST.6-8.2, WRST.6-8.4

802 A.D. Khmer empire, based in what is now Cambodia, rules much of region

939 Vietnam becomes semi-independent from China after 1,000 years of domination

c. 1150 King Suryavarman II has the Angkor Wat temple built in Cambodia

1565 The Spanish establish their first settlement in the Philippines

1000 1100 1500

148 Chapter 5

(t to b) ©Jose Fuste Raga/Corbis; Mariano Pozo/age fotostock; ©Pascal Deloche/Godong/Corbis

---

Project-Based Learning ✋

Hands-On

Creating Time Lines
Students will work in groups to create illustrated time lines of a country in Southeast Asia. Time lines should list facts about the country's history and include current events. Time lines might contain photos from the Internet that reflect events in the country's history. Each group will present their time lines to the class. Display completed time lines in a hallway or other public area in the school.

Digital Hands-On

Creating Digital Presentations
Students will work in groups to prepare web-based notes on a collaborative, online writing platform about the countries of Southeast Asia. Each group should then create a collaborative digital presentation that includes photos with captions and videos. Students will share their projects with each group, and groups will then leave audio or text comments on each other's presentation.

edtechteacher
21st Century Learning

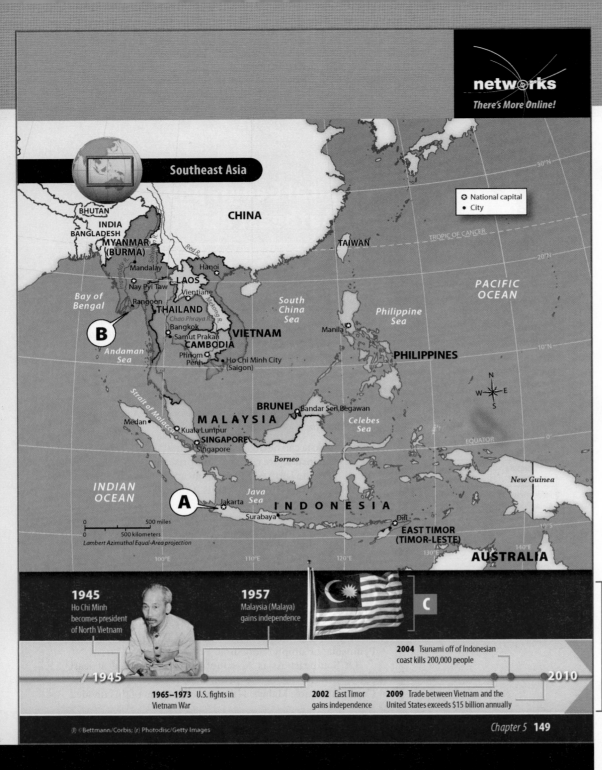

Southeast Asia

- National capital
- City

BHUTAN
INDIA
BANGLADESH
MYANMAR
(BURMA)
CHINA
TAIWAN
Mandalay
Hanoi
LAOS
Nay Pyi Taw
Vientiane
Bay of
Bengal
Rangoon
THAILAND
Chao Phraya R.
PACIFIC
OCEAN
B
Bangkok
Samut Prakan
CAMBODIA
VIETNAM
South
China
Sea
Philippine
Sea
Andaman
Sea
Phnom
Penh
Ho Chi Minh City
(Saigon)
Manila
PHILIPPINES
Strait of Malacca
BRUNEI
Bandar Seri Begawan
MALAYSIA
Celebes
Sea
Medan
Kuala Lumpur
SINGAPORE
Singapore
EQUATOR
Borneo
New Guinea
INDIAN
OCEAN
Java
Sea
A
Jakarta
INDONESIA
Surabaya
Dili
EAST TIMOR
(TIMOR-LESTE)
AUSTRALIA

0   500 miles
0   500 kilometers
Lambert Azimuthal Equal-Area projection

1945
Ho Chi Minh
becomes president
of North Vietnam

1957
Malaysia (Malaya)
gains independence

C

2004 Tsunami off of Indonesian
coast kills 200,000 people

1945   2010

1965–1973 U.S. fights in
Vietnam War

2002 East Timor
gains independence

2009 Trade between Vietnam and the
United States exceeds $15 billion annually

(l) ©Bettmann/Corbis; (r) Photodisc/Getty Images

Chapter 5 **149**

Step Into the Time

V Visual Skills

Reading a Time Line Have students review the time line and images. As a class, discuss its major points of interest. **Ask:**

- **What can you infer about relations between Vietnam and China in the early part of the first century (1000 A.D.)?** *(Sample response: Relations between the two countries were probably tense as Vietnam had just gained its independence.)*
- **When did the Spanish set up their first settlement in the Philippines?** *(1565)*
- **How many years did United States troops fight in the Vietnam War?** *(eight years)* **BL** **Logical/Mathematical**

C Critical Thinking Skills

Making Inferences Point out the item on the time line dated 1957. Explain to students that Malaysia contained a number of British territories, including the island of Singapore. In 1965 the island of Singapore seceded, or broke away, from Malaysia and became its own country, ruled as an independent republic. Have students consider what challenges a newly independent country might face. **Ask: What challenges do you think Singapore faced when it became an independent country?** *(Students should infer that Singapore may have struggled with its new independent status having been under British and Malaysian rule.)*

Tell students that in an effort to bring economic stability to the region, Singapore joined other countries in forming the Association of Southeast Asian Nations (ASEAN) in 1967.
BL **Verbal/Linguistic**

V

CLOSE & REFLECT

Formulating Questions Have students generate a list of questions they have about Southeast Asia based on the chapter introduction. Tell students to fill in the answers to these questions as they read the chapter.

TIME LINE AND MAP

Reading a Time Line and Map

Analzying Maps Display the interactive time line and map on the whiteboard. Have volunteers read each event as it is revealed on the time line. Ask students to identify where in Southeast Asia the event took place and find its location on the map. **AL** **ELL** **Visual/Spatial**

See page 147B for other online activities.

ENGAGE

🔔 **Bellringer** Note that Southeast Asia contains many islands. Guide a class discussion about the various challenges faced by people who live on an island. **Ask: How might living on an island influence the way people live?** (*Answers will vary but might mention factors such as tides and storms, transportation costs, isolation, or industries such as fishing.*) Then read the Essential Question and the "It Matters Because" statement. Have students brainstorm some challenges people might face when living in island communities of Southeast Asia.

TEACH & ASSESS

C Critical Thinking Skills

Making Inferences Remind students that Southeast Asia is made up of mainland landforms as well as many islands. **Ask:**

- **What advantages might people have when living on the mainland?** (*Possible response: The mainland is closer to China and India, which might make it easier to trade and communicate with those two countries.*)
- **What advantages might people have when living in the island communities of Southeast Asia?** (*Possible response: Being on an island located near waterways may help shipping and trade because of easy access to ports.*)
  BL Visual/Spatial, Logical/Mathematical

R Reading Skills

Applying Point out the word *insular* and read the parenthetical information aloud to students. Explain that in addition to the technical meaning of insular as it pertains to geography, the word has other meanings. Have students look up the word in a dictionary and identify the other definitions. **Ask: How do the other meanings relate to the technical meaning of *insular* in terms of geography?** (*The meanings "remote, or detached" and "isolated or separated" relate to islands, which also can be described as "remote, detached, or isolated."*) Have students use the term *insular* in a sentence that does not relate to the geographical meaning of the word. **AL** **ELL** Verbal/Linguistic

---

ANSWER, p. 150

Taking Notes Indochinese Peninsula and Malay Peninsula: Cambodia, Laos, Malaysia, Myanmar (Burma), Thailand, and Vietnam; Singapore, which occupies an island connected by a causeway to the peninsula's southern tip, could also be included; **Borneo:** Indonesia, Malaysia, and Brunei; **New Guinea:** Indonesia and Papua New Guinea; **Java:** Indonesia; **Timor:** Indonesia and East Timor; **Luzon:** The Philippines.

---

networks

There's More Online!

- ☑ **IMAGE** Indonesian Tsunami
- ☑ **MAP** Malaysia/Indonesian Islands
- ☑ **SLIDE SHOW** Wildlife of Southeast Asia
- ☑ **VIDEO**

Reading HELPDESK

Academic Vocabulary RH.6-8.4
(Tier Two Words)
- **commodity**

Content Vocabulary RH.6-8.4
(Tier Three Words)
- **insular**
- **flora**
- **fauna**
- **endemic**

TAKING NOTES: *Key Ideas and Details* RH.6-8.1, RH.6-8.7

Identify As you read the lesson, use a graphic organizer like this one to identify the countries that occupy or share the region's main peninsulas and islands.

Peninsula or Island	Country or Countries
Indochinese and Malay Peninsulas	
Borneo	
New Guinea	
Java	
Timor	
Luzon	

150

Lesson 1
Physical Geography of Southeast Asia

ESSENTIAL QUESTION · *How does geography influence the way people live?*

IT MATTERS BECAUSE

Southeast Asia is like a challenging puzzle. Some of its main pieces, its countries, are divided into smaller pieces. Learning how the region's pieces fit together will help you answer a question geographers ask: What makes it a region?

Landforms and Resources

C

R

GUIDING QUESTION *How are the landforms of Southeast Asia's mainland different from the landforms of its islands?*

Southeast Asia can be divided into two main parts: a mainland area and an **insular** area, an area comprised of islands. (*Insular* comes from the Latin word *insula*, meaning "island." Another term that comes from *insula* is *peninsula*, which means "almost an island.")

The mainland sits at the southeastern corner of the Asian continent, bordering the world's two most populous countries: China and India. In this area, where the Indian Ocean meets the Pacific, thousands of islands stretch across miles of tropical waters.

Peninsulas and Islands

Most of the mainland occupies a large peninsula that juts southward from the Asian continent. Located between India and China, this extension of land is known as the Indochinese Peninsula, or simply Indochina.

Of Southeast Asia's 11 countries, 6 are located at least partly on the mainland peninsulas. These countries are Cambodia, Laos, Malaysia (the western region of this divided

---

networks *Online Teaching Options*

▶ VIDEO

Around the World—Borneo

Evaluating Use this video about the physical geography, climate, and wildlife of Borneo, located in Southeast Asia, to introduce the lesson. After watching the video, have students evaluate the information presented. In pairs, ask students to share one or two key facts that they found interesting or surprising. **AL** Visual/Spatial

See page 147C for other online activities.

country), Myanmar (also known as Burma), Thailand, and Vietnam. The tiny island country of Singapore sits just off the southern tip of the Malay Peninsula. A bridge connects Singapore's main island to the peninsula.

The region's other four countries, along with the eastern part of Malaysia, occupy islands in the vast Malay Archipelago. Larger in area than any other island group in the world, it contains more than 24,000 islands, stretching from mainland Southeast Asia to Australia. Among the islands are 7 that rank among the 20 largest in the world: New Guinea, Borneo, Sumatra, Sulawesi, Java, Luzon, and Mindanao.

More than 17,000 of the islands in the Malay Archipelago are part of Indonesia, which is by far the largest country in Southeast Asia. Indonesia shares the islands of Timor, New Guinea, and Borneo with other countries. East Timor, one of the world's newest countries, occupies the eastern half of Timor. Malaysia's eastern region spreads across northern Borneo and surrounds the small country of Brunei.

The northernmost islands in the Malay Archipelago are the Philippines, which form their own archipelago east of the mainland. The Philippines are a country of more than 7,000 islands and islets.

Mountains and Volcanoes

Much of the land in Southeast Asia is rugged and mountainous. On the mainland, mountain ranges generally have a north-south orientation. They include a group of ranges along the western edge of Myanmar that follow the border between Myanmar and Thailand and form the backbone of the Malay Peninsula. The Annamese Cordillera, a range that stretches through Laos and Vietnam, runs parallel to the mainland's eastern coast.

Many of the mountains on Southeast Asia's islands have volcanic origins. The islands lie along the Ring of Fire, a seismically active zone that encircles much of the Pacific Ocean. Most of the world's earthquakes and volcanic eruptions occur within this belt.

Cyril Ruoso/National Geographic Stock

This aerial view of Komodo National Park in Indonesia reveals that mountainous islands are a major part of the landscape in Southeast Asia.

Identifying What Southeast Asian island group has a larger area than any other island group in the world?

Chapter 5 **151**

R1 Reading Skills

Defining Review with students the meaning of *archipelago* (a group of islands). Have students identify the Malay Archipelago on a map. **AL** **Visual/Spatial**

R2 Reading Skills

Identifying Students may have trouble pronouncing the names of islands in Southeast Asia. Read aloud the seven largest islands, modeling correct pronunciation (noo GIH-nee, BORN ee-yo, soo MAH-tra, soo lah WAY-see, JAH-vah, \lü-zän\, min də-nä-ō). Have student volunteers identify and point to the location on the political map as you say the name of each island. **ELL** **Verbal/Linguistic**

V Visual Skills

Interpreting and Calculating Have students work in pairs to make an educated guess as to how many miles of coastline the islands of Southeast Asia include. Tell students to refer to the bar scale on the political map of Southeast Asia in the chapter opener to calculate the mileage. **Ask: Which country in Southeast Asia has the most miles of coastline?** *(Indonesia)* **Logical/Mathematical, Visual/Spatial**

C Critical Thinking Skills

Making Inferences Have students analyze the photograph, noting the various mountain ranges and their location. **Ask:**

- **How do you think living in regions along the Ring of Fire affect daily life?** *(Students' responses will vary but should discuss how the close proximity of mountain ranges to bodies of water would likely cause tsunamis during seismic activity such as earthquakes.)*
- **What is one way that island communities can be ready for a tsunami?** *(Students' responses may vary. Students may infer that coastal communities have alarms sound when a tsunami is approaching, or they may have emergency preparedness drills to map the quickest routes to higher ground, and so on.)* **Logical/Mathematical**

MAP

Malaysia/Indonesian Islands

Listing Use the map to help students visualize the regions of Malaysia and the Indonesian Islands. Guide a class discussion to help students understand some of the unique features of these landforms. Make a list of the features on the board. Then end the discussion by asking volunteers to point out each of the features listed. **ELL** **Visual/Spatial, Verbal/Linguistic**

See page 147C for other online activities.

ANSWER, p. 151

Identifying the Malay Archipelago, containing more than 24,000 islands, stretching from mainland Southeast Asia to Australia

C Critical Thinking Skills

Determining Cause and Effect Have students describe the cause and effect of all the tension and pressure on Earth's crust in Southeast Asia. *(Cause: Four major plates meet in this region. Effect: The plates have broken up and created many islands and volcanoes.)* **BL** Logical/Mathematical

R Reading Skills

Summarizing Help students summarize the information about Indonesia's active volcanoes by focusing on their impact. **Ask:**

• What happened in 1883? *(The famous volcano Krakatoa erupted and collapsed into the sea, causing a tsunami that killed about 36,000 people.)*

• What happened as a result of the earthquake in 2004? *(A devastating tsunami hit the coast, killing more than 230,000 people.)* **AL** Verbal/Linguistic

W Writing Skills

Informative/Explanatory Have students imagine they are news reporters at the scene of one of the deadly tsunamis mentioned in the text. Tell students to write a news report detailing the devastation. Students may need to do research for additional information to include. **Verbal/Linguistic**

T Technology Skills

Researching on the Internet and Using Visual Aids Assign small groups to research countries in Southeast Asia to identify which natural resources are prevalent and scarce in their assigned country. Have students use a software presentation program to present visuals and facts about their assigned region's natural resources. Encourage students to show pictures demonstrating how the resources are used. Students' research should answer a self-generated question as well as the following questions:

• **What items are made from natural resources in this region?**

• **How has the production of these natural resources impacted the region?**

• **What are some local businesses that benefit from the natural resources?**

• **What are some ways that the country protects its natural resources?** **BL** Naturalist

---

ANSWERS, p. 152

CRITICAL THINKING Volcanic flows leave rich, fertile soil suitable for growing crops.

✓ **READING PROGRESS CHECK** Because of the location along the Ring of Fire, the area is rich in natural resources, such as metals and gemstones. This wealth has helped in the development of the region.

A farmer tends to his rice crop near Mount Mayon, the most active volcano in the Philippines.
▶ **CRITICAL THINKING**
Analyzing Despite the dangers, how do farmers in the region benefit from volcanic eruptions?

T

Academic Vocabulary

commodity a material, resource, or product that is bought and sold

In Southeast Asia, four major plates meet: the Eurasian Plate, the Indo-Australian Plate, the Pacific Plate, and the Indian Plate. The pressures and tensions produced by the meeting of these plates have fractured Earth's crust into many smaller plates across the region. This action has also produced the many islands and the fractured geography, as well as the volcanoes.

C

Indonesia has more than 100 active volcanoes—more than any other country in the world. Most are in a long arc along the country's southern edge. One of the most famous volcanoes, Krakatoa, lies between the islands of Sumatra and Java. In 1883 Krakatoa erupted and collapsed into the sea, triggering tsunamis that claimed about 36,000 lives.

R

An even deadlier tsunami occurred in Indonesia in 2004. A powerful undersea earthquake off the coast of Sumatra produced huge waves that slammed into coastal areas of Southeast and South Asia, causing more than 230,000 deaths.

W

Natural Resources

Southeast Asia possesses a rich variety of mineral resources, including tin, copper, lead, zinc, gold, and gemstones such as rubies and sapphires. Indonesia, Malaysia, and Thailand rank among the world's top tin producers, with Indonesia accounting for roughly a fourth of the total world production of this **commodity**.

Teak, mahogany, ebony, and other hardwood trees that grow in Southeast Asia's tropical forests have long been in high demand. Many of the region's countries export wood and wood products. To combat deforestation, some countries have restricted logging.

Southeast Asia is also rich in fossil fuels. Indonesia and Malaysia rank among the top 30 countries in the world in oil reserves and production. They rank among the top 15 in natural gas reserves and production.

✓ **READING PROGRESS CHECK**

Analyzing What effect has the Ring of Fire had on the formation of the region?

Bodies of Water

GUIDING QUESTION *Why does Southeast Asia have so many different seas?*

Bodies of water are key parts of Southeast Asia's geography and identity. The region encompasses about 5 million square miles (13 million sq. km), but only a third of the area is land.

Per-Andre Hoffmann/Picture Press/Getty Images

---

netw⊙rks *Online Teaching Options*

MAP

Volcanoes in Southeast Asia

Discussing Use the map to lead a class discussion that focuses on the density of volcanoes in Southeast Asia and the statistics of volcanoes in the region. Have students review and explain the characteristics of a volcanic explosion and how it affects the surrounding communities.
AL Naturalist, Interpersonal

See page 147C for other online activities.

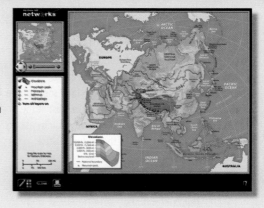

Oceans and Seas

The Malay Peninsula and Indonesia's Sunda Isles represent the boundary between two oceans. To the west and south lies the Indian Ocean, and to the north and east lies the Pacific Ocean. The region's largest seas are the South China Sea and the Philippine Sea. West of the Malaysian Peninsula lies the Andaman Sea.

Some of the busiest lanes in the world pass through Southeast Asia's seas and their waterways. About a quarter of the world's trade, including half of all sea shipments of oil, goes through the Strait of Malacca, which links the South China and Andaman Seas. As a result, Singapore, which controls the Strait of Malacca, has become one of the most important ports in the world.

V₁

River Systems

Southeast Asia's longest and most important rivers are on the mainland. Most rain flows into one of five major rivers. From west to east, the rivers are the Irrawaddy, Salween, Chao Phraya, Mekong, and Red. Each river generally flows from highlands in the north to lowlands in the south before emptying into the sea.

The Irrawaddy, Salween, and Mekong begin high on the Plateau of Tibet. The Irrawaddy flows almost straight south through a valley in Myanmar's center. The river plays a major role in the region's transportation system. Its vast fertile delta is important for farming.

V₂

The Salween runs southward through the eastern part of Myanmar, forming part of that country's border with Thailand. Like the Irawaddy, it drains into the Andaman Sea. The Mekong is Southeast Asia's longest river. It twists and turns for about 2,700 miles (4,345 km) through or near Myanmar, Thailand, Laos, Cambodia, and Vietnam. The river's drainage basin is twice the size of California, and its enormous delta is one of the world's most productive agricultural regions.

The port city of Banda Aceh in Indonesia suffered great damage from a tsunami that struck on December 26, 2004.

☑ **READING PROGRESS CHECK**

Analyzing Why do you think Southeast Asia's longest rivers are found on the mainland and not on islands?

Eugene Hoshiko/AP Images

Chapter 5 **153**

IMAGE

© Image Source/Getty Images

Indonesian Tsunami

Determining Cause and Effect Use the interactive image of the destruction in Indonesia post-tsunami to discuss the damage that this natural disaster can cause. Ask a small group of volunteers to research deadly tsunamis that have occurred over the last twenty years. Then use the groups' research to guide a class discussion about the causes of tsunamis *(land and underwater earthquakes)* and the effects of tsunamis *(damage to coastal areas, homes, boats, loss of life, etc.)* **BL**
Logical/Mathematical, Interpersonal

See page 147C for other online activities.

Interactive Photos

V₁ Visual Skills

Creating Visuals Have students visualize the different bodies of water and where they are located. **Ask: What are the two largest seas in the region?** *(the South China Sea and the Philippine Sea)*

Have students create a simple sketch of each body of water mentioned in the text. Tell students not to write the name of the body of water, but to label nearby landforms and other bodies of water as clues. Have students work with a partner to play "Where's That Body of Water?" in which partners quiz each other using their sketches. **Visual/Spatial**

V₂ Visual Skills

Creating Charts As students read the information about Southeast Asia's important rivers, have them create and complete a three-column chart like the one below to organize the information in the text. Have students conduct online research to find more information about the rivers to complete the chart. **Visual/Spatial**

River	Location and Flow	Importance
Irrawaddy	*high on plateau of Tibet, flows south through Myanmar; drains into Andaman Sea*	*major transportation route, fertile delta good for farming*
Salween	*high on plateau of Tibet, flows south forming part of border with Thailand; drains into Andaman Sea*	
Chao Phraya	*high on plateau of Tibet*	
Mekong	*winds through or near Myanmar, Thailand, Laos, Cambodia, and Vietnam*	*longest river in Southeast Asia; delta is productive agricultural region*
Red	*from highlands in north to lowlands in south*	

ANSWER, p. 153

☑ **READING PROGRESS CHECK** The region's mainland area is significantly larger than even the largest island, Borneo. Also, some rivers on the mainland flow long distances through China before they even enter Southeast Asia. Lastly, most of the region's islands have mountainous centers, and rivers are limited in length by the distance from the mountains where they originate to the coast.

C Critical Thinking Skills

Sequencing Have students analyze the photograph and read the caption. **Ask: What is latex?** *(a milky liquid harvested from rubber tree plants)*

C

Have students use reliable online sources to research the process of latex harvesting in Indonesia. Tell students to create a flow chart that shows the sequence of events in the harvesting process. Encourage students to include pictures or other types of diagrams in their flow charts. Ask volunteers to present their charts to the class. **BL** **Logical/Mathematical**

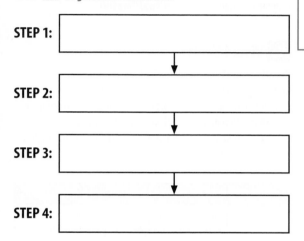

STEP 1: [ ]

↓

STEP 2: [ ]

↓

STEP 3: [ ]

↓

STEP 4: [ ]

R1 Reading Skills

Explaining As they read the section "A Tropical Region," have students visualize the different air currents discussed. **Ask:**

- **What brings rain and warm air to islands and the mainland?** *(The sun's direct rays and low pressure bring monsoon winds, as well as warm air and rain to the region.)*
- **How does the sea affect temperature?** *(It makes the temperature milder.)*
- **Why are there glaciers in Puncak Jaya even though it is near the Equator?** *(It has a high elevation.)* **Verbal/ Linguistic**

R2 Reading Skills

Identifying After reading "A Tropical Region," have students identify comparative and superlative words. *(hottest, most, cooler, drier, highest)* Explain that these words show comparison. Model an example such as, "The temperature in this room is *cooler* than it is outside." Have students work in pairs to practice using these and other words that show comparisons. **ELL** **Verbal/Linguistic**

ANSWER, p. 154

CRITICAL THINKING Climates in Southeast Asia are generally hot and humid, allowing for an abundance of plant life, including rubber trees.

A plantation worker in Indonesia gathers latex, a milky liquid tapped from rubber trees. The latex is eventually refined into useable rubber.

▶ **CRITICAL THINKING**
Analyzing Why do rubber trees and plants grow so well in Indonesia and other parts of Southeast Asia?

Climate, Vegetation, and Wildlife

GUIDING QUESTION *In what ways does Southeast Asia's location shape its climate?*

Climates in Southeast Asia are generally hot and humid. Much of the region receives more than 60 inches (152 cm) of rain fall each year. Because of these weather conditions and the variety of habitats in Southeast Asia, the region is home to an astonishing abundance of plant and animal life.

A Tropical Region

Latitude and air currents play major roles in shaping Southeast Asia's climates. Nearly the entire region lies within the Tropics—the zone that receives the hottest, most direct rays of the sun. From November to March, the direct rays of the sun are south of the Equator in the Southern Hemisphere. This produces areas of low pressure that draw monsoon winds that blow across the region from the northeast to the southwest. These winds bring cooler, drier air to much of the mainland but deliver heavy rains to the southern Malay Peninsula and to the islands. From May to September, the pattern reverses. The direct rays of the sun and the associated low pressure are north of the Equator. This causes monsoon winds to blow from the southwest to the northeast, bringing warm air and rain to the islands and the mainland.

R1

Most of the region's land is surrounded or nearly surrounded by the sea, which has a moderating effect on air temperatures. Elevation also affects weather conditions. Temperatures in the highland areas are generally cooler than in the lowland areas. At the top of Indonesia's highest peak, Puncak Jaya (PUHN-chock JAH-yuh), which is close to the Equator, glaciers are visible.

R2

(vertical text) JUSTIN GUARIGLIA/National Geographic Stock

154 Chapter 5

---

networks   *Online Teaching Options*

SLIDE SHOW

Wildlife of Southeast Asia

Describing Use the slide show of various plants and animals to discuss the wildlife of the region. Then tell students to guide a "Southeast Asian Safari" in which they pretend to spot one of the plants or animals in the wild. Acting as the safari tour guide, students should describe characteristics of the plant or animal to the class. Students may wish to conduct additional research about their chosen plant or animal. **AL** **Kinesthetic**

Slide Show

(vertical text) (l) ©Ocean/Corbis, ©Kryssia Campos/Getty Images, (tr) Erica Simone Leeds, (br) ©JG Photography/Alamy

See page 147C for other online activities.

The sea, the elevation, and air currents combine to create four climate zones. The southern Malay Peninsula, the southern Philippines, and most of Indonesia have a tropical rain forest climate. A tropical monsoon climate, with rainy and dry seasons, prevails in the northern Philippines, the northern Malay Peninsula, and coastal areas of the mainland. Most inland areas fall within a tropical savanna climate zone with less distinct rainy and dry seasons. The northernmost mainland has a humid subtropical climate in which summers are hot and wet and winters are mild and dry.

Weather in Southeast Asia sometimes turns deadly. Intense tropical storms called typhoons form over warm Pacific Ocean waters and slowly spin westward, often targeting the Philippines. With winds that can exceed 150 miles (241 km) per hour and torrential rains that sometimes continue for days, typhoons can wipe out homes and buildings, cause devastating floods, destroy crops, and kill large numbers of people.

Plants and Animals

Few places in the world rival Southeast Asia in diversity of **flora**, or plant life. Indonesia, for example, has more than 40,000 species of flowering plants, including about 5,000 species of orchids and more than 3,000 species of trees.

Blanketing much of the region are either tropical rain forests or forests with a mix of evergreen and deciduous trees. In coastal areas, forests of mangrove trees, which have aboveground roots, form a border between land and sea.

Southeast Asia's **fauna**, or animal life, consists of a wide variety of animals. Many species, including mammals, birds, fish, and insects, are **endemic**, or found nowhere else in the world. Fires, logging, mining, agriculture, and poaching have reduced the habitat of many animals.

☑ **READING PROGRESS CHECK**

Identifying What are three factors that affect climate in Southeast Asia?

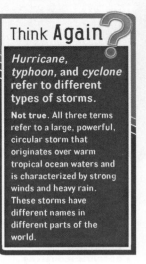

Think Again?

Hurricane, typhoon, and *cyclone* refer to different types of storms.

Not true. All three terms refer to a large, powerful, circular storm that originates over warm tropical ocean waters and is characterized by strong winds and heavy rain. These storms have different names in different parts of the world.

FOLDABLES
Study Organizer

Include this lesson's information in your Foldable®.

LESSON 1 REVIEW (CCSS)

Reviewing Vocabulary (Tier Three Words)
1. What peninsula forms a long bridge between mainland and *insular* Southeast Asia? RH.6-8.4

Answering the Guiding Questions
2. *Identifying* What are some of Southeast Asia's most important mineral resources? RH.6-8.1

3. *Analyzing* Why are most of Indonesia's volcanoes located along its southern edge? RH.6-8.1

4. *Analyzing* What is the connection between Singapore's status as one of the most important ports in the world and its location at the southern end of the Strait of Malacca? RH.6-8.1

5. *Describing* How do monsoon winds cause wet and dry seasons on Southeast Asia's mainland? RH.6-8.5

6. *Argument Writing* Write a persuasive letter urging the government leaders of Southeast Asia to take urgent action to protect the region's tropical forests from uncontrolled logging. Discuss the importance of the forests and the consequences of deforestation. WHST.6-8.1, WHST.6-8.4

Chapter 5 **155**

LESSON 1 REVIEW ANSWERS

Reviewing Vocabulary

1. the Malay Peninsula

Answering the Guiding Questions

2. *Identifying* Possible answers include tin, copper, lead, zinc, gold, and gemstones such as rubies and sapphires.

3. *Analyzing* The country's southern edge lies along the boundary between two tectonic plates.

4. *Analyzing* The strait is a busy and important waterway. An estimated one-quarter of the world's trade and half of all sea shipments of oil pass through it.

5. *Describing* From November to March, monsoon winds blow across the mainland, which makes the air cool and dry. From May to September, the winds blow across the warm ocean waters, bringing abundant rainfall.

6. *Argument Writing* Students' answers should be supported by information about the effects of deforestation included in the text.

V Visual Skills

Simulating Help students visualize the different climate zones in Southeast Asia. Organize students into four groups and give each group a folded piece of paper with one of the four climate zones written on it: *tropical rain forest, tropical monsoon, tropical savanna,* and *humid subtropical.* Using labeled paper on desks to specify certain regions or countries, organize the classroom into a map of Southeast Asia *(southern Malay peninsula, northern Malay peninsula, Philippines, and so on)*. Have groups use information in the text about Southeast Asia's climate zones to arrange themselves in the proper location. For example, students in the tropical rain forest group should stand at the southern Malay Peninsula, the southern Philippines, and Indonesia. After all zones have been filled, discuss the climate in each region. **Kinesthetic**

W Writing Skills

Argument Have students write a paragraph to answer the following prompt: **Should some of Southeast Asia's rain forest be designated as protected land? Why or why not?** Tell students to support their arguments using research-based evidence. **BL** **Verbal/Linguistic**

Content Background Knowledge

Orangutans The Southeast Asian islands of Sumatra and Borneo are home to orangutans, large apes that live in the rain forests. Like gorillas and chimpanzees, orangutans are intelligent and have the ability to reason and problem solve. Much of their time is spent looking for fruit and insects by swinging through the forests from limb to limb with their long, strong arms. Adult male orangutans can grow to over four feet tall and can weigh almost three hundred pounds. The word orangutan in Malaysian means "person of the forest." Orangutans are threatened with extinction because of human activity such as logging and mining.

CLOSE & REFLECT

Summarizing Have students consider this lesson's Essential Question: *How does geography influence the way people live?* Tell students to look back at the images in this lesson and write a brief summarizing answer to the question. Encourage students to think about how landforms and waterways, climate, and natural resources affect the way people live.

ANSWER, p. 155

☑ **READING PROGRESS CHECK** Possible answers include latitude, air currents/monsoon winds, water, and elevation.

History of Southeast Asia

ENGAGE

Bellringer Tell students that this lesson discusses the history of Southeast Asia. Have students preview the lesson by skimming the headings and looking at the map and photographs. Help students make connections to the previous lesson about Southeast Asia's geography. **Ask:** How do you think Southeast Asia's history might connect to its geography and natural resources? *(Students may note that the region's wealth of natural resources, including valuable oil reserves in Indonesia and Malaysia, may have led to widespread trade and economic growth.)*

TEACH & ASSESS

C Critical Thinking Skills

Making Inferences Ask a volunteer to read the "It Matters Because" statement. Point to Southeast Asia on a map, noting its proximity to China and India. **Ask:**

• Why might Southeast Asia get "less attention" than China and India? *(Possible answer: The larger countries of China and India have huge populations, produce more goods, and have rich histories.)*

• Why do you think Southeast Asia may play a bigger role in world history in the future? *(Possible answer: With thriving seaports, growing cities, and valuable natural resources, countries in Southeast Asia are apt to play a bigger economic role.)* **AL** Logical/Mathematical, Interpersonal

Making Connections Display a map that shows the proximity of China and India to Southeast Asian countries. Share this information with students:

• Different culture groups occupied Southeast Asia from 800 to 1200, causing conflict among their kingdoms. Indian and Chinese cultures impacted the region with the spread of Hinduism and Buddhism. The Angkor Kingdom controlled the region that is now the southern portion of the Indochina Peninsula. The Khmer kingdom of Angkor advanced into a long-lasting civilization.

• In the 1600s, the Dutch began to colonize Indonesia. From 1942 to 1945, Indonesia was occupied by Japan. In 1949, the country became independent after the Japanese surrendered at the end of World War II.

ANSWER, p. 156

Taking Notes Answers should include important events in the selected country's history. Example of answers for Singapore: gains independence, becomes major industrial center, becomes one of the world's most prosperous countries, joins ASEAN

---

networks

There's More Online!

☑ **IMAGE** Angkor Wat

☑ **MAP** History of Southeast Asian Civilizations

☑ **VIDEO**

Reading HELPDESK

Academic Vocabulary RH.6-8.4
(Tier Two Words)
• ultimate

Content Vocabulary RH.6-8.4
(Tier Three Words)
• **sultan**
• **plantation**
• **absolute monarchy**
• **constitutional monarchy**

TAKING NOTES: *Key Ideas and Details* RH.6-8.1, RH.6-8.7

Describe Select one of the countries from the lesson. As you read, describe three important events in that country's history on a web diagram like the one below.

Country:

Lesson 2
History of Southeast Asia

ESSENTIAL QUESTION • *How does geography influence the way people live?*

IT MATTERS BECAUSE

C *Southeast Asia sometimes gets less attention than its two giant neighbors, China and India. The region has played an important role in world history in recent centuries, however, and it is likely to play an even larger role in the future.*

Kingdoms and Empires

GUIDING QUESTION *What role has trade played in Southeast Asia's history?*

Southeast Asia is known as "the Crossroads of the World" because it is located along important maritime trade routes. Trade has exposed the region to many different cultural influences. It also has made the region prey for foreign powers seeking to increase wealth and power by controlling the routes.

Prehistoric Cultures

Humans have lived in Southeast Asia for at least 40,000 years. For much of this period, the region looked quite different from today. Earth was in the grip of an ice age, so sea levels were lower. Much of the continental shelf lay above water as dry land. This land connected the mainland to many areas that are now islands, including Borneo, Sumatra, and Java. The mainland area, therefore, was much larger than it is now, and the island area was much smaller. As the ice age waned, the seas began to rise. They reached their present levels about 8,000 years ago.

Throughout the prehistoric period, Southeast Asia's inhabitants survived by hunting and gathering. They used stone tools and weapons. Around 6,000 years ago, people had begun practicing agriculture, growing rice in fertile river

(l to r) ©Jose Fuste Raga/Corbis; ©badz/age fotostock; Manfred Bail/Alamy; Keystone/Hulton Archive/Getty Images

---

networks *Online Teaching Options*

VIDEO

Around the World—Malaysia

Analyzing Visuals Use this video about the various aspects of life in Malaysia, located in Southeast Asia, to introduce the lesson. Ask students to share what they learned from the video and if anything surprised them. Guide a class discussion about how Southeast Asia's geographical location may have influenced trade, the growth of tourism, and the spread of different cultures. Have students consider why Southeast Asia is known as "the Crossroads of the World." **BL** Interpersonal

See page 147D for other online activities.

BBC Motion Gallery Education

valleys and deltas. Agriculture allowed for a more settled existence and led to the development of complex societies.

Powerful Societies Emerge

Several thousand years ago, early metalworking societies arose in Southeast Asia. Using sophisticated techniques, these cultures produced bronze tools, weapons, ornaments, and ceremonial drums. The most famous of these cultures, the Dong Son, was centered in northern Vietnam.

In the middle of the 100s B.C., China and India began to exert a powerful influence. China conquered the Red River delta in the northeast and made Vietnam a province of the Han empire. For the next 1,000 years, Vietnam remained under Chinese control. Chinese culture became embedded in the cultures of Vietnam and its neighbors.

People from India came to Southeast Asia as traders and missionaries. India's culture and its religions, Hinduism and Buddhism, spread along trade routes from India into Southeast Asia. Societies with Indian roots began to develop throughout the region.

R

Trading Societies

V

Funan, one of the first important trade-based states in the region, was established in the A.D. 100s. It covered parts of what are now Cambodia, Thailand, and Vietnam. Its people traded with China and India, but its cultural influences were mostly Indian.

Around the A.D. 600s, a kingdom called Srivijaya arose on the island of Sumatra and gained control of the Strait of Malacca. This waterway connecting the Pacific and Indian oceans was important because of the many trade goods that had passed through it by boat.

W

The main Hindu temple at Angkor Wat displays ancient building styles of India and Southeast Asia. Angkor Wat forms the largest single religious site in the world. Today, it is the national symbol of Cambodia, and the main temple appears on that country's flag.

Identifying How did Hinduism spread to Southeast Asia?

©Jose Fuste Raga/Corbis

Chapter 5 **157**

R Reading Skills

Determining Central Ideas Remind students of China and India's proximity to Southeast Asia. Have students locate the two countries on a map. Use the following questions to help students identify the main ideas about the emergence of powerful societies. **Ask:**

- **When did China and India begin to exert their power over Southeast Asia?** *(in the middle of the second century B.C.)*
- **What regions in Southeast Asia did China control?** *(the Red River delta in the northeast and later all of Vietnam)*
- **What religions spread to Southeast Asia, and how were they spread?** *(Hinduism and Buddhism; along trade routes)* **AL Verbal/Linguistic**

V Visual Skills

Creating Time Lines Have students work in small groups to create time lines showing when different trading societies emerged in Southeast Asia. Students should organize dates and locations referred to in the text and visually integrate the information from the text. Challenge students to research the types of goods that were traded and add a visual representation of those goods to their time lines (spices, silk, etc.). Have students present their time lines to the class. **BL Logical/Mathematical, Visual/Spatial**

W Writing Skills

Narrative Help students make the connection between trade and the spread of ideas. Tell students to think about people who traveled to Southeast Asia thousands of years ago. **Ask:** How do you think ideas and religions spread as a result of trade activity? *(Students' answers will vary but may include mention of traders discussing their beliefs with people who traded goods with them.)*

In class, have students write a rough draft of a story about a person or people who belonged to one of the trading societies mentioned in the text. Have students skim the lesson or get ideas from photographs. As homework, have students create their final draft, which may be a story or a script detailing the trade that occurred. Students' narratives should reflect an understanding of the goods traded, how they were traded, and how ideas were spread. **Verbal/Linguistic, Interpersonal, Intrapersonal**

ANSWER, p. 157

Identifying Traders and missionaries who traveled along trade routes from India to Southeast Asia helped spread Hinduism.

V Visual Skills

Analyzing Images/Comparing and Contrasting Have students recall what they learned about Angkor Wat from the video. Then have students analyze the photographs of Angkor Wat and the modern mosque in the text. Have students consider why people in past and present civilizations are inspired to build such grand structures. **Ask: What are some similarities and differences between Angkor Wat and the mosque shown on this page?** *(Students' answers will vary but might include similarities such as the fact that they are both large and honor their respective religions. Differences include that Angkor Wat is much larger and honors Hinduism; the mosque is on the water and honors Islam.)* **Visual/Spatial**

T Technology Skills

Researching on the Internet Discuss with students the significance of agricultural societies in Southeast Asia. Explain that rice was and is a key crop in regions such as the Philippine Islands. For homework, direct students to research rice terraces using reliable online sources. Review with students reliable web resources for agricultural information. These could include The World Bank for statistics, websites of well-known nonprofit organizations with specialized databanks, or online encyclopedia sites, other than Wikipedia. Have students write a short research report that describes the process of how rice terraces are constructed, as well as how the terraces have changed over time. **BL Verbal/Linguistic**

W Writing Skills

Narrative Have students write a short narrative that takes place in one of the agricultural societies described on the page. Students' narratives should be set between 600 and 1000 years ago, and should reflect some aspect of life described in the text. *(For example, a story set in Pagan should mention the people of the Irawaddy delta and how they grew rice.)* **Verbal/Linguistic, Intrapersonal**

V

This modern mosque built on stilts is located near the port city of Malacca in Malaysia. When the tide is high and the water level rises, the building appears to be floating.

▶ **CRITICAL THINKING**
Describing How did the religion of Islam reach Southeast Asia?

This included much of the spice trade, which connected China and Southeast Asia with India, Southwest Asia, Africa, and Europe. By controlling trade, Srivijaya grew into an empire that dominated commerce in the region for 600 years. Its capital, Palembang, became an important center of Buddhism.

Agricultural Societies

T

Southeast Asia's major agricultural societies developed where rice could be grown. The Pagan kingdom sprang up in Myanmar's Irrawaddy delta; Vietnamese society took root in the Red River delta; and the Khmer empire was centered near a large lake called Tonle Sap in Cambodia. The Khmer invented a water-management system to improve crops. The empire is also known for architecture, especially the temple complexes Angkor Wat and Angkor Thom. Built 800 years ago, the complexes still stand, drawing millions of visitors annually.

W

Islamic States

Islam, the religion of Muslims, could have reached Southeast Asia as early as the A.D. 800s or A.D. 900s when traders from the Middle East or western India traveled the sea route to China. By the 1200s, two Islamic kingdoms had been established in northern Sumatra. From there, Islam gradually spread eastward. By the 1400s, other Islamic kingdoms had risen near ports located along the main trade route through the region's waterways. By the 1600s, Islam had become the dominant religion across the Malay Archipelago.

©badz/age fotostock

158 Chapter 5

net**w**orks   *Online Teaching Options*

VIDEO

Islam in Southeast Asia

Analyzing Visuals Use the video of the mosque in Singapore to discuss the development of Islam in Southeast Asia. Guide a class discussion about the importance of religious structures in Southeast Asia. Have students consider the architecture of the mosque and how it can represent a culture. **BL Interpersonal**

See page 147D for other online activities.

Interactive Photos

© Image Source/Getty Images

ANSWER, p. 158

CRITICAL THINKING Traders from the Middle East and India brought Islam to Southeast Asia by way of the sea route to China.

The most important Islamic kingdom was centered on the port of Malacca on the Malay Peninsula. Founded in about 1400, Malacca capitalized on its location along the Strait of Malacca and developed into a powerful trading empire. Its **sultans**, or kings, ruled over much of the peninsula and the island of Sumatra across the strait.

☑ **READING PROGRESS CHECK**

Identifying What are some ways in which India influenced Southeast Asia?

C

Western Colonization

GUIDING QUESTION *How did European colonization change Southeast Asia?*

During the period known as the Age of Discovery, European explorers made long voyages in search of gold, silver, spices, and other sources of wealth. They also sought to spread Christianity and to map the world. The arrival of European ships in Southeast Asia marked the beginning of conquest and colonization that would leave the region dramatically changed.

European Traders

From ancient times through the Middle Ages, spices from Southeast Asia had reached Europe through Chinese, Indian, and Arab traders. Europeans used spices such as ginger, cinnamon, cloves, nutmeg, and mace to flavor food, to preserve meat, and to make perfumes and medicines. The demand was great and supplies were limited, so traders were able to charge high prices. Some spices were worth more than gold. The fabulous wealth of the spice trade led European powers to seek ocean routes to the source of the spices, and to gain control of the trade.

T

These spices on display on the Indonesian island of Bali include nutmeg, lemon grass, and cinnamon.
▶ **CRITICAL THINKING**
Describing Why did Europeans value Southeast Asian spices?

Manfred Bail/Alamy

Chapter 5 **159**

MAP

The Spice Islands

Discussing Use the map to identify and discuss the Spice Islands. Guide students to understand the impact spices had on the region and how spices brought wealth to different European powers. Make a connection to the importance of spices by having students consider the amount of aisle and shelf space that spices occupy in a grocery store. **ELL** Visual/Spatial

See page 147D for other online activities.

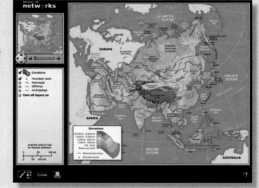

C **Critical Thinking Skills**

Making Connections Have students read the first paragraph on this page. Ask them to consider how Malaccan rulers took advantage of their location. **Ask: Why do you think Malacca developed into such a powerful trading empire?** *(Students' answers will vary but should include that its location along the Strait of Malacca made it a viable trading region and that wealth from trade allowed it to maintain power.)* **Logical/Mathematical**

T **Technology Skills**

Collaborating and Researching on the Internet Organize students into five trading groups: Chinese, Indian, Arab, European, and Southeast Asia. Have students use information in the text as well as reliable online sources to research their chosen trade group. Tell students to identify and take notes about specific goods that were traded during the Middle Ages. Have students work in small groups to present an Agricultural Fair in which groups trade with one another. You may wish to set up desks to serve as "booths" from which students can market their goods. **ELL** **Kinesthetic**

V

V **Visual Skills**

Creating Maps Have students read the text about European trade and look at the image on this page. Have students work with a partner to create a map that shows different trade goods and where they were traded. Direct students to create a key with icons to represent different trade items. Have students share their maps with the class. **ELL** Visual/Spatial

Making Connections A common misconception about spices and their use in the Middle Ages was that they were widely used to preserve meat or disguise the taste of meat that had spoiled. While salting was, and still is, one way to preserve meat, the process of pickling, smoking, or drying meat was also common. Regardless of how tasty spices are, they will rarely mask the taste of rotten meat!

ANSWERS, p. 159

☑ **READING PROGRESS CHECK** Traders and missionaries brought India's rich culture and its main religions, Hinduism and Buddhism, to the region. Agricultural and trading societies with Indian roots developed throughout the region.

CRITICAL THINKING Spices flavored food and were used as perfumes and medicine.

History of Southeast Asia

V Visual Skills

Creating Maps Help students visualize routes through Southeast Asia taken by European explorers from Portugal and Spain. Have students work in pairs to create a map that shows where explorers traveled and from which country their voyages originated. Students may wish to research other explorers that came to the region during the 1500s, such as English explorer Sir Francis Drake (1577–1580). Have students assign a different colored route for each explorer on their maps. Students can also use a key to show the countries represented by the different explorers. **ELL** Visual/Spatial **C2**

C1 Critical Thinking Skills

Synthesizing Have students read the section, "European Traders" with a partner. **Ask:**

- Why do you think the Netherlands became involved with the spice trade? *(Students should infer that Dutch rulers likely saw a way to gain a profit.)*
- Why did the Dutch navigate a new trade route to the Spice Islands? *(The Portuguese controlled the Strait of Malacca, so the Dutch charted a new route to use for trade.)*
- What was the result of this new trade route? *(The Dutch replaced the Portuguese as the dominant trading power.)* **AL** Verbal/Linguistic

C2 Critical Thinking Skills

Sequencing/Creating Time Lines To help students understand the sequence, have them create a time line with key dates and events from the text as well as the map. **Ask:**

- What was the first Southeast Asian country to gain its independence, and when did it become independent? *(the Philippines, 1946)*
- Who ruled Indonesia before it became independent? *(the Netherlands)*
- Which Southeast Asian country gained its independence most recently, and when did it become fully independent? *(East Timor; it declared independence in 1975, but was invaded by Indonesia; after years of violent rule, it gained independence in 2002.)* Visual/Spatial, Logical/Mathematical

---

ANSWERS, p. 160

MAP SKILLS

1. Thailand; it was never colonized because it opened trade with rival European powers.
2. Indonesia is made up of many islands separated from each other by great distances.

Independence of Southeast Asian Countries

(1984, from U.K.) Date of independence, ruling power

MYANMAR (BURMA) (1948, from U.K.)
LAOS (1949, from France)
THAILAND (independent)
VIETNAM (1954, from France)
CAMBODIA (1953, from France)
PHILIPPINES (1946, from U.S.)
BRUNEI (1984, from U.K.)
MALAYSIA (1957, from U.K.)
SINGAPORE (1965, from Malaysia)
INDONESIA (1953, from the Netherlands)
EAST TIMOR (TIMOR-LESTE) (2002, from Indonesia)

Lambert Azimuthal Equal-Area projection

MAP SKILLS

1. **PLACES AND REGIONS** Which Southeast Asian country does not have an independence date? Why?

2. **PHYSICAL GEOGRAPHY** Why might Indonesia find it difficult to achieve a sense of national unity?

In the early 1500s, Portuguese navigators discovered they could reach India and Southeast Asia by sailing around the southern tip of Africa. In 1511 the Portuguese conquered Malacca. That same year, they discovered the sources of cloves, nutmeg, and mace: the Moluccas and the Banda Islands, which became known as the Spice Islands. Through much of the 1500s, wealth generated by spices enriched Portugal's monarchy.

Meanwhile, other European powers sought alternate routes that would allow them to profit from the spice trade. The explorer Ferdinand Magellan commanded five Spanish ships that reached the Philippines by sailing across the Pacific Ocean from Mexico. Soon the Philippines became a Spanish colony.

At the beginning of the 1600s, Holland (known today as the Netherlands) jumped into the spice trade. Because the Portuguese controlled the Strait of Malacca, the Dutch charted a new route to the Spice Islands. By the middle of the century, they replaced the Portuguese as the dominant trading power.

Colonial Rule

During the 1800s and early 1900s, European countries gained control over other parts of Southeast Asia. Burma and Malaysia became colonies of Great Britain, and Vietnam, Laos, and Cambodia

160 Chapter 5

---

net**w**orks   *Online Teaching Options*

MAP

History of Southeast Asian Civilizations

Analyzing Maps Display the map that identifies early civilizations of Southeast Asia to begin a discussion with students to help them understand the significance and impact of early civilizations in Southeast Asia. Discuss with students the colonization of different countries in the region. Guide a discussion about the reasons why countries may desire to seek their independence. **AL** Interpersonal

See page 147D for other online activities.

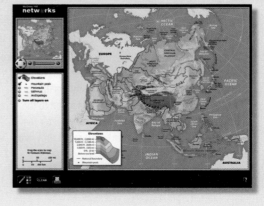

became colonies of France. In addition to the spice trade, European countries developed tin and coal mines and built factories to process the raw materials. They also established **plantations**, or large farms on which a single crop is grown for export. Plantation crops included tea, coffee, tobacco, and rubber trees. Thousands of laborers were brought in from China and India to work in the mines and on plantations. Many of them stayed on as permanent residents of the colonies.

Thailand (Siam)

Thailand, then known as Siam, was the only state in Southeast Asia that Europeans did not colonize. It was ruled by an **absolute monarchy** from the mid-1300s until 1932. In an absolute monarchy, one ruler has **ultimate** governing power over the country. The rulers of Siam had resisted threats from Burma since the 1500s. When the British declared war there, Siam's leaders agreed to allow free trade with Great Britain and other Western countries. This admission allowed the country to remain independent, acting as a buffer state between British and French possessions.

Academic Vocabulary

ultimate most extreme or greatest

☑ **READING PROGRESS CHECK**

Identifying In what ways did European powers gain wealth from their colonies in Southeast Asia?

Independent Countries

GUIDING QUESTION *What events ended the colonial era in Southeast Asia?*

In the early 1900s, nearly all of Southeast Asia was under the control of foreign powers. Colonial rule was often harsh, unjust, and exploitive, and sometimes it was met with violent resistance by the region's people. It was not this resistance, however, that ended colonialism. Instead, it was dramatic events that unfolded elsewhere in the world.

Dawn of Freedom

The first Southeast Asian colony to glimpse independence was the Philippines, which had been ruled by Spain since the 1500s. The United States took control of the colony in 1898 after defeating Spain in the Spanish-American War. During World War II, Japan sent its military forces to take control of Southeast Asian lands.

A Buddhist monk (right) in Cambodia casts his vote in a local election held in 2012. Today, Cambodia is struggling to build a democracy after years of civil war.
▶ **CRITICAL THINKING**
Describing Why were the 1970s a difficult decade for Cambodia's people?

Chapter 5 **161**

VIDEO

Vietnam War Memorial

Analyzing Visuals Use the video on the Vietnam Memorial to discuss the Vietnam War as both a regional event and as an important event in United States history. Guide a class discussion about the lasting effects of the war on the region. **AL** Interpersonal, Intrapersonal

See page 147D for other online activities.

T Technology Skills

Collaborating and Making Presentations Assign each of several student groups one of the trade items or crops mentioned in the text. Have groups research their assigned item to answer the following questions:

• **Where was the item grown or produced?**
• **What products were made from this item?**
• **Where was this product exported?**

After students have had time to conduct research and take notes about their topic, have them present a summary of their findings to the class. **Verbal/Linguistic, Interpersonal**

R Reading Skills

Determining Word Meanings Have students brainstorm synonyms for the word *absolute*. *(total, complete)* To help students understand the meaning of the word *monarchy*, tell them to think of other words with the prefix mono- *(monopoly, monologue, monorail, etc.)* Point to the term *absolute monarchy*. **Ask:** What can you infer about a country that is an *absolute monarchy*? *(Sample response: The country is ruled by only one leader who has complete control.)* **AL** **ELL** **Verbal/Linguistic**

C Critical Thinking Skills

Identifying Central Issues Ask students to consider the description of colonialism in Southeast Asia and the fact that it was outside events that determined the fate of these nations. **Ask:**

• **What does this type of colonialism suggest about the way that the colonies were viewed by the colonizing nations?** *(The colonies were seen as a way to make money for the colonizer, and were also seen as a political tool or asset that could be traded to make peace with other nations.)*

• **What challenges do you think newly independent countries might have faced after being under colonial rule?** *(Students' responses may vary but might include the challenges of forming a new government and protecting the rights of the people.)* **AL** **ELL** **Interpersonal**

ANSWERS, p. 161

☑ **READING PROGRESS CHECK** They made money off the spice trade because spices were in such high demand in Europe. They also mined resources like tin and coal and built factories to manufacture goods from these resources. They established plantations to export agricultural products such as tea, coffee, tobacco, and rubber.

CRITICAL THINKING Cambodians suffered from brutal treatment, military rule, and armed conflict.

V Visual Skills

Creating Visuals To help students comprehend the many dates and facts presented in the text, have them work in pairs to read and visualize the information in these paragraphs. **Ask: How is the information in these paragraphs presented?** *(sequentially, by different regions)* As students read the text, have them work with a partner to create a flow chart or time line to visualize key events. **AL** **Visual/Spatial**

T Technology Skills

Analyzing News Media Review the information in the text about the struggle for democracy in different Southeast Asian countries. Guide a class discussion about the significance of elections in newly democratic societies. Assign the following activity for homework:

Have students conduct online research to find information about the Cambodian elections held in 2012. Students should identify and analyze at least three articles from Web sites managed by news organizations, such as *The New York Times,* CNN, *The Washington Post,* Reuters, TIME, etc. Direct students to assess the credibility and accuracy of each source based on the information found in their research. Have students note any articles they found that presented conflicting or inaccurate information. Tell students to compile their findings in a short essay, describing the elections, their outcome, and how the information was presented by different news media. **BL** **Logical/Mathematical**

C Critical Thinking Skills

Hypothesizing Have students consider how and why the United States found itself deeply involved in the Vietnam War. Explain that American involvement began when a few American military advisors were sent to the region by President Eisenhower in the 1950s and that decision led to a full-scale military conflict that resulted in the deaths of 58,272 American soldiers whose names are listed on the Vietnam War Memorial. Explain also that countless more were injured and many are still missing and unaccounted for. American involvement finally ended in January 1973 with the Paris Peace Accords. **Ask: Why do you think the United States committed itself to such an expensive and long-drawn out war?** *Students' responses may vary but might include that American leadership, through several presidents, was fearful of a Communist takeover that would spread through all of Southeast Asia.* **Interpersonal**

Viet cong fighters patrol a waterway in the Mekong Delta during the Vietnam War. The Viet cong carried out armed attacks on U.S. and South Vietnamese forces. Their goal was to unite all of Vietnam under Communist rule.

▶ **CRITICAL THINKING**
Predicting What was the outcome of the Vietnam War?

Japan's nearness to Southeast Asia was a great advantage. The Japanese hoped to use the region's oil, rubber, and timber to help its economy and enable it to continue the war. Japan's rule lasted four years and caused the region's people great hardship.

The war ended in 1945, and the United States granted independence to the Philippines in 1946. Soon, other Southeast Asian colonies began to break free of European rulers. Myanmar negotiated its independence from Britain in 1948, and Indonesia was freed from the Netherlands in 1949. In the 1950s, Vietnam, Laos, and Cambodia freed themselves from French rule, and Malaysia and Singapore became independent of Britain.

The last country to gain its freedom was East Timor, sometimes called by its Portuguese name, Timor-Leste (TEE-mor LESS-tay). After being ruled by Portugal since the 1500s, East Timor declared independence in 1975 but was invaded by Indonesia. Indonesia's harsh, violent rule lasted there until 2002.

Regional Conflicts

The newly independent countries of Southeast Asia faced many challenges. Wars, revolutions, and dictatorships tested the new leaders. In Vietnam, Communist forces defeated the French in 1954 and ruled the northern part of the country. The United States supported leaders in the south. Fighting led to the Vietnam War, which lasted until 1975 and took more than 2 million lives. After the war ended, North Vietnam united the country under Communist rule.

162 *Chapter 5*

Keystone/Hulton Archive/Getty Images

---

net‌works   *Online Teaching Options*

VIDEO

Modern Buddhist Monks

Comparing and Contrasting Use the video about modern Buddhist monks to discuss the daily lives of today's Buddhist monks in different regions of Southeast Asia. Ask students to consider the similarities and differences of today's monks with those who lived in past Southeast Asian civilizations. Have students think about how modern Buddhist monks face different challenges. **BL** **Verbal/Linguistic**

See page 147D for other online activities.

Fresh photos from all over the world/Getty Images

ANSWER, p. 162

CRITICAL THINKING Two million lives were lost, and North Vietnam united the country under Communist rule.

The Vietnam War affected other parts of Southeast Asia. In Laos, a conflict pitted the government of Laos against nationalists allied with Vietnamese communists. In 1975 the government of Laos collapsed, and many people fled to other countries.

In 1970, Cambodia's military took over the government. Five years later, a rural communist movement, called the Khmer Rouge, overthrew this government. The country's new leaders began a brutal campaign of terror and destruction. Between 1975 and 1979, at least 1.5 million people died or were killed. In 1978 Vietnamese forces invaded Cambodia and installed a new government controlled by Vietnam, sparking almost 13 years of civil war.

Modern Southeast Asia

The economic growth of East Asian countries such as China and Taiwan in the late 1900s helped some countries in Southeast Asia. Thailand, Malaysia, Indonesia, the Philippines, and Vietnam became centers of manufacturing in the region. Textiles and tourism are important parts of Cambodia's economy. Singapore, which gained independence from Great Britain in 1959 and then from Malaysia in 1965, is one of the world's most prosperous countries.

Thailand has been a **constitutional monarchy** since 1932. A constitutional monarchy's ruler is legally bound by a constitution and government. Thailand's government has often been threatened by the military. Numerous military coups took place in the 1900s. By the 1980s, Thailand had combined a tradition of monarchy with democratic reforms, and it enjoyed high rates of economic growth through the 1990s.

Myanmar has struggled since gaining independence. In 1962 the military seized power and established a socialist government. Since then, leaders have closed off the country to outside influences. Even a cyclone in 2008 that killed more than 100,000 people did not persuade the government to open its borders to allow aid from abroad.

FOLDABLES
Study Organizer

Include this lesson's information in your Foldable®.

☑ **READING PROGRESS CHECK**

Identifying What colonial power ruled Vietnam before 1954?

V Visual Skills

Diagramming Help students organize information about the Vietnam War and the years of warfare in Cambodia. Have students work in pairs to create a Venn diagram comparing conflicts in each region. Have students share their diagrams with the class. **Ask:**

- **How is the Vietnam War similar to the conflicts endured by Cambodia in the 1970s?** *(Students' responses may vary but should include that both countries suffered enormous loss of life and involved foreign military powers.)*

- **How did they differ?** *(Students might mention that the United States or NATO did not send military troops to Cambodia to try and end the violence.)* **Visual/Spatial**

T Technology Skills

Collaborating and Making Presentations Assign each of several student groups a different country in Southeast Asia. Tell students they will "produce" a talk show titled "Southeast Asia Today," in which a host interviews historians and economists about the current economy in their assigned country. Student "hosts" should prepare a list of questions relating to the region's economic growth or decline; students being interviewed should answer the questions, acting as "expert" panelists. If time allows, have students conduct outside research about their respective countries. Following each group's presentation, allow the "studio audience" to ask questions of panelists. **BL Kinesthetic, Interpersonal**

CLOSE & REFLECT

Creating Charts Have students work in pairs to create a three-column chart labeled *Region/Country, History,* and *Conflict.* As a lesson review, have students complete the chart with information from the lesson. Then guide a class discussion about the lasting effects of some of these conflicts.

LESSON 2 REVIEW (CCSS)

Reviewing Vocabulary (Tier Three Words)
1. What crops were grown on *plantations* in Southeast Asian colonies? RH.6-8.4

Answering the Guiding Questions
2. *Describing* How did the geography of Southeast Asia change as a result of a rise in sea level? RH.6-8.5

3. *Analyzing* What made the Strait of Malacca such an important waterway? RH.6-8.1

4. *Determining Central Ideas* Why did European countries want to control the spice trade? RH.6-8.2

5. *Analyzing* How could the resources of Southeast Asia help Japan's economy and its ability to continue fighting in World War II? RH.6-8.1

6. *Informative/Explanatory Writing* Knowing about the history of colonization in Southeast Asia, write a paragraph in which you answer these questions: What are the dangers of resisting colonization? What are the consequences of not resisting? WHST.6-8.2, WHST.6-8.4

Chapter 5 **163**

LESSON 2 REVIEW ANSWERS

Reviewing Vocabulary

1. tea, coffee, tobacco, rubber trees

Answering the Guiding Questions

2. *Describing* Areas that had been connected to the mainland—such as Borneo, Java, and Sumatra—became islands.

3. *Analyzing* Much of the spice trade as well as other trade between India and China passed through the strait, which connects the Pacific and Indian oceans. Control of the waterway meant control of regional trade.

4. *Determining Central Ideas* Spices were highly valued in Europe, and traders were able to charge high prices for them. Some were even more expensive than gold. The spice trade could therefore bring a tremendous amount of wealth to any country that controlled it.

5. *Analyzing* Oil could be used to create energy that would power factories or war planes and ships. Resources such as rubber and timber could be used to make items to sell or to use in the war.

6. *Informative/Explanatory Writing* Students' answers should be supported by the history of colonization in the region. Accept all reasonable answers.

ANSWER, p. 163

☑ **READING PROGRESS CHECK** France

ENGAGE

Bellringer Have students preview the lesson by scanning the headings, guiding question, and photographs. Ask students to reflect on the previous lesson and what they learned about colonial rule and regional conflicts in Southeast Asia. Have students consider how these issues might affect the current culture groups inhabiting the region. Tell students to think about the positive and negative consequences of many different cultural groups living in the same area. Students should consider the Essential Questions as they read this lesson: *What makes a culture unique? Why does conflict develop?*

TEACH & ASSESS

R Reading Skills

Paraphrasing Have students work in pairs to paraphrase the section, "Population Profile." Tell students to focus on the main ideas of the text. Circulate to provide guidance to ensure that students include numbers and percentages. **Ask: Why do you think Indonesia has such a large population?** *(Answers will vary but students might infer that large families are the cultural norm there.)* **Verbal/Linguistic**

C Critical Thinking Skills

Analyzing Information Explain that Java contains about half of Indonesia's population even though it is only the country's fourth largest island. **Ask: Why do you think the relatively small island of Java has such a large population?** *(Answers will vary but students might infer that the island's location and busy ports bring industry and jobs to the region. For those who do not live in cities, the volcanic soil is fertile for farming.)*

Point out that the population of the United States is about 350 million. Provide a world map and have students compare the land area of the United States to that of Indonesia to help them get a sense of how densely populated the region is. **BL** **Logical/Mathematical**

ANSWER, p. 164

Taking Notes Answers include: urbanization is changing region; Cambodia remains rural; Philippines, Indonesia undergo great population change; region has many ethnic groups; many languages are spoken.

---

networks

There's More Online!

☑ **IMAGE** Minority Groups in Southeast Asia

☑ **MAP** Urban Southeast Asia

☑ **VIDEO**

Reading HELPDESK CCSS

Academic Vocabulary RH.6-8.4
(Tier Two Words)

• exploit

Content Vocabulary RH.6-8.4
(Tier Three Words)

• primate city
• minority
• Pacific Rim
• subsistence farming
• ecotourism

TAKING NOTES: Key Ideas and Details RH.6-8.7, RH.6-8.8

Identify As you read, use a graphic organizer like this one to note key facts about the people of Southeast Asia.

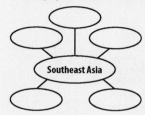

Southeast Asia

Lesson 3
Life in Southeast Asia

ESSENTIAL QUESTIONS • *What makes a culture unique?* • *Why does conflict develop?*

IT MATTERS BECAUSE
Southeast Asia is one of the most culturally diverse regions in the world. Learning about this diversity will lead to a better understanding of the region.

People and Places

GUIDING QUESTION *How is Southeast Asia's population shifting?*

In population size, Southeast Asia has fewer people than its neighbors, China and India. Compared to other areas, however, Southeast Asia's population is high. This lesson describes where the region's people live. The lesson also discusses how the population is expanding and changing.

Population Profile
Southeast Asia is home to about 625 million people. Indonesia has a population of approximately 250 million, which is 40 percent of the regional total.

Many Southeast Asian countries experienced rapid population growth in the 1900s, but today the region's growth rate is only slightly above the world average. Population is not evenly distributed. The highest densities generally are found in areas where good soil and abundant water allow agriculture to thrive. These areas include coastal plains, river valleys, and deltas. One of the greatest population densities is on the island of Java, whose volcanic soils are exceptionally fertile.

People on the Move
Historically, Southeast Asian societies were mostly rural. Since World War II, however, people have moved steadily from rural areas to cities. This movement is called

(l to r) ©FRANCIS R. MALASIG/epa/Corbis; LatitudeStock - Nadia Mackenzie/Gallo Images/Getty Images; PAUL CHESLEY/National Geographic Stock; Dondi Tawatao/Getty Images News/Getty Images; ©Reed Kaestner/Corbis

---

networks *Online Teaching Options*

VIDEO

Thai Economy is Booming

Comparing and Contrasting Use this video about the booming industrial economy in Thailand, one country located in Southeast Asia, to introduce the lesson. Have students write a paragraph about an aspect of daily life in the region that they found interesting. Guide a class discussion about how life in modern-day Southeast Asia is similar to or different from the students' own communities. **BL** **Verbal/Linguistic**

See page 147E for other online activities.

BBC Motion Gallery Education

urbanization. Urbanization is occurring most rapidly in countries that recently were or are currently the most rural.

Urbanization has produced explosive population growth in some cities. Manila, the capital of the Philippines, is home to more than 11 million people. Manila is a **primate city**—a city so large and influential that it dominates the rest of the country. Like many large cities, Manila suffers from overcrowding. More than a third of its inhabitants live in slums, where people are desperately poor and most dwellings are crudely built shacks.

Rapid population growth in and around Jakarta, the capital of Indonesia, has created a continuous urban chain of cities that were once separated. This megalopolis, as such areas are called, is one of the largest in the world, with more than 26 million people.

☑ **READING PROGRESS CHECK**

Identifying What types of geographical areas in Southeast Asia have the highest population densities?

People and Cultures

GUIDING QUESTION *How have China and India influenced Southeast Asian cultures?*

Peoples from other regions have migrated to Southeast Asia for more than 2,000 years for many different reasons. As a result, Southeast Asia has a rich mix of peoples and cultures.

Southeast Asia's cities provide contrasts in the ways people live. In Manila, the Philippines (left), residents crowd into slum areas not far from the city's modern business center. Singapore's Chinatown district (right) is known for its restored historic buildings and numerous shops and restaurants.

▶ **CRITICAL THINKING**
Describing How have Southeast Asia's cities changed since World War II?

Chapter 5 **165**

(l) ©FRANCIS R. MALASIG/epa/Corbis; (r) LatitudeStock - Nadia Mackenzie/Gallo Images/Getty Images

R Reading Skills

Determining Word Meanings Tell students that understanding the meaning of a base word can help them identify the meaning of an unfamiliar word. **Ask:**

- What is the base word of *urbanization?* *(urban)*
- What other words can you think of that have the same root as the word *primate?* *(Samples: primary, primal, primeval, primitive)*
- What clues do these words give about the meaning of the word *primate?* *(Possible answer: These words all relate to being first, original, or dominant, so primate must relate to being dominant or important.)* **AL ELL Verbal/ Linguistic**

W Writing Skills

Informative/Explanatory Tell students to use information in the text about the effects of population growth to write an essay about living in a primate city such as Manila or a megalopolis like Jakarta. Students should include information about the pros and cons of living in such an environment. After students have written a first draft, allow time for a peer-review session in which students swap essays with a partner and supply a constructive critique. For homework, have students edit and revise their essays as needed. **BL Verbal/ Linguistic**

V Visual Skills

Analyzing Images/Comparing and Contrasting Have students work in pairs or small groups to analyze and compare and contrast the two photographs shown on this page. Tell students to use a graphic organizer, such as a Venn diagram, in which to compile their notes. **Ask:** What can you infer about life in Southeast Asia's cities based on these images? *(Students should indicate that city life varies from crowded slums to neighborhoods with well-maintained, attractive buildings.)* **AL ELL Visual/Spatial**

MAP

Urban Southeast Asia

Determining Cause and Effect Use the interactive map to discuss the urban areas of Southeast Asia with students. Guide students to understand the cause-effect relationship between urbanization and issues that plague modern-day cities, such as overpopulation, crime, and poverty. **BL Logical/Mathematical**

See page 147E for other online activities.

ANSWERS, p. 165

☑ **READING PROGRESS CHECK** The highest densities are on coastal plains and in river valleys and deltas.
CRITICAL THINKING Since World War II, Southeast Asian cities have grown as a result of movement from rural areas to urban centers. Because of the tremendous population increase, many cities are overcrowded. Other cities, such as Jakarta, have grown in size, creating large metropolitan areas made up of cities once separate from each other.

T Technology Skills

Collaborating and Making Presentations Briefly discuss with students the way that archeologists study objects from the past to learn about past cultures and civilizations. Organize students into seven small groups and assign them one of the following ethnic groups mentioned in the text: Burmese *(Myanmar)*; Siamese *(Thailand)*; Malay *(Malaysia)*; Mon-Khmer *(Laos, Cambodia)*; Vietnamese *(Vietnam)*; Javanese *(Indonesia)*; and Tagalog *(Philippines)*. Tell students they will give a presentation as if they are archeologists in the future who are looking back at evidence from today.

Have students use information from the text and online research to learn about their assigned ethnic group. Students may wish to assign members of their group a specific element to research, such as language, clothing, food, and music. Have students present a summary of their findings to the class as if addressing a team of archaeologists. Encourage students to include music and visual displays to clarify information about their culture group. **BL Interpersonal, Auditory/Musical**

R Reading Skills

Determining Word Meanings Remind students that understanding word parts can help provide clues to a word's meaning. Point out the term *indigenous*. Have students work with a partner to identify the word's parts to understand its meaning. **Ask: How can identifying word parts help you understand the meaning of the word *indigenous*?** *(gen = birth; ous = relating to)* Have students practice using the term *indigenous* in a sentence. *(Sample: Certain palm trees are indigenous to the state of Florida.)* **ELL Verbal/Linguistic**

W Writing Skills

Informative/Explanatory Have students write an informative paragraph that describes daily life in either a rural or urban community in Southeast Asia. Encourage students to use sensory adjectives to make their descriptions precise and vivid, and to provide a concluding statement. **AL Verbal/ Linguistic**

A woman of the Padaung ethnic group drives a car in Myanmar near Yangon (Rangoon). Many Southeast Asians today blend traditional and modern ways.
▶ **CRITICAL THINKING**
Describing What is a major characteristic of peoples and cultures in Southeast Asia?

Ethnic and Language Groups

Southeast Asia's population consists of many ethnic groups. Five main groups dominate the mainland: the Burmese in Myanmar, the Siamese in Thailand, the Malay in Malaysia, the Mon-Khmer in Laos and Cambodia, and the Vietnamese in Vietnam. The largest group in Indonesia is the Javanese, and the largest group in the Philippines is the Tagalog. Many smaller groups, sometimes called **minorities**, also live in each country.

The people of Southeast Asia speak many languages. Traveling throughout Indonesia, one could encounter several hundred different languages. Most of the region's languages are indigenous, or native to the region. Others, including English, Spanish, and French, arrived with trade and colonialism.

Religion and the Arts

Buddhism is the most widely practiced religion across most of the mainland. Islam is dominant on the southern Malay Peninsula and across the Indonesian islands. In the Philippines and East Timor, most people are Roman Catholic. In some remote areas, people practice animist religions. Animism is based on the belief that all natural objects, such as trees, rivers, and mountains, have spirits.

When people from India brought Buddhism and Hinduism to the region, they also brought rich traditions in architecture, sculpture, and literature. Some of the greatest architecture and sculpture are Hindu and Buddhist temples built centuries ago.

The wide variety of art forms that flourish in Southeast Asia reflect the region's great diversity of cultures. In Thailand, plays known as *likay* feature singing, dancing, and vibrantly colored costumes. Actors improvise song lyrics, dialogue, and plots. In the popular shadow-puppet theater in Indonesia, Malaysia, and Cambodia, one puppeteer sings, chants, and controls the puppets behind a screen that is lit from the back. An orchestra of metal instruments provides music.

Daily Life

Although Southeast Asian cities are growing rapidly, three-fourths of the region's people live in rural areas. Many rural people move to the cities, but some leave the region to work in other countries. The money they send home helps their families survive.

PAUL CHESLEY/National Geographic Stock

166 *Chapter 5*

netw⊙rks   *Online Teaching Options*

IMAGE

Minority Groups in Southeast Asia

Analyzing Visuals Use the interactive image of the minority groups in Southeast Asia to discuss the different people who live in the region. Have students write a paragraph describing the various minority groups. **AL Verbal/Linguistic, Interpersonal, Intrapersonal**

See page 147E for other online activities.

Interactive Photos

This region has many diverse types of landscapes. Land forms range from mountains to grasslands. Waterways include rivers, lakes, and shorelines. Vegetation varies depending on the soil quality and access to water within the specific area. Animal life has adapted to take advantage of what the region has to offer.

© Image Source/Getty Images

ANSWER, p. 166

CRITICAL THINKING There is a rich mix of people and cultures. In each country, there is typically a dominant group and a number of minority ethnic groups.

Education and literacy rates vary across the region. The highest literacy rate is in Vietnam, where 94 percent of the people can read and write. At the other extreme are East Timor, Laos, and Cambodia, all of which have literacy rates below 75 percent. Roughly 95 percent of the schools in East Timor were destroyed during the country's fight for independence from Indonesia. The government of the new country is working to build new schools.

Many sports are popular in Southeast Asia. Some are traditional and generally unknown outside the region, while others—including soccer, badminton, martial arts, and volleyball—are international. All 11 countries in the region participate in the Southeast Asian Games that take place every two years. The countries take turns hosting the games, which include Olympic sports and traditional regional sports like *sepaktakraw*, a kind of volleyball played with the feet, knees, head, and chest.

☑ **READING PROGRESS CHECK**

Identifying Which religions are most widespread in Southeast Asia?

Issues in Southeast Asia

GUIDING QUESTION *In what ways have human activities affected the environment in Southeast Asia?*

Southeast Asia is a region in transition. In recent decades, the rapid economic growth along much of the **Pacific Rim**—the area bordering the Pacific Ocean—has brought great changes to some of the region's countries. With these changes, however, have come new challenges and problems.

Residents of Manila, the Philippines, celebrate a religious festival that has its roots in the culture of Spain. The Philippines was part of the Spanish Empire from the 1500s to the late 1800s.

Dondi Tawatao/Getty Images News/Getty Images

GRAPHIC ORGANIZER

Challenges in Southeast Asia

Making Connections Lead a discussion concerning the economic, environmental, and political challenges facing Southeast Asia. Use the Graphic Organizer to list student contributions to the discussion. Then ask students to consider the relationships that these challenges may have to each other. Allow students to share their ideas. **Logical/Mathematical, Visual/Spatial, Verbal/Linguistic**

See page 147E for other online activities.

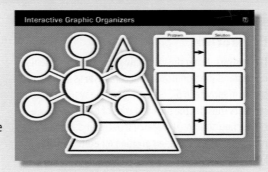

Interactive Graphic Organizers

T Technology Skills

Analyzing Data/Researching on the Internet Guide a brief discussion about varied literacy rates in different regions of Southeast Asia. Organize students into small groups, assigning each a country mentioned in the text. Have students in each group research their assigned country to determine its specific literacy rate. Students' research should also provide employment rates. **Ask: Do you think there is a connection between the country's literacy rate and its employment rate? If so, explain the connection, providing statistical support.** *(Students' answers will vary but should include relevant responses supported by their analysis. For example, students may determine that a country's employment rate is high due to a higher literacy rate, and therefore, a better educated population.)*
BL Logical/Mathematical

C Critical Thinking Skills

Drawing Conclusions Have students think about what it would be like to lose 95% of the schools in your community and your state. Guide students in a discussion about the different issues facing the new government of East Timor. **Ask:**

- **What are some of the early steps the government would need to take in order to replace so many of the country's schools?** *(Possible answer: decide where the schools should be located, make sure there are roads or access to the schools, hire teachers, decide which schools to build first)*
- **What are some challenges the schools will face when they reopen?** *(Children will be behind because they could not go to school for a long time, families will need to readjust to sending their children to school, children may want to come from other areas if their schools are not ready yet)* **Verbal/Linguistic**

R Reading Skills

Expressing Have students read the paragraph that outlines various sports played in Southeast Asia. Tell students to choose a sport discussed in the text to act out for their classmates. **Ask: How are sports in Southeast Asia similar to or different from sports played in the United States?** *(Students' answers will vary but should include comparisons to soccer, badminton, martial arts, and volleyball.)* **AL ELL** Verbal/Linguistic, Kinesthetic

ANSWER, p. 167

☑ **READING PROGRESS CHECK** Buddhism, Islam, Christianity

Life in Southeast Asia

C1 Critical Thinking Skills

Transferring Knowledge Lead a discussion about the different ways that people earn a living in Southeast Asia. After students read this page, assign one way that people earn a living to each of several student groups or pairs. Tell students they will conduct a Southeast Asian Job Fair in which each group sets up a "booth" to highlight its job prospects. Have students arrange desks in a half circle and attempt to "recruit" job seekers. Students may want to prepare a short script to entice potential employees to pursue their livelihood or industry. After all students have participated in the job fair, facilitate a class discussion about ways to earn a living in Southeast Asia. **BL** **Verbal/Linguistic, Kinesthetic**

R Reading Skills

Listing To help students comprehend the information about different crops, have them work with a partner to list the crops and indicate where they are grown:

- Rice *(main product in the region, but Thailand and Vietnam are world leaders in exporting rice)*
- Natural rubber and palm oil *(Malaysia, Indonesia, southern Thailand)*
- Coconuts and sugar *(Philippines)*
- Cacao, coffee, spices *(region's other top export crops)*
  AL **Verbal/Linguistic**

C2 Critical Thinking Skills

Making Inferences Have students refer to the Chapter Opener map and locate the country of Singapore in relation to the other countries mentioned in this section. **Ask: Why do you think the small country of Singapore has grown to become a major industrial center?** *(Singapore is located on the Strait of Malacca and one quarter of the world's trade goods pass through the strait making Singapore's port one of the world's busiest.)* **Verbal/Linguistic**

Content Background Knowledge

A famous landmark in Singapore is a statue called the Merlion, a combination of a mermaid and a lion. The statue was built to honor the city's early days as a fishing village. The statue, unveiled in 1972, weighs approximately 70 tons and now sits in the city's Merlion Park.

ANSWER, p. 168

Identifying Commerce, finance, communication, and information technology have made great strides in Southeast Asia. The region provides a large, driven, and generally inexpensive workforce for U.S., Japanese, and European industries.

A young American visitor poses with a produce seller on a busy street in Hanoi, Vietnam. Tourism is a growing industry in Vietnam and many other Southeast Asian countries.

C2

Identifying What other new industries have developed in Southeast Asia in recent decades?

Earning a Living

C1

Farming remains the most common livelihood in most countries. Many rural villages depend on rice, the most important food staple in the region, as a cash crop. Rice is by far the most widely grown crop. Two of the region's countries, Thailand and Vietnam, lead the world in rice exports. Plantations located in Malaysia, Indonesia, and southern Thailand produce natural rubber and palm oil, while coconuts and sugar are important crops in the Philippines. Southeast Asia's other top export crops include cacao, coffee, and spices.

R

Many farmers grow food only to feed themselves and their families. This is called **subsistence farming**. Some practice subsistence farming but also work seasonally to earn money.

Since the end of the colonial period, many countries have focused on industry. The tiny country of Singapore has developed into a major industrial center. Mining contributes to the economies of some countries in the region. Indonesia, Malaysia, and Thailand together produce more than half of the world's tin. Large deposits of copper and gold are mined on the Indonesian portion of the island of New Guinea.

Fishing is an important livelihood in Thailand, Indonesia, Malaysia, and the Philippines. Tourism is a growing industry in countries such as Cambodia, Thailand, and Vietnam. An important part of this industry is **ecotourism**, or touring natural environments such as rain forests and coral reefs.

Finance, communication, and information technology have also improved greatly in the region. Many people in the cities use cell phones and have access to the Internet. Due to its large and generally inexpensive labor force, many U.S., Japanese, and European industries employ workers in the region.

Making Connections

In 1968, Indonesia, Malaysia, the Philippines, Singapore, and Thailand joined together to form the Association of Southeast Asian Nations (ASEAN). The organization seeks to increase economic development, social progress, and cultural development in the region. All the countries in the region except East Timor are members. Although many countries have experienced economic growth since the late 1960s, Cambodia, Laos, Myanmar, and Vietnam rank among the poorest countries in the world.

©Reed Kaestner/Corbis

168 *Chapter 5*

---

networks *Online Teaching Options*

IMAGE

Ecotourism

Defending Using the interactive image, help students understand the significance of ecotourism as a growing source of income in different parts of the world. Have students consider the pros and cons of ecotourism, conducting additional research if necessary, and write a paragraph defending their position on ecotourism in Southeast Asia. **BL** **Naturalist**

See page 147E for other online activities.

Interactive Photos

© Image Source/Getty Images

Economic and Environmental Challenges

Southeast Asia faces many challenges. The gap between rich and poor has widened in recent decades. Economic growth has helped some people out of poverty, but many still struggle to meet daily needs. In Manila, Jakarta, and other big cities, rapid urbanization has led to overcrowding and water shortages.

Protecting the environment is another challenge. Industries provide an economic boost, but they sometimes **exploit** and harm the environment. Tin mining has created huge wastelands in Malaysia, Thailand, and Indonesia. Commercial logging and farming destroy the tropical forests at an alarming rate. Indonesia and Malaysia recently introduced laws to slow deforestation while still promoting economic growth.

Dams along the Mekong River create hydroelectric power, but that also has created problems for the fishing industry. Vietnam, Cambodia, Laos, and Thailand established the Mekong River Commission to encourage safe management and usage of the river and its resources. Conflict over control of oil and gas resources in the South China Sea is another challenge. Vietnam, the Philippines, and Malaysia surround the sea. The countries' claims on the resources are in dispute.

Political Challenges

Since the end of the colonial era, economic and social progress have been slowed by political instability. After the military took over the government of Myanmar in 1962, the country slid into isolation, poverty, and brutality. The government has refused democratic elections and limits any protest by its people. Some people in Myanmar have tried to bring democracy to the country. In 2011 the military government began to allow more freedom for its people. In 2012 the United States reestablished diplomatic ties with Myanmar and assigned an ambassador to the country for the first time in more than 20 years.

✓ **READING PROGRESS CHECK**

Determining Central Ideas What is the mission of the Association of Southeast Asian Nations (ASEAN)?

Academic Vocabulary

exploit to use a person, a resource, or a situation unfairly and selfishly

FOLDABLES
Study Organizer
Include this lesson's information in your Foldable®.

LESSON 3 REVIEW CCSS

Reviewing Vocabulary (Tier Three Words)
1. ***Identifying*** What are some of the problems that a *primate city* might experience? RH.6-8.4

Answering the Guiding Questions
2. ***Analyzing*** Why might the literacy rate in East Timor soon begin to rise? RH.6-8.1
3. ***Determining Central Ideas*** What are some of the environmental problems facing Southeast Asia? RH.6-8.2

4. ***Analyzing*** What might happen to agricultural production in Southeast Asia if the urbanization trend continues? RH.6-8.1
5. ***Determining Word Meanings*** What is *animism*, and where is it practiced in Southeast Asia? RH.6-8.4
6. ***Argument Writing*** Imagine that your class is trying to pick a destination for an overseas field trip. Write a letter to your classmates encouraging them to select Southeast Asia. Give specific reasons why this region would make a good destination. WHST.6-8.1, WHST.6-8.4

Chapter 5 **169**

LESSON 3 REVIEW ANSWERS

Reviewing Vocabulary

1. overcrowding, slums, disease, unemployment

Answering the Guiding Questions

2. ***Analyzing*** The government is working to build new schools.

3. ***Determining Central Ideas*** air and water pollution, wastelands created by mining, deforestation, loss of habitat

4. ***Analyzing*** Agricultural production might drop, because there would be fewer people to work the land.

5. ***Determining Word Meanings*** Animism is a type of religion based on the belief that all natural objects have spirits. Animist religions are practiced in many areas of Southeast Asia, including northern Myanmar, northern Laos, and the interior of the island of Borneo.

6. ***Argument Writing*** Students' letters should emphasize such things as the region's climate, beaches and tropical islands, historical sites and monuments, foods, and rich cultural traditions.

V1 Visual Skills

Creating Charts Help students organize information about the economic and environmental challenges faced by countries in Southeast Asia. Tell students to create a two-column chart with the left column labeled *City/Country/Region* and the right column labeled *Challenges*. Have students work with a partner to fill in the chart. A sample response for Manila is shown below.

City/Country/Region	Challenges
Manila, Philippines	Overcrowding, water shortages

Visual/Spatial

V2 Visual Skills

Creating Time Lines/Sequencing Help students understand the sequence of events presented in this "Political Challenges" paragraph. Have them work with a partner to create a time line of events. After students have had time to create their time lines, **ask: What key event happened to repair United States relations with Myanmar, and when did it take place?** *(In 2011 the military government began to allow more freedom for its people; the United States reestablished diplomatic ties in 2012 and assigned an ambassador to the country. President Obama visited Myanmar after his reelection in 2012 and addressed the people encouraging them to continue to expand their economic and political freedoms and offering American support.)* **Visual/Spatial, Logical/Mathematical**

CLOSE & REFLECT

Naming To close the lesson, note that Southeast Asia is made up of many islands, each with various cultures, religions, and languages. Name a country and call on different students to describe the country and tell one way that it is different from where they live and one way that it is similar. Continue to name countries and call on students, making sure that every student has a chance to participate.

ANSWER, p. 169

✓ **READING PROGRESS CHECK** ASEAN seeks to increase economic development, social progress, and cultural development and to promote peace and security across the region.

CHAPTER REVIEW ACTIVITY

Have students create a four-column chart like the one below. Have students list *Physical Geography, Resources, History and Culture,* and *Daily Life* as column headings. Tell students to complete the chart for each category with key information and examples from the text. *(Students' answers may vary but should include key concepts discussed in each of the three lessons in the chapter.)*

Southeast Asia			
Physical Geography	Resources	History and Culture	Daily Life

REVIEW THE ENDURING UNDERSTANDINGS

Review this chapter's Enduring Understanding with students:

• *People, places, and ideas change over time.*

Now pose the following questions in a class discussion to apply it to this chapter.

• **What are some of Southeast Asia's natural resources, and where are they located?** *(Southeast Asia is rich in mineral resources, such as copper, lead, zinc, and gold, as well as gemstones such as rubies and sapphires. Tin is produced in Indonesia, Malaysia, and Thailand. Rain forests are home to valuable hardwood trees, such as teak, mahogany, and ebony. Southeast Asia also has valuable fossil fuels including oil and natural gas reserves.)*

• **How would you describe Southeast Asia's governments during the 1900s?** *(Sample answer: For a little more than the first half of the century, most of Southeast Asia's countries were under colonial rule, which was often harsh, violent, and unjust. This period of colonialism led to a quest for independence by many Southeast Asian countries.)*

• **Describe the concept of urbanization and explain how it has impacted Southeast Asian cities.** *(Sample answer: Urbanization has caused population growth to explode in a number of Southeast Asian cities such as Manila in the Philippines, and Jakarta, Indonesia. This rapid population growth has resulted in issues such as overcrowding and unemployment.)*

Directions: Write your answers on a separate piece of paper.

❶ Use your **FOLDABLES** to explore the Essential Question.
INFORMATIVE/EXPLANATORY WRITING Explain in a paragraph where Southeast Asia's agricultural societies began and why they originated in those locations. WHST.6-8.2, WHST.6-8.10

❷ **21st Century Skills**
ANALYZING Research information to write about the economies of Vietnam and Cambodia. Discuss which country you think will undergo stronger economic development in the next decade. WHST.6-8.7, WHST.6-8.8

❸ **Thinking Like a Geographer** RH.6-8.7
IDENTIFYING The population of the Greater Jakarta, Indonesia, metropolitan area reached 26 million people. How many large U.S. cities, including the largest city in your state, would have to be combined to reach a population of 26 million? Use the chart to list several American cities and their respective populations. Add the totals until you reach approximately 26 million.

City	Population

❹ **GEOGRAPHY ACTIVITY**

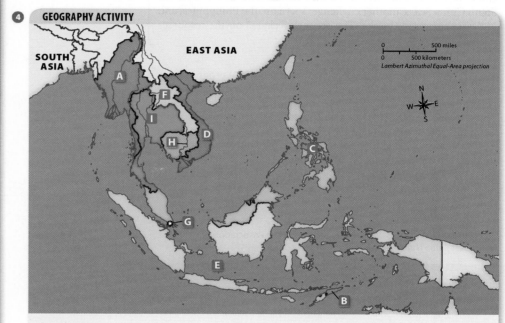

Locating Places
Match the letters on the map with the numbered places below. RH.6-8.7

1. Philippines
2. Thailand
3. Laos
4. Java Sea
5. Myanmar
6. Singapore
7. Mekong River
8. East Timor (Timor-Leste)
9. Vietnam

ACTIVITIES ANSWERS

Exploring the Essential Question

❶ **INFORMATIVE/EXPLANATORY WRITING** Southeast Asia's agricultural societies grew up in areas that were good for growing rice. Rice grows in water so these areas are located in river deltas or other wet places like the Irrawaddy delta in Myanmar, the Red River Valley in Vietnam, or near a lake such as the Tonle Sap, in Cambodia.

21st Century Skills

❷ **ANALYZING** Student responses will vary, but should address the prompt about the economies of Vietnam and Cambodia, choosing between the two countries and providing support for their answer through research and documentation using reliable online or print resources.

REVIEW THE GUIDING QUESTIONS

Directions: Choose the best answer for each question.

1 The region of Southeast Asia consists mainly of RH.6-8.4
   A.   constitutional monarchies.
   B.   Singapore.
   C.   peninsulas and islands.
   D.   war-ravaged countries.

2 Which country has the greatest number of active volcanoes in the world? RH.6-8.1
   F.   Indonesia
   G.   Vietnam
   H.   Krakatoa
   I.   Thailand

3 Why did foreign powers begin to colonize Southeast Asian countries? RH.6-8.5
   A.   to defeat local uprisings
   B.   to control the profitable spice trade
   C.   to test new oceangoing navigation instruments
   D.   to enslave the Southeast Asian peoples

4 In which country did the Khmer Rouge arise? RH.6-8.1
   F.   the Philippines
   G.   Laos
   H.   Myanmar
   I.   Cambodia

5 Forty percent of the population of Southeast Asia live in RH.6-8.1
   A.   Manila.
   B.   Brunei.
   C.   Indonesia.
   D.   Malaysia.

6 What is one of the greatest challenges Southeast Asian countries face? RH.6-8.2
   F.   loss of trade
   G.   environmental damage
   H.   loss of cottage industries
   I.   devaluation of their monetary systems

Chapter 5 **171**

Thinking Like a Geographer

3 **IDENTIFYING** Choices will vary considerably but must include the most populous city in their state and students should come up with a list of additional American cities whose population totals add up to approximately 26 million people.

Geography Activity

4 **LOCATING PLACES**

   1. C
   2. I
   3. F
   4. E
   5. A
   6. G
   7. H
   8. B
   9. D

ASSESSMENT ANSWERS
Review the Guiding Questions

1 **C** For this question, students may recall the term *insular*, which refers to an area comprised of islands. They should also recall the two main peninsulas in Southeast Asia: the Malay Peninsula and the Indochinese Peninsula. Refer students to the "Landforms and Resources" section in Lesson 1 for help.

2 **F** Students should be able to eliminate choice H immediately, as it refers to the name of a famous volcanic mountain. Students should recall that Indonesia has more than 100 active volcanoes. Have students reread the "Mountains and Volcanoes" section in Lesson 1 for further understanding.

3 **B** Students should recognize choice C as a distractor, as testing navigation instruments was not a motive for colonization. Students should recall that spices were a valuable trade item in Southeast Asia during the era of colonization. If students answered incorrectly, refer them to the section "European Traders" in Lesson 2 for help.

4 **I** To answer this question, students need to recall the information about the rural communist movement called Khmer Rouge in Lesson 2 in the "Regional Conflicts" section. Students may recall the violent campaign of terror and Cambodia's long period of civil war.

5 **C** Remembering that Indonesia is the largest country in Southeast Asia, with over 17,000 islands, should help students find the correct answer. Students should instantly recognize choice A as a distractor, as Manila is a city, not a country. Refer students to the Lesson 1 "Peninsulas and Islands" section for clarification.

6 **G** Students should recall the environmental problems facing Southeast Asian countries, which are a direct result of human activity. Refer students to Lesson 3 to review the environmental issues in Southeast Asia.

DBQ Analyzing Documents

7 B The building of the Suez Canal and invention of steamships are both examples of technological change, not political, cultural, or geographical changes. If students answer incorrectly, have them give examples of political, cultural, and geographical changes to emphasize the difference.

8 G The tin referred to in the passage was most likely mined in Southeast Asia, since it would need to be transported from that region for Singapore to benefit from a growing demand.

Short Response

9 Possible answer: Leaders of Vietnam would emphasize cultural differences with China in an effort to convince the Vietnamese people to join in their revolts by seeing the Chinese as an alien, conquering power, not as a friend or ally with a similar culture.

10 Possible answer: The Vietnamese people resisted control by China early in their history and they fought against the French to gain independence after World War II. In the 1960s and 1970s, North Vietnam, and its communist government, backed by China, fought against South Vietnam which was supported by the United States. U.S involvement was an attempt to prevent the spread of Communism in Southeast Asia.

Extended Response

11 Students' essays should present statistics about poverty and education levels in Vietnam (and elsewhere in Southeast Asia, when relevant) and offer opinions about child-labor practices and the effects of public financial support for companies that rely on child labor for high-profit goods. Essays should be grammatically correct and use transition words so that they flow smoothly.

DBQ ANALYZING DOCUMENTS

7 IDENTIFYING Read the following passage:

> "The opening of the Suez Canal in 1869 and the advent of steamships launched an era of prosperity for Singapore as . . . trade expanded. . . . In the 20th century, the automobile industry's demand for rubber from Southeast Asia and the packaging industry's need for tin helped make Singapore one of the world's major ports."
>
> —from U.S. State Department, "Singapore: History" (2011)

What kind of change was the initial cause of Singapore's growth? **RH.6-8.1, RH.6-8.10**

A. political
B. technological
C. cultural
D. geographical

8 ANALYZING Where was the tin mentioned in the passage most likely mined? **RH.6-8.1, RH.6-8.10**

F. southern Africa
G. Southeast Asia
H. East Asia
I. Oceania

SHORT RESPONSE

> "The Chinese conquerors referred to Vietnam as Annam, the 'pacified south.' But it was not peaceful. . . . Revolts recurred chronically [regularly], and . . . [leaders] stressed that Vietnam's customs, practices, and interests differed from those of China."
>
> —from Stanley Karnow, *Vietnam: A History* (1983)

9 IDENTIFYING POINT OF VIEW Why would leaders of Vietnamese revolts emphasize that Vietnam's culture was different from China's? **RH.6-8.6, RH.6-8.10**

10 ANALYZING How were the events that took place early in Vietnam's history, described here, similar to its later history? **RH.6-8.1, RH.6-8.10**

EXTENDED RESPONSE

11 INFORMATIVE/EXPLANATORY WRITING Vietnam has one of the highest literacy rates in Southeast Asia and one of the highest poverty rates. With this in mind, research online and at the library to write about this seeming contradiction. In your essay, explore the effects of poverty on child labor. What impact does the purchase of high-priced consumer goods made in factories staffed by children have on the practice of child labor? **WHST.6-8.6, WHST.6-8.9**

Need Extra Help?

If You've Missed Question	1	2	3	4	5	6	7	8	9	10	11
Review Lesson	1	1	2	2	3	3	3	1	2	2	3

From VIETNAM: A HISTORY, by Stanley Karnow, Copyright © 1983 by WGBH Educational Foundation and Stanley Karnow. Used by permission of Viking Penguin, a division of Penguin Group (USA) Inc. Reprinted by permission of SLL/Sterling Lord Literistic, Inc. Copyright by Stanley Karnow

---

net**w**◉rks   *Online Teaching Options*

Practicing 21st Century Skills

Practicing Skills Your students can practice important 21st Century skills such as geography, reading, writing, and critical thinking by using resources found in the Skills Builder tab of the online Student Learning Center. Resources include templates, handbooks, and slide shows. These same resources are also available in the Resource Library of the Teacher Lesson Center. **AL**

South Asia Planner

UNDERSTANDING BY DESIGN®

Enduring Understandings

- *People, places, and ideas change over time.*

Essential Questions

- *How does geography influence the way people live?*
- *How do governments change?*
- *What makes a culture unique?*

Predictable Misunderstandings

- *South Asia has the same landscape as the other places in Asia.*
- *The people of South Asia have the same language and culture as the rest of Asia.*
- *South Asia has a recent history due to colonization from other countries.*

Assessment Evidence

Performance Tasks:

- *Project-Based Learning Digital Hands-On Chapter Project*
- *Project-Based Learning Hands-On Chapter Project*

Other Evidence:

- *Critical Thinking Skills Activity*
- *Primary Sources Reading Skills Activity*
- *GeoLab Activity*
- *Participation in Interactive Whiteboard Activities*
- *Contribution to small-group activities*
- *Interpretation of slide show images and special purpose maps*
- *Participation in class discussions about cultural and economic topics*
- *Lesson Reviews*
- *Chapter Assessments*

SUGGESTED PACING GUIDE

Introducing the Chapter	1 Day	Lesson 3	2 Days
Lesson 1	2 Days	Chapter Wrap-Up and Assessment	1 Day
Lesson 2	2 Days		

TOTAL TIME   8 Days

Key for Using the Teacher Edition

SKILL-BASED ACTIVITIES

Types of skill activities found in the Teacher Edition.

* **V** **Visual Skills** require students to analyze maps, graphs, charts, and photos.

W **Writing Skills** provide writing opportunities to help students comprehend the text.

R **Reading Skills** help students practice reading skills and master vocabulary.

C **Critical Thinking Skills** help students apply and extend what they have learned.

T **Technology Skills** require students to use digital tools effectively.

*Letters are followed by a number when there is more than one of the same type of skill on the page.

DIFFERENTIATED INSTRUCTION

All activities are written for the on-level student unless otherwise marked with the leveled labels below.

BL Beyond Level
AL Approaching Level
ELL English Language Learners

All students benefit from activities that utilize different learning styles. Many activities are marked as below when a particular learning style is highlighted.

Intrapersonal	Naturalist
Logical/Mathematical	Kinesthetic
Visual/Spatial	Auditory/Musical
Verbal/Linguistic	Interpersonal

National Geography Standards covered in Chapter 6

Learners will understand:

I. The World in Spatial Terms

Standard 1: How to use maps and other geographic representations, geospatial technologies, and spatial thinking to understand and communicate information

Standard 3: How to analyze the spatial organization of people, places, and environments on Earth's surface

II. Places and Regions

Standard 4: The physical and human characteristics of places

Standard 5: That people create regions to interpret Earth's complexity

Standard 6: How culture and experience influence people's perceptions of places and regions

IV. Human Systems

Standard 9: The characteristics, distribution, and migration of human populations on Earth's surface

Standard 10: The characteristics, distribution, and complexity of Earth's cultural mosaics

Standard 11: The patterns and networks of economic interdependence on Earth's surface

Standard 12: The processes, patterns, and functions of human settlement

Standard 13: How the forces of cooperation and conflict among people influence the division and control of Earth's surface

V. Environment and Society

Standard 14: How human actions modify the physical environment

Standard 15: How physical systems affect human systems

VI. The Uses of Geography

Standard 17: How to apply geography to interpret the past

Standard 18: How to apply geography to interpret the present and plan for the future

CHAPTER OPENER PLANNER

Students will know:

- *that South Asia has a varying landscape.*
- *that the people of South Asia have cultures and languages unique to them.*
- *that South Asia has a long history that stretches back thousands of years.*

Students will be able to:

- *analyze a world map to identify countries of South Asia.*
- *use a time line to discuss various events in the history of South Asia.*

UNDERSTANDING
BY DESIGN®

☑ *Print Teaching Options*

V **Visual Skills**

☐ **P. 174** Students use the map to reinforce map skills.
AL Visual/Spatial

☐ **P. 175** Students review the time line and discuss its major points of interest. Visual/Spatial

☑ *Online Teaching Options*

☐ **MAP** **Reading a Map**—Students identify aspects and locations of the region on a map.

☐ **TIME LINE** **Reading a Time Line and Map**—Students learn about where and when historical events occurred in South Asia. Visual/Spatial

☐ **MAP** **Interactive World Atlas**—Students use the interactive world atlas to identify the region and describe its terrain.

☑ *Printable Digital Worksheets*

☐ **WORKSHEET** **Primary Sources Reading Skills: Climbing Mount Everest**—Students can use this worksheet to learn more about the exploration of Everest and the explorers of the peak.

☐ **WORKSHEET** **GeoLab: Indian Textiles**—Students can use this worksheet to understand the process of making natural textile dyes.

☐ **WORKSHEET** **Critical Thinking Skills: Call Centers in India**—Students can use this worksheet to discuss the advantages and disadvantages of outsourcing jobs to other countries.

Project-Based Learning

Hands-On

Create a Simulated News Broadcast

Students will work in small groups to create a simulated news broadcast about South Asia. Each group should write stories about South Asia's physical features, history, cultures, or current events. Each story will be presented in 30 second increments. The groups will plan the order of each segment to create a cohesive news broadcast that transitions from story to story. The news broadcasts will be presented live in the classroom to an audience of classmates.

Digital Hands-On

Create a Video Documentary

Students will work in pairs to produce a video documentary about South Asia's physical features. Videos should integrate photos, narration, and background music. Have students search online for copyright free photos and information to incorporate into their documentary. Videos can be shared within the class or online.

Print Resources

ANCILLARY RESOURCES
These ancillaries are available for every chapter and lesson.

- **Reading Essentials and Study Guide Workbook** **AL** **ELL**
- **Chapter Tests and Lesson Quizzes Blackline Masters**

PRINTABLE DIGITAL WORKSHEETS
These printable digital worksheets are available for every chapter and lesson!

- **Hands-On Chapter Projects**
- **What Do You Know? Activities**
- **Chapter Summaries (English and Spanish)**
- **Vocabulary Builder Activities**
- **Quizzes and Tests**
- **Reading Essentials and Study Guide (English and Spanish)** **AL** **ELL**
- **Guided Reading Activities**

More Media Resources

SUGGESTED VIDEOS
NOTE: Be sure to preview videos to ensure they are age-appropriate.

- **Everest—50 Years on the Mountain** (90 min.)
- **Ganges (from the Himalayas through India and Bangladesh)** (150 min.)
- **India One Country A Million Worlds** (53 min.)

SUGGESTED READING
- *Monsoon Summer,* by Mitali Perkins **BL**
- *Mohandas Gandhi,* by Kem Knapp Sawyer **AL**
- *India: the Land, the People, the Culture (series of three books),* by Bobbie Kalman

PHYSICAL GEOGRAPHY OF SOUTH ASIA

Students will know:
- *that South Asia has a varying landscape.*

Students will be able to:
- **describe** *South Asia's different physical features.*
- **describe** *the various climates of South Asia.*
- **describe** *important natural resources in the region.*

UNDERSTANDING
BY DESIGN®

☑ *Print Teaching Options*

V Visual Skills

☐ **P. 176** Students create a word square for each vocabulary word they encounter, beginning with the word *subcontinent.* **AL** **ELL** Visual/Spatial, Verbal/Linguistic

☐ **P. 177** Students draw conclusions about the homes of the individuals shown in the photograph. Visual/Spatial

☐ **P. 179** Students analyze a map of seasonal rain and wind patterns. **AL** Visual/Spatial

☐ **P. 180** Students describe what is happening in the photograph to better understand the water resource issues that affect South Asia. Visual/Spatial

☐ **P. 181** Students create charts listing the mineral, energy, and forest resources of South Asia by country. Visual/Spatial

W Writing Skills

☐ **P. 181** Students write a short report on an endangered species' habitat, reasons for endangered status, and efforts to save it. **BL** Visual/Spatial, Naturalist

R Reading Skills

☐ **P. 176** Students locate on a classroom map the mountain ranges of South Asia's northern boundary, Mount Everest, and Khyber Pass. **AL** Visual/Spatial, Verbal/Linguistic

☐ **P. 178** Students summarize information about South Asia's climates. **ELL** Verbal/Linguistic

☐ **P. 179** Students summarize how two large temperate climate zones are created by the mountains of South Asia. **BL** Verbal/Linguistic

C Critical Thinking Skills

☐ **P. 177** Students identify the main ideas about the landforms and rivers of South Asia. Visual/Spatial, Verbal/Linguistic

☐ **P. 180** Using a T-chart, students identify the central issues and pros/cons of the development of hydroelectric projects in India. Naturalist, Verbal/Linguistic

T Technology Skills

☐ **P. 178** Students use the Internet to look up the weather forecast for a city in India. **BL** Logical/Mathematical

---

☑ *Online Teaching Options*

V Visual Skills

☐ **ANIMATION** **Rivers in South Asia**—Students use the animation to discuss and analyze the three major rivers of South Asia. Visual/Spatial

☐ **IMAGE** **Mount Everest**—Use the interactive image of Everest to discuss this landform.

☐ **MAP** **Physical Geography: South Asia**—Use the physical geography layer on the Chapter Opener map to review the various landforms and waterways of South Asia.

☐ **MAP** **Climates: South Asia**—Use the climate layer on the Chapter Opener map to review the various climates of the region.

☐ **INFOGRAPHIC** **Salt Water vs. Freshwater**—Reuse the infographic about salt water and freshwater to review water accessibility.

☐ **MAP** **Resources: South Asia**—Use the resources layer of the Chapter Opener map to review the other resources in the region.

☐ **IMAGE** **Teak Wood**—Use the interactive image to discuss the resources unique to the region.

W Writing Skills

☐ **DIAGRAM** **Water Wells**—Students analyze the diagram of a water well and research problems associated with wells. **AL** Naturalist, Logical/Mathematical

R Reading Skills

☐ **LECTURE SLIDE** **Weather Extremes in South Asia**—Use the lecture slide about weather extremes to review how people have adapted to such extremes.

☐ **LECTURE SLIDE** **Hurricanes, Cyclones, and Typhoons**—Use the lecture slide to review the different natural disasters and why they have regional names.

C Critical Thinking Skills

☐ **VIDEO** **Around the World—Bhutan**—Students watch the video and compare and contrast the geography of Bhutan with the geography of their own region. **BL** Logical/Mathematical

☐ **SLIDE SHOW** **Geographic Features of South Asia**—Use the interactive slide show to make connections to the physical features of the region.

☐ **GAME** **Drag-and-Drop: Adapting to Climate**—Students explain how people adapt to the climate and rainfall changes. **ELL** Interpersonal

T Technology Skills

☐ **MAP** **Monsoons**—Students use the map to discuss monsoons and use the Internet to determine if the United States has monsoons. **BL** Verbal/Linguistic, Naturalist

☐ **ONLINE SELF-CHECK QUIZ** **Lesson 1**—Students receive instant feedback on their mastery of lesson content.

☑ *Printable Digital Worksheets*

W Writing Skills

☐ **WORKSHEET** **Primary Sources Reading Skills: Climbing Mount Everest**—Students can use this worksheet to learn more about the exploration of Everest and the explorers of the peak.

HISTORY OF SOUTH ASIA

Students will know:
- that South Asia has a long history that stretches back thousands of years.

Students will be able to:
- **discuss** the early history of South Asia.
- **describe** religious traditions of South Asia.
- **explain** the three Indian empires.
- **describe** modern South Asia.

UNDERSTANDING
BY DESIGN®

☑ *Print Teaching Options*

V Visual Skills

☐ **P. 184** Students create a chart to list the chief aspects of Hinduism, Jainism, and Buddhism. **Visual/Spatial, Verbal/Linguistic**

☐ **P. 185** Students analyze the photograph of the Taj Mahal and describe its style. **AL Visual/Spatial**

☐ **P. 186** Students use the map at the bottom of the page to discuss the British takeover and rule of India and make connections to U.S. history. **AL Visual/Spatial**

☐ **P. 187** Students analyze the photograph of Jawaharlal Nehru and Mohandas Gandhi for striking or unusual aspects of the two men depicted. **AL Visual/Spatial**

W Writing Skills

☐ **P. 187** Students write a short biography of Jawaharlal Nehru or Mohandas Gandhi, describing roles in India's independence, religious and political beliefs, and Nehru's accomplishments as prime minister. **Verbal/Linguistic**

R Reading Skills

☐ **P. 183** Students complete a definition tree for vocabulary words. **ELL Visual/Spatial, Verbal/Linguistic**

☐ **P. 185** Students determine the main ideas about the three Indian empires of the Mauryas, the Guptas, and the Mughals. **Verbal/Linguistic**

☐ **P. 187** Students discuss the effect of geography on communication. **AL Visual/Spatial, Interpersonal**

C Critical Thinking Skills

☐ **P. 182** Students use visual and text clues to theorize about the Indus Valley civilizations. **BL Verbal/Linguistic, Logical/Mathematical**

☐ **P. 183** Students determine the main ideas about the Aryan migration. **Verbal/Linguistic**

☐ **P. 186** Students discuss the idea of boycotting. **AL Verbal/Linguistic**

T Technology Skills

☐ **P. 184** Interested students research the Eightfold Path and give an oral report comparing Buddhism with other religions. **BL Verbal/Linguistic, Interpersonal**

☑ *Online Teaching Options*

V Visual Skills

☐ **VIDEO Visions of India**—Days of Raj—Students watch the video about Rajasthan, the land of palaces and forts in northern India, sharing what they have learned. **AL Visual/Spatial**

☐ **IMAGE Sanskrit**—Students use the interactive image to analyze Sanskrit and familiarize students with this language.

☐ **VIDEO Mohenjo-Daro**—Students watch the video about Mohenjo-Daro and share what they find most interesting about the Indus Valley civilization. **AL Intrapersonal**

☐ **IMAGE 360° View: Taj Mahal**—Students examine the photograph and identify the elements that make the Taj Mahal such a unique and beautiful monument. **BL Visual/Spatial**

☐ **MAP The British in India**—Students use the interactive map to discuss the British colonization of India and India's independence movement. **AL Visual/Spatial**

☐ **MAP Kashmir**—Students use the physical map focusing in on Kashmir to discuss the dispute there.

W Writing Skills

☐ **GRAPHIC ORGANIZER Three Indian Empires**—Students can use the interactive graphic organizer to review the three major empires of India.

R Reading Skills

☐ **LECTURE SLIDE Caste System Organization**—Students use the lecture slide to review the main categories of the caste system.

☐ **LECTURE SLIDE Nuclear Threat**—Students can use the lecture slide on India and Pakistan relations and the idea of nuclear proliferation to discuss this conflict.

C Critical Thinking Skills

☐ **GRAPHIC ORGANIZER Major Religions of South Asia**—Students use the interactive graphic organizer to compare and contrast the major religions of South Asia. **BL Interpersonal**

☐ **CHART Buddhist Eightfold Path**—Students can use the chart of the Eightfold Path to discuss what each path means and the basic principles of Buddhism.

T Technology Skills

☐ **ONLINE SELF-CHECK QUIZ Lesson 2**—Students receive instant feedback on their mastery of lesson content.

☑ *Printable Digital Worksheets*

W Writing Skills

☐ **WORKSHEET GeoLab: Indian Textiles**—Students can use this worksheet to understand the process of making natural textile dyes.

LIFE IN SOUTH ASIA

Students will know:
- that the people of South Asia have cultures and languages unique to them.

Students will be able to:
- **describe** population patterns in South Asia.
- **describe** people and cultures in the region.
- **explore** religion, the arts, and daily life in the region.
- **examine** economic issues in South Asia.
- **describe** conflict in the region.

UNDERSTANDING
BY DESIGN®

☑ *Print Teaching Options*

V **Visual Skills**

☐ **P. 189** Students analyze information on a population graphic. **Visual/Spatial**

☐ **P. 190** Students create a two-column chart to identify the various languages spoken in each country of the region. **ELL**

☐ **P. 191** Students discuss the cultural life of South Asia by completing a concept web on the board. **AL** **Visual/Spatial, Verbal Linguistic**

R **Reading Skills**

☐ **P. 192** Students apply what they know and have learned about unreliable phone service to the areas of health care, business, and other areas.

☐ **P. 193** Students answer questions to focus on the central issues facing South Asia. **AL** **Verbal/Linguistic**

C **Critical Thinking Skills**

☐ **P. 188** Students discuss the human and environmental issues related to India's rapid population growth and propose possible solutions. **AL**

☐ **P. 189** Students compare and contrast differences between India and the United States in terms of the rural/urban population split. **AL** **Verbal/Linguistic**

☐ **P. 192** Students identify the central issues facing South Asians today. **Verbal/Linguistic**

T **Technology Skills**

☐ **P. 192** Students use the Internet to research ecotours of the region and present photographs of their chosen destination to the class. **BL** **Verbal/Linguistic**

☑ *Online Teaching Options*

V **Visual Skills**

☐ **MAP** **Population: South Asia**—Students use the population layer of the Chapter Opener map to discuss the population of the region.

☐ **MAP** **India**—Students can use the political layer of the Chapter Opener map to discuss the urban/rural centers of India.

☐ **IMAGE** **Outsourcing**—Students use the interactive photograph to discuss the impact outsourcing jobs to India has on Indians and Americans. **AL** **Visual/Spatial**

W **Writing Skills**

☐ **SLIDE SHOW** **Culture Groups in South Asia**—Students view a slide show about South Asian culture and write a paragraph about what they would like to see if they were to visit South Asia and why. **AL** **Visual/Spatial, Intrapersonal, Verbal/Linguistic**

R **Reading Skills**

☐ **GRAPHIC ORGANIZER** **Languages and Cultures of South Asia**—Students use the interactive graphic organizer to discuss the languages and cultural groups of South Asia.

☐ **GRAPHIC ORGANIZER** **Issues in South Asia Today**—Students can use the interactive graphic organizer to review the major issues in South Asia today.

C **Critical Thinking Skills**

☐ **VIDEO** **Should Elephants Weep?**—Students watch the video about how India's burgeoning population threatens elephant habitats and their very survival in the wild and discuss possible solutions to the problem. **AL** **Visual/Spatial**

☐ **GRAPHS** **Population Pyramid: India**—Students can use the population pyramids of India and the United States to compare populations across age and gender. **ELL** **Visual/Spatial**

☐ **CHART** **Comparing Urban Population in India and the United States**—Students use the chart to compare populations of major cities in India and the United States. **BL** **Logical/Mathematical**

☐ **CHART** **Conflict in South Asia**—Students use the cause and effect chart to discuss the India/Pakistan conflict, Nepal, and the Pakistan-Afghanistan border issue.

T **Technology Skills**

☐ **ONLINE SELF-CHECK QUIZ** **Lesson 3**—Students receive instant feedback on their mastery of lesson content.

INTERVENTION AND REMEDIATION STRATEGIES

LESSON 1 Physical Geography of South Asia

Reading and Comprehension

Students may find some of the content vocabulary words in this lesson confusing, such as the term *alluvial plain*. Students may also be confused by the difference between a monsoon and a cyclone. Have students work with a partner to research these terms to learn how or if they differ from a hurricane. Then have students make flashcards of each content vocabulary term and quiz each other. Circulate to provide corrective guidance to clarify meaning and pronunciation of terms as needed.

Text Evidence

Have students work in groups to research the climate and natural resources found in regions of South Asia discussed in this lesson: northern mountains and plains, central and southern highlands, and islands. Tell students to present an analysis of their findings, and to summarize the information supported by evidence found in their research. Remind students that a summary includes only the main points and leaves out minor details.

LESSON 2 History of South Asia

Reading and Comprehension

Have students work in pairs to use each content vocabulary word in sentences that show the meaning of the words. Then have students choose a term from the list and explain to their partner how it relates to a lesson concept. For example, students might explain that the caste system is the way social classes are organized in South Asia. Circulate to provide corrective guidance.

Text Evidence

Have students work in small groups to write a summary about the different segments of South Asia's history. You may wish to use the lesson's headings and subheadings to assign students their topic titles: "Early Civilizations," "Religious Traditions," "Three Indian Empires," "The British in South Asia," "Achieving Independence," and "India and Pakistan." Have students collaborate to find evidence in the text on which to base their summaries and present them to the class.

LESSON 3 Life in South Asia

Reading and Comprehension

As a lesson review, have students work in pairs to outline important aspects of daily life in South Asia. Tell partners to take turns summarizing portions of the text, dividing the text into segments using the lesson's headings and subheadings. To ensure comprehension of the concepts in this lesson, have students write two or three sentences describing life in South Asia today.

Text Evidence

Have small groups of students create a cause-effect chart that shows the cause of various challenges faced by people in South Asia and their effect. Students may wish to indicate on their charts if the issue is ongoing, and what is being done to remedy these challenges. Tell students they may conduct additional research about these problems using reliable online sources. After groups have presented their charts to the class, discuss the causes and effects of outsourcing.

Online Resources

Level Reader

Use this online lower-level text that corresponds directly to the text in the online Student Edition.

Guided Reading Activities

This resource uses graphic organizers and guiding questions to help students with comprehension.

Assessing Background Knowledge

Use these worksheets to pre-assess students' background knowledge before they read the chapter.

Reading Essentials and Study Guide Workbook

This resource offers writing and reading activities for the approaching-level student.

Self-Check Quizzes

This online assessment tool provides instant feedback for students to check their progress.

SOUTH ASIA

networks
There's More Online about South Asia.

CHAPTER **6**

Lesson 1
Physical Geography
of South Asia

Lesson 2
History of South Asia

Lesson 3
Life in South Asia

ESSENTIAL QUESTIONS · How does geography influence the way people live?
· How do governments change? · What makes a culture unique?

A man in traditional clothes
celebrates at a Hindu festival in
northern India.

The Story Matters...

The landscape of South Asia is one of contrasts—from lowlands only a few feet above sea level to the Himalaya, the highest mountains in the world. Many of the rivers of South Asia begin in the Himalaya and flow down onto valleys and plains, providing the fertile soils needed for farming. Many of the countries of South Asia have their roots in ancient civilizations and religions that developed in these river valleys.

FOLDABLES
Study Organizer

Go to the Foldables® library in the back of your book to make a Foldable® that will help you take notes while reading this chapter.

173

Letter from the Author

Dear Geography Teacher,

The United States has a growing relationship with India. As a result, parts of American culture have spread to India, and characteristics of Indian culture are woven into American culture. To help students understand India's influence in American culture today, ask students to interview two adults for homework. Have them identify and record examples of evidence of Indian culture in the U.S. Then have students list each example on a sticky note and attach it to a map of South Asia. The number of notes on the map will reveal the importance of India in students' lives today.

Richard G. Boehm

CHAPTER 6
South Asia

ENGAGE

Bellringer To orient students to the region, tell them that South Asia consists of India and several nearby countries. Then create a T-chart on the board. On one side write "What We Know About South Asia." For five minutes have students brainstorm everything they know about the geography, history, and culture of South Asia. For example, students might mention a large population, crowded cities, the Himalaya, or Ganges River. Assign one student the task of making a copy of the chart. After five minutes, add the second column heading: "What We Learned About South Asia." Tell students that they will complete this side of the chart after they finish the chapter. Then have students read "The Story Matters..." and the photograph caption.

What We Know About South Asia	What We Learned About South Asia

Content Background Knowledge

Many men in India wear turbans for a variety of reasons. In some cases, turbans indicate a person's class, caste, religion, or profession. In the Sikh religion, men do not cut their hair so they wrap their long hair up in turbans. In addition, many Sikhs also do not cut their beards. Sikhism is a religion that began in India and Pakistan in the 1400s. Wearing turbans is also common among Muslims. Among specific groups there are rules or customs that determine the color or type of turban. In addition, turbans are generally different based upon the region or country.

FOLDABLES
Study Organizer

Go to the Foldables® library for a chapter-based Foldable® activity that your students can use to help take notes and prepare for assessment.

TEACH & ASSESS

Step Into the Place

V₁ Visual Skills

Analyzing Maps Direct students' attention to the map and tell them that South Asia consists of seven countries. **Ask:**

- **What countries make up South Asia?** *(India, Pakistan, Nepal, Bhutan, Bangladesh, Sri Lanka, Maldives)*
- **How would you rank these countries from largest to smallest?** *(India, Pakistan, Bangladesh, Nepal, Sri Lanka, Bhutan, Maldives)*
- **What is the latitude range for these countries?** *(from about 5° North to about 35° North)*

Tell students that the Himalaya extend across northern Pakistan and India and across Nepal and Bhutan. Remind students that "The Story Matters..." mentioned rivers that begin in the Himalaya and flow through valleys and plains, where ancient civilizations and religions developed. **Ask:**

- **What three rivers shown on the map begin in the Himalaya?** *(Indus, Ganges, Brahmaputra)*
- **What countries do these three rivers flow through?** *(The Indus River flows through India and Pakistan. The Ganges and Brahmaputra rivers flow through India and Bangladesh.)*

Then have students answer the Step Into the Place questions.
AL Visual/Spatial

V₂ Visual Skills

Analyzing Images Have students look at the picture of the road along the Khyber Pass (Picture A). **Ask:**

- **What challenges would invaders taking this route face?** *(It is physically challenging and attackers/defenders would be able to look down on the area to see them coming.)*
- **What does the layout of this route suggest about South Asia's connection to the North and West?** *(South Asia is mostly isolated from these areas.)* **AL** Visual/Spatial

---

V₁ The northern part of South Asia is separated from the rest of Asia by mountains. The southern part of South Asia juts out of the Asian continent and into the waters of the Arabian Sea, Indian Ocean, and Bay of Bengal.

V₂

Step Into the Place

MAP FOCUS Use the map to answer the following questions.

1 PLACES AND REGIONS What is the capital of Bangladesh?

2 THE GEOGRAPHER'S WORLD What are the two island countries of South Asia?

3 PHYSICAL GEOGRAPHY Which South Asian countries are landlocked?

4 CRITICAL THINKING Analyzing Use the scale bar to estimate the distance between Mumbai and New Delhi.

MOUNTAIN GATEWAY A road winds through the Khyber Pass at the border between Pakistan and Afghanistan. Invaders and traders of long ago used the pass to enter South Asia from the northwest.

HISTORIC MONASTERY Built in the 1600s, this Buddhist monastery overlooks Thimphu, the capital of Bhutan. Today, the monastery holds government offices and the throne room of Bhutan's king.

Step Into the Time

TIME LINE Choose two events from the time line and explain the connection between those events and their effects on the people of South Asia today. WHST.6-8.2, WHST.6-8.4

c. 3000 B.C. Indus River Valley civilization emerges

1500 B.C. Aryans migrate south into India

c. 500s B.C. Buddhism emerges in South Asia

A.D. 1526 Mughal Empire begins reign

B.C. A.D.

174 Chapter 6

Project-Based Learning

Hands-On

Writing a News Broadcast
Students will work in small groups to create a simulated news broadcast about South Asia. Each group should write stories about South Asia's physical features, history, cultures, or current events. Each story will be presented in 30 second increments. The groups will plan the order of each segment to create a cohesive news broadcast that transitions from story to story. The news broadcasts will be presented live in the classroom to an audience of classmates.

Digital Hands-On

Creating a Video Documentary
Students will work in pairs to produce a video documentary about South Asia's physical features. Videos should integrate photos, narration, and background music. Have students search online for copyright free photos and information to incorporate into their documentary. Videos can be shared within the class or online.

ANSWERS, p. 174

STEP INTO THE PLACE
1. Dhaka
2. Sri Lanka and Maldives
3. Nepal and Bhutan
4. **CRITICAL THINKING** 715 miles (1152 km)

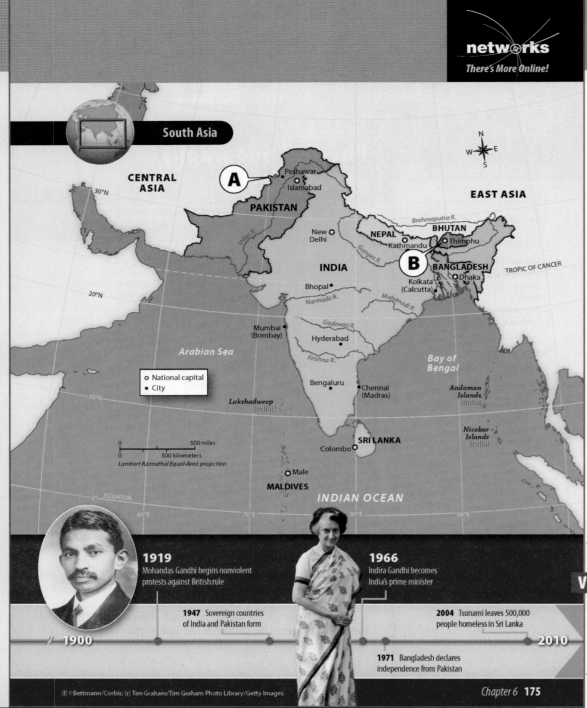

CHAPTER 6
South Asia

South Asia

CENTRAL ASIA

EAST ASIA

PAKISTAN

NEPAL   BHUTAN

New Delhi

Kathmandu   Thimphu

INDIA   BANGLADESH

TROPIC OF CANCER

Bhopal   Kolkata (Calcutta)   Dhaka

Narmada R.   Mahanadi R.

Arabian Sea   Godavari R.

Mumbai (Bombay)   Hyderabad

Krishna R.

Bay of Bengal

Bengaluru   Chennai (Madras)   Andaman Islands (India)

○ National capital
● City

Lakshadweep (India)

Nicobar Islands (India)

SRI LANKA
Colombo

500 miles
500 kilometers
Lambert Azimuthal Equal-Area projection

● Male
MALDIVES

INDIAN OCEAN

EQUATOR

1919 Mohandas Gandhi begins nonviolent protests against British rule

1966 Indira Gandhi becomes India's prime minister

1947 Sovereign countries of India and Pakistan form

2004 Tsunami leaves 500,000 people homeless in Sri Lanka

1900   2010

1971 Bangladesh declares independence from Pakistan

(l) ©Bettmann/Corbis; (r) Tim Graham/Tim Graham Photo Library/Getty Images

Chapter 6 **175**

Step Into the Time

V Visual Skills

Interpreting Have students use the time line to answer the following questions. **Ask:**

- How far back does civilization date in South Asia? *(more than 5,000 years)*
- In what century did India, Pakistan, and Bangladesh become independent countries? *(20th century)*
- How long after Mohandas Gandhi began his protests against British rule did India and Pakistan become sovereign countries? *(28 years)*
- How do the two photographs on the opposite page relate to the time line? *(The top photograph shows the Khyber Pass, through which the Aryans mentioned in the time line, might have passed. The lower photograph shows a Buddhist monastery, and the time line mentions Buddhism emerging in South Asia about 500 B.C.)* **AL** Visual/Spatial

Content Background Knowledge

As students examine the time line, share with them the following information, which is expanded upon later in the chapter.

- The Indus River Valley civilization is one of the world's oldest known civilizations. The civilization arose near the Indus River in what is now Pakistan.
- The Aryans were a group of people who settled in India around 1500 B.C. and strongly influenced the culture of the region. Historians are not sure of their origins, but think that they came from the northwest.
- The religion of Buddhism was founded in India by a holy man called "the Buddha."
- The Mogul Empire was led by Muslim rulers. They introduced Islam into South Asia.
- Mohandas Gandhi is probably the most famous Indian leader. Known for his practice of nonviolent resistance, he was instrumental in gaining India's independence from Great Britain.
- Indira Gandhi was the daughter of Jawaharlal Nehru, another leader of India's independence movement. Indira Gandhi was the first woman to serve as prime minister of India.

CLOSE & REFLECT

Formulating Questions Based on their introduction to South Asia, have students make a list of questions they have about the region. Call on volunteers to share their questions. Then suggest that students look for answers to their questions as they study the chapter.

TIME LINE AND MAP

Reading a Time Line and Map

Analyzing Visuals Display the time line and map on the whiteboard. Have volunteers read each event as it is revealed on the time line. Ask students to identify the country or countries where the event took place, if possible, and find its location on the map. **ELL**

See page 173B for other online activities.

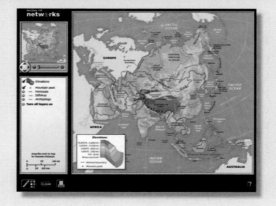

ENGAGE

Bellringer Display a physical map of South Asia for students to examine. Give students five minutes to write a paragraph describing the main features of the region's geography based on what they see on the map. Call on volunteers to read their descriptions. Then tell students that they will learn more about the physical geography of South Asia in this lesson, including information they cannot gain from the map, such as details on the climate and natural resources.

TEACH & ASSESS

V Visual Skills

Creating Word Squares Suggest that students create word squares for each vocabulary word. *(Sample answers for subcontinent: a geographically or politically unique part of a larger continent; India is part of the subcontinent of South Asia; draw a landmass with a large section of it shaded; larger than a region and smaller than a continent)* **ELL** **AL** Visual/Spatial, Verbal/Linguistic

Definition		Illustration
	Vocabulary Word	
Sentence		Characteristics

R Reading Skills

Locating Ask a volunteer to locate on a physical map the three mountain ranges that form South Asia's northern boundary: the Hindu Kush, the Karakoram, and the Himalaya. Call on another volunteer to locate Mount Everest and the Khyber Pass. Note that these mountains are still being built up by the movement of Earth's plates. **Ask:**

• **How is Mount Everest distinctive?** *(It is the highest mountain in the world.)*

• **Why is the Khyber Pass important?** *(It is one of the few openings in the mountain ranges that separate South Asia from the rest of Asia.)* **AL** Visual/Spatial, Verbal/Linguistic

---

ANSWER, p. 176

TAKING NOTES Students should list any three main ideas from the lesson. Examples: Three large mountain ranges form the northern boundary of South Asia. The Ganges and Brahmaputra rivers form the largest delta on Earth, which is also one of the world's most fertile farming regions. South Asia's annual monsoon rains provide water for crops, helping to support the large population.

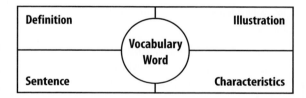

networks

There's More Online!

☑ **CHART/GRAPH** Water Wells

☑ **MAP** Monsoons

☑ **ANIMATION** Rivers in South Asia

☑ **VIDEO**

Reading **HELP**DESK (CCSS)

Academic Vocabulary RH.6-8.4
• annual *(Tier Two Words)*

Content Vocabulary RH.6-8.4
• **subcontinent** *(Tier Three Words)*
• **alluvial plain**
• **delta**
• **atoll**
• **monsoon**
• **cyclone**

TAKING NOTES: *Key Ideas and Details* RH.6-8.2, RH.6-8.7

Organize As you read the lesson, identify at least three facts about the physical geography of South Asia and write them in a graphic organizer like the one below.

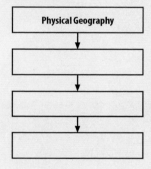

Physical Geography

↓

↓

↓

176

Lesson 1
Physical Geography of South Asia

ESSENTIAL QUESTION • *How does geography influence the way people live?*

IT MATTERS BECAUSE
South Asia is a land of contrasts, with snowcapped mountains towering over parched deserts. More than one-sixth of the world's people live in this region.

South Asia's Physical Features

GUIDING QUESTION *What physical features make South Asia unique?*

V South Asia forms a **subcontinent**. A subcontinent is a geographically or politically unique part of a larger continent. Seven countries make up the region of South Asia. Of these, India is by far the largest. The other six countries are Pakistan, Nepal, Bhutan, Bangladesh, Maldives, and Sri Lanka.

Northern Mountains and Plains

R Three mighty mountain ranges form South Asia's northern border. They are the Hindu Kush, the Karakoram, and the Himalaya. The Himalaya range includes the highest mountain in the world: Mount Everest, at 29,028 feet (8,848 m). The mountain ranges form a physical barrier. Invaders and traders could enter South Asia through only a few openings, such as the Khyber Pass between Afghanistan and Pakistan. Plate tectonics created the ranges millions of years ago. Today, the mountains are still rising. Plate movements also cause earthquakes throughout South Asia.

Three major rivers begin as small streams from the mountain ranges. The rivers are the Indus, the Ganges, and the Brahmaputra. The Indus flows southward through

---

networks *Online Teaching Options*

VIDEO

Around the World—Bhutan

Comparing and Contrasting Use this video about the landscape, lifestyle, climate, and wildlife of Bhutan to preview the lesson content. Have students compare and contrast the geography of South Asia with the geography of their own region. **BL** Logical/Mathematical

See page 173C for other online activities.

Pakistan to the Arabian Sea. The Ganges and the Brahmaputra flow east and southeast to the Bay of Bengal.

The three rivers cross a vast plains area, where their annual flooding has deposited rich soil for growing crops. One-tenth of the world's people now live in the **alluvial plain** created by the Ganges River. This alluvial plain, or area of fertile soil deposited by floodwaters, is the world's longest.

C

The Brahmaputra and the Ganges come together and form the largest **delta** on Earth. Deltas are places where rivers deposit soil at the mouth of a river. The Brahmaputra/Ganges delta has some of the world's richest farmland.

Central and Southern Highlands

Mountains and rivers also dominate central and southern parts of South Asia. They physically and culturally separate India into northern and southern parts. Much of southern India is a high, flat area called the Deccan Plateau. Two low mountain ranges, the Western and Eastern Ghats, form the plateau's edges. A narrow coastal plain lies between each mountain range and the seacoast. The soils of the plain are rich and fertile.

Islands of South Asia

Sri Lanka and Maldives are the two island countries of South Asia. Sri Lanka, shaped like a teardrop, lies off the southeastern tip of India. Maldives lies southwest of India's tip and is made up of numerous islands. Many of the islands are small, ring-shaped islands called **atolls**.

☑ **READING PROGRESS CHECK**

Describing Describe the main physical regions of South Asia.

People wash clothes along the banks of the Ganges River in Varanasi, India. The Ganges is important for daily activities, but to Hindus it is also sacred. The city of Varanasi draws religious pilgrims from all over India.

▶ **CRITICAL THINKING**
Describing How does the Ganges help India's economy?

V

©Frederic Soltan/Sygma/Corbis

Chapter 6 **177**

C Critical Thinking Skills

Finding the Main Idea Pose the following questions to help students identify the main ideas about the landforms and rivers of South Asia. As students answer the questions, have them locate the landforms and rivers on a classroom map. **Ask:**

- **What three major rivers begin in the mountains of northern South Asia and flow across plains?** *(Indus, Ganges, and Brahmaputra)*
- **What is an alluvial plain, and what is unique about the alluvial plain of the Ganges River?** *(An alluvial plain is an area of fertile soil deposited by floodwaters. The alluvial plain of the Ganges River is the longest in the world.)*
- **What is a delta, and what is unique about the delta formed by the Brahmaputra and Ganges rivers?** *(A delta is an area where rivers deposit soil at the mouth of a river. The Brahmaputra/Ganges delta is the largest delta on Earth.)*
- **What landform dominates southern India?** *(the Deccan Plateau)*
- **What mountain ranges border the plateau?** *(the Western and Eastern Ghats)*
- **Where are the two island countries of South Asia located?** *(Sri Lanka lies off the southeastern tip of India; Maldives lies southwest of India's tip.)* **Visual/Spatial, Verbal/Linguistic**

V Visual Skills

Interpreting Direct students' attention to the photograph at the bottom of the page. **Ask:**

- **Based on the activity shown in this photograph, what conclusion can you draw about these people's homes?** *(They probably do not have running water in their homes. They may not have electricity to run a washing machine. It is probably very inexpensive to pay someone to wash their clothes for them.)*
- **What are some likely effects of using the river to wash clothes?** *(The river will be polluted by the detergents used to clean the clothes. This will affect the fish and wildlife in the water as well as the soil on the riverbed further downstream.)* **AL Visual/Spatial**

ANIMATION

Rivers in South Asia

Analyzing Use the animation to discuss and analyze the three major rivers of South Asia. Have students create 3-column comparision charts to synthesize the information that they gain from this activity. Discuss with students which river may be the most important and why.
BL Visual/Spatial

See page 173C for other online activities.

ANSWERS, p. 177

☑ **READING PROGRESS CHECK** The main physical regions are the northern mountains and plains, the central and southern highlands, and the islands.
CRITICAL THINKING Annual flooding of the Ganges provides fertile soil for growing crops.

R Reading Skills

Summarizing Use the following questions to help students summarize the information about South Asia's climates. **Ask:**

- **What kind of climate dominates the southern half of South Asia, and what kind of climate dominates the northern half?** *(tropical in the southern half and warm temperate in the northern half)*

- **What are monsoons?** *(seasonal wind patterns that bring heavy rainfall)*

- **What are the advantages and disadvantages of the monsoons?** *(They bring rain for farms to grow food, but they cause floods that damage property and kill people.)*

- **What are cyclones, and where do they occur?** *(large, swirling storms with violent winds and heavy rains; they occur along the coast of the Bay of Bengal)*

- **Why are cyclones so destructive?** *(Their strong winds push water far inland and flood the low-lying delta lands of the Brahmaputra and Ganges rivers.)*

- **What is the main difference between a tropical wet/dry climate and a tropical wet climate?** *(A tropical wet/dry climate has wet and dry seasons, while a tropical wet climate has rain year-round.)*

- **What parts of South Asia are dry?** *(parts of the Deccan Plateau in India and the Thar Desert between Pakistan and India)* **ELL** Verbal/Linguistic

T Technology Skills

Researching on the Internet To give students an idea of the typical temperatures in South Asia, suggest that they look up the weather forecast for a city in India on the Internet. Students will probably need to convert the temperatures from Celsius to Fahrenheit. They can use an online conversion site to make the conversions. While studying this chapter, you might ask a student to give a daily report on the temperature in a northern and a southern city in India and compare it with the temperature in your community. **BL** Logical/Mathematical

---

Visual Vocabulary

Atoll An atoll is a small, ring-shaped island formed when coral builds up around the edges of an ancient, underwater volcano. **R**

T

Academic Vocabulary

annual yearly or each year

South Asia's Climates

GUIDING QUESTION *How does climate affect people's lives in South Asia?*

Climate is closely related to the physical features of the region. Because the physical features of South Asia are so diverse, the region's climate is diverse, too. About half of South Asia has a tropical climate, with different kinds of plant life. Much of the northern half of the region enjoys a warm temperate climate. You can also find cool highlands in the north and scorching deserts to the west.

Monsoons

Much of South Asia's climate is a result of seasonal wind patterns called **monsoons**. Most of the region has little or no rainfall for eight months of the year. Then, beginning in May and early June, temperatures begin to rise sharply. Heated air causes a change in wind direction. Winds from the Indian Ocean carry moisture inland, bringing heavy rains and flooding. Most areas along the coast get at least 90 inches (229 cm) of rain per year. Millions of family farms depend on rain for survival.

The annual monsoon rains support South Asia's large population. Without the rains, the region could not grow enough food for its people. The floods come at a cost, though—they damage property and can cause loss of life.

Other natural hazards include tropical **cyclones**. These large, swirling storms often slam into the coast along the Bay of Bengal. Their violent winds and heavy rains can cause devastation. The strong winds push water from the Bay of Bengal to the shore, flooding low-lying areas far inland. One cyclone can kill tens of thousands of people. The delta lands of the Brahmaputra and Ganges rivers are especially vulnerable to flooding.

Tropical and Dry Areas

Much of South Asia has a tropical wet/dry climate with just three seasons—hot, wet, and cool. The hot and cool seasons are dry. The three seasons are a result of the monsoon wind patterns.

Tropical wet climates are found along the western coast of India, southern Sri Lanka, and the Ganges Delta in Bangladesh. These areas get plenty of rain year-round and have thick, green vegetation.

Not all of South Asia gets drenched by seasonal monsoons. Some places are dry. Parts of the Deccan Plateau, for example, get little rain, because the Western Ghats block the winds and rains of the wet-season monsoons.

Northwestern South Asia has the region's driest climate. The Thar Desert straddles the border between Pakistan and India. The area gets relatively little rain; **annual** rainfall is less than 20 inches (51 cm). The vegetation is mostly low, thorny trees and parched grasses.

---

netw⊙rks *Online Teaching Options*

MAP

Monsoons

Analyzing Maps Use the map about monsoons to discuss this weather feature. Have volunteers explain how a monsoon works or have a group of students demonstrate how a monsoon functions. Suggest that students conduct Internet research to find out if the United States has monsoons. *(Yes, the southwestern United States does.)* **BL** Verbal/Linguistic, Naturalist

See page 173C for other online activities.

Highland and Temperate Climates

The tops of the huge mountain ranges on South Asia's northern border are covered year-round in snow. The mountains affect the climate of lower-lying areas. In winter, the Himalaya block the cold winds sweeping down from Central Asia. This forms a large temperate zone that stretches across Nepal, Bhutan, northern Bangladesh, and northeastern India. Farther south, the elevation of the Deccan Plateau combined with the wind-blocking effect of the Western and Eastern Ghats creates another temperate climate area.

R

✓ **READING PROGRESS CHECK**

Analyzing What positive and negative effects do the monsoons have on the lives of people in South Asia?

South Asia's Natural Resources

GUIDING QUESTION *Which natural resources are most important to South Asia's large population?*

South Asia has many natural resources, but they are not evenly distributed. As South Asia's largest country, India has the most productive land, as well as water and mineral resources.

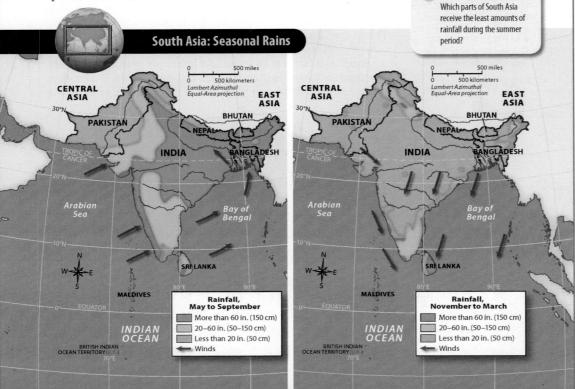

South Asia: Seasonal Rains

Rainfall, May to September
- More than 60 in. (150 cm)
- 20–60 in. (50–150 cm)
- Less than 20 in. (50 cm)
- ← Winds

Rainfall, November to March
- More than 60 in. (150 cm)
- 20–60 in. (50–150 cm)
- Less than 20 in. (50 cm)
- ← Winds

MAP SKILLS

1 PHYSICAL GEOGRAPHY
What time of year brings wet weather to much of South Asia? What time of year brings drier weather? Why?

2 PLACES AND REGIONS
Which parts of South Asia receive the least amounts of rainfall during the summer period?

GAME

Drag-And-Drop: Adapting to Climates

Reviewing Using the drag-and-drop game, discuss the concepts of droughts and monsoons further. Then, ask students to explain ways in which people adapt to the climate. In addition, use the game to highlight ways people adapt to climate and extreme weather. **AL** Intrapersonal

See page 173C for other online activities.

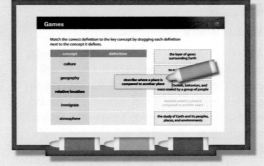

V Visual Skills

Analyzing Maps Direct students' attention to the map of seasonal rain and wind patterns at the bottom of the page and use the following questions to help students analyze the maps.
Ask:

- **What two seasons do these maps show?** *(a wet season and a dry season)*
- **During the monsoon, or wet season, how do the winds blow?** *(from the ocean toward the land)*
- **Why do you think these winds bring rain?** *(because they pick up moisture from the ocean)*
- **Which map shows the dry season? How do you know?** *(the map on the right because it is mostly beige and the key says that the area in beige gets less than 20 inches/50 centimeters of rain)*
- **What months form the dry season?** *(November to March)*
- **Which months are missing from both maps? Why do you think that is?** *(April and October; possible answer is that both April and October are neither really rainy or really dry)*
- **What is the wind pattern during the dry season?** *(The wind blows south across the land toward the ocean.)*
- **What areas of South Asia still receive a fair amount of rain during this season?** *(the southwestern coast of India, the tip of India, most of the eastern coast of India, Sri Lanka, parts of Bangladesh, and a small section of northern Pakistan and India)*
- **What do most of these areas have in common?** *(Most of the areas are near the ocean.)* **AL** Visual/Spatial

V

R Reading Skills

Explaining Invite a student or students to explain how two large temperate climate zones are created by the mountains in South Asia. *(The Himalaya block cold winds from Central Asia, forming a large temperate zone across Nepal, Bhutan, northern Bangladesh, and northeastern India. The wind-blocking effect of the Western and Eastern Ghats help create another temperate climate zone on the Deccan Plateau.* **BL** Verbal/Linguistic

---

ANSWERS, p. 179

MAP SKILLS

1. May to September is wetter. November to March is drier. The amount of rain is affected by the wind patterns.
2. Northeastern area (near border of India and Pakistan) and south central India

✓ **READING PROGRESS CHECK** Monsoons provide the rain for growing food. The storms, though, can cause severe flooding, property damage, and loss of life.

V Visual Skills

Analyzing Images Ask students to describe what is happening in the photograph at the bottom of the page and what it indicates about water resources in this Indian village. *(a crowd of people are trying to draw water from a well by dropping buckets tied to ropes deep into the well; It indicates that many people depend on this well for water, and the water is very low or scarce.)* ELL Visual/Spatial

Making Connections Most Americans have no experience with the kind of water problems that people in much of South Asia live with. In India, for example, more than two-thirds of the people do not have access to treated drinking water, and more than half of the households do not have toilet facilities. However, more than 50 percent of households do have cell phones. What might this suggest about the challenges of getting clean water? *(Examples: The per-person cost of a cell phone may be much less than the per-person cost of providing clean water to a community. Communities may not have leadership that is able to pool people's resources to accomplish such a monumental task.)* Logical/Mathematical, Interpersonal

C Critical Thinking Skills

Identifying Central Issues To help clarify the central issues surrounding the development of hydroelectric projects, create a T-chart on the board. Call on students to identify the pros and cons of damming rivers in India. *(Pros: will provide water for drinking, irrigation, electricity; Cons: will flood land, displace millions of people, affect ecosystems)* **Ask:**

- What alternatives do opponents of the dam projects offer? *(small-scale projects and traditional ways to manage water needs)*
- Do you think this sounds like a reasonable alternative? Why or why not? *(Students' opinions may vary, but students should give reasons for their opinions. Students may recognize the need for more details to judge the viability of the alternative.)* Naturalist, Verbal/Linguistic

Dam Projects in India

Pros	Cons

ANSWER, p. 180

CRITICAL THINKING dry climate; a large desert area called the Thar; the vegetation is mostly low, thorny trees, and parched grasses

---

Water Resources

South Asians depend on rivers for irrigation, drinking and household water, and transportation. Water in rivers is also considered sacred in Hinduism, the principal religion in India. Hindus revere the Ganges, named for the goddess Ganga.

Today, water is an important source of energy for South Asia. Mountains provide swift-flowing rivers that can be used to generate electricity. Several dams, such as the Narmada River project, are being built, but hundreds more are planned. The Indian government argues that the projects will provide water for drinking, irrigation, and electricity. Opponents point out that areas must be flooded to build dams. This will displace millions of people and destroy ecosystems. They favor smaller-scale projects and traditional ways to manage water needs.

Mineral and Energy Resources

India has most of South Asia's mineral resources. These include iron ore, manganese, and chromite, all used in making steel. India also has large quantities of mica, a rock used to manufacture electrical equipment.

Nepal's natural resources include mica and copper. To the south, Sri Lanka boasts some of the world's finest gemstones, including sapphires and rubies. Sri Lanka also has large quantities of graphite. This is the "lead" that is used in pencils. Graphite is also used in batteries and as a lubricant.

South Asia has several important petroleum reserves. They are located in northern Pakistan and near the Ganges Delta. Exploration in the Arabian Sea has yielded some oil. One offshore oil field was

Villagers in northwestern India try to get water from a large well. When this region is affected by drought, dams, wells, and ponds often go dry.
▶ CRITICAL THINKING
Describing What are the physical characteristics of northwestern India?

©Amit Dave/Reuters/Corbis

networks *Online Teaching Options*

DIAGRAM

Water Wells

Analyzing Diagrams Display the diagram of a water well and call on a volunteer to explain how the well works and how people tap it. Tell students that wells can vary greatly in depth, in complexity, and in the quality and quantity of water they provide. Interested students might research some of the problems associated with wells.
AL Naturalist, Logical/Mathematical

See page 173C for other online activities.

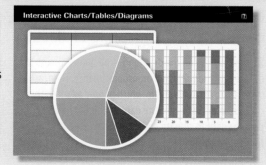

Interactive Charts/Tables/Diagrams

discovered in the mid-1970s about 100 miles (161 km) west of the Mumbai (Bombay) coast. The field accounted for a large portion of India's domestic oil production. Overall, though, South Asia depends on imported oil. Natural gas fields are found in southern Pakistan and in Bangladesh. India also has an important deposit of uranium north of the Eastern Ghats. The uranium is used in the country's nuclear power plants.

Forests and Wildlife

Like rivers, forests have greatly influenced the history of South Asia. In colonial times, when the British ruled much of the subcontinent, forests were admired for their beauty but exploited for their commercial value. Important timber resources then included teak, sal, and sandalwood. The woods are still valuable today. There is much debate about how they should be used or whether they should be conserved.

Each kind of wood has qualities that make it valuable. Teak is a strong, attractive wood used to make high-quality furniture. Sal is a hardwood used for construction. Sandalwood, with its sweet scent, is often used to make decorative objects.

Forests are, however, more than resources for wood products. They take in carbon dioxide—a greenhouse gas—and release oxygen. Tree roots hold soil in place, reducing erosion. People live in the forests and depend on leaves and fruits for food. Forests also provide habitat for much of South Asia's unique wildlife. Indian forests, for example, are home to three of Earth's most endangered mammals: the tiger, the Asian elephant, and the one-horned rhinoceros. South Asians are working to reverse some of the region's wildlife losses. The creation of wildlife reserves and laws controlling hunting and logging have started to make a difference.

☑ **READING PROGRESS CHECK**

Analyzing Think about how people use rivers in South Asia. How is it similar to how rivers are used in other parts of the world?

©David Pickford/Robert Harding World Imagery/Corbis

A porter in Nepal uses a headband to carry a heavy load in the snowy, high altitudes of the Himalaya.
▶ **CRITICAL THINKING**
Explaining Why are Himalaya snows important to people living in the plains areas of South Asia?

V

W

FOLDABLES
Study Organizer

Include this lesson's information in your Foldable®.

LESSON 1 REVIEW CCSS

Reviewing Vocabulary (Tier Three Words)
1. Why is a *delta* often used as an agricultural area? RH.6-8.4

Answering the Guiding Questions
2. ***Analyzing*** Why was the Khyber Pass so important to South Asia for centuries? RH.6-8.1

3. ***Determining Central Ideas*** What might happen in South Asia if there were no monsoons? RH.6-8.2

4. ***Analyzing*** What might be the consequences of cutting down a forest in South Asia? RH.6-8.1

5. ***Informative/Explanatory Writing*** Take notes about the physical features of the countries of South Asia. Use your notes to write about the features. Use descriptive terms to contrast the mountains, deserts, plains, and rivers of the region. WHST.6-8.2, WHST.6-8.4

Chapter 6 **181**

LESSON 1 REVIEW ANSWERS

Reviewing Vocabulary

1. The sand and silt that a river deposits at its delta make the soil rich for farming.

Answering the Guiding Questions

2. ***Analyzing*** It was one of only a few narrow passes through the mountains that allowed people to travel between South Asia and the area to the northwest.

3. ***Determining Central Ideas*** There would be much less fresh water because monsoons supply most of the rain for the region. Crops would fail, and people would go thirsty and starve.

4. ***Analyzing*** Many kinds of animals would lose their habitats. People who live in the forest would have to move elsewhere and might even have to develop a new way of life. Soil erosion would increase. The atmosphere would contain more carbon dioxide and less oxygen.

5. ***Informative/Explanatory Writing*** Students' responses should be supported by facts from the textbook.

V **Visual Skills**

Creating Charts Suggest that students create charts listing the mineral, energy, and forest resources of South Asia by country. (**India:** *iron ore, manganese, chromite, mica, oil, uranium;* **Nepal:** *mica, copper;* **Sri Lanka:** *gemstones, graphite, teak, sal, sandalwood;* **Pakistan:** *petroleum, natural gas;* **Bangladesh:** *natural gas*) **Visual/Spatial**

Mineral, Energy, and Forest Resources of South Asia
India:
Nepal:
Sri Lanka:
Pakistan:
Bangladesh:

W **Writing Skills**

Informative/Explanatory Divide students into three groups. Have each group research the status of one of the three endangered species mentioned in the text: the tiger, Asian elephant, or one-horned rhinoceros. Assign students to write a one- or two-page report describing the species' habitat and home range, reasons for its endangered status, and efforts to save it from extinction. **BL** **Verbal/Linguistic, Naturalist**

CLOSE & REFLECT

Describing Remind students that at the beginning of this lesson they spent five minutes writing a paragraph describing the main features of South Asia's geography. Tell students to repeat the assignment, now that they have learned more about the region's geography. Call on a few volunteers to read their "before" and "after" paragraphs.

ANSWERS, p. 181

CRITICAL THINKING The snows, when melted, supply water that feeds into rivers, which are used by people in the plains for irrigation, drinking and household needs, and transportation.
☑ **READING PROGRESS CHECK** Rivers are used in South Asia and throughout the world for drinking, washing, transportation, irrigation, and hydroelectricity. They also provide habitat for wildlife.

History of South Asia

ENGAGE

 Bellringer To introduce the lesson, ask students to write three questions they have about the history of India or Pakistan. Call on volunteers to share their questions. Then tell students to save their questions and to look for answers as they read this lesson about the history of South Asia. Encourage students to preview the lesson by skimming the guiding questions, headings, visuals, and captions.

TEACH & ASSESS

C Critical Thinking Skills

Theorizing Note that the Indus Valley civilization was one of the world's earliest civilizations, along with those of Mesopatamia and ancient Egypt. Point out the location of the two major cities, Mohenjo-Daro and Harappa, on a map. Have students consider what people have learned about the Indus Valley civilization from the objects that archeologists have uncovered. **Ask:**

- What are some things we might learn about the civilization when we decipher their written language? *(customs; family, government, and legal structures)*
- How would artifacts show that people traveled over long distances? *(the objects may be made from materials that are not found in the region; the objects may be almost identical to those found/made in a region that is far away)*

BL Verbal/Linguistic, Logical/Mathematical

Content Background Knowledge

The large cities of the Indus Valley civilization were remarkably well-planned and technologically advanced. They were the first cities in the world to have sanitation systems. In fact, the ancient Indus sewage systems were more efficient than the systems in use in some parts of Pakistan and India today. Unlike today, every house had a bathroom with a drain and access to water from a well.

ANSWER, p. 182

TAKING NOTES Students may include the following events on their time lines: **Beginning of Indus Valley civilization:** 3500 B.C.; **Migration of Aryans to India:** 1500 B.C.; **Rig Veda takes shape, laying foundations for Hinduism:** 1200 B.C.; **Fall of Aryan civilization:** 500 B.C.; **Rise of Jainism and Buddhism:** 500 B.C.; **Rise of Mauryan Empire:** 300 B.C.; **Rise of Mughal Empire:** 1500s; **British establish settlements in India:** 1600s; **Rebellion in northern India against British rule:** 1857; **Indian National Congress formed:** 1885; **Much of South Asia split into India and Pakistan, granted independence:** 1947

---

networks

There's More Online!

- ☑ **IMAGE** Taj Mahal
- ☑ **MAP** The British in India
- ☑ **VIDEO**

Reading HELPDESK **CCSS**

Academic Vocabulary RH.6-8.4
(Tier Two Words)
- policy

Content Vocabulary RH.6-8.4
(Tier Three Words)
- caste
- reincarnation
- Raj
- boycott
- civil disobedience
- nuclear proliferation

TAKING NOTES: *Integration of Knowledge and Ideas* RH.6-8.5, RH.6-8.7

Sequence As you read about the history of South Asia, use a time line like this one to order events from the beginning of the Indus Valley civilization to independence.

3500 B.C.   2000 B.C.

Lesson 2
History of South Asia

ESSENTIAL QUESTION · *How do governments change?*

IT MATTERS BECAUSE
South Asia is home to one of the oldest known civilizations. You will learn about the birth of a civilization and the struggle for independence by studying its rich history.

Early South Asia

GUIDING QUESTION *How did South Asia's early history lay the foundation for modern life in the region?*

The history of South Asia stretches back thousands of years. The region has experienced much change, yet many social structures and religious beliefs are steeped in tradition.

Early Civilizations

In the early 1920s, archaeologists in South Asia discovered the remains of one of the oldest known civilizations. Because of its location near the Indus River, this culture is known as the Indus Valley civilization. Its origins date back to 3500 B.C. The Indus Valley civilization formed about the same time as other river-valley civilizations around the world.

Two major centers of Indus Valley culture were located at Harappa and Mohenjo-Daro in modern-day Pakistan. These were large cities. Archaeologists have also discovered dozens of smaller settlements.

Written records by the Indus Valley people—mainly strings of symbols—have never been fully deciphered, but archaeological excavations indicate that the civilization was advanced. City streets were laid out in a grid-like pattern. Most houses were made of brick and had their own wells. Houses even had bathrooms and drains. Although most residents were farmers, craftsmanship flourished, as is evident

(l to r) JAMES L. STANFIELD/National Geographic Stock; ©Keren Su/Corbis; Robert Harding Picture Library Ltd/Alamy; LORI EPSTEIN/National Geographic Stock; ©Bettmann/Corbis

---

networks *Online Teaching Options*

VIDEO

Visions of India—Days of Raj

Informative/Explanatory Writing Use this video about the history of India, including the British influence on the country, to generate interest in the lesson content. Ask students to share new information they learned in a written paragraph. **AL** Visual/Spatial

See page 173D for other online activities.

BBC Motion Gallery Education

from toys and other artifacts. Some of the same artifacts show that people traded over long distances.

The Indus Valley culture lasted for about 1,000 years. What brought it to an end? No one knows for sure. A natural disaster such as an earthquake may have occurred. Disease or enemy invasions might have played a part in bringing down the civilization.

Equally mysterious are the beginnings of the Aryans, a group that swept into what is now India about 1500 B.C. They came from the northwest, probably from southern Russia and central Asia. Were they invaders, migrants, or wandering nomads? There are different theories about the Aryans. They likely herded sheep, cows, and other livestock in their homeland. Once in India, they settled down to become farmers.

The Aryan civilization lasted for about 1,000 years. It left behind two important legacies for South Asians. The first legacy was social. Aryans believed that society could be successful only if people followed strict roles and tasks. So, they established a system of *varnas*, or castes. **Castes** were social classes. The top class was made up of Brahmans, or priests. Next came the warriors. Third were the merchants. The bottom class consisted of laborers and peasants.

The caste system had a deep impact on South Asia for thousands of years, causing much inequality. If they were born into a lower caste, people could not move up in society, regardless of their talents. After India won its independence in 1947, the new country outlawed the caste system. Some effects of the system are still present though.

The second major legacy of the Aryans was literary. Recall that scholars have not been able to fully decipher the Indus Valley writing. In contrast, the Aryans composed long poetic texts, called the Vedas, in the ancient Sanskrit language. Sanskrit is the parent language of Hindi, one of the most important languages in modern India. Sanskrit also greatly influenced the development of ancient Greek and Latin.

A worker replaces broken bricks with new ones at the ruins of the ancient city of Mohenjo-Daro in Pakistan.
▶ **CRITICAL THINKING**
Describing What have archaeological digs revealed about the Indus Valley civilization and its large cities?

Chapter 6 **183**

V Visual Skills

Integrating Visual Information   Ask students to study the photograph of the ruins of Mohenjo-Daro at the bottom of the page. **Ask: What is striking about this city?** *(Sample answers: All the buildings and walls are made of the same kind of brick; the buildings look very uniform; the streets appear very narrow; and there seems to be no space for trees or other plants.)* **Visual/Spatial**

C Critical Thinking Skills

Finding the Main Idea   Pose the following questions to help students focus on the main ideas about the Aryan migration into South Asia. **Ask:**

- **Who were the Aryans, and when did they migrate to South Asia?** *(Historians are not sure who they were. They probably were herders from southern Russia and central Asia. They came to India about 1500 B.C.)*
- **What did the Aryans do when they came to India?** *(They became farmers.)*
- **What are two major legacies of the Aryan civilization?** *(the caste system and the Sanskrit language, which is the parent language of Hindi)*
- **The Indus Valley civilization and the Aryan civilization both lasted the same number of years. How many years did each last?** *(about 1,000 years)* **Verbal/Linguistic**

V

R Reading Skills

Defining and Expressing   Direct students in completing a definition tree like the one below for each vocabulary word they encounter in this lesson, beginning with the word *caste*. Call on volunteers to share the sentences they generate. Use the opportunity to correct any misconceptions students may have about the meaning or use of each word. *(Sample answer: social class; The family belonged to the lowest caste, so the son had no hope of becoming a doctor.)* **ELL** **Visual/Spatial, Verbal/Linguistic**

caste	**Definition:**
	Sentence:

IMAGE

Mohenjo-Daro

Describing   After students view the interactive image, call on volunteers to share what they find most interesting about the Indus Valley civilization. Ask students to imagine living in Mohenjo-Daro. **Ask: What would they have liked about their life? What would they have disliked?** **AL** **Intrapersonal**

See page 173D for other online activities.

Interactive Photos

ANSWER, p. 183

CRITICAL THINKING   The civilization was advanced. In the large cities, streets were laid out in a grid-like pattern, with mostly brick houses that had wells, drains, and bathrooms. Craftsmanship flourished, and the people traded over long distances.

V1 Visual Skills

Creating Charts Suggest that students create a chart to take notes on the chief aspects of Hinduism, Jainism, and Buddhism and then use the chart as a study aid. (*Hinduism: caste system, way of life, no founder, no holy book, no central set of core beliefs, belief in reincarnation and possibility of nirvana; Jainism: rejects caste system, based on Hindu principle of non-injury, followers turn from farming to commerce to avoid having to kill or injure living creatures; Buddhism: founded by Siddhartha Gautama or Buddha, belief in Four Noble Truths, rejects caste system*) **Visual/Spatial, Verbal/Linguistic**

Major Religions of South Asia		
Hinduism	**Jainism**	**Buddhism**

V2 Visual Skills

Analyzing Images Have students examine the photographs of the Hindu temple and Buddhist statue. **Ask:**

- **How would you describe the style of the temple?**
  (*Possible responses: colorful, complex, ornate*)
- **How would you describe the style of the statue?**
  (*Possible responses: simple, dramatic*)

Explain that the Buddha is often portrayed in this pose of meditation and that meditation is a basic practice in Buddhism. Call on volunteers to share what they know about meditation. **Visual/Spatial**

T Technology Skills

Researching on the Internet Ask interested students to research the Eightfold Path and give an oral report to the class on what is meant by right view, right intention, right speech, right action, right way of living, right effort, right mindfulness, and right concentration. Encourage a class discussion of similarities and differences between Buddhism and other religions with which students are familiar. **BL**
Verbal/Linguistic, Interpersonal

A steplike Hindu temple (top) and a wall statue of the Buddha (bottom) show the effects of Hinduism and Buddhism on South Asia's architecture and art.

The Vedas were religious hymns handed down orally for many centuries before they were written down. The *Rig Veda* [rihg vay•duh] likely took shape around 1200 B.C. This poem is a series of hymns in honor of Aryan deities. The hymns are full of vivid imagery and philosophical ideas. This poem laid the foundation for the growth of Hinduism.

Religious Traditions

South Asia is the birthplace of several major religions. The first of these is Hinduism. Often described as a way of life, Hinduism has no founder, no holy book, and no central set of core beliefs. Hindus usually pay respect to the Vedas and take part in religious rituals, either at home or in a local temple.

Hindus believe in **reincarnation**, or the rebirth of a soul in another body. Related to this idea is karma—the belief that actions in this life can affect your next life. After many lifetimes, an enlightened soul can be released from the reincarnation cycle of birth, death, and rebirth. Then the soul enters nirvana, a state of eternal bliss.

Around 500 B.C., two new religions arose in South Asia in response to Hinduism and its emphasis on the caste system. The first was Jainism. This religion was based on the Hindu principle of ahimsa, or noninjury. Followers of Jainism turned from farming to commerce so they would not have to kill or injure any living creature.

The second new religion began in northeastern India. It was founded by a noble prince named Siddhārtha Gautama. When he was 29 years old, Siddhārtha gave up his wealthy lifestyle and traveled in poverty, searching for spiritual truth. He reached his goal at the age of 35 and became known as "the Buddha," or "the enlightened one." He passed on to his followers what he believed to be the Four Noble Truths:

- Life is full of suffering.
- The cause of suffering is selfish desire.
- Suffering can be stopped by conquering desire.
- Desire can be conquered by following the Eightfold Path: right view, right intention, right speech, right action, right way of living, right effort, right mindfulness, and right concentration.

184 *Chapter 6*

(t) ©Keren Su/Corbis; (b) Robert Harding Picture Library Ltd/Alamy

network**s** *Online Teaching Options*

GRAPHIC ORGANIZER

Major Religions of South Asia

Comparing and Contrasting Use the interactive graphic organizer to review and discuss the major religions of South Asia. With a partner, ask students to identify similarities and differences among the religions. **BL Interpersonal**

See page 173D for other online activities.

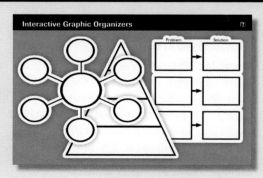

Interactive Graphic Organizers

Buddhists, like Jains, largely rejected the caste system. Hinduism remains the major religion throughout India today. Buddhism has spread to other Asian countries, while Jainism remains a small but vibrant religion in India.

Three Indian Empires

The Aryan civilization faded by 500 B.C. Around 200 years later, another power arose: the Mauryas. The Mauryas conquered much of South Asia. Their most famous ruler was named Ashoka. A highly successful warrior, he converted to Buddhism around 260 B.C. and adopted a life of nonviolence. His conversion influenced many people throughout the subcontinent. Trade and culture thrived under his rule.

Hundreds of years later, another empire, the Guptas, managed to unify much of northern India. Under the ruler Chandragupta I, science, medicine, mathematics, and the arts flourished. Gupta scholars developed the decimal system in mathematics that we still use today.

Finally, during the 1500s and 1600s, India witnessed the flowering of a third great empire: the Mughals. In contrast to earlier emperors, Mughal rulers were Muslim rather than Hindu. They were the first Indian emperors to be members of a minority religion. During this era, many South Asians converted to Islam.

Some of the Mughals were tolerant. Akbar the Great, who ruled from 1556 to 1605, was a devoted Muslim, but he encouraged freedom of religion. He regularly held discussions with religious scholars. As with the Mauryas and the Guptas, culture, science, and the arts flourished under the Mughals. The architectural monument known as the Taj Mahal was constructed by the fifth Mughal emperor, Shah Jahan, in memory of his beloved wife.

✔ **READING PROGRESS CHECK**

Identifying What two especially important legacies did the Aryans leave behind?

A reflecting pool leads to the magnificent Taj Mahal in Agra, northern India. Built of white marble, the Taj Mahal is considered the greatest example of Muslim architecture in South Asia.

▶ **CRITICAL THINKING**
Describing What was the purpose of the Taj Mahal?

R

Modern South Asia

GUIDING QUESTION *How has conflict in South Asia led to change?*

Since their early history, South Asians have been no strangers to conflict. Then, beginning in the late 1800s, a combination of internal and external factors led to great changes in the region.

Chapter 6 **185**

LORI EPSTEIN/National Geographic Stock

IMAGE

360° View: The Taj Mahal

Analyzing Images Using the 360° image, have students examine and identify the elements that make the Taj Mahal such a unique and beautiful monument. Encourage students to do independent research to find out more about the history of this palace. **BL** Visual/ Spatial

See page 173D for other online activities.

Interactive Photos

This region has many diverse types of landscapes. Land forms range from mountains to grasslands. Waterways include rivers, lakes, and shorelines. Vegetation varies depending on the soil quality and access to water within the specific area. Animal life has adapted to take advantage of what the region has to offer.

V Visual Skills

Analyzing Images Have students examine the photograph of the Taj Mahal and share with them the information in the Content Background Knowledge below. **Ask: How would you describe the style of the Taj Mahal?** *(Possible responses: simple, elegant, balanced)* **AL** Visual/Spatial

V

R Reading Skills

Determining Central Ideas Pose the following questions to help students identify the main ideas about the three Indian empires of the Mauryas, the Guptas, and the Mughals. Explain that each of these names represents a dynasty, a succession of rulers from one family. **Ask:**

- **When did the Mauryas come to power in India?** *(about 300 B.C.)*
- **Who was the most famous ruler of the Mauryas, and what did he accomplish?** *(Ashoka; his conversion to Buddhism influenced many people, also trade and culture thrived under his rule.)*
- **When did the Guptas come to power, and what did they accomplish?** *(The Guptas came to power hundreds of years after the Mauryas. They unified much of north India and developed the decimal system. The arts and sciences flourished during their reign.)*
- **When did the Mughals rule India?** *(during the 1500s and 1600s)*
- **What was unique about the Mughals?** *(They were Muslim rather than Hindu and the first Indian emperors to be members of a minority religion.)*
- **What happened during the reign of the Mughals?** *(Many South Asians converted to Islam; some rulers encouraged freedom of religion; culture, science, and the arts flourished; and the Taj Mahal was built.)* **Verbal/Linguistic**

Content Background Knowledge

The Taj Mahal is one of the most famous buildings in the world and considered by some to be the most beautiful. It serves as the tomb for Mumtaz Mahal, the wife of the Mughal emperor Shah Jahan. The queen died in childbirth, and Shah Jahan intended the tomb to represent the queen's house in paradise. It was built by 20,000 laborers over a period of 22 years.

ANSWERS, p. 185

CRITICAL THINKING The Taj Mahal was built by the fifth Mughal emperor Shah Jahan, as a memorial of his wife.

✔ **READING PROGRESS CHECK** They left the concept of the caste system, or social classes. They also left the Vedas, or sacred texts, which led to the development of Hinduism.

V Visual Skills

Analyzing Maps Use the map at the bottom of the page to discuss the British takeover and rule of India. **Ask:**

- In the 1600s, British traders established settlements in India. Where were these early settlements? *(along the eastern coast of India and extending inland from the mouths of the Ganges and Brahmaputra rivers)*

- By about how much did the British increase their territory in India between 1767 and 1805? *(They more than doubled it.)*

- During what period did the British empire increase the most in size? *(1805 to 1857)* **AL** Visual/Spatial

Making Connections Help students connect this period in Indian history with events in American history. Remind students that the British had colonies in what is now the United States during the 1600s and up until the colonies declared their independence in 1776. The American Revolutionary War lasted until 1783. Point out that Indians had even more reason than Americans to resent British rule since Indians had occupied their lands for hundreds of years.

C Critical Thinking Skills

Synthesizing Tell students that boycotting British goods was not as simple as it sounds. The colonial system often took the raw products (resources) back to the home country where they were manufactured into finished goods. Those finished goods would then be sent back to the orginal country. The price was much higher than if the goods had been manufactured locally. Ghandi promoted the use of homespun rather than buying cloth that had been manufactured in England. This meant that people had to spin their own cloth. **Ask: Why might people be reluctant to boycott English fabric?** *(It would be a lot of work to spin their own fabric and make their own clothing. The cotton farms may have been owned by colonists who might not sell them the cotton for spinning.)* **AL** Verbal/Linguistic

The British in South Asia

Beginning in the 1500s, European countries used improved ships and maps in exploration. In the 1600s, British traders established settlements in India. With the decline of the Mughal Empire, the traders became a powerful presence in South Asia. The British were especially interested in textiles, timber, and tea.

After a bloody rebellion in northern India in 1857, the British government took direct control of most of South Asia. They ruled over what is today India, Pakistan, and Bangladesh. The British used the name India to refer to the entire area. By this time, India was a British colony rather than a trading partner. Although the British built railways, schools, and ports, Indians resented a foreign presence in their land. In the late 1800s, an independence movement began.

Achieving Independence

In 1885, less than 30 years after the rebellion of 1857, Indian supporters of independence formed the Indian National Congress. The British, however, were reluctant to give up the **Raj**, as their imperialist rule of India was called. The Congress responded by endorsing a **boycott**. A boycott means refusing to buy or use certain goods—in this case, Indians refused to buy imported British goods.

In the early 1900s, two members of the Congress became leaders. The first was Mohandas K. Gandhi. Often called "Mahatma," which

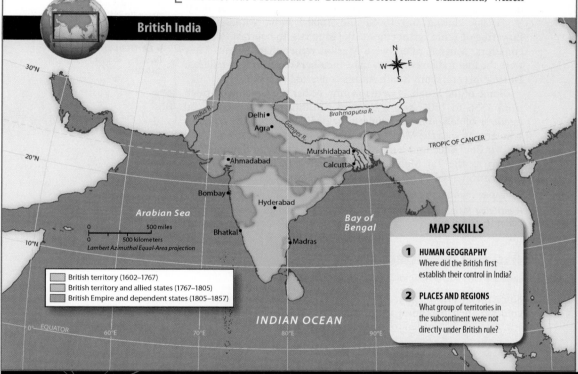

British India

British territory (1602–1767)
British territory and allied states (1767–1805)
British Empire and dependent states (1805–1857)

MAP SKILLS

1. **HUMAN GEOGRAPHY**
   Where did the British first establish their control in India?

2. **PLACES AND REGIONS**
   What group of territories in the subcontinent were not directly under British rule?

networks   *Online Teaching Options*

MAP

The British in India

Analyzing Maps Use the map to discuss the British colonization of India and India's independence movement. Guide students through a class discussion on sections of India that started as British colonies and later gained independence. Ask students to explain what inferences they can make based on the map. **AL** Visual/Spatial

See page 173D for other online activities.

ANSWERS, p. 186

MAP SKILLS

1. The British built trading forts along the coasts.
2. British rule was indirect in the Indian states under the rule of princes.

means "great soul," Gandhi studied law. He practiced law in South Africa, where the racist **policies** shocked and angered him. He returned to India determined to fight for independence from the British.

Gandhi was deeply opposed to violence. His most powerful weapon against British rule was **civil disobedience**, or nonviolent resistance. He was joined by a younger leader, Jawaharlal Nehru. Also trained as a lawyer, Nehru was the son of one of the original leaders of the Congress. Gandhi and Nehru finally succeeded in persuading the British to leave South Asia and surrender colonial rule. India became independent in August 1947. Conflicts between Hindus and Muslims, however, divided the subcontinent.

India and Pakistan

Since Mughal times, South Asia has been troubled by religious and cultural divisions between Hindus and Muslims. In 1947, as part of the independence settlement, the British negotiated a division of the subcontinent. Two countries were created: India (mainly Hindu) and Pakistan (mainly Muslim). To complicate matters, Pakistan was divided into western and eastern sectors. In the 1970s, East Pakistan achieved independence after a civil war and became the country of Bangladesh.

Tensions between India and Pakistan did not die down. The two countries have fought several wars and are involved in a dispute over the region of Kashmir, located in the Himalaya and Karakoram mountain ranges. In the late 1990s, both countries developed nuclear weapons. Because of this **nuclear proliferation**, or the spread of enormously powerful atomic weapons, conflict between the two countries could prove dangerous.

☑ READING PROGRESS CHECK

Describing What countries were created out of the South Asia subcontinent? What religions do the people of these countries follow?

©Bettmann/Corbis

Jawaharlal Nehru (left) and Mohandas K. Gandhi (right) were the main leaders of India's independence movement during the 1930s and 1940s.

▶ **CRITICAL THINKING**
Describing What method did Gandhi and Nehru use to get the British to leave India?

Academic Vocabulary

policy plan or course of action

FOLDABLES
Study Organizer

Include this lesson's information in your Foldable®.

LESSON 2 REVIEW **CCSS**

Reviewing Vocabulary (Tier Three Words)
1. How has the *caste* system influenced life in South Asia? RH.6-8.4

Answering the Guiding Questions
2. ***Describing*** How are the religions of Jainism and Buddhism alike? How are they different? RH.6-8.5

3. ***Determining Central Ideas*** Why are Hindu-Muslim conflicts in South Asia so significant to the history of the region? RH.6-8.2

4. ***Narrative Writing*** You are a time traveler whose machine can transport you to any one of the following: the Indus Valley cities of Harappa or Mohenjo-Daro; the empires of Ashoka or Akbar the Great; or the struggle for independence by the Indian National Congress under the leadership of Mohandas Gandhi. Write a brief story describing what you see and hear in the time and setting of your choice. WHST.6-8.4, WHST.6-8.10

Chapter 6 **187**

LESSON 2 REVIEW ANSWERS

Reviewing Vocabulary

1. Beginning in Aryan times, the concept of caste dictated the occupations and tasks an individual could undertake according to his or her birth and position in society.

Answering the Guiding Questions

2. ***Describing*** Both religions arose in response to Hinduism and its emphasis on the caste system. Jainism is based on the principle of non-injury. Buddhism is based on the Four Noble Truths and other teachings of its founder, Buddha.

3. ***Determining Central Ideas*** Religious conflicts caused much of South Asia to be divided into the nations of India (mainly Hindu) and Pakistan (mainly Muslim) following independence. The nations are still in conflict, notably in a dispute over Kashmir. Both countries have nuclear weapons, so the stakes are high.

4. ***Narrative Writing*** Sample answer: Student stories should include the main ideas and supporting details given in this lesson, such as accurate dates, names, and locations. If time permits, allow students to conduct further research on the topic of their choice.

V Visual Skills

Analyzing Images Have students examine the photograph of Jawaharlal Nehru and Mohandas Gandhi. **Ask: What do you find striking or unusual about the photograph?** *(Possible responses: The two men are sitting on the floor, even though there are chairs in the room. Gandhi's chest, arms, and legs are bare. Gandhi appears very thin.)*

Suggest that students might find explanations for the unusual aspects of the photograph as they research the lives of these two men for the writing assignment that follows. **AL** **Visual/Spatial**

W Writing Skills

Informative/Explanatory Have students conduct Internet research and write a two-page biography of either Jawaharlal Nehru or Mohandas Gandhi. Tell students to focus on their roles in India's independence movement, their religious and political beliefs, and Nehru's accomplishments. Select a biography of each leader to read aloud to the class. **Verbal/Linguistic**

R Reading Skills

Discussing Have students locate Bangladesh and Pakistan on the map. Remind students that these were one country for quite some time. Lead students in a discussion about what it would be like to have a country that is divided by a landmass in the middle, particularly when the border country is not a friend. Have students consider that there were no cell phones and there was no Internet during any of the years that Pakistan was divided into two sections. **AL** **Visual/Spatial, Interpersonal**

CLOSE & REFLECT

Discussing After discussing the conflict between India and Pakistan, close the lesson by reminding students of the questions they formulated about the history of India and Pakistan at the beginning of the lesson. Ask if students have found answers to their questions, and call on volunteers to share the answers they have discovered.

ANSWERS, p. 187

CRITICAL THINKING They used civil disobedience, or non-violent resistance to British rule.
☑ READING PROGRESS CHECK India and Pakistan: Indian people are mainly Hindu. Pakistani people are mainly Muslim.

Chapter 6 **187**

ENGAGE

🔔 **Bellringer** Ask students to think about what they have learned so far about the geography and history of South Asia. Then tell them to think about life in this region and write down one way in which life in South Asia is different from life in the United States. Ask volunteers to read their statements aloud. Then tell students that they will learn more about the people and culture of South Asia in this lesson. Have students preview the lesson by skimming the headings, guiding questions, and visuals.

TEACH & ASSESS

C Critical Thinking Skills

Problem-Solving Emphasize the fact that South Asia has about half the area of the lower 48 states, but has five times the population of the United States. On a classroom map of the United States, mark off half of it and tell students to imagine moving ALL the population to the other half and then multiplying that population by five. On a map of Asia, call attention to the difference in size between China and India. Then ask students to imagine India with more people than China. **Ask:** What problems do you think India might face with its projected population growth? *(Possible responses: not enough resources to feed and shelter so many people, widespread poverty and hunger, social unrest, environmental degradation, political instability)* **AL** **Logical/Mathematical, Verbal/Linguistic**

Content Background Knowledge

Of the 10 most populous countries in the world, 10 of them are in South Asia: India, Pakistan, and Bangladesh. Only India and China have populations above 1 billion. The third most populous nation is the United States with 314 million. Pakistan is 6th largest with 190 million and Bangladesh is 8th with 161 million.

ANSWER, p. 188

Taking Notes Sample answers: **Urban growth**—Urban areas in India showed more growth than rural areas for the first time in the 2011 census. **Languages**—Although the two official languages of India are Hindi and English, 15 other languages are spoken by millions of people. **Religion**—The six main religions in South Asia are Hinduism, Islam, Buddhism, Jainism, Sikhism, and Christianity.

---

networks

There's More Online!

☑ **CHART/GRAPH** Population of India

☑ **SLIDE SHOW** Culture Groups in South Asia

☑ **VIDEO**

Reading **HELP**DESK (CCSS)

Academic Vocabulary RH.6-8.4
(Tier Two Words)
- **establish**

Content Vocabulary RH.6-8.4
(Tier Three Words)
- **sitar**
- **green revolution**
- **cottage industry**
- **outsourcing**
- *dalit*

TAKING NOTES: *Key Ideas and Details* RH.6-8.2, RH.6-8.7

Describe As you read the lesson, create a chart like the one below and write one key fact about each topic.

Urban growth	
Languages	
Religion	

188

Lesson 3
Life in South Asia

ESSENTIAL QUESTION · *What makes a culture unique?*

IT MATTERS BECAUSE
By 2030, India will become the most populous country on the planet. Among the challenges India faces are raising the standard of living of its people.

People and Places

GUIDING QUESTION *What are the population patterns of South Asia?*

C South Asia is about half the size of the lower 48 states of the United States, but more than 1.5 billion people live in the region. That is about five times the size of the American population.

Population Profile
The largest countries in South Asia—in geographical area and in population—are India, Pakistan, and Bangladesh. The estimated population of India is 1.22 billion. This makes it the world's second-most-populous country, after China. India's birth rate, though, is higher than China's. By 2030, India will be the world's most populous country. Today, India alone has about 17.3 percent of all the world's people. The median age of Indians is 25 years old.

Pakistan's population is about 190 million. It is the world's sixth-largest country. The population of Bangladesh is about 160 million. By 2025, that number could grow to 205 million.

Where People Live
South Asians live mainly in areas that are good for farming. This means, for example, that a high percentage of Indians live in the fertile Ganges Plain in the north-central and northeastern parts of the country.

---

networks *Online Teaching Options*

VIDEO

Should Elephants Weep

Discussing Use this video about the dangers that elephants in India face to discuss human-environment interactions and current challenges for both human and animal populations in South Asia. Ask students if they are aware of any other animals, either in South Asia or in the region where they live, that are at risk for becoming endangered or extinct due to human-environment interactions. **AL** **Visual/Spatial**

See page 173E for other online activities.

Agriculture plays a major role in India's economy. This is also true of other countries in South Asia. Although India has many large cities, about 7 of every 10 people live in the country's small villages. In contrast, the United States was already more urban than rural as early as 1920. Today, more than 7 of every 10 U.S. residents live in urban areas.

Population trends are changing, though, as more and more Indians leave their villages every year. The 2011 census showed more growth in urban areas than in rural areas—a first for India. People migrate to big cities, called "metros," in hopes of finding better jobs and a higher standard of living. Major cities in India include Mumbai, New Delhi (the capital city), Chennai (Madras), Kolkata (Calcutta), Bengaluru (Bangalore), and Hyderabad.

Census data show that Indian cities are experiencing rapid growth. For example, Mumbai is the business center of the country. The population of Mumbai and its surrounding urban area has grown from a few million around the time of independence to about 20 million. That makes Mumbai India's largest city and the fourth-largest city in the world. Bengaluru, India's third-largest city and a center for technology industries, is growing rapidly, as well.

C

GRAPH SKILLS ›

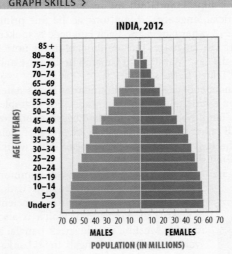

INDIA, 2012

AGE (IN YEARS): 85+, 80–84, 75–79, 70–74, 65–69, 60–64, 55–59, 50–54, 45–49, 40–44, 35–39, 30–34, 25–29, 20–24, 15–19, 10–14, 5–9, Under 5

70 60 50 40 30 20 10 0 10 20 30 40 50 60 70
MALES   FEMALES
POPULATION (IN MILLIONS)

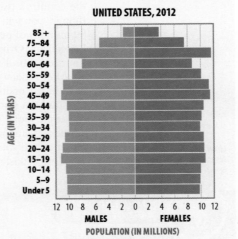

UNITED STATES, 2012

AGE (IN YEARS): 85+, 75–84, 65–74, 60–64, 55–59, 50–54, 45–49, 40–44, 35–39, 30–34, 25–29, 20–24, 15–19, 10–14, 5–9, Under 5

12 10 8 6 4 2 0 2 4 6 8 10 12
MALES   FEMALES
POPULATION (IN MILLIONS)

V

Source: U.S. Census Bureau, Statistical Abstract of the United States: 2012

POPULATION PYRAMIDS
Population pyramids use bar graphs to show a country's population by age and gender. A population pyramid shaped like India's indicates high birthrates and short life expectancy. A population pyramid shaped like the United States's indicates low birthrates and long life expectancy.

▶ **CRITICAL THINKING**
1. **Analyzing** How many males and females in India are between 10 and 14 years of age? How many in the United States?
2. **Analyzing** Compare the *Population in Millions* numbers at the bottom of each pyramid. What do the numbers tell you about the total population of India and the United States?

Chapter 6 **189**

C **Critical Thinking Skills**

Comparing and Contrasting Emphasize that India is still largely a rural nation. Use the following questions to focus students' attention on the differences between India and the United States in terms of the rural/urban population split. **Ask:**

- **About what percentage of Indians live in rural areas and what percentage live in urban areas?** *(about 70 percent live in rural areas and about 30 percent live in urban areas)*
- **How does that compare to the percentage in the United States?** *(It is just the opposite. About 30 percent of Americans live in rural areas, and more than 70 percent live in urban areas.)*
- **How is India becoming more like the United States?** *(More Indians are now moving to the cities, and the cities are growing rapidly.)*
- **Why are Indians migrating to large cities?** *(They hope to find better jobs and a higher standard of living.)* **AL** Verbal/Linguistic

Making Connections From an economic perspective, the standard of living is a measure of income against the cost of living. This can show how much money an earner has available after paying for the basic expenses, such as food, clothing, and shelter. This is also described as "real income." This is one reason that looking at the average household income in South Asia is not as telling as the standard of living. Have students consider their possessions and way of life to see how they could compare the standard of living, for example, what type/size home they live in, the number of pairs of shoes and other clothing items they own, the value of all of their electronic gadgets, etc.

V **Visual Skills**

Analyzing Graphs Have students read the caption in the graph skills and compare the two population pyramids. Then have students analyze the information and answer the Critical Thinking questions. In addition, **ask:**

- **How do the top three age groups in the two countries compare?** *(The number of elderly people is greater in the United States.)*
- **How many more preteens and teenagers are there in India than the United States?** *(about 178 million more; there are about 220 million preteen and teenagers in India compared to about 42 million in the United States.)* **Visual/Spatial**

CHART

Population Pyramid: India

Interpreting Use the population pyramid to guide students in a class discussion on the population distribution across age and gender in India. Point out where India's highest and lowest population distribution lies on the age/gender scale. Then, with a partner, have students exchange and write down other facts about the region they have learned from the chart. To reinforce the information, display the population density map from the Chapter Opener as you discuss population distribution and density. **ELL** Visual/Spatial

See page 173E for other online activities.

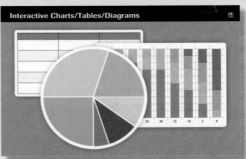
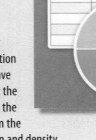
Interactive Charts/Tables/Diagrams

ANSWERS, p. 189

CRITICAL THINKING
1. Between 115 million and 120 million; about 20 million
2. Based on the numbers, India has a much larger population than the U.S.

Making Connections The chart below shows the top ten cities by population density. In comparison to these cities, Los Angeles, the American city with the highest population density, ranked 90th *(with 2,750 people per sq km)* and New York City ranked 114th *(with 2,050 people per sq km)*.

Ranking of World's Cities by Population Density		
City	**Country**	**Population Density (people per sq km)**
Mumbai	India	29,650
Kolkata	India	23,900
Karachi	Pakistan	18,900
Lagos	Nigeria	18,150
Shenzhen	China	17,150
Seoul/Incheon	South Korea	16,700
Taipei	Taiwan	15,200
Chennai	India	14,350
Bogota	Colombia	13,500
Shanghai	China	13,400

V Visual Skills

Creating Charts Have students create a chart like the one below to help them see the diversity of languages spoken in South Asia. (**Northern India:** *Punjabi;* **Eastern India:** *Bengali, Oriya;* **Western India:** *Marathi, Gujarati;* **Southern India:** *Kannada, Tamil, Telugu;* **Pakistan:** *Urdu, English;* **Bangladesh:** *Bangla;* **Sri Lanka:** *Sinhalese, Tamil*) **ELL** **Visual/Spatial**

Language Groups in South Asia	
Country and/or Region	**Languages**
Northern India	
Eastern India	
Western India	
Southern India	
Pakistan	
Bangladesh	
Sri Lanka	

ANSWERS, p. 190

☑ **READING PROGRESS CHECK** Possible response: Indian's median age is 25. This means that most of the population is of childbearing/childrearing age.
Identifying Hindi and English

Population *density* is the number of people who live in a given unit of area. In Mumbai, the population density is 80,100 per square mile (30,900 per sq. km)—seven times the world's average.

The rapid growth of South Asia has put a strain on its resources. Cities struggle to provide essential services to all people, some of whom live in slums surrounding the city centers. Air and water pollution have increased with overcrowded conditions.

☑ **READING PROGRESS CHECK**

Citing Text Evidence Why is India projected to overtake China as the most populous country by 2030?

People and Cultures

GUIDING QUESTION *How are the diverse cultures in South Asia rooted in ethnic and religious traditions?*

The cultures of South Asia are highly diverse. We think of the United States as a "melting pot" or a "nation of immigrants." The same might be said of South Asia.

Academic Vocabulary

establish to set up

Ethnic and Language Groups

If you look at an Indian currency note, you will see that all the important information appears in Hindi and in English. These are the country's two official languages. If you look at the fine print, though, you will find 15 other languages. Each language is spoken by millions of people. The languages include Punjabi in the north; Bengali and Oriya in the east; Marathi and Gujarati in the west; and Kannada, Tamil, and Telugu in the south.

After India won independence in 1947, boundaries for its states were based mainly on ethnic groups and languages. For example, the southern state of Tamil Nadu was **established** because most of its people spoke Tamil rather than Hindi. Indians are proud of their ethnic and language heritage. In fact, many who speak Tamil would rather talk to you in English than in Hindi.

Most Pakistanis are Muslim. The country's most common languages are Urdu and English. Urdu, like Hindi, developed from ancient Sanskrit. In Bangladesh, which is also mainly Muslim, people speak Bangla, a variation of Indian Bengali. In Sri Lanka, most people speak Sinhalese. This language has its own unique alphabet. An important minority in Sri Lanka speaks Tamil, mainly because Sri Lanka is so close to the southern state of India, called Tamil Nadu.

Indian currency note with portrait of Mohandas K. Gandhi

Identifying What two official languages appear on Indian currency notes?

©Jeremy Horner/Corbis

networks   *Online Teaching Options*

CHART

Comparing Urban Populations in India and the United States

Analyzing Information Ask students what conclusions they can draw from comparing the population size of India's major cities to the population size of major cities in the United States. Have students create a 2-column chart that shows the comparison of each of the countries' largest cities. Expand the activity by discussing the types of problems students might expect to find in India's large cities. **BL** **Logical/Mathematical**

See page 173E for other online activities.

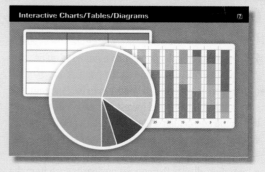
Interactive Charts/Tables/Diagrams

Religion and the Arts

South Asia's diversity is also apparent in religion and the arts. Six main religions are practiced in the region: Hinduism, Islam, Buddhism, Jainism, Sikhism, and Christianity. You have already learned about the first four religions. Sikhism developed in the 1500s, nearly 2,000 years after Buddhism and Jainism. Yet it, too, was a reaction to Hinduism—by and large, Sikhs reject the Hindu caste system. Sikhs deeply respect their original guru, or teacher. Like Muslims and Christians, they are *monotheists*, meaning they believe in only one God.

Artistic expression is rich in South Asia. Two great epic poems of ancient India, the *Ramayana* and the *Mahabharata*, embody Hindu social and religious values. Their impact extends far beyond the Hindu community, though. South Asian children of all religions can tell you about the plots and characters of these epics. They are part of the region's heritage.

South Asia also is a center for classical dance. Music is a thriving art, and many of the region's musicians, singers, and composers are popular. Ravi Shankar was probably the best-known Indian musician and composer. He performed on the **sitar**, a stringed instrument. Motion pictures first arrived in India in 1896. The country now has the largest film industry in the world. The Hindi film industry, nicknamed "Bollywood," is based in Mumbai. Kolkata is also a filmmaking center.

Daily Life

Life in South Asia centers on family. Several generations of family members often live together. They share household chores and finances. Within the family, age and gender play important roles. Elders are respected, and females are often subordinate to males.

Arranged marriages are still common for many South Asians, but less so than in the past. Parents often introduce couples to each other but allow them to decide whether to marry. When couples meet independently of their parents, it is still important to get approval to marry from their parents.

A typical, South Asian family meal would include rice, legumes, and flatbreads. Curry is a combination of spices that is part of many dishes. South Asians do not eat a great deal of meat, in part because of religious guidelines.

☑ **READING PROGRESS CHECK**

Describing How do South Asian culture and American culture compare?

A South Asian family enjoys a meal of dishes of their region.

Identifying What foods make up a typical meal in South Asian homes?

V

Thinking Like a Geographer

What's In a Name?

Why have the names of many Indian cities been changed? National pride sparked Indians to discard names linked to colonial history. For example, the name Bombay came from the Portuguese *bom baia*, meaning "good bay." The city was renamed Mumbai in 1995 in honor of an ancient Hindu goddess.

Chapter 6 **191**

(l) ©Christopher Pillitz/In Pictures/Corbis

V Visual Skills

Creating Visuals On the board, begin a concept web on the topic of South Asian culture and add information as you discuss the cultural life of South Asia with the class. You might include such major categories as religion, arts, family, marriage, and food. (*Religion:* Hinduism, Islam, Buddhism, Jainism, Sikhism, Christianity; *Arts:* Epic poems Ramayana and Mahabharata, classical dance, sitar music of Ravi Shankar, Bollywood movies; *Family:* extended families live together, elders respected, females subordinate to males; *Marriage:* arranged marriages common, parental approval essential; *Food:* meals of rice, legumes, flatbreads; curry a common spice; not much meat) **AL**
Visual/Spatial, Verbal/Linguistic

Culture of South Asia

Content Background Knowledge

As you discuss the various aspects of South Asian cultural life, you might share with students the following information:

- An epic is a long poem that narrates the deeds and adventures of a legendary hero. Two major epics of Western culture are Homer's *The Iliad* and *The Odyssey.*
- Legumes are a class of vegetables that provide protein and are considered a healthy substitute for meat. They include beans, peas, lentils, soybeans, and peanuts.
- Flatbreads are just what they sound like: breads made from flattened dough. Pita bread, naan, and tortillas are all flatbreads. A variety of flatbreads are common in the Middle East, South Asia, and East Asia.
- Among the six main religions in South Asia, only Jainism requires its followers to be vegetarians. Many Hindus, Buddhists, and Sikhs practice vegetarianism because of their belief in nonviolence toward all living creatures.

Culture Groups in South Asia

Evaluating Use the slide show to demonstrate the unique aspects of South Asian culture, including its dance, music, and festivals. Ask students to describe what they find most appealing about the culture. Then have students write a paragraph of what they would like to see if they were to visit South Asia, including why they would like to see this. **AL** **Visual/Spatial, Intrapersonal, Verbal/Linguistic**

See page 173E for other online activities.

Slide Show

ANSWERS, p. 191

Identifying A typical meal would include rice, legumes, and flatbread. Curry, a combination of spices, is usually a part of many dishes. South Asians, however, do not eat much meat, partly because of religious guidelines.

☑ **READING PROGRESS CHECK** Sample answer: Both are extremely diverse. South Asian family life and marriage customs differ from those in America. While South Asian households often consist of extended families, American households are more likely to be nuclear. Arranged marriages are common in South Asia but rare in the United States. Females are less likely to be subordinate to males in the United States than they are in South Asia. Diets also differ. Americans tend to eat a lot of meat, while South Asians do not.

Life in South Asia

C Critical Thinking Skills

Identifying Central Issues Pose the following questions to focus students' attention on the central issues facing South Asians today. **Ask:**

- **What is the green revolution, and how is it important to Indians?** *(The green revolution consists of agricultural advances, such as the use of irrigation, fertilizers, and high-yielding crops that help increase food production. It has helped Indians produce enough food to feed themselves without having to import food since the 1970s.)*

- **Why might the benefits of the green revolution fall short in the future?** *(With a growing population, India has an increased need for food. Green revolution methods are not producing ever-increasing yields.)*

- **In what occupations besides farming do South Asians make their living?** *(from mining and fishing; from such cottage industries as textile weaving, jewelry-making, furniture-making, and wood carving; as computer specialists, engineers, and software designers; from ecotourism)* **Verbal/Linguistic**

T Technology Skills

Researching on the Internet Suggest that students research ecotours in South Asia and choose a trip they would like to take. Have students describe their trips to the class, telling where they will go, what they will see and do, and where they will stay. Students might share Internet photographs of places they plan to visit. **BL Verbal/Linguistic**

R Reading Skills

Applying Have students consider the different ways that unreliable landline phones would impact the country. Present a chart with the following areas and ask students to identify specific problems that might arise without reliable phone service: the economy, healthcare, government, and emergency services. *(Students should recognize the businesses need to communicate with suppliers, customers, sales representatives, and so on. For healthcare, doctors and other providers need to be able to communicate with labs, x-ray and radiology technicians, pharmacists, and so on. Communication is critical to government functions, enabling the leaders to know what is happening "on the ground." Emergency services must have reliable phone service because people do not plan for their emergencies.)* **Ask: How have cell phones helped India?** *(Possible response: Cell phones have helped the people of India to communicate over long distances when landline phones have not been reliable.)*

ANSWER, p. 192

CRITICAL THINKING Indians have access to the Internet; many foreign companies, especially in English-speaking countries outsource work to South Asia, which has a large number of English speakers.

Customers can apply for visas, check e-mail and Web sites, and receive computer instruction at a cybercafe in Bengaluru, India.
▶ **CRITICAL THINKING** **C**
Describing How has South Asia been affected by the global revolution in communications?

Issues in South Asia

GUIDING QUESTION *What impact do economic and environmental issues have on life in South Asia?*

South Asia is a region of rapid growth. As the population grows, it will be ever more important for South Asians to work together to resolve their differences and jointly address the issues they face.

Earning a Living

One of the biggest challenges for South Asians is making a living. Many people are farmers, but good cropland is scarce. Yet South Asians have managed to grow enough food to feed their huge population. How do they do it?

Agricultural advances known as the **green revolution** have helped increase crop yields. The green revolution involves the use of irrigation, fertilizers, and high-yielding crops. Because of these improvements, India has not had to import food to feed its people since the 1970s. This situation might change, however. Green revolution methods are no longer yielding increases in crop productivity to meet the growing need.

In addition to farming, some South Asians make a living from mining or fishing. Others own or work for **cottage industries**—small businesses that employ people in their homes. Cottage industries include textile weaving, making jewelry and furniture, and wood carving. These small businesses help traditional crafts survive.

Advanced technology is a fast-growing part of the South Asian economy. Entire cities have grown up around the high-tech field. Indian computer specialists, engineers, and software designers are in high demand throughout the world, including the United States.

Another growing part of South Asia's economy is ecotourism. Ecotourism combines recreational travel and environmental awareness.

Making Connections

The efficiency of communication systems varies. Newspapers are thriving, cheap, and widely read, but landline phones are often unreliable. Cell phones have helped ease communication problems.

Because of its vast numbers of English speakers, India is well suited for **outsourcing**. Outsourcing occurs when a company hires an outside company or individual to do work. U.S. companies often outsource to foreign countries where workers may be more flexible or willing to work for lower wages. A U.S. resident who calls customer service with a laptop problem might speak to an agent in India.

192 *Chapter 6*

©Steve Raymer/Corbis

---

net**w**orks *Online Teaching Options*

IMAGE

Outsourcing

Determining Effects Use the interactive image to discuss the outsourcing of jobs to India and its effects on both Indians and Americans. *(While Indians gain jobs, Americans lose them.)* Explain that call center services, computer programming, data entry, and web design services are a few examples of the many kinds of jobs that can be outsourced.
AL Visual/Spatial

See page 173E for other online activities.

Interactive Photos

This region has many diverse types of landscapes. Land forms range from mountains to grasslands. Waterways include rivers, lakes, and shorelines. Vegetation varies depending on the soil quality and access to water within the specific area. Animal life has adapted to take advantage of what the region has to offer.

©Image Source/Getty Images

Meeting Challenges

Despite South Asia's rich resources, the region faces a number of challenges. One challenge is the long-standing conflict between India and Pakistan over the largely Muslim territory of Kashmir. The area containing the headwaters of the Indus River is one source of conflict. Both countries want to control the source of the river. Today, control of Kashmir is divided between the two countries.

Sometimes, political conflicts have resulted in tragedy. Two of India's prime ministers have been assassinated in recent decades: Indira Gandhi (the daughter of Jawaharlal Nehru) in 1984, and her son Rajiv Gandhi in 1991. Both prime ministers were killed by extremists who opposed their views. Another issue in India involves oppression of the *dalits*, or so-called "untouchables." For centuries, these people have been discriminated against as outcasts, barely clinging to the lowest rung on the social ladder.

Other South Asian countries also face challenges. In Sri Lanka, Buddhists and Hindus engaged in a civil war that lasted several decades and cost more than 60,000 lives. In Nepal, a rebel group has been struggling since 1996 to overthrow democracy and establish a communist government. Tribal people control large parts of the Pakistan-Afghanistan border.

Other challenges involve health and environmental issues. Rapid population growth and lack of infrastructure have led to water pollution and air pollution in many parts of South Asia. Deforestation is also a major problem. Most of India's forests have been cut down for timber or development. Water quality, wildlife habitats, and climate have been affected as a result.

South Asia has achieved some success in meeting the challenges. The civil war in Sri Lanka has ended, restoring peace to that island country. India has implemented stricter controls on air and water pollution. Government expenditures for wildlife conservation have increased many times over.

R

FOLDABLES
Study Organizer

Include this lesson's information in your Foldable®.

☑ **READING PROGRESS CHECK**

Analyzing Why might a U.S. company outsource its customer-service operations to a company in South Asia?

LESSON 3 REVIEW

Reviewing Vocabulary (Tier Three Words)
1. Why has the *green revolution* been important for South Asians? RH.6-8.4

Answering the Guiding Questions
2. *Determining Central Ideas* Why might population growth in South Asia be a major problem in the years ahead? RH.6-8.2
3. *Determining Word Meanings* Why is South Asia sometimes called a religious and ethnic "melting pot"? RH.6-8.4

4. *Identifying* Give two examples of environmental issues confronting South Asia today. RH.6-8.1
5. *Informative/Explanatory Writing* Assume you are a seventh-grader in India, Pakistan, Bangladesh, Sri Lanka, or another South Asian country. Write a journal entry describing your typical day. Include some information about your family, as well as your friends and your favorite hobbies. WHST.6-8.2, WHST.6-8.4

Chapter 6 **193**

LESSON 3 REVIEW ANSWERS

Reviewing Vocabulary

1. The green revolution allowed for agricultural advancements which increased crop yields. South Asians no longer have to import food. They can grow enough to feed their population.

Answering the Guiding Questions

2. *Determing Central Ideas* Rapid population growth in the region may put a great burden on human and natural resources.

3. *Determining Word Meanings* There are six major religions in South Asia and numerous ethnic and language groups.

4. *Identifying* Examples include air and water pollution and deforestation.

5. *Informative/Explanatory Writing* A sample entry might describe a student who lives with his or her extended family in a rural village. They eat mainly vegetarian food spiced with curry. The student likes to watch movies and chat with friends on a cell phone.

R Reading Skills

Determining Central Ideas Focus students' attention on the central issues facing South Asia by posing the following questions. **Ask:**

- **What is one reason for the conflict between India and Pakistan over Kashmir?** *(Both countries want control of the source of the Indus River, which is in this region.)*
- **What two Indian prime ministers were assassinated in recent decades?** *(Indira Gandhi in 1984 and Rajiv Gandhi in 1991)*
- **What two groups fought each other for several decades in Sri Lanka's civil war?** *(Buddhists and Hindus)*
- **What poses a threat to democracy in Nepal?** *(A rebel group has been struggling since 1996 to overthrow the democracy and establish a Communist government.)*
- **What health and environmental issues does South Asia face?** *(water pollution, air pollution, deforestation)*
- **What progress has South Asia made recently in meeting its challenges?** *(Civil war ended in Sri Lanka. India has implemented stricter controls on air and water pollution and increased funding for wildlife conservation.)* **AL** Verbal/ Linguistic

Content Background Knowledge

In the Hindu caste system, the *dalits* formerly could only work in the lowest-status jobs, and they had to stay separate from upper-caste people. They could not drink water from the same wells or walk on the same streets as the upper caste. Not only could they not touch an upper-caste person, they could not even look the person in the eye. When India became independent, the new constitution banned such practices and instituted affirmative action for *dalits* in education and government jobs. But the traditional practices remained for many years and still survive in some remote areas. As India's economy has expanded since 1991, many *dalits* have started their own businesses and have raised their income and social status. A small but growing number of *dalits* have become wealthy and achieved social acceptance.

CLOSE & REFLECT

Creating Charts To close the lesson, remind students of the T-chart that they started at the beginning of the chapter. Give students five minutes to brainstorm a list of new things they have learned about the geography, history, and culture of South Asia. Ask students to add these items to the second column heading: "What We Learned About South Asia."

ANSWER, p. 193

☑ **READING PROGRESS CHECK** The workers would likely be more flexible or willing to work for lower wages than workers in the United States.

CHAPTER REVIEW ACTIVITY

To summarize the chapter, direct students to complete a concept web on each of the three lessons in the chapter. Tell students to identify five important ideas about each subject. Call on volunteers to share their completed concept webs. *(Students' answers may vary but should reflect the main ideas covered in each of the three lessons of the chapter.)*

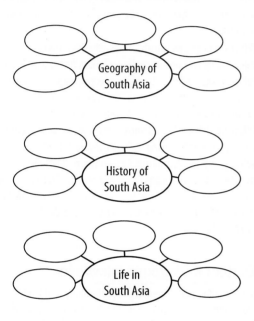

REVIEW THE ENDURING UNDERSTANDINGS

Review this chapter's Enduring Understanding with students:

• *People, places, and ideas change over time.*

Pose the following questions in a class discussion to apply this idea to the chapter.

• **How have people changed the natural environment in South Asia?** *(Sample answer: They have polluted the rivers and the air, cut down forests, dammed rivers, developed mines, killed wildlife, and built up urban areas.)*

• **How has the government of India changed over time?** *(Sample answer: For about 1,000 years, India was ruled by Aryans. Three dynasties—the Mauryas, Guptas, and Mughals—followed about 200 years later. In the 1800s, the British made India a colony. In 1947, after a long struggle of nonviolent opposition, India achieved independence and the country established a democracy.)*

• **The majority of India's people still live in small villages. How are population trends in India changing?** *(Sample answer: India's population is growing rapidly and India will soon replace China as the most populated nation on Earth. More and more Indians are leaving their villages every year for work in urban areas, and urban areas are now growing faster than rural areas for the first time in the history of the country.)*

Directions: Write your answers on a separate piece of paper.

1 Use your **FOLDABLES** to explore the Essential Questions.
INFORMATIVE/EXPLANATORY WRITING Choose one of the countries that make up South Asia. Compare the physical and population maps of that country found in the front of the chapter. Explain in two or more paragraphs how the geographical features of that country influence where people live. WHST.6-8.2, WHST.6-8.4

2 **21st Century Skills**
ANALYZING Use the Internet and print resources to find three or more facts about the economy of one of the South Asian countries. Present your facts in a chart. Then write at least two paragraphs explaining the effects physical geography has on the country's economy. WHST.6-8.7, WHST.6-8.8

3 **Thinking Like a Geographer**
INTEGRATING VISUAL INFORMATION Use a web graphic organizer like the one shown here to list the six main religions practiced by people in South Asia, along with one fact you think is important to remember about each one. RH.6-8.2, RH.6-8.7

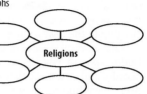

4 **GEOGRAPHY ACTIVITY**

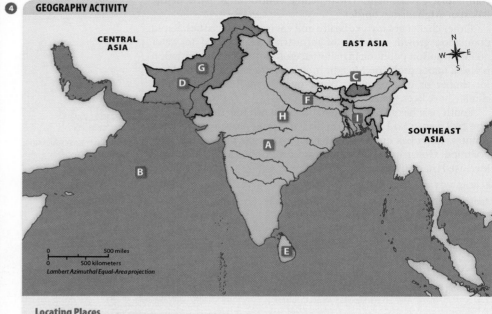

Locating Places
Match the letters on the map with the numbered places listed below. RH.6-8.7

1. Ganges River	**3.** Sri Lanka	**5.** Kathmandu	**7.** Indus River	**9.** India
2. Bhutan	**4.** Arabian Sea	**6.** Pakistan	**8.** Bangladesh	

ACTIVITIES ANSWERS

Essential Question

1 **INFORMATIVE/EXPLANATORY WRITING** One observation might be that people tend to live in river valleys and coastal plains where they have access to water and fertile soil and where there are fewer obstacles to transportation.

REVIEW THE GUIDING QUESTIONS

Directions: Choose the best answer for each question.

1 The subcontinent of South Asia is separated from the rest of Asia by the RH.6-8.2
- A. Bay of Bengal.
- B. Ganges River.
- C. Hindu Kush, the Karakoram Range, and the Himalaya.
- D. Thar Desert.

2 Much of South Asia's weather is directly influenced by wind patterns called RH.6-8.1, RH.6-8.4
- F. cyclones.
- G. northerlies.
- H. doldrums.
- I. monsoons.

3 Which ancient Indian civilization was responsible for establishing the caste system? RH.6-8.2
- A. Mauryans
- B. Aryans
- C. Guptas
- D. Mughals

4 In what year did India finally obtain its independence from Great Britain? RH.6-8.2
- F. 1885
- G. 1918
- H. 1947
- I. 1960

5 Which South Asian nation is expected to become the most heavily populated country on Earth within the next 15 to 20 years? RH.6-8.2
- A. Pakistan
- B. India
- C. Bangladesh
- D. Sri Lanka

6 Which area has been the source of political conflict and violence between India and Pakistan? RH.6-8.2
- F. Nepal
- G. Kashmir
- H. Tibet
- I. Bhutan

Chapter 6 **195**

21st Century Skills

2 **ANALYZING** Students should draw some connections between a country's natural resources, its location, the level of education of its people, and its access to deep water ports for trade and its economy.

Thinking Like a Geographer

3 **INTEGRATING VISUAL INFORMATION** Facts will vary, but the six main religions practiced in South Asia are Hinduism, Jainism, Buddhism, Islam, Sikhism, and Christianity.

Geography Activity

4 **LOCATING PLACES**

1. H
2. C
3. E
4. B
5. F
6. G
7. D
8. I
9. A

ASSESSMENT ANSWERS

Review the Guiding Questions

1 **C** A physical map of South Asia would show that these three mountain ranges—the Hindu Kush, Karakoram Range, and Himalaya—separate South Asia from the rest of the Asian continent.

2 **I** Students can eliminate answers G and H because northerlies and doldrums are not mentioned in this chapter. Answer F can also be eliminated because cyclones are large, swirling storms with violent winds and heavy rains that often slam into the South Asian coast along the Bay of Bengal. Monsoons, the correct answer, are seasonal wind patterns that bring heavy rains to South Asia during the summer months and cool dry winds during the winter months.

3 **B** Lesson 2 identifies the Aryans as the group that established a system of varnas, or castes, in South Asia. The Aryans settled in what is now India about 1500 B.C. and ruled until about 500 B.C. The caste system became deeply entrenched in India, and its effects linger on today.

4 **H** India did not gain its independence from Great Britain until 1947, but unlike the United States did not have to endure a war to do so. India achieved its independence through nonviolent resistance. If students had difficulty answering this question, refer them to Lesson 2 and have them reread the "India and Pakistan" section in their text.

5 **B** Experts project that India will overtake China as the most populous country on Earth within the next 15 to 20 years. If students had difficulty answering this question refer them to the infographic in Lesson 3 for further analysis or have them reread the "Population Profile" section in Lesson 3.

6 **G** Kashmir is a largely Muslim territory that is divided between Pakistan and India. Both countries want to control the source of the Indus River, which lies within Kashmir. For centuries, Kashmir was part of the Indian kingdoms ruled by princes and maharajas. When this land was declared to be part of Pakistan, the region's Hindu prince fled to Delhi, where he signed his state over to India. India claims the legal right to Kashmir, but Pakistan insists that it would be a better cultural fit for Kashmir's Muslim residents. The result has been decades of tension and occasional fighting between these two nuclear-armed countries.

DBQ Analyzing Documents

7 C Pakistan's population is growing at a rapid rate. Population growth means increased demand for energy. Answers A and D can be eliminated; though both are demands on electricity, neither answer causes the same mass concern on its own. Answer B is a distractor, but since an aging population is on the rise, this concern will effect the future and not necessarily the present as widely.

8 I Machinery that cannot work without electricity would shut down factory operations, resulting in an economic loss. The other examples are all personal inconveniences but not economic losses. Review the differences between economic loss and personal inconvenience. Remind students that a personal inconvenience means that people can live without it, but that the convenience supplies comfort and an easier path.

Short Response

9 The Buddhist belief in rebirth is similar to the same belief in other Indian religions.

10 Possible answer: Since the circumstances of a person's next life depend on his or her karma, and karma reflects both good and bad actions, it should be possible for a person to be born in circumstances that are worse than a previous life if bad actions mean he or she does not deserve a better life. This inference may cause difficulty for some students; a discussion of karma may need to take place in a small group setting to grasp the concept.

Extended Response

11 Students' responses should show a reasonable amount of thought and offer a solution to one of the region's problems. Some suggestions of the challenges for the leader might include: the growth of the population; the continuing conflict in the region; the distribution of wealth and/or class structure; lack of food and water needed to sustain life; increasing demands for electricity; pollution and environmental damage caused by rapid industrialization; disruption of the extended family support system that occurs when some members migrate to urban areas for work.

DBQ ANALYZING DOCUMENTS

7 ANALYZING Read the following passage:

"*Because it cannot produce enough electricity to meet demand, [Pakistan's] government shuts off power for extended periods of time. These chronic blackouts, called load-shedding, sometimes last up to 18 hours a day and hamper economic activity, particularly affecting the country's textile industry, and leave people across a wide socio-economic spectrum in sweltering heat.*"

—from Azmat Khan, "You Aren't Hearing About Pakistan's Biggest Problems" (2011)

How is Pakistan's population related to this problem? RH.6-8.1, RH.6-8.10

A. The large number of young people creates high demand for electricity.

B. The aging population relies on energy-demanding health care.

C. A growing population causes growing demand for electricity.

D. Consumers' demand for electric cars means an increase in energy needs.

8 IDENTIFYING Which of the following is an example of an economic problem that can result from a loss of electricity? RH.6-8.2, RH.6-8.10

F. lack of power for cooking meals

G. people being unable to recharge electronics

H. lack of hot water for cleaning

I. factory machinery that cannot run

SHORT RESPONSE

"*Buddhism, like other faiths of India, believes in a cycle of rebirth. Humans are born many times on earth, each time with the opportunity to perfect themselves further. And it is their own karma—the sum total of deeds [actions in life], good and bad—that determines the circumstances of a future birth.*"

—from Vidya Dehejia, "Buddhism and Buddhist Art"

9 ANALYZING How does the Buddhist belief in rebirth fit in the broader culture of India? RH.6-8.1, RH.6-8.10

10 CITING TEXT EVIDENCE In Buddhism, is a person always reborn into better circumstances in a new life? Why or why not? RH.6-8.1, RH.6-8.10

EXTENDED RESPONSE

11 INFORMATIVE/EXPLANATORY WRITING What do you think is the biggest challenge facing South Asia in the twenty-first century? In several paragraphs, explain what you would do to meet that challenge if you were a leader in that region of the world. WHST.6-8.2, WHST.6-8.10

Need Extra Help?

If You've Missed Question	❶	❷	❸	❹	❺	❻	❼	❽	❾	❿	⓫
Review Lesson	1	1	2	2	3	3	3	3	2	2	3

---

networks   *Online Teaching Options*

Evaluation and Assessment

Assessing Use eAssessment to create your own tests from hundreds of available questions. eAssessment helps you design assessments that meet the needs of different types of learners.

CHAPTER 7
Central Asia, the Caucasus, and Siberian Russia Planner

UNDERSTANDING BY DESIGN®

Enduring Understandings

- People, places, and ideas change over time.

Essential Questions

- How does geography influence the way people live?
- How do governments change?

Predictable Misunderstandings

- The countries in this region all share the same landscape.
- There is a shared culture among the people of this region.
- There is a shared history among the people of this region.

Assessment Evidence

Performance Tasks:

- Project-Based Learning Digital Hands-On Chapter Project
- Project-Based Learning Hands-On Chapter Project

Other Evidence:

- Technology Skills Activity
- Geography Skills Activity
- Participation in Interactive Whiteboard Activities
- Contribution to small-group activities
- Interpretation of slide show images and special purpose maps
- Participation in class discussions about cultural and economic topics
- Lesson Reviews
- Chapter Assessments

SUGGESTED PACING GUIDE

Introducing the Chapter . . . . 1 Day	Lesson 3 . . . . .2 Days
Lesson 1 . . . . .2 Days	Chapter Wrap-Up and Assessment . . . . . . 1 Day
Lesson 2 . . . . .2 Days	

TOTAL TIME   8 Days

Key for Using the Teacher Edition

SKILL-BASED ACTIVITIES

Types of skill activities found in the Teacher Edition.

* **V** **Visual Skills** require students to analyze maps, graphs, charts, and photos.

W **Writing Skills** provide writing opportunities to help students comprehend the text.

R **Reading Skills** help students practice reading skills and master vocabulary.

C **Critical Thinking Skills** help students apply and extend what they have learned.

T **Technology Skills** require students to use digital tools effectively.

*Letters are followed by a number when there is more than one of the same type of skill on the page.

DIFFERENTIATED INSTRUCTION

All activities are written for the on-level student unless otherwise marked with the leveled labels below.

BL Beyond Level
AL Approaching Level
ELL English Language Learners

All students benefit from activities that utilize different learning styles. Many activities are marked as below when a particular learning style is highlighted.

Intrapersonal	Naturalist
Logical/Mathematical	Kinesthetic
Visual/Spatial	Auditory/Musical
Verbal/Linguistic	Interpersonal

National Geography Standards covered in Chapter 7

Learners will understand:

I. The World in Spatial Terms

Standard 1: How to use maps and other geographic representations, geospatial technologies, and spatial thinking to understand and communicate information

Standard 3: How to analyze the spatial organization of people, places, and environments on Earth's surface

II. Places and Regions

Standard 4: The physical and human characteristics of places

Standard 5: That people create regions to interpret Earth's complexity

Standard 6: How culture and experience influence people's perceptions of places and regions

IV. Human Systems

Standard 9: The characteristics, distribution, and migration of human populations on Earth's surface

Standard 10: The characteristics, distribution, and complexity of Earth's cultural mosaics

Standard 11: The patterns and networks of economic interdependence on Earth's surface

Standard 12: The processes, patterns, and functions of human settlement

Standard 13: How the forces of cooperation and conflict among people influence the division and control of Earth's surface

V. Environment and Society

Standard 14: How human actions modify the physical environment

Standard 15: How physical systems affect human systems

VI. The Uses of Geography

Standard 17: How to apply geography to interpret the past

Standard 18: How to apply geography to interpret the present and plan for the future

CHAPTER OPENER PLANNER

Students will know:
- that Central Asia, the Caucasus, and Siberian Russia share a harsh landscape.
- that countries within the region have different climates even though they share a harsh landscape.

Students will be able to:
- **analyze** a world map to identify Siberian Russia as well as the countries of Central Asia and the Caucasus.
- **use** a time line to discuss various events in the history of Central Asia, the Caucasus, and Siberian Russia.

UNDERSTANDING
BY DESIGN®

☑ *Print Teaching Options*

V Visual Skills

☐ **P. 198** Students use the map to reinforce map skills.

☐ **P. 199** Students review the time line and discuss its major points of interest. **Visual/Spatial**

W Writing Skills

☐ **P. 199** Students choose an event on the time line and write a paragraph to describe the effects that event might have on the people of the region. **Verbal/Linguistic**

R Reading Skills

☐ **P. 198** Students make a chart with the phonetic spellings of the names of countries in this subregion and practice their pronunciation. **AL ELL**

☑ *Online Teaching Options*

☐ **MAP** **Reading a Map**—Students identify aspects and locations of the region on a map.

☐ **TIME LINE** **Reading a Time Line and Map**—Students learn about where and when historical events occurred in Russia and Siberia. **AL Visual/Spatial**

☐ **MAP** **Interactive World Atlas**—Students use the interactive world atlas to identify the region and describe its terrain.

☑ *Printable Digital Worksheets*

☐ **WORKSHEET** **Geography Skills: Time Zones**—Students can use the worksheet to understand the reasons behind the establishment of the Time Zones and also practice the skill of reading the Time Zones.

☐ **WORKSHEET** **Technology Skills: Analyzing Data**—Students can use this worksheet to analyze information about land area of countries in this region.

Project-Based Learning

Hands-On

Create a Quilt Square

As students learn about Central Asia and Siberian Russia, they will create a quilt square (cloth or paper depending on time and materials at hand) highlighting facts and themes about the people living in these regions. Students might focus on a region's physical features, climate, conflicts, history, and culture. After reviewing with peers, students will create a quilt square that illustrates this information. Quilt squares should be taped or pinned together to make one quilt and might be displayed in a public area.

Digital Hands-On

Create an Audio Travel Journal

Students will create an audio travel journal that compares and contrasts Central Asia and Siberian Russia. Students should write a script that describes the physical features, history, and culture of this region. The script should also highlight similarities and differences found throughout the region. Students will edit the script with help from classmates and make an audio recording of the journal. Have students share their journals with the class.

Print Resources

ANCILLARY RESOURCES

These ancillaries are available for every chapter and lesson.

- **Reading Essentials and Study Guide Workbook** **AL ELL**
- **Chapter Tests and Lesson Quizzes Blackline Masters**

PRINTABLE DIGITAL WORKSHEETS

These printable digital worksheets are available for every chapter and lesson!

- **Hands-On Chapter Projects**
- **What Do You Know? Activities**
- **Chapter Summaries (English and Spanish)**
- **Vocabulary Builder Activities**
- **Quizzes and Tests**
- **Reading Essentials and Study Guide (English and Spanish)** **AL ELL**
- **Guided Reading Activities**

More Media Resources

SUGGESTED VIDEOS

NOTE: Be sure to preview videos to ensure they are age-appropriate.

- **History—Modern Marvels: The Trans-Siberian Railroad** (50 min.)
- **Lake Baikal—The Earth's Blue Diamond** (57 min.)
- **Globe Trekker—Georgia & Armenia** (55 min.)

SUGGESTED READING

- ***Between Shades of Gray,*** by Ruta Sepetys **BL**
- ***The Endless Steppe: Growing Up in Siberia,*** by Esther Hautzig
- ***Tales Told in Tents: Stories from Central Asia,*** by Sally Pomme Clayton **AL**

PHYSICAL GEOGRAPHY OF THE REGIONS

Students will know:
- that Central Asia, the Caucasus, and Siberian Russia share a harsh landscape.
- that the countries in the region have different climates even though they share a harsh landscape.
- that the countries in the region have different resources.

Students will be able to:
- **describe** the physical features of Central Asia, the Caucasus, and Siberian Russia.
- **describe** the various climates of the regions.
- **describe** important natural resources in the regions.

UNDERSTANDING BY DESIGN®

☑ Print Teaching Options

V Visual Skills

☐ **P. 200** Students locate and compare the size of Russian Siberia and Canada on a globe. **AL ELL**

☐ **P. 201** Students locate Turkmenistan, Uzbekistan, Kyrgyzstan, and Tajikistan and make visual comparisons of their sizes to U.S. states. **ELL Visual/Spatial**

☐ **P. 202** Students compare the size of Texas with the combined areas of the Kyzyl Kum and the Kara-Kum deserts and use this information to discuss how the landscape would affect food production in the area. **AL**

W Writing Skills

☐ **P. 204** Students write an informative essay explaining interesting facts they learn about a waterway.

R Reading Skills

☐ **P. 203** Students use text evidence from "A Variety of Climates" to answer questions about the climate of the plains and deserts. **Verbal/Linguistic**

☐ **P. 204** Students identify why the forests of Siberia are not of economic value to the region.

☐ **P. 205** Students discuss why rivers are an important resource in Central Asia. **Logical/Mathematical**

C Critical Thinking Skills

☐ **P. 202** Students infer how the landscape of Siberia and Central Asia might affect the population growth.

☐ **P. 203** Students make inferences about climate and food production. **Logical/Mathematical**

☐ **P. 205** Students give examples of deciduous trees.

☐ **P. 205** Students identify problems that workers on the oil pipelines or in the coalfields in Siberia might face.

T Technology Skills

☐ **P. 201** Students research the question *Why are earthquakes common in the Caucasus and Central Asia?* and report their findings to the class. **Interpersonal**

☐ **P. 202** Students use the Internet to research the characteristics of tundra, taiga, and steppe and use digital tools to make a chart to present their findings.

☑ Online Teaching Options

V Visual Skills

VIDEO Adapting to Climates—Use the video to review how people and animals adapted to the environment. **Visual/Spatial**

MAP Climates: Central Asia—Use the climate layer of the Chapter Opener map to discuss the various climates of the region. **Visual/Spatial**

IMAGE Breaking Ice—Use the interactive image about ice breakers to connect to the discussion and photo in the text and learn more about why this is needed.

IMAGE Russian Forests—Students study the interactive image to learn about forests and their uses and make a list of forest products they use. **AL Interpersonal, Verbal/Linguistic**

IMAGE Taiga Tree—Use the interactive image of a larch tree to discuss this type of tree that is in high demand.

MAP Resources: Central Asia—Use the resources layer of the Chapter Opener map to review the other resources in this vast region. **Naturalist**

W Writing Skills

VIDEO Ancient Sites—Siberia—Students watch the video about Siberian Russia and write three questions they have about this subregion. **Visual/Spatial, Verbal/Linguistic**

IMAGE 360° View: Siberia's Climate and Vegetation—Students use the 360° image and review the different layers of land and how plant life has adapted and write a paragraph explaining how adaptations help plant life survive in a harsh climate. **BL Visual/Spatial**

MAP World Record Waterways in Central Asia—Students identify different waterways and compare them with other waterways presented in previous chapters. They choose two waterways and write a paragraph comparing and contrasting their characteristics. **BL**

R Reading Skills

LECTURE SLIDE Country Names—Use the lecture slide with the names of the countries to discuss the use of the suffix "stan" and its meaning.

GAME Drag-and-Drop: Landforms of Siberia, Central Asia, and the Caucasus—Use the game to review the regions and the landforms discussed in the lesson; additional bank for climate included.

C Critical Thinking Skills

MAP Understanding the Region—Students locate specific countries using cardinal directions as clues on the political layer of the Chapter Opener map. **AL ELL Visual/Spatial**

T Technology Skills

ONLINE SELF-CHECK QUIZ Lesson 1—Students receive instant feedback on their mastery of lesson content.

☑ Printable Digital Worksheets

W Writing Skills

WORKSHEET Technology Skills: Analyzing Data—Students can use this worksheet to analyze information about land area of countries in this region.

HISTORY OF THE REGIONS

Students will know:
- that the countries in this region have unique cultures with many different ethnic groups.

Students will be able to:
- **discuss** the early history of Siberia, Central Asia, and the Caucasus.
- **explain** the changes in rulers and governments in the regions.

UNDERSTANDING BY DESIGN®

☑ *Print Teaching Options*

V **Visual Skills**

☐ **P. 207** Students explain the benefits of the Trans-Siberian Railroad. **Verbal/Linguistic**

☐ **P. 209** Students study the image of a dam and debate the pros and cons of dams. **Visual/Spatial**

W **Writing Skills**

☐ **P. 208** Students write a persuasive essay on whether government use of prison labor is good for a country.

R **Reading Skills**

☐ **P. 206** Students discuss what natural landforms would make crossing into Siberia from Europe difficult.

☐ **P. 208** Students explain why the Silk Road was prized by conquerors and why nomad groups live in the deserts.

☐ **P. 210** Students use the antonym *simple* to find the meaning of *complex*. **AL** **Verbal/Linguistic**

☐ **P. 211** Students explain why the Soviet Union punished some of the people in the Caucasus after World War I.

C **Critical Thinking Skills**

☐ **P. 207** Students draw conclusions about why Siberia would be a good place of exile for prisoners.

☐ **P. 209** Students reason why cotton production was important to the Russians and how irrigating would increase cotton production. **Logical/Mathematical**

☐ **P. 210** Students think about problems young people face when leaving home for the first time and connect them to problems faced by republics after declaring independence.

☐ **P. 211** Students interpret what the people of the Caucasus lost when the Soviets took over the region.

T **Technology Skills**

☐ **P. 210** Student groups research facts on the early history of Georgia or Armenia and present at least three facts orally or use a software presentation program.

☐ **P. 211** Students use the Internet to research the Armenian Genocide and use a software presentation program to present what they have learned.

☑ *Online Teaching Options*

V **Visual Skills**

☐ **VIDEO** **Planet Wild—Lake Baikal**—Students watch the video and share whether anything that they learned surprised them. **AL** **ELL** **Visual/Spatial**

☐ **IMAGE** **360° View: Samarkand**—Students use the 360° photo of Samarkand to discuss this city in the region. **Visual/Spatial**

☐ **IMAGE** **A Gulag**—Students can use the interactive image to discuss what it might have been like to be imprisoned in a gulag. **Visual/Spatial**

W **Writing Skills**

☐ **MAP** **Influences on Central Asia**—Students make a two-column chart with the heads *Empires* and *Influences* and complete the chart. **Visual/Spatial, Verbal/Linguistic**

☐ **GRAPHIC ORGANIZER** **History of the Caucasus**—Students use a graphic organizer to compare and contrast the development of the Caucasus with other regions they have studied. **AL** **Visual/Spatial, Verbal/Linguistic**

R **Reading Skills**

☐ **GRAPHIC ORGANIZER** **Settling Siberia**—Students use the interactive graphic organizer to review the history of settlement in Siberia.

C **Critical Thinking Skills**

☐ **MAP** **Trans-Siberian Railroad**—Students identify the route of the Trans-Siberian Railroad from Moscow to Vladivostok on the animated map and discuss the use of this route for trade and travel. **AL** **ELL** **Visual/Spatial**

☐ **IMAGES** **How Dams Work**—Students use the images about dams to learn about dams, hydroelectric power, and irrigation to write a paragraph about three things they learned and to compare the region's dams to other dams from previous chapters. **BL**

☐ **MAP** **The Soviet Union**—Students use the map about the Soviet Union and its breakup into individual states to discuss the impact of this political change to this region. **Visual/Spatial**

T **Technology Skills**

☐ **ONLINE SELF-CHECK QUIZ** **Lesson 2**—Students receive instant feedback on their mastery of lesson content.

LIFE IN THE REGIONS

Students will know:
- that the countries in this region have unique cultures with many different ethnic groups.

Students will be able to:
- **describe** population patterns in Siberian Russia, Central Asia, and the Caucasus.
- **describe** people and cultures in the region, including languages and religion.
- **discuss** ethnic unrest in the region.
- **describe** daily life in the region.
- **explain** challenges that lie ahead for the region.

UNDERSTANDING BY DESIGN®

☑ Print Teaching Options

V Visual Skills

☐ **P. 214** Students analyze a population density map.

☐ **P. 216** Students identify characteristics of rural daily life based on a photograph. **Visual/Spatial**

☐ **P. 217** Students create drawings of each of the house types explained in the text. **Visual/Spatial**

W Writing Skills

☐ **P. 215** Students write an essay that explains how a religion reflects the life and beliefs of the people.

☐ **P. 219** Students write a persuasive essay supporting the side of one country in territorial issues and reasons why.

R Reading Skills

☐ **P. 213** Students use the text to illustrate an oasis. **AL**

☐ **P. 216** Students use context clues to define *homogenous*.

☐ **P. 216** Students discuss the conflicts between countries within Central Asia and the Caucasus. **Interpersonal**

☐ **P. 218** Students distinguish facts from opinions about public health in Central Asia. **Verbal/Linguistic**

C Critical Thinking Skills

☐ **P. 212** Students determine what affect the czars and Soviets had on Siberia. **AL** **Logical/Mathematical**

☐ **P. 215** Students read about the Caucasus and write three questions based on the content.

☐ **P. 218** Students determine negative effects of emigration and positive effects of schooling. **AL** **ELL**

☐ **P. 219** Students determine causes and effects of the shrinking Aral Sea. **AL** **ELL**

T Technology Skills

☐ **P. 213** Students research the ten largest cities in Central Asia and create a chart and map to show results. **BL**

☐ **P. 217** Students research the constitution of an assigned country to determine ideas the constitution addresses.

☐ **P. 218** Students use the Internet to find images that show before, after, and current photos of the Aral Sea.

☑ Online Teaching Options

V Visual Skills

VIDEO **Cities in Central Asia**—Students view the video about the largest cities in Central Asia and discuss how and why these cities developed in specific areas. **ELL** **Visual/Spatial**

IMAGE **The Armenian Apostolic Church**—Students use the interactive image to discuss religions in the region and identify which regions have high populations of followers. **AL** **ELL**

W Writing Skills

VIDEO **World's Wonders—Trading Domes of Bukhara**—Students watch the video about life in the regions and write three examples of what they learned. **ELL** **Visual/Spatial**

IMAGES **The Aral Sea**—Students analyze before and after images of the Aral Sea and write theories as to how the changes may have occurred. **Visual/Spatial, Logical/Mathematical**

SLIDE SHOW **Daily Life in Central Asia**—Students view the slide show and write central ideas about the lives of people shown and discuss the daily life of people in the different countries. **ELL**

R Reading Skills

GRAPHIC ORGANIZER **Languages and Religions in Central Asia**—Students use the interactive graphic organizer to review the languages and religions in the region.

GRAPHIC ORGANIZER **Challenges in Central Asia**—Students use the graphic organizer to review challenges in Central Asia and write events in chronological order. **AL** **Visual/Spatial**

C Critical Thinking Skills

MAP **Understanding Time Zones**—Students use the animated map to identify their time zone and calculate the current time of day it is in Tashkent, Uzbekistan. **Visual/Spatial**

MAP **Population: Central Asia**—Students use the population layer on the Chapter Opener map to discuss the population distributions in this region.

IMAGE **Living in a Yurt**—Students use the interactive image of the yurt interior to discuss how people live in this dwelling and compare it to the nomadic people who do not live in yurts and how they survive the rough terrain and climate.

T Technology Skills

ONLINE SELF-CHECK QUIZ **Lesson 3**—Students receive instant feedback on their mastery of lesson content.

☑ Printable Digital Worksheets

W Writing Skills

WORKSHEET **Geography Skills: Time Zones**—Students can use the worksheet to understand the reasons behind the establishment of the Time Zones and also practice the skill of reading the Time Zones.

LESSON 1   Physical Geography of the Regions

Reading and Comprehension

Challenge students to use each of this lesson's content vocabulary words in a paragraph about people, places, and cultures in Central Asia, the Caucasus, and Siberian Russia. Have students take turns reading their paragraphs to a partner. Then have students add one or two sentences that summarize other important information in the lesson. Guide a question-answer session in which students are called upon to summarize different sections of text.

Text Evidence

Have students work in small groups to identify and describe issues in many Caucasus and Central Asian countries. Tell students to present an analysis of their findings that answers this question: *What government and economic issues do these regions face?* Tell students they may conduct online research to find out more about the issues, and to use evidence in the text and from their research to support their answer. After groups have presented their reports, discuss some of the problems faced by countries in Central Asia, the Caucasus, and Siberian Russia.

LESSON 2   History of the Regions

Reading and Comprehension

To help students make connections between the settlement, invasion, and conquests discussed in this lesson, have students look for signal words as they read. Tell students that sequence is often signaled by words such as *first, then, next,* and *finally.* Words such as *like* and *as* indicate comparison, and the words *but, however,* and *though* indicate concepts being contrasted. Have students skim the lesson to look for signal words and note which concepts and ideas are being compared or contrasted, or discussed chronologically.

Text Evidence

Assign student pairs two of the countries discussed in the lesson to research and analyze, drawing comparisons to information presented in the text. Tell students to note information found in their research about each country's government that supports or conflicts with evidence in the text. As students research each country's government, have them note key ideas and details to answer the essential question: *How do governments change?* Have students present their findings to the class.

LESSON 3   Life in the Regions

Reading and Comprehension

Have students skim the lesson to identify words that may be unfamiliar or confusing, such as *hinterlands, czars, indigenous,* and *pastoral.* Have students use print or online dictionaries to define the words. Then have students take turns explaining how each word relates to a concept in the lesson. Guide a class discussion about complex concepts and terms, such as *free-enterprise economies* or *ethnic-related disputes.*

Text Evidence

Organize students into small groups and tell students to research a territorial issue in the Caucasus, Central Asia, or Siberian Russia that exists today. Have groups use evidence from the text and additional research to identify the issue, how it started, what people it has affected, and if it is being resolved. Have groups present their reports to the class, using visuals to clarify concepts and ideas.

Online Resources

Level Reader

Use this online lower-level text that corresponds directly to the text in the online Student Edition.

Guided Reading Activities

This resource uses graphic organizers and guiding questions to help students with comprehension.

Assessing Background Knowledge

Use these worksheets to pre-assess students' background knowledge before they read the chapter.

Reading Essentials and Study Guide Workbook

This resource offers writing and reading activities for the approaching-level student.

Self-Check Quizzes

This online assessment tool provides instant feedback for students to check their progress.

CENTRAL ASIA, THE CAUCASUS, AND SIBERIAN RUSSIA

ESSENTIAL QUESTIONS · How does geography influence the way people live?
· How do governments change?

©Strunin Anatoly/ITAR-TASS/Photo/Corbis

A woman of northwestern Siberia in traditional dress

net**w**rks

There's More Online about Central Asia, the Caucasus, and Siberian Russia.

CHAPTER **7**

Lesson 1
Physical Geography of the Regions

Lesson 2
History of the Regions

Lesson 3
Life in the Regions

The Story Matters...

Central Asia, the Caucasus, and Siberian Russia share a harsh land. Siberia is an enormous and cold land, but it contains vast and economically important oil and natural gas resources. The mountainous terrain, semiarid steppes, and vast deserts of Central Asia are home to many ethnic groups, some with roots in ancient cultures. Throughout history, people living in Central Asia have been affected by conflicts in the region, as well as expansion of the Russian Empire and the Soviet Union.

FOLDABLES
Study Organizer

Go to the Foldables® library in the back of your book to make a Foldable® that will help you take notes while reading this chapter.

197

CHAPTER 7
Central Asia, the Caucasus, and Siberian Russia

ENGAGE

Think-Pair-Share Have students brainstorm a list of synonyms for the word *harsh* and have them list people, places, and things that could be described as being *harsh*. Students might cite language, weather conditions, or consequences as being harsh. Then have students read "The Story Matters..." about Central Asia, the Caucasus, and Siberian Russia, a region with a harsh landscape.

Use the following questions to guide students in a discussion about the resources and climate of the region. **Ask:**

- **How would vast oil and natural gas resources affect a region's economy?** *(The region could become an important exporter of these resources, providing the resources locally, nationally, and internationally.)*
- **How might the harsh landscape and a cold climate affect the ability to develop those natural resources?** *(The climate might pose challenges in developing or accessing the resources. These challenges might also make it more expensive to develop the resources. However, people might still find it economically advantageous to pursue the development.)*
- **How do strong ties to cultures of the past influence ethnic groups?** *(Ties to the past often determine culture and traditions. These ties may also affect the way that the culture changes.)*

Comparing and Contrasting Have students compare and contrast the clothes worn by the Siberian girl to the clothes worn by Americans who live in cold winter climates. Students can take notes in a chart like the one shown below. Have volunteers use the Internet to research the kinds of clothing to wear during a cold Siberian winter and present a slide show to the class using presentation software.

Siberian Clothing   American Clothing

FOLDABLES
Study Organizer

Go to the Foldables® library for a cumulative chapter-based Foldable® activity that your students can use to help take notes and prepare for assessment.

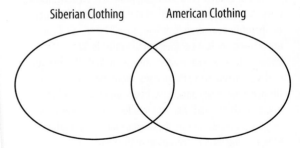

Letter from the Author

Dear Geography Teacher,

In this chapter, students will learn about the fascinating northward flowing rivers in Siberia. The banks of the giant rivers, the Ob, Lena, and Yenisey, overflow every spring because ice at their sources in the south thaws. The northerly mouths of these rivers, however, are still clogged with ice. Flooding occurs because there is nowhere for the water to flow. The spring floods in Russia create vast marshes and swamps and render potentially productive land unusable for agriculture.

TEACH & ASSESS

Step Into the Place

V Visual Skills

Reading a Map Use the following questions to reinforce students' understanding of the Chapter Opener map. **Ask:**

- **How many countries make up this region? Identify them.** *(Nine: Russia, Kazakhstan, Uzbekistan, Kyrgyzstan, Tajikistan, Turkmenistan, Azerbaijan, Armenia, and Georgia)*
- **In which cardinal direction from the Ural Mountains does most of this region lie?** *(east)*
- **Based on the latitude of the northern part of Russia, what conclusions can you draw about its climate?** *(Possible answer: The northern part of Russia is near the Arctic Circle. This area would have a subarctic climate with very cold winters.)* **Visual/Spatial, Verbal/Linguistic**

R Reading Skills

Pronouncing Difficult Words Help students to correctly pronounce the names of the countries in this region by making a chart with the phonetic spellings of the names. Practice saying the names aloud with students: **Kazakhstan**, (kuh-zahk-STAHN); **Uzbekistan**, (ooz-beh-kih-STAN); **Kyrgyzstan**, (keer-gih-STAN); **Tajikistan**, (tah-jih-kih-STAN); **Azerbaijan**, (a-zur-by-JAHN); **Russia**, (RUH-shuh); **Turkmenistan**, (turk-MEH-nih-stan); **Armenia**, (ar-MEAN-ee-uh); **Georgia**, (JOR-juh) **ELL** **AL** **Auditory/Musical, Verbal/Linguistic**

Content Background Knowledge

The city of Yakutsk (yah-KOOTSK), located in Eastern Siberia, is the coldest city on Earth. During its eight-month winter, temperatures can drop to as low as −83°F (−64°C). People are warned not to wear their glasses outside during the winter. The severe cold makes the metal on the frames stick to skin, and removing the glasses might tear off chunks of flesh. People wear coats, hats, boots, and other clothing made of rabbit, Arctic fox, and reindeer to keep warm. In July, their hottest month, the average high temperature is 65°F, causing locals to complain of the heat!

ANSWERS, p. 198

STEP INTO THE PLACE
1. Kazakhstan and Uzbekistan
2. Kazakhstan
3. Armenia
4. **CRITICAL THINKING** Most flow south to north because rivers follow the path of least resistance. In this case, the rivers flow into the seas north of Russia.

Chapter 7 **CENTRAL ASIA, THE CAUCASUS, AND SIBERIAN RUSSIA**

Siberian Russia, the Central Asian countries, and the Caucasus region make up a large area. The regions were once part of the Soviet Union.

Step Into the Place

MAP FOCUS Use the map to answer the following questions.

1 PHYSICAL GEOGRAPHY The Aral Sea extends into which two countries?

2 THE GEOGRAPHER'S WORLD Which country borders Kyrgyzstan to the north?

3 PLACES AND REGIONS Yerevan is the capital city of which country?

4 CRITICAL THINKING Analyzing In which direction do most Siberian rivers flow? Why do you think this is so?

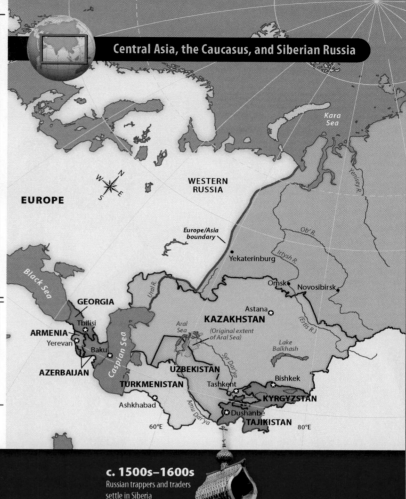

Central Asia, the Caucasus, and Siberian Russia

Step Into the Time

TIME LINE Choose one event on the time line and describe what effects that event might have on the people of the region. WHST.6-8.2, WHST.6-8.4

c. A.D. 900s–1450s Mongol khans rule southern Siberia

c. 1500s–1600s Russian trappers and traders settle in Siberia

c. 1600s Russia expands to Pacific coast

198 Chapter 7

Bruno Morandi/Robert Harding World Imagery/Getty Images

Project-Based Learning 🖐

Hands-On

Creating a Quilt Square

As students learn about Central Asia and Siberian Russia, they will create a quilt square (cloth or paper depending on time) highlighting facts and themes about the people living in these regions. Students might focus on a region's physical features, climate, conflicts, history, and culture. After reviewing their ideas with peers, students will create a quilt square that illustrates this information. Quilt squares should be taped or pinned together to make one quilt and might be displayed in a public area.

Digital Hands-On

Creating an Audio Travel Journal

Students will create an audio travel journal that compares Central Asia and Siberian Russia. Students should write a script that describes the physical features, history, and culture of this region and highlights similarities and differences found throughout the region. Students will edit the script and make an audio recording of the journal. Have students share their journals with the class.

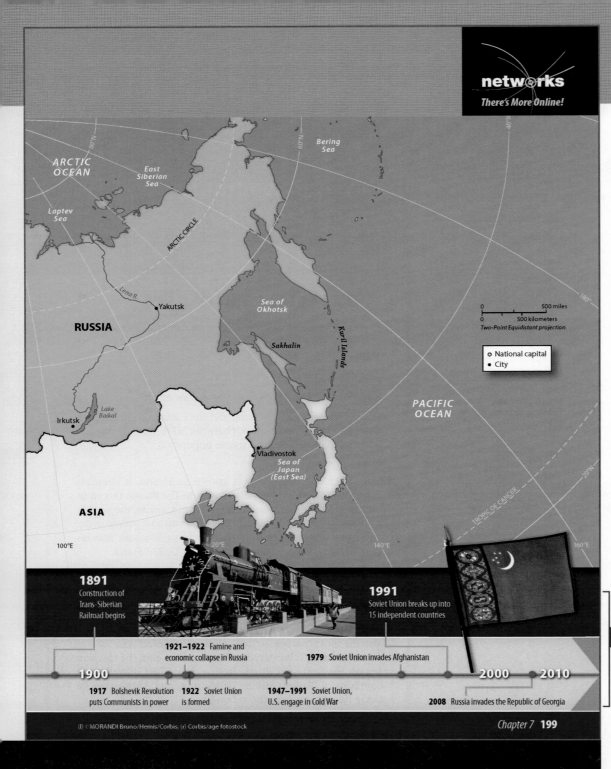

RUSSIA

ASIA

PACIFIC OCEAN

1891
Construction of Trans-Siberian Railroad begins

1991
Soviet Union breaks up into 15 independent countries

1921–1922 Famine and economic collapse in Russia

1979 Soviet Union invades Afghanistan

1900

1917 Bolshevik Revolution puts Communists in power

1922 Soviet Union is formed

1947–1991 Soviet Union, U.S. engage in Cold War

2000 **2010**

2008 Russia invades the Republic of Georgia

(l) ©MORANDI Bruno/Hemis/Corbis; (r) Corbis/age fotostock

Chapter 7 **199**

TIME LINE AND MAP

Reading a Time Line and Map

Integrating Visual Information Display the time line and map on the whiteboard. Have volunteers read each event as it is revealed on the time line. Ask students to identify where in the world the event took place and find its location on the map. **AL Visual/Spatial**

See page 197B for other online activities.

Step Into the Time

V Visual Skills

Reading a Time Line Have students review the time line and as a class, discuss its major points of interest. **Ask:**

- **What period of time is shown on the time line?** *(from 900s to 2008)*
- **Which events contributed to the formation of the Soviet Union?** *(1917, Bolshevik Revolution; 1921–1922, famine and economic collapse in Russia)*
- **During what time in history did Russia expand its territory all the way to the Pacific Ocean?** *(1600s)*
- **What helped Russians transport natural resources from the cold lands of Siberia to factories in the west?** *(the Trans-Siberian Railroad)*

Ask students to list some historical events that could be added to the time line. *(Student answers will vary but should include accurate event placement.)* **Visual/Spatial, Verbal/Linguistic**

W Writing Skills

Informative/Explanatory Use the activity described at the beginning of the time line as a writing prompt. Before writing their paragraphs, have students use events on the time line to brainstorm ideas about how the expansion of Siberian Russia affected Central Asia. Have students share their completed paragraphs with the class. **Logical/Mathematical, Verbal/Linguistic**

V

CLOSE & REFLECT

Making Inferences Have students use the events on the time line to make an inference about the influence Russian trappers and traders had on Russian expansion. *(Possible answer: Trappers and traders were the first people to discover and make known the riches in the east.)* **Ask:** **Why do you think Russia wanted to expand its territory across Siberia to the Pacific Ocean?** *(Possible answer: Expansion through Siberia to the Pacific Ocean would give Russia access to a warm ocean port; Siberia might be rich in natural resources that would benefit the Russian economy.)* **Verbal/Linguistic, Logical/Mathematical**

ENGAGE

Bellringer Before students begin the lesson, have them brainstorm a list of places they know or have read about that have extremely cold winters. Students may cite Alaska or the Scandinavian countries of Norway, Sweden, and Finland or the northern part of Western Russia. **Ask:** How does the cold climate and the proximity to the North Pole affect the growing season and human outdoor activities in these areas? *(The growing season is much shorter in the Arctic regions, and fewer crops are able to grow there. People may still spend time outdoors, but the activities they do will be different from those in warm climates and people will dress differently, wearing more layers and warmer clothes.)*

Then make a connection between students' answers and the Essential Question: *How does geography influence the way people live?*

TEACH & ASSESS

R Reading Skills

Summarizing Summarizing helps students remember and better understand what they have read. Have students summarize the information in this paragraph. *(Possible answer: Siberia covers a large area of the world from the Ural Mountains to the Pacific Ocean, but few people live there because of its harsh climate and difficult terrain.)* **Verbal/Linguistic**

V Visual Skills

Reading a Globe Have students locate the eastern part of Russia known as Siberia and the country of Canada to make a visual size comparison of the two areas. Then have them locate Siberia's Pacific coast, the city of Moscow, and the state of Maine in the United States on a globe. Have volunteers use a tape measure and the Key to determine the distances between the coast and Moscow and the coast and Maine. Also ask volunteers to determine the distance across Siberia from the Ural Mountains to the Pacific Ocean. **ELL** **AL** **Visual/ Spatial, Logical/Mathematical**

ANSWER, p. 200

Taking Notes Notes should include facts from each section, such as: the three regions and the countries of Central Asia and the Caucasus; the West Siberian Plain and central Siberian plateau, the mountains and climates of each region; rivers and other waterways of each region; and each region's important natural resources.

---

networks

There's More Online!

☑ **IMAGE** Breaking Ice
☑ **MAP** Understanding the Region
☑ **VIDEO**

Reading **HELP**DESK

Academic Vocabulary RH.6-8.4
(Tier Two Words)
• define

Content Vocabulary RH.6-8.4
(Tier Three Words)
• tundra
• taiga
• permafrost
• steppe
• deciduous

TAKING NOTES: *Key Ideas and Details* RH.6-8.2, RH.6-8.7

Summarize As you read the lesson, list important details for each topic of the lesson on a graphic organizer like the one below.

Topic	Details
Regions	
Landforms and Climates	
Waterways	
Natural Resources	

200

Lesson 1
Physical Geography of the Regions

ESSENTIAL QUESTION · *How does geography influence the way people live?*

IT MATTERS BECAUSE
Russian Siberia, the Central Asian countries, and the Caucasus make up a large area. The regions cover about one-ninth of the world's total land area.

Regions

GUIDING QUESTION *Which countries make up the regions?*

Siberian Russia, Central Asia, and the Caucasus are separate regions. They share certain characteristics, such as rugged terrain, harsh climate, and sparse population.

Siberian Russia

R The eastern part of Russia is known as Siberia. It stretches from the Ural Mountains in the west to the Pacific Ocean in the east. Siberia is 25 percent larger than Canada, the world's second-largest country. The region is so vast that people living on Siberia's Pacific coast are farther from Moscow, Russia's capital, than they are from Maine in the United States.

V

Central Asia
Central Asia is made up of five countries: Kazakhstan, Turkmenistan, Uzbekistan, Kyrgyzstan, and Tajikistan. Kazakhstan is the northernmost and largest country in Central Asia and the ninth-largest country in the world. It is also the most sparsely settled country in Central Asia.

Kazakhstan is bordered by China on the east, the Caspian Sea on the west, and Russia to its north. The Central Asian countries of Turkmenistan, Uzbekistan, and Kyrgyzstan lie along Kazakhstan's southern border.

---

networks   *Online Teaching Options*

VIDEO

Ancient Sites—Siberia

Formulating Questions Use this video about the physical geography and wildlife of Siberia to introduce the lesson. Ask students to write three questions they have about this region or its wildlife after watching the video. Collect the questions and discuss them as a class after reading the lesson. **Visual/Spatial, Verbal/Linguistic**

See page 197C for other online activities.

Turkmenistan and Uzbekistan are about the same size. Both are about twice the size of Minnesota. Turkmenistan has the smallest population in Central Asia, and Uzbekistan has the largest.

Kyrgyzstan and Tajikistan form Uzbekistan's eastern border. Both are small countries with small populations. Kyrgyzstan is about the size of South Dakota, and the smaller Tajikistan is about the size of Iowa.

Turkmenistan, Kyrgyzstan, and Tajikistan are Central Asia's southernmost countries. South of the countries lie China, Pakistan, Afghanistan, and Iran.

The Caucasus Region

Between the Caspian Sea and the Black Sea and south of the Caucasus Mountains is a region called the Caucasus. Its three small countries—Georgia, Azerbaijan, and Armenia—together total about the size of North Dakota. To their north lies Russia. Turkey and Iran border the Caucasus region to the south.

☑ READING PROGRESS CHECK

Analyzing Why is Kazakhstan, which has a larger population than Turkmenistan, more sparsely settled than Turkmenistan?

Landforms and Climates

GUIDING QUESTION *What are the major landforms and climates of Siberia, Central Asia, and the Caucasus region?*

The variety of landforms and climates that characterize the Caucasus, Central Asia, and Siberia make for one of the most geographically interesting regions of the world.

Mountains

The Caucasus Mountains **define** the Caucasus region. These mountains generally mark the border between Europe and Asia. Many of the mountains in this range are volcanoes. Although they have not erupted in thousands of years, the forces that formed them make the region prone to frequent earthquakes.

To the east, two high mountain ranges lie along Central Asia's border with China. The rugged Tian Shan cover most of Kyrgyzstan and extend into eastern Kazakhstan and Uzbekistan. On their southwestern edge is a smaller range called the Pamirs. They cover most of Tajikistan. Like the Caucasus, the Tian Shan and the Pamirs are an earthquake zone.

©Irina Popova/Corbis

Academic Vocabulary

define to describe the nature or extent of something

Musicians perform in a mountain village in the Caucasus of southern Russia.
Identifying Where is the Caucasus located?

Chapter 7 **201**

MAP

Understanding the Region

Locating Display the political layer of the Chapter Opener map to review the countries located in this region. Have volunteers locate each country as you name them. Review the pronunciation of the countries' names. Then ask students to locate specific countries using the cardinal directions as clues. For example: **Which country lies mainly to the southeast of Uzbekistan?** *(Tajikistan)* **ELL** **AL** **Visual/Spatial, Verbal/Linguistic**

See page 197C for other online activities.

V Visual Skills

Integrating Visual Information Display a political map of the world and have students locate Turkmenistan, Uzbekistan, Kyrgyzstan, and Tajikistan and the American states of Minnesota, South Dakota, and Iowa. Have them use the information in the text to compare visually the sizes of the countries to these states in the United States. Continue making visual comparisons with the combined countries in the Caucasus region to the size of the state of North Dakota. **ELL** **Visual/Spatial**

R Reading Skills

Determining Word Meanings Remind students to add academic and content vocabulary words to their lists. Tell them to write their own definitions for the words and to include drawings if desired. **ELL** **AL** **Verbal/Linguistic**

T Technology Skills

Researching on the Internet Have students work in small groups to research the question: **Why are earthquakes common in the Caucasus and Central Asia?** Have groups report their findings to the class. Encourage them to use presentation software or create visuals to aid in their explanations. **Verbal/Linguistic, Interpersonal**

Content Background Knowledge

Share these facts about Central Asia with students:

- Many believe that Mt. Ararat in the Caucasus is the final resting place for Noah's Ark.
- Mt. Elbrus, an inactive volcano, is the highest mountain in the Caucasus and the tenth highest in the world. It is also considered one of the world's most deadliest peaks with about 30 climbers a year being killed.
- The Tian Shan Mountains cover an area approximately equal to that of the Rockies. Issyk-Kol, in western Tian Shan, is one of the world's largest mountain lakes. It is slightly salty and is ice-free in winter.
- *Pamir* means "U-shaped valley." The Pamirs are snow-capped throughout the year.
- Marco Polo used the Terak Pass in the Pamir Mountains on his way to China in 1271.
- *Ural* is a Turkish word meaning "Stone Belt."

ANSWERS, p. 201

☑ READING PROGRESS CHECK Kazakhstan covers a much larger area than Turkmenistan does, so its population density is lower.
Identifying in the mountainous region that borders Europe and Asia

C Critical Thinking Skills

Making Inferences Explain to students that plains and deserts cover much of Siberia and Central Asia. **Ask: How might the landscape of Siberia and Central Asia affect the population growth of the area?** *(Students' answers may vary but should include characteristics of the plains and deserts found in the region and make the inference that not many people would choose to live in the harsh landscape.)* **Verbal/Linguistic**

T Technology Skills

Using Digital Tools Have small groups of students work together to use the Internet to research the characteristics of tundra, taiga, and steppe. Then have them use digital tools to make a chart to present their findings. Tell students to individually use the information on their charts and the information in the text to compare and contrast Siberia's geography. Have them write short reports explaining the similarities and contrasts between different areas in Siberia. **BL** **Visual/Spatial, Logical/Mathematical**

V Visual Skills

Integrating Visual Information Display a political map of the United States. Have a volunteer locate the state of Texas. Have students make a visual comparison of the size of Texas with the combined areas of the Kyzyl Kum and the Kara-Kum deserts in Central Asia. Have students use this information to discuss how the landscape would affect food production in the area. **AL** **Visual/Spatial, Logical/Mathematical**

Content Background Knowledge

The Nenet people herd reindeer and migrate seasonally with those reindeer, traveling about 1,000 kilometers in each direction. The reindeer and the migratory patterns are critical to their way of life. The reindeer provide food, shelter, and clothing. During the years of communist rule, the Nenet people were not free to migrate, but had to live and work on collective farms, which were required to pay taxes to the Russian government in the form of reindeer meat. The government took the children and sent them to state-run boarding schools. Not only were the Nenet children taken from their families, but they were not allowed to speak their own language at school. Today the Nenet are politically free, but their way of life faces new challenges. Their long-established migratory patterns are affected by Earth's climate change, which causes the ice to melt earlier in the spring and freeze later in the fall. At the same time, development of the region related to oil extraction (pipelines, roads, railroads) also affects their migration.

ANSWER, p. 202

CRITICAL THINKING grassland plains, mountain plateaus, coastal lowlands, and deserts

---

The Ural Mountains, which run north and south through Russia, are yet another border range. These heavily forested mountains are much lower in elevation than the other ranges. Geographers consider the Ural Mountains to be a boundary between Europe and Asia. The Urals also mark the western border of Russia's Siberia region. The eastern third of Siberia is another mountainous region that extends south along Russia's border with Mongolia.

Plains and Deserts

Plains and deserts also characterize the regions. In Siberia, the west Siberian plain extends from the Ural Mountains east to the Yenisey River. Covering an area of almost 1 million square miles (2.6 million sq. km), the west Siberian plain is one of the world's largest and flattest plains. Its lowland areas are poorly drained, with many swamps and marshes. East of the Yenisey River, the land rises to form the central Siberian plateau, a rugged region of hills cut by deep river gorges.

Siberia's geography changes from north to south as well as from west to east. Extreme northern Siberia is mostly **tundra**—a treeless zone found near the Arctic Circle or at high mountain elevations. Northern Siberia is a harsh environment of bare, rocky ground with patches of small shrubs, mosses, and lichens.

South of the tundra lies a vast area of **taiga**—a zone of coniferous forest. Siberia's taiga is swampy, because, like the tundra, the region is covered in **permafrost**, a layer of permanently frozen ground that lies beneath the surface soil and rocks. Permafrost covers about two-thirds of Siberia. Southern portions of the western plains and central plateau contain dry grasslands called **steppe;** the steppe extends into Kazakhstan in Central Asia.

Central Asia is made up of lowland mountains and dune-covered deserts. Most of Kazakhstan consists of dry grassland plains and plateaus, with lowlands on its coast along the Caspian Sea. In eastern Kazakhstan, the Kyzyl Kum desert stretches south into Uzbekistan. Another desert, the Kara–Kum, extends over most of nearby Turkmenistan. Together, they form a harsh region, nearly the size of Texas, consisting of sand ridges, scattered grasses, and desert plants.

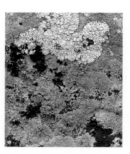

Visual Vocabulary

Lichen a plantlike organism that consists of algae and fungus

Nomadic people live in Siberia and Central Asia. A family, including reindeer and a dog, gather outside their home (left). A shepherd and his flock (right) cross the steppe near a Central Asian mountain range in Kazakhstan.

▶ **CRITICAL THINKING**
Describing What landscapes are found in much of Central Asia?

netw♦rks *Online Teaching Options*

IMAGE

360° View: Siberia's Climate and Vegetation

Explaining Display the 360° image of the Siberian tundra. Use the image to review with students the different layers of land in the region and how the plant life has adapted to the climate. Have students write a paragraph explaining how the adaptations help the plants survive in a harsh climate. **BL** **Visual/Spatial, Naturalist**

See page 197C for other online activities.

Interactive Photos

DIAGRAM SKILLS >

BELOW GROUND IN SIBERIA
This cutaway diagram shows how permafrost penetrates below ground in Siberia.

Active Layer— Soil that freezes and thaws seasonally

Permafrost— Soil that remains frozen year-round

Unfrozen Soil—

▶ **CRITICAL THINKING**

1. **Identifying** What is the active layer?

2. **Describing** How might climate change affect permafrost?

A Variety of Climates

The regions have many climates, ranging from arctic climates in Siberia to desert climates in Central Asia. Dry conditions prevail across much of Central Asia, characterizing what is called an arid climate. The steppe of southwest Siberia and northern Kazakhstan receives a little more rain and has a semiarid climate. Moving north and east, summers become shorter and cooler, and the winters become colder. Summer in the Siberian tundra, for example, lasts only two months. Temperatures rarely rise above 50°F (10°C). Summers in the mountain valleys of eastern Siberia are longer and milder. Eastern and central Siberia have some of the coldest winters on Earth. There, the temperature has reached as low as –96°F (–71°C). The west Siberian plain experiences heavy snows, but elsewhere snowfall is light.

The mountain areas of Central Asia have a humid continental climate. Temperatures and precipitation in these areas vary according to location and elevation. Mountain valleys have hot, dry summers and cold winters. Rainfall varies from 4 inches to 20 inches (10 cm to 51 cm) per year. Mountain foothills are cooler and get more rain. The high elevations are even colder, with more rain and snow.

The Caucasus Mountains give Georgia, Azerbaijan, and Armenia a climate much like the mountains of eastern Central Asia. The presence, however, of two large bodies of water—the Caspian Sea and the Black Sea—makes the region's summers cooler and winters warmer. The Black Sea gives Georgia's coastal lowlands a humid subtropical climate, with up to 100 inches (254 cm) of rainfall in a year. Farther east, in the mountains and mountain valleys, the climate is much drier.

R

C

Chapter 7 **203**

MAP

World Record Waterways in Central Asia

Discussing Display the map that shows extreme waterways in this region. Have students identify the different waterways and make comparisons with other waterways presented in previous chapters. Have them choose two waterways—one from this region and one presented in previous chapters—and write a paragraph comparing and contrasting their characteristics.

BL Visual/Spatial, Verbal/Linguistic

See page 197C for other online activities.

R Reading Skills

Citing Text Evidence Have students read the section, "A Variety of Climates." Then have them use text evidence to answer the following questions about the climate of this region. Students should answer the questions then read, or cite, the sentence or sentences in the text that support their answers. **Ask:**

- **What is the difference between an arid and semi-arid climate?** *(Conditions in an arid climate are dry with very little to no rainfall. Semi-arid climates receive a bit more rain than arid climates.)*

- **What is summer like in the Siberian tundra?** *(Summer lasts only two months with the temperature rarely rising above 50°F.)*

- **How might you describe winters in eastern and central Siberia?** *(The winters are some of the coldest on Earth with temperatures as low as –96°F.)*

- **What kind of climate do the mountain areas of Central Asia have?** *(humid continental climate)*

- **How is the climate in mountain valleys in Central Asia different from the climate in the mountain foothills?** *(Mountain valleys have hot, dry summers and cold winters with 4–20 inches of rainfall per year. Mountain foothills are cooler and get more rain.)*

- **How does the Caspian Sea and the Black Sea affect the climates in the Caucasus?** *(They make the region's summers cooler and winters warmer. The Black Sea gives Georgia's coastal lowlands a humid subtropical climate with a high amount of rainfall.)* **Verbal/Linguistic, Naturalist**

C Critical Thinking Skills

Making Inferences As students consider the content of this page, use the text and the vegetation layer of the Chapter Opener map to discuss the following questions with students. **Ask:**

- **How might the climate in Siberia affect food production in the area?** *(Possible answer: Because of the short growing season, food production would be minimal.)*

- **How might the people in Siberia get their food?** *(Possible answer: Most of the people's food would need to be transported to the area. The people are dependent on others to produce what they eat.)*

- **How might the climate in Georgia's coastal lowlands affect food production?** *(With a humid subtropical climate and a lot of rain, food production should be good. However, soil conditions and other factors would also affect the production)* **Logical/Mathematical**

ANSWERS, p. 203

DIAGRAM SKILLS

1. The active layer is ground that seasonally freezes and thaws.

2. Warming trends might thaw permafrost in some areas.

R1 Reading Skills

Citing Text Evidence As you read the section called "Waterways" to students, have them write down key words or phrases that can help them identify the main idea. Then, **ask:**

- **What kind of water is in the Caspian Sea and the Aral Sea?** *(salt water)*
- **How is the water in these seas different from the water in Lake Baikal?** *(The water in Lake Baikal is fresh.)* **Verbal/Linguistic, Logical/Mathematical**

W Writing Skills

Informative/Explanatory Waterways are important to this region. Have students choose one of the waterways cited in the text to research. Then have them write an informative essay explaining interesting facts they learn about their chosen waterways. Review with students good paragraph structure including a main idea sentence and the inclusion of supporting details. Ask volunteers to share their essays with the class. **Naturalist, Verbal/Linguistic**

R2 Reading Skills

Identifying Problems Siberia contains about 20 percent of all the world's trees. **Ask: Why isn't this vast resource an economic value to the region?** *(Siberia is mainly covered with permafrost, which limits the kind of trees that can grow there. Most of the trees in Siberia are larch. Since larch wood is of poor quality, there is not much demand for larch wood and its products.)* **Logical/Mathematical**

Content Background Knowledge

Legend has it that during the Bolshevik Revolution, a train containing part of Czar Nicholas II's treasure derailed and sunk to the bottom of Lake Baikal. The train was under the command of Admiral Alexander Kolchak, a World War I hero and a leader of the White Russians fighting against the Bolsheviks. Kolchak was arrested by Lenin and executed by firing squad in 1920. His body was hidden under the ice of the Angara River, which flows out of Lake Baikal. No treasure was ever recovered. However, in 2010, a mini-sub conducting mapping exercises in Lake Baikal, reportedly located pieces of a train, ammunition boxes, and rectangular blocks with a metallic gleam 1,200 feet below the surface of the lake. The treasure, if real, could be worth billions of dollars.

ANSWERS, p. 204

☑ **READING PROGRESS CHECK** mountainous
CRITICAL THINKING Ice in the north blocks the north-flowing rivers from emptying into the Arctic Ocean, resulting in floods. Temperatures are warmer where the rivers begin in the south than at their mouths in the north.

Waterways

The Caspian Sea separates the Caucasus and Central Asia. At nearly the size of California, this saltwater lake is the largest inland body of water in the world. To the east, the Aral Sea, a much smaller saltwater lake, straddles the Kazakhstan-Uzbekistan border. Once the world's fourth-largest lake, the Aral has been shrinking for decades.

Lake Baikal, in southeastern Siberia, is the world's largest freshwater lake by volume. It holds about 20 percent of all the freshwater on Earth. With a maximum depth of more than 1 mile (0.6 km), Lake Baikal is also the deepest lake in the world.

The dry climate forces many people in Central Asia to depend heavily on the region's two major rivers, the Syr Dar'ya and the Amu Dar'ya. The rivers flow from mountains across deserts and are used for irrigation. In Siberia, four great rivers—the Ob', the Irtysh, the Yenisey, and the Lena—flow north to empty into the Arctic Ocean. They are among the world's largest river systems. The north-flowing Siberian rivers flood vast areas in the spring. Temperatures are warmer where the rivers begin in the south than at their mouths in the north. Ice in the north blocks the rivers from emptying into the Arctic Ocean, resulting in floods.

Unlike other main Siberian rivers, the Amur River drains eastward. Some of it forms the border between Russia and China. Affected by summer winds, the Amur river valley is warmer than the rest of Siberia. It is Siberia's main food-producing area.

The nuclear-powered ship *Rossiya* breaks through Arctic Sea ice to open passageways for other ships. Nuclear-powered icebreakers like *Rossiya* can travel only in cold water because their reactors need to be kept cool.

▶ **CRITICAL THINKING**
Describing How are Siberia's rivers affected by the ice in the far north?

☑ **READING PROGRESS CHECK**
Citing Text Evidence What type of terrain is common in Siberia, Central Asia, and the Caucasus region?

Natural Resources

GUIDING QUESTION *Which natural resources of Siberia, Central Asia, and the Caucasus are economically important?*

Siberia holds some of the greatest wealth in natural resources on Earth. The Caucasus is also rich in natural resources. Central Asia is rich in natural resources too, but the area has little water.

Vast Forests

Siberia's vast taiga contains about 20 percent of all the world's trees. The economic value of this resource is limited, however. One reason is that a lack of roads makes logging

Patrick Landmann/Photo Researchers

204 Chapter 7

---

netw⊕rks   *Online Teaching Options*

Russian Forests

Analyzing Images Display the interactive image of the forests in Russia. Discuss with students how forests are a valuable resource and use the interactive image to learn about their availability and uses. Make connections with students to the forests of Russia and the forests of the United States and how climate may affect tree growth. Have students make a list of wood or forest products they use.
AL Interpersonal, Verbal/Linguistic

See page 197C for other online activities.

Interactive Photos

©Image Source/Getty Images

in the region difficult. Another is that most of the taiga's trees are larch, one of the few species that will grow on permafrost. Because the quality of larch wood is poor, it is not in demand. Central Asia has few trees because of the arid climate. Parts of the Caucasus are forested. Oak and other **deciduous** trees are found in some lowlands and at lower mountain elevations. Higher in the mountains, pine, fir, and other coniferous trees grow.

C1

Energy and Mineral Resources

C2

All three regions are important producers of oil and natural gas. Fields in the tundra and taiga of Siberia's Ob' River basin make Russia a major provider of these fuels. The Central Siberian Plateau supplies most of Russia's coal. Other huge coal deposits exist in the Lena River valley in southeast Siberia. These areas are so remote, however, that most of their resources remain untapped. Eastern Siberia also holds most of Russia's gold, lead, and iron ore. The tundra region near the mouth of the Yenisey River is one of the world's leading producers of nickel and platinum.

Important oil and gas resources are found in Kazakhstan, Uzbekistan, and Turkmenistan in Central Asia. Large coal deposits are present in Kazakhstan, Tajikistan, and Uzbekistan. Kazakhstan is a major producer of uranium. The mountains of Tajikistan and Kyrgyzstan contain rich mineral resources, as do the eastern mountain areas of Kazakhstan and Uzbekistan. Gold, mercury, copper, iron, tin, lead, zinc, and other metals are mined there.

Most of the Central Asian countries have harnessed their rivers, especially in mountain areas, to produce electricity. The same is true of the Caucasus region, which does not have the rich energy resources of Siberia or Central Asia. Only Azerbaijan is a major oil and gas producer, mainly from fields near or in the Caspian Sea.

R

☑ **READING PROGRESS CHECK**

Identifying Which three resources are economically important in all three regions?

A worker welds a pipeline at the Urengoy gas field in northwestern Siberia. The Urengoy is one of the largest gas fields in the world. Its natural gas is sent by pipeline to customers as far away as Western Europe.

Identifying What minerals other than natural gas are found in Siberia?

FOLDABLES
Study Organizer

Include this lesson's information in your Foldable®.

Dmitry Beliakov/Bloomberg/Getty Images

LESSON 1 REVIEW (CCSS)

Reviewing Vocabulary (Tier Three Words)
1. How does the *permafrost* affect the geography of Siberian Russia? RH.6-8.4

Answering the Guiding Questions
2. *Identifying* What countries make up the Caucasus region and Central Asia? RH.6-8.2

3. *Identifying* Where are Siberia's lowlands and mountains? RH.6-8.2

4. *Identifying* What geographic feature separates the Caucasus and Central Asia? RH.6-8.2

5. *Analyzing* Why are so many of Siberia's vast resources undeveloped? RH.6-8.1

6. *Informative/Explanatory Writing* Write a paragraph to answer the question: How do you think climate affects the way people of the regions make a living? WHST.6-8.2, WHST.6-8.10

Chapter 7 **205**

LESSON 1 REVIEW ANSWERS

Reviewing Vocabulary

1. It creates swamps and limits the types of trees that can grow.

Answering the Guiding Questions

2. *Identifying* The Caucasus region consists of Georgia, Armenia, and Azerbaijan. Kazakhstan, Uzbekistan, Turkmenistan, Tajikistan, and Kyrgyzstan make up Central Asia.

3. *Identifying* The lowland areas are the West Siberian Plains and the lowlands north of the Central Siberian Plateau. The Ural Mountains separate western Siberia from the rest of Russia. Other mountain ranges are in eastern and southeastern Siberia.

4. *Identifying* the Caspian Sea

5. *Analyzing* They are located in remote areas that do not have good transportation networks.

6. *Informative/Explanatory* Answers will vary. Responses should note that cold weather in much of the regions limit the time that can be spent outside as well as the amount of work that can be done effectively.

C1 Critical Thinking Skills

Giving Examples Review the definition of *deciduous*. *(type of plant or tree that sheds its leaves in certain seasons or at certain stages in its life cycle)* Have students give examples of deciduous trees. Students may cite trees such as oak, maple, and ash. **Ask: What is the difference between a deciduous tree and a coniferous one?** *(Coniferous trees have cones; most have needles instead of leaves; they stay green year round.)* **Naturalist**

C2 Critical Thinking Skills

Identifying Problems Have students apply what they have read about the climate in Siberia to accessing the natural resources of the region. **Ask: What problems might workers on the oil pipelines or in the coal fields in Siberia face?** *(Answers should include problems relating to the extremely cold weather and harsh climate.)* **Logical/Mathematical**

R Reading Skills

Identifying Have students consider the multiple uses of rivers that they have learned about in previous chapters. **Ask: Why are rivers an important resource?** *(Possible answer: Power plants using hydroelectric, or waterpower, produce electricity to be used by the people in an area.)* **Verbal/Linguistic, Logical/Mathematical**

Content Background Knowledge

Uranium was used as early as 79 A.D. to add color to ceramic glazes. It was not discovered to be radioactive until 1896. It is an element that occurs naturally at low levels in almost all rock, soil, and water. Uranium ores are mined and converted for use in industry. The military uses uranium metal to protect Army tanks, to power nuclear submarines, and to make nuclear weapons. Nuclear power plants, some lighting fixtures, some chemicals used in photography, and phosphate fertilizers all use uranium.

CLOSE & REFLECT

Formatting Questions To close and review this lesson, have students write questions based on the information presented in this lesson about landforms and waterways, climates, and natural resources. Collect the questions and answer them as a class. Post the questions that still need answers and add responses as students continue their study and increase their knowledge of the region. Have volunteers do research to add responses to any unanswered questions.

ANSWERS, p. 205

Identifying oil, coal, gold, lead, zinc, iron ore, nickel, and platinum.
☑ **READING PROGRESS CHECK** coal, oil, natural gas

History of the Regions

ENGAGE

Bellringer The U.S.S.R, made up of Russia and its satellite countries, was a communist dictatorship during much of the 20th century. But by 1991, the Soviet Union was dissolved and all the republics became independent countries. Communism is an economic system inspired by the writings of Karl Marx. Explain that Marx was a communist and that he believed all property should belong to the community or the state, not to private individuals. **Ask: Why do you think people were eager to end communist control in their countries?** *(Students' answers will vary but should include an understanding of the lack of individual freedoms and ability to work to better self and family under communist rule.)*

Then make a connection between students' answers and the Essential Question: *How do governments change?*

TEACH & ASSESS

R1 Reading Skills

Applying Review with students what they may know about Beringia, the ancient land bridge between Russia and Alaska. Beringia was a flat, grassy, treeless plain that connected Asia with North America. Many animals and people used this land bridge to travel between the continents. **Ask:**

- **What natural landforms would make crossing into Siberia from Europe or from central and eastern Asia difficult for people?** *(Mountains: Ural, Caucasus, Tian Shan, and Pamir)*
- **Why would nomads migrate to southern Siberia from central and eastern Asia?** *(Possible response: People followed food sources and migrated to areas that provided food for both people and animals.)* **Verbal/Linguistic**

R2 Reading Skills

Determining Word Meanings Remind students that knowing the meaning of related words can help them understand the meanings of unknown words. **Ask: What is a pasture?** *(a grassy field on which animals can graze or feed)* Have students connect the meaning of *pasture* to the meaning of *pastoral*. *(Both have something to do with grazing animals.)* **Verbal/Linguistic**

ANSWER, p. 206

Taking Notes (Siberia alone) Tartars; (Siberia-Central Asia) Manchurians, Huns; (Central Asia-Caucasus) Greeks, Arabs, Timur; (Caucasus alone) Romans, Ottoman Turks; (Siberia-Central Asia-Caucasus) Russians, Mongols, Persians

---

networks

There's More Online!

☑ **IMAGE** Samarkand
☑ **MAP** The Soviet Union
☑ **ANIMATION** Trans-Siberian Railroad
☑ **VIDEO**

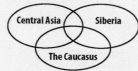

Reading HELPDESK ⓒⓒⓢⓢ

Academic Vocabulary RH.6-8.4
(Tier Two Words)
- **inhibit**
- **complex**

Content Vocabulary RH.6-8.4
(Tier Three Words)
- **pastoral**
- **collective**
- **irrigate**

TAKING NOTES: Key Ideas and Details RH.6-8.1, RH.6-8.4

Categorize As you read about the histories of Siberia, Central Asia, and the Caucasus, use a graphic organizer like this one to keep track of the invaders who conquered each region.

Central Asia   Siberia
The Caucasus

Lesson 2
History of the Regions

ESSENTIAL QUESTION · How do governments change?

IT MATTERS BECAUSE
Under communism, the Soviet Union was the main force in the regions. Today, the republics of Russia, the Caucasus, and Central Asia are running their own affairs.

Siberia

GUIDING QUESTION *How did the settlement of Siberia progress over time?*

R1 Scientists are uncertain exactly when the first humans arrived in Siberia and whether they came from Europe or from central and eastern Asia. What is more certain is that thousands of years ago, some of them crossed from eastern Siberia to what is now Alaska to become the first people in the Americas.

Settlement, Invasion, and Conquest
After about 1000 B.C., Turkic, Iranian, Mongol, and Chinese people began migrating into southern Siberia from central and eastern Asia. These early people were nomads who lived in small groups. Some were hunter-gatherers. Others were **R2** **pastoral**; their lives were based on herding animals.

In the 200s B.C., invaders from Manchuria in northeast China drove many groups north onto the central Siberian plateau. The invaders from Manchuria were the first of several peoples to conquer parts of Siberia and add it to their empire. Other invaders included the Huns, Mongols, and Tartars. The Tartars were defeated by the Russians, who had been coming into Siberia to trade for furs.

Russian Siberia
As they pushed east, Russian traders built small forts and trading posts. Some of these sites eventually became towns.

---

networks   *Online Teaching Options*

VIDEO

Planet Wild - Lake Baikal

Interpreting Use this video about the largest freshwater lake in the world, Lake Baikal, to introduce the lesson. Ask students to share what they learned from the video about the variety of wildlife that lives in Lake Baikal and this lake's impact on the region. Ask students if anything surprised them. **ELL** **AL** **Visual/Spatial**

See page 197D for other online activities.

Some Siberian groups welcomed the Russians. Groups that resisted eventually were subdued. By 1700, Russian control extended to the Pacific Ocean, and some 230,000 Russians were living in Siberia. The czars who were the rulers of Russia also used Siberia as a place of exile for political prisoners.

Lack of roads and other transportation links **inhibited** Siberia's development until the Trans-Siberian Railroad was built across the region between 1891 and 1905. To encourage settlement, the czar began offering settlers free land. By 1914, more than 3 million people had settled in Siberia.

The railroad allowed easier export of products from the region. Coal mines were opened in several locations. Modern farming methods were introduced, and the farmers began producing dairy products and large amounts of grain.

Revolution and Development

When the czar was overthrown and the Communists took control in 1917, some Siberian leaders resisted the new government. In 1922 the Communists brought Siberia under control. Siberia became part of the Union of Soviet Socialist Republics (also called the Soviet Union and USSR)—the country they formed from the Russian Empire.

C

Academic Vocabulary

inhibit to restrict or prevent a process or an action

A richly decorated train station stands in the city of Irkutsk, a major stopping point on the Trans-Siberian Railroad.

©John Warburton-Lee Photography/Alamy

Trans-Siberian Railroad

ARCTIC OCEAN

Baltic Sea

Moscow
Nizhniy Novgorod
Yekaterinburg
Omsk
Novosibirsk
Krasnoyarsk
Irkutsk
Lake Baikal
YABLONOVYY MTS.
Vladivostok

RUSSIA

URAL MOUNTAINS

Ob R.

Angara R.

Black Sea
Aral Sea

Bering Sea

Sea of Okhotsk

PACIFIC OCEAN

Sea of Japan (East Sea)

Trans-Siberian Railroad
Capital city
City

1,000 miles
1,000 kilometers
Two-Point Equidistant projection

MAP SKILLS

1 **THE GEOGRAPHER'S WORLD** What areas are linked by the Trans-Siberian Railroad?

2 **ENVIRONMENT AND SOCIETY** How did the Trans-Siberian Railroad affect settlement?

C Critical Thinking Skills

Recognizing Relationships Explain to students that when someone is exiled, the person is forced to leave and cannot return to his or her native country. When the czars exiled a person to Siberia it was like putting him or her in prison for life. **Ask: What do you know about Siberia that would make it a good place of exile for prisoners?** *(Students' answers will vary but should include an understanding of the hostile environment that almost ensures no escape.)* **Verbal/Linguistic, Logical/Mathematical**

V Visual Skills

Explaining Have students study the map at the bottom of the page. **Ask: What were the benefits of the Trans-Siberian Railroad?** *(Possible answers: easier exporting of products, allowed for ease of travel so that the opening of coal mines could happen, direct route from Moscow to the warm water port of Vladivostok, helped with the spread of modern farming methods to the area)* **Verbal/Linguistic**

V

Content Background Knowledge

Ivan IV, better known as Ivan the Terrible, made Siberia part of the Russian Empire. His successor, Boris Godunov, was the first to use Siberia as a place of exile. He sent rioters from the village of Uglich to Siberia for protesting the suspicious deaths of Ivan's wife and son. A public bell from the town was also exiled to Siberia because the bell was used to call the townspeople to the riot. Later Czar Alexis sent people who disagreed with the teachings of the Russian Orthodox Church to Siberia. Disagreement with the church was also thought to be disagreement with the czar.

MAP

Trans-Siberian Railroad

Integrating Visual Information Display the map of the Trans-Siberian Railroad. Have students identify stops along its route from Moscow to Vladivostok. Discuss with students the use of this route for trade and travel. Have students use the features of the map to figure out how long the railroad is and what countries it travels through. **ELL AL Visual/Spatial**

See page 197D for other online activities.

ANSWERS, p. 207

MAP SKILLS

1. The railroad connects Moscow and other major cities in western Russia with cities in Siberia and ultimately with the Russian Far East and the Sea of Japan. Branch lines go to Mongolia and China.

2. The railroad has brought people and goods into and out of the region, linked mineral sites with centers of production, encouraged the rise of farms and settlements along its track, and generally promoted the development of Siberia.

W Writing Skills

Argument The Soviets forced people who were imprisoned in Siberian gulags to work on government projects such as the Trans-Siberian Railroad. Have students gather in small groups to brainstorm reasons why a government might use forced prison labor. Then have each student write a persuasive essay to answer the question: **Is government use of forced prison labor in the best interests of the country?** *(Students' essays will vary but should include a claim and specific supporting details.)* **Logical/Mathematical**

R Reading Skills

Explaining Read aloud the Guiding Question under the "Central Asia" header and remind students that they should consider this question as they read through this section. Then have a volunteer read the first paragraph in this section. **Ask:**

- Why was the Silk Road prized by conquerors of central Asia? *(The Silk Road was a valuable trade route that linked Europe and China.)*
- Why did many nomad groups go to live in the deserts and dry plains of this region? *(The nomads wanted to be free and not to be ruled by any of the conquerors.)* **Verbal/ Linguistic**

Content Background Knowledge

The Soviets first established their gulags in 1919 in the remote regions of Siberia. By the 1930s, these forced labor camps held millions of political and religious dissenters along with murderers, thieves, and other common criminals. Prisoners endured harsh conditions including too little food, not enough clothing, severe weather, long working hours, and physical abuse by the guards. The death rate for prisoners was high. The prisoners were forced to work on projects that helped the Soviet economy including the White Sea-Baltic Canal, the Moscow-Volga Canal, the Baikal-Amur main railroad line, many hydroelectric stations and roads. Gulags existed into the 1980s.

W Soviet leaders increased mining and industry in the region, especially along the Trans-Siberian Railroad. Much of this expansion came through the use of forced labor. Labor camps called gulags spread across Siberia in the 1930s. Millions of people who disagreed with Communist government policies were imprisoned in gulags. The Communists also combined the lands of small farmers into large, government-run farms called **collectives**. Farmers who resisted giving up their land were sent to the gulags.

When Germany invaded Russia during World War II, Soviet leaders relocated some factories to Siberia to keep them from being captured by German forces. Siberian industry continued to grow after the war. In the late 1990s, oil production increased but has not reached the levels of the late 1980s. Yet oil prices have risen, giving the Russian government a steady source of income. China's increased need for oil has led to calls to develop eastern Siberia's untapped reserves.

✔ **READING PROGRESS CHECK**

Determining Central Ideas How did control of Siberia change over time?

The city of Samarqand, in present-day Uzbekistan, was Central Asia's major political and cultural center during the 1300s and 1400s. Many buildings from this period, such as this mosque and burial site, still stand today.
▶ **CRITICAL THINKING**
Describing Why did Samarqand become an important center of the Islamic world during the 1300s and 1400s?

MARTIN GRAY/National Geographic Stock

Central Asia

GUIDING QUESTION *How have invaders affected Central Asia's history and culture?*

For most of their history, the countries of Central Asia have been part of outside empires. In the 300s B.C., the region was the eastern border of the Greek empire created by Alexander the Great. In the centuries that followed, the Chinese, Huns, and other groups took turns ruling Central Asia. For many conquerors, the greatest prize was control of the Silk Road, the network of trade routes that linked China and Europe. Nomad groups that could not defeat the invaders often retreated into the region's deserts and dry plains, where they continued to live in freedom.

The Influence of Islam
The Arab conquest of Central Asia in the early A.D. 700s brought the religion of Islam to the region, where it remains the main religion today. The Arabs were soon replaced by the Persians, who ruled until the Mongols conquered the region in the early 1200s. In the mid-1300s, a Central Asian conqueror, Timur, overthrew the Mongol rulers. His armies soon conquered a huge region that stretched from the Caucasus to India.

The Silk Road city of Samarqand was the capital of Timur's empire. He made the city a center of culture by bringing in artists and

208 *Chapter 7*

netw⊚rks   *Online Teaching Options*

MAP

Influences on Central Asia

Integrating Visual Information Display the map of the empires in Central Asia. Review with students the history of the empires and their influence over the region. Ask students to make a two-column chart with the heads: ***Empires*** and ***Influences***; then have students fill in the chart using the information from the review. **Visual/ Spatial, Verbal/Linguistic**

See page 197D for other online activities.

scholars from other parts of the empire. His successors continued his support of the arts and sciences by establishing madrassas, Islamic centers of learning. Samarqand became a major center for the study of astronomy and mathematics.

Russian Rule and After

Czar Peter the Great began expanding the Russian Empire into Central Asia in the 1700s. By the mid-1800s, most of the region was under Russian control. The Russians' main interest was to grow cotton in Kazakhstan and Uzbekistan. To increase production, they began to **irrigate** the land. They also expanded the railroads to link the region with Russia.

When the Russian Revolution began in 1917, parts of Central Asia took advantage of the unrest to declare their independence. By 1920, Communist forces from Russia had regained control. Under a treaty of union, five of the Central Asian countries became part of the Soviet Union.

Soviet rule brought great change. The Soviets built dams on rivers to generate electric power and collect water for irrigation. They built one of the world's longest canals, the Kara-Kum Canal, to carry water from the Amu Dar'ya River more than 500 miles (805 km) to irrigate desert land near the Caspian Sea. They also increased industry by opening mines and factories to develop the region's mineral wealth.

The changes also had negative impacts. Soviet leaders resettled large numbers of Russians and other Europeans in the region. Local farmers and nomadic herders were forced onto collectives. The Soviets tried to uproot local cultures. They closed mosques to end the practice of Islam in the region.

ALEXANDER NEMENOV/AFP/Getty Images

The Sayano-Shushenskaya Dam, in south central Siberia, was built during the Soviet era. For many years, it was Russia's largest hydroelectric project. In 2009 an accident at the dam's power plant caused flooding that killed 78 people and destroyed much property.

▶ **CRITICAL THINKING**
Describing What economic changes did Soviet rule bring to Central Asia?

Chapter 7 **209**

IMAGES

How Dams Work

Discussing Display the interactive images about how dams work to discuss the importance of dams, hydroelectric power, and the use of water for irrigation. Have students write a paragraph about three things they have learned about dams. Have volunteers research comparisons between the Sayano-Shushenskaya Dam in south central Siberia and the Hoover Dam in the southwestern United States. **BL** Verbal/Linguistic

See page 197D for other online activities.

Interactive Photos

C Critical Thinking Skills

Reasoning Have students read the first paragraph of the section, "Russian Rule and After." Explain that Peter the Great's goal was to make Russia a great nation. **Ask:**

- **Why do you think cotton production was important to the Russians?** *(Students' answers will vary but should demonstrate an understanding of the many uses for cotton and the large Russian population that could benefit from its production.)*
- **How would irrigating the land increase cotton production?** *(Possible answer: Irrigating the land supplies water to the cotton plants to help them grow. Bigger and healthier plants can produce more cotton.)* **Logical/ Mathematical**

V Visual Skills

Collaborating After students study the photo and text about building dams, divide the class into two groups to debate the pros and cons of building dams on rivers to generate electric power and collect water for irrigation. Have groups use the Internet to find information about positive and negative effects of dams and other photos of areas before and after dams were built. Have groups present their findings in a class debate with the goal of persuading peers to their point of view. **Verbal/ Linguistic, Naturalist**

Content Background Knowledge

The Kara-Kum Canal was constructed in the 1950s in Turkmenistan to carry water from the Amu Dar'ya River south to the capital in Ashgabat. Over the years, agricultural chemicals and pesticides have contaminated the river's surface water and groundwater. Irrigation in the flood plains along the canal has left salt deposits that make the soil infertile. Irrigation has also decreased the amount of water from the river that enters the Aral Sea. Consequently, the Aral Sea has shrunk.

ANSWER, p. 209

CRITICAL THINKING The Soviets built dams for electric power and irrigation, constructed the Kara-Kum Canal to irrigate desert lands, and promoted industry by opening mines and factories to develop mineral wealth.

History of the Regions

C Critical Thinking Skills

Identifying Central Issues Being part of the Soviet Union meant that the republics were tied to the decisions made by the communist government in Moscow, sometimes referred to as "Mother Russia." Moscow's decisions affected the economy, laws, and other apsects of daily life in each of the republics. **Ask: What are some challenges the newly independent countries faced in creating new economies after leaving the Soviet Union?** *(Possible answer: They needed to decide if they would have a free market, a communist economy, or some mix of both. They needed to create laws that enabled businesses to form, and they also had to create a banking system.)* **Logical/Mathematical, Verbal/ Linguistic**

R Reading Skills

Determining Word Meanings Remind students that knowing the meaning of an antonym of a word can help them understand the meaning of an unfamiliar word. **Ask: How can the meaning of** *simple* **help you understand the meaning of** *complex***?** *(Possible answer:* Simple *means "easy or uncomplicated." Knowing that* complex *means the opposite helps me to understand that* complex *means "not easy, complicated, or difficult.")* **Logical/Mathematical**

T Technology Skills

Researching on the Internet Have students work in groups of two or three and use the Internet to research facts on the early history (from ancient times to the 1700s) of either Georgia or Armenia. Have groups present at least three facts to the class either orally or using a software presentation program. As classmates listen to each presentation, have them formulate questions that the facts may prompt. Allow other groups to answer the questions if they are able. Have students research answers to the unanswered questions and post them. **Verbal/ Linguistic, Logical/Mathematical**

ANSWERS, p. 210

☑ READING PROGRESS CHECK Many of its peoples were nomads who could move to remote areas and continue to live independently.

CRITICAL THINKING With too many government controls, the system did not take into account what people wanted and needed. It could not respond quickly or easily to changes in the global economy.

When the Soviet Union collapsed in 1991, the republics declared their independence. The region's present-day countries were formed. Most of the countries are still struggling with problems that arose after Soviet rule. Among the problems are modernizing their economies and dealing with ethnic tensions and dictatorial rulers.

☑ READING PROGRESS CHECK

Analyzing Why was Central Asia difficult to conquer and control completely?

After independence, Georgia ended government economic controls and allowed free enterprise. As a result, many inefficient, Soviet-built factories were abandoned and left to decay.
▶ **CRITICAL THINKING**
Determining Central Ideas Why did the Soviet economic system fail?

Academic Vocabulary

complex having interrelated parts that are difficult to understand or separate

The Caucasus

GUIDING QUESTION *How did the countries of Georgia, Armenia, and Azerbaijan develop?*

The Caucasus are a crossroads between Europe and Asia. This region has drawn conquerors since ancient times. It was part of the ancient Persian, Greek, and Roman empires. Later, Persians, Turks, and Russians dominated the region. This history of conquests and migrations makes the Caucasus one of the most ethnically **complex** places in the world today.

Early History

Georgia and Armenia have each had periods of self-rule during their long histories. Both existed briefly as powerful kingdoms in ancient times but came under the control of powerful neighbors. Around the year A.D. 300, each threw off Persian rule and established kingdoms again. They became two of the earliest countries to convert to the Christian religion. Beginning in the A.D. 600s, Muslim conquerors brought Islam to the Caucasus.

Later, much of the region was conquered by the Mongols in the 1200s and became part of Timur's Central Asian empire in the late 1300s. The Byzantines—Christians who controlled the eastern part of the old Roman Empire—and Persians also sought control of the region. By the late 1400s, the struggle had shifted to the Persians and a new power in Southwest Asia—the Ottoman Turks. The Ottomans and Persians competed for the Caucasus for the next 300 years.

Russian and Soviet Rule

The Christian Armenians and Georgians suffered under Persian and Turkish control. In the early 1700s, they turned to Russia for protection from their Muslim rulers. By the early 1800s, Russia had

Tim E White/Photolibrary/Getty Images

---

netw⊙rks *Online Teaching Options*

GRAPHIC ORGANIZER

History of the Caucasus

Discussing Display the interactive graphic organizer about the history of the Caucasus. Discuss with students how this region developed. Have students use the interactive graphic organizer to compare and contrast the development of the region with other regions they have studied. **AL Visual/ Spatial, Verbal/Linguistic**

See page 197D for other online activities.

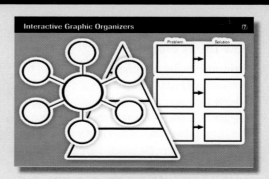

Interactive Graphic Organizers

annexed most of the region. Only part of Armenia remained in the Ottoman Empire.

During World War I, hundreds of thousands of Armenians died at the hands of Ottoman troops, and Russia took the rest of Armenia. Then, the Russian Revolution gave the entire Caucasus the chance to break free of Russian control. Georgia, Armenia, and Azerbaijan briefly formed independent states. Following the Communist victory in Russia's civil war, the Soviet Union annexed the Caucasus in 1922 and eventually created three Soviet socialist republics from the region—the present-day countries of Georgia, Armenia, and Azerbaijan. **T**

The Caucasus benefited but also suffered under Soviet rule. Communists transformed the Caucasus from a largely agricultural area to an urban and industrial one. Soviet power finally ended centuries of invasion and instability, but crushed all opposition. Then during World War II, Germany invaded the Caucasus.

Some of the region's ethnic groups were accused of helping the German invaders. After the war, these groups were broken apart and resettled in various other republics of the USSR. The Soviets also punished other Caucasus people for showing pride in and loyalty to their ethnic identity and culture. Persecution eased after the death of the brutal Soviet dictator Joseph Stalin in 1953. Caucasus leaders took steps toward freedom when the Soviet Union began falling apart in the late 1980s. Non-Communists were already in power in Armenia and Georgia when the Soviet Union dissolved in 1991. **C**

Like the Central Asian republics, Georgia, Armenia, and Azerbaijan declared their independence in 1991. As in Central Asia, though, their 70-some years under Soviet control continue to affect these countries. Since independence, these countries have struggled with economic changes, ethnic tensions, and border conflicts.

☑ **READING PROGRESS CHECK**

Citing Text Evidence Which Caucasus country did not have a history of independence before the end of Soviet rule?

FOLDABLES Study Organizer

Include this lesson's information in your Foldable®.

LESSON 2 REVIEW

Reviewing Vocabulary (Tier Three Words)
1. How did Soviet *collectives* change agriculture in Siberia and Central Asia? **RH.6-8.4**

Answering the Guiding Questions
2. ***Describing*** What factors contributed to Siberia's economic growth and development? **RH.6-8.5**

3. ***Analyzing*** How might Central Asia's culture and history have been different if Arabs had not been among the region's many conquerors? **RH.6-8.1**

4. ***Determining Central Ideas*** Why are the countries of the Caucasus so culturally complex? **RH.6-8.2**

5. ***Argument Writing*** Do you believe that the Soviet Union's persecution of groups for their ethnic loyalty and pride was a good policy? Why or why not? **WHST.6-8.2, WHST.6-8.4**

Chapter 7 **211**

LESSON 2 REVIEW ANSWERS

Reviewing Vocabulary

1. They combined the lands of individual small farmers into large, government-run farms.

Answering the Guiding Questions

2. ***Describing*** Russian traders built forts and trading posts that eventually became towns. The Russians' pacification of the nomads encouraged further settlement, as did the completion of the Trans-Siberian Railroad. The railroad also encouraged agriculture and development of Siberia's natural resources, as did economic planning under Communist rule. The Communists brought industry to Siberia.

3. ***Analyzing*** Islam and Islamic culture might not have been introduced to the region, and Samarkand might not have become a center of culture and learning.

4. ***Determining Central Ideas*** They have been the object of many invasions over the centuries as well as the related political and religious conflicts that developed. This history makes the region home to many diverse ethnic groups.

5. ***Argument Writing*** Students should weigh the cultural issues against the political, sovereignty, and security issues.

T **Technology Skills**

Making Presentations Genocide is the organized and deliberate killing of a group of people with the intent of putting an end to their existence. The Turkish government planned and carried out genocide against the Armenian people during World War I. Have students work in small groups to use the Internet to research the Armenian Genocide. Then have them use a software presentation program to present what they have learned to the class. Circulate to answer questions and watch for sensitive material. **Visual/Spatial, Verbal/Linguistic**

C **Critical Thinking Skills**

Interpreting Explain to students that Soviet rule benefited the people of the Caucasus, but the region also suffered under it. **Ask: What did the people of the Caucasus lose when the Soviets took over the region?** *(The people lost their freedom to rule themselves and voice their opposition to the Communists.)* **Verbal/Linguistic**

Content Background Knowledge

During World War I, the Ottoman Empire—an independent Islamic power from 1300 to 1923—aligned itself with Germany and the Central Powers. Between 1915 and 1918, the Empire carried out mass killings of Christian Armenians. The genocide was meant to undermine the growth of Armenian nationalism and to stop the spread of ideas about civil rights. Armenian men were forced into service in the Ottoman army and then killed. Adult men who were left in the towns were arrested, taken out of town, and then killed. Women, children, and older men were deported to isolated areas, but many died on the journey or suffered cruelties and physical abuse. More massacres began in 1920, and by 1922 the Armenians were effectively wiped out of their homeland. Towns, villages, and historical sites were destroyed; churches were desecrated; and libraries were burned. The 3,000-year-old heritage of the Armenians was wiped out. Survivors sought refuge in other countries. The largest Armenian community is now found in the United States.

CLOSE & REFLECT

Evaluating To close this lesson, have students think about all the hardships that the people of Central Asia and the Caucasus endured before gaining their freedom from Soviet rule in the early 1990s. Ask them to think about how important freedom is in their lives and if it is something they would risk fighting for.

ANSWER, p. 211

☑ **READING PROGRESS CHECK** Azerbaijan

ENGAGE

 Bellringer Review with students that Siberian Russia is a huge region with a location and landforms that greatly affect how the people live there. The region is so large that people living on Siberia's Pacific coast are farther from Moscow than they are from the United States. Then have students imagine what it would be like to actually live there. Have students discuss whether or not they would choose to live in rural Siberia if they were given free land that they would own. Place students in small groups based on their answers. Have groups who would live in Siberian Russia work together to create a chart listing the positives for the move. Have groups who would not move there create a chart listing the negatives to living in the region.

Post the charts on a bulletin board in the classroom; these charts will be referred to again at the end of this lesson. Then read aloud the It Matters Because statement. Explain to students that they will be reading about the culture and daily life in Siberian Russia, Central Asia, and the Caucasus. As they read, they should think about the Essential Question: *How does geography influence the way people live?* and about the group charts that they created.

TEACH & ASSESS

R Reading Skills

Specifying Have volunteers read aloud the first two paragraphs of the section, "Siberian Russia." **Ask: Where do most of Siberians live?** *(In cities and towns along the Trans-Siberian Railroad)*

Review with students what they have learned about the Trans-Siberian Railroad. Then, **ask: Why do you think the city of Vladivostok is a major port for shipping?** *(Students' answers should reflect the understanding that the city is located at the end of the Trans-Siberian Railroad and is located on the Sea of Japan. This location makes the city ideal for shipping by either boat or train.)* **Logical/Mathematical**

C Critical Thinking Skills

Determining Cause and Effect Have a volunteer read aloud the last paragraph of the section "Siberian Russia." **Ask: What effect did the czars and Soviets have on the region?** *(The czars offered people resettlement programs so many Russian people relocated to Siberia.)* **AL Verbal/Linguistic, Logical/Mathematical**

ANSWER, p. 212

TAKING NOTES Notes should include information, such as: which people live in each region and where they live; the important languages, religions, and cultural issues in each region; and the domestic and international political challenges the countries in each region face.

---

netw⊕rks

There's More Online!

☑ **IMAGES** Living in a Yurt
☑ **MAP** Understanding Time Zones
☑ **VIDEO**

Reading **HELP**DESK (CCSS)

Academic Vocabulary RH.6-8.4
(Tier Two Words)
- **significant**

Content Vocabulary RH.6-8.4
(Tier Three Words)
- **oasis**
- **homogeneous**
- **yurt**

TAKING NOTES: *Key Ideas and Details* RH.6-8.2, RH.6-8.7

Summarize As you read the lesson, list important details for each region using a graphic organizer like the one below.

Siberian Russia	1. 2.
The Caucasus	1. 2.
Central Asia	1. 2.

212

Lesson 3
Life in the Regions

ESSENTIAL QUESTION · *How does geography influence the way people live?*

IT MATTERS BECAUSE
To live in these regions, people must adjust to a harsh and mountainous landscape.

People and Places

GUIDING QUESTION *Who are the peoples of Siberia, Central Asia, and the Caucasus, and where do they live?*

Siberia and most of Central Asia share much the same settlement pattern—the regions have a few large cities and sparsely settled remote areas. The Caucasus is a more urban region, and its rural areas are more densely populated.

Siberian Russia

More than half of Siberians live in the hundreds of cities and towns in the region. Most are alongside or south of the route of the Trans-Siberian Railroad, especially on the west Siberian plain. Novosibirsk, a city of nearly 1.5 million, is located there. It is Siberia's largest city and the third largest in Russia.

A few small cities and many towns also exist along the Ob', the Yenisey, and the Lena rivers and their tributaries, as well as along Siberia's eastern coast. Vladivostok, a city of 500,000 on the Sea of Japan in extreme southeastern Siberia, is located at the eastern end of the Trans-Siberian Railroad. It is a major port for shipping goods into and out of all of Russia.

The resettlement programs of the czars and Soviets have made Siberia's population overwhelmingly Russian. There are still populations of Mongol and Turkic groups, as well as other indigenous peoples. Most people have settled on farms or in cities and towns. A few in the north still live as pastoral nomads.

(l to r) TIGRAN MEHRABYAN/AFP/Getty Images; AFP/Stringer/AFP/Getty Images; ©dbimages/Alamy; ©IGOR KOVALENKO/epa/Corbis; ©Robert Harding World Imagery/Alamy

---

netw⊕rks *Online Teaching Options*

VIDEO

World's Wonders—Trading Domes of Bukhara

Giving Examples Use this video about trading in Bukhara, located in Uzbekistan, to discuss the importance of trade throughout history. Be sure to highlight the ancient techniques for making goods and trading. After students watch the video, ask them to write three examples of what they learned from the video about the importance of trade in Bukhara. Then have them share these examples of the people and places presented in the video in a guided class discussion. **ELL Visual/Spatial**

See page 197E for other online activities.

BBC Motion Gallery Education

Central Asia

T
Kazakhstan is the only country in Central Asia with a largely urban population. About two-thirds of the people are ethnic Kazakhs. Another 25 percent are Russians. Most of the Russians and many Kazakhs live in Alma-Ata. With 1.4 million people, it is the country's largest city and industrial center. About 40 percent of Kazakhstan's people live in rural areas. Most live in the small towns and farm villages that are scattered across the lowlands and plateaus of the steppe.

R1

R2
Turkmenistan is about evenly divided between people who live in cities and large towns and those who live in rural settlements. The greatest number of people live along the Amu Dar'ya and in **oasis** areas in the south. An oasis is a green area by a water source in a dry region. Ethnic Turkomans make up about three-fourths of the population. Russians, at about 10 percent, form the second-largest ethnic group. Most Turkomans live in villages. Most Russians live in the capital, Ashkhabad, which has a population of about 850,000, and in Turkmenistan's two smaller cities.

Most people in Uzbekistan live in the eastern half of the country, almost two-thirds of them in rural areas. Heavily populated oases are covered with orchards, farm fields, and irrigation canals. Most rural people are Uzbeks. Most of the city dwellers are Russian and Kazakh. Uzbekistan's capital city, Tashkent, is home to more than 2 million people. It is Central Asia's largest city and its economic and cultural center.

Thinking Like a Geographer

World Time Zones

The world has 24 official time zones, each 15° of longitude apart. The Prime Meridian is the reference for measuring time at 0°. Traveling east from 0°, the time is one hour later in each time zone. Traveling west from 0°, the time is one hour earlier. When crossing the International Date Line at 180° longitude from west to east, one day is lost; when crossing from east to west, one day is gained.

MAP SKILLS

PLACES AND REGIONS How many time zones are in the area from the Caucasus to Siberia's easternmost point at the International Date Line?

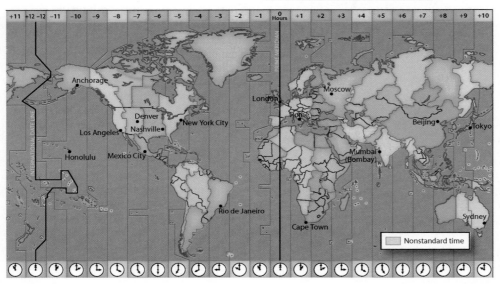

Chapter 7 **213**

MAP

Understanding Time Zones

Analyzing Visuals Display the map of the time zones. Have students identify the time zone in which they live. Explain that the history of the development of the time zones involves mass transportation and the need to have schedules that made sense to people along the route. Have students utilize the animated map by calculating the current time of day it is where they live, with the current time of day it is in Tashkent, Uzbekistan. Students may need help locating the city of Tashkent on the map. **Visual/Spatial, Logical/Mathematical**

See page 197E for other online activities.

CHAPTER 7, Lesson 3
Life in the Regions

T Technology Skills

Collaborating Explain to students that Central Asia is a region where most of its people live in rural areas; however, there are some larger cities. Have a small group of volunteers work together to research and list the ten largest cities in the region. Students should include the name, location, and population of the ten cities. Allow the group time to research the Internet for the information. Then ask them to create a chart listing their results and to print out a map marking the cities. Display the finished products in the classroom. **BL Verbal/Linguistic**

R1 Reading Skills

Calculating Have students independently read the first paragraph in the section, "Central Asia." **Ask:**

- **What percent of people in Kazakhstan are not Russian?** *(75%)*

- **What percent of Kazakhstan's people live in cities?** *(60%)*

If students are having difficulty reversing percentages, remind them that the total is always 100%, so they should subtract the percentage given in the text from 100%. **AL Logical/Mathematical**

R2 Reading Skills

Illustrating Write out the words *oasis* and *oases* on the board. Point out both words in the text. Tell students that the word *oasis* has an irregular plural spelling, which is *oases*.

Invite students to explain what they think an oasis looks like. After a few students have had a chance to explain their ideas, have them draw pictures of an oasis. Student drawings could include orchards, trees, farm fields, rural settlements, and irrigation canals. Have volunteers present their illustrations to the class by explaining the different features in their drawings and why they chose to include these features. **AL Visual/Spatial**

ANSWER, p. 213

MAP SKILLS 8 time zones

Life in the Regions

V Visual Skills

Interpreting In pairs, have students study the population density map. **Ask:**

- Which countries are located around the Caspian Sea? *(Turkmenistan, Kazakhstan, and Azerbaijan)*
- Which three countries on the map are the most densely populated? *(Azerbaijan, Armenia, Georgia)*
- Consider what you have learned about Kazakhstan in earlier lessons. Why does Kazakhstan have so many unpopulated areas? *(The mountains and harsh climate make it hard for people to live there.)*

Have partners continue their study of the map by having them answer the Map Skills questions. **Visual/Spatial**

C Critical Thinking Skills

Speculating Emphasize the text, which states that Georgia contains *significant* minorities, and the Caucasus has *over 50 small ethnic groups*. Lead a class discussion about cultural diversity. Have students relate what they know about concerns over varying cultures living in close proximity to one another. **Ask:** What are some challenges and benefits of having so many different groups of people living in the Caucasus? *(**Challenges include:** religious differences may lead to clashes; language differences may lead to communication concerns; differences in customs and beliefs may lead to misunderstandings. **Benefits include:** learning from people with different ideas and perspectives.)* **Verbal/Linguistic**

Content Background Knowledge

Georgia is known as the dividing line between Asia and Europe. It is still seen as an ancient country filled with harsh, rugged mountains and people who are very determined. Georgia suffered under communist rulers until 1991, when it declared its independence from Russia. Soon after declaring its independence, civil war disrupted the country. Finally, in 2003, the people of Georgia opposed the parliamentary elections and forced the president to resign. This was called the Rose Revolution. Since the Rose Revolution, the leaders of Georgia have strengthened and improved the country's economy. Today Georgia has become a favorite international tourist spot, especially along the Black Sea. It has also become famous for its agricultural land, which produces grapes for its fine wines.

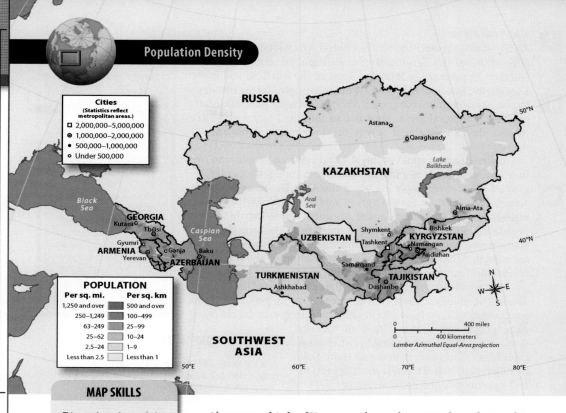

Population Density

Cities
(Statistics reflect metropolitan areas.)
- ▫ 2,000,000–5,000,000
- ⊙ 1,000,000–2,000,000
- ● 500,000–1,000,000
- ○ Under 500,000

POPULATION	
Per sq. mi.	Per sq. km
1,250 and over	500 and over
250–1,249	100–499
63–249	25–99
25–62	10–24
2.5–24	1–9
Less than 2.5	Less than 1

MAP SKILLS

This map shows the population density and major cities of Central Asia and the Caucasus.

1. **HUMAN GEOGRAPHY**
   What city on the map has the largest population?

2. **PLACES AND REGIONS**
   How does population density in Armenia compare with Turkmenistan's?

Academic Vocabulary

significant a noticeably large amount; important

About two-thirds of Kyrgyzstan's people are Kirghiz. The Kirghiz were once nomads who were settled onto collectives during Soviet rule. They remain largely rural today.

Less than 40 percent of the population live in cities and towns. Most of the town dwellers are Uzbeks and Russians. Tajikistan is also mainly rural, but the country's largely mountainous terrain causes its settled areas to be densely populated. Villages dot the foothills and mountain valleys. In dry regions, irrigation has created densely populated oases. About 80 percent of the people are ethnic Tajiks. Most of the rest are Uzbeks.

The Caucasus

C Nearly all of Armenia's people are ethnic Armenians. Most of Azerbaijan's people are ethnic Azeris. Georgia is largely ethnic Georgian but has a population that contains **significant** minorities—mainly Armenians and Azeris. The Caucasus is also home to about 50 smaller ethnic groups.

About half the region's people are urban, and half are rural. Armenia, however, has a larger urban population overall. Two-thirds of Armenians live in cities and towns.

214 Chapter 7

netw⊙rks *Online Teaching Options*

VIDEOS

Cities in Central Asia

Integrating Visual Information Have students view the videos highlighting cities in the region. Then display a map of the area and have students identify and mark each of the large cities referred to in the video. Guide students in a class discussion about how and why these large cities developed in the specific areas. **ELL** **Visual/Spatial, Verbal/Linguistic**

See page 197E for other online activities.

Fresh photos from all over the world/Getty Images

ANSWER, p. 214

MAP SKILLS
1. Tashkent
2. Armenia is more densely populated than is Turkmenistan.

The region's rural population is not evenly distributed. Mountain valleys and foothills and some parts of the mountains are heavily settled. Few people live above 6,000 feet (1,829 m). The area along Georgia's Black Sea coast is also densely populated. At the same time, one of every four Georgians lives in Tbilisi, its capital city of 1.1 million.

Armenia's Ararat plain, near the country's border with Turkey and Iran, is its most heavily populated region. The plain and the surrounding foothills and mountains are Armenia's economic and cultural center. Yerevan, its capital city of 1.1 million people, is located there.

Azerbaijan's most densely populated area is around its capital, Baku, on a peninsula in the Caspian Sea. Baku, with about 2 million people, is the largest city and most important industrial center in the Caucasus. Azerbaijan's most heavily settled rural region is in the extreme southeast, between the Caspian Sea and its border with Iran.

☑ **READING PROGRESS CHECK**

Identifying Where does most of Central Asia's Russian population live?

People and Cultures

GUIDING QUESTION *How are the cultures of Central Asia and the Caucasus alike and different?*

Siberia, Central Asia, and the Caucasus not only have different population distributions, their cultures are also very different. In parts of Central Asia, Soviet rule left lasting Russian influences. In parts of the Caucasus, Russian influences are strong but less widespread.

Language and Religion

Russian is the main language in Siberia, and Christianity, mainly Russian Orthodox, is the dominant religion, along with Buddhist and Muslim minorities. Russian is widely spoken in Central Asia. In Kazakhstan and Kyrgyzstan, Russian is an official language, in addition to the language of the country's ethnic majority. Russian is often used in business. In Kazakhstan, 95 percent of the population speaks it, mostly as a second language.

About half of Kazakhstan's people are Christians, and half are Muslims. In the rest of Central Asia, between 75 percent and 90 percent of the people practice Islam, and most of the rest are Christians.

In the Caucasus, most Armenians and Georgians are Christians, and most Azerbaijanis are Muslims. Georgia has a significant Muslim minority as well. In each country, the language of its ethnic majority is the official language and is widely spoken.

AFP/Stringer/AFP/Getty Images

Armenia was the first country in the world to adopt Christianity as its official religion—in A.D. 301. Today, most Armenians belong to the Armenian Apostolic Church.

Identifying Which country in the Caucasus has a large Muslim minority?

IMAGE

The Armenian Apostolic Church

Discussing Use the interactive image of the Armenian Apostolic Church to lead a class discussion about the various religions within the region. Have students review and identify which regions contain high populations of followers for each of the religions. **ELL** **AL** Visual/Spatial

See page 197E for other online activities.

Interactive Photos

C1 Critical Thinking Skills

Reasoning Review with students what they have learned about temperature and climate at higher elevations and how these conditions affect where people live. **Ask: Based on what you know about climate, why do you think most people in this region live below 6,000 feet (1,829cm)?** *(The climate can be very cold and harsh at higher altitudes, so most people would probably prefer to live at lower elevations.)* **Logical/Mathematical**

C2 Critical Thinking Skills

Formulating Questions With a partner, have students reread the section, "The Caucasus," that begins on the previous page. Have each student write three questions based on the content in the section. Have pairs exchange questions, and have students write answers for their partner's questions. Call on pairs to share their questions and answers with the class. **Verbal/Linguistic**

W Writing Skills

Informative/Explanatory As a class, read aloud the "Language and Religion" section. Have volunteers write the names of each country and each of the religions that are practiced in that country on the board. Have students consider the importance of religion in people's lives. Ask students to think about the way that the diversity of religions has affected the countries of Central Asia, and compare that with the way that it affects the United States. **Ask: What are some of the ways that diverse religions can affect a nation?** *(They can make national unity difficult. They can cause people to value religious freedom. They can create conflicts because people have very different views about what is right and wrong.)*

Have students conduct research to learn more about one of the religions practiced within a particular country as listed in this section. Make sure students are using reliable sources, and have them list the sources that they use. Then have students write an essay that explains how the religion reflects the life and beliefs of the people in the chosen country. **Verbal/Linguistic**

ANSWERS, p. 215

☑ **READING PROGRESS CHECK** in cities and towns
Identifying Georgia

R1 **Reading Skills**

Using Context Clues Remind students that it is helpful to find the meaning of words by using the context of the sentence and reading the other words around the unknown word or words. Have a volunteer pronounce the word *homogeneous*. Have another volunteer identify the words in the same sentence that provide help in defining it. *(of the same kind)* **ELL** Verbal/Linguistic

R2 **Reading Skills**

Stating Discuss the numerous conflicts between countries within the region, as metioned in the section, "Ethnic Unrest."
Ask:

- **What countries are enemies with the Armenians?** *(the Turks and Azeris)*

- **In the late 1800s, who was fighting against the spread of the Islamic religion, and who were they fighting?** *(The Christian Armenians were fighting the Azeris living in Iran and the Caucasus.)*

- **Who have the Armenians been fighting more recently, and what are they presently fighting for?** *(The Armenians have been fighting the Azeris over control of Nagorno-Karabakh.)*

- **Why has Russia helped Georgian rebels?** *(Russia wants to increase its influence over Georgia.)*

- **What is the reason that many people were killed or fled from Tajikistan before 1997?** *(After the Soviet rule ended, the country was torn by civil war. 10,000 people were killed and 500,000 people had fled by 1997 when a peace agreement was reached.)* **Logical/Mathematical**

V **Visual Skills**

Analyzing Images Direct students' attention to the photograph of the women making a rug. **Ask: What characteristics of daily life in rural areas do you see in this photo?** *(It shows that in the rural area women work together. It is not clear if the women are working in a home, but the location is very sparse and the women are sitting on blankets on a bench propped up with bricks. This suggests that they live simple lives and are probably not wealthy.)* **Visual/Spatial**

ANSWER, p. 216

CRITICAL THINKING The growth of industry has led to the mass production of goods and the increase in demand for manufactured products. This development has decreased the sale of hand-made goods.

Visual Vocabulary

Yurt a round tent with a domed roof covered with heavy, waterproof wool felt or animal skins

Village women in Uzbekistan and other parts of Central Asia have traditionally woven carpets and rugs. After years of decline under the Soviets, the art of carpet weaving is now being taught at workshops in some urban areas.
► **CRITICAL THINKING**
Analyzing What economic change has affected the making of traditional goods by hand?

Ethnic Unrest

Compared to the rest of the Caucasus, Armenians are **homogeneous**, or of the same kind. The Turks and Azeris, who live in the countries bordering Armenia, historically have been the Armenians' enemies. In the 1890s and again during World War I, the Turks massacred millions of Armenians who were living under Turkish rule. Meanwhile, Christian Armenians were fighting the influence of Islam being spread by Azeris living in the Caucasus and Iran.

More recently, Armenians and Azeris have been fighting over Nagorno-Karabakh, a region with an Armenian majority that is part of Azerbaijan. In 1988 Armenia seized Nagorno-Karabakh and the territory that connected it to Azerbaijan. As tensions and violence increased, many Azeris fled the region. The dispute remains unsettled.

Georgia also has experienced much ethnic unrest. Its Armenian minority has long sought greater self-rule. In 1992 ethnic minority groups in Georgia's Abkhaz Republic region revolted for independence. In 2008 other minorities in its South Ossetia region did the same. Russia sent troops to each region to help the rebels and increase its influence over Georgia. Pressure from other countries caused the Russians to withdraw from South Ossetia, but tensions over both regions continue.

In Central Asia, Tajikistan was torn by civil war after Soviet rule ended. Tajik Communists, backed by Russian troops, fought Islamic groups and their allies. Some 10,000 people were killed and 500,000 were forced to flee before a peace agreement was reached in 1997.

Culture and Daily Life

Most urban Kazakhs live and dress like Europeans. Rural Kazakhs, women especially, continue to wear the heavily embroidered and colorful traditional Kazakh clothing. Many rural Kazakhs also live in **yurts**. Colorful embroidered rugs decorate traditional Kazakh homes. Such rugs are typical of most Central Asian cultures.

Some Kirghiz and other rural Central Asians also live in sturdy yurts. Rural Kirghiz women stay at home caring for their children while the men tend to the family's crops and livestock. Raising and racing horses are important in most Central Asian cultures.

Uzbek families are often large. Family relationships are close, and parents have great authority. Children help with tasks around the home. In cities and towns, most families live in

---

netw⦿rks *Online Teaching Options*

SLIDE SHOW

Daily Life in Central Asia

Determining Central Ideas As a class, view the slide show about daily life in the region. Have students write down the central ideas about the lives of people and the arts in the region that are highlighted in the images. Then discuss the daily life of the people in the different countries discussed in the chapter. Have students add notes from the discussion to their earlier writing.
ELL Interpersonal

See page 197E for other online activities.

Slide Show

houses with a courtyard, where they spend much of their leisure time. Uzbeks also decorate their homes with colorful rugs, but most wear Western-style clothing.

Most Tajiks live in the western half of the country in the valleys that lie between the steep mountains. They live in villages of 200 to 700 flat-roofed houses along an irrigation canal or a river. A mud fence surrounds each house and the orchard or vineyard next to it. In mountain communities, the villages are smaller. On steep slopes, the houses' flat roofs are the yards for the houses above them.

In a nomad camp, Kirghiz herders tend to their horses. Equestrian sports (sports with horses), such as racing and a form of polo, are important parts of the culture of Central Asia's nomadic people.

V₂

✔ **READING PROGRESS CHECK**

Citing Text Evidence What ethnic unrest exists in the Caucasus today?

Relationships and Challenges

GUIDING QUESTION *What challenges lie ahead for the regions?*

Most Caucasus and Central Asian countries have struggled to establish stable, democratic governments since the end of Soviet rule. They are also trying to develop free-enterprise economies after years of Communist government controls.

R

The Soviet Legacy

The countries of the Caucasus and Central Asia adopted new constitutions after they gained independence. The constitutions created democratic governments, gave the people rights and freedoms, and set the stage for free market economies. In practice, however, the promises were hard to keep.

T

©IGOR KOVALENKO/epa/Corbis

Chapter 7 **217**

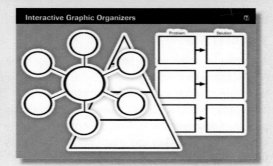

Life in the Regions

T Technology Skills

Using Visual Aids Have a student read the caption under the photograph. Guide students in a class discussion about the photograph, the caption, and the Critical Thinking question and answer. Then invite a small group of volunteers to find other visual images of the Aral Sea using the Internet or other news media sources. Encourage students to find a variety of images from different time periods showing before, after, and current photos of the shrinking Aral Sea. Remind students that they should give credit to their sources for photographs as well as text, and to include a list of sources for the images they collect. Display the images in the classroom. **Naturalist**

C Critical Thinking Skills

Determining Cause and Effect Work with students to understand the reasons people from Central Asia, the Caucasus, and Siberian Russia are choosing to leave. **Ask:**

- **Why have Russians been leaving Central Asia?** (*Student answers should include: unstable or corrupt governments; to gain religious freedom; poor economic conditions; civil war; political or religious wars; high levels of pollution; environmental disasters*)
- **What is one of the negative effects that emigration has had on countries?** (*Emigration has deprived countries of skilled workers.*)
- **What is one of the positive effects of schooling?** (*Nearly all adults in Central Asia and the Caucasus can read and write.*) **AL ELL Interpersonal**

R Reading Skills

Depicting Have students reread the last two paragraphs of the section, "The Soviet Legacy." Have students find examples in the two paragraphs that depict either hope or great concern for the people and the environment of the region. (*Hope: Young people are filling the void of skilled workers. Nearly all adults can read and write. Concern: High levels of pollution are creating health risks and have damaged the environment.*) **Verbal/Linguistic**

ANSWER, p. 218

CRITICAL THINKING In pushing for more industry and agriculture, the Soviets ignored environmental concerns, resulting in high levels of pollution and related health risks. Also, irrigation needed for new farms drew heavily on the rivers leading to the Aral Sea. As a result, not enough water reached the Aral Sea to replace the water lost to evaporation. The sea's water level then dropped, and its shoreline receded.

Old rusting ships lie in the sand where the Aral Sea used to be. The Aral Sea supported a major fishing industry before its water level dropped.

▶ **CRITICAL THINKING**
Analyzing How have Soviet policies of the past affected Central Asia's environment today?

In Azerbaijan and Kyrgyzstan, former Communists came to power and were reluctant to change their authoritarian ways. Uzbekistan's Communist party stayed in control by changing its name. In Tajikistan and Georgia, civil war and government corruption brought hardships to citizens.

Turkmenistan's first leader was not a Communist. He seized all power, however, declared himself president for life, and showed little concern for the people. The country's first real elections were not held until a year after his death in 2006. Most other countries in the two regions are now also moving slowly toward democracy.

Russians have been leaving Central Asia gradually since the end of Soviet rule. This emigration has deprived some countries of workers with the skills needed to run the mines, factories, and other businesses created during the Soviet era. Students who are graduating from the many universities, scientific and technical institutes, trade schools, and public schools the Soviets created are closing the gap. Another benefit of schooling is that nearly all adults in Central Asia and the Caucasus can now read and write.

Public health in Central Asia has suffered. The Soviets' carelessness in developing agriculture and industry has resulted in high levels of pollution and related health risks. The environmental disaster they created in the Aral Sea is a good example.

The Shrinking Aral Sea

The Aral Sea was once the fourth-largest inland lake in the world. Today it has lost about 90 percent of its water. Towns that were once important fishing ports are now dozens of miles from the sea.

©Robert Harding World Imagery/Alamy

218 *Chapter 7*

---

netw⊙rks   *Online Teaching Options*

IMAGES

The Aral Sea

Analyzing As a class, use the before and after image of the Aral Sea to analyze the changes that occurred to the sea in the pictures. You may also consider using the images provided by students in the Technology Skills activity on this page. In small groups, have students make comparisons between the images. Then have groups write out theories as to how the changes may have occurred. **Visual/Spatial, Logical/Mathematical**

See page 197E for other online activities.

Interactive Photos

©Image Source/Getty Images

The problem began in the 1960s, when the Soviets built huge farms in the desert and steppes; they dug long canals to irrigate them. Not enough water from the Amu Dar'ya and Syr Dar'ya reached the sea to replace the water lost to evaporation and irrigation. The sea's water level dropped, and its shoreline receded.

What was once the seafloor became dry land filled with salt and farm chemicals from decades of runoff from the irrigated fields. Winds whipping across this polluted wasteland carried salt and chemicals hundreds of miles away into people's lungs. Lung diseases and cancer rates rose as a result.

Kazakhstan is now trying to raise the sea's water level again; some improvement has resulted. Uzbekistan and Turkmenistan have not been able, however, to agree on ways to reduce their use of the Amu Dar'ya's water. Without a regional solution, restoring the sea might not be possible.

Territorial Issues

The dispute over the Amu Dar'ya is just one of several regional issues caused by Soviet rule. When the Soviets created the borders of their Central Asian and Caucasus republics, they paid little attention to where each region's ethnic groups lived. Ethnic-related disputes exist along every shared boundary in Central Asia.

Azerbaijan, Iran, Russia, Turkmenistan, and Kazakhstan also cannot agree on how to share the surface and seabed of the Caspian Sea. At stake is access to minerals such as oil and natural gas, fishing rights, and transportation for the landlocked countries of Azerbaijan and Turkmenistan. Russia and Japan have a long-running dispute over the Kuril Islands, an island chain that extends south from Siberia's Kamchatka peninsula. Japan still claims rights to the southernmost islands, which it lost to the Soviet Union during World War II.

FOLDABLES
Study Organizer

Include this lesson's information in your Foldable®.

☑ **READING PROGRESS CHECK**

Determining Central Ideas Why were the Caucasus and Central Asia slow to establish democratic governments when the Soviet Union collapsed?

LESSON 3 REVIEW CCSS

Reviewing Vocabulary (Tier Three Words)
1. Why are *oases* important in Central Asia? RH.6-8.4

Answering the Guiding Questions
2. ***Describing*** Why does most of Siberia's population live along the Trans-Siberian Railroad? RH.6-8.5

3. ***Identifying*** What cultural characteristics do many of Central Asia's main ethnic groups share? RH.6-8.2

4. ***Analyzing*** How have ethnic tensions affected relationships in the Caucasus and Central Asia? RH.6-8.1

5. ***Narrative Writing*** Create a journal entry describing a day on the Trans-Siberian Railroad or in a rural community in Central Asia. WHST.6-8.4, WHST.6-8.10

Chapter 7 **219**

LESSON 3 REVIEW ANSWERS

Reviewing Vocabulary

1. They provide fields for growing crops and places of settlement for people living in dry areas.

Answering the Guiding Questions

2. ***Describing*** The railroad provides an easy means to get people and goods into Siberia and the products its people produce out to market.

3. ***Identifying*** Most live in rural areas. Many of them live in yurts. Colorful and embroidered clothing and rugs are traditional, especially among rural populations.

4. ***Analyzing*** They have led to secessionist movements in Georgia, conflict between Azerbaijan and Armenia, and boundary disputes between every country in Central Asia.

5. ***Narrative Writing*** Students' journal entries should accurately reflect the culture and daily life of the region and people observed.

C **Critical Thinking Skills**

Determining Cause and Effect Discuss the importance of identifying causes and effects with students. Then have students read "The Shrinking Aral Sea" section silently looking for causes and effects. **Ask:**

• **What are two reasons listed in the text that have caused the Aral Sea to shrink?** *(water lost to evaporation and irrigation used to supply water to farms)*

• **How have the changes to the Aral Sea affected public health?** *(Lung disease and cancer rates have risen because winds whip across the polluted area that was once the sea, and people breathe in the chemicals and salt that the winds pick up.)*

• **What is causing a delay in restoring water to the Aral Sea?** *(Uzbekistan and Turkmenistan cannot agree on ways to reduce their use of Amu Dar'ya's water)* **AL** **ELL**

W **Writing Skills**

Argument Have students research one of the territorial issues between a set of countries listed in the text. Encourage students to begin their research with an open mind, but then to choose one side of the territorial issue based on their research. Then have students write a persuasive essay stating their opinion supporting the side of one country and the reasons that convinced them to choose this side of the issue. **Interpersonal**

CLOSE & REFLECT

Evaluating To close this lesson, have students think about the charts they created at the beginning of the lesson on whether or not they would live in Siberian Russia if their families were given free land. Ask students to explain if they still agree with their earlier decision. Have students write a paragraph re-evaluating their initial decision with specific reasons from the text that reinforce their initial decision or that caused them to change their mind.

ANSWER, p. 219

☑ **READING PROGRESS CHECK** Many of their first leaders as independent nations were the same Soviet leaders or other former Soviet officials.

CHAPTER REVIEW ACTIVITY

Have students create a three-circle Venn diagram to compare and contrast the geography in Siberia from its north to its south. Have them label the circles tundra, taiga, steppe. Tell students to list unique characteristics of each kind of geography in the outer circles and to list shared characteristics of two or more kinds of geography in the appropriate intersecting space. *(Possible answers: **tundra**—treeless, bare, rocky ground, small shrubs, mosses, lichens; **taiga**—coniferous forest, swampy; **steppe**—dry grasslands; intersection of tundra and taiga—covered in permafrost)* **Visual/Spatial, Logical/Mathematical**

Geography of Siberia

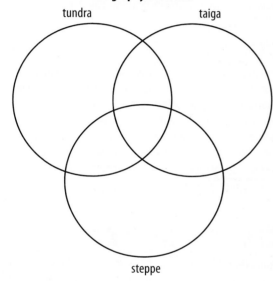

tundra   taiga

steppe

REVIEW THE ENDURING UNDERSTANDINGS

Review this chapter's Enduring Understanding with students:

• *People, places, and ideas change over time.*

Now pose the following questions in a class discussion to apply this to this chapter.

• **How does the climate of this region change as you travel from northern Siberia to the southern Caucasus?** *(Possible answer: Northern Siberia has a mostly arctic climate that becomes semiarid as you go southwest into Central Asia. Central Asia has mostly an arid climate, but in the mountain areas the climate is humid continental as is the climate in the mountainous area in the Caucasus. The coastal lowlands in the Caucasus have a humid subtropical climate. Overall, temperatures become warmer as you travel south.)*

• **How did Siberia change after the Communists overthrew the czar in Russia?** *(Sample answer: Siberia experienced increased mining and industry; gulags were built to house political prisoners and criminals.)*

• **How have the countries in Central Asia and the Caucasus changed after becoming independent of Russia?** *(Students' answers will vary but should include relevant details such as increased ethnic unrest, civil wars, territorial disputes, establishment of democratic governments, development of free enterprise, attainment of rights and freedoms for the people.)*

Chapter 7 **ACTIVITIES**

Directions: Write your answers on a separate piece of paper.

① Use your **FOLDABLES** to explore the Essential Questions.
INFORMATIVE/EXPLANATORY WRITING Review the population map at the beginning of this unit. Explain why some areas are heavily populated. Describe factors that influenced this pattern of settlement in three or more paragraphs. WHST.6-8.2, WHST.6-8.4

② **21st Century Skills**
INTEGRATING VISUAL INFORMATION Research to find a a primary source and a secondary source on the collapse of the Soviet Union. Read and discuss the two documents. Answer the questions: What kind of information is provided by the primary source? Is it different from information provided by the secondary source? How? Which source provides information that is more accurate? Why? RH.6-8.9, RH.6-8.10

③ **Thinking Like a Geographer**
INTEGRATING VISUAL INFORMATION Create a time line. List five key events in the history of the region. Include the entries on your time line. RH.6-8.2, WHST.6-8.10

④ **GEOGRAPHY ACTIVITY**

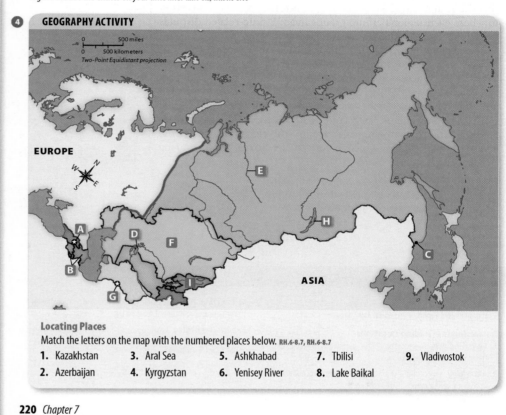

Locating Places
Match the letters on the map with the numbered places below. RH.6-8.7, RH.6-8.7

1. Kazakhstan	3. Aral Sea	5. Ashkhabad	7. Tbilisi	9. Vladivostok
2. Azerbaijan	4. Kyrgyzstan	6. Yenisey River	8. Lake Baikal	

220 *Chapter 7*

ACTIVITIES ANSWERS

Exploring the Essential Question

① **INFORMATIVE/ EXPLANATORY WRITING** Students' essays should include relevant and specific details to explain and describe the influences on population patterns. Essays should be a minimum of three paragraphs and meet standards for spelling and grammar.

21st Century Skills

② **INTEGRATING VISUAL INFORMATION** Answers discussing the two documents should be analytical, and, where appropriate, include examples to support their conclusions.

REVIEW THE GUIDING QUESTIONS

Directions: Choose the best answer for each question.

① Natural resources found in Siberian Russia and Central Asia include huge deposits of RH.6-8.2
- A. oil and natural gas.
- B. lead and antimony.
- C. copper and tungsten.
- D. bauxite and iron.

② What is the name of the mountain chain that divides Europe from Asia? RH.6-8.4
- F. Ural Mountains
- G. Caucasus Mountains
- H. Syr Dar'ya
- I. Tien Shan

③ What technological development opened up Siberia for settlement and aided economic expansion? RH.6-8.1
- A. the telephone
- B. the steam engine
- C. the Trans-Siberian Railroad
- D. the Moscow to Novosibirsk Canal

④ What benefits did the Caucasus countries of Armenia, Georgia, and Azerbaijan gain from the years they were part of the Soviet Union? RH.6-8.1
- F. Roads and airports were built.
- G. They profited greatly from the Cold War arms race.
- H. Soviet military power reduced ethnic tensions and brought peace to the region.
- I. The Soviets encouraged the development of the area's natural resources.

⑤ Which large inland lake nearly dried up because of mismanagement and too much irrigation? RH.6-8.2
- A. Caspian Sea
- B. Aral Sea
- C. Black Sea
- D. Red Sea

⑥ The two most popular religions practiced by the people who live in Central Asia, the Caucasus, and Siberia are RH.6-8.2
- F. Protestantism and Catholicism.
- G. Islam and Hinduism.
- H. Hinduism and Christianity.
- I. Christianity and Islam.

Chapter 7 **221**

Thinking Like a Geographer

③ **INTEGRATING VISUAL INFORMATION** Time lines should include at least five events. Possible entries include: Mongolian invaders capture much of Siberia—early 1200s; completion of the Trans-Siberian Railroad 1905; Czar Nicholas of Russia is overthrown 1917; Communists control Central Asia 1920; Soviet Union annexes the Caucasus 1922; Soviet Union collapses 1991; Georgia, Armenia, and Azerbaijan declare independence 1991.

Geography Activity

④ **LOCATING PLACES**

1. F
2. B
3. D
4. I
5. G
6. E
7. A
8. H
9. C

ASSESSMENT ANSWERS

Review the Guiding Questions

① **A** To answer this question, students need to remember that oil and natural gas are energy resources that are found in all three areas of this region. Recognizing that antimony, tungsten, and bauxite are natural resources not frequently mentioned in the text will help students eliminate choices B, C, and D. Refer students to the "Energy and Mineral Resources" section in Lesson 1.

② **F** The Ural Mountains divide Europe from Asia. Refer students who answer incorrectly to review Lesson 1.

③ **C** Clue words in the question include *settlement* and *economic expansion*. Both terms imply movement of either people or goods. Knowing this helps to eliminate choices A and D. Since a steam engine can be used to pull a train but is just part of a railroad, choosing C, Trans-Siberian Railroad, would be the logical choice. If students answer incorrectly, refer them to the "Revolution and Development" section of Lesson 2.

④ **H** To answer this question, students need to remember that the people of the Caucasus turned to Russia for protection from Muslim rulers, which brought peace to the region. Remembering that the Cold War was between the U.S.S.R. and the U.S. and that the area has little in the way of natural resources helps to eliminate choices G and I. If students are having difficulty answering the question, have students reread Lesson 2 section "The Caucasus" for help.

⑤ **B** Knowing that the Red Sea is not in this region helps to eliminate choice D. Remembering that both the Black Sea and the Caspian Sea, choices A and C, have thriving sea ports and are used for transporting imports and exports, helps to eliminate them. Refer students to reread Lesson 3 "The Shrinking Aral Sea" to fully understand and answer the question.

⑥ **I** To answer this question, students need to remember that Russian Orthodox is a Christian religion but is not the same as Protestantism and Catholicism. This helps eliminate choice F. Also remembering that many of the people in the area are Muslims who practice Islam will help students pair Islam with Christianity and choose **I** for the answer. Have students reread the "Language and Religion" section in Lesson 3 for help.

DBQ Analyzing Documents

7 **A** The purpose of the caravans along the Silk Road in Central Asia in ancient times was to carry out the trade of silk and other goods, using this trade route between the Far East and Europe.

8 **H** The Sogdians were important for their cultural impact, as their alphabet influenced the alphabets developed by other peoples and they spread two religions to new areas.

Short Response

9 "Co-financing" means that Kazakhstan is joining with USAID in providing funds for the economic development projects in the country.

10 Possible answer: Students can infer that Kazakhstan's economy has improved from its condition as a "once-underdeveloped" economy when USAID first began financing projects in that nation because it now has enough resources to help provide funding for new development projects. Students may also explain that Kazakhstan's leaders are still interested in promoting their nation's economic development or else they would not bother to fund such projects.

Extended Response

11 Students' essays should reflect thoughtful consideration when comparing and contrasting the building of the Trans-Siberian Railroad in Russia with the construction of America's transcontinental railroad. Students should make clear connections between the two and clear distinctions of the settlement patterns and economic growth each railroad brought to the area. Grammar and spelling in essays should meet your standards.

DBQ ANALYZING DOCUMENTS

7 **IDENTIFYING** Read the following passage about the Sogdians, a group of people who were important during the early history of Central Asia:

"*The Sogdians were the major participants in the Silk Road caravans, ... their alphabet the source of later alphabets to the east, they carried with them such religions as Zoroastrianism . . . and Nestorian Christianity.*"

—from Albert Dien, "The Glories of Sogdiana"

What was the purpose of caravans along the Silk Road in ancient times? **RH.6-8.1, RH.6-8.10**

A. to carry out trade of valuable goods

B. to achieve military conquest

C. to spread Sogdian culture to new areas

D. to enrich the Sogdian rulers

8 **ANALYZING** The Sogdians were important because they **RH.6-8.1, RH.6-8.10**

F. built the silk road.

G. organized the caravans.

H. had a strong cultural impact.

I. ruled the region for many centuries.

SHORT RESPONSE

The following passage discusses the work of USAID, a U.S. government agency that provides humanitarian aid and assistance for development to other countries:

"*When USAID arrived in Kazakhstan in 1992, . . . the country's centrally controlled [economic] system lay in ruins. No one could have imagined that, less than 15 years later, this once-underdeveloped . . . republic would be co-financing USAID's economic development work in the country.*"

—from Geoff Minott and Leanne McDougall, "One Part U.S., Two Parts Kazakhstan" (2012)

9 **DETERMINING WORD MEANINGS** What do the authors mean when they say that now Kazakhstan is "co-financing" USAID projects? **RH.6-8.4**

10 **ANALYZING** What can you infer about Kazakhstan's economy from this report? **RH.6-8.1, RH.6-8.10**

EXTENDED RESPONSE

11 **INFORMATIVE/EXPLANATORY WRITING** Research to find out about the construction of America's transcontinental railroad. In an essay, compare the building of that railroad with the building of the Trans-Siberian Railroad in Russia. In your writing, describe the effects each railroad had on settlement patterns and economic growth. **WHST.6-8.2, WHST.6-8.4**

Need Extra Help?

If You've Missed Question	**1**	**2**	**3**	**4**	**5**	**6**	**7**	**8**	**9**	**10**	**11**
Review Lesson	1	1	2	2	3	3	2	2	3	3	2

From "THE GLORIES OF SOGDIANA," by Albert E. Dien. Silkroad Foundation ©1997–2000. http://www.silk-road.com/art/sogdian.shtml

netw⊙rks *Online Teaching Options*

Remediation and Assessment

Evaluating The *Assess* tab in the online Teacher Lesson Center includes resources to help students improve their test-taking skills. It also contains many project-based rubrics to help you assess students' work.

National Geography Standards covered in Chapter 8

Learners will understand:

I. The World in Spatial Terms

Standard 1: How to use maps and other geographic representations, geospatial technologies, and spatial thinking to understand and communicate information

Standard 3: How to analyze the spatial organization of people, places, and environments on Earth's surface

II. Places and Regions

Standard 4: The physical and human characteristics of places

Standard 5: That people create regions to interpret Earth's complexity

Standard 6: How culture and experience influence people's perceptions of places and regions

IV. Human Systems

Standard 9: The characteristics, distribution, and migration of human populations on Earth's surface

Standard 10: The characteristics, distribution, and complexity of Earth's cultural mosaics

Standard 11: The patterns and networks of economic interdependence on Earth's surface

Standard 12: The processes, patterns, and functions of human settlement

Standard 13: How the forces of cooperation and conflict among people influence the division and control of Earth's surface

V. Environment and Society

Standard 14: How human actions modify the physical environment

Standard 15: How physical systems affect human systems

VI. The Uses of Geography

Standard 17: How to apply geography to interpret the past

Standard 18: How to apply geography to interpret the present and plan for the future

UNDERSTANDING BY DESIGN®

Enduring Understandings

- *People, places, and ideas change over time.*

Essential Questions

- *How does geography influence the way people live?*
- *Why do civilizations rise and fall?*
- *How does religion shape society?*

Predictable Misunderstandings

- *Southwest Asia has a similar physical landscape to the rest of Asia.*
- *People of Southwest Asia have a similar religion and culture to the rest of Asia.*
- *Southwest Asia has limited resources because of its location.*
- *Southwest Asia has a small population because of its location and climate.*

Assessment Evidence

Performance Tasks:

- *Project-Based Learning Digital Hands-On Chapter Project*
- *Project-Based Learning Hands-On Chapter Project*

Other Evidence:

- *Technology Skills Activity*
- *Geography and Economics Activity*
- *Participation in Interactive Whiteboard Activities*
- *Contribution to small-group activities*
- *Interpretation of slide show images and special purpose maps*
- *Participation in class discussions about cultural and economic topics*
- *Lesson Reviews*
- *Chapter Assessments*

SUGGESTED PACING GUIDE

Introducing the Chapter............... 1 Day	Lesson 3 .... 2 Days
Lesson 1 .... 2 Days	What Do You Think? .... 3 Days
Lesson 2 .... 2 Days	Chapter Wrap-Up and Assessment...... 1 Day

TOTAL TIME   11 Days

Key for Using the Teacher Edition

SKILL-BASED ACTIVITIES

Types of skill activities found in the Teacher Edition.

* **V** **Visual Skills** require students to analyze maps, graphs, charts, and photos.

W **Writing Skills** provide writing opportunities to help students comprehend the text.

R **Reading Skills** help students practice reading skills and master vocabulary.

C **Critical Thinking Skills** help students apply and extend what they have learned.

T **Technology Skills** require students to use digital tools effectively.

*Letters are followed by a number when there is more than one of the same type of skill on the page.

DIFFERENTIATED INSTRUCTION

All activities are written for the on-level student unless otherwise marked with the leveled labels below.

BL **Beyond Level**
AL **Approaching Level**
ELL **English Language Learners**

All students benefit from activities that utilize different learning styles. Many activities are marked as below when a particular learning style is highlighted.

Intrapersonal	Naturalist
Logical/Mathematical	Kinesthetic
Visual/Spatial	Auditory/Musical
Verbal/Linguistic	Interpersonal

CHAPTER OPENER PLANNER

Students will know:
- *that Southwest Asia has a unique landscape when compared to the rest of Asia.*
- *how the region's features, resources, and cultures have influenced the large population that live in this region.*

Students will be able to:
- *analyze a world map to identify countries of Southwest Asia.*
- *use a time line to discuss various events in the history of Southwest Asia.*

UNDERSTANDING BY DESIGN®

☑ *Print Teaching Options*

V **Visual Skills**

☐ **P. 224** Students use the map of Southwest Asia to reinforce map skills. **Visual/Spatial**

☐ **P. 225** Students review the time line and discuss its major points of interest. **Visual/Spatial**

W **Writing Skills**

☐ **P. 225** Students choose an event from the time line and write a paragraph explaining its effect on the region and world. **Verbal/Linguistic**

☑ *Online Teaching Options*

☐ **MAP** **Reading a Map**—Students identify aspects and locations of the region on a map.

☐ **TIME LINE** **Reading a Time Line and Map**—Students learn about where historical events occurred in the region and identify the places where events took place on the map. **ELL**

☐ **MAP** **Interactive World Atlas**—Students use the interactive world atlas to identify the region and describe its terrain.

☑ *Printable Digital Worksheets*

☐ **WORKSHEET** **Geography and Economics: Oil**—Students can use the worksheet to review the location of oil reserves around the world and the process of extracting oil, the price of oil, and the conflicts that can develop over this resource.

☐ **WORKSHEET** **Technology Skills: Using Visuals**—Students use this worksheet to analyze visuals to learn more about the history of the Kurds

---

Project-Based Learning

Hands-On

Create an Illustrated Encyclopedia

Students will work independently to create an illustrated encyclopedia page about Southwest Asia. Each student will be assigned a specific topic about Southwest Asia to research. Each illustrated encyclopedia page will include visuals, descriptions of the visuals, and content information. The encyclopedia pages can then be compiled into one illustrated encyclopedia about Southwest Asia.

Digital Hands-On

Create a Video Documentary

Students will work in groups to create a short video documentary about Southwest Asia. Each group will be assigned a specific topic about Southwest Asia: physical geography, early history, modern history, people, cultures, and current day challenges. The video documentary will consist of still images with narrated voice-overs by students. The documentary videos can be created using a free, web-based video creation site.

21ˢᵗ Century Learning

Print Resources

ANCILLARY RESOURCES

These ancillaries are available for every chapter and lesson.

- **Reading Essentials and Study Guide Workbook** **AL** **ELL**
- **Chapter Tests and Lesson Quizzes Blackline Masters**

PRINTABLE DIGITAL WORKSHEETS

These printable digital worksheets are available for every chapter and lesson!

- **Hands-On Chapter Projects**
- **What Do You Know? Activities**
- **Chapter Summaries (English and Spanish)**
- **Vocabulary Builder Activities**
- **Quizzes and Tests**
- **Reading Essentials and Study Guide (English and Spanish)** **AL** **ELL**
- **Guided Reading Activities**

More Media Resources

SUGGESTED VIDEOS

NOTE: Be sure to preview videos to ensure they are age-appropriate.

- **Occupation 101—Voices of the Silent Majority** (documentary, 90 min.)
- **Globe Trekker: Istanbul** (48 min.)
- **Inside Mecca, National Geographic** (60 min.)

SUGGESTED READING 📚

- ***Purple Heart,*** by Patricia McCormick **BL**
- ***Nasgreen's Secret School: A True Story From Afghanistan,*** by Jeanette Winter **AL**
- ***Tasting the Sky: A Palestinian Childhood,*** by Ibtisam Barakat
- ***Where the Streets Had a Name,*** by Randa Abdel-Fattah

PHYSICAL GEOGRAPHY OF SOUTHWEST ASIA

Students will know:
- that Southwest Asia has a unique landscape when compared to the rest of Asia.
- that water is a scarce resource for Southwest Asia but most of the world's oil and gas reserves are in this region.

Students will be able to:
- **describe** the physical features of Southwest Asia.
- **describe** the various climates of this region.
- **discuss** important natural resources in this region.

UNDERSTANDING
BY DESIGN®

☑ Print Teaching Options

V Visual Skills

☐ **P. 227** Students draw an outline map of the Arab Peninsula and mark landforms and bodies of water.

☐ **P. 229** Students create and complete a flowchart about climate causes and effects in Southwest Asia.

W Writing Skills

☐ **P. 230** Students brainstorm what they might pack to travel to one of the regions based on the time of year.

☐ **P. 231** Students research threats to marine life and write a paragraph to defend or refute the idea that offshore oil drilling in the Persian Gulf is vital to the economy. **AL**

R Reading Skills

☐ **P. 228** Students determine the meaning of *alluvial plain*.

☐ **P. 228** Students make connections between the Dead Sea and the Caspian Sea.

☐ **P. 229** Students identify the descriptive language used in a paragraph about Southwest Asia's climates. **AL ELL**

☐ **P. 230** Students use prefixes to understand *semi-arid*.

C Critical Thinking Skills

☐ **P. 226** Students discuss positive and negative aspects of the Hindu Kush mountain range and effects of passes. **AL**

☐ **P. 227** Students compare and contrast the physical features of Iran and Turkey. **AL**

T Technology Skills

☐ **P. 228** Students conduct research about one of the seas located in this region and prepare and present a slide show.

☐ **P. 230** Students conduct research about the climate, summarize key facts, and use visuals to support findings.

☐ **P. 231** Students conduct online research to determine the size of petroleum deposits in each country in Southwest Asia and specific revenues generated from exporting petroleum. **BL**

☑ Online Teaching Options

V Visual Skills

☐ **VIDEO** **Israel/Palestine Water**—Students watch the video about the water crisis in Israel and Palestine and share one or two key facts they found interesting. **AL** Visual/Spatial

☐ **MAP** **Physical Geography: Southwest Asia**—Students discuss waterways and landforms of the region using the physical geography layer of the Chapter Opener map. Visual/Spatial, Naturalist

☐ **DIAGRAM** **Oases**—Students use the diagram and chart to discuss oases and describe how oases form. **AL** Naturalist

☐ **MAP** **Resources: Southwest Asia**—Students use the resources layer of the Chapter Opener map to discuss the other resources available in the region.

☐ **MAP** **Climates: Southwest Asia**—Students use the climate layer on the Chapter Opener map to analyze the climate in the region and discuss various ways people may have to adapt to it.

W Writing Skills

☐ **GRAPHIC ORGANIZER** **Southwest Asia as a Region**—Students use the interactive graphic organizer to discuss and review the landforms and waterways of the region.

C Critical Thinking Skills

☐ **MAP** **Bodies of Water in Southwest Asia**—Students analyze photos of the bodies of water, discuss the qualities of each, and infer how these bodies of water impact people living in the surrounding region. **BL** Verbal/Linguistic

☐ **MAP** **Vegetation: Southwest Asia**—Students use the vegetation layer on the Chapter Opener map to discuss the landscape of the region and its influence on development and how people live.

☐ **GRAPH** **Oil Reserves in the World**—Students use the circle graph to compare the region's oil supply to that of the rest of the world.

T Technology Skills

☐ **ANIMATION** **Why Much of the World's Oil Supply is in Southwest Asia**—Students watch the animation and discuss why this region is a rich source of oil. **BL** Verbal/Linguistic

☐ **ONLINE SELF-CHECK QUIZ** **Lesson 1**—Students receive instant feedback on their mastery of lesson content.

☑ Printable Digital Worksheets

W Writing Skills

☐ **WORKSHEET** **Geography and Economics: Oil**—Students can use the worksheet to review the location of oil reserves around the world and the process of extracting oil, the price of oil, and the conflicts that can develop over this resource.

HISTORY OF SOUTHWEST ASIA

Students will know:
- *that three major world religions developed in this region.*
- *how the region's features, resources, and cultures have influenced the large population that lives in this region.*

Students will be able to:
- **discuss** the early history of Southwest Asia.
- **examine** the religions that developed in the region, including Islamic expansion.
- **explore** conflicts in the region, including civil wars and terrorism.

UNDERSTANDING
BY DESIGN®

☑ *Print Teaching Options*

V Visual Skills

☐ **P. 233** Students create a three-column chart to take notes on three major religions. **AL**

☐ **P. 235** Students create a graph that shows the rise and fall of Islam in Southwest Asia. **Visual/Spatial**

☐ **P. 238** Students create a flow chart to visualize key events in the Arab-Israeli conflict. **Visual/Spatial**

W Writing Skills

☐ **P. 234** Students write a blog for a Southwest Asian travel and tourism web site. **BL**

☐ **P. 238** Students research what each U.S. president did or did not do to resolve the Arab-Israeli conflict, and write an argumentative essay about why the United States has an obligation to help bring peace to the Middle East.

R Reading Skills

☐ **P. 232** Students identify synonyms for *civilization* and why it is important to learn about past civilizations.

☐ **P. 233** Students identify the meaning of *polytheism* and *monotheism* and find words with same prefixes. **ELL**

☐ **P. 237** Students determine the meaning of the word *mandate* and how a mandate system might cause conflict.

C Critical Thinking Skills

☐ **P. 232** Students describe the rise of civilization in Mesopotamia and make connections to today's cities.

☐ **P. 233** Students discuss what a civilization's belief system can reveal about its society and values.

☐ **P. 238** Students consider the impact of years of conflict in the West Bank and East Jerusalem.

☐ **P. 239** Students identify causes and effects of conflict in the Persian Gulf.

T Technology Skills

☐ **P. 236** Students research and give oral reports on present-day issues facing Southwest Asia focusing on either the role of conflict and leadership or how natural resources bring both wealth and conflict. **BL**

☐ **P. 237** Students research how Turkish Armenians were treated by the Young Turk government during and after World War I.

☑ *Online Teaching Options*

V Visual Skills

☐ **VIDEO** **Mesopotamia**—Students watch the video about the history of Mesopotamia and discuss how Southwest Asia's geographical location may have influenced trade and the spread of different cultures. **AL**

☐ **IMAGE** **Cuneiform**—Students use the interactive image of cuneiform to discuss the examples and definition of this early form of writing. **Visual/Spatial**

☐ **MAP** **Islamic Expansion**—Students use the map to discuss Islamic expansion and understand the impact that Islam had on people in different regions. **AL** **Verbal/Linguistic**

☐ **IMAGE** **The Kurds**—Students analyze dress, belongings, and the faces of the Kurds using the interactive photograph and discuss how the Kurds' quest for their own independent country has led to conflicts in the region. **BL** **Verbal/Linguistic**

☐ **VIDEO** **Temple Mount, Jerusalem**—Students use the video of the temple with the western wall and dome to discuss the importance of this region to the three major religions.

W Writing Skills

☐ **MAP** **Israel and Palestine**—Students analyze the map and discuss the division of the territory between Israel and Palestine and the development of Israel as an independent nation and write a paragraph about the lasting effects of conflict on the region. **BL** **Interpersonal**

C Critical Thinking Skills

☐ **DIAGRAM** **Ziggurats**—Students use the interactive diagram of the ziggurat to analyze the purpose of this type of building and its architecture. **Visual/Spatial**

☐ **MAP** **Conflicts in Southwest Asia**—Students use the map to discuss the conflicts that have developed in this region over time. **Visual/Spatial**

☐ **CHART** **Three Major Religions**—Students use the chart of the three major religions to discuss their similarities, differences, and reasons for expansion. **Interpersonal**

☐ **TIME LINE** **Independence of Southwest Asia**—Students use the time line to understand the significance and impact of independence in various Southwest Asian countries. **AL** **Verbal**

T Technology Skills

☐ **ONLINE SELF-CHECK QUIZ** **Lesson 2**—Students receive instant feedback on their mastery of lesson content.

☑ *Printable Digital Worksheets*

W Writing Skills

☐ **WORKSHEET** **Technology Skills: Using Visuals**—Students use this worksheet to analyze visuals to learn more about the history of the Kurds.

LIFE IN SOUTHWEST ASIA

Students will know:
- *that three major world religions developed in this region.*
- *that water is a scarce resource for Southwest Asia but a great deal of the world's oil and gas reserves are in this region.*
- *how the region's features, resources, and cultures have influenced the large population that live in this region.*

Students will be able to:
- *describe population patterns in Southwest Asia.*
- *describe people and cultures in the region, including languages and religion.*
- *examine the connection between religion and the arts in the region.*
- *describe daily life in the region.*
- *explore issues in Southwest Asia, such as oil dependency and control, changing governments, and water concerns.*

UNDERSTANDING
BY DESIGN®

☑ *Print Teaching Options*

V Visual Skills

☐ **P. 241** Students create a graph about population density.

☐ **P. 242** Students organize ethnic groups in a chart.

☐ **P. 244** Students create a visual representation of information about the different livelihoods discussed. **BL**

☐ **P. 247** Students create a diagram or other visual that explains the process of extracting fossil water.

W Writing Skills

☐ **P. 241** Students write a paragraph about an aspect of city life for the assigned city for their group.

☐ **P. 244** Students read and summarize a story from *The Thousand and One Nights*.

R Reading Skills

☐ **P. 240** Students identify the main ideas in the text. **AL**

☐ **P. 242** Students find meaning by how a word is used.

☐ **P. 245** Students discuss the meaning of "breaking fast" and its relation to the word *breakfast*. **AL** **ELL**

☐ **P. 246** Students use context clues to find meaning. **AL**

C Critical Thinking Skills

☐ **P. 240** Students discuss factors that cause people to live in certain regions and where most people live.

☐ **P. 242** Students consider the consequences of so many different ethnic groups living across Southwest Asia.

☐ **P. 245** Students consider the challenges faced by people in different regions as a result of petroleum production.

☐ **P. 247** Students consider the challenges faced by regions that are reliant on freshwater sources of water.

T Technology Skills

☐ **P. 243** Students research different ethnic groups.

☐ **P. 244** Students research one of Southwest Asia's cultural aspects and make a presentation for a "cultural fair."

☐ **P. 246** Students research the Arab Spring. **BL**

☑ *Online Teaching Options*

V Visual Skills

☐ **MAP** **Population: Southwest Asia**—Students study the population layer on the Chapter Opener map with a partner and discuss the population density of each region. **AL** Logical

☐ **IMAGES** **Cities Along the Tigris and Euphrates**—Use the images to show the development of major cities like those in Dubai. Visual/Spatial

☐ **VIDEO** **Arabic Fast Food**—Use the video to discuss the westernization of the region and how western influences create challenges for the people of the region. **AL** Visual/Spatial

W Writing Skills

☐ **VIDEO** **Around the World - Oman** —Students watch the video about the culture of the country of Oman and discuss how the westernization of their culture is one of the current issues facing the region of Southwest Asia.

☐ **SLIDE SHOW** **Art of Southwest Asia**—Students take notes as they view the slide show about art in Southwest Asia. Interpersonal, Intrapersonal

☐ **VIDEO** **Burning Oil in Kuwait**—Students discuss the influence of oil on global economies and write a paragraph about the influence oil has on interactions between Kuwait and the rest of the world. **BL** Logical/Mathematical, Interpersonal

C Critical Thinking Skills

☐ **CHART** **English Words with Roots in Languages of Southwest Asia**—Students use the chart of American words that originate from Arabic, Hebrew, and Farsi to analyze how language has spread and changed around the world and discuss how the spread of languages has impacted communication among groups of people in Southwest Asia and other parts of the world. **ELL**

☐ **IMAGE** **Foods of Ramadan**—Students discuss the similarities and differences of various holiday traditions and foods after learning about the foods of Ramadan using the interactive photograph. **AL** Verbal/Linguistic

☐ **MAP** **Resources: Southwest Asia**—Use the resources layer of the Chapter Opener map to discuss the importance of oil and its role in the current challenges and relationships in the region.

T Technology Skills

☐ **GAME** **Life in Southwest Asia**—Students use the drag-and-drop game to reinforce their knowledge of life in Southwest Asia. Kinesthetic, Visual/Spatial

☐ **ONLINE SELF-CHECK QUIZ** **Lesson 3**—Students receive instant feedback on their mastery of lesson content.

INTERVENTION AND REMEDIATION STRATEGIES

LESSON 1 Physical Geography of Southwest Asia

Reading and Comprehension

Students may have trouble with the meaning and pronunciation of some of the content vocabulary words, such as *alluvial* and *wadi*. Have student pairs play a guessing game in which one person gives clues about a content vocabulary term, and the other student tries to guess it. Have pairs compete against other pairs to see who can guess the most terms correctly in a certain amount of time. As a "bonus" question, have each team use the academic vocabulary term *vary* correctly in a sentence.

Text Evidence

Have students work in small groups to analyze the impact of one of the landforms or waterways described in the lesson. Students should describe key aspects of their feature covered in the text, or they may wish to conduct additional research. For example, students may wish to examine the mountain ranges in Iran. Or they might analyze the Arabian Sea or the Strait of Hormuz as they relate to transportation. Tell students to present an analysis of their findings, including answers to the following questions: *Where is this landform or waterway located? How does it impact the people who live in that region? What are some of its unique characteristics?*

LESSON 2 History of Southwest Asia

Reading and Comprehension

Have students skim the lesson to look for unfamiliar or confusing words. Tell students to write down what they think the word might mean based on context clues in the text. Then have students look up each word in the dictionary to find the definition of each word. Have students count how many definitions they guessed correctly. Discuss the word parts *poly-* and *mono-* to help students fully understand the meaning of the content vocabulary terms *polytheism* and *monotheism*.

Text Evidence

Have student groups create a flow chart or time line showing how Southwest Asia's early civilizations developed through the years. Flow charts or time lines should depict facts about groups of people based on evidence in the text, or from additional research, and should answer the following questions: *How were people affected by the practice of agriculture? What role did religion play in Southwest Asia's history? What conflicts developed through the years? Do any still exist today?* Have groups present their findings to the class.

LESSON 3 Life in Southwest Asia

Reading and Comprehension

Have students skim the lesson to find challenging or unfamiliar words, such as *urbanization* and *uninhabited*, and try to determine each word's meaning by using context clues. Then have students look up the words' definitions using an online or print dictionary to clarify the meanings. Have students work in pairs to practice using these words in sentences. Then ask students to explain a concept in this lesson using one of the academic vocabulary terms. Discuss the word parts in the content vocabulary terms *dependency* and *hydropolitics* to help students comprehend each word's meaning.

Text Evidence

Assign student pairs or groups one of the Southwest Asian countries discussed in this lesson. Tell students to write a summary explaining their assigned country's population profile, ethnic and language groups, culture, and daily life. Students may wish to conduct research using Web sites such as https://www.cia.gov/library/publications/the-world-factbook/ to learn about each country's history. After students have had time to compile and summarize information from their research, have them present their summaries to the class.

Online Resources

Level Reader

Use this online lower-level text that corresponds directly to the text in the online Student Edition.

Guided Reading Activities

This resource uses graphic organizers and guiding questions to help students with comprehension.

Assessing Background Knowledge

Use these worksheets to pre-assess students' background knowledge before they read the chapter.

Reading Essentials and Study Guide Workbook

This resource offers writing and reading activities for the approaching-level student.

Self-Check Quizzes

This online assessment tool provides instant feedback for students to check their progress.

SOUTHWEST ASIA

ESSENTIAL QUESTIONS · How does geography influence the way people live?
· Why do civilizations rise and fall? · How does religion shape society?

Wathiq Khuzaie/Getty Images News/Getty Images

A woman in Baghdad, Iraq, displays her inked fingers, showing that she has just voted in the election.

Lesson 1
Physical Geography of Southwest Asia

Lesson 2
History of Southwest Asia

Lesson 3
Life in Southwest Asia

The Story Matters...

The area between the Tigris and Euphrates rivers in Southwest Asia is known as the Fertile Crescent. Here, fertile soil and water for irrigation supported the growth of an early civilization—Mesopotamia. Three major world religions—Judaism, Christianity, and Islam—began in this region. From ancient to modern times, the region's physical features, resources, and cultures have greatly influenced how people live.

FOLDABLES
Study Organizer

Go to the Foldables® library in the back of your book to make a Foldable® that will help you take notes while reading this chapter.

223

ENGAGE

Bellringer Point to a political map of Southwest Asia, clarifying the location of the countries that will be discussed in this chapter: Turkey, Syria, Lebanon, Israel, Jordan, Saudi Arabia, Yemen, Oman, the United Arab Emirates, Qatar, Bahrain, Kuwait, Iraq, Iran, and Afghanistan. Have students point to the region known as the Middle East. **Ask:**

- **Why do you think the region between the Tigris and Euphrates rivers is known as the Fertile Crescent?** *(Sample response: The region has fertile soil and is formed in the shape of a moon sliver, or crescent.)*
- **Why is the region sometimes referred to as the "cradle of civilization"?** *(Sample response: Some of the world's earliest civilizations began there, like a baby in a cradle.)*

Have students read "The Story Matters…." Have students recall what they may have learned about the region known as the Fertile Crescent. Point out that this region is the birthplace of three major religions: Judaism, Christianity, and Islam. **Ask: How might having three major religions begin in Southwest Asian countries shape its societies?** *(Students may infer that this region is home to diverse cultures and that may mean there is conflict over religious beliefs.)*

Tell students that they will learn more about the unique features and cultures of countries in Southwest Asia in this chapter.

Content Background Knowledge

In some of the countries in this region, women have had the right to vote since the countries were formed. In other countries, women still do not have the right to vote.

- Women in Kuwait do not have the right to vote.
- Women in Saudi Arabia will be able to vote in 2015.
- In Qatar, women gained the right to vote in 1999.
- In Iraq, women had the legal right to vote in 1958, but this was not exercised until 1980. In Jordan the same was true from 1974 to 1989.
- In Afghanistan, women's right to vote (and many other rights) were taken away from 1996 to 2001.

FOLDABLES
Study Organizer

Go to the Foldables® library for a cumulative chapter-based Foldable® activity that your students can use to help take notes and prepare for assessment.

Letter from the Author

Dear Geography Teacher,

The study of Southwest Asia allows students to see the role of geography in political decisions, or *geopolitics*. One example of this is seen in the Strait of Hormuz, which is important to the transfer of Southwest Asia's oil to world markets. The world's countries have placed economic sanctions on Iran to force it to abandon nuclear enrichment efforts. In response, Iran has threatened to block the Strait of Hormuz, disrupting the flow of oil to markets and wreaking havoc on the world economy.

TEACH & ASSESS

Step Into the Place

V Visual Skills

Reading a Map Have students read the introductory paragraph and look at the map. Explain that this map shows the countries of Southwest Asia. Have students use the map to answer the Step Into the Place questions. Then **ask:**

- What Southwest Asian country is located the farthest south? *(Yemen)*
- What is the capital of Oman? *(Masqat)*
- What countries share a border with Iraq? *(Iran, Kuwait, Saudi Arabia, Jordan, Syria, and Turkey)* **Visual/Spatial**

Making Connections Have students look at the photographs on this page. Explain that while Southwest Asian countries have a rich history that dates back to ancient times, they are also home to modern cities. To help students make connections between the past and present of the region, read the following information:

- Some of the world's largest known oil reserves are located in Southwest Asian countries. These top oil-producing countries include Saudi Arabia, Iran, Iraq, the United Arab Emirates, and Kuwait, and are part of a region often referred to as the Middle East.
- The city of Dubai in the United Arab Emirates is home to the world's tallest building. Known as Burj Khalifa, the building stretches 2,717 feet (828 meters) high. Opened in January 2010, the building has 162 floors with an observation deck on the 124th floor.
- Sports such as soccer and horse racing are popular in various Southwest Asian countries. Camel racing is a traditional sport in countries such as Saudi Arabia, Kuwait, Qatar, and the United Arab Emirates.
- Salt from the Dead Sea is used in cosmetic products, such as lotions and body scrubs, that are sold worldwide.

ANSWERS, p. 224

STEP INTO THE PLACE
1. Damascus
2. Saudi Arabia and Oman
3. the Red Sea
4. **CRITICAL THINKING** northwest

Chapter 8

SOUTHWEST ASIA

> Southwest Asia lies where the continents of Asia, Africa, and Europe meet. Some of the world's earliest civilizations started here.

Step Into the Place

MAP FOCUS Use the map to answer the following questions.

1. **PLACES AND REGIONS** What is the capital city of Syria?
2. **THE GEOGRAPHER'S WORLD** What countries border Yemen?
3. **THE GEOGRAPHER'S WORLD** What body of water lies west of Saudi Arabia?
4. **CRITICAL THINKING** **Describing** In which direction would you travel from the Persian Gulf to the city of Ankara?

BEACH RESORT Vacationers gather at a beach along the Dead Sea. Because of the high salt content of the water, people who bathe in the Dead Sea can float on its surface without effort.

PORT CITY Modern buildings tower over the city of Jaffa, along Israel's Mediterranean coast. One of the world's oldest cities, Jaffa is known for its historic areas, fragrant gardens, and sprawling flea market.

Step Into the Time

TIME LINE Choose an event from the time line and write a paragraph explaining its effect on the region and the world.
WHST.6-8.2, WHST.6-8.4

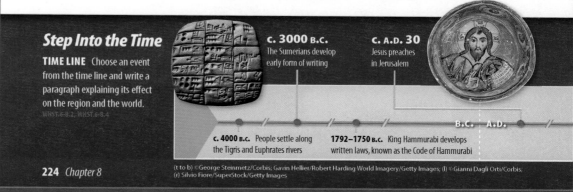

c. 3000 B.C. The Sumerians develop early form of writing

c. A.D. 30 Jesus preaches in Jerusalem

c. 4000 B.C. People settle along the Tigris and Euphrates rivers

1792–1750 B.C. King Hammurabi develops written laws, known as the Code of Hammurabi

224 *Chapter 8*

(t to b) ©George Steinmetz/Corbis; Gavin Hellier/Robert Harding World Imagery/Getty Images; (l) ©Gianni Dagli Orti/Corbis; (r) Silvio Fiore/SuperStock/Getty Images

---

Project-Based Learning

Hands-On

Create an Encyclopedia Page

Students will work independently to create an illustrated encyclopedia page about Southwest Asia. Each student will be assigned a specific topic about Southwest Asia to research. Each illustrated encyclopedia page will include visuals, descriptions of the visuals, and content information. The encyclopedia pages can then be compiled into one illustrated encyclopedia about Southwest Asia.

Digital Hands-On

Create a Video Documentary

Groups will create a short video documentary on a specific topic about Southwest Asia, such as: physical geography, early history, modern history, people, cultures, and current-day challenges. The video documentary will consist of still images with narrated voice-overs (by students) and can be created using a free, web-based video creation site.

edtechteacher
21st Century Learning

Southwest Asia

RUSSIA

Black Sea

Aral Sea

CENTRAL ASIA

Caspian Sea

TURKEY

Ankara

AFGHANISTAN

Kabul

Tehran

Mediterranean Sea

SYRIA

Beirut

LEBANON

Damascus

Tel Aviv-Jaffa

Jerusalem

ISRAEL

JORDAN

Arbil

Baghdad

IRAQ

IRAN

A

B

AFRICA

TROPIC OF CANCER

KUWAIT

Kuwait

Persian Gulf (Arabian Gulf)

SAUDI ARABIA

BAHRAIN

Manama

QATAR

Doha

Abu Dhabi

UNITED ARAB EMIRATES

Gulf of Oman

Masqat

SOUTH ASIA

Riyadh

OMAN

Red Sea

Makkah (Mecca)

o National capital
• City

0   500 miles
0   500 kilometers
Lambert Azimuthal Equal-Area projection

YEMEN

Sanaa

INDIAN OCEAN

Gulf of Aden

2003   The Iraq War begins

1290   The Ottoman Empire begins; lasts until 1922

1948   Israel is founded

1900

2010

A.D. 600s Muhammad begins preaching the teachings of Islam

1938   Oil is discovered in Saudi Arabia

1990   Persian Gulf War begins

2010   Arab Spring revolts take place in the Middle East

©GORAN TOMASEVIC/Reuters/Corbis

Chapter 8 **225**

Step Into the Time

V Visual Skills

Reading a Time Line Have students review the time line and images. As a class, discuss its major points of interest. **Ask:**

- **How long after oil was discovered in Saudi Arabia was Israel founded?** *(10 years)*
- **How long did the Ottoman Empire last?** *(over 600 years)* **Visual/Spatial**

W Writing Skills

Informative/Explanatory Read aloud the activity described at the beginning of the time line, asking students to write a paragraph about a time line event. Use the following questions to help students consider the effects of the different events on the time line before they begin to write. **Ask:**

- **How would the development of writing affect future civilizations?** *(Sample response: The impact was likely dramatic, as people now had a way to record important information and keep written records.)*
- **How do you think the Code of Hammurabi impacted society at the time? What kind of long-term impact would this have on future societies or civilizations?** *(Sample response: It gave people a different view of the law because it was written down and could be discussed and argued about. Once people experienced what it was like to have laws that were written down, they would not be likely to want to have laws that were "in the head" of the rulers rather than codified.)*

Have students share their completed paragraphs with the class. **Verbal/Linguistic, Interpersonal**

V

CLOSE & REFLECT

Summarizing Have students briefly review the photographs, map, and time line, and think about what they have learned so far about Southwest Asia. Have students turn to a partner and summarize key information about the region.

MAP AND TIME LINE

Reading a Time Line and Map

Identifying Display the time line and map on the whiteboard. Have volunteers read each event as it is revealed on the time line. Ask students to identify where in Southwest Asia the event took place and find its location on the map. ELL Visual/Spatial

See page 223B for other online activities.

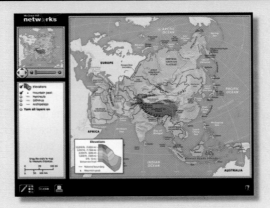

ENGAGE

Bellringer Note that Southwest Asia's location is unique because it is situated where the continents of Asia, Africa, and Europe converge. Refer to a physical map of the region. **Ask:** How might the location of the countries in the region impact people who live there? *(Answers will vary but might mention that people living in the region are exposed to different cultures.)* Then read the "It Matters Because" statement and tell students to think about how people have been influenced by Southwest Asia's physical features.

TEACH & ASSESS

C Critical Thinking Skills

Theorizing Explain that the Hindu Kush is a large mountain range that stretches about 500 miles across portions of Southwest Asia. The mountain system runs from the northeast to the southwest and reaches up to 150 miles wide in some parts. **Ask:**

- What do you think are positive and negative aspects of this vast mountain range for the people who live in the region? *(Sample answer: **positive**—the mountains create a natural barrier to protect people from enemy invasions; **negative**—the mountains may limit travel and trade.)*
- How did the creation of mountain passes impact people who live along the Hindu Kush mountain range? *(Mountain passes made it easier for people to travel throughout the region, so it made trade with other countries easier.)* **AL** Visual/Spatial

Content Background Knowledge

Camels are especially well suited to the deserts of Southwest Asia. They are able to cope with the arid climate, the heat, and sandstorms. The Arabian Camel has just one hump, and that hump stores fat—up to 80 pounds of it—which the camel is able to convert to energy. This allows them to survive for several months without food. Camels can go a week without water and then drink 32 gallons of it at one time. Camels are also incredibly strong pack animals and can carry 200 pounds while walking 20 miles a day. Camels have special adaptations for dealing with desert sand. They have nostrils that can close, two sets of extra long eyelashes to protect their eyes, and a second clear inner eyelid that protects the eye while letting enough light in for the camels to see. .

ANSWER, p. 226

Taking Notes **Mountains:** Hindu Kush, Ararat; **Deserts:** Arabian Desert, the Empty Quarter; **Natural Resources:** oil, natural gas

---

netw**rks**

There's More Online!

☑ **CHART/GRAPH** Oases

☑ **MAP** Bodies of Water in Southwest Asia

☑ **ANIMATION** Why Much of the World's Oil Supply is in Southwest Asia

☑ **VIDEO**

Reading **HELP**DESK (CCSS)

Academic Vocabulary RH.6-8.4
(Tier Two Words)
- **vary**

Content Vocabulary RH.6-8.4
(Tier Three Words)
- **alluvial plain**
- **oasis**
- **wadi**
- **semiarid**

TAKING NOTES: *Key Ideas and Details* RH.6-8.2, RH.6-8.7

Identify As you read the lesson, complete the graphic organizer by listing the physical features found in this region.

Southwest Asia	Examples
Mountains	
Deserts	
Natural Resources	

Lesson 1
Physical Geography of Southwest Asia

ESSENTIAL QUESTION · *How does geography influence the way people live?*

IT MATTERS BECAUSE

Southwest Asia is characterized by a complex physical geography that influences its people, history, and importance in the world today.

Southwest Asia's Physical Features

GUIDING QUESTION *What are the main landforms and resources in Southwest Asia?*

Southwest Asia comprises 15 countries that lie in the area where Asia meets Europe and Africa. Similarities in physical geography help unite these countries into a single region. Mountains and plateaus formed by active plate tectonics can be seen throughout the region. Dry, desert climates are also widespread.

Mountains and Plateaus

Mountains and plateaus dominate the landscape of Southwest Asia. They have been created over the past 100 million years by collisions between four tectonic plates. This movement also caused earthquakes.

Southwest Asia's loftiest mountains rise in the Hindu Kush range, which stretches across much of Afghanistan and along Afghanistan's border with the South Asian country of Pakistan.

The Hindu Kush and neighboring ranges form natural barriers to travel and trade. As a result, mountain passes have been important in this area. One of the world's most famous

(l to r) ©Yannis Kontos/Sygma/Corbis; ©Dean Conger/Corbis; ©Eric Nathan/arabianEye/Corbis

---

netw**rks** *Online Teaching Options*

VIDEO

Israel/Palestine Water

Evaluating Use this video about physical geography, climate, and the fight over a scarce water supply between Israel and Palestine to introduce the content of this lesson. After watching the video, have students evaluate the information presented. Ask students to share with a partner one or two key facts that they found interesting or that surprised them. **AL** Visual/Spatial

See page 223C for other online activities.

BBC Motion Gallery Education

passes is the Khyber Pass. It links the cities of Kabul, Afghanistan, and Peshawar, Pakistan. The pass has served as a route for trade and invading armies for thousands of years.

A vast plateau, covering much of Iran, is encircled by high mountain ranges. The mountains of western Iran merge with those of eastern Turkey. Close to the border rises Turkey's highest peak, Ararat, a massive, snowcapped volcano that last erupted in 1840. An elevated area known as the Anatolian Plateau spreads across central and western Turkey.

The Arabian Peninsula consists of Saudi Arabia, Yemen, Oman, and several other countries. It is a single, vast plateau that slopes gently from the southwest to the northwest. Long mountain ranges that parallel the peninsula's southwestern, northwestern, and southeastern coasts are actually the deeply eroded edges of the plateau.

Bodies of Water

The region of Southwest Asia has thousands of miles of coastline. Turkey has coasts on the Mediterranean and Black seas. Syria, Lebanon, Jordan, and Israel have coasts on the Mediterranean Sea. Jordan, Saudi Arabia, and Yemen border the long, narrow Red Sea. The Red Sea has been one of the world's busiest waterways since Egypt's Suez Canal, connecting the Red Sea and the Mediterranean, was completed in 1869. To the southeast of the Arabian Peninsula lies a part of the Indian Ocean called the Arabian Sea. Yemen and its neighbor Oman have coasts along this sea.

A deadly earthquake in 1999 left widespread destruction in Turkey.
► **CRITICAL THINKING**
Describing What causes earthquakes throughout Southwest Asia?

©Yannis Kontos/Sygma/Corbis

Chapter 8 **227**

MAP

Physical Geography: Southwest Asia

Making Connections Use the physical geography layer of the Chapter Opener map to discuss the landforms and waterways of the region. Guide a class discussion to help students make connections between these landforms and waterways and their impact on trade and commerce. Encourage them to fill out or create a graphic organizer that will allow them to review this information before an assessment. **Visual/Spatial, Naturalist**

See page 223C for other online activities.

C Critical Thinking Skills

Comparing and Contrasting Review the meaning of the word *plateau* with students: an extensive land area with a fairly level surface. Emphasize the fact that a plateau covers much of Iran. Then have students turn to a partner and compare and contrast the physical features of Iran and Turkey. **Ask:**

- **What physical features do Iran and Turkey share?** *(The regions of western Iran and eastern Turkey both have high mountain ranges.)*
- **What landform is unique to Turkey?** *(Mount Ararat, the country's highest peak, is historically important to Christians and thought to be the landing point of Noah's Ark.)* **AL** **Verbal/Linguistic**

V₁ Visual Skills

Creating Maps Have students work with a partner to draw an outline map of the Arabian Peninsula. As they read the paragraph, have them label the map with countries and landforms. Tell students to take notes on the physical features of each region directly on the map. **ELL** **Visual/Spatial**

V₂ Visual Skills

Interpreting Have students work with a partner to interpret the information in the paragraph, using the outline maps they created to mark landforms. As students read the information one sentence at a time, their partner should indicate on the outline map where each body of water is located. **Ask:**

- **On what body of water do Syria, Lebanon, Jordan, and Israel have coasts?** *(the Mediterranean Sea)*
- **Why is the Red Sea a busy waterway?** *(Egypt's Suez Canal which opened in 1869, connected the Red Sea to the Mediterranean Sea making it an important sea passage connecting trade routes between three continents.)* **Interpersonal**

T Technology Skills

Researching The Suez Canal has been important to the region and the world. Have students research the construction of the canal, the Suez Canal Crisis (1956), or some of the treaties and agreements regarding its use. Allow students to present their findings to the class. **Verbal/Linguistic**

ANSWER, p. 227

CRITICAL THINKING Earthquakes are caused by four colliding plates that slowly lift mountains and plateaus higher and higher.

T Technology Skills

Researching on the Internet/Using Visual Aids Have small groups of students conduct research to locate photographs of and information about one of the seas listed in the section. Have students prepare and present a slide show describing the sea and some of its unique characteristics. Presentations should use photographs to enhance and support key information. Provide the following questions to serve as a launch point for students' research:

- **What is the location of the sea?**
- **Is there anything unique about the sea?**
- **How did the sea get its name?**
- **Can people swim in the sea? If so, what is it like? If not, explain why.**
- **What is boat travel like on the sea?** *(shipping, recreational, fishing, tourist)* **Visual/Spatial**

R Reading Skills

Determining Word Meanings Help students understand the term *alluvial plain* by having them find synonyms for the word *alluvial* in a print or online thesaurus *(muddy, sandy, grainy, sedimentary)*. Have students recall the term "Fertile Crescent" used in the Chapter Opener. **Ask: How does the alluvial plain that covers Iraq and parts of Syria and Turkey relate to the Fertile Crescent?** *(The alluvial plain was created by deposits of fertile silt and soil along the Tigris and Euphrates rivers, which is where the term Fertile Crescent originated.)*
ELL Verbal/Linguistic

Making Connections Remind students that they read about the Caspian Sea in previous chapters. Have students locate both the Caspian Sea and the Dead Sea on a map. **Ask:**

- **How is the Dead Sea similar to the Caspian Sea?** *(They are both really lakes, but are called seas because they are large lakes with salty water.)*
- **How are these two seas different?** *(The Caspian Sea is bordered by many nations. The Dead Sea is completely within Israel's borders.)*

Remind students that previous chapters described the different countries that are disputing control of the Caspian Sea and its resources. Challenge students to find out more about the uses for the minerals found in both of these seas as well as the different disputes surrounding the Caspian Sea's resources.

ANSWER, p. 228

CRITICAL THINKING Enormous oil deposits are found in the countries that border the Persian Gulf. Ships carrying oil exports from these countries rely on the Strait of Hormuz to remain open in order to reach their destinations.

Oil tankers pass through the Strait of Hormuz. The strait is the only sea passage from the Persian Gulf to the open ocean.
▶ **CRITICAL THINKING**
Analyzing Why is the Strait of Hormuz considered a strategic waterway?

Thinking Like a Geographer

Characteristics of Seas

The word *sea* is most often used to describe a large body of salt water that is part of, or connected to, an ocean. The Black Sea and the Mediterranean Sea, both of which are connected to the Atlantic Ocean, meet this description, as does the Red Sea, a narrow extension of the Indian Ocean. The landlocked Caspian and Dead seas, however, do not. They best fit the description of *lake*. Large lakes with salty water, however, are sometimes called seas.

228 Chapter 8

In the northeast, the Arabian Peninsula is shaped by the Persian Gulf, which is connected to the ocean by a strategic waterway called the Strait of Hormuz. The Persian Gulf has become tremendously important in world affairs since the middle of the 1900s.

Eight of Southwest Asia's 15 countries border the Persian Gulf: Oman, the United Arab Emirates, Saudi Arabia, Qatar, Bahrain, Kuwait, Iraq, and Iran. In the north, Iran also borders the landlocked Caspian Sea.

The Dead Sea, which lies between Israel and Jordan, is also landlocked. It is far smaller than the region's other seas. At 1,300 feet (396 m) below sea level, it ranks as the world's lowest body of water, and its shore represents the lowest land elevation.

Southwest Asia's two longest and most important rivers are the Tigris and the Euphrates, which are often considered parts of the same river system. The rivers begin within 50 miles (80 km) of each other in the mountains of eastern Turkey. In their lower courses, they flow parallel to one another across a broad **alluvial plain**, a plain created by sediment deposited during floods. The plain covers most of Iraq as well as eastern Syria and southeastern Turkey. This area has been known since ancient times as Mesopotamia, which is Greek for "land between the rivers." Thousands of years ago, one of the world's earliest civilizations took root in the fertile lands of Mesopotamia.

Deserts

Desert landscapes spread across most of Southwest Asia. The Arabian Desert, which covers nearly the entire Arabian Peninsula, is the largest in the region and one of the largest in the world. It is made up of rocky plateaus, gravel-covered plains, salt-crusted flats, flows of black lava, and sand seas, which are unbroken expanses of sand.

©Dean Conger/Corbis

---

networks   *Online Teaching Options*

MAP

Bodies of Water in Southwest Asia

Integrating Visual Information Use the visuals of the bodies of water to discuss the different qualities of each body of water in Southwest Asia. Have students use the information presented in the visuals to infer how these bodies of water impact people who live in each surrounding region. **BL Verbal/Linguistic**

See page 223C for other online activities.

In the southern part of the peninsula lies the largest sand sea in the world: the Rub' al-Khali, or Empty Quarter. Winds have sculpted its reddish-orange sands into towering dunes and long, winding ridges. The climate is so dry and hot that this starkly beautiful wilderness cannot support permanent human settlements. In some areas, nomadic people known as the Bedouin keep herds of camels, horses, and sheep.

The Arabian Desert is a harsh environment, but plants thrive in oases. An **oasis** is an area in a desert where underground water allows plants to grow throughout the year.

☑ **READING PROGRESS CHECK**

Analyzing How has tectonic activity—that is, movement of Earth's crustal plates—helped shape landforms in Southwest Asia?

Southwest Asia's Climates

GUIDING QUESTION *What are some ways that mountains, seas, and other physical features affect climate in Southwest Asia?*

A single type of climate dominates most of Southwest Asia. The only parts of the region with greater climatic variety lie in the northwest and northeast.

An Arid Region

Although this region is surrounded by seas and gulfs, water is a scarce resource here. Most of the region falls within an arid, or very dry, climate zone. Deserts—areas that receive less than 10 inches (25 cm) of annual rainfall—cover nearly the entire Arabian Peninsula as well as large parts of Iran. These deserts are part of a broad band of arid lands that stretch from western North Africa to East Asia. Southwest Asia's arid lands can be brutally hot in the summer. Temperatures in the Arabian Desert can soar as high as 129°F (54°C).

Mountain springs provide a constant flow of water through the Bani Wadi Khalid riverbed in northern Oman. Along the stream's course are large rock formations and shimmering pools of turquoise water.

▶ **CRITICAL THINKING**
Analyzing What feature makes the Bani Wadi Khalid area different from most other landscapes in the Arabian Peninsula?

©Eric Nathan/arabianEye/Corbis

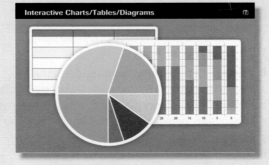

R Reading Skills

Identifying/Paraphrasing Help students identify and comprehend the descriptive language used in the second paragraph of the section, "Deserts." Have students work in pairs to find and list verbs in the paragraph. *(lies, sculpted, keep)* Have them identify descriptive adjectives, looking up words they may not understand in a dictionary. *(largest, reddish-orange, towering, long, dry, hot, starkly, beautiful, permanent, nomadic)* Then have students turn to their partner and paraphrase the information in the paragraph using their own words. **ELL** **AL**
Verbal/Linguistic

V Visual Skills

Creating Charts Read aloud the Guiding Question and remind students that physical features can affect climate, which can in turn affect the region. Have students read the information about Southwest Asia's climate. As they read, have students create and complete a chart like the one below. Have them identify the dominant climate in Southwest Asia along with the characteristics of that climate in the box on the left. Then in the box on the right, have students list the effects of this dominant regional climate on the region. *(Water is scarce throughout the region. Temperatures are extremely hot in the summer.)* **Visual/Spatial, Logical/Mathematical**

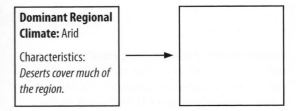

Dominant Regional Climate: Arid

Characteristics:
Deserts cover much of the region.

T Technology Skills

Researching Have students think about how they dress when it is hot in the summer and compare their dress to the dress of the people of Southwest Asia. Have students research why the people of Southwest Asia dress the way they do and which type of dress better protects the person from the sun. **Interpersonal**

ANSWERS, p. 229

☑ **READING PROGRESS CHECK** Tectonic activity created the mountain ranges and plateaus. It also causes earthquakes.
CRITICAL THINKING Water flows readily in the Bani Wadi Khalid area, while most of the Arabian Peninsula's surface is made up of dry desert landscape.

R **Reading Skills**

Determining Word Meanings Point out the word *semiarid* to students. Explain that understanding word parts can help them define confusing words. The prefix *semi-*, for example, means "half" or "partial." **Ask: What other words can you think of that begin with the prefix *semi-*?** *(Samples: semifinal, semicircle, semiformal)* `ELL` `AL` **Verbal/Linguistic**

W **Writing Skills**

Narrative Tell students to imagine that they will travel to one of the regions discussed in this lesson. Have students brainstorm what they might pack for their trip based on the time of year they will travel and the region they will visit. Then have students write a narrative paragraph explaining what they will bring based on the climate described in the text. Students may wish to conduct additional research to explore variations in weather patterns in their region. Encourage students to consider what would be helpful to bring on their trip in addition to clothing. *(Students' narratives will vary but should list appropriate clothing and items for their region at a particular time of year. For example, students may choose to bring hiking boots and sweaters if they plan to travel in the Hindu Kush mountain range, as well as camping gear, water, a GPS, a flashlight, and so on.)* **Verbal/Linguistic**

T **Technology Skills**

Researching on the Internet/Using Visual Aids Organize students into small groups and have each group conduct online research to find images that relate to the climate of a specific region in Southwest Asia. Remind students that websites with the suffix ".gov" are often reliable, such as http://earthobservatory.nasa.gov, as well as websites ending in ".org". Have students locate information and images relating to a climate-related event, such as the dramatic dust storm that hit southern Afghanistan in December 2011. Tell groups to summarize key facts about the climate of their region and present a short report to the class. Students should use visuals to support their findings. **Visual/Spatial**

ANSWERS, p. 230

CRITICAL THINKING Saudi Arabia, Iran, Iraq, Kuwait, United Arab Emirates
☑ **READING PROGRESS CHECK** Farmers can probably grow crops without irrigation in wetter parts of the region, which include areas along the Mediterranean and Aegean coasts, western Turkey, and areas along the Black Sea in Turkey and the Caspian Sea in Iran.

INFOGRAPHIC

OIL: RESERVES AND CONSUMPTION
KEEPING US ON THE MOVE
The countries of Southwest Asia have some of the largest reserves of oil in the world.

LARGEST OIL RESERVES (in barrels)

1	Saudi Arabia	262,600,000,000
2	Venezuela	211,200,000,000
3	Canada	175,200,000,000
4	Iran	137,000,000,000
5	Iraq	115,000,000,000
6	Kuwait	104,000,000,000
7	United Arab Emirates	97,800,000,000
8	Russia	60,000,000,000

TOP OIL CONSUMERS (Consumption in barrels per day)

1	United States	19,150,000
2	China	9,400,000
3	Japan	4,452,000
4	India	3,182,000
5	Saudi Arabia	2,643,000
6	Germany	2,495,000
7	Canada	2,209,000
8	Russia	2,199,000

Oil reserves are estimates of the amount of crude oil located in a particular economic region. Oil consumption is the amount of oil an economic region uses.

▶ **CRITICAL THINKING**

Describing Which Southwest Asian countries are among the countries with the largest oil reserves?

Although rain is scarce in this region, rainfall can quickly transform the desert landscapes. Torrents of water race through **wadis** (WAH-deez), or streambeds that are dry. Buried seeds sprout within hours, carpeting barren gravel plains in green.

R At the margins of Southwest Asia's dry zones lie areas that are considered **semiarid** (seh-mee-AIR-id), or somewhat dry. These areas are found in the highlands and mountain ranges of the region.

W A Mediterranean climate prevails along Southwest Asia's Mediterranean and Aegean coasts and across much of western Turkey. Winds blowing off the seas bring mild temperatures and moderate amounts of rainfall during the winter months. The summer months are warm and dry.

Academic Vocabulary

vary to show differences between things

T Mountainous areas of eastern Turkey, western Iran, and central Afghanistan have continental climates in which temperatures **vary** greatly between summer and winter. The mountains of the Hindu Kush range in far eastern Afghanistan fall within a highland climate zone, and glaciers are found among the soaring peaks.

☑ **READING PROGRESS CHECK**

Identifying In what parts of Southwest Asia could farmers grow crops without irrigation?

230 *Chapter 8*

netw⊙rks *Online Teaching Options*

`ANIMATION`

Why Much of the World's Oil Supply Is in Southwest Asia

Discussing Use the animation to guide a class discussion about why this region is a rich source of oil. Guide students to understand the dependency issues facing nations that rely on oil reserves from the region. Extend the discussion by asking students to relate the discussion to the United States' dependency on oil. Have students write a paragraph that summarizes the information from the class discussion and the global impact of oil. `BL` **Verbal/Linguistic**

See page 223C for other online activities.

Natural Resources

GUIDING QUESTION *How do natural resources influence the lives of people in Southwest Asia?*

Scarcity of water has shaped this region's human history and settlement patterns. Other natural resources, however, are found in abundance. The most important resources are two fossil fuels for which the world has a seemingly unquenchable thirst: oil and natural gas.

The gaseous form of petroleum is called natural gas, and the liquid form is called crude oil, or simply oil. Crude oil is refined to produce energy sources such as gasoline, diesel fuel, heating oil, and industrial fuel oil. Petroleum is also the basic raw material used to make many other products, such as plastics, bicycle tires, and cloth fibers.

The world's largest known deposits of petroleum are in Southwest Asia. Most are concentrated around and under the Persian Gulf. Together, five countries that border the gulf—Saudi Arabia, Iran, Iraq, Kuwait, and United Arab Emirates—hold more than half the oil that has been discovered in the world.

Most of the petroleum produced by these countries is exported to industrialized countries. Petroleum revenues have brought tremendous wealth to a few people in the exporting countries. But only in a relatively few areas has the wealth been used to improve the lives of the people or bring about modernization.

Southwest Asia also has a great variety of mineral resources. Large coal deposits are found in Turkey and Iran. Phosphates, used to make fertilizers, are mined in Iraq, Israel, and Syria. Between 2006 and 2010, American geologists conducting a survey of Afghanistan discovered enormous deposits of iron, copper, gold, cobalt, lithium, and other minerals such as rare earth elements used to make electronic devices.

FOLDABLES
Study Organizer

Include this lesson's information in your Foldable®.

✓ **READING PROGRESS CHECK**

Identifying Five countries that border the Persian Gulf hold more than half the oil that has been discovered in the world. Name three of the countries.

LESSON 1 REVIEW

Reviewing Vocabulary (Tier Three Words)
1. Describe the difference between a *wadi* and an *oasis*. RH.6-8.4

Answering the Guiding Questions
2. ***Identifying*** What makes the Dead Sea distinct? RH.6-8.1
3. ***Describing*** What are the major physical geography features of the Arabian Peninsula? RH.6-8.1

4. ***Describing*** If you were to travel across the Arabian Desert, what are two types of landscapes or landforms you might see? RH.6-8.2
5. ***Citing Text Evidence*** The United Nations ranks Afghanistan as one of the world's poorest countries. How might recent discoveries change that situation? RH.6-8.1
6. ***Narrative Writing*** Imagine that you are spending a few days exploring the area of the Arabian Desert called the Rub' al-Khali. Write a one-paragraph journal entry describing the experience. WHST.6-8.4, WHST.6-8.9

Chapter 8 **231**

W **Writing Skills**

Argument Discuss the impact of petroleum revenues for people in Southwest Asia. Explain that while the petroleum industry has improved the quality of life for many people in countries bordering the Persian Gulf, offshore drilling can harm the environment and potentially threaten and hurt marine life.

Have students conduct research about the potential threats to marine life in the Persian Gulf and write a paragraph to defend or refute the following prompt: **Offshore oil drilling in the Persian Gulf is vital to sustaining a strong economy.** Tell students to support their arguments using evidence based on research from reliable online sources. You may wish to recommend specific sites that offer reliable facts on both sides of the issue, such as https://www.cia.gov/library/publications/the-world-factbook/ and http://www.offshore-mag.com/oilfield-development/middleeast/middleeast-oilfield-news.html. Challenge students to offer solutions to United States' dependency on imported oil. Suggest students find online articles to help give them ideas, such as http://livinggreenmag.com/2012/01/24/energy-ecology/end-offshore-drilling-and-oil-imports-prize-winning-plan-describes-how-to-reduce-u-s-reliance-on-oil/. *(Students' arguments will vary but should include a claim either for or against offshore oil drilling in the Persian Gulf and should defend their arguments with supporting evidence.)* **AL** **Verbal/Linguistic, Naturalist**

T **Technology Skills**

Analyzing Data Assign five student groups one of the five countries that border the Persian Gulf. Tell students to conduct research using reliable online sources, such as https://www.cia.gov/library/publications/the-world-factbook/index.html, to determine the size of petroleum deposits in each country and specific revenues generated from exporting petroleum. Have students compile the data, integrate the information visually by creating a graph or chart, and summarize the information in a presentation to the class. **BL** **Logical/Mathematical**

CLOSE & REFLECT

Recognizing Relationships Tell students to review the images in this lesson and write questions they may still have about countries in Southwest Asia. Encourage students to consider how a region's natural resources affect the way people live. Guide a discussion about the relationship between countries bordering the Persian Gulf and the United States with regard to oil dependency.

ANSWER, p. 231

✓ **READING PROGRESS CHECK** Accept any three of the following: Saudi Arabia, Iran, Iraq, Kuwait, and the United Arab Emirates.

LESSON 1 REVIEW ANSWERS

Reviewing Vocabulary

1. A wadi is a desert streambed that is dry except during a heavy rain. An oasis is a small area in a desert where water and vegetation are found.

Answering the Guiding Questions

2. **Identifying** It is the world's lowest body of water, and its shores represent the lowest land elevation.

3. **Describing** The peninsula is a vast plateau. Mountain ranges along the coasts are the eroded edges of the plateau.

4. **Describing** Accept any two of the following: Rocky plateaus, gravel-covered plains, salt-crusted flats, flows of black lava, sand seas, sand dunes.

5. **Citing Text Evidence** Untapped mineral deposits were discovered between 2006 and 2010. Exploitation of these resources could help lift the country out of poverty.

6. **Narrative Writing** Journal entries should be written in first person and include one or more interesting details about the area.

ENGAGE

Bellringer Before students begin this lesson, have them recall the unique characteristics of Southwest Asia's physical features. Discuss how the region's physical geography might relate to the history of the region. Guide students to make the connection between the fertile land in the region and the ability for early agrarian civilizations to take hold.

TEACH & ASSESS

R Reading Skills

Explaining Ask a student volunteer to read aloud the "It Matters Because" statement. Point out the word *civilization*. Ask students to brainstorm and identify synonyms for words that relate to or have similar word parts as the word *civilization*, using a dictionary or thesaurus if needed. *(civil/courteous, civilized/cultured, civilian/citizen)* **Ask: Why do you think it is important to learn about past civilizations?** *(Possible answer: Studying past civilizations can help us learn how people lived and how different cultures developed.)* **AL** **ELL** **Intrapersonal**

C Critical Thinking Skills

Sequencing Point to Southwest Asia on a physical map, reminding students of its nickname "the Fertile Crescent." **Ask: What factors contributed to the rise of civilization in Mesopotamia?** *(When humans changed from hunter-gatherers to living in farming societies, villages began to emerge. Over time, they grew into cities.)* **Verbal/Linguistic**

Making Connections Help students make the connection between the development of cities in early civilizations and those that we have today. Share this information with students:

- The earliest civilizations did not inhabit a large country, as we do today. Instead, people were ruled by city-states, which encompassed the city and the surrounding area. Based on the analysis of ancient written tablets, historians have determined that temples and palaces were the central focus of ancient city-states.
- Modern-day examples of city-states include Monaco, which is a principality ruled as a constitutional monarchy on the southern border of France; and Singapore, a parliamentary republic in Southeast Asia.

ANSWER, p. 232

Taking Notes Possible time line entries: **2000 B.C.**—Monotheism grows; **A.D. 100**—Christianity grows; **A.D. 600**—Islam spreads; **A.D. 1400**—Mongols conquer large area

---

---

networks

There's More Online!

☑ **CHART/GRAPH** Ziggurats
☑ **IMAGES** The Kurds
☑ **MAP** Islamic Expansion
☑ **VIDEO**

Reading HELPDESK CCSS

Academic Vocabulary RH.6-8.4

(Tier Two Words)
- expand
- collapse

Content Vocabulary RH.6-8.4

(Tier Three Words)
- polytheism
- millennium
- monotheism

TAKING NOTES: *Key Ideas and Details* RH.6-8.5, RH.6-8.7

Sequence As you read about Southwest Asia's history, use a time line to put key events and developments in order.

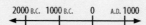

2000 B.C.　1000 B.C.　0　A.D. 1000

232

Lesson 2
History of Southwest Asia

ESSENTIAL QUESTION · *Why do civilizations rise and fall?*

IT MATTERS BECAUSE

R *Southwest Asia has played a large role in human history. The world's earliest civilization developed here, and three major religions were born. Great empires that arose in the region grew to cover parts of three continents.*

Early Southwest Asia

GUIDING QUESTION *What are some of the most important advancements that occurred in Southwest Asia in ancient times?*

Mesopotamia

Throughout most of human history, people lived as hunter-gatherers. In small groups, they hunted wild animals and searched for wild fruits, nuts, and vegetables. They were nomadic, frequently moving from place to place. About 10,000 years ago, though, a dramatic change began to occur: People started practicing agriculture—raising animals and growing crops. One of the first places this agricultural revolution unfolded was in Mesopotamia. Mesopotamia was a fertile plain between the Tigris and Euphrates rivers in present-day Iraq.

C With the shift to agriculture came a shift to a more settled lifestyle. Villages began to appear in Mesopotamia. Because food was plentiful, some villagers were freed up from farming and could undertake toolmaking, basket weaving, or record keeping. Over time, some villages grew into large, powerful cities that had their own governments and military forces. These cities represent the world's first civilizations.

Over thousands of years, Mesopotamian societies such as the Sumerians and the Babylonians invented sophisticated

(l to r) ©nik wheeler/Alamy; ©Nathan Benn/Ottochrome/Corbis; General Photographic Agency/Hulton Archive/Getty Images; ©Nik Wheeler/Corbis

---

networks　*Online Teaching Options*

VIDEO

Mesopotamia

Evaluating Use this video about the history of the ancient civilizations in Mesopotamia to introduce the lesson. Ask students to write three questions to clarify anything that was not called out in the video. Instruct students to not put their name on the questions. Collect the questions and answer a few, then redistribute the questions and have student volunteers answer some of the questions they receive. **AL** **Verbal/Linguistic**

See page 223D for other online activities.

BBC Motion Gallery Education

irrigation and farming methods. They built huge, pyramid-shaped temple towers, and made advances in mathematics, astronomy, government, and law. Using a writing system called cuneiform (kew-NAY-ih-form), they produced great works of literature, including a poem known as the *Epic of Gilgamesh*. Mesopotamia's achievements helped shape later civilizations in Greece, Rome, and Western Europe.

Birthplace of World Religions

Southwest Asia is also a cradle of religion. Three of the world's major religions originated there. In ancient times, most people in the region worshiped many gods. This practice is known as **polytheism**. During the second millennium B.C., a new religion arose. A **millennium** is a period of a thousand years. This new religion was based on **monotheism**—the belief in just one God—and developed among a people called the Israelites. This religion came to be known as Judaism and its followers as Jews.

Jews believe the father of the Israelite people was Abraham. According to the Hebrew Bible, God called Abraham to leave his home in Mesopotamia and found a new nation in a land called Canaan, between the Jordan River and the Mediterranean Sea. The area is shared today by Israel, the Palestinian territories, and Lebanon.

About A.D. 30, a Jewish teacher named Jesus began preaching in this area. The teachings of Jesus led to the rise of Christianity. This new religion spread rapidly throughout the Mediterranean world and into Europe. It also spread across Southwest Asia.

Then, in the A.D. 600s, Islam—the religion of Muslims—arose in the Arabian Peninsula. Muhammad, regarded by Muslims as the last and greatest of the prophets, announced his message in the desert city of Makkah (Mecca). Many of the teachings of Islam are similar to those of Judaism and Christianity. For example, all three religions are monotheistic and regard Abraham as the messenger of God who first taught this belief.

The Ziggurat of Ur was a temple built in Mesopotamia during the 2000s B.C. It served as the political and religious center of the city of Ur.

▶ **CRITICAL THINKING**
Determining Word Meanings
Why is early Mesopotamia called a civilization?

Chapter 8 **233**

V Visual Skills

Creating Charts Have students create a three-column chart to take notes on the three major religions discussed in the text. Encourage students to add information they may know about each religion, such as different places of worship and holidays. Students may wish to organize the information in a compare-contrast diagram to note how the religions are similar and different. **AL** Visual/Spatial

Judaism	Christianity	Islam
• *monotheistic*	• *monotheistic*	• *monotheistic*
• *Jerusalem, holy city*	• *Jerusalem, holy city*	• *Jerusalem, holy city*
• *2000 B.C.*	• *1st century A.D.*	• *600s A.D.*
• *Abraham*	• *Jesus*	• *Muhammad*
• *Canaan*	• *Nazareth*	• *Makkah (Mecca)*
• *Jews*	• *Christians*	• *Muslims*

R Reading Skills

Determining Word Meanings Have students identify the meaning of the terms *polytheism* and *monotheism*. Have students brainstorm other words with the prefixes *poly-* and *mono-*. Write the words on the board under the headings *poly* and *mono* as students call them out. Have students write a sentence using one of the words from each list that demonstrates an understanding of each word's meaning. **ELL** Verbal/Linguistic

C Critical Thinking Skills

Making Connections Tell students to review the information about Judaism, Christianity, and Islam. **Ask: What can a civilization's belief system reveal about its society and values?** (*Students' answers will vary but might include that religions formed in Southwest Asian civilizations valued belief systems that honor one god. The fact that these religions spread, indicates their influence and popularity and shows the value placed on belief systems.*) Verbal/Linguistic

DIAGRAM

Ziggurats

Analyzing Visuals Use the diagram of the ziggurat to help students analyze the purpose of this type of building and its architecture. Discuss the structure's size and what it reveals about the significance of religion in Southwest Asia around 2000 B.C. Have students compare the Ziggurat to other large structures that have been previously discussed in other chapters. **Visual/Spatial**

See page 223D for other online activities.

Interactive Charts/Tables/Diagrams

ANSWER, p. 233

CRITICAL THINKING It developed features of a civilization, such as city life, government and law, military forces, sophisticated farming methods, advances in mathematics and astronomy, and a writing system.

Chapter 8   233

V Visual Skills

Creating Time Lines Have students recall the information about the formation of Islam. Then have students work with a partner to read these paragraphs and create a time line that highlights key events relating to the foundation and expansion of Islam. *(Students' time lines should include most of the following key events: began in the A.D. 600s with the preaching of Muhammad; Muhammad dies in A.D. 632; A.D. 800 Islam spreads across most of Southwest Asia, Spain, Portugal, and northernmost Africa.)* **Logical/Mathematical, Interpersonal**

C Critical Thinking Skills

Making Inferences Have students consider Southwest Asia's physical geography with regard to the spread of Islam. **Ask: Why do you think Islam spread so quickly and so far?** *(Students' answers will vary but might include that because Southwest Asia sits at the convergence of three continents, traders and missionaries across the region may have been responsible for spreading the faith.)* **Verbal/Linguistic**

W Writing Skills

Informative/Explanatory Discuss the golden age of Islamic society. Explain that the cultural contributions during this time reflected different regions and groups of people.

For homework, have students write a blog for a Southwest Asian travel and tourism Web site that highlights information about various contributions of Islamic culture. Students may choose from a topic discussed in the text, such as architecture, math, or science, or may research other cultural aspects such as art, literature, and music. Students' blogs should provide examples of specific cultural offerings related to their topic and should answer the following question: **How did the region's cultural flowering during the golden age influence people in Southwest Asia?**

Remind students to introduce their topic clearly, using precise language and domain-specific vocabulary and to inform potential visitors to the region about the cultural offerings to Islamic society during the golden age. Ask volunteers to read their blogs to the class. Discuss the impact of the golden age on Islamic society. **BL Verbal/Linguistic**

Southwest Asia is the birthplace of Judaism, Christianity, and Islam. The three religions still influence the region today. (left) A Jewish teenager carries a scroll of the Hebrew Bible at the Western Wall in Jerusalem. (center) Muslims circle the Kaaba, a cube-shaped shrine, at the Grand Mosque in Makkah, Saudi Arabia. (right) Christian clergy lead a procession held in Jerusalem shortly before Easter.

▶ **CRITICAL THINKING** V
Describing How is the influence of Judaism, Christianity, and Islam reflected in Southwest Asia today?

Academic Vocabulary

expand to increase or enlarge

C

W

Islamic Expansion

The religion that Muhammad preached was relatively simple and direct. It focused on the need to obey the will of Allah, the Arab word for God. It obligated followers to perform five duties, which became known as the Pillars of Islam: promising faith to God and accepting Muhammad as God's prophet, praying five times daily, fasting during the month of Ramadan (RAHM-uh-don), aiding the poor and unfortunate, and making a pilgrimage to the holy city of Makkah.

In its first several years, Islam attracted few converts. By the time of Muhammad's death, however, in A.D. 632, it had **expanded** across the Arabian Peninsula. Under Muhammad's successors, known as caliphs (KAY-lifs), Arab armies began spreading the religion through military conquests. It was also spread by scholars, by religious pilgrims, and by Arab traders.

By about A.D. 800, Islam had spread across nearly all of Southwest Asia, including Persia (present-day Iran) and part of Turkey. It also extended into most of Spain and Portugal and across northernmost Africa. It later expanded to northern and eastern Africa, Central Asia, and South and Southeast Asia.

Islamic society was enriched by knowledge, skills, ideas, and cultural influences from many different peoples and areas. The influences contributed to a flowering of Islamic culture that lasted for centuries. During this period, great works of architecture were built, and centers of learning arose. Arab scholars made advances in math and science. This golden age was to have a lasting impact on every place it touched.

234 Chapter 8

CHART

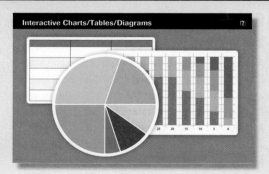
Interactive Charts/Tables/Diagrams

Three Major Religions

Discussing Use the chart of the three major religions to review the development of each religion in the Southwest Asia region. Remind students of the definitions of *polytheism* and *monotheism*. Guide a class discussion about their similarities, differences, and the reasons that religions spread throughout a region. Be sure to point out how trade and the exchange of ideas through trade can influence the spread of religion. **Interpersonal**

See page 223D for other online activities.

ANSWER, p. 234

CRITICAL THINKING The modern country of Israel is a Jewish state, several Southwest Asian countries have sizeable Christian communities, and Islam is the major religion throughout most of the region.

During the 1100s and 1200s, crusaders from Western Europe set up Christian states along Southwest Asia's Mediterranean coast. The Muslims fought back and gained control of these territories by 1300. However, in other areas, Muslim military power weakened.

In the middle of the 1200s, a Central Asian people known as the Mongols, led by the grandson of the famous leader Genghis Khan, conquered Persia and Mesopotamia. These areas became part of a vast Mongol empire that stretched across much of Eurasia.

As a result of the Mongol attacks, the Islamic world was fragmented and fell into decay. Soon, however, a new era of Islamic expansion began. At its heart were the Ottomans, a group of Muslim tribes who began building an empire on the Anatolian Peninsula in the early 1200s. By the mid-1300s, the Ottoman Empire had grown to include much of western Southwest Asia and parts of southeastern Europe and northern Africa. At its height, it was one of the world's most powerful states. It endured for six centuries before finally **collapsing** in the early 1900s.

☑ **READING PROGRESS CHECK**
Determining Central Ideas What are some ways in which Islam was spread?

R

C

V

Academic Vocabulary

collapse to break down completely

R Reading Skills

Determining Word Meanings Have students work in pairs to identify words they may find unfamiliar or confusing as they read this page. Tell students to list the words and use print or online dictionaries to determine each word's meaning and write it down next to each word. Then have students write a sentence for each word on the list that shows the word's meaning. **ELL** Verbal/Linguistic, Interpersonal

C Critical Thinking Skills

Determining Cause and Effect Have students read the first two paragraphs on this page. Ask them to identify the reasons that Islamic expansion slowed by the 1200s. **Ask:**

- **What first caused the expansion of Islam to diminish?** (Arab military and political power weakened, and crusaders from Western Europe set up Christian states along Southwest Asia's Mediterranean coast.)
- **What contributed to this decline in the middle of the 1200s?** (A Central Asian people known as the Mongols conquered much of Persia and Mesopotamia.) Verbal/Linguistic

V Visual Skills

Creating Graphs Have students review the information about Islamic expansion and then read the text about its decline on this page. Have students work with a partner to create a line or bar graph that shows the rise and fall of Islam in Southwest Asia. Tell students their graphs should depict the expansion of Islam beginning with Islam's first years to the collapse of the Ottoman Empire in the early 1900s. You may wish to show students examples of graphs, suggesting they use graph paper and mark their graphs with evenly spaced time periods. Ask student pairs to share their graphs with the class. Visual/Spatial, Logical/Mathematical

MAP SKILLS

1 **THE GEOGRAPHER'S WORLD** How far did Islam spread by A.D. 750?

2 **PLACES AND REGIONS** Why did Muslims from Arabia conquer lands such as Syria, Persia, and Egypt?

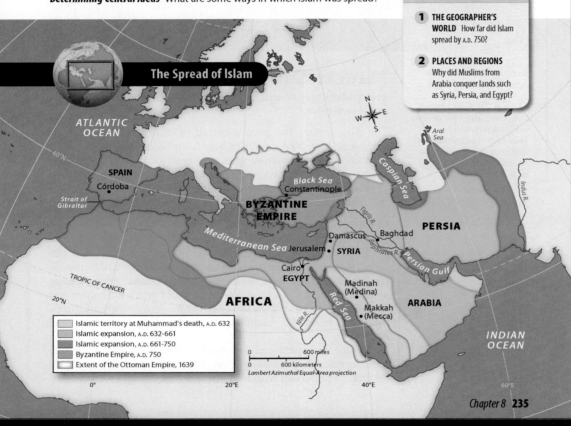

The Spread of Islam

ATLANTIC OCEAN

40°N

SPAIN
Córdoba

Strait of Gibraltar

ATLANTIC OCEAN

Black Sea
Constantinople
BYZANTINE EMPIRE

Mediterranean Sea
Jerusalem
Cairo
EGYPT

TROPIC OF CANCER

20°N

AFRICA

Aral Sea

Caspian Sea

Tigris R.
Damascus   Baghdad   PERSIA
SYRIA   Euphrates R.
Persian Gulf

Indus R.

Madinah (Medina)

Makkah (Mecca)

ARABIA

Red Sea
Nile R.

INDIAN OCEAN

Islamic territory at Muhammad's death, A.D. 632
Islamic expansion, A.D. 632–661
Islamic expansion, A.D. 661–750
Byzantine Empire, A.D. 750
Extent of the Ottoman Empire, 1639

0   600 miles
0   600 kilometers
Lambert Azimuthal Equal-Area projection

0°   20°E   40°E   60°E

Chapter 8   235

MAP

Islamic Expansion

Analyzing Visuals Use the map to discuss Islamic expansion with students. Have students add information to the charts that they worked on earlier using information shown in the map and discussed in class. Guide students to understand the impact that Islam had on people in different regions. **AL** Verbal/Linguistic, Interpersonal

See page 223D for other online activities.

ANSWERS, p. 235

☑ **READING PROGRESS CHECK** It was spread through military conquests by Arab armies. It was also spread by scholars, religious pilgrims, and Arab traders.
MAP SKILLS
1. Spain, Morocco, and southeastern Europe
2. These areas were richer and more culturally and economically developed than Arabia.

History of Southwest Asia

V Visual Skills

Making Inferences Have students look at the image and read the caption on this page. **Ask: Why do you think General Mustapha Kemal was called "Father of the Turks"?** *(Sample answer: He likely earned that nickname because Turks considered him a hero and were thankful that he introduced reforms to modernize the country.)* **Visual/Spatial**

T Technology Skills

Researching on the Internet Read aloud the Guiding Question to students. Have students use reliable online sources to conduct research about present-day issues facing Southwest Asia. Tell students to focus their research on one of these two topics: the role of conflict and leadership in the quest for independence or how natural resources can play a part in bringing wealth but also in creating conflict. Remind students to assess the credibility and accuracy of online sources before using them in their research. Ask students to give brief oral reports on their findings, which should be supported by evidence from their research. **BL Verbal/Linguistic**

C Critical Thinking Skills

Speculating Discuss the various reasons that countries might want to seek their independence and the results of their struggle for independence. **Ask:**

- **How did World War I affect the Ottoman Empire?** *(After the war ended, the Ottoman Empire was dissolved.)*
- **What do you think were some advantages of Turkey becoming independent from its former rule by the Ottoman Empire?** *(Students' answers will vary but might include that Turkey wanted to escape from harsh or corrupt rule.)*
- **What negative consequences might Southwest Asian countries face after becoming independent?** *(Students' answers will vary but might include that countries may become unstable depending on the strength of their military, leadership, economies, and governments.)* **Verbal/Linguistic**

V

General Mustafa Kemal reviews Turkish troops during the war that led to the creation of a Turkish republic in 1923. Kemal, a military hero, became Turkey's first president and introduced reforms to modernize the country. In honor of his achievements, Kemal was later called Atatürk, meaning "Father of the Turks."

Modern Southwest Asia

T

GUIDING QUESTION *What present-day issues facing Southwest Asia have their roots in ancient times?*

The past century has been a period of change and conflict for Southwest Asia. New countries have been born, new borders have been drawn, and numerous wars have been fought. Vast petroleum reserves discovered during this period have brought great wealth to some of the region's countries but have also created new tensions and conflicts.

Independent Countries

C

After reaching the peak of its power in the 1500s, the Ottoman Empire began to decline. The decline worsened in the 1800s and early 1900s. During that time, the empire lost African and European territories through wars, treaties, and revolutions. After fighting alongside the losing Central Powers in World War I, the empire was formally dissolved. A few years later, the modern country of Turkey was founded on the Anatolian Peninsula, where the empire had been born.

European interest and influence in Southwest Asia had been growing since the 1869 completion of the Suez Canal, which quickly became an important world waterway. In the peace settlement that

236 Chapter 8

---

networks *Online Teaching Options*

TIME LINE

Independence of Southwest Asia

Analyzing Time Lines Use the time line to help students understand the significance and impact of independence sought by various Southwest Asian countries. Guide a discussion about the reasons that led to the independence of countries in the region. Encourage students to research a particular country in the region and its fight for independence. **AL Verbal/Linguistic**

See page 223D for other online activities.

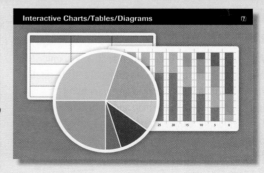

Interactive Charts/Tables/Diagrams

ended World War I, Britain and France gained control over the Ottoman Empire's former territories under a mandate system. In this arrangement, the people of these territories were to be prepared for eventual independence. **R**

Dividing up their territories, the British and French created new political boundaries that showed little regard for existing ethnic, religious, political, or historical divisions. These boundaries would take on deep importance when the territorial units became independent countries and when new discoveries of petroleum deposits were made.

T Long-simmering resentment toward the European colonial powers soon grew into strong nationalist movements among Arabs, Persians, Turks, and other groups. Between 1930 and 1971, one country after another won its independence, and the map of Southwest Asia began to take its present form.

Arab-Israeli Conflict

One of the mandates received by Britain after World War I was the territory called Palestine. It roughly corresponded to the Land of Israel, which was the area inhabited by the Jewish people in ancient times. Most of the people living in Palestine at the time of the mandate were Muslim Arabs. During the same period, growing numbers of Jewish immigrants seeking to escape persecution had been arriving from Europe and other parts of the world. As the Jewish population increased, tensions between Palestinian Arabs and Jews deepened.

Jewish nationalists called for the reestablishment of their historic homeland in Palestine. This movement gained support as a result of the Holocaust—the systematic murder of 6 million European Jews by Nazi Germany during World War II. Hundreds of thousands of Jews who survived the Holocaust were now refugees in search of a place to live.

In 1947 the United Nations decided on the issue of Palestine. The United Nations voted to divide the territory into two states, one Arab and one Jewish. The proposal was rejected by the Arabs.

MAP SKILLS

1 HUMAN GEOGRAPHY How does Israel's territory today compare with Israel's territory in 1967?

2 PHYSICAL GEOGRAPHY What feature is unique about the land area of the Palestinian territories?

Territorial Changes

Original Jewish state under U.N. Partition Plan 1947
Territory acquired by Israel in 1948
Territory acquired by Israel in 1967
Areas of partial Palestinian self-rule
— Present-day border of Israel
— Present-day border of West Bank and Gaza Strip
◇ Capital city
• City

Chapter 8 **237**

R **Reading Skills**

Determining Word Meanings Point out the word *mandate* to students and have them look up the word in a dictionary to determine its meaning and identify synonyms. *(order, command, instruction)* Tell students that the word *mandate* has specific connotations as it relates to governments. In the case of territories settled after World War I, the term *mandate* has a precise meaning as it relates to explicit orders and boundaries involving those territories. Have students turn to a partner and use the word *mandate* in a sentence. **Ask: How might a mandate system cause conflict between countries?** *(Sample response: Countries' rulers and governments may have different motives and ideas about how territories should be divided.)* **Verbal/Linguistic**

T **Technology Skills**

Collaborating and Making Presentations Tell students that the country of Armenia, which shares a border with northeastern Turkey, was the first nation to establish Christianity as its official religion. Have students consider how this may have led to later conflict as it relates to "long-simmering resentment."

As homework, have students work in small groups to research how Turkish Armenians were treated by the Turkish government during and after World War I. Have groups formulate questions to focus their research such as:

• **What caused the conflict?**
• **Who did the conflict involve?**
• **Where did it take place? How long did it last?**

You may suggest specific Web sites to help groups narrow their research, such as: http://www.britannica.com/EBchecked/topic/35178/Armenia/44272/Ottomans-and-Safavids and https://www.cia.gov/library/publications/the-world-factbook/geos/am.html.

After students have had time to conduct research and take notes, have groups present a summary of their findings to the class. **BL** **Verbal/Linguistic, Interpersonal**

MAP

Territorial Changes in Israel and Palestine

Collaborating In pairs, have students work together to analyze the map. Then, guide a discussion about the division of the territory between Israel and Palestine and the development of Israel as an independent nation. Have the partners write a paragraph about the lasting effects of conflict on the region and the struggles to maintain peace in the region. Circulate to answer questions and guide student learning. **BL** **Interpersonal**

See page 223D for other online activities.

ANSWER, p. 237

MAP SKILLS

1. In 1967, Israel acquired the West Bank, Gaza Strip, Golan Heights, and the Sinai Peninsula. Today, Israel no longer controls the Sinai Peninsula but still has the Golan Heights. Partial self-rule has been given to the Palestinians in the West Bank and the Gaza Strip.
2. The Palestinian Territories are made up of two parts—the West Bank and the Gaza Strip—separated by Israeli territory.

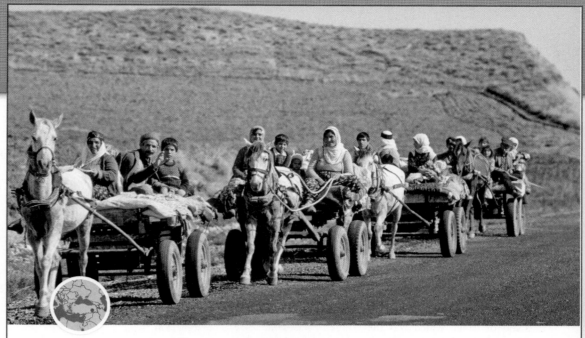

V Visual Skills

Creating Visuals To help students comprehend the series of events presented in the text, have them work in pairs to visualize the reading. **Ask: How many years after Israel captured the Sinai Peninsula did it withdraw from the region?** *(15 years)*

As students read the text, have them work with a partner to create a flow chart to visualize key events. Encourage students to add key dates and events to the Taking Notes time line at the beginning of this lesson. Challenge students to find out more about the Six-Day War, using Web sites such as these: www.jewishvirtuallibrary.org/jsource/History/67_War.html; www.sixdaywar.co.uk. **AL Visual/Spatial, Interpersonal**

C Critical Thinking Skills

Hypothesizing Have students consider the impact of years of conflict in the West Bank and East Jerusalem. **Ask: Why do you think a resolution to the Arab-Israeli conflict has been unsuccessful?** *(Students' responses may vary but might include that each side may be unwilling to compromise.)* **Verbal/ Linguistic**

W Writing Skills

Argument Explain that various attempts by United States presidents have been made to resolve the Arab-Israeli conflict and that since Israel declared its independence in 1948, peace has eluded the region. Have students consider the impact years of conflict in the West Bank and East Jerusalem has had on the people who live in the region.

As homework, have students conduct online research to determine what each United States president did or did not do to resolve the Arab-Israeli conflict, beginning with the presidency of Richard Nixon to the present administration. Have students write out notes on the various attempts by specific presidents.

Then tell students to write an argumentative essay on whether or not the United States has an obligation to help bring peace to the region. Students should support their argument with logical reasoning and relevant data and evidence from reliable online sources. **BL Verbal/Linguistic, Interpersonal**

Kurdish families travel by cart over a modern road in southeastern Turkey. The Kurds are a Sunni Muslim people with their own language and culture. Living in the mountains north of Southwest Asia, the Kurds have been ruled by other people throughout history.

▶ **CRITICAL THINKING**
Analyzing Why has the demand of the Kurds for their own independent country been difficult to achieve?

The Arabs did not want to give up land. On the day in 1948 that Israel, the Jewish state, declared its independence, armies from neighboring Arab countries invaded. Hundreds of thousands of Palestinian Arabs became refugees after fleeing the violence. That war ended with a truce in 1948. Other major Arab-Israeli wars were fought, however, in the 1950s, 1960s, and 1970s.

During a brief 1967 war, Israel captured areas known as the West Bank, East Jerusalem, the Sinai Peninsula, the Gaza Strip, and Golan Heights. Its control of these areas was opposed by Palestinian Arabs and neighboring Arab countries, which led to further conflict. Israel withdrew from the Sinai Peninsula in 1982 and from the Gaza Strip in 2005. It continues to control the West Bank and East Jerusalem. Numerous attempts have been made to find a peaceful solution to the Arab-Israeli conflict, but so far none have been successful.

Civil Wars

In addition to the strife between Arabs and Israelis, Southwest Asia has seen numerous other conflicts since World War II. Ethnic, religious, and political differences have fueled many conflicts. So has the rise of Islamist movements that consider Islam to be a political system as well as a religion. The desire to control large oil fields has also caused, or contributed to, many of the conflicts.

Civil wars have torn apart Lebanon, Afghanistan, and Yemen. The Kurds, a fiercely independent people living in eastern Turkey, northern Iraq, and western Iran, have fought to gain their own

©Nik Wheeler/Corbis

---

networks *Online Teaching Options*

IMAGE

The Kurds

Analyzing Visuals Use the image of the Kurds to help students learn more about this group of people. Have students analyze different aspects of the image and make connections to the representations of their culture, like their dress. Guide a class discussion about how the Kurds' quest for their own independent country has led to conflicts in the region. **BL Verbal/Linguistic**

See page 223D for other online activities.

Interactive Photos

© Image Source/Getty Images

ANSWER, p. 238

CRITICAL THINKING The Kurdish population is divided among several countries (Turkey, Iraq, Iran, and Syria), all of which oppose a Kurdish independent state that would be created from some of their territories.

country. A revolution in Iran in the late 1970s resulted in the overthrow of that country's monarchy and the establishment of an Islamic republic. Iraq invaded Iran in 1980, touching off an eight-year-long war. A decade later, Iraq invaded and annexed its small but oil-rich neighbor, Kuwait. This invasion triggered the Persian Gulf War, in which a coalition led by the United States quickly liberated Kuwait.

Conflict and Terrorism

On September 11, 2001, an Islamist organization called al-Qaeda carried out terrorist attacks on U.S. soil that killed nearly 3,000 people. The United States determined that Afghanistan's Islamist ruling group, the Taliban, was supporting al-Qaeda and sheltering its leaders. In October, forces led by the United States and the United Kingdom invaded Afghanistan and removed the Taliban from power.

Two years later, the Second Persian Gulf War began when forces from the United States and the United Kingdom invaded Iraq and overthrew the government of Saddam Hussein. Hussein was accused of possessing weapons of mass destruction, a suspicion that eventually was proved to be untrue.

Looking to the Future

Despite the many conflicts, there is hope for a more peaceful and brighter future in Southwest Asia. Revenue from petroleum has brought prosperity and modernization to oil-rich countries of the Persian Gulf. In 2010 and 2011, a popular uprising in Tunisia inspired democratic movements in Yemen, Bahrain, and Syria.

On the other hand, militant Islamic political movements limit the growth of democracy and civil rights. In addition, throughout the region, major gaps still exist in standards of living between the oil-rich countries and poorer countries.

☑ **READING PROGRESS CHECK**

Determining Central Ideas What event in Europe helped spur the creation of a Jewish state in Southwest Asia?

Think Again?

The Middle East and Southwest Asia are two names for the same region.

Not true. According to most authorities, the Middle East includes all or part of North Africa as well as all or most of Southwest Asia. Some authorities also consider the countries of Central Asia to be part of the Middle East.

FOLDABLES Study Organizer

Include this lesson's information in your Foldable®.

LESSON 2 REVIEW CCSS

Reviewing Vocabulary (Tier Three Words)
1. What is the difference between *monotheism* and *polytheism*? RH.6-8.4

Answering the Guiding Questions
2. *Identifying* What is one of the Pillars of Islam? RH.6-8.2

3. *Describing* What change in Mesopotamia around 10,000 years ago resulted in a less nomadic lifestyle? RH.6-8.5

4. *Identifying* What are two developments that occurred during Islam's golden age? RH.6-8.2

5. *Citing Text Evidence* What empire represented a second period of Islamic expansion, and where did that empire begin? RH.6-8.1

6. *Determining Central Ideas* How did the 2001 terrorist attacks on the United States lead to a U.S. invasion of Afghanistan? RH.6-8.2

7. *Informative/Explanatory Writing* Some conflicts in Southwest Asia relate to the struggle for a homeland by groups such as the Jews, the Palestinians, and the Kurds. Write a short essay discussing what a homeland is and why groups are willing to fight for one. WHST.6-8.2, WHST.6-8.4

Chapter 8 **239**

LESSON 2 REVIEW ANSWERS

Reviewing Vocabulary

1. Monotheism is the belief in one god, and polytheism is the belief in many gods.

Answering the Guiding Questions

2. **Identifying** Accept any one of the following: making declarations of faith, praying five times each day, fasting during the month of Ramadan (RAHM-uh-don), giving aid to the poor and unfortunate, making a pilgrimage to Makkah.

3. **Describing** People began practicing agriculture. Instead of surviving by hunting and gathering, they grew crops and raised animals.

4. **Identifying** Accept any two of the following: Great works of architecture were built, centers of learning arose throughout the Islamic world, Arab scholars made significant advances.

5. **Citing Text Evidence** The Ottoman Empire, which began on the Anatolian Peninsula

6. **Determining Central Ideas** The United States accused Afghanistan's Islamist ruling group, the Taliban, of supporting the terrorist organization al-Qaeda and sheltering its leaders.

7. **Informative/Explanatory Writing** Responses should provide explanation of what constitutes a homeland and valid reasons for loyalty to one's homeland.

C Critical Thinking Skills

Determining Cause and Effect Have a volunteer read aloud the first paragraph on this page. In a class discussion, ask students to identify the causes and effects of conflict in the Persian Gulf. **Ask:**

- **What was the effect of revolution in Iran in the late 1970s?** (*Iran's monarchy was overthrown and an Islamic republic was established.*)
- **What caused an eight-year-long war between Iraq and Iran?** (*Iraq invaded Iran in 1980.*)
- **What was the effect of Iraq's invasion and annexation of Kuwait?** (*It triggered the Persian Gulf War.*)
- **What was the result of the Persian Gulf War?** (*A coalition led by United States forces quickly liberated Kuwait.*) **Verbal/Linguistic**

T Technology Skills

Researching on the Internet Have small groups of students research the events of September 11, 2001. You may want to assign each of the groups one of the sites that the terrorists attacked that day to research: World Trade Center Tower One, World Trade Center Tower Two, the Pentagon, and Flight 93 that crashed into a field in Pennsylvania instead of striking a site in Washington, DC. **Logical/Mathematical, Interpersonal**

Content Background Knowledge

Osama bin Laden, a radical leader of the militant Islamist group al-Qaeda, was considered the mastermind behind the terrorist attacks on September 11, 2001 on the United States. After a man-hunt that lasted almost 10 years, bin Laden was killed by a team of United States Navy SEALs (an acronym for Sea, Air, and Land) who invaded bin Laden's compound in Pakistan during a pre-dawn raid in May 2011.

CLOSE & REFLECT

Have students recall what they learned about the birthplace of world religions in Southwest Asia. Have them consider how this and other factors led to instability and conflict among different regions. Guide a class discussion about the impact these conflicts have had on people who live in Southwest Asia.

ANSWER, p. 239

☑ **READING PROGRESS CHECK** The Holocaust, in which six million Jews were killed.

ENGAGE

Bellringer Ask students to brainstorm words that come to mind based on what they have learned about Southwest Asia so far. Write the words on the board as students call them out. Have students skim through the photographs in this lesson and have them consider how Southwest Asia's history might influence societies that live there now. **Ask: Would you ever want to visit Southwest Asia? If so, what region would you most like to visit and why? If not, what are your reasons?** *(Students' answers will vary but may cite the attraction of modern cities or the war-torn regions of the region as a deterrent.)*

TEACH & ASSESS

C Critical Thinking Skills

Determining Cause and Effect Ask a volunteer to read the "It Matters Because" statement. Point to Southwest Asia on a map, noting that even though it is smaller, its population is larger than that of the United States. **Ask:**

- **What factors do you think cause people to live in certain regions?** *(Answers will vary. Possible answer: Factors might include living near a body of water, which can be used for transportation as well as the fishing industry. People might live near areas that have natural resources or fertile land to benefit agriculture.)*
- **Judging from the map and what you have learned about the physical geography of the region, where do you think most people live in Southwest Asia?** *(Answers will vary. Possible answer: Most people likely live in major cities that have growing economies and employment opportunities.)* **Verbal/Linguistic**

R Reading Skills

Determining Central Ideas Help students identify and understand the main ideas in the text. **Ask:**

- **Which countries in Southwest Asia have the largest populations?** *(Iran and Turkey)*
- **In which region of Southwest Asia is the population rising? Why?** *(the Persian Gulf; those countries have an abundance of oil, which helps bring jobs to the region)* **AL** **Verbal/Linguistic**

ANSWER, p. 240

Taking Notes Where people live in the region depends on the availability of water and natural resources. Three world religions began in Southwest Asia. Some countries in the region greatly depend on oil.

---

networks

There's More Online!

☑ **IMAGES** Foods of Ramadan
☑ **VIDEO**

Reading **HELP**DESK (CCSS)

Academic Vocabulary RH.6-8.4

- **widespread** *(Tier Two Words)*

Content Vocabulary RH.6-8.4

- **hydropolitics** *(Tier Three Words)*
- **fossil water**

TAKING NOTES: *Key Ideas and Details* RH.6-8.2, RH.6-8.7

Determine the Main Idea As you read the lesson, write the main idea for each section on a graphic organizer like the one below.

Main Ideas

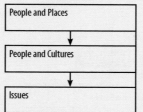

Main Ideas
People and Places
↓
People and Cultures
↓
Issues

240

Lesson 3
Life in Southwest Asia

ESSENTIAL QUESTION · *How does religion shape society?*

IT MATTERS BECAUSE

C *Because of its strategic location at the convergence of three continents, its huge petroleum reserves, and the deep-rooted conflicts that divide its people, Southwest Asia occupies a central place in world affairs.*

People and Places

GUIDING QUESTION *In what parts of Southwest Asia do most people live?*

Southwest Asia's population is slightly greater than that of the United States, although the region is only about three-fourths as large as the United States in area. Throughout history, population patterns in Southwest Asia have been shaped largely by the availability of water. In recent times, another resource—petroleum—has also played an important role.

Population Profile

Southwest Asia is home to about 330 million people. Iran and Turkey, its most populous countries, each have about 80 million people. Some oil-rich countries around the Persian Gulf are experiencing population booms as their fast-growing economies attract foreign workers. Qatar has had one of the world's highest population growth rates in recent years.

R Today, many countries of Southwest Asia are highly urbanized. In Israel, Saudi Arabia, and Kuwait, for example, more than four of every five people live in cities. In Afghanistan and Yemen, however, more than two-thirds of the people live in rural areas. However, these countries have the region's highest annual urbanization rate as people move to the cities. As a whole, the region has a rapidly growing population and a high percentage of people below 15 years of age.

(l to r) ©Charles Bowman/Robert Harding World Imagery/Corbis; ©Jose Fuste Raga/Corbis; ©ATEF HASSAN/Reuters/Corbis; ©Peter Turnley/Corbis

---

networks *Online Teaching Options*

VIDEO

Around the World—Oman

Analyzing Visuals Use this video about Oman, a country in Southwest Asia, to introduce the lesson. Have students write a paragraph about an aspect of life in Oman or Southwest Asia that they find intriguing or appealing, or one that they want to know more about. Tell students to think about the images shown in this video as they read the lesson. **AL** **Visual/Spatial**

See page 223E for other online activities.

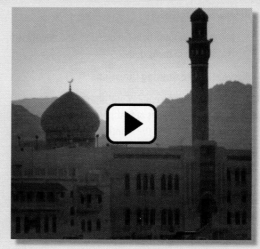

BBC Motion Gallery Education

Where People Live

Population is not evenly distributed across Southwest Asia. The highest densities are in the region's northern and western parts and in its southern tip. These areas include parts of Turkey, Iraq, Iran, and Afghanistan; the countries along the coast of the Mediterranean Sea; and the highlands of southern Saudi Arabia and southwestern Yemen. Most of these areas have relatively higher rainfall.

Areas with dry or somewhat dry climates are more sparsely populated. These areas include the Arabian Desert and the desert lands that spread across central and eastern Iran. Some desert areas are almost completely uninhabited. One exception is Mesopotamia, the land between the Tigris and Euphrates rivers in Iraq. Although its climate is relatively dry, the area supports high population density because the rivers provide abundant water for irrigating crops.

Southwest Asia has metropolises, such as Istanbul, Damascus, Tehran, and Baghdad, that are home to millions of people. Gleaming modern cities, such as Dubai, Abu Dhabi, and Riyadh, rise from the sands of oil-rich Persian Gulf countries. Tel Aviv, Israel's largest city after Jerusalem, is a thriving urban center. These cities stand in sharp contrast to ancient rural villages that seem untouched by the passing of time. In some of the region's desert areas, nomads, known as Bedouins, sleep in tents and raise herds of camels, sheep, goats, and cattle.

V

W

At a height of more than 2,700 feet (823 m), the Burj Khalifa (left) is the tallest building in the world. The building is located in Dubai, United Arab Emirates. (right) Adobe storage buildings stand along Al-Assad Lake, a reservoir on the Euphrates River in Syria. A network of canals carries water from the lake to irrigate land on both sides of the Euphrates.

✔ READING PROGRESS CHECK

Citing Text Evidence Why do some countries around the Persian Gulf have rapidly growing populations?

Chapter 8 **241**

V Visual Skills

Creating Graphs Have students work in small groups to create a bar or line graph based on information in the text about population distribution and density in Southwest Asia. Students should organize locations or regions and their populations to visually integrate the information from the text. Suggest that students enhance their graphs by using the CIA World Factbook Web site (https://www.cia.gov/library/publications/the-world-factbook/) to research recent population figures in countries discussed in the text. Have students present their graphs to the class. **Logical/Mathematical, Visual/Spatial**

W Writing Skills

Informative/Explanatory Help students understand the sharp contrast between the thriving modern cities and the sparsely populated rural villages in Southwest Asia. Organize students into small groups and assign each group one of the cities discussed in the text.

In class, have groups assign different aspects of city life to each member, suggesting topics such as culture, commerce, education, transportation, and lifestyle. As homework, have group members research their assigned topic and write an informative paragraph about what they learned. Then have students compile their findings as a group in class. Conduct a "City Seminar" in which group members present their paragraphs. Students' paragraphs should reflect an understanding of their assigned topic and city.

After students present their paragraphs, guide a class discussion about the different lifestyles people have in cities with those who live in rural communities. **Ask: What are some advantages and disadvantages of living in a large city?** *(Students' answers will vary but might mention that large cities offer more employment opportunities, better transportation, and more cultural offerings. Disadvantages include that cities may be overcrowded and may face issues such as crime and pollution.)* **Verbal/Linguistic, Interpersonal**

MAP

Population: Southwest Asia

Making Connections Have students study the population layer on the Chapter Opener map with a partner to discuss the population distribution and density of each region. Guide students to understand why some areas are more densely populated than others, citing examples from the text and the map. Have students make connections between where people settle and the locations of landforms and bodies of water.

AL **Logical/Mathematical**

See page 223E for other online activities.

ANSWER, p. 241

✔ READING PROGRESS CHECK Their growing economies are attracting large numbers of workers from other countries.

Life in Southwest Asia

V Visual Skills

Creating Charts Help students comprehend the information about ethnic groups by having them organize the information in a chart as shown below.

Group	Countries
Arabs	Saudi Arabia, Syria, Jordan, others
Turks	Turkey
Persians	Iran
Jews	Israel
Kurds	Turkey, Iran, Iraq (Kurdistan)

After students have completed their charts, **ask: How does this demonstrate that Southwest Asia is a "crossroads of humanity"?** *(The region holds many different people from various ethnic groups who speak different languages.)* **Visual/Spatial**

C Critical Thinking Skills

Predicting Consequences Have students consider the consequences of so many different ethnic groups living across Southwest Asia. **Ask: What could be positive and negative consequences of many different cultural groups living in the same region?** *(Students' answers will vary, but students may say that a positive consequence could be the sharing of different cultures and ideas; a negative consequence could be that different beliefs and religions across Southwest Asia could cause conflict.)* **Interpersonal**

R Reading Skills

Determining Word Meanings Have students locate the academic vocabulary word *widespread* and write it on the board. Ask a volunteer to guess what the word means based on how the word sounds and how it is used in the sentence. Then have students use a dictionary to find the word's definition. Have students practice using the word in sentences of their own. Provide corrective feedback and additional sample sentences as needed, to clarify both the word's meaning and usage. **AL** **Verbal/Linguistic**

ANSWER, p. 242

MAP SKILLS
1. Semitic languages
2. Indo-European and Turkic language

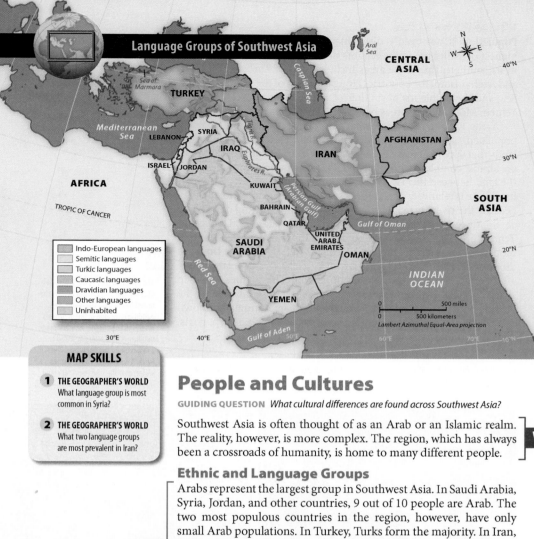

Language Groups of Southwest Asia

- Indo-European languages
- Semitic languages
- Turkic languages
- Caucasic languages
- Dravidian languages
- Other languages
- Uninhabited

MAP SKILLS

1 **THE GEOGRAPHER'S WORLD** What language group is most common in Syria?

2 **THE GEOGRAPHER'S WORLD** What two language groups are most prevalent in Iran?

Academic Vocabulary

widespread spread out

People and Cultures

GUIDING QUESTION *What cultural differences are found across Southwest Asia?*

Southwest Asia is often thought of as an Arab or an Islamic realm. The reality, however, is more complex. The region, which has always been a crossroads of humanity, is home to many different people. **V**

Ethnic and Language Groups

Arabs represent the largest group in Southwest Asia. In Saudi Arabia, Syria, Jordan, and other countries, 9 out of 10 people are Arab. The two most populous countries in the region, however, have only small Arab populations. In Turkey, Turks form the majority. In Iran, which once was the historical region called Persia, most people are Persian.

In Israel, which was founded as a Jewish state, Jews account for about three-fourths of the population. Kurds, who have no country of their own, represent significant minorities in Turkey, Iran, and Iraq. The region they inhabit is traditionally known as Kurdistan.

Arabic, spoken by Arabs, is the most **widespread** language in Southwest Asia. Other important languages include Turkish and Farsi, the language of Persians. Hebrew is the official language of Israel, and Kurdish is spoken by Kurds. **R**

242 Chapter 8

---

netw⊙rks   *Online Teaching Options*

CHART

English Words with Roots in Languages of Southwest Asia

Analyzing Information In a class discussion, use the chart of American words that originate from Arabic, Hebrew, and Farsi to analyze how language has spread and changed around the world. Discuss the concept of assimilation as it relates to the spread of languages. Have students consider how the spread of languages has impacted communication among different groups of people in Southwest Asia and other parts of the world. **ELL** **Verbal/Linguistic**

See page 223E for other online activities.

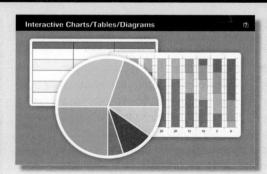

Interactive Charts/Tables/Diagrams

Some of the region's countries have complex ethnic and linguistic makeups. Afghanistan, for example, is home to Pashtuns, Tajiks, Hazaras, Uzbeks, Aimaks, Turkmen, and Balochs. In addition to the official languages of Afghanistan—Pashto and Afghan Persian—the Afghani people speak Uzbek and more than 30 other languages.

The presence of so many ethnic and language groups in one country presents a challenge to national unity. Many people in Southwest Asia identify with their ethnic group more strongly than with the country they live in. This is clearly evident in countries such as Afghanistan, where people identify themselves as Pashtun or Hazari rather than as Afghani. Even in countries that are mostly Arab, such as Syria and Iraq, people identify with tribes that are based on family relationships. Tribal identity is often stronger than national identity.

Religion and the Arts

From its birthplace in the cities of the Arabian Peninsula, Islam spread across Southwest Asia some 1,300 years ago. It remains the region's dominant religion, helping to unite people of different ethnicity and languages. It is practiced by Arabs, Turks, Persians, Kurds, and many other groups.

Islam has two main branches, Sunni and Shia. Most of Southwest Asia's Muslims are Sunnis. In Iran, however, Shias—Muslims of the Shia branch—outnumber Sunnis nine to one.

Judaism is practiced by about three-fourths of the people in Israel. Christians represent about 40 percent of the population in Lebanon and 10 percent in Syria.

An Iranian woman copies the tile design on a wall at a mosque in Eşfahān, Iran. Islam discourages showing living figures in religious art, so Muslim artists often work in colorful geometric patterns, floral designs, and calligraphy. Passages from the Quran decorate the walls of many mosques.

▶ CRITICAL THINKING
Analyzing Why would Muslim artists use passages from the Quran in calligraphy?

©Jose Fuste Raga/Corbis

Chapter 8 **243**

SLIDE SHOW

Art of Southwest Asia

Discussing Have students take notes as they view the slide show about art in Southwest Asia. Instruct the students to make detailed notes describing the images shown in the slide show and how that particular piece of art connects to the culture of Southwest Asia. Guide a class discussion about the importance of art in different societies and what it can reveal about different cultures. **Intrapersonal, Interpersonal**

See page 223E for other online activities.

Slide Show

T1 **Technology Skills**

Collaborating Organize students into small groups and assign them one of the ethnic groups from Afghanistan mentioned in the text. Tell students to research the ethnic group and give an oral report to the class. Students' reports should answer the following questions:

- **In what region of Afghanistan is this group primarily concentrated?**
- **What is the main language?**
- **What are some unique features about this ethnic group, such as clothing, food, and music?**

Encourage students to enhance their oral reports with graphics, maps, and audio clips to clarify information. **Verbal/ Linguistic, Auditory/Musical**

T2

C **Critical Thinking Skills**

Making Inferences Ask students to consider the types of challenges having so many different ethnic and language groups in the region might present. **Ask:** What sort of problems might occur as a result of people identifying with their own ethnic group instead of the country in which they live? *(Possible response: Since people are not united by national identity, there may be more tension and conflict between different groups.)* **Interpersonal**

T2 **Technology Skills**

Evaluating a Web Site Draw students' attention to the image on this page and read aloud the caption. Ask students to consider why Islam discourages showing living figures in religious art. Explain that it is a belief in the Islam religion that crafting living forms is exclusive only to God, or "Allah" in Arabic.

For homework, have students go on a "virtual museum visit" by visiting the Metropolitan Museum of Art's online Islamic art exhibit. Direct students to the following Web site: http://www.metmuseum.org/toah/hd/figs/hd_figs.htm. Tell students to view the slide show of Islamic art displayed on the museum's Web site and read the information about "figural representation" in Islamic art. Have students write a paragraph that answers the following question: **How does art reflect cultural values and traditions?** Have students present their findings, using copies of images to clarify information. **BL** **Verbal/Linguistic**

ANSWER, p. 243

CRITICAL THINKING Muslims revere the Quran as their holy book and turn to its passages for inspiration.

T Technology Skills

Collaborating Organize students into seven groups and assign them one of Southwest Asia's cultural aspects: *art/architecture, calligraphy, mosaics, weaving, storytelling/poetry/literature, film/stage,* and *music/dance.* Have groups research their assigned topic to make a presentation for a "cultural fair." Tell students to explain the history of their assigned cultural facet and its significance in Southwest Asian society or religion.

After students have had time to conduct research and take notes about their topic, have them present a summary of their findings to the class. Encourage students to include multimedia components in their presentations, such as images and music, to clarify information. **Auditory/Musical, Interpersonal**

W Writing Skills

Informative/Explanatory Tell students that *The Thousand and One Nights* is a collection of stories, including some that students may be familiar with. Assign students to read one of the stories and write a summary of the story. If students have heard the story before, ask them to compare and contrast the different versions. *(The stories are available for free online at www.bartleby.com.)* **Verbal/Linguistic**

V Visual Skills

Drawing Guide a class discussion about daily life across Southwest Asia. Have students create a visual representation of information about the different livelihoods discussed in the text. Students may wish to create a poster or multimedia display depicting one or more of the ways people earn a living in Southwest Asia. As a challenge, encourage students to create a map showing where certain livelihoods are practiced. Have them create a key with icons that illustrate where certain industries are prevalent. For example, students might draw an oil well to represent petroleum production. **BL** **Visual/Spatial**

A family in Iraq eats a pre-dawn meal before fasting on the second day of the Muslim holy month of Ramadan. Muslims believe that fasting will help people focus on God and on living better lives. According to the Quran, Muhammad first received teachings from God during the month of Ramadan.
▶ **CRITICAL THINKING**
Describing How does religion affect daily life in Southwest Asia?

T Religion and art have been closely tied in Southwest Asia throughout history. Some of the region's most magnificent works of architecture are mosques, temples, and other religious structures. Sacred texts such as the Hebrew and Christian Bibles and Islam's Quran stand as works of literature as well as guides to their followers.

The region also has other rich artistic traditions, including calligraphy, mosaics, weaving, storytelling, and poetry. Colorful, handwoven carpets from Persia, or present-day Iran, have been famous for centuries, as has the collection of folktales known as *The Thousand and One Nights.* **W**

Daily Life

Across Southwest Asia, daily life varies greatly. Some people live in cities, some live in villages, and a few live as nomads. Throughout the region's history, most people practiced traditional livelihoods such as farming, raising livestock, or fishing. In recent times, more people have been leaving the land to work in petroleum production, food processing, auto manufacturing, textiles, and construction. **V**

Religion plays a central role in the daily lives of many people in Southwest Asia. Islam is a complete way of life, with rules regarding diet, hygiene, relationships, business, law, and more. To Muslims, families are the foundation of a healthy society; maintaining family ties is an important duty.

©ATEF HASSAN/Reuters/Corbis

244 Chapter 8

---

networks   *Online Teaching Options*

IMAGE

Foods of Ramadan

Comparing and Contrasting Use the interactive image about the different foods that are served during Ramadan to help students understand the significance of how, why, and when they are served. Guide a discussion about similarities and differences of various holiday traditions and foods observed in different religions. Encourage students to create charts or graphic organizers to record the similarities and differences discussed. **AL** **Verbal/Linguistic**

See page 223E for other online activities.

Interactive Photos

© Image Source/Getty Images

ANSWER, p. 244

CRITICAL THINKING Religion influences daily life because it guides people's decisions about relationships, the foods they eat, the way they dress, and even how they conduct business.

Ramadan, the ninth month of the Muslim calendar, is a holy month of fasting. Between dawn and dusk, Muslims are obligated to refrain from eating and drinking. After ending their fast with prayer each evening, people enjoy festive meals. The end of Ramadan is marked by a three-day celebration called *Eid al-Fitr*, which translates as Festival of Breaking Fast. **R**

✓ **READING PROGRESS CHECK**

Identifying What is the major ethnic group in Iran, and what language does that group speak?

Issues

GUIDING QUESTION *How have oil wealth and availability of natural resources created challenges for countries of Southwest Asia?*

The period since World War II has brought a great deal of change and conflict to Southwest Asia. Looking to the future, the region faces many difficult issues. Some of them relate to resources and others to ethnic, religious, and cultural divisions. Some are new, and others are rooted in the distant past.

Oil Dependency and Control

The discovery in the mid-1900s of vast petroleum deposits in Southwest Asia had a strong impact on the region. Exports of petroleum products have brought great wealth to countries around the Persian Gulf, where the largest deposits are found. With this wealth came modernization in some countries. In other countries, little has changed, especially for the average person.

C Petroleum has brought new challenges. Many people living in modern cities in oil-producing countries grew up living in tents and practicing traditional farming and herding. Some Muslims believe that increased exposure to Western ways is corrupting the region's people. Another issue is the growing gap between rich and poor countries. Qatar and Kuwait, for example, rank among the wealthiest countries in the world; Afghanistan ranks among the poorest. The struggle to control oil has led to tension and wars. It has also resulted in increased intervention in Southwest Asia by foreign powers.

©Peter Turnley/Corbis

In 1991 U.S.-led forces pushed Iraqi invaders out of Kuwait. As Iraqi troops left, they set fire to more than 600 oil wells. Tons of thick oil smoke filled the air, and unburned oil spilled into the Persian Gulf. This environmental disaster took place in the area around Kuwait. The air and the soil were polluted, and animal and sea life were destroyed.

Chapter 8 **245**

VIDEO

Burning Oil in Kuwait

Recognizing Relationships After students have viewed the video of the burning oil field in Kuwait, discuss the influence of this resource on global economies. Then have students write a paragraph about the influence this valuable resource has on interactions between this region and the rest of the world. **BL** Logical/Mathematical, Interpersonal

See page 223E for other online activities.

R Reading Skills

Determining Word Meanings Draw students' attention to the last sentence of the first paragraph and the term "Festival of Breaking Fast." **Ask: What word can you think of that sounds like this phrase?** *(breakfast)*

Explain that the word *fast* has different meanings. Have students look up the word in a dictionary and identify its different meanings and parts of speech. To ensure comprehension, review what adjectives are and have students write a sentence using the word as an adjective. *(Sample response: The word* fast *can mean "quick or speedy" as in "She is a fast runner." It can also mean "stuck or tight" as in "The dog held the ball fast in his mouth." It also means "loyal or true" as in "They became fast friends.")*

Clarify for students that in the phrase *breaking fast*, the word *fast* is used as a noun, meaning "a period or practice of not eating food." Tell students that the word can also be used as a verb meaning "to refrain from eating food." Tell students that many different religions endorse fasting for different reasons, such as Ramadan in the Muslim faith, Yom Kippur in the Jewish faith, or Lent in the Christian faith. **ELL AL** Verbal/Linguistic

C Critical Thinking Skills

Identifying Problems Have students consider the challenges faced by people in different regions as a result of petroleum production as volunteers read aloud the first two paragraphs of this section. Discuss the transition people in the Persian Gulf have made in recent years as a result of this valuable, non-renewable resource. **Ask:**

- **What are some issues that people living in cities might face as a result of rapid modernization?** *(Possible answer: People who were accustomed to living in tents as farmers would probably have a difficult time adjusting to the new, more modern way of life. They might feel their traditional culture could be threatened by increased exposure to more Western ways of life.)*

- **How might petroleum production cause a rift between certain segments of the population?** *(Possible answer: While some people grow wealthy in oil-rich regions like the Persian Gulf, others, such as in Afghanistan, remain poor.)* **AL** Verbal/Linguistic

---

ANSWER, p. 245

✓ **READING PROGRESS CHECK** Persians are Iran's major ethnic group. Farsi is the dominant language.

Because of irrigation, farming is possible in some dry areas of Saudi Arabia. This wheat farm in Saudi Arabia's Nejd region is supported by center-pivot irrigation. This method involves a long pipe of sprinklers that moves in a circle around a deep well that supplies the water.

▶ **CRITICAL THINKING**
Determining Central Ideas Why is fossil water valuable to Saudi Arabia?

R | Reading Skills

Using Context Clues Help students comprehend the significance of oil dependency by having them use context clues in the text to determine word meanings. **Ask:**

- **What does it mean to be** *dependent* **on something?** *(It means to rely on it, or count on it.)*
- **What would it look like when a country would "thrive" due to higher oil prices?** *(The country's economy would grow. More people would have jobs. More people would be able to buy and sell the things they need and want.)*
- **What does it mean when a resource is not** *renewable*? *(It means that it cannot be renewed or restored. Once it is gone, it cannot be replaced.)*
- **What does it mean when something is** *depleted*? *(It means that it is used up.)* **AL Verbal/Linguistic**

T | Technology Skills

Analyzing News Media Review the information in the text about the Arab Spring. Guide a class discussion about the turmoil that resulted in various regions as a result of pro-democracy protests. Assign the following activity for homework:

Have students conduct online research to find information about the Arab Spring and how it started. In their research, students should identify and analyze how social media contributed to the uprising. Tell students to locate and analyze an article from a United States-based news organization, such as *The New York Times, The Washington Post,* or CNN, and an article from a news organization based in Southwest Asia, such as Al Jazeera.

Direct students to assess how the events of the Arab Spring were reported by the media. Have students note any articles they found that presented conflicting or inaccurate information and if any information appeared biased. Tell students to compile their findings in an essay, describing the events, their outcome, and how the information was presented by different news media. Have students also find out if any of the governments worked to stop the flow of information (or change/control the information) that people were getting. Ask volunteers to present their findings to the class. **BL Logical/Mathematical**

Oil dependency is also an issue. Exporting countries thrive when oil commands high prices, but they suffer when worldwide prices drop. Further, oil is not a renewable resource, and the countries have already depleted some of their reserves. To lessen their dependency on oil, exporting countries have invested money in other industries. Countries that import oil are investigating alternatives to oil.

R

Changing Governments

More than six decades after it began, the Arab-Israeli conflict continues as one of the biggest issues facing Southwest Asia. At the heart of the conflict are the Gaza Strip and West Bank territories, which Israel captured in 1967. Eruptions of violence have hampered progress toward a peaceful solution.

T The years 2010 and 2011 marked the beginning of the Arab Spring, a wave of pro-democracy protests and uprisings in North Africa and Southwest Asia. Protests against authoritarian rulers broke out in Tunisia, Egypt, Libya, Yemen, Bahrain, Syria, Jordan, and Oman in early 2011.

By the end of the year, leaders in Tunisia, Egypt, Libya, and Yemen were overthrown. Protests in Bahrain were quashed by security forces, but the government later agreed to implement reforms. Syria fell into upheaval when the government used armed force to stop protests. More peaceful reform efforts are underway in Jordan and Oman.

Ray Ellis/Photo Researchers

246 *Chapter 8*

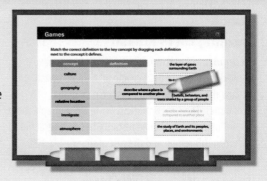

netw✪rks   *Online Teaching Options*

GAME

Life in Southwest Asia

Identifying Use the drag-and-drop game to reinforce the content of this lesson. After students have taken turns dragging the correct responses to fill in the blanks, divide the class into six groups and assign each group a number from one to six. Ask each group to write an additional "fill-in the-blank" statement that supplements or expands upon the information in the numbered statement corresponding to their group number. **AL Kinesthetic, Visual/Spatial**

See page 223E for other online activities.

ANSWER, p. 246

CRITICAL THINKING Saudi Arabia has no rivers that flow year-round. Fossil water, trapped thousands of years ago below ground, can be pumped to the surface and used to turn areas of barren desert into farmland.

Water Concerns

Scarcity of freshwater has plagued Southwest Asia throughout history. Dramatic population growth has produced greater demand for this precious resource, making the situation more dire and increasing the importance of **hydropolitics**, or politics related to water usage and access.

Water from the saltwater seas that surround Southwest Asia can be made into freshwater through desalination, or the removal of salt. Unfortunately, this process is expensive and therefore not practical for meeting the region's water needs.

Saudi Arabia, which has no rivers that flow year-round, has tapped into **fossil water**. This term refers to water that fell as rain thousands of years ago, when the region's climate was wetter, and is now trapped between rock layers deep below ground. By pumping the water to the surface for irrigation, Saudi Arabia has transformed areas of barren desert into productive farmland. Fossil water is not a renewable resource, however, and the underground reservoirs could soon run dry.

The region's greatest source of freshwater is the Tigris-Euphrates river system. From their sources in the mountains of eastern Turkey, the Tigris and Euphrates rivers flow southeastward through the desert plains of Syria and Iraq.

The three countries depend heavily on the rivers and their tributaries. In recent decades, all have built dams to control flooding, to generate electricity, and to capture water for irrigation. Syria and Iraq, which are downstream from Turkey, have bitterly opposed an ambitious, decades-long dam-building project in Turkey that threatens to reduce river flow.

☑ READING PROGRESS CHECK

Describing What was the Arab Spring? What countries in Southwest Asia were involved?

FOLDABLES
Study Organizer

Include this lesson's information in your Foldable®.

LESSON 3 REVIEW (CCSS)

Reviewing Vocabulary (Tier Three Words)
1. What is *fossil water*? RH.6-8.4

Answering the Guiding Questions
2. ***Identifying*** What are Southwest Asia's two most populous countries, and approximately how many people live in each country? RH.6-8.2
3. ***Determining Word Meanings*** What is hydropolitics? RH.6-8.4
4. ***Analyzing*** How might dams built on the Tigris and Euphrates rivers in Turkey affect agriculture in Syria and Iraq? RH.6-8.1
5. ***Identifying*** What are the two main branches of Islam, and to which branch do most Muslims in Southwest Asia belong? RH.6-8.2

6. ***Identifying Point of View*** How might Persian Gulf countries be affected if oil-importing countries begin turning to alternate energy sources? RH.6-8.6
7. ***Describing*** Who are the Bedouin? RH.6-8.4
8. ***Narrative Writing*** Imagine that have you spent your whole life in a poor village somewhere in Southwest Asia. Then, one day you visit Dubai, a bustling, modern city of skyscrapers and shopping malls. Write a letter to a friend or a family member back in your village describing your experience in Dubai. WHST.6-8.4, WHST.6-8.10

Chapter 8 **247**

LESSON 3 REVIEW ANSWERS

Reviewing Vocabulary

1. This is water that fell as rain thousands of years ago and is trapped deep underground. Saudi Arabia uses this to irrigate desert lands for farming.

Answering the Guiding Questions

2. **Identifying** The region's two most populous countries are Turkey and Iraq. They each have a population of around 80 million people.

3. **Determining Word Meanings** politics related to water access and usage

4. **Analyzing** Syria and Iraq are located downstream from Turkey. If the dams reduce the flow of the rivers, Syria and Iraq will have less water for irrigation.

5. **Identifying** The two main branches are Sunni and Shia. Most Southwest Asia Muslims belong to the Sunni branch.

6. **Identifying Point of View** Greater use of alternate energy sources could cause a drop in oil exports. A drop would hurt the economies of the oil-exporting Persian Gulf countries.

7. **Describing** The Bedouin are nomadic people who live in desert areas of Southwest Asia and raise animals.

8. **Narrative Writing** Student letters should provide information about Dubai, along with interesting and accurate descriptions based on evidence in the text.

Ⅴ Visual Skills

Creating Visuals Help students organize information in the text about fossil water to comprehend the process. Have students work in pairs to create a diagram or other visual that explains the process of extracting fossil water. Have students share their diagrams with the class. **Ask:**

- **What is a potentially negative impact from tapping into fossil water?** *(Fossil water is not renewable, so the underground reservoirs could run dry.)*
- **What are some of the problems that will arise if the underground reservoirs run dry?** *(The farms will not be able to produce food for the people of the country. The people working the farms will need to find a new way of life. The country will need to import a much greater portion of the food that is needed to feed the people. This will change the way the country depends on other nations, creating a different type of interdependent relationship with other nations.)* **Visual/Spatial**

C Critical Thinking Skills

Finding the Main Idea Ask students to consider the challenges faced by regions in Southwest Asia that are reliant on freshwater sources. **Ask:**

- **Which countries in Southwest Asia are the most heavily dependent on the Tigris-Euphrates river system?** *(Turkey, Syria, and Iraq)*
- **Why have these countries built dams in recent decades?** *(to control flooding, to generate electricity, and to capture water for irrigation)*
- **Why have Syria and Iraq opposed a major dam-building project in Turkey?** *(Syria and Iraq are both downstream from Turkey, so a dam would threaten the flow of water from the river to their countries.)* **Verbal/Linguistic**

CLOSE & REFLECT

To close the lesson, have students work in pairs to create a three-column chart labeled with the headings *Culture, Oil,* and *Water.* As a lesson review, have students complete the chart with information from the lesson. Then guide a class discussion about the issues related to cultural differences and natural resources across Southwest Asia.

ANSWER, p. 247

☑ READING PROGRESS CHECK protests against authoritarian rule; Tunisia, Libya, Yemen, Bahrain, Syria, Jordan, and Oman

ENGAGE

🔔 **Bellringer** Before students read the What Do You Think? feature, make sure they understand the concept of sanctions. Explain that sanctions, or trade restrictions, are often used as a tool of foreign policy. Put the concept into terms students can understand by drawing parallels between sanctions and restrictions that parents may impose on their children. For example, ask students how they would be impacted if their parents took their cell phones away until they spent each night doing homework. Ask students to consider how imposing sanctions on countries might impact their actions, except on a much larger scale. Tell students that this feature presents two views on the issue of sanctions and their use and effectiveness at changing government policies.

TEACH & ASSESS

R Reading Skills

Determining Word Meanings Have students read the introductory paragraph and the *Yes!* viewpoint. Help students understand the consequences of sanctions by explaining the meaning of trade restrictions. Have students look up the word *restriction* in the dictionary. **Ask:**

- What does it mean to *restrict* something or someone? *(to control or limit)*
- What example can you think of in which a country might want to control or limit actions by another country? Give an example. *(Student answers will vary but should include that a country might want to control or limit actions by another country if it wants that country to do or not do something. For example, if a country is involved in a civil war, and innocent people are getting killed, other countries might place restrictions on that country, demanding it stop fighting and change its policies.)* **AL** **Verbal/Linguistic**

C Critical Thinking Skills

Analyzing Primary Sources/Identifying Points of View Have students turn to a partner and paraphrase the first sentence under the *Yes!* paragraph in their own words. **Ask:** Based on this statement, what is the author's opinion about sanctions? *(Sample response: The author thinks sanctions are a good idea. He thinks they can help change policies and help divide the cost of sanctions among cooperating countries against countries that are uncooperative.)* **Verbal/Linguistic**

What Do You Think? CCSS

Are Trade Restrictions Effective at Changing a Government's Policies?

R Sometimes, one country restricts trade with another country as a way to force it to change its policies. For example, if the U.S. government wants a country to give its citizens more democratic rights, it might not allow that country to sell goods in the United States. Although the U.S. government often applies trade restrictions on countries, opinions differ about their effectiveness.

Yes !

PRIMARY SOURCE

C " Sanctions aimed at achieving major policy objectives have the strongest chance of success if applied by a multilateral coalition [many countries]; it helps that the multilateral approach also shares the cost.... Smart sanctions have their use in tightening the screws on a recalcitrant [stubborn] or defiant [openly disobedient] regime [government] without inflicting collateral [additional] damage on the population.... And even when sanctions don't achieve stated objectives, they nonetheless signal resolve [determination], and may in fact be essential to prepare the political ground at home and abroad for military action against the target. "

—Gordon Kaplan, "Making Economic Sanctions Work"

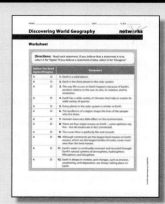

248 Chapter 8

TEXT: from "Making Economic Sanctions Work" © 2010 by Gordon Kaplan. Published by UT San Diego, August 20, 2010; PHOTO: (t) Justin Guariglia/Corbis; (b) ©Monty Rakusen/cultura/Corbis

---

networks *Online Teaching Options*

WORKSHEET

Discovering World Geography networks

Worksheet

How to Analyze a Primary Source

Distinguishing Fact from Opinion Have student pairs use this worksheet to analyze and critique the opinion stated by each writer. Instruct students to review each primary source by first noting all the facts stated, and then all the opinions. Tell students to note which opinions are supported by evidence. Have students collaborate to draw conclusions about the effectiveness of each document. **BL** **Verbal/Linguistic**

Rows of cargo containers await shipment at Singapore, a city-state in Southeast Asia. Singapore depends on international trade for its survival. Its port is one of the busiest cargo shipping centers in the world.

C Critical Thinking Skills

Analyzing Visuals Have students look at the photograph of cargo containers in Singapore. Guide students to view the photograph with respect to how many different jobs are being shown. For example, people drive the trucks, operate the forklifts, and so on. **Ask: How might sanctions impact businesses and their employees in Singapore?** *(Student answers will vary but should include that a port city like Singapore, which is reliant on international trade, would be negatively impacted by sanctions, even on other countries, because it would mean fewer goods would be exported to those countries.)* **Visual/Spatial**

C

W Writing Skills

Argument Have students imagine they are either a leader of a country that wants to impose sanctions on another country, or the leader of a country that does not want to comply with sanctions imposed by another country. Have students write a speech for a television address by the leader to citizens of that country explaining his or her opinion. Tell students in writing their arguments to provide valid reasons each leader might use for having the stated opinion about sanctions. *(Students' speeches should show an understanding of why leaders might have strong opinions about either the restrictions and economic hardships that sanctions might cause, or the effectiveness their implementation might cause.)* **Intrapersonal, Verbal/Linguistic**

No!

PRIMARY SOURCE

" Imposing sanctions…are not only an act of war according to international law, they are most often the first step toward a real war starting with a bombing campaign. We should be using diplomacy rather than threats and hostility. Nothing promotes peace better than free trade. Countries that trade with each other generally do not make war on each other, as both countries gain economic benefits they do not want to jeopardize. Also, trade and friendship applies much more effective persuasion to encourage better behavior, as does leading by example. "

—Ron Paul, "The Folly of Sanctions"

A port security worker checks cargo at a warehouse in London, England. Ships from all over the world pass through major international ports, such as London.

What Do You Think? DBQ

1. **Identifying Point of View** According to Kaplan, why are sanctions effective even if they do not achieve their objectives?
RH.6-8.6, RH.6-8.10

2. **Identifying Point of View** Why does Paul think that free trade is better than economic sanctions for promoting peace?
RH.6-8.6, RH.6-8.10

3. **Analyzing** Who do you think makes the stronger argument, Kaplan or Paul?
RH.6-8.1, RH.6-8.8

Chapter 8 **249**

CLOSE & REFLECT

Have students choose one of the primary sources and write a paragraph explaining why they agree or disagree with the writer's opinion. Encourage students to consider the impact of the sanctions on the country's private citizens as well as on the country's leadership. Tell students to cite specific evidence they find compelling or that they feel can be refuted. **Intrapersonal, Interpersonal**

WORKSHEET

Making an Outline

Determining Cause and Effect Have students work in pairs to outline each excerpt using the worksheet. Ask students to work together to find the main idea and supporting statements for each excerpt. Then, have student pairs use the outline to either write a paragraph summarizing the viewpoints or to write their own viewpoint based on their opinion, using the outline to compare and contrast their ideas to the original excerpts. **ELL** **Interpersonal, Intrapersonal**

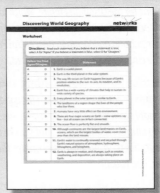

ANSWERS, p. 249

DBQ What Do You **Think?**

1. Sanctions prepare people for the possibility that military action will be used against a stubborn or disobedient government.

2. Paul believes that countries that trade with each other will not go to war because they do not want to jeopardize losing the economic benefits they enjoy.

3. Student answers will vary, but should clearly explain what makes the given argument stronger.

CHAPTER REVIEW ACTIVITY

Have students create a four-column chart like the one below with the headings *Physical Geography, Resources, History and Culture*, and *Challenges/Conflicts*. Tell students to complete the chart for each category with key information and examples from the text. Direct students to explain how one topic, such as resources, might relate to another topic, such as challenges and conflicts. *(Students' answers should include key concepts discussed in each of the three lessons in the chapter, such as **Physical Geography:** Mountains and plateaus dominate the region including the Hindu Kush range. The Mediterranean, Black, and Red seas shape the region. Other water is scarce and the Arabian Desert covers nearly the entire Arabian Peninsula. **Resources:** oil and natural gas; minerals such as coal, phosphates, iron, copper, gold, cobalt, lithium. **History and Culture:** birthplace of three religions; Ottoman Empire reached its peak in 1500s; European influence after World War I; division of Palestine and creation of Israel. **Challenges/Conflicts:** conflicting ethnic groups have led to civil wars and terrorist attacks. The Arab League works to promote cooperation among countries. Students might mention that resources such as petroleum and water can cause conflicts in various regions due to dependency issues.)*

Southwest Asia			
Physical Geography	Resources	History and Culture	Challenges/Conflicts

REVIEW THE ENDURING UNDERSTANDINGS

Review this chapter's Enduring Understanding with students:

- *People, places, and ideas change over time.*

Now pose the following questions in a class discussion to apply this to this chapter.

- **How does petroleum have both a positive and negative impact on certain regions in Southwest Asia?** *(positive: The gaseous and liquid forms of petroleum can be produced for energy sources such as fuel and heating oil, and can be used to create products such as certain plastics. Revenues generated from petroleum exports have brought wealth to several regions in Southwest Asia; negative: The discovery of petroleum reserves has created tensions and conflicts in some regions.)*

- **How would you describe the Ottoman Empire in the 1800s and early 1900s?** *(This period marked a major decline for the Ottoman Empire, which lost African and European territories through wars, treaties, and revolutions. After fighting and losing to the Central Powers in World War I, the empire was eventually dissolved.)*

- **Describe the makeup of ethnic and language groups in Southwest Asia.** *(Though Southwest Asia is primarily considered an Arab region, the makeup of people and cultures is quite varied. Arabs make up the largest group, but there are also other groups that live in Turkey, Iran, and Israel.)*

Chapter 8 ACTIVITIES

Directions: Write your answers on a separate piece of paper.

1. Use your **FOLDABLES** to explore the Essential Question.
   INFORMATIVE/EXPLANATORY WRITING Choose one of the countries in this region and learn about its natural resources. Then write an essay to answer: Is the country using its resources wisely? WHST.6-8.2, WHST.6-8.8

2. **21st Century Skills**
   INTEGRATING VISUAL INFORMATION Working in small groups, identify one problem facing the countries of Southwest Asia. Research its effects on the people of the region and offer possible solutions. Produce a slide show or build a visual display to share your findings. WHST.6-8.7, WHST.6-8.6

3. **Thinking Like a Geographer**
   IDENTIFYING Identify five countries of Southwest Asia. List the countries and their capital cities. Then write one interesting fact about each country. RH.6-8.2, WHST.6-8.9

4. **GEOGRAPHY ACTIVITY**

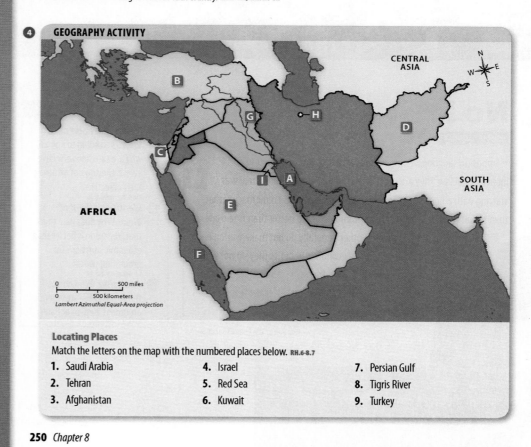

Locating Places
Match the letters on the map with the numbered places below. RH.6-8.7

1. Saudi Arabia
2. Tehran
3. Afghanistan
4. Israel
5. Red Sea
6. Kuwait
7. Persian Gulf
8. Tigris River
9. Turkey

ACTIVITIES ANSWERS

Exploring the Essential Question

1. **INFORMATIVE/EXPLANATORY WRITING** Students' work will vary, but should be well-researched, organized, and answer the questions. It should meet established standards for spelling and grammar.

21st Century Skills

2. **INTEGRATING VISUAL INFORMATION** Topics students might choose include the Palestinian-Israeli conflict; water shortages; revolutions; fighting over control of rich oil fields; ethnic rivalries; political and religious differences, the rise of religious fundamentalism; and terrorism.

REVIEW THE GUIDING QUESTIONS

Directions: Choose the best answer for each question.

1 Which scarce resource has most directly shaped Southwest Asia's history and settlement patterns? RH.6-8.2
A. rich soil
B. natural gas
C. water
D. forests

2 Southwest Asia's physical geography can be described as one of RH.6-8.1
F. high mountains.
G. extremes.
H. little variety.
I. sandy deserts.

3 How long ago did humans convert from living as hunter-gatherers to living in settlements and practicing agriculture? RH.6-8.2
A. a million years ago
B. 10,000 years ago
C. 50,000 years ago
D. 100,000 years ago

4 Which three major world religions originated in Southwest Asia? RH.6-8.2
F. Sikhism, Hinduism, Judaism
G. Christianity, Judaism, Hinduism
H. Islam, Judaism, Christianity
I. Judaism, Islam, Hinduism

5 What twentieth-century discovery brought great wealth to some countries in Southwest Asia? RH.6-8.2
A. the cell phone
B. vast petroleum deposits
C. gold
D. rubies and emeralds

6 The population of Southwest Asia is RH.6-8.1
F. growing rapidly.
G. declining.
H. aging.
I. leaving to find work in India.

Chapter 8 **251**

Students' work should reflect thoughtful research and fully explain the nature of the problem.

Thinking Like a Geographer

3 **IDENTIFYING** While the facts listed will vary, the countries and their capitals are: Afghanistan-Kabul; Bahrain-Manama; Iran-Tehran; Iraq-Baghdad; Israel-Tel Aviv; Jordan-Amman; Kuwait-Kuwait; Lebanon-Beirut; Oman-Muscat; Qatar-Doha; Saudi-Arabia-Riyadh; Syria-Damascus; Turkey-Ankara; United Arab Emirates-Abu Dhabi; and Yemen-Sana'a.

Geography Activity

3 **LOCATING PLACES**

1. E
2. H
3. D
4. C
5. F
6. I
7. A
8. G
9. B

ASSESSMENT ANSWERS
Review the Guiding Questions

1 **C** For this question, students should recall where people live based on climate and rainfall. Students may be confused by choice A, which relates to the agricultural societies that formed as a direct result of the fertile plain between the Tigris and Euphrates rivers. Refer students to Lesson 3 "People and Places" section for help.

2 **G** Students should be able to eliminate choice H immediately, as the text describes a variety of physical geography throughout Southwest Asia. Students should recall that regions in Southwest Asia have both high mountains (choice F) and sandy deserts (choice I). If students are having difficulty, have them reread the section "Southwest Asia's Physical Features" section in Lesson 1 for help.

3 **B** Students should recognize choice B as the correct answer based on information presented about nomadic hunter-gatherer societies shifting to agrarian communities. To help clarify the dramatic change during this time period, refer students to the section about Mesopotamia in Lesson 2.

4 **H** To answer this question, students need to recall the information about the birthplace of world religions in Lesson 2. While choices G and I may be confusing as they contain two correct choices, students should recall that Islam, Judaism, and Christianity are the three major religions that originated in Southwest Asia. Refer students to Lesson 2 to reread the "Birthplace of World Religions" section for further information.

5 **B** Students should be able to eliminate choice A immediately, as the text does not refer to cell phones as a 20th century discovery. Students should recognize choice B as the correct choice, as petroleum deposits and petroleum production are discussed throughout Lesson 3. Have students reread "Issues in Southwest Asia" in Lesson 3 for clarification.

6 **F** Students should recall information in Lesson 3 about the rapid population growth in various regions of Southwest Asia, particularly urban areas. Refer students to both the "Population Profile" and "Where People Live" sections to review population issues in Southwest Asia.

DBQ Analyzing Documents

7 A Biomedical equipment, like electronics, is a high-technology industry. Students should recognize that they may eliminate choices **B** and **C** because neither answer has to do with technology in the reading. Though tourism is referenced as an industry, it does not have anything to do with technology advancements. If students are having difficulty with the terminology in the passage, explain the meaning of each of the industry sectors listed.

8 H The most reasonable inference is that tourists stopped traveling to Israel out of concern for their safety due to the violence. If students have answered incorrectly, read aloud the last section of the passage, stressing the words *Prior to violence.* Reinforce that a concern for safety is an important factor to consider whenever traveling and that sometimes the United States government issues warning to travelers when there is a threat to people's safety.

Short Response

9 "Decline rates" mean the rate at which production of oil from existing wells goes down, or declines, from one year to the next. Remind students to look for context clues, or other words nearby, when trying to define a word or phrase in a sentence. In this passage, students should recognize the word *add* and the bracketed phrase *make up* demonstrate that production is behind or lower than needed.

10 Possible answer: The decline rates could be caused by the existing wells running out of oil or the oil in them becoming more difficult to reach using the existing technology.

Extended Response

11 Essays will vary in topic and perspective, but should all be well-organized, thoughtful, and well-written as well as meeting your standards for grammar and spelling. Students may touch on some of the following: discovery of vast petroleum deposits have brought wealth to some but have not alleviated poverty for many others; culture clashes brought on by modern versus traditional societies; fear of western influences; religious intolerance; religious extremism; political disagreements; territorial disputes; centuries old ethnic and territorial disputes.

Chapter 8 ASSESSMENT (continued)

DBQ ANALYZING DOCUMENTS

7 CITING TEXT EVIDENCE Read the following passage about Israel's economy:

"*Israel has a diversified, technologically advanced economy. . . . The major industrial sectors include high-technology electronic and biomedical equipment, metal products, processed foods, chemicals, and transport equipment. . . . Prior to the violence that began in September 2000, [Israel] was a major tourist destination.*"

—from U.S. State Department Background Notes, "Israel"

Which detail supports the idea that Israel's economy is technologically advanced? RH.6-8.2, RH.6-8.10

A. biomedical equipment industry

B. processed food industry

C. transport equipment industry

D. tourism industry

8 ANALYZING What inference can you draw about the decline of tourism to Israel after 2000? RH.6-8.1, RH.6-8.10

F. Economic hard times reduced tourism to all locations.

G. Other places became more fashionable as tourist destinations.

H. Tourism declined because people were worried about their safety.

I. Lower prices for air travel would revive tourism to Israel.

SHORT RESPONSE

"*One challenge the Saudis face in achieving their strategic vision to add production capacity is that their existing fields experience 6 to 8 percent annual 'decline rates' on average . . . , meaning that the country needs around 700,000 [billion barrels per day] in additional capacity each year just to [make up] for natural decline.*"

—from Energy Information Administration, *Saudi Arabia*

9 DETERMINING WORD MEANINGS Based on this passage, what do the "decline rates" refer to? RH.6-8.4, RH.6-8.10

10 ANALYZING What could cause these decline rates? RH.6-8.1, RH.6-8.10

EXTENDED RESPONSE

11 INFORMATIVE/EXPLANATORY WRITING Write an essay explaining why you think conflict in this part of the world since the end of World War II has increased so dramatically. Consider how conflict and wars in this part of the world affect you and your family. WHST.6-8.2, WHST.6-8.4

Need Extra Help?

If You've Missed Question	1	2	3	4	5	6	7	8	9	10	11
Review Lesson	1	1	2	2	3	3	3	3	1	1	2

---

networks *Online Teaching Options*

Evaluation and Assessment

Assessing Use eAssessment to create your own tests from hundreds of available questions. eAssessment helps you design assessments that meet the needs of different types of learners.

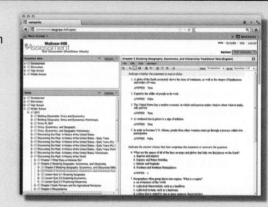

UNDERSTANDING BY DESIGN®

Enduring Understandings

- *People, places, and ideas change over time.*

Essential Questions

- *How do people adapt to their environment?*
- *How does religion shape society?*
- *Why do conflicts develop?*
- *Why do people trade?*
- *How does physical geography influence the way people live?*
- *How does technology change the way people live?*
- *Why do people make economic choices?*
- *How do new ideas change the way people live?*
- *What makes a culture unique?*

Students will know:

- *that Africa has a very diverse geography and how geography shaped the development of Africa's civilization.*
- *that Africa has an ancient history.*
- *how trade brought different cultures, languages, and religions to Africa.*
- *that the waterways in Africa have had a large impact on the development of civilizations in Africa.*
- *the main exports and imports of several African countries.*
- *present-day issues that affect Africans and other people throughout the world.*

Students will be able to:

- ***identify*** *how physical geography affected the locations of settlements in Africa.*
- ***describe*** *the various climates of Africa.*
- ***discuss*** *the value of the natural resources in various regions in Africa.*
- ***describe*** *colonization of Africa.*
- ***describe*** *people and cultures of Africa, including languages and religion.*
- ***describe*** *daily life in the region.*
- ***explore*** *issues that present challenges to the countries of Africa.*

Predictable Misunderstandings

- *The desert forms the majority of the landscape in North Africa.*
- *North Africa has a low population due to the landscape.*
- *The landscape of East Africa is the same as in North Africa.*
- *The culture, language, and religion of East Africa are the same as North Africa.*
- *The geography of Central Africa is affected by North Africa's geography.*
- *Resources of Central Africa have had no effect on the history of the region.*
- *West Africa shares similar geography to North and Central Africa.*

- *The region's history is relatively current.*
- *Southern Africa has limited resources that do not affect the economy of the region.*
- *Southern Africa has little impact on the global economy.*

Assessment Evidence

Performance Tasks:

- *Unit GeoLab Activity*
- *Environmental Case Study*

Other Evidence:

- *Physical Location GeoQuiz*
- *Political Location GeoQuiz*
- *City Location GeoQuiz*
- *Physical Geography Activity*
- *Cultural Geography Activity*
- *Geography and History Activity*
- *Geography and Economics Activity*
- *Reading Skills Activity*
- *Geography Skills Activity*
- *Critical Thinking Skills Activity*
- *Technology Skills Activity*
- *Writing Skills Activity*
- *Participation in Interactive Whiteboard Activities*
- *Analysis of graphic organizers, graphs, and charts*
- *Lesson Reviews*
- *Chapter Assessments*

Key for Using the Teacher Edition

SKILL-BASED ACTIVITIES

Types of skill activites found in the Teacher Edition.

* **V** **Visual Skills** require students to analyze maps, graphs, charts, and photos.

W **Writing Skills** provide writing opportunities to help students comprehend the text.

R **Reading Skills** help students practice reading skills and master vocabulary.

C **Critical Thinking Skills** help students apply and extend what they have learned.

T **Technology Skills** require students to use digital tools effectively.

*Letters are followed by a number when there is more than one of the same type of skill on the page.

DIFFERENTIATED INSTRUCTION

All activities are written for the on-level student unless otherwise marked with the leveled labels below.

BL Beyond Level

AL Approaching Level

ELL English Language Learners

All students benefit from activities that utilize different learning styles. Many activities are marked as below when a particular learning style is highlighted.

Intrapersonal	Naturalist
Logical/Mathematical	Kinesthetic
Visual/Spatial	Auditory/Musical
Verbal/Linguistic	Interpersonal

SUGGESTED PACING GUIDE

Introducing the Unit . . . . 3 Days
Chapter 9: North Africa . . . . 8 Days
Chapter 10: East Africa . . . . 8 Days
Chapter 11: Central Africa . . . . 8 Days
Chapter 12: West Africa . . . . 8 Days
Chapter 13: Southern Africa . . . . 8 Days
Global Connections . . . . 3 Days
What Do You Think? . . . . 3 Days

TOTAL TIME   49 Days

PLANNER

☑ *Print Teaching Options*

V Visual Skills

☐ **P. 255** Students discuss the shape, size, and location of Africa seen in the satellite image. **BL**

☐ **P. 256** Students analyze the features of a physical map of Africa, noting elevations. **AL**

☐ **P. 257** Students read a political map of Africa. **ELL** Visual/Spatial

☐ **P. 258** Students use a population density map to describe Africa's cities. **AL** Logical/Mathematical

☐ **P. 259** Students use the land use and resource map to discuss Africa's resources. **AL** Visual/Spatial

☐ **P. 260** Students use a climate map to discuss Africa's climates. **AL** Visual/Spatial

W Writing Skills

☐ **P. 260** Students write a short narrative imagining life in the deserts of Africa. **BL** Naturalist

R Reading Skills

☐ **P. 254** Students explain the text about Africa. **ELL**

☐ **P. 254** Students describe some of the challenges of attaining natural resources. **AL**

☐ **P. 255** Students determine central ideas about biomes of Africa. **AL** Verbal/Linguistic

C Critical Thinking Skills

☐ **P. 254** Students analyze how bodies of water affect life in Africa. Verbal/Linguistic

☐ **P. 255** Students evaluate economic ties of the United States and the countries of Africa.

☐ **P. 256** Students evaluate the importance of the Suez Canal to commerce. **BL**

☐ **P. 257** Students use a political map to reason why borders of countries formed. **BL**

☐ **P. 258** Students use a population density map to integrate visual information. **ELL** Logical/Mathematical

☐ **P. 259** Small groups use a resource map to discuss the relationships between resources and a region's wealth. **BL** Interpersonal

T Technology Skills

☐ **P. 258** Students search the Internet for recent news articles about political events and natural disasters of Africa. **BL**

☑ *Online Teaching Options*

V Visual Skills

☐ **MAP** **Physical Map: Africa**—Students identify areas of elevation and physical regions on a physical map. **AL** Kinesthetic

☐ **MAP** **Political Map: Africa**—Students use the political map to calculate the distances between locations on the map. **ELL** Kinesthetic, Logical/Mathematical

☐ **MAP** **Regional Map**—Students make connections between the images in the unit and their location on the interactive map. Visual/Spatial

☐ **MAP** **Climates Map: Africa**—Students work in groups to create wall murals describing a particular regional land use based on climate. **AL** Visual/Spatial

☐ **MAP** **Population Map: Africa**—Students can use the population layer on the Unit Opener map to review the population distribution and density.

W Writing Skills

☐ **MAP** **Resources Map: Africa**—Students discuss the resource map, and then do further research about specific resources found in a country of Africa. **ELL** Verbal/Linguistic

C Critical Thinking Skills

☐ **VIDEO** **Video Tour of Africa**—Students analyze information in a video montage highlighting Africa and create a list of interesting details about Africa. **AL** Visual/Spatial

T Technology Skills

☐ **GAME** **Political Boundaries: Africa Game**—Students play a drag-and-drop game to identify and place countries, cities, and islands of Africa. Kinesthetic

☑ *Printable Digital Worksheets*

☐ **WORKSHEETS** **Environmental Case Studies: Global Health**—Students read and learn about assessing the global health of a region and the planet. **BL**

☐ **QUIZ** **Physical Location GeoQuiz**—Use the Physical Location GeoQuiz as a pre- or post-assessment of students' knowledge of Africa's landforms and bodies of water.

☐ **QUIZ** **Political Location GeoQuiz**—Use the Political Location GeoQuiz as a pre- or post-assessment of students' knowledge of Africa's countries.

☐ **QUIZ** **City Location GeoQuiz**—Use the City Location GeoQuiz as a pre- or post-assessment of students' knowledge of Africa's major cities.

☐ **QUIZ** **Physical Geography Activity**—Students will analyze an elevation profile of the region.

☐ **QUIZ** **Cultural Geography Activity**—Students will read about the culture of the region and answer questions related to the excerpt.

AFRICA

UNIT **3**

Chapter 9	Chapter 10	Chapter 11	Chapter 12	Chapter 13
North Africa	East Africa	Central Africa	West Africa	Southern Africa

Thomas Marent/National Geographic Stock

Global Connections

The Global Connections issue for this unit gives students an opportunity to learn about the challenges faced by the people of Sudan. Students will read about the region's history and learn about the conflict in Darfur. Students also will consider the effects of conflicting religious beliefs on the political and economic stability of the region, and think about the impact of regional warfare on the people of Sudan and neighboring countries. Students will work independently and in small groups to present what they have learned.

AL Verbal/Linguistic

ENGAGE

Bellringer Direct students' attention to the Unit Opener image. Point out the contrasts between landscapes in your local region and the landscapes of Africa. **Ask:**

- What do you notice about the landscape? *(Possible answer: low grassy land, trees with thick trunks and few branches, and large puddles of water)*
- What type of climate might this region experience? *(Students may speculate that this is a hot, humid climate.)*
- What land use might dominate this region of Africa? *(Students may speculate from the oxen and wagon in the image that this region is dominated by simple agricultural practices.)*

Have students share their knowledge of Africa's landscapes, languages, and cultures. Guide them to understand that Africa is very large, and just as the United States has varying landscapes and climates, so does Africa. **Ask: What do you think is true about the landscapes, languages, and cultures found in Africa?** *(Student answers may vary, but students should speculate that great diversity is found in Africa among its people and land.)*

Making Connections Have students connect what they already know with the following facts on Africa.

- Africa is the second largest continent covering approximately 22% of Earth's total land area.
- It is comprised of 54 independent nations.
- It has a population of approximately one billion people, with half of the population under the age of 25.
- Both the Prime Meridian and Equator pass through Africa.
- More than 2,000 languages are spoken. Several dialects of Arabic combine to make it the most common language in Africa.
- Africa has more than 3,000 distinct ethnic groups.
- Lake Victoria is the second-largest freshwater lake in the world.
- The Nile River is the longest river in the world.
- The Sahara in northern Africa is the largest desert in the world.

Tell students they will be learning more about Africa's rich history and great cultural diversity. They will also learn about the economic and environmental challenges faced by the people of Africa. Unit Six highlights five regions in Africa: North Africa, East Africa, Central Africa, West Africa, and Southern Africa.

TEACH & ASSESS

R1 Reading Skills

Explaining Have a student volunteer read the introductory paragraph aloud. Then ask students to explain what they have read. **Ask:**

- How much of Earth's total land area is covered by Africa? *(about one-fifth)*
- Which landforms of Africa influence how people utilize Earth's resources to survive? *(the Sahara, Congo River, and Great Rift Valley)*
- How large is Africa in comparison to Asia? *(second to Asia in total land area)*
- How many independent political units are there in Africa? *(54)* **ELL** Verbal/Linguistic

R2 Reading Skills

Describing Have students describe what they see in the photo associated with the paragraph, "Natural Resources." Then, have a volunteer read the paragraph. **Ask:**

- What activity does the photo show? *(gold mining)*
- What are some challenges faced by gold miners? *(hard labor, work underground, environmental hazards)*

Have students identify the types of natural resources that are of great economic value. Then, **ask:**

- Which natural resources found in Africa have particularly high value throughout the world? *(gold, uranium, diamonds)*
- What are three countries in Africa where these minerals are found? *(South Africa, Botswana, Democratic Republic of the Congo)* **AL** Verbal/Linguistic

C Critical Thinking Skills

Analyzing Have students explain what is meant by, "the uplifting of the land," as described in the paragraph titled, "Bodies of Water." **Ask:**

- How is land uplifted? *(by tectonic plate movement, earthquakes)*
- When did Africa's huge basins form as a result of the uplifting of the land? *(millions of years ago)*
- What role do water bodies, such as Lake Victoria and the Nile River, play in the life of Africans? *(Students should recognize that availability of water is vital to life and the economy of different regions in Africa.)* **Naturalist**

R1 EXPLORE the CONTINENT

AFRICA The continent of Africa covers about one-fifth of Earth's total land area. Africa is the world's second-largest continent, after Asia. For the 54 independent countries located in Africa, physical features such as the Sahara, the Congo River, and the Great Rift Valley have greatly influenced how people live in this environment.

R2 ① **NATURAL RESOURCES** The region has an abundance of minerals. South Africa, Botswana, and the Democratic Republic of the Congo are among the countries that have valuable deposits of gold, uranium, diamonds, and other minerals. These miners work in one of the world's deepest gold mines in South Africa.

C ② **BODIES OF WATER** Many of Africa's lakes lie in huge basins formed millions of years ago by the uplifting of the land. The Nile, the world's longest river, flows from the East African highlands through Egypt to the Mediterranean Sea.

254 *Unit 3*

---

networks *Online Teaching Options*

VIDEO

Video Tour of Africa

Analyzing Images Display the video montage highlighting Africa. Prior to starting the video, have students identify with their name on a sticky note an area of Africa that is of particular interest to them and attach the sticky note to a map of Africa. As students watch the video, have them write down any information provided about their identified location. Following the video, have students individually remove their sticky notes from the map and share what they have learned about their chosen areas. Create a list of "Details about Africa" on the board as students share information. **AL** Visual/Spatial

3 LANDFORMS Africa's geography is made up of a variety of landforms. Step-like plateaus rise from the coasts to inland mountains. Tropical grasslands with scattered trees cover almost one half of the continent. These giraffes are among the millions of animals—zebras, gazelles, lions, and cheetahs—that roam East Africa's Serengeti, one of the world's largest plains.

R

C

FAST **FACT**

Africa is three times the size of the United States.

Unit 3 255

V Visual Skills

Interpreting Direct student attention to the satellite image at the top of the page. Have students discuss the shape and size of Africa. Remind students that both the Prime Meridian and the Equator cross Africa, dividing the land area among all four hemispheres: Northern, Southern, Western, and Eastern. **Ask:**

- **From the satellite image, what can you tell about climates found in Africa?** *(vast areas of arid regions in the northern third of the continent, regions of vegetation along the coastlines and central interior of the continent)*
- **What do you notice about the land and bordering bodies of water?** *(Students should notice that Africa is surrounded by water with the exception of a small land bridge at the northeast point of Africa.)* **BL** **Visual/Spatial**

R Reading Skills

Determining Central Ideas Direct students' attention to the large photo of giraffes on the grasslands and allow for comments. Ask a volunteer to read the paragraph titled, "Landforms." **Ask:**

- **What biome covers almost half of the continent?** *(tropical grasslands)*
- **Why are tropical grasslands important to Africa?** *(home to millions of animals)*

Have students speculate on the importance of animal diversity to the region. **Ask: What value does animal diversity offer the region?** *(Possible answer: diversity allows for complex ecosystems to form and provides food opportunities for animals and humans.)* **AL**

C Critical Thinking Skills

Evaluating Have students read the Fast Fact and locate the framed area placed on Africa. Have students compare the size of Africa to the size of the United States. **Ask: Why would the United States want to maintain strong economic ties with countries in Africa?** *(Possible answers: as a source of natural resources, as a region of economic development, and for trade with American companies)* **Verbal/Linguistic**

WORKSHEET

Environmental Case Study

Evaluating The Environmental Case Study for this unit is about assessing the global health of the region and the planet. This topic will help students understand both the affects of the changes to the physical world and to the animals in the region. Divide the students into groups and distribute the case study, allowing some in-class time for planning. Have groups share their findings with the class. **BL** **Logical/Mathematical**

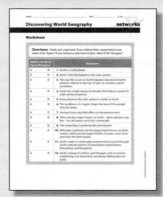

V Visual Skills

Reading a Map Have students work in pairs to analyze the features of the physical map. Discuss the map as a group, noting the difference between elevations. Ask students to note where the highest elevations occur in Africa and speculate on regions where most settlement and land use occurs. Point out the Red Sea as a strategic transportation route between Europe and southern Africa and southern Asia. **Ask:**

• **Where are regions of highest elevation found in Africa?** (Atlas Mountains, Ethiopian Highlands, Great Rift Valley, Bie Plateau, Drakensberg Range)

• **Into which body of water does the Nile River empty?** (Mediterranean Sea)

• **What is the elevation of Mt. Kilimanjaro?** (19,341 ft., or 5,895 m)

• **On which river is the Aswan High Dam found?** (Nile River)

• **What is the elevation of the Congo Basin?** (between 1,000 and 2,000 ft., or between 300 and 600 m)

• **Which mountain range borders the Strait of Gibraltar?** (Atlas Mountains)

• **Near which body of water is the Nubian Desert found?** (Red Sea)

Have students identify regions on the physical map. **Ask:** Which region dominates northern Africa? (Sahara) **Ask:** What types of regions are found in the southern part of Africa? (desert and mountain) **AL** Visual/Spatial

C Critical Thinking Skills

Evaluating Have students focus on the Sinai Peninsula. Have students identify the elevation and discuss the importance of its location. **Ask:**

• **What makes the Suez Canal a strategic point for commerce?** (The canal allows the passage of vessels from the Mediterranean Sea to the Red Sea without having to go completely around the continent.)

• **Without the Suez Canal, what route would be necessary for ships to travel from the Mediterranean Sea to the Indian Ocean?** (along the west coast of Africa and around the Cape of Good Hope) **BL** Visual/Spatial

---

ANSWERS, p. 256

MAP SKILLS
1. Atlas Mountains
2. Lake Malawi
3. Kilimanjaro

256

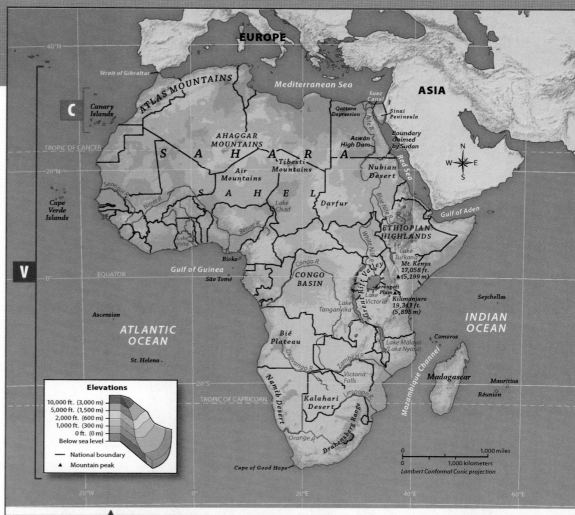

AFRICA

PHYSICAL

MAP SKILLS

1. **PLACES AND REGIONS** What is the major mountain range of North Africa?

2. **THE GEOGRAPHER'S WORLD** Which of Africa's largest lakes lies farthest to the south?

3. **PHYSICAL GEOGRAPHY** What is the highest mountain in Africa?

256 Unit 3

networks *Online Teaching Options*

MAP

Africa: Physical Map

Displaying Use the interactive Physical Map of Africa to help students identify Africa's various regions and features. Divide the class into small groups. Have students find Lake Victoria. Each group should plot the most feasible route from Lake Victoria to the Atlantic Ocean. Have each group present its route on the whiteboard and explain why it is the most feasible of all choices. Have the class select the route that appears to take greatest advantage of available landforms, and the quickest route to the Atlantic Ocean. **AL** Kinesthetic, Naturalist

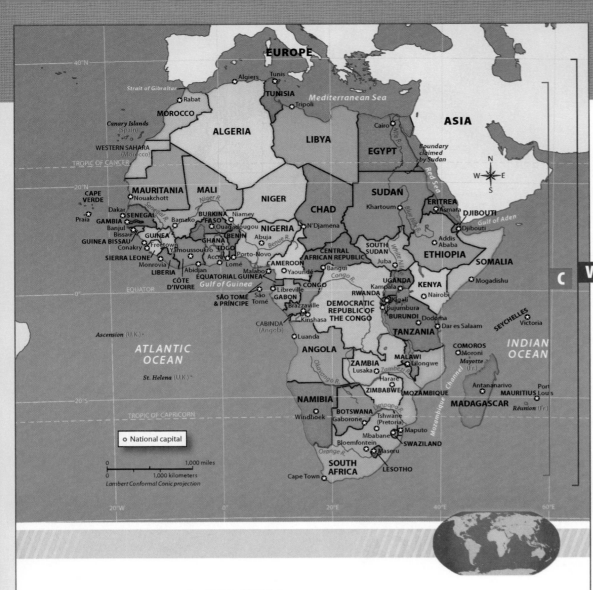

POLITICAL

MAP SKILLS

1 **PLACES AND REGIONS** Which country in the region of North Africa is the largest in area?

2 **PLACES AND REGIONS** Name three island countries of Africa.

3 **THE GEOGRAPHER'S WORLD** Which countries border Namibia in Southern Africa?

Unit 3 **257**

V Visual Skills

Reading a Map Direct students' attention to the political map. Point out the map key and scale. Ask students for general comments about the map, including size and shape of countries, number of countries, and the location of countries that are part of current news events. **Ask:**

- **Which African countries border the Mediterranean Sea?** *(Morocco, Algeria, Tunisia, Libya, Egypt)*
- **Which African countries border the Indian Ocean?** *(Somalia, Kenya, Tanzania, Mozambique, South Africa)*
- **Which island country is located in the Indian Ocean?** *(Madagascar)*
- **In which country is the Suez Canal located?** *(Egypt)*
- **Which three countries appear to have the largest land areas?** *(Algeria, Sudan, Democratic Republic of the Congo)*
- **What is the capital of Nigeria?** *(Abuja)*
- **Which country is found on Africa's west coast and is crossed by the Equator?** *(Gabon)* **ELL** **Visual/Spatial**

C Critical Thinking Skills

Reasoning Direct students' attention to the shape of the different countries. **Ask:**

- **What do you think formed the borders of these countries?** *(Students answers may vary, but should focus on either the natural landforms or political agreements following conflict or warfare.)*
- **What do you think offers the most advantage for an African country: size, available natural resources, or location along a coastline? Why?** *(Student answers will vary but should be supported with sound reasoning.)*
- **Three countries border Lake Victoria. What types of challenges might that impose on the three countries regarding the lake's management?** *(Possible answers: cooperation on the lake's health and management of its resources)* **BL** **Verbal/Linguistic**

GAME

Political Boundaries: Africa Game

Identifying Display the Political Map of Africa. As a class, play the drag-and-drop game to identify country and city names on the map. Then have volunteers use whiteboard tools to circle national capitals, draw a line from one capital to another, and calculate the distance. Ask students to recall the types of landforms being crossed as they draw lines across the map. Provide students with the names of national capitals. **ELL** **Kinesthetic**

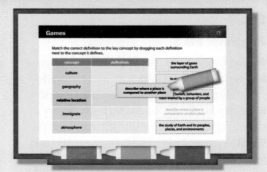

ANSWERS, p. 257

MAP SKILLS

1. Algeria
2. Cape Verde (north west); São Tomé and Príncipe (central west); Comoros, Madagascar, Mauritius, Seychelles (east)
3. Angola, Zambia, Botswana, and South Africa

C Critical Thinking Skills

Integrating Visual Information Ask students about their first impressions of the population density in Africa based on what they observe on the map. **Ask:**

- **Which regions have the highest population densities, and which physical characteristics attract development?** *(near the Mediterranean coast and along water ways; availability of water attracts development)*

- **Which regions have low population densities, and which physical characteristics discourage development?** *(interior and desert regions are sparsely populated; deserts are barren, with little water for agriculture; transportation to and from deep interiors of the continent may be difficult)* **ELL Logical/Mathematical**

V Visual Skills

Reading a Map Direct students' attention to the cities and population map keys. **Ask:**

- **How many cities in Africa exceed 5 million people?** *(three: Cairo, Lagos, Kinshasa)*

- **What is the range of population density for regions in Africa shown on the map as shades of yellow?** *(Less than 2.5 to 24 persons per sq. mi., or less than 1–9 persons per sq. km)*

- **What is the population density of Casablanca?** *(between 2 million and 5 million people)*

- **For the most part, what is the population density around Lake Victoria?** *(between 63 and 1,249 people per sq. mi., or between 25 and 499 people per sq. km)* **AL Logical/Mathematical**

T Technology Skills

Analyzing News Media Ask students to search the Internet for recent news articles about Africa. Topics could include political uprisings, land or resource disputes, climate-related problems, and natural disasters. Have students read some of the news articles out loud in class. Use these articles to lead a class discussion on current events in Africa. **BL**

ANSWERS, p. 258

MAP SKILLS

1. desert regions of the Sahara, the Kalahari, and the Namib
2. Almost all are near inland waterways or ocean shores.
3. Cairo, Egypt; Lagos, Nigeria; Kinshasa, Democratic Republic of the Congo

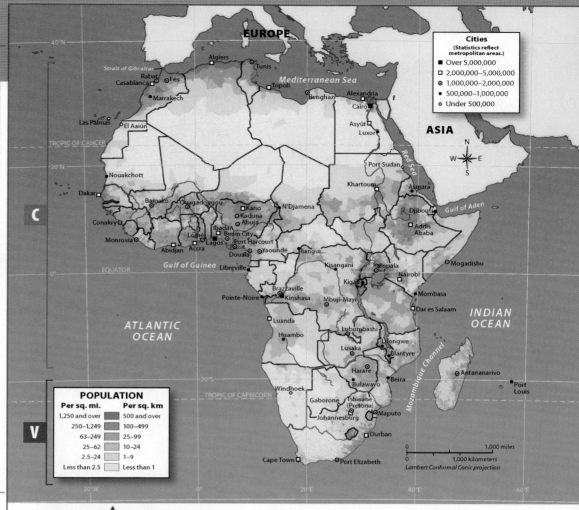

AFRICA

POPULATION DENSITY

MAP SKILLS

1. **PLACES AND REGIONS** Which areas of Africa have the lowest population density?

2. **THE GEOGRAPHER'S WORLD** Generalize about the areas of Africa with the highest population densities. What can you say about these places?

3. **PLACES AND REGIONS** What are the largest cities in Africa?

258 Unit 3

networks Online Teaching Options

Regional Map

Making Connections Display the interactive regional map to students. Select some of the images that are connected to the map and place them in the context of the map and the unit. Guide a discussion helping students to identify the content of the images and then to make a connection between the image and the map location. **Visual/Spatial**

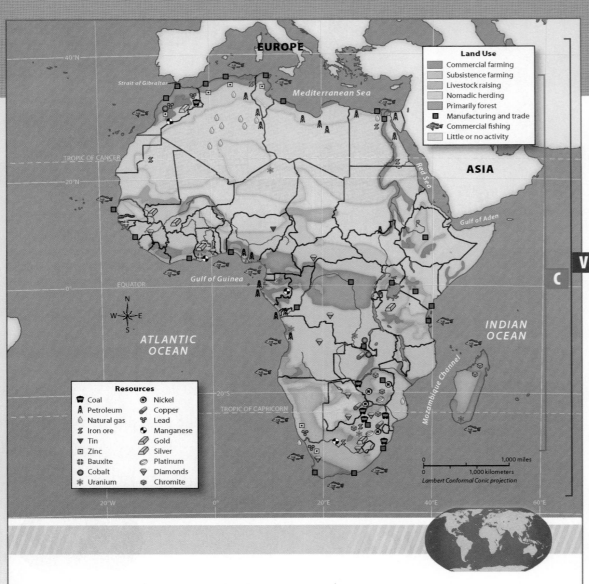

Land Use

- Commercial farming
- Subsistence farming
- Livestock raising
- Nomadic herding
- Primarily forest
- ■ Manufacturing and trade
- 🐟 Commercial fishing
- Little or no activity

Resources

Coal	⊙ Nickel
Petroleum	Copper
Natural gas	Lead
Iron ore	Manganese
▼ Tin	Gold
☐ Zinc	Silver
Bauxite	Platinum
● Cobalt	Diamonds
✳ Uranium	Chromite

0 1,000 miles
0 1,000 kilometers
Lambert Conformal Conic projection

ECONOMIC RESOURCES

MAP SKILLS

1. **ENVIRONMENT AND SOCIETY** Where are precious minerals mined in different areas of Africa?

2. **HUMAN GEOGRAPHY** What is the most common type of farming in Africa?

3. **PLACES AND REGIONS** Why do you think the Nile River valley specializes in commercial farming?

Unit 3 **259**

Africa: Resources Map

Analyzing Information Display the interactive Resource Map and allow students time to review and discuss the region as each layer is revealed. Then assign a country to each student. Students should research the dominant industries, agricultural products, imports, and exports of their countries by accessing their assigned country on the Central Intelligence Agency World Factbook at https://www.cia.gov/library/publications/the-world-factbook/. Group students by land use regions as shown on the Resources Map to share what they have learned. **ELL** Visual/Spatial

V Visual Skills

Reading a Map Review the Land Use and Resources Map keys for the Economic Resources map. **Ask:**

- **What are the dominant land uses in Africa?** *(nomadic herding and subsistence farming)*
- **Where is there little or no land use?** *(in desert regions)*
- **Where does most commercial fishing occur?** *(along Africa's west coast in the Atlantic Ocean)*

Then have pairs answer the following questions. **Ask:**

- **Where are oil reserves found in Africa?** *(along the west central and northern coastlines)*
- **Where does manufacturing take place in Africa?** *(northern and central regions, as well as the southern tip region)*
- **Where has zinc been located?** *(southwest tip and along the northwest coastline region)*
- **Where has uranium been discovered?** *(in the northern desert region and central region)*
- **What are the dominant land uses practiced on the island nation of Madagascar?** *(livestock raising and commercial farming)*
- **Where has bauxite been located?** *(far western coasts)*
- **Where are reserves of natural gas found?** *(northwestern region of the Sahara Desert)*
- **Where are Africa's forests located?** *(within the central area near the Equator)*
- **Where are diamonds found in Africa?** *(central and southern regions)* **AL** Visual/Spatial

C Critical Thinking Skills

Transferring Knowledge Explain that natural resources bring wealth, economic independence, and global importance to some countries in Africa. As a class, discuss how the sale of natural resources, such as oil, natural gas, lumber, uranium or diamonds, can result in dependent relationships between countries that have resources and countries that need resources. Organize students into groups, each representing an advertising agency promoting an important natural resource. Direct each group to come up with a printed advertisement or a commercial that can be acted out promoting the resource. Have each group present to the class. **BL** Interpersonal, Kinesthetic

---

ANSWER, p. 259

MAP SKILLS

1. The precious metals gold, silver, and platinum are mined in southern Africa. Gold is also mined in eastern Africa (Tanzania) and western Africa (Mali and Ghana).
2. Subsistence farming
3. Answers will vary but could include that the Nile is one of the world's largest fertile regions. This allows Egyptians to produce many crops in the region around the Nile River valley.

V Visual Skills

Reading a Map Have students locate the Equator while reviewing the climate map. **Ask:**

- **What two climate types cover large regions in Africa?** *(arid and tropical savanna)*
- **Where are tropical rain forests found on the African mainland?** *(deep central region)*
- **About how much of Africa is affected by a desert climate?** *(about one-third)*
- **What types of climate are found near the Victoria Falls?** *(humid subtropical and semi-arid)*
- **What type of climate separates the northern desert region from the central tropical savanna?** *(semi-arid)*
- **Aside from the southern tip of Africa, what other regions experience a Mediterranean climate?** *(northwest coastal region and sections of the north coastline)*
- **Aside from the deep central region of Africa, what other region is impacted by a tropical rain forest climate?** *(east coast of Madagascar)* **AL** Visual/Spatial

W Writing Skills

Narrative Have students write a short narrative imagining life in the deserts of Africa. Tell them to explain how the heat, sun, sand, and lack of water would influence their daily activities. **BL** Naturalist

CLOSE & REFLECT

Making a Presentation Have students reflect on what they have learned so far about Africa. Divide the class into small groups. Assign a country to each group. Each group will create a slide show on the "People of Africa" that includes the languages, religions, foods, music, art, and traditions of the assigned country. Encourage students to research several sites on the Internet to obtain images and information about the people of their assigned country. Each group should create a PowerPoint or other multimedia presentation on the assigned country. **AL** Interpersonal

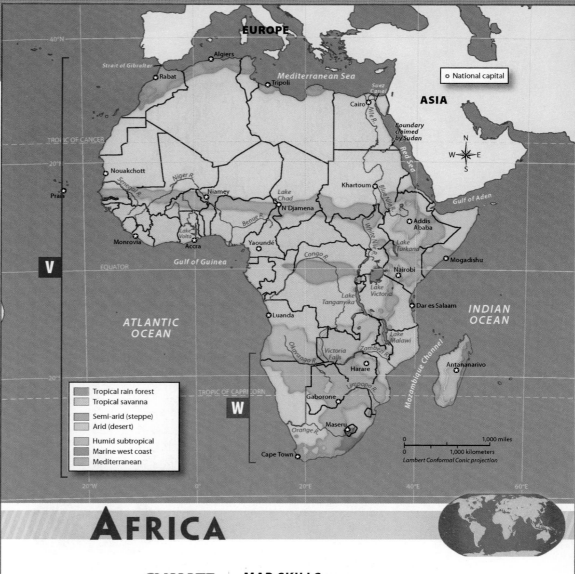

CLIMATE

MAP SKILLS

1 **PLACES AND REGIONS** In the area of Africa south of the Sahara, what is the predominant climate?

2 **PHYSICAL GEOGRAPHY** What climate types are in the area around the Congo River?

3 **PLACES AND REGIONS** What is the climate of Cape Town, South Africa?

260 *Unit 3*

netw⊙rks *Online Teaching Options*

MAP

Africa: Climates Map

Organizing Have students use the interactive Climate Map to discuss the variety of climates in Africa. Organize students into small groups. Assign a type of climate to each group. Students should research the types of land uses possible within the assigned climate type. Create a classroom climate wall mural. Divide large mural paper into seven sections to reflect the seven climate types. Have students in each climate group work together to creatively label their section and add art to the mural that reflects land use possibilities in Africa for their assigned climate type. Display the wall mural. **AL**

ANSWER, p. 260

MAP SKILLS
1. Semi-arid or steppe
2. Tropical and tropical savanna
3. Mediterranean

UNDERSTANDING BY DESIGN®

Enduring Understandings

- *People, places, and ideas change over time.*

Essential Questions

- *How do people adapt to their environment?*
- *How does religion shape society?*
- *Why do conflicts develop?*

Predictable Misunderstandings

- *The desert forms the majority of the landscape in North Africa.*
- *North Africa has a low population due to the landscape.*

Assessment Evidence

Performance Tasks:

- *Project-Based Learning Digital Hands-On Chapter Project*
- *Project-Based Learning Hands-On Chapter Project*

Other Evidence:

- *Critical Thinking Skills Activity*
- *Technology Skills Activity*
- *Reading Skills Activity*
- *Participation in Interactive Whiteboard Activities*
- *Contribution to small-group activities*
- *Interpretation of slide show images and special purpose maps*
- *Participation in class discussions about cultural and economic topics*
- *Lesson Reviews*
- *Chapter Assessments*

SUGGESTED PACING GUIDE

Introducing the Chapter............... 1 Day	Lesson 3 ....2 Days	
Lesson 1 ....2 Days	Chapter Wrap-Up and Assessment...... 1 Day	
Lesson 2 ....2 Days		

TOTAL TIME   8 Days

Key for Using the Teacher Edition

SKILL-BASED ACTIVITIES

Types of skill activities found in the Teacher Edition.

V Visual Skills require students to analyze maps, graphs, charts, and photos.

W Writing Skills provide writing opportunities to help students comprehend the text.

R Reading Skills help students practice reading skills and master vocabulary.

C Critical Thinking Skills help students apply and extend what they have learned.

T Technology Skills require students to use digital tools effectively.

*Letters are followed by a number when there is more than one of the same type of skill on the page.

DIFFERENTIATED INSTRUCTION

All activities are written for the on-level student unless otherwise marked with the leveled labels below.

BL Beyond Level
AL Approaching Level
ELL English Language Learners

All students benefit from activities that utilize different learning styles. Many activities are marked as below when a particular learning style is highlighted.

Intrapersonal	Naturalist
Logical/Mathematical	Kinesthetic
Visual/Spatial	Auditory/Musical
Verbal/Linguistic	Interpersonal

National Geography Standards covered in Chapter 9

Learners will understand:

I. The World in Spatial Terms

Standard 1: How to use maps and other geographic representations, geospatial technologies, and spatial thinking to understand and communicate information

Standard 3: How to analyze the spatial organization of people, places, and environments on Earth's surface

II. Places and Regions

Standard 4: The physical and human characteristics of places

Standard 5: That people create regions to interpret Earth's complexity

Standard 6: How culture and experience influence people's perceptions of places and regions

IV. Human Systems

Standard 9: The characteristics, distribution, and migration of human populations on Earth's surface

Standard 10: The characteristics, distribution, and complexity of Earth's cultural mosaics

Standard 11: The patterns and networks of economic interdependence on Earth's surface

Standard 12: The processes, patterns, and functions of human settlement

Standard 13: How the forces of cooperation and conflict among people influence the division and control of Earth's surface

V. Environment and Society

Standard 14: How human actions modify the physical environment

Standard 15: How physical systems affect human systems

VI. The Uses of Geography

Standard 17: How to apply geography to interpret the past

Standard 18: How to apply geography to interpret the present and plan for the future

CHAPTER OPENER PLANNER

Students will know:
- that the population of North Africa uses the waterways available to them for trade and farming.
- that these waterways have had a large impact on the development of civilizations in North Africa.
- how trade routes along waterways allowed for the development of religion.

Students will be able to:
- *analyze* a world map to identify countries of North Africa.
- *use* a time line to discuss various events in the history of North Africa.

UNDERSTANDING BY DESIGN®

☑ *Print Teaching Options*

V Visual Skills

☐ **P. 262** Students use the map to answer the Step Into the Place questions. **Visual/Spatial**

☐ **P. 263** Students review the time line and images and discuss the major points of interest. **Visual/Spatial**

C Critical Thinking Skills

☐ **P. 263** Students speculate on how the dicovery of oil has impacted the country of Libya. **Verbal/Linguistic**

☑ *Online Teaching Options*

☐ **MAP** **Reading a Map**—Students identify aspects and locations of the region on a map.

☐ **TIME LINE** **Reading a Time Line and Map**—Students learn about where and when historical events occurred in North Africa. **Visual/Spatial**

☐ **MAP** **Interactive World Atlas**—Students use the interactive world atlas to identify the region and describe its terrain.

☑ *Printable Digital Worksheets*

☐ **WORKSHEET** **Technology Skills: Comparing Canals**—Students can use this worksheet to compare the Suez to other canals.

☐ **WORKSHEET** **Reading Skills: Geography of Cairo**—Students can use this worksheet to understand more about the human and physical geography of Cairo, Egypt.

Project-Based Learning

Hands-On

Creating Map Overlays
Working in pairs or small groups, students will research information about North Africa's natural resources, climate, languages, religions, and historical events. Students will sketch maps of North Africa and use clear plastic sheets of paper to create map overlays that contain the research information. Students will use the overlays to answer the chapter's Essential Questions. Students will present and discuss their data findings to the class.

Digital Hands-On

Conducting a Virtual Archeological Dig
Students will conduct a virtual archeological dig as they learn about the countries in North Africa. Students will research important physical features and historical events of the region by using virtual online museums to obtain information. Students should then write a short description of the "artifacts" and provide a photo or image to document their virtual archeological dig. Students will then create an online presentation of their findings. Once they are completed, students will uncover what their classmates discovered by viewing each other's presentations.

edtechteacher
21st Century Learning

Print Resources

ANCILLARY RESOURCES
These ancillaries are available for every chapter and lesson.
- **Reading Essentials and Study Guide Workbook** AL ELL
- **Chapter Tests and Lesson Quizzes Blackline Masters**

PRINTABLE DIGITAL WORKSHEETS
These printable digital worksheets are available for every chapter and lesson.
- **Hands-On Chapter Projects**
- **What Do You Know? Activities**
- **Chapter Summaries (English and Spanish)**
- **Vocabulary Builder Activities**
- **Quizzes and Tests**
- **Reading Essentials and Study Guide (English and Spanish)** AL ELL
- **Guided Reading Activities**

More Media Resources

SUGGESTED VIDEOS
NOTE: Be sure to preview any clips to ensure they are age-appropriate.
- **The Sahara: The Forgotten History of the World's Harshest Desert** (2 discs 190 min.)
- **Unlocking the Great Pyramid, National Geographic** (50 min.)
- **Globe Trekker: Northern Africa** (165 min.)

SUGGESTED READING
- *Lights on the Nile,* by Donna Jo Napoli
- *Ancient Egypt: Tales of Gods and Pharaohs,* by Marcia Williams AL
- *Ali, Child of the Desert,* by Jonathan London AL

PHYSICAL GEOGRAPHY OF NORTH AFRICA

Students will know:
- *that the waterways in North Africa have had a large impact on the development of civilizations in North Africa.*

Students will be able to:
- *describe* the physical features of North Africa including important waterways.
- *describe* the various climates of this region.
- *discuss* important natural resources in this region.

UNDERSTANDING
BY DESIGN®

☑ *Print Teaching Options*

V Visual Skills

☐ **P. 264** Students use the text to describe one natural feature that provides water for a farmer's wheat.

☐ **P. 265** Students describe what is unusual about the Atlas Mountain range. **Visual/Spatial**

☐ **P. 268** Students diagram the rain shadow effect. **Visual**

☐ **P. 270** Students speculate about the source of water in a photograph and how it is used. **Visual/Spatial**

W Writing Skills

☐ **P. 268** Students write letters as if they were tourists in the Sahara Desert. **ELL** **Verbal/Linguistic**

☐ **P. 271** Students write an argument about the use of fossil water in the desert. **BL** **Verbal/Linguistic**

R Reading Skills

☐ **P. 265** Students use context clues to find meaning. **ELL**

☐ **P. 265** Students calculate the differences in terrain. **AL**

☐ **P. 266** Students find synonyms. **BL** **Verbal/Linguistic**

☐ **P. 267** Students discuss advantages and disadvantages of the Aswan High Dam. **Logical/Mathematical**

☐ **P. 268** Students discuss the Sahara as a barrier. **AL**

C Critical Thinking Skills

☐ **P. 264** Students infer the advantages and disadvantages of the Mediterranean Sea to North Africa.

☐ **P. 265** Students discuss the image of a village in the Atlas Mountains and discuss its climate. **Logical/Mathematical**

☐ **P. 266** Students infer why the seasonal flooding of the Nile benefited Egypt. **Verbal/Linguistic**

☐ **P. 267** Students identify problems a community might have after long hot periods without rain. **Naturalist**

☐ **P. 270** Students make inferences about resources. **ELL**

T Technology Skills

☐ **P. 266** Students make a chart showing data about three rivers.

☑ *Online Teaching Options*

V Visual Skills

☐ **VIDEO** **Wild Worlds: The Sahara Desert**—Students watch the video about the Sahara Desert in North Africa and share one or two key facts they found interesting. **ELL** **Visual/Spatial**

☐ **IMAGE** **360° View: Cairo on the Nile**—Students use the 360° view of the city of Cairo and discuss why this major city would develop on an often flooding river.

☐ **MAP** **Climates: North Africa**—Students use the map to discuss the climates of this region.

☐ **MAP** **Resources: North Africa**—Students use the map to discuss the resources of the region.

W Writing Skills

☐ **MAP** **Physical Geography: North Africa**—Students use the physical geography map to make a list of the landforms and waterways of North Africa. **AL** **Naturalist**

☐ **IMAGE** **Mediterranean Climates and Agriculture**—Students write a paragraph about the importance of the Mediterranean climate to the agricultural economies of the region. **BL**

R Reading Skills

☐ **GRAPHIC ORGANIZER** **Resources in North Africa**—Students outline resources in North Africa.

C Critical Thinking Skills

☐ **MAP** **The Nile River**—Students use the animated map to explain the characteristics of the Nile and how it affects the surrounding communities. **AL** **Verbal/Linguistic**

☐ **MAP** **Climates: North Africa**—Students compare and contrast the different climates of North Africa. **Visual/Spatial, Verbal/Linguistic**

☐ **IMAGE** **The Suez Canal**—Students suggest the advantages of the Suez Canal. **AL**

☐ **MAP** **Making Connections: Mediterranean Climates**—Students discuss the meaning of "Mediterranean climate."

☐ **INFOGRAPHIC** **Fresh Water vs. Saltwater**—Students use this infographic to discuss the need to tap wells in the region and remind students about the lack of fresh water.

T Technology Skills

☐ **ONLINE SELF-CHECK QUIZ** **Lesson 1**—Students receive instant feedback on their mastery of lesson content.

HISTORY OF NORTH AFRICA

Students will know:
- that the population of North Africa uses the waterways available to them for trade and farming.
- that the waterways in North Africa have had a large impact on the development of the civilizations in North Africa.
- how trade routes along waterways allowed for the development of religion.

Students will be able to:
- **discuss** the importance of Ancient Egypt, including its religion, culture, and influence.
- **describe** the Middle Ages and the rise of Islam.
- **explore** the modern era of North Africa, including colonization and independence, and recent unrest.

UNDERSTANDING
BY DESIGN®

☑ *Print Teaching Options*

V Visual Skills

☐ **P. 273** Students reinforce their map skills using a map of ancient Egypt. **Visual/Spatial**

☐ **P. 278** Students draw a vertical time line to show when North African countries gained their independence.

W Writing Skills

☐ **P. 275** Students write a paragraph arguing for the idea that the Internet will bring about a better understanding between cultures. **AL** **Verbal/Linguistic**

☐ **P. 276** Students write an argument about whether religion and customs bind people together.

R Reading Skills

☐ **P. 272** Students identify central ideas. **AL** **Verbal**

☐ **P. 273** Students discuss how the word *polytheism* defines itself. **Verbal/Linguistic**

☐ **P. 274** Students discuss how the styles and building of Egyptian tombs changed over time. **AL** **Verbal/Linguistic**

☐ **P. 276** Students compare rulers of ancient Egypt and the Muslim empire.

☐ **P. 278** Students discuss trade and the Suez Canal. **AL**

☐ **P. 279** Students identify when and where the Arab Spring revolts began. **Verbal/Linguistic**

C Critical Thinking Skills

☐ **P. 272** Students make inferences about rulers of ancient Egypt. **BL** **Verbal/Linguistic**

☐ **P. 273** Students identify evidence that supports an inference. **BL** **Logical/Mathematical**

☐ **P. 275** Students evaluate the benefits of libraries.

☐ **P. 276** Students infer why the Berbers are just one ethnic group of many to live in North Africa. **Logical**

T Technology Skills

☐ **P. 274** Students use Web sites to translate simple phrases into hieroglyphics and give a presentation. **BL**

☐ **P. 277** Students research the building of the Suez Canal. **BL** **Interpersonal**

☑ *Online Teaching Options*

V Visual Skills

☐ **SLIDE SHOW** **Egyptian Artifacts**—Students watch a slide show about Egyptian artifacts and describe the materials and skills used in making the artifacts. **Visual/Spatial, Interpersonal**

☐ **IMAGE** **360° View: Ancient Egypt**—Students use the 360° image of ancient Egypt to show how this civilization relied heavily on the Nile River for a vast variety of elements.

W Writing Skills

☐ **VIDEO** **Gift of the Nile**—Students watch the video about life in ancient Egypt and write a few sentences explaining what they learned. **AL** **ELL**

☐ **ANIMATION** **How the Pyramids Were Built**—Students watch an animation about the building of the pyramids and write a brief essay about how they were built. **ELL** **Visual/Spatial**

☐ **MAP** **Compare Independence Movements**—Students use the map to write paragraphs to compare independence movements of individual countries in North Africa. **BL** **Verbal/Linguistic**

R Reading Skills

☐ **GRAPHIC ORGANIZER** **Roman and Islamic Empires in North Africa**—Students record information about the two different empires and their influence on the region.

☐ **GRAPHIC ORGANIZER** **Europeans in North Africa**—Students use the interactive graphic organizer to identify which European country had a presence in the region and why.

☐ **LECTURE SLIDE** **How Do You Spell Qadaffi?**—Students use the lecture slide about translating words from one language to another to discuss the difficulty of translating Arabic to English.

C Critical Thinking Skills

☐ **IMAGE** **Islam**—Students use the interactive photograph to discuss how Islam affects Muslims' daily life. **ELL** **Verbal/Linguistic**

☐ **MAP** **The Punic Wars**—Students learn about the Punic Wars using the interactive map and make a chart to classify information from the map. **ELL** **AL** **Visual/Spatial**

☐ **GAME** **Drag-and-Drop: Governments and Dictatorships**—Students play the game to make connections between a country's economy, geographic position, history, and the kind of government it has. **AL** **Kinesthetic**

T Technology Skills

☐ **ONLINE SELF-CHECK QUIZ** **Lesson 2**—Students receive instant feedback on their mastery of lesson content.

LIFE IN NORTH AFRICA

Students will know:
- how trade routes along waterways allowed for the development of religion.

Students will be able to:
- **describe** the people of North Africa, their daily life, and culture.
- **discuss** challenges in North Africa, including economic and social issues.
- **examine** North Africa's future in terms of political issues and relations with other nations.

UNDERSTANDING
BY DESIGN®

☑ *Print Teaching Options*

V Visual Skills

☐ **P. 284** Students use a map to discuss why people from Morocco, Algeria, and Tunisia move to Spain and France.

☐ **P. 285** Students create a chart to compare types of government. **Visual/Spatial**

W Writing Skills

☐ **P. 282** Students write an essay about where they would want to live in North Africa. **Verbal/Linguistic**

☐ **P. 285** Students write a paragraph about why literacy is important. **Intrapersonal**

R Reading Skills

☐ **P. 280** Students use a base word to determine meaning. **AL** **ELL**

☐ **P. 281** Students use context clues to understand terms.

☐ **P. 284** Students cite text evidence to support the statement that Morocco's economy is diversified.

☐ **P. 287** Students discuss current issues in North Africa.

C Critical Thinking Skills

☐ **P. 281** Students infer why streets in North Africa might be narrow and curving and the problems this might cause.

☐ **P. 282** Students identify foods they have eaten that are common in North Africa. **Intrapersonal**

☐ **P. 282** Students draw conclusions about why artists whose work is criticized in Algeria might want to leave.

☐ **P. 283** Students debate the pros and cons of censorship.

☐ **P. 284** Students identify problems that inadequate health care might cause in the region. **Logical**

☐ **P. 286** Students compare the Civil War in the United States to the unrest in the Middle East. **BL** **Logical**

T Technology Skills

☐ **P. 281** Students research Egyptian street markets. **ELL**

☐ **P. 283** Student groups research newspaper articles about Qaddafi's death. **Verbal/Linguistic**

☐ **P. 286** Students research the progress Egypt is making on writing a new constitution. **Verbal/Linguistic**

☑ *Online Teaching Options*

V Visual Skills

☐ **SLIDE SHOW** **Artisans of North Africa**—Students view the slide show and discuss the development of art and culture in North Africa. **Visual/Spatial**

☐ **LECTURE SLIDE** **Islamic Art Patterns**—Students use the lecture slide with examples of typical Islamic patterns to discuss this art style and complete their own pattern.

☐ **MAP** **Population: North Africa**—Students can use the population map to visually display the population distribution in the region.

☐ **CHARTS** **Population Pyramids: North Africa**—Students can use the population pyramids to talk about the aging population as a social and economic issue.

W Writing Skills

☐ **VIDEO** **Egypt Internet Freedom**—Students watch the video about the Arab Spring movement in North Africa. Then students write a paragraph about why this would be of interest to them. **ELL**

☐ **IMAGE** **360° View: Algiers**—Students write a short paragraph about something they find fascinating about Algiers. **AL** **Intrapersonal**

☐ **IMAGE** **Cuisine of North Africa**—Students discuss the varieties of food in North Africa and write a short paragraph about which food they find most appealing, and why. **ELL** **Verbal**

C Critical Thinking Skills

☐ **GRAPHIC ORGANIZER** **Economies of North African Countries**—Students use the graphic organizer to rank the economies of the region from most likely to least likely to grow. **Visual**

☐ **GRAPH** **Oil Reserves in the World**—Students can use the circle graph comparing oil reserves in the region with those in the rest of the world.

☐ **CHART** **Literacy Rates Around the World**—Students use the chart to compare literacy rates around the world to literacy rates in North Africa and analyze how they might affect the region.

☐ **IMAGE** **Arab Spring**—Students use the interactive image to discuss the events of the Arab Spring in the context of political and social changes taking place and speculate whether the changes will be good or bad and if they will be long lasting. **BL** **Visual/Spatial, Verbal/Linguistic**

T Technology Skills

☐ **ONLINE SELF-CHECK QUIZ** **Lesson 3**—Students receive instant feedback on their mastery of lesson content.

☑ *Printable Digital Worksheets*

W Writing Skills

☐ **WORKSHEET** **Reading Skills: The Geography of Cairo**—Students can use this worksheet to understand more about the human and physical geography of Cairo, Egypt.

INTERVENTION AND REMEDIATION STRATEGIES

LESSON 1 Physical Geography of North Africa

Reading and Comprehension

To ensure comprehension of the concepts in this lesson, have students write sentences using the lesson vocabulary. Tell students that their sentences should show an understanding of the meaning of each word and how it applies to the lesson content. Have students work in pairs to conduct a peer review, by sharing their sentences and checking each word's meaning. Circulate to provide corrective guidance. Then have students collaborate to write one or two paragraphs using each content vocabulary term that demonstrates their understanding of landforms and waterways in North Africa.

Text Evidence

Organize students into four groups and assign each group one of the following topics: Landforms, Waterways, Climate, and Resources. Tell students they will play a game of "True or False?" to test their knowledge of the lesson. Have members of each group write one sentence about their assigned topic, and note whether it is true or false. Then have students take turns quizzing other members of their group. When each group has had time to answer the questions, call out "Switch!" and have groups swap questions so that each topic is reviewed by each group.

LESSON 2 History of North Africa

Reading and Comprehension

Have students scan the lesson to identify cause-and-effect relationships that relate to the history of civilizations in North Africa. For example, students may note that the rise of Egypt led to increased trade, which in turn resulted in the expansion of Egypt. Tell students to look for signal words as they read. Remind students that words and phrases such as *because, since, result of, due to, therefore, consequently,* and *effect on* all indicate cause or effect. Have students work with a partner to practice using these words to explain concepts and cause-and-effect relationships in this lesson.

Text Evidence

Have students work in pairs or small groups to research facts about the history of North Africa. Assign groups one of the following topics discussed in this lesson: Religion and Culture in Ancient Egypt, Influence of Carthage and Rome, Rise of Islam, Foreign Rule, and Recent Decades. Tell students to use information from the text and from their research to answer questions generated by their group as well as this lesson's essential question: *How does religion shape society?* Have students present their findings to the class. Encourage students to use visual displays to enhance their presentations.

LESSON 3 Life in North Africa

Reading and Comprehension

To ensure comprehension of the concepts in this lesson, have students write a paragraph that explains how people in North Africa are experiencing political changes. As a launch point for students' paragraphs, read aloud the essential question: *Why do conflicts develop?* Tell students to write a few sentences using at least one of the content and academic vocabulary terms to explain how political issues have affected specific regions in North Africa. Students may wish to conduct online research to enhance their paragraphs.

Text Evidence

To help students make the connection between social issues and the way of life in different regions of North Africa, have students work in small groups to create a visual representation of the issues facing regions discussed in this lesson. For example, students may choose to create a flow chart or diagram that shows the impact of economic issues in Libya, or the effect of population growth in Libya and Egypt. Have students in each group work together to summarize how these issues impact daily life for people living in the region. Encourage students to use content vocabulary terms in their summaries.

Online Resources

Approaching Level Reader

Use this online lower-level text that corresponds directly to the text in the online Student Edition.

Guided Reading Activities

This resource uses graphic organizers and guiding questions to help students with comprehension.

Assessing Background Knowledge

Use these worksheets to pre-assess students' background knowledge before they read the chapter.

Reading Essentials and Study Guide Workbook

This resource offers writing and reading activities for the approaching-level student.

Self-Check Quizzes

This online assessment tool provides instant feedback for students to check their progress.

NORTH AFRICA

networks
There's More Online about North Africa.

CHAPTER 9

ESSENTIAL QUESTIONS · *How do people adapt to their environment?*
· *How does religion shape society?* · *Why do conflicts develop?*

Tips Images/SuperStock

Souks, or markets, such as this one in Esna, Egypt, carry a wide assortment of goods.

Lesson 1
The Physical Geography of North Africa

Lesson 2
The History of North Africa

Lesson 3
Life in North Africa

The Story Matters...

Because of the fertile soil in the Nile River valley, ancient Egyptians created a farming society that developed into an empire thousands of years ago. Their great achievements had a tremendous impact on later civilizations in the region. Other waterways influenced the development of trade and communications among Africa, Asia, and Europe. Waterways and trade routes were also important to the spread of ideas and religion, including Islam.

FOLDABLES
Study Organizer

Go to the Foldables® library in the back of your book to make a Foldable® that will help you take notes while reading this chapter.

	Know	Learned
Geography		
History		
Economy		

261

ENGAGE

Bellringer Point to the political map of North Africa and ask students to locate each country. Point out that the Atlantic Ocean, the Mediterranean Sea, and the Red Sea border this region and that the Nile River runs through it. Use the following questions to help students recognize the causes and effects of the Mediterranean on the way of life in North Africa.
Ask:

- **What effects might these bodies of water have on North African countries?** *(Sample responses: the Atlantic isolates the countries on its borders from other continents; the Nile provides water to the countries it runs through and it might provide transportation to and from some parts of Africa; the Mediterranean Sea provides a waterway from Africa to Southern Europe; the Red Sea is narrower and provides less of a barrier than does the Mediterranean; all bodies of water make it possible for people living on their shores to fish.)*

- **How might these bodies of water have influenced ways of life in North African countries?** *(Sample responses: The Nile made farming and fishing possible in Egypt and other countries along its banks; North African and European cultures may have developed differently because the Atlantic and the Mediterranean separate the regions; the Red Sea, being narrow, may have promoted travel and trade between North Africa and the Middle East.)*

Making Connections Have students read "The Story Matters..." and call on volunteers to explain why the soil along the Nile was more fertile than in other areas of North Africa. *(Rivers deposit soil from other fertile areas along their banks.)* Encourage students to discuss the reasons that good farming conditions often form the basis of civilizations. **Ask: How else do bodies of water make the rise of civilizations possible?** *(Students may point out that access to seaports and rivers make it possible to exchange goods, ideas, and people with other areas.)*

Tell students that they will learn more about the unique features and cultures of countries in North Africa in this chapter.

Letter from the Author

Dear Geography Teacher,

Discuss the Arab Spring with students as they read this chapter. The Arab Spring refers to the popular demonstrations throughout several North African countries that began in December, 2010. People organized demonstrations using social media to protest their authoritarian and totalitarian governments. These protests led to elections and new leadership in Egypt, Tunisia, and Libya in 2012. The effect that the Arab Spring will have on this region is still unknown.

FOLDABLES
Study Organizer

Go to the Foldables® library for a cumulative chapter-based Foldable® activity that your students can use to help take notes and prepare for assessment.

	Know	Learned
Geography		
History		
Economy		

TEACH & ASSESS

Step Into the Place

V Visual Skills

Reading a Map Have students read the introductory paragraph and look at the map. Explain that this map shows the countries of North Africa. Have students use the map to answer the Step Into the Place questions. **Ask:**

- **Which countries have shores on the Mediterranean Sea?** *(Morocco, Algeria, Tunisia, Libya, Egypt)*
- **Which country is connected by land to the Middle East?** *(Egypt)*
- **Which country is closest to Europe?** *(Morocco)* Visual/Spatial

Content Background Knowledge

- The Sahara Desert is a distinctive landform in North Africa. Because its environment is so harsh, it has only 2.5 million inhabitants. Most of the people who live there are nomads who herd camels and goats. Due to the Sahara's increasing aridity and heat, these herders find it more and more difficult to maintain their traditional way of life.

- The Nile River brings fertile soil to the farmlands along its banks during its seasonal flooding. The ingenuity of the farmers makes this flooding a benefit rather than a disaster. They have constructed canals and basins that prevent the soil from being sucked away when the Nile recedes. These canals and basins also hold the water for future irrigation of the crops.

- Several of the governments of the countries in North Africa have had major upheavals in recent years. For example, in 2011, Morocco's King Mohammed VI addressed the demands that his people made during the Arab Spring demonstrations. He proposed to his electorate such constitutional amendments as a ban on torture and other inhuman treatment as well as imprisonment without cause, and he called for more freedom for women. The king, however, did not propose any limits on his own power.

ANSWERS, p. 262

STEP INTO THE PLACE

1. Rabat
2. Red Sea
3. Algeria
4. The capitals are located near bodies of water.

NORTH AFRICA CCSS

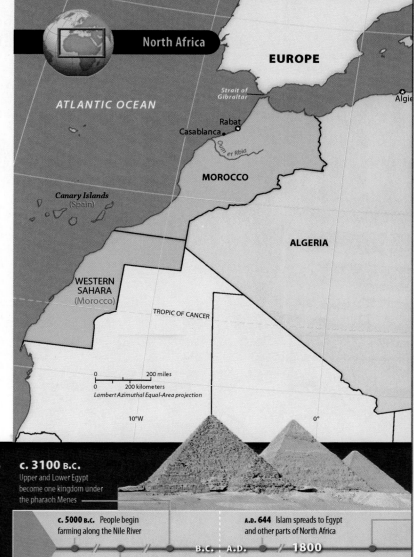

V *The countries of North Africa border the Mediterranean Sea. They make up one region of the African continent. To their south, the Sahara crosses Africa, and to the south of the Sahara lie the other regions of the second-largest continent.*

Step Into the Place

MAP FOCUS Use the map to answer the following questions.

1. **PLACES AND REGIONS** What is the capital of Morocco?

2. **THE GEOGRAPHER'S WORLD** What body of water flows to the east of Egypt?

3. **THE GEOGRAPHER'S WORLD** Which North African country has the largest land area?

4. **CRITICAL THINKING**
   Analyzing What do the capitals of the North African countries have in common geographically?

0 200 miles
0 200 kilometers
Lambert Azimuthal Equal-Area projection

10°W   0°

Step Into the Time

TIME LINE Choose an event from the time line and write a paragraph explaining the social, economic, or environmental effects of that event on the region and the world.
WHST.6-8.2, WHST.6-8.4

c. 3100 B.C.
Upper and Lower Egypt become one kingdom under the pharaoh Menes

c. 5000 B.C. People begin farming along the Nile River

c. 3200 B.C. Ancient Egyptians develop hieroglyphic writing

A.D. 644 Islam spreads to Egypt and other parts of North Africa

B.C. A.D. 1800

262 *Chapter 9*

©Jose Fuste Raga/Corbis

Project-Based Learning

Hands-On

Creating Map Overlays

Working in pairs or small groups, students will research information about North Africa's natural resources, climate, languages, religions, and historical events. Students will sketch maps of North Africa and use clear plastic sheets to create map overlays that contain the research information. Students will use the overlays to answer the chapter's Essential Questions. Students will present and discuss their data findings to the class.

Digital Hands-On

Conducting a Virtual Dig

Students will conduct a virtual archeological dig about the countries in North Africa by using virtual online museums to obtain information. Students should write a short description of the "artifacts," provide a photo or image to document their virtual archeological dig, and create an online presentation of their findings. Students will uncover what their classmates discovered by viewing each other's presentations.

edtechteacher
21ˢᵗ Century Learning

1830
Algeria, Tunisia, and Morocco become part of the French Empire

1969
Muammar al-Qaddafi seizes power in Libya

1956 Oil is discovered in Libya

2010–2011 Pro-democracy revolts known as the Arab Spring take place in Tunisia, Egypt, and Libya

1900

1859–1869 The Suez Canal is built, linking the Mediterranean and Red seas

1970 The Aswän High Dam is completed

2003 Earthquake in northern Algeria leaves 200,000 people homeless

2000

2011 Egyptian president Mubarak leaves office

(l) Apic/Hulton Archive/Getty Images; (r) Victor Sokolowicz/Bloomberg/Getty Images

Chapter 9 **263**

Step Into the Time

V Visual Skills

Reading a Time Line Have students review the time line and images. As a class, discuss its major points of interest. **Ask:**

- **What date and event on the time line first signals a developing civilization?** *(Ancient Egyptians developed hieroglyphic writing in 3200 B.C.)*
- **When did Islam begin to spread throughout North Africa?** *(A.D. 644)*
- **Look at the map. Why might France have colonized Algeria, Morocco, and Tunisia rather than other North African countries?** *(Students may observe that these countries are closer to France than other North African countries.)* **Visual/Spatial**

C Critical Thinking Skills

Speculating Have students discuss the discovery of oil in Libya, as referenced on the time line. **Ask:**

- **When was oil discovered in Libya?** *(1956)*
- **What were some of the likely immediate results of this discovery?** *(The location where oil was discovered probably became a boom town, with people and businesses growing up almost overnight. The country's economy probably benefited right away because the oil could be used to provide energy in the country and it could be exported for revenue.)*
- **How might the discovery of oil have changed the country over time?** *(It would likely have given the country more power as a trading partner in the world.)* **Verbal/Linguistic**

V

CLOSE & REFLECT

Formulating Questions Have students generate a list of questions they have about North Africa based on the chapter introduction. Tell students to look for answers to these questions as they read the chapter.

TIME LINE AND MAP

Reading a Time Line and Map

Identifying Display the time line and map on the whiteboard. Have volunteers read each event as it is revealed on the time line. Ask students to identify where in North Africa the event took place and find its location on the map. **Visual/Spatial**

See page 261B for other online activities.

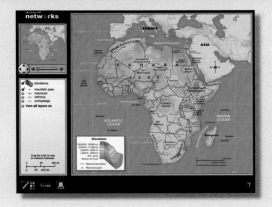

ENGAGE

Bellringer Point out to students that North Africa is a hot, dry region that has several important resources. **Ask: What features do you think North Africa has in common with the southwestern United States?** *(Students' answers will vary but should include the ideas that both regions have a hot, dry climate and stretches of desert. Some students may know that both regions have reserves of oil.)*

TEACH & ASSESS

V Visual Skills

Creating Visuals Have a volunteer read the first paragraph. Note that Hassan is an Egyptian farmer. Point out that one of a country's main concerns is providing enough food for its population. Of the five North African nations, conditions in Egypt are most favorable for agriculture because Egypt has sufficient water for growing crops. **Ask: What is one natural feature that provides water for Hassan's wheat?** *(the Nile River)*

Explain that Egyptians built canals to increase the area irrigated by Nile water early in their history and continue to do so today. Have students research Egyptian canals. Then have them draw pictures, diagrams, or maps showing a typical canal in Egypt. **Visual/Spatial**

C Critical Thinking Skills

Making Inferences Display the Chapter Opener map that shows the physical geography of North Africa. Have students look at the locations of the various bodies of water that surround the region. Then, **ask: Why might the Mediterranean Sea have been a disadvantage early in the history of North African countries?** *(Possible response: Because means of transportation were not as advanced as they are today; it kept Europe and North Africa apart, thus making cultural exchanges and trade between the two areas difficult. At the same time, it provided a waterway to North Africa for advancing armies.)* **Logical/Mathematical, Verbal/Linguistic**

ANSWER, p. 264

Taking Notes Atlas Mountains—In western North Africa; near coast; two mountain ranges; affects climate through rain shadow. **Sahara**—Covers most of inland North Africa; very dry; very hot in summer; has ergs, hamadas, oases. **Qattara Depression**—In northwestern Egypt; below sea level; vehicles cannot drive through it. **Nile River**—flows through Egypt; forms large delta; supports farming; home to most of Egypt's people. **Suez Canal**—Human-made; connects Mediterranean and Red Seas; links Europe and Indian and Pacific Oceans; saves transportation time and cost.

---

networks

There's More Online!

- ☑ **IMAGE** Berber Homes
- ☑ **MAP** Mediterranean Climates
- ☑ **VIDEO**

Reading HELPDESK CCSS

Academic Vocabulary RH.6-8.4
(Tier Two Words)

- margin
- channel

Content Vocabulary RH.6-8.4
(Tier Three Words)

- **delta**
- **silt**
- **wadi**
- **erg**
- **nomad**
- **phosphate**
- **aquifer**

TAKING NOTES: *Key Ideas and Details* RH.6-8.7, WHST.6-8.9

Organize Information As you read about North Africa's physical geography, take notes using the graphic organizer below. Add rows to list more features and their characteristics.

Feature	Characteristic
Atlas Mountains	

Lesson 1
The Physical Geography of North Africa

ESSENTIAL QUESTION · *How do people adapt to their environment?*

IT MATTERS BECAUSE
The Sahara, in North Africa, is the world's largest hot desert. The desert extends over almost the entire northern one-third of the continent of Africa.

Landforms and Waterways

GUIDING QUESTION *How have physical features shaped life in the region?*

Hassan is an Egyptian farmer. In winter, when temperatures are milder than during the summer, he grows wheat. Rainfall is scarce in Egypt, however. How does Hassan get the water he needs to grow his wheat? He draws it from a canal. Canals carry water from the Nile River to the country's farms around the river. Just as they did thousands of years ago, Egypt's farmers still depend on the waters of the Nile.

Countries of the Region

Egypt is the easternmost country in North Africa. The Sinai Peninsula, a triangle of land across the Red Sea from Africa, belongs to Egypt but it is considered a part of Southwest Asia.

North Africa includes five countries. All, like Egypt, sit on the southern shore of the Mediterranean Sea. Libya is to Egypt's west. Tunisia and Algeria are west of that country. Farthest west is Morocco, which has a small Mediterranean coast and a longer coast along the Atlantic Ocean. South of Morocco lies an area called Western Sahara. Morocco claims this area, although the United Nations does not recognize its ownership of this land.

---

networks   *Online Teaching Options*

VIDEO

Wild Worlds—The Sahara Desert

Evaluating Use this video about the physical geography, climate, and wildlife of the Sahara Desert in North Africa to introduce the content of this lesson. After watching the video, have students evaluate the information presented. Ask students to share with a partner one or two key facts they found interesting or that surprised them. **ELL Visual/Spatial**

See page 261C for other online activities.

North Africa is a large region. If you placed North Africa over the 48 connected states of the United States, it would reach from Maine to Washington state and cover the northern half of the country.

Coastal Plains and Mountains

R1 In North Africa, low, narrow plains sit on the **margins**, or edges, of the Mediterranean and Atlantic coasts. In the west, the high Atlas Mountains rise just behind this coastal plain. These mountains extend about 1,200 miles (1,931 km) across Morocco and Algeria into Tunisia. They form the longest mountain chain in Africa and greatly influence the region's climate.

The Atlas Mountains are actually two sets of mountains that run alongside each other. A high plateau sits between them. The southern chain is generally higher than the one to the north. It includes Mount Toubkal in Morocco. At 13,665 feet (4,165 m), it is the highest peak in North Africa.

South of these mountains is a low plateau that reaches across most of North Africa. The land rises higher in a few spots formed by isolated mountains. In Egypt, the southern reaches of the Nile River cut through a highland area to form a deep gorge, or valley. Southeastern Egypt has low mountains on the shores of the Red Sea. The southern part of Egypt's Sinai Peninsula is also mountainous. This area includes Egypt's highest point, Gebel Katherina. It reaches 8,652 feet (2,637 m) high. Another set of low mountains lies in northeastern Libya, near the coast.

Lowlands

Northwestern Egypt has a large area of lowland. Called the Qattara Depression, it sinks 440 feet (134 m) below sea level. This area is nearly the size of New Jersey. Marshes and lakes prevent cars and trucks from passing through it.

©Amar Grover/JAI/Corbis

Academic Vocabulary

margin an edge

V

A village stands at the foot of a large granite formation in the Atlas Mountains of Morocco.
▶ **CRITICAL THINKING**
Describing How many sets of mountains make up the Atlas Mountains? What landform separates the sets of mountains?

R2

Chapter 9 265

MAP

Physical Geography: North Africa

Locating Have students use the physical geography layer on the Chapter Opener map to make a list of the landforms and waterways of this region. When completed, have students share their lists with a partner to discuss and check each other's lists. Discuss with students which landform or waterway they feel would be most significant to the people of North Africa. **AL** **Naturalist**

R1 Reading Skills

Using Context Clues Have a volunteer read the first sentence in the section "Coastal Plains and Mountains." **Ask: Which word or words in this sentence help define the word** *margin?* (edge and/or coasts) **ELL** **Verbal/Linguistic**

V Visual Skills

Describing Have students find the Atlas Mountains on the Chapter Opener map that shows the physical geography of North Africa. **Ask: What is unusual about the Atlas Mountain range?** (It is formed by two sets of mountains with a plateau between them.) **Visual/Spatial**

C

R2 Reading Skills

Calculating Have students consider the vast differences in the heights and depths of the terrain in North Africa. **Ask:**

- **What is the difference between the heights of Mount Toubkal in Morocco and Gebel Katherina in Egypt?** (5,013 feet or 1,528 meters)
- **What is the difference between Egypt's highest point and its lowest point?** (8,212 feet or 2,503 meters. If students have difficulty figuring this out, explain that they need to subtract the depth of the Qattara Depression from the height of Gebel Katherina. Remind them that any time they are asked to find the difference between two numbers they must subtract.) **AL** **Logical/Mathematical**

C Critical Thinking Skills

Analyzing Visuals Have students study the photograph on the bottom of this page. **Ask:**

- **What kind of climate do you think this village has?** (Students should infer from the lack of vegetation that the climate is dry.)
- **What features shown in the photograph might cause a dry climate?** (Students may infer that the mountains surrounding the village may be blocking rainfall there. Or the mountains may be separating the area from a body of water.) **Logical/Mathematical**

ANSWER, p. 265

CRITICAL THINKING The Atlas Mountains are two sets of mountains that run alongside each other. A high plateau sits between them. The southern chain is generally higher than the one to the north.

T **Technology Skills**

T Technology Skills

Researching on the Internet Assign pairs to work together to research three important world rivers, such as the Nile, Amazon, and Yangtze. Then ask them to make charts showing these rivers' lengths, the continents they run through, the various features in the areas they run through, and what features make them unique. Ask volunteers to give presentations about the rivers and explain why they chose the rivers they did. **Interpersonal, Visual/Spatial**

R Reading Skills

Applying Point out the word *channel* and the Academic Vocabulary definition. Explain that in addition to the technical meaning as it pertains to geography, the word has different but related meanings. Have students look up and identify synonyms for the word. **Ask:** What synonym refers to the technical meaning of channel as it relates to geography? *(Conduit is a synonym for* channel.*)*

Have students use the term *channel* in different sentences to help them understand each of the different meanings of the word. **BL** **Verbal/Linguistic**

C Critical Thinking Skills

Making Inferences Ask a volunteer to read aloud the last paragraph in the section "Waterways." Explain that typically when an area floods at the same time each year it is called seasonal flooding. **Ask:** Why was the seasonal flooding of the Nile a benefit to Egypt? *(This made the soil fertile and provided water for crops.)*

Continue by discussing the attributes of a civilization. Guide students to reinforce what they have learned by discussing that the attributes of a civilization often include written records, a government, an organized religion, art, and technology. **Ask:** Why did the ability to grow plentiful food lead Egyptians to form a civilization? *(Responses will vary, but should include that the ability to easily produce plentiful food gave people the wealth and leisure to develop the attributes of civilization.)* **Verbal/Linguistic**

ANSWER, p. 266

CRITICAL THINKING Egyptians today control the waters of the Nile. With dams and man-made lakes, they now have a predictable and steady supply of water year-round to grow crops. The downside is that the silt no longer settles on the land to enrich the soil's fertility and they must use fertilizers.

Lush green farmland contrasts sharply with the vast desert areas that stretch for hundreds of miles on either side of the Nile River.
▶ **CRITICAL THINKING**
Analyzing How is the relationship of Egyptians to the Nile River today different from the relationship of ancient Egyptians to the river?

Academic Vocabulary

channel course

Waterways

For centuries, North Africa has been linked by the Mediterranean Sea to other lands. The sea has brought trade, new ideas, and conquering armies.

Next to the Mediterranean, the most important body of water in the region is the Nile River. At 4,160 miles (6,695 km), the mighty Nile is the longest river in the world. It begins far south of Egypt at Lake Victoria in East Africa. That lake sits on the border of Uganda and Tanzania. The river flows northward, joined by several tributaries. The most important of them is the Blue Nile, which begins in the highlands of Ethiopia.

The Nile has a massive delta at its mouth. A **delta** is an area formed by soil deposits that build up as river water slows down. Many deltas form where a river enters a larger body of water. The Nile delta is found where the Nile meets the Mediterranean Sea. Here, at the mouth of the river, the Nile's delta covers more than 9,500 square miles (24,605 sq. km)—larger than the size of New Hampshire. The river once took seven different **channels**, or courses, to reach the sea. Today, only two remain. The others have been filled with soil.

The Nile brings life to dry Egypt. In ancient times, filled by rains to the south, the Nile flooded each year. These floods left **silt**—a fine, rich soil that is excellent for farming—along the banks of the river and in the delta. Farmers used the soil to grow crops. Because they could grow large amounts of food, they were able to support the growth of a great civilization. Ancient Egypt was called "the gift of the Nile."

266 *Chapter 9*

©B. Anthony Stewart/National Geographic Society/Corbis

---

netw⊙rks *Online Teaching Options*

MAP

The Nile River

Discussing Using the map that highlights the Nile River and delta, lead a class discussion of the changes that have taken place to the tributaries and the river itself over time. Discuss the changes that happen to the river and delta during the seasons. Have students review and explain the characteristics of the Nile and how it affects the surrounding communities. **AL** **Verbal/Linguistic**

See page 261C for other online activities.

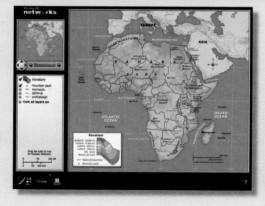

Today, several dams control the floods. The largest is Aswān High Dam. These dams hold back the high volume of water produced in the rainy season. The water can then be released during the year. An important benefit is that Egypt's farmers today can grow crops year-round. This is the water the farmer Hassan uses to grow his wheat. Another benefit of the dams is that people in Egypt have security from floods. One negative consequence of the dams is that the silt no longer settles on the land and enriches the soil.

Egypt controls another important waterway. This one, the Suez Canal, is human-made. The canal connects the Mediterranean Sea to the Red Sea. As a result, it links Europe and North Africa to the Indian and Pacific oceans. International trade depends on this canal. Using it enables ships traveling between Asia and Europe to avoid going all the way around Africa. The Suez Canal saves many days of travel time and much costly fuel.

✓ **READING PROGRESS CHECK**

Citing Text Evidence Why was ancient Egypt called "the gift of the Nile"?

Climate

GUIDING QUESTION *How do people survive in a dry climate?*

What would it be like if it hardly ever rained? That is the situation that many North Africans face. Large areas of the region receive only a few inches of rainfall each year—if that much.

A container ship passes through Egypt's Suez Canal, one of the world's most heavily used shipping lanes. Opened in 1869, the canal has been enlarged over the years to handle much bigger ships.

▶ **CRITICAL THINKING**
Describing What advantages does the Suez Canal provide for ship travel?

Frederic Neema/Workbook Stock/Getty Images

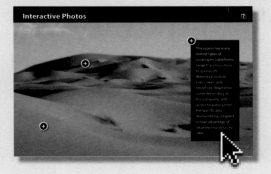

IMAGE

The Suez Canal

Integrating Visual Information Use the interactive image to discuss information about the Suez Canal with students. Call on volunteers to suggest the advantages of this human-made waterway as you list them on the board. Have students copy the list of these advantages in their notebooks. Encourage students to make comparisons to other human-made waterways discussed in previous chapters. **AL** Verbal/Linguistic

See page 261C for other online activities.

Lissa Harrison

Interactive Photos

R **Reading Skills**

Specifying Explain that the Nile remains important to Egypt's economy, even today. To enhance its benefits, modern Egyptians have built several dams along the Nile. **Ask:**

- **What are some of the advantages of the dams?** *(Advantages: farmers can raise crops all year long; floods are no longer a danger.)*

- **What are the disadvantages of the dams?** *(The Nile no longer deposits rich silt on its banks so farmers must use chemical fertilizers which pollute the river.)* **Logical/Mathematical**

C1 **Critical Thinking Skills**

Recognizing Relationships Encourage students to discuss ways in which technology has improved communications between different regions, such as the building of roads and railroads. Remind them that explorers, as well as engineers, have sought ways to shorten distances between places and people. **Ask:**

- **Why did engineers build the Suez Canal?** *(to make it easier for traders and travelers to get to Asia)*

- **What benefits did the Suez Canal bring to trade?** *(It resulted in a shorter route into the Indian and Pacific Oceans so that international trading became easier between Asia and Europe. The canal also saves fuel and time travel, which would make traded items less costly. Overall, this would increase trade between Asia and Europe.)* **BL** **Verbal/Linguistic**

C2 **Critical Thinking Skills**

Identifying Problems Point out that nearly everyone likes warm, sunny weather but that too much heat and sun can have drawbacks. **Ask:** **What are some of the problems a community might have after long hot periods without rain?** *(Answers will vary but may include restrictions against watering lawns and gardens, fewer and more expensive fruits and vegetables, the closing of public pools and fountains, air pollution, and the increased risk of wildfires.)* **Naturalist**

ANSWERS, p. 267

✓ **READING PROGRESS CHECK** Sample answer: Ancient Egypt was called the "gift of the Nile" because the river's waters made farming in the dry region possible.
CRITICAL THINKING It enables ships traveling between Asia and Europe to avoid going all the way around Africa, saving many days of travel time and costly fuel.

C Critical Thinking Skills

Determining Cause and Effect Review the different landforms found in the countries of North Africa. Have students identify which landforms can be found in each country. **Ask:**

- **What effect might the North African mountains have on the climate in the areas south of them?** *(They can affect the climates by blocking rainfall in areas on their southern slopes.)*

- **What is another explanation for inland North Africa's hot, dry climate?** *(High pressure air systems bring hot, dry air from the south to inland North Africa, where it remains for much of the year.)* **Logical/Mathematical**

V Visual Skills

Diagramming Have students diagram the rain shadow effect. Students may use the description of this effect, located in a previous chapter of the text, or you can provide them with online references for further information. Provide a completed diagram version for students to check their diagrams. **BL Visual/ Spatial**

W Writing Skills

Narrative Encourage students to imagine that they are tourists traveling through the Sahara Desert. Have them write a letter to a friend or family member describing what they see. Have them include the words *erg*, *oasis*, *hamada*, and *nomad* in their narratives. Explain the meanings of these words if students are having difficulty. **ELL Verbal/Linguistic**

R Reading Skills

Listing Guide students in a discussion about how the Sahara desert forms a barrier between North Africa and Africa's more southern areas. **Ask:**

- **What are some of the most important problems in traveling through the Sahara?** *(Possible answers may include: its vast size, dust storms, shifting sand dunes, heat, little to no water)*

- **Why would this barrier have been more significant in the past, such as before the early 1900s?** *(Possible answer: Before air travel, the only way to get past the desert was to travel through it or around it.)* **AL Verbal/Linguistic**

ANSWER, p. 268

CRITICAL THINKING Sand dunes are formed by strong winds that also change the shape and size of the dunes.

Causes of North Africa's Climates

C The Atlas Mountains play a major role in controlling the climate in the western part of North Africa. These mountains create the rain shadow effect. Moist air blows southward from the Atlantic Ocean **V** and the Mediterranean Sea toward the mountains. As the air rises up the northern slopes, it cools and releases rain. By the time it passes over the mountains, the air is dry. This dry air reaches the interior. Inland areas, then, remain arid.

The vast inland area of North Africa is dry for another reason. High-pressure air systems descend over areas to the south of the region for much of the year. They send hot, dry air blowing to the north. This air mass dries out the land. On the rare occasions when it does rain in the desert, the southern winds soon follow. They dry the land and leave behind **wadis**, or dry streambeds.

Desert and Semiarid Areas

Landscapes in the Sahara include rugged mountains, stony plains, and large sand dunes. A traveler (left) leads a camel caravan past towering dunes in the Moroccan part of the Sahara. Farther east, Egypt's part of the Sahara (right)—called the Libyan Desert—has rocky surfaces.
▶ **CRITICAL THINKING**
Describing How are sand dunes formed?

W Much of North Africa, then, is covered by a desert: the Sahara. Imagine a vast expanse of space, like an ocean, but covered in sand and rock. That is what the Sahara looks like. Spreading across more than 3.5 million square miles (9.1 million sq. km), the Sahara is as large as the entire United States. It covers most of North Africa and spills into three other regions of Africa, as well.

R The Sahara's vast stretches of sand are called **ergs**. Strong winds blow the sand about, creating huge dust storms that choke people and animals that are caught outside. The winds also build towering sand dunes. When new winds blow, they can change the shape and size of those dunes.

netw⊙rks *Online Teaching Options*

MAP

Climates: North Africa

Comparing and Contrasting Display the climate layer of the Chapter Opener map to review and discuss the various climates found in the region. Click on each climate for more information. Have students compare and contrast the different climates to each other and to those in other nations previously discussed. **Visual/Spatial, Verbal/Linguistic**

See page 261C for other online activities.

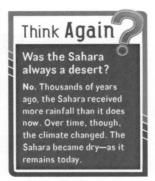

Hemis/Photoshot

Ergs cover only about a quarter of the Sahara. In other areas, rocky plateaus called *hamadas* and rocks eroded by wind are common. Some areas contain oases, areas fed by underground sources of water. Plants can grow in oases and trade caravans that cross the desert stop at them for needed water. **Nomads**, people who move about from place to place in search of food, rely on these oases during their travels. They use the plants to graze herds of sheep or other animals. Some people live on oases and grow crops.

In the North African part of the Sahara, temperatures soar during the day in the summer. They can reach as high as 136°F (58°C). During the winter, though, daytime temperatures can drop as low as 55°F (13°C).

Coastal areas of North Africa have a Mediterranean climate that is well suited for growing cereal crops, citrus fruits, grapes, olives, and dates.

C

Mediterranean and Other Climates

North of the desert are different climate zones. A band of steppes encircle the desert immediately to the north. Temperatures here are high, and rainfall is slightly greater than in the desert. This band extends to the eastern coast. Coastal cities in Libya receive only 10 inches to 15 inches (25 cm to 38 cm) of rain per year. Alexandria, near Egypt's coast, generally receives only 7 inches (18 cm) of rainfall per year.

R

A Mediterranean climate dominates the western coast. This climate gives the region warm, dry summers and mild, rainy winters. More rain falls along the coast than in the dry interior. Rain amounts are higher in the west than in the east. In the west, they are higher on the mountain slopes than along the coast. Coastal areas of Morocco receive 32 inches (81 cm) or less of rain per year.

Think Again?

Was the Sahara always a desert?

No. Thousands of years ago, the Sahara received more rainfall than it does now. Over time, though, the climate changed. The Sahara became dry—as it remains today.

Chapter 9 **269**

Lissa Harrison

IMAGE

Mediterranean Climates and Agriculture

Summarizing As a class, use the interactive image of agriculture in the region to discuss the Mediterranean climate zone that exists in some areas of North Africa. Call on volunteers to suggest ways that the climate in each area might affect shelter, food, and livestock. Have students write a brief paragraph summarizing the importance of the Mediterranean climate to the agricultural economies of the countries that are located in this climate zone. Encourage students to review a climate map as a reference. Volunteers may read their paragraphs to the class.

BL Verbal/Linguistic, Naturalist

See page 261C for other online activities.

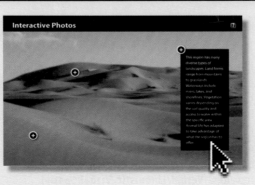

Interactive Photos

C Critical Thinking Skills

Giving Examples Review with students the hazards of the desert. **Ask:**

- What are some examples of desert features that make it possible for people to survive in the Sahara? *(oases, underground sources of water)*
- What aspects of this way of life might be important to the nomads of the Sahara desert? *(Possible responses: This is their traditional lifestyle and the only one they have ever known. They are familiar with the environment and how to survive there. They have strong ties to their families and friends there. They may have cultural traditions that are related to life in the desert.)* **BL** Interpersonal, Intrapersonal

R Reading Skills

Identifying Point out to students that not all of North Africa is desert. Nearer to the coast, the climate changes. Have students read the text, then discuss the information about the climate zones. **Ask:**

- What climate does the area just north of the desert have? *(Steppe area just north of the desert has high temperatures and slightly more rain than the desert area.)*
- What is the yearly rainfall for cities in Libya near the coast? *(They receive 10 to 15 inches (25 cm to 38 cm) of rain per year.)*
- What is the yearly rainfall for cities in Egypt near the coast? *(Alexandria receives 7 inches (18 cm) of rain per year.)*
- What type of climate does the western coast have? *(The western coast has a Mediterranean climate with mild, rainy winters, and warm dry summers)*
- What is the yearly rainfall in coastal areas with a Mediterranean climate? *(Coastal cities, like Morocco, receive about 32 inches (81 cm) of rain per year.)*
- Using your prior knowledge skills about climates, what do you predict the climate is like in the mountainous areas of North Africa? *(Students' answers will vary, but should predict that since these areas have a higher elevation they will have lower temperatures and more rain.)* **Verbal/ Linguistic**

V Visual Skills

Speculating Have students study the photograph on this page. Help them to understand that it shows a desert environment and review facts about desert climates. Then, point out the pump. Encourage students to speculate about the source of this water and how they think it is used. Have them read the section "Water" to check their predictions. **Visual/ Spatial, Logical/Mathematical**

V

C Critical Thinking Skills

Making Inferences Help students see that an uneven distribution of resources among countries makes some countries dependent on others. Use the resources map from the Chapter Opener to help students understand the distribution of resources. **Ask:**

- **What principle resources are found in North Africa?** *(oil and gas)*
- **Which North African country has the most oil?** *(Libya)*
- **What important resource does North Africa need?** *(water)*
- **Why are North Africa's oil and natural gas reserves desired by many other countries?** *(Oil and gas provide most of the energy needed for the world's factories, transportation, and homes, and many countries do not have enough oil and gas to meet their energy needs.)* **ELL**

T Technology Skills

Analyzing News Media Explain to students that a country's resources are important economically and politically. They are a measure of a country's wealth and position in the world. Have them use the Internet to research the effect the discovery of oil reserves had on North Africa's status in the world. Ask them to find news items that discuss how problems with a country such as Libya might affect the price of oil and its availability in the United States. Have them make a slide show of these news items. Ask volunteers to accompany their slide show with brief talks to the class. **BL Intrapersonal**

As North Africa's population grows, the demand for water increases. This pump provides water from deep underground to people living in a Sahara environment.
▶ **CRITICAL THINKING**
Describing Why is so much water available underground in parts of the Sahara?

Mountain areas with highland climates also receive more rainfall—as much as 80 inches (203 cm) per year. Highland climates are found within the mountains. Morocco's Atlas Mountains often are covered by snow in the winter. As hard as it might be to believe, just a few hundred miles north of the Sahara, people can snow ski.

☑ **READING PROGRESS CHECK**

Analyzing Where do you think most people in North Africa live? Explain why this might be so.

Resources

GUIDING QUESTION *What resources does North Africa have?*

Oil and natural gas are resources that we use to power our cars and trucks and to generate electricity and heat. Some countries of North Africa have these resources in large quantities. All five countries in the region, though, struggle to get enough of another precious resource—water.

Oil, Gas, and Other Resources

Libya is the most oil-rich country in North Africa. Its oil reserves are ranked ninth in the world and it exports more oil than all but 15 other countries. Libya also has natural gas, but in lesser amounts. The money Libya earns from oil has fueled its economy.

Algeria has large reserves of natural gas—more than all but nine other countries. It also has large supplies of oil. These two resources make up nearly all of its exports.

©Inge Yspeert/Corbis

270 *Chapter 9*

netw⚙rks   *Online Teaching Options*

GRAPHIC ORGANIZER

Resources in North Africa

Illustrating Have students study the interactive graphic organizer about natural resources in North Africa. Then guide them in a discussion and review what they have learned. Encourage them to use the resources map from the Chapter Opener for review while working to complete this organizer as a class. Illustrate how to create an outline to organize the information about North Africa's resources. **Verbal/Linguistic, Visual/Spatial**

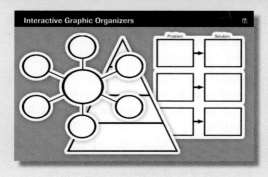

Interactive Graphic Organizers

ANSWERS, p. 270

☑ **READING PROGRESS CHECK** Sample answer: Most people in North Africa probably live along the coasts, where rainfall is highest, and along the Nile, which can support farming.

CRITICAL THINKING Underground water is trapped by layers of rock and is available for tapping.

Like Algeria, Egypt has larger reserves of natural gas than oil. Still, it has enough oil to supply most of what it consumes each year. Egypt even sells a small amount to other countries.

Tunisia's main resources are iron ore and phosphates. **Phosphates** are chemical compounds that are often used in fertilizers. These products are important in Morocco, as well. In addition, rich fishing grounds off Morocco's coast are a vital resource. Fish is one of that country's leading exports.

Water

Limited rainfall and high temperatures in this region leave little freshwater on the surface. Rains can be heavy when they come, but the sandy soil soon absorbs the water. Dry winds evaporate the rest. Only the Nile is a reliable source of water for farming throughout the year.

How vital is the Nile? Ninety-five out of every 100 Egyptians live within 12 miles (19 km) of the Nile River or its delta. Yet this narrow river valley and the large delta make up only a small part of Egypt's total area. Without the waters of the Nile, Egypt's people could not survive.

Outside of the Nile valley, most of the region's water needs are met with water that comes from oases and aquifers. **Aquifers** are underground layers of rock in which water collects. People use wells to tap into this water. Libya, for instance, relies on aquifers to meet almost all of its water needs. However, nearly half of Libya's people have no access to water that has been treated to be sure it meets health standards.

A growing population in this region poses problems for the future. Demand for the water in an aquifer shared by Algeria, Libya, and Tunisia has increased ninefold in recent years. In North Africa, aquifers take a long time to refill. If people continue to take water out at a high rate, the aquifers might not be able to refill quickly enough and the region's water problem will become much worse.

W

FOLDABLES
Study Organizer
Include this lesson's information in your Foldable®.

✔ **READING PROGRESS CHECK**

Analyzing Why would aquifers take a long time to fill up in North Africa?

LESSON 1 REVIEW **CCSS**

Reviewing Vocabulary (Tier Three Words)
1. In which desert feature can people live year-round, a *wadi* or an oasis? Why? RH.6-8.4

Answering the Guiding Questions
2. *Describing* How has the Mediterranean Sea affected the region? RH.6-8.5
3. *Analyzing* Does the northern or the southern chain of the Atlas Mountains receive more rainfall? Why? RH.6-8.1

4. *Determining Central Ideas* Which nations in the region are likely to import energy resources? Why? RH.6-8.2
5. *Analyzing* How can governments in the region prevent aquifers from being used up? RH.6-8.1
6. *Informative/Explanatory Writing* Write a paragraph comparing and contrasting the climates of Egypt and Morocco. WHST.6-8.2, WHST.6-8.4

Chapter 9 **271**

LESSON 1 REVIEW ANSWERS

Reviewing Vocabulary

1. People can live year-round on oases because water is always present. *Wadis* are streambeds that fill with water only when it rains and dry up soon after.

Answering the Guiding Questions

2. **Describing** The Mediterranean Sea has linked North Africa to other lands for centuries. It also provides warm, moist air that produces rain on the north side of the Atlas Mountains.

3. **Analyzing** The northern chain of the Atlas Mountains receive more rainfall because the warm, moist air of the Mediterranean flows over them. By the time the air reaches the southern chain, it is already dry.

4. **Determining Central Ideas** Tunisia and Morocco, which do not have oil or gas, probably need to import energy resources. Libya, Algeria, and Egypt all have enough of these resources to export some.

5. **Analyzing** Possible answer: To prevent aquifers from drying up, governments might have to limit the amount of water people can use. They might try finding other sources of water.

6. **Informative/Explanatory** Students' paragraphs should emphasize the overall dryness of Egypt, which includes only dry steppe and desert climates, with the more varied climates of Morocco, which have those two climate zones and also a Mediterranean climate along the coast and highland climates in the mountains.

C **Critical Thinking Skills**

Comparing Point out that several North African countries have similar kinds and amounts of resources. **Ask: In what way are Egypt's resources similar to those of Algeria?** *(They both have large reserves of oil but larger reserves of natural gas than of oil.)* **AL** Verbal/Linguistic

W **Writing Skills**

Argument Ask students to form pairs and have each pair member write an argument about the wisdom of using water from underground desert sources. Students should note that its use as a resource may draw more people to live in the desert and consider how that will affect water reserves. They should consider wherther or not anyone knows for certain how much water is available from these underground reservoirs. They should also question wether or not it is appropriate to restrict or regulate how this water can be used. For example, should developers be able to move in and build golf courses and swimming pools? What might happen if the sources were to suddenly dry up? **BL** Verbal/Linguistic

Content Background Knowledge

Phosphates have other uses besides making fertilizer. Some of these are:

- To make water-based paints
- To make polishes for aluminum
- To make various materials flame resistant
- To make water safe for drinking

CLOSE & REFLECT

Have students consider this lesson's Essential Question: *How does geography influence the way people live?* Tell students to look back at the images in this lesson. Encourage students to think about how landforms and waterways, climates, and natural resources affect the way people live.

ANSWER, p. 271

✔ **READING PROGRESS CHECK** Sample answer: Aquifers in North Africa take a long time to fill up because low rainfall means there is little water provided to add to them.

The History of North Africa

ENGAGE

Bellringer Help students appreciate how long ago Egyptian civilization began. Tell them that it began before the religions of Judaism, Christianity, and Islam were founded and before the ancient Roman and Greek civilizations had started. Have students discuss what they would see if they could travel back in time to ancient Egypt. Point out that not only Egypt, but also the other North African countries have long and varied histories. Have students write lists about what they would like to know about North Africa. Post the lists on a bulletin board in the classroom; these lists will be referred to again at the end of this lesson.

TEACH & ASSESS

R1 Reading Skills

Determining Central Ideas Read aloud the first paragraph of the section "The Rise of Egypt." **Ask: What idea is the most important in this paragraph?** *(Some Egyptians began to do jobs other than farming.)* Guide students to understand that plentiful food made it unnecessary for everyone to farm, thus giving some people the opportunity to become craftspeople, soldiers, and rulers. **AL Verbal/Linguistic**

C Critical Thinking Skills

Making Inferences Have a volunteer read aloud the last paragraph of the section "The Rise of Egypt." **Ask: What words in this paragraph suggest that the rulers of ancient Egypt governed undemocratically?** *(Students should note that the text reads that the people were made to work on projects and were forced to join the army, suggesting that they had no choice but to obey.)* **BL Verbal/Linguistic**

R2 Reading Skills

Using Context Clues Explain that it is often unnecessary to use a dictionary to understand a new word because the context, or surrounding words, may define it. **Ask: What words in sentences two and three of the second paragraph in "The Rise of Egypt" explain the word *pharaoh*?** *(king and ruled)*

ANSWER, p. 272

Taking Notes About 3000 B.C.: Two kingdoms of Egypt united. **About 1500 B.C.:** Egypt begins to expand its empire. **600s B.C.:** Carthage founded, begins rise to power **100s B.C.:** Rome gains control of North Africa. **A.D. 642–705:** Muslim conquest of North Africa completed. **1500s:** Foreigners seize parts of North Africa. **1952–1962:** North African nations gain independence. **2011:** Arab Spring revolts unseat governments in Tunisia, Egypt, Libya and bring about changes in Algeria, and Morocco.

---

networks

There's More Online!

☑ **IMAGES** Islam

☑ **MAP** The Punic Wars

☑ **ANIMATION** How the Pyramids Were Built

☑ **SLIDE SHOW** Egyptian Artifacts

☑ **VIDEO**

Reading HELPDESK (CCSS)

Academic Vocabulary RH.6-8.4
(Tier Two Words)
- project
- demonstrate

Content Vocabulary RH.6-8.4
(Tier Three Words)
- pharaoh
- myrrh
- hieroglyphics
- convert
- monotheism
- caliph
- regime
- fundamentalist
- civil war

TAKING NOTES: Key Ideas and Details RH.6-8.2, RH.6-8.7

Summarize As you read about the history of North Africa, note key events and their importance using a graphic organizer like the one below.

Year, Event	Importance

Lesson 2

The History of North Africa

ESSENTIAL QUESTION · *How does religion shape society?*

IT MATTERS BECAUSE
One of the world's first civilizations arose in North Africa thousands of years ago.

Ancient Egypt

GUIDING QUESTION *Why was ancient Egypt important?*

Egypt, in North Africa, was one of the earliest known civilizations. Egyptian civilization arose along the Nile River, and Egyptians depended on the Nile for their livelihood. They built cities, organized government, and invented a writing system to keep records and create literature.

The Rise of Egypt

People have been living along the banks of the Nile River for thousands of years. As many as 8,000 years ago, people settled in the area to farm. The rich floodwaters of the Nile allowed farmers to produce enough food to support a growing population. Over time, some members of this early society began to do other things besides farming. Some made pottery. Others crafted jewelry. Some became soldiers. A few became kings.

About 5,000 years ago, two kingdoms along the Nile were united into one. For most of the next 3,000 years, kings called **pharaohs** ruled the land. The great mass of people farmed the land. They paid a share of their crops to the government. The government's leaders also made them work on important **projects**, or planned activities. These projects included building temples and other monuments. Sometimes the people had to fight in the pharaoh's armies.

(l to r) KENNETH GARRETT/National Geographic Stock; Guenter Fischer/Getty Images; Khaled Desouki/AFP/Getty Images

---

networks *Online Teaching Options*

VIDEO

Gift of the Nile

Giving Examples Use this video about the life of ancient Egyptians and their use of the Nile River to introduce the lesson. As they watch the video, ask students to write down what they learned from the video about how people lived during ancient times. Then have them provide examples of ancient ways of life in a guided class discussion.
ELL Visual/Spatial

See page 261D for other online activities.

BBC Motion Gallery Education

The Expansion of Egypt

R1
For centuries, Egypt traded with nearby lands. Merchants carried Egyptian grain and other products to the south. There they traded for luxury goods like gold, ivory, and incense. They also traded to the east for wood from what is now Lebanon.

Around 1500 B.C., the Egyptians decided to expand their area. They took control of lands to the south that held gold and seized areas along the Red Sea that had **myrrh**. This plant substance gives off a pleasing scent. Priests burned it in religious ceremonies. Egypt also conquered the eastern shores of the Mediterranean. That gave them control of the timber there. Egypt's kings gained wealth by taxing conquered peoples.

C

Religion and Culture in Ancient Egypt

The pharaoh was the head of Egyptian society. He was seen as more than a man. He was thought to be the son of the sun god. The Egyptians practiced polytheism, which is the belief in many gods. The sun god was one of the most important of their gods. His daily journey through the sky brought the warmth needed to grow crops. The pharaoh, Egyptians believed, connected them to the gods. He made sure that they would flourish as a people.

R2

KENNETH GARRETT/National Geographic Stock

Academic Vocabulary

project a planned activity

One of the most famous Egyptian pharaohs was the boy-king Tutankhamen. At 10 years of age, Tutankhamen became ruler of Egypt, but he died unexpectedly nine years later.
▶ **CRITICAL THINKING**
Describing Based on the map, describe the area controlled by ancient Egypt.

Ancient Egypt

Mediterranean Sea

Dead Sea

NILE DELTA
LOWER EGYPT
30°N
Great Pyramid and Sphinx • Giza • Memphis

N W E S

EASTERN DESERT

WESTERN DESERT

UPPER EGYPT

Red Sea

☐ Nile Valley

25°N

• Thebes

First Cataract

TROPIC OF CANCER

NUBIA

0   100 miles
0   100 kilometers
Lambert Azimuthal Equal-Area projection

Second Cataract

30°E   35°E

(l) ©Ocean/Corbis, ©Kryssia Campos/Getty Images, (t) Erica Simone Leeds, (b) ©IG Photography/Alamy

SLIDE SHOW

Egyptian Artifacts

Describing Have students view the slide show about Egyptian artifacts. Explain that the objects shown were made by Egyptian artists and craftspeople. Point out that art and craftsmanship is an important aspect of a civilization. Encourage students to describe the objects shown in each slide in terms of the skill and materials used in making them. Have students explain what this tells them about certain aspects of Egyptian culture. **Visual/Spatial, Interpersonal**

See page 261D for other online activities.

Slide Show

R1 Reading Skills

Specifying Ask a volunteer to read the first paragraph of "The Expansion of Egypt" aloud. **Ask:**

- **What did Egyptian traders exchange for foreign goods?** *(Egyptian grain)*
- **What did they receive in exchange?** *(luxury goods)*
  AL **Verbal/Linguistic**

C Critical Thinking Skills

Identifying Evidence Point out to students that trade with other countries can lead to attempts to gain more power and wealth. **Ask: What evidence is given in this paragraph that this occurred in ancient Egypt?** *(Around 1500 B.C. Egyptians began to conquer areas that contained such valuable goods as gold, timber, and myrrh.)* **BL** **Logical/ Mathematical, Interpersonal**

R2 Reading Skills

Defining Ask students to look at the word *polytheism*. Have a volunteer read the definition that follows this word. Have students find the word in a dictionary to learn what each separate syllable of the word means. **Ask: How does this word define itself?** *(Sample answer: "poly" means many, "theos" means god, and "-ism" refers to a belief. Therefore* polytheism *means the belief in many gods.)* **Verbal/Linguistic**

V Visual Skills

Reading a Map Have students study the map of ancient Egypt. Explain that it shows two geographical features that gave Egypt access to other areas. **Ask:**

- **Where is the land connection between Egypt and Southwest Asia located?** *(in northeast Egypt between the Mediterranean and Red Seas)*
- **What waterway gave Egypt access to lands to its south?** *(the Nile River)* **Visual/Spatial**

ANSWER, p. 273

CRITICAL THINKING Ancient Egypt had a wide delta area near the Mediterranean and a long, stem-like territory that extended south along the Nile River.

R1 Reading Skills

Specifying Point out that customs changed over time. For example, Egyptians made different kinds of tombs over the ages. **Ask:**

- **What were the first tombs like?** *(They were low structures built of bricks.)*
- **When did Egyptian workers begin building pyramids as tombs?** *(2600 B.C.)*
- **What building material was used for these tombs?** *(rock)*
- **What was the final form of Egyptian tombs?** *(They were caves that workers carved from rocky cliffs.)* **AL** **Verbal/ Linguistic**

T Technology Skills

Making Presentations Tell students that they can learn to decode words written in hieroglyphics. Divide them into small groups and ask each group to find a reputable Web site on the Internet that shows how to translate their names or simple phrases into hieroglyphics. Then have them write their words or phrases in Egyptian hieroglyphics large enough to display to the class. Call on volunteers to give brief talks comparing the ancient Egyptian system of writing with the alphabet system that we use in English today. **BL**
Interpersonal, Verbal/Linguistic

R2 Reading Skills

Determining Central Ideas Have students study the infographic at the bottom of the page. Circulate to review the information and answer any questions. Then, **ask:**

- **How did the tombs built for pharaohs show that Egyptians believed in life after death?** *(Possible answers: the tombs were furnished with all the things the pharaohs might use in their daily lives, such as food; the pharaohs' bodies were preserved as mummies.)*
- **What are the three theories of how the pyramids were built shown in the infographic? Which do you think is most likely?** *(The three theories are ramps on the outside of the pyramid, the use of cranes, and ramps on the inside of the pyramid. Students should pick one theory and explain why they think it is the best.)* **Interpersonal**

ANSWER, p. 274

CRITICAL THINKING Pyramid building required planning and measurement. Those who came after built on the Egyptians' architectural knowledge, used tools that the Egyptians developed, and planned their buildings according to mathematical equations for figuring distance, time, and weight to transport heavy material.

R1 Egyptians believed in life after death. Because of this belief, the pharaohs had vast tombs built for themselves. The tombs were filled with riches, food, and other goods. These goods were meant to support the pharaohs in the afterlife. When the pharaoh died, his body was preserved as a mummy and placed in the tomb.

At first the tombs were low structures built of bricks. Around 2600 B.C., the first pyramid was built as a tomb. These huge tombs, made of rock, were built by thousands of workers. Later, the pharaohs stopped building pyramids. Instead, workers carved their tombs out of rocky cliffs.

T Historians know much about ancient Egypt because the Egyptians had a system of writing. The system, called **hieroglyphics**, used pictures to represent sounds or words.

Influence of Ancient Egypt

Academic Vocabulary

demonstrate to show

The Egyptians made many advances in mathematics and science. They used mathematics to measure farm fields and to figure out taxes. Their studies of the stars and planets led to advances in astronomy. They were masters of engineering as **demonstrated** by their great pyramids and temples.

R2

INFOGRAPHIC

HOW DID THEY DO THAT?
PYRAMIDS OF EGYPT
The pyramids, the tombs of the pharaohs, were engineering marvels for their time. Several theories exist on how the ancient Egyptians were able to build these massive structures.

Workers moved huge stone blocks on ramps built on the outside of the pyramids.

Cranes were used to lift the stone blocks during construction.

Workers moved the stone blocks on ramps built on the inside of the building.

BUILDING THE PYRAMIDS
Thousands of people were involved in building a pyramid. Much of the work was done by farmers during the Nile floods, when they could not tend their fields. Surveyors, engineers, carpenters, and stonecutters also lent their skills.

▶ **CRITICAL THINKING**
Analyzing How might the building of the pyramids have led to advances in science and mathematics?

---

net**w**orks   *Online Teaching Options*

ANIMATION

How the Pyramids Were Built

Integrating Visual Information Have students view the animation depicting the building of the pyramids. Help students understand such technical information as the measurements used for creating the pyramids. For example, explain that a cubit equals 45.72 cm. After viewing and discussing the animation, have students write a brief essay about the building of the pyramids. Encourage them to conduct research as needed to strengthen their essays. **ELL** **Visual/Spatial, Logical/Mathematical**

See page 261D for other online activities.

Guenter Fischer/Getty Images

C Some of this knowledge was spread to other areas through trade and conquest. Later, Egypt had one of the world's earliest libraries. It was built in the 200s B.C., when Greece conquered and ruled Egypt. The library stored many important works of ancient literature.

☑ READING PROGRESS CHECK

Determining Central Ideas Why is it important to know about ancient Egypt?

The Middle Ages

GUIDING QUESTION *How was North Africa connected to other areas?*

Today, people use the Internet to contact each other anywhere in the world. In ancient times, people had to make contact in person. The people of North Africa used the Mediterranean Sea to make this contact with other peoples. Sometimes they were joined by trade. Other times they were joined by conflict. **W**

Carthage and Rome

Western North Africa was first visited by other Mediterranean peoples in the 600s B.C. At that time, traders from what is now Lebanon sailed southwest across the Mediterranean. They built new settlements in many areas. One was a city in what is now Tunisia. They called it Carthage. Within about 200 years, the city had grown powerful. It controlled North Africa from modern Tunisia to Morocco. It also ruled parts of modern Spain and Italy. **R**

In the 200s B.C. and 100s B.C., Carthage fought three wars with the Roman Empire. In the last war, Rome defeated Carthage and destroyed the city. Rome, then, came to control western North Africa. Eventually, Rome conquered Egypt, as well.

The waters of a Roman bath reflect the ruins of the city of Leptis Magna in Libya. The Romans made Leptis Magna one of the most beautiful cities in North Africa during the A.D. 100s.

Identifying What ancient city fought Rome for control of much of North Africa?

Chapter 9 **275**

MAP

The Punic Wars

Creating a Chart Tell students that the wars fought between Rome and Carthage were called the Punic Wars. Use the map about the Punic Wars to teach the influence of Roman culture on North Africa. This map also shows the human-environment interaction with regard to geographic limitations and military movements. Make a chart on the chalkboard with the headings *Roman Influence on North Africa* and *Geographic Limitations on Military Movements*. As you discuss the map, have volunteers fill in the appropriate information under each heading. **ELL** **AL** **Visual/Spatial**

See page 261D for other online activities.

V Visual Skills

Making Inferences Lead students to discuss different ways that people react to new groups of people who have different cultural values or ideas. *(Students should identify the three main possibilities: to fully adopt the new ideas or behaviors, to fully reject the new group and its ideas, and to incorporate some of the ideas while holding on to some of the old ways.)* Have students study the photo and read the caption. **Ask: Why might you infer that each civilization influenced the other?** *(Possible answer: The columns and sculptures both show influences of Roman architecture. These influences can also be seen in the pyramids in Egypt, suggesting that some Egyptians were influenced by the Roman Empire.)* **BL**

C Critical Thinking Skills

Evaluating Point out that for most of history, people could only read books if they were in printed format. This meant that people needed to have access to the printed books. Libraries have played an important role in this. **Ask:**

- **Which country occupied Egypt when the first library was established?** *(Greece)*
- **What are some benefits of libraries?** *(They allow people to learn about the ideas and events of the past.)* **Verbal/Linguistic**

W Writing Skills

Argument As a class, read aloud the section called "To the Middle Ages." Ask students if they have friends abroad with whom they keep in touch through the Internet. Ask them if they think that close contact will help bring about better understanding between different cultures. Have them write a paragraph explaining why they think it will or will not. **AL** **Verbal/Linguistic**

R Reading Skills

Citing Text Evidence Have the class read aloud the first two paragraphs of the section "Carthage and Rome." **Ask:**

- **From which country did the founders of Carthage come?** *(from Lebanon)*
- **Which part of North Africa did Carthage dominate?** *(from Tunisia to Morocco)*
- **About when did Rome defeat Carthage and take control of western North Africa?** *(about 100 B.C.)*

ANSWERS, p. 275

☑ READING PROGRESS CHECK Possible answer: It is important to know about ancient Egypt because its people made many advances in knowledge and its culture influenced other lands.
Identifying Carthage

C Critical Thinking Skills

Making Inferences Lead students in a discussion about why people might reject some aspects of a foreign culture and accept others. **Ask:**

- **What was the main effect of the Roman conquest of North Africa?** *(Many North Africans became Christians.)*
- **Why do you think the original natives, the Berbers, are just one ethnic group of many in North Africa?** *(North African countries were conquered and occupied by other nations. Inhabitants of these other nations migrated to North Africa.)* **Logical/Mathematical**

R Reading Skills

Compare and Contrast Have students consider how the Muslim empire was organized politically. Then have students compare this with what they have just read about how ancient Egypt was ruled. **Ask:**

- **Who ruled in the Muslim empire?** *(the caliph)*
- **How did the caliph compare to the pharaohs of ancient Egypt?** *(they were both religious leaders)*
- **How were the caliph and pharaohs different?** *(The caliph had religious and politial authority, but he was not considered to be a god in the way that the pharoahs had been.)* **Verbal/Linguistic**

W Writing Skills

Argument Help students understand that Islamic rulers had trouble controlling North Africa because the individual Berber kingdoms were in constant conflict with one another. Point out that when a powerful kingdom arose in Cairo, Egypt, most of the people there converted to Islam. Ask students to write a paragraph arguing for the idea that a common religion and similar customs can bind people together. *(Students' arguments might include the idea that a common religion and similar customs make a group of people feel like a family. Like family members, they are inclined to help and defend each other and to work toward common goals. In addition, when people have common views, they are more likely to agree on the laws.)* **Verbal/Linguistic**

ANSWERS, p. 276

CRITICAL THINKING Islam spread outside of Arabia as its followers conquered other lands, especially in North Africa. Islamic rulers built empires and helped unite the peoples of Southwest Asia and North Africa.

☑ READING PROGRESS CHECK Possible answer: The Islamic empire had more impact on North Africa than the Roman Empire. Most North Africans adopted Islam and the Arabic language. Previously, only some North Africans had converted to Christianity under the Roman Empire; otherwise, that empire affected them very little.

Religion plays a central role in the lives of most North Africans today. These Muslim women gather for prayer in the main square of El Mansûra, a city in Egypt's Nile delta.
▶ **CRITICAL THINKING**
Describing How did Islam develop during the century after Muhammad?

During Roman times, many North Africans **converted**, or changed, religions. Because the Roman Empire had adopted Christianity, many North Africans converted to this religion. Others followed their native religions. Except for religion, Roman rule had little effect on native North Africans. Most people continued to live as before. Millions of Berbers who live in western North Africa today are descended from these native people.

Rise of Islam

The Roman Empire fell in the A.D. 400s. Afterward, several local kingdoms formed in North Africa. In the A.D. 600s, though, a new influence emerged in the region. The religion of Islam was founded on the Arabian Peninsula by the prophet Muhammad in A.D. 632. Followers of this religion—called Muslims—began to conquer other lands. By A.D. 642, they had conquered Egypt. By A.D. 705, they ruled all of North Africa. Islam, like Judaism and Christianity, is a monotheistic religion. **Monotheism** means belief in just one god.

Islamic Rule

The Muslim empire was ruled by the **caliph**. This figure had political and religious authority. Caliphs had trouble keeping control over North Africa, however. By the A.D. 800s, separate Berber kingdoms had arisen in parts of the region. These kingdoms often fought one another. Some gained control of most of North Africa. Others only ruled parts of the area.

An Islamic group known as the Fatamids arose in Egypt in the A.D. 1000s. Its rulers expanded Cairo and made it their capital. The city became a center of Muslim learning and trade.

Islamic Culture

At first, Berbers and Egyptians resisted the Islamic religion. By the A.D. 1000s, though, most of them had converted. They also adopted the Arabic language. This language and Islamic learning linked North Africa to the Muslim world. It also helped unite the cultures and people of North Africa and Southwest Asia. Considerable similarities between the regions exist to this day, more than 1,000 years later.

☑ READING PROGRESS CHECK

Identifying Point of View Did the Roman or the Islamic empire have more impact on North Africa? Why do you think so?

---

netw⊙rks   *Online Teaching Options*

IMAGE

Islam

Determining Central Ideas Have the class study the interactive image highlighting the religion of Islam. Call on volunteers to read the information provided about Islam given in the image and write significant facts on the board. Then have them use this information to discuss Islam's cultural influence on North Africa and its effects on Muslims' daily life. **ELL** **Visual/Linguistic, Interpersonal**

See page 261D for other online activities.

Interactive Photos

The Modern Era

GUIDING QUESTION *What leads people to revolt against a government?*

North Africans formed their own countries in the late 1900s. In recent decades, these countries have changed in far-reaching ways. Often, unrest accompanied the changes.

Foreign Rule

In the 1500s, North Africa began to fall under the rule of foreign armies. The Portuguese and Spanish captured parts of Morocco. The Ottoman Empire, based in modern Turkey, took the rest.

The 1800s saw Ottoman power weaken and Europeans move into North Africa. France began to conquer Algeria in 1830. Although it took several decades, by the late 1800s France controlled that area and Tunisia, too. Some Europeans who settled in these areas grew wealthy. Muslim natives, though, were largely poor. In the early 1900s, France and Spain split control of Morocco. At about the same time, Italy seized Libya.

C

Egypt kept its independence for much of the 1800s. Its kings tried to build a more modern state. One of the accomplishments was completing construction of the Suez Canal in 1869.

T

MAP SKILLS

1 **PLACES AND REGIONS**
Which North African country was the first to become independent?

2 **HUMAN GEOGRAPHY**
How was Libya governed before independence?

North African Independence

(1962, from France) Date of independence, ruling power

0 500 miles
0 500 kilometers
Lambert Azimuthal Equal-Area projection

MOROCCO (1956, from France)

WESTERN SAHARA (Morocco)

TUNISIA (1956, from France)

ALGERIA (1962, from France)

LIBYA (1951, from United Nations trusteeship, administered by British and French governors)

EGYPT (1922, from U.K.)

C Critical Thinking Skills

Making Inferences Lead a discussion about how the people of one nation might react to being ruled by a group of foreigners. Help them understand that foreign rulers might divide a country without regard to its population's sense of identity, use the natives as a source of cheap labor, exploit its resources, and impose customs that are contradictory to the native people's basic beliefs. **Ask: Why do you think that North Africans resented European rule?** *(Students' answers should be based on the statements in the text that Europeans who settled in North Africa were rich while the natives were poor and that France and Spain split Morocco between them. Answers might include reasons given in the class discussion.)* Have students study the map showing North African independence. Then have students answer the Map Skills questions. **BL** Verbal/Linguistic

T Technology Skills

Using and Citing Information Have groups of students use the Internet to research the building of the Suez Canal. They should learn what two bodies of water it connects, its purposes and advantages, and how it affected Egypt's independence. Ask a member of one group to present the information found. Then ask representatives of other groups to add to that information or correct it. Make sure each group cites the information and lists the Web sites that they used to gain their information. **BL** Interpersonal, Verbal/Linguistic

Content Background Knowledge

Foreign Occupations of Morocco Morocco is the North African country located closest to Europe. The Strait of Gibraltar made it highly vulnerable to early European invaders.

- **146 B.C.:** Morocco was conquered by the Romans
- **7th century:** Arabs began to control Morocco
- **1500s:** Spain and Portugal took over portions of Morocco
- **Mid 19th century:** Various European countries vied to control Morocco
- **1911:** France ruled Morocco
- **1953:** Morocco obtained independence

MAP

Compare Independence Movements

Comparing and Contrasting Use the map to compare the independence movements of the individual countries of North Africa. As a class, discuss which European countries colonized the North African countries and why. Then, with a partner, have students write paragraphs describing the similarities and differences of the independence struggles in each country. **BL** Verbal/Linguistic

ANSWERS, p. 277
MAP SKILLS
1. Egypt
2. Italy controlled Libya.

The History of North Africa

Thomas Hartwell/Time & Life Pictures/Getty Images

R Reading Skills

Stating Review the importance of the Suez Canal. Guide students to discuss its importance to the trade industry. Have students refer to Lesson 1 if they want further information. **Ask:**

- **When did Egypt lose its independence?** *(in 1882)*
- **What country took control of Egypt at that time?** *(Britain)*
- **Why do you think the British took control of Egypt?** *(Britain wanted to control the Suez Canal.)* **AL** **Verbal/Linguistic**

V Visual Skills

Creating a Time Line Have students read the section "Independence." Then, have them draw a vertical time line showing the sequence in which North African countries gained their independence. Encourage them to add any details given in the text about each country and its new government and to include illustrations about the events. When students have finished their time lines, display them on the wall. **Visual/Spatial, Kinesthetic**

Content Background Knowledge

French Colonialism in Algeria Describe the colonial period in Algeria for students.

- The Algerian people were ruled by the French military.
- French settlers in Algeria had representatives in government in France. The Algerian people had no such representation.
- French settlers built schools and hospitals, but very few Algerians went to school or benefited from French medical care.
- French settlers took much of the best land. Over time, many Algerian people moved onto less desirable land.
- About 200,000 Algerians fought on the side of the French during World War I. After the war, many soldiers stayed in France.

In 1987 soldiers marched in a parade in Tripoli, Libya's capital, to celebrate the rule of Muammar al-Qaddafi. Opponents finally overthrew the military dictator in 2011.

R

▶ **CRITICAL THINKING**
Analyzing Why was Qaddafi able to rule Libya for so long? Why was he finally overthrown?

The Suez Canal quickly became a vital waterway. Because of the canal's importance, though, other nations wanted to control Egypt. In 1882 Britain sent troops to Egypt. Kings continued to rule, but the British were the real power in the country.

Independence

Many North Africans resented European control. Independence movements arose across the region in the early 1900s. They gained strength after World War II. Italy had been defeated in the war, and France and Britain were severely weakened.

Egypt broke free of foreign control first. In 1952 a group of Egyptian army officers revolted against the king and the British. They created an independent republic, and they put the government in charge of the economy.

V

Algerians had to fight long and hard for independence. They rebelled against French rule starting in 1954. Not until 1962 did they succeed in ousting the French. Many Europeans fled the country after independence was achieved.

Military leaders also took control of Libya in 1969. They were led by Muammar al-Qaddafi. He remained in control of the nation—and its oil wealth—for more than 40 years. Tunisia and Morocco have avoided military rule. Tunisia has been a republic since gaining independence in 1959. Morocco has had a monarchy since gaining freedom from France in 1956.

Recent Decades

Independence has not always led to success for the countries of North Africa. Algeria has been plagued by unrest among Islamic

---

netw⊙rks   *Online Teaching Options*

GAME

Drag-and-Drop: Governments and Dictatorships

Making Connections Have students play the drag-and-drop game to learn about the governments and dictatorships in North Africa. Use this activity to introduce and to provide context for the development of independence movements. Help students make the connection between a country's economy, geographic position, history, and the kind of government it has. **AL** **Visual/Spatial, Kinesthetic**

See page 261D for other online activities.

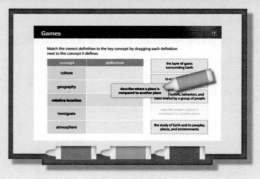

ANSWER, p. 278

CRITICAL THINKING Muammar al-Qaddafi used military rule to control Libya. The people revolted against his harsh regime.

political groups. Tunisia's government was often accused by the U.S. government of neglecting the rights of the nation's people. Libyan leader Qaddafi had a harsh **regime**, or style of government. Dissent was suppressed, and the government controlled all aspects of life. Qaddafi angered other nations by supporting terrorist groups.

Meanwhile, other problems built up in these nations. High population growth strained their economies. Corrupt governments fueled unrest. In recent years, Muslim **fundamentalists** have led a movement for the people and government to follow the strict laws of Islam. They also reject Western influences on Muslim society.

These problems came to a head in late 2010 in a series of revolts called the Arab Spring. The revolts began in Tunisia, where widespread unrest succeeded in convincing the longtime president to step down from power early in 2011. Tunisians celebrated as a new government took office.

Emboldened by this success, many Egyptians took to the streets. For more than two weeks, thousands of Egyptians turned out every day in Cairo and other cities to protest the government. This revolt also succeeded. In February 2011, Egypt's longtime president Hosni Mubarak gave up power. A group of officers took control and promised to create a new government run by civilians. In 2012 Egyptians voted in the first free presidential election in the country's history.

Unrest also arose in Morocco. There, the king agreed to several reforms that would give more power to the people.

The Arab Spring revolt also reached Libya. The government cracked down on protests. That response angered more Libyans. A **civil war**, or a fight for control of the government, broke out. After months of fighting, the rebels succeeded in taking control of the country. In October of 2011, they killed Qaddafi, and his remaining supporters gave up.

☑ READING PROGRESS CHECK

Determining Central Ideas How did the people of North Africa react to European control of the region? Compare that reaction to how North Africans reacted to rule by the Islamic Empire.

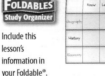

FOLDABLES
Study Organizer

Include this lesson's information in your Foldable®.

CHAPTER 9, Lesson 2
The History of North Africa

R1 Reading Skills

Defining Explain that the second paragraph in the section, "Recent Decades," is about Muslim fundamentalists. Lead students to understand that proponents of other belief systems can also be fundamentalists. **Ask: What is a Muslim fundamentalist?** *(A follower of Islam who wants the government to conform strictly to Islamic law and rejects foreign influences.)* **Verbal/Linguistic**

R2 Reading Skills

Summarizing Have students discuss the Arab Spring revolts. **Ask:**

- **When and where did the Arab Spring revolts begin?** *(late 2010; in Tunisia)*

- **How did the Arab Spring change life in Egypt?** *(The country had its first free elections. The people chose a new leader.)*

- **How was Morocco's experience different from the other three countries?** *(In Morocco, the government was not overthrown. Instead, the king agreed to several reforms in the government.)*

- **How does what happened in Tunisia compare (or contrast) with what happened in Libya?** *(In Tunisia, the president stepped down from power. In Libya, Qaddafi refused to step down and in fact responded with a crack-down. In the end, Qadaffi was killed. In both cases, a new government was created. In Morocco there was much less bloodshed.)* **Verbal/Linguistic**

CLOSE & REFLECT

Evaluating To close this lesson, have students look at the lists that they made at the beginning of the lesson. Ask each student to add things about North Africa's history that they have learned. Then have students write a paragraph describing what they learned, along with any personal responses that they may have to the historical events described.

LESSON 2 REVIEW CCSS

Reviewing Vocabulary (Tier Three Words)
1. How were the *pharaohs* of ancient Egypt and the *caliphs* of the Muslim empire similar? How were they different? RH.6-8.4

Answering the Guiding Questions
2. *Identifying Point of View* Why did the people of Egypt not revolt against the pharaoh even though they had to pay high taxes and work on major building projects? RH.6-8.6

3. *Integrating Visual Information* Look at a map of the world. What routes do you think the people of North Africa traveled to trade with the people of Southwest Asia in the Middle Ages? RH.6-8.7

4. *Determining Central Ideas* What has caused unrest in North Africa in recent years? RH.6-8.2

5. *Informative/Explanatory Writing* Write a summary of the events and results of the Arab Spring. WHST.6-8.2, WHST.6-8.4

Chapter 9 **279**

LESSON 2 REVIEW ANSWERS

Reviewing Vocabulary

1. Pharaohs and caliphs were similar in that they both held religious and political power. They were different in that pharaohs were thought to be the sons of the sun god and caliphs were not.

Answering the Guiding Questions

2. **Identifying Point of View** Ancient Egyptians thought the pharaoh, as the son of the sun god, was needed to ensure that all the people would flourish. That belief discouraged them from doing anything to harm the pharaoh.

3. **Integrating Visual Information** People could travel between Southwest Asia and North Africa

overland across the Sinai Peninsula and by water across the Mediterranean Sea.

4. **Determining Central Ideas** Poor economies, harsh governments, and Islamic fundamentalists' anger over growing western influence all led to growing unrest.

5. **Informative/Explanatory Writing** Students' paragraphs should include the protests in Tunisia and their results; the continuing protests in Egypt, the downfall of Hosni Mubarak, and the replacement by a new government; the civil war in Libya and Muammar Qaddafi's fall and death; and the reforms in Algeria and Morocco.

ANSWER, p. 279

☑ **READING PROGRESS CHECK** North Africans wanted some degree of independence from both the Islamic Empire and the Europeans of the 1800s and 1900s.

ENGAGE

Bellringer Before students begin the lesson, ask them to think about activities they do on a daily basis and who or what influences them to do the daily actions. **Ask:** What is something that you must do every day? How do you feel if for some reason you are not able to do it? *(Students' answers will vary but should include specific details about daily activities or rituals that they perform.)*

TEACH & ASSESS

C Critical Thinking Skills

Making Connections Read the Guiding Question with students. Explain that daily life for many in North Africa is based on certain tenets of the religion of Islam. Read the first paragraph and discuss the practices of Islam. **Ask:** Do you think the practices of Islam would be difficult to follow in the United States? Explain. *(Students' answers will vary but should include a serious, informed, and logical reason why the practice would be difficult to follow due to cultural differences and demands made on individuals' time including work and school schedules.)* **Interpersonal, Verbal/Linguistic**

R Reading Skills

Determining Word Meanings Tell students that knowing the meaning of a base word can help them to identify the meaning of an unfamiliar word. **Ask:**

• What is the base word of *urbanization*? *(urban)*
• What does *urban* mean? *(city or town)*
• What context clue helps you to confirm the meaning of *urban*? *(city dwellers)* **ELL Verbal/Linguistic**

Content Background Knowledge

Ramadan is the ninth month of the lunar calendar and is the holiest time in the Islamic year. Muslims believe that God revealed the Quran to the Prophet Muhammad in A.D. 610 during this time. Muslims do not eat or drink from sunup to sundown during the entire month. The purpose of fasting is to lessen believers' dependence on material goods, purify their hearts, and to strengthen their compassion for the poor.

ANSWER, p. 280

Taking Notes Sample answers: **Daily Life**—Strong influence of Islam; Differences between urban and rural life; **Culture**—Visual arts influenced by Islam; Films important in Algeria and Egypt; Egypt known for literature; **Society**—Need for economic growth; High population growth; Literacy issues; Push for democracy; Rise of Islamic fundamentalism

---

networks

There's More Online!

☑ **IMAGES** Cuisine of North Africa
☑ **VIDEO**

Reading **HELP**DESK CCSS

Academic Vocabulary RH.6-8.4
(Tier Two Words)
• emphasis
• factor

Content Vocabulary RH.6-8.4
(Tier Three Words)
• souk
• fellaheen
• couscous
• diversified
• constitution

TAKING NOTES: *Key Ideas and Details* RH.6-8.2, RH.6-8.7

Summarize As you read about daily life, culture, and society in the region, take notes using the graphic organizer below.

Daily Life	Culture	Society
•	•	•
•	•	•

280

Lesson 3
Life in North Africa

ESSENTIAL QUESTION • *Why do conflicts develop?*

IT MATTERS BECAUSE
North Africa is experiencing political changes.

Culture of North Africa

GUIDING QUESTION *What is daily life like in North Africa?*

The vast majority of people in North Africa practice the Islamic religion. Five times a day, the call to prayer rings out from mosques across North Africa, and devout Muslims stop what they are doing to say prayers. Each week on Friday, millions assemble in the mosques for Friday prayer and to hear a sermon. Once a year during Ramadan, the ninth month of the Islamic calendar, Muslims fast (do not eat) from dawn to dusk.

The People
Three main groups—Egyptians, Berbers, and Arabs—make up the population of North Africa. The region has a varied culture. Egypt's ancient heritage looms over that nation just as the pyramids tower over some of its cities. French influence can be seen from Morocco to Tunisia. Although Arab Muslim culture dominates, some Berber traditions continue.

Although most people are Muslims, some Christians and Jews also live in the region. One in 10 of Egypt's people are Christians. Most of them belong to the Coptic Christian church, which formed in the A.D. 400s.

Of the North African nations, Libya has the highest rate of urbanization. More than three of every four Libyans live in an urban area. Only about half of Egypt's people are city dwellers.

(l to r) Franz Marc Frei/Lonely Planet Images/Getty Images; Andrew Woodley/Alamy; ©Adam Reynolds/Corbis; ©Claudia Wiens/Corbis; ©Nichole Sobecki/Corbis

---

networks *Online Teaching Options*

VIDEO

Egypt Internet Freedom

Narrative Use this video about the role of social media and the Internet in the recent civilian uprisings in Egypt to introduce the lesson about daily life and current issues in North Africa. Have students write a paragraph about one aspect of the video that was interesting to them. **ELL Intrapersonal**

See page 261E for other online activities.

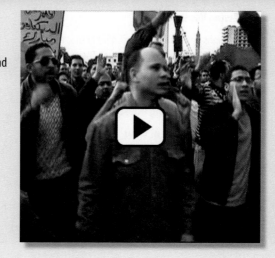

BBC Motion Gallery Education

Daily Life

Patterns of daily life differ between the cities and the countryside. The region's cities tend to be busy, bustling centers of industry and trade. They also are a blend of traditional cultures and modern life.

Towns and cities of North Africa show no signs of having been planned. Instead, they have grown steadily over the centuries. Streets are narrow and curving. Some built-up areas extend into the surrounding rural farming areas.

Cairo, Egypt, is by far North Africa's largest city, with more than 9.3 million people. The next three largest cities are Algiers, Algeria; Casablanca, Morocco; and Tunis, Tunisia. Combined they have fewer people than Cairo.

Cairo's buildings reflect its more than 1,000-year history. The waterfront along the Nile River boasts gleaming modern skyscrapers and parks. Throughout the city are historic mosques—Islamic places of worship. Tourists flock to the city's famous museums, though they have to endure traffic jams to get there. A jumble of old apartment buildings spreads to the west. Beyond them, a million or so people live in mud huts in a massive poor neighborhood called "the City of the Dead."

An important feature of North African cities is the **souk**, or open-air market. Here, businesspeople set up stalls where they sell food, craft products, and other goods. Singers and acrobats perform here and there in the markets, especially at night.

Life in rural areas follows a different pattern. Farming villages in rural Egypt can be as small as 500 people. Families live in homes built of mud brick with few windows. Each morning, the **fellaheen**—poor farmers of Egypt—walk to work in the fields outside the village.

Spices are among the many products sold at the Khan el-Khalili, the largest souk in Cairo, Egypt. Founded in 1382, the marketplace is a network of streets lined with shops, coffeehouses, and restaurants.

R ► **CRITICAL THINKING**
Describing How did cities in North Africa develop?

Chapter 9 **281**

IMAGE

360° View: Algiers

Analyzing Visuals Display the 360° photo of Algiers for students. Discuss with students the layout of this large city and aspects of daily life in rural and urban North Africa. Have students create a travel brochure that highlights some of the interesting features of North Africa for the purpose of encouraging tourism to the region.
AL Intrapersonal

See page 261E for other online activities.

Interactive Photos

C1 **Critical Thinking Skills**

Contrasting After reading the content of the "Daily Life" section, have students discuss the contrasts between living in a city in North Africa and living in a rural area. **Ask: Using one word for each, how could you summarize the difference between urban and rural life in North Africa?** *(Possible answer: modern vs. old-fashioned)* **Verbal/Linguistic, Logical/Mathematical**

C2 **Critical Thinking Skills**

Making Inferences Have students use what they know about how American streets and roads were made and how they looked before automobiles were invented to make inferences about why streets and roads look like they do in North Africa. **Ask:**

- **Why might many streets in North African cities be narrow and curving?** *(Possible answer: The streets were made before modern vehicles were invented and only had to accommodate people and animals.)*
- **What problems might narrow streets cause?** *(Possible answer: Cars and other modern vehicles would have a difficult time using the streets.)* **Logical/Mathematical**

T **Technology Skills**

Researching on the Internet and Making Presentations Divide the class into four small groups and assign each group one of the following topics: the history of the Khan el-Khalili in Cairo; products sold at the Egyptian Khan el-Khalili; the history of the American Khan el-Khalili in Falls Church, Virginia; and products sold at the American Khan el-Khalili. Have each group make an oral presentation of its findings and use a software presentation program to show photos of the markets. After the presentations conclude, have students compare and contrast the two markets. Draw a Venn diagram on the board and list the students' comparisons in the appropriate sections.
ELL **Visual/Spatial, Verbal/Linguistic**

R **Reading Skills**

Using Context Clues Remind students to use the words and phrases around an unfamiliar word to help them understand it. **Ask: What context clues help you understand that** *fellaheen* **are poor farmers?** *(They walk to work, use hand tools, and use muscle power or animal power.)* **Verbal/Linguistic**

ANSWER, p. 281

CRITICAL THINKING Cities show no signs of planning but have grown steadily over the centuries. Streets are narrow and curving. Some built-up areas extend into farmland. Cities are busy centers of industry and trade. They also show the blend of traditional and modern ways of life.

W Writing Skills

Informative Have students gather in small groups to brainstorm reasons why living in Cairo, on a farm in Libya or Morocco, or as a nomad would be desirable. Then have each student write a narrative essay explaining his or her answer to the question: **Where in North Africa would you prefer to live?** Tell students that their essays should be in a five-paragraph format with an introductory paragraph, which includes a topic sentence that answers the question, three supporting paragraphs explaining the reasons for their choice, and a concluding paragraph. Have students share their essays with the class. **Intrapersonal, Verbal/Linguistic**

C1 Critical Thinking Skills

Making Connections Have students discuss different regional foods of the United States. Then have students discuss the types of foods that they have eaten that are common to Morocco and discuss their flavors and textures. Then discuss any unusual foods that students have eaten. **Ask:** Would you be interested in sampling pigeon? What do you think it would taste like? *(Students' answers will vary but should include valid reasons.)* **Intrapersonal, Verbal/Linguistic**

C2 Critical Thinking Skills

Drawing Conclusions Have a volunteer read the section "Arts" aloud. **Ask:** Why might artists in Algeria whose work is harshly criticized leave the country? *(Possible answer: Artists want the freedom to create and express what they want, so they go to a country where they can have that freedom.)* **Interpersonal, Intrapersonal**

Content Background Knowledge

Islamic art is controlled by strict religious beliefs and follows guidelines established in the *Quran*. The art is decorative and does not depict religious figures because Muslims are afraid that the use of figures may lead to idolatry, which is extreme love or admiration of a person. Idolatry is forbidden by the *Quran*. Muslims also believe that God is unique, cannot be compared to humans, and cannot be portrayed. It is also forbidden to portray the Prophet Mohammad. Calligraphy—a form of decorative handwriting—appears frequently in Islamic art along with arabesques (intertwined flowing lines), scrollwork, and complex geometric designs. Secular, or non-religious, Islamic art is found on objects used in daily life, such as bowls, carpets, and cushions.

A family enjoys a meal at home in the town of Matmata in southern Tunisia. The Berber town is known for its dwellings that are built underground in cave-like structures. To create a home, a resident digs a wide pit in the ground and then hollows out caves around the pit's edge. The caves serve as rooms, which are connected by trench-like corridors.

Many use hand tools and rely on muscle power or animal power. At day's end, they return home.

Farms in Libya are clustered around oases. These communities are small because so little land can be farmed. In Morocco, many farmers live in the well-watered highland areas. They build terraces on steep hillsides to plant their crops.

Some rural dwellers still live like nomads. This is the same kind of life Berbers have followed for centuries. They tend herds of sheep, goats, or camels. They move from place to place in search of food and water for their herds. Some settle in one area for part of the year to grow grains.

Food

Moroccan food has gained fame around the world for its rich and complex flavors. The base of many Moroccan meals is **couscous**, small nuggets of semolina wheat that are steamed. Rich stews of meat and vegetables are poured over it. This style of cooking is also common in Algeria and Tunisia.

Sandwiches in this region are often made with flat pieces of pita bread. They might include grilled pieces of lamb, chicken, or fish. Falafel is made from ground, dried beans and formed into cakes and fried. Pigeon is also popular in Egypt and Morocco.

Arts

The arts in North Africa reflect the influence of Islam. The Islamic religion forbids art that shows the figures of animals or humans. Folk art, like weaving and embroidery, has intricate patterns but no figures. These patterns are also used to decorate buildings.

Many young people in North Africa are attracted to Western

282 Chapter 9

Andrew Woodley/Alamy

---

netw⊕rks   *Online Teaching Options*

IMAGE

Cuisine of North Africa

Integrating Visual Information Display the interactive image of the cuisine of North Africa. Discuss with students the different varieties of food in the region and how the flavors and spices that are available influence the cuisine. Have students write a short paragraph about which food they find most appealing and why. **ELL** **Verbal/ Linguistic, Intrapersonal**

See page 261E for other online activities.

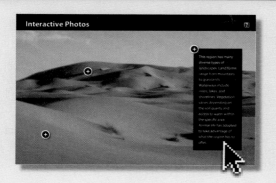

Interactive Photos

Lissa Harrison

music and movies. This has provoked an angry response among some strict Muslims. In Algeria, some artists have left the country because of harsh criticism. Egypt has long been a center of television and film production. Its shows and movies are seen throughout the Arab world.

C

Languages and Literature

Arabic is the official language of all five countries in North Africa. French is prominent in Morocco, Algeria, and Tunisia. French and English are most often heard in the region's cities, but Berber languages are more common in rural areas.

As the largest Arabic-speaking country, Egypt has played an important part in the literature of the region. Egyptian writers have explored themes like the impact of influences from Western culture. Novelist Naguib Mahfouz, who wrote more than 30 novels and hundreds of stories, achieved worldwide recognition when he won the Nobel Prize for Literature in 1988.

☑ READING PROGRESS CHECK

Identifying What is an example of the influence of Islam on daily life in North Africa?

Challenges in North Africa

GUIDING QUESTION *What challenges face North Africa?*

Standards of living vary widely across the region and even within countries. In addition to economic issues, the region faces significant social challenges.

Economic Issues

T₂

When oil was discovered in Libya, Muammar al-Qaddafi, the leader of the country, said that a major goal was to provide social benefits to everyone. That did not happen. The income gained from selling oil did not reach most of the country's people. When Qaddafi fell from power in 2011, Libyans hoped that their lives would improve, but progress started slowly.

Algeria has tried to shift its economy away from the **emphasis** on the sale of oil and natural gas. The government keeps tight control of businesses, however. As a result, companies from other countries are not willing to invest there.

©Adam Reynolds/Corbis

Academic Vocabulary

emphasis importance

T₁

A craftsperson in Cairo, Egypt, uses copper thread to embroider Arabic writing onto fabric. Muslims prize the art of beautiful writing, which they use to express the words of the Quran, the Islamic holy book.
▶ **CRITICAL THINKING**
Determining Central Ideas
How has Islam influenced the arts of North Africa?

Chapter 9 **283**

C Critical Thinking Skills

Defending Explain to students that *censorship* occurs when media, such as books, movies, and music, are examined closely by a government or a group with a specific agenda to determine if people should have access to them. Every year in the United States, parents challenge hundreds of books that they think are inappropriate for use in school curriculums or to have in school libraries. The challenges are based mainly on sex, drugs, foul language, and graphic descriptions. Have students compare and contrast the censorship of books in our country with the angry response among strict Muslims to Western music and movies. Have students debate the pros and cons of censorship and when it may or may not be appropriate. **Verbal/Linguistic, Interpersonal**

T₁ Technology Skills

Transferring Knowledge Have small groups of students use the Internet to research sites that teach how to write and pronounce some Arabic words. Have groups present to the class two or three words that they learned by correctly writing the word on the board, pronouncing it, and telling what it means in English. **ELL** **Verbal/Linguistic, Kinesthetic**

T₂ Technology Skills

Analyzing News Media After months of violent fighting in Libya, Muammar al-Qaddafi was killed on October 20, 2011. This ended the 42-year rule of one of the world's longest-lasting dictators. Divide the class into two groups. Have one group use the Internet to research newspaper articles that appeared on October 21, 2011, about Qaddafi's death. Have the other group research information presented on Internet news sites the same day. After groups present their findings to the class, have students analyze the information presented in both mediums to judge their effectiveness. **Logical/Mathematical, Verbal/Linguistic**

(l) ©Ocean/Corbis, ©Kryssia Campos/Getty Images, (tr) Erica Simone Leeds, (br) ©JG Photography/Alamy

SLIDE SHOW

Artisans of North Africa

Discussing Show students the slide show about the artisans of North Africa. Have volunteers read the captions about the artisans, crafts, and arts of the region. Discuss with students the development of art and culture in the region. Be sure to make connections between art and religion. Working in pairs, have students discuss three things they have learned about artisans in North Africa. **Visual/Spatial**

See page 261E for other online activities.

Slide Show

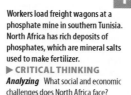

R Reading Skills

Citing Text Evidence Remind students of the importance of using text evidence to answer questions. **Ask: What text evidence supports the statement that Morocco's economy is diversified?** *(The people of the country engage in mining, some manufacturing, farming, and tourism.)*

V Visual Skills

Integrating Visual Information Display a political map of the world to students. **Ask: Why would most of the people who leave Morocco, Algeria, and Tunisia move to Spain and France?** *(Possible answer: The people of Morocco, Algeria, and Tunisia speak French so there would be no language barrier when moving to France. Spain is a short distance across the Mediterranean Sea from these North African countries.)* **Visual/Spatial, Verbal/Linguistic, Logical/Mathematical**

C Critical Thinking Skills

Identifying Problems Explain to students that one of the social issues faced by the people in North Africa is inadequate health care. **Ask: What problems might inadequate health care cause in this region?** *(Possible answers: the spread of disease, early death, birth defects)* **Verbal/Linguistic, Logical/Mathematical**

T Technology Skills

Analyzing News Media Images Have students watch a video of Secretary of State Hillary Clinton giving her speech on February 25, 2012. They can view the speech online at www.tunisia-live.net/2012/02/25/secretary-of-state-hillary-clinton-town-hall-live-from-tunis. Ask students why it might be important to the people of Tunisia to hear from the United States' Secretary of State. *(Possible answer: The United States is a powerful nation and is also a symbol of democracy. People who are trying to create a democratic government will want to know that the United States believes in what they are doing.)* **ELL Auditory/Musical, Interpersonal**

ANSWER, p. 284

CRITICAL THINKING widespread poverty; overreliance on one product, such as oil; lack of outside investment because of tight government controls; migration to Europe; high population growth

---

R Morocco's economy is the most **diversified**. A diversified economy includes a mix of many different economic activities. The people of the country engage in mining, some manufacturing, farming, and tourism. Poverty and unemployment are widespread in Morocco, however.

V In recent years, thousands have left the region for Europe. They move mostly to Spain and France looking for jobs. Morocco, Algeria, and Tunisia have lost the most people.

Social Issues

C High population growth is a major concern in Libya and Egypt. This growth rate contributes to crowding and inadequate health care, as well as poverty. A large share of the population in the region is 14 years old or younger. This is especially true in Egypt and Libya. These countries will have to work hard to develop their economies so that today's young people can find jobs in the future.

T In February 2012, U.S. Secretary of State Hillary Clinton addressed young people in Tunisia and across the region. She cited the work they did to bring about the massive changes of the Arab Spring. Clinton warned, though, that it would take a long time and hard work to build the country's economy and increase jobs for young people. The U.S. government has pledged money to several countries to help them accomplish these goals.

Another issue is literacy. Libya has the highest literacy rate in the region: 89 percent of Libyans can read and write. The literacy rate is

Workers load freight wagons at a phosphate mine in southern Tunisia. North Africa has rich deposits of phosphates, which are mineral salts used to make fertilizer.
▶ **CRITICAL THINKING**
Analyzing What social and economic challenges does North Africa face?

mediacolor's/Alamy

284 Chapter 9

---

netw⬤rks *Online Teaching Options*

GRAPHIC ORGANIZER

Economies of North African Countries

Identifying Display the graphic organizer about the economies of North African countries. Have volunteers identify and complete the information contained on the graphic organizer. Lead a class discussion reviewing the various economies of the region. As a class, rank the economies in order from most likely to grow to least likely to grow. **Visual/Spatial**

See page 261E for other online activities.

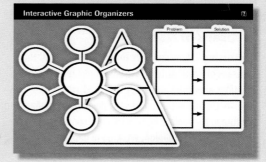

Interactive Graphic Organizers

W

C

much lower in the other North African countries. Literacy is most serious in Morocco, where little more than one-half of Moroccans can read and write. A very low literacy rate among women is a major **factor**, or cause, for this trend. More than 65 percent of Moroccan men can read and write; less than 40 percent of that nation's women can. Literacy among women is about 20 percent lower than among men in the other four countries of the region, as well. This gap hinders the ability of the countries to build strong economies.

Women students meet for class at Cairo, Egypt's Al-Azhar University, the world's chief center for Islamic learning. In Egypt, women may work outside the home, attend universities, vote, and run for office. However, opportunities for women still lag behind those for men in education and the labor market.
▶ **CRITICAL THINKING**
Analyzing How does the issue of women's literacy affect economies in North Africa?

☑ **READING PROGRESS CHECK**

Identifying Point of View What might happen in North Africa if young people grow impatient with the slow rate of economic growth? Why?

North Africa's Future

GUIDING QUESTION *How will North Africa address the problems it faces?*

Powerful new social movements have swept through the region of North Africa in recent years. They have led to major political changes in three countries and put pressures on the governments of the other two.

Academic Vocabulary

factor a cause

Political Issues

V

Two political forces are strong in the region of North Africa. One is a push for democracy. Many North Africans have grown more and more frustrated with their leaders. They think the leaders focused more on building their own power than on building the economy and improving their countries. Many question the government's harsh treatment of people who criticize their countries' leaders. Some leaders are calling for the different groups to learn to work together to avoid the conflicts that pull societies apart.

Chapter 9 **285**

Literacy Rates Around the World

Analyzing Display the chart that compares literacy rates around the world to literacy rates in North Africa. Have volunteers read the information presented on the chart. Have students analyze how low literacy rates along with an aging population might affect the region. Have students write three things they learned from the information in the chart. **Visual/Spatial, Verbal/ Linguistic**

See page 261E for other online activities.

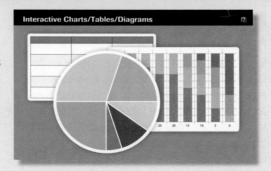

Interactive Charts/Tables/Diagrams

W **Writing Skills**

Explanatory Have students brainstorm ideas about why literacy, or the ability to read and write, is important. Then have students individually write a paragraph to answer the question: **Why is literacy important to me?** Remind students that their paragraphs should include a topic sentence and a concluding sentence along with at least three sentences that contain specific reasons or details. **Intrapersonal**

C **Critical Thinking Skills**

Making Inferences Have students consider how they would feel if girls were not taught how to read and write in the United States. Then have them compare attitudes toward women here and in North Africa. **Ask:**

- **Why do you think fewer women than men can read and write?** *(Students' answers will vary but should demonstrate an understanding of women's perceived roles in the regional society.)*
- **How do men and women both suffer when there is a low literacy rate for women?** *(If women are not able to read and write, then they are not able to fully participate in the economic and political structure. This means that the society will not have the benefit of all of the ideas, knowledge, and input from half of the people.)* **Interpersonal**

V **Visual Skills**

Creating a Chart Have students discuss the characteristics of a democracy and a dictatorship. Draw a T-chart on the board and list their ideas. **Ask: What might you conclude about why the people in this region are pushing for democracy?** *(Students' answers will vary but should include relevant details such as wanting personal freedoms like free speech.)* **AL Verbal/Linguistic**

Democracy	Dictatorship

ANSWERS, p. 285

☑ **READING PROGRESS CHECK** Young people might become so frustrated by slow economic growth that they lead new revolts against the governments of North African nations.

CRITICAL THINKING The fact that many women in North Africa cannot read and write hinders the ability of nations to build strong economies.

Life in North Africa

C1 Critical Thinking Skills

Making Inferences Review with students the principle of separation of church and state as found in the United States Constitution. Discuss with students the different role religion plays in our government and in the governments of the countries in North Africa. **Ask:**

- **Why would some strict Muslims want to see an end to Western influences on their culture?** *(Students' answers will vary but should demonstrate an understanding of the principles of Islam and the Islamic belief that secular or Western influences are bad.)*

- **How might our government respond to outside influences on American culture?** *(Students' answers will vary.)* **Logical/Mathematical, Verbal/Linguistic**

T Technology Skills

Researching on the Internet Have volunteers use the Internet to research the progress Egypt is making on writing a new constitution and the aftereffects of the Arab Spring revolts. Ask them to give a short verbal report to the class. **Verbal/Linguistic**

C2 Critical Thinking Skills

Comparing and Contrasting Have students compare and contrast the Civil War in the United States with the Arab Spring revolts in Algeria and Morocco. **Ask: How was the Civil War similar to and different from the Arab Spring revolts?** *(Possible answers: The Civil War and the Arab Spring revolts were violent and caused death and destruction. Both involved making changes to their countries' governments. The Civil War was the direct result of some states wanting to separate from the Union; the Arab Spring sought to unite the people under new, democratic governments. The Civil War involved disputes about states' rights, but the Arab Spring involved disputes about human rights and personal freedoms.)*
BL Verbal/Linguistic, Logical/Mathematical

Content Background Knowledge

Religious fundamentalists believe strongly and passionately in the principles of their faith, are often intolerant of other religious views, and oppose ideas that are not specifically spelled out or part of their religion (secular). Often fundamentalists follow strict behavior guidelines.

ANSWER, p. 286

CRITICAL THINKING The victorious rebels set up a new government and worked to rebuild the war-torn country; however, they faced the problems of keeping the country together and avoiding another conflict.

Young people in Benghazi, Libya, yell protest slogans against dictator Muammar al-Qaddafi. Clashes between street demonstrators and armed government forces in February 2011 led to much bloodshed. A civil war broke out, and rebel groups eventually overthrew Qaddafi.
► CRITICAL THINKING
Describing What happened in Libya after the fall of Qaddafi?

The second force was an increase in Islamic fundamentalism. Some strict Muslims want laws changed to conform to the rules of Islam. They want to see an end to Western influences on their culture. The political party of the Muslim Brotherhood gained a majority in Egypt's parliament in the 2011 elections. It also won a majority in Morocco and a large share of seats in Tunisia. These forces helped bring about the Arab Spring of 2010 and 2011. They have left conditions across the region uncertain.

Egypt began writing a new **constitution** in 2012. A constitution is a set of rules for a nation and its government. Egypt's new government could give more power to the parliament, the lawmaking body. It is not clear how well this new government will work or what groups will control it, though.

For nearly 20 years, Algeria has undergone brutal conflict between Islamist groups and the government and its forces. As many as 100,000 people have died in the fighting. As in Morocco, the government was able to keep power after the Arab Spring, but it had to promise to reform the political system.

By 2012, Libya's victorious rebels were working on making a new government. They also faced the need to rebuild much of the country after the civil war. In 2012, leaders in eastern Libya said they wanted self-rule in their part of the country. Although they said that they did not wish to divide the country or to keep their area's oil wealth for themselves, the move raised the possibility of continued conflict in Libya.

286 Chapter 9

---

netw⊙rks *Online Teaching Options*

IMAGE

Arab Spring Protests

Speculating Display the interactive image about the Arab Spring protests. Discuss with students the sequence of events in the Arab Spring protests in the context of the political and social changes taking place in this region. Have students use what they know to speculate about whether the changes will be good or bad for the region and if they will be long lasting. **BL Visual/Spatial, Verbal/Linguistic**

See page 261E for other online activities.

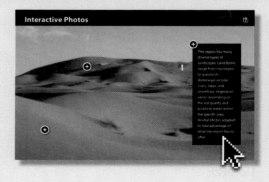

Interactive Photos

Islam in the Modern World

Many Muslims in the region worry about the impact of Western culture on their lands. They think that Western entertainment conflicts with Islamic values. They also disagree with Western ideas about women's rights.

Women in North Africa generally have more rights than those in other Muslim lands. In Tunisia, for instance, they can own businesses and have their own bank accounts. About half of all university students in Tunisia are women. Women may lose some of these rights if extreme Muslim leaders take control of the governments.

Several million of Egypt's Coptic Christians have grown more worried about their position in recent years as well. Some Muslim extremists have attacked them and bombed churches. Early in 2012, the longtime head of the Coptic church died. He had led the church for nearly 40 years in relative peace until near the end of his life. His death increased the uncertainty for Copts in that area.

Relations with Other Nations

Egypt broke ranks with other Muslim nations in 1979 when it signed a peace treaty with Israel. It has also developed close ties with the United States since then. That friendship has come under increasing criticism from Muslim fundamentalists. Morocco has also had close relations with the United States. Its government has been criticized for this as well.

These situations raise more questions about what will happen if Muslim conservatives gain power. Will the new governments reject close ties with the United States? Will they take steps against Israel?

The situations in Algeria and Libya also are uncertain. Will new governments there be less willing to sell oil to the United States? For what purposes will they use the money they earn from selling oil? The answers to these questions will help to shape the future of North Africa and the world.

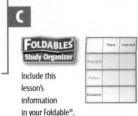

FOLDABLES
Study Organizer

Include this lesson's information in your Foldable®.

☑ **READING PROGRESS CHECK**

Analyzing Why were the results of the Arab Spring different in Algeria and Morocco compared with the other countries of the region?

LESSON 3 REVIEW (CCSS)

Reviewing Vocabulary (Tier Three Words)
1. Is it important for an economy to be *diversified*? Why or why not? RH.6-8.4

Answering the Guiding Questions
2. *Determining Central Ideas* Why do you think many Muslims worry about the impact of Western culture on their lands? RH.6-8.2

3. *Describing* How is the relatively young population connected to the economic issues in these nations? RH.6-8.5

4. *Analyzing* About half of Egypt's people live in rural areas. Most of them are farmers. What impact does that have on Egypt's economy? Why? RH.6-8.1

5. *Identifying Point of View* Why is the political situation in North Africa important to the United States? RH.6-8.6

6. *Argument Writing* Do you think the most serious issues facing North Africa are political, social, or cultural? Write a paragraph explaining why. WHST.6-8.1, WHST.6-8.4

Chapter 9 **287**

LESSON 3 REVIEW ANSWERS

Reviewing Vocabulary

1. Economies that are diversified, rather than those that rely solely on one good or few goods, provide economic stability, more jobs, and grow faster.

Answering the Guiding Questions

2. **Determining Central Ideas** Answers will vary but responses should indicate that Muslims believe the values of Western culture undermine Muslim values and tenets of Islam.

3. **Describing** Sample answer: The relatively young population means there is a large group of people who will need jobs in the future, which will put serious pressure on the nations' economies.

4. **Analyzing** Possible answer: The high percentage of farmers in Egypt will hamper the nation's ability to grow the economy rapidly because agriculture usually does not result in rapid economic growth.

5. **Identifying Point of View** Egypt and Morocco have been close to the United States for many years. If new governments in either nation are less friendly, that could hurt the ability of the government of the United States to rely on their support. Changes in Algeria and Libya could also result in the loss of energy resources.

6. **Argument Writing** Students' paragraphs should take one side of the issue, explain their position clearly, and give supporting arguments.

R Reading Skills

R **Reading Skills**

Explaining After students have read the section "Islam in the Modern World," **ask:**

- Why are many Muslims worried about the impact of Western culture on their lands? *(They think Western culture, including music, television, movies, education, and art, conflicts with Islamic values, and they disagree with Western ideas about women's rights and the roles women play in society.)*
- What rights do many women in Tunisia have that women in other Muslim lands might not have? *(Women in North Africa can own businesses, have their own bank accounts, and attend college.)*
- What worries Egypt's Coptic Christians? *(Muslim extremists have attacked Coptic Christians and bombed their churches. The long-time leader of the Coptic church died.)* **AL**

C **Critical Thinking Skills**

Speculating Have volunteers read aloud each of the four questions posed in the last two paragraphs. Have students work in small groups to discuss their views on what the answers might be or what outcomes might happen. Tell students to use what they know about the political and economic situations in North Africa and the rest of the world to formulate and support their answers. Have each group take notes and come to a consensus on their ideas, noting any strong dissenting opinions as well. Then have groups share their thoughts with the class. **Verbal/Linguistic, Logical/Mathematical**

CLOSE & REFLECT

Synthesizing To close this lesson, refer students back to the Essential Question: *Why do conflicts develop?* Remind them about the political changes that continue to face the countries of North Africa. Then, have each student write an answer to the question. Collect the answers and post them. Tell students to be aware of news stories about these countries and report to the class any breaking news they hear or read about further political developments or further conflict.

ANSWER, p. 287

☑ **READING PROGRESS CHECK** In Algeria and Morocco, governments agreed to make reforms that apparently satisfied their nations' people, since protests for further change ended. In the other three nations, revolts continued until their regimes fell.

CHAPTER REVIEW ACTIVITY

Have students create a Venn diagram to compare and contrast the urban area of Cairo, Egypt, with rural areas in North Africa. Have them label the circles *urban area: Cairo* and *rural areas*. Tell students to list the unique characteristics of each area in the outer circles and to list the shared characteristics of the two areas in the intersecting space. *(Possible answers: **urban area: Cairo**—center of industry and trade for Egypt, home to more than 9 million people, contains old and modern buildings, Nile waterfront contains modern skyscrapers and parks, historic mosques, museums, a great deal of traffic and tourists, souks, wealthy and poor neighborhoods, and entertainment areas; **both**—people live and work there, most people have similar religious beliefs, most people speak the same language, most people long for political freedom; **rural areas**—small farming villages, mud brick homes, fields for farming, hand tools, work animals, some farms clustered around oases or terraced on steep hillsides, some people live like nomads)* **Visual/Spatial, Logical/Mathematical**

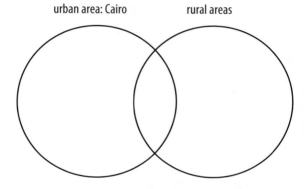

urban area: Cairo   rural areas

REVIEW THE ENDURING UNDERSTANDINGS

Review this chapter's Enduring Understanding with students:

• *People, places, and ideas change over time.*

Now pose the following questions in a class discussion to apply this Enduring Understanding to this chapter.

• **How does the physical geography of Morocco change as you travel inland and south from the Mediterranean Sea?** *(Along the coast of the Mediterranean Sea are low narrow plains in the country of Morocco. As you travel south, you cross the Atlas Mountains with a high plateau between the two mountain ranges. Further south of these mountains is a low plateau.)*

• **How did the acceptance of Islam change the culture of the region of North Africa?** *(Most people changed their religion to Islam and adopted the Arabic language. These changes helped to unite the cultures and people of North Africa and Southwest Asia. Cairo became a center of Muslim learning and trade.)*

• **How have the uprisings of the Arab Spring changed the political landscape of the region?** *(Dictators have been overthrown and new governments with democratic tendencies have been formed.)*

Directions: Write your answers on a separate piece of paper.

1 Use your **FOLDABLES** to explore the Essential Question.
INFORMATIVE/EXPLANATORY WRITING Briefly describe the population distribution in the region of North Africa and suggest a likely reason for the distribution. WHST.6-8.2, WHST.6-8.4

2 **21st Century Skills**
INTEGRATING VISUAL INFORMATION With a partner, create a set of flash cards showing an outline of the five North African countries combined and outlines of the individual countries. Make five separate cards with the names of the capital cities. Devise a game using the flash cards, and exchange games with another pair of classmates. After playing both games, work with the other pair to turn the flash card games into a computer game. WHST.6-8.6, WHST.6-8.10

3 **Thinking Like a Geographer**
INTEGRATING VISUAL INFORMATION On an outline map of North Africa, indicate the region's climates. Include the rain shadow areas on the map key. RH.6-8.7, WHST.6-8.10

4 **GEOGRAPHY ACTIVITY**

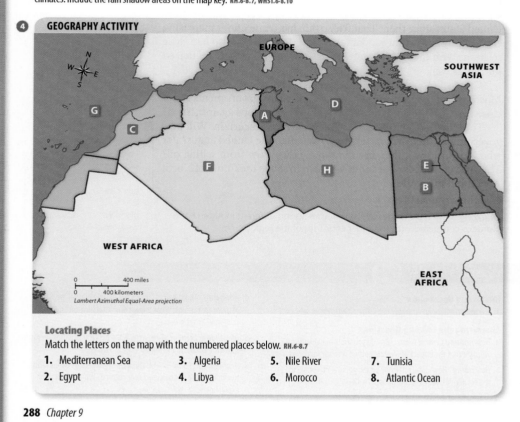

Locating Places
Match the letters on the map with the numbered places below. RH.6-8.7

1. Mediterranean Sea
2. Egypt
3. Algeria
4. Libya
5. Nile River
6. Morocco
7. Tunisia
8. Atlantic Ocean

ACTIVITIES ANSWERS
Exploring the Essential Question

1 **INFORMATIVE/EXPLANATORY WRITING** The populations of the five countries of North Africa tend to group along the edge of the Mediterranean Sea. Similarly, 95 percent of Egypt's population lives near the Nile or its delta. Although the area near the sea does not receive abundant rainfall, it gets more rain than the vast Sahara to the south, so farming is possible, and people tend to live where they can make a livelihood.

REVIEW THE GUIDING QUESTIONS
Directions: Choose the best answer for each question.

1 One nickname for ancient Egypt was RH.6-8.4
   A. serpent of the sea.
   B. wadi of the floods.
   C. gift of the Nile.
   D. delta dawn.

2 Of the North African countries, Libya has the most RH.6-8.1
   F. olives.
   G. oil.
   H. water.
   I. cedarwood.

3 Hieroglyphics were RH.6-8.4
   A. equipment used for building pyramids.
   B. Muslim political and religious leaders.
   C. pictures that represented sounds or words.
   D. spices burned for religious ceremonies.

4 The Berbers and Egyptians became linked to the Muslim world in the A.D. 1000s by RH.6-8.2
   F. the defeat at Carthage.
   G. the power of the caliphs.
   H. the Arabic language and Islamic learning.
   I. the pharaoh's desire for more territory.

5 The official language of the five North African nations is RH.6-8.4
   A. Coptic.
   B. French.
   C. Afrikaner.
   D. Arabic.

6 Today's Islamic fundamentalists in North Africa want to RH.6-8.5
   F. return to their families' farms.
   G. convert the citizens of Israel.
   H. end Western influence on the Islamic culture.
   I. turn around the Tunisian economy.

Chapter 9 **289**

21st Century Skills

2 **INTEGRATING VISUAL INFORMATION** Students' cards should accurately indicate the general outline of the region and the political boundaries of the five countries that make up the region. Capital cities should be named and spelled correctly on the game cards. The games should be creative and fun. Students should all play an active role in collaborating and completing this assignment.

Thinking Like a Geographer

3 **UNDERSTANDING MAPS** Students should show the arid sections of North Africa, including the Sahara. They should also indicate the rain-shadow effect of the Atlas Mountains.

Geography Activity

4 **LOCATING PLACES**

   1. D
   2. B
   3. F
   4. H
   5. E
   6. C
   7. A
   8. G

ASSESSMENT ANSWERS
Review the Guiding Questions

1 **C** To answer this question, students need to remember that the Nile River is the most important body of water in the region and is also the longest river in the world. This knowledge will help them zero in on choice C. Refer students to Lesson 1 "The Waterways" for help.

2 **G** To answer this question, students need to remember that much of North Africa, including Libya, is covered by a desert and has a semiarid climate. This knowledge will help them eliminate choices F, H, and I. If students are having difficulty answering the question, have them read the "Oil, Gas, and Other Resources" section in Lesson 1.

3 **C** To answer this question, students need to remember that the ancient Egyptians used a system of writing called hieroglyphics. Knowing this will help students eliminate choices A, B, and D. Associating sounds and words with writing will help students choose choice C. Refer students to Lesson 2 under the "Religion and Culture in Ancient Egypt" section for help.

4 **H** To answer this question, students need to remember that by the A.D. 1000s most Berbers and Egyptians had converted to Islam and were speaking Arabic. Knowing that Rome defeated Carthage and that Romans were Christians helps eliminate choice F, that caliphs had trouble keeping control over North Africa helps eliminate choice G, and that the pharaohs ruled in ancient times helps eliminate choice I. Have students reread the "Rise of Islam" section in Lesson 2 for additional help in answering this question.

5 **D** Students should eliminate choice C immediately because an Afrikaner is a member of a South African ethnic group descended from 17th century European colonists. Though French is a prominent language in Morocco, Algeria, and Tunisia, it is not the official language. Remembering that most people in North Africa are Muslims who speak Arabic will help students answer the question. Refer students to Lesson 3 "Languages and Literature" for help.

6 **H** Although many Muslims in North Africa worry about their governments, they also worry about the impact of Western culture on the Islamic way of life. Many Muslims believe that Western styles of dress, music, and entertainment conflict with Islamic values.

DBQ Analyzing Documents

7 **C** Since the TNC had as its goals overthrowing the Qaddafi regime and guiding Libya to the creation of a democratic government, it saw itself as having only a temporary role in leading Libya. Have students reread the passage if they are having difficulty answering the question. Further explain that the phrase *with the stated aim* refers to the goal of the Transitional National Council.

8 **I** Since the United Nations recognized the TNC as the new legitimate government of Libya, the old government—the Qaddafi regime—had probably lost power by that time. Have students cite exact text to help find the answer. Point to the section starting with *captured the capital*. Help students understand the meaning of this phrase.

Short Response

9 The main idea of this passage is that Moroccan culture shows the influence of several other cultures as a result of the complex history of the land. If students are having difficulty finding the main idea, remind them that often the main idea is located in the beginning of the passage, just as each paragraph starts with a topic sentence.

10 Moroccan culture was influenced by other cultures as a result of contact caused by invasion (the Arab invasion), trade (with Senegal and sub-Saharan states), and learning (the Arabs learned cooking secrets from the Persians). Point out the words *strongly influenced*. Then have students reread the passage for specific details about the types of influences. This will help them describe each of the influences.

Extended Response

11 Students should research reliable sources to gather information, such as online Internet sources and in newspapers and magazines, about the 2011 Arab Spring as well as the current conditions in the region. They will need to give examples to support their opinions regarding the success of the uprisings and the current quality of life. Students should keep track of the sources they used for their writing and cite them as sources.

DBQ ANALYZING DOCUMENTS

7 **CITING TEXT EVIDENCE** Read the following passage about recent changes in Libya's government:

"*In March 2011, a Transitional National Council (TNC) was formed . . . with the stated aim of overthrowing the Qaddafi regime and guiding the country to democracy. . . . Anti-Qaddafi forces in August 2011 captured the capital, Tripoli. In mid-September, the [United Nations] General Assembly voted to recognize the TNC as the legitimate interim governing body of Libya.*"

—from CIA World Factbook, "Libya"

How did the Transitional National Council view its role in Libya? **RH.6-8.6, RH.6-8.10**

A. as an ally of Qaddafi
B. as supporters of Libya's former king
C. as a temporary government
D. as social reformers

8 **ANALYZING** What happened to the Qaddafi government in 2011? **RH.6-8.1, RH.6-8.10**

F. It remained in control of the country.
G. It relocated to a new capital.
H. It forged an alliance with the TNC.
I. It fell out of power.

SHORT RESPONSE

"*Morocco, on account of the invasions of Arabs and the exterior adventures of Moorish kings, was strongly influenced by Middle Eastern culture and the culture of the Andaluz [Muslim-ruled Spain]. The Arabs learned [cooking] secrets from the Persians and brought them to Morocco; from Senegal and other lands south of the Sahara came caravans of spices. Even the Turks made a contribution.*"

—from Paula Wolfert, *Couscous and Other Good Food From Morocco* (1973)

9 **DETERMINING CENTRAL IDEAS** What is the main idea of this passage? **RH.6-8.2, RH.6-8.10**

10 **DESCRIBING** What kinds of contact by different groups led to these influences on Moroccan culture? **RH.6-8.5, RH.6-8.10**

EXTENDED RESPONSE

11 **INFORMATIVE/EXPLANATORY WRITING** Research the Arab Spring of 2011. Write an essay contrasting the current situation in the countries that were involved in the Arab Spring with their situation before the upheaval. Did the "spring" last? Did the citizens of these countries gain or lose what they were trying to achieve? Are their lives better or worse today than they were before 2011? Do any of them now have a stable, democratic government? **WHST.6-8.2, WHST.6-8.7**

Need Extra Help?

If You've Missed Question	❶	❷	❸	❹	❺	❻	❼	❽	❾	❿	⓫
Review Lesson	1	1	2	2	3	3	2	2	2	2	2

---

netw⊙rks *Online Teaching Options*

Evaluation and Assessment

Assessing Use eAssessment to create your own tests from hundreds of available questions. eAssessment helps you design assessments that meet the needs of different types of learners.

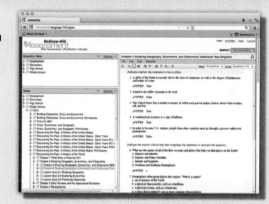

National Geography Standards covered in Chapter 10

Learners will understand:

I. The World in Spatial Terms

Standard 1: How to use maps and other geographic representations, geospatial technologies, and spatial thinking to understand and communicate information

Standard 3: How to analyze the spatial organization of people, places, and environments on Earth's surface

II. Places and Regions

Standard 4: The physical and human characteristics of places

Standard 5: That people create regions to interpret Earth's complexity

Standard 6: How culture and experience influence people's perceptions of places and regions

III. Physical Systems

Standard 7: The physical processes that shape the patterns of Earth's surface

IV. Human Systems

Standard 9: The characteristics, distribution, and migration of human populations on Earth's surface

Standard 10: The characteristics, distribution, and complexity of Earth's cultural mosaics

Standard 11: The patterns and networks of economic interdependence on Earth's surface

Standard 12: The processes, patterns, and functions of human settlement

Standard 13: How the forces of cooperation and conflict among people influence the division and control of Earth's surface

V. Environment and Society

Standard 14: How human actions modify the physical environment

Standard 15: How physical systems affect human systems

VI. The Uses of Geography

Standard 17: How to apply geography to interpret the past

Standard 18: How to apply geography to interpret the present and plan for the future

---

UNDERSTANDING BY DESIGN®

Enduring Understandings

- *People, places, and ideas change over time.*

Essential Questions

- *How does geography influence the way people live?*
- *Why do people trade?*
- *Why does conflict develop?*

Predictable Misunderstandings

- *The landscape of East Africa is the same as that in North Africa.*
- *The culture, language, and religion of East Africa are the same as North Africa.*

Assessment Evidence

Performance Tasks:

- *Project-Based Learning Digital Hands-On Chapter Project*
- *Project-Based Learning Hands-On Chapter Project*

Other Evidence:

- *GeoLab Activity*
- *Geography and Economics Activity*
- *Participation in Interactive Whiteboard Activities*
- *Contribution to small-group activities*
- *Interpretation of slide show images and special purpose maps*
- *Participation in class discussions about cultural and economic topics*
- *Lesson Reviews*
- *Chapter Assessments*

SUGGESTED PACING GUIDE

Introducing the Chapter	1 Day	Lesson 3	2 Days
Lesson 1	2 Days	Global Connections	3 Days
Lesson 2	2 Days	Chapter Wrap-Up and Assessment	1 Day

TOTAL TIME   11 Days

Key for Using the Teacher Edition

SKILL-BASED ACTIVITIES

Types of skill activities found in the Teacher Edition.

* **V Visual Skills** require students to analyze maps, graphs, charts, and photos.

W Writing Skills provide writing opportunities to help students comprehend the text.

R Reading Skills help students practice reading skills and master vocabulary.

C Critical Thinking Skills help students apply and extend what they have learned.

T Technology Skills require students to use digital tools effectively.

*Letters are followed by a number when there is more than one of the same type of skill on the page.

DIFFERENTIATED INSTRUCTION

All activities are written for the on-level student unless otherwise marked with the leveled labels below.

BL Beyond Level
AL Approaching Level
ELL English Language Learners

All students benefit from activities that utilize different learning styles. Many activities are marked as below when a particular learning style is highlighted.

Intrapersonal	Naturalist
Logical/Mathematical	Kinesthetic
Visual/Spatial	Auditory/Musical
Verbal/Linguistic	Interpersonal

CHAPTER OPENER PLANNER

Students will know:
- that trade in East Africa brought different cultures, languages, and religions to the region.
- that East Africa has a diverse landscape.

Students will be able to:
- *analyze* a world map to identify countries of East Africa.
- *use* a time line to discuss various events in the history of East Africa.

UNDERSTANDING
BY DESIGN®

☑ *Print Teaching Options*

V Visual Skills

☐ **P. 292** Students analyze photos of East Africa.
AL ELL Visual/Spatial

☐ **P. 293** Students review the time line and discuss its major points of interest. **Visual/Spatial**

W Writing Skills

☐ **P. 293** Students use at least two events on the time line to write a paragraph describing how trade influenced the development of East Africa. **Verbal/Linguistic, Logical/Mathematical**

☑ *Online Teaching Options*

☐ **MAP** **Reading a Map**—Students identify aspects and locations of the region on a map.

☐ **TIME LINE** **Reading a Time Line and Map**—Students learn about where and when historical events occurred in East Africa. **Visual/Spatial**

☐ **MAP** **Interactive World Atlas**—Students use the interactive world atlas to identify the region and describe its terrain.

☑ *Printable Digital Worksheets*

☐ **WORKSHEET** **GeoLab: Make a Glacier**—Students can use this worksheet to learn more about glaciers and how they are created.

☐ **WORKSHEET** **Geography and Economics: Trading in Ancient Kingdoms of East Africa**—Students can use this worksheet to understand trade routes and the impact of trade on the ancient kingdoms of East Africa.

Project-Based Learning

Hands-On

Making a 3-D Model
Have students work in groups to construct a 3-D model of East Africa and specifically, the Great Rift Valley. Students will use clay, salt dough, or other materials to create the region according to its physical features, adding in color and texture to detail specific landforms and bodies of water.

Digital Hands-On

Creating Online Quizzes
Students will work in pairs to create quizzes about the physical features, history, and cultures of East Africa using an online poll, survey, or quiz creation tool. Students should write questions about photos, maps, and videos that should be incorporated into the quiz. Quizzes will be taken online by fellow classmates and then graded. Review the correct answers with the class.

Print Resources

ANCILLARY RESOURCES
These ancillaries are available for every chapter and lesson.
- **Reading Essentials and Study Guide Workbook** **AL ELL**
- **Chapter Tests and Lesson Quizzes Blackline Masters**

PRINTABLE DIGITAL WORKSHEETS
These printable digital worksheets are available for every chapter and lesson.
- **Hands-On Chapter Projects**
- **What Do You Know? Activities**
- **Chapter Summaries (English and Spanish)**
- **Vocabulary Builder Activities**
- **Quizzes and Tests**
- **Reading Essentials and Study Guide (English and Spanish)** **AL ELL**
- **Guided Reading Activities**

More Media Resources

SUGGESTED VIDEOS
NOTE: Be sure to preview videos to ensure they are age-appropriate.
- **The Great Rift: Africa's Greatest Story** (150 min.)
- **Africa the Serengeti** (40 min.)
- **Cosmos Global Documentaries East Africa—Kenya, Tanzania** (53 min.)

SUGGESTED READING
- *Burn My Heart,* by Beverly Naidoo
- *Lost Boy, Lost Girl: Escaping Civil War in Sudan,* by John Bul Dau and Martha Arual Akech **BL**
- *Only the Mountains Do Not Move: A Maasai Story of Culture and Conservation,* by Jan Reynolds **AL**
- *Growing Up Maasai on the African Savannah,* by Joseph Lemasolai Lekuton

PHYSICAL GEOGRAPHY OF EAST AFRICA

Students will know:
• *that trade in East Africa brought different cultures, languages, and religions to the region.*
• *East Africa has a diverse landscape.*

Students will be able to:
• **describe** *the physical features of East Africa.*
• **describe** *the various climates of this region.*
• **discuss** *important natural resources in this region.*

UNDERSTANDING
BY DESIGN®

☑ *Print Teaching Options*

V **Visual Skills**

☐ **P. 294** Students use cardinal directions and the map to state directions. **ELL**

☐ **P. 294** Students visualize how Africa was once connected to the Arabian Peninsula. **Visual/Spatial**

☐ **P. 301** Students diagram food eaten by migrating species.

W **Writing Skills**

☐ **P. 296** Students write an essay about the country they researched in the Technology Skills Activity.

☐ **P. 297** Students debate and write an argument whether the Jonglei Canal should be completed. **ELL** **Verbal**

☐ **P. 299** Students research and write about the crops of Tanzania. **BL** **Verbal/Linguistic**

R **Reading Skills**

☐ **P. 297** Students read about the bodies of water in East Africa and answer questions. **Logical/Mathematical**

☐ **P. 300** Students paraphrase text. **AL**

☐ **P. 300** Students use word parts to find meaning. **ELL**

☐ **P. 301** Students define *geothermal* using Greek roots. **Verbal/Linguistic**

C **Critical Thinking Skills**

☐ **P. 298** Students connect the amount of rainfall in their area to the amount in East Africa. **Logical/Mathematical**

☐ **P. 299** Students identify what makes desertification an urgent issue. **Verbal/Linguistic**

☐ **P. 300** Students make connections between the economy, way of life, and natural resources.

T **Technology Skills**

☐ **P. 295** Students research photos of the Great Rift system and present a slide show. **Visual/Spatial**

☐ **P. 296** Students research an assigned country and prepare a slide show. **Visual/Spatial**

☐ **P. 300** Students research uses for salt.

☑ *Online Teaching Options*

V **Visual Skills**

☐ **IMAGE** **360° View: Lake Bogoria in Great Rift Valley**—Students make connections to the text with this 360° view of the Great Rift Valley.

☐ **MAP** **Geo Facts: East Africa**—Students use the Geo Facts map to highlight the unique geography of the region.

☐ **MAP** **Resources: East Africa**—Students use the resources map to highlight the other resources in the region.

W **Writing Skills**

☐ **VIDEO** **Wild Wonders: Ethiopia**—Students watch the video about Ethiopia and write three questions they have about East Africa. **AL** **Visual/Spatial**

☐ **IMAGE** **The Great Rift Valley Viewed from Space**—Students discuss the unique landforms in East Africa and write a paragraph about which landforms they find most interesting when viewed from space. **AL** **Intrapersonal, Naturalist**

☐ **IMAGE** **Lake Victoria**—Students use the interactive photo to discuss geographical features of Lake Victoria and write three things they learned. **ELL** **Visual/Spatial, Naturalist**

☐ **IMAGE** **Glaciers in East Africa**—Students learn about glaciers in East Africa and write a short paragraph explaining why most people would not associate snow and ice with the continent of Africa. **Visual/Spatial, Verbal/Linguistic**

R **Reading Skills**

☐ **GRAPHIC ORGANIZER** **Diverse Physical Features of East Africa**—Students use the interactive graphic organizer to review the variety of landforms and bodies of water in the region.

C **Critical Thinking Skills**

☐ **SLIDE SHOW** **The Nile River's Source**—Students watch the slide show about the Nile River and discuss why it is an important body of water for all of Africa. **Visual/Spatial, Verbal/Linguistic**

☐ **MAP** **The Nile River**—Students use the map to discuss the changes that took place to the Nile River and its channels over time and then explain the characteristics of the Nile as well as how it affects all the communities along its banks. **AL** **Verbal/Linguistic**

☐ **MAP** **Desertification of the Sahel**—Students discuss desertification of the Sahel and identify problems that desertification causes. **Visual/Spatial, Naturalist**

☐ **GRAPHIC ORGANIZER** **Alternative Energy Sources in Africa**—Students discuss and analyze the alternative energy sources being developed in Africa. **BL** **Interpersonal**

T **Technology Skills**

☐ **ONLINE SELF-CHECK QUIZ** **Lesson 1**—Students receive instant feedback on their mastery of lesson content.

☑ *Printable Digital Worksheets*

W **Writing Skills**

☐ **WORKSHEET** **GeoLab: Making a Glacier**—Students can use this worksheet to learn more about glaciers.

HISTORY OF EAST AFRICA

Students will know:
- that trade in East Africa brought different cultures, languages, and religions to the region.

Students will be able to:
- **discuss** how the history of trade has impacted East Africa.
- **examine** the colonial era and its effect on East Africa.
- **describe** independence movements and independence for East African countries.
- **explore** instability in East Africa.

UNDERSTANDING
BY DESIGN®

☑ *Print Teaching Options*

V Visual Skills

☐ **P. 303** Students use map to discuss trading states.

☐ **P. 304** Students describe why they think Kilwa was successful in trading. **Logical/Mathematical**

☐ **P. 305** Students trace the sea route from Europe to India and discuss trade and geography. **Visual/Spatial**

W Writing Skills

☐ **P. 306** Students write a persuasive essay about motivators for going to war—religion or the economy.

R Reading Skills

☐ **P. 302** Students discuss the results of trade in the ancient kingdoms in East Africa. **Verbal/Linguistic**

☐ **P. 306** Students use context clues to find meaning. **AL**

☐ **P. 307** Students cite text evidence to support what helped Ethiopia remain an independent country. **Logical**

☐ **P. 307** Students explain what caused Europeans to grant East African colonies their independence in the 1960s.

☐ **P. 309** Students discuss the issues of civil war in Sudan.

C Critical Thinking Skills

☐ **P. 303** Students research words in Swahili. **BL Auditory**

☐ **P. 304** Students infer why Kilwa was a walled city.

☐ **P. 306** Students infer why the emperor of Ethiopia would not want his country to be a protectorate of Italy. **Logical**

☐ **P. 307** Students evaluate British colonization of Kenya.

☐ **P. 308** Students consider governments and genocide.

☐ **P. 309** Students make connections between the American Civil War and the civil war in Somalia.

T Technology Skills

☐ **P. 304** Students research the places that Ibn Battuta visited in his lifetime and plot them on a map.

☐ **P. 305** Students research Stanley's journey to locate Livingstone. **Verbal/Linguistic**

☐ **P. 308** Students analyze facts about Idi Amin.

☑ *Online Teaching Options*

V Visual Skills

☐ **VIDEO** **Postcards from Kenya**—Students watch the video about Kenya and East Africa and share what they learned from the video. **Visual/Spatial, Intrapersonal**

☐ **IMAGE** **Vasco de Gama**—Students use this interactive photo to discuss this explorer and his role in African colonization and imperialism.

☐ **IMAGE** **The Nile River's Source**—Students use the interactive photo from lesson 1 to discuss Livingstone and the historical quest for the source of the Nile.

W Writing Skills

☐ **GRAPHIC ORGANIZER** **Reviewing: East African Independence**—Students use the interactive graphic organizer to review the information about East African independence.

☐ **SLIDE SHOW** **Ancient Africa**—Students discuss groups that lived in ancient Africa and the evidence that proves their existence and write a paragraph about the evidence. **AL Verbal**

☐ **IMAGE** **Battle at Omdurman**—Students discuss the battle at Omdurman and write a paragraph about why they think the use of modern guns helped defeat the Mahdist army. **BL**

☐ **MAP** **East African Colonization**—Students discuss which European nations colonized which part of East Africa and write a paragraph explaining which nation they think was most successful.

R Reading Skills

☐ **GRAPHIC ORGANIZER** **African Trade**—Students use the graphic organizer to review African trade.

C Critical Thinking Skills

☐ **MAP** **African Trade Routes and Goods**—Students discuss the various routes and goods that were traded using the animated map. **BL Visual/Spatial, Logical/Mathematical**

☐ **MAP** **East African Independence**—Students discuss the historical changes that resulted from European colonization and the movement to end colonization using the map. **AL Visual**

☐ **IMAGE** **Refugee Camps: South Sudan**—Students discuss the genocide and forced relocation in South Sudan and share their thoughts and feelings.

☐ **MAP** **Resources: East Africa**—Students can use the resources map to discuss the oil that is located in Sudan and how this plays a role in the historical events of that country.

☐ **IMAGE** **Ethiopian Freedom and the Battle of Adwa**—Students use the interactive photo of this battle to discuss its historical significance and compare it to the Battle at Khartoum.

T Technology Skills

☐ **ONLINE SELF-CHECK QUIZ** **Lesson 2**—Students receive instant feedback on their mastery of lesson content.

☑ *Printable Digital Worksheets*

W Writing Skills

☐ **WORKSHEET** **Geography and Economics: Trading in Ancient Kingdoms of East Africa**—Students use worksheet to understand trade in the ancient kingdoms of East Africa.

LIFE IN EAST AFRICA

Students will know:
- that trade in East Africa brought different cultures, languages, and religions to the region.

Students will be able to:
- **describe** population density in East Africa.
- **describe** people and cultures in the region, including languages and religion.
- **describe** daily life in the region.
- **explore** challenges in East Africa, including economic, environmental, and health issues.

UNDERSTANDING
BY DESIGN®

☑ *Print Teaching Options*

W Writing Skills

☐ **P. 313** Students write a letter to a fictional friend in Nairobi as though they were a new resident in the country. **Naturalist**

☐ **P. 317** Students write a report about the lack of electricity and its impact on deforestation. **BL** **Verbal/Linguistic**

R Reading Skills

☐ **P. 311** Students relate the term *extended family* to the term *clan*. **Verbal/Linguistic**

☐ **P. 312** Students determine the meaning of the word *Nilotic*. **Verbal/Linguistic**

☐ **P. 315** Students list the three most serious challenges to East African agriculture. **Naturalist**

☐ **P. 316** Students identify food crops and cash crops. **AL**

C Critical Thinking Skills

☐ **P. 310** Students compare the populations of the countries in East Africa. **Logical/Mathematical**

☐ **P. 311** Students infer why most Sudanese people live along the Nile River. **Verbal/Linguistic**

☐ **P. 312** Students determine effects of diversity in languages. **BL** **Interpersonal**

☐ **P. 314** Students analyze oral traditions. **AL** **Verbal/Linguistic**

☐ **P. 315** Students identify evidence in the text that human beings originated in East Africa. **Verbal/Linguistic**

☐ **P. 316** Students reason why low literacy rates hurt a nation's economy. **BL**

☐ **P. 317** Students determine why East Africa set up national parks. **AL** **Naturalist**

T Technology Skills

☐ **P. 311** Student groups use the Internet to research different ethnic groups from Kenya. **Interpersonal**

☐ **P. 315** Student groups research and prepare a report about one of East Africa's national parks. **Naturalist**

☑ *Online Teaching Options*

V Visual Skills

☐ **VIDEO** **America's Gift**—Students watch the video about American foreign aid going to Uganda to fight HIV/AIDS. **Interpersonal**

☐ **MAP** **Islam in Africa**—Students use the map about the spread of Islam in Africa to discuss how this religion developed in this region.

☐ **VIDEO** **Nairobi**—Students compare the advantages and disadvantages of Nairobi to a large city with which they are familiar. **Visual/Spatial, Verbal/Linguistic**

☐ **MAP** **Population: East Africa**—Students use the population map to discuss the population density and distribution of the region.

☐ **MAP** **Museums: Preserving Kenya's Heritage and Culture**—Students use the map of Kenya that focuses on the regional museums to discuss the desire to preserve cultural heritage.

☐ **IMAGES** **Animal Poaching**—Students use the interactive images about animal poaching to discuss the hunting of endangered species and the demand for these items.

W Writing Skills

☐ **IMAGES** **360º Views: Masai and Kenya**—Students use the 360º views to discuss the differences between urban and rural life in East Africa and write a paragraph. **ELL** **Visual**

☐ **GRAPHIC ORGANIZER** **Issues in East Africa Today**—Students create an essay outline of the information on the interactive graphic organizer with a partner. **AL** **Interpersonal**

R Reading Skills

☐ **CHART** **Language in East Africa**—Students use the language chart to discuss the various languages spoken in East Africa.

C Critical Thinking Skills

☐ **CHART** **Official Languages in East Africa**—Students discuss the communication problems resulting when inhabitants of a region speak many different languages. **Verbal/Linguistic, Interpersonal**

☐ **GRAPHIC ORGANIZER** **Urban and Rural Life in East Africa**—Students use the interactive graphic organizer to make comparisons about urban and rural life in East Africa.

☐ **GAME** **Fill-in-the-Blank Game**—Students play a fill-in-the-blank game and write a short paragraph developing a topic addressed in the activity. **Verbal/Linguistic**

☐ **CHART** **Literacy Rates Across Africa**—Students use the chart to examine the literacy rates of African nations.

☐ **CHART** **Life Expectancy Across Africa**—Students discuss how health issues have affected the economy of Africa and brainstorm methods that Africans can use to improve their life expectancy rates. **BL**

T Technology Skills

☐ **ONLINE SELF-CHECK QUIZ** **Lesson 3**—Students receive instant feedback on their mastery of lesson content.

INTERVENTION AND REMEDIATION STRATEGIES

LESSON 1 Physical Geography of East Africa

Reading and Comprehension

Organize students into five groups. Assign the academic vocabulary word or one of the four content vocabulary words for this lesson to each group. Challenge students in each group to write a paragraph using their assigned term to explain a concept in the lesson. Then have groups switch words until all groups have worked with each term. Challenge students to use the word *rift* as both a noun and a verb, checking its meaning in a print or online dictionary. Provide guidance as needed, ensuring that students have used each term correctly and demonstrate an understanding of lesson concepts.

Text Evidence

Have students review the lesson and use the headings and subheadings to create an outline to better comprehend lesson concepts. Briefly review with students the proper format of an outline. Have students write key words and phrases in their notebooks to remind them about important content under each heading and subheading. Then have students conduct a peer review by switching outlines with a partner. Encourage students to make revisions and additions to their outlines as needed.

LESSON 2 History of East Africa

Reading and Comprehension

To ensure comprehension of the academic and content vocabulary words in this lesson, have students work in mixed-ability pairs to review each word. Have students say each word while their partner writes down a definition based on context clues in the text. Have partners quiz each other on the terms, clarifying meanings by locating the definitions in a dictionary. Challenge students to identify and use the different nuances in meanings of the words *impact* (verb and noun) and *tribute*.

Text Evidence

Have students work in pairs to identify word parts to improve their understanding of content vocabulary terms. Have students choose a term, such as *genocide*, to break down into word parts and their meanings (*gen-* = birth, race, produce; *-cide* = to kill). To increase their understanding of the terms, challenge pairs to come up with other words with the same prefixes or suffixes (*genetics, suicide,* etc.). Then have partners write a paragraph using content vocabulary to explain a lesson concept. Tell students to cite specific evidence from the text to support their reasoning.

LESSON 3 Life in East Africa

Reading and Comprehension

To ensure comprehension of the concepts explained in this lesson, have students work in small groups and take turns acting as the teacher. Tell students the assignment to teach is titled "People, Culture, and Conflict in East Africa." Students should choose a concept, place, or vocabulary word from the lesson and explain it to the rest of their group. Encourage student "teachers" to draw diagrams or charts on the board to help their "class" visualize key concepts from the lesson. Have "teachers" assess students' understanding by posing the essential question: *Why does conflict develop?*

Text Evidence

Organize students into five groups to create a visual representation of an aspect of life in East Africa discussed in this lesson. Assign groups the following topics to depict in their visual displays: Where People Live, Ethnic Groups, Languages and Religion, Daily Life, and Arts and Culture. Students may choose to create a poster, a graphic organizer, or diagram as well as photographs they find online to enhance their displays. Have students present their displays to the class, using evidence from the text to support their visuals.

Online Resources

Level Reader

Use this online lower-level text that corresponds directly to the text in the online Student Edition.

Guided Reading Activities

This resource uses graphic organizers and guiding questions to help students with comprehension.

What Do You Know?

Use these worksheets to pre-assess students' background knowledge before they read the chapter.

Reading Essentials and Study Guide Workbook

This resource offers writing and reading activities for the approaching-level student.

Self-Check Quizzes

This online assessment tool provides instant feedback for students to check their progress.

EAST AFRICA

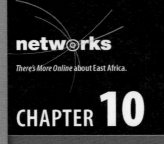

ESSENTIAL QUESTIONS · *How does geography influence the way people live?* · *Why do people trade?* · *Why does conflict develop?*

Ariadne Van Zandbergen/Lonely Planet Images/Getty Images

Teenage girl from the East African country of Somalia

Lesson 1
Physical Geography of East Africa

Lesson 2
History of East Africa

Lesson 3
Life in East Africa

The Story Matters...

Some of Africa's earliest kingdoms developed in East Africa, where trade in gold and ivory brought great wealth. Since ancient times, thriving trade has fostered interaction among different cultures, influencing language and religion and creating much ethnic diversity across the region. The landscape of East Africa also has great diversity—from the Serengeti Plain and the Great Rift Valley to the highlands in Ethiopia and Kilimanjaro in Kenya.

FOLDABLES
Study Organizer

Go to the Foldables® library in the back of your book to make a Foldable® that will help you take notes while reading this chapter.

291

ENGAGE

Bellringer Explain to students that elephant tusks are made of ivory and then have students brainstorm a list of uses for ivory. Students might cite statues, beads, decorative boxes, hairpins, buttons, and piano keys. Tell students that to get ivory, people must first kill an elephant and then cut off its tusks. Today, it is illegal to kill an elephant for ivory, and items like piano keys are now made from plastic. Then have students read "The Story Matters. . ." about East Africa, an area with a diverse landscape.

Use the following questions to guide the class in a discussion about how thriving trade routes can be beneficial to a region.

- **In addition to goods, what else might be traded?**
- **Why would trade in gold and ivory bring great wealth to a region?**
- **What does having a diverse landscape mean and how might it affect a region?**

Tell students that in this chapter they will learn about the countries of East Africa.

Making Connections Have students look at the picture, read the caption, and locate the country of Somalia on the Chapter Opener map. Explain that Somalia has a semiarid climate with hot temperatures and little rainfall. Tell students that a little over a third of the Somali people over the age of 15 can read and write. Children average only about three years of schooling. There is a high risk of being infected with a major disease, such as HIV/AIDS, and life expectancy at birth is only 50.8 years.

Have volunteers use the Internet to research comparable facts about people in the United States. (*United States: 99% of people over the age of 15 can read and write; children average 12 years of school; there is a low risk for infectious diseases; life expectancy at birth is 78.49 years.*) **Ask:** How might your future be different from the future of a teenager in Somalia? (*Students' answers will vary but should demonstrate an understanding of the health and education advantages that United States teenagers have. Some students may also have background knowledge about famine and civil war in the area.*) **Logical/Mathematical, Intrapersonal**

Letter from the Author

Dear Geography Teacher,

This chapter is rich with geographic information about East African countries. After students have studied the chapter, have them write an essay that describes reasons it has been difficult for East African countries to form a national identity. Help your students organize the topics of their essays by identifying some of the issues that challenge these countries, including history, language, religion, land and climate, resources, and lack of economic cooperation.

Richard H. Boehm

FOLDABLES
Study Organizer

Go to the Foldables® library for a cumulative chapter-based Foldable® activity that your students can use to help take notes and prepare for assessment.

TEACH & ASSESS

Step Into the Place

V Visual Skills

Integrating Visual Information Have students look at the image of Mount Kilimanjaro (photo A) and read the caption. Explain that an inactive volcano is a dormant volcano—it has not erupted for a long period of time. However, it could erupt again. Inactive volcanoes are also called sleeping volcanoes. **Ask:** What information does the snow at the top of the volcano tell you? *(Possible answer: The mountain has a high elevation and temperatures near the top are below freezing.)*

Next have students look at the image of the war-torn city (photo B) and read the caption. Have them locate Mogadishu, Somalia, on the map. **Ask:** What information can you infer about Mogadishu from this image? *(Possible answer: It is a country that has experienced a lot of war; these buildings were once large and resort like, but not anymore.)* **AL** Visual/Spatial, Verbal/Linguistic

Content Background Knowledge

Pronouncing Difficult Words Help students to correctly pronounce the names of the countries in East Africa by making a chart with the phonetic spellings of the names. Practice saying the names aloud with students. Then have partners say the names together.

Sudan	soo-DAN
South Sudan	south soo-DAN
Eritrea	air-ih-TREE-uh
Djibouti	jih-BOOT-ee
Somalia	so-MAH-lee-uh
Ethiopia	eeth-ee-OE-pee-uh
Kenya	KEN-yuh
Tanzania	tan-zuh-NEE-uh
Uganda	yoo-GAHN-dah
Rwanda	ruh-WAHN-duh
Burundi	buh-ROON-dee

ELL Auditory/Musical, Verbal/Linguistic

Some of Africa's important early civilizations flourished in East Africa. Many of the countries have been scarred by conflict in recent years.

Step Into the Place

MAP FOCUS Use the map to answer the following questions.

1 THE GEOGRAPHER'S WORLD Which three East African countries share Lake Victoria?

2 PLACES AND REGIONS What is the capital city of Kenya?

3 THE GEOGRAPHER'S WORLD The Tekeze is a major river in what country?

4 CRITICAL THINKING Integrating Visual Information What country is cut off from the sea by Eritrea, Djibouti, and Somalia?

V

INACTIVE VOLCANO Snowcapped Kilimanjaro looms over savanna plains near the border of Tanzania and Kenya. The mountain is made up of three volcanic cones, all inactive.

B

WAR-TORN CITY Ruined buildings line an Indian Ocean beach in Mogadishu, the capital of Somalia. Since the early 1990s, various armed groups have fought over Somalia.

Step Into the Time

TIME LINE Using at least two events on the time line, write a paragraph describing how trade influenced the development of East Africa.
WHST.6–8.2, WHST.6-8.4

800 B.C. Kingdom of Kush develops along the Nile River

A.D. 400 Kingdom of Aksum prospers from trade

B.C. | **A.D.**

30,000–20,000 B.C. Ancient people live in what is now Sudan

1100s Muslim settlements multiply in East Africa

292 *Chapter 10*

(t to b) ©Fridmar Damm/Corbis: John Moore/Getty Images News/Getty Images; Patrick Syder/Lonely Planet Images/Getty Images

---

Project-Based Learning ✋

Hands-On

Creating a 3-D Model
Have students work in small groups to construct a 3-D model of East Africa and specifically, the Great Rift Valley. Students will use clay, salt dough, or other materials to create the region according to its physical features, adding in color and texture to detail specific landforms and bodies of water.

Digital Hands-On

Creating Online Quizzes
Students will work in pairs to create quizzes about the physical features, history, and cultures of East Africa using an online poll, survey, or quiz creation tool. Students should write quiz questions about photos, maps, and videos. Quizzes will be taken online by fellow classmates and then graded. Review the correct answers with the class.

edtech**teacher**
21st Century Learning

ANSWERS, p. 292

STEP INTO THE PLACE
1. Kenya, Uganda, and Tanzania
2. Nairobi
3. Ethiopia
4. **CRITICAL THINKING** Ethiopia

networks
There's More Online!

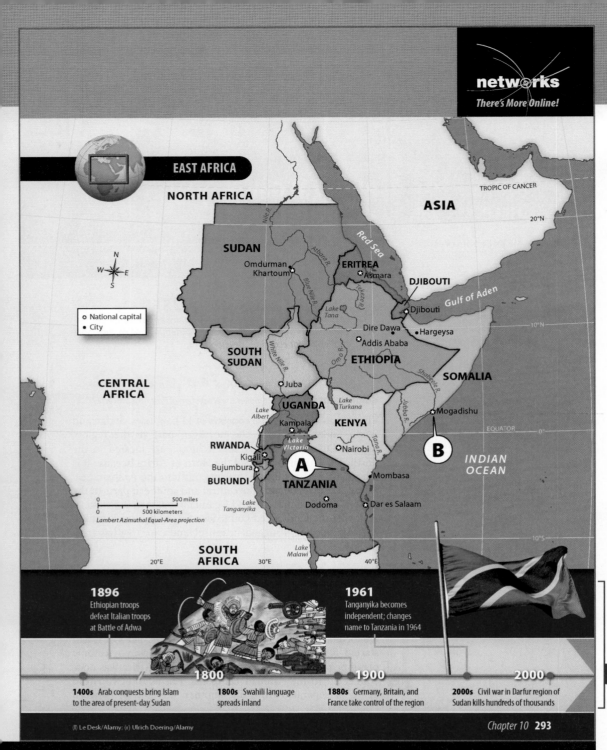

EAST AFRICA

NORTH AFRICA

ASIA

TROPIC OF CANCER

20°N

SUDAN

Omdurman
Khartoum

ERITREA

Asmara

DJIBOUTI

Djibouti

Gulf of Aden

Red Sea

Dire Dawa

Hargeysa

o National capital
• City

Lake
Tana

SOUTH
SUDAN

Addis Ababa

ETHIOPIA

SOMALIA

CENTRAL
AFRICA

Juba

Lake
Albert

Lake
Turkana

UGANDA

Kampala

KENYA

Mogadishu

EQUATOR   0°

RWANDA

Kigali

Lake
Victoria

Nairobi

B

INDIAN
OCEAN

Bujumbura

A

BURUNDI

TANZANIA

Mombasa

500 miles

Lake
Tanganyika

Dodoma

Dar es Salaam

0   500 kilometers
Lambert Azimuthal Equal-Area projection

SOUTH
AFRICA

Lake
Malawi

10°S

20°E   30°E   40°E

1896
Ethiopian troops
defeat Italian troops
at Battle of Adwa

1961
Tanganyika becomes
independent; changes
name to Tanzania in 1964

1800

1900

2000

1400s Arab conquests bring Islam
to the area of present-day Sudan

1800s Swahili language
spreads inland

1880s Germany, Britain, and
France take control of the region

2000s Civil war in Darfur region of
Sudan kills hundreds of thousands

(l) Le Desk/Alamy; (r) Ulrich Doering/Alamy

Chapter 10 **293**

Reading a Time Line and Map

Integrating Visual Information Display the interactive
time line and map on the whiteboard. Have volunteers
read each event as it is revealed on the time line. Ask
students to specify the date and the country in which the
event took place and find its location on the map.
AL Visual/Spatial

See page 291B for other online activities.

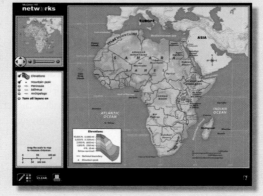

Step Into the Time

V Visual Skills

Reading a Time Line Have students review the time line and
as a class, discuss its major points of interest. **Ask:**

- **What period of time is shown on the time line?** *(from
  30,000 B.C. to A.D. 2000)*
- **When did people start living in what is now Sudan?**
  (30,000 B.C.)
- **During what time in history did Germany, Britain, and
  France control the region?** *(1880s)*
- **Who won the Battle of Adwa in 1896?** *(Ethiopian troops)*
- **When did Tanzania become the official name of a
  country in East Africa?** *(1964)*
- **What happened in the Darfur region of Sudan in the
  2000s?** *(Civil war killed hundreds of thousands of people.)*

Ask students to list some historical events that could be
added to the time line. *(Student answers will vary but should
include accurate event placement.)* **Visual/Spatial, Verbal/
Linguistic**

W Writing Skills

Informative/Explanatory Read aloud the activity described
at the beginning of the time line. Before writing their
paragraphs, have students review the time line events and
choose the two they wish to write about. Have students who
choose the same events work together to brainstorm ideas
about how trade influenced the development of East Africa.
Have students share their completed paragraphs with the
class. **Logical/Mathematical, Verbal/Linguistic**

V

CLOSE & REFLECT

To close, review the names of the countries in East Africa and
explain that these countries have been scarred by conflict. **Ask:**
**Why do you think Germany, Britain, and France took
control of the region in the 1880s?** *(Possible answer: They
may have wanted to profit from the trade routes.)*

Discuss that many African countries have extensive natural
resources, such as minerals, that have been the source of some
of the conflicts. Have students write three predictions about
East Africa. Tell them to check their predictions as they read the
chapter. **Verbal/Linguistic, Logical/Mathematical**

ENGAGE

 Bellringer Before students begin the lesson, have them brainstorm a list of the possible landscapes and climates found in East Africa. Have students use their list of possible landforms and climates of East Africa throughout the lesson, correcting misconceptions as they move through the content. Have students make a connection between their lists and the Essential Question and "It Matters Because" statement.

TEACH & ASSESS

V1 Visual Skills

Reading a Map As students read, have them use the Chapter Opener map to locate the countries by using the cardinal directions given in the text. Review with students what a *peninsula* is *(a piece of land surrounded by water on three sides)* and what *landlocked* means. *(surrounded by land and having no coastline or seaport)* Also review the correct pronunciations of the countries' names. **ELL** **Visual/Spatial**

R Reading Skills

Defining Review with students how Earth's crust is changing. **Ask:**

- What is a geological fault? *(a break in the rocks that make up Earth's crust, along which rocks on either side have moved past each other)*
- What are tectonic plates? *(huge, irregularly-shaped slabs of solid rock that make up the foundation of Earth's crust)*

Have volunteers use the Internet to find pictures of these geological features. Then have students use context clues to determine the meaning of *rifted. (separated from one another)* **ELL** **AL** **Verbal/Linguistic**

V2 Visual Skills

Visualizing To help students visualize how Africa was once connected to the Arabian Peninsula, reproduce the Chapter Opener map and cut apart Africa and the Arabian Peninsula to make two puzzle pieces. Demonstrate how the two pieces can fit together. Display the pieces on an overhead projector and then move them together. **Visual/Spatial, Kinesthetic**

ANSWER, p. 294

Taking Notes **Landforms:** Great Rift Valley, plains, plateaus, mountains; **Water:** Nile River, Lake Victoria, Lake Tanganyika, Lake Malawi (Nyasa), Jonglei Canal

---

---

networks

There's More Online!

☑ **IMAGES** Glaciers in East Africa

☑ **MAP** Desertification of the Sahel

☑ **SLIDE SHOW** The Nile River's Source

☑ **VIDEO**

Reading HELPDESK CCSS

Academic Vocabulary RH.6-8.4
(Tier Two Words)
- consist

Content Vocabulary RH.6-8.4
(Tier Three Words)
- rift
- desertification
- hydroelectric power
- geothermal energy

TAKING NOTES: *Key Ideas and Details* RH.6-8.2, RH.6-8.7

Identifying As you study the lesson, use a web diagram like this one to list information about the land and water features of the region.

Land and Water Features → Landforms, Water

294

Lesson 1
Physical Geography of East Africa

ESSENTIAL QUESTION · *How does geography influence the way people live?*

IT MATTERS BECAUSE
East Africa offers a rugged, beautiful landscape and different climates. The region provides variety, potential, and considerable challenges for economic development.

Land and Water Features

GUIDING QUESTION *What makes the ecosystem of East Africa diverse?*

V1 The region of East Africa **consists** of 11 countries. Sudan and South Sudan dominate the northern part of the region. Eritrea, Djibouti, Somalia, and Ethiopia are located in the northeast. This area is called the Horn of Africa because it is a horn-shaped peninsula that juts out into the Arabian Sea. Three countries occupy the central and southern parts of the region: Kenya, Tanzania, and Uganda. Finally, in the western sector lie the landlocked countries of Rwanda and Burundi. East Africa offers a rugged, beautiful landscape that has great variety.

Landforms

R The Great Rift Valley is the most unusual feature of East Africa's physical geography. Sometimes it is called the Great Rift system because it is not one single valley. Rather, it is a series of large valleys and depressions in Earth's surface. These are formed by long chains of geological faults. The Great Rift started forming about 20 million years ago when tectonic **V2** plates began to tear apart from one another. Africa was once connected to the Arabian Peninsula. But as the two **rifted** apart, or separated from one another, the land in between

(l to r) ©Hemis/Alamy; ©Michael Freeman/Corbis; ©John Warburton-Lee Photography/Alamy; Bruno Zanzottera/Parallelozero/Aurora Photos; ©Nigel Pavitt/JAI/Corbis

---

networks *Online Teaching Options*

VIDEO

Wild Wonders—Ethiopia

Formulating Questions Use this video about the landforms, waterways, climate, and wildlife of Ethiopia to introduce the lesson. Ask students to write three questions they have about East Africa after watching the video. Collect the questions and discuss them as a class after the lesson. **AL** **Naturalist, Verbal/Linguistic**

See page 291C for other online activities.

BBC Motion Gallery Education

sank and was filled by the Red Sea. Eventually, all of East Africa will separate from the rest of Africa, and the Red Sea will fill the rift.

The Great Rift system's northern end is in Jordan in Southwest Asia. From Jordan, it stretches about 4,000 miles (6,437 km) to its southern end in Mozambique in southeastern Africa. The rift has an average width of 30 miles to 40 miles (48 km to 64 km).

The rift system has an eastern and western branch in East Africa. The eastern Rift Valley—the main branch—runs from Southwest Asia along the Jordan River, Dead Sea, and Red Sea. It continues through the Danakil plain in Ethiopia. It is one of the hottest and driest places on Earth, and earthquakes and volcanic activity occur here regularly. Long, deep cracks develop in Earth's surface as the tectonic plates rift apart.

As the eastern Rift Valley continues south from the Danakil plain, the conditions are not as severe. It takes the form of deep valleys as it extends into Kenya and Tanzania, and down to Mozambique. The shorter western Rift Valley stretches from Lake Malawi in the south through Uganda in the north through a series of valleys. A chain of deep lakes that includes Lake Tanganyika, Lake Edward, and Lake Albert marks the western rift's northward path.

Along the branches of the Great Rift Valley, much volcanic and seismic activity occurred. The largest volcanoes are located on the eastern Rift. These include Mount Kenya and Kilimanjaro. Kilimanjaro is on the border between Kenya and Tanzania. With a summit of 19,341 feet (5,895 m), Kilimanjaro is the tallest mountain in Africa. Its summit is covered with snow year-round, even though the mountain is near the Equator.

Sudan is home to vast plains and plateaus. The northern part of the country is desert covered in sand or gravel. Somalia lies in the eastern part of the region, along the Indian Ocean.

©Hemis/Alamy

Academic Vocabulary

consist to be made up of

R

This aerial view shows a section of the floor of the eastern Rift Valley in Kenya. Many fault lines appear in the valley. Hardened lava from volcanoes and openings in the ground also mark the landscape.

▶ CRITICAL THINKING
Describing How will East Africa eventually be affected by the Rift's tectonic plate activity?

Chapter 10 **295**

Lissa Harrison

IMAGE

The Great Rift System Viewed From Space

Discussing Display the image of the Great Rift Valley taken from space. Discuss with students the unique landforms that can be seen in East Africa. Ask volunteers to locate the landforms as they are identified. Use the physical geography layer of the Chapter Opener map to review the landforms and waterways of East Africa with students. Then, have students write a paragraph explaining which landform looks the most interesting to them.

AL Intrapersonal, Naturalist

See page 291C for other online activities.

Interactive Photos

This region has many diverse types of landscapes. Land forms range from mountains to grasslands. Waterways include rivers, lakes, and shorelines. Vegetation varies depending on the soil quality and access to water within the specific area. Animal life has adapted to take advantage of what the region has to offer.

R Reading Skills

Identifying Allow time for students to read the text on the page silently and study the image at the bottom of the page. Then as a class, discuss the following questions about the Great Rift system. **Ask:**

• **In what direction does the Great Rift system run?** *(north to south)*

• **How would you describe the Danakil Plain in Ethiopia?** *(The eastern Rift Valley runs through the plain. It is one of the hottest and driest places on Earth. It is an area where earthquakes and volcanic activity occur regularly. As the tectonic plates rift apart, long, deep cracks develop in the plain's surface.)*

• **How far south does the eastern Rift Valley go?** *(south to Mozambique)*

• **What landforms can be found in the western Rift Valley?** *(valleys and lakes)*

• **Where in the Great Rift Valley can you find the largest volcanoes?** *(on the eastern Rift)* **Verbal/Linguistic**

T Technology Skills

Using Visual Aids Have volunteers use the Internet to find additional photos of the Great Rift system. Then have them use a software presentation program to present a slide show of the photos to the class. Suggest that they write captions to display with the photos and credit their sources. **Visual/Spatial**

T

Content Background Knowledge

Share these facts about Mt. Kilimanjaro with students:

• Mt. Kilimanjaro is the tallest mountain in Africa.

• The names of the mountain's three volcanic cones are Kibo, Mawenzi, and Shira.

• Kilimanjaro National Park, which surrounds the mountain, is a UNESCO World Heritage site.

• A German geographer, Hans Meyer, and an Austrian mountain climber, Ludwig Purtscheller, were the first to reach the mountain's summit in 1889.

• Around 25,000 climbers per year try to reach the mountain's summit.

• Examples of these ecosystems are found on the mountain: glacier, snowfields, deserts, alpine moorland, savannah, and tropical jungle.

ANSWER, p. 295

CRITICAL THINKING Possible answer: All of East Africa will separate from the rest of Africa, and the Red Sea will fill the rift.

T Technology Skills

Using Visual Aids Divide the class into eleven small groups and assign each group a country in East Africa to research. Have groups use the Internet to gather photos that show the landscape of their country. Using a software presentation program, have groups make a slide show to present their visuals along with captions for the photos. Tell students to sequence their photos to show the landscape from north to south. Combine the presentations into a travelogue of East Africa. **Visual/Spatial, Logical/Mathematical**

W Writing Skills

Informative/Explanatory Have the groups write a five-paragraph essay about the landscape of the country they researched with their small group. Groups' essays should include an introductory paragraph listing at least three characteristics of the country's landscape. The body of the essay should include three paragraphs, each detailing one of the characteristics mentioned in the introductory paragraph. Specific examples of landforms can be included. The final paragraph should be a summary of the country's landscape. Have volunteers share their essays with the class. **Verbal/Linguistic**

Make Connections Tell students that although the Amazon River is shorter than the Nile, it carries more freshwater than any other river in the world. Have students compare the Nile to other rivers previously discussed in other chapters. **Verbal/Linguistic, Logical/Mathematical**

V Visual Skills

Reading a Map After students have read the section, "Bodies of Water," use the Chapter Opener map to trace the Blue Nile from its headwaters at Lake Tana in northern Ethiopia and the White Nile from its headwaters at Lake Victoria in Uganda to their convergence in Khartoum, Sudan. Then have students continue to trace the Nile River until it empties into the Mediterranean Sea. **Ask:** In which cardinal direction does the Nile River flow? *(north)* **ELL Visual/Spatial, Logical/Mathematical**

The palace of Sudan's president in Khartoum stands near where the Blue Nile joins the White Nile. The White Nile is named for the light-colored clay sediment found in its waters. The Blue Nile's name comes from the river's appearance during flood season when the water level is high.

▶ **CRITICAL THINKING**
Describing Where do each of the two Nile tributaries begin?

Somalia is also an extremely dry area. The country is made up largely of savanna and semidesert. To the north of Somalia lies the small country of Djibouti. Located on the coast between the Red Sea and the Gulf of Aden, Djibouti displays a highly diverse landscape. It has rugged mountains and desert plains.

South of Sudan, at the western edge of Uganda, the Ruwenzori Mountains divide that country from the Democratic Republic of the Congo. These peaks are sometimes called the "Mountains of the Moon." Mountains give way to hills in small, landlocked Rwanda. It is known as the "land of a thousand hills" for its beautiful landscape.

Bodies of Water

The longest river in the world is the Nile (4,132 miles or 6,650 km). The Nile Basin includes parts of many countries in the East African region: Tanzania, Burundi, Rwanda, Kenya, Uganda, Ethiopia, South Sudan, and the Sudan. Beginning in the 1800s, European explorers made numerous expeditions in attempts to find the source of the Nile River. The great river was discovered to have two sets of headwaters. One of them, the Blue Nile, rises in the northern highlands of Ethiopia. The other source, the White Nile, begins in Lake Victoria and runs through Lake Albert. The White Nile then passes through the swampy wetlands of central South Sudan, a huge area called the Sudd.

In northern Sudan, the Blue Nile and the White Nile meet at the city of Khartoum. The great river then runs northward through Egypt and empties into the Mediterranean Sea. Other than the Nile,

©Michael Freeman/Corbis

296 *Chapter 10*

netw⊙rks *Online Teaching Options*

SLIDE SHOW

The Nile River's Source

Discussing Use the slide show highlighting the historical search for the Nile River's source to discuss the various dangers that a person searching for the source of the Nile River could face. Then, discuss with students why this is an important body of water for all of Africa. Have students write three facts that they learned about the river. **Visual/Spatial, Verbal/Linguistic**

See page 291C for other online activities.

Slide Show

(l) ©Ocean/Corbis, ©Kryssia Campos/Getty Images, (tr) Erica Simone Leeds, (br) ©IG Photography/Alamy

ANSWER, p. 296

CRITICAL THINKING **Blue Nile:** northern highlands of Ethiopia; **White Nile:** Lake Victoria and Lake Albert

East Africa has few important rivers. This is due to the intermittent rainfall and the high temperatures in many areas of the region.

In the late 1970s, the swampy Sudd was the focus of a huge construction project called the Jonglei Canal. This channel was designed to avoid the Sudd. The goal was to allow the headstreams of the White Nile to flow more freely. Instead of the water spreading across the Sudd and slowly moving through it, the canal would allow more water to flow downstream and reach Sudan and Egypt. That would support more agriculture and better city services in those countries. But it would also damage the wetland environment of the Sudd. Fisheries could collapse and go extinct. Construction was suspended in 1983. The project could not continue because civil war in Sudan made it too dangerous. **W**

Many of the lakes in East Africa are located near the Great Rift Valley. The largest lake on the continent of Africa is Lake Victoria. This lake lies between the western and the eastern branches of the Great Rift. The lake stretches into three countries: Uganda and Kenya in the north and Tanzania in the south. With an area of 26,828 square miles (69,484 sq. km), Lake Victoria is the second-largest freshwater lake in the world, after Lake Superior in the United States. For such a large body of water, Lake Victoria is relatively shallow. Its greatest known depth is about 270 feet (82 m). The lake is home to more than 200 species of fish. Of these, tilapia has the most economic value.

Another important lake in the region is Lake Tanganyika. This long, narrow body of water is located south of Lake Victoria, between Tanzania and the Democratic Republic of the Congo. The lake is only 10 to 45 miles (16 km to 72 km) wide, but very long. Measuring 410 miles (660 km) north to south, it is the world's longest freshwater lake. With a maximum depth of 4,710 feet (1,436 m), it is also the second deepest. Only Lake Baikal in Russia is deeper than Lake Tanganyika. **R**

Farther south is Lake Malawi. It is the third-largest lake in the East African Rift Valley. The lake lies mainly in Malawi and forms part of that country's border with Tanzania and Mozambique.

☑ READING PROGRESS CHECK

Identifying What caused the striking physical features of the Great Rift Valley in East Africa?

Fishers leave the eastern shore of Lake Victoria by boat early in the morning to fish for tilapia and Nile perch. With its many fish species, Lake Victoria supports Africa's largest inland fishery.

©John Warburton-Lee Photography/Alamy

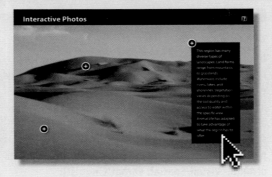

Chapter 10 **297**

W Writing Skills

Argument Have students discuss the construction of the Jonglei Canal. **Ask:**

- **What were the benefits in constructing the Jonglei Canal?** *(The headstreams of the White Nile would flow more freely and allow more water to flow downstream and reach Sudan and Egypt. This would support more agriculture and better city services in those countries.)*
- **What were the disadvantages in constructing the Jonglei Canal?** *(The canal would damage the wetland environment, eventually making the fisheries extinct.)*
- **Why was the canal never completed?** *(Civil war in Sudan, beginning in 1983, made it too dangerous to continue work.)*

Have students work in small groups to debate the question: **If peace arrives in the region, should the Jonglei Canal be completed?** Then have students individually write an argument to answer the question. Students should make a claim either for or against resuming construction of the canal and present at least three reasons to support their claim. Pair English language learners and approaching level students with proficient students to write a joint argument. **ELL Verbal/Linguistic**

R Reading Skills

Citing Text Evidence In pairs, have students finish reading about the bodies of water in the region. Then have students use text evidence from the entire section to answer the following questions. **Ask:**

- **Other than the Nile, why does East Africa have few important rivers?** *(There is not much rain in the region and the temperatures are very high in many areas.)*
- **Where are many of the lakes in East Africa located?** *(near the Great Rift Valley)*
- **Is tilapia a freshwater or a saltwater fish?** *(It is a freshwater fish because it is found in Lake Victoria, which is the second-largest freshwater lake in the world.)*
- **What distinguishes Lake Tanganyika from other lakes in the world?** *(It is the longest freshwater lake in the world and the second-deepest lake in the world.)*
- **Where is Lake Malawi located?** *(The lake lies mainly in Malawi and forms part of that country's border with Tanzania and Mozambique.)* **Verbal/Linguistic, Logical/Mathematical**

Lissa Harrison

IMAGE

Lake Victoria

Discussing Display the interactive image of Lake Victoria to students. Tell students to locate the lake on the Chapter Opener map and use cardinal directions to describe its relative location. *(Lake Victoria is located in southeastern Uganda and northern Tanzania. A small part of the lake is in southwestern Kenya.)* Have volunteers read the information presented. Discuss with students the geographical features of this body of water. Have students write three things they learned about Lake Victoria.
ELL Visual/Spatial, Naturalist

See page 291C for other online activities.

Interactive Photos

ANSWERS, p. 297

☑ READING PROGRESS CHECK the movement of tectonic plates millions of years ago

R Reading Skills

Explaining Display the climate map of Africa from the Unit Opener and have students focus on East Africa. **Ask: Why does the climate in East Africa vary from one local area to another?** *(because of different latitudes, altitudes, distances from the sea, and terrains in the region)* **Logical/Mathematical**

C1 Critical Thinking Skills

Drawing Conclusions Have volunteers read the section, "Temperatures," aloud. Discuss why the climate and geography are extremely varied. **Ask:**

• Why would Sudan, Djibouti, and Somalia have high temperatures for much of the year? *(The countries are located on the coast where temperatures tend to be warmer.)*

• Why would glaciers be found on high mountains? *(High mountains have elevations where temperatures are low enough to support ice and snow conditions.)*

• What is the climate of the highlands of Kenya and Uganda? *(The climate is always spring-like.)* **AL** **Logical/ Mathematical**

T Technology Skills

Using Visual Aids Read aloud the caption and the Critical Thinking question for the students to answer. Discuss their answers and the image in the photo. Then have students choose three or more countries in East Africa and research their average high and low temperatures. Encourage them to use a software program to create a graph of the information. Many software programs, including word-processing and spreadsheet programs, can be used to make charts and then turn those charts into circle, line, or bar graphs. Have students present their graphs to the class. If students have used different types of graphs, have them discuss how each graph displays the information differently and which type of graph works best for displaying this type of information. **BL** **Logical/ Mathematical**

C2 Critical Thinking Skills

Making Connections Ask students to identify the time of year when rainfall is plentiful in the region where they live. Have them discuss what influences the amount of rain that falls, such as latitude, mountains, and temperatures. Then have them make connections between the amount of rainfall in their area to the amount of rainfall in areas in East Africa. **Verbal/ Linguistic, Logical/Mathematical**

ANSWER, p. 298

CRITICAL THINKING Interior areas of East Africa are made of highlands and are cooler despite closeness to the Equator.

298

Climates of East Africa

GUIDING QUESTION *How does climate vary in East Africa?*

R Climate varies widely in the East African region. Temperature and rainfall can be quite different from one local area to another. The major factors explaining these variations include latitude, altitude, distance from the sea, and the type of terrain, such as mountains, highlands, desert, or coastal plains.

Temperatures

The diverse physical features of East African geography are matched by an extremely varied climate. In general, temperatures tend to be warmer toward the coast and cooler in the highlands. Sudan, Djibouti, and Somalia have high temperatures for much of the year. High mountains such as Kilimanjaro and the peaks of the Ruwenzori Range have had glaciers for thousands of years. Due to climate change, however, these glaciers are melting. Some experts predict that the glaciers of Kilimanjaro will completely disappear over the next 20 years.

C1 The climate is always spring-like in the highlands of Kenya and Uganda. As a whole, however, Kenya and Uganda display considerable variations in climate. These variations depend on factors such as latitude, elevation, wind patterns, and ocean currents.

Rainfall

In many parts of East Africa, rainfall is seasonal. This is especially true close to the Equator. Wet seasons alternate with dry ones. For **C2** example, on the tropical grasslands, or savannas, of Kenya and

T The Savoia glacier is located along the border of Uganda and the Democratic Republic of the Congo. Many scientists are concerned about the effects of climate change on the Ruwenzori glaciers. Around 1900, some 43 glaciers were distributed over 6 mountains in the range. Today, fewer than half of these glaciers still exist, on only 3 of the mountains. The rest have melted.

▶ **CRITICAL THINKING**
Analyzing Why do temperatures tend to be cool in inland East Africa despite the region's closeness to the Equator?

298 *Chapter 10*

Bruno Zanzottera/Parallelozero/Aurora Photos

---

networks   *Online Teaching Options*

IMAGE

Glaciers in East Africa

Integrating Visual Information Display the interactive image of the glaciers in East Africa and discuss the cause and effects of melt, age, and height. Have students research images or video of Mt. Kilimanjaro to discuss this landform and its relationship to the glaciers of East Africa. Have students write a short paragraph explaining why most people would not associate snow and ice with the continent of Africa. **Visual/Spatial, Verbal/Linguistic**

See page 291C for other online activities.

Interactive Photos

Lissa Harrison

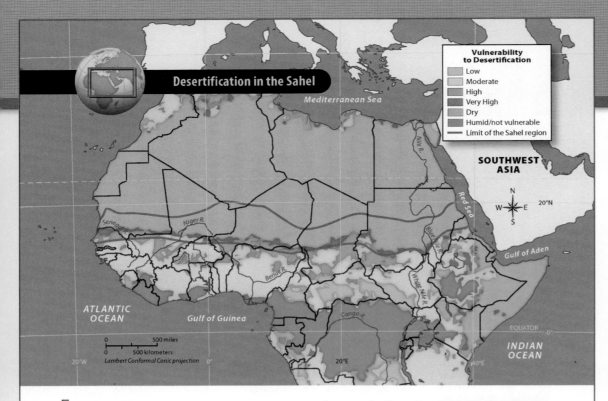

Desertification in the Sahel

Vulnerability to Desertification

- Low
- Moderate
- High
- Very High
- Dry
- Humid/not vulnerable
- Limit of the Sahel region

Mediterranean Sea

SOUTHWEST ASIA

Nile R.

Red Sea

Senegal R.

Niger R.

Gulf of Aden

Benue R.

Blue Nile R.

White Nile R.

ATLANTIC OCEAN

Gulf of Guinea

Congo R.

EQUATOR

INDIAN OCEAN

0   500 miles
0   500 kilometers
Lambert Conformal Conic projection

W

Tanzania, two rainy seasons occur in most years. These are the "long rains" of April and May and the "short rains" of October and November. The months in between these periods are dry, with little or no rainfall.

Rainfall in the region, however, can be unpredictable. Sparse rainfall can result in severe drought. In 2011, for example, Somalia suffered one of the worst droughts in its history. Political instability in that country made the effects of the drought especially severe. Observers estimated that 13 million people struggled to survive in the countries of Somalia, Ethiopia, Djibouti, and Kenya.

Another urgent issue in the region is **desertification**, or the process by which agricultural land is turned into desert. This process occurs when long periods of drought and unwise land use destroy vegetation. The land is left dry and barren. During the past half century, desertification has affected much of the Sahel. The Sahel is the "edge," or border area, between the Sahara and the countries farther to the south. Two such border nations in East Africa are Sudan and South Sudan.

C

☑ **READING PROGRESS CHECK**

Determining Central Ideas What generalization can you make about the variations in temperature in East Africa?

MAP SKILLS

1 **PLACES AND REGIONS** Based on the legend, most of the Sahel is at what level of desertification?

2 **THE GEOGRAPHER'S WORLD** What causes desertification?

MAP

Desertification of the Sahel

Speculating Display the map about the desertification of the Sahel to students. Remind students of the definition of desertification. Discuss with students the changes to the area in vegetation and climate. Ask students to identify problems that desertification causes and to speculate about what may happen in the future to this area. Compare the desertification of the Sahel to the Sahara. **Visual/Spatial, Naturalist**

See page 291C for other online activities.

W **Writing Skills**

Informative/Explanatory Tell students that the climate of Tanzania is ideal for growing food crops. In fact, the Tanzanian economy is based on agriculture. Irrigation is used to help crops grow during the dry seasons. Most farmers are peasants who cultivate the land by hand hoe. Some use ploughs pulled by oxen and about 10 percent of peasants use tractors. Even people who live in the cities have urban gardens for growing vegetables. Ask a small group of volunteers to research the types of crops grown in Tanzania. Have them create a graphic organizer of their researched information that includes short written descriptions, and share their findings with the class. **BL** **Verbal/Linguistic, Logical/Mathematical**

C **Critical Thinking Skills**

Identifying Problems Tell students that *Sahel* means "shore" in Arabic. **Ask: What makes desertification an urgent issue?** *(Students' answers will vary but should demonstrate an understanding of the process and why destroying vegetation in an area negatively impacts living things.)*

Ask volunteers to use the Internet to research current projects designed to solve the problems in the Sahel, such as the OASIS project (Organizing to Advance Solutions in the Sahel) based at the University of California at Berkeley. **Verbal/Linguistic**

Content Background Knowledge

The drought of 2011 in Somalia caused tens of thousands of people to flee the area on foot and seek food and shelter in refugee camps in Kenya and Ethiopia. Many of the refugees walked 50 miles or more across hazardous terrain. No rain fell in the area for two years and food prices rose. Livestock died and farms turned to dust. Civil war in Somalia made it too dangerous for humanitarian relief workers to bring in aid. A militant group banned most Western aid workers from entering part of southern Somalia and blocked villagers from leaving. However, in February 2012, the United Nations declared that the famine in Somalia had ended because of a successful harvest and emergency food deliveries. But the fighting continues in much of the country, and thousands of people are still starving and dying. Humanitarian efforts are on-going.

ANSWERS, p. 299

MAP SKILLS

1. Dry

2. long periods of drought and poor land use

☑ **READING PROGRESS CHECK** In general, areas nearer the coast and the Equator have warmer temperatures, and cooler temperatures prevail in the highlands of the interior.

C Critical Thinking Skills

Making Connections Have students think about regions in our country where the economy and people's way of life are linked to its natural resources. **Ask:**

- What might happen in a region when natural resources run out or are damaged in some way? Give an example. *(Possible answer: The economy is hurt and is weakened, such as when the BP oil disaster polluted the Gulf region.)*
- What might happen to natural resources in a region when there are political issues such as a dictatorship or a civil war? *(Students' answers may vary but should include relevant details such as war slowing the ability to exploit natural resources.)* **Verbal/Linguistic**

T Technology Skills

Using and Citing Information Salt has many uses in the home as well as in the production of industrial chemicals, plastics, fertilizers, and soaps. Divide students into small groups and have them use the Internet to research the uses of salt, both in the home and in industry. Have groups make a list of the various uses for salt. **Logical/Mathematical**

R1 Reading Skills

Paraphrasing Ask students to use their own words to explain the phrase, "East Africa's energy potential has yet to be realized." *(Possible answer: East Africa has energy resources that are not being used as much as they could be.)* **Verbal/Linguistic**

R2 Reading Skills

Determining Word Meanings Point out the Greek root *hydro* meaning "water" in the word *hydroelectric*. Remind students that knowing the meaning of Greek and Latin roots can help them understand the meanings of unfamiliar words. **ELL Verbal/Linguistic**

Content Background Knowledge

Lake Assal is the saltiest lake on Earth, even saltier than the Dead Sea and ten times saltier than the ocean. It is located at the head of the Great Rift Valley on the lowest point of land on the continent of Africa. It is in the Danakil Desert. The area's extremely hot temperatures and strong winds cause the water in the lake to evaporate quickly. This leaves a ring of salt minerals around the shoreline.

ANSWER, p. 300

Identifying gold, gemstones (sapphires and diamonds), tin, and lumber

---

Workers collect salt at Lake Assal in Djibouti. Salt covers everything, so very little vegetation is able to grow along the lake's shoreline. Located in the hot desert, the lake's area has summer temperatures as high as 126°F (52°C).

Identifying What other mineral resources are found in East Africa?

C

Resources of East Africa

GUIDING QUESTION *Which natural resources are important in East Africa?*

The natural resources of a region are closely linked to its economy and people's way of life. Settlement patterns in a geographical area have often been shaped by that area's natural resources. Important resources in East Africa are minerals, energy sources, landscapes, and wildlife. The ability of some countries to exploit these resources, however, has been hampered by political issues.

Mineral Resources

Mineral resources in East Africa include small gold deposits along the rifts in Kenya, Uganda, and Tanzania; gemstones like sapphires and diamonds in Tanzania; and tin in Rwanda. Ethiopia and Uganda produce lumber. Lake Assal in Djibouti, located about 500 feet (152 m) below sea level, is the world's largest salt reserve, with more than 1 billion tons of salt. This lake is located at the lowest point in Africa.

T

Energy Resources

Energy resources in East Africa include coal in Tanzania, as well as petroleum in Uganda, South Sudan, and northwestern Kenya. East Africa's energy potential has yet to be realized, though. For example, Sudan has the opportunity to develop **hydroelectric power**, or the production of electricity through the use of falling water. Hydroelectric power is already used in Kenya and Tanzania.

R1

R2

©Nigel Pavitt/JAI/Corbis

netw⊕rks   *Online Teaching Options*

GRAPHIC ORGANIZER

Alternative Energy Sources in Africa

Analyzing Display the interactive graphic organizer about alternative energy sources in Africa. Discuss and analyze with students the different alternative energy sources that are being developed in Africa. Have students write a short paragraph explaining which alternative energy source they believe will be most effective. **BL Interpersonal**

See page 291C for other online activities.

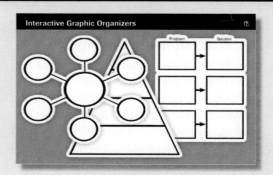

Interactive Graphic Organizers

R Likewise, Kenya and Djibouti are favorable locations for the development of **geothermal energy**. This type of energy comes from underground heat sources, such as hot springs and steam. In Kenya, an international group of companies is working with the government to develop geothermal energy sources. If they are successful, 30 percent of the country's energy needs could be met by geothermal energy by the year 2030. In Djibouti, geothermal energy production is expected to begin by the year 2014.

C In East Africa, management of energy resources and energy use often has been inconsistent and uneven. Major cities gobble up much of the energy that is produced. Energy is often unavailable in rural areas.

Land and Wildlife

Besides mineral and energy resources, East Africa's land and wildlife are important assets. The soils in the region are not especially rich for agriculture, and farming is challenging. The breathtaking scenery of the Great Rift Valley, however, is an important tourist resource.

East Africa is also home to the greatest assemblage of wildlife in the world. Many national parks and wildlife sanctuaries are found in the region. Perhaps the most well-known wildlife reserves are located in Kenya and Tanzania. An outstanding example is the Serengeti Plain; this vast area, larger than the state of Connecticut, consists of tropical savanna grasslands. Two internationally famous national parks are located in East Africa—Serengeti National Park in Tanzania and the Masai Mara National Reserve in Kenya. These parks harbor lions, leopards, cheetahs, giraffes, zebras, elephants, and dozens of species of antelope.

Every year, thousands of tourists pour in from all over the world to see the marvel of the Great Migration. In this mass movement, more than 1 million animals travel hundreds of miles in search of fresh grazing land. The spectacular wildlife of East Africa makes an important contribution to the economy of the region.

☑ READING PROGRESS CHECK

Identifying What two promising alternatives might help improve energy supplies in the East African region?

Think Again?

Animals involved in the Great Migration on the Serengeti Plain travel together.

Not True. Nature employs a more sophisticated system. The three major migrating species are zebras, wildebeests, and Thomson's gazelles. These species migrate in a succession. First come the zebras. They consume crude, coarse, high grasses. Then the wildebeests follow, grazing on the lower shoots exposed by their predecessors. Last are the smaller Thomson's gazelles, antelopes that eat tender, fine shoots close to the ground.

V

FOLDABLES
Study Organizer

Include this lesson's information in your Foldable®.

LESSON 1 REVIEW **CCSS**

Reviewing Vocabulary (Tier Three Words)
1. What causes the process of *desertification*? RH.6-8.4

Answering the Guiding Questions
2. ***Describing*** What are the differing characteristics that make Lake Victoria and Lake Tanganyika noteworthy bodies of water, both in East Africa and in the world as a whole? RH.6-8.5

3. ***Analyzing*** How might desertification affect the economy in a region? RH.6-8.1

4. ***Identifying*** How are energy supplies distributed in East Africa? RH.6-8.2

5. ***Informative/Explanatory Writing*** Write a letter to a friend or a relative explaining why you want to visit East Africa to see the region's wildlife. WHST.6-8.2, WHST.6-8.4

LESSON 1 REVIEW ANSWERS

Reviewing Vocabulary

1. The process of desertification is caused by drought and by human overuse of the land.

Answering the Guiding Questions

2. **Describing** Lake Victoria is the largest lake in Africa and the second-largest freshwater lake in the world. Lake Tanganyika is the longest freshwater lake in the world and the second-deepest lake in the world.

3. **Analyzing** When land becomes dry and barren, it is no longer suitable for agricultural purposes.

4. **Identifying** Cities consume the majority of available energy supplies, leaving little for rural areas.

5. **Informative/Explanatory Writing** Answers will vary, but students should reference animals that live on the grasslands of East African countries and why they would be interesting species to observe.

ENGAGE

R Reading Skills

Determining Word Meanings Point out the word *geothermal,* and have students identify the Greek roots and their meanings. *(Geo means "earth" and therm means "heat.")* **Ask:** Using the meanings of the Greek roots, how could you define *geothermal*? *(Possible answer: the heat of the earth)* **Verbal/Linguistic**

C Critical Thinking Skills

Making Inferences Have students summarize the last paragraph in the section, "Energy Resources." Then, **ask:** What can you infer about life in rural areas, knowing that energy is often unavailable there? *(Students' answers will vary but should include relevant details on activities that cannot be done without electricity.)* **BL** **Logical/Mathematical**

V Visual Skills

Diagramming Display photos of zebras, wildebeests, and Thomson's gazelles. After reading the Think Again feature, have students work with partners to diagram the sequence of food consumed by the migrating species. *(Diagrams should show the following sequence: high grasses, lower shoots, and fine shoots that are close to the ground.)* Display the diagrams and have students discuss how nature's system for the Great Migration ensures that the animals have what they need as they travel. **Kinesthetic, Visual/Spatial**

CLOSE & REFLECT

Formatting Questions To close this lesson, have students write questions based on the information presented in this lesson about landforms and waterways, climates, and natural resources. Collect the questions and answer them as a class. Post the questions that still need answers and add responses as students continue their study and increase their knowledge of the region. Have volunteers do research to add responses to any unanswered questions.

ANSWER, p. 301

☑ READING PROGRESS CHECK Two promising alternatives are hydroelectric power and geothermal energy.

ENGAGE

Bellringer Have students think about something they would really like to have but do not have enough money to buy. Have them brainstorm legal ways to get the item, including working for money or bartering. Point out that working is a form of trading—work for money. Help students connect their answers to the Essential Question.

TEACH & ASSESS

R Reading Skills

Citing Text Evidence Have students read the "It Matters Because" statement. Remind students that one by-product of trade is the exchange of ideas, beliefs, and customs. **Ask: What were some of the results of trade in the ancient kingdoms in East Africa?** *(Trade brought together people from different civilizations and resulted in the spread of Christianity and Islam into the region.)* **Verbal/Linguistic**

V Visual Skills

Interpreting Have students plot the ancient region of Nubia on their Chapter Opener maps. Read aloud the information about the location of this region, emphasizing the cardinal directions. **ELL AL Visual/Spatial, Kinesthetic**

Content Background Knowledge

In the beginning, the nobles of Nubia thought and acted like the Egyptians, dressing like them, building similar homes, and worshiping the same gods. After moving their capital further south on the Nile, the nobles acted more like the people in South Sahara Africa, even changing the style of jewelry they wore. Nubia was the only kingdom in the area that had iron, and it was a major producer of gold. Nubia traded iron for Egyptian cotton. Over time, Nubia could not meet the demand for iron so traders went to other places. When trade diminished, the country weakened.

ANSWER, p. 302

Taking Notes Nubia/Kush: Kush arose around 1050 B.C., Kush conquered Egypt mid 700s B.C., Moved capital after Assyrian invasion in 600 B.C., Iron-making, Conquered by Aksum around A.D. 350; **Aksum:** Greatest trading market in NE Africa, Gold and ivory, Possibly slaves, 4th century—Christianity, Written language (Ge'ez), Declined after Muslims conquered Persia and Adulis; **Coastal City-States:** Arabs settled on coast beginning around 10th century, Settlements grew into towns/cities, formed trading states

---

networks

There's More Online!

☑ **IMAGE** British at Omdurman

☑ **MAP** African Trade Routes and Goods

☑ **SLIDE SHOW** Ancient Africa

☑ **VIDEO**

Reading **HELP**DESK **CCSS**

Academic Vocabulary RH.6-8.4
(Tier Two Words)
• **impact**

Content Vocabulary RH.6-8.4
(Tier Three Words)
• **tribute**
• **imperialism**
• **genocide**
• **refugee**

TAKING NOTES: *Key Ideas and Details* RH.6-8.7

Organizing As you study the lesson, use a chart like this one to list important facts about the places.

Place	Facts
Nubia/Kush	
Aksum	
Coastal City-States	

Lesson 2
History of East Africa

ESSENTIAL QUESTION • *Why do people trade?*

IT MATTERS BECAUSE
East Africa has been a center of trade since ancient times. Throughout much of its history, East Africa has attracted people from many other continents.

R Kingdoms and Trading States

GUIDING QUESTION *How has the history of trade impacted the region?*

Trade was important in the ancient kingdoms in East Africa. Contact between East Africa and other areas brought together people from different civilizations. Trade also resulted in the spread of Christianity and Islam into the region.

Ancient Nubia
The ancient region of Nubia was located in northeastern Africa, below ancient Egypt. The region stretched southward along the Nile River valley almost to what is now the Sudanese city of Khartoum. The region was bounded by the Libyan Desert in the west and by the Red Sea in the east. The Nile River was the pathway by which Nubia and the powerful empire of Egypt interacted.

V In about 1050 B.C., a powerful civilization arose in Nubia. This was known as Kush. The Egyptians traded extensively with the Kushites, purchasing copper, gold, ivory, ebony, slaves, and cattle. The Kushites, in turn, adopted many Egyptian customs and practices. For example, they built pyramids to mark the tombs of their rulers and nobles.

During the final centuries of their civilization, the Kushites were isolated from Egypt. As a result, they turned increasingly to other African people south of the Sahara for trade and cultural contact. Around A.D. 350, Kush was

---

netw⊙rks *Online Teaching Options*

VIDEO

Postcards from Kenya

Interpreting Use this video about some of the unique aspects of the country of Kenya to introduce the history of East Africa. Ask student volunteers to share what they learned from the video about aspects of Kenya. Ask students if anything about the landscape, history, or daily life of Kenya surprised them. **Visual/Spatial, Intrapersonal**

See page 291D for other online activities.

BBC Motion Gallery Education

conquered by Aksum, a powerful state in what is now northern Ethiopia.

Aksum

The date of Aksum's establishment is uncertain but it might have been around 1000 B.C. The people of Aksum derived their wealth and power primarily from trade. Aksum was strategically located, and it controlled the port city of Adulis on the Red Sea. At its height of power, Aksum was the most important trading center in the region. Its trading connections extended all the way to Alexandria on the Mediterranean Sea. Aksum traders specialized in sea routes that connected the Red Sea to India.

Through the port of Adulis flowed gold and ivory, as well as raw materials. It is possible that Aksum sold captives for the slave trade. Aksum traded glue, candy, and gum arabic, a substance from acacia trees that today is used in the food industry. Christianity spread from its origin in Jerusalem along the trade routes. The Aksum kings adopted Christianity as their religion.

Trade Cities

Beginning around the A.D. 900s, after the decline of Aksum, Arabs settled on the East African coast of the Indian Ocean. The religion of Islam grew steadily more important in the region. At the same time, the Arabic and Bantu languages mingled to create a new language. This language is known as Swahili. The name comes from an Arabic word meaning "coast dwellers." Swahili is widely spoken today in Tanzania and Kenya, as well as in some other countries.

Gradually, the coastal settlements formed independent trading states. From coastal Somalia southward, along the shores of Kenya and Tanzania, these city-states prospered. They included Mogadishu, Lamu, Malindi, and Mombasa.

Many of the pyramids of ancient Kush still stand in present-day Sudan. Near the pyramids, the Kushites built a capital city called Meroë. Archaeologists have uncovered some of the remains of Meroë, including a royal palace, temples, and mud-brick homes.

▶ **CRITICAL THINKING**
Determining Central Ideas What do the pyramids of Meroë reveal about Kushite culture?

Chapter 10 **303**

C₁ Critical Thinking Skills

Drawing Conclusions Have students work in pairs to read the section, "Aksum." Then, **ask: What advantage did Aksum have that made it a great trading market?** *(Possible answer: Aksum's location on the Red Sea and its control of the port city of Adulis helped it have trading connections on the Mediterranean Sea, the Red Sea, and all the way to India.)* **Verbal/Linguistic**

C₂ Critical Thinking Skills

Making Connections Tell students that if they have seen the movie or stage musical of *The Lion King* they already know some words or phrases in the Swahili language. For example, in Swahili, *simba* means "lion," *rafiki* means "friend," and *hakuna matata* means "no problems or no worries." Have volunteers use the Internet to find other words or phrases in the Swahili language, along with their pronunciations, to teach to the class. Or teach the class the Swahili words for *hello*—jambo (JAHM-boh) and *goodbye*—kwaheri (kwah-HAIR-ree). Challenge students to use the Swahili language in their conversations. Tell them that the Swahili language is part of many college curriculums. **BL Verbal/Linguistic, Auditory/Musical**

V Visual Skills

Integrating Visual Information Have students use the historical trade route map on the following page to locate the independent trading states of Mogadishu, Lamu, Malindi, and Mombasa. **Ask: What helped to make these independent trading states successful?** *(their location on the Indian Ocean)* **Visual/Spatial, Logical/Mathematical**

Content Background Knowledge

Aksum (also spelled *Axum*) was both the name of the kingdom and its capital. Its capital still exists in northern Ethiopia. Today, the city of Aksum is a tourist destination. In its central square are 126 tall, granite obelisks, some standing and some lying broken on the ground. A fallen obelisk that measures 110 feet (34 m) is thought to be the tallest obelisk ever made.

Ancient Africa

Describing Show the slide show about ancient Africa to students. Discuss with students the various groups that lived in this region during the time and the evidence that exists today that proves their existence. Have students write a short paragraph describing the evidence they find most unusual or fascinating. **AL Verbal/ Linguistic, Intrapersonal**

See page 291D for other online activities.

Slide Show

ANSWER, p. 303

CRITICAL THINKING The Kushites had close cultural links to the Egyptians, adopting practices such as the building of pyramids to mark the tombs of rulers and nobles.

(l) ©Ocean/Corbis, ©Kryssia Campos/Getty Images, (tr) ©Erica Simone Leeds, (br) ©JG Photography/Alamy

Nigel Pavitt/AWL Images/Getty Images

History of East Africa

V Visual Skills

Integrating Visual Information Have students locate the trading city of Kilwa on the historical trade route map. **Ask: Why do you think this city was successful in trading?** *(Possible answer: It was located near the coast of East Africa, which gave trading ships easy access to it, and the city traded items that were in high demand such as copper, iron, ivory, and gold.)* **Visual/Spatial, Logical/Mathematical**

C Critical Thinking Skills

Making Inferences Ask students to describe what a "walled city" is and if anyone has ever visited or seen a walled city. **Ask: Why do you think Kilwa was a walled city?** *(Students' answers will vary but should demonstrate an understanding of walls around a city being used as a means of protection and defense along with the realization that most traders to Kilwa were probably strangers, not all of whom had honest intentions.)*

Discuss the use of walls, moats, or other protective features that cities, villages, or manors used for protection. **Logical/Mathematical, Verbal/Linguistic**

T Technology Skills

Using Visual Aids Born in Tangier, Morocco, Ibn Battuta was the son of a rich, Muslim family. He traveled for almost 30 of his 64 years. He started traveling at 20 years of age in A.D. 1325 with a trip east from Morocco to Mecca, the Muslim holy city that all Muslims, if able, are supposed to visit at least once in their lifetimes. In the course of his travels, he covered land all the way east to China, south down the coast of East Africa to Kilwa, north to Turkey, and west to Mali. Along the way he became sick many times, was attacked by bandits, was shipwrecked, traveled with Mongol Khan, was a teacher and a judge in India, and rented a camel to tour Yemen.

Have volunteers research all the places that Ibn Battuta visited in his lifetime and plot them on a map of the world. Display the map for the class to see. Ask volunteers to present any interesting anecdotes that they discovered during their research. **Visual/Spatial, Verbal/Linguistic**

ANSWERS, p. 304

MAP SKILLS

1. The city-states were located on the Indian Ocean coast and linked inland Africa with distant markets in India and China. They were valuable go-betweens in the trade of the Indian Ocean region.

2. Inland areas of Africa supplied enslaved people, beads, incense, and ivory for export out of East African ports.

☑ **READING PROGRESS CHECK** The coastal cities and the kingdom of Aksum accumulated great wealth from trade.

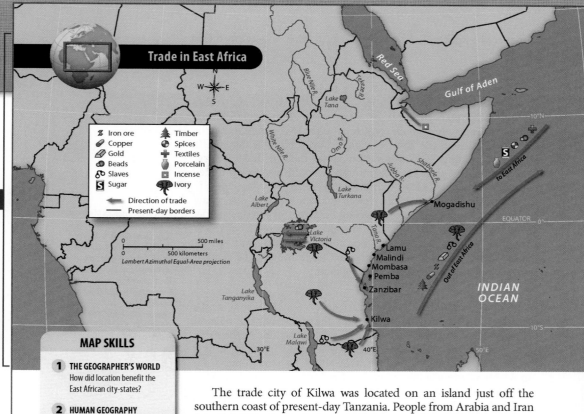

Trade in East Africa

Iron ore
Copper
Gold
Beads
Slaves
Sugar
Timber
Spices
Textiles
Porcelain
Incense
Ivory

Direction of trade
Present-day borders

0   500 miles
0   500 kilometers
Lambert Azimuthal Equal-Area projection

MAP SKILLS

1. **THE GEOGRAPHER'S WORLD** How did location benefit the East African city-states?

2. **HUMAN GEOGRAPHY** What part did inland Africa play in the region's trade?

The trade city of Kilwa was located on an island just off the southern coast of present-day Tanzania. People from Arabia and Iran founded Kilwa in the late A.D. 900s. The merchants of Kilwa dealt in copper, iron, ivory, and gold. They exchanged these goods for products from many lands, including Chinese porcelain and Indian cotton.

C **T** Kilwa was a walled city. Its ruler lived in an impressive palace. For two centuries, the city was probably the wealthiest trading center in East Africa. The fourteenth-century traveler Ibn Battuta praised Kilwa as a beautiful city. At the time of Ibn Battuta's visit, Kilwa was ruled by Abu al-Mawahib. The sultan was so generous that people called him "the father of gifts."

☑ **READING PROGRESS CHECK**

Identifying Compare the economies of the coastal city-states in East Africa to those of the kingdom of Aksum.

The Colonial Era

GUIDING QUESTION *What was the effect of colonization on East Africa?*

Until the late 1800s, most Europeans knew little or nothing about Africa. Two of the continent's most famous explorers were Henry Morton Stanley and David Livingstone. In 1878 Stanley published a

304 Chapter 10

---

netw⊙rks *Online Teaching Options*

MAP

African Trade Routes and Goods

Analyzing Information Display the map of African trade routes and goods. Discuss with students the various routes and the goods that were traded. Have students tell which routes they think were most prosperous, which goods they think were the most valuable, and why people would want those goods. *(Possible answer: The routes where iron ore was traded because iron was used to make tools and weapons.)*
BL **Visual/Spatial, Logical/Mathematical**

See page 291D for other online activities.

popular travel book about his adventures in Africa. The book's title was *Through the Dark Continent*. The goal of Stanley's journey was to locate Livingstone, a medical missionary. Livingstone had traveled to Africa in the hope of locating the source of the Nile River.

European Traders

Just before 1500, the European age of discovery began to **impact** East Africa. Among the European countries, Portugal took the lead in overseas exploration. Along with other Europeans, the Portuguese established a sea route to India. From Europe, they sailed south along the west coast of Africa and then along the east coast of Africa. Then, they sailed along the coast of Arabia and on to India. This was a much easier and less expensive way to trade with India than any of the overland trade routes. In this way, the Portuguese were able to bring back many valuable spices from India.

As trade increased, the Portuguese began to demand **tribute**, or a regular tax payment, from the East African trading cities. The Portuguese had religious as well as economic motives; they believed that Christianity should replace Islam as the region's religion. Portuguese influence in the region did not last long, however. The Portuguese could not withstand attacks by African groups in the region. Other European countries became interested in colonizing Africa.

European Colonial Rule

In the late 1800s, European leaders set out a plan to dominate and control the continent of Africa. The action by which one nation is able to control another smaller or weaker nation is known as **imperialism**.

Academic Vocabulary

impact an effect or an influence

The Battle of Omdurman was fought in Sudan in 1898. In this battle, British and Egyptian forces—equipped with modern guns—defeated a much larger Mahdist army that used older weapons.

▶ **CRITICAL THINKING**
Integrating Visual Information
How does Hale's painting present the battle scene? What view of imperialism does it seem to support?

IMAGE

British at Omdurman

Discussing Display the interactive image about the British at Omdurman. Have volunteers read the information presented. Discuss the significance of the battle. Have students write a paragraph about why they think the use of modern guns helped to defeat the larger Mahdist army. **BL** **Visual/Spatial**

See page 291D for other online activities.

Interactive Photos

R1 **Reading Skills**

Citing Text Evidence Have students finish reading the first paragraph in the section, "The Colonial Era." Then, **ask:**

- **Why did Stanley explore Africa?** *(to find Livingstone, a medical missionary, who was missing)*
- **Why was Livingstone in Africa?** *(He was hoping to locate the source of the Nile River.)* **Logical/Mathematical**

T **Technology Skills**

Researching on the Internet In October 1869, Dr. David Livingstone had been missing for four years somewhere in the interior of Africa. Livingstone was a popular British explorer and medical missionary, famous for charting the unknown continent of Africa. An American newspaper editor wanted to boost the circulation of his newspaper and thought that an article about finding Livingstone would make a good cover story to increase sales. Thus, the editor sent Henry Morton Stanley on an expedition to Africa to find Livingstone.

Divide students into small groups and have them research information about Stanley's journey to locate Livingstone and to find out if Stanley really said, "Dr. Livingstone, I presume," when finally encountering the medical missionary. Tell students to list at least five things they learned about the two men and report their findings to the class. **Verbal/Linguistic**

V **Visual Skills**

Interpreting Display a map of the world. Ask volunteers to trace the sea route from Europe to India as they read. **Ask:**

- **What geographic location did European traders have to pass on the route they sailed from the west coast of Africa to the east coast of Africa?** *(the Cape of Good Hope)*
- **Why would a water route to India be better than an overland trade route?** *(A water route was easier and less expensive.)* **Visual/Spatial, Verbal/Linguistic**

R2 **Reading Skills**

Citing Text Evidence Read the first paragraph in the section, "European Colonial Rule," to students. Then, **ask: What would European countries gain by colonizing Africa?** *(economic profit, access to raw materials, the opening of new markets, increased national pride, the protection of sea routes)* **AL** **Verbal/Linguistic, Interpersonal**

ANSWER, p. 305

CRITICAL THINKING Hale's painting places the British soldiers in a heroic, superior position ready to overwhelm the Mahdists. It implies that Europeans had a right to rule over other people and to put down any resistance to the spread of their civilization.

Argument Divide students into small groups to discuss what motivates countries to go to war. Remind them that Portugal had both religious and economic motives for attacking some of the city-states on the east coast of Africa. Then have students individually write a five-paragraph persuasive essay to answer the question: **Which do you think is a stronger motivator for going to war—religion or the economy?** **Logical/ Mathematical, Verbal/Linguistic**

R **Reading Skills**

Using Context Clues Remind students that sometimes the definitions of words are included in nearby text. Using these context clues can help them figure out the meanings of unknown words. **Ask: What does the word** *Mahdi* **mean?** *(redeemer of Islam)*

Further explain to students that if they encounter an unfamiliar word in a definition, such as *redeemer,* they may need to use a dictionary to find its meaning. Tell students that in this case, they would need to find the definition of the base word— *redeem.* Ask a volunteer to use a dictionary to find its meaning. *(to save)* **Ask: Why would Ahmad want to "save Islam"?** *(Possible answer: Since the British were Christians, many people in the region may have converted from Islam to Christianity under British rule. Ahmad wanted the people to return to Islam.)*
AL **Verbal/Linguistic, Logical/Mathematical**

C **Critical Thinking Skills**

Making Inferences Have students work in pairs to review the section, "Independent Ethiopia." Then, have students summarize the information in the paragraphs. **Ask: Why would the emperor of Ethiopia not want his country to be a protectorate of Italy?** *(Possible answer: The emperor wanted Ethiopia to be independent. If Ethiopia was a protectorate of Italy, Italy would control it and it would lose its independence.)* **Logical/Mathematical**

A painting in traditional Ethiopian style shows King Menelik II receiving ammunition for his army. Menelik worked to bring modern ways to Ethiopia. He especially wanted to prepare his army to successfully resist European invaders.

Africa was carved up into colonies. The reasons for colonization included economic profit, access to raw materials, and the opening of new markets. These reasons also included national pride, the protection of sea routes, the maintenance of the balance of power, and a quest to convert Africans to Christianity.

Occasional rebellions challenged European colonial rule. An especially bloody rebellion occurred against British and Egyptian domination in Sudan. Muhammad Ahmad, a religious and military leader, declared that he was the Mahdi, or redeemer of Islam. Mahdist forces succeeded in capturing Khartoum, the Sudanese capital. They established a new state there. In 1898 the British succeeded in reasserting their control of the region.

Independent Ethiopia

The revolt against foreign influence in Sudan eventually resulted in failure. In Ethiopia, however, the desire for independence prevailed. Italy had colonized the neighboring territory of Eritrea along the Red Sea coast. In 1889 the Italians signed a treaty with the Ethiopian emperor, Menelik II. Over the next few years, Italy claimed that, according to one provision of this treaty, it had the right to establish a "protectorate" in Ethiopia.

Menelik firmly denied these claims. He rejected the treaty in 1893. The Italian governor of Eritrea finally launched a major military attack in response in 1896. At the Battle of Adwa on March 1 of that year, Menelik defeated the Italian army. This conflict was

Sabena Jane Blackbird/Alamy

netw⊚rks *Online Teaching Options*

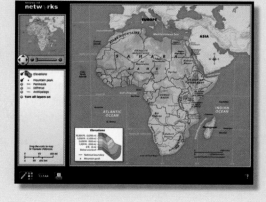

MAP

East African Colonization

Defending Display the map about the colonization of East Africa. Discuss with students which European nations colonized which part of East Africa and why they did so. Then have students write a short paragraph explaining which European nation they think profited the most from colonizing East Africa. Students should include details that defend the European nation they choose. **Interpersonal, Logical/Mathematical**

See page 291D for other online activities.

one of the most important battles in African history. After the Battle of Adwa, the European powers had no choice but to recognize Ethiopia as an independent state. Physical geography played an important role in Ethiopia's ability to remain independent. Rugged mountains with difficult terrain provided a barrier that was difficult for attacking forces to overcome.

☑ READING PROGRESS CHECK

Explaining What was the significance of Menelik II's victory at the Battle of Adwa in 1896?

Independence

GUIDING QUESTION *How did the countries of East Africa gain their independence?*

After the end of World War II in 1945, a movement ensued to end colonialism in Africa, Asia, and Latin America. In East Africa, particularly, Europeans were seen as disrupting traditional life. In addition, European countries were weakened by the fighting in World War II. Because of these pressures, Europeans granted East African colonies their independence in the 1960s. However, many of the former colonies faced difficulties in establishing their own countries.

New Nations Form

The early 1960s was a turning point for East Africa. During the period from 1960 to 1963 alone, six East African countries obtained independence: Somalia, Kenya, Uganda, Tanzania, Rwanda, and Burundi.

The achievement of independence in Kenya and Tanzania was especially important. Kenya had been a British colony for about 75 years. British plantation owners dominated the economy. They disrupted the traditional East African agricultural system. Local village agriculture was replaced by the production of cash crops, such as coffee and tea, on a large scale. Native people, such as the Kikuyu, were driven off the land. The British also controlled the government.

A nationalist named Jomo Kenyatta led the political protest movement in Kenya and negotiated the terms of independence for his country. In late 1963, Kenya became independent. Jomo Kenyatta served as the country's first prime minister and later as its president.

Tanzania also sought independence. Before independence, the country was called Tanganyika.

As independent Kenya's first leader, Jomo Kenyatta brought stability and economic growth to the country. When appearing in public, Kenyatta often carried a fly whisk, a symbol of authority in some traditional African societies.

▶ CRITICAL THINKING

Describing How did Kenya win its independence from British rule?

©Bettmann/Corbis

Chapter 10 **307**

MAP

East African Independence

Summarizing Display the colonization map with the dates of East African independence added. Have volunteers read the information on the map. Discuss with students the historical changes in the region that resulted from the European colonization of the area and then the movement to end colonization and gain independence. Have students summarize three things they learned about East African independence. **AL** Visual/Spatial

See page 291D for other online activities.

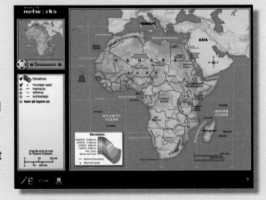

R1 Reading Skills

Citing Text Evidence Review the content of the section, "Independent Ethiopia," with students. Display the physical geography map from the Chapter Opener and review the geography of Ethiopia. **Ask:** What helped Ethiopia to remain an independent country? *(The rugged mountains and difficult terrain surrounding Ethiopia provided a barrier that was difficult for attacking forces to overcome.)* **Verbal/Linguistic, Logical/Mathematical**

R2 Reading Skills

Explaining Have students read the, "Independence," section. Remind that at one time many European countries controlled parts of South America and Africa from afar. **Ask:** What European events led to East African colonies gaining independence in the 1960s? *(European colonizers were pressured by other world countries who considered Europeans to be disrupting traditional life in the colonies; European economies were weakened after World War II.)* **Verbal/Linguistic**

C Critical Thinking Skills

Evaluating Ask student volunteers to name other countries that were British colonies at one time. Make sure students understand how large the British Empire was at one point. **Ask:** Why was British colonization not a good thing for the people of Kenya? *(The traditional East African agricultural system was disrupted by British plantation owners. They replaced the local village agriculture with the production of cash crops. Under British rule, people were driven off the land, and the British controlled the government.)* **Logical/Mathematical, Interpersonal**

Content Background Knowledge

A political protest movement in Kenya began in the 1920s. In the 1950s, the British government arrested Jomo Kenyatta on the charge of association with a terrorist organization called the Mau Mau movement. Kenyatta strongly denied the charge, but he was convicted and sentenced to imprisonment. After his release from prison, Kenyatta took the lead in negotiating the terms of independence for his country.

ANSWERS, p. 307

☑ **READING PROGRESS CHECK** Menilek II defeated a major Italian military force, thus ensuring independence for Ethiopia and gaining international recognition.

CRITICAL THINKING Political protests led to the formation of the Mau Mau Movement, and conflict broke out. Jomo Kenyatta took the lead in negotiating independence for Kenya, which came in late 1963.

C Critical Thinking Skills

Make Connections As students read about the genocide of the Tutsi, remind them about the genocide of the Jewish people by the Nazis or the genocide of the Armenians by the Turkish Empire. Point out that while genocide has occurred in many places and times, there have also been people who opposed the action. Yad Vashem, the Holocaust memorial in Israel, has as part of its mission to honor those who risked everything to help the Jewish people during World War II. **Ask: Why it is important to memorialize those who risked everything to save others?** *(It shows that there will always be some people who do what is right. It celebrates the best of humanity in the worst of situations.)* **Interpersonal**

T Technology Skills

Evaluating a Web Site Explain to students that Idi Amin was known as the "Butcher of Uganda." He was a brutal dictator who sent out "killer squads" to hunt down and murder his opponents. Divide students into small groups and have them find three web sites with information about Amin. Have them identify facts that appear on all three sites, facts that only appear on one or two of the sites, and contradicting facts. Tell students to evaluate each web site for trustworthiness and to report their findings to the class. Circulate to clarify content and to watch for age-appropriate content. **Verbal/Linguistic, Logical/Mathematical**

Content Background Knowledge

When Tanganyika merged with Zanzibar, the new name Tanzania was created by combining Tan(ganyika) + Zan(zibar) + -ia (suffix for country). The country's official name is the United Republic of Tanzania. On April 26 of each year, the people of Tanzania celebrate the unification of Zanzibar and Tanganyika with Union Day festivities. The largest city, Dar es Salaam, served as the country's government center, but in 1974 the city of Dodoma was selected as the official capital. That move was completed in 1996, but Dar es Salaam is still considered to be the commercial capital. In 2012 the population of Tanzania was estimated to be nearly 47 million, with about 75% of the residents living in rural areas. Kiswahili (Swahili), the native language of the Bantu people, is the official language of Tanzania.

ANSWER, p. 308

CRITICAL THINKING Political boundaries set during colonial times did not work well for some African territories after independence. In some cases, the boundaries often separated members of particular ethnic groups from each other. In other cases, they grouped together people of different, often rival, ethnic groups in one country. As a result, national unity became difficult to achieve.

Villagers in South Sudan try to put out fires after warplanes from neighboring Sudan raided the area in early 2012. A year earlier, South Sudan had gained independence from Sudan following years of civil war. However, tensions remained high and conflict continued.
▶ **CRITICAL THINKING**
Describing Why have some African countries after independence faced civil wars and conflicts with neighboring countries?

When Germany was defeated in World War I, Tanganyika came under British control. Independence was the ultimate goal for Tanganyika—a goal it reached in late 1961. Three years later, the country merged with Zanzibar, and its name was changed to Tanzania.

Highland Countries
The Highland areas had a difficult road to independence. Many ethnic groups in the former colonies were often in conflict with one another. Ethnic tensions have long simmered in Rwanda and Burundi. These countries are home to two rival ethnic groups. The Hutu are in the majority there, and the Tutsi are a minority. In the 1990s, the Hutu-dominated government of Rwanda launched an attack on the Tutsi that amounted to **genocide**—the slaughter of an entire people on ethnic grounds. Hundreds of thousands of people were killed.

Bloodshed also stained the history of Uganda after independence. From 1971 to 1979, the country was ruled by the military dictator Idi Amin. Cruelty, violence, corruption, and ethnic persecution marked Amin's regime. Human rights groups estimate that hundreds of thousands of people lost their lives under his rule. Amin was finally forced to flee into exile. He died in 2003.

The Horn of Africa
The history of Somalia since independence in 1960 offers another example of the problems East African countries have faced. Since the 1970s, Somalia has been scarred by civil war. Border disputes with Ethiopia have also increased instability. Rival clan factions have

Michael Onyiego/AP Images

308 *Chapter 10*

---

netw⊙rks   *Online Teaching Options*

IMAGE

Refugee Camps: South Sudan

Expressing Display the photo of the refugee camps in South Sudan. Discuss with students the genocide and forced relocation in South Sudan. Have students share their thoughts and feeling about genocide with a partner. Be sure to discuss with students the lasting impact that violence and forced relocation can have on the culture of a civilization. **Visual/Spatial, Interpersonal**

See page 291D for other online activities.

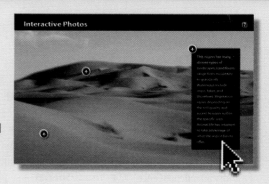

Interactive Photos

Lissa Harrison

engaged in bitter feuds. Drought has brought famine to much of the country. In late 1992, the United States led a multinational intervention force in an effort to restore peace to the country. The civil war in Somalia, however, remained unresolved.

The instability, misery, and violence in Somalia also have affected neighboring countries. Thousands of **refugees**, for example, have made their way into Kenya. A refugee is a person who flees to another country for safety.

Elsewhere in the Horn of Africa, more than 30 years of fighting have marked the recent history of Eritrea. This country achieved independence in 1993 after a long struggle with Ethiopia. Access to the sea was an important territorial issue in this conflict. In the years since independence, Eritrea has undertaken military conflicts with Yemen and resumed attacks on Ethiopia. The country is unable to provide enough food for its people. Furthermore, economic progress has been limited because many Eritreans serve in the army rather than in the workforce.

A New Nation

Africa's newest country emerged as a result of civil war. Sudan won independence from Egyptian and British control in 1956. Leaders in southern Sudan were angered because the newly independent Sudanese government had failed to carry out its promise to create a federal system. Southern leaders also feared that the new central government would try to establish an Islamic and Arabic state.

Religion was also an issue that generated conflict. Most people in Sudan are Muslim, but in the southernmost 10 provinces, most people follow traditional African religious practices or the Christian religion. Economic issues are also a problem. The southern provinces hold a large share of the area's petroleum deposits. As a result of the civil war, the country of South Sudan became independent from Sudan in 2011.

 R

FOLDABLES
Study Organizer

Include this lesson's information in your Foldable®.

☑ **READING PROGRESS CHECK**

Determining Central Ideas How has civil war played an important part in the recent history of East Africa?

LESSON 2 REVIEW **CCSS**

Reviewing Vocabulary (Tier Three Words)
1. What were some of the factors that led European nations to practice *imperialism* in Africa? **RH.6-8.3, RH.6-8.4**

Answering the Guiding Questions
2. *Identifying* Discuss two important events that occurred in the history of the Ethiopian kingdom of Aksum. **RH.6-8.2**
3. *Identifying* Which two countries took the lead in the European colonization of East Africa in the late 1800s? **RH.6-8.2**

4. *Describing* What have been some of the major problems that East African countries have faced in building their nations after achieving independence? **RH.6-8.5**

5. *Narrative Writing* You are a modern-day Ibn Battuta, traveling through East Africa. Write a series of journal or diary notes telling about the people you meet and the sights you see there. **WHST.6-8.4, WHST.6-8.10**

LESSON 2 REVIEW ANSWERS

Reviewing Vocabulary

1. Factors contributing to imperialism included national pride, economic profit, a quest for raw materials and new markets, concern for maintaining the balance of power, and religious zeal.

Answering the Guiding Questions

2. **Identifying** the adoption of Christianity and the invention of a written and spoken language, known as Ge'ez

3. **Identifying** Great Britain and Germany

4. **Describing** Many countries in the region have suffered civil war, famine and drought, lack of economic development, and political instability.

5. **Narrative Writing** Students' responses will vary but should include information from the text on the economic, political, religious, and cultural issues facing East African countries as well as the physical sights enjoyed.

C Critical Thinking Skills

Making Connections Have students recall what they know about the American Civil War. They may say that it was a war between the North and the South or a war over slavery. Ask them to think about how the American people would have reacted if a multinational force intervened in that war in an effort to restore peace to our country. **Ask: Why do you think the civil war in Somalia has remained unresolved even with the intervention by a multinational force?** *(Students' answers will vary but should demonstrate an understanding of the conditions in Somalia and the reasons for the civil war.)* **Logical/Mathematical, Verbal/Linguistic**

R Reading Skills

Identifying Ask a volunteer to read aloud the last sentence under, "A New Nation." Have students discuss the issues that brought about the civil war. **Ask: What issues caused South Sudan to become independent from Sudan?** *(issues over the system of government created by Sudan, religion, and economics)* **Verbal/Linguistic**

Content Background Knowledge

Today, the new nation of South Sudan finds itself in an economic bind. It stands to benefit from oil wealth if it can get its oil to the coast to export via a pipeline that runs through Sudan. Currently, however, it is one of Africa's least developed countries. The price it has paid for independence is steep. Observers have estimated that at least 1.5 million people lost their lives in the long conflict with Sudan, while more than 4 million were displaced and became refugees.

CLOSE & REFLECT

Evaluating To close this lesson, have students think about all the conflict that has occurred in this region for the past hundreds of years and how this conflict has led to changes, both good and bad. Ask them to think about the lasting effects of conflict in a region.

ANSWER, p. 309

☑ **READING PROGRESS CHECK** Civil war has scarred the recent history of countries such as Sudan and South Sudan, Somalia, Eritrea, and Ethiopia.

ENGAGE

Bellringer Lead students in a discussion about a neighborhood they know that has many different ethnic groups or a small town that has families from different ethnic backgrounds. Pose the following questions for discussion:

- Do the different groups of people in this town or neighborhood share elements of each other's culture?
- Are the people from the different ethnic groups friendly with each other?

Have students discuss the differences among such groups. Then help students see the connection between their answers and the Essential Question and "It Matters Because" statement.

TEACH & ASSESS

R Reading Skills

Identifying Remind students that throughout history, most cities have been founded near bodies of water or other kinds of commonly traveled routes. **Ask:**

- Near what body of water are Mogadishu, Mombasa, and Dar es Salaam located? *(the Indian Ocean)*
- Which cities grew out of important trading centers? *(Nairobi and Addis Ababa)* **AL** **Verbal/Linguistic**

C Critical Thinking Skills

Comparing Have a volunteer read the second paragraph of, "Where People Live." Then, **ask:**

- Which of the eleven East African countries has the largest population? *(Ethiopia)*
- Which has the smallest? *(Djibouti)*
- What is the numerical difference between their populations? *(about 79 million)* **Logical/Mathematical**

ANSWER, p. 310

Taking Notes **The People of East Africa:** different ethnic groups in one country; local African languages—many are spoken in one country; Christian or Muslim, also traditional African faiths; **Daily Life and Culture:** most people live in rural settings, but cities are growing; industry in cities and agriculture in rural areas; electricity and other modern conveniences in cities, but not in rural areas; oral traditions, textiles, anthropology and ecology; **Challenges:** poor soil, drought, unpredictable climate, limited resources, wildlife management, poaching, deforestation, HIV/AIDS

---

netw⊛rks

There's More Online!

- ☑ **IMAGES** Animal Poaching
- ☑ **MAP** Museums: Preserving Kenya's Heritage and Culture
- ☑ **VIDEO**

Reading HELPDESK **CCSS**

Academic Vocabulary RH.6-8.4
(Tier Two Words)
- **diverse**

Content Vocabulary RH.6-8.4
(Tier Three Words)
- **population density**
- **clan**
- **subsistence agriculture**
- **oral tradition**
- **poaching**

TAKING NOTES: Key Ideas and Details RH.6-8.2, RH.6-8.7

Summarizing As you read about East African populations, daily life, culture, and challenges today, use a web diagram like the one here to list facts and details about each important idea.

Cultures of East Africa

The People of East Africa — Challenges — Daily Life and Culture

310 Chapter 10

Lesson 3
Life in East Africa

ESSENTIAL QUESTION · *Why does conflict develop?*

IT MATTERS BECAUSE

East Africa is a region of great diversity in ethnicity, religion, and language—not only across the region, but also within individual countries.

The People of East Africa

GUIDING QUESTION *What ethnic groups contribute to the diversity of the population?*

East African countries typically are home to many ethnic groups. Another striking feature in this region is the split between urban and rural populations. Languages and religions make up a mosaic of many different elements.

Where People Live

The population of East Africa is split between large cities and rural areas. Many large cities are on or near the coast of the Indian Ocean (for example, Mogadishu in Somalia, Mombasa in Kenya, and Dar es Salaam in Tanzania). Some large cities, however, developed from important trading centers. Such cities include Nairobi, the capital of Kenya, and Addis Ababa, the capital of Ethiopia.

Of the 11 countries in the region, Ethiopia has the largest population (about 80 million), and Djibouti has the smallest (about 1 million). People are distributed unevenly in East Africa. **Population density** measures how many people live in a given geographical area. A thickly settled area has a high population density. In thinly settled areas, the density is low. In Tanzania, population density varies greatly from one area to another. Overall, Rwanda has the highest population density in the region. Somalia has the lowest.

(l to r) Tom Cockrem/age fotostock; ©Cameron Davidson/Corbis; Harry Hook/Stone/Getty Images; Charles O. Cecil/Alamy; Zhao Yingquan/Newscom

---

netw⊛rks *Online Teaching Options*

VIDEO

America's Gift

Listing Use this video to discuss the role that American foreign aid plays in treating the victims of the HIV/AIDS epidemic and controlling the spread of the disease in places like Uganda and other nations in East Africa. Ask students how this aid is perceived among the people who receive it and how it affects America's reputation abroad. Then ask if they think that Americans facing financial crisis at home and cutbacks to domestic programs will continue to fund and support programs like this or foreign aid in general. **Interpersonal**

See page 291E for other online activities.

BBC Motion Gallery Education

In Ethiopia, the majority of people live in the central highlands. The warmer and drier areas of lower elevations are thinly inhabited. In Sudan, most people live along the Nile River. Arid parts of the country are thinly populated. In Somalia, most people are nomadic or seminomadic.

Ethnic Groups

The populations of Kenya, Tanzania, and Ethiopia are **diverse** in terms of ethnicity. Sometimes competition among different ethnic groups has led to political and economic conflict. Ethnic identity is closely linked to language and also to geography.

In Kenya, for example, the Kikuyu, Kamba, Meru, and Nyika people inhabit the fertile highlands of the Central Rift. The Luhya live in the Lake Victoria basin. The rural Luo people are located in the lower parts of the western plateau. The Masai people tend their herds of cattle in the south, along the Kenya-Tanzania border. Like the Masai, the Samburu and the Turkana are pastoralists. They live in the arid northwestern region of Kenya.

Another type of ethnic identity is the **clan**. A clan is a large group of people sharing a common ancestor in the far past. A group of related clans is called a clan family. Smaller groups of related people within a clan are called subclans. In Somalia, the basic ethnic unit is the clan.

Academic Vocabulary

diverse having or exhibiting variety

Nairobi, the capital of Kenya, was founded in 1899 as a railway stop between plantations in Uganda and ports on the Kenyan coast. Today, Nairobi is one of East Africa's largest cities, with a population of about 3 million.

▶ **CRITICAL THINKING**
Describing Why are most East African cities located either along the Indian Ocean coast or in inland, highland areas?

Tom Cockrem/age fotostock

VIDEO

Nairobi

Comparing/Contrasting Use the video about Nairobi to generate a discussion about this large city in East Africa and its population. After watching the video, ask students to point out the advantages and disadvantages of this city compared to a large city with which they are familiar. Chart these advantages and disadvantages on the chalkboard. Use the population layer of the Chapter Opener map to reinforce the information contained in the video. **Visual/Spatial, Verbal/Linguistic**

See page 607E for other online activities.

©Digital Vision/Getty Images

C1 Critical Thinking Skills

Making Inferences Review with students the advantages of living near a body of water. Display the population density map of Africa from the Unit Opener to help students make these connections. **Ask: Why do you think that most Sudanese people live along the Nile River?** (*Answers should include these ideas: the river provides such advantages as fishing, irrigation for growing crops, and a method of travel.*) **Verbal Linguistic**

C2 Critical Thinking Skills

Recognizing Relationships Point out to students that people become more competitive when sharing the same space and goods and, in such a conflict, choose people most like themselves as allies. **Ask: Why might a common or close geographical location cause economic and political conflict among different ethnic groups?** (*Possible answers: the groups might compete for use of the land and resources; they might compete for political control and power; they might feel that other groups' belief systems and customs threaten their own.*) **BL Logical/Mathematical**

T Technology Skills

Researching on the Internet Divide the class into eight groups and have each group choose a different ethnic group from Kenya to research. Tell each group to use the Internet to learn more about their group's location, language, method of earning a living, and any unique traditions. Have students use presentation software to present information about their group to the class. **Interpersonal, Verbal/Linguistic**

R Reading Skills

Paraphrasing Point out to students that the word *clan* is derived from the Scottish word *clan* that means *family*. Explain to students that many national groups recognize clan relationships. **Ask: Why might the phrase *extended family* be another term for *clan*?** (*because the members of a clan all have a single ancestor*) **Verbal/Linguistic**

ANSWER, p. 311

CRITICAL THINKING Coastal areas provide outlets for trade by sea; highland areas have mild climates and produce agricultural products that require nearby trading centers.

C1 Critical Thinking Skills

Determining Cause and Effect Have students brainstorm the characteristics of a close-knit family and how those characteristics also apply to one's ethnic group. **Ask: What characteristics might reinforce a person's allegiance to his or her ethnic group?** *(Answers will vary but should include a shared homeland, a strong sense of family connections, loyalty to group, similar customs and traditions, a common history, common goals, and a common language.)* **Verbal/Linguistic, Interpersonal**

C2 Critical Thinking Skills

Identifying Problems Ask students what they think it might be like to live in a small country where people speak about 100 different languages. Have students brainstorm a list of different places and aspects of life that would be negatively affected by not being able to speak the same language. *(Examples include school, religious services, government decrees and laws, shopping, and going to the doctor.)* **Ask: What might be some of the overarching effects of diversity in languages?** *(Answers will vary. It may cause misunderstanding among different groups, it might lead to inefficiency in business and poor communication in business relationships, and the lack of one traditional mother tongue might lessen cohesiveness among a country's inhabitants.)* **BL Verbal/Linguistic, Interpersonal**

R Reading Skills

Determining Word Meaning Tell students that although 100 different languages are spoken in Ethiopia, some of these languages have common characteristics. The languages can be placed into four different categories according to these characteristics. The name of each category refers to a shared location or extended ethnic group. Point out the first syllable of the word *Nilotic*. **Ask: To what area of Africa do you think this word refers?** *(the area around the Nile River)* **Verbal/Linguistic**

In the A.D. 1100s, an Ethiopian king had the Church of St. George carved from solid red volcanic rock. Today, St. George and 10 similar churches in the town of Lalibela attract Ethiopian Christian worshippers as well as tourists from around the world.

Identifying What are the major religions in East Africa today?

In countries that have many diverse ethnic groups, building a sense of national identity is difficult. People often feel a stronger attachment and allegiance to their ethnic group than to their country. A Somali, for example, might feel a greater attachment to his or her clan than to the country of Somalia. **C1**

Languages

East Africa is a region where many African languages are spoken. For example, Ethiopians speak about 100 distinct languages. Kenya also has a wide variety of spoken languages. Swahili and English are used by large numbers of people to communicate. Those two languages are the official languages of the Kenyan legislature and of the courts. **R**

Swahili is almost universal in Tanzania. The geographical location and colonial history of East African countries have often made an impact on the languages spoken there. For example, in Somalia the official language is Somali. However, Arabic is widely spoken in the northern area of the country, and Swahili is widespread in the south. In Somalia's colleges and universities, it is not uncommon to hear people speaking English or Italian. In Djibouti, Arabic and French are important languages.

Religion

Most people of East Africa follow either the Christian or Muslim faith. However, a number of traditional African religions also thrive in the region. Traders and missionaries from the Mediterranean region brought Christianity to Ethiopia in the A.D. 300s. The Ethiopian Orthodox Church is one of the world's oldest Christian churches. Today, about 60 percent of Ethiopians are Christians.

©Cameron Davidson/Corbis

netw⊙rks *Online Teaching Options*

CHART

Official Languages in East Africa

Making Connections Use the chart of the "Official Languages in East Africa" to begin a discussion about the communication problems that result when inhabitants of a region speak many different languages. Ask students to share an experience they have had while trying to communicate with someone whose language was different from their own. Continue the discussion by asking what strategies students used to overcome the language barrier and effectively convey their messages.
Verbal/Linguistic, Interpersonal

See page 291E for other online activities.

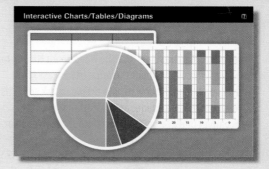

Interactive Charts/Tables/Diagrams

ANSWER, p. 312

Identifying Christianity, Islam, and traditional African religions

R In Kenya, the constitution guarantees freedom of religion. Christianity first arrived in Kenya with the Portuguese in the 1400s. But the religion was not practiced for several hundred years, until colonial missionaries arrived in Kenya in the late 1800s. Muslims are an important religious minority in Kenya. Today, Christianity is practiced by more than two-thirds of Kenya's population.

Tanzania is evenly split among Christianity, Islam, and traditional African religions. About one-third of the population follows each one of these three religious traditions.

☑ **READING PROGRESS CHECK**

Analyzing In a region with such diverse languages, how do you think East Africans can communicate with people outside their own language group?

Life and Culture

GUIDING QUESTION *What is daily life like for people in East Africa?*

In East Africa, traditional customs, as well as the impact of modernization, can be seen in daily life and culture. Culture in East Africa often displays a blend of African and European ways of life.

Daily Life

The rhythms of daily life are varied in East Africa. One factor is where people live: in cities or in rural areas. Most East Africans live in the countryside. But cities are growing rapidly, due to the economic opportunities they provide.

Nairobi is Kenya's capital and most important industrial city. The city is home to more than 3 million people. This makes Nairobi the most populous city in East Africa. It is a city of contrasts. High-rise business and apartment buildings sit near slums built of scrap material.

Daily life in rural areas is quite different from life in the cities. A rural family's housing, for example, might consist of a thatched-roof dwelling with very little in the way of modern or sanitary conveniences. Often, no electricity is available. Some rural people practice **subsistence agriculture**, growing crops to feed themselves and their families. Other rural people grow cash crops to sell.

A Masai mother and son (top) stand outside their home built of mud, sticks, and grass. The Masai people herd cattle on the inland plains of Kenya and Tanzania. A mosque and Islamic-style buildings (bottom) crowd the harbor of Mombasa, a city on Kenya's Indian Ocean coast.

▶ **CRITICAL THINKING**
Describing How do ways of life differ in East Africa depending on location and culture?

Chapter 10 **313**

(t) Harry Hook/Stone/Getty Images; (b) Nigel Pavitt/AWL Images/Getty Images

Lissa Harrison

IMAGES

360° Views: Masai and Kenya

Contrasting Use the 360° views of the Masai and Kenya to engage students in a discussion of the differences between urban and rural life in East Africa. Lead students in a discussion of the advantages and disadvantages of both ways of life. Have students write a paragraph contrasting either city or rural life in East Africa with city or rural life in the United States. **ELL**
Visual/Spatial, Verbal/Linguistic

See page 291E for other online activities.

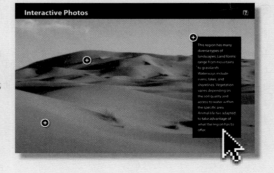

Interactive Photos

R Reading Skills

Citing Text Evidence Have students use text evidence to answer the following questions about religion in Kenya and Tanzania. **Ask:**

- **What group established Christianity in Kenya? When?** *(colonial missionaries; in the late 1800s)*
- **What role does Islam play in Kenya?** *(It is an important religious minority there.)*
- **What is the breakdown of religions in Tanzania?** *(One third of Tanzanians follow Christianity; one third follow Islam; one third follow traditional African beliefs.)* **AL** **Verbal/Linguistic, Logical/Mathematical**

W Writing Skills

Narrative Ask students to write a letter as though they were a Kenyan who moved from the country to Nairobi, where they have taken a job at the airport. The letter should be written to a fictional friend living in the country. Students should describe the city and ask them to contrast their lives in the city with the ones they knew in the country. Have them include information about their new job at the airport and their daily life. Then ask them to describe things that they miss about home, such as the nearness of friends and relatives, the traditional ceremonies, and the closeness to nature. Call on volunteers to read their letters. **Naturalist**

C Critical Thinking Skills

Differentiating Tell students that cash crops are crops that are grown for a profit, but do not feed the people of the country. Examples of cash crops are coffee and sugar. Subsistence farming is when a farmer only grows enough to feed his family. **Ask:**

- **What is the difference between subsistence farming and growing cash crops?** *(Subsistence farmers grow just enough crops to meet their families' needs; cash crop farmers grow crops to sell.)*
- **How do cash crop farmers feed their families?** *(They use the money they earn from selling their cash crops to buy food.)* **Logical/Mathematical**

ANSWERS, p. 313

☑ **READING PROGRESS CHECK** They use working or official languages, such as English and Swahili.

CRITICAL THINKING In rural interior areas, people such as the Masai follow traditional African lifestyles and often herd cattle; in urban and coastal areas, people follow more modern lifestyles and have jobs based on commerce, shipping, and industry; in coastal areas, some residents are influenced by the Islamic cultural heritage brought by Arab traders centuries ago.

Life in East Africa

G1 Critical Thinking Skills

Speculating Have students read the description of the lives of the Masai. Discuss that the government wants the Masai to end their nomadic lifestyle. Have students speculate what the Masai would gain or have to give up by changing their nomadic culture. **Ask:** How will life change for the Masai if they are no longer nomadic? *(What they might have to give up: independent lifestyle; cultural traditions; close family relationships. What they might gain: access to food sources and clean drinking water; access to good medical care; modern education)* **Verbal/Linguistic**

C2 Critical Thinking Skills

Analyzing Remind students that a phrase's meaning can often be determined by analyzing its components. **Ask:**

- **What does** *oral* **mean?** *(by mouth)*
- **What does** *tradition* **mean?** *(a custom or piece of folklore handed down through the generations)*
- **What is the most logical way to put these meanings together?** *(An oral tradition is a custom or piece of folklore handed down through the generations by word of mouth.)*
- **Besides family and local histories, what are some examples of oral tradition?** *(Possible answers: fairy tales, fables, poems, and the lyrics of folk songs)*
- **Why do you think oral tradition was used to support independence?** *(Possible response: Oral traditions are used to teach important ideas and values. Using oral tradition to pass on hymns of praise for independence showed that it was important to the people.)* **AL** **Verbal/Linguistic, Interpersonal**

T Technology Skills

Using Digital Tools Have students form pairs and ask them to research *tarab* music from Tanzania or *benga* music from Kenya on the Internet. Have students download different songs from copyright-free sites. Tell students to create a presentation in which they play the songs for the class. Students can choose pictures or scenes that can be displayed while the songs are playing. Challenge students to find out about the different instruments that are featured in tarab orchestras as well. **BL** **Auditory/Musical**

ANSWER, p. 314

CRITICAL THINKING East African culture is a blend of many cultures—African, European, Islamic, and Indian—because of trade, migrations, and different contacts with people in other parts of the world, especially in the Indian Ocean area.

A tarab orchestra performs in Zanzibar, an Indian Ocean island that is part of Tanzania. Tarab is a form of music that began in Zanzibar and spread to other areas. The musician (left) plays a *qanun*, a stringed instrument believed to have been first used in Islamic Persia during the A.D. 900s.

▶ **CRITICAL THINKING** **C2**
Determining Central Ideas
What does a form of music like tarab reveal about East African culture?

In Tanzania, groups such as the Sukuma farm the land south of Lake Victoria. The Chaggas grow coffee in the plains around Kilimanjaro.

The Masai are a nomadic people who live in Tanzania and Kenya. They wander from place to place throughout the year as they tend herds of cattle. Their cattle provide the Masai with most of their diet. **C1**

The Masai have developed a unique way of living. Groups of four to eight families build a kraal, or a circular thornbush enclosure. The kraal shelters their herds of livestock. The families live in mud-dung houses inside the kraal.

The governments of Kenya and Tanzania have set up programs to persuade the Masai to abandon their nomadic lifestyle. The governments want to conserve land and protect wildlife, but the Masai have resisted. They want to preserve their way of life.

Arts and Culture

East African culture is deeply influenced by **oral tradition**. This means that stories, fables, poems, proverbs, and family histories are passed by word of mouth from one generation to the next. Folktales and fables offer good examples of oral tradition. In Kenya, the oral tradition functioned in a political way. Hymns of praise were passed on to support independence.

The small country of Djibouti is well known for its colorful dyed clothing. This includes a traditional piece of cloth that men wear around their waist like a skirt. It is common clothing for herders.

A leading novelist in East Africa is Kenya's Ngugi wa Thiong'o. His novel *Weep Not, Child* (1964) is considered the first important English-language novel written by an East African. This book is a story about the effects of conflict on families in Kenya. He also has authored works in the Bantu language of Kenya's Kikuyu people.

In Tanzania, an appealing and popular form of music is *tarab*. This type of music combines African, Arab, and Indian elements and instruments. Tarab has developed an international following. In Kenya, a popular musical style is *benga*. This pop style emerged in the 1960s in the area near Lake Victoria, which is inhabited by the Luo ethnic group. **T**

314 *Chapter 10*

Charles O. Cecil/Alamy

---

net**w**orks   *Online Teaching Options*

GAME

Fill-in-the-Blank Game

Identifying Use the fill-in-the-blank game to review the content of this lesson. Once students have completed this activity, ask them to choose one of the statements and use it as the topic sentence for a short paragraph they will write and later share with their classmates. **Verbal/Linguistic**

See page 291E for other online activities.

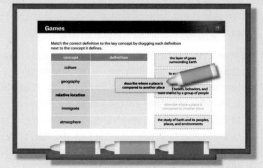

East Africa is also linked to important findings in the fields of anthropology and ecology. Evidence indicates that East Africa is where human beings originated. The earliest known human bones come from Kenya and Ethiopia. The fossil beds of Olduvai Gorge in northern Tanzania have furnished us with an important record of 2 million years of human evolution.

[C]

In the domain of ecology, the national park systems of East Africa have no equal in the world. Protected areas like the Masai Mara National Reserve and Samburu National Reserve in Kenya, the Serengeti National Park in Tanzania, Queen Elizabeth National Park in Uganda, and Volcanoes National Park in Rwanda are preserving a precious inheritance.

[T]

✅ **READING PROGRESS CHECK**

Describing Compare and contrast urban and rural daily life in East Africa.

Challenges

GUIDING QUESTION *How do economic, environmental, and health issues affect the region today?*

Today, the people of East Africa face many complex, challenging issues. Some of the most important challenges involve economic development, the environment, and health.

Economic Development

[R]

Agriculture is the main economic activity in East Africa. Farmers in the region, however, face difficult challenges. First, the soils in East Africa are not especially fertile. Second, climate conditions are often unpredictable. Rainfall can be intermittent. Drought can severely damage crops.

Government policies in some countries of East Africa also favor the production of cash crops such as coffee for export. Such policies harm subsistence farmers who attempt to produce enough food to meet local needs. Much of this pattern of growing cash crops results from colonialism. Even after the countries of East Africa gained independence, the practice of growing cash crops for sale continued.

Self-sufficiency is a challenge in East Africa. The region is one of the poorest in the world. In addition, the population of many countries there is growing at a faster rate than the world's average. Industrialization has come slowly for East Africa.

Students view an exhibit of African wildlife at the Kenya National Museum in Nairobi. The museum's purpose is to collect, preserve, study, and present Kenya's cultural and natural heritage.

▶ **CRITICAL THINKING**
Describing How do East Africans protect living wildlife?

Zhao Yingquan/Newscom

Chapter 10 **315**

GRAPHIC ORGANIZER

Issues in East Africa Today

Reviewing Display the interactive graphic organizer. Tell students that they can use it to help them summarize the various issues faced by East Africans. With a partner, have students create an outline of the information on the organizer. Encourage them to discuss and review the information with their partners. **AL Interpersonal**

See page 291E for other online activities.

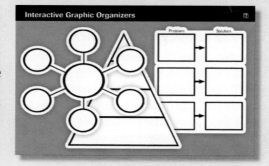

Interactive Graphic Organizers

C Critical Thinking Skills

Identifying Evidence Tell students that anthropology is the study of human beings and their ancestors through time and space. Tell them that fossils are the remains or impressions of prehistoric organisms preserved in petrified form or as molds in rock. Help them understand how anthropologists use fossils to learn about early humans. **Ask:** What evidence does the text give that human beings originated in East Africa? *(The earliest known human bones were found in Kenya and Ethiopia; northern Tanzania contains fossil beds that have furnished us with an important record of human evolution over the past 2 million years.)*

Ask volunteers to use the Internet to find other pieces of evidence showing that human beings originated in East Africa. **Verbal/Linguistic**

T Technology Skills

Researching on the Internet Tell students that because tourists are drawn to East Africa's beautiful national parks, they are a benefit to that region's economy. The parks also preserve valuable areas of Africa's environment. Divide students into five groups and have each group choose one of the parks mentioned in the text. Ask students to find information about ways in which their chosen park has helped Africa's ecology and to write a three-paragraph report on their findings. Students should include in their reports the name of the country in which their park is located, the size of the park, animals unique to their park, and any other remarkable details for which their park is known. **Naturalist**

R Reading Skills

Listing Help students understand why agriculture is East Africa's main economic activity in spite of serious issues faced by that region's farmers. **Ask:** What are the three most serious challenges to East African agriculture? *(1. East African soils are not especially fertile; 2. droughts are frequent; 3. government policies favor farmers that raise cash crops rather than subsistence farmers.)* **Naturalist**

ANSWERS, p. 315

✅ **READING PROGRESS CHECK** Life in a city might involve working in an office or a factory. Life in rural areas would probably involve farming except among the Masai. Housing in cities might have modern conveniences, while housing in rural areas might be restricted to thatched-roof huts with unreliable or no electric power.

CRITICAL THINKING They have set up national parks in various areas to protect living wildlife.

Life in East Africa

C1 Critical Thinking Skills

Making Connections Review with students that attitudes left over from colonialism still influence government agricultural policies. For example, government policies favor cash crop production over subsistence farming. **Ask:**

- How does colonialism affect government policies concerning East African industries? *(The government still makes policies favoring industries that once made money for the colonial powers.)*
- Why did the colonial powers set up these policies? *(They saw their East African colonies as sources of wealth for them. Therefore, the colonial powers forced the people in their colonies to grow crops and produce goods that could be traded on the world market.)* **Verbal/Linguistic, Logical/ Mathematical**

R Reading Skills

Identifying Point out to students that subsistence crops raised on subsistence farms are more varied than cash crops. **Ask:**

- What are some important East African food crops? *(corn, millet, barley, potatoes, and cassava)*
- What are some important East African cash crops? *(coffee and cotton)* **AL Verbal/Linguistic**

C2 Critical Thinking Skills

Reasoning Call on a volunteer to read the last two sentences in the section, "Economic Development." Then, **ask: Why might low literacy rates hurt a nation's economy?** *(Answers will vary. Students' ideas may include: if a large number of a country's citizens are unable to read or write, they will be unable to hold high-level jobs; therefore, they will not be able to pay enough taxes to support and develop the country. Then, too, they will not be in a position to contribute ideas for new businesses and national projects.)* **BL Verbal/Linguistic**

Scores of elephant tusks, seized from illegal poachers, are burned in Kenya. The purpose of the burning was symbolic: to point out the need to keep ivory from reaching international markets and to stop the illegal killing of elephants for their tusks.

Necessary resources such as trained workers, new facilities, and equipment have been lacking. In Ethiopia, for example, manufacturing amounts to only about 10 percent of the economy. Most of Ethiopia's exports are agricultural products. Its most important export is coffee.

C1 The emphasis on primary industries that harvest or extract raw material, such as farming, mining, and logging, is also derived from colonialism. Colonial powers developed their colonies to provide products for the powers. Even after independence, the former colonies continue to produce the same products.

R In Tanzania, the economy is mostly agricultural. Many farmers practice subsistence agriculture. Corn (maize), rice, millet, bananas, barley, wheat, potatoes, and cassava are among the important crops. Coffee and cotton are the most important cash crops. Gold is Tanzania's most valuable export.

C2 In parts of East Africa, the economy has suffered because of civil war and political instability. The economy also is linked to the availability of transportation, communication, and education. One key indicator of progress in education is a country's literacy rate. Literacy rates across the region range from a low of 38 percent in Somalia to a high of 87 percent in Kenya.

Environmental Issues

East Africa faces challenging issues related to the environment. The region's lack of electric power has quickened the pace of deforestation. People are cutting down trees to meet their energy needs at an

©Andrew Holbrooke/Corbis

net❂rks *Online Teaching Options*

CHART

Life Expectancy Across Africa

Discussing Display the chart about the life expectancy of people across Africa. Discuss with students the ways in which the low life expectancy may be affecting the economy. Encourage students to research and review the population pyramids for the countries of East Africa and compare their life expectancy using a different visualization of information. Lead a class discussion about ways that foreign aid, along with improvments in economies and governments, are improving life expectancy. **BL**

See page 291E for other online activities.

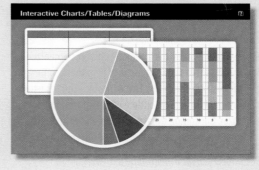

Interactive Charts/Tables/Diagrams

alarming rate. They use the wood to cook food and heat their homes. Along with deforestation, desertification poses serious problems in countries like Sudan.

By setting up national parks and wildlife sanctuaries, the countries of East Africa are hoping that this will boost their economies and preserve their heritage. Ecotourism is tourism for the sake of enjoying natural beauty and observing wildlife. Revenue from ecotourism is important to the East African economy.

Wild animals such as elephants and lions also face the threat of **poaching**. Poaching is the trapping or killing of protected wild animals for the sake of profit in the illegal wildlife trade. African elephants are especially vulnerable to poaching; they are killed for their ivory tusks.

Health Issues

In East Africa, poor nutrition continues to be a difficult problem to overcome. One of the main causes of hunger and malnutrition in the region has been war. Since 1990, conflict in several East African countries has halted economic development and caused widespread starvation. Large numbers of refugees have poured across international borders.

HIV/AIDS is a serious and often fatal disease affecting people in the region. AIDS is an abbreviation that stands for "acquired immune deficiency syndrome." AIDS is caused by a virus that spreads from person to person. This disease continues to be a major health issue in Kenya, Tanzania, and Ethiopia. The resources required for medical education and treatment have put a further strain on East African economies.

Deaths from AIDS have cut the average life expectancy in East Africa. Drought and famine also have an impact on life expectancy. In East Africa, life expectancy at birth is 58 years in Rwanda and 62 years in Sudan. In Kenya, it is 63 years. By contrast, life expectancy in the United States is now about 78.5 years.

✓ **READING PROGRESS CHECK**

Citing Text Evidence What is one major cause of deforestation in the region of East Africa?

FOLDABLES
Study Organizer
Include this lesson's information in your Foldable®.

LESSON 3 REVIEW

Reviewing Vocabulary (Tier Three Words)
1. How might *poaching* affect the economies of some East African countries? RH.6-8.4

Answering the Guiding Questions
2. ***Determining Central Ideas*** What general statements can you make about the ethnic groups and where people live in East Africa? RH.6-8.2

3. ***Identifying*** Identify two ways in which trade has played a central role in the history of East Africa. RH.6-8.2

4. ***Describing*** What are two of the most important challenges confronting East Africa today? RH.6-8.1

5. ***Informative/Explanatory Writing*** Write a paragraph or two in which you explain some of the environmental issues that confront East Africa today. WHST.6-8.2, WHST.6-8.4

Chapter 10 **317**

LESSON 3 REVIEW ANSWERS

Reviewing Vocabulary

1. Poaching, or the illegal trapping or killing of wildlife, endangers one of the region's most valuable natural resources: its wildlife. Wildlife contributes to the East African economy by attracting thousands of tourists each year.

Answering the Guiding Questions

2. **Determining Central Ideas** Larger cities tend to be located on or near the coast. Some large cities developed from early trading centers. Population density varies. There are many different ethnic groups in East Africa. There are many different spoken languages.

3. **Identifying** Trade made ancient kingdoms such as Aksum in Ethiopia extremely wealthy. Trade attracted Arab settlers from the Arab Peninsula, as well as the Portuguese in the late 1400s. Finally, trade was an important component in European colonization in the late 1800s.

4. **Describing** Important challenges include economic development and conquering malnutrition.

5. **Informative/Explanatory Writing** Answers will vary, but students should include information from the text about environmental challenges in East Africa, such as deforestation, poaching, and wildlife management.

W Writing Skills

Informative/Explanatory Lead students to discuss a serious consequence of undeveloped electrical power in East Africa—deforestation. Help them understand that East Africans are cutting down their trees because burning wood is one of the few ways they have to heat their homes and cook their food. Ask students to research the problem on the Internet. Ask them to explore the following aspects of the problem: the rate that deforestation is taking place in East Africa, how it is contributing to desertification, and the effects that deforestation is predicted to have on East Africa's economy. Then ask students to search the Internet for solutions proposed by ecologists to slow down deforestation. Have them write a report with four paragraphs, the first to introduce the topic, the second and third to describe the problem and propose solutions, and the last to summarize their ideas. **BL** Verbal/Linguistic

C Critical Thinking Skills

Drawing Conclusions Have students review the image on the previous page and read the last two paragraphs in the section, "Environmental Issues." **Ask:** Why did the countries of East Africa set up national parks and wildlife sanctuaries? *(to promote ecotourism and preserve their heritage of wildlife)* **AL** Verbal/Linguistic, Naturalist

R Reading Skills

Identifying Read the section, "Health Issues," to students. Then, **ask:**

- **What are two of the main causes for East Africa's health issues?** *(war, which causes malnutrition; and a disease called HIV/AIDS that is passed from person to person)*
- **How have East Africa's health issues affected the life expectancy of its people?** *(In some East African countries, life expectancy is about 20 years less than in the United States.)*

CLOSE & REFLECT

To close this lesson, have students discuss ways that conflicts may occur when groups with different cultures and loyalties compete for resources. Also help students review that in the recent past, colonizing powers have exploited East African resources and have failed to educate its labor force or to develop its industrial facilities.

ANSWER, p. 317

✓ **READING PROGRESS CHECK** Because electric power is not widely available in rural areas, people living in the countryside cut down trees to meet their energy needs.

ENGAGE

🔔 **Bellringer** Before students read the Global Connections feature on the country of Sudan, explain that the feature provides information on a country that has experienced warfare and extreme political upheaval and social unrest. Help students understand that civil war affects both the country and the region. Talk about the global impact of civil war as other countries search for a solution to regional conflict. Help students understand what a refugee is and what might happen to people when they are displaced or driven out of their own countries.

TEACH & ASSESS

V Visual Skills

Creating Visuals Create a graphic organizer on the board by writing *Sudan* as the title, with the two columns labeled: *Northern Sudan* and *Southern Sudan*. Have students read the introductory paragraph. Then, **ask: What facts would you add under the "Northern Sudan" column of the graphic organizer?** *(Arab Muslim, live in cities)*

Add the information to the graphic organizer. **Ask: What facts would you add under the "Southern Sudan" column of the graphic organizer?** *(African, rural famers, African traditional religions, Christianity)*

Add the information that students suggest to the graphic organizer. As you continue this lesson, add additional facts showing the difference between Northern and Southern Sudan. **AL** Visual/Spatial

R Reading Skills

Specifying After students read the first paragraph in column one, add a box linked to the title of the graphic organizer on the board and write the facts about Sudan as students list them. **Ask: What are four facts about the country of Sudan?** *(sixteenth-largest nation, third largest country in Africa, population 33.4 million people, forty-fourth in land area)*

Then have students read the section "Northern Control." **Ask: What created conflict between northern Sudan and the people of southern Sudan?** *(government in northern Sudan wanted to unify Sudan under Arabic and Islamic rule)*

Draw an arrow on the graphic organizer from the northern part to the southern part and label the arrow with the identified conflict. **Verbal/Linguistic**

Sudan Refugees and Displacement

V | Sudan has been involved in civil war for many years. Most people in the northern part of Sudan are Arab Muslim and live in cities. People in the southern part are African, rural farmers, and follow either African traditional religions or Christianity.

R | **Geography** Sudan is the sixteenth-largest country in the world in area and the third-largest country in Africa. It was the largest before South Sudan gained independence. Sudan's population is 33.4 million. South Sudan has approximately half that number. In land area, South Sudan ranks forty-fourth in the world.

Northern Control As an independent country, northern Sudan and its leaders controlled the government. They wanted to unify Sudan under Arabic and Islamic rule. In opposition were non-Muslims and the people of southern Sudan.

By the end of 2010, about 43.7 million people of the world did not have a home.

Violence Continues When South Sudan became an independent country on July 9, 2011, many people hoped to start a new, peaceful life. However, several violent conflicts broke out, including continued conflict in Darfur.

C1 | **Conflict in Darfur** Darfur is a region in western Sudan. In 2003 Darfur rebel groups rose up against the Sudanese government. The rebels demanded that the government stop its unjust social and economic policies. The government reacted by raiding and burning villages. In the long conflict that followed, thousands were killed, and many were forced from their homes.

Refugees and IDPs Refugees are people who have left their country because they are in danger or have been victims of persecution. A major problem also exists with internally displaced persons (IDPs). An IDP is someone who is forced to flee his or her home because of danger, but who remains in his or her country. **C2**

World Refugee Day The United Nations (UN) World Refugee Day is observed every year on June 20. The events call attention to the problems refugees face.

People of South Sudan move to a new refugee camp to escape conflict and hunger. ▶

Paula Bronstein/Getty Images News/Getty Images

---

networks *Online Teaching Options*

ANIMATION

Refugees

Collaborating Use the animation to discuss the movement of refugees and the possible reasons for that movement. Divide the class into groups of three. Have each group generate a list of ten adjectives that they believe describe the refugees' experience. Have each group share its list. Make a master list on the board. Discuss why the plight of refugees is difficult not only for the refugees, but for the country accepting the refugees as well. **ELL** Interpersonal

REFUGEE CAMP CONDITIONS AND DAILY LIFE

Nichole Sobecki/Corbis

THERE'S MORE ONLINE

SEE a timeline of the crisis in Darfur • WATCH the Red Cross help refugees

G1 Critical Thinking Skills

Determining Cause and Effect Have students work with a partner to read and create a flow chart of the events that occurred in Darfur in 2003. Allow class time for students to complete the chart. **Ask:**

- **What happened first?** *(Rebels rose up against the government.)*
- **What happened next?** *(Rebels made demands of the government.)*
- **Then what happened?** *(Government raided and burned down villages.)*
- **What was the effect of all of these events on the people of Darfur?** *(Thousands were killed or forced from their homes.)* **AL** **Logical/Mathematical**

V

C2 Critical Thinking Skills

Problem-Solving As a class, read aloud the sections "Refugees and IDPs" and "World Refugee Day" and discuss the problems that challenge the region and possible solutions. **Ask:**

- **How does World Refugee Day address the world's concern about refugees and IDPs?** *(Students might suggest that it brings the attention and resources of the world to the problems faced by displaced people.)*
- **In what ways might governments and the private sector work together to solve the problem of refugees and IDPs?** *(Possible answers: provide needed financial resources to help refugees; governments could work with a country's ambassador to help stop the conflict or concern.)*
- **What do you think are the most critical needs of refugees and IDPs?** *(Students' answers will vary but should include basic needs such as food, shelter, medical attention, clean water, safety.)* **Verbal/Linguistic**

V Visual Skills

Analyzing Images Have students analyze the full page image of refugees. **Ask:**

- **What word would you use to describe how these refugees feel?** *(Answers will vary but could include scared, horrified, sad, grief-stricken, hurried, terrified.)*
- **Why do you think refugees would leave their homes and land, rather than stand up to their governments?** *(Possible answers: lack of the resources to attempt a viable resistance; fear for their or their family's safety)* **ELL** **Visual/Spatial, Intrapersonal**

(l) ©Ocean/Corbis, ©Kryssia Campos/Getty Images, (tr) ©Erica Simone Leeds, (br) ©IG Photography/Alamy

SLIDE SHOW

Refugee Camps

Discussing Use the slide show of refugee camps around the world to discuss the conditions of these camps. Have students work in small groups to research the difficulties faced by refugees on the Internet. Then have groups propose solutions to the problems. Have students share their research and solutions in an oral or visual presentation to the class. **BL** **Visual/Spatial**

Slide Show

GLOBAL CONNECTIONS //////////

R Reading Skills

Citing Text Evidence As students read each of the statistic headlines on the page, have them cite text evidence to explain each statistic. List the facts on the board. **Ask: Given all of these facts, what do you conclude are the issues driving the conflict in Sudan?** (*strong differences in religion and culture, the economics of oil production, problems associated with a displaced population, political discord and instability*) **ELL**

C Critical Thinking Skills

Identifying Central Issues Review the statistical facts listed on the board and have students identify central issues. **Ask:**

- **Why are the problems in Sudan not just problems for Sudan and South Sudan, but a regional problem, as well?** (*Possible answer: Refugees cause social, political, and financial difficulties for neighboring countries. Armed conflict could spread into the region.*)

- **In what ways are the issues facing Sudan a global issue?** (*Students might mention that economic and political ties with Sudan or South Sudan affect relationships with nations in other regions of the world and test the resolve of the United Nations to address regional issues.*) **BL** **Logical/Mathematical**

V Visual Skills

Synthesizing Remind students that images often provide many important details. Direct student's attention to the image at the bottom right of the page. Discuss the details shown in this image. **Ask: What information does this photo provide?** (*possible age of rebels, how they are armed, perhaps a sense of desperation or weight of the cause shown in the rebel's facial expression*)

Have students refer to the image in the middle of the page of the soldier and the young boy. **Ask:**

- **What did the photographer capture in this image?** (*Possible answers: a greeting, an extension of friendship, a request for help, two individuals passing, a recognition of authority*)

- **What does the presence of the soldier indicate?** (*Students might respond that the soldier is there to help keep the peace, protect refugees.*)

Then lead a class discussion asking students: **How do you think peace could be brought to the region?** Help students to conclude that there are no simple solutions for the Sudanese people. **BL** **Visual/Spatial, Verbal/Linguistic**

These numbers and statistics can help you learn about the problems the Sudanese people face.

R

$1.25 a day

Although a peace agreement in 2005 brought some stability to the people of South Sudan, many terrible problems exist. More than 80 percent of the residents live on less than $1.25 a day. The country has the world's highest maternal mortality rate. About 50 percent of elementary school-age children do not attend school.

two million

South Sudan seceded from Sudan in 2011 as a result of a peace treaty that ended decades of war that had killed 2 million people. The two countries have come close to war again. Disputes over control of territory led to armed conflict.

75%

Oil is a source of conflict between Sudan and South Sudan. About 75 percent of the oil is in South Sudan, but all the pipelines run north to Sudan. When disputes over oil erupted in 2012, Sudan bombed oil fields in South Sudan.

300,000

In 2003 rebellion broke out in Darfur, a region in western Sudan. Government militia attacked Darfur and the rebels. The United Nations estimates that as many as 300,000 people died in five years of conflict in Darfur. Violence still erupts at times, breaking the fragile peace.

V

43.7 MILLION

By the end of 2010, about 43.7 million people of the world did not have a home. The number of refugees is the highest in 15 years.

C

More than 500,000

Refugees are people who have left their country because they are in danger or have been victims of persecution. In January 2011, 178,000 refugees were in Sudan, and 387,000 Sudanese who were living in other countries.

one point six million

In January 2011, more than 1.6 million Sudanese people were internally displaced.

(t) ©WOLFGANG RATTAY/Reuters/Corbis; (tr) MCT/McClatchy-Tribune/Getty Images; (bl) ASHRAF SHAZLY/AFP/Getty Images; (br) ©Lynsey Addario/VII/Corbis

320 *Chapter 10*

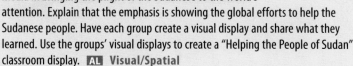

netw⚬rks *Online Teaching Options*

VIDEO

Scene at a Refugee Camp

Transferring Knowledge Use the video to analyze a scene at a refugee camp. Have students describe the elements of the scene. Divide the class into small groups. Have each group research the efforts of private agencies and individuals to aid the people of Sudan, including the people of Darfur. Have one group research the impact of social media in bringing the plight of the Sudanese to the world's attention. Explain that the emphasis is showing the global efforts to help the Sudanese people. Have each group create a visual display and share what they learned. Use the groups' visual displays to create a "Helping the People of Sudan" classroom display. **AL** **Visual/Spatial**

©Digital Vision/Getty Images

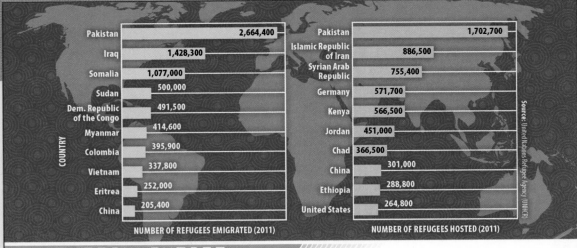

COUNTRY	NUMBER OF REFUGEES EMIGRATED (2011)
Pakistan	2,664,400
Iraq	1,428,300
Somalia	1,077,000
Sudan	500,000
Dem. Republic of the Congo	491,500
Myanmar	414,600
Colombia	395,900
Vietnam	337,800
Eritrea	252,000
China	205,400

	NUMBER OF REFUGEES HOSTED (2011)
Pakistan	1,702,700
Islamic Republic of Iran	886,500
Syrian Arab Republic	755,400
Germany	571,700
Kenya	566,500
Jordan	451,000
Chad	366,500
China	301,000
Ethiopia	288,800
United States	264,800

Source: United Nations Refugee Agency (UNHCR)

GLOBAL IMPACT

MIGRATION OF REFUGEES Refugees are people who flee to another country because of wars, political unrest, food shortages, or other problems. The graph on the left lists the 10 major source countries of refugees and the number of refugees who emigrated from those countries in 2011.

The graph on the right lists the 10 major host countries. A host country is the country a refugee moves to. For example, more than 1.7 million refugees immigrated to Pakistan in 2011.

Sudan and South Sudan

The map shows the two countries, their national capitals, and disputed areas.

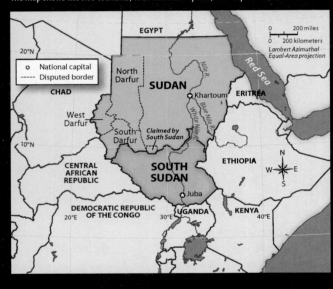

- o National capital
- ----- Disputed border

EGYPT
20°N
North Darfur
CHAD
SUDAN
Khartoum ◊
ERITREA
Red Sea
West Darfur
South Darfur
Claimed by South Sudan
Blue Nile
White Nile
Nile R.
10°N
CENTRAL AFRICAN REPUBLIC
SOUTH SUDAN
ETHIOPIA
Juba ◊
DEMOCRATIC REPUBLIC OF THE CONGO
20°E
UGANDA
KENYA
30°E
40°E

0   200 miles
0   200 kilometers
Lambert Azimuthal Equal-Area projection

Thinking Like a Geographer

1. **The Geographer's World** What are the major differences between Sudan and South Sudan?

2. **Human Geography** Why is oil a major factor in the conflict between Sudan and South Sudan?

3. **Human Geography** Imagine you are from Sudan and you come to live in the United States. Write a story about how you and your family learn to live in an American community.

V

Chapter 10 **321**

MAP

Crisis in Darfur

Creating Time Lines Use the map and the time line associated with it to discuss the sequence of events with regard to the crisis in Darfur. Have students discuss when and how it started, and if it is resolved. Have students create their own time line of the events for review. Encourage students to research the Internet or to read media accounts of past and/or current events in Darfur to add to their time lines. **Visual/Spatial**

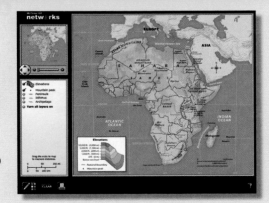

C

C Critical Thinking Skills

Drawing Conclusions Have students study the graphs showing the global impact of refugees. **Ask:**

- What does the graph on the left show? *(the number of refugees leaving these countries)*

- What does the graph on the right show? *(the number of refugees hosted or received into these countries)*

- Where does Sudan rank in the graph on the left? *(Sudan has the fourth highest number of refugees leaving the country.)*

- Look at the map below. Which of the countries in the graph on the right are most likely hosting the majority of Sudan's refugees? *(Kenya, Chad, and Ethiopia)* **Verbal/Linguistic**

V Visual Skills

Reading a Map Have students analyze the map. **Ask:**

- What is the capital of Sudan? *(Khartoum)*
- What is the capital of South Sudan? *(Juba)*
- What countries border both Sudan and South Sudan? *(Central African Republic, Ethiopia)*
- What body of water is near Sudan? *(the Red Sea)*
- Why is there a disputed border? *(South Sudan thinks that part of the land belongs to them and Sudan disagrees.)* **ELL Visual/Spatial**

CLOSE & REFLECT

Divide the class into two teams. Assign one team Sudan. Assign the other team South Sudan. Each team will organize its members to research the political, military, economic, religious, and social conditions of its assigned country. The teams should discuss and refine their research efforts into workable sections.

Each team will choose three to five individuals to represent its group at a mock United Nations summit. Each team will present its plan for peace between the two countries. The "summit," comprised of 6 students, will moderate the presentations of the two "countries" and based on what it hears draft a peace plan for the region to be voted on by the class, as the "body" of the United Nations. **BL Verbal/Linguistic, Interpersonal**

ANSWERS, p. 321

THINKING LIKE A GEOGRAPHER

1. Sudan is bigger than South Sudan; South Sudan has half the population of Sudan; People in South Sudan did not want to be under Arabic and Islamic rule.

2. About three-fourths of the oil is in South Sudan but all of the pipelines run north to Sudan

3. Stories will vary but should include the differences between living in Sudan and living in America.

CHAPTER REVIEW ACTIVITY

Have students create a two-column chart to list the characteristics of the climates of East Africa. Have them label the columns *Temperatures, Rainfall*. Tell students to list unique characteristics of each in the appropriate column. *(Possible answers:* **Temperatures***—warmer toward the coast, cooler in the highlands, cold on high mountains, temperatures dependent on latitude, elevation, wind patterns, and ocean currents;* **Rainfall***—seasonal with wet and dry seasons alternating, unpredictable with sparse rainfall resulting in severe drought and causing desertification)* **Visual/Spatial, Logical/ Mathematical**

Climates of East Africa	
Temperatures	**Rainfall**

REVIEW THE ENDURING UNDERSTANDINGS

Review this chapter's Enduring Understanding with students:

• *People, places, and ideas change over time.*

Now pose the following questions in a class discussion to apply this to this chapter.

• **How are the high mountains in East Africa changing?** *(Because of climate change, the glaciers that cover the high mountains in East Africa are melting.)*

• **How did the end of World War II change European colonies in East Africa?** *(Possible answer: After the war, many East African colonies gained independence.)*

• **How did European colonization change the region?** *(Possible answers: European missionaries introduced Christianity and converted many in the area to the faith; Europeans changed the agricultural system from one of subsistence to the production of cash crops. It led to political boundaries that were not based on cultural or social factors.)*

Chapter 10 ACTIVITIES (CCSS)

Directions: Write your answers on a separate piece of paper.

① Use your **FOLDABLES** to explore the Essential Question.
INFORMATIVE/EXPLANATORY WRITING Review the population map of East Africa at the beginning of the chapter. In two or more paragraphs, explain why people have settled in the locations indicated on the map.

② **21st Century Skills**
INTEGRATING VISUAL INFORMATION Conduct research and write a paragraph about one of the national park systems in East Africa. Review a partner's paragraph using these questions to guide you: Did the paragraph include relevant details? Was there anything missing that you expected to find in the paragraph? Discuss the review of your paragraph with your partner. Revise your paragraph as needed.

③ **Thinking Like a Geographer**
IDENTIFYING Choose 1 of the 11 countries of East Africa. In a graphic organizer like the one shown, identify the capital city of the country and write two geographical facts about the country.

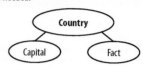

④ **GEOGRAPHY ACTIVITY**

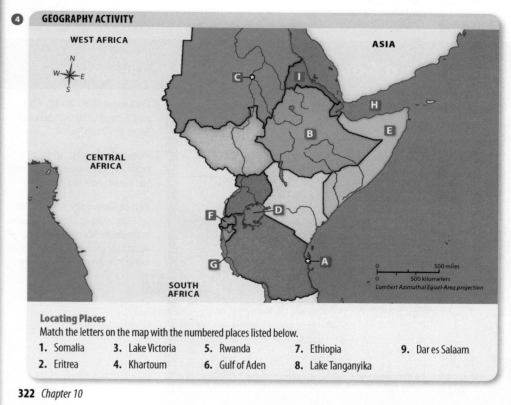

Locating Places
Match the letters on the map with the numbered places listed below.

1. Somalia	**3.** Lake Victoria	**5.** Rwanda	**7.** Ethiopia	**9.** Dar es Salaam
2. Eritrea	**4.** Khartoum	**6.** Gulf of Aden	**8.** Lake Tanganyika	

ACTIVITIES ANSWERS

Exploring the Essential Question

① **INFORMATIVE/EXPLANATORY WRITING** Students' work should reflect careful observation and the ability to read the population map correctly. Students should also use what they have learned about locations meeting the needs of the population to explain why people have settled where they have. Paragraphs should be well organized and meet your expectations for spelling and grammar.

21st Century Skills

② **INTEGRATING VISUAL INFORMATION** Students should choose one national park located in East Africa. They should include the park's name and location, as well as details that list when and why it was converted to a national park. Paragraphs should reflect thorough research using reliable resources, be interesting, informative, and well organized, and meet your expectations for spelling and grammar.

REVIEW THE GUIDING QUESTIONS

Directions: Choose the best answer for each question.

1 The physical geography and landscape of East Africa are dominated by a series of geological faults collectively known as
   A. the Ruwenzori Mountains.
   B. the Great Rift Valley.
   C. Kilimanjaro.
   D. Jonglei.

2 Because of long periods of drought and overgrazing, agricultural land has turned into desert in a process called
   F. irrigation.
   G. desertification.
   H. urbanization.
   I. defoliation.

3 Throughout history, the countries of East Africa have been centers of
   A. trade.
   B. revolution.
   C. oil exploration.
   D. the slave trade.

4 Most countries in East Africa earned their independence from European colonial powers during which decade of the twentieth century?
   F. the 1950s
   G. the 1980s
   H. the 1940s
   I. the 1960s

5 What is the name of the nomadic people who herd cattle and build their mud-dung houses inside a kraal?
   A. Samburu
   B. Masai
   C. Kamba
   D. Meru

6 What is the main economic activity in East Africa?
   F. manufacturing
   G. tourism
   H. agriculture
   I. oil and gas production

Chapter 10 **323**

ASSESSMENT ANSWERS
Review the Guiding Questions

1 B To answer this question, students need to remember that Kilimanjaro is a mountain and Jonglei is a canal. This knowledge will eliminate answers C and D. Remembering that the Great Rift system is a series of large valleys and depressions formed by long chains of geological faults will help them eliminate answer A and choose answer C. Refer students to the "Landform" section in Lesson 1 for help.

2 G The clue word in this question is *desert*. The word is also the base word in the answer choice G, *desertification*. Connecting the words *desert* and *drought* in the question will also help eliminate choice F (*irrigation* connects to watering something), choice H (*urbanization* connects to cities), and choice I (*defoliation* connects to loss of leaves). Refer students to reread the "Climate" section in Lesson 1 for additional help.

3 A To answer this question, students need to remember that the ancient kingdoms in the region were centers of trade. It was for that trade that the Europeans eventually colonized the region. This knowledge will help them eliminate choices B, C, and D. If students are having difficulties answering this question, have them reread the "Trade Cities" section in Lesson 2.

4 I To answer this question, students need to remember that independence from European colonial powers occurred after World War II which ended in 1945. This knowledge will help them eliminate choice H. Remembering that in the early 1960s six East African countries gained independence will help them choose the correct decade from the remaining answers. Refer students to the "Independence" section in Lesson 2 for help.

5 B The clue words in this question are *nomadic* and *kraal*. Connecting a kraal to the Masai, a nomadic people, will help students choose the correct answer, B. Have students review the "Daily Life" section in Lesson 3.

6 H Remembering that most of the people in East Africa are farmers will help students make the connection to agriculture. Refer students to Lesson 3. Have them reread the "Economic Development" section for further information.

Thinking Like a Geographer

3 IDENTIFYING Facts listed will vary. Countries and their capital cities are:

Sudan—Khartoum

South Sudan—Juba

Eritrea—Asmara

Ethiopia—Addis Ababa

Djibouti—Djibouti

Somalia—Mogadishu

Kenya—Nairobi

Uganda—Kampala

Rwanda—Kigali

Burundi—Bujumbura

Tanzania—Dodoma

Geography Activities

4 LOCATING PLACES

1. E
2. I
3. D
4. C
5. F
6. H
7. B
8. G
9. A

DBQ Analyzing Documents

7 **A** Since the author contrasts the success of Kenyan farmers growing fruits, vegetables, and flowers with traditional crops such as coffee and tea, these three crops are probably products in demand. Explain that the context clue "a figure that dwarfs" eliminates answer B. And it is Rwanda, not Kenya, that the passage states imported food, eliminating answer D.

8 **F** The other sectors of Rwanda's economy might also have seen success, but the author only cites evidence of the success of its agricultural sector. Remind students to pay close attention to each word and to eliminate answer choices that are not found in the text.

Short Response

9 A refugee camp was needed because the thousands of Somalis fleeing a civil war in their homeland had entered Kenya and the people there needed shelter. Review the aspects of civil war. Also review that many women and children would need protection/shelter from the fighting.

10 Possible answer: A refugee camp as large Dadaab would need many of the facilities found in any city of a similar size—housing, water and sewage facilities, places to distribute food, medical facilities, schools for the children, energy to power lighting and heating, police to maintain order, and so on.

Extended Response

11 Students' essays should show evidence of research, consideration of the topic, and exhibit good grammar and spelling as well as stating a preference for which country they would prefer living in. Check that the factors posed in the writing assignment are addressed in students' essays.

DBQ ANALYZING DOCUMENTS

7 **ANALYZING** Read the following passage about economies in Africa:

"*Kenyan farmers, mostly small, are responsible for $1 billion in annual exports of fruits, vegetables, and flowers, a figure that dwarfs the country's traditional coffee and tea exports. . . . Rwanda, . . . long an importer of food, now grows enough to satisfy the needs of its people, and even exports cash crops such as coffee for the first time.*"

—from G. Paschal Zachary, "Africa's Amazing Rise and What It Can Teach the World" (2012)

What statement best explains the success of Kenya's farmers? RH.6-8.1, RH.6-8.10

A. They produced a variety of crops that were in demand.
B. They produced more coffee and tea.
C. They exported cash crops for the first time.
D. They imported food from Rwanda.

8 **CITING TEXT EVIDENCE** Which sector of Rwanda's economy has seen success? RH.6-8.1, RH.6-8.10

F. agriculture
G. industry
H. mining
I. service industries

SHORT RESPONSE

"*The world's biggest refugee camp, Dadaab, in northeastern Kenya marks its 20th anniversary this year. The camp, which was set up to host 90,000 people, now shelters nearly one-half million refugees. . . . The [United Nations] set up the first camps in Dadaab between October 1991 and June 1992, following a civil war [in Somalia] that continues to this day.*"

—from Lisa Schlein, "World's Biggest Refugee Camp in Kenya Marks 20th Anniversary" (2012)

9 **DETERMINING CENTRAL IDEAS** Why was a refugee camp needed? RH.6-8.2, RH.6-8.10

10 **ANALYZING** What kinds of facilities would officials need to create to take care of tens of thousands of people? RH.6-8.1, RH.6-8.10

EXTENDED RESPONSE

11 **INFORMATIVE/EXPLANATORY WRITING** In an essay, compare and contrast the countries of Somalia and Kenya. Use your text and Internet research to examine each country's physical geography, culture, average income, education levels, type of government, employment, and other factors that affect the way people live. Of the two, which country would you rather live in? WHST.6-8.6, WHST.6-8.7

Need Extra Help?

If You've Missed Question	1	2	3	4	5	6	7	8	9	10	11
Review Lesson	1	1	2	2	3	3	3	3	2	2	3

From "Africa's Amazing Rise and What It Can Teach the World" by G. Paschal Zachary, Feb 25, 2012, http://www.theatlantic.com/international/archive/2012/02. Copyright © G. Paschal Zachary; "World's Biggest Refugee Camp in Kenya Marks 20th Anniversary," by Lisa Schlein, February 21, 2012. *Voice of America,* http://voanews.com

---

netw⊙rks *Online Teaching Options*

Remediation and Assessment

Evaluating The *Assess* tab in the online Teacher Lesson Center includes resources to help students improve their test-taking skills. It also contains many project-based rubrics to help you assess students' work.

UNDERSTANDING BY DESIGN®

Enduring Understandings

- *People, places, and ideas change over time.*

Essential Questions

- *How do people adapt to their environment?*
- *How does technology change the way people live?*
- *Why do people make economic choices?*

Predictable Misunderstandings

- *The geography of Central Africa is affected by North Africa's geography.*
- *Resources of Central Africa have had no effect on the history of the region.*

Assessment Evidence

Performance Tasks:

- *Project-Based Learning Digital Hands-On Chapter Project*
- *Project-Based Learning Hands-On Chapter Project*

Other Evidence:

- *Geography Skills Activity*
- *Reading Skills Activity*
- *Writing Skills Activity*
- *Participation in Interactive Whiteboard Activities*
- *Contribution to small-group activities*
- *Interpretation of slide show images and special purpose maps*
- *Participation in class discussions about cultural and economic topics*
- *Lesson Reviews*
- *Chapter Assessments*

SUGGESTED PACING GUIDE

Introducing the Chapter	1 Day	Lesson 3	2 Days
Lesson 1	2 Days	What Do You Think?	3 Days
Lesson 2	2 Days	Chapter Wrap-Up and Assessment	1 Day

TOTAL TIME   11 Days

Key for Using the Teacher Edition

SKILL-BASED ACTIVITIES

Types of skill activities found in the Teacher Edition.

* **V Visual Skills** require students to analyze maps, graphs, charts, and photos.

W Writing Skills provide writing opportunities to help students comprehend the text.

R Reading Skills help students practice reading skills and master vocabulary.

C Critical Thinking Skills help students apply and extend what they have learned.

T Technology Skills require students to use digital tools effectively.

*Letters are followed by a number when there is more than one of the same type of skill on the page.

DIFFERENTIATED INSTRUCTION

All activities are written for the on-level student unless otherwise marked with the leveled labels below.

BL Beyond Level
AL Approaching Level
ELL English Language Learners

All students benefit from activities that utilize different learning styles. Many activities are marked as below when a particular learning style is highlighted.

Intrapersonal	Naturalist
Logical/Mathematical	Kinesthetic
Visual/Spatial	Auditory/Musical
Verbal/Linguistic	Interpersonal

Learners will understand:

I. The World in Spatial Terms

Standard 1: How to use maps and other geographic representations, geospatial technologies, and spatial thinking to understand and communicate information

Standard 3: How to analyze the spatial organization of people, places, and environments on Earth's surface

II. Places and Regions

Standard 4: The physical and human characteristics of places

Standard 5: That people create regions to interpret Earth's complexity

Standard 6: How culture and experience influence people's perceptions of places and regions

IV. Human Systems

Standard 9: The characteristics, distribution, and migration of human populations on Earth's surface

Standard 10: The characteristics, distribution, and complexity of Earth's cultural mosaics

Standard 11: The patterns and networks of economic interdependence on Earth's surface

Standard 12: The processes, patterns, and functions of human settlement

Standard 13: How the forces of cooperation and conflict among people influence the division and control of Earth's surface

V. Environment and Society

Standard 14: How human actions modify the physical environment

Standard 15: How physical systems affect human systems

VI. The Uses of Geography

Standard 17: How to apply geography to interpret the past

Standard 18: How to apply geography to interpret the present and plan for the future

CHAPTER OPENER PLANNER

Students will know:

- that the geography of Central Africa is very different than that of North Africa because of rainforests.
- that the Congo River, not the Nile, creates the rainforests of Central Africa.

Students will be able to:

- *analyze* a world map to identify countries of Central Africa.
- *use* a time line to discuss various events in the history of Central Africa.

UNDERSTANDING
BY DESIGN®

☑ *Print Teaching Options*

V Visual Skills

☐ **P. 326** Students use the map of Central Africa to reinforce map skills. **Visual/Spatial**

☐ **P. 327** Students review the time line and discuss its major points of interest. **Visual/Spatial**

W Writing Skills

☐ **P. 327** Students choose two events to describe the cause-effect relationship between natural resources and the slave trade. **Verbal/Linguistic**

R Reading Skills

☐ **P. 326** Students use context clues to define *sultan*. **ELL** **Verbal/Linguistic**

C Critical Thinking Skills

☐ **P. 326** Students analyze the significance of music and dance in Central Africa. **Auditory/Musical**

☑ *Online Teaching Options*

☐ **MAP** **Reading A Map**—Students identify aspects and locations of the region on a map.

☐ **TIME LINE** **Reading a Time Line and Map**—Students learn about where and when historical events occurred in Central Africa. **Visual/Spatial**

☐ **MAP** **Interactive World Atlas**—Students use the interactive world atlas to identify the region and describe its terrain.

☑ *Printable Digital Worksheets*

☐ **WORKSHEET** **Geography Skills: Resources in Central Africa**—Students can use this worksheet to discuss and learn more about the resources of Central Africa.

☐ **WORKSHEET** **Reading Skills: The Agricultural Revolution of Africa**—Students can use this worksheet to understand more about the agricultural revolution.

☐ **WORKSHEET** **Writing Skills: Population Growth and the Environment**—Students can use this worksheet to understand trade routes and the impact of population growth on the environment.

Project-Based Learning

Hands-On

Creating Thematic Maps

Students will work in groups to create thematic maps for countries in Central Africa. Maps for each country should use colors or graphics to illustrate a major theme, such as the number of cell phone or Internet users or the amount of roadways and airports found in each country. Students might refer to the online CIA World Factbook for reliable statistics. Once the students have created their maps, have them present their findings to the class.

Digital Hands-On

Creating Digital Infographics

Have students work in pairs or small groups to create digital infographics on one or more of the following topics in Central Africa: Diversity, Art and Music, History, Daily Life, Climate, and Natural Resources. Once students have selected a topic(s), they will conduct online research to find information, photos, charts, and maps to include in their infographics. Have students present their infographics to the class.

Print Resources

ANCILLARY RESOURCES

These ancillaries are available for every chapter and lesson.

- **Reading Essentials and Study Guide Workbook** **AL** **ELL**
- **Chapter Tests and Lesson Quizzes Blackline Masters**

PRINTABLE DIGITAL WORKSHEETS

These printable digital worksheets are available for every chapter and lesson!

- **Hands-On Chapter Projects**
- **What Do You Know? Activities**
- **Chapter Summaries (English and Spanish)**
- **Vocabulary Builder Activities**
- **Quizzes and Tests**
- **Reading Essentials and Study Guide (English and Spanish)** **AL** **ELL**
- **Guided Reading Activities**

More Media Resources

SUGGESTED VIDEOS

NOTE: Be sure to preview videos to ensure they are age-appropriate.

- **Amazon Instant Videos, Wild Africa, Season 1 Episode 6, "Lakes and Rivers"** (59 min.)
- **Amazon Instant Videos, Wild Africa, The Jungle** (59 min.)
- **Amazon Instant Videos, Wild Africa, The Savannah** (59 min.)

SUGGESTED READING

- *Africa,* by Mike Graf **AL**
- *A Walk Through a Rain Forest,* by David Jenike and Mark Jenike
- *African Journey,* by John Chiasson **BL**

PHYSICAL GEOGRAPHY OF CENTRAL AFRICA

Students will know:
- *that the geography of Central Africa is very different than North Africa because of rain forests.*
- *that the Congo River, not the Nile, creates the rain forests of Central Africa.*

Students will be able to:
- **describe** *the landforms and waterways in Central Africa.*
- **describe** *the climate and vegetation of this region.*
- **discuss** *important natural resources in this region.*

UNDERSTANDING
BY DESIGN®

☑ *Print Teaching Options*

V Visual Skills

- ☐ **P. 328** Students create a visual representation of their Taking Notes graphic organizer. **AL** Visual/Spatial

- ☐ **P. 330** Students create a weather map that depicts information from the text. **ELL** Visual/Spatial, Kinesthetic

- ☐ **P. 331** Students diagram the impact of sunlight on rain forests. Visual/Spatial

- ☐ **P. 332** Students create a graphic organizer to organize information about mineral resources. Visual/Spatial

W Writing Skills

- ☐ **P. 332** Students write a paragraph about whether slash-and-burn agriculture is vital to sustaining agriculture in Central Africa. **BL** Verbal/Linguistic

R Reading Skills

- ☐ **P. 329** Students use context clues to determine meaning. **AL** **ELL** Verbal/Linguistic

- ☐ **P. 330** Students identify cause-and-effect relationships in the text. Verbal/Linguistic

- ☐ **P. 331** Students define slash-and-burn agriculture. **ELL** **AL** Verbal/Linguistic

- ☐ **P. 333** Students cite text evidence to list reasons that Central Africa's mineral resources have remained underdeveloped. **AL** Verbal/Linguistic

C Critical Thinking Skills

- ☐ **P. 329** Students predict the impact of cataracts on the Congo River. **BL** Verbal/Linguistic

T Technology Skills

- ☐ **P. 333** Students conduct research and prepare a short presentation about their assigned country and its natural resources. **BL** Visual/Spatial, Logical/Mathematical

☑ *Online Teaching Options*

V Visual Skills

- ☐ **VIDEO** **The Kuwait of Africa**—Students watch the video about the discovery and production of oil in Equatorial Guinea and share two key facts they found interesting. **ELL** Interpersonal

- ☐ **MAP** **Physical Geography: Central Africa**—Students can use the physical geography map to highlight the landforms and waterways of Central Africa.

- ☐ **VIDEO** **Congo River**—Students can use the video of the Congo to extend the content and highlight the watershed, the cataracts, and the size of the river.

- ☐ **MAP** **Climates: Central Africa**—Students can use the climate map to discuss the climates of Central Africa.

- ☐ **MAP** **Resources: Central Africa**—Students can use the resources map to highlight other resources and their relative locations in the region.

W Writing Skills

- ☐ **MAP** **The Route of the Congo**—Students study a map showing the Congo River and write a paragraph comparing it to the Nile River. **AL** Verbal/Linguistic

R Reading Skills

- ☐ **LECTURE SLIDE** **Rain Forest and Savannah**—Students can use the lecture slide to review the features of the rain forest and the savannah and their relation to each other.

- ☐ **LECTURE SLIDE** **Developing Resources**—Students can use the lecture slide to discuss the reasons this region struggles to develop its resources.

C Critical Thinking Skills

- ☐ **IMAGE** **Rain Forest of Gabon**—Students discuss how rain forests developed and the change from the Sahara to the rain forest. **AL** Visual/Spatial, Verbal/Linguistic

- ☐ **IMAGE** **Slash-and-Burn Agriculture**—Students discuss the pros and the cons of slash-and-burn agriculture and whether it is justified. **AL** Verbal/Linguistic

- ☐ **IMAGE** **Mining for Gold**—Students discuss how resources in the region are developed or mined and at what cost. **AL** Verbal/Linguistic

T Technology Skills

- ☐ **ONLINE SELF-CHECK QUIZ** **Lesson 1**—Students receive instant feedback on their mastery of lesson content.

☑ *Printable Digital Worksheets*

W Writing Skills

- ☐ **WORKSHEET** **Geography Skills: Resources in Central Africa**—Students can use this worksheet to discuss and learn more about the resources of Central Africa.

HISTORY OF CENTRAL AFRICA

Students will know:
- that climate change led to the development of agriculture in Central Africa.
- that contact from Europeans brought different cultures, languages, and religions to the region.

Students will be able to:
- *discuss* early settlement and the development of agriculture in Central Africa.
- *examine* European contact and its effects including the slave trade and colonialism.
- *describe* independence movements and independence for Central African countries.

UNDERSTANDING
BY DESIGN®

☑ *Print Teaching Options*

V Visual Skills

- ☐ **P. 336** Students diagram triangular trade. **Visual/Spatial**

- ☐ **P. 337** Students create a visual representation of the word *colonialism* as it relates to Central Africa. **ELL Visual/Spatial**

W Writing Skills

- ☐ **P. 335** Students write a persuasive essay about whether or not more palm oil plantations should be built in Cameroon. **Verbal/Linguistic**

R Reading Skills

- ☐ **P. 334** Students sequence events relating to changes in agriculture. **AL Logical/Mathematical**

- ☐ **P. 335** Students use a dictionary to determine connotations and multiple meanings. **ELL Verbal/Linguistic**

- ☐ **P. 336** Students use word parts to determine meaning. **ELL Verbal/Linguistic**

- ☐ **P. 338** Students use context clues to understand the word *exploitation*. **AL Verbal/Linguistic**

- ☐ **P. 339** Students paraphrase paragraphs about independence in Central Africa. **Verbal/Linguistic**

C Critical Thinking Skills

- ☐ **P. 334** Students determine how Earth's climate changes affect people's ability to survive. **AL Verbal/Linguistic**

- ☐ **P. 335** Students compare and contrast stone and iron as materials for tools. **Logical/Mathematical**

- ☐ **P. 338** Students formulate questions about the countries shown on the map and their governments.

- ☐ **P. 338** Students make inferences about the colonization of Central Africa.

- ☐ **P. 339** Students determine the effects of independence on Central African countries. **BL Logical/Mathematical**

T Technology Skills

- ☐ **P. 337** Students research where corn is grown and its uses in Central Africa and prepare a presentation based on their findings. **Interpersonal**

☑ *Online Teaching Options*

V Visual Skills

- ☐ **VIDEO Congo Civil War**—Students watch the video about the history of the civil war in the Congo and evaluate the information presented in the video. **AL Verbal/Linguistic**

- ☐ **VIDEO Harvest in Central Africa**—Students can use the video of harvesting palm oil to discuss the different types of plants used by people of the region.

W Writing Skills

- ☐ **MAP Triangular Trade**—Students use the map to discuss the triangular trade and its impact on Africa. Then they create a flow chart that depicts the process. **AL Visual/Spatial**

- ☐ **MAP Resistance to Colonization**—Students use the animated map and write a cause-effect paragraph explaining colonization and resistance to colonization. **BL Verbal/Linguistic**

R Reading Skills

- ☐ **GAME Drag-and-Drop: Historical Changes in Central Africa**—Students use the drag-and-drop game to review countries in Central Africa. **AL Kinesthetic**

- ☐ **MAP Independence in Central Africa**—Students can use the map of independence in Central Africa to review the dates that the countries in the region became independent nations.

C Critical Thinking Skills

- ☐ **SLIDE SHOW Harvest in Central Africa**—Students learn about the crops grown by farmers of Central Africa and make connections to farming in or near their community. **Verbal/Linguistic, Naturalist**

- ☐ **CHART Impact of the African Slave Trade**—Students can use the chart to discuss the facts with regard to the African slave trade and its impact on Africa.

T Technology Skills

- ☐ **ONLINE SELF-CHECK QUIZ Lesson 2**—Students receive instant feedback on their mastery of lesson content.

☑ *Printable Digital Worksheets*

W Writing Skills

- ☐ **WORKSHEET The Agricultural Revolution of Africa**—Students can use this worksheet to understand more about the agricultural revolution of Africa.

LIFE IN CENTRAL AFRICA

Students will know:
- that contact from Europeans brought different cultures, languages, and religions to the region.

Students will be able to:
- **describe** the makeup of the population in Central Africa and where people live.
- **describe** people and cultures in the region, including languages and religion.
- **describe** daily life in the region.
- **explore** regional issues that present challenges to the region.

UNDERSTANDING BY DESIGN®

☑ Print Teaching Options

V Visual Skills

☐ **P. 341** Students create a diagram or chart to compare and contrast information about rural and urban areas. **AL** Visual/Spatial

☐ **P. 342** Students use a software program to create a graph that shows the population percentages of Central African countries. **Logical/Mathematical**

☐ **P. 343** Students create a graph showing city populations and the diversity of religions in the Democratic Republic of Congo. **Visual/Spatial**

W Writing Skills

☐ **P. 341** Students write a three-paragraph proposal with suggestions on how to deal with three anticipated issues of two large capital cities being located so close together. **BL** Verbal/Linguistic

☐ **P. 345** Students write an argumentative essay based on their response to information about growth and the environment in Central Africa. **BL** Verbal/Linguistic

R Reading Skills

☐ **P. 341** Students use base words to determine meaning. **AL ELL** Verbal/Linguistic

☐ **P. 343** Students summarize the information about daily life in Central Africa. **AL** Verbal/Linguistic

C Critical Thinking Skills

☐ **P. 340** Students make connections between Central Africa and the United States based on the ages of their populations. **BL** Interpersonal

☐ **P. 344** Students identify problems and describe why modernization has been slow to come to some parts of Central Africa. **Verbal/Linguistic**

☐ **P. 345** Students discuss challenges facing Central Africa and suggest solutions. **Logical/Mathematical**

T Technology Skills

☐ **P. 344** Students research the different languages of Central Africa and create a map showing where certain languages are spoken. **BL** Visual/Spatial

---

☑ Online Teaching Options

V Visual Skills

☐ **MAP** **Population: Central Africa**—Students can use the population map to discuss the population distribution and density.

☐ **IMAGE** **360° View: Brazzaville**—Students can use the 360° view of the city of Brazzaville in Central Africa to highlight the larger cities in Central Africa.

☐ **SLIDE SHOW** **Types of Housing in Central Africa**—Students view different types of housing in Central Africa and create a chart to organize the information. **ELL** Visual/Spatial

☐ **VIDEO** **Music of Central Africa**—Students can use the video of the Kinshasa symphony to discuss the arts of Central Africa.

W Writing Skills

☐ **VIDEO** **Kings of the Congo**—Students watch the video about the gorillas in the Congo, the threats to their habitats, and human-environment interaction and write a paragraph. **AL**

☐ **IMAGE** **Rural and City Life in Central Africa**—Students use the photographs to compare and contrast rural and city life and write a paragraph. **AL** Verbal/Linguistic

R Reading Skills

☐ **LECTURE SLIDE** **Defining: Trade Languages**—Students can use the lecture slide to review the meaning of trade languages.

☐ **GRAPHIC ORGANIZER** **Subsistence Farming in Central Africa**—Students use the graphic organizer to review the crops and livestock that are part of subsistence farming in Central Africa.

C Critical Thinking Skills

☐ **GRAPH** **Population of Central Africa**—Students discuss the cause-effect relationship between population changes and issues that affect cities. **BL** Visual/Spatial

☐ **MAP** **Cultural Influences on Central Africa**—Students can use the colony map and the information to review the European and African influences on culture in Central Africa.

☐ **CHART** **Social Issues in Central Africa**—Students compare hospitals in Central Africa to hospitals in the United States and discuss ways to improve social issues in Central Africa. **AL**

T Technology Skills

☐ **ONLINE SELF-CHECK QUIZ** **Lesson 3**—Students receive instant feedback on their mastery of lesson content.

☑ Printable Digital Worksheets

W Writing Skills

☐ **WORKSHEET** **Writing Skills: Population Growth and the Environment**—Students can use this worksheet to understand the impact of population growth on the environment.

INTERVENTION AND REMEDIATION STRATEGIES

LESSON 1 Physical Geography of Central Africa

Reading and Comprehension

Have students work in pairs to outline landforms and waterways of Central Africa. Tell students to divide the lesson into sections, and then each write a sentence or two about each subtopic. For example, one student might write a sentence about the Congo River's importance while his or her partner writes about the significance of rain forests in the region. Ask volunteers to share their sentences with the class as a review of concepts in the lesson.

Text Evidence

Organize students into four groups, and assign groups the following topics regarding Central Africa: waterways, landforms, climate and vegetation, and resources. Have groups collaborate to create a visual display about their assigned topic. Encourage students to describe their topic in the form of a poster, time line, or digital slide presentation. Tell students to present an analysis of their topic using evidence from the text to support the concepts presented in their displays.

LESSON 2 History of Central Africa

Reading and Comprehension

Review with students how using signal words can help them organize information. Tell students that a sequence is often signaled by words such as *first, then, next, later, last,* and *finally.* Words that signal examples will follow include *such as, for example, in particular,* and *the following.* Have students review the lesson and note which concepts are presented sequentially, or in order, and which indicate examples. For instance, students might note the sequence of events regarding the development of agriculture or the slave trade. Or they might list examples of new crops to show the effect of farming.

Text Evidence

Organize students into three groups and assign groups the following topics: Group 1/Early Settlement, Group 2/European Contact and Afterward, and Group 3/Independent Countries. Have students collaborate to write a summary of their topic. Tell students their summaries should answer the guiding questions: Group 1/*How did agriculture and trade develop in Central Africa?*, Group 2/*How did colonization by foreign countries affect Central Africa?*, and Group 3/*What effects did gaining independence have on the countries of Central Africa?* Have a member of each group read the group's summary to the class.

LESSON 3 Life in Central Africa

Reading and Comprehension

Have students skim the lesson to identify and review terms they may not fully understand, such as *ethnic, median, savanna, subsistence farming,* and *metropolis.* Have students work with a partner to create flash cards for each of the terms by writing the word on one side and the definition on the other. Students may also draw sketches to serve as clues to each word's meaning. Have pairs use their flashcards to take turns quizzing each other. Then have them practice using the words in sentences to explain concepts in the lesson.

Text Evidence

Students may have trouble grasping the contrast that exists between rural and city life in Central African countries today. Organize students into small groups and have each group research a different country in Central Africa. Tell students to use the text and information from their research to identify the country's population density and where it is concentrated. Encourage students to find facts about the country's education, economy, and challenges. After groups present their findings, discuss various issues facing Central African countries today.

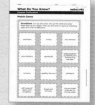

CENTRAL AFRICA

There's More Online about Central Africa.

CHAPTER 11

ESSENTIAL QUESTIONS · How do people adapt to their environment? · How does technology change the way people live? · What makes a culture unique?

A Congolese woman wears the traditional hairstyle that originated in the area long ago.

Andrew McConnell/Robert Harding World Imagery/Getty Images

Lesson 1
Physical Geography of Central Africa

Lesson 2
History of Central Africa

Lesson 3
Life in Central Africa

The Story Matters...

The region of Central Africa straddles the Equator, which creates tropical climates that support the growth of rain forests and savannas. The Congo River—Africa's second-longest river—has so many tributaries that it forms Africa's largest system of waterways. Abundant natural resources in Central Africa greatly influenced its history. Today, the resources are vital to helping nations in the region achieve and maintain stability.

FOLDABLES®
Study Organizer

Go to the Foldables® library in the back of your book to make a Foldable® that will help you take notes while reading this chapter.

325

ENGAGE

Think-Pair-Share Have students think of a nearby river, lake, or other large body of water they know about. Have student pairs brainstorm a list of reasons why this body of water might be important to nearby communities. Students may list recreational activities and tourism as well as fishing, agriculture, and transportation. Have students compare their lists. Then have students read "The Story Matters. . . ."

Making Inferences Display a political map of Central Africa or use the one on the following pages. Ask a volunteer to locate the Congo River. Guide students to understand the Congo River's size and importance to its surrounding regions. Help students make the connection between the Congo River and the people of this region. **Ask: What type of activities do you think the Congo River supports?** *(Sample response: The Congo River probably supports agriculture by providing water for irrigation of nearby farmland or it may be used for trading.)*

Making Connections Point out that there are two countries in Central Africa with similar names: Congo and Democratic Republic of the Congo (DRC). Explain that a Congolese person such as the woman in the photograph is most likely from Congo. Help students differentiate the countries by explaining the meaning of a democratic republic by comparing this form of government to that of the United States. **Ask: What is the type of government that the United States has?** *(It has a federal republic based on the United States Constitution and amendments. The president is elected the leader of the government.)*

Explain that the Democratic Republic of the Congo has had several constitutions over the years, and its power is primarily assigned to the president, who nominates a prime minister as head of government. **AL** **Verbal/Linguistic**

Letter from the Author

Dear Geography Teacher,

Students should use the information from this chapter to write a report about the barriers to modern development in Central Africa. Emphasis will vary by country but population growth should be a common topic among the reports. Other issues students might cite include difficulties like poor political leadership, different religious practices, language barriers, cultural differences, poor transportation, a lagging educational system, and a cycle of rural poverty.

Richard H. Boehm

FOLDABLES®
Study Organizer

Go to the Foldables® library for a cumulative chapter-based Foldable® activity that your students can use to help take notes and prepare for assessment.

TEACH & ASSESS

Step Into the Place

V Visual Skills

Reading a Map Have students read the introductory paragraph and look at the map. Explain that this map shows the countries in Central Africa. **Ask:**

- **How many countries share a border with Gabon?** *(three)* **Identify them.** *(Equatorial Guinea, Cameroon, and Congo)*
- **What is the capital of Equatorial Guinea?** *(Malabo)*
- **What is the smallest country in Central Africa?** *(São Tomé and Príncipe)*
- **What is the largest?** *(Democratic Republic of the Congo)*

Then have students use the map to answer the Step Into the Place questions. **Visual/Spatial**

C Critical Thinking Skills

Analyzing Visuals Have students review photograph B. **Ask: What do you think is the significance of music and dance in some Central African cultures?** *(Sample response: Music and dancing likely play important roles as they are used in ceremonies to honor leaders as well as in social gatherings.)* **Verbal/Linguistic, Auditory/Musical**

R Reading Skills

Using Context Clues Remind students that using context clues can help them understand the meaning of unknown words. **Ask:**

- **What is a *sultan*?** *(a king or ruler)*
- **What context clues helped you determine its meaning?** *(palace)*

Explain that a sultan is a king or ruler usually of a Muslim country or state. **ELL** **Verbal/Linguistic**

ANSWERS, p. 326

STEP INTO THE PLACE

1. seven
2. São Tomé and Príncipe
3. They are close together.
4. **CRITICAL THINKING** Libreville and Port-Gentil in Gabon and Douala in Cameroon. Trade is most likely very important because of the coastal locations.

Chapter 11
CENTRAL AFRICA (CCSS)

V *Central Africa's many rivers are a source of life for people of the region. The geography of the region is dominated by the rain forest basin of the Congo River.*

Step Into the Place

MAP FOCUS Use the map to answer the following questions.

1. **THE GEOGRAPHER'S WORLD** How many countries make up the region of Central Africa?
2. **THE GEOGRAPHER'S WORLD** What island country is part of the region?
3. **PLACES AND REGIONS** What is unusual about the capitals of Congo and the Democratic Republic of the Congo?
4. **CRITICAL THINKING** **Analyzing** Which cities in Gabon and Cameroon are located along the coasts? Think about their locations. What economic activities do you think are important in those cities?

A **ISLAND PARADISE** A highway circles the scenic coast of São Tomé, a volcanic island, off the western coast of Central Africa. São Tomé forms part of São Tomé and Príncipe, a small island nation.

B **SULTAN'S COURT MUSICIANS** Musicians perform traditional music at a palace of a sultan in Foumban, Cameroon. Music and dance are an important part of ceremonies and social gatherings in Central Africa.

Step Into the Time

TIME LINE Choose at least two events from the time line to describe the cause-and-effect relationship between natural resources and the slave trade in Central Africa. *RH.6-8.5, WHST.6-8.2*

1000 B.C. Iron Age spreads to Central Africa

1000 B.C.–A.D. 1100 Bantu people migrate to Congo rain forest

1470s São Tomé becomes the first port of the Atlantic slave trade

1700s Slave trade spreads to interior of continent

326 Chapter 11

Project-Based Learning ✋

Hands-On

Making Thematic Maps

Students will work in groups to create thematic maps for countries in Central Africa. Maps for each country should use colors or graphics to illustrate a major theme, such as number of cell phone or Internet users or amount of roadways and airports in each country. Students might refer to the online CIA World Factbook for reliable statistics. Once the students have created their maps, have them present their findings to the class.

Digital Hands-On

Creating Digital Infographics

Have pairs or small groups create digital infographics on one or more of the following topics in Central Africa: Diversity, Art and Music, History, Daily Life, Climate, and Natural Resources. They will conduct online research to find information, photos, charts, and maps for their infographics. Have them present their infographics to the class.

edtech teacher
21st Century Learning

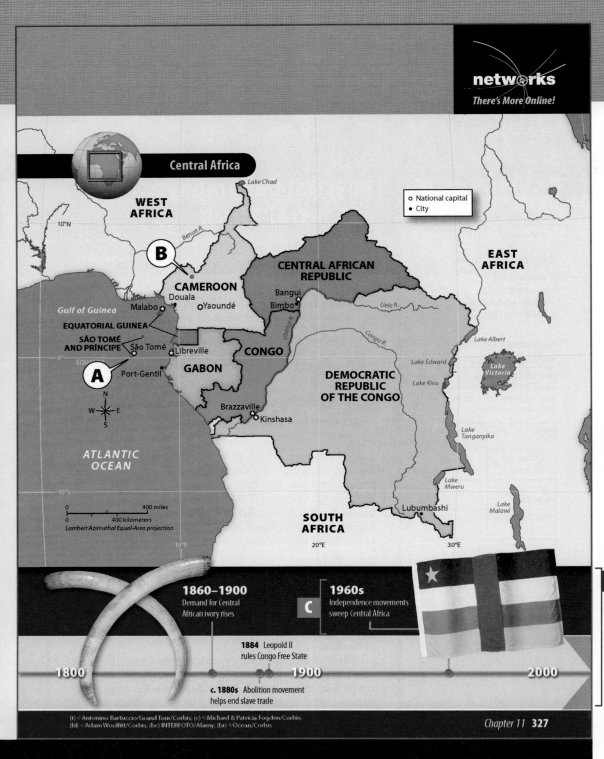

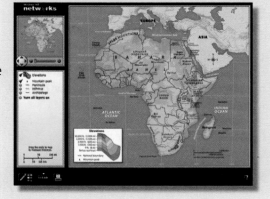

Central Africa

National capital
City

WEST AFRICA

10°N

Lake Chad

Benue R.

B

CENTRAL AFRICAN REPUBLIC

CAMEROON
Douala
Malabo
Yaoundé
Bangui
Bimbo

EAST AFRICA

Gulf of Guinea

Uele R.

EQUATORIAL GUINEA

Ubangi R.

Congo R.

Lake Albert

SÃO TOMÉ AND PRÍNCIPE
São Tomé
Libreville

CONGO

Lake Edward

Lake Victoria

EQU

A

GABON

Port-Gentil

DEMOCRATIC REPUBLIC OF THE CONGO

Lake Kivu

N
W   E
S

Brazzaville
Kinshasa

ATLANTIC OCEAN

Lake Tanganyika

10°S

Lake Mweru

Lake Malawi

0   400 miles
0   400 kilometers
Lambert Azimuthal Equal-Area projection

SOUTH AFRICA

Lubumbashi

20°E

30°E

1860–1900
Demand for Central African ivory rises

1960s
Independence movements sweep Central Africa

C

1800

1884 Leopold II rules Congo Free State

1900

2000

c. 1880s Abolition movement helps end slave trade

(t) ©Antonino Bartuccio/Grand Tour/Corbis; (c) ©Michael & Patricia Fogden/Corbis; (bl) ©Adam Woolfitt/Corbis; (bc) INTERFOTO/Alamy; (br) ©Ocean/Corbis

Chapter 11   **327**

Step Into the Time

V Visual Skills

Reading a Time Line Have students review the time line and images. As a class, discuss its major points of interest. **Ask:**

- **When did the Bantu people migrate to the Congo rain forest?** (They migrated to the Congo rain forest between 1000 B.C. and A.D. 1100.)

- **What did Leopold II do?** (He ruled Congo Free State beginning in 1884.)

- **When did the demand for Central Africa ivory increase?** (between 1860 and 1900)

- **Why do you think the demand rose during this time?** (Sample response: European explorers likely realized that ivory was a valuable natural resource, and they wanted to increase their wealth through trade.) **Visual/Spatial**

C Critical Thinking Skills

Making Inferences Point out the item on the time line dated 1960s. **Ask: Why do you think a series of independence movements swept across Central Africa during the 1960s?** (Sample response: With the increase in independence movements around the world, people living in Central Africa likely wanted their own independence from colonial rule.)
BL Verbal/Linguistic

V

W Writing Skills

Informative/Explanatory Read aloud the activity described at the beginning of the time line. Before students write their paragraphs, have them consider events on the time line that show a cause-and-effect relationship. For example, as a result of São Tomé becoming the first port of the Atlantic slave trade, the slave trade eventually spread to the continent's interior regions. Have students share their completed paragraphs with the class. **Verbal/Linguistic**

CLOSE & REFLECT

Summarizing Have students briefly review the photographs, map, and time line and think about what they have learned so far about countries in Central Africa. Have students turn to a partner and summarize key information about the region.

TIME LINE AND MAP

Reading a Time Line and Map

Analyzing Visuals Display the time line and map on the whiteboard. Ask volunteers to read events on the time line and identify where in Central Africa the event took place. Have them find its location on the map. Ask students to consider each country's importance based on its size on the map and the events shown on the time line. **AL Visual/Spatial**

See page 325B for other online activities.

ENGAGE

 Bellringer Before students begin the lesson, have them brainstorm a list of places they may have visited or have read about that are warm and tropical with abundant rainfall. Students may cite Florida, the Virgin Islands, South America, Hawaii, and so on. Read the Essential Question aloud and discuss how living in such a warm climate might affect the way people live. **Ask:**

- **How might the hot and wet climate in Central Africa and its proximity to the equator affect different crops grown in the region?** (Students' answers will vary but should include relevant details about the effects of an equatorial climate on living things.)

- **How might this type of climate impact human activities in the region?** (Sample response: People who live in the region probably dress in light clothing that protects them from the sun and from mosquitos and other bugs. People who visit the region may need to adjust to the temperatures and humidity.)

Tell students that they will learn more about Central Africa's climate and physical features in this lesson.

TEACH & ASSESS

V Visual Skills

Visualizing Have student pairs create a visual representation of the Taking Notes graphic organizer. Tell students to create simple drawings to identify specific characteristics about each topic. For example, students may draw the Congo River and a plain to represent the Congo Basin. As they read the section, "Landforms and Waterways," students may use their charts and drawings to note how Central Africa's physical geography is similar and different. **Ask: What physical features do you think are the most important to the region?** (the Congo River and its watershed) **AL** Visual/Spatial

---

ANSWER, p. 328

Taking Notes Sample answer: **Landforms and Waterways: Main idea:** Congo River and tributaries; **Details:** transportation; irrigation; not always navigable; **Climate and Vegetation: Main idea:** warm and wet climate along the Equator; **Details:** high temperatures, high humidity, rain falls all year; **Natural Resources: Main idea:** minerals; Congo River; **Details:** manganese; gold; diamonds; cobalt; hydroelectric power

---

networks

There's More Online!

☑ **IMAGES** Slash and Burn Agriculture

☑ **VIDEO**

Reading HELPDESK CCSS

Academic Vocabulary RH.6-8.4
(Tier Two Words)
- **potential**

Content Vocabulary RH.6-8.4
(Tier Three Words)
- **watershed**
- **estuary**
- **slash-and-burn**
- **biodiversity**

TAKING NOTES: *Key Ideas and Details* RH.6-8.2, RH.6-8.7

Find the Main Idea As you study the lesson, write a main idea about each topic on a graphic organizer. Then write details that support the main idea.

Topic	Main Idea/Detail
Landforms and Waterways	
Climate and Vegetation	
Natural Resources	

328

Lesson 1
Physical Geography of Central Africa

ESSENTIAL QUESTION · *How do people adapt to their environment?*

IT MATTERS BECAUSE

Central Africa is smaller than many regions, but it holds a tremendous variety of geographic features. These features include a vast rain forest–covered basin, one of the world's greatest river systems, soaring mountains, and a deep rift valley marking the line along which Africa is splitting apart.

Landforms and Waterways

GUIDING QUESTION *What makes some landforms and waterways so important to the region?*

Central Africa is located in Earth's equatorial zone—that is, the area along and near the Equator. The region consists of seven countries. The largest of these is the Democratic Republic of the Congo (DRC). It dwarfs its neighbors, which are the Central African Republic, the Republic of the Congo, Cameroon, Gabon, Equatorial Guinea, and the island country of São Tomé and Príncipe.

Landforms

V The dominant landform of Central Africa is the **watershed** of the Congo River. A watershed is the land drained by a river and its system of tributaries. At the center of the watershed is a depression called the Congo Basin. A rolling plain spreads across the center of the basin, and high plateaus rise on most of its sides.

The region's eastern edge runs along the Great Rift Valley, also known as the Great Rift System. Here, rugged mountain ranges soar above a broad, deep valley that holds several long, narrow lakes. Margherita Peak, which rises from a range

(l to r) ©Per-Anders Pettersson/Corbis; ©Ian Nichols/National Geographic Society/Corbis; ©Nigel Pavitt/JAI/Corbis; ©FINBARR O'REILLY/Reuters/Corbis

---

networks *Online Teaching Options*

VIDEO

The Kuwait of Africa

Evaluating Use this video about the growing economy in Equatorial Guinea, and the natural resources that economy is based on, to introduce the lesson. After watching the video, have students evaluate the information presented. Ask students to share with a partner one or two key facts they found interesting or that surprised them.
ELL Interpersonal

See page 325C for other online activities.

BBC Motion Gallery Education

called the Ruwenzori (ROO-un-ZO-ree), reaches the lofty height of 16,763 feet (5,109 m). Margherita Peak is the highest summit in the region and the third highest on the entire continent, ranking after Kilimanjaro and Mount Kenya.

Along the Atlantic coast of Central Africa stretches a narrow lowland. Off the coast lie several important islands. Two of these islands form the country of São Tomé and Príncipe. Two other islands, called Bioko and Pagalu, belong to Equatorial Guinea. This country also includes several smaller islands, as well as a territory on the mainland known as Mbini.

Waterways

Six of the seven countries in Central Africa have coasts on the Atlantic Ocean. The Central African Republic is the region's only landlocked country.

The Congo River and its tributaries account for most of Central Africa's inland waterways. The source of the Congo lies in East Africa between Lake Tanganyika and Lake Malawi (also called Lake Nyasa). From there, the river flows about 2,900 miles (4,667 km) to its mouth on the Atlantic Ocean. Among African rivers, only the Nile is longer than the Congo. When measured by water flow, the Congo tops every river in the world except South America's Amazon.

Difficult Navigation

No other river system in Africa offers as many miles of navigable waterways as the Congo and its tributaries. A navigable river is one on which ships and boats can travel. The Congo River is not navigable for its entire course, however. Several series of cataracts and rapids interrupt the passage of ships on the river.

Perhaps the most significant of these interruptions occurs rather close to the mouth of the Congo River. Only about 100 miles (161 km) from the Atlantic Ocean lie cataracts that block seagoing ships from traveling farther inland. The seaport city of Matadi is found here. Downstream from Matadi, in the final part of its journey, the river widens into an **estuary**, a passage in which freshwater meets salt water.

©Per-Anders Pettersson/Corbis

Fishers in the Democratic Republic of the Congo use bamboo supports to lower their nets into the waters along the rapids of the Congo River.

▶ **CRITICAL THINKING**
Describing What makes navigation difficult on parts of the Congo River?

Chapter 11 **329**

R Reading Skills

Determining Word Meanings After reading the section, "Waterways," aloud, have students point to the word *tributaries* in the text. Ask students to determine the word's meaning based on context clues in the sentence. **Ask:**

- **Based on this sentence, what are *tributaries*?** *(a system of waterways that flow into a larger body of water, such as the Congo River)*
- **What context clue in the sentence helped you determine the meaning of the word *tributaries*?** *(waterways)*
- **What word can you think of that shares the same root word as *tributaries*?** *(contribute)*
- **How does this word relate to the meaning of *tributaries*?** *(Sample response: The smaller networks of waterways contribute to the larger body of water—in this case, the Congo River.)* **AL** **ELL** **Verbal/Linguistic**

C Critical Thinking Skills

Predicting Consequences Have students read the section, "Difficult Navigation." Then review the meaning of the word *cataracts* with students: a large waterfall or steep rapids. Emphasize the fact that there are a series of cataracts at the mouth of the Congo River and that they block many ships from heading further inland. **Ask:**

- **How do you think the region might be impacted by cataracts that are at the mouth of the Congo River?** *(Sample response: Transportation of goods upriver may be a challenge. This may cause businesses to transport goods by land.)*
- **How do you think the port city of Matadi might be impacted by cataracts?** *(Sample response: Matadi is probably a bustling port city that is thriving economically because large ships are unable to go further upstream.)*
BL **Verbal/Linguistic**

MAP

The Route of the Congo River

Comparing and Contrasting Display the map which highlights the route of the Congo River to students. Have volunteers point out where it seems to start, where it stops, and the countries it flows through. Be sure that students understand that the map shows that the Congo is not navigable all the way through. Have students write a paragraph comparing the Congo River to the Nile River.
AL **Verbal/Linguistic**

See page 325C for other online activities.

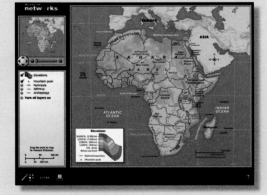

ANSWER, p. 329

CRITICAL THINKING The Congo River is navigable, but not for its entire course, because of cataracts and rapids that block the movement of ships.

330

R Reading Skills

Determining Cause and Effect Remind students to look for signal words as they read to help them identify cause-and-effect relationships. Tell students to be on the lookout for words that indicate a cause—*because, since, resulted from, due to.* The words *therefore, consequently, so,* and *as a result* indicate an effect. Have students work in pairs to identify the cause-and-effect relationships in the section, "Climate and Vegetation." **Ask:**

- What is the cause of the tropical climate in Central Africa? *(It is centered on the Equator.)*
- Why is the variation in length of days minimal from season to season in Central Africa? *(It is near the Equator.)*
- Identify two effects of Central Africa's location? *(Temperatures are warm to hot, and rainfall is plentiful.)*

Encourage students to identify signal words that indicate other cause-and-effect relationships as they read this page. **Verbal/Linguistic**

V Visual Skills

Creating Maps Have students work in small groups to create a weather map that depicts the information presented in the section, "Climate Zones." After groups have had time to prepare their maps, ask volunteers to present the information as if they are delivering a weather forecast for a television station in Central Africa. Encourage students to use different colors and images to represent higher and lower temperatures and the amount of rainfall in different regions.

As you refer to a map of Central Africa, guide a class discussion about the variation in climate as it relates to proximity to the Equator. **Ask: Which regions in Central Africa experience less rainfall based on their proximity to the Equator?** *(southern portions of the Democratic Republic of the Congo, northern parts of the Central African Republic, and northern Cameroon)* **ELL Visual/Spatial, Kinesthetic**

ANSWERS, p. 330

☑ **READING PROGRESS CHECK** It provides a livelihood for people living nearby; it is an important transportation artery; it is a source of hydroelectric power.

CRITICAL THINKING Camera traps enable researchers to obtain information about animals without disturbing or endangering the animals or their habitats.

A scientist and animal trackers analyze camera trap video of gorillas in a Central African rain forest. A camera trap is a camera equipped with a special sensor that captures images of wildlife on film, when humans are not present.
▶ **CRITICAL THINKING**
Analyzing How might camera traps aid in protecting Central African wildlife?

The Congo River is important to Central Africa for several reasons. First, it provides a livelihood for people who live along its banks. They use the river's water for agriculture and depend on its fish for food. Second, the river is a vital transportation artery. Although the cataracts and rapids prevent ships from navigating the entire river, ship traffic connects people and places along various sections of the river. Finally, dams on the river generate hydroelectric power.

☑ **READING PROGRESS CHECK**

Identifying Give two reasons for the Congo River's importance to Central Africa.

Climate and Vegetation

GUIDING QUESTION *What are the prevailing climates in Central Africa?*

Because Central Africa is centered on the Equator, the climate in much of the region is tropical. Temperatures are warm to hot, and rainfall is plentiful. The amount of rainfall generally decreases as distance from the Equator increases. In the northern and southern parts of the region, dry seasons alternate with wet seasons.

Climate Zones

The belt of Central Africa that lies along the Equator has a warm, wet climate. Because of its location, this zone experiences little seasonal variation in weather and length of daylight. The midday sun is directly or almost directly overhead every day, and daytime temperatures are always high. Rainfall is abundant throughout the year, with totals greater than 80 inches (203 cm) in some areas.

To the north and the south of the region's equatorial zone lie tropical wet-and-dry climate zones. As the name suggests, these zones have both rainy and dry seasons. There is great climate variation within the zones. In the areas nearest the Equator, the dry season typically lasts about four months. In the areas farthest from the Equator, it might last as long as seven months.

Rain Forest

A tropical rain forest, the second largest in the world, covers more than half of Central Africa. In this rain-soaked realm, closely packed trees soar as high as 15-story buildings. The forest also holds a

©Ian Nichols/National Geographic Society/Corbis

netw⊙rks   *Online Teaching Options*

IMAGE

Rain Forests of Gabon

Discussing Using the interactive image of the rain forests in Gabon, discuss with students how these rain forests developed. Guide a class discussion about the change from the Sahara to the rain forest. Help students make the connection to desertification of the Sahara and the Sahel as the development of deserts where there was once rain forests. Encourage students to make comparisons to rain forests previously described in other chapters and the dangers all rain forests face due to human-environment interaction. **AL Visual/Spatial, Verbal/Linguistic**

See page 325C for other online activities.

Interactive Photos

Lissa Harrison

tremendous variety of other plants, some of which are used in traditional medicines. Scientists think that only a fraction of the plant species in the forest have been identified. Most remain to be discovered.

The trees and other plants in the rain forest compete for survival. The interwoven crowns of the trees create a dense canopy, or roof, that blocks nearly all of the sunlight, leaving the lower levels in gloom. A tree seedling or sapling can only grow tall if a mature tree dies or if wind blows down some of its branches, creating an opening in the canopy. Because of the lack of sunlight, the forest floor has few of the small plants found in other types of forests. Instead, the forest floor is covered by dead leaves that decompose rapidly in the warm, wet conditions.

V

Savannas

In the northern and southern areas of Central Africa, rain forests give way to savannas, or areas with a mixture of trees, shrubs, and grasslands. The exact mix of vegetation depends on the length of the dry seasons. Human activity over thousands of years might be responsible for an increase in the size of the savanna areas. Experts believe that the change of forestland into savanna could be the result of clearing land through **slash-and-burn** agriculture.

R

This form of farming involves turning forestland into cropland. Trees and shrubs are cut down and burned in order to make the soil more fertile, at least temporarily.

©Nigel Pavitt/JAI/Corbis

Garamba National Park in the Democratic Republic of the Congo is home to the few surviving Northern white rhinoceroses.

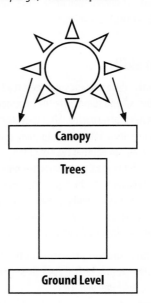

Chapter 11 **331**

Lissa Harrison

IMAGE

Slash-and-Burn Agriculture

Comparing Display the interactive image about slash-and-burn agriculture to discuss the pros and cons of this traditional method of agriculture. Lead a class discussion to compare this method to more modern day methods of clearing fields and on whether or not the method of slash-and-burn agriculture is harmful or beneficial to the environment. **AL** Verbal/Linguistic

See page 325C for other online activities.

Interactive Photos

V **Visual Skills**

Diagramming Have student volunteers read the section, "Rain Forest," aloud in class. Emphasize one of the main ideas in the section about the competition for sunlight in Central Africa's rain forests. After they read, have students work in pairs to create a drawing or diagram such as the one below. Remind students to look for cause-and-effect relationships as they read. **Ask:**

- **What is the effect of lack of sunlight at ground level in a rain forest?** *(Few plants can grow there, so the ground consists mostly of decomposing leaves.)*
- **What can help the growth of tree seedlings and saplings?** *(Wind damage or the death of a mature tree can create an opening in the canopy, allowing sunlight to reach seedlings and saplings.)* **Visual/Spatial**

| Canopy |
| Trees |
| Ground Level |

R **Reading Skills**

Defining Have students work in pairs to identify the definition of the term *slash-and-burn agriculture*, as it is used in the section, "Savannas." **Ask: How does the term slash-and-burn agriculture give you a clue about its meaning?** *(The term sounds like what it means: slashing trees and burning them to clear land.)* **ELL** **AL** Verbal/Linguistic

Argument Discuss the pros and cons of clearing land through slash-and-burn agriculture. Explain that this method allows farmers to make the soil temporarily more fertile, but it destroys forestland and pollutes the air.

Have students conduct research to learn more about the benefits and drawbacks of slash-and-burn agriculture. Tell students to write a paragraph to defend or refute the following prompt: **Slash-and-burn agriculture is vital to sustaining agriculture in Central Africa.**

Tell students to support their arguments using evidence based on research from reliable online sources. You may wish to recommend specific sites that offer facts on both sides of the issue, such as: http://www.eoearth.org/article/Slash_and_burn. Ask volunteers to read their argumentative paragraphs to the class. **BL** **Verbal/Linguistic**

Creating Visuals Have student volunteers read the section, "Natural Resources," and summarize the information about Central Africa's mineral resources. After they read, have students work in pairs to relate the information visually by creating a web diagram or other type of graphic organizer. Students may wish to organize the information according to region, in a center oval, with the type of mineral resources found in that region in surrounding ovals. Or, they may prefer to write a resource in a center oval, with regions where the resource is abundant in surrounding ovals. **Ask:**

- What mineral resources are found in the province of Katanga in the Democratic Republic of the Congo? *(cobalt, copper, gold, and uranium)*
- What are some of the minerals found in other areas of the Democratic Republic of the Congo? *(diamonds, iron ore, and limestone)*
- What type of metal is produced in Gabon? *(manganese)* **Visual/Spatial**

Miners search for gold in an open-pit mine in the northeastern part of the Democratic Republic of the Congo. For more than a decade, rival groups in the DRC have fought each other for control of the country's rich natural resources, such as gold, diamonds, and timber.

Within a few years, the soil becomes depleted and farmers move on. The plots of land are left so that trees and shrubs can return. Then the farmers return and repeat the process of cutting, burning, and farming. Sometimes plots remain fallow—that is, not planted—for as long as 20 years.

Slash-and-burn agriculture provides a livelihood for many people. Others, however, point out that it destroys plant and animal habitat, creates air pollution, and is causing the world's tropical forests to shrink at an alarming rate.

Those who support protecting the environment worry that activities that harm rain forests threaten biodiversity. **Biodiversity** refers to the wide variety of life on Earth. These conservationists argue that if ecosystems are wiped out, numerous valuable species will be lost forever.

W

✔ **READING PROGRESS CHECK**

Describing Imagine that you live in northern Cameroon. You decide to move to a location in the Republic of the Congo very near the Equator. What changes in climate can you expect?

Natural Resources

GUIDING QUESTION *Which natural resources are important in Central Africa?*

Central Africa is rich in mineral, energy, and other resources. However, many of these resources have not yet been developed.

Mineral Resources

V The greatest abundance of mineral resources in Central Africa is found in the Democratic Republic of the Congo. Within that country, the area richest in mineral resources is a province called Katanga. Katanga holds deposits of more than a dozen minerals, including cobalt, copper, gold, and uranium. Minerals mined in other areas of the country include diamonds, iron ore, and limestone.

Gabon produces more than a tenth of the world's supply of manganese. This hard, silvery metal is used in the manufacture of iron and steel. The country also produces uranium, diamonds, and gold, and it holds reserves of high-quality iron ore.

©FINBARR O'REILLY/Reuters/Corbis

IMAGE

Mining for Gold

Discussing Display the interactive image about gold mining to discuss with students the manual process of mining for gold. Have students describe what they are seeing in the image. Use this image to begin a class discussion about different resources in the region. Have students consider how each resource is developed or mined, and at what cost to the environment. **AL** **Verbal/Linguistic**

See page 325C for other online activities.

Interactive Photos

Lissa Harrison

ANSWERS, p. 332

✔ **READING PROGRESS CHECK** It will be warmer and wetter in the new location.

Bauxite and cobalt are among Cameroon's most significant mineral resources. Equatorial Guinea has deposits of uranium, gold, iron ore, and manganese. Most of these deposits have yet to be exploited. Diamond mining is an important industry in the Central African Republic. Rich deposits of uranium, gold, and other minerals could bring the country wealth in the future.

Why have the mineral resources in some parts of Central Africa remained underdeveloped? Political instability, civil conflict, and the high costs of investment have played a role. Perhaps the most important reason, however, is that the region lacks good transportation networks. In the Democratic Republic of the Congo, for example, the Congo River still serves as the major transportation artery. The landlocked Central African Republic also must use rivers for transport. It has few paved roads and no railways. Similarly, most roads in Equatorial Guinea are unpaved and there is no railway system. **R**

Other Resources

The region is rich in resources other than minerals. In the Democratic Republic of the Congo, for example, rapids and waterfalls on the Congo River and its tributaries offer vast **potential** for hydroelectric power. The forest reserves of the DRC are rivaled by few countries in the world. Fish from the ocean and its fresh water systems provide another important resource.

Developing these resources, however, will affect the environment. Damming rivers for hydroelectric power results in large changes to river ecosystems. Deforestation and habitat change occur when forests are cut. **T**

In the 1990s, large reserves of petroleum and natural gas were discovered under the seafloor off Equatorial Guinea's Atlantic Coast. The export of oil and gas products have boosted the country's economy.

Likewise, petroleum has been Cameroon's leading export since 1980. The country also has natural gas deposits, but the high cost of development has kept them untapped. Nearly all of Cameroon's energy comes from dams that generate hydroelectricity.

☑ **READING PROGRESS CHECK**

Identifying Central Issues What are two of the factors that have slowed development of Central Africa's rich natural resources?

Academic Vocabulary

potential possible; capable of becoming

FOLDABLES
Study Organizer
Include this lesson's information in your Foldable®.

LESSON 1 REVIEW (CCSS)

Reviewing Vocabulary (Tier Three Words)
1. Why might *slash-and-burn agriculture* be harmful to a country's land in the long term? RH.6-8.4

Answering the Guiding Questions
2. *Analyzing* What comparisons can you make between the Congo River in Central Africa and two of the other great rivers of the world: the Nile and the Amazon? RH.6-8.1

3. *Describing* What conclusion can you make about the prevailing climate conditions in areas near the Equator? RH.6-8.1

4. *Analyzing* How would you evaluate Central Africa's hydroelectric potential? RH.6-8.1

5. *Argument Writing* Write a letter to a friend to persuade him or her to invest in mineral production in Central Africa. In your letter, use some of the information you have learned in this lesson. WHST.6-8.1, WHST.6-8.9

Chapter 11 **333**

LESSON 1 REVIEW ANSWERS

Reviewing Vocabulary

1. Slash-and-burn agriculture destroys plant and animal habitat, pollutes the air, requires long fallow periods, and causes forests to shrink.

Answering the Guiding Questions

2. **Analyzing** The Congo is Africa's second-longest river, after the Nile; in terms of the rate of flow, the Congo is second in the world to the Amazon.

3. **Describing** Temperatures are extremely warm, and rainfall is constant and plentiful throughout the year.

4. **Analyzing** Central Africa possesses very high potential for hydroelectricity due to the rapids and waterfalls on the region's rivers.

5. **Argument Writing** The letter should mention some of the mineral sources found in Central Africa, and it should discuss the fact that most of the resources have not been exploited yet. It could also discuss obstacles to exploitation, which include political instability, civil conflict, high investment costs, and the lack of good transportation networks.

R Reading Skills

Citing Text Evidence Point out that the last paragraph in the section, "Mineral Resources," begins by asking a question. Tell students that this structure often indicates the answer to the question will follow. Have students work in pairs to identify text evidence by listing reasons that Central Africa's mineral resources have remained underdeveloped. *(political instability, civil conflict, high investment costs, lack of good transportation networks)* **Ask: What is an example of poor transportation in Central Africa?** *(Students should list one of the following examples: The Central African Republic has no access to the sea, few paved roads, and no railways; Equatorial Guinea has few paved roads and no railways.)* **AL** **Verbal/Linguistic**

T Technology Skills

Researching on the Internet Have students consider how a country's resources can affect its economy. Organize students into seven groups and assign each group a Central African country discussed in this lesson. Then, have student groups conduct online research to find additional information about resources in their assigned country. Direct them to find statistics about the country's natural resources and figures related to importing and exporting resources. Tell groups to interpret the information from their research in visual displays, such as charts or graphs. Students should prepare a short presentation in which they summarize their country's resources and economy using visuals to support their findings. **BL** **Visual/Spatial, Logical/Mathematical**

CLOSE & REFLECT

Recognizing Relationships Tell students to review the images in this lesson and write questions they may still have about Central Africa's physical geography. Have students think about the challenges that physical features present to its inhabitants. Encourage students to consider how people in Central African countries adapt to their environment. Guide a discussion about the relationship between a country's natural resources and the way people live.

ANSWER, p. 333

☑ **READING PROGRESS CHECK** Factors include political instability, civil conflict, high investment costs, and the lack of good transportation networks.

ENGAGE

Bellringer Tell students that this lesson discusses Central Africa's history, which involved the quest for independence after European colonization. Have students preview the lesson by skimming the headings, looking at the photographs, and reading the Guiding Questions. **Ask:** Based on your preview of this lesson, what issues have Central African countries struggled with over the years? *(Students may note that Central Africa has struggled with slavery and with obtaining freedom from colonial rule by European countries.)*

Tell students that they will learn more about the history of Central Africa in this lesson.

TEACH & ASSESS

C Critical Thinking Skills

Determining Cause and Effect Explain that before the development of agriculture, early people were hunters and gatherers who moved from place to place in search of food. **Ask:**

- **What happened as a result of the Earth's climate entering a dry phase?** *(Vegetation patterns changed and that led to the movement of people.)*
- **How did Earth's climate changes affect people's ability to survive?** *(People were forced to find food from a smaller area of their environment.)* **AL Verbal/Linguistic**

R Reading Skills

Sequencing Remind students that looking for time-order signal words can help them sequence events in a text. This can help them better understand events and their relationship to one another. Words such as *first, next, also, then, eventually, finally, furthermore,* and *last* show a continuation of time. Have students read the paragraphs in the section, "Development of Agriculture," and list words and phrases that indicate time order. *(Around 10,000 years ago, also, gradually, this led to, over time)* **Ask:**

- **What started the agricultural revolution?** *(People began to collect plants.)*
- **What happened next?** *(People developed and refined tools that were specially designed for digging. People also learned how to grow roots and tubers.)*
- **What happened over time?** *(The hunters and gatherers turned into farmers.)* **AL Logical/Mathematical**

ANSWER, p. 334

Taking Notes Products—palm oil and cassava;
European Contact—adoption of new crops

netw⊙rks

There's More Online!

☑ VIDEO

Academic Vocabulary RH.6-8.4 (Tier Two Words)
- **foundation**

Content Vocabulary RH.6-8.4 (Tier Three Words)
- **millet**
- **palm oil**
- **cassava**
- **colonialism**
- **missionary**
- **coup**

TAKING NOTES: *Key Ideas and Details* RH.6-8.2, RH.6-8.7

Organize Use a diagram like this one to note important information about the history of Central Africa, adding one or more facts to each of the boxes.

Topic	Information
Products	Millet Sorghum
European contact	Slave trade

334

Lesson 2
History of Central Africa

ESSENTIAL QUESTION · *How does technology change the way people live?*

IT MATTERS BECAUSE
Central Africa's past is a fascinating and often tragic story involving migrations, slavery, exploitation by foreign powers, and the struggle for independence, stability, and prosperity.

Early Settlement

GUIDING QUESTION *How did agriculture and trade develop in Central Africa?*

Through most of the prehistoric period, the people of Central Africa were hunters and gatherers who survived on wild game and wild plants. Eventually, climate changes forced the people to develop new ways of life.

Development of Agriculture
Around 10,000 years ago, Earth's climate entered a dry phase. Vegetation patterns changed in response and led to the movement of people. The changes also intensified the struggle for survival. The region's inhabitants were forced to find ways to get more food from a smaller area of their environment.

Gradually, a transformation that historians call the agricultural revolution swept through the region, beginning in the north. People began to collect plants—especially roots and tubers—on a more regular basis. They developed and refined tools such as stone hoes that were specially designed for digging. They discovered that if they planted a piece of a root or tuber in fertile soil, a new plant would grow from it. Over time, the hunters and gatherers turned into farmers.

Cereal farming was the next agricultural development in Central Africa. In the savannas of the north, people began cultivating **millet** and sorghum, two wild grasses that produce edible seeds. Millet proved to be especially well-suited to the

(l to r) Gary John Norman/Alamy; Mary Evans Picture Library/Alamy; UPPA/Photoshot; INTERFOTO/Personalities/Alamy

---

netw⊙rks *Online Teaching Options*

VIDEO

Congo Civil War

Giving Examples Use this video about the history of civil war in the Congo to introduce the lesson. As students watch the video, have them evaluate the information presented and write down key facts that they learned about Central Africa's history. Guide a class discussion in which students are asked to cite examples of topics discussed in the video. **AL Verbal/Linguistic, Interpersonal**

See page 325D for other online activities.

BBC Motion Gallery Education

area's climate. The crop thrives in high temperatures and is resistant to drought.

In addition to growing crops, Central Africa's early farmers cultivated trees and gathered their fruit. From the fruit of oil palms they made a cooking oil that was rich in proteins and vitamins. The nutrition boost provided by **palm oil** helped people to become healthier, and improved health brought about population growth.

W

The increase in the food supply from the practice of agriculture meant that people could live in larger, more settled communities. The agricultural revolution laid the **foundation** for village life and also for the development of items used in daily life.

R

Using Mineral Resources
Since early times, people in Central Africa have made tools from stone. Around 3,000 years ago, they began using a new material that was far better in many ways: iron. Iron tools were expensive and could only be made by skilled artisans, but they were far more efficient and less brittle than stone tools.

C

In addition to iron, people in ancient Central Africa made use of other minerals, especially copper and salt. These resources played an important role in trade.

☑ READING PROGRESS CHECK

Determining Central Ideas Why was the agricultural revolution so important for the development of Central Africa as a region?

European Contact and Afterward

GUIDING QUESTION *How did colonization by foreign countries affect Central Africa?*

Regular contact with Europeans, which began in the 1400s, marked the start of a new era in Central Africa's history.

The Slave Trade
As European ships began reaching the Atlantic coast of Central Africa in the 1400s, the region began developing into one of the busiest hubs of the slave trade. The trade was driven because European colonizers demanded a large workforce for their huge plantations in the Americas. The slave trade would continue and grow for more than three centuries.

The first European country to become actively involved in the slave trade was Portugal. In the late 1400s, the Portuguese established a colony on the island of São Tomé in order to grow sugar.

Academic Vocabulary

foundation the basis of something

A woman in Cameroon carries fruit from oil palm trees to market. The pulp from this fruit is used to make cooking oil. Some environmentalists fear that the creation of more palm oil plantations in the country will endanger the livelihood of small farmers and lead to the destruction of existing rain forests.

Gary John Norman/Alamy

Chapter 11 **335**

W **Writing Skills**

Argument Have students look at the photograph on this page and read the caption and second paragraph on this page. **Ask: What is a benefit of palm oil?** *(Students should mention that palm oil can be used for cooking and the proteins and vitamins in the oil have nutritional benefits.)*

Have students write a persuasive essay to answer the following question: **Should more palm oil plantations be created in Cameroon?** Tell students that they may conduct online research to support their arguments. *(Students' arguments should present a valid claim that is supported by evidence from the text and/or their research. Arguments in favor of additional plantations should cite benefits of palm oil. Arguments in favor of fewer plantations should show evidence of endangering the livelihood of small farmers and the destruction of rain forests in the region.)* **Verbal/Linguistic**

R **Reading Skills**

Determining Word Meanings Tell students that many words in the English language have different definitions as well as different connotations or shades of meaning. Have students work in pairs to look up the meaning of the word *foundation*. Have them list the word's different meanings and take turns using the word in a sentence. **Ask: How does the foundation of a house relate to the agricultural revolution?** *(Sample answer: The foundation of a house is its base or support, just like the agricultural revolution served as a base for village life in Central Africa.)* **ELL Verbal/Linguistic**

C **Critical Thinking Skills**

Comparing and Contrasting After reading the section, "Using Mineral Resources," make sure students understand the significance of the step from stone tools to iron tools by comparing and contrasting them. **Ask: How are stone and iron similar and different?** *(Both materials could be used to make tools, but iron tools could only be made by skilled artisans.)* **Logical/Mathematical**

SLIDE SHOW

Harvest in Central Africa

Making Connections After students view the slide show about crops that are important to Central Africa, have them identify crops grown by the farmers in their area. Lead a discussion about what food products are derived from these crops, and discuss agricultural practices such as organic gardening and genetic engineering. Have interested students use the Internet to research the practice of genetic engineering and the controversy surrounding genetically modified organisms (GMOs) and then present their findings to the class. **Verbal/Linguistic, Naturalist**

See page 325D for other online activities.

Slide Show

© Ocean/Corbis; Kryssia Campos/Flickr RF/Getty Images; Erica Simone Leeds; © IG Photography/Alamy

ANSWER, p. 335

☑ **READING PROGRESS CHECK** The agricultural revolution allowed people to settle down and build communities that were larger, more stable, and self-sufficient.

History of Central Africa

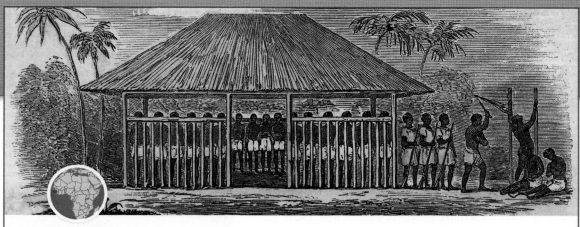

R Reading Skills

Determining Word Meanings Students may have trouble with some of the vocabulary in the section, "European Contact and Afterward." Have students read the paragraphs in the section, "The Slave Trade," and write down words they find confusing or do not understand, such as *estuary, enclosures,* and *barracoons.* Remind students that identifying word parts can help them better understand a word's meaning. For example, the prefix *en-* means "within" as in *encircle,* or "to put within a circle." **Ask:**

- **What word parts help you understand the meaning of** *enclosures***?** *(The prefix* en- *means "within or put into" and* close *means to shut or block, so enclosures are things that shut something in.)*
- **What English word is similar to the word** *barracoons***?** *(barricade or barrier)*
- **How does the meaning of the English word help you understand the meaning of barracoons?** *(A barricade is used to block something or close something in and barracoons were used to keep enslaved people in.)* **ELL Verbal/ Linguistic**

V Visual Skills

Interpreting Discuss the concept of triangular trade. Have partners interpret how triangular trade worked with a drawing, flow chart, or diagram. Encourage students to be creative but as accurate as possible in drawing visual representations of textual information. For example, to show how the stages of the trade "followed the direction of prevailing winds," students may draw a boat's billowing sails with an arrow indicating the wind's direction. **Ask:**

- **Where did ships travel in the first stage of triangular trade, and what goods did they carry?** *(from Europe to Africa; manufactured goods such as cloth, beads, metal goods, guns, and liquor)*
- **What did ships bring back in the last stage of triangular trade?** *(rum and goods such as tobacco, molasses, and cotton that were produced on slave-labor plantations)* **Visual/Spatial, Interpersonal**

Slave traders held people who were captured for slavery in *barracoons,* or sheds. There, the captives stayed for several months before they were sold and shipped to the Americas. During imprisonment, the captives were chained by the neck and legs and often beaten.
▶ **CRITICAL THINKING**
Determining Word Meaning What was the Middle Passage?

R

Later, this island became a staging area for the transportation of African slaves to Portugal's main conquest in the Western Hemisphere: Brazil in South America.

Gabon served as one of the most important centers of the slave trade. Slaves were gathered in the country's interior and taken on boats to a coastal inlet called the Gabon Estuary. Some of these slaves were people who had been cast out of their own societies. Others had been captured in warfare. At settlements on the estuary, the slaves were held in enclosures known as barracoons until European ships arrived.

V

The slave trade was part of what is sometimes called the "triangular trade," named for the triangular pattern formed by the three stages of the trade. In the first stage, ships would sail to Africa with cargoes of manufactured goods such as cloth, beads, metal goods, guns, and liquor. These goods would be traded for slaves. In the second stage, known as the Middle Passage, the ships would carry their human cargo to the Americas. There, the slaves would be exchanged for goods such as rum, tobacco, molasses, and cotton that were produced on slave-labor plantations. In the third stage, the ships would return to Europe. Ships of the time were powered by wind, and each stage followed the direction of prevailing winds.

Adoption of New Crops

After European countries established colonies in the Americas, they brought some of the native plants back to Europe and to Africa. Two plants in particular had an important effect on farming and diet in Central Africa. These were cassava and maize.

The **cassava** plant has thick, edible roots known as tubers. Rich in nutritious starch, the tubers are used to make flour, breads, and tapioca. The plant thrives in hot, sunny climates and is able to survive droughts and locust attacks. Historians believe that Portuguese ships brought cassava to Africa from Brazil. Today, cassava is a staple food for many of Africa's people.

Mary Evans Picture Library/Alamy

netw⊙rks *Online Teaching Options*

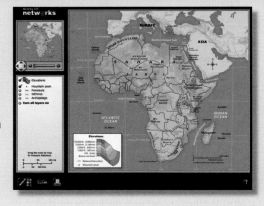

MAP

Triangular Trade

Discussing Display the map about triangular trade to students. Guide a class discussion about history of the African slave trade and its lasting impact on Central Africa. Ask student volunteers to create a flow chart on the board that depicts the process of triangular trade and its impact on Central Africa. **AL Visual/Spatial**

See page 325D for other online activities.

ANSWER, p. 336

Determining Word Meaning It was the second stage of the triangular trade. Enslaved people were shipped from Africa to the Americas.

Maize, often called corn, is one of the most important staple grains of the Western Hemisphere. Today it is the most widely grown grain crop in the Americas. Maize was domesticated in prehistoric times, probably in Central America. It was carried around the world by Europeans after their discovery of the Americas.

T

Colonialism

Colonialism is the political and economic rule of one region or country by another country, usually for profit. European countries began to practice colonialism in the 1500s and 1600s. They first founded colonies in the Americas for economic gain.

V

Colonialism came much later to Central Africa. Exploration and settlement by Europeans was impeded by the difficulty of transportation, the presence of tropical diseases like malaria, and other challenges. In the second half of the 19th century, however, European presence in the region began to grow sharply.

In 1884–1885, Germany hosted a landmark conference of European countries in the city of Berlin. The countries attending the conference agreed on a plan for dividing Africa into colonies that could be exploited for European profit.

King Leopold II of Belgium was among the strongest supporters of the conference. He believed that a fortune could be made from rubber plants. Rubber was one of the most plentiful and valuable natural resources of Central Africa. After 1885, King Leopold took over a vast area that came to be known as the Congo Free State. The king held the area as a personal possession, and he did indeed make a fortune.

Belgium's King Leopold II (oval) turned his privately owned Congo territory into a large labor camp for the harvesting of rubber. African workers (below) were overseen by European officials. Nearly 10 million Africans died of overwork or cruelty under Leopold's direct rule.

Chapter 11 **337**

T **Technology Skills**

Researching on the Internet Discuss the importance of maize, or corn, as a staple grain. Organize students into small groups and assign the following activity for homework. Have each group conduct online research to identify where corn is grown in the Americas and its various uses. Have groups prepare a presentation based on their findings that includes a summary and visuals. Encourage students to find a variety of products made from corn. Tell students to identify the products, such as ethanol and corn syrup, and list their benefits and potential hazards. Share the Content Background Knowledge with students to provide context for the controversy surrounding high-fructose corn syrup. After groups have made their presentations, guide a class discussion about the uses of corn. **Ask:**

- **What is corn syrup?** *(Corn syrup is made from cornstarch and is used as a sweetener.)*
- **What is ethanol and how is it used?** *(It is a grain alcohol made from corn and other starches that can be added to gasoline for cars.)* **Logical/Mathematical, Interpersonal**

V **Visual Skills**

Creating Visuals Have partners work together to create a visual representation of the word *colonialism* as it relates to Central Africa. For example, students may draw a flow chart or web diagram with the word *colonialism* in the center and arrows pointing to other words or names of countries.

Encourage students to think of a way to show colonialism with an equation, such as: **Colonialism = Political and Economic Rule of a country or region + Profit.** Then, **ask: Why did European countries practice colonialism in Central Africa?** *(They sought economic gain from resources in other countries.)* **ELL** **Visual/Spatial, Interpersonal**

Content Background Knowledge

Share the following information with students to provide some context for understanding the controversy surrounding high-fructose corn syrup.

- Scientific studies have shown that consuming high-fructose corn syrup, a sweetener made from corn, can cause weight gain. Studies have linked consumption of the sweetener to obesity due to significant weight gain in lab animals.
- In a meal purchased from a fast-food restaurant, most of the products consumed are made from or produced with corn: corn-fed beef in hamburgers, high fructose corn syrup in the bun and sauce, French fries fried in corn oil, and the corn syrup in sodas.

MAP

Resistance to Colonization

Integrating Visual Information Display the map of the European colonies in Central Africa. Have students write a cause-and-effect paragraph explaining what encouraged the countries of Europe to colonize, what happened as a result of colonization, and why the people of Central Africa were resistant. Use the map's features to place the countries that were colonized in chronological order. **BL** **Verbal/Linguistic**

See page 325D for other online activities.

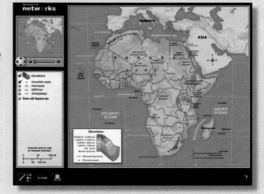

History of Central Africa

C1 Critical Thinking Skills

Formulating Questions Before students answer the Map Skills questions, have them work with a partner to analyze the map. Tell students to write down any questions they have about the various countries shown on the map. For example, students may want to know how certain countries got their names.

Guide students to understand that a republic is a form of government in which citizens are ruled by elected officials. The Republic of the Congo has a president and two legislative houses, the Senate and the National Assembly. **Ask: How is the government of the Republic of the Congo similar to that of the United States?** *(The United States is also a republic led by a president with two legislative houses, but the United States has a senate and a house of representatives.)* **Verbal/Linguistic**

R Reading Skills

Using Context Clues Ask a volunteer to read aloud the second paragraph on this page. Have students work in pairs to determine the meaning of *exploitation* based on context clues in the sentence. **Ask: What context clues in the sentence help you understand the meaning of the word *exploitation*?** *(justified, claiming)* Guide students to understand that exploitation, in this case of Africa, refers to the mistreatment or abuse of something or someone. **AL Verbal/Linguistic**

C2 Critical Thinking Skills

Making Inferences Discuss the colonization of Central Africa by Europeans with students. **Ask:**

- **How do you think Central Africans felt about Europeans?** *(Sample answer: They probably resented Europeans for trying to convert them to Christianity and for treating African workers poorly.)*
- **What do you think Central Africans did in response to European colonization?** *(Sample answer: They probably made attempts to seek independence from Europeans' harsh rule.)* **Verbal/Linguistic**

ANSWERS, p. 338

✓ **READING PROGRESS CHECK** At the conference, European countries agreed on a plan to divide up and exploit Central Africa.

MAP SKILLS

1. Both lands are affected by the Congo River and its tributaries. Each land was once ruled by a different European power—Congo (France) and the Democratic Republic of the Congo (Belgium) and became independent under the same name.
2. The Central African Republic is landlocked, with no direct access to the ocean.

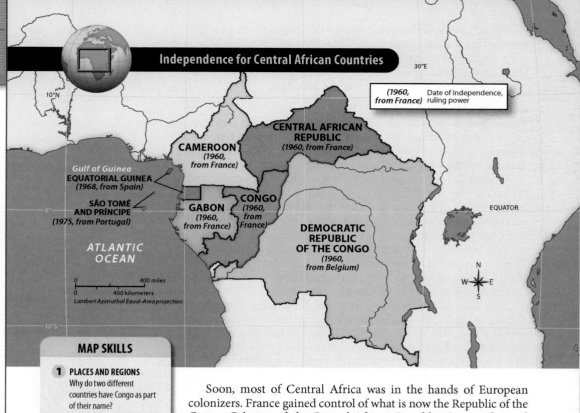

Independence for Central African Countries

(1960, from France) Date of independence, ruling power

CENTRAL AFRICAN REPUBLIC (1960, from France)

CAMEROON (1960, from France)

Gulf of Guinea

EQUATORIAL GUINEA (1968, from Spain)

SÃO TOMÉ AND PRÍNCIPE (1975, from Portugal)

GABON (1960, from France)

CONGO (1960, from France)

ATLANTIC OCEAN

DEMOCRATIC REPUBLIC OF THE CONGO (1960, from Belgium)

EQUATOR

0   400 miles
0   400 kilometers
Lambert Azimuthal Equal-Area projection

MAP SKILLS

1 **PLACES AND REGIONS** Why do two different countries have Congo as part of their name?

2 **THE GEOGRAPHER'S WORLD** What country of Central Africa is landlocked?

Soon, most of Central Africa was in the hands of European colonizers. France gained control of what is now the Republic of the Congo, Gabon, and the Central African Republic. Spain colonized what is now Equatorial Guinea, while Germany ruled Cameroon. Portugal retained possession of São Tomé and Príncipe.

Europeans often justified their economic exploitation of Africa by claiming that their goal was to promote civilization and to spread Christianity. Europeans sent many **missionaries** to Africa in order to convert the native people.

At the same time, Europeans often treated the African workers under their control harshly. By the early 1900s, small revolts against French rule and the plantation-based economy were common. In the Congo Free State, the people suffered severe hardships and cruel treatment under King Leopold. Pressured by growing outrage from around the world, the Belgian parliament took over the vast area from King Leopold. It became an official colony of Belgium and was known as the Belgian Congo.

☑ **READING PROGRESS CHECK**

Determining Central Ideas How was Central Africa affected by a conference held in Germany in the mid-1880s?

338 Chapter 11

---

networks   *Online Teaching Options*

GAME

Drag-and-Drop: Historical Changes in Central Africa

Displaying Using the drag-and-drop game, have student pairs review the countries in Central Africa including the name of each country, the European country to colonize the Central African nation, the date that each country in Central Africa was colonized, and the date each Central African country achieved its independence. Use this activity to review the content of this lesson. **AL Kinesthetic**

See page 325D for other online activities.

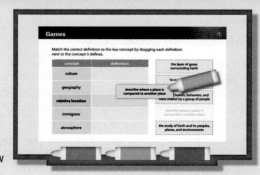

Independent Countries

GUIDING QUESTION *What effects did gaining independence have on the countries of Central Africa?*

Near the middle of the 20th century, European countries became willing to grant independence to their African colonies. All seven of Central Africa's countries gained their independence in the period from 1960 to 1975.

A Wave of Independence

In 1960 France was the most important European colonial power in Central Africa. That year witnessed the independence of four French colonies: Gabon, the Republic of the Congo, the Central African Republic, and Cameroon, which France had gained from Germany during World War I. In the same year, the Democratic Republic of the Congo won independence from Belgium.

Many of these new countries experienced hard times after independence. Their people suffered through periods of ethnic conflict, harsh rule, and human rights abuses. In the Central African Republic, military officer Jean-Bédel Bokassa staged a **coup**. He ruled as a dictator and proclaimed himself the country's emperor. He brutally punished anyone who protested against his rule.

There have also been success stories, such as Gabon. Thanks in large part to its plentiful natural resources, Gabon has become one of the wealthiest and most stable countries in Africa.

Smaller Countries

Equatorial Guinea won independence from Spain in 1968. The country's first president, Francisco Macías Nguema, soon took over the government and became a ruthless dictator. In 1979, he was ousted by his nephew, who also ruled with an iron hand.

Portugal granted independence to São Tomé and Príncipe in 1975. With independence came great hope for the future. Like many of its neighbors, however, the country has been plagued by political instability and corruption.

☑ **READING PROGRESS CHECK**

Identifying Since the countries of the region gained independence, list at least two factors that have limited their political and economic progress.

FOLDABLES
Study Organizer

Include this lesson's information in your Foldable®.

LESSON 2 REVIEW CCSS

Reviewing Vocabulary (Tier Three Words)
1. Why was *millet* a suitable grain for planting in Central Africa? RH.6-8.4

Answering the Guiding Questions
2. *Determining Central Ideas* Why might tools made from iron be superior to tools made from stone? RH.6-8.2
3. *Identifying* What were two major motivations for the European colonization of Central Africa? RH.6-8.1

4. *Analyzing* In what way was the rule of Bokassa in the Central African Republic similar to the rule of Nguema in Equatorial Guinea? RH.6-8.1
5. *Informative/Explanatory Writing* Write a few paragraphs explaining the development of the slave trade in Central Africa. WHST.6-8.2, WHST.6-8.10

Chapter 11 **339**

LESSON 2 REVIEW ANSWERS

Reviewing Vocabulary

1. Millet thrives in high temperatures and is resistant to drought.

Answering the Guiding Questions

2. **Determining Central Ideas** They might have used iron tools to dig holes for planting, to dig up roots and tubers, and to chop down trees and shrubs.

3. **Identifying** European countries were motivated by the desire to gain economic profit, promote civilization in undeveloped areas, and spread Christianity.

4. **Analyzing** They both ruled as dictators.

5. **Informative/Explanatory Writing** Essays should discuss when the slave trade began, why and where slaves were in demand, and triangular trade.

C1 Critical Thinking Skills

Identifying Central Issues Discuss the independence movement that swept across Central Africa in the 1960s by having students summarize the section, "A Wave of Independence." Then, **ask:**

- **What role did France play in Central Africa in 1960?** *(France was the most important European colonial power in Central Africa in 1960.)*
- **Which colonies in Central Africa became independent at that time?** *(Gabon, the Republic of the Congo, the Central African Republic, and Cameroon became independent from France, and the Democratic Republic of the Congo became independent from Belgium.)* **Verbal/Linguistic**

C2 Critical Thinking Skills

Determining Cause and Effect Guide a class discussion about the transition from colonization to independence for Central African countries. Have students consider the expectations people who lived under colonial rule might have had after gaining their independence. **Ask:**

- **What was the effect of independence on some of the new countries in Central Africa?** *(They experienced hard times, and their people suffered through periods of ethnic conflict, harsh rule, and human rights abuses.)*
- **How was the Central African Republic ruled after gaining independence?** *(Military officer Jean-Bédel Bokassa ruled as a dictator and punished anyone who protested against his rule.)* **BL Logical/Mathematical**

R Reading Skills

Paraphrasing Have students work in pairs to read about the transition from colonial rule to independence in Central Africa. Tell partners to take turns paraphrasing each paragraph in the section "A Wave of Independence." **Ask:** Which Central African country has become one of Africa's wealthiest and most stable countries, and why? *(Gabon has become relatively wealthy and stable by taking advantage of its plentiful natural resources.)* **Interpersonal**

CLOSE & REFLECT

Evaluating To close this lesson, have students think about all the hardships that the people of Central Africa have endured, both before and after gaining their freedom from colonial rule. Guide students to consider the pros and cons of independence.

ANSWER, p. 339

☑ **READING PROGRESS CHECK** Factors include political instability, harsh rule, corruption, ethnic conflict, and human rights abuses.

ENGAGE

 Bellringer Review with students the effects that gaining independence had on countries in Central Africa. Explain that the battle to win independence by most Central African countries was relatively recent. Ask students to consider how this newfound independence might influence Central African countries today. Have students write down any positive and negative consequences they predict might result from this newly gained independence with regard to a country's political, economic, and social progress.

TEACH & ASSESS

C Critical Thinking Skills

Making Connections Discuss the figures cited in the text relating to Central Africa's population growth rates. Explain that "median age" refers to the middle or average age in that country. Guide students to understand the relationship between a region's population makeup and its economic and social impact. **Ask:**

- What might be some issues facing Central Africa with regard to the age of its population? *(Sample answer: Central Africa likely faces issues with schools and how to best educate its large population of young people. Businesses may also face challenges with having an adequate work force due to the number of young people who are not old enough to work yet.)*

- How might these needs differ from those of the United States? *(Sample answer: The needs of Central Africa's population relate more to young people, whereas the United States' population is older. The United States' population likely has more of an impact on housing and employment opportunities than issues related to schools and education.)*

  BL Interpersonal

ANSWER, p. 340

Taking Notes People—mosaic of numerous groups; many different languages; relatively low density; majority of people live in rural areas except in countries such as Gabon; **Daily Life and Culture**—subsistence farming in the country; gendered activities; blend of traditional ways with modern lifestyles; activity in the visual, verbal, and performance arts

---

netw🌐rks

There's More Online!

☑ **SLIDE SHOW** Types of Housing in Central Africa

☑ **VIDEO**

Reading HELPDESK CCSS

Academic Vocabulary RH.6-8.4

- **characteristic** (Tier Two Words)
- **depict**

Content Vocabulary RH.6-8.4

- **refugee** (Tier Three Words)
- **trade language**

TAKING NOTES: *Key Ideas and Details* RH.6-8.2, RH.6-8.7

Find the Main Idea As you study the lesson, create a chart like this one, and fill in at least two key facts about each topic.

Topic	Fact #1	Fact #2
People		
Daily Life and Culture		

Lesson 3
Life in Central Africa

ESSENTIAL QUESTION · *What makes a culture unique?*

IT MATTERS BECAUSE
Central Africa is characterized by tremendous diversity in terms of its people, population patterns, languages, arts, and daily life.

The People of Central Africa

GUIDING QUESTION *What are some of the differences found among the people of Central Africa?*

Many different ethnic groups live in Central Africa. Each group is united by a shared language and culture.

Makeup of the Population

Central Africa is home to around 105 million people, which is roughly one-third as many as the United States has. The Democratic Republic of the Congo is by far the most populous country: It holds more than two-thirds of the region's people. Compared to other parts of the world, Central Africa does not have a large population or a high population density. However, its countries have high population growth rates. In all seven countries, the median age is below 20, which means that children and teenagers make up about half of the population. By comparison, the median age in the United States is about 37.

Life expectancy at birth for the people of the region varies considerably. In the Central African Republic, for example, life expectancy is about 50 years, while in Equatorial Guinea and São Tomé and Príncipe, it is around 63.

Hundreds of ethnic groups live in the region. Cameroon and the DRC each are home to more than 200 different groups. Some groups spread into two or more countries. One

(l to r) MJ Photography/Alamy; Eye Ubiquitous/Glow Images; Junior D. Kannah/AFP/Getty Images; ©Pascal Deloche/Godong/Corbis

---

netw🌐rks *Online Teaching Options*

VIDEO

The Kings of the Congo

Use this video about the mountain gorillas of the Congo, and the dangers they face due to human-environment interaction, to introduce the lesson. Have students write a paragraph about an aspect of life for the gorillas and the people in the Congo that they found interesting or that surprised them. Guide a class discussion about how the needs of daily life in modern-day Central Africa pose risks to the wildlife and the people that live there. **AL** Verbal/Linguistic

See page 325E for other online activities.

BBC Motion Gallery Education

such group is called the Fang. Historians believe the Fang once dwelled on the savanna. In the late 18th century, they began a migration into the rain forests. Today they live in mainland Equatorial Guinea, northern Gabon, and southern Cameroon.

Another people found in the region is the Bambuti, sometimes called the Mbuti. The Bambuti live in densely forested areas of the Democratic Republic of the Congo. They are extremely short in stature: Adults average less than 4 feet 6 inches (137 cm) in height. They were probably the earliest inhabitants of an area known as the Ituri Forest. Historical records show that the Bambuti have lived in this area for at least 4,500 years as nomadic hunters and gatherers.

The population of Central Africa also includes many refugees. **Refugees** are displaced people who have been forced to leave their homes because of war or injustice. Between 1997 and 2003, for example, a brutal civil war devastated the Democratic Republic of the Congo. A huge number of refugees fled the conflict.

R

City and Country

Most of Central Africa's people live in the rural areas and make their living through subsistence farming. In the DRC, for example, almost two-thirds of the people live in the country.

Large urban areas dot the region, however. More importantly, the ratio of city-dwellers to rural residents is changing rapidly. For example, every year, the DRC's urban areas gain about 4.5 percent of the population. Many of the chief cities of the region are capitals of countries. Kinshasa, the capital of the DRC, has grown into a sprawling metropolis with around 9 million inhabitants. Just across the Congo River from Kinshasa sits Brazzaville, the capital of the Republic of the Congo. Brazzaville is home to about 1.6 million people.

V

MJ Photography/Alamy

Government buildings surround a busy central square in Brazzaville, capital of the Republic of the Congo. Brazzaville is located on the north bank of the Congo River, just across from Kinshasa, the capital of the neighboring Democratic Republic of the Congo. This is the only place in the world where two national capital cities are located on opposite sides of a river, within sight of each other.

Chapter 11 341

R Reading Skills

Determining Word Meanings Point out the content vocabulary word *refugees* in the section, "Makeup of the Population." Remind students that understanding the meaning of a base word can help them identify the meaning of an unfamiliar word. **Ask:**

- **What is the base word for the word *refugees*?** *(refuge)*
- **How might this word provide a clue to the meaning of *refugees*?** *(Sample answer: A refuge is a safe haven and refugees are people who are looking for a safe place to live.)*
  AL **ELL** **Verbal/Linguistic**

W

V Visual Skills

Comparing and Contrasting Discuss the differences between life in Central Africa's rural and urban areas. Have student pairs work together to create a diagram or chart that organizes the information in the section, "City and Country." Suggest that students label one side of their diagram "Urban" and the other "Rural." **Ask:**

- **How does the population of the Democratic Republic of the Congo change each year?** *(Every year its urban areas gain about 4.5 percent of the population.)*
- **How do Central Africa's rural areas compare to its cities?** *(Most people in Central Africa live in rural areas, but Central Africa does have major cities, many that are capitals of countries and are home to many people.)* **AL** **Visual/Spatial**

W Writing Skills

Argument Have students analyze the photograph and read the caption on this page. Tell students that the capital cities of Kinshasa and Brazzaville are likely to become one of the world's largest metropolitan areas by 2025. Have students consider the issues that might result from two large capital cities being located so close together and then write a three-paragraph proposal to one of the city's governing bodies with suggestions on how to deal with three anticipated issues. Student arguments should provide positive suggestions for handling future problems. **BL** **Verbal/Linguistic**

GRAPHS

Population of Central Africa

Determining Cause and Effect Display the graphs that show the different aspects of population in Central Africa to discuss the changes, population distribution, and population density in the region. Guide students to understand the cause-and-effect relationship between population changes and issues that impact today's cities, such as crime, a shortage of services, and overcrowding. **BL** **Visual/Spatial**

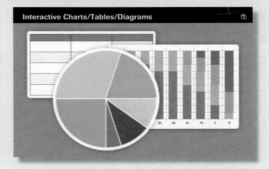

Interactive Charts/Tables/Diagrams

See page 325E for other online activities.

Life in Central Africa

V Visual Skills

Creating Graphs Have students work with a partner to create a graph that depicts information presented in the section, "City and Country." Have students use a software program to create a bar, circle, or line graph that shows the population percentages of Central African countries mentioned in the text.

Review with students the steps to convert a percent into a fraction. For example, tell students that 50% is written as 50/100, which can be simplified to 5/10, or 1/2. Then have students convert the information about Central African countries' population percentages into fractions. **Ask:**

- **Approximately what fraction of Gabon's population lives in cities?** *(86/100 or 43/50)*
- **What fraction of the Central African Republic's population lives in cities?** *(62/100 or 31/50)*
- **What fraction of Cameroon's population are city dwellers?** *(58/100 or 29/50)* **Logical/Mathematical**

T Technology Skills

Creating Maps Discuss the ethnic diversity of Central Africa's population, as described in the section, "Language and Religion." **Ask: Why do you think Cameroon is described as an "ethnic crossroads"?** *(It is home to many different ethnic groups who speak several different languages.)*

Have students create a map that shows the different languages spoken in different parts of Cameroon. Students may wish to conduct online research to find specific regions where certain languages are spoken. Tell students to use poster board and colored pencils or markers to show regions where each language is spoken. Have students present their posters along with a short paragraph that summarizes the ethnic and linguistic makeup of Cameroon. **BL Visual/Spatial**

Village women of the Hutu ethnic group prepare a meal in the eastern part of the Democratic Republic of the Congo. The Hutu are one of hundreds of ethnic groups in Central Africa.
▶ **CRITICAL THINKING**
Describing Why did trade languages emerge in Central Africa?

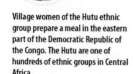

In a few countries in this region, more than half the people live in cities. In Gabon, for example, city-dwellers account for 86 percent of the total population. In the Central African Republic, the figure is 62 percent, and in Cameroon it is 58 percent. Cameroon's two major cities, Douala and Yaoundé, each have populations of around 2 million, roughly the population of Houston or Philadelphia.

Language and Religion

Because Central Africa's population is made up of hundreds of different ethnic groups, it is not surprising that hundreds of different languages are spoken across the region. Cameroon, which has been described as an ethnic crossroads, serves as an example of the region's linguistic diversity. Three main language families are used in Cameroon. In the north, where Islam has been a significant influence, the languages spoken are in the Sudanic family. The Sudanic-speaking people in this part of Cameroon include the Fulani, the Sao, and the Kanuri. The Fulani are Muslims. They began migrating into Cameroon from what is now Niger more than 1,000 years ago. In the southern part of Cameroon, people speak Bantu languages. In the west are found semi-Bantu speakers, such as the Bamileke and the Tikar.

During the colonial era, people searched for common linguistic ground, especially when they traded with one another. Certain **trade languages** emerged. Because France and Belgium had the most widespread interest in the region, French became the most common trade language of Central Africa.

---

networks *Online Teaching Options*

IMAGES

Rural and City Life in Central Africa

Comparing and Contrasting Display the interactive images that compare rural and city life in Central Africa to students. Have students write a paragraph describing the similarities and differences between rural and city life in Central African countries. **AL Verbal/Linguistic**

See page 325E for other online activities.

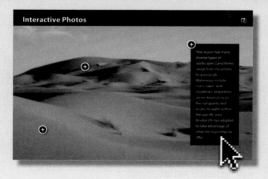

Interactive Photos

Central Africa is also diverse in terms of religion. In the Democratic Republic of the Congo, for example, roughly 50 percent of the people are Roman Catholic, 20 percent are Protestant, 10 percent are Muslim, and 10 percent belong to a local sect called the Kimbanguist Church. The remaining 10 percent follow traditional African religions, which are based on a core set of beliefs, including the existence of a supreme being, the presence of spirits in the natural world, and the power of ancestors and magic.

V

☑ **READING PROGRESS CHECK**

Describing Where do most of Central Africa's people live? How do they make their living?

How People Live

GUIDING QUESTION *What are some of the key aspects of daily life and culture in Central Africa?*

In Central Africa, daily life and culture reflect the variety of influences to which the region has been exposed.

Daily Life

C

Daily life in Central Africa is a blend of traditional and modern **characteristics**. This combination results mainly from the impact of colonialism. It also reflects the urban-rural division of the population.

In the countryside, most people practice subsistence farming. On small plots of land, they grow crops such as cassava, maize, and millet, and they raise livestock. They strive to grow enough crops and raise enough animals to feed themselves and their families. If any surplus remains, they may sell it for small amounts of cash. Most people in the countryside live in small houses that they have built themselves. Building materials include mud, sundried mud bricks, wood, bark, and cement. For roofs, people typically use palm fronds woven together or sheets of corrugated iron.

One of the most common methods of constructing houses is known as wattle-and-daub. Poles driven into the ground are woven with slender, flexible branches or reeds to create the wattle. The finished wattle is plastered with mud or clay, known as daub. Then, a palm-frond roof is placed on top of the house.

R

In much of rural Central Africa, women carry out the gathering, production, and preparation of food for the household. The men hunt, trap, and fish. In addition to growing food to eat, men and women may also grow crops for sale, such as coffee, cotton, and cocoa.

Okra, corn, and yams are staple vegetables in the diets of many Central Africans. Other important foods are cassava, sweet potatoes, rice, beans, and plantains. Game is popular, as are fish-based dishes. Peanuts, milk, and poultry add protein to many dishes.

Academic Vocabulary

characteristic a quality or an aspect

Chapter 11 **343**

V Visual Skills

Creating Graphs Have students create a graph showing city populations and the diversity of religions among the people in the Democratic Republic of the Congo. Before they create their graphs, tell students to convert the percentages to fractions. *(DRC = 1/2 Roman Catholic, 1/5 Protestant, 1/10 Muslim, 1/10 members of Kimbanguist Church, and 1/10 belong to traditional African religions)* **Visual/Spatial**

C Critical Thinking Skills

Determining Cause and Effect Have student volunteers provide some of the main ideas about the history of Central Africa that they learned about in Lesson 2. **Ask:**

- **Based on what you know about the history of the region, what has had a lasting impact on Central Africa?** *(Sample answer: The influence of colonialism has had a major impact on the daily life of people who live in the region.)*

- **What has been another cause of Central Africa's unique blend of characteristics?** *(The urban-rural division of the population has caused daily life to be a blend of both traditional and modern ways.)* **AL Logical/Mathematical**

R Reading Skills

Summarizing Have students work in pairs to summarize the information in the section, "Daily Life," about farming, housing, and life in Central Africa. Remind students that a summary includes only main ideas and should not include minor details. **Ask:**

- **What is the main idea of how people support themselves?** *(People use subsistence farming to support themselves.)*

- **What are some materials that the people of Central Africa use for building houses?** *People use mud, sundried mud bricks, wood, bark, and cement. For roofs, they typically use woven palm fronds or sheets of corrugated iron.)* **AL Verbal/Linguistic**

SLIDE SHOW

Types of Housing in Central Africa

Classifying Display the slide show of various types of housing in Central Africa to students. Review the images and have volunteers describe what they see. Discuss with students the material used and the way each house is constructed. Have students create a chart to organize the information presented in the text and the slide show. **ELL Visual/Spatial**

See page 325E for other online activities.

Slide Show

ANSWER, p. 343

☑ **READING PROGRESS CHECK** in rural areas; through subsistence farming

C

C Critical Thinking Skills

Identifying Problems Discuss with the class how many African cities are moving from traditional ways of life to more contemporary lifestyles. **Ask: Why do you think modernization has been slow to come to some parts of Central Africa?** *(Central Africa has little infrastructure, so it lacks modern facilities such as adequate health care facilities and efficient transportation. Educational systems are also poor in regions that have been undeveloped.)* **Verbal/Linguistic**

T Technology Skills

Making Presentations Guide a class discussion about the different cultures of Central Africa and how people there express themselves artistically. After students read the section, "Culture and Arts," organize them into small groups and assign each group a particular aspect of Central African culture and arts. Then have groups complete the following activity for homework:

Tell students to research their cultural or artistic aspect for a Central African Culture Fair in which each group will highlight an aspect of Central African culture. Have students conduct online research to find more information about their assigned cultural aspect. In preparation for the Culture Fair, encourage students to find samples of music, dance, theater, and literature. They may also wish to share traditional food dishes with the class. Tell students their presentations should answer this question: **What is unique about your assigned Central African cultural aspect or form of artistic expression?**

Students who are musically and theatrically inclined may wish to perform a sampling of traditional music by playing an instrument, singing a traditional song, or performing a traditional dance. After groups have made their presentations, facilitate a class discussion about the cultural diversity in Central Africa. **BL Auditory/Musical, Kinesthetic**

Many food-related customs of Central Africa may seem surprising. In some areas, for example, males eat in one room while females eat in another. Generosity and hospitality are so deeply ingrained in some cultures that hosts might offer guests an abundance of food while remaining hungry themselves.

In many Central African cities, traditional ways of life are yielding to contemporary lifestyles. Modernization, however, has not always come easily. Central Africa has little infrastructure, which includes the fundamental facilities and systems that serve a city, an area, or a country. In the Central African Republic, for example, only a few cities and towns have modern health care facilities. Other obstacles to modernization include poor transportation and educational systems.

Culture and Arts

The visual, verbal, and performing arts are important to the cultures of many ethnic groups in Central Africa. In the southwestern part of the DRC, for example, the people known as the Kongo produce wooden statues in which nails and other pieces of metal are embedded. The Yaka create highly decorative masks and figurines. The Luba people of the southeastern part of the country are known for their skillful carvings that **depict** women and motherhood. The Mangbetu people of the northeast are known internationally for their pottery and sculpture.

In the field of literature, several modern Congolese authors are internationally recognized as poets, playwrights, and novelists. They include Clémentine Madiya Faik-Nzuji, Kama Kamanda, Ntumb Diur, and Timothée Malembe.

The DRC's capital city of Kinshasa is known around the world for its thriving music scene. The most popular style is African jazz, known as OK jazz. This style originated in the nightclubs of Kinshasa in the 1950s.

In northern Cameroon, the Fulani people decorate leather items and gourds with elaborate geometric designs. In music, the country's southern forest region is known for its drumming. In the north, the focus is on flute music.

Equatorial Guinea was formerly a colony of Spain, and Spanish influence can be tasted in the country's cuisine. In Malabo, the capital city, Spanish styles are found in the architecture. The country has produced several writers whose Spanish-language works have become known around the world.

Musicians of the Congolese Symphony Orchestra perform in Kinshasa, capital of the DRC.
▶ **CRITICAL THINKING**
Describing Why is Kinshasa widely regarded as one of the music centers of the world?

Junior D. Kannah/AFP/Getty Images

☑ **READING PROGRESS CHECK**
Determining Word Meanings What is the main goal of subsistence farmers?

---

netwrks   *Online Teaching Options*

CHART

Social Issues in Central Africa

Discussing Using the chart with information about hospitals in Central Africa, work with students to compare that information to the statistics about hospitals in the United States. Guide a class discussion about the education levels, income levels of people in the Central Africa, health concerns, and economic struggles, and possible ways to improve these social issues.
AL Interpersonal

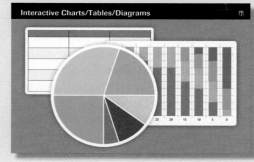

Interactive Charts/Tables/Diagrams

See page 325E for other online activities.

ANSWERS, p. 344

☑ **READING PROGRESS CHECK** to grow enough crops and raise enough animals to feed themselves and their families

Regional Issues

C

GUIDING QUESTION *What are the greatest challenges confronting Central Africa?*

Central Africa's people and governments face many complex issues. Among the issues are the economy, the environment, political stability, and population growth.

Growth and the Environment

W

With great population growth comes the need for economic development. The economies of many countries in the region depend heavily on agriculture, logging, and mining. Central African countries such as Gabon and Equatorial Guinea export significant amounts of valuable hardwoods, including mahogany, ebony, and okoumé.

In general, economic development depends on economic growth. Economic growth usually means that more resources are used and more pollution and waste are produced. In Central Africa, economic activities such as mining and logging are taking place in areas of high biodiversity. Some conservationists fear that this biodiversity is being lost in the rush to exploit resources.

The result is tension between the forces of economic growth and the forces of environmental conservation. In some areas, these tensions have at times led to conflict between local people and outside groups.

Development in Central Africa also raises other questions. Should the profits from economic activities go to foreign corporations and investors, or should they remain with the national governments? How should the profits and economic benefits be shared by the people?

☑ **READING PROGRESS CHECK**

Describing Why are some people critical of mining and logging activities in the region?

A nurse checks a patient's treatment chart at a clinic in Brazzaville, Republic of the Congo.

©Pascal Deloche/Godong/Corbis

FOLDABLES
Study Organizer

Include this lesson's information in your Foldable®.

LESSON 3 REVIEW (CCSS)

Reviewing Vocabulary (Tier Three Words)
1. Why was the use of a trade language helpful in Central Africa? RH.6-8.4

Answering the Guiding Questions
2. ***Describing*** What are two distinctive features of the Bambuti people, who live in the rain forests of the Democratic Republic of the Congo? RH.6-8.1

3. ***Determining Central Ideas*** What are some of the customs in Central Africa related to food? RH.6-8.2

4. ***Analyzing*** Why has the lack of political stability posed major problems for development in some Central African countries? RH.6-8.1

5. ***Informative/Explanatory Writing*** Write a paragraph or two in which you explain some of the economic issues confronting Central Africa. WHST.6-8.2, WHST.6-8.4

Chapter 11 **345**

C Critical Thinking Skills

Suggesting a Solution Guide a class discussion about the greatest challenges facing Central Africa, as discussed in the section, "Regional Issues." **Ask:**

• **What are the main issues facing Central Africa's people and governments?** *(economy, environment, political stability, and population growth)*

• **Based on what you have learned about Central African countries so far, what might be a solution to one of these problems?** *(Sample answer: Central African regions that have an abundance of natural resources, such as trees and minerals, should try to develop and export these resources to improve the economy.)* **Logical/Mathematical**

W Writing Skills

Argument Have students prepare an argumentative essay based on their response to information in the section, "Growth and the Environment" about changes in Central Africa. Ask students to choose one of the issues in the text to either support or refute, backing up their essays with evidence from the text. Students may wish to conduct additional research online to find supporting evidence for their essays. Have students present their essays to the class.

CLOSE & REFLECT

Summarizing To close the lesson, remind students that Central Africa has a long history of colonization and has a diverse population with a variety of ethnic groups and languages. Have students write a few sentences about a region in Central Africa they might like to visit. Tell students to provide an interesting fact they learned about that region.

LESSON 3 REVIEW ANSWERS

Reviewing Vocabulary

1. The use of a common language—French in many cases—was economically beneficial because everyone could understand each other while trading.

Answering the Guiding Questions

2. **Describing** The Bambuti are unusually short in stature, and they are nomadic hunter-gatherers.

3. **Determining Central Ideas** In some areas, males and females eat separately, and people show great generosity and hospitality.

4. **Analyzing** Political instability has blocked economic progress and development in health and education. It has also paved the way for corruption.

5. **Informative/Explanatory Writing** Students should mention that rapid population growth has put pressure on the economies of the region's countries. They should also discuss the region's economic dependence on agriculture, logging, and mining, and the fact that these activities raise environmental concerns. Lastly, they could discuss the struggle to control profits, which pits governments against foreign corporations and investors.

ANSWER, p. 345

☑ **READING PROGRESS CHECK** These economic activities destroy or limit biodiversity.

ENGAGE

Bellringer Before students read the What Do You Think? feature, make sure they understand what the United Nations is and its role in global affairs. Explain that the United Nations was formed in 1945 to help keep peace and preserve international law and to promote human rights around the world. While the UN Security Council tries to maintain peace and security with "peacekeeping missions," it has faced scrutiny from some critics who have questioned the council's effectiveness in recent years. Ask students to consider the challenges faced by the UN Security Council. Tell students that this feature presents two views on the issue of the UN's effectiveness at reducing conflict in Africa. Then have students read the introductory paragraph and the *No!* viewpoint.

TEACH & ASSESS

R1 Reading Skills

Determining Word Meanings Have students work in pairs to read the *No!* viewpoint. As they read, have partners write down words they find confusing or do not understand. Tell students to look up the words in a dictionary and share the definitions with their partner.

Remind students to identify word parts to help them understand unfamiliar words. Use the word *unprecedented* as an example by writing its word parts on the board: *un-* = not; *pre-* = before; *cede-* = go; *ent-* = something that performs the action; *ed-* = having the qualities or characteristics of. **Ask:** What does it mean if the number of missions were *unprecedented*? *(The number of missions had not occurred ever before, meaning there were many missions that occurred in the post-Cold War era.)* **AL** Verbal/Linguistic

R2 Reading Skills

Analyzing Primary Sources Use the following questions to help students analyze and understand the *No!* viewpoint on this page. **Ask:**

- What evidence does the author use to support the claim about UN peacekeeping missions? *(The author supports the claim that the UN has treated Africa like a "giant laboratory" by listing specific events in Angola, Somalia, and Rwanda that highlight failed attempts at peacekeeping.)*
- Do you think the author's argument is compelling? If so, cite specific evidence from the text that supports your opinion. If not, explain why. *(Students who agree with the author's argument presented in the* No! *viewpoint might cite the list of "disasters" in regions mentioned by the author. Students who disagree with the argument may say that setbacks are inevitable due to the ongoing violence in those regions.)* **Logical/Mathematical**

What Do You Think?

Has the United Nations Been Effective at Reducing Conflict in Africa?

The 53 independent states of Africa share one continent, but the vast land holds different people and varied resources and economies. During the past six decades, armed political conflict, either within a nation or between nations, has been the norm rather than the exception for many Africans. Since 1945, the United Nations (UN) Security Council, in its resolve to maintain international peace and security, has mounted 29 peacekeeping missions in Africa. Have the efforts of the United Nations been effective?

No !
PRIMARY SOURCE

R1 " Africa has thus been a giant laboratory for UN peacekeeping and has repeatedly tested the capacity and political resolve of an often self-absorbed Security Council. . . . Under the loose heading of peacekeeping, the UN launched an unprecedented number of missions in the post–Cold War era. But . . . hard times appeared after disasters in Angola in 1992, when warlord Jonas Savimbi brushed aside a weak UN peacekeeping mission to return to war after losing an election; in Somalia in 1993, when the UN withdrew its peacekeeping mission after the death of eighteen U.S. soldiers; and in Rwanda in 1994, when the UN shamefully failed to halt genocide against about eight hundred thousand **R2** people and instead withdrew its peacekeeping force from the country. These events scarred the organization and made its most powerful members wary of intervening in Africa: an area generally of low strategic interest to them. "

—Adekeye Adebajo, Director, Centre for Conflict Resolution, University of Cape Town, South Africa, in *UN Peacekeeping in Africa: From the Suez Crisis to the Sudan Conflicts*

A militiaman stands guard with a machine gun in Somalia. The East African country has had political upheaval since 1991. Islamic militia forces and UN-backed government forces compete for control of Somalia.

346 *Chapter 11*

TEXT: From UNITED NATIONS SECURITY COUNCIL SPECIAL REPORT REPORT NUMBER 2 THE PEACEBUILDING COMMISSION 17 November 2009. <www.securitycouncilreport.org/site/c.glKWLeMTIsG/b.5023589/k.1023/Special_Research_No_2brThe_Peacebuilding_Commissionbr17_November_2009.htm> PHOTO: © Sean Meridel/Corbis

---

netw⊙rks   *Online Teaching Options*

WORKSHEET

How to Analyze a Primary Source

Distinguishing Fact from Opinion Organize students into small groups and have each group use this worksheet to analyze and critique each viewpoint. Instruct groups to review each primary source by first noting all the facts stated and then all the opinions. Circulate among groups to help students settle debates about the difference between fact and opinion. Have groups present concluding statements about the effectiveness of each document and discuss them as a class. **AL** Verbal/Linguistic, Logical/Mathematical

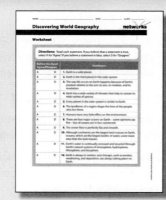

Troops from Thailand have contributed to UN–African Union peacekeeping efforts in the war-torn Darfur region of Sudan. In Darfur, the Thai troops conducted patrols and provided protection to civilians and humanitarian aid workers.

TEXT: From UN PEACEKEEPING IN AFRICA: FROM THE SUEZ CRISIS TO THE SUDAN CONFLICTS, by Adekeye Adebajo. Copyright ©2011 by Lynne Rienner Publishers, Inc. Used with permission by the publisher. PHOTO: ©Albert Gonzalez Farran/Demotix/Corbis

Yes !
PRIMARY SOURCE

❝ Bearing in mind the relatively young period of existence of the PBC [Peacebuilding Commission] (and the fact that inevitably it was experimenting in its first two years), Sierra Leone and Burundi—the first two countries placed on the PBC agenda—seem to have achieved some real success in consolidating peace. Burundi has made headway with its peace process, including the gains relating to its inclusive political dialogue. Sierra Leone has also chalked up significant milestones and emerged as a post conflict state on the tracks of peace consolidation, with clear reforms in socioeconomic and security sector aspects. Both countries have also had to deal with some potentially serious setbacks and in both cases it seems that the proactive involvement of the PBC has added value in overcoming those problems. ❞

—Security Council Report, Special Research Report No. 2, The Peacebuilding Commission, 17 November 2009

What Do You Think? **DBQ**

1 *Identifying Point of View* What evidence does the Yes answer contain to support its viewpoint? What evidence does the No answer contain to support its viewpoint?
RH.6-8.6

2 *Distinguishing Fact From Opinion* The two sources state facts and opinions. Identify one fact and one opinion from each source.
RH.6-8.8

Critical Thinking

3 *Analyzing* Weigh the evidence. Africa has had 29 peacekeeping missions in roughly 60 years. If the United Nations has to keep going back, have the missions been effective? Why or why not?
RH.6-8.1, RH.6-8.10

Chapter 11 **347**

V Visual Skills

Analyzing Images Have partners read the *Yes!* viewpoint and discuss whether the photograph on this page supports the evidence outlined in the *Yes!* viewpoint. **Ask:** Based on the photograph, what is the author's opinion about UN peacekeeping missions? *(Sample response: The author believes that the UN peacekeeping missions are achieving success as evidenced in the photograph.)* **AL** Visual/Spatial

W Writing Skills

Argument Have students write a persuasive argument that presents their own viewpoint on the issue of UN peacekeeping missions in Africa. Students should support their viewpoint with text evidence from the feature as well as any research they conduct on the issue. Students should include a list of reliable resources. *(Students' paragraphs should show an understanding of the purpose of UN peacekeeping missions and their degree of success in Africa.)* **BL** Intrapersonal, Verbal/Linguistic

CLOSE & REFLECT

Comparing and Contrasting Have students write a paragraph to compare and contrast each viewpoint and to discuss which argument they found the most persuasive. Tell students to cite specific evidence they find compelling or that they feel could be more convincing.

ANSWERS, p. 347

DBQ What Do You **Think?**

1. **Yes:** Sierra Leone and Burundi "achieved some real success in consolidating peace" in spite of setbacks. **No:** "Disasters" occurred in Angola, where a warlord thwarted a peacekeeping mission; in Somalia, where the UN withdrew after 18 US soldiers were killed; and in Rwanda, where the UN "shamefully failed to halt genocide."

2. Sample responses: **Yes: Fact**—Sierra Leone and Burundi were the first countries in which the PBC conducted missions. **Opinion**—Sierra Leone and Burundi "seem" to have achieved success in consolidating peace. **No: Fact**—In Angola in 1992, Jonas Savimbi lost an election and started a war. **Opinion**—The Security Council is "self-absorbed"; the 1992 peacekeeping mission in Angola was "weak."

3. Answers will vary. Possible response: Africa is a huge place, and each of the 53 countries probably has its own issues and problems. One country might be very violent, making the success of a peacekeeping mission very difficult. Another country might be able to achieve and maintain peace because the leaders and the people are willing to talk and compromise. What may be most important is that someone be there trying to make peace.

WORKSHEET

Critical Thinking Skills: Analyzing Peacekeeping Missions

Predicting Consequences Have students conduct online research to analyze the missions cited in each excerpt. Remind students to use reliable sources. Ask students to consider the causes and consequences of peacekeeping missions. **BL** Verbal/Linguistic

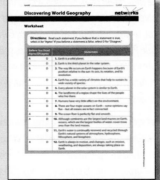

CHAPTER REVIEW ACTIVITY

To review the chapter, have students create a flow chart like the one below. Have students label each box as shown to demonstrate an understanding of the cause-effect relationships presented in the chapter. Tell students to complete the flow chart for each category with key information and examples from the text. *(Students' answers may vary but should include key concepts discussed in each of the three lessons in the chapter and their relationship to one another. For example, students might list the development of tools, which led to agrarian communities, and that most people in rural areas today make their living through subsistence farming. Students might also mention that Central Africa's history of colonization caused a blend of modern and traditional characteristics in daily life.)*

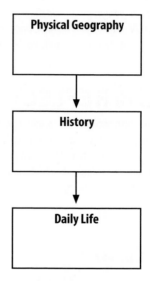

REVIEW THE ENDURING UNDERSTANDINGS

Review this chapter's Enduring Understanding with students:

- **People, places, and ideas change over time.**

Now pose the following questions in a class discussion to apply this to this chapter.

- **What role has the Congo River and its tributaries played in Central Africa?** *(The Congo River provides a livelihood for people who live along its banks, it is a vital transportation artery, and dams on the river generate large amounts of hydroelectric power.)*

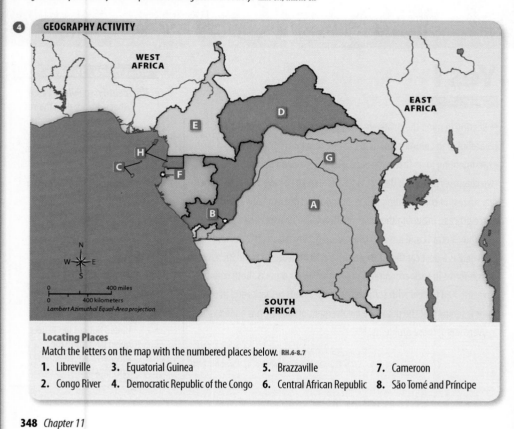

Directions: Write your answers on a separate piece of paper.

1 Use your **FOLDABLES** to explore the Essential Question.
INFORMATIVE/EXPLANATORY WRITING Some geographers believe the area of Central Africa that is now savanna was at one time forestland. What might have changed the physical composition of this area? Write a short essay discussing this hypothesis. How does this relate to the concept of people adapting to the environment? WHST.6-8.2, WHST.6-8.4

2 21st Century Skills
IDENTIFYING Use the text and the Internet to find information about one of the countries of Central Africa. List important resources for that country. WHST.6-8.6, WHST.6-8.8

3 Thinking Like a Geographer
ANALYZING Much of Central Africa depends on agriculture as a main economic activity. Why is a good transportation system important to an agricultural society? RH.6-8.1, WHST.6-8.9

4 GEOGRAPHY ACTIVITY

Locating Places
Match the letters on the map with the numbered places below. RH.6-8.7

1. Libreville
2. Congo River
3. Equatorial Guinea
4. Democratic Republic of the Congo
5. Brazzaville
6. Central African Republic
7. Cameroon
8. São Tomé and Príncipe

- **How would you describe Central Africa's system of triangular trade?** *(Triangular trade was a system of trade that relied on prevailing winds that powered ships and involved three stages: ships that brought goods such as cloth, metal, beads, tobacco and guns from Europe to Africa; the Middle Passage, in which slaves were shipped from Africa to the Americas; and the third stage, in which ships returned from America to Europe with rum and goods such as tobacco, molasses, and cotton)*

- **How would you describe the makeup of Central Africa's population and places where people live?** *(Central Africa's population has hundreds of different ethnic groups and as a result, many different languages are spoken. Most people live in rural areas, but Central Africa has a number of large cities where the population is quickly growing.)*

ACTIVITIES ANSWERS

Exploring the Essential Question

1 **INFORMATIVE/EXPLANATORY WRITING** Students should describe the process of slash-and-burn agriculture as the possible reason for the change from forestland to savanna and the continuing deforestation. If the scientists' theory is correct, it demonstrates how native people adapted to the land due to the need to grow food for their families where forests were incompatible with farming.

REVIEW THE GUIDING QUESTIONS

Directions: Choose the best answer for each question.

1 Choose Central Africa's primary landform. RH.6-8.4
- A. islands
- B. caves
- C. Congo River watershed
- D. steppes

2 Because Central Africa is centered on the Equator, its climate is RH.6-8.2
- F. Mediterranean.
- G. tropical.
- H. arid.
- I. mild.

3 Why were Europeans slow to establish colonies in Central Africa? RH.6-8.1
- A. The area had no worthwhile natural resources to exploit.
- B. They couldn't decide how to share the African countries.
- C. Transportation was difficult, and they feared malaria and other diseases.
- D. They didn't want to convert people.

4 The Republic of the Congo was a colony of which country? RH.6-8.2
- F. Spain
- G. France
- H. Portugal
- I. England

5 Most of the population of Central Africa makes a living by means of RH.6-8.2
- A. subsistence farming.
- B. factory labor.
- C. crafting.
- D. foreign trade.

6 Identify an obstacle to developing a modern economy in Central Africa. RH.6-8.1
- F. diverse populations
- G. commitment to traditional religions
- H. primitive housing construction
- I. insufficient infrastructure, poor transportation, and poor education

Chapter 11 **349**

21st Century Skills

2 IDENTIFYING Responses should include key resources for the selected African country using information from the text and reliable sources from the Internet.

Thinking Like a Geographer

3 ANALYZING Good transportation is needed to be able to deliver the crops quickly to markets before food spoils.

Geography Activities

4 LOCATING PLACES

1. F
2. G
3. H
4. A
5. B
6. D
7. E
8. C

ASSESSMENT ANSWERS
Review the Guiding Questions

1 C For this question, students may be confused initially by the term *Congo River watershed,* as the Congo River is a waterway, not a landform. But they should recall that the *Congo River watershed* is a vast region covered with rain forests. Refer students to first section of Lesson 1 for help.

2 G Students should be able to eliminate choice H immediately, as rainfall is plentiful in regions along the Equator. Students should recall that the belt of Central Africa that lies along the Equator has a tropical climate that is warm and wet. If students need clarification, direct them to the section on climate in Lesson 1.

3 C Students should recognize choice A as a distractor, as many regions in Central Africa have plentiful natural resources. Students should recall Europeans were not eager to found settlements in Central Africa due to the transportation difficulties and the threat of tropical diseases. Refer students to the section, "Colonialism," in Lesson 2 for help.

4 G To answer this question, students need to recall the map in Lesson 2, "Independence for Central African Countries." Choice F may confuse students, as Spain colonized what is now Equatorial Guinea. However, students should recall the control that France gained of different Central African territories including the Republic of the Congo.

5 A Students should remember that most of Central Africa's people live in rural areas and make their living through subsistence farming. Students should recognize choice B as a distractor, as factories are not discussed in the text. Refer students to the section, "City and Country," in Lesson 3 for clarification.

6 I Students should recall concepts related to Central Africa's economic challenges, which are discussed in the section, "How People Live," in Lesson 3. Students may find choice F confusing, as Central Africa is made up of hundreds of ethnic groups with different languages, but should recognize choice G as a distractor, as Central Africa also has religious diversity.

DBQ Analyzing Documents

7 C Lamb blames European colonial governments, which, he says, "virtually ensured" that Africans would have difficulty governing themselves after independence. If students do not understand that "colonial administrations" refers to the European countries that colonized Africa, have them review Lesson 2.

8 H The tribes that were favored became entrenched in power and interested in maintaining their power. The tribes that were out of favor became entrenched in powerlessness and could grow resentful of their lower status. Have students who answer incorrectly, reread the passage and note that nothing is said about resources *(option F)* or allies outside the country *(option I)*.

Short Response

9 Sample answer: The main idea of this passage is that the Republic of the Congo is rich in resources, which help drive the economy.

10 Possible answer: The government of the Republic of the Congo can benefit in several ways by developing its other resources. First, the other resources will provide additional jobs, and the earnings of those workers can help add to economic growth. Second, sale of these other minerals can add to the nation's wealth, also promoting economic growth. Third, having additional products to sell reduces the country's reliance on oil, giving it some protection against economic disaster if oil prices fall or its oil reserves run out.

Extended Response

11 Students should note that colonists in Central Africa and in the Americas established plantations for farming. Plantations required large workforces, and plantation owners wanted cheap labor. Students should refer to the triangular trade to show the similarities in colonial establishment of the slave trade in Central Africa and the Americas.

DBQ ANALYZING DOCUMENTS

7 ANALYZING INFORMATION Read the following passage about European colonial rule in Africa:

> "*The manner in which colonial administrations governed virtually ensured the failure of Africa's transition into independence. Their practice of 'divide and rule'—favoring some tribes to the exclusion of others—served to [heighten] the ethnic divisiveness that had been pulling Africa in different directions for centuries.*"
>
> —from David Lamb, *The Africans* (1984)

What group does Lamb blame for the problems African nations have had creating stable governments since independence? RH.6-8.1, RH.6-8.10

A. the groups that led independence movements in Africa
B. the wealthy, more-developed nations of the world today
C. European colonial governments
D. African leaders since independence

8 IDENTIFYING POINT OF VIEW Why would favoring some tribes over others cause problems?
RH.6-8.6, RH.6-8.10
F. by draining the country of valuable resources
G. by making disfavored tribes dependent on the colonial government
H. by creating inequality that becomes entrenched
I. by forcing tribes to find allies outside their country

SHORT RESPONSE

> "*The Congo's economy is based primarily on its petroleum sector, which is by far the country's greatest revenue earner.... A new potash mine ... is expected to produce 1.2 million tons of potash ... [used in fertilizer] per year by 2013. This will make Congo the largest producer of potash in Africa.... [One new iron ore mine] is thought to have ore reserves enough to be the world's third-largest iron ore mine.*"
>
> —from "Republic of the Congo," State Department Background Notes

9 DETERMINING CENTRAL IDEAS What is the main idea of this passage? RH.6-8.2, RH.6-8.10

10 IDENTIFYING POINT OF VIEW If oil is so valuable, why would the government of the Republic of the Congo bother developing potash and iron ore mines? Explain your answer. RH.6-8.6, RH.6-8.10

EXTENDED RESPONSE

11 ANALYZING How was slavery in Central Africa and in the Americas similar? WHST.6-8.2, WHST.6-8.4

Need Extra Help?

If You've Missed Question	**1**	**2**	**3**	**4**	**5**	**6**	**7**	**8**	**9**	**10**	**11**
Review Lesson	1	1	2	2	3	3	2	2	3	3	2

---

networks *Online Teaching Options*

Practicing 21st Century Skills

Practicing Skills Your students can practice important 21st Century skills such as geography, reading, writing, and critical thinking by using resources found in the Skills Builder tab of the online Student Learning Center. Resources include templates, handbooks, and slide shows. These same resources are also available in the Resource Library of the Teacher Lesson Center.

CHAPTER 12
West Africa Planner

UNDERSTANDING BY DESIGN®

Enduring Understandings
- *People, places, and ideas change over time.*

Essential Questions
- *How does physical geography influence the way people live?*
- *How do new ideas change the way people live?*
- *What makes a culture unique?*

Predictable Misunderstandings
- *West Africa shares similar geography to North and Central Africa.*
- *The region's history is relatively current.*
- *The issues that occur in West Africa today are similar to the rest of the region.*

Assessment Evidence
Performance Tasks:
- *Project-Based Learning Digital Hands-On Chapter Project*
- *Project-Based Learning Hands-On Chapter Project*

Other Evidence:
- *Critical Thinking Skills Activity*
- *Geography and History Activity*
- *Participation in Interactive Whiteboard Activities*
- *Contribution to small-group activities*
- *Interpretation of slide show images and special purpose maps*
- *Participation in class discussions about cultural and economic topics*
- *Lesson Reviews*
- *Chapter Assessments*

SUGGESTED PACING GUIDE

Introducing the Chapter............... 1 Day	Lesson 3 ....2 Days
Lesson 1 ....2 Days	Chapter Wrap-Up and Assessment...... 1 Day
Lesson 2 ....2 Days	

TOTAL TIME   8 Days

Key for Using the Teacher Edition

SKILL-BASED ACTIVITIES

Types of skill activities found in the Teacher Edition.

V **Visual Skills** require students to analyze maps, graphs, charts, and photos.

W **Writing Skills** provide writing opportunities to help students comprehend the text.

R **Reading Skills** help students practice reading skills and master vocabulary.

C **Critical Thinking Skills** help students apply and extend what they have learned.

T **Technology Skills** require students to use digital tools effectively.

*Letters are followed by a number when there is more than one of the same type of skill on the page.

DIFFERENTIATED INSTRUCTION

All activities are written for the on-level student unless otherwise marked with the leveled labels below.

BL Beyond Level
AL Approaching Level
ELL English Language Learners

All students benefit from activities that utilize different learning styles. Many activities are marked as below when a particular learning style is highlighted.

Intrapersonal	Naturalist
Logical/Mathematical	Kinesthetic
Visual/Spatial	Auditory/Musical
Verbal/Linguistic	Interpersonal

National Geography Standards covered in Chapter 12

Learners will understand:

I. The World in Spatial Terms
Standard 1: How to use maps and other geographic representations, geospatial technologies, and spatial thinking to understand and communicate information

Standard 3: How to analyze the spatial organization of people, places, and environments on Earth's surface

II. Places and Regions
Standard 4: The physical and human characteristics of places

Standard 5: That people create regions to interpret Earth's complexity

Standard 6: How culture and experience influence people's perceptions of places and regions

IV. Human Systems
Standard 9: The characteristics, distribution, and migration of human populations on Earth's surface

Standard 10: The characteristics, distribution, and complexity of Earth's cultural mosaics

Standard 11: The patterns and networks of economic interdependence on Earth's surface

Standard 12: The processes, patterns, and functions of human settlement

Standard 13: How the forces of cooperation and conflict among people influence the division and control of Earth's surface

V. Environment and Society
Standard 14: How human actions modify the physical environment

Standard 15: How physical systems affect human systems

VI. The Uses of Geography
Standard 17: How to apply geography to interpret the past

Standard 18: How to apply geography to interpret the present and plan for the future

CHAPTER OPENER PLANNER

Students will know:

- *that West Africa has a diverse landscape, which includes deserts, steppe, savanna, and rain forests.*
- *that West Africa has an ancient history, which was influenced by herding societies and trading kingdoms.*

Students will be able to:

- **analyze** *a world map to identify countries of West Africa.*
- **use** *a time line to discuss various events in the history of West Africa.*

UNDERSTANDING
BY DESIGN®

☑ *Print Teaching Options*

V **Visual Skills**

- ☐ **P. 352** Students use the map of West Africa to reinforce map skills.

- ☐ **P. 353** Students review the time line and discuss its major points of interest. **Visual/Spatial**

W **Writing Skills**

- ☐ **P. 353** Students write a paragraph to explain why a place would have been set up for freed slaves. **Verbal/Linguistic**

C **Critical Thinking Skills**

- ☐ **P. 353** Students relate the two events that happened around 1300 on the time line to Islam. **Logical/Mathematical**

☑ *Online Teaching Options*

- ☐ **MAP** **Reading a Map**—Students identify aspects and locations of the region on a map.

- ☐ **TIME LINE** **Reading a Time Line and Map**—Students learn about where and when historical events occurred in West Africa. **Visual/Spatial**

- ☐ **MAP** **Interactive World Atlas**—Students use the interactive world atlas to identify the region and describe its terrain.

☑ *Printable Digital Worksheets*

- ☐ **WORKSHEET** **Geography and History: Bantu Migration**—Students can use this worksheet to understand more about the Bantu migration.

- ☐ **WORKSHEET** **Critical Thinking Skills: Slave Trade with Europeans**—Students can use this worksheet to understand more about the slave trade with Europeans.

Project-Based Learning

Hands-On

Designing Flags

After studying West Africa, students will work in pairs to design and illustrate a flag for each country in the region. Using colors, symbols, and words, the flags will illustrate historical events and cultural elements of the country. Students will present their flags to the class. Flags will be displayed with a map of West Africa in a prominent location in the classroom.

Digital Hands-On

Creating a Video Newscast

Students will produce a video newscast about West Africa using a web-based movie program. Working on a shared online document, groups of students will research West Africa, write scripts, and collaboratively produce the newscast. The newscast should be uploaded to a Web site and be available for all students to view.

21st Century Learning

Print Resources

ANCILLARY RESOURCES

These ancillaries are available for every chapter and lesson.

- **Reading Essentials and Study Guide Workbook** **AL** **ELL**
- **Chapter Tests and Lesson Quizzes Blackline Masters**

PRINTABLE DIGITAL WORKSHEETS

These printable digital worksheets are available for every chapter and lesson!

- **Hands-On Chapter Projects**
- **What Do You Know? Activities**
- **Chapter Summaries (English and Spanish)**
- **Vocabulary Builder Activities**
- **Quizzes and Tests**
- **Reading Essentials and Study Guide (English and Spanish)** **AL** **ELL**
- **Guided Reading Activities**

More Media Resources

SUGGESTED VIDEOS

NOTE: Be sure to preview videos to ensure they are age-appropriate.

- *Abidgan* (34 min.)
- **Amazon Instant Video, *Coasts*** (59 min.)

SUGGESTED READING

- ***The Benin Kingdom of West Africa,*** by John Peffer-Engels **AL**
- ***Liberia: A Question and Answer Book,*** by Muriel L. DuBois
- ***Festivals of the World: Nigeria,*** by Elizabeth Berg

PHYSICAL GEOGRAPHY OF WEST AFRICA

Students will know:
- *that the resources of West Africa also helped to spread religion throughout the region.*

Students will be able to:
- *describe* the landforms and waterways in West Africa.
- *describe* the climate and vegetation of this region, including dry zones and wet zones.
- *discuss* important natural resources in this region and how West Africa provides for its energy needs.

UNDERSTANDING
BY DESIGN®

☑ *Print Teaching Options*

V   Visual Skills

☐ **P. 354** Students create a mental map of West Africa and discuss challenges of landlocked countries. **Visual/Spatial**

☐ **P. 357** Students draw a sketch of the Sahel and discuss dry and wet climate zones. **ELL Visual/Spatial**

W   Writing Skills

☐ **P. 356** Students write a multi-paragraph essay arguing what they think the main factor is in the shrinking of Lake Chad. **BL Verbal/Linguistic**

R   Reading Skills

☐ **P. 355** Students determine meanings of *nomadic* and *seminomadic*. **ELL Verbal/Linguistic, Kinesthetic**

☐ **P. 359** Students use context clues to define *hydroelectric*. **ELL Verbal/Linguistic**

C   Critical Thinking Skills

☐ **P. 355** Students identify main ideas about bodies of water and compare with a partner. **AL Interpersonal**

☐ **P. 356** Students draw a Venn diagram to compare and contrast the Senegal and Black and White Volta Rivers. **Visual/Spatial**

☐ **P. 358** Students make connections between natural resources around Lake Chad and the decreasing size of Lake Chad. **Logical/Mathematical**

☐ **P. 359** Students make a list of resources and classify them in a chart by country. **AL Visual/Spatial**

T   Technology Skills

☐ **P. 357** Students create a bar graph that compares the amount of rainfall in dry zones and wet zones. **AL Logical/Mathematical**

☐ **P. 358** Students work in groups to deliver an oral presentation about an assigned energy type on the infographic. **Interpersonal, Verbal/Linguistic**

☑ *Online Teaching Options*

V   Visual Skills

☐ **VIDEO Wild Wonders: Africa—Desert Camels**—Students watch the video about the desert camels of Africa and describe one country they would like to visit. **AL Verbal/Linguistic**

☐ **MAP Geo Facts: West Africa**—Students can use the geo facts map to discuss the interesting geographic facts of the region.

☐ **MAP Physical Geography: West Africa**—Students can use the physical geography map to highlight the landforms and bodies of water in the region.

☐ **MAP Climates: West Africa**—Students can use the climate map to discuss the various climate zones of the region.

W   Writing Skills

☐ **IMAGE Lake Chad**—Students use the interactive photo to make a list of the effects of water use from the Niger River on Lake Chad. **AL Visual/Spatial**

☐ **SLIDE SHOW West Africa's Variety of Land**—Students watch the slide show, and then choose a landform and create a poem about it.

☐ **IMAGE Wet vs. Dry Zones**—Students use the side-by-side photos of the wet and dry zones to write a paragraph to contrast the two climates. **AL Verbal/Linguistic**

☐ **MAP Resources: West Africa**—Students use the map to discuss the locations of important resources in West Africa and create a jingle to remember the resources. **Visual/Spatial, Auditory/Musical**

R   Reading Skills

☐ **GRAPHIC ORGANIZER Landlocked vs. Coastline**—Students can use the interactive graphic organizer to discuss the nations that are landlocked or on the coastline.

☐ **LECTURE SLIDE Offshore Drilling**—Students can use the lecture slide of offshore drilling to discuss the reasons it is done and the costs of this location and process.

C   Critical Thinking Skills

☐ **CHART Comparing Rivers**—Students can use the interactive chart to compare the Nile, the Congo, and the Niger Rivers.

T   Technology Skills

☐ **ONLINE SELF-CHECK QUIZ Lesson 1**—Students receive instant feedback on their mastery of lesson content.

THE HISTORY OF WEST AFRICA

Students will know:
- that West Africa has an ancient history, which was influenced by herding societies and trading kingdoms.
- how the colonial rule and slave trade of the Europeans had an impact on West Africa, which continues to today.

Students will be able to:
- *describe* the life of ancient herders in West Africa.
- *discuss* trading kingdoms.
- *describe* colonization of West Africa.
- *explore* how West African colonies gained independence.
- *discuss* civil war in West Africa.

UNDERSTANDING
BY DESIGN®

☑ *Print Teaching Options*

V **Visual Skills**

☐ **P. 362** Students use a map and infer why many kingdoms grew near Timbuktu. **Logical/Mathematical**

☐ **P. 363** Students describe why they think Mansa Musa is on his throne in a photo. **ELL** **Visual/Spatial**

☐ **P. 364** Students analyze the image of Freetown to infer why the British government chose this location. **ELL**

☐ **P. 365** Students analyze the map of Triangular Trade. **BL** **Logical/Mathematical**

W **Writing Skills**

☐ **P. 362** Students write an argument supporting whether they agree it was acceptable for the Almoravids to conquer other regions to spread their religion. **Verbal/Linguistic**

R **Reading Skills**

☐ **P. 360** Students explore how sentences from the text can be used as text evidence. **AL** **Logical/Mathematical**

☐ **P. 362** Students explain whether they think it was wise for the kingdom of Ghana to rely heavily on the gold trade. **Logical/Mathematical, Verbal/Linguistic**

☐ **P. 363** Students cite text evidence to answer questions about the Songhai empire. **Verbal/Linguistic**

☐ **P. 364** Students use context clues to gain understanding and determine word meanings. **AL**

C **Critical Thinking Skills**

☐ **P. 361** Students infer why the Bantu did not migrate to North Africa. **ELL** **Logical/Mathematical**

☐ **P. 363** Students analyze why salt was traded in exchange for gold. **Logical/ Mathematical**

☐ **P. 366** Students determine the effects of Ghana's independence. **AL**

☐ **P. 367** Students make connections between the United States' civil war and civil wars in West Africa. **BL**

T **Technology Skills**

☐ **P. 367** Students research online for information about the conflicts in Liberia or Sierra Leone and write an evaluation of the information presented on the Web site with the news story. **Interpersonal, Verbal/Linguistic**

☑ *Online Teaching Options*

V **Visual Skills**

☐ **MAP** **The First Trading Kingdoms**—Students use the animated map to discuss which goods were most valuable and why certain trade routes were better than others. **Visual/Spatial, Logical/Mathematical**

☐ **IMAGE** **Freetown, Sierra Leone**—Students use the interactive photo to compare and contrast the history of Freetown using a Venn diagram.

W **Writing Skills**

☐ **VIDEO** **Freedom in French African Countries**—Students watch the video about the history of colonialism and slavery in West Africa and write three questions they have about the region. **ELL** **AL** **Verbal/Linguistic**

☐ **SLIDE SHOW** **The Salt Trade**—Students view the slide show about the salt trade and write a paragraph describing the importance of the salt trade to the development of the region. **AL** **ELL** **Verbal/Linguistic**

☐ **SLIDE SHOW** **Mansa Musa**—Students discuss the importance of Mansa Musa and write three interview questions and answers for Mansa Musa to assess his contributions. **Interpersonal, Verbal/Linguistic**

R **Reading Skills**

☐ **LECTURE SLIDE** **Uses for Salt**—Student can use the lecture slide to highlight ancient and modern uses of salt.

☐ **MAP** **Slavery in West Africa**—Students use the static map of the triangular trade to discuss West Africa's place in this trade route.

☐ **IMAGE** **Kwame Nkrumah**—Students discuss the role of Kwame Nkrumah in the fight for independence in Ghana. **BL** **Logical/Mathematical**

C **Critical Thinking Skills**

☐ **GAME** **Drag-and-Drop: Trade in West Africa**—Students can use the drag-and-drop game to highlight how trade changed the region of West Africa.

☐ **MAP** **Imperialism and Independence in West Africa**—Students use the map of imperialism to discuss the change from the interactions between Europe and West Africa during the slave trade and during imperialism and colonization. **Visual/Spatial, Verbal/Linguistic**

T **Technology Skills**

☐ **ONLINE SELF-CHECK QUIZ** **Lesson 2**—Students receive instant feedback on their mastery of lesson content.

☑ *Printable Digital Worksheets*

W **Writing Skills**

☐ **WORKSHEET** **Geography and History: Bantu Migration**—Students can use this worksheet to understand the Bantu Migration.

☐ **WORKSHEET** **Critical Thinking Skills: Slave Trade with Europeans**—Students can use this worksheet to understand more about the slave trade with Europeans.

LIFE IN WEST AFRICA

Students will know:

- *that the resources of West Africa also helped to spread religion throughout the region.*
- *that the colonial rule and slave trade of the Europeans had an impact on West Africa, which continues today.*

Students will be able to:

- *describe* the makeup of the population in West Africa and where people live.
- *describe* settlement patterns in the region.
- *describe* daily life in the region.
- *explore* challenges including government and economics, and health and education.

UNDERSTANDING
BY DESIGN®

☑ *Print Teaching Options*

V Visual Skills

☐ **P. 368** Students analyze a map of West Africa that shows colonial borders. **AL** Visual/Spatial

☐ **P. 371** Students sketch a pattern or design for a kente cloth. **ELL** Visual/Spatial

☐ **P. 372** Students analyze how the image of the steel plant represents economic diversity in West Africa and why shipbuilding is a good industry to develop. **AL** Visual/Spatial

W Writing Skills

☐ **P. 370** Students write an informative essay about the different religions practiced in West Africa. **BL** Verbal/Linguistic

R Reading Skills

☐ **P. 368** Students define the words *national unity* as single words and as a phrase. **ELL**

☐ **P. 369** Students review the difference between *pidgin* and *creole*. Logical/Mathematical, Verbal/Linguistic

☐ **P. 371** Students define *nuclear* and *extended family* and compare the meanings. **AL** Verbal/Linguistic

C Critical Thinking Skills

☐ **P. 369** Students brainstorm ways Nigeria and Benin can help make the Yoruba people feel more connected to their country. **ELL** Interpersonal

☐ **P. 372** Students review why the European countries colonized Africa. **BL** Verbal/Linguistic, Logical

☐ **P. 373** Students speculate on the effects of political corruption in West Africa. **AL** Verbal/Linguistic

T Technology Skills

☐ **P. 370** Students analyze data from a population chart and answer questions related to the data. **AL**

☐ **P. 373** Students research a viral disease that affects many people in West Africa and present their findings digitally to the class. **BL** Verbal/Linguistic

☑ *Online Teaching Options*

V Visual Skills

☐ **VIDEO** **Mosque at Djenne**—Students can use the video of the mosque to discuss religion in the region.

☐ **IMAGE** **360° Views: Lagos, Nigeria**—Students use the views of Lagos, Nigeria to discuss rural and urban settlements and population distribution and identify details that illustrate an urban area. **ELL** Visual/Spatial

☐ **IMAGE** **West African Art**—Students use the interactive photo to discuss different traditions in West African art and explain orally how two of the traditions are similar and different. **ELL**

☐ **MAP** **Population: West Africa**—Students can use the population map to discuss breakdown and distribution of population in the region.

☐ **VIDEO** **Daily Life in West Africa**—Students can use the video to highlight and make connections about certain aspects of daily life in the region.

W Writing Skills

☐ **VIDEO** **Benin Child Slaves**—Students watch a video about this current issue in West Africa and explain what is being done to save young children from being exploited for cheap labor. **AL**

☐ **CHART** **Ethnic Groups in West Africa**—Students use the interactive chart to discuss the ethnic population distribution across West Africa and write about the ethnic groups in any one country. **AL** **ELL** Visual/Spatial

R Reading Skills

☐ **GRAPHIC ORGANIZER** **Challenges in West Africa**—Students use the graphic organizer to review current issues and challenges that West Africa faces. Visual/Spatial, Verbal/Linguistic

☐ **LECTURE SLIDE** **Infrastructure**—Students can use the lecture slide about infrastructure to discuss how this development is important for the future of West Africa.

C Critical Thinking Skills

☐ **IMAGES** **Contrasting Settlements**—Students can use the images to discuss the differences in extended family vs. nuclear family and rural environments vs. urban environments.

T Technology Skills

☐ **ONLINE SELF-CHECK QUIZ** **Lesson 3**—Students receive instant feedback on their mastery of lesson content.

INTERVENTION AND REMEDIATION STRATEGIES

LESSON 1 Physical Geography of West Africa

Reading and Comprehension

Help students visualize concepts from this lesson by acting as tour guides through West Africa. You may wish to organize students into groups according to these topics: the Sahara, the Sahel, the savanna, and the rain forest. Students should work in pairs or small groups to plan their journey, noting points of interest along the way. Tell students to write a paragraph describing their trip, demonstrating knowledge of vocabulary words' meaning as they are used in the text. Students should also refer to specific landforms and waterways discussed in the text.

Text Evidence

Organize students into small groups and have each group create a two-column chart with the headings *Now* and *Then*. Tell students to review the text to fill in their graphic organizers with facts about West Africa's landforms, waterways, and resources. Students should list facts in each column about a topic as it existed in the past, and as it is now. For example, students might list Lake Chad and write "shrinking" under the *Now* column and "one of the largest bodies of water in Africa" under the *Then* column. Have students share their charts with the class.

LESSON 2 History of West Africa

Reading and Comprehension

Have students skim the lesson to find challenging or unfamiliar words and try to determine each word's meaning by using context clues. Tell students to look up the words' definitions using an online or print dictionary to clarify their meanings. Have students work in pairs to create flashcards and quiz each other. Then ask students to explain a concept in this lesson using one of the academic vocabulary terms. For example, students might use the word *displace* to explain the migration of the Bantu.

Text Evidence

Organize students into small groups. Tell students they will create a list of reasons why one of the three ancient empires in West Africa—the Ghana, the Mali, or the Songhai—is important. Each group should prepare a short presentation that addresses the essential question: *What makes a culture unique?* In preparing their presentations, students should explain why the empire was powerful and unique. Remind students to support their reasoning with evidence from the text.

LESSON 3 Life in West Africa

Reading and Comprehension

Review the academic and content vocabulary words with students, clarifying pronunciation. To ensure comprehension of the concepts in this lesson, have students write sentences using the terms to show their understanding of each word's meaning. Then have students conduct a peer review by exchanging their papers with a partner. Challenge student pairs to write a paragraph using all the academic and vocabulary terms that demonstrate their knowledge of concepts in this lesson.

Text Evidence

Assign student groups one of the West African countries discussed in this lesson. Tell students to write a summary explaining their assigned country's ethnic groups, languages, religions, cultures, and challenges. Suggest that students assign one of these topics for each group member to write a sentence. Then have groups compile the sentences to create a rough draft of their summary. Encourage students to create a visual to accompany their summaries, such as a poster or graphic organizer. Have students present their summaries and visuals to the class.

Online Resources

Level Reader

Use this online lower-level text that corresponds directly to the text in the online Student Edition.

Guided Reading Activities

This resource uses graphic organizers and guiding questions to help students with comprehension.

What Do You Know?

Use these worksheets to pre-assess students' background knowledge before they read the chapter.

Reading Essentials and Study Guide Workbook

This resource offers writing and reading activities for the approaching-level student.

Self-Check Quizzes

This online assessment tool provides instant feedback for students to check their progress.

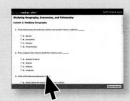

WEST AFRICA

ESSENTIAL QUESTIONS · *How does physical geography influence the way people live?* · *How do new ideas change the way people live?* · *What makes a culture unique?*

Young woman wears dress of traditional Kente cloth at a cultural festival in Ghana

Anadne Van Zandbergen/Alamy

Lesson 1
Physical Geography of West Africa

Lesson 2
The History of West Africa

Lesson 3
Life in West Africa

The Story Matters...

West Africa's diverse landscape includes desert, steppe, savanna, and tropical rain forests. Ancient rock paintings in Chad reveal details of the early herding societies who lived in this region. With rich deposits of gold and salt, trading kingdoms developed in Ghana and Mali. Trade also spread Islamic culture through much of the region. Gold attracted Europeans, whose colonial rule and slave trade impacted West Africa. Many of the independent nations of West Africa still struggle with civil war.

FOLDABLES
Study Organizer

Go to the Foldables® library in the back of your book to make a Foldable® that will help you take notes while reading this chapter.

351

ENGAGE

Think-Pair-Share To orient students to the region, draw a chart on the board with the headings of *Desert, Steppe, Savanna,* and *Tropical Rain Forest*. Have students brainstorm adjectives to describe these landforms and resource areas to remind them what each area is like. *(Possible answers: Desert: arid, hot, little vegetation; Steppe: dry, scrubby vegetation; Savanna: grassland, fertile soil; Tropical Rain Forest: humid, much rainfall, hot)* Then ask students to work with a partner to make a list of the resources that might be found in each of the areas. Have pairs share their lists with the class. Direct students to read "The Story Matters. . ." and add any resources that they did not include in their lists.

Making Inferences Based on what they have read, ask students to think of how these resources affected the rise of civilizations in West Africa. **Ask: How did resources influence where people settled, what they traded, and how they lived?** *(Answers will vary, but students may infer that people settled near the areas where gold and salt were located, and those were major trade goods. They also may infer that these trade goods made civilizations very wealthy but also vulnerable.)*

Remind students what they have already learned about European colonialism and the slave trade. Tell students that European domination in Africa was not limited to a small section of the continent, but was pervasive during the colonial period. **Ask: How do you think the location of West African countries along the Atlantic Ocean affected their involvement in the slave trade?** *(Students may conclude that it was easier for European countries to take over West African countries because they were close to the ocean and were susceptible to invaders.)*

T Technology Skills

Using Digital Tools Have students research the origins of Kente cloth, as well as how the patterns and colors differ by region. Ask students to use a digital presentation program to create a presentation that includes pictures of different examples of Kente cloth. **Visual/Spatial**

Letter from the Author

Dear Geography Teacher,

The Sahel is a vast area on the southern edge of the Sahara and includes several West African countries. For almost two decades, desertification has been an on-going concern in this region. As students learn about this region today, discuss the following questions with them: Why is desertification a critical problem in countries such as Mali, Chad, Niger, and Burkina Faso? Will humans ever be able to stop desertification in the Sahel?

FOLDABLES
Study Organizer

Go to the Foldables® library for a cumulative chapter-based Foldable® activity that your students can use to help take notes and prepare for assessment.

TEACH & ASSESS

Step Into the Place

V Visual Skills

Reading a Map Have students read the introductory paragraph and look at the map. Explain that this map shows the countries of West Africa. Have students use the map to answer the Step Into the Place questions. **Ask:**

- **Which countries in West Africa are landlocked?** *(Mali, Burkina Faso, Niger, and Chad)*

- **How many capital cities in West Africa lie along the Atlantic Ocean?** *(ten)*

- **How would you describe the availability of water in Chad?** *(The country is landlocked and the only water shown is Lake Chad which is on its western border. Most of the country does not have any major river or body of water.)*

- **How does this compare to Ghana?** *(Ghana not only lies along the Atlantic Ocean, but also has many large rivers that run through it.)* **AL Visual/Spatial**

Making Connections Explain to students that many European countries colonized most of Africa in the 1800s, but that one country in West Africa, Liberia, was able to resist European colonialism. Today, all of the countries in West Africa are independent. To help students make connections between the past and present of the region, share the following information:

- British West Africa included the territories of Sierra Leone, Gambia, the Gold Coast, and Nigeria. These colonies gained their independence from Great Britain in the 1950s and '60s.

- The American Colonization Society sent free African Americans to a colony in western Africa in the early 1800s. **W** This colony became the nation of Liberia in 1847. It was never under European colonial rule and remained independent since its founding.

- Benin, Niger, Burkina Faso, Cote d'Ivoire, and Chad all won their independence from France in August 1960.

- The former Portuguese colonies of Cape Verde and Guinea-Bissau did not gain their independence until the mid-1970s.

ANSWERS, p. 352

STEP INTO THE PLACE
1. Lake Chad and Lake Volta
2. Burkina Faso
3. Monrovia
4. **CRITICAL THINKING** northwest

STEP INTO THE TIME
1847; Freetown was founded to provide a place for freed slaves.

WEST AFRICA CCSS

V West Africa presents a rich variety of ethnic groups who speak many languages. Over the past 50 years, a number of the countries in the region have gained independence.

West Africa
TROPIC OF CANCER

Step Into the Place

MAP FOCUS Use the map to answer the following questions.

1 **THE GEOGRAPHER'S WORLD** What are the two major lakes shown on the map?

2 **THE GEOGRAPHER'S WORLD** Which of the following countries is landlocked: Senegal, Burkina Faso, or Benin?

3 **PLACES AND REGIONS** What is the capital city of Liberia?

4 **CRITICAL THINKING Integrating Visual Information** If you are traveling from the capital city of Togo to the city of Bamako, in which direction are you traveling?

o National capital

Step Into the Time

TIME LINE View the time line to answer these questions: In what year did Liberia declare independence? What event occurred in 1787?
RH.6-8.7

1300s Timbuktu is a center of Islamic culture

1000 B.C. Bantu people of West Africa begin migrations south and east

250 B.C. Mali becomes center for trade

1324 Mansa Musa makes pilgrimage to Mecca

1000 — B.C. — A.D. — 1000 — 1300

352 Chapter 12

Jordi Cami/Cover/Getty Images

Project-Based Learning ✋

Hands-On

Designing a Flag
After studying West Africa, students will work in pairs to design and illustrate a flag for each country in the region. Using colors, symbols, and words, the flags will illustrate historical events and cultural elements of the country. Students will present their flags to the class. Flags will be displayed with a map of West Africa in a prominent location in the classroom.

Digital Hands-On

Producing a Video Newscast
Students will produce a video newscast about West Africa using a web-based movie program. Working on a shared online document, groups of students will research West Africa, write scripts, and collaboratively produce the newscast. The newscast should be uploaded to a Web site and be available for all students to view.

edtechteacher
21st Century Learning

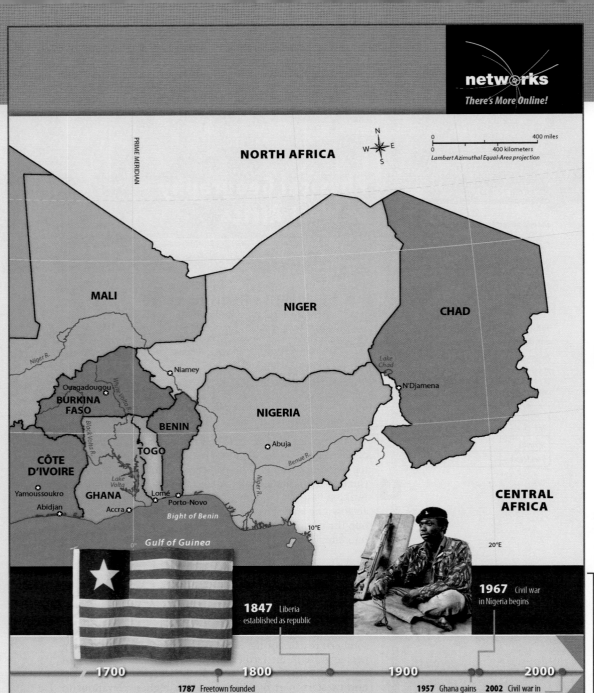

NORTH AFRICA

MALI

NIGER

CHAD

Niamey

N'Djamena

Lake Chad

OUAGADOUGOU

BURKINA FASO

NIGERIA

BENIN

TOGO

Abuja

CÔTE D'IVOIRE

Lake Volta

Niger R.

Benue R.

CENTRAL AFRICA

Yamoussoukro

GHANA

Lomé

Porto-Novo

Abidjan

Accra

Bight of Benin

Gulf of Guinea

10°E

20°E

PRIME MERIDIAN

Niger R.

White Volta R.

Black Volta R.

0   400 miles
0   400 kilometers
Lambert Azimuthal Equal-Area projection

1847 Liberia established as republic

1967 Civil war in Nigeria begins

1700   1800   1900   2000

1787 Freetown founded as haven for freed slaves

1957 Ghana gains independence

2002 Civil war in Sierra Leone ends

(l) Stockbyte/Getty Images; (r) Baileys History Archive/The Image Works

Chapter 12 **353**

networks
There's More Online!

Step Into the Time

V Visual Skills

Reading a Time Line Have students review the time line and images. As a class, discuss its major points of interest. **Ask:**

- **What kingdom became a center of trade around 250 B.C.?** *(Mali)*
- **How long had Ghana been independent when Sierra Leone's civil war ended?** *(45 years)*
- **For what is Timbuktu known?** *(as a center of Islamic culture in the 1300s)* **Visual/Spatial**

C Critical Thinking Skills

Comparing Point out to students the two events that are listed on the time line around the year 1300. **Ask: How do both of these events relate to Islam?** *(Sample response: Muslims make a pilgrimage to Mecca. With Timbuktu being a center of Islamic culture, Mansa Musa adopted Islam and followed the practice of making a pilgrimage to Mecca.)* **Logical/ Mathematical**

W Writing Skills

Informative/Explanatory Read aloud the questions at the beginning of the time line. Before students write their answers, ask them to think about the connection between the founding of Freetown and the independence of Liberia. Ask them to write a paragraph to explain why a place would have been set up for freed slaves. **Verbal/Linguistic**

V

CLOSE & REFLECT

Summarizing Have students briefly review the photographs, map, and time line, and think about what they have learned so far about West Africa. Have students turn to a partner and summarize key information about the region.

TIME LINE

Reading a Time Line and Map

Analyzing Visuals Display the time line and map on the whiteboard. Have volunteers read each event as it is revealed on the time line. Ask students to identify where in West Africa the event took place and find its location on the map. **Visual/Spatial**

See page 351B for other online activities.

ENGAGE

Bellringer Before students begin the lesson; invite volunteers to describe what kind of clothing they would wear and activities they might do in the following places: desert, mountains, and savannah. Then ask students to consider how being near a body of water might affect the activities and the climate of the area. **Ask: How are dry and wet climates different, and how do they affect the activities of a region?** *(Students' answers will vary but should include relevant details about how rainfall is limited in a dry climate. This results in limited agriculture and means that people must take careful measures to collect and conserve water. People also must modify their activities to adapt to the dry climate. Wet climates provide much more rainfall and can be more moderate. They allow a better potential for agriculture, but too much rain can wipe out crops. Again, people may modify their activities to adapt to the amount of rainfall in the region.)*

TEACH & ASSESS

V Visual Skills

Creating Maps Have students create a mental map of West Africa, including the countries mentioned in the text. Point out to them that they may use the Chapter Opener map as a reference.

As they read this section, have students think about which countries are on the Atlantic Ocean and which countries are landlocked. **Ask: What challenges might a landlocked country face that a country near the coast would not? Explain.** *(Possible response: Being on the coast gives a country better access to transportation and trade. If a landlocked country wants to access the coast, it must maintain good relations with a country that lies on the coast. The landlocked country might have to spend more money to access the coast since it has to cross another country to reach it. It will also need to pay for the ability to have ships dock in the ports.)* **Visual/Spatial**

ANSWER, p. 354

Taking Notes Sample answer: **Sahara:** little rainfall, average of just 3 inches per year. Shrubs and other small plants that live in the Sahara go long periods without freshwater; **Sahel:** semiarid region, short rainy season, annual rainfall between 8 and 20 inches. Low grasses, thorny shrubs, few trees. Livestock, such as cattle, sheep, camels, and pack ox graze on the grasses. Crops of millet and peanuts; **Savanna:** Thick grasses and scattered trees. Annual rainfall from 31 to 59 inches; **Rain forest:** Known for broad-leaved evergreen trees and rich biodiversity. Rainfall as much as 200 inches per year.

---

networks

There's More Online!

☑ **IMAGE** Lake Chad

☑ **SLIDE SHOW** West Africa's Variety of Land

☑ **VIDEO**

Reading HELPDESK CCSS

Academic Vocabulary RH.6-8.4
(Tier Two Words)
• volume

Content Vocabulary RH.6-8.4
(Tier Three Words)
• basin
• harmattan

TAKING NOTES: *Key Ideas and Details* RH.6-8.2, RH.6-8.7

Organize As you read the lesson, fill in a chart like this one, discussing the dryness and vegetation in these different regions.

Sahara	
The Sahel	
Savanna	
Rain forest	

Lesson 1

Physical Geography of West Africa

ESSENTIAL QUESTION · *How does physical geography influence the way people live?*

IT MATTERS BECAUSE

West Africa has a varied landscape. Its vast grasslands are bounded on the north by the world's largest desert and on the south by coastal rain forests. West Africa provides an example of how cultures adapt to different climates and landforms.

Landforms and Bodies of Water

GUIDING QUESTION *In what ways do major rivers contribute to the economies of West African countries?*

West Africa is a land of broad contrasts. Many of the countries of the region have Atlantic coastlines. Four places in the region—Cape Verde, St. Helena, Ascension, and Tristan da Cunha—are islands in the Atlantic. Mali, Niger, Chad, and Burkina Faso are landlocked countries, or countries entirely enclosed by land. The southern reaches of the Sahara extend into the northern regions of the steppe, and savannas merge into rain forests in the south.

Landforms

Erosion has worn most of the land of West Africa into a rolling plateau that slopes to sea level on the coasts. West Africa has no major mountain ranges, but it has highland regions and isolated mountains. The Air, also known as the Air Massif, is a group of mountains in central Niger, along the southern reaches of the Sahara. The livestock of the Tuareg people graze in the fertile valleys between the mountains of the Air Massif. The Tibesti Mountains, located mostly in the northwestern part of Chad, have the highest elevations in

(l to r) George Holton/Photo Researchers; NASA/Photo Researchers; ©FLORIN IORGANDA/X02105/Reuters/Corbis

---

networks *Online Teaching Options*

VIDEO

Wild Wonders: Africa—Desert Camels

Describing Use the video about the physical geography and climate of West Africa to introduce the lesson. Lead a class discussion about how the camel is used in the desert and why. After watching the video, have students describe one unique aspect of camels and caravans and ask if anything surprised them. **AL** **Verbal/Linguistic**

See page 351C for other online activities.

BBC Motion Gallery Education

West Africa. The highest peak is Emi Koussi, an extinct volcano standing 11,204 feet (3,415 m) above sea level.

Southeast of the Tibesti Mountains, near Chad's eastern border, is an arid desert plateau region called the Ennedi. There are abundant wild game animals in the Ennedi. These animals attract a small population of seminomadic people who live here with their livestock during the rainy season. The Jos Plateau in central Nigeria is mostly open grassland and farmland.

In central Guinea is a highland region of savanna and deciduous forest known as the Fouta Djallon. It extends southeast to become the Guinea highlands, a humid, densely forested region.

Bodies of Water

The Niger River, West Africa's longest and most important river, originates at an elevation of 2,800 feet (853 m) in the Guinea highlands. It flows northeast toward the Sahara. Just beyond the town of Mopti in Mali, the Niger River enters the "inland delta." This is an area where the river spreads out across the relatively flat land into many creeks, marshes, and lakes that are connected to the river by channels. During the rainy season, the area floods completely. In the dry season, however, the waters recede, leaving fertile farmland.

As the Niger flows past Timbuktu, along the southern edges of the Sahara, the inland delta ends and the river returns to a single channel. As it flows through Niger and Nigeria, it joins its most important tributary, the Benue River, which doubles its **volume** of water. Where the Niger River reaches the Gulf of Guinea, it forms the Niger delta. This large area is a great **basin**, a lower area of land drained by a river and its tributaries. Along its 2,600-mile (4,184-km) course, the Niger provides water for irrigation and hydroelectric power. It is the main source of Mali's fishing industry, and it serves as an important route for transporting crops and goods.

R

C

Academic Vocabulary

volume an amount

Tuareg people lead their camels and goats to an oasis. The nomadic group tend to their livestock in the valleys of mountains. At one time, the Tuareg controlled the caravan trade routes across the Sahara.

George Holton/Photo Researchers

Chapter 12 **355**

SLIDE SHOW

West Africa's Variety of Land

Comparing and Contrasting Show the slide show about the variety of landforms in West Africa to students. Have them choose one landform that interests them and create a poem about it. They should draw a sketch of the landform and attach the poem that describes its features. **Verbal/Linguistic, Naturalist**

See page 351C for other online activities.

Slide Show

R Reading Skills

Determining Word Meanings Ask students what the word *nomadic* means. Then point out the word *seminomadic* in the text. Ask students what the prefix *semi-* (half, part) means. Then have two volunteers model the two words, showing how the meanings of the words are different. **Ask:**

- **Based on your understanding of the prefix *semi-*, what does the word *semi-arid* mean?** *(somewhat dry but not fully dry)*
- **What other words can you think of that use the prefix *semi-* that could describe the climate, lifestyle, or environment of West Africa?** *(Possible answers: semi-humid, semi-tropical, semi-domesticated)*
- **Why is using the prefix *semi-* to describe the climate, lifestyle, and environment of West Africa appropriate?** *(Sample response: The environment and people of West Africa are varied and distinct. People have had to adapt to the changing conditions of the environment. In some cases, being adaptable means not fully committing to one lifestyle or the other.)* **ELL** **Verbal/Linguistic**

C Critical Thinking Skills

Finding the Main Idea Have students read the section, "Bodies of Water." Explain to students that sometimes a section has more than one main idea. Have them identify more than one main idea in the section. Then ask them to share their answers with a partner. **Ask: Were the main ideas that you found similar or different than the ones of your partner? How did finding the main ideas help provide a better understanding of the bodies of water of West Africa?** *(Sample response: They were similar. I know that the most important river is the Niger because it is the lifeline of the region.)* **AL** **Interpersonal**

Content Background Knowledge

Explain to students that the Tuareg people of West Africa live mainly in Mali and Niger. Sometimes they are called the "Blue Men" because of the clothing they wear. To protect from the blowing winds and sand, men wear veils to cover their faces. The veils are dyed in blue indigo, and some of this dye rubs off on their faces. Drought in the Sahel has decreased the number of Tuareg in the region. Some have settled in cities where they have had to change their nomadic ways of life. In some cases, this change in lifestyle, integration with urban dwellers, and general discontent with the government has led to conflict.

C Critical Thinking Skills

Comparing and Contrasting After students read the text about the Senegal and Black and White Volta Rivers, ask them to draw a Venn diagram. Have them complete the Venn diagram by writing details about the rivers that are similar to and different from each other. **Ask:**

- **How are the rivers used differently by the people of West Africa?** (*The Black and White Volta Rivers meet at a point at which there is a dam. Therefore, people are controlling the flow of the water for electricity and irrigation. The Senegal River serves as a border between two countries.*)
- **The flow of the Senegal is northwest. Use the Chapter Opener map to decide which direction the Black and White Volta Rivers flow.** (*The flow is southerly to southeast.*)

If needed, encourage students to also use a physical map of West Africa to help them determine the flow of these rivers. **Visual/Spatial**

W Writing Skills

Argument Ask students to do some additional research to learn more about the shrinking of Lake Chad and its effect on the plants, animals, and humans who depend on it. Organize students into two teams: one representing the farmers who need water for their properties; the other representing scientists who say the lake cannot sustain increased use due to drought and climate change. Have groups write their arguments using facts and details to support their stand. Then set up a mock debate with teams arguing their side of the issue. Allow them to address counterarguments. Assign three students to judge the debate. **BL Verbal/Linguistic**

Content Background Knowledge

The Akosombo Dam was completed in 1965 and was paid for by the United States, Great Britain, Ghana, and the World Bank. The dam generates about 900 megawatts of electricity, which is enough for the country of Ghana to both meet its own electric needs and sell power to its neighbors. Construction of the dam was part of the Volta River Project, which also included building the aluminum smelter that is in the area.

ANSWERS, p. 356

CRITICAL THINKING a series of droughts

✓ READING PROGRESS CHECK West Africa is ancient. Erosion has worn most of the rock into a rolling, low-lying plateau. Much of West Africa is a vast, open savanna. It is bounded to the north by the Sahara Desert and to the south by the equatorial rain forests.

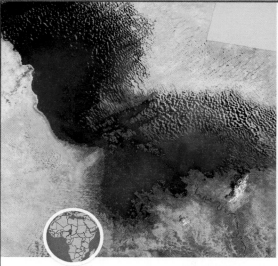
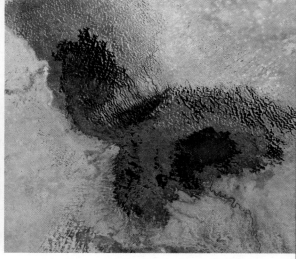

Satellite images show the Lake Chad area. Lake water is shown in blue, vegetation in red, and the surrounding desert in brown. The lake once was one of the largest bodies of water in Africa. The image on the left shows Lake Chad as it appeared in 1973. By 2007 (right), the lake had dramatically decreased in size.

▶ **CRITICAL THINKING**

Analyzing Taking water from the lake to use for irrigation is one reason that Lake Chad is smaller. What is another major cause of the lake shrinking in size?

The Senegal River rises in the Fouta Djallon in Guinea. Then it flows northwest to the Atlantic Ocean. For about 515 miles (829 km), the course of the Senegal River marks the border between the countries of Mauritania and Senegal.

The Black Volta River and the White Volta River originate in Burkina Faso and flow into Ghana. At a point near where the two rivers once met is the Akosombo Dam, which forms one of the world's largest artificial lakes—Lake Volta. The dam provides most of Ghana's electrical needs, and the lake provides water for irrigation.

Lake Chad covers portions of Niger, Nigeria, Chad, and Cameroon along the south part of the Sahara. The size of the lake varies from season to season, depending on the rainfall that feeds its tributaries. A series of droughts helped cause Lake Chad to shrink. Another cause was the amount of water taken from the lake and from the rivers that feed it to use for irrigating crops. People may be taking more water than water systems will be able to replace.

✓ READING PROGRESS CHECK

Describing Describe the landforms of West Africa.

Climate

GUIDING QUESTION *How do amounts of rainfall differ throughout West Africa?*

The climate of West Africa is diverse, from the harsh, arid Sahara in the north to the lush, coastal rain forests in the south. In between are vast stretches of grassland—the dry, semiarid Sahel and the lush, rainier savanna. The key characteristic of the climates throughout the region is its two distinct seasons: the wet season and the dry season.

NASA/Photo Researchers

---

netw⊙rks   *Online Teaching Options*

IMAGE

Lake Chad

Analyzing Images Use the interactive image of Lake Chad to discuss with the class how human use and climate affect physical features. After viewing the before and after images, have students make a list of the effects of water use from the Niger River on Lake Chad. Invite students to offer solutions. **AL Visual/Spatial**

See page 351C for other online activities.

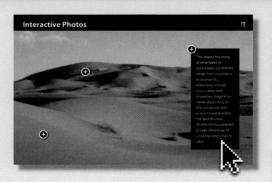

Interactive Photos

Lissa Harrison

Dry Zones

The Sahel is a semiarid region that runs between the arid Sahara and the savanna. Beginning in northern Senegal and stretching west into East Africa, the Sahel has a short rainy season. Annual rainfall ranges from only 8 inches to 20 inches (20 cm to 51 cm). This climate supports low grasses, thorny shrubs, and a few trees. The grasses are plentiful enough to support grazing livestock, such as cattle, sheep, camels, and pack oxen. It is important, however, that the herds do not grow too large. Too many animals leads to overgrazing and permanent damage to the grasslands. Overgrazing and too much farming result in desertification, the process in which semiarid lands become drier and more desert-like.

North of the Sahel is the Sahara. Daytime high temperatures are often more than 100°F (38°C) in the summer, though temperatures at night can drop by as much as 50°F. The few shrubs and other small plants that live in the Sahara must go for long periods without water. Some plants send long roots to water sources deep underground. After a rainfall, plants that have waited many months will suddenly flower, carpeting the desert with color.

From late November until mid-March, the dry, hot wind known as the **harmattan** blows through the Sahara with intensity. It carries thick clouds of dust that can extend hundreds of miles over the Atlantic Ocean, where it settles on the decks of ships. Harmattan winds contribute to the process of desertification.

V

Wet Zones

South of the Sahel, rains are more plentiful and feed the fuller, lusher plant life of the savanna. The savanna has two seasons—rainy and dry. The rainy season usually extends from April to September, and the rest of the year is dry. Annual rainfall reaches between 31 inches and 59 inches (79 cm and 150 cm). In some locations, though, annual rainfall can be as little as 20 inches (51 cm). This wide variability in rainfall makes human activity difficult.

T

The hot, dry wind that streams in from the northeast or east in the western Sahara is called the harmattan.

▶ **CRITICAL THINKING**
Describing During what months is the harmattan the strongest?

©FLORIN IORGANDA /X02105/Reuters/Corbis

Chapter 12 **357**

IMAGE

Wet vs. Dry Zones

Contrasting Use the side-by-side interactive image of the wet and dry zones to compare the two climates and discuss their influence on West Africa. Have students write a paragraph that summarizes the differences between the wet and dry zones. **AL** Logical/ Mathematical

See page 351C for other online activities.

Interactive Photos

This region has many diverse types of landscapes. Land forms range from mountains to grasslands. Waterways include rivers, lakes, and shorelines. Vegetation varies depending on the soil quality and access to water within the specific area. Animal life has adapted to take advantage of what the region has to offer.

T Technology Skills

Making Presentations As a class review the infographic. Next divide the class into four groups and assign each group one of the energy types displayed in the infographic. Ask each group to expand on what the infographic illustrates about their assigned energy type. Have each student group use reliable resources to research the energy resource as it relates to West Africa. Then have groups deliver an oral presentation about their section of the infographic. **Interpersonal, Visual/Linguistic**

C Critical Thinking Skills

Making Connections Review the difference between renewable (can be replaced fairly quickly and easily) and nonrenewable (cannot be replaced and will run out over time) resources. Then discuss the terms *exhaustible* and *inexhaustible* when referring to resources. Invite volunteers to share examples of both kinds of resources and list them on the board. **Ask:**

• **What mineral resource is important around Lake Chad?** *(petroleum)*

• **Based on what you have read about Lake Chad, how might the fact that it is decreasing in size affect access to this resource?** *(Possible answer: With the shrinking of Lake Chad, the people in the region may be better able to access petroleum. However, with less available water in the lake, it may not be possible to sustain life in the region.)*

• **What can you infer about the cost of getting to the oil in Ghana as compared to the cost of getting the oil in Nigeria and other countries in the region?** *(It is most likely much more expensive to get to Ghana's oil because it was not worth exploiting until the price of oil went up.)*

• **What prediction can you make about the importance of petroleum in this region of West Africa?** *(It will continue to remain important to the region's economy, but the people of the region will need to prepare for the resource to run out and have alternative energy sources prepared as well as a more diverse economy to avoid reliance on petroleum.)* **Logical/Mathematical**

ANSWERS, p. 358

CRITICAL THINKING Solar power
✔ **READING PROGRESS CHECK** The dry, semiarid Sahel and the lush, rainier savanna.

INFOGRAPHIC

WEST AFRICAN ENERGY

West Africa is relatively rich in energy resources. These resources are not, however, equally developed. Also, each form of energy has benefits and drawbacks.

KEY: Pros Cons

HYDROELECTRIC
Sustainable, adjustable, safe
Initial expense, restricts sediment flows, effects on ecosystems

SOLAR POWER
Renewable, low environmental effect, can reach poor and remote populations
Low efficiency, high costs, weather dependent

OIL
Well-developed technology, easily transported, relatively inexpensive
Non-renewable, pollution

NATURAL GAS
Less pollution than oil or coal, efficient
Requires expensive pipelines, highly combustible, non-renewable

West Africa is rich in energy resources. Because of the increasing demand for energy, West Africa's importance as an energy supplier to world markets continues to grow.

▶ **CRITICAL THINKING**
Analyzing What form of energy has little or no effect on the environment?

Farther to the south, tropical rain forests cover the land. The rain forests, known for their broad-leaved evergreen trees and rich biodiversity, receive plenty of rain. Rain forests in Sierra Leone and Liberia can receive as much as 200 inches (508 cm) of rain per year.

✔ **READING PROGRESS CHECK**
Identifying What are the two major grassland areas of West Africa?

Resources

GUIDING QUESTION *How do West African countries provide for their energy needs?*

West Africa contains many resources, but some countries lack the money to develop their resources into industries.

Energy Resources
Nigeria is the region's biggest producer of petroleum. In 2010 Nigeria ranked among the top 10 in the world, producing oil at a rate of almost 2.5 million barrels per day. The petroleum industry has not been as quick to tap the country's vast natural gas reserves.

Chad has oil fields in the area north of Lake Chad. Benin has offshore oil fields, as does Ghana. The oil in Ghana was considered too expensive to extract until increases in oil prices made it profitable to drill.

---

netw⊙rks *Online Teaching Options*

MAP

Resources: West Africa

Analyzing Maps Use the resources layer of the Chapter Opener map to discuss the locations of the important resources in West Africa. Have students take turns pointing to areas that are rich in different resources and naming them. Challenge students to write a jingle to remember the vital resources of the region. **Musical/Auditory**

See page 351C for other online activities.

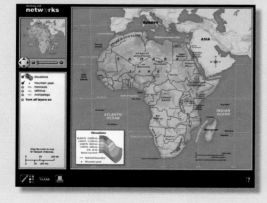

Ghana's main sources of electricity are two dams on the Volta River: the Akosombo Dam and the dam at Kpong. The Organization for the Development of the Senegal River, which is made up of several countries of the region, manages the river's resources, including hydroelectric stations. The Senegal River provides about half of the energy used in Mauritania today. Hydroelectric power is vital to meeting the energy needs in Togo and Nigeria.

 R

Other Resources

The gold trade attracted Portuguese explorers, who first visited the region in 1471. For centuries afterward, the country was simply called the Gold Coast and Europeans lived and worked there, building trading posts and forts. Gold mining remains important to the economy of Ghana, along with the mining of diamonds, manganese, and bauxite. Ghana also has unmined deposits of limestone and iron ore.

Gold is mined in Mali, Burkina Faso, and Nigeria, too. Togo mines phosphate and limestone, which are used as fertilizers and to make paper, glass, paint, and other everyday products. Togo also has promising gold deposits, but so far no gold-mining industry. Niger has a salt-mining industry. In addition to its important gold industry, Mali also mines salt and limestone, but many of Mali's mineral resources are untapped. These include iron ore and manganese, which are important in making steel.

Mauritania mines copper and iron ore, but many of the iron ore deposits have been depleted. Nigeria mines iron ore, tin, limestone, and small quantities of other minerals. Burkina Faso is one of the world's leading sources of manganese. Benin has deposits of iron ore, limestone, chromium ore, gold, and marble. Benin is a leader in the production of hardwoods, but most of the rain forests where this wood comes from have been cleared.

 C

FOLDABLES®
Study Organizer

Include this lesson's information in your Foldable®.

☑ **READING PROGRESS CHECK**

Analyzing Why is Benin's hardwood industry at risk? What is another industry in this region that has faced a similar problem?

LESSON 1 REVIEW **CCSS**

Reviewing Vocabulary (Tier Three Words)
1. How can the *harmattan* winds influence climate and vegetation? RH.6-8.4

Answering the Guiding Questions
2. ***Describing*** Why has Lake Chad changed in size over time? RH.6-8.5
3. ***Determining Central Ideas*** Why is desertification an issue in West Africa? RH.6-8.2

4. ***Identifying*** Why did the government in Ghana change its mind about its offshore oil deposits? RH.6-8.1
5. ***Informative/Explanatory Writing*** Explain how desertification occurs and why it is such an important environmental issue in West Africa. WHST.6-8.2, WHST.6-8.4

Chapter 12 **359**

LESSON 1 REVIEW ANSWERS

Reviewing Vocabulary

1. Harmattan winds blow warm, dry, dusty air from desert regions into the savanna, which can cause the spread of desert like conditions.

Answering the Guiding Questions

2. **Describing** In the second half of the 1900s, Lake Chad shrank because of a series of droughts and because water was being taken from the lake and its feeders to irrigate crops. The size of Lake Chad also changes from season to season, depending on the amount of rainfall and the amount of water usage.

3. **Determining Central Ideas** Desertification causes the desert to spread, which will result in less rainfall, less vegetation, and less land for growing crops.

4. **Identifying** The price of oil went up, which meant that there would still be a profit after investing the money to get the oil.

5. **Informative/Explanatory Writing** Responses should mention that if the Sahara spreads southward, turning the Sahel and parts of the savanna into desert, many animals and plants will no longer be able to survive. Paragraphs should mention how harmattan winds and clearing land for agriculture are two causes of desertification.

R **Reading Skills**

Using Context Clues Ask students to read the paragraph on Ghana's sources of electricity. Point out the word *hydroelectric*. **Ask:**

- **What are some context clues that help you understand the meaning of *hydroelectric*?** (*Ghana's main sources of electricity are the two dams on the Volta River*)
- **What does *hydroelectric* mean?** (*Possible answer: It is electric power produced from the flow of water.*)

Have students locate on a map the general area on the Volta River where the Akosombo Dam and the dam at Kpong are located. Ask them to identify and locate the countries that benefit from the hydroelectricity. (*Mauritania, Togo, Nigeria, Ghana*) **BL** **ELL** **Verbal/Linguistic**

C **Critical Thinking Skills**

Classifying Have students read the section titled, "Other Resources." Discuss with them how the discovery of resources encouraged European exploration of the region. Then ask students to make a list of the resources and classify them in a chart by country. **Ask:**

- **What resource is the most common?** (*gold*)
- **What resources are unique to one country?** (*chromium ore, marble, hardwoods*)
- **What important factor affects a country's ability to economically benefit from a resource?** (*It has to be able to develop an industry from the resource, which involves mining or harvesting it.*) **AL** **Visual/Spatial**

CLOSE & REFLECT

Summarizing Tell students to review the images and headings in this lesson and then write a summary of West Africa's physical geography. Have students think about the challenges that the people of West Africa face now and will in the future. Invite volunteers to share their summaries with the class. Then guide a class discussion about potential solutions to the challenges within the region.

ANSWER, p. 359

☑ **READING PROGRESS CHECK** The rain forests where the hardwoods come from have mostly been cleared. The hardwood industry will grow smaller, just as the iron industry in Mauritania grew smaller after most of the iron had been depleted.

ENGAGE

 Bellringer Before students begin the lesson, provide an opportunity for them to think about what it is like to have freedom. Have them explore the difference between having freedom and living under the control of someone else. Then have them brainstorm ways that someone might change after being given his or her freedom, and how it might be challenging to live in freedom when one formerly did not. Point out that many of the countries of West Africa lived under European control for a long time. After they gained their freedom from European rule, the countries and their citizens faced challenges that they continue to overcome today.

TEACH & ASSESS

R Reading Skills

Citing Text Evidence Remind students that when they answer questions, they should strive to cite text evidence to support their answers. Point out the sentence about rock drawings. **Ask: How did the Sahara change over time? What text evidence shows this?** *(The area grew drier and had fewer animals. The text describes the animals that used to live there as well as how it used to look.)* **AL** **Logical/ Mathematical**

C Critical Thinking Skills

Drawing Conclusions After students read the section titled, "Ancient Herders," discuss with them why herding animals was a good activity in the desert for nomadic people. **Ask:**

- **Why were camels the perfect animal to live and work in the Sahara?** *(They could survive without water for a long time and carry heavy loads for long distances.)*
- **How were they an ideal animal for seminomadic people?** *(Seminomadic people often moved from place to place. Since camels could carry heavy loads for long distances, they could handle the moving from place to place and carrying the belongings of the seminomadic people.)* **Verbal/Linguistic**

ANSWER, p. 360

Taking Notes Ghana: made iron weapons, had major deposits of gold, prospered through trade; **Mali:** ruled by Mansa Musa, center of Islam, built wealth through salt trade; **Songhai:** largest of the three empires, conquered Timbuktu and Djenne, organized into governmental provinces

---

netw⊙rks

There's More Online!

☑ **IMAGES** Freetown, Sierra Leone
☑ **MAP** The First Trading Kingdoms
☑ **VIDEO**

Reading **HELP**DESK CCSS

Academic Vocabulary RH.6-8.4
(Tier Two Words)
- displace
- element
- revenue

Content Vocabulary RH.6-8.4
(Tier Three Words)
- **imperialism**
- **secede**

TAKING NOTES: *Key Ideas and Details* RH.6-8.2, RH.6-8.7

Describe On a chart like this one, write at least two different facts about the three ancient empires of Ghana, Mali, and Songhai.

Ghana	Mali	Songhai

360

Lesson 2
The History of West Africa

ESSENTIAL QUESTION · *How do new ideas change the way people live?*

IT MATTERS BECAUSE
West Africa was under the control of a series of wealthy trading kingdoms until the late 1800s, when Europeans seized control of their lands. Regaining their independence from Europe and establishing themselves in the modern world has been a challenge.

Ancient Times

GUIDING QUESTION What opportunities did Muslims from North Africa see in West Africa?

Early civilizations in West Africa learned to thrive in a variety of climates and landscapes, from the Sahara to the tropical rain forests. Throughout its history, the region was open to many migrations and invasions because of its resources.

Ancient Herders

We think of the Sahara as a hot, intensely dry place where few living things can survive. Ten thousand years ago, the Sahara was a much different place. Rock drawings from 8000 B.C. depict a world that looks more like a savanna than a desert. Drawings include lakes, forests, and large animals not seen in the Sahara in modern times: ostriches, giraffes, elephants, antelope, and rhinoceroses. Seminomadic people herded cattle and hunted wild animals. As the climate grew drier, fewer species of plants and animals survived the harsh environment. Many people moved south, following the retreat of the grasslands and the rain. During this period of desertification, people discovered that camels can survive without water for longer periods than cattle, sheep, or goats. Camels also can carry heavy loads for long distances. They were perfect domesticated animals for desert dwellers.

(l to r) John Elk/Lonely Planet Images/Getty Images; Abraham Cresques/The Bridgeman Art Library/Getty Images; Chris Jackson/Getty Images News/Getty Images

---

netw⊙rks *Online Teaching Options*

VIDEO

Freedom in French African Countries

Interpreting Use this video about the history and influence of French colonization in West Africa to introduce the lesson. Ask students to write three questions that they have about the historical events mentioned in the video. Then have them return to the questions after reading the lesson to see if their questions were answered. **ELL** **AL** **Verbal/Linguistic**

See page 351D for other online activities.

BBC Motion Gallery Education

Movement of People

The Bantu people inhabited West Africa in ancient times. They had developed farming as early as 2000 B.C. A vast migration of Bantu people out of West Africa began around 1000 B.C. and continued for hundreds of years. Their farming practices allowed them to expand rather easily into areas occupied by hunter-gatherer groups. The Bantu became the dominant population in most of East and South Africa. The Bantu might have reached the East African coast as early as the A.D. 200s. They **displaced** many of the people who had lived on these lands before them. **C**

Wherever the Bantu moved, they spread their culture, including three vital **elements**. First, the Bantu cultivated bananas, taro, and yams, which were originally from Malaysia. These crops thrived in the humidity of the tropical rain forests. Second, the Bantu spread their languages everywhere they settled. Today, more than 500 distinct Bantu languages are spoken by 85 million Africans. Third, the Bantu brought iron-smelting technology. They could create tools and weapons unlike any the native people had ever seen.

Academic Vocabulary

displace to take over a place or position of others

element an important part or characteristic

Trade Across the Sahara

For thousands of years, the Sahara was a barrier to contact between West Africa and North Africa. By the A.D. 700s, Arab Muslims had crossed the Sahara and conquered most of North Africa. They dominated the southern Mediterranean and controlled trade in that region, as well as Saharan trade routes into West Africa. Arab geographers slowly learned about Africa south of the Sahara. They realized that the region offered opportunities, not only in trade, but also in adding converts to Islam. One of the West African kingdoms they learned about was Ghana. **R**

Ghana controlled the gold trade in the region. It traded gold for salt that Arab traders brought in from the Sahara. Salt was a very important trade good. It was the best preserver of food, and it was rare and difficult to acquire.

The Berber people had lived in North Africa long before the Arabs arrived. The Berbers resisted Islam for a while, but in time they converted. Several groups of Islamic Berbers joined together to become the Almoravids. They were fierce fighters, and they wanted to spread their new faith.

Merchants sell slabs of salt in a market town in central Mali. Salt is plentiful in the Sahara. These conditions gave rise to the African salt trade of ancient times.

▶ CRITICAL THINKING

Describing Why was salt a valuable item for trade?

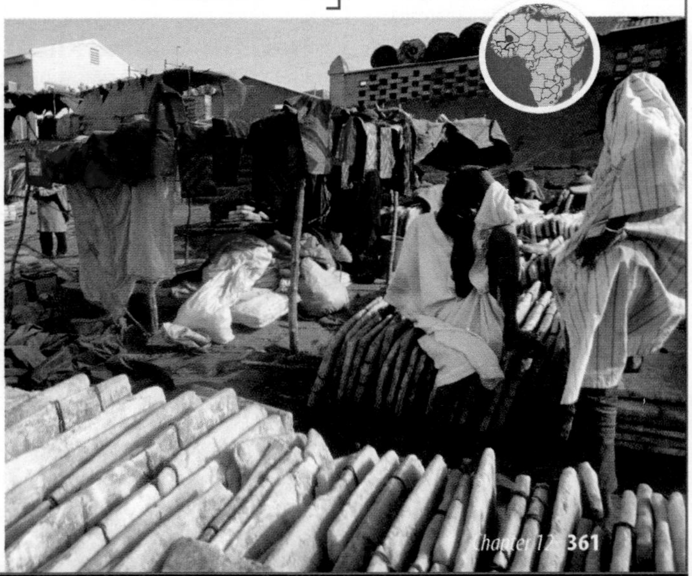

John Elk/Lonely Planet Images/Getty Images

Chapter 12 361

C Critical Thinking Skills

Making Inferences Review with students the migration of the Bantu. **Ask: Why do you think the Bantu did not migrate to North Africa?** *(Possible answer: The region might have been under the control of another group or the climate and physical geography of the Sahara were too harsh to endure.)* **ELL Logical/Mathematical**

R Reading Skills

Explaining Discuss with students how the Arab Muslims did cross the Sahara, despite the harsh climate, and conquered North Africa, where the Bantu did not migrate. **Ask: How did new ideas bring change to the people of West Africa and North Africa when the Arab Muslims came to the region?** *(Possible answer: Many people in North Africa and West Africa converted to Islam and realized that there were other civilizations beyond Africa with whom they could trade and from whom they could learn new ideas.)* **AL Verbal/Linguistic**

V Visual Skills

Analyzing Images Have students examine the image of the people with many tablets of salt. **Ask: What can you infer about salt from analyzing this image, and how does that compare to the value of salt long ago?** *(Possible answer: The area must have salt mines nearby which produce plentiful supplies of salt, which are still valuable but no longer as valuable as gold because if they were, the salt would be better protected than it is in the photograph.)* **Visual/Spatial, Logical/Mathematical**

V

Content Background Knowledge

Salt is not an important trade commodity in West Africa anymore. The United States and China are the leaders in salt production today. Together they produce about 40 percent of all the world's salt. Ghana and Senegal are the main salt-producing countries in West Africa today. However, their reserves are not developed, which has led to low production. A lack of modern technology is the main reason that nations in West Africa lag behind the United States and China.

LECTURE SLIDES

The Salt Trade

Integrating Visual Information Use the lecture slide presentation about the salt trade in the West African kingdoms to lead a discussion with students about the importance of salt to the early trade and history of the region. Have students write a paragraph describing the importance of the salt trade in the development of the region. **AL ELL Verbal/Linguistic**

See page 351D for other online activities.

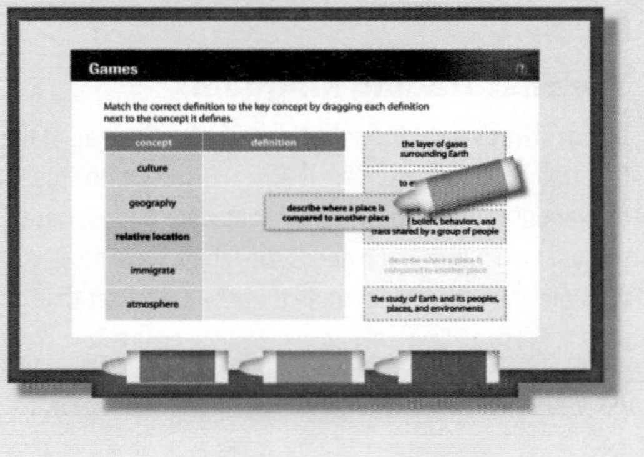

ANSWER, p. 361

CRITICAL THINKING Salt was rare in many areas and hard to acquire, and it was the best preserver of food.

The History of West Africa

V Visual Skills

Integrating Visual Information Have students locate the trading city of Timbuktu on the map. Then have students study the map key. **Ask: Why do you think so many kingdoms grew near this city?** *(Possible answer: It was a major trading center, and through trade, the kingdoms could thrive. Timbuktu was also located along trade routes and near a river, which provided options for transportation to and from the kingdoms.)* **Visual/Spatial, Logical/Mathematical**

R Reading Skills

Applying Review with students how Ghana relied on trade, especially the gold trade. Explain that gold made the kingdom rich, but the kingdom did not develop its economy in any other area. **Ask: Do you think it was wise for the kingdom of Ghana to rely so much on the gold trade? Explain.** *(Possible answer: No, the kingdom was too reliant on the gold trade. Even though gold made the kingdom rich, it did not help the country prepare for the future. When Ghana was invaded, the gold trade declined, and the kingdom did not have any other industry or economic base that would support the people, not even agriculture.)* **Logical/Mathematical, Verbal/Linguistic**

W Writing Skills

Argument The Almoravids were so avid about their faith that they conquered other lands in order to spread their religion.

Have students use the follwing question as a writing prompt and to support their argument with facts and details. **Ask: Do you think that it was acceptable for the Almoravids to conquer other regions in order to spread their religion?**

Point out additional text and online resources that students may use to gather support for their argument. Remind them to address counterarguments and to clearly state their argument in the introduction and conclusion. Have students take turns reading their arguments to a partner who chose the other side. Provide an opportunity for pairs to debate. **Verbal/Linguistic, Intrapersonal**

ANSWERS, p. 362

MAP SKILLS
1. Timbuktu
2. buy and trade for other goods, create strong empires

☑ READING PROGRESS CHECK The Almoravids conquered Ghana, which damaged trade activities. To feed the large population of Almoravids, Ghana needed more food. The increase in agriculture resulted in desertification. Once Ghana was weak, the kingdoms it had conquered were able to break free of Ghana's rule.

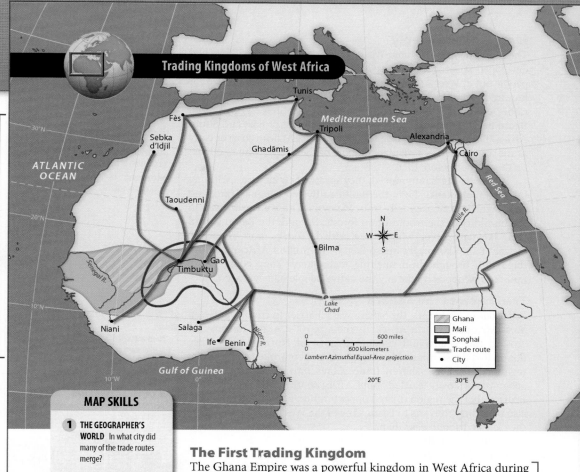

Trading Kingdoms of West Africa

Map legend:
- Ghana
- Mali
- Songhai
- Trade route
- City

0 – 600 miles
0 – 600 kilometers
Lambert Azimuthal Equal-Area projection

MAP SKILLS

1 THE GEOGRAPHER'S WORLD In what city did many of the trade routes merge?

2 PLACES AND REGIONS The early African kingdoms developed near gold-rich areas. What did a plentiful supply of gold allow them to do?

The First Trading Kingdom

The Ghana Empire was a powerful kingdom in West Africa during the Middle Ages. It had grown wealthy from its control of the gold trade. As the empire grew wealthy, it conquered many of its neighbors, including gold-rich lands to the south. Ghana built a strong trade with Muslim countries in North Africa.

In the A.D. 1000s, the Almoravids conquered Ghana. Almoravid rule over Ghana lasted only a few years, but that was long enough to damage the trade that kept the empire alive. With the arrival of so many Almoravids, there was now a larger population to feed. The dry climate could not support the sudden increase in agriculture, and this resulted in desertification: Land that at one time was fertile became desert. Ghana became weak, and its conquered neighbors began to break away.

☑ READING PROGRESS CHECK

Determining Central Ideas Why did the Ghana Empire collapse?

---

net**w**⊙rks   *Online Teaching Options*

MAP

The First Trading Kingdoms

Integrating Visual Information Display the map of the first trading kingdoms of West Africa. Discuss with students the various routes and the goods that were traded. Have students tell which trade goods they think were most valuable and why certain trade routes were better than others. **Visual/Spatial, Logical/Mathematical**

See page 351D for other online activities.

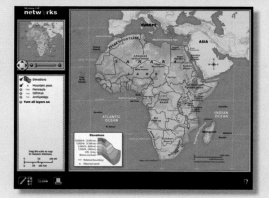

West African Kingdoms

GUIDING QUESTION *Why was the city of Timbuktu important to different trading kingdoms in West Africa?*

Several West African kingdoms sought to take control of the trade the fallen Ghana Empire had established in the region. Islam was taking hold in northern West Africa, and the most powerful of the new trading kingdoms were Muslim: Mali and Songhai.

Mali

The trading kingdom of Mali came after Ghana. Mali grew rich from the gold-for-salt trade. Its rulers conquered neighboring lands and built an empire.

The empire of Mali reached its height under the emperor Mansa Musa. The city of Timbuktu, which was already an important trading post, became a center for Islamic culture. Mansa Musa went on a historic pilgrimage to Mecca. By the time Mansa Musa returned home, the Islamic world knew there was a new and powerful Islamic kingdom south of the Sahara.

C

Songhai

R

After Mansa Musa's death, Songhai replaced Mali as the most powerful West African empire. A well-trained army and a navy that patrolled the Niger River made Songhai the largest of the three trading empires. Songhai now controlled the region's trade routes, had salt mines in the Sahara, and sought to turn their empire into the center for Islamic learning. The Songhai Empire eventually fell to the Moroccans, who seized the salt mines and destroyed the empire by the end of the 1500s.

Coastal Kingdoms

Slavery had been practiced in Africa for centuries. Muslims from North Africa and Asia had been buying enslaved people from south of the Sahara. As European colonists established colonies in the Western Hemisphere, they purchased enslaved people to do their labor. Small African kingdoms along the Atlantic coast became trading partners with Portugal, Spain, and Great Britain. Trade in enslaved persons became highly profitable in these kingdoms. When Europeans outlawed the slave trade, the kingdoms' economies began to fail.

☑ **READING PROGRESS CHECK**

Identifying How did the slave trade in West Africa change after the arrival of the Europeans?

Mansa Musa is shown sitting on his throne in this map of Africa from an atlas created in 1375.

Abraham Cresques/The Bridgeman Art Library/Getty Images

Chapter 12 **363**

C Critical Thinking Skills

Analyzing After students read the section titled "Mali," review with them how salt was used in ancient times. Encourage students to analyze the value of salt and compare it to the value of gold. **Ask:**

- **Why was salt traded in exchange for gold?** *(Possible answer: Since salt was used to preserve food, people who had no access to salt needed it.)*

- **Was it a good trade?** *(In some ways it was a good trade because salt enabled people to preserve food, which is necessary for survival. In other ways, it was not a good trade because salt goes bad or can be ruined if it gets wet. Gold does not get ruined in the same way.)* **Logical/Mathematical**

R Reading Skills

Citing Text Evidence Explain to students that going back to the text to find an answer to a question is not the only way to respond to a question. However, citing the wording from the text in a response is more explicit. Provide the following questions and have students practice using the skill. **Ask:**

- **What enabled Songhai to become the largest of the three trading empires of West Africa?** *(The Songhai empire had a well-trained army and a navy.)*

- **What led to the empire's downfall?** *(Songhai fell to the Moroccans, who seized the salt mines and destroyed the empire.)* **Verbal/Linguistic**

V

V Visual Skills

Interpreting Ask students to examine the image of Mansa Musa. Discuss with students how Mansa Musa is shown in a map. **Ask: Why do you think Mansa Musa is portrayed in this way?** *(Possible answer: He was a great ruler who brought much wealth through the gold trade to Mali. The image of Mansa Musa is on a map and he is depicted holding gold. This image portrays a powerful ruler.)* **ELL** **Visual/Spatial**

(l) ©Ocean/Corbis, ©Kryssia Campos/Getty Images, (tr) Erica Simone Leeds, (br) ©JG Photography/Alamy

SLIDE SHOW

Mansa Musa

Assessing Use the slide show on Mansa Musa to discuss with students the importance of this ruler in early West African history. Have students write three interview questions and answers for Mansa Musa that assess his importance and contributions. Then, with a partner, have them ask Mansa Musa the questions. Invite volunteers to perform their interview in front of the class.

Interpersonal, Verbal/Linguistic

Slide Show

See page 351D for other online activities.

ANSWER, p. 363

☑ **READING PROGRESS CHECK** The slave trade became highly profitable for the West African kingdoms that traded with the Europeans.

C Critical Thinking Skills

Determining Cause and Effect Review with students what abolitionism was and how the movement toward the abolition of slavery in the United States was gaining strength during the early 1800s. **Ask:** What effect did the founding of the British colony of Freetown have on slavery? *(It led to the ban of the slave trade in 1807 by the British government and America's founding of Liberia for freed American slaves.)*

Have students work in small groups to write a paragraph that expresses the changing views on slavery and the move toward the abolition of slavery. Invite volunteers to share their writing with the class. **Interpersonal, Verbal/Linguistic**

R Reading Skills

Using Context Clues Remind students that to find the meaning of an unfamiliar word, they can look at other words in the sentence to help gain understanding. **Ask:** What does the word *revenue* mean? *(income that is collected)*

Then explain to students that if they are unfamiliar with a word that is provided in a definition they may need to use a dictionary or thesaurus to find its meaning. Ask a volunteer to use a dictionary to find its meaning. *(money gained or earned).* **Ask:** Why was it important to replace the revenue that would have been gained from slave trade with something else? *(In order to truly end the slave trade, it was important for slave traders to have another way to earn money. This was also important to the other businesses in the region because the slave trade was a large part of the economy.)* **AL Logical/Mathematical**

V Visual Skills

Visualizing Point to the image of Freetown, and allow ample time for students to study it. **Ask:** Why do you think the British government chose this location for freed slaves? *(Possible answer: It is near the coast, where freed slaves would have access to the ocean, which could provide transportation and trade.)*

Have students visualize what it was like for former slaves to arrive in Freetown. Ask them to make a list of adjectives that might describe their feelings. Then have them make a list of resources and opportunities newly freed slaves would have had in Freetown based on the physical features in the photograph. Using their lists, instruct students to make a travel brochure for Freetown. **ELL Visual/Spatial**

ANSWER, p. 364

CRITICAL THINKING Freetown was founded as a colony for runaway and freed enslaved persons.

European Domination

GUIDING QUESTION *What were some of the factors that aroused European interest in exploring and colonizing Africa?*

In the late 1800s, several European countries were eager to expand into Africa with its many natural resources. After hundreds of years of self-rule, West Africans lost control of their lands to the Europeans.

Changing Trade

C The British government outlawed the slave trade in 1807. Great Britain tried but could not keep other European countries from continuing to export slaves. The British founded the colony of Freetown in Sierra Leone in 1787 as a safe haven for runaway or freed enslaved persons. The Americans followed suit in 1822, founding Liberia as a home for freed American slaves.

Academic Vocabulary

revenue income

R The British encouraged development of the palm oil trade to make up for the loss of **revenue** from the slave trade. British traders and missionaries familiarized themselves with the trading culture of the Niger River. The British started to profit from their growing role in West African trade. Before long, France took notice.

Creating Colonies

Before the mid-1800s, the British and French posted military in North Africa, and the British and Dutch had settled in South Africa. In 1869 two events increased Europe's interest in Africa. First, the Suez Canal—an artificial waterway connecting the Mediterranean Sea to the Red Sea—opened. Second, diamonds were discovered in South Africa.

Freetown, the largest city in Sierra Leone, is located in the western part of the country along the Atlantic coast.
▶ **CRITICAL THINKING**
Describing What is unique about how Freetown was founded?

364 Chapter 12

Chris Jackson/Getty Images News/Getty Images

---

networks   *Online Teaching Options*

IMAGE

Freetown, Sierra Leone

Comparing and Contrasting Display the interactive image of Freetown, Sierra Leone, for students. Discuss its historical significance, as well as the current development of the city. Have students review the development of Freetown using the captions in the image and encourage them to create a graphic organizer for later review. **Visual/Spatial, Verbal/Linguistic**

See page 351D for other online activities.

Interactive Photos

Lissa Harrison

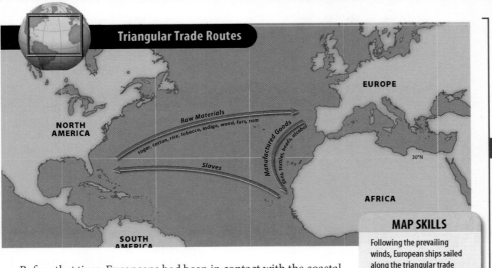

Triangular Trade Routes

NORTH AMERICA

EUROPE

Raw Materials
sugar, cotton, rice, tobacco, indigo, wood, furs, rum

Manufactured Goods
guns, textiles, beads, alcohol

30°N

Slaves

AFRICA

SOUTH AMERICA

MAP SKILLS

Following the prevailing winds, European ships sailed along the triangular trade route.

1 THE GEOGRAPHER'S WORLD Why were raw materials from the Americas shipped to Europe rather than to other parts of the world?

2 PLACES AND REGIONS Most European trade with Africa was conducted in West Africa. Why do you think this was so?

Before that time, Europeans had been in contact with the coastal kingdoms, but few had ventured into the interior of West Africa. This began to change as Great Britain, France, Portugal, Belgium, and the new, unified country of Germany began planning to carve out empires in Africa. Europeans followed a policy of **imperialism**, or seizing political control of other places to create an empire. At the Berlin Conference of 1884–1885, the European powers established rules for partitioning Africa.

The French and British claimed the most territory in West Africa. The modern countries of Benin, Burkina Faso, Chad, Côte d'Ivoire, Guinea, Mali, Mauritania, Niger, and Senegal were French colonies. Gambia, Ghana, Nigeria, Sierra Leone, and St. Helena were British colonies. Togo started out as a German possession, but Germany lost it in World War I.

Some colonies were ruled more harshly than others, but one thing was true about all of them: Europeans made the important decisions about how Africans lived. Settlers from Europe could set up farms on the most fertile land, even if Africans were forced off that land. Africans resisted, sometimes violently.

☑ **READING PROGRESS CHECK**

Describing What was the purpose of the Berlin Conference?

New Countries

GUIDING QUESTION *How does a ruler gain and hold political power?*

West African colonies began gaining independence in the late 1950s. The struggle for economic and political success was difficult because of the complex ethnic makeup of these countries.

Chapter 12 **365**

V **Visual Skills**

Analyzing Maps Provide time for students to study and review the map. **Ask:**

- **Why do you think that South America was not part of the Triangular Trade?** *(Possible answer: The triangular trade route developed as a way for Europe and North America to trade goods between themselves and take slaves and resources from Africa.)*
- **Why would natural resources be shipped from West Africa and manufactured goods be shipped back to West Africa?** *(Possible answer: There were no manufacturing facilities in Africa at the time. This was likely a result of Europeans deciding what would happen in Africa—it was more profitable for Europeans if the goods were manufactured by European companies back home. Also, the manufacturing companies now had more customers—West Africans.)*
- **How do you think the independence of the United States in the late 1700s affected Britain's supply of raw materials from North America? Explain.** *(Possible answer: It probably cut back on Britain's supply from what became the United States, but Britain still had raw materials coming in from Canada. It probably also meant that the United States would become a strong trading partner with Britain once they were through fighting each other.)* **BL** **Logical/Mathematical**

Content Background Knowledge

Imperialism was not a new concept when the European powers met at the Berlin Conference to divide Africa. In the modern sense of the term, it was first used in 1800. However, imperialism had existed since ancient times, as empires in Asia and Southwest Asia expanded and conquered others. In the nineteenth century the term took on a new meaning. It was a "new" imperialism, practiced globally and not just by Europeans. Colonizing different parts of the world became a competition, many times at the price of those who were colonized. European colonization of Africa would cause challenges for many African nations as independence movements began in the late 1950s.

MAP

Imperialism and Independence in West Africa

Integrating Visual Information Display the map of imperialism to discuss the changes that resulted from the interactions between Europe and West Africa. Begin the discussion with the slave trade, then move on to the influence of imperialism on the colonization of the region by European nations. Have students write three statements about the information on the map, including anything that surprised them, such as the dates of independence. **Visual/Spatial, Verbal/Linguistic**

See page 351D for other online activities.

ANSWERS, p. 365

MAP SKILLS

1. European countries had colonies in the Americas. The colonies provided raw materials to Europe.
2. Possible response: It was easier for ships doing business in Africa to get to Europe and North America if they traveled to/from West Africa.

☑ **READING PROGRESS CHECK** European countries met to decide how to divide Africa among themselves.

G1 Critical Thinking Skills

Making Generalizations Review with students some of the challenges that the countries of West Africa faced upon achieving independence, such as ethnic makeup and corrupt leadership. **Ask: How are the challenges that the nations of West Africa faced after independence a result of European colonization?** *(Possible answer: They are largely a result of European colonization because European countries established political boundaries (nations) that had nothing to do with the cultural or ethnic regions. West Africans experienced corrupt leadership under European rule, which is probably why many of the African leaders who held power after independence were corrupt.)* **AL** **Logical/Mathematical**

V Visual Skills

Creating Time Lines Have students read the section titled, "Ghana Leads the Way." Direct students to work with a partner to create a time line of the history of Ghana from European interaction to a democratic government. Suggest that students enhance their time lines by doing additional research to fill any large time gaps with significant events in the country's history. Invite volunteers to share their time lines with the class. **ELL** **Visual/Spatial, Interpersonal**

C2 Critical Thinking Skills

Determining Cause and Effect Provide an opportunity for students to read the section on the former French colonies and to take time to think about Ghana's influence in the region. **Ask:**

- **How did Ghana's independence affect other countries in West Africa?** *(They influenced other independence movements in the French colonies in the region.)*
- **Did the countries in West Africa under French control gain independence differently than those under British control? Explain.** *(France gave its colonies a form of self-rule, unlike the British. However, it did not work. The colonies under French rule wanted complete independence like the Gold Coast and Ghana achieved.)* **AL** **Verbal/Linguistic**

The leader of Ghana, Kwame Nkrumah (center), meets with a citizen in 1959. Bediako Poku (standing) headed the Convention People's Party (CPP), a political party Nkrumah started. A referendum election in 1964 made the CPP the nation's only legal party, and Nkrumah was installed as president of Ghana for life. The military and police ousted Nkrumah from power in 1966.

Another factor working against political stability was the actions taken by the leaders. Often, they seized power and then used force to stay in power. **C1**

Ghana Leads the Way

The Gold Coast had been important to European trade since Portugal set up its first fort there in 1487. By the early 1800s, it was under British control, and in 1874 the Gold Coast became a British colony. The most important industries were gold, forest resources, and a newly introduced crop—the cocoa bean from which chocolate is made. By the 1920s, the Gold Coast supplied more than half the world's cocoa. **V**

After the end of World War II, Dr. Kwame Nkrumah led protests calling for independence. Protests flared throughout the colony. In 1957 the Gold Coast gained its independence and became the Republic of Ghana. For many years, Ghana was troubled by conflict. In 1992 Ghana approved a new constitution that established a multiparty democracy. Since then, presidential elections have been peaceful, and Ghana has become a model of political reform in West Africa.

Former French Colonies

Throughout the 1950s, France made concessions to its West African colonies, many of which had instituted some form of self-rule. The independence of Ghana excited and inspired Africans, however. Cries for independence began erupting all over Africa. French Sudan and Senegal united to become the Republic of Mali, but Senegal broke away the following year, and Mali declared its own independence. In 1960 Mauritania, Niger, Côte d'Ivoire, Gambia, and Burkina Faso declared their independence. By 1961, all of France's colonies in West Africa were independent. **C2**

Nigeria

Nigeria had never been a country before the British combined two of their colonies to form the Nigerian Protectorate in 1914. Several different ethnic groups lived in this new territory. The Yoruba and Edo people had distinct territories in the south. The Hausa people were Muslims who lived in the north. The Igbo people were farmers who began to migrate east after British colonization.

When Nigeria gained its independence in 1960, tensions grew between ethnic groups. Because Britain had concentrated most of its development, including building schools, in southern Nigeria,

Mark Kauffman/Time & Life Pictures/Getty Images

---

netw⊕rks   *Online Teaching Options*

IMAGE

Kwame Nkrumah

Applying Display the interactive image of Kwame Nkrumah. Discuss with students his role in the fight for independence in Ghana. Ask students if they can think of other independence movements in other parts of the world that were led by a leader such as Nkrumah. If needed, allow students some time to work in small groups to research other examples. Have a class discussion on their findings, and compare and contrast the situations and personalities. **BL** **Interpersonal**

See page 351D for other online activities.

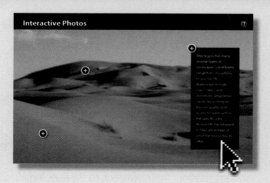

Lissa Harrison

most well-educated Nigerians lived in the south. They became leaders of the new government. Many of them were Igbo, who were mostly Christian. When they ventured north to govern the Hausa, they were met with hostility. Conflicts among the three major ethnic divisions in the country—the Hausa, the Yoruba, and the Igbo—grew violent. Thousands of Igbo living in northern Nigeria were massacred. As many as a million more fled to a region dominated by the Igbo. In 1967 the eastern region **seceded**, or withdrew formally, from Nigeria and announced that it was now the independent republic of Biafra. Nigerian forces invaded Biafra, and after more than two years of war, Biafra was in ruins. Starvation and disease may have killed more than 1 million people.

For long periods since then, the military has controlled the country's government. A new constitution was written in 1978. A year later, a democratically elected civilian government took office. That ended in a military coup in 1983. It was not until 1999 that another democratically elected president was able to rule Nigeria.

Civil War

Sometimes a military coup erupts into civil war. In late 1989, Charles Taylor led an invasion of Liberia. His aim was to depose the president, Samuel Doe. Ethnic conflict was at the heart of this struggle. Taylor and his rebels were of the Mano and Gio peoples. President Doe belonged to the Krahn people. After Doe's arrest and execution, Liberia endured seven years of civil war.

Conflict spilled over Liberia's borders into neighboring Sierra Leone. Thousands of civilians died, and many were forced to leave their homes. The civil war in Sierra Leone did not end until 2002. Estimates are that 50,000 died and another 2 million people lost their homes in the civil war. In 2012 Charles Taylor was brought to trial by a special court. He was found guilty of war crimes and crimes against humanity for his part in Sierra Leone's civil war.

☑ **READING PROGRESS CHECK**

Determining Central Ideas What reason might the French have had for letting their African colonies declare independence?

Thinking Like a Geographer

Religious Rivalry

In the A.D. 700s, Muslim people converted many West Africans to Islam. Over time, Islam became the dominant religion in northern parts of the region. Many West Africans along the coastal areas adopted Christianity after the arrival of the Europeans in the 1500s. Others continue to practice traditional African religions. Relations between these different religious groups have not always been good.

FOLDABLES Study Organizer

Include this lesson's information in your Foldable®.

LESSON 2 REVIEW CCSS

Reviewing Vocabulary (Tier Three Words)

1. How did the Berlin Conference of 1884–1885 help achieve the goals of European *imperialism*? RH.6-8.4

Answering the Guiding Questions

2. *Determining Central Ideas* How did the Bantu culture influence the parts of Africa to which the Bantu migrated? RH.6-8.2

3. *Identifying* How did the Islamic world become aware of the wealth of the Mali Empire? RH.6-8.2

4. *Describing* Why did the British encourage development of the palm oil trade in African kingdoms on the Atlantic coast? RH.6-8.5

5. *Analyzing* Why did Nigeria face so many challenges when becoming an independent country? RH.6-8.1

6. *Argument Writing* Write a speech to the French government in the late 1950s about how important the independence of Ghana is and why France should release its colonies. WHST.6-8.1, WHST.6-8.4

Chapter 12 **367**

C Critical Thinking Skills

Making Connections Review with students the meaning of *secede* and make connections to how South Carolina and the Southern states seceded from the Union. Remind them that this action instigated the American Civil War in the 1860s. Invite volunteers to explain why the Southern states seceded (*states' rights and slavery*). **Ask:**

• **How were the circumstances that Nigeria experienced during its civil war and the United States during the American Civil War similar and different?** (*Similar: There were many deaths in both conflicts, as well as destruction after the conflicts ended; Different: In Nigeria, the eastern region seceded because of ethnic divisions, while in the United States the issue was more political. In Nigeria, the conflict erupted in the 1960s, while the American Civil War took place in the 1860s.*)

• **How were the results similar and different?** (*Possible answer: There was some degree of political change in both conflicts. In Nigeria a new constitution was written, while in the United States, the constitution was amended. In the case of Nigeria, it took a while for a democratic election to take place, while in the United States democratic elections took place at their regular intervals.*) **BL** **Logical/Mathematical**

T Technology Skills

Evaluating a Web Site Have students work in small groups to find a news story that covered the conflicts in Liberia or Sierra Leone. Ask them to compare and contrast the information in their text with the information that they read online. Then ask students to each write an evaluation of the information presented on the Web site with the news story. Ask them to include in their evaluations if the news story cited source information, used quotations from key people involved, presented both sides of the event or issue, and used facts to support the point of view. **Interpersonal, Verbal/Linguistic**

CLOSE & REFLECT

Expressing To close this lesson, have students think about how new ideas that were brought to West Africa changed the way people lived. Ask them to think about the positive and negative effects of these ideas. Have students write a topic sentence that expresses the effects of the ideas and then list at least three relevant details that describe specific examples from the lesson.

ANSWER, p. 367

☑ **READING PROGRESS CHECK** Sample answer: There was much ethnic and political conflict in the French colonies, so the French might have thought that it would be better to allow the colonies to declare independence rather than trying to resolve the conflict.

LESSON 2 REVIEW ANSWERS

Reviewing Vocabulary

1. At the Berlin Conference, European countries divided Africa among themselves, with the aim of taking political and economic control.

Answering the Guiding Questions

2. **Determining Central Ideas** The Bantu brought bananas, taro, and yams to the tropical rain forest regions. They spread their languages everywhere they settled, so now 85 million Africans speak more than 500 distinct Bantu languages. The Bantu had iron-smelting technology and were able to create tools and weapons the indigenous peoples had not seen before.

3. **Identifying** Mansa Musa went on a pilgrimage to Mecca and took along thousands of his subjects, plus 80 camels loaded with gold.

4. **Describing** The British encouraged development of the palm oil trade to make up for the loss of revenue from the slave trade.

5. **Analyzing** Several different groups of ethnic Africans lived in the British-created colony. The groups were a mix of Christians, Muslims, and followers of traditional African religions. Conflicts among ethnic groups turned violent.

6. **Argument Writing** Students' responses should include information from the text about Ghana's struggle for independence and about France's many colonies and their wish for independence.

ENGAGE

Making Connections Show students a picture or an actual sample of a kente cloth. Explain that this is an example of traditional weaving done by the Ashanti people of Ghana. The Ashanti use the kente cloth for special celebrations. It represents their history, culture, beliefs, values, and ideas.

Ask: Is there a special tradition or type of artwork that is important to your culture or a culture that you know well? How is it similar and different? *(Answers will vary. Students should demonstrate an understanding of cultural traditions and how they are similar and different yet unique.)*

TEACH & ASSESS

V Visual Skills

Analyzing Maps Show students a current political map of West Africa. Then display a map of West Africa before 1950, preferably one that shows colonial borders. **Ask:**

- **How are the borders of West African countries in both maps similar and different?** *(They appear to be similar.)*
- **Why do you think there are few to no differences?** *(Possible answer: When West African nations became independent, it was easier to maintain the same borders.)*
- **What challenges would an ethnically diverse country face that a more homogenous one would not?** *(More ethnically diverse countries might have to deal with more disputes among different groups. Ethnic groups may have different ways of life. In a country with less diversity, people would most likely have fewer conflicts.)* **AL** Visual/Spatial

R Reading Skills

Defining Read aloud the sentence in the section, "Ethnic Groups," that includes the words *national unity*. Discuss the meanings of each word with students. Ask them to think about how the words are different when they are combined, *national* and *unity* versus *national unity*. Have students write a paragraph about what *national unity* means and how it relates to West Africa. Provide an opportunity for students to read their paragraphs to the class. **ELL** Verbal/Linguistic

---

ANSWER, p. 368

Taking Notes **City:** people more likely to wear Western-style clothing and live and work in Western-style buildings; a wide variety of people from different ethnic groups, other races, and other countries; more likely to speak the country's official language; life usually built around nuclear family; **Rural:** people more likely to wear traditional clothing; life built around extended family; ethnicity and tradition still important; devotion to traditional values keeps languages and cultures alive even as the country itself is changing.

---

networks

There's More Online!

☑ **SLIDE SHOW** Daily Life in West Africa

☑ **VIDEO**

Reading **HELP**DESK **CCSS**

Academic Vocabulary RH.6-8.4
(Tier Two Words)
- **diverse**

Content Vocabulary RH.6-8.4
(Tier Three Words)
- **pidgin**
- **creole**
- **animist**
- **extended family**
- **nuclear family**
- **kente**
- **infrastructure**

TAKING NOTES: *Key Ideas and Details* RH.6-8.2, RH.6-8.7

Compare and Contrast Use a graphic organizer like the one below to show some of the differences between life in a West African city and life in a rural area of West Africa.

City	Rural
•	•
•	•
•	•
•	

Lesson 3
Life in West Africa

ESSENTIAL QUESTION · *What makes a culture unique?*

IT MATTERS BECAUSE
West African countries have faced many challenges in the decades since they achieved independence. Even as they struggle to modernize and improve their economies, West Africans have been able to spread their artistic gifts to people around the world.

The People of the Region

GUIDING QUESTION Why are two or more languages spoken in some West African countries?

West Africa is the most populous region of Africa. Many different ethnic groups live here, and each group brings something unique to their country's culture.

Ethnic Groups

European countries that carved up Africa to add to their overseas empires had their own reasons for setting colonial borders where they did. They did not consider the borders of the different ethnic groups of the Africans who already lived on the land they colonized. As a result, the European colonies in Africa contained populations that were ethnically **diverse**. When African countries declared independence, the new national borders closely followed the old colonial borders, preserving that diversity.

Establishing a sense of national unity is difficult, however. Many people have a stronger identification with their ethnic group than with the country they live in. For example, the Hausa are citizens of Nigeria, but many feel closer ties to the people and culture of the Hausa than to the country of Nigeria.

(l to r) Glen Allison/Photodisc/Getty Images; ©Carlos Cazalis/Corbis; Olivier Asselin/Alamy; African/The Bridgeman Art Library/Getty Images; ©nabil zorkot/dpa/Corbis

---

networks *Online Teaching Options*

VIDEO

Benin Child Slaves

Comparing and Contrasting Use the video about the current issue of human trafficking and child slavery in Benin to discuss just one of the social issues and challenges in West Africa. Have students create a chart while they watch the video and take notes on the information mentioned in the video. Ask them to identify ways that this issue is being fought and how this issue impacts the rest of the world. **AL** Interpersonal

See page 351E for other online activities.

BBC Motion Gallery Education

Another factor working against national unity is that a West African ethnic group does not typically live in only one country. Some Yoruba people, for example, live in Nigeria. Other Yoruba live in Benin. No matter where they live, the Yoruba feel a closer connection to other Yoruba people than to Nigeria or Benin.

Languages

When West African countries achieved independence, the majority held on to the European language that had been used most in business and government during the colonial period. The European languages—English, Portuguese, and French—became the official languages of West African countries. In some cases, Arabic is also an official language.

Most ethnic groups retain their traditional languages, and many use that language more than they do the official European language. In some places, European and African languages have intermixed to form a **pidgin** language. A pidgin is a simplified language used by people who cannot speak each other's languages but need a way to communicate. Sometimes two or more languages blend so well that the mixture becomes the language of the region. This is called a **creole** language. Crioulo is the language spoken most often in Cape Verde. It is a creole language, part Portuguese and part African dialect.

Religion

Islam was introduced to North Africa in the A.D. 600s, and it spread southward with trade. It was well established in many parts of West Africa long before the arrival of Christian missionaries from Europe. Today, a sizable portion of West African populations are Muslim.

Glen Allison/Photodisc/Getty Images

Academic Vocabulary

diverse comprised of many distinct and different parts

C

Women talk near the Great Mosque in Djenne, Mali. The Great Mosque is the largest mud-brick building in the world. The first mosque on this site was built in the 1200s. The current mosque was built in 1907.
▶ **CRITICAL THINKING**
Describing In what region of Africa was Islam first introduced?

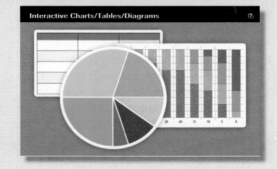

Chapter 12 **369**

CHART

Ethnic Groups in West Africa

Analyzing Charts Use the chart of different ethnic groups in West Africa to discuss the ethnic population distribution across the region. Have students take turns identifying nations in which an ethnic group dominates or nations in which there is such diversity that it is difficult to determine if there is a majority group. Ask students to choose one country and write about the different ethnic groups that comprise its population.
AL **ELL** **Verbal/Linguistic**

See page 351E for other online activities.

C Critical Thinking Skills

Speculating Have students think of how they feel when they are part of a team or group. Brainstorm words that are associated with this feeling. *(Possible words include belonging, connected, understanding, welcoming.)*

Now tell them they are part of a group of students being transferred to a rival school, and it is their first day at the new school. Brainstorm words that are associated with this feeling. *(Possible words include fear, loneliness, isolation, sadness.)*

Ask them to think if they would be more likely to eat lunch on the first day with the group of students transferred from their old school or with new students from the rival school. **Ask:** Why do you think that the Yoruba have more of a connection to their own people than to the country in which they live? *(They want to be with people who are like themselves, other Yoruba, no matter where they are. They feel a stronger connection to their group than to their country, just as we would feel a stronger connection to a group of old friends than to a new school.)* **ELL** **Interpersonal**

R Reading Skills

Naming After students read the section titled, "Languages," review with them the difference between *pidgin* and *creole*. **Ask:**

- Crioulo is an example of which kind of language? *(creole)*
- A language that is part French and part African would be what kind of language? *(creole or pidgin)*
- If two groups speak different languages, they may speak which kind of language to communicate? *(pidgin)*
- Why do you think pidgin and creole languages developed? *(Possible answer: Colonialism played a large part in the development of pidgin and creole languages since different cultures were grouped together that spoke different languages yet needed to communicate. Also, colonial powers needed to communicate with the indigenous people of the areas they colonized and did not speak the language.)* **Logical/Mathematical, Verbal/Linguistic**

ANSWER, p. 369

CRITICAL THINKING North Africa

Life in West Africa

W Writing Skills

Informative/Explanatory Have students write an essay about the different religions practiced in West Africa. Point out additional print and electronic resources that students can use to learn about the different religions and where they are practiced. Tell students that they should plan out their paragraphs and organize the information they gathered from research before they begin writing. Review the proper way to cite sources and remind students that they must give proper credit to avoid plagiarism. **BL Verbal/Linguistic**

T Technology Skills

Analyzing Data Copy the following data on population density and urban population percentages by country for West Africa on the board.

Country	Population Density (per square km)	% Living in Urban Areas
Benin	77	40
Burkina Faso	51	18
Cote d'Ivoire	57	45
Gambia	150	54
Ghana	94	48
Guinea	39	33
Guinea Bissau	44	30
Liberia	34	58
Mali	11	30
Mauritania	3	40
Niger	12	17
Nigeria	145	48
Senegal	60	42
Sierra Leone	79	41
Togo	111	40

Ask: Is there a connection between population density and the percentage of the population that lives in cities? *(Not necessarily. For example, Burkina Faso has a higher population density than Mali, but a lower percentage of people living in urban areas.)* **AL Logical/Mathematical**

ANSWERS, p. 370

CRITICAL THINKING No. While Africa has a few megacities and some large cities, most settlements are scattered villages.

☑ READING PROGRESS CHECK Most people still speak the traditional language of their ethnic group. Some people still practice traditional African religions.

Lagos is Nigeria's largest city and ranks among the fastest-growing megacities in the world. During the 2000s, about 600,000 people have moved to Lagos every year.
▶ CRITICAL THINKING
W *Describing* Are megacities the most common form of settlement in West Africa? Explain.

In some countries, however, Christianity is just as dominant as Islam, or more so. Even in countries where Christianity or Islam is dominant, many people still practice traditional African religions. These religions have their own rituals and celebrations that tie communities together. The beliefs are not written on paper but passed on from one generation to another. Often, the people believe in a supreme creator god and are **animists**, which means they believe in spirits—spirits of their ancestors, the air, the earth, and rivers.

Settlement Patterns

West Africa had few large towns until the colonial period. Even today, the most common settlement patterns in West Africa consist of scattered villages. Villages represent the homesteads of **extended families**, or families made up of parents, children, and other close relatives, often of more than two generations. The size of the villages and the population density depend on how much human activity the land can sustain. Water is an issue in the northern parts of West **T** Africa, so populations are small and spread out.

Most of the largest cities in West Africa are capital cities, like Bamako, Mali, which more than tripled in population between 1960 and 1970, when droughts caused people to migrate from the countryside. The largest city in West Africa is Lagos in Nigeria, with an estimated 10.5 million people. Lagos was Nigeria's capital until 1991; Abuja is now Nigeria's capital city.

☑ READING PROGRESS CHECK

Determining Central Ideas What are two ways traditions have survived in West Africa?

---

net**w**◉rks   *Online Teaching Options*

IMAGE

360° View: Lagos, Nigeria

Locating Use the 360° view of Lagos, Nigeria, to engage students in a discussion about rural and urban settlements and population distribution. Ask students to point out details in the image that illustrate an urban area. Have students use these details to identify other urban areas that are familiar to them and to share those locations and descriptions in small groups. **ELL Visual/Spatial**

See page 351E for other online activities.

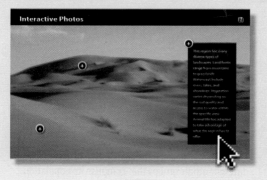

Life and Culture in the Region

GUIDING QUESTION *Why are traditions more important in rural areas of West Africa than they are in West African cities?*

A variety of cultures thrive in West Africa, some of them traditional and some contemporary. Countries in the north—such as Mali, Mauritania, and Niger—are more influenced by the culture of North Africa than are their neighboring countries.

Daily Life

West Africa, with its complicated history and rich mixture of ethnicities, has a diverse culture. English or French may be the language of the cities, or of business and politics, but hundreds of other languages are still spoken. People in cities are more likely to wear Western-style clothing and to live and work in Western-style buildings. Far from the city, many people retain the traditions of their ancestors. These people are more likely to wear traditional clothing. Life in rural villages is built around the extended family. In cities, the **nuclear family**—parents with their children—is the more common family structure.

City dwellers are far more likely to deal with a wide variety of people over the course of a day than are rural dwellers. Capital cities teem with people from different ethnic groups, races, and countries. They are more likely to speak the official language because that is the language they all have in common. In rural areas, ethnicity and tradition are still important. Devotion to traditional values keeps those languages and cultures alive even as the country is changing. The downside is that ethnic pride sometimes results in conflicts between neighboring ethnic groups.

The Arts

West Africans have created numerous unique and important works of art in many artistic fields. Traditional artwork, such as carved masks from Nigeria and Sierra Leone, are world famous. Another well-known traditional art form is **kente**, a colorful, handwoven cloth from Ghana. One of West Africa's most important artist-figures is the griot, a musical storyteller who is part historian and part spiritual advisor.

Dance is the most popular form of recreation in West Africa. Workers use dance to celebrate their skills and accomplishments; professional guilds have their own dances. Dance is used for its healing qualities, but people also dance to popular music in clubs.

A worker weaves kente cloth in Ghana (above). The painted wood mask (below) comes from Burkina Faso.

(t) Olivier Asselin/Alamy; (b) African/The Bridgeman Art Library/Getty Images

Chapter 12 **371**

IMAGES

West African Art

Comparing and Contrasting Use the interactive images about West African art to highlight different traditions in art and the role of art in daily life. Have students choose and examine two traditions that are illustrated in the photo and explain orally how they are similar and different. **ELL** **Visual/Spatial, Verbal/ Linguistic**

Interactive Photos

See page 351E for other online activities.

V Visual Skills

Creating Visuals Point out the image of a weaver weaving kente cloth. Review with students that a kente cloth can reveal a lot about a group's history, traditions, culture, beliefs, and so forth. Have students sketch out a pattern or design for their own kente cloth and to include descriptions of what the patterns or colors represent. Invite students to share their sketches with the class. **ELL** **Visual/Spatial**

V

R Reading Skills

Determining Word Meanings After students read the first paragraph of the section on daily life, point out the term *nuclear family*. Ask volunteers to define the word *nuclear*. *(central)* Then ask volunteers to say in their own words the definition of *extended family*. **Ask:**

- **How are the meanings of both terms similar and different?** *(Extended families are made up of parents, children, and more distant relatives. A nuclear family is just made up of parents and children; therefore, relatives are not central to a nuclear family.)*
- **How does a rural versus urban area affect the family structure in West Africa?** *(Possible answer: Families in urban areas are more likely to include nuclear families, while families in rural areas are more likely to focus on extended families.)* **AL** **Verbal/Linguistic**

Content Background Knowledge

Daily Life in Rural West Africa Explain to students that daily life in rural West Africa can vary by country and ethnic group but that some characteristics are similar.

- Some villagers live in mud brick houses with roofs made of tin and dried grasses.
- In front of some houses there is often an area for a fireplace or fire pits and benches. This area is used for family activities and events.
- Most cooking is done outdoors in fire pits by women in the extended family. Women help raise chickens and goats and gather wood for the fire.
- Men or women may be field workers, or they may sell handmade crafts or locally grown produce in markets. Men may work as carpenters or teachers.
- Children may attend school or may be needed to help their parents work in the fields. They also may not be able to attend school because they need to look after their younger siblings while their parents work.

V Visual Skills

Analyzing Images Explain to students that despite the many challenges that West African countries face with regard to ethnic tensions, they are striving to diversify their economies. **Ask:**

- **How does this image represent economic diversity in West Africa?** *(Possible answer: It shows how the Ivory Coast is working to expand its manufacturing industry.)*
- **Why is shipbuilding a good industry for the country to develop?** *(Possible answer: The Ivory Coast is situated on an ocean. The country can easily test ships that it builds.)* **AL** **Visual/Spatial**

C Critical Thinking Skills

Drawing Conclusions Review with students why the European countries colonized Africa. **Ask:**

- **What does** *infrastructure* **mean?** *(underlying framework)*
- **How was the infrastructure built in Africa during colonization?** *(It was built with a focus on using the resources, such as minerals and crops, for the benefit of the colonists.)*
- **How did reliance on these resources affect African countries after colonization ended?** *(Reliance on these resources meant that the economies of West Africa would be hurt if the price fluctuated greatly in the global market.)*
- **Why do you think European countries just focused on building the colonies' economies around resources?** *(Possible answer: They were not concerned about the long-term well-being of the countries. They were only interested in making the mother nations wealthy.)*
- **Why would it be difficult to change the economic focus of the newly independent countries?** *(In order to change an economic focus, the people must have the education and skills needed for the new industries. Also, there must be someone who has money to invest in building new businesses.)*
BL **Verbal/Linguistic, Logical/Mathematical**

Workers are on the job at a steel plant in Côte d'Ivoire. Like many other countries in the region, Côte d'Ivoire is developing its industries. Major manufacturing industries include bus and truck assembly and shipbuilding.

West African music blends a variety of many sounds, combining traditional and modern instruments. The Arabic influences of North African music mix with the music of sub-Saharan Africa, as well as with American and European rock and pop music.

West Africa has produced some of the world's finest writers. The most widely read of all African novels is *Things Fall Apart* by Chinua Achebe of Nigeria. Senegal's first president, Léopold Senghor, was a famous poet and lecturer on African history and culture.

☑ **READING PROGRESS CHECK**

Identifying Point of View Select an artistic field that you think best shows the culture of West Africa, and explain why you believe it does.

Challenges Facing the Region

GUIDING QUESTION *How did West African countries build up so much debt?*

Many West African countries face serious problems. To improve their situations, they must deal with these challenges and more: bad economies, corrupt governments, out-of-control population growth, disease, and poorly funded schools.

Government and Economics

The European powers that colonized Africa built the colonies' economies on a few key resources, such as petroleum, gold, peanuts, or copper. The **infrastructure**, or underlying framework of the colonies, was built around those key resources. Once the colonies achieved independence, it became important for them to develop a variety of different industries. Otherwise, any drop in the world price of a key resource would greatly affect a country's economy. Many foreign governments invested money in developing the

©nabil zorkot/dpa/Corbis

372 *Chapter 12*

---

netw⊕rks *Online Teaching Options*

GRAPHIC ORGANIZER

Challenges in West Africa

Listing Review current issues and challenges that West Africa faces using the interactive graphic organizer. Allow students to take turns citing examples. Have students vote on one issue or challenge they think is most difficult and then brainstorm a list of potential solutions. **Logical/ Mathematical, Interpersonal**

See page 351E for other online activities.

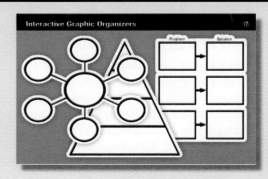
Interactive Graphic Organizers

ANSWER, p. 372

☑**READING PROGRESS CHECK** Answers should reflect something specific about West African artistic culture as discussed in this chapter.

industrial base of the new African countries. In many cases, money from the loans was not used wisely. As a result, the invested money did not yield high returns. West African countries were not only dealing with struggling economies but also faced enormous debt.

The International Monetary Fund and the World Bank have declared that no poor or developing country should have to pay a debt it cannot possibly manage. Debt relief has been important for countries such as Ghana, which suffered from bad economic choices and political instability. Ghana is now a model for economic and political reform in West Africa. Nigeria benefited from debt relief as well, and was able to pay off the remainder of what it owed in 2006.

A major challenge for the region is that, as the population grows, the demand for food and jobs grows. An economy does not have a chance to grow if it cannot meet the needs of a growing population.

Health and Education

Thirty-four million people in the world are living with the HIV virus, and 22.9 million of them live in sub-Saharan Africa. Dealing with such a large number of HIV-infected people presents several challenges. The first challenge is to supply health care to the growing number of people who carry the virus. The second challenge is to reduce the number of new HIV infections, usually through education. The third challenge is to deal with the families and communities hurt by AIDS-related deaths.

West Africa has a high birthrate, and the population is growing quickly, but life expectancy is still short compared to other parts of the world. Health care is an issue in large cities, but it is an even greater issue in rural areas.

The population of West Africa is young. For West Africa to have a sound future, educational systems must effectively prepare young people for economic and social development. A lack of education funding means that some countries cannot afford to make updates or improvements to their schools.

☑ READING PROGRESS CHECK

Analyzing Why is education such an important issue for the future of West Africa?

FOLDABLES®
Study Organizer

Include this lesson's information in your Foldable®.

LESSON 3 REVIEW **CCSS**

Reviewing Vocabulary (Tier Three Words)
1. How did the *infrastructure* of West African colonies lead to poor economies when they became independent countries? RH.6-8.4

Answering the Guiding Questions
2. *Analyzing* What are the advantages of a pidgin language? RH.6-8.1

3. *Describing* What is one potential downside to preserving traditional values in rural West Africa? RH.6-8.2

4. *Identifying* What are three major challenges to fighting AIDS in West Africa? RH.6-8.2

5. *Narrative Writing* Select a West African country and write a letter to the government of the country about the importance of investing in education. Explain how education will help solve the problems discussed in this lesson and how it will help preserve West African culture. RH.6-8.4, RH.6-8.10

Chapter 12 **373**

LESSON 3 REVIEW ANSWERS

Reviewing Vocabulary

1. The West African countries' infrastructure, or framework, depended on a few key resources and industries. They did not develop a variety of resources and industries. As a result, when the market for the key resources and industries dropped, their entire economies struggled.

Answering the Guiding Questions

2. **Analyzing** They allow people who do not speak the same language to have simple conversations.

3. **Describing** Ethnic pride is an important traditional value, but it sometimes causes conflicts between neighboring ethnic groups.

4. **Identifying** 1) Supplying health care to the growing number of people carrying the virus; 2) Reducing new HIV infections, usually through education; 3) Dealing with families and communities hurt by AIDS-related deaths.

5. **Narrative Writing** Students' responses should include information from the text about how education in West Africa will lead to a better overall healthy and a strong economy.

C Critical Thinking Skills

Speculating After students read about the use and abuse of loans in West African countries, discuss with them the affect of political corruption on the region. **Ask:**

- **Why do you think there is some corruption among government leaders who use loans for their own purposes and interests?** *(Possible answer: They may want personal gain or fortune. They may not be thinking about how their actions hurt other people.)*

- **Why do you think some money was not wisely invested?** *(Possible answer: The government may not have had the experience or know-how of sound investing.)* **AL** Verbal/Linguistic

T Technology Skills

Using and Citing Information Have students work in pairs or small groups to research a disease or virus (besides HIV), such as yellow fever, that is affecting a large percentage of the population in West Africa. Ask them to find statistics to track the progress of the number of people who have contracted the disease as well as progress on controlling the disease or virus in sub-Saharan Africa. Point out that the World Health Organization Web site often publishes such statistics and information. In addition, the Bill and Melinda Gates Foundation is doing work in vaccinating people against some of the common illnesses in the region.

Review with students how to use and cite information. Then ask students to present their findings digitally, including the sources they used. Discuss as a class what diseases and viruses seem to be more under control than others and which ones will be real challenges for the countries of West Africa in the future. **BL** Verbal/Linguistic

CLOSE & REFLECT

To close this lesson, have students discuss different challenges facing West Africa today, including ethnic diversity, poverty, lack of education, and poor healthcare. Ask students to think of different solutions for these challenges.

ANSWER, p. 373

☑ **READING PROGRESS CHECK** If West Africa is to have a sound future, the people need to be educated enough to solve the many problems that hurt this region. The people need to have an education in order to build businesses and perform higher level jobs.

CHAPTER REVIEW ACTIVITY

Have pairs of students create a time line to illustrate the history of West Africa. Write the following list of events on a piece of paper without including the dates. Leave room between each item in the list. Make copies and have volunteers cut the lists into strips and make one set for each pair of students. Ask pairs to put the strips of events in the correct sequence and find the date of each event. Then have pairs make a time line showing the events in the correct order:

- Bantu migration *(1000 B.C.)*
- Mali becomes a center for trade. *(250 B.C.)*
- The Almoravids conquer the kingdom of Ghana. *(A.D. 1000s)*
- The kingdoms of Mali followed by Songhai thrive from the gold-for-salt trade. *(A.D. 1100–1300s)*
- The Moroccans conquer the Songhai Empire. *(end of the A.D. 1500s)*
- Britain sets up Freetown, a colony in Sierra Leone, for free enslaved people. *(1787)*
- Britain bans the slave trade. *(1807)*
- European powers carve up Africa into colonies at the Berlin Conference. *(1884–85)*
- Independence movements break out across the region. *(1950s)*
- All former French colonies in the region are free. *(1961)*

The History of West Africa

1000 B.C.   1961

REVIEW THE ENDURING UNDERSTANDINGS

Review this chapter's Enduring Understanding with students:

- *People, places, and ideas change over time.*

Now pose the following questions in a class discussion to apply this to this chapter.

- **How has the warm, dry climate of part of the region of West Africa affected its physical geography?** *(People have had to use more water from Lake Chad for irrigation. The dryness in the Sahara, in addition to desertification, makes it difficult to live in the Sahel. Strong winds blow, and once semiarid lands are more like a desert.)*

- **What discoveries encouraged outside interest in Africa, both in ancient and modern times?** *(Resources such as gold and diamonds attracted groups from northern Africa and Asia in ancient times and Europeans in modern times.)*

- **How have West African countries tried to stabilize and diversify their economies post-independence?** *(Possible answer: They have tried to diversify their economies by developing other industries such as manufacturing.)*

Directions: Write your answers on a separate piece of paper.

1 Use your FOLDABLES to explore the Essential Question.
INFORMATIVE/EXPLANATORY WRITING Choose any three countries in this region and take a closer look at how the people who live there earn their living. Use the CIA Factbook or another Internet resource to list the top five occupations in each of the three countries and the average annual wage people earn for each. Arrange your data in a chart. Are any of those occupations directly related to the physical geography of the area? Explain in one or two paragraphs. WHST.6-8.2, WHST.6-8.6

2 **21st Century Skills**
INTEGRATING VISUAL INFORMATION In small groups, research the problems facing one of the countries of West Africa. Discuss possible solutions to one of the problems. Create a bulletin board display with pictures and captions to illustrate your solution to the problem. WHST.6-8.7, WHST.6-8.8

3 **Thinking Like a Geographer**
DETERMINING CENTRAL IDEAS After reviewing the chapter, choose five of the most important events in the history of West Africa. Place those events and their dates on a time line. RH.6-8.2, WHST.6-8.10

4 **GEOGRAPHY ACTIVITY**

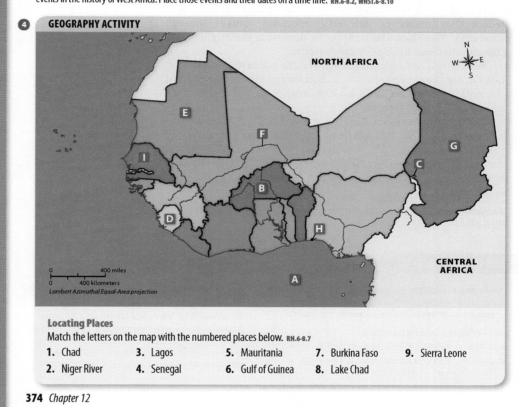

Locating Places
Match the letters on the map with the numbered places below. RH.6-8.7

1. Chad
2. Niger River
3. Lagos
4. Senegal
5. Mauritania
6. Gulf of Guinea
7. Burkina Faso
8. Lake Chad
9. Sierra Leone

ACTIVITIES ANSWERS

Exploring the Essential Question

1 **INFORMATIVE/EXPLANATORY WRITING** Students' charts should list the top five occupations (along with the salaries) for each of the three countries they chose. Paragraphs should discuss the relationship between the jobs listed and the geography of the country. Paragraphs should be well organized and be free of grammar and spelling errors.

21st Century Skills

2 **INTEGRATING VISUAL INFORMATION** Students' work should be well researched and thoughtful. The problems are great, so the bulletin board may include many different ideas for solutions to the problem students choose to research.

REVIEW THE GUIDING QUESTIONS

Directions: Choose the best answer for each question.

1 The climate of northern West Africa can best be described as RH.6-8.4
  A. desert.
  B. savannah.
  C. tropical rain forest.
  D. marine west coast.

2 What attracted Portuguese explorers to Ghana in 1471? RH.6-8.1
  F. salt
  G. petroleum
  H. lithium
  I. gold

3 What did wealthy North African Muslim traders want from the people of West Africa? RH.6-8.2
  A. gold and converts to Islam
  B. salt and gold
  C. diamonds and emeralds
  D. ivory and camels

4 At the Berlin Conference of 1884–1885, France, Germany, Great Britain, Portugal, and Belgium decided to RH.6-8.1
  F. fund secondary schools and universities in West Africa.
  G. restrict the trade of enslaved people.
  H. heavily tax coffee and cocoa grown in West Africa.
  I. build empires by carving up and taking political control of African lands for themselves.

5 Traditional African religions are RH.6-8.2
  A. the dominant religions in West Africa.
  B. no longer practiced.
  C. only practiced in Mali.
  D. practiced, even in countries where Christianity or Islam is dominant.

6 When two or more languages blend and become the language of a region, the result is called a RH.6-8.4
  F. pidgin language.
  G. blended language.
  H. creole language.
  I. diverse language.

Chapter 12 **375**

Thinking Like a Geographer

3 **DETERMINING CENTRAL IDEAS** Time lines should include factual information. Sample entries: **A.D. 1000**—Ghana is conquered; **1471**—Portuguese explorers reach West Africa; **1822**—Liberia founded; **1967**—Biafra declares independence; **1992**—Ghana approves new constitution

Geography Activity

4 **LOCATING PLACES**

1. G
2. F
3. H
4. I
5. E
6. A
7. B
8. C
9. D

ASSESSMENT ANSWERS
Review the Guiding Questions

1 **A** To answer this question, students should remember that the Sahara Desert occupies most of northern West Africa, leading to A as the correct answer. Students can eliminate C tropical rain forest and D marine west coast, since neither of these climates are mentioned in the chapter. Remind students that B savanna is located south of the Sahel. Refer students to the, "Dry Zones," section of Lesson 1 for help.

2 **I** Even though petroleum and lithium were resources that attracted outsiders later, these answer choices (G and H) can be eliminated because the question is asking about the year 1471. Ask students to consider the two remaining answer choices. Which resource would have attracted a European country to travel all the way to Africa? Gold, answer choice I, was more important. Refer students to the ,"Other Resources," section in Lesson 1 for additional help.

3 **A** Remind students that they already know that gold attracted outsiders to West Africa, thereby eliminating answer choices C and D. However, the key word in this question is *Muslim*—they wanted to spread the religion of Islam. Refer students to the, "Trade Across the Sahara," section in Lesson 2 for additional help.

4 **I** To answer this question students need to know what happened at the Berlin Conference. Refer students to the, "Creating Colonies," section in Lesson 2 for help. The European countries did not want to fund universities in their colonies, so answer F does not make sense. Slavery was outlawed in Europe before this time, making G incorrect. Answer H would make the exports from West Africa too expensive so this can be ruled out.

5 **D** The clue word in this question is *traditional*. Since many of the countries are predominantly Christian or Muslim, answer A is incorrect. Choices B and C suggest that these are not practiced throughout the region, which is incorrect. Have students review the, "Religion," section in Lesson 3 for additional help.

6 **H** Remembering that creole and pidgin languages are common in Africa should help students eliminate answers G and I. Students will need to recall that a creole language is one that started out as pidgin but became so commonly used in a region that it was adopted and then called a creole language. Refer students to Lesson 3. Have them reread the, "Languages," section for reinforcement.

Chapter 12 **ASSESSMENT** *(continued)*

DBQ Analyzing Documents

7 **B** The passage means that nomads who move into new areas follow their traditional patterns of land use, which is actually "land abuse" according to the passage, and those patterns of the nomads turn those new areas into desert.

8 **I** In pointing out that arid and semiarid lands can recover from drought when the rains come, as long as those lands are well managed, this passage provides evidence for the idea that droughts alone do not cause desertification.

Short Response

9 Sample answer: One of the difficulties new democracies face is the willingness of those who held office to give up that office when they lose an election. The ability of Ghana's leaders to repeatedly do so shows that the country strongly follows a basic principle of democracy, which is to allow free elections and then abide by the results of those elections.

10 Sample answer: President Obama thinks the achievement of building a strong democracy is even more important than winning independence because without it, a country could fall into the conflict and chaos of a civil war or break apart into separate countries if ethnic groups decide to form their own nation. Winning independence gives a people a chance to forge a country; building a strong democracy means that country will survive.

Extended Response

11 Students' papers about ecotourism as a way that developing nations can use their natural resources should show evidence of thoughtful research using reliable resources. Students should present an opinion—pro or con, cite text evidence to support their opinion, be clear and concise, and meet grade-level appropriate standards for spelling and grammar.

DBQ ANALYZING DOCUMENTS

7 **DETERMINING WORD MEANINGS** Read the following passage about the problem of desertification:

> "*Nomads are trying to escape the desert, but because of their land-use practices, they are bringing the desert with them. It is a misconception that droughts cause desertification. Droughts are common in arid and semiarid lands. Well-managed lands can recover from drought when the rains return. Continued land abuse during droughts, however, increases land degradation.*"
>
> —from United States Geological Survey, "Desertification"

What does the passage mean in saying that nomads "are bringing the desert with them"? RH.6-8.1, RH.6-8.10

A. Nomads bring their desert customs wherever they move.

B. Nomads create desert in new areas because of their land-use practices.

C. Nomads have the skills they need to survive in the desert.

D. Nomads can teach their way of life to other people.

8 **IDENTIFYING** What evidence does the passage give that droughts alone do not cause desertification? RH.6-8.1, RH.6-8.10

F. the movement of nomads to new areas

G. the rate at which desertification takes place

H. droughts prevent desertification

I. the ability of lands to recover from drought

SHORT RESPONSE

> "*The people of Ghana have . . . put democracy on a firmer footing, with repeated peaceful transfers of power. . . . This progress . . . will ultimately be more significant [than the struggle for independence]. For just as it is important to emerge from the control of other nations, it is even more important to build one's own nation.*"
>
> —from President Barack Obama, "Remarks to the Ghanian Parliament" (2009)

9 **DETERMINING CENTRAL IDEAS** How do "repeated peaceful transfers of power" show that democracy in Ghana is on a "firmer footing"? RH.6-8.2

10 **IDENTIFYING POINT OF VIEW** Why does President Obama think this achievement is more important than winning independence? RH.6-8.6

EXTENDED RESPONSE

11 **ARGUMENT WRITING** Ecotourism is often mentioned as a way that developing nations can use their natural resources to produce income while preserving those resources for future generations. Research the pros and cons of the topic, and decide whether or not ecotourism would be good for the countries of West Africa. Present your response in an essay. WHST.6-8.1, WHST.6-8.4

Need Extra Help?

If You've Missed Question	**1**	**2**	**3**	**4**	**5**	**6**	**7**	**8**	**9**	**10**	**11**
Review Lesson	1	1	2	2	3	3	1	1	2	2	3

From "Desertification," http://pubs.usgs.gov/gip/deserts/desertification, Department of the Interior/United States Geological Survey, The USGS home page is http://www.usgs.gov.

netw⊙rks *Online Teaching Options*

Evaluation and Assessment

Assessing Use eAssessment to create your own tests from hundreds of available questions. eAssessment helps you design assessments that meet the needs of different types of learners.

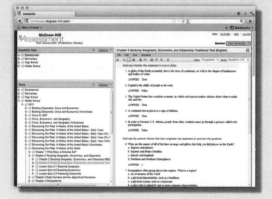

CHAPTER 13
Southern Africa Planner

 National Geography Standards covered in Chapter 13

Learners will understand:

UNDERSTANDING BY DESIGN®

Enduring Understandings
- *People, places, and ideas change over time.*

Essential Questions
- *How does physical geography influence the way people live?*
- *How do new ideas change the way people live?*

Predictable Misunderstandings
- *Southern Africa has a similar geography to the rest of Africa.*
- *Southern Africa has limited resources that do not affect the economy of the region.*
- *Southern Africa has little impact on the global economy.*

Assessment Evidence
Performance Tasks:
- *Project-Based Learning Digital Hands-On Chapter Project*
- *Project-Based Learning Hands-On Chapter Project*

Other Evidence:
- *Technology Skills Activity*
- *Geography and Economics Activity*
- *Participation in Interactive Whiteboard Activities*
- *Contribution to small-group activities*
- *Interpretation of slide show images and special purpose maps*
- *Participation in class discussions about cultural and economic topics*
- *Lesson Reviews*
- *Chapter Assessments*

I. The World in Spatial Terms
Standard 1: How to use maps and other geographic representations, geospatial technologies, and spatial thinking to understand and communicate information

Standard 3: How to analyze the spatial organization of people, places, and environments on Earth's surface

II. Places and Regions
Standard 4: The physical and human characteristics of places

Standard 5: That people create regions to interpret Earth's complexity

Standard 6: How culture and experience influence people's perceptions of places and regions

IV. Human Systems
Standard 9: The characteristics, distribution, and migration of human populations on Earth's surface

Standard 10: The characteristics, distribution, and complexity of Earth's cultural mosaics

Standard 11: The patterns and networks of economic interdependence on Earth's surface

Standard 12: The processes, patterns, and functions of human settlement

Standard 13: How the forces of cooperation and conflict among people influence the division and control of Earth's surface

V. Environment and Society
Standard 14: How human actions modify the physical environment

Standard 15: How physical systems affect human systems

VI. The Uses of Geography
Standard 17: How to apply geography to interpret the past

Standard 18: How to apply geography to interpret the present and plan for the future

---

SUGGESTED PACING GUIDE

Introducing the Chapter . . . . 1 Day	Lesson 3 . . . . .2 Days
Lesson 1 . . . . .2 Days	Chapter Wrap-Up and Assessment . . . . . . 1 Day
Lesson 2 . . . . .2 Days	

TOTAL TIME   8 Days

Key for Using the Teacher Edition

SKILL-BASED ACTIVITIES

Types of skill activities found in the Teacher Edition.

V **Visual Skills** require students to analyze maps, graphs, charts, and photos.

W **Writing Skills** provide writing opportunities to help students comprehend the text.

R **Reading Skills** help students practice reading skills and master vocabulary.

C **Critical Thinking Skills** help students apply and extend what they have learned.

T **Technology Skills** require students to use digital tools effectively.

*Letters are followed by a number when there is more than one of the same type of skill on the page.

DIFFERENTIATED INSTRUCTION

All activities are written for the on-level student unless otherwise marked with the leveled labels below.

BL Beyond Level
AL Approaching Level
ELL English Language Learners

All students benefit from activities that utilize different learning styles. Many activities are marked as below when a particular learning style is highlighted.

Intrapersonal	Naturalist
Logical/Mathematical	Kinesthetic
Visual/Spatial	Auditory/Musical
Verbal/Linguistic	Interpersonal

CHAPTER OPENER PLANNER

Students will know:
- *that Southern Africa has a unique geography that draws tourists to the region.*
- *that Southern Africa is rich in natural resources, including diamonds.*
- *that Southern Africa and its resources are important to the global economy.*
- *how control over the resources in Southern Africa influences the region today.*

Students will be able to:
- **use** *a world map to identify countries of Southern Africa.*
- **use** *a time line to discuss various events in the history of Southern Africa.*

UNDERSTANDING
BY DESIGN®

☑ *Print Teaching Options*

V Visual Skills

- ☐ **P. 378** Students use the map of Southern Africa to reinforce map skills. **Visual/Spatial**

- ☐ **P. 379** Students review the time line and discuss its major points of interest. **Logical/Mathematical**

T Technology Skills

- ☐ **P. 378** Students research animals of Southern Africa and make a poster or picture book to share.

☑ *Online Teaching Options*

- ☐ **MAP** **Reading a Map**—Students identify aspects and locations of the region on a map.

- ☐ **TIME LINE** **Reading a Time Line and Map**—Students learn about where and when historical events occurred in Southern Africa. **Visual/Spatial**

- ☐ **MAP** **Interactive World Altas**—Students use the interactive world atlas to identify the region and describe its terrain.

☑ *Printable Digital Worksheets*

- ☐ **WORKSHEET** **Technology Skills: Collaborating Online**—Students can use this worksheet to find safe ways to collaborate online.

- ☐ **WORKSHEET** **Geography and Economics: Population Distribution and Economy**—Students can use this worksheet to make connections between population distribution and economy.

Project-Based Learning

Hands-On

Creating a Board Game

Students will work in groups to research, design, and create a board game based on information about Southern Africa. Using information from the chapter and other sources, students will design the game board, define the rules of the game, and create any trivia or question cards. Once completed, groups will take turns playing the games that their classmates created.

Digital Hands-On

Adding QR Codes to a Map

Have students add QR codes to an outline map of Southern Africa. Through online research, students will select photos, video, current event articles, and maps related to the physical geography, history, and culture of the region. Then students will create and affix the codes to digitally annotate the map. Maps can be displayed and scanned with a QR reader by students and adults for a multimedia-rich tour of the region.

21ˢᵗ Century Learning

Print Resources

ANCILLARY RESOURCES

These ancillaries are available for every chapter and lesson.

- **Reading Essentials and Study Guide Workbook** **AL** **ELL**
- **Chapter Tests and Lesson Quizzes Blackline Masters**

PRINTABLE DIGITAL WORKSHEETS

These printable digital worksheets are available for every chapter and lesson!

- **Hands-On Chapter Projects**
- **What Do You Know? Activities**
- **Chapter Summaries (English and Spanish)**
- **Vocabulary Builder Activities**
- **Quizzes and Tests**
- **Reading Essentials and Study Guide (English and Spanish)** **AL** **ELL**
- **Guided Reading Activities**

More Media Resources

SUGGESTED VIDEOS

NOTE: Be sure to preview videos to ensure they are age-appropriate.

- **White Lion** (88 min.)

SUGGESTED READING

- *Out of the Shadows,* by Jason Wallace **BL**
- *Nelson Mandela: Long Walk to Freedom,* by Chris van Wyk **AL**

PHYSICAL GEOGRAPHY OF SOUTHERN AFRICA

Students will know:
- that Southern Africa has a unique geography that draws tourists to the region.
- that Southern Africa is rich in natural resources, including diamonds.
- that Southern Africa and its resources are important to the global economy.
- how control over the resources in Southern Africa influences the region today.

Students will be able to:
- **describe** the landforms and bodies of water in Southern Africa.
- **describe** the various climates of the region.
- **discuss** important natural resources in this region, including minerals and energy resources.

UNDERSTANDING
BY DESIGN®

☑ *Print Teaching Options*

V Visual Skills

☐ **P. 382** Students draw the three major rivers of Southern Africa on outline maps of the region. **Visual/Spatial**

☐ **P. 383** Students create charts to take notes on the climates of Southern Africa. **Verbal/Linguistic**

☐ **P. 386** Students create charts listing the mineral, energy, and other natural resources of Southern Africa by country. **Kinesthetic, Interpersonal**

W Writing Skills

☐ **P. 381** Students describe one of the deserts in South Africa in an informative paper. **Verbal/Linguistic**

☐ **P. 383** Students conduct research and write an essay about one of the following physical features: Lake Malawi, Great Rift Valley, or Etosha Pan. **BL Verbal/Linguistic**

R Reading Skills

☐ **P. 381** Students create word squares for each vocabulary word they encounter. **ELL AL Visual/Spatial**

☐ **P. 382** Students discuss the importance of large river systems and summarize information about Southern Africa's rivers. **Verbal/Linguistic**

☐ **P. 385** Students explain climatic conditions in the desert regions of Southern Africa. **Verbal/Linguistic**

C Critical Thinking Skills

☐ **P. 380** Students compare and contrast Southern African countries by size. **Visual/Spatial**

☐ **P. 384** Students relate information about Southern Africa's climate zones to their own experience. **Logical**

☐ **P. 387** Students analyze information on how minerals can be used to fund wars. **AL Verbal/Linguistic**

T Technology Skills

☐ **P. 384** Students look up the weather forecast for each capital city in Southern Africa on the Internet. **ELL Verbal/Linguistic, Logical/Mathematical**

☐ **P. 387** Students research Etosha National Park in Namibia and create a graphic organizer to display the information. **Verbal/Linguistic, Visual/Spatial**

☑ *Online Teaching Options*

V Visual Skills

☐ **VIDEO** **Around the World—Botswana**—Students use the video to compare the physical geography of Botswana and the geography of the United States. **AL Visual/Spatial**

☐ **MAP** **Africa's Size**—Students compare the sizes of countries in Africa, Asia, and Europe.

☐ **IMAGE** **Drakensberg Mountains**—Students use the image to highlight this landform.

☐ **VIDEO** **Seychelles**—Students use the video of the Seychelles to discuss this island country.

☐ **MAP** **Physical Geography: Southern Africa**—Students study the physical geography layer of the map and then create posters of the landforms and waterways in Southern Africa. **AL**

☐ **VIDEO** **Victoria Falls**—Students use the video of the falls to make connections.

☐ **IMAGE** **360° View: Etosha Pan**—Students can use the image to discuss this landform.

☐ **MAP** **Resources: South Africa**—Students use the map to discuss the resources of the region.

R Reading Skills

☐ **LECTURE SLIDE** **Namibia Plateaus**—Students can use the video to highlight this landform.

☐ **LECTURE SLIDE** **Escarpment**—Students use the slide to review the definition of *escarpment*.

☐ **LECTURE SLIDE** **Tropic of Cancer and Capricorn**—Students can use the lecture slide to discuss these two latitude lines and what it means to have a tropical climate.

☐ **GAME** **Drag-and-Drop: Climate Zones in Southern Africa**—Students can use the drag-and-drop game to review the climate zones of the region.

☐ **CHART** **Making Diamonds into Jewelry**—Students use the chart to discuss the different cuts of a diamond and the different aspects of the cuts to extend the discussion from the text.

C Critical Thinking Skills

☐ **MAP** **Climates: Southern Africa**—Students discuss climate zones in Southern Africa. **AL**

☐ **MAP** **Monsoons**—Students discuss the positive and negative effects of monsoons. **AL**

☐ **IMAGE** **Kalahari Dunes**—Students research how wildlife adapted to desert conditions. **AL**

☐ **SLIDE SHOW** **Diamonds**—Students discuss processes of turning diamonds into jewelry. **ELL**

☐ **IMAGES** **Hydroelectric Power**—Students discuss hydroelectric power as an energy resource.

☐ **CHART** **Wildlife Preserves in South Africa**— Students discuss African wildlife.

T Technology Skills

☐ **ONLINE SELF-CHECK QUIZ** **Lesson 1**—Students receive instant feedback on their mastery of lesson content.

HISTORY OF SOUTHERN AFRICA

Students will know:

- that Southern Africa has a unique geography that draws tourists to the region.
- that Southern Africa is rich in natural resources, including diamonds.
- that Southern Africa and its resources are important to the global economy.
- how control over the resources in Southern Africa influences the region today.

Students will be able to:

- **describe** the rise of kingdoms in Southern Africa.
- **discuss** colonization in Southern Africa by European countries.
- **explore** how South African colonies gained independence.
- **discuss** apartheid and equal rights in South Africa.

UNDERSTANDING BY DESIGN®

☑ *Print Teaching Options*

V Visual Skills

☐ **P. 389** Students follow a sequence chart showing the events and prominent groups involved in the fall of the Kingdom of Zimbabwe. **AL** Visual/Spatial

☐ **P. 389** Students integrate the visual information in the photograph of the ruins of the Great Enclosure of the city of Great Zimbabwe. Visual/Spatial

☐ **P. 391** Students create a map key for an outline map of Southern Africa and label the countries in the region and color them based on which European nation once controlled them. **ELL** **AL** Visual/Spatial

☐ **P. 391** Students examine and analyze the photograph of the siege of Mafeking. Visual/Spatial

☐ **P. 392** Students create time lines showing the dates that the countries of Southern Africa became independent. Visual/Spatial

W Writing Skills

☐ **P. 393** Students conduct Internet research and write a biography of Nelson Mandela. **BL** Verbal/Linguistic

R Reading Skills

☐ **P. 388** Students summarize the main features of the advanced civilization in the Kingdom of Zimbabwe in Southern Africa. **ELL** Verbal/Linguistic

☐ **P. 393** Students summarize the history of South Africa after World War II. Verbal/Linguistic

C Critical Thinking Skills

☐ **P. 390** Students focus on the main ideas about the European colonization of Southern Africa. Logical/Mathematical

☐ **P. 391** Students evaluate the European takeover of Southern Africa. Verbal/Linguistic

T Technology Skills

☐ **P. 392** Students research the move for independence of one of the countries of Southern Africa. Interpersonal

☑ *Online Teaching Options*

V Visual Skills

IMAGE **The Boer War**—Students make connections between the Boer War and other conflicts stemming from a nation's desire to gain control of another region's valuable natural resources. Logical/Mathematical, Verbal/Linguistic, Intrapersonal

MAP **Colonization and Independence of Southern Africa**—Students can use the map to focus on the independence movement of the region.

W Writing Skills

VIDEO **Comrade Capitalist**—Students watch the video about the history of Southern Africa and write three predictions about Southern Africa's history. **ELL** Verbal/Linguistic

MAP **Colonization and Independence of Southern Africa**—Students use the map to discuss the colonization of Southern Africa and write a response to answer how the natural resources of Southern Africa have affected its history. **BL** Visual/Spatial

R Reading Skills

GAME **Drag-and-Drop: Early History of Southern Africa**—Students can use the drag-and-drop game to review the history of Southern Africa.

C Critical Thinking Skills

IMAGES **The Boer War**—Students can use the interactive photo to discuss the Boer War and its significance in the history of Southern Africa.

TIME LINE **History of Apartheid**—Students use the interactive time line to discuss apartheid, its impact, and how it was abolished. **BL** Verbal/Linguistic

T Technology Skills

ONLINE SELF-CHECK QUIZ **Lesson 2**—Students receive instant feedback on their mastery of lesson content.

LIFE IN SOUTHERN AFRICA

Students will know:
- *how control over the resources in Southern Africa influences the region today.*

Students will be able to:
- **describe** *the population distribution in Southern Africa.*
- **describe** *ethnic and culture groups, religions, and languages in the region.*
- **describe** *daily life in the region.*
- **explore** *social, economic, and political challenges in the region.*

UNDERSTANDING
BY DESIGN®

☑ *Print Teaching Options*

V Visual Skills

☐ **P. 395** Students study the population density map and practice their map skills. **Visual/Spatial**

☐ **P. 397** Students analyze the photograph of Luanda in Angola and compare it to other cities. **Visual/Spatial**

☐ **P. 398** Students analyze a photograph of an outdoor market. **Intrapersonal**

W Writing Skills

☐ **P. 399** Students research an aspect of village life in Southern Africa today and write a three-paragraph paper on their findings. **BL** **Verbal/Linguistic**

R Reading Skills

☐ **P. 396** Students identify the main religions of Southern Africa. **AL** **ELL** **Verbal/Linguistic**

☐ **P. 398** Students discuss and summarize the urban environment in Southern Africa. **ELL**

☐ **P. 399** Students determine central ideas and describe the way of life in rural areas of Southern Africa. **Verbal**

☐ **P. 401** Students summarize the section on progress and growth and identify the continuing problems that Southern Africa faces.

C Critical Thinking Skills

☐ **P. 394** Students answer questions about population patterns in Southern Africa. **AL** **Verbal/Linguistic**

☐ **P. 397** Students predict possible consequences of the people speaking so many different languages in Southern Africa. **BL** **Verbal/Linguistic**

☐ **P. 398** Students connect the lingering effects of apartheid to the region today. **Logical/Mathematical**

☐ **P. 400** Students identify health problems that people in Southern Africa face. **Verbal/Linguistic**

T Technology Skills

☐ **P. 396** Students choose an ethnic group to research on the Internet and prepare a brief oral report about the group. **Visual/Spatial, Verbal/Linguistic**

⊠ *Online Teaching Options*

V Visual Skills

☐ **MAP** **Population: Southern Africa**—Students study the population map and discuss density and distribution of population in Southern Africa. **ELL** **Verbal/Linguistic**

☐ **IMAGE** **Markets in Southern Africa**—Students use the interactive photograph to discuss the diversity of goods at markets and make a list of items they can identify. **ELL**

☐ **MAP** **Malaria Deaths**—Students use a map depicting malaria deaths in Africa as a springboard for a discussion of health issues that are prevalent in Southern Africa. **AL** **Visual/Spatial, Logical/Mathematical, Verbal/Linguistic**

☐ **IMAGE** **360° View: Johannesburg, South Africa**—Students can use the image of Johannesburg to further extend the text.

W Writing Skills

☐ **VIDEO** **South African Community**—Students watch the video and create a chart to compare and contrast ways of life in the video with ways of life in other regions of Africa. **AL**

R Reading Skills

☐ **GRAPHIC ORGANIZER** **Challenges in Southern Africa**—Students can use the interactive graphic organizer to review the content of the lesson.

C Critical Thinking Skills

☐ **CHARTS** **Population Pyramid: Southern Africa**—Students can use the chart to discuss how population breaks down from male to female and across age ranges.

☐ **IMAGE** **Urban vs. Traditional Life**—Students use the side-by-side photographs to discuss urban and rural life and make a list of the benefits and drawbacks of each way of life. **Verbal**

☐ **CHART** **Health Issues in Southern Africa**—Students can use the chart to discuss the life expectancy and health issues of Southern Africa and why health issues are so prevalent.

☐ **CHART** **Ethnic and Cultural Groups in Southern Africa**—Students discuss the diverse cultures in the region and speculate on how European colonialism affected this diversity. **AL**

☐ **CHART** **Religions and Languages of Southern Africa**—Students can use the chart of religions and languages to connect to the chart discussed in the text.

☐ **SLIDE SHOW** **Cities in Southern Africa**—Students view the slide show of urban areas in Southern Africa and compare and contrast cities there with cities in the United States. **AL**

T Technology Skills

☐ **ONLINE SELF-CHECK QUIZ** **Lesson 3**—Students receive instant feedback on their mastery of lesson content.

☑ *Printable Digital Worksheets*

W Writing Skills

☐ **WORKSHEET** **Geography and Economics: Population Distribution and Economy**—Students can use this worksheet to make connections between population distribution and economy.

☐ **WORKSHEET** **Technology Skills: Collaborating Online**—Students can use this worksheet to find safe ways to collaborate online.

INTERVENTION AND REMEDIATION STRATEGIES

LESSON 1   Physical Geography of Southern Africa

Reading and Comprehension

Organize students into five groups. Assign a different content vocabulary word to each group. Have students in each group work together to create a paragraph about a concept in the lesson, using their assigned term. For example, students may use the term *landlocked* in a paragraph about Southern Africa's landforms. After groups have completed their paragraphs, ask a volunteer from each group to read the paragraph. Provide guidance as needed, ensuring that students have used each term correctly.

Text Evidence

Have students review the lesson and use the headings and subheadings to create an outline of the lesson. If students need help organizing information, guide them to break down each section into key points, or main ideas. Then have students write key words and phrases in their notebooks to remind them about important content under each heading and subheading. Have students work in teams to quiz each other using the words and phrases from their notebooks.

LESSON 2   History of Southern Africa

Reading and Comprehension

Have students work in teams to play "vocabulary charades." Tell students to write down each vocabulary term on a separate, folded piece of paper and place the papers on a desk. Students may also add other names and concepts from the lesson such as Great Zimbabwe, Zulu, and Nelson Mandela. Have two students from a team pick one of the papers and silently give clues by acting out the term for their team to guess. Assign one point for each correct guess; the team with the most points wins. You may wish to use a timer to keep the game moving.

Text Evidence

Organize students into small groups. Tell students they will create a cause-and-effect flow chart to depict a key concept from the lesson. Tell students their charts should answer the essential question: *How do new ideas change the way people live?* To avoid duplication, you may wish to assign each group a specific key concept. Have groups present their charts along with a brief summary, citing textual evidence that supports their visuals.

LESSON 3   Life in Southern Africa

Reading and Comprehension

Organize students into small groups. Have groups outline key facts about Southern Africa related to one of the following topics: population patterns, ethnic and culture groups, and religion and languages. To ensure comprehension of the topics, conduct a question/answer session in which students from each group answer questions about their topic.

Text Evidence

Assign each of the lesson's guiding questions to student groups. Have each group create a slide show or poster to visually answer the question. For example, to answer the question *How do the various people of Southern Africa live?* students might show images of cities and busy street markets, as well as small rural villages. Students may wish to download and print images from the Internet, or draw their own illustrations.

Online Resources

Level Reader

Use this online lower-level text that corresponds directly to the text in the online Student Edition.

Guided Reading Activities

This resource uses graphic organizers and guiding questions to help students with comprehension.

Assessing Background Knowledge

Use these worksheets to pre-assess students' background knowledge before they read the chapter.

Reading Essentials and Study Guide Workbook

This resource offers writing and reading activities for the approaching-level student.

Self-Check Quizzes

This online assessment tool provides instant feedback for students to check their progress.

SOUTHERN AFRICA

ESSENTIAL QUESTIONS · *How does geography influence the way people live?*
· *How do new ideas change the way people live?*

Gallo Images · LK15/Getty Images

**Miner from Johannesburg,
South Africa**

networks
There's More Online about Southern Africa.

CHAPTER 13

Lesson 1
*Physical Geography of
Southern Africa*

Lesson 2
History of Southern Africa

Lesson 3
Life in Southern Africa

The Story Matters...

From the steep slopes of the Great Escarpment to the plunging Victoria Falls, Southern Africa is filled with magnificent scenery and wildlife, which draw tourists from around the world. Southern Africa is also the continent's richest region in natural resources, including gold and diamonds. Many of Southern Africa's natural resources have become important to the global economy. Control over these vital resources has brought many great economic, political, and social changes to the region.

FOLDABLES®
Study Organizer

Go to the Foldables® library in the back of your book to make a Foldable® that will help you take notes while reading this chapter.

377

ENGAGE

Bellringer Ask students to think for a few minutes about what they have learned so far about the various regions of Africa. Then tell students that they will now begin the study of Southern Africa. Ask students to formulate questions about this region's geography, history, and culture, and assign one student to make a chart listing the questions that the class generates. Tell the class that you will save the questions and review them at the end of the chapter to see if the students can answer them. Then have students read "The Story Matters..." and share with them the information in the Content Background Knowledge.

Southern Africa

Questions	Answers

Content Background Knowledge

- The Great Escarpment consists of steep slopes separating the interior plateaus of southern Africa from the lower, narrow coastal plains.
- Victoria Falls is one of the largest and most impressive waterfalls in the world. It lies on the border between Zambia and Zimbabwe, where the Zambezi River plunges over the edge of a plateau into the gorges below.
- Southern Africa is home to such wildlife as baboons, elephants, giraffes, hippopotami, zebras, leopards, lions, and cheetahs.

Letter from the Author

Dear Geography Teacher,

Southern Africa is vast in size and natural resources, but its path to modern development has been slowed by physical and human geographic factors. After reading this chapter, discuss with students if they think any of the problems the countries face in this region can be resolved. Will disease and poor nutrition lessen? Will racial, religious, and tribal tensions ease? How will the large number of orphaned children in the region affect further economic development?

FOLDABLES®
Study Organizer

Go to the Foldables® library for a chapter-based Foldable® activity that your students can use to help take notes and prepare for assessment.

TEACH & ASSESS

Step Into the Place

V Visual Skills

Analyzing Maps Have students read the introductory paragraph and study the map. Explain that Southern Africa includes ten mainland countries and four island countries. Have students identify each of the countries and list them on the board. (**Mainland:** *Angola, Namibia, Zambia, Botswana, South Africa, Zimbabwe, Mozambique, Malawi, Swaziland, and Lesotho;* **Island:** *Madagascar, Comoros, Seychelles, and Mauritius*) **Ask:**

- **Which country is embedded within South Africa?** (*Lesotho*)
- **What is the latitude range for these countries?** (*from about 5° South to about 35° South*)
- **How would you expect this latitude range to affect the climate?** (*This latitude range begins close to the Equator, which would most likely result in a warm and humid climate, and then progresses to a temperate climate further south.*)
- **What two oceans meet off the coast of South Africa?** (*Indian Ocean and Atlantic Ocean*)
- **Which of the mainland countries are landlocked?** (*Zimbabwe, Malawi, Zambia, Botswana, Lesotho, and Swaziland*)
- **Where is Cape Town located within South Africa?** (*on the southwestern coast of the country*)

Then have students answer the Step Into the Place questions. **Visual/Spatial**

T Technology Skills

Researching on the Internet Have interested students research animals found in Southern Africa, such as the meerkats found in Namibia. Have them make posters or picture books of interesting facts and photographs of the animals that they find online. Remind students to use reliable sources and to credit the sources of the photographs they use. Posters and picture books can be shared with a younger class. **Visual/Spatial**

ANSWERS, p. 378

STEP INTO THE PLACE
1. Angola
2. South Africa
3. Zambia, Mozambique, South Africa, and Botswana
4. Gaborone

STEP INTO THE TIME
Students may note that the region's economy, government, and culture have likely been heavily influenced by long years of colonial rule by the Dutch and British. They also may note that colonial rule ended comparatively recently in Southern Africa.

Chapter 13
SOUTHERN AFRICA CCSS

> **V** Most of inland Southern Africa is rich in resources and home to a wide variety of ethnic groups. The region's coastal and island countries are struggling to develop their economies.

Step Into the Place

MAP FOCUS Use the map to answer the following questions.

1. **PLACES AND REGIONS**
Luanda is the capital city of what country?

2. **THE GEOGRAPHER'S WORLD**
What country is located on the southern tip of the African continent?

3. **THE GEOGRAPHER'S WORLD**
What countries share a border with Zimbabwe?

4. **CRITICAL THINKING**
Integrating Visual Information Which of these places is the smallest in area: Lesotho, Gaborone, or Malawi?

A

PROVINCIAL CAPITAL The flat-topped Table Mountain overlooks the city of Cape Town, South Africa. Cape Town serves as the capital of the Western Cape province.

T

B

DESERT MAMMAL The meerkat is a member of the mongoose family. Only about 1 foot tall (30 cm), the meerkat stands by using its long tail for balance.

Step Into the Time

TIME LINE Based on events on the time line, predict the effects of Southern Africa's colonial past on the economy, government, and culture of the region.
WHST.6-8.10

A.D. 900 Kingdom of Great Zimbabwe established

1400s Mutapa Empire flourishes

1652 Dutch establish Cape Colony

1806 Britain gains control of Cape Colony

1800

(t to b) ©Bob Krist/Corbis; ©Nigel J. Dennis; Gallo Images/Corbis; Brian Perry/Alamy

---

Project-Based Learning ✋

Hands-On

Creating a Board Game

Students will work in groups to research, design, and create a board game based on information about Southern Africa. Using information from the chapter and other sources, students will design the game board, define the rules of the game, and create any trivia or question cards. Once completed, groups will take turns playing the games that their classmates created.

Digital Hands-On

Adding QR Codes to a Map

Have students add QR codes to an outline map of Southern Africa. Through online research, students will select photos, video, current event articles, and maps related to the physical geography, history, and culture of the region. Then students will create and affix the codes to digitally annotate the map. Maps can be displayed and scanned with a QR reader by students and adults for a multimedia-rich tour of the region.

edtechteacher
21st Century Learning

Southern Africa (map)

CENTRAL AFRICA
EAST AFRICA
CABINDA (Angola)
Luanda
ANGOLA
Huambo
Lake Tanganyika
SEYCHELLES • Victoria
Kitwe
Lilongwe
Lake Malawi (Lake Nyasa)
Moroni • COMOROS
• Mayotte
Mamoudzou (Fr.)
ZAMBIA
Lusaka
Zambezi R.
MALAWI
Okavango R.
Rundu
Lake Kariba
Harare
ZIMBABWE
• Bulawayo
MOZAMBIQUE
MADAGASCAR
• Toamasina
Antananarivo
MAURITIUS
Port Louis
Réunion (Fr.)
B Francistown
NAMIBIA
Windhoek
BOTSWANA
Gaborone
Tshwane (Pretoria)
Johannesburg
Soweto
Mbabane
Maputo
Matola
SWAZILAND
Mozambique Channel
Umpopo R.
TROPIC OF CAPRICORN
INDIAN OCEAN
ATLANTIC OCEAN
Bloemfontein
Maseru LESOTHO
Orange R.
A SOUTH AFRICA
Cape Town

○ National capital
◦ Departmental capital
• City

0 500 miles
0 500 kilometers
Lambert Azimuthal Equal-Area projection

EQUATOR

Timeline
1910 Boers establish independent Union of South Africa
1960s Colonies gain independence and self-rule
1979 Birth of Zimbabwe
1900
2000
1886 World's largest gold deposits discovered
1962 Nelson Mandela sentenced to life in prison
1993 Interim constitution enumerates rights for all people

(l) Bob Thomas/Popperfoto/Getty Images; (r) Stockbyte/Getty Images

Chapter 13 **379**

TIME LINE

Reading a Time Line and Map

Analyzing Visuals Display the time line and map on the interactive whiteboard. Have volunteers read each event as it is revealed on the time line. Ask students to identify the location on the map where an event took place. **Visual/Spatial**

See page 377B for other online activities.

CHAPTER 13
Southern Africa

Step Into the Time

V Visual Skills

Interpreting Have students study the time line. Note that there are few events that happen between the years 1800–1900. Then point to the date of 1886, when gold deposits were discovered. Discuss how this discovery lead to further development of Southern Africa. Also **ask:**

- During what period of time did indigenous people rule a powerful kingdom and empire in Southern Africa? *(between A.D. 900 and the 1400s)*
- In what decade did the colonies in Southern Africa gain independence and self-rule? *(1960s)*
- About how many centuries earlier did the American colonies gain independence? *(about two centuries earlier)* **Logical/Mathematical**

Content Background Knowledge

As students examine the time line, share with them the following information, which is expanded upon later in the chapter.

- Great Zimbabwe was the capital of a wealthy, powerful kingdom established by indigenous people called the Shona in what is now Zimbabwe and Mozambique. It flourished between A.D. 900 and 1400.
- The Mutapa empire of the Shona followed the Kingdom of Great Zimbabwe but was gradually taken over by the Portuguese during the 1500s and 1600s.
- The Portuguese and other Europeans began establishing trading posts in Southern Africa around 1500. Colonies came later. The Dutch established Cape Colony on the southern tip of what is now South Africa in 1652.
- The Dutch were known as Boers, which means farmers.
- Nelson Mandela is a black South African who fought against racial discrimination in his country and was imprisoned for many years before being elected the first black president of South Africa.

CLOSE & REFLECT

Formulating Questions Based on this introduction to Southern Africa, have students add to the list of questions they generated earlier about the region. Suggest that students look for answers to their questions as they study the chapter.

ENGAGE

Bellringer To introduce the lesson, display both a physical and a political map of Southern Africa and tell students to choose a country in the region that they would like to visit. Give students a few minutes to write a paragraph describing the features of the country's geography based on what they can tell from the physical map, including landforms and bodies of water. Ask students to save their paragraphs. Then tell students that they will learn more about the physical geography of the countries of Southern Africa in this lesson.

TEACH & ASSESS

C1 Critical Thinking Skills

Drawing Conclusions Using the physical map of Africa from the unit opener, point out the location of the Cape of Good Hope on the southern tip of Africa. Explain that this cape was first named Cape of Storms, but that name was thought to be too negative. Note that this spot is considered the meeting place of the Atlantic and Indian oceans. **Ask:**

• Is there a clear dividing line between the Atlantic and Indian oceans, or between any of the oceans? *(no)*
• What conclusion can you draw about the world oceans? *(They form one large global ocean.)* **AL** Visual/Spatial

C2 Critical Thinking Skills

Comparing and Contrasting Suggest that students refer to a map of Southern Africa as they finish reading the section, "Landforms and Bodies of Water." On the board, create a three-column chart like the one below and call on volunteers to place the countries of the region into the three categories based on size. Students should use the information in the text as well as on their own examination of the map. *(**Fairly large:** Angola, South Africa, Namibia, Mozambique, Zambia, Botswana, Madagascar; **Medium:** Zimbabwe, Malawi; **Tiny:** Swaziland, Lesotho, Comoros, Mauritius, Seychelles)* Visual/Spatial

Countries of Southern Africa by Size		
Fairly Large	**Medium**	**Tiny**

ANSWER, p. 380

Taking Notes Depending on the countries selected, notes should include information about a country's physical geography, such as the plateaus and deserts of Namibia and Botswana or the plateaus and coastal plains of Mozambique; the tropical, temperate, and/or arid climate of a country; important resources such as diamonds, gold, and platinum in Namibia and South Africa or copper and emeralds in Zambia.

---

networks

There's More Online!

☑ **IMAGES** Etosha Pan
☑ **SLIDE SHOW** Diamonds
☑ **VIDEO**

Reading **HELP**DESK (CCSS)

Academic Vocabulary RH.6-8.4
• **network** *(Tier Two Words)*

Content Vocabulary RH.6-8.4
(Tier Three Words)
• **escarpment**
• **landlocked**
• **reservoir**
• **blood diamonds**
• **poaching**

TAKING NOTES: *Key Ideas and Details* RH.6-8.2, RH.6-8.7

Summarize As you read, list important details about two countries of Southern Africa in a graphic organizer like the one below.

Country:		
Physical Geography		
Climate		
Natural Resources		

Lesson 1
Physical Geography of Southern Africa

ESSENTIAL QUESTION • *How does geography influence the way people live?*

IT MATTERS BECAUSE
Southern Africa is the world's leading producer of gold, platinum, chromium, and diamonds. Other minerals the region supplies, including uranium and copper, are also important in the global economy.

Landforms and Bodies of Water

GUIDING QUESTION *What are the dominant physical features of Southern Africa?*

The region of Southern Africa consists of the 10 southernmost countries on the African continent. It also includes four independent island countries and two French island territories in the Indian Ocean off Africa's east coast.

Southern Africa is bordered by the Indian Ocean on the east and the Atlantic Ocean on the west. The Cape of Good Hope at the southern tip of the continent is considered the place where the two oceans meet.

Several of the region's countries are fairly large. Angola and South Africa are each nearly the size of Western Europe and are the continent's seventh- and ninth-largest countries, respectively. Along with Namibia, Mozambique, Zambia, and Botswana, Angola and South Africa rank in the top 25 percent of the world's countries in land area.

The country of Madagascar occupies the world's fourth-largest island, also called Madagascar. The region's three other island countries—Comoros, Mauritius, and Seychelles—are tiny. Their combined area of 1,800 square miles (4,662 sq. km) makes them smaller than the state of Delaware.

(l to r) ©Martin Harvey/Corbis; ©Roger De La Harpe; Gallo Images/Corbis; ©Paul A. Souders/Corbis Per-Andes Petersson/PDPd Party-Agents/Getty Images; ©George Steinmetz/Corbis

---

networks *Online Teaching Options*

VIDEO

Around the World—Botswana

Comparing and Contrasting Use this video about the physical geography, climate, and wildlife of Botswana, located in Southern Africa, to preview the lesson content. Have students compare and contrast the geography of Southern Africa with the geography of the United States. **AL** Naturalist

See page 377C for other online activities.

BBC Motion Gallery Education

Landforms

If Southern Africa's physical geography had to be described with one word, that word would be *high*. A series of plateaus that range in elevation from 3,000 feet to 6,000 feet (914 m to 1,829 m) cover most of the region. The northern plateaus extend from Malawi across Zambia and Angola. These plateaus are largely forested. Farther south, the plateaus are covered mainly by grasslands.

The plateau's outer edges form a steep slope called the Great Escarpment. In Angola, the **escarpment**, a steep cliff between a higher and a lower surface, runs parallel to the Atlantic Coast and continues through Namibia. Between the escarpment and the Atlantic Ocean lies a strip of desert called the Namib that is 80 miles to 100 miles (129 km to 161 km) wide. The Namib runs 1,200 miles (1,931 km) from southern Angola to western South Africa, where it merges with another desert, the Kalahari.

The Kalahari Desert is a vast, sand-covered plateau that sits some 3,000 feet (914 m) above sea level. It is bordered by even higher plateaus. The Kalahari covers much of eastern Namibia and most of Botswana. In some places, long chains of sand dunes rise as much as 200 feet (61 m) high. The sand in some areas is red because of minerals that coat the grains of sand.

South of the Kalahari Desert, much of the rest of Southern Africa is covered by a huge plateau that slopes from about 8,000 feet (2,438 m) in the east to 2,000 feet (610 m) in the west. At the southern tip of this plateau, the Great Escarpment breaks into several small, low mountain ranges. This group of ranges is known as the Cape Ranges. The ranges are separated from each other by dry basins called the Great Karoo and the Little Karoo.

As the Great Escarpment follows South Africa's coastline, it forms the Drakensberg Mountains. This is the most rugged part of the escarpment. Mountain peaks rise to more than 11,000 feet (3,353 m). A narrow coastal plain lies between the mountains and the Indian Ocean.

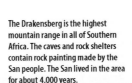
The Drakensberg is the highest mountain range in all of Southern Africa. The caves and rock shelters contain rock painting made by the San people. The San lived in the area for about 4,000 years.

©Martin Harvey/Corbis

R1 Reading Skills

Defining Suggest that students create word squares like the one below for each vocabulary word they encounter, beginning with the word *escarpment*. Review the four sections of the word square as needed making sure students understand the difference between the definition of a word and the characteristics of the word. *(Sample answers for escarpment:* **definition:** *a steep cliff between a higher and a lower surface;* **sentence:** *The escarpment rose almost 5,000 feet above the coastal plain.* **Illustration:** *students might draw a steep cliff;* **characteristics:** *steep, made of rock and soil, divides two areas of land)*

Definition		Illustration
	escarpment	
Sentence		Characteristics

ELL AL Visual/Spatial

W Writing Skills

Informative/Explanatory Have students select one of the two deserts described in the section and use the Internet to find out more information about their choice. In a three or four paragraph informative report, students should include information on the size of the desert, unusual landforms within the desert, rainfall amounts, plants, wildlife, and any other known resources. Call on volunteers to share their reports with the class. BL Verbal/Linguistic

R2 Reading Skills

Summarizing Remind students that writing a summary of a section is a great way to take notes. To help students summarize the information about Southern Africa's landforms, **ask: What geographical terms would you use to characterize the landscape of Southern Africa?** *(Possible answer: plateau, escarpment, desert, coastal plain)* **Visual/Spatial**

MAP

Africa's Size

Analyzing Maps Display the infographic-style map and highlight and discuss the sheer size of Africa, using the countries placed in its borders to discuss just how large the continent is. Allow students time to study the map. Tell students that Africa is the second largest continent after Asia. Lead a class discussion comparing the sizes of the various countries in Africa, Asia, and Europe. **Visual/Spatial**

See page 377C for other online activities.

V Visual Skills

Creating Maps After handing out outline maps of Africa, direct students to draw the three major rivers in Southern Africa—the Zambezi, Limpopo, and Orange—on the outline maps. Encourage students to use a color that is easily identifiable—such as blue—to represent water. Have students add other details and notes to the map as they continue to read. **Visual/Spatial**

T Technology Skills

Researching on the Internet After students read the text about Victoria Falls, read the Content Background Knowledge below to them and discuss which trail they would most likely take to see Victoria Falls. Have interested students research the difference in accessing the trails and report back to the class. Encourage students to add these trails to their outline maps.

R Reading Skills

Summarizing Ask a volunteer to finish reading the section, "Bodies of Water," out loud. Discuss the importance of large river systems to emphasize the significance of water as a natural resource. Then have students summarize the information about Southern Africa's rivers. **Ask:**

• What is the longest river in Southern Africa? *(Zambezi River)*

• What is the second longest river in Southern Africa, and what is its course? *(Orange River; It begins in the highlands of Lesotho and flows westward to the Atlantic Ocean.)*

• What is the course of the Limpopo River? *(It flows eastward along South Africa's border with Botswana and Zimbabwe, drops over the Great Escarpment, crosses the plains of southern Mozambique, and empties into the Indian Ocean.)*
Verbal/Linguistic

Content Background Knowledge

One of the seven natural wonders of the world, Victoria Falls is the largest waterfall in the world based on a combination of its width and height together. Located on the border between Zambia and Zimbabwe, the waterfall is protected by national parks in the two countries. Trails lead to the waterfall on both sides of the border. However, viewers can see only about 30 percent of the waterfall from the Zambian side and about 80 percent from the Zimbabwean side. The Scottish explorer Dr. David Livingstone named Victoria Falls after Queen Victoria of England.

ANSWER, p. 382

CRITICAL THINKING along the Zambezi River on the border between Zambia and Zimbabwe

---

As rivers spill from one plateau to the next, they create thundering waterfalls, such as the spectacular Victoria Falls.
▶ **CRITICAL THINKING**
Describing Where are the falls located?

The Drakensberg mountains parallel the Indian Ocean coastline for some 700 miles (1,127 km) through Lesotho and Swaziland, two **landlocked** countries in Southern Africa. Near Swaziland, the escarpment pulls back from the coastline to create a broad coastal plain that covers much of Mozambique. Northwestern Mozambique and the neighboring countries of Zimbabwe, Zambia, and Malawi lie at higher elevations west of the escarpment, on the plateau.

Bodies of Water

V Three major river systems—the Zambezi, Limpopo, and Orange—drain most of Southern Africa. The Zambezi, which stretches for 2,200 miles (3,541 km), is the region's longest river. On the Zambia-Zimbabwe border, midway through its course, the Zambezi plunges over the spectacular Victoria Falls into a narrow gorge. Roughly a mile (1.6 km) wide and 350 feet (107 m) high, the falls are about **T** twice the width and height of Niagara Falls in North America. Because of the heavy veil of mist that rises from the gorge, the area's indigenous people named the falls *Mosi-oa-Tunya* ("The Smoke That Thunders").

The Orange River is Southern Africa's second-longest river. It begins in the highlands of Lesotho and flows westward to reach the Atlantic Ocean. Its course marks the southern boundary of the Kalahari Desert. The region's third-longest river, the Limpopo, flows **R** eastward in a large arc along South Africa's border with Botswana and Zimbabwe. The river then drops over the Great Escarpment to cross the plains of southern Mozambique to the Indian Ocean.

©Roger De La Harpe/Gallo Images/Corbis

---

networks   *Online Teaching Options*

MAP

Physical Geography: Southern Africa

Interpreting Visual Information Allow time for pairs of students to study the physical geography layer of the Chapter Opener map. Then have partners create a poster of the landforms and waterways of Southern Africa. Posters should include drawings or images and text that identifies and describes the region's major landforms and bodies of water. **AL Visual/Spatial**

See page 377C for other online activities.

These three rivers, their tributaries, and Southern Africa's other rivers have carved a **network** of canyons and gorges across the plateaus. Dams have been built in the area to store water. Lake Kariba, Southern Africa's second-largest lake, is really a **reservoir**, or an artificial lake created by a dam.

The region's largest lake—and the third largest in all of Africa—is Lake Malawi (also known as Lake Nyasa), which forms Malawi's border with Mozambique and Tanzania. It is the southernmost lake of the Great Rift Valley which stretches for thousands of miles. Lake Malawi fills a depression, or hollow, that follows one of the rifts, or tears, in Earth's crust. Because of the great depth of the depression, Lake Malawi is one of the deepest lakes in the world.

A number of flat basins, called pans, can be found in Southern Africa. The salt deposits they contain provide nourishment for wild animals. Etosha Pan, in northern Namibia, is an enormous expanse of salt that covers 1,900 square miles (4,921 sq. km). It is the largest pan in Africa, and it is the center of Etosha National Park. The park is home to some of the greatest numbers of lions, elephants, rhinoceroses, and other large animals in the world.

☑ **READING PROGRESS CHECK**

Identifying Which type of landform is common in Southern Africa?

Climate

GUIDING QUESTION *What is the climate of Southern Africa?*

Southern Africa has a wide variety of climates, ranging from humid to arid to hot to cool. Nearly all of the region's climates have distinct seasons, with certain seasons receiving most of the rain.

Tropical Zone

The Tropic of Capricorn crosses the middle of Southern Africa. This places the northern half of the region in the Tropics. Northern Angola and northern Mozambique have a tropical wet-dry climate. Each area gets as much as 70 inches (178 cm) of rain per year. Most of it falls in the spring, summer, and fall—from October to May. The high elevation makes temperatures cool.

©Paul A. Souders/Corbis

Thinking Like a **Geographer**

Pans

Pans are believed to be the beds of ancient lakes whose water evaporated over time. They are among the flattest known landforms. Small amounts of rain can flood large areas of their surface. It is this flooding that causes and maintains their flatness. Salt deposits form as rainwater pools slowly evaporate. *Why can a small amount of rain flood a large area of a pan?*

Academic Vocabulary

network a complex, interconnected chain or system of things such as roads, canals, or computers

Zebras are among the many animals that live in the national park that is part of the Etosha Pan.
▶ CRITICAL THINKING
Describing What is unique about the Etosha Pan?

MAP

Climates: Southern Africa

Analyzing Maps Display the climate layer of the Chapter Opener map for students and discuss the climate zones of Southern Africa. As you focus on each area, call on volunteers to describe the temperature and rainfall patterns of each type of climate. **AL Visual/Spatial**

See page 377C for other online activities.

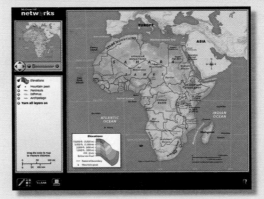

W Writing Skills

Informative/Explanatory Have students conduct Internet research to write an informative essay about one of the following topics: Lake Malawi, Great Rift Valley, or Etosha Pan. Make sure all three topics are selected. Call on volunteers to share their essays with the class and to answer questions about the topic. **BL Verbal/Linguistic, Naturalist**

V₁ Visual Skills

Creating Charts Suggest that students begin a chart like the one below to take notes on the varied climates of Southern Africa as they progress through the section, "Climates." *(Example: Area: Northern Angola, Northern Mozambique; Description of Climate: Tropical wet-dry; 70 inches of rain per year, mostly from October to May; cool temperatures ranging from upper 60s°F to upper 70s°F, but warmer along coasts)* Have students continue to fill in their charts as they read the rest of the section on the next two pages. **Verbal/Linguistic**

Climates of Southern Africa	
Area	**Description of Climate**
	Tropical wet-dry
	Temperate
	Desert

V₂ Visual Skills

Evaluating As a class, evaluate the photo on this page. Remind students that photos can tell a story about places. **Ask:**

• **How would you describe the vegetation, landforms, and climate in this photograph?** *(Possible answers: sparse, it looks very dry and flat, no trees or water, it looks very hot)*

• **What is surprising about the kinds of animals that this land supports?** *(Possible answer: The animals are large, grazing mammals, and the vegetation appears too sparse to support such animals.)* **AL Visual/Spatial**

ANSWERS, p. 383

Thinking Like a Geographer because the land is so flat
☑ **READING PROGRESS CHECK** plateaus
CRITICAL THINKING The area contains an enormous amount of salt deposits.

People struggle to wade through the waters after a heavy rainfall in the coastal city of Maputo in southwestern Mozambique.
▶ **CRITICAL THINKING**
Describing How does the length of the rainy season in western Mozambique compare with the length in the northern part of the country?

Daily average temperatures range from the upper 60s°F (upper 10s°C) to the upper 70s°F (mid-20s°C). Along the coasts, temperatures are warmer.

Much of northern Mozambique's coastline is watered by rain-bearing winds called monsoons that sweep in from the Indian Ocean during the summer months. More than 70 inches (178 cm) of annual rainfall is common.

Parts of Angola and Mozambique have humid subtropical climates, as do Malawi, Zambia, and northeastern Zimbabwe. The rainy season here is shorter than in the tropical wet/dry zone, and also brings less rainfall. Most places average 24 inches to 40 inches (61cm to 102 cm) per year. Average temperatures are also slightly cooler. Nighttime frosts are not uncommon in July on the high plateaus of Zambia and Malawi. Temperatures on summer days in lowland areas, however, can exceed 100°F (38°C).

Temperate Zones

Much of South Africa, central Namibia, eastern Botswana, and southern Mozambique have temperate, or moderate, climates that are not marked by extremes of temperature. Most of these areas are semiarid. Summer days are warm—from 70°F to 90°F (21°C to 32°C), depending on elevation. Winters are cool, with frosts and sometimes freezing temperatures on the high plateaus.

Annual rainfall varies from 8 inches (20 cm) in some areas to 24 inches (61 cm) in others. Most of the rain falls during the summer, with very little the rest of the year. Droughts are common; in some places, they last for several years.

Lesotho, Swaziland, and eastern South Africa, including the Indian Ocean coastline, are much wetter. Temperatures are like those in the semiarid regions, but ocean currents and moist ocean air bring up to 55 inches (140 cm) of rain annually. Like elsewhere in the region, most of this rain falls in the summer.

Desert Regions

Western South Africa, western Namibia, and much of Botswana are arid. Along the coast, the Namib gets very little rain. In some years, no rain falls. But fog and dew provide small plants with the moisture they need to survive. Temperatures along the coast are mild, however, with daily averages ranging from 48°F to 68°F (9°C to 20°C). The

Per-Anders Petersson/PDFd Party-Agents/Getty Images

netw⊙rks *Online Teaching Options*

MAP

Monsoons

Understanding Visuals Display the map on monsoons to discuss with students the effect of this natural disaster on Southern Africa. Lead a class discussion on the positive and negative effects of monsoons on the people of Southern Africa. Encourage students to create a graphic organizer to review the information about climates in Southern Africa. **AL** Verbal/Linguistic

See page 377C for other online activities.

ANSWER, p. 384

CRITICAL THINKING The rainy season is shorter in western Mozambique.

aridity, the fog, and the mild temperatures result from the cold Benguela Current that flows along the coast. This area is sometimes called the "Skeleton Coast" because many ships used to lose their way in the fog and run aground. Once ashore, the sailors rarely survived because of the lack of water in the sandy desert.

In inland areas of the Namib Desert, temperatures are hotter with summer highs from the upper 80s°F to more than 100°F (30°C to 38°C). In winter, freezing temperatures sometimes occur. During wet years, desert grasses and bushes appear. Much of the time, however, the Namib is home to vast areas of barren sand. **R**

The Kalahari's location—farther inland than the Namib—and dry air make its temperatures more extreme than in the Namib. The Kalahari also gets a little more precipitation than the Namib.

☑ **READING PROGRESS CHECK**

Describing Why are temperatures in Southern Africa's tropical countries generally not hot?

Natural Resources

GUIDING QUESTION *What natural resources are found in Southern Africa, and why are they important?*

Southern Africa is the continent's richest region in natural resources. Mineral resources have helped the Republic of South Africa, in particular, to build a strong economy. In other countries, like Angola and Namibia, such resources provide the only source of wealth. **C**

The landscape of the Skeleton Coast is made up of sand dunes, rocky canyons, and mountains. Dense fogs and cool sea breezes are characteristic of the area.

▶ **CRITICAL THINKING**
Describing How did the Skeleton Coast get its name?

©George Steinmetz/Corbis

Chapter 13 **385**

Lissa Harrison

IMAGE

The Kalahari Dunes

Researching on the Internet Display the interactive image of the Kalahari Desert. As a class, discuss the desert climate zone in Southern Africa and the number of countries this climate zone crosses. Have interested students research how wildlife has adapted to the desert conditions and give oral reports to the class. **AL**
Naturalist

See page 377C for other online activities.

R **Reading Skills**

Explaining Use the following questions to help students find explanations for climate conditions in the desert regions of Southern Africa. **Ask:**

- If no rain falls in the Namib Desert in some years, how do plants survive? *(They get the moisture they need from dew and fog.)*
- What causes the aridity, fog, and mild temperatures along the coast of Namibia? *(the cold Benguela Current that flows along the coast)*
- Why does the Kalahari have more extreme temperatures than the Namib? *(It is located farther inland and has dry air.)* **Verbal/Linguistic**

C **Critical Thinking Skills**

Making Comparisons As needed, have students look back through the previous chapters in the unit on Africa to recall the resources of the other regions of the continent in order to compare them to the resources of Southern Africa. Also, have students use the resources map of Africa in the Unit Opener as they read the section, "Natural Resources," to make comparisons among the regions. **Ask:** Why are natural resources important to a country's economy? *(They are often the basis of industry and a country's exports.)* **Logical/Mathematical**

Content Background Knowledge

About a third of Namibia's foggy coastline lies within Skeleton Coast National Park. Despite the aridity and bleakness of this desert area, the park is home to many mammals who have adapted to the desert environment including elephants, black rhinos, lions, cheetahs, giraffes, zebras, and hyenas. Cape fur seals and seabirds inhabit the many shipwrecks along the coast. In the off-shore waters are Benguela dolphins, killer whales, and humpback whales. Tourists can book safaris to view the wildlife.

ANSWERS, p. 385

☑ **READING PROGRESS CHECK** because of their high elevations

CRITICAL THINKING Many ships lost their way because of the heavy fog and ran aground there.

V1 Visual Skills

Integrating Visual Information Emphasize that many people in Southern Africa are employed in the mining industry because the region has large deposits of many valuable minerals. **Ask: What do you think are some drawbacks of working in a mine?** *(Answers will vary. Students may note that the work is dirty and dangerous and often poses health risks.)* **Visual/Spatial**

V2 Visual Skills

Creating Charts Have students work with a partner to read and discuss the sections about the resources of the region on this page and the next. Then have pairs create charts listing the mineral, energy, and other resources of Southern Africa by country. **Kinesthetic, Interpersonal**

Natural Resources of Southern Africa	
Country	**Natural Resources**
Republic of South Africa	*platinum, chromium, gold, diamonds, coal, iron ore, uranium, copper*
Zimbabwe	*coal, hydroelectric power, gold, agricultural land*
Botswana	*coal, diamonds*
Mozambique	*coal, natural gas, tantalite, gold, platinum, diamonds, iron ore, copper*
Angola	*natural gas, oil, diamonds*
Namibia	*oil, natural gas, tin, zinc, copper, gold, silver, uranium*
Zambia	*hydroelectric power, copper, cobalt, gold, silver, iron ore, emeralds*
Malawi	*hydroelectric power, rubies, sapphires, semiprecious gems, fertile soil*
Lesotho	*few natural resources*
Swaziland	*few natural resources*

More than one-half of the world's diamonds are harvested from mines, such as this one, in Southern Africa. Diamonds were formed deep in Earth thousands of years ago under extreme heat and pressure. Volcanic pressure brings them to Earth's surface.

South Africa's Resources

The Republic of South Africa has some of the largest mineral reserves in the world. It is the world's largest producer of platinum, chromium, and gold, and one of the largest producers of diamonds—both gems and industrial diamonds, or diamonds used to make cutting or grinding tools. These resources, along with important deposits of coal, iron ore, uranium, copper, and other minerals, have created a thriving mining industry. This industry has attracted workers and investments from other countries that have helped South Africa's industries grow.

Energy Resources

The Republic of South Africa, Zimbabwe, Botswana, and Mozambique mine and burn coal from their own deposits to produce most of their electric power. Mozambique has large deposits of natural gas as well, as does Angola. Angola is also one of Africa's leading oil producers. Namibia has oil and natural gas deposits, too, and they are slowly being developed. Oil and gas must be refined, or changed into other products, before they can be used.

The region's rivers are another resource for providing power. Zimbabwe and Zambia get electricity from the huge Kariba Gorge dam on the Zambezi River. Malawi's rivers and falls generate power for that country. Deforestation, however, allows more sediment to enter the rivers, which reduces the water flow and the electricity that the rivers produce. Mozambique, Zimbabwe, and Angola have not made full use of their rivers to provide power. Economic development and the standard of living in those countries have suffered as a result.

©Herve Collart/Sygma/Corbis

386 *Chapter 13*

---

networks *Online Teaching Options*

SLIDE SHOW

Diamonds

Integrating Visual Information Use the slide show to discuss the processes of turning this mineral into jewelry and of adapting it for industrial purposes. Explain that diamonds have become valuable partly because they are fairly rare and are considered beautiful by a large majority of people. Lead a class discussion about the mining and use of diamonds and the consequences of mining for this mineral. **ELL Verbal/Linguistic**

Slide Show

See page 377C for other online activities.

(l) ©Ocean/Corbis, ©Kryssia Campos/Getty Images, (tr) Erica Simone Leeds, (br) ©IG Photography/Alamy

Minerals and Other Resources

Namibia is one of Africa's richest countries in mineral resources. It is an important producer of tin, zinc, copper, gold, silver, and uranium. It also ranks with South Africa and Botswana as a leading world supplier of diamonds. In the 1990s, rebels captured Angola's mines and sold the diamonds to continue a 20-year-old civil war against the government. In countries outside Southern Africa, groups have also mined diamonds to pay for rebellions and other violent conflicts. Diamonds used for this purpose are called **blood diamonds**.

Gold is a leading export for Zimbabwe. Mozambique has the world's largest supply of the rare metal tantalite, which is used to make electronic parts and camera lenses. Gold, platinum, and diamonds are mined there too, as are iron ore and copper. Much of Zambia's economy is based on copper and cobalt, although gold, silver, and iron ore are also mined. Zambia has some of the largest emerald deposits in the world. A small amount of rubies, sapphires, and a variety of semiprecious gems are mined in neighboring Malawi.

Malawi's most important natural resource is its fertile soil. The country's economy is based mainly on agriculture. Tobacco is its most important export. Exporting farm products is also a major economic activity in Zimbabwe. Lesotho and Swaziland have few natural resources. Most of their people practice subsistence farming, growing only enough to meet their needs.

C

Wildlife

Southern Africa is known for its variety of animal life. Wildebeests, lions, zebras, giraffes, and many other animals are found across the region. They live within and outside the many national parks and wildlife reserves that nearly every country has created to protect them. Tourists come from throughout the world to see these animals. **Poaching**, or illegally killing game, is a problem. Poachers shoot elephants for their valuable ivory tusks and rhinoceroses for their horns. Others kill animals to sell their skins and meat and to protect livestock and crops.

T

FOLDABLES®
Study Organizer

Include this lesson's information in your Foldable®.

☑ **READING PROGRESS CHECK**

Describing How does deforestation affect the energy supply in the region?

LESSON 1 REVIEW

Reviewing Vocabulary (Tier Three Words)
1. Why is *poaching* against the law? RH.6-8.4

Answering the Guiding Questions
2. *Describing* How has damming Southern Africa's rivers benefited the people and countries of the region? RH.6-8.5

3. *Identifying* What are the rainfall and temperature differences between Southern Africa's tropical, temperate, and arid regions? RH.6-8.1

4. *Describing* For what resources is Southern Africa known throughout the world? RH.6-8.1

5. *Narrative Writing* Create a journal entry recording your observations and experiences during one day of a photo safari at Etosha National Park. WHST.6-8.4, WHST.6-8.10

Chapter 13 **387**

LESSON 1 REVIEW ANSWERS

Reviewing Vocabulary

1. Poachers kill animals that are protected by law and sell ivory and other parts for their own gain.

Answering the Guiding Questions

2. **Describing** Dams create lakes to store water for use during dry periods and to generate electricity for homes and industries.

3. **Identifying** Tropical areas are rainy but not very hot. Temperate areas get less rain than tropical areas and have warm summers and cool winters. Arid areas get the least rain and have mild temperatures along the coast, though inland areas have hot summers.

4. **Describing** The region is the world's leading producer of platinum, chromium, gold, and diamonds. Its wildlife draws tourists.

5. **Narrative Writing** Journal entries should be consistent with the physical geography of that part of Namibia and the wildlife in the national park.

C **Critical Thinking Skills**

Analyzing Information After students have read the secton, "Minerals and Other Resources," direct them to do additional research on the value and importance of the various minerals. Then lead a class discussion on how minerals can lead to wars. **Ask: Should people mine minerals to fund wars? Why or why not?** (*Answers will vary but should include thoughtful conclusions.*)

Further discussion should compare mining for valuable resources in the United States with mining in Africa. **Ask: Are there any conflicts in the United States over mining products or mining itself?** (*Student answers will vary but may include the idea that some people do not want mines because they say mining can hurt the environment.*) **AL** **Verbal/Linguistic**

T **Technology Skills**

Researching on the Internet In preparation for completing the narrative writing assignment in the Lesson 1 Review, have students conduct Internet research on Etosha National Park in Namibia. Suggest that students look for information about the park's landscape, vegetation, climate, and wildlife. Encourage them to study photographs of the park. Have students work in pairs to relate the information visually by creating a concept web or other type of graphic organizer. **Verbal/Linguistic, Visual/Spatial**

CLOSE & REFLECT

Identifying Central Ideas Remind students of the paragraph they wrote at the beginning of this lesson describing the geography of Southern Africa based on a physical map of the region. Suggest that students take ten minutes to jot down the most important things they have learned about the region's physical geography and use these to revise their paragraphs. Call on volunteers to share their lists of important ideas and their revised paragraphs.

ANSWER, p. 387

☑ **READING PROGRESS CHECK** People are destroying trees to create farm fields and to obtain wood for cooking fuel.

ENGAGE

Bellringer To introduce the lesson, ask students to write down what they already know about the history of Southern Africa. Call on volunteers to share what they have written. Then tell students that they will learn more about the history of the region in this lesson. Encourage students to preview the lesson by skimming the Guiding Questions, headings, visuals, and captions.

TEACH & ASSESS

R Reading Skills

Summarizing Have students read the sections on this page and the top of the next page. Emphasize that people have lived in Southern Africa for thousands of years, developing a variety of cultures. Explain that Great Zimbabwe was the center of an advanced civilization called the Kingdom of Zimbabwe. Pose the following questions to help students summarize the main features of the civilization. **Ask:**

- **Where was the Kingdom of Zimbabwe?** *(in what is now Zimbabwe and Mozambique)*
- **What does the name *Zimbabwe* mean?** *(stone houses)*
- **How many people lived in the capital city of Great Zimbabwe and the surrounding valley?** *(as many as 20,000 people)*
- **How did Great Zimbabwe become wealthy?** *(It was a great commercial center where gold was collected from nearby mines and then taken to ports to trade with Arabs.)*
- **Why are the buildings of Great Zimbabwe so impressive?** *(Some buildings were more than 30 feet high and were made of large stones cut to fit and stay in place without mortar to hold them together.)*
- **What is one theory explaining why Great Zimbabwe was abandoned in the 1400s?** *(Its growing population had exhausted the water and food supply.)*
- **How long did the Kingdom of Zimbabwe last?** *(about 500 years, from about A.D. 900 to the 1400s)*

AL **ELL** Verbal/Linguistic

ANSWER, p. 388

Taking Notes Key events and dates include: **A.D. 900:** Shona builds powerful kingdom; **1300s:** Great Zimbabwe is commercial center; **late 1600s:** Portuguese driven out of the region; **1879:** Zulu War; **1652:** Cape Colony founded; **1899:** Boer War begins; **1910:** Union of South Africa formed; **1960s:** Several African colonies gain independence; **1990:** South Africa repeals apartheid rules; **1993:** new constitution extends South Africans' rights; **1994:** Mandela elected president.

networks

There's More Online!

☑ VIDEO

Reading HELPDESK (CCSS)

Academic Vocabulary RH.6-8.4
(Tier Two Words)
- exploit
- grant

Content Vocabulary RH.6-8.4
(Tier Three Words)
- apartheid
- civil disobedience
- embargo

TAKING NOTES: *Key Ideas and Details* RH.6-8.5, RH.6-8.7

Sequence Create a time line like this one. Then list five key events and their dates in the history of the region.

←—+——+——+——+——→

388

Lesson 2
History of Southern Africa

ESSENTIAL QUESTION · *How do new ideas change the way people live?*

IT MATTERS BECAUSE
Many of Southern Africa's resources have become important parts of the global economy. Political instability and unrest have sometimes disrupted the flow of products to world markets. Much of the instability and unrest is directly or indirectly the result of the region's colonial history.

Rise of Kingdoms

GUIDING QUESTION What major events mark the early history of Southern Africa?

Southern Africa's indigenous people have inhabited the region for thousands of years. Some lived as hunter-gatherers. Others farmed and herded cattle. Trade among the groups flourished. Ivory, gold, copper, and other goods moved from the interior to the east coast. There such goods were exchanged for tools, salt, and luxury items including beads, porcelain, and cloth from China, India, and Persia.

Great Zimbabwe

Around the year A.D. 900, the Shona people built a wealthy and powerful kingdom in what is now Zimbabwe and Mozambique. The capital was a city called Great Zimbabwe. (*Zimbabwe* is a Shona word meaning "stone houses.") As many as 20,000 people lived in the city and the surrounding valley.

Great Zimbabwe was the largest of many similar cities throughout the region. By the 1300s, it had become a great commercial center, collecting gold mined nearby and trading it to Arabs at ports on the Indian Ocean.

Great Zimbabwe was abandoned in the 1400s, possibly because its growing population exhausted its water and food

(l to r) ©Christine Osborne/Corbis; Hulton Archive/Getty Images; ©dpa/dpa/Corbis; ©David Turnley/Corbis; ©Louise Gubb/Corbis SABA

---

networks *Online Teaching Options*

VIDEO

Comrade Capitalist

Understanding Content Use this video to generate interest in the history of Southern Africa by discussing the life of the post-apartheid leader mentioned in the video. After students watch the video, have them share what they found most interesting. Then ask each student to write three aspects about Southern Africa's history they learned from the video. Refer back to the aspect at the end of this lesson to see if students connect the information to the content of the lesson. **ELL** Verbal/Linguistic

See page 377D for other online activities.

BBC Motion Gallery Education

resources. The city's ruins show the Shona's skill as builders. Some structures were more than 30 feet (9 m) high. Their large stones were cut to fit and stay in place without mortar to hold them together.

The Mutapa Empire

In the late 1400s, the Shona conquered the region between the Zambezi and Limpopo rivers from Zimbabwe to the coast of Mozambique. Like Great Zimbabwe, the Mutapa Empire thrived on the gold it mined and traded for goods from China and India.

The Portuguese arrived and took over the coastal trade in the 1500s. They gradually gained control over the empire and forced its people to mine gold for them. In the late 1600s, Mutapa kings allied with the nearby Rozwi kingdom to drive out the Portuguese. Instead, the Rozwi conquered the Mutapa's territory and ruled it until the early 1800s, when it became part of the Zulu Empire.

Other Kingdoms

The Zulu leader Shaka united his people in the early 1800s to form the Zulu Empire in what is now South Africa. He built a powerful army and used it to expand the empire by conquering neighboring people. Shaka was killed in 1828, but his empire survived until the British destroyed it in the Zulu War of 1879.

A series of kingdoms rose and fell on the island of Madagascar from the 1600s to the 1800s. Some of the early kingdoms were influenced by Arab and Muslim culture. In the early 1800s, one king allied with the British on the nearby island of Mauritius to prevent the French from taking control of Madagascar. He eventually conquered most of the island and formed the Kingdom of Madagascar. French troops invaded the kingdom in 1895 and made it a French possession.

☑ READING PROGRESS CHECK

Identifying Which outsiders traded with Southern Africans before the Europeans arrived?

V1

Shown are remnants of the walls of the Great Enclosure of the city of Great Zimbabwe. According to historians, houses of the royal family were located within the walls.

Identifying How did Great Zimbabwe become an important center of trade?

Christine Osborne/Corbis

Chapter 13 **389**

See page 377D for other online activities.

IMAGE

360° View: Zimbabwe Ruins

Analyzing Images Display the 360° view of the Zimbabwe Ruins to students and introduce aspects of the early history of Southern Africa and emphasize the skill of the Shona builders. Tell students that the first Europeans to see the ruins refused to believe that indigenous people had the skill to build the structures. Ask students to write a paragraph describing the ruins as if they were a tourist viewing them for the first time. **AL** Verbal/Linguistic

Lissa Harrison

V1 Visual Skills

Creating Charts To help students follow the sequence of events following the fall of the kingdom of Zimbabwe, create a sequence chart on the board like the one below. Tell students to focus on the fact that various groups controlled the territory over this period of time, including Europeans. **AL** Visual/Spatial

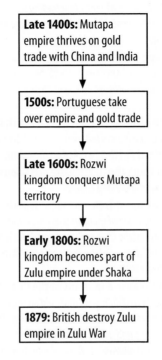

Late 1400s: Mutapa empire thrives on gold trade with China and India

↓

1500s: Portuguese take over empire and gold trade

↓

Late 1600s: Rozwi kingdom conquers Mutapa territory

↓

Early 1800s: Rozwi kingdom becomes part of Zulu empire under Shaka

↓

1879: British destroy Zulu empire in Zulu War

V2 Visual Skills

Integrating Visual Information Ask students to study the photograph of the ruins of the Great Enclosure of the city of Great Zimbabwe at the bottom of the page. Have a volunteer read the caption and answer the question. Then, **ask:**

- **Do you notice anything unusual about the walls and the enclosure?** *(The walls appear to be curved rather than straight, and the enclosure appears to be circular rather than rectangular.)*
- **Would curved walls be easier or harder to construct than straight walls?** *(harder)*

Discuss the fact that back when these walls were constructed, the people did not have machines and trucks to build and transfer materials such as are used today. Invite students to comment on the difficulty of building these walls by hand or with simple tools. **Visual/Spatial**

ANSWERS, p. 389

Identifying by mining gold and trading it to Arab traders
☑ READING PROGRESS CHECK Arab traders

History of Southern Africa

C Critical Thinking Skills

Finding the Main Idea Read the Guiding Question and the section with students. Then pose the following questions to focus students' attention on the main ideas about the European colonization of Southern Africa. **Ask:**

- **From the 1500s to about the 1800s, what kind of involvement did European countries generally have with Southern Africa?** *(They had trading posts and supply stations along the coast, and ships stopped there on their way to and from Asia.)*

- **How was Cape Colony an exception?** *(At Cape Colony, the Dutch founded a settlement and established farms on which slaves from India, Southeast Asia, and other parts of Africa worked.)*

- **How did the Africans respond to the Dutch invasion?** *(They fought against them but were defeated. Some Africans then fled north while others worked on the colonists' farms.)*

- **Why do you think the Dutch were victorious?** *(probably because they had superior weapons)*

- **What was the Great Trek, and what was the cause of it?** *(It was a migration of thousands of Boers from Cape Colony to an area north of the Orange River. Great Britain had gained control of Cape Colony, and the Boers resented British rule and wanted to escape it.)*

- **What was the cause and result of the Boer War?** *(The Boers discovered diamonds and gold on their territory, and the British wanted control of these resources. The British defeated the Boers and gained control over them again. In 1910 Great Britain allowed the Boer colonies to join the Cape Colony and form the Union of South Africa, an independent country.)* **Verbal/Linguistic**

Content Background Knowledge

The European colonization of Africa was primarily motivated by economic gain. To feed their industries, the major European powers needed the raw materials that Africa had in abundance. In addition, European countries sought to solve their problems of unemployment and poverty partly by establishing settler colonies and exporting some of their population to Africa. Although most African societies fought against the European invasion, they did not have the political organization or the technology to match the Europeans. For the most part, the Africans armed themselves with spears, bows and arrows, swords, and old rifles, while the Europeans had newer rifles, machine guns, and artillery guns.

Three Zulu leaders are shown holding shields and wearing traditional attire. The Zulu built a great empire, but during the 1800s, European settlers took control of their grazing and water resources. The Zulu population is about 9 million today, making them the largest ethnic group in the Republic of South Africa.

Academic Vocabulary

exploit to make use of something, sometimes in an unjust manner for one's own advantage or gain

European Colonies

GUIDING QUESTION *How did Southern Africa come under European control?*

Around 1500, Portugal and other European countries began establishing settlements along the African coast. The first settlements were trading posts and supply stations at which ships could stop on their way to and from Asia. As time passed, the Europeans grew interested in **exploiting** Africa's natural resources and, as a source of labor, its people.

Clashes in South Africa

During the 1600s till about the 1800s, Europeans set up trading posts but did not establish colonies, which are large territories with settlers from the home country. One exception was Cape Colony, founded by the Dutch in 1652 at the Cape of Good Hope on the southern tip of what is now South Africa. The Dutch became known as Boers, the Dutch word for farmers. They grew wheat and raised sheep and cattle. Enslaved people from India, Southeast Asia, and other parts of Africa provided much of the labor.

The Africans did not like the Dutch pushing into their land, and soon they started fighting over it. By the late 1700s, the Africans had been defeated. Some fled north into the desert. Others became workers on the colonists' farms.

The Union of South Africa

Wars in Europe gave Britain control of the Cape Colony in the early 1800s. Thousands of British settlers soon arrived. The Boers resented British rule. Many decided to seek new land beyond the reach of British control. Beginning in the 1830s, thousands of Boers left the colony in a migration called the Great Trek and settled north of the Orange River.

In the 1860s, the Boers discovered diamonds in their territory. Then, in 1886, they found the world's largest gold deposits. British efforts to gain these resources led to the Boer War in 1899. The Boers were defeated and again came under British control. In 1910 Britain allowed the Boer colonies to join the Cape Colony in forming an independent country—the Union of South Africa. The small African kingdoms of Lesotho and Swaziland remained under British control.

Hulton Archive/Getty Images

390 Chapter 13

net**w**orks *Online Teaching Options*

IMAGE

The Boer War

Making Connections Display the image of Boer soldiers fighting from the trenches at the siege of Mafikeng. Remind students that the Boer War resulted from Britain's efforts to gain control of the diamond and gold deposits discovered in the territory settled by the Boers. Ask students to recall from previous chapters other regions that came under attack by outsiders who were intent on gaining control of a valuable natural resource. Then begin a discussion by asking whether a nation is ever justified in starting a war for this reason. **Logical/Mathematical, Verbal/Linguistic, Intrapersonal**

See page 693D for other online activities.

Lissa Harrison

Colonialism in Other Areas

While the British and the Boers competed for South Africa, other European countries were competing over the rest of Africa. In 1884 representatives of these countries met in Berlin, Germany, to divide the continent among themselves.

In Southern Africa, Britain gained control over what is now Malawi, Zambia, Zimbabwe, and Botswana. The Berlin Conference decided Portugal had rights to Angola and Mozambique. Germany received what is now Namibia, although South Africa seized the colony during World War I. Besides Madagascar, France controlled what is now Comoros. Mauritius and Seychelles were British colonies.

C

European control in Southern Africa continued for about the next 80 years. Not until the 1960s did the region's colonies begin to gain independence and self-rule.

V₁

☑ READING PROGRESS CHECK

Analyzing Which European country claimed the most territory in Southern Africa in the 1800s?

Independence and Equal Rights

GUIDING QUESTION *What challenges did Southern Africans face in regaining freedom and self-rule?*

French rule in Madagascar ended in 1960, making it the first Southern African country to gain independence. Britain **granted** independence to Malawi and Zambia in 1964 and to Botswana and Lesotho in 1966. Swaziland and Mauritius gained their freedom in 1968, and Seychelles in 1976. Elsewhere, however, freedom was more difficult to achieve.

©dpa/dpa/Corbis

Academic Vocabulary

grant to permit as a right, a privilege, or a favor

Boer soldiers fight from trenches at the siege of Mafeking in 1900. The siege, lasting more than 200 days, resulted in an important victory for British forces.

▶ **CRITICAL THINKING**
Describing Who were the Boers? Why were the Boer Wars fought?

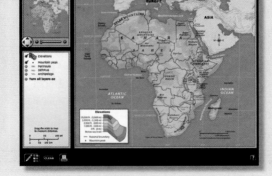

MAP

Colonization and Independence of Southern Africa

Synthesizing Display the map about colonization and independence in Southern Africa to lead a discussion on these historical events. Explain to students that there were many clashes between the Boers and the British during the struggle for colonization and independence, along with many other clashes. Ask students to write a response to this question: **How have the natural resources of Southern Africa affected its history?**
BL Visual/Spatial

See page 377D for other online activities.

C Critical Thinking Skills

Evaluating Explain that there were many European countries competing for Southern African territories. As a class, discuss the European takeover of Africa. **Ask:**

- **How did European countries divide up Southern Africa?** *(They held a conference in Berlin in 1884 to divide the continent among themselves.)*
- **Do you think the European countries had the right to take control of Southern Africa? Why or why not?** *(Answers will vary, but students should give reasons for their answers.)*
- **How is the European takeover of Southern Africa similar to or different from the European takeover of North and South America?** *(Students may note that in both cases Europeans took land by force from native people, but the takeovers occurred in different centuries.)* **Verbal/Linguistic**

V₂

V₁ Visual Skills

Creating Maps Have students use the outline maps of Southern Africa from Lesson 1 to show how European countries divided up the region. Direct students to create a map key with a color for each of the following countries: Great Britain, Germany, France, and Portugal. Tell students to label the African countries and color them based on which European nation controlled them. (**Great Britain:** *Malawi, Zambia, Zimbabwe, Botswana, Mauritius, Seychelles;* **Portugal:** *Angola, Mozambique;* **Germany:** *Namibia;* **France:** *Madagascar, Comoros)* **ELL**
AL Visual/Spatial

V₂ Visual Skills

Analyzing Images Have students examine the photograph of the siege of Mafikeng at the bottom of the page. **Ask:**

- **What kind of trenches are the men fighting from?** *(small dirt embankments)*
- **How are the men dressed?** *(in casual pants, jackets, and hats)*
- **What kind of weapons are they using?** *(rifles)*
- **What is your impression of this kind of fighting?** *(Answers will vary. Students may note that the trenches and clothing provide little protection and the style of warfare is much simpler than modern warfare.)* **Visual/Spatial**

ANSWERS, p. 391

☑ READING PROGRESS CHECK Great Britain
CRITICAL THINKING Dutch settlers in South Africa; they resented British rule

V Visual Skills

Creating Time Lines Using the text from the previous page and this page and Internet research, have students create time lines showing the dates that the countries of Southern Africa became independent and the country from which each one gained independence. You might have students create individual time lines or construct one class time line on the board. *(Possible answers: **1910:** South Africa (Great Britain); **1960:** Madagascar (France); **1964:** Malawi and Zambia (Great Britain); **1966:** Botswana and Lesotho (Great Britain); **1968:** Swaziland and Mauritius (Great Britain); **1975:** Angola and Mozambique (Portugal); **1976:** Seychelles (Great Britain); **1979:** Zimbabwe (Great Britain))* Since the text does not give some of the dates, students can research them or you may want to share the following information: Comoros gained its independence from France in 1975. Namibia gained its independence in 1990 from South Africa. **Visual/Spatial**

T Technology Skills

Researching on the Internet Have interested students research one of the civil wars of Angola or Mozambique or the guerrilla war in Rhodesia, which became Zimbabwe. Have students identify and explain the groups that were fighting in the country, why the war took as long as it did to resolve, how many people died in the conflicts, and how it impacted the economy of the country. Have students share their research with the class. Then discuss why peace can be so difficult between different cultures. **Interpersonal**

Making Connections As you discuss the history of Southern Africa, help students make connections with similar aspects of United States history. For example, in both North America and in Africa, Europeans viewed their culture as being superior to native cultures. They promoted the idea that they were "civilizing" indigenous people as they took over their land. In addition, like Southern Africa, some states in the United States had laws that enforced racially segregated public places until the mid-1900s.

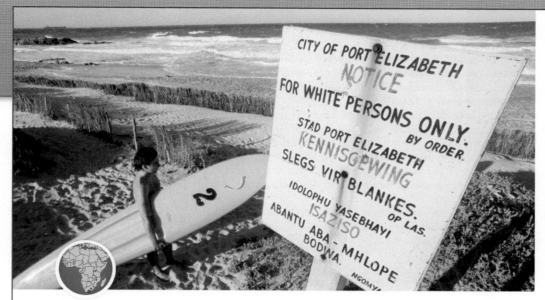

Laws in South Africa limited the political rights of black Africans and set up separate parks, beaches, and other public places.

▶ **CRITICAL THINKING**
Describing Who controlled South Africa's government until World War II? Who controlled the government beginning in 1948?

V

The End of Portuguese Rule

While other European nations gave up their African colonies, Portugal refused to do so. Revolts for independence broke out in Angola in 1961 and in Mozambique in 1964. The thousands of troops Portugal sent to crush these revolts failed to do so.

By 1974, the Portuguese had grown tired of these bloody and expensive wars. Portuguese military leaders overthrew Portugal's government and pulled the troops out of Africa. Angola and Mozambique became independent countries in 1975 as a result. Fighting continued, however, as rebel groups in each country competed for control. Mozambique's long civil war ended when a peace agreement was reached in 1994. Peace was not finally achieved in Angola until 2002.

The Birth of Zimbabwe

T

After granting Malawi and Zambia independence, Britain prepared to free neighboring Zimbabwe, then called Southern Rhodesia. The colony's white leaders, who controlled the government, instead formed a country they called Rhodesia and continued to rule.

Rhodesia's African population demanded the right to vote. When the government resisted, a guerrilla war began. In 1979 the government finally agreed to hold elections in which all Rhodesians could take part. Rebel leader Robert Mugabe was elected president, and Rhodesia's name was changed to Zimbabwe.

Equal Rights in South Africa

After independence, the growth of South Africa's mining and other industries depended on the labor of black Africans, who greatly

©David Turnley/Corbis

netw⊙rks *Online Teaching Options*

TIME LINE

History of Apartheid

Reading Time Lines Display the time line to discuss how apartheid developed, its impact on Southern Africa, and how it was abolished. Lead a class discussion on the effects of apartheid on the citizens of Southern African countries. As the students discuss the affects, list them on the board. **BL** **Interpersonal**

See page 377D for other online activities.

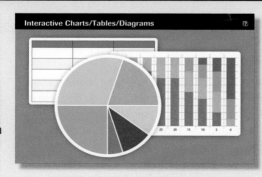

Interactive Charts/Tables/Diagrams

See page 377D for other online activities.

ANSWER, p. 392

CRITICAL THINKING English South Africans; Afrikaners *(descendants of the Dutch Boers)*

outnumbered the country's whites. The white minority government stayed in power by limiting the black population's educational and economic opportunities and political rights.

English South Africans controlled the government until the end of World War II. Then a strike by more than 60,000 black mine workers frightened white voters into electing an Afrikaner government in 1948 that promised to take action. (Afrikaners are the descendants of the Boers. They speak a language called Afrikaans, which gives them their name.)

R

The new government leaders began enacting laws that created a system called **apartheid**—an Afrikaans word meaning "apartness." Apartheid limited the rights of blacks. For example, laws forced black South Africans to live in separate areas called "homelands." People of non-European background were not even allowed to vote. The African National Congress (ANC), an organization of black South Africans, began a campaign of **civil disobedience**, disobeying certain laws as a means of protest. The government's violent response to peaceful protests caused the ANC to turn to armed conflict. In 1962 ANC leader Nelson Mandela was arrested and sentenced to life in prison.

By the 1970s, apartheid-related events in South Africa had gained world attention. Countries began placing **embargos**, or bans on trade, on South Africa. Meanwhile, the struggle in South Africa grew more intense. In 1989 South Africa's president, P.W. Botha, was forced to resign. In 1990 the government, under Botha's successor, F.W. de Klerk, began repealing the apartheid laws. Mandela was released from prison in 1991. In 1993 a new constitution gave South Africans of all races the right to vote. The ANC easily won elections held in 1994, and Mandela became the country's president.

In 1995 the new government created a truth and reconciliation commission. Its task was to ease racial tensions and heal the country by uncovering the truth about the human rights violations that had occurred under apartheid.

By 1994, South Africa's policy of apartheid was officially over. Nelson Mandela became the first black person to be elected president of South Africa. Mandela is shown voting for the first time in his life on April 27, 1994.

©Louise Gubb/Corbis SABA

☑ **READING PROGRESS CHECK**

Determining Central Ideas Why do you think South Africa's government created the apartheid system?

FOLDABLES
Study Organizer

Include this lesson's information in your Foldable®.

R Reading Skills

Summarizing Explain that war and conflict have been a major component to the lives of many in Southern Africa. Help students summarize the history of South Africa after World War II. **Ask:**

- **How did whites maintain power in South Africa when they were in the minority?** *(They limited the educational and economic opportunities and political rights of the black majority.)*

- **How did white voters react to a strike by 60,000 black miners at the end of World War II?** *(They elected an Afrikaner government in 1948 that promised to take action.)*

- **What actions did the new Afrikaner government take?** *(The new government enacted laws establishing apartheid. The laws forced blacks to live in separate homelands, and they were not allowed to vote.)*

- **How did black Africans react to the government's actions?** *(They organized the African National Congress and began a campaign of civil disobedience.)*

- **How did foreign countries aid the anti-apartheid movement?** *(They placed embargos on South Africa.)*

- **What role did Nelson Mandela play in South Africa's history?** *(As an ANC leader, he was imprisoned from 1962 to 1991. After a new constitution in 1993 gave all races the right to vote, he was elected South Africa's president.)* **Verbal/Linguistic**

W Writing Skills

Informative/Explanatory Have students conduct Internet research and write a one-page biography of Nelson Mandela. Tell students to focus on his role in the African National Congress, his political beliefs, his imprisonment and release, and his accomplishments as president of South Africa. **BL Verbal/Linguistic**

LESSON 2 REVIEW CCSS

Reviewing Vocabulary (Tier Three Words)
1. Why might some people disapprove of *civil disobedience* as a means of protest and of achieving change? RH.6-8.4

Answering the Guiding Questions
2. *Analyzing* How did some of Southern Africa's early people benefit from the region's natural resources? RH.6-8.1

3. *Identifying* Name five present-day countries in Southern Africa that were once controlled by Britain. RH.6-8.2

4. *Determining Central Ideas* Why was gaining independence especially difficult for Angola and Mozambique? RH.6-8.2

5. *Argument Writing* Write a paragraph explaining whether actions against the governments of Rhodesia and South Africa were justified. WHST.6-8.1, WHST.6-8.4

Chapter 13 **393**

LESSON 2 REVIEW ANSWERS

Reviewing Vocabulary

1. because it involves breaking the law

Answering the Guiding Questions

2. **Analyzing** They traded gold and ivory for tools, salt, and such luxury items as beads, porcelain, and cloth from China, India, and Persia.

3. **Identifying** Accept any five: Botswana, Lesotho, Malawi, Mauritius, Seychelles, South Africa, Swaziland, Zambia, Zimbabwe

4. **Determining Central Ideas** Unlike the British, the Portuguese opposed independence for their colonies and used force to prevent it. Long rebellions were required to gain freedom. Long civil wars followed independence, as rebel groups fought among themselves for control of the new country.

5. **Argument Writing** Answers should focus on the fact that white minority governments in those countries restricted the freedom, opportunities, rights, equality, and political power of the black African majorities.

CLOSE & REFLECT

Describing Close the lesson by asking students to imagine themselves as a native Southern African during the colonial period. Direct them to write a paragraph describing how they feel about the political situation in their country after learning about the unrest in Southern Africa. Call on volunteers to share their paragraphs.

ANSWER, p. 393

☑ **READING PROGRESS CHECK** so the white minority could control the country

ENGAGE

Bellringer As you point to a map of the region, remind students that the ten mainland countries of Southern Africa are Angola, Namibia, Zambia, Botswana, South Africa, Zimbabwe, Mozambique, Malawi, Swaziland, and Lesotho and the four island countries are Madagascar, Comoros, Seychelles, and Mauritius. Ask students to choose one country and write a geographic or historical fact about the country that they learned in the previous two lessons and speculate on how this fact might affect the people's lives in the chosen country. Call on volunteers to share their facts and speculations.

Have students save their writing to see if any of their speculations are confirmed as they read this lesson. Then direct students to preview the lesson by skimming the headings, guiding questions, and visuals.

TEACH & ASSESS

C Critical Thinking Skills

Identifying Central Issues Explain that the population density in the countries of Southern Africa varies greatly, just as there are many different ethnic and cultural groups among these countries. Use the following questions to help students focus on the most important information about the population patterns. **Ask:**

- **What group makes up the majority in every country of Southern Africa?** *(black Africans)*
- **What percentage of the population is white?** *(from 10 percent in South Africa to less than 1 percent in almost all the other countries)*
- **Which country has the most people?** *(South Africa)*
- **How does geography affect where people live in Botswana and Namibia?** *(Most people live away from the desert and arid areas.)* **AL** **Verbal/Linguistic**

ANSWER, p. 394

Taking Notes Notes should include at least two key points about each topic, such as the following: **Population:** In Angola and South Africa most people live in cities. Malawi is the region's most rural, most densely populated, and poorest nation; **Culture groups:** One of the largest culture groups is the Shona, who make up more than 80 percent of the population of Zimbabwe. The largest ethnic group in South Africa is the Zulu; **Health Issues:** Most people in Southern Africa do not live beyond age 55. Common diseases include malaria, dysentery, cholera, tuberculosis, and HIV/AIDS.

net works

There's More Online!

☑ **SLIDE SHOW** Cities in Southern Africa

☑ **VIDEO**

Reading HELPDESK CCSS

Academic Vocabulary RH.6-8.4
(Tier Two Words)
- **contact**
- **trend**

Content Vocabulary RH.6-8.4
(Tier Three Words)
- **utility**
- **thatch**
- **periodic market**

TAKING NOTES: *Key Ideas and Details* RH.6-8.2, RH.6-8.7

Summarize Create a chart like this one. Then list information about Southern Africa on these three topics.

Population	
Culture Groups	
Health Issues	

Lesson 3
Life in Southern Africa

ESSENTIAL QUESTION · *How does geography influence the way people live?*

IT MATTERS BECAUSE
Control over Southern Africa's vast and vital natural resources has been passed on to new leadership. Great economic, political, and social changes and challenges have accompanied this transfer.

The People of the Region

GUIDING QUESTION *Where do people live in Southern Africa?*

The population of Southern Africa is overwhelmingly black African. The largest white minority is in the country of South Africa, where whites represent 10 percent of the population. In almost every other country, whites and Asians make up less than 1 percent of the population. The region's black African population is made up of many different ethnic and culture groups.

Population Patterns
Southern Africa's countries vary widely in population. Fewer than 2 million people live in the small countries of Lesotho and Swaziland. South Africa, which surrounds both of them, has the region's largest population—about 49 million.

Population depends heavily on geography and economics. For example, Botswana and Namibia are much larger than Swaziland and Lesotho, but their populations are only slightly larger. Most Batswana, as the people of Botswana are called, live in the northeast, away from their country's desert areas. Similarly, most Namibians live in the northern part of their country, away from the arid south and west.

South Africa and Angola are about the same size. South Africa, the region's most industrialized nation, has three times as many people. In both countries, most people live in

394

(l to r) ©STR/Reuters/Corbis; Ken Gerhardt/Gallo Images/Getty Images; Tom Cockrem/Photolibrary/Getty Images; ALEXANDER JOE/AFP/Getty Images

---

net works *Online Teaching Options*

VIDEO

South African Community

Comparing and Contrasting Use this video about daily life and current issues in Southern Africa to preview the lesson content. Lead a class discussion in which students compare and contrast the ways of life portrayed in the video with what they have learned about the ways of life in other regions of Africa. Draw a T-Chart on the board with the labels *Similarities/Differences* and have students supply the content. **AL** **Interpersonal**

See page 377E for other online activities.

BBC Motion Gallery Education

cities. Angola's rural areas are thus much more thinly populated than rural areas in South Africa.

Mozambique, which is slightly smaller than Namibia and much smaller than Angola, has a population greater than those two countries combined. Most of Mozambique's 23 million people are engaged in farming, mainly along the fertile coastal plain.

Zambia is twice as big as Zimbabwe. Zimbabwe, with a population of about 12 million, has only 2 million fewer people. Both countries are largely rural, with only about one-third of their people living in cities. Large parts of Zambia are thinly populated.

Malawi is just one-third the size of Zimbabwe and one-sixth the size of Zambia, yet it exceeds both in population. With some 16 million people living in an area roughly the size of Pennsylvania, it is the region's most densely populated country. On average, every square mile holds more than 250 people.

Surprisingly, Malawi is also Southern Africa's most rural nation. Only 20 percent of its people live in cities. Its small size and large rural population mean that most of its farms are small. Most farm villages are not able to produce much more than what they need. As a result, Malawi is the region's poorest country. The average Malawian earns less than $350 per year.

C

MAP SKILLS

1 **PLACES AND REGIONS** What do the cities of Johannesburg, Durban, and Cape Town have in common?

2 **THE GEOGRAPHER'S WORLD** In general, which area of Southern Africa is more densely populated: eastern or western?

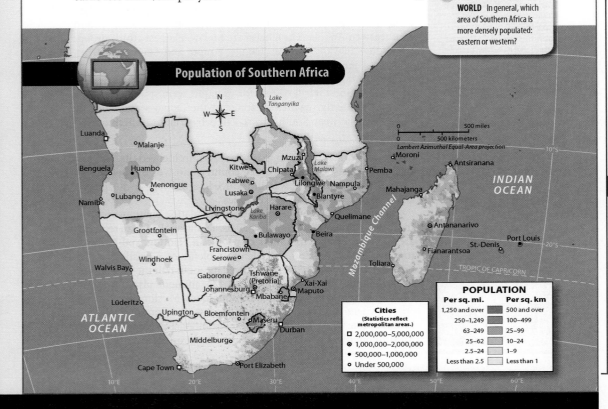

Population of Southern Africa

C Critical Thinking Skills

Comparing and Contrasting Discuss the population density of the local area and have students compare it with other areas of the United States. Explain that in most countries there are areas that are densely populated and other areas that are sparsely populated. Then discuss the similarities and differences in population patterns among the countries of Southern Africa. **Ask:**

- **In which two countries of Southern Africa do most of the people live in cities?** *(South Africa and Angola)*
- **Which countries are largely rural?** *(Mozambique, Zambia, Zimbabwe, and Malawi)*
- **How are the population patterns in Zambia and Zimbabwe similar?** *(In both countries, most of the people live in rural areas. Only about a third of the people live in cities.)*
- **How do the population patterns in Zambia and Zimbabwe differ?** *(The population density in the two countries differs. Zimbabwe has almost as many people as Zambia, even though it is about half the size. That means Zimbabwe is more densely populated than Zambia.)*
- **Which country in Southern Africa is the most densely populated, the most rural, and also the poorest?** *(Malawi)* **Logical/Mathematical**

V

V Visual Skills

Analyzing Maps Allow time for students to study the population density map at the bottom of the page. Have them answer the Map Skills questions. Then, **ask:**

- **Why are large areas of South Africa, Botswana, and Namibia so sparsely populated?** *(because of the desert and arid lands)*
- **Which countries are the most densely populated?** *(Malawi, Mozambique, and Zimbabwe)*
- **Why does the population density of a country matter?** *(It may affect the people's standard of living and quality of life. If a large number of people live in a small area, the country may not have enough natural resources to adequately support the population.)* **Visual/Spatial**

MAP

Population: Southern Africa

Listing Display the population layer of the Chapter Opener interactive map to students and discuss the density and distribution of population in Southern Africa. With a partner, have students create a list of issues that dense population areas may experience. Discuss the completed lists as a class. **ELL** **Verbal/Linguistic**

See page 377E for other online activities.

ANSWERS, p. 395
MAP SKILLS
1. Each city has a population greater than 2 million.
2. eastern

Life in Southern Africa

T

T Technology Skills

Researching on the Internet On the board, list the following ethnic groups of Southern Africa:

- Shona of Zimbabwe
- Zulu of South Africa
- Xhosa of South Africa
- Khoekhoe of South Africa
- Tsonga of South Africa, Zimbabwe, and Mozambique
- Tswana of Botswana
- Ovimbundu of Angola
- Mbundu of Angola
- Ambo of Angola and Namibia
- San of Namibia, Botswana, and Angola
- Chewa of Malawi

Have students choose one of the groups and conduct Internet research to learn about the group's culture. Ask students to prepare brief oral reports and to share the information with the class. **Visual/Spatial, Verbal/Linguistic**

C Critical Thinking Skills

Identifying Problems Draw students' attention to the fact that Europeans divided Southern Africa into colonies and countries without considering the territorial areas of the various indigenous groups. **Ask: What kinds of problems might result from such an oversight?** *(The various groups within a country might differ in their systems of government, they might compete for control of the country, and the conflicts might result in wars.)*

Tell students that such problems did result because Europeans largely ignored the territorial areas of the various ethnic groups. **Interpersonal**

R Reading Skills

Identifying Remind students that religion may shape cultural beliefs and that this was a goal for many Christian missionaries sent to Africa during the colonial era. Because of this, Christianity is the major religion of most people in Southern Africa. Help students identify the main religions of Southern Africa. **Ask: What other religions are important in the region?** *(traditional African religions, Islam, and Hinduism)* **AL**
ELL Verbal/Linguistic

Members of the Nazareth Baptist Church in South Africa take part in their annual pilgrimage to the mountain of Nhlangakazi. The church is also called the Shembe Church after its founder, Isaiah Shembe.

Think Again ?

Southern Africa's large island country of Madagascar was settled by African people.

Not true. Most of Madagascar's people speak Malagasy, a language related to those spoken in Indonesia, the Philippines, and islands in the South Pacific. The language of Madagascar indicates that the island's early inhabitants probably came from that part of the world.

Ethnic and Culture Groups

Africans are not a single people. Southern Africa is home to many ethnic and cultural groups who speak several different languages. One group, the Shona, makes up more than 80 percent of the population of the country of Zimbabwe. South Africa's 9 million Zulu make up that country's largest ethnic group. More than 7 million Xhosa also live there, as do the Khoekhoe. Some 4.5 million Tsonga people are spread among the countries of South Africa, Zimbabwe, and Mozambique.

About 4 million Tswana form the major population group in Botswana. A similar number of Ovimbundu and 2.5 million Mbundu make up approximately two-thirds of Angola's population. A smaller group, the Ambo, live in Angola and Namibia. About half of Namibia's people belong to this ethnic group. The San, a nomadic people, live mainly in Namibia, Botswana, and southeastern Angola. The Chewa are Malawi's largest ethnic group.

Groups like the Chewa, Tsonga, Ambo, and San illustrate an important point about Southern Africa's history. When Europeans divided the region, they paid little attention to its indigenous people. The Chewa and their territory, for example, were split among four colonies. Similarly, the area inhabited by the Tsonga was divided by the borders between South Africa, Zimbabwe, and Mozambique.

C

Religion and Languages

Southern Africa's colonial past has also influenced its people's religious beliefs. In almost every country, most of the people are Christians. Christianity was introduced to the region during the colonial era by Christian missionaries.

In Angola, however, nearly half the population continues to hold traditional indigenous religious beliefs. Traditional African religions are followed by large numbers of people in Namibia and Lesotho, too. In Zimbabwe and Swaziland, a blend of Christianity and traditional religious beliefs is followed by about half the population.

R

Swaziland, Zambia, Malawi, and Mozambique also have large Muslim populations. Most of Mozambique's Muslims live on the coast, where **contact** with Arab traders led long ago to the introduction of Islam. Immigration from Asia explains Zambia's Muslim population, as well as its large Hindu minority.

©STR/Reuters/Corbis

396 Chapter 13

---

networks *Online Teaching Options*

CHART

Ethnic and Cultural Groups in Southern Africa

Analyzing Charts Display the chart of the ethnic and cultural groups of Southern Africa to students and lead a class discussion about the many cultures in this diverse region. Ask students to speculate on how European colonialism affected the diversity of ethnic groups and culture. **AL Verbal/Linguistic**

See page 377E for other online activities.

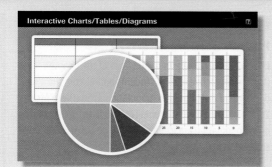

Interactive Charts/Tables/Diagrams

Portuguese remains the official language in Angola and Mozambique. English is an official language in most of the former British colonies. Its use, however, is mainly limited to official and business communications; nowhere is it widely spoken by the people. Instead, most speak indigenous languages. South Africa has 10 official languages besides English; Zambia has 7.

Academic Vocabulary

contact communication or interaction with someone

C1

✓ **READING PROGRESS CHECK**

Determining Central Ideas What is the main religion practiced in Southern Africa?

Life in Southern Africa

GUIDING QUESTION *How do the various people of Southern Africa live?*

As in other regions of Africa, life differs from city to countryside. Many rural people continue to follow traditional ways of life. At the same time, urban and economic growth are challenging and changing many of the traditional ways.

Urban Life

Although most people in the region of Southern Africa live in the countryside, migration to cities grows because of job opportunities. Harare, Zimbabwe, has grown to more than 1.5 million, as have Lusaka, Zambia, and Maputo, Mozambique. Luanda, Angola's capital, is even larger: It holds some 4.5 million people. South Africa has four cities—Durban, Ekurhuleni, Cape Town, and Johannesburg—with populations of around 3 million or more.

C2

Shown here is a high-rise building under construction in the city of Luanda in Angola. Luanda is the country's main seaport and government center.

Ken Gerhardt/Gallo Images/Getty Images

C1 Critical Thinking Skills

Predicting Consequences Draw students' attention to the fact that most of the people of Southern Africa speak indigenous languages and that the use of English is mostly limited to government and business communications. South Africa has ten official languages besides English and Zambia has seven. **Ask: What do you think might be the consequences of people speaking so many different languages?** *(Sample answers: The various ethnic groups might be more likely to retain their own distinctive cultures; people might feel more loyalty to other members of their ethnic group than to the country as a whole; there might be strong divisions between the various groups; people might have problems working together; there might be communication barriers.)* **BL Verbal/Linguistic**

C2 Critical Thinking Skills

Contrasting As you discuss the content of the section, "Life in Southern Africa," have student volunteers answer the following questions. **Ask:**

- **Where do most of the people in Southern Africa live?** *(in the countryside)*
- **How does that contrast with the situation in the United States and other developed nations?** *(Most people live in cities in the United States and other developed nations.)* **Interpersonal**

V

V Visual Skills

Analyzing Images Direct students' attention to the photograph at the bottom of the page. **Ask: How is the city of Luanda in Angola similar to cities in many other parts of the world, including the United States?** *(It has many high-rise buildings; the buildings are close together and divided into blocks with roads in-between; cars appear to be an important method of transportation.)* **Visual/Spatial**

SLIDE SHOW

Cities in Southern Africa

Comparing and Contrasting Display the slide show that highlights cities of Southern Africa. Have students write down three facts about the urban environments of Southern Africa as they view the images and captions. Have volunteers share their facts. Then, lead a class discussion in which students compare and contrast cities in Southern Africa with cities in the United States. **AL Verbal/Linguistic**

Slide Show

See page 377E for other online activities.

ANSWER, p. 397

✓ **READING PROGRESS CHECK** Christianity

Life in Southern Africa

V Visual Skills

Analyzing Images Direct students' attention to the colorful photograph of an outdoor market and all its goods at the top of the page. **Ask:**

- If you were a tourist in Lusaka, Zambia, what items in this market might interest you? *(Answers will vary.)*
- What purpose do outdoor markets like this one serve? *(They give local people a venue to sell their products and earn money to support their families.)* **Intrapersonal**

V

R Reading Skills

Summarizing Use the section, "Urban Growth and Change," to discuss with students the urban environment in Southern Africa. **Ask: How has the rapid growth of cities contributed to the spread of diseases in Southern Africa?** *(The cities cannot provide adequate trash collection and sewage and water treatment. Some cities cannot provide enough clean water for all the people. Outbreaks of cholera and other diseases have resulted from polluted drinking water.)* **ELL Logical/Mathematical**

C Critical Thinking Skills

Making Connections Remind students that South Africa had an apartheid system that kept blacks and whites separate until 1990. **Ask:**

- In what kind of communities do most blacks in Johannesburg live? *(Most blacks live in "townships" at the city's edge, many of which have no electricity, clean water, or sewer facilities.)*
- How does Johannesburg show the lingering effects of apartheid? *(For the most part, the races still live in separate communities.)*
- What do you think are some consequences of this situation? *(Answers will vary. Students may suggest that racial tension and conflict probably remain high.)* **Logical/Mathematical**

At an outdoor market in Lusaka, vendors come to sell handcrafted items. Food and entertainment are also available.

▶ **CRITICAL THINKING**
R
Describing What are periodic markets?

Urban Growth and Change

The rapid growth of some cities has strained public **utilities**—services such as trash collection, sewage treatment, and water distribution. Luanda, for example, has had many problems providing enough clean water for its many people. Outbreaks of cholera and other diseases have resulted from drinking polluted water.

The region's cities have a mix of many ethnic groups and cultures. An example is Johannesburg, where the wealth from nearby gold fields helped build one of the most impressive downtowns in all of Africa. Outside the central city are the white neighborhoods where about 20 percent of the city's population live. Some black South Africans have moved into these neighborhoods since the end of apartheid. Most, however, live in "townships" at the city's edge. These areas often have no electricity, clean water, or sewer facilities. Most of the region's large cities have shantytowns.

C

Johannesburg's role as a mining, manufacturing, and financial center has attracted people from around the world. Every black ethnic group in Southern Africa is present, as well. The white community is mainly English and Afrikaner. Large Portuguese, Greek, Italian, Russian, Polish, and Lebanese populations also live there. Indians, Filipinos, Malays, and Chinese live mainly in the townships. At least 12 languages are heard on city streets.

Tom Cockrem/Photolibrary/Getty Images

398 *Chapter 13*

---

netw⊙rks *Online Teaching Options*

IMAGE

Markets in Southern Africa

Analyzing Images Display the interactive image to discuss with students the diversity of goods bought and sold in the markets of Southern Africa. Have students make lists of all the items they can identify in the photograph, perhaps competing to see which student can identify the most. Have students make comparisons between this market to an experience that they may have had in a farmer's market or grocery store. **ELL Verbal/Linguistic**

See page 377E for other online activities.

Lissa Harrison

ANSWER, p. 398

CRITICAL THINKING open-air trading markets held regularly along major travel routes or in cities

Family and Traditional Life

People who move to the cities must adjust to new experiences and a different way of life. In the countryside, traditional ways of life remain strong.

Rural villages are often small—consisting of perhaps 20 or 30 houses. Building materials, which vary by ethnic group, include rocks, mud bricks, woven sticks and twigs packed with clay, and **thatch**—straw or other plant material used to cover roofs.

In many cultures, all the people in a village are related by blood or marriage to the village's headman or chief. Men often have more than one wife. They provide a house for each wife and their children. Growing food crops is the main economic activity. Many families raise cattle as well, mainly for milk and as a symbol of wealth.

People in the countryside practice subsistence farming, growing the food they need to survive. Artwork sometimes provides a family with a source of cash. Wood and ivory carving are art forms that are generally practiced by men. Pottery-making is usually a woman's craft. In some cultures, both men and women make baskets. They sell the products in cities or at **periodic markets**—open-air trading markets held regularly at crossroads or in larger towns.

In recent times, more and more men have been leaving their villages to work at jobs in cities or mines. Although the money they send home helps support their families, this **trend** has greatly changed village life. Many villages now consist largely of women, children, and older men. Women have increasingly taken on traditional male roles in herding, family and community leadership, and other activities.

R

Academic Vocabulary

trend a general tendency or preference

W

Members of South Africa's Ndebele tribe attend a gathering of traditional leaders from all over the country in November 2009 to honor former President Nelson Mandela.

☑ **READING PROGRESS CHECK**

Citing Text Evidence Where in their countries do most Southern Africans live?

Southern Africa Today

GUIDING QUESTION *What challenges and prospects do the countries of Southern Africa face?*

Southern Africa's wealth of mineral, wildlife, and other resources may be the key to its future. Still, the region faces serious social, economic, and political challenges.

Health Issues

Life expectancy in Southern Africa is low. In the majority of countries, most people do not live beyond age 50 to 55. Lack of good rural health care is one reason, although many countries are trying to build or improve rural clinics.

ALEXANDER JOE/AFP/Getty Images

Chapter 13 **399**

IMAGES

Urban vs. Traditional Life

Analyzing Images Display the side-by-side photographs as you discuss urban and rural life in Southern Africa with students. Ask students to make a list of the benefits and drawbacks of each way of life. As students make their lists, use their comments to create a Venn diagram highlighting the benefits and drawbacks of urban and traditional life. **Verbal/Linguistic**

See page 377E for other online activities.

Interactive Photos

R **Reading Skills**

Determining Central Ideas Remind students that the majority of people in Southern Africa live in rural areas, so the way of life described in the section, "Family and Traditional Life," applies to a large number of people. **Ask:**

- **What does a typical rural village look like?** *(20 or 30 houses with thatch roofs and walls made of rocks, mud bricks, or woven sticks and twigs packed with clay)*
- **How are the people in a typical village related?** *(by blood or marriage to the headman or chief)*
- **What is family life like?** *(Men often have more than one wife and provide a hut for each wife and their children.)*
- **How do villagers support themselves?** *(They grow their own food, and many raise cattle for milk. Men make wood and ivory carvings, women make pottery, and both make baskets to sell in periodic markets.)*
- **How has village life changed in recent years?** *(More men have been leaving their villages to work at jobs in cities or mines, so many villages consist largely of women, children, and older men. Women have taken on traditional male roles as herders and as family and community leaders.)* **Verbal/Linguistic**

W **Writing Skills**

Informative/Explanatory Have students conduct Internet or library research using reliable resources to learn more about village life in Southern Africa as it is today. Students should select a cultural topic such as education, music, food, village leadership, or entertainment. Encourage students to consider if their findings show that village life has been impacted by globalization or if their research shows that the villagers have stayed with traditional ways of life. Have students write a three-paragraph report on their findings and include photographs, audio clips, or examples such as recipes. Students may also present brief oral reports to the class. **BL** **Verbal/Linguistic, Auditory/Musical**

ANSWER, p. 399

☑ **READING PROGRESS CHECK** rural areas

Making Connections To help students appreciate how low the life expectancy in Southern Africa is (age 50 to 55), share these statistics on the countries with the world's highest life expectancies. You might note that the United States ranks 51st with a life expectancy of 78.49 years.

Country	Life Expectancy
Monaco	89.68
Macau	84.43
Japan	83.91
Singapore	83.75
San Marion	83.07
Andorra	82.50
Guernsey	82.24
Hong Kong	82.12
Australia	81.90
Italy	81.86

C Critical Thinking Skills

Identifying Problems Pose the following questions to focus students' attention on the health problems that people in Southern Africa face. **Ask:**

- What is one reason for the low life expectancy in Southern Africa? *(lack of good rural health care)*
- What diseases with environmental causes are common in Southern Africa, and what are their causes? *(malaria, which is caused by mosquitoes, and dysentery and cholera, which are caused by bacteria in water)*
- Which two conditions or diseases kill many infants and young children in Southern Africa? *(malnutrition and HIV/AIDS)*
- Which countries have the highest HIV/AIDS rates in the world, and what is the rate? *(Swaziland, Botswana, Lesotho, South Africa; about one in every four adults)* **Logical/Mathematical**

Reported Malaria Deaths, 2009

	More than 20,000
	10,001–20,000
	1,001–10,000
	500–1,000
	Fewer than 500
	No data

MAP SKILLS

1 THE GEOGRAPHER'S WORLD On what continent has malaria been responsible for the greatest number of deaths?

2 THE GEOGRAPHER'S WORLD In what regions of the world has malaria been responsible for the fewest deaths?

Disease

Malaria, a tropical disease carried by mosquitoes, is a problem in several countries. Dysentery and cholera, potentially fatal diseases caused by bacteria in water, are also widespread. So is tuberculosis. Malnutrition is a cause of death for many infants and young children.

Southern Africa has some of the highest rates of infant death in the world. In Angola, Malawi, and Mozambique, about 100 to 120 of every 1,000 children die in infancy. Elsewhere in the region, the figure is 40 to 60 per 1,000. (The infant death rate in the United States is 7 per 1,000.)

A major cause of death in children and adults is HIV/AIDS. Southern Africa has a higher HIV/AIDS rate than any other region in Africa. Swaziland, Botswana, Lesotho, and South Africa have the highest rates in the world. About one of every four adults (25 percent) in these countries is infected with this sexually transmitted disease, which women pass on to their children at birth. In the rest of the region, the adult HIV/AIDS rate averages between 11 and 14 percent. (In the United States, the rate is 0.6 percent.)

The high incidence of HIV/AIDS has disrupted the labor force by depriving countries of needed workers. It has also disrupted families through death, inability to work, or AIDS-related family issues. The disease has created millions of AIDS orphans, children whose mother and father have died from AIDS. The huge number of AIDS orphans is a major social problem.

400 Chapter 13

netw⊙rks   *Online Teaching Options*

MAP

Malaria Deaths

Analyzing Maps Display the map depicting *Reported Malaria Deaths, 2009*. Ask students to use the map's key to identify the continent that experienced the greatest number of deaths from malaria in 2009. Then lead a discussion about why Africa, when compared with other continents, might have a disproportionate number of deaths. Continue your discussion by addressing other health issues prevalent in the countries of Southern Africa. **AL** **Visual/Spatial, Logical/Mathematical, Verbal/Linguistic**

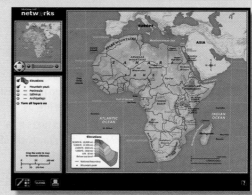

See page 377E for other online activities.

Progress and Growth

Angola and Mozambique continue to rebuild the cities and towns, industries, railroads, and communications systems that have been damaged or destroyed by years of civil war. Oil exports in Angola and aluminum exports in Mozambique help finance this effort. So does the tourism that peace and stability have brought back to the beautiful beaches and resorts along Mozambique's coast.

Tourism at national parks has grown with the establishment of stable, democratic governments. Zambia and Malawi replaced one-party rule with more democratic forms of government in the 1990s. Botswana and Namibia have been strong democracies, respecting and protecting human rights, since independence. Only Zimbabwe and Swaziland continue to suffer economic decline and political unrest, largely due to repressive leaders.

R

Help From Other Countries

The United States has used economic aid to strengthen democracy in Southern Africa. Other U.S. programs have provided billions of dollars to pay for medications and care for AIDS sufferers and AIDS orphans.

Other countries and international organizations have also made huge investments in the region. Taiwan's development of a textile industry in Lesotho, for example, is giving some of that poor country's workers an alternative to employment in South Africa's mines.

Foreign investment, workers, and tourists have also returned to South Africa as it continues to recover from the effects of apartheid. South Africa remains the region's most industrial and wealthiest country. It also faces serious economic challenges. Many of its traditional African farming communities struggle in poverty, growing few if any cash crops. Its heavy reliance on the export of mineral and agricultural goods places it at risk if world demand or prices for the goods fall. These problems mirror the challenges that many other countries in Southern Africa also confront.

FOLDABLES
Study Organizer

Include this lesson's information in your Foldable®.

☑ **READING PROGRESS CHECK**

Analyzing Why is life expectancy in Southern Africa so low?

LESSON 3 REVIEW

Reviewing Vocabulary (Tier Three Words)
1. What did rural Southern Africans use clay and *thatch* for? RH.6-8.4

Answering the Guiding Questions
2. *Determining Central Ideas* How did colonialism and contact with traders influence religious beliefs in Southern Africa? RH.6-8.2

3. *Describing* What are rural and city life like for Southern Africa's black population? RH.6-8.5

4. *Analyzing* How and why has Southern Africa benefited from the growth of democracy in the region? RH.6-8.1

5. *Argument Writing* Write a letter to the editor of a Southern African newspaper explaining whether the region should continue to work for change. WHST.6-8.1, WHST.6-8.4

Chapter 13 **401**

LESSON 3 REVIEW ANSWERS

Reviewing Vocabulary

1. Rural people use clay and thatch for building houses.

Answering the Guiding Questions

2. **Determining Central Ideas** European missionaries introduced Christianity during the colonial era. Today, in almost every Southern African country, most people are Christians.

3. **Describing** The rural population lives in huts in small villages where everyone is related. People farm, raise cattle, make crafts, and live in traditional ways. Most urban people live in shantytowns or townships on the edges of cities and work at wage-earning jobs. Cultures and traditions are blended and weakened,

and people must adjust to different ways of life. In both city and countryside, most people are poor.

4. **Analyzing** Democratic governments have brought black majority rule to the region. Democracy and stability have also resulted in economic growth as tourism has returned and foreign countries have invested in the region's economic development.

5. **Argument Writing** Letters should consider economic, public health, and social conditions.

R **Reading Skills**

Summarizing Have student volunteers take turns reading the section, "Progress and Growth." It is important that students understand the progress that has been made and the continuing problems that Southern Africa faces. Have students summarize both of these elements. **Ask:**

• **How are Angola and Mozambique financing the rebuilding of cities, towns, industries, railroads, and communication systems damaged by years of civil war?** *(through oil exports in Angola and aluminum exports and tourism in Mozambique)*

• **What has led to the growth of tourism in the region's national parks?** *(the establishment of stable, democratic governments)*

• **Which two countries still suffer from economic decline and political unrest under repressive leaders?** *(Zimbabwe and Swaziland)* Read the Content Background Knowledge below to students to help them understand.

Then have students read "Help from Other Countries." **Ask:**

• **What problems does South Africa share with other countries in the region?** *(Many traditional African farming communities are poor. Overreliance on the export of mineral and agricultural goods is risky because world demand or prices could fall.)* **Verbal/Linguistic**

Content Background Knowledge

Swaziland is ruled by a king and is one of the few absolute monarchies left in the world. King Mswati II has ruled over his subjects since 1986, when he took over for his father, who had ruled for nearly 61 years. Most of the people of Swaziland belong to one tribe and follow a traditional way of life in the countryside. They live in poverty and often face food shortages.

CLOSE & REFLECT

Drawing Conclusions To close the lesson, remind students of the questions they formulated at the beginning of the chapter about the region's geography, history, and culture. Review the chart of questions and have students answer as many of the questions as they can.

ANSWER, p. 401

☑ **READING PROGRESS CHECK** Low life expectancy results from poor rural health care, high infant death rates, and the high incidence of disease, especially HIV/AIDS.

CHAPTER REVIEW ACTIVITY

To summarize the chapter, divide the class into three groups and assign each group one of the lessons in the chapter. Have the group for the first lesson complete the first chart below on the physical geography, the group for the second lesson fill in the time line putting historical events in order, and the group for the third lesson complete the final chart on life in Southern Africa. Have groups focus on the main ideas in each of the lessons and then present their chart to the class to review the information with everyone. *(Students' answers should reflect the main ideas covered in each of the three lessons of the chapter.)*

Physical Geography of Southern Africa				
Country	Landforms	Bodies of Water	Climate	Resources

History of Southern Africa

Life in Southern Africa			
Country	People	Urban and Rural Life	Current Issues

REVIEW THE ENDURING UNDERSTANDING

Review this chapter's "Enduring Understanding" with students:

- *People, places, and ideas change over time.*

Pose the following questions in a class discussion to apply this idea to this chapter.

- **How have people affected the wildlife of Southern Africa?** *(Sample answer: People have killed many animals to sell their tusks, horns, skin, and meat and to protect livestock and crops. Others have established national parks and wildlife reserves where the animals are protected and help promote the economy by drawing tourists.)*

- **How did Europeans affect the political boundaries of Southern Africa?** *(European nations divided up the region among themselves, largely ignoring the territorial areas of indigenous people. European colonies later became countries.)*

- **How did colonialism affect the religious beliefs of people in Southern Africa?** *(Sample answer: Because of contact with Europeans, most people in Southern Africa are now Christians, although some people still practice traditional African religions or a blend of African religions and Christianity.)*

Directions: Write your answers on a separate piece of paper.

1 Use your FOLDABLES to explore the Essential Question.
INFORMATIVE/EXPLANATORY WRITING Write two paragraphs explaining how Southern Africa's resources place the region in a favorable position to develop trade with other countries. WHST.6-8.2, WHST.6-8.10

2 21st Century Skills
DESCRIBING Using information from the text and online, create a brief slide show of Southern Africa's energy resources and how the region uses the resources. Narrate the slide show, identifying the different countries' means of generating power. WHST.6-8.8, WHST.6-8.9

3 Thinking Like a Geographer
DETERMINING CENTRAL IDEAS As a geographer, would you favor setting aside more or less land for game preserves in Southern Africa? Use a T-chart to list your pro and con arguments. WHST.6-8.1, WHST.6-8.4

4 **GEOGRAPHY ACTIVITY**

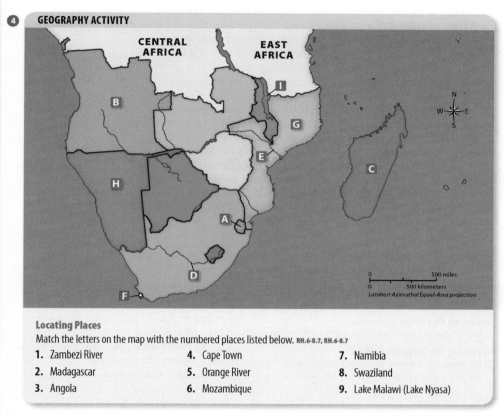

Locating Places
Match the letters on the map with the numbered places listed below. RH.6-8.7, RH.6-8.7

1. Zambezi River
2. Madagascar
3. Angola
4. Cape Town
5. Orange River
6. Mozambique
7. Namibia
8. Swaziland
9. Lake Malawi (Lake Nyasa)

ACTIVITIES ANSWERS

Essential Question

1 **INFORMATIVE/EXPLANATORY WRITING** Students' paragraphs might include the following points: In several countries of Southern Africa, such as Angola and Namibia, natural resources are the country's only source of wealth. South Africa's large mineral reserves have enabled it to develop a strong economy based on mining and manufacturing. As the world's largest producer of platinum, chromium, and gold, it has a superior position in supplying these minerals to other countries. It also produces many of the world's diamonds, both gems and industrial diamonds.

REVIEW THE GUIDING QUESTIONS

Directions: Choose the best answer for each question.

❶ The country of Madagascar is RH.6-8.2
- A. a large plateau.
- B. Southern Africa's regional capital city.
- C. the world's fourth-largest island.
- D. the world's largest exporter of coconut milk.

❷ Which is the longest river in Southern Africa? RH.6-8.4
- F. Kariba
- G. Congo
- H. Great Karoo
- I. Zambezi

❸ Western South Africa, western Namibia, and Botswana have what climate zone in common? RH.6-8.1
- A. tropical
- B. desert
- C. Mediterranean
- D. steppe

❹ The amount of hydroelectric power in this region has been reduced by RH.6-8.5
- F. deforestation.
- G. droughts.
- H. monsoons.
- I. civil disturbances.

❺ South Africa's Afrikaners are descended from which population group? RH.6-8.2
- A. native Africans
- B. Boers
- C. Portuguese colonists
- D. Zambians

❻ Which is the most densely populated country in Southern Africa? RH.6-8.2
- F. Zambia
- G. the Republic of South Africa
- H. Madagascar
- I. Malawi

Chapter 13 **403**

21st Century Skills

❷ DESCRIBING Slide shows should include images of the types of power generated in each country, such as burning coal or harnessing river waters to generate hydroelectric power. Students should accurately identify the main source of energy in each Southern African country and should clearly narrate their slide show.

Thinking Like a Geographer

❸ DETERMINING CENTRAL IDEAS More land: need to protect endangered animals and to promote ecotourism for economic growth; less land: people living in the region need to work the land to support themselves

Geography Activities

❹ LOCATING PLACES

1. E
2. C
3. B
4. F
5. D
6. G
7. H
8. A
9. I

ASSESSMENT ANSWERS
Review the Guiding Questions

❶ C The first page of Lesson 1 identifies Madagascar as the world's fourth-largest island. Students should be able to eliminate answer D since coconut milk is not one of the major resources of Southern Africa. There was also no mention in the chapter of a region having a capital city, so B should be easily eliminated. If students recall correctly, they should realize that plateaus are common throughout the region.

❷ I Students need to recall which rivers were highlighted within the region. They should then easily eliminate all answers except I. Have students who answer incorrectly review Lesson 1, which states that the Zambezi is the longest river in Southern Africa.

❸ B Students should recall that the countries mentioned are not close to the Equator, so they would not have a tropical climate. Refer students to Lesson 1, in which it states that western South Africa, western Namibia, and much of Botswana are arid. The Namib and Kalahari deserts cover this area.

❹ F Students should remember that monsoons, answer H, bring more rain, which would increase the flow in rivers. They should also be able to eliminate answer I, since civil disturbances would not affect river flows. Answer G may confuse some students, but in Lesson 1 the text states that deforestation allows more sediment to enter the rivers, which reduces the water flow and the electricity that the rivers produce.

❺ B Students will have to remember that the Boers were Dutch farmers who settled in South Africa. They should easily eliminate answer D, since Zambians would be from Zambia, not South Africa. Lesson 2 states that Afrikaners are the descendants of the Boers.

❻ I Students will have to recall that Zambia, South Africa, and Madagascar are all fairly large countries. Malawi is the smallest of the four choices, and it also has a large population, making it the most densely populated country of the four. Lesson 3 identifies Malawi as the region's most densely populated country.

DBQ Analyzing Documents

7 **C** Since the Okavango includes a delta, students should infer that the Okavango is a river. Also, since the floods are annual, the Okavango River floods the Kalahari Desert more or less every year. If students are having difficulty understanding or defining all of the vocabulary in the passage, remind them to look for context clues to help them. For the word *annual*, point out the context clue *in wetter years*.

8 **G** Because the floodwaters of the Okavango are generally shallow rather than deep, the land of the Kalahari must be mainly flat, with few valleys or other depressions that would allow water to accumulate. Students should note the key words in this passage that provide details about the land, *vast areas . . . only a few inches of water.*

Short Response

9 Mandela and the others who engaged in both the nonviolent campaign and the attempt at an armed uprising were trying to tear down the apartheid system of South Africa that limited the rights of nonwhites.

10 Possible answer: Those opposing apartheid eventually succeeded when their nonviolent efforts were combined with external pressure. International support for their efforts and sanctions against the white government forced those in the government to negotiate.

Extended Response

11 Student essays should describe the geography and animal life of one or more countries in the region. Students should imagine what it would be like to stay out of doors on a safari with tents and outdoor cooking facilities. Their essays should meet your standards for correct grammatical expression and spelling.

DBQ ANALYZING DOCUMENTS

7 **ANALYZING** Read the following passage about the area around the Okavango River and the Kalahari Desert.

"*During dry periods [the Okavango Delta] is estimated to cover at least 6,000 square miles, but in wetter years, with a heavy annual flood, the Okavango's waters can spread over 8,500 square miles of the Kalahari's sands. Deep water occurs in only a few channels, while vast areas of reed beds are covered by only a few inches of water.*"

—from Cecil Keen, *Okavango*

As described in the reading, the Okavango is a RH.6-8.1, RH.6-8.10

A. desert.   C. river.

B. mountain.   D. reed bed.

8 **ANALYZING** What can you infer about the land of the Kalahari from this passage? RH.6-8.1, RH.6-8.10

F. It is sandy because it absorbs most of the water fairly quickly.

G. It is fairly flat because more of the water is shallow than deep.

H. It is wet most of the time because it lets the floodwaters stand.

I. It tilts to the west because that is where the deep channels form.

SHORT RESPONSE

"*Discouraged about the lack of results from their nonviolent campaign, Nelson Mandela and others called for an armed uprising . . . that paralleled the nonviolent resistance. That, too, failed to tear down the apartheid system, and in the end a concerted grassroots nonviolent civil resistance movement [together] with international support and sanctions [against the government] forced the white government to negotiate.*"

—from Lester R. Kurtz, "The Anti-Apartheid Struggle in South Africa"

9 **DETERMINING CENTRAL IDEAS** What were Mandela and others trying to achieve? RH.6-8.2, RH.6-8.10

10 **ANALYZING** How did they eventually succeed? RH.6-8.1, RH.6-8.10

EXTENDED RESPONSE

11 **INFORMATIVE/EXPLANATORY WRITING** Southern Africa has an abundance of wildlife, including animals, birds, fish, and exotic plant life. Tourists come from all over the world to see the animals, which live on animal preserves and in the wild. Do some research on travel in Southern Africa, then write an essay describing the experience of going on safari. Talk about which areas of the region you visited and what you saw, and what kind of accommodations you had on your safari. WHST.6-8.2, WHST.6-8.7

Need Extra Help?

If You've Missed Question	❶	❷	❸	❹	❺	❻	❼	❽	❾	❿	⓫
Review Lesson	1	1	1	1	2	3	1	1	2	2	3

---

netw⦿rks *Online Teaching Options*

Remediation and Assessment

Evaluating The *Assess* tab in the online Teacher Lesson Center includes resources to help students improve their test-taking skills. It also contains many project-based rubrics to help you assess students' work.

Oceania, Australia, New Zealand, and Antarctica Planner

UNDERSTANDING BY DESIGN®

Enduring Understandings

- *People, places, and ideas change over time.*

Essential Questions

- *How does physical geography influence the way people live?*
- *Why does conflict develop?*
- *What makes a culture unique?*

Students will know:

- *that Oceania, Australia, New Zealand, and Antarctica each have a unique physical geography.*
- *that Oceania, Australia, and New Zealand have both indigenous populations and immigrants from Europe and other countries, creating diverse cultures.*
- *that Oceania, Australia, and New Zealand have important resources.*
- *that Antarctica does have some resources, but it is hard to access them.*
- *that the climate of Antarctica is unlike any other region.*
- *that Antarctica plays a role in the climate of the Earth and in global issues today.*

Students will be able to:

- ***analyze a map*** *to identify countries, cities, and geographic features of Oceania, Australia, New Zealand, and Antarctica.*

- ***use*** *a time line to discuss important events in the history of the regions.*
- ***identify*** *landforms and waterways in the regions.*
- ***describe*** *the various climates in the regions.*
- ***describe*** *important resources found in the regions.*
- ***discuss*** *the migration of Europeans to Oceania, Australia, and New Zealand.*
- ***describe*** *colonial times in Australia and New Zealand.*
- ***describe*** *the cultures of indigenous people.*
- ***discuss*** *religion, daily life, and culture.*
- ***discuss*** *economies in each of the regions.*
- ***describe*** *the major concerns in each of the regions.*
- ***discuss*** *the role of Antarctica in global issues.*

Predictable Misunderstandings

- *The geography of Australia and New Zealand is the same as other islands in the Pacific.*
- *The culture of Australia and New Zealand has not been impacted by Europe in a similar way as the rest of the world.*
- *Oceania's geography is mostly ice.*
- *There are no resources in this region.*
- *Antarctica's physical geography is unimpressive because it is mostly ice.*
- *There are no resources in Antarctica.*

Assessment Evidence

Performance Tasks:

- *Environmental Case Study*

Other Evidence:

- *Physical Location GeoQuiz*
- *Political Location GeoQuiz*
- *City Location GeoQuiz*
- *Physical Geography Activity*
- *Cultural Geography Activity*
- *Geography and History Activity*
- *Geography and Economics Activity*
- *Reading Skills Activity*
- *Geography Skills Activity*
- *Critical Thinking Skills Activity*
- *Technology Skills Activity*
- *Participation in Interactive Whiteboard Activities*
- *Contribution to small group activities*
- *Interpretation of slide show images*
- *Participation in class discussions*
- *Analysis of graphic organizers, graphs, and charts*
- *Lesson Reviews*
- *Chapter Assessments*

Key for Using the Teacher Edition

SKILL-BASED ACTIVITIES

Types of skill activites found in the Teacher Edition.

* **V Visual Skills** require students to analyze maps, graphs, charts, and photos.

W Writing Skills provide writing opportunities to help students comprehend the text.

R Reading Skills help students practice reading skills and master vocabulary.

C Critical Thinking Skills help students apply and extend what they have learned.

T Technology Skills require students to use digital tools effectively.

*Letters are followed by a number when there is more than one of the same type of skill on the page.

DIFFERENTIATED INSTRUCTION

All activities are written for the on-level student unless otherwise marked with the leveled labels below.

BL Beyond Level

AL Approaching Level

ELL English Language Learners

All students benefit from activities that utilize different learning styles. Many activities are marked as below when a particular learning style is highlighted.

Intrapersonal	Naturalist
Logical/Mathematical	Kinesthetic
Visual/Spatial	Auditory/Musical
Verbal/Linguistic	Interpersonal

SUGGESTED PACING GUIDE

Introducing the Unit	3 Days
Chapter 14: Australia and New Zealand	8 Days
Chapter 15: Oceania	8 Days
Chapter 16: Antarctica	6 Days
Global Connections	3 Days
What Do You Think?	3 Days

TOTAL TIME   31 Days

PLANNER

☑ Print Teaching Options

V Visual Skills

☐ **P. 406** Students discuss the land use and energy resources of New Zealand as shown in a photograph.
AL Visual/Spatial

☐ **P. 407** Students discuss what they see in a satellite image of the region. **AL** Visual/Spatial

☐ **P. 408** Students analyze features on the physical map.
AL Visual/Spatial, Naturalist

☐ **P. 409** Students analyze the political map of Oceania, Australia, New Zealand, and Antarctica. **ELL** Visual

☐ **P. 410** Students analyze the population density map of the regions. **AL** Logical/Mathematical

☐ **P. 411** Students compare the regional land uses in Australia to those in Oceania and Antarctica.

☐ **P. 412** Students analyze the climate map of the region.

W Writing Skills

☐ **P. 412** Students research how the tourism industry takes advantage of unique qualities of a country, island group, or continent in the region. Verbal/Linguistic

R Reading Skills

☐ **P. 406** Students identify main ideas in the introductory paragraph about the region. **ELL** Verbal/Linguistic

☐ **P. 407** Students discuss the meanings of *monolith* and *archipelago*. **ELL** Verbal/Linguistic

C Critical Thinking Skills

☐ **P. 405** Students make inferences about the landscapes, languages, and cultures found in Australia, New Zealand, Oceania, and Antarctica.

☐ **P. 407** Students compare the land area of the 48 contiguous United States with the land area of Australia. Visual/Spatial

☐ **P. 408** Students discuss the physical features and predict population density of Australia. **BL** Visual/Spatial

☐ **P. 410** Students use the maps to connect the physical geography of Australia to its population. **BL**

☐ **P. 411** Students use the map to write five questions about natural resources and their importance. **AL**

☐ **P. 412** Students determine cause and effect relationships relating to how climate impacts economy. **BL**

T Technology Skills

☐ **P. 406** Student groups research aspects of the formation of the islands of Oceania and how life is affected by the volcanic activity there. **AL** Verbal/Linguistic

☑ Online Teaching Options

V Visual Skills

☐ **MAP** **Regional Map**—Students use the regional map to connect images to their locations.
AL Visual/Spatial

☐ **MAP** **Climates Map: Australia, New Zealand, Oceania, and Antarctica**—Students use the map to discuss climates and then explore climate research in New Zealand and create a visual display highlighting what they learn. **AL** Interpersonal

☐ **MAP** **Population Density Map: Australia, New Zealand, Oceania, and Antarctica**—Students identify the regions' population density and distribution.

☐ **MAP** **Political Map: Australia, New Zealand, Oceania, and Antarctica**—Students identify the regions' political boundaries.

W Writing Skills

☐ **VIDEO** **Video Tour of Australia, New Zealand, Oceania, and Antarctica**—Students watch a video montage highlighting Oceania, Australia, New Zealand, and Antarctica and write five questions they have. **AL** Visual/Spatial

C Critical Thinking Skills

☐ **MAP** **Physical Map: Australia, New Zealand, Oceania, and Antarctica**—Students identify the regions' various physical features, analyze sizes of continents and islands, and calculate distances. **AL** Kinesthetic

T Technology Skills

☐ **GAME** **Political Boundaries: Australia, New Zealand, Oceania, and Antarctica Game**—Students play a drag-and-drop game to identify and place countries, cities, and islands of the regions. **ELL** Kinesthetic

☐ **MAP** **Economic Resources Map: Australia, New Zealand, Oceania, and Antarctica**—Students use the map to discuss resources and then research the importance of a resource on a global scale, creating a visual presentation. **AL** Logical/Mathematical

☑ Printable Digital Worksheets

☐ **WORKSHEET** **Environmental Case Study**—Students will use the environmental case study worksheets to understand how climate change is affecting different areas of Earth. **BL** Logical/Mathematical

☐ **QUIZ** **Physical Location GeoQuiz**—Use the Physical Location GeoQuiz as a pre- or post-assessment of students' knowledge of the regions' landforms and bodies of water.

☐ **QUIZ** **Political Location GeoQuiz**—Use the Political Location GeoQuiz as a pre- or post-assessment of students' knowledge of the regions' countries.

☐ **QUIZ** **City Location GeoQuiz**—Use the City Location GeoQuiz as a pre- or post-assessment of students' knowledge of the regions' major cities.

☐ **WORKSHEET** **Physical Geography Activity**—Students will analyze an elevation profile of the regions.

☐ **WORKSHEET** **Cultural Geography Activity**—Students will read about the culture of one of the regions and answer questions related to the excerpt.

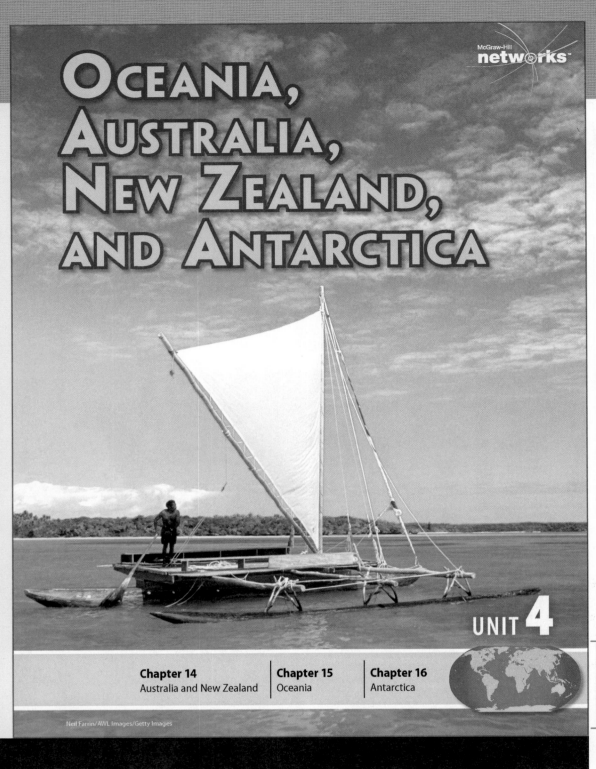

OCEANIA, AUSTRALIA, NEW ZEALAND, AND ANTARCTICA

McGraw-Hill networks™

| Chapter 14 | Chapter 15 | Chapter 16 |
| Australia and New Zealand | Oceania | Antarctica |

UNIT 4

Neil Farrin/AWL Images/Getty Images

Global Connections

The Global Connections issue for this unit gives students an opportunity to learn about the environmental and economic impact of invasive species, such as wild rabbits and cane toads found in Australia. They will learn how invasive species can upset existing ecologies to the point of endangering existing species, and will consider the connection between invasive species and the extinction of native species. Students will work independently and in small groups to present what they learn. **Logical/Mathematical**

ENGAGE

Bellringer Direct student attention to the image of the sailboat. Have them consider the construction of the sailboat and the landscape beyond it. **Ask:**

- What do you notice about the construction of the sailboat? *(Students' answers will vary.)*
- What resources do you think this individual uses for survival? *(Students might suggest that the individual uses available wood, plants, and seafood for survival.)*
- What do you notice about the landscape? *(Students should note that the land is flat and seems to be surrounded by water.)*

Making Connections Have students connect what they know about Oceania, Australia, New Zealand, and Antarctica with the following unit facts:

- New Zealand ranks as the 76th country in size in the world and is about the size of the state of Colorado.
- Challenges in New Zealand include deforestation, soil erosion, and animal and plant invasive species.
- Australia is the smallest continent and ranks as the 6th country in size in the world, slightly smaller in land area than the 48 contiguous states of the United States.
- Australia's climate is mostly arid to semi-arid.
- Australia accounts for about 29 percent of the world's coal exports.
- Australia is the only continent that has no glaciers.
- Oceania is a region in the Pacific Ocean containing thousands of islands, most of which are small and many of which are uninhabited.
- The continent of Antarctica covers about 14 million sq. km and is the 5th largest continent.
- Antarctica contains no permanent cropland.
- Antarctica is governed by international treaties.

C

C Critical Thinking Skills

Making Inferences Have students look at the area covered in the unit on a globe or a world map and make inferences about the two continents and the islands. **Ask: What do you think is true about the landscapes, languages, and cultures found throughout this region? Why?** *(Students may speculate that great diversity is found throughout the region due to the fact that it is made up of two continents and many islands, some of which are great distances apart.)*

Tell students they will be learning about the differing climates and the economic and environmental challenges faced by the people throughout this expansive region that reaches from north of the Equator to the South Pole. Unit Seven highlights four regions: Australia, New Zealand, Oceania, and Antarctica.

TEACH & ASSESS   **R**

R Reading Skills

Identifying Have a student volunteer read the introductory paragraph aloud and identify main ideas. **Ask:**

- In which hemisphere is this region almost entirely found? *(in the Southern Hemisphere)*
- What contrasts exist in the landforms in this region? *(from large continents to tiny islands)*
- How far south does the region extend? How far north does the region extend? *(to the South Pole; north of the Equator)* **ELL** Verbal/Linguistic

V Visual Skills

Interpreting Have students interpret what they see in the photograph associated with the paragraph, "Natural Resources." Have a student volunteer read the paragraph. **Ask:**

- In what way do the people of New Zealand use the land? *(farming and the raising of livestock)*
- What type of renewable energy resource is being used in the photo? How do you know? *(wind; presence of the windmill)*
- What other type of energy resource is important for the people of New Zealand? Where does this energy resource come from? *(geothermal; from the volcanic activity in the region)* **AL** Visual/Spatial

T Technology Skills

Researching on the Internet Have a group of students do Internet research using reliable resources on how islands are formed from underwater volcanoes. Have another group locate the islands of Oceania on the world map of the Ring of Fire from the Chapter 2 Opener and research how their location impacts life there. Have a third group research when most of the islands of Oceania were formed. Have them find photographs of erupting volcanoes that are still forming islands today and share them with the class. **AL** Verbal/Linguistic

EXPLORE the CONTINENT

THIS region lies almost entirely in the Southern Hemisphere, reaching from north of the Equator to the South Pole. The countries that make up this region contain an amazing variety of landforms and range in size from tiny islands to large continents.

① NATURAL RESOURCES This region holds abundant natural resources. New Zealand's North Island has good farmland and pasture for grazing sheep and other animals. The location of New Zealand along the Ring of Fire provides geothermal energy. Australia is rich in precious metals, oil and natural gas, and fertile farmland. In Oceania, wind and solar energy are plentiful, as are fish and other seafood.

② ISLANDS AND REEFS Oceania is made up of thousands of islands with different physical features. These islands were formed millions of years ago by underwater volcanoes. Coral islands, called atolls, are made up of reef islands surrounding lagoons. Off Australia's northeastern shore lies the spectacular Great Barrier Reef. By contrast, the water surrounding Antarctica's coasts freezes into thick plains of ice during winter. Other huge ice formations include glaciers and icebergs.

406 Unit 4

net**w**rks   *Online Teaching Options*

VIDEO TOUR

Video Tour of Oceania, Australia, New Zealand, and Antarctica

Interpreting Visual Information Display the video montage highlighting Oceania, Australia, New Zealand, and Antarctica. Prior to starting the video, have students sitting near each other generate five questions about the geography, resources, climate, and/or people of the region. Have the same students revisit their questions after the video. Have students share their questions and answers. Categorize information on the board under four headings: geography, resources, climate, people. List any unanswered questions on chart paper. Have students fill in the answers as they progress through the unit. **AL** Visual/Spatial

③ **LANDFORMS** Physical landscapes vary throughout the region. In New Zealand, the towering mountains of the Southern Alps rise on South Island. Australia is mostly flat. The Central Lowlands, however, contain a massive stone monolith known as Ayers Rock, or *Uluru* to the Aboriginal people of Australia. Antarctica is made up of one large, icy landmass and an archipelago of rocky islands.

FAST FACT

Australia is slightly smaller than the 48 U.S. states.

Unit 4 **407**

V Visual Skills

Interpreting Direct students' attention to the satellite image of the region at the top of the page. Explain that this unit covers two continents and many islands. **Ask:**

- **Which continent is labeled number 1?** *(Australia)*
- **What area is labeled number 2?** *(the islands of Oceania)*
- **Which continent is labeled number 3? How do you know?** *((Antarctica; Antarctica is covered with snow and ice; that is why it appears all white.)* **AL** **Visual/Spatial**

R Reading Skills

Determining Word Meanings Ask a volunteer to read the paragraph, "Landforms," and discuss word meanings in the text. **Ask:**

- **What can be said about the landscapes of the region?** *(The landscapes are quite varied from lowlands to mountains to rocky islands.)*
- **What is a monolith?** *(a single massive rock)*
- **What is an archipelago?** *(a chain or cluster of islands)*
- **Which words in the text explain the landscape shown in the photograph under the text?** *(large, ice landmass)* **Verbal/Linguistic**

C Critical Thinking Skills

Evaluating Have students read the Fast Fact and compare the land area of the 48 contiguous United States with the land area of Australia. **Ask:**

- **How does the land area of Australia compare with the land area of 48 of the states that make up the United States?** *(Australia is slightly smaller.)*
- **How might Australia's physical location benefit it economically?** *(Australia is close to Asia and can have ports open to countries to the north, the south, the east, and to the west)* **Visual/Spatial**

WORKSHEET

Environmental Case Study

Evaluating The Environmental Case Study worksheet for this unit is about climate change. This topic will help students understand how climate change is affecting vastly different areas of Earth, such as Oceania and Antarctica. Divide the students into groups and distribute the case study, allowing some in-class time for planning. Have groups share findings with the class.
BL **Logical/Mathematical**

Oceania, Australia, New Zealand, and Antarctica

V Visual Skills

Reading a Map Have students work in pairs to analyze the features of the physical map. Discuss the map as a group, noting the difference between elevations. Ask students to note how Antarctica is shown as an inset on the map and the two different scales on the map. Have students find the Hawaiian Islands. Remind students that the Hawaiian Islands joined the United States as the 50th state in 1959. Point out the three regions of Oceania: Micronesia, Melanesia, Polynesia. **Ask:** V

- **Which region is found north of the Equator?** *(Micronesia)*
- **What is the highest point in New Guinea?** *(Mt. Wilhelm at 14,762 ft, or 4,500 m)*
- **Where are the Cook Islands found?** *(in Polynesia)*
- **Which bodies of water are found along the Australian coastline?** *(Coral Sea, Tasman Sea, Great Australian Bight)*
- **What is the highest mountain found on the Great Dividing Range in Australia?** *(Mt. Kosciuszko at 7,310 ft, or 2,228 m)*
- **Where is the Great Barrier Reef located?** *(in the Coral Sea near the northeastern shore of Australia)*
- **Which oceans surround Antarctica?** *(Atlantic Ocean, Pacific Ocean, Indian Ocean)*
- **How much of Antarctica falls within the Antarctic Circle?** *(all of it with the exception of the tip of the Antarctic Peninsula)*
- **In which region are the highest elevations found?** *(in East Antarctica)* **AL** Visual/Spatial, Naturalist

C Critical Thinking Skills

Evaluating Have students focus on the continent of Australia. **Ask:**

- **What can be stated about the physical features labeled on western Australia?** *(mostly deserts)*
- **In which areas would you expect the population to be most dense in Australia?** *(most likely near Lake Eyre, at major port areas along the coast, and along the Murray River and Darling River)* **BL** Visual/Spatial

---

ANSWERS, p. 408

MAP SKILLS

1. southeast Australia
2. Elevations are much higher in Antarctica.
3. Great Sandy Desert, Gibson Desert, and Great Victoria Desert

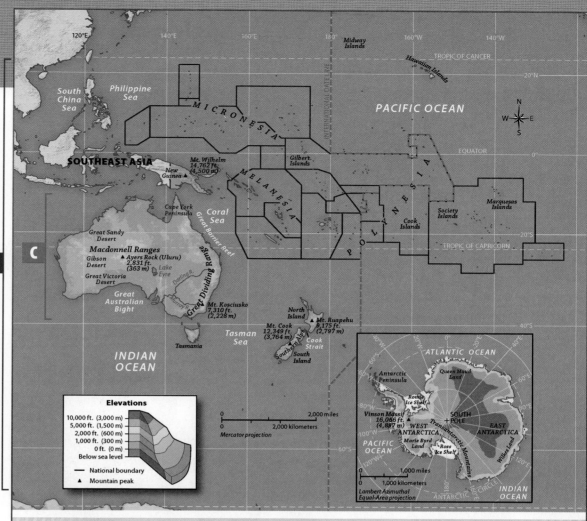

OCEANIA, AUSTRALIA, NEW ZEALAND, AND ANTARCTICA

PHYSICAL

MAP SKILLS

1. **THE GEOGRAPHER'S WORLD** Where are the region's major rivers located?

2. **PLACES AND REGIONS** How is the land elevation in Antarctica different from elevations elsewhere in the region?

3. **PHYSICAL GEOGRAPHY** Which deserts are found in Australia?

408 Unit 4

---

networks *Online Teaching Options*

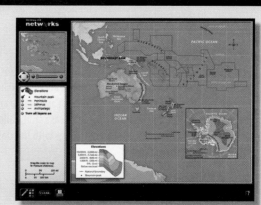

MAP

Physical Map: Oceania, Australia, New Zealand, and Antarctica

Displaying Use the physical interactive map to help students identify the region's various physical features. Divide the class into small groups. Have students build the region by first placing in the two continents and then building the island nations of Oceania as if placing puzzle pieces into the Pacific Ocean. Have students add New Zealand to their regional puzzle. Have students measure the distance between Australia and New Zealand and compare that with the diameter of Antarctica from east to west and from north to south. **AL** Kinesthetic

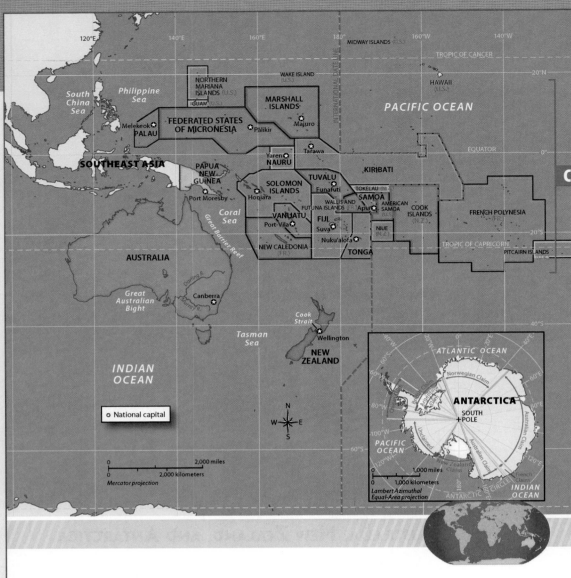

POLITICAL

MAP SKILLS

1 **THE GEOGRAPHER'S WORLD** How far is Wellington, New Zealand, from Canberra, Australia?

2 **PLACES AND REGIONS** Which country controls Guam and the Northern Mariana Islands?

3 **PLACES AND REGIONS** Which country is located on half of a major island?

Unit 4 **409**

V Visual Skills

Reading a Map Have students study the political map. Have a volunteer explain the boxes drawn around groups of the islands of Oceania. **Ask:**

- **What do you notice about the political ties of some of the islands and island nations in Oceania?** *(They have political ties to France, New Zealand, the United Kingdom, and the United States.)*
- **What is the capital of the Federated States of Micronesia?** *(Palikir)*
- **What happens to the International Date Line as it crosses Oceania?** *(It changes longitude as it moves around Kiribati, Samoa, Tonga, and New Zealand.)*
- **What is the capital of New Zealand?** *(Wellington)*
- **What is the capital of Australia?** *(Canberra)*
- **What countries claim territory in Antarctica?** *(Great Britain, Norway, Australia, France, New Zealand, Chili, Argentina)*
- **Which country claims the largest amount of land area in Antarctica?** *(Australia)* **ELL** Visual/Spatial

C Critical Thinking Skills

Reasoning Have students discuss the island nations of Oceania. Direct student attention to the shapes of the different political boundaries of Oceania. **Ask:**

- **What do you think determined the varied shapes of the political boundaries found in Oceania?** *(political agreements, conquest, and location of islands in the Pacific Ocean)*
- **What would you speculate about the cultures and languages found in Oceania? Why?** *(quite varied due to each island's history and political ties)*
- **Why do some island groups, such as French Polynesia, not show a national capital?** *(Students might suggest that the governmental affairs of those island groups are controlled abroad.)* **BL** Logical/Mathematical

---

GAME

Political Boundaries: Oceania, Australia, New Zealand, and Antarctica Game

Organizing Information Display the interactive political map of Oceania, Australia, New Zealand, and Antarctica. As a class, play the drag-and-drop game to study the political boundaries of countries. Then have volunteers use whiteboard tools to circle national capitals, draw a line from one capital to another, and calculate the distance. Have students use whiteboard tools to group islands that have political ties to other countries. **ELL** Kinesthetic

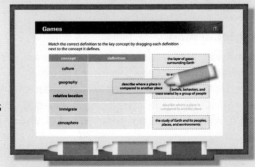

ANSWERS, p. 409

MAP SKILLS

1. approximately 1,500 miles (2,414 km)
2. United States
3. Papua New Guinea

Oceania, Australia, New Zealand, and Antarctica

V1 Visual Skills

Integrating Visual Information Have students state their general expectations of population density for the region, and then use the population density map to check their predictions. **Ask:**

- **Are the population densities shown on the map located where you expected them to be? Why or why not?** *(Students might say that expectations were met because population densities are usually highest near coastal regions, and/or that they did not expect anyone lived in Antarctica.)*

- **How might tourism play a role in the higher populations of some of the islands?** *(More people are needed to meet the demands of service industries, such as hotels and restaurants for tourists.)* **BL**

V2 Visual Skills

Reading a Map Direct students' attention to the cities and population map keys. **Ask:**

- **Where are the region's largest cities located?** *(eastern Australia)*

- **Which cities have populations over 2 million people?** *(Sidney, Melbourne)*

- **How does the population of Perth compare to the population of Newcastle?** *(within the same range of 1 to 2 million people)*

- **What is the population of Port Moresby in Papua New Guinea?** *(under 500,000 people)*

- **What is the population density of much of New Zealand?** *(2.5 to 24 people per square mi., or 1 to 9 people per square km)*

- **How many cities in New Zealand have populations greater than 1 million people?** *(one—Auckland)* **AL** **Logical/Mathematical**

C Critical Thinking Skills

Reasoning Have students refer back to the physical map of the region and connect the physical geography of Australia with its population. **Ask: What would account for low population densities in Australia's central and western regions?** *(mostly desert regions)* **What might explain the high population density of Melbourne?** *(port city, tourism, commercial center for the region)* **BL**

ANSWERS, p. 410

MAP SKILLS

1. climate and industry
2. The North Island is more densely populated than the South Island.
3. extreme cold and lack of plant life for food

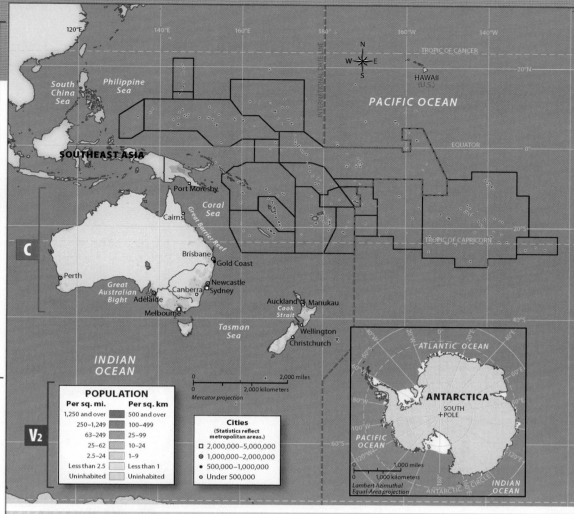

OCEANIA, AUSTRALIA, NEW ZEALAND, AND ANTARCTICA

POPULATION DENSITY

MAP SKILLS

1 **ENVIRONMENT AND SOCIETY** Why do you think most people in Australia live along the country's east coast?

2 **PLACES AND REGIONS** How do population densities compare on New Zealand's South and North Islands?

3 **ENVIRONMENT AND SOCIETY** Why do you think Antarctica has no permanent human residents?

410 Unit 4

---

netw⊙rks *Online Teaching Options*

MAP

Regional Map

Identifying Use this interactive Regional Map where the images introduced throughout the unit are pinned/connected to the map at the correct location, so students can see the location of the image in context to the map. Have students identify each of the locations. **AL** Visual/Spatial

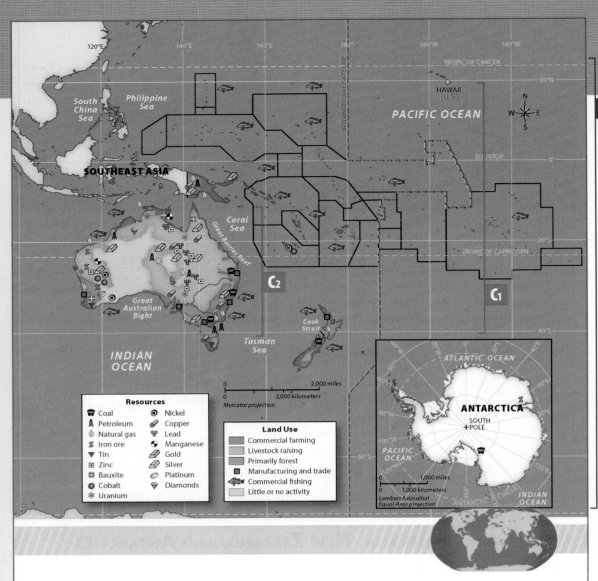

Resources

🏴 Coal	⊗ Nickel
⚑ Petroleum	⚑ Copper
◊ Natural gas	⚑ Lead
⚒ Iron ore	⚘ Manganese
▽ Tin	⚑ Gold
⊡ Zinc	⚑ Silver
⊞ Bauxite	⊘ Platinum
◉ Cobalt	⚑ Diamonds
✳ Uranium	

Land Use

- Commercial farming
- Livestock raising
- Primarily forest
- Manufacturing and trade
- Commercial fishing
- Little or no activity

ECONOMIC RESOURCES

MAP SKILLS

1. **ENVIRONMENT AND SOCIETY** How is much of the land in Australia used?

2. **PHYSICAL GEOGRAPHY** What mineral resources are found in New Zealand?

3. **HUMAN GEOGRAPHY** What are the primary economic activities in Oceania north of New Zealand?

Unit 4 **411**

MAP

Economic Resources Map: Oceania, Australia, New Zealand, and Antarctica

Analyzing Maps Display the interactive resource map and allow students time to review and discuss the region as each layer is revealed. Then assign each student a resource. Students should research the importance of the resource on a global scale. For example: *How valuable and of what importance is bauxite to the global economy?* Have students assigned the same resource share their research. Students should create a visual of the resource and add a marketing phrase that captures the global economic importance of the resource. **AL** Logical/Mathematical

UNIT 4
Oceania, Australia, New Zealand, and Antarctica

V

V Visual Skills

Reading a Map Review the Land Use and Resources map keys. Have students compare the regional land uses in Australia to those in Oceania and Antarctica. **Ask:**

- **Where is commercial farming done in Australia?** *(near the east and west coasts)*
- **Where does most commercial fishing occur?** *(in Oceania and along the coasts of Australia and New Zealand)*
- **Where is there little or no land use activity?** *(Antarctica and the desert regions of Australia)* **Visual/Spatial**

C1 Critical Thinking Skills

Formulating Questions Have pairs of students use the map to write five questions about the natural resources and the economic importance of those resources for Oceania, Australia, New Zealand, and Antarctica. Have them write the answers on a separate piece of paper. Then have pairs exchange and answer each other's questions. Possible questions could include:

- **Where have gold reserves been identified?** *(in Papua New Guinea and in Australia)*
- **Where does most manufacturing occur?** *(southern and eastern coastal cities of Australia and in northern New Zealand)*
- **Where has zinc been located?** *(central and western Australia)*
- **What has been discovered in the interior of Australia?** *(oil, natural gas, gold, copper, zinc, silver, lead)*
- **In which country have diamonds been discovered?** *(Australia)*
- **Where is coal mined?** *(Australia, New Zealand)*
- **Where has cobalt been discovered?** *(western Australia)*
- **Which countries have identified iron ore as an available resource?** *(Australia, New Zealand)*
- **Where has uranium been found?** *(Australia, New Zealand)*
- **Which country has identified platinum as an available resource? (Australia)** **AL** Visual/Spatial

C2 Critical Thinking Skills

Synthesizing Help students understand economic importance of natural resources for Australia. **Ask: Which natural resources found in Australia might be sought on a global scale and attract foreign investment?** *(Students might speculate all of Australia's natural resources in one way or another would be sought by other countries, especially its gold, silver, diamonds, natural gas, coal, and copper.)* **BL** Logical/ Mathematical

ANSWERS, p. 411

MAP SKILLS
1. for livestock raising
2. coal, iron ore, uranium
3. commercial fishing

Unit 4   411

V Visual Skills

Analyzing a Map Review with students the size of Australia in relationship to the United States. **Ask:**

• Which two climates impact most of Australia? *(arid and semi-arid)*

• How would life be different in the United States if most of our country had an arid and semi-arid climate? *(We would not be able to grow the amount of food that we now grow and would not be able to support our population.)* **Logical/Mathematical**

C Critical Thinking Skills

Determining Cause and Effect Have students use what they have learned about how climate impacts a country's economy to determine cause-and-effect relationships. **Ask:**

• How might climate affect the tourism industry in Oceania? *(People visit the region to enjoy the warm weather, available recreation, plants, and animals of rain forest climates.)*

• Which type of climate presents the greatest economic hardship for a region? Why? *(Students may speculate that an arid environment such as is found in Australia creates the greatest economic hardship because it limits land use; others will say that even an arid climate is better than the extreme cold of Antarctica.)*

• What must a country rely on for economic health if its land use is limited? *(trade, manufacturing, and the export of its natural resources)* **BL** **Logical/Mathematical**

CLOSE & REFLECT

Narrative Have students reflect on what they have learned so far about Australia, Oceania, New Zealand, and Antarctica. Divide the class into teams. Assign each team a country, island group found in Oceania, or the continent of Antarctica. Students should research how the tourism industry takes advantage of the unique qualities of region, such as photographic excursions and cruises. Have student teams collaborate on a two-page narrative describing how tourism impacts their assigned location. **Verbal/Linguistic**

ANSWERS, p. 412

MAP SKILLS
1. tropical savanna and semi-arid
2. marine west coast
3. Oceania

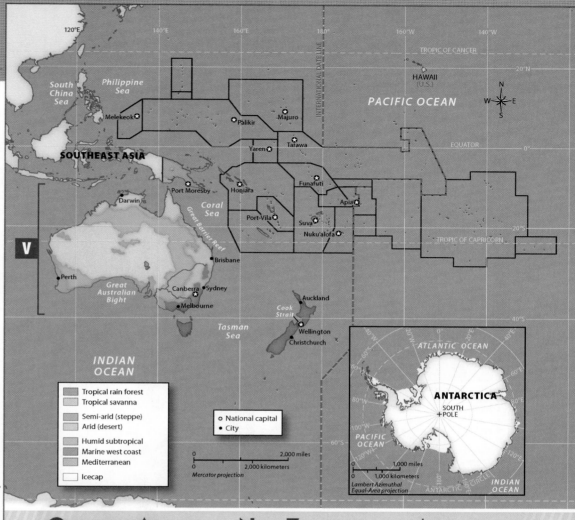

OCEANIA, AUSTRALIA, NEW ZEALAND, AND ANTARCTICA

CLIMATE

MAP SKILLS

1 **PLACES AND REGIONS** What climate zones are found in northern Australia?

2 **PLACES AND REGIONS** What climate zone is found throughout New Zealand?

3 **ENVIRONMENT AND SOCIETY** In what parts of the region could tropical crops be grown?

412 *Unit 4*

---

networks *Online Teaching Options*

MAP

Climate Map: Oceania, Australia, New Zealand, and Antarctica

Making Presentations Have students use the interactive climate map to discuss the variety of climates found throughout the region. Have small groups learn about new climate research being conducted in Antarctica by several countries. Assign each group a different research station. Have a "Share a Day in Antarctica With Us" class. Each group should share what the international science community has learned from the work being conducted at its assigned research station through a visual display highlighting the information. Invite parents, the local newspaper, and staff to visit the class and speak to the students about their displays. **AL** **Interpersonal**

CHAPTER 14
Australia and New Zealand Planner

National Geography Standards covered in Chapter 14

Learners will understand:

UNDERSTANDING BY DESIGN®

Enduring Understandings
- *People, places, and ideas change over time.*

Essential Questions
- *How does physical geography influence the way people live?*
- *Why does conflict develop?*
- *What makes a culture unique?*

Predictable Misunderstandings
- *The geography of Australia and New Zealand is the same as other islands in the Pacific.*
- *The culture of Australia and New Zealand has not been impacted by Europe in a similar way as the rest of the world.*

Assessment Evidence

Performance Tasks:
- *Project-Based Learning Digital Hands-On Chapter Project*
- *Project-Based Learning Hands-On Chapter Project*

Other Evidence:
- *Reading Skills Activity*
- *Geography Skills Activity*
- *Participation in Interactive Whiteboard Activities*
- *Contribution to small-group activities*
- *Interpretation of slide show images and special purpose maps*
- *Participation in class discussions about cultural and economic topics*
- *Lesson Reviews*
- *Chapter Assessments*

I. The World in Spatial Terms
Standard 1: How to use maps and other geographic representations, geospatial technologies, and spatial thinking to understand and communicate information

Standard 3: How to analyze the spatial organization of people, places, and environments on Earth's surface

II. Places and Regions
Standard 4: The physical and human characteristics of places

Standard 5: That people create regions to interpret Earth's complexity

Standard 6: How culture and experience influence people's perceptions of places and regions

III. Physical Systems
Standard 8: The characteristics and spatial distribution of ecosystems and biomes on Earth's surface

IV. Human Systems
Standard 9: The characteristics, distribution, and migration of human populations on Earth's surface

Standard 10: The characteristics, distribution, and complexity of Earth's cultural mosaics

Standard 11: The patterns and networks of economic interdependence on Earth's surface

Standard 12: The processes, patterns, and functions of human settlement

Standard 13: How the forces of cooperation and conflict among people influence the division and control of Earth's surface

V. Environment and Society
Standard 14: How human actions modify the physical environment

Standard 15: How physical systems affect human systems

Standard 16: The changes that occur in the meaning, use, distribution, and importance of resources

VI. The Uses of Geography
Standard 17: How to apply geography to interpret the past

Standard 18: How to apply geography to interpret the present and plan for the future

SUGGESTED PACING GUIDE

Introducing the Chapter	1 Day
Lesson 1	2 Days
Lesson 2	2 Days
Lesson 3	2 Days
Global Connections	3 Days
Chapter Wrap-Up and Assessment	1 Day

TOTAL TIME   11 Days

Key for Using the Teacher Edition

SKILL-BASED ACTIVITIES

Types of skill activities found in the Teacher Edition.

V **Visual Skills** require students to analyze maps, graphs, charts, and photos.

W **Writing Skills** provide writing opportunities to help students comprehend the text.

R **Reading Skills** help students practice reading skills and master vocabulary.

C **Critical Thinking Skills** help students apply and extend what they have learned.

T **Technology Skills** require students to use digital tools effectively.

*Letters are followed by a number when there is more than one of the same type of skill on the page.

DIFFERENTIATED INSTRUCTION

All activities are written for the on-level student unless otherwise marked with the leveled labels below.

BL Beyond Level
AL Approaching Level
ELL English Language Learners

All students benefit from activities that utilize different learning styles. Many activities are marked as below when a particular learning style is highlighted.

Intrapersonal	Naturalist
Logical/Mathematical	Kinesthetic
Visual/Spatial	Auditory/Musical
Verbal/Linguistic	Interpersonal

CHAPTER OPENER PLANNER

Students will know:
- *that Australia and New Zealand have unique geographies and climates.*
- *that the resources of Australia and New Zealand attracted European colonists.*
- *that the Europeans and indigenous populations create diverse cultures in Australia and New Zealand.*

Students will be able to:
- **analyze** *a world map to identify the countries of Australia and New Zealand.*
- **use** *a time line to discuss various events in the history of Australia and New Zealand.*

UNDERSTANDING BY DESIGN®

☑ *Print Teaching Options*

V Visual Skills

☐ **P. 414** Students use the map of Australia and New Zealand to reinforce map skills.

☐ **P. 414** Students use the time line to discuss major events in the history of Australia and New Zealand.

R Reading Skills

☐ **P. 414** Students determine the meaning of *spectacle*.
AL **ELL** **Verbal/Linguistic**

W Writing Skills

☐ **P. 415** Students write an informative paragraph about a cause-and-effect relationship in the time line of events.

☑ *Online Teaching Options*

☐ **MAP** **Reading a Map**—Students identify aspects and locations of the region on a map.

☐ **TIME LINE** **Reading a Time Line and Map**—Students learn about where and when historical events occurred in Australia and New Zealand using the time line and map.

☐ **MAP** **Interactive World Atlas**—Students use the interactive world atlas to identify the region and describe its terrain.

☑ *Printable Digital Worksheets*

☐ **WORKSHEET** **Geography Skills: Reading a Climate Map**—Students use a climate map of Australia and New Zealand to study the region and make predictions.

☐ **WORKSHEET** **Reading Skills: The Maori in New Zealand**—Students can use this worksheet to learn more about the Maori.

Project-Based Learning

Hands-On

Debating a Current Issue
Students will work in groups to research a controversial current issue related to Australia and New Zealand. As a class, decide on which issues to debate and organize the class into groups to debate an issue assigned to them. Each sub-group must research and develop arguments for its position. Have the class hold a classroom debate. The debate will be moderated by the teacher. Have students who are not participating in that specific debate vote on which group best defended its position.

Digital Hands-On

Researching Conservation Efforts
Students will research preservation efforts to sustain the Great Barrier Reef as a natural resource. Working in groups, students will research information about the reef using online resources. Each group will contact an environmental organization as part of their research. Groups will write questions and submit them to the organization. In a classroom discussion, students will talk online with members of the organization to discuss conservation efforts to preserve the Great Barrier Reef.

Print Resources

ANCILLARY RESOURCES
These ancillaries are available for every chapter and lesson.
- **Reading Essentials and Study Guide Workbook** **AL** **ELL**
- **Chapter Tests and Lesson Quizzes Blackline Masters**

PRINTABLE DIGITAL WORKSHEETS
These printable digital worksheets are available for every chapter and lesson!
- **Hands-On Chapter Projects**
- **What Do You Know? Activities**
- **Chapter Summaries (English and Spanish)**
- **Vocabulary Builder Activities**
- **Quizzes and Tests**
- **Reading Essentials and Study Guide (English and Spanish)** **AL** **ELL**
- **Guided Reading Activities**

More Media Resources

SUGGESTED VIDEOS
NOTE: Be sure to preview videos to ensure they are age-appropriate.
- **The Sundowners** (133 min.)
- **Animal Planet—Great Barrier Reef** (100 min.)
- **Australia: The Last Barrier** (Cousteau 48 min.)
- **New Zealand—The Smoldering Sea**

SUGGESTED READING
- *The Fatal Shore: The Epic of Australia's Founding,* by Robert Hughes **BL**
- *In a Sun Burnt Country,* by Bill Bryson **BL**
- *Over in Australia: Amazing Animals Down Under,* by Marianne Collins Burkes
- *Australia & Oceania (True Books),* by Mel Friedman **AL**
- *Carnivorous Nights on the Trail of the Tasmanian Tiger,* by Margaret Mittelbach & Michael Crewdson **BL**
- *Cousteau: An Adventure in New Zealand,* by the Cousteau Society

ⓔdtechteacher
21ˢᵗ Century Learning

PHYSICAL GEOGRAPHY

Students will know:
- *that Australia and New Zealand have unique geographies and climates.*
- *that the resources of Australia and New Zealand attracted European colonists.*

Students will be able to:
- **describe** *the landforms and waterways of Australia and New Zealand.*
- **describe** *the various climates of the region.*
- **discuss** *plant and animal life in the region.*

UNDERSTANDING BY DESIGN®

☑ *Print Teaching Options*

V Visual Skills

- ☐ **P. 417** Students create a chart to describe different landforms. **Visual/Spatial**
- ☐ **P. 418** Students create a flow chart or diagram about the formation of the Great Barrier Reef. **Interpersonal**
- ☐ **P. 421** Students use outline maps of countries in opposite hemispheres and label the seasons at certain times. **AL**

W Writing Skills

- ☐ **P. 420** Students write a compare-contrast essay about New Zealand's two main islands. **Verbal/Linguistic**
- ☐ **P. 423** Students imagine they are a tour guide in Australia or New Zealand and write a narrative essay. **Intrapersonal**

R Reading Skills

- ☐ **P. 416** Students specify the difference between an island and a continent. **AL ELL Verbal/Linguistic**
- ☐ **P. 417** Students use word parts to find meaning. **AL ELL Verbal/Linguistic**
- ☐ **P. 419** Students use Latin and Greek roots to determine the meanings of *lithosphere* and *hydrosphere*. **ELL Verbal**
- ☐ **P. 421** Students show understanding of climates by non-verbal communication. **ELL Kinesthetic**
- ☐ **P. 422** Students summarize New Zealand's climates.

C Critical Thinking Skills

- ☐ **P. 419** Students discuss how volcanoes can be both good and bad. **BL Logical/Mathematical**
- ☐ **P. 421** Students locate the Ring of Fire and predict what it would be like to live someplace where earthquakes occur. **Logical/Mathematical**
- ☐ **P. 423** Students discuss and predict animal adaptations.

T Technology Skills

- ☐ **P. 421** Students research to find impacts of El Niño on their assigned contine nt and prepare a short presentation. **BL**

☑ *Online Teaching Options*

V Visual Skills

- ☐ **MAP Physical Geography: Australia and New Zealand**—Students use the physical geography layer of the Chapter Opener map to review the landforms and waterways of this region.
- ☐ **IMAGE 360° View: Windjana Gorge**—Students use the 360° image of Windjana Gorge to extend the content of the unique variety of landforms in this region.
- ☐ **MAP The Great Barrier Reef**—Students use the map to discuss length and size of environmental issues occurring in the Great Barrier Reef. **AL**
- ☐ **MAP Climates: Australia and New Zealand**—Students use the climate layer of the Chapter Opener map to discuss climate zones in Australia and New Zealand.
- ☐ **MAP Vegetation: Australia and New Zealand**—Students use the vegetation layer of the Chapter Opener map to discuss the vegetation and how it may promote the wildlife of the region.

W Writing Skills

- ☐ **VIDEO World's Best Hot Creatures—Australia**—Students watch the video about the physical geography of the region and make flashcards using topics and terms from the lesson.
- ☐ **SLIDE SHOW Views of Australia and New Zealand**—Students use the slide show to discuss the unique geography and make a two-column chart to compare and contrast landforms and waterways in Australia and New Zealand.
- ☐ **VIDEO A Geyser in New Zealand**—Students view the video, discuss geothermal events in New Zealand, and write a cause-effect paragraph to explain why the geyser occurs and its effects.
- ☐ **GRAPHIC ORGANIZER Landforms and Waterways of New Zealand**—Students use the interactive graphic organizer to review and assess the topic discussed in this lesson.
- ☐ **VIDEO Kangaroos in the Grasslands**—Students view the video about kangaroos in the grassland and categorize the different animals discussed in the video and in the text. **BL Visual**

C Critical Thinking Skills

- ☐ **IMAGE Fjords**—Students use the interactive photo to discuss fjords, why they are unique, and how they form. **BL**
- ☐ **IMAGES Comparing Geysers**—Students use the images on geysers to compare the geysers of Iceland and Yellowstone with the geysers of New Zealand.
- ☐ **IMAGE Volcanoes**—Students use the photo of volcanoes to compare them to geysers.
- ☐ **IMAGE 360° View: Australia's Outback**—Students use the 360° image of the Australian Outback to discuss this unique region of Australia and the climate in this region.
- ☐ **LECTURE SLIDE Problems with Kangaroos**—Students use the lecture slide to discuss the interactions between humans and kangaroos to highlight the human-environment interaction.

T Technology Skills

- ☐ **ONLINE SELF-CHECK QUIZ Lesson 1**—Students receive instant feedback on their mastery of lesson content.

☑ *Printable Digital Worksheets*

W Writing Skills

- ☐ **WORKSHEET Geography Skills: Reading a Climate Map**—Students use a climate map of Australia and New Zealand to study the region and make predictions.

HISTORY OF AUSTRALIA AND NEW ZEALAND

Students will know:
- that the resources of Australia and New Zealand attracted European colonists.
- that the Europeans and indigenous populations create diverse cultures in Australia and New Zealand.

Students will be able to:
- **describe** the first people of Australia and New Zealand.
- **discuss** colonial times in the region.
- **describe** the challenges presented by introduced species.
- **explore** the region today.

UNDERSTANDING
BY DESIGN®

☑ *Print Teaching Options*

V Visual Skills

☐ **P. 424** Students create illustrations depicting human migration to Australia. **Visual/Spatial**

☐ **P. 426** Students create a poster about the Maori way of life. **Visual/Spatial**

☐ **P. 428** Students create time lines for a century in the history of Australia and New Zealand. **Visual/Spatial**

W Writing Skills

☐ **P. 425** Students write an informative essay on a topic related to the Aboriginal culture. **BL Verbal/Linguistic**

☐ **P. 429** Students write a narrative essay about what life was like in southeastern Australia in the 1800s. **Verbal/Linguistic**

R Reading Skills

☐ **P. 426** Students summarize information about Maori beliefs and traditions. **Verbal/Linguistic**

☐ **P. 429** Students discuss why animals not native to Australia were brought there. **AL Verbal/Linguistic**

C Critical Thinking Skills

☐ **P. 425** Students compare and contrast Aboriginal people who were nomadic and those who settled in one location. **Verbal/Linguistic**

☐ **P. 429** Students make connections between the discovery of gold and Australia's change from a prison colony to a nation. **Logical/Mathematical**

☐ **P. 430** Students compare and contrast the impacts of foreign settlers on the Maori and the impact of foreign settlers on Native Americans. **BL Logical/Mathematical**

T Technology Skills

☐ **P. 427** Students conduct research and make a presentation on a specific aspect of Maori culture. **Auditory/Musical, Interpersonal**

☐ **P. 431** Students research either Maori or Aboriginal rights and "produce" a talk show in which a host interviews historians and representatives from both groups. **Kinesthetic, Interpersonal**

☑ *Online Teaching Options*

W Writing Skills

☐ **VIDEO** **Ancient Lives—Aborigines**—Students watch the video about the history of Australia and New Zealand and write three facts they learned. **ELL Verbal/Linguistic**

☐ **MAP** **History of Australia**—Students use the interactive map and time line to explore Australian history and write a brief essay about one of the lasting effects of an event in Australia's history.

R Reading Skills

☐ **LECTURE SLIDE** **Tikanga**—Students use the lecture slide to review Maori culture.

☐ **GAME** **Drag-and-Drop: Australian History**—Students use the drag and drop game to review aspects of Australian history.

☐ **GRAPHIC ORGANIZER** **Comparing Aborigines and Maori**—Students use the interactive graphic organizer to review and compare the Aborigines to the Maori and make a Venn diagram to compare the two groups. **AL Visual/Spatial**

☐ **IMAGE** **Maori Culture**—Students use the interactive image about Maori culture to further extend the content.

☐ **TIME LINE** **Australian Gold Rush**—Students use the time line to discuss how the desire for gold affected the population of Australia.

C Critical Thinking Skills

☐ **MAP** **The Maori of New Zealand**—Students use the map to discuss the movement of the Maori to New Zealand. **ELL**

☐ **IMAGE** **Australia in World War II**—Students consider how Australia's involvement in World War II affected its relations with New Zealand and the United States. **Interpersonal**

☐ **IMAGE** **360° View: Aboriginal Rock Paintings**—Students use the photo to discuss the culture of Aborigines in this region and make connections between the Aboriginal culture and Native American beliefs.

☐ **IMAGE** **Dingoes**—Students use the interactive image of dingoes to discuss this wild dog and the controversy about domesticating them.

T Technology Skills

☐ **ONLINE SELF-CHECK QUIZ** **Lesson 2**—Students receive instant feedback on their mastery of lesson content.

☑ *Printable Digital Worksheets*

W Writing Skills

☐ **WORKSHEET** **Reading Skills: The Maori in New Zealand**—Students can use this worksheet to learn more about the Maori.

LIFE IN AUSTRALIA AND NEW ZEALAND

Students will know:

- that the resources of Australia and New Zealand attracted European colonists.
- how the Europeans and indigenous populations create diverse cultures in Australia and New Zealand.

Students will be able to:

- **describe** the diverse populations of Australia and New Zealand.
- **compare** urban and rural life in the region.
- **describe** Aboriginal and Maori culture.
- **describe** natural resources and economies of Australia and New Zealand.
- **explore** current issues in the region such as indigenous rights.

UNDERSTANDING BY DESIGN®

☑ Print Teaching Options

V Visual Skills

- ☐ **P. 432** Students create a circle graph of the populations of Australia and New Zealand. **Logical/Mathematical**

- ☐ **P. 437** Students draw a diagram or flow chart to show the step-by-step process of using geothermal energy. **Visual/Spatial, Interpersonal**

- ☐ **P. 438** Students use information about indigenous rights to stage a mock protest. **BL Verbal/Linguistic**

W Writing Skills

- ☐ **P. 433** Students write a short narrative about a day in the life of a person who lives either in a rural or an urban area of Australia. **Verbal/Linguistic, Interpersonal**

- ☐ **P. 435** Students write a short argumentative essay supporting or refuting the idea that living in the Outback is socially isolating for school-aged children. **Verbal/Linguistic, Interpersonal**

R Reading Skills

- ☐ **P. 433** Students calculate using the formula for converting percentages to fractions. **Mathematical**

- ☐ **P. 435** Students determine the meaning of *revival*. **Verbal/Linguistic**

- ☐ **P. 436** Students use word parts to find meanings. **ELL**

- ☐ **P. 439** Students explain population rates in Australia and New Zealand. **AL Logical/Mathematical**

C Critical Thinking Skills

- ☐ **P. 434** Students discuss some of the nicknames and slang given in the text. **AL Verbal/Linguistic**

- ☐ **P. 438** Students recall what they learned about the history of the Maori. **Verbal/Linguistic**

T Technology Skills

- ☐ **P. 434** Students research information about specific universities in New Zealand and Australia.

- ☐ **P. 435** Students give a short oral presentation on an aspect of Aboriginal or Maori culture. **ELL Auditory/Musical, Kinesthetic**

☑ Online Teaching Options

V Visual Skills

- **SLIDE SHOW** **Sports of Australia**—Students use the slide show to discuss popular sports that take place in the daily lives of Australians.

- **IMAGE** **360° Views: Sydney Opera House Outside and Inside**—Students use photos to discuss the Sydney Opera House, its location and construction, and its contributions to culture.

- **VIDEO** **Didgeridoo**—Students use the video of the man playing this instrument to discuss cultural influences on music and the arts.

- **IMAGE** **Wool Processing**—Students use the photograph to discuss the economies and resources of the region.

- **IMAGE** **Aboriginal and Maori Protests**—Students discuss the differing viewpoints people have about indigenous rights. **BL Interpersonal**

W Writing Skills

- **VIDEO** **Around the World—Eastern Australia**—Students watch the video about life in Australia and New Zealand and write a paragraph about an aspect of each country. **ELL Verbal**

R Reading Skills

- **LECTURE SLIDE** **Comparing of Football Around the World**—Students use the lecture slide to compare different aspects and rules between football, soccer, and rugby.

- **CHART** **Australian and New Zealand Universities**—Students use the chart to discuss the role of universities in the educational system and consider what it might be like to attend a university in Australia or New Zealand.

- **LECTURE SLIDE** **Slang in Australia and New Zealand**—Students use the lecture slide to discuss slang in Australia and New Zealand and compare it to slang in the United States and UK.

- **GAME** **Drag-and-Drop: Australian and New Zealand's Economies**—Students use the drag and drop game to review and compare the economies of Australia and New Zealand.

C Critical Thinking Skills

- **MAP** **Population: Australia and New Zealand**—Students use the population layer of the Chapter Opener map to discuss population distribution and density in the region.

- **CHART** **Australia's Economy**—Students use the interactive chart to review Australia's economy by sector, the employment rate, and their imports and exports.

- **CHARTS** **Population Pyramids: Australia and New Zealand**—Students use the interactive charts (population pyramids) to discuss the distribution of population across age and gender. They analyze the low birth rate and the life expectancy of the region and discuss how this could impact the economies of the region.

- **MAP** **Resources: Australia and New Zealand**—Students use the resources layer of the Chapter Opener map to make a Venn diagram to compare and contrast resources found in each country. **AL**

T Technology Skills

- **ONLINE SELF-CHECK QUIZ** **Lesson 3**—Students receive instant feedback on their mastery of lesson content.

INTERVENTION AND REMEDIATION STRATEGIES

LESSON 1 Physical Geography

Reading and Comprehension

Help students understand and pronounce content vocabulary terms that may be confusing. Have students work in pairs to create fill-in-the-blank flashcards. On one side, students should write the term; on the other, they should write a sentence with a blank space where the word should go. For example, for the term *Outback*, students might write "Water is difficult to find in the isolated part of Australia known as the _____." To ensure comprehension of the terms, have students take turns quizzing each other.

Text Evidence

Have students work in pairs to compare and contrast the physical geography of Australia and New Zealand. Assign pairs one of the following topics: landforms, waterways, climates, plant and animal life. Have one student in each pair find key information about the topic for Australia, and the other find information about the topic for New Zealand. Then have partners compare their notes to determine the similarities and differences of the physical geography in each country.

LESSON 2 History of the Region

Reading and Comprehension

Help students visualize concepts from this lesson by mapping an imaginary trip to Australia and New Zealand. Tell students to work with a partner to plan their journey and then write a paragraph describing their trip. Have pairs use at least two content vocabulary terms in their paragraphs to demonstrate knowledge of the vocabulary words' meaning as used in the text. For example, students may describe how they saw a dingo while in the Outback, or how they witnessed a ceremony involving Kapahaka.

Text Evidence

Organize students into small groups, and assign one of the following topics to each group: Aboriginal culture, Maori culture, British Australia, introduced species, and British New Zealand. Have students collaborate to research their topic using the text and online sources. Tell students to trace specific claims about their topic and complete a two-column chart that lists each claim and whether or not the author provides evidence to support it. Ask groups to present their findings to the class.

LESSON 3 Life in Australia and New Zealand

Reading and Comprehension

To help students grasp the main concepts in this lesson, have them work in pairs or small groups to paraphrase a portion of the text. You may wish to assign students sections of text under a subheading. Challenge students to condense one or two paragraphs into one summarizing sentence. Remind students that a summary includes main ideas, not details. Then, call on students to say their sentences aloud. After all students have had a turn, tell students to work individually to write two or three sentences describing life in Australia and New Zealand.

Text Evidence

To ensure that students have grasped the concepts in the lesson, tell students they will play a "Jeopardy" style game show, with you acting as the host. Allow students time to review the lesson while you prepare topics and statements, which students will respond to in the form of a question. You may wish to organize topics from the content using headings and subheadings as "categories." Tell students they may only respond by raising their hand. You may wish to assign points for each question and give students "bonus points" for additional questions they answer correctly.

Online Resources

Approaching Level Reader

Use this online lower-level text that corresponds directly to the text in the online Student Edition.

Guided Reading Activities

This resource uses graphic organizers and guiding questions to help students with comprehension.

Assessing Background Knowledge

Use these worksheets to pre-assess students' background knowledge before they read the chapter.

Reading Essentials and Study Guide Workbook

This resource offers writing and reading activities for the approaching-level student.

Self-Check Quizzes

This online assessment tool provides instant feedback for students to check their progress.

AUSTRALIA AND NEW ZEALAND

ESSENTIAL QUESTIONS · *How does geography influence the way people live?* · *Why does conflict develop?* · *What makes a culture unique?*

Penny Tweedie/The Image Bank/Getty Images

A baby kangaroo nuzzles a young boy. The name "kangaroo" stems from aboriginal language.

netw⚬rks
There's More Online about Australia and New Zealand.

CHAPTER 14

Lesson 1
Physical Geography

Lesson 2
History of the Region

Lesson 3
Life in Australia and New Zealand

The Story Matters...

Thousands of years ago, Asian and Pacific people began migrating to Australia and New Zealand. People from different European countries later migrated to the region because of its abundant natural resources. These diverse cultures are woven into the fabric of Australia and New Zealand.

FOLDABLES
Study Organizer

Go to the Foldables® library in the back of your book to make a Foldable® that will help you take notes while reading this chapter.

413

ENGAGE

Think-Pair-Share Ask students if they have ever moved to a new place. Call on volunteers to share their experiences. Provide guiding questions such as: **Were you excited or nervous about moving? If so, why? What were some differences between the place you moved to and your previous location? What were some challenges about moving to a new place?**

Tell students to brainstorm a list of reasons people move from one place to another. Students may list a parent's new job or military relocation, better educational opportunities, to be closer to extended family members, and so on. Have students read "The Story Matters..." and discuss the idea of migration, as well as the reasons for migration described in the text. **Ask:**

- **How is migration similar to moving (relocation)?** *(It is what happens when people move to a new place. Sometimes they move or migrate permanently. Other times they migrate seasonally.)*

- **How is it different from moving?** *(Moving also describes a local relocation or small move, but immigration usually implies moving over a longer distance.)*

- **What does the text say is one reason that people moved from Europe to this region?** *(the abundant natural resources)*

- **What does that suggest about other reasons that people move?** *(They might move because their own homeland does not provide for their needs. Also, if they need to move for other reasons, they will look for a place that has resources to support them.)*

Making Inferences Have students find Australia and New Zealand on a political world map. **Ask: Why do you think Australia is sometimes referred to as a region "down under"?** *(Sample responses: Australia is located close to the South Pole, so on a globe it appears to be "down under" other continents on Earth. The region gets that nickname because Australia and New Zealand are completely south of (or under) the Equator.)*

Tell students that in this chapter they will learn about physical, historical, and current characteristics of Australia and New Zealand.

FOLDABLES
Study Organizer

Go to the Foldables® library for a cumulative chapter-based Foldable® activity that your students can use to help take notes and prepare for assessment.

Letter from the Author

Dear Geography Teacher,

The original inhabitants of Australia and New Zealand are fascinating examples of how humans have adapted to their physical surroundings. Using a graphic organizer such as a Foldable®, ask students to compare and contrast the Aborigines of Australia to the Maori of New Zealand. Make sure that this comparison includes information about modern times. For example, students might list how each of these groups has been integrated into their country's economy, political system, educational system, and so on.

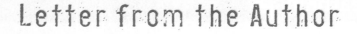

TEACH & ASSESS
Step Into the Place

V Visual Skills

Reading a Map Have students read the introductory paragraph and look at the map. Explain that this map shows the countries of Australia and New Zealand. Have students use the map to answer the Step Into the Place questions. **Ask:**

- What is the capital city of New Zealand? *(Wellington)*
- Where is it located? *(on the southern tip of New Zealand's North Island)*
- What part of the world lies to the north of Australia and New Zealand? *(Southeast Asia)*
- Which islands are located off the coast of Australia? *(the Coral Sea Islands, Norfolk Island, and Tasmania)*
- Which island is the largest? *(Tasmania)*
- Which islands sit to the east of New Zealand? *(the Chatham Islands)* **Visual/Spatial**

R Reading Skills

Determining Word Meanings Ask students to look at the photograph of the hiker (image B) and read the caption. **Ask: Based on what you see in the photograph, what is a *spectacle*?** *(an unusual, notable, or eye-catching scene or sight)*

Have students offer sentences using the word *spectacle*. Ask: **What words can you think of that have the root *spec-* in them?** *(Sample responses: spectator, spectacles, spectacular)*

Tell students that knowing Greek and Latin roots can help them better understand word meanings. **Ask: Based on the words you listed with the root *spec-*, what do you think it means?** *(look, see)*

Tell students that many words with similar definitions may have different connotations, or shades of meaning, depending on how they are used. Provide students with these sentences to show them the different shades of meaning between *spectacle* and *view*: The fresh snowfall was a welcome spectacle for skiers on the mountain. The view from my bedroom was blocked by the moving van. **AL** **ELL** **Verbal/Linguistic**

Chapter 14
AUSTRALIA AND NEW ZEALAND (CCSS)

V As the only place on Earth that is a continent and a country, Australia is unique. Located 1,200 miles (1,931 km) southeast of Australia, two large islands make up most of New Zealand's landmass.

Step Into the Place

MAP FOCUS Use the map to answer the following questions.

1 **PLACES AND REGIONS**
What city is Australia's national capital?

2 **THE GEOGRAPHER'S WORLD**
What sea separates Australia and New Zealand?

3 **THE GEOGRAPHER'S WORLD**
What reef lies off the northeastern coast of Australia?

4 **CRITICAL THINKING** **Integrating Visual Information** Look at the map. What can you infer from the location of Australia's major cities about where most Australians live?

A HARBOR VIEW A view from the harbor's bridge provides a magnificent view of Sydney, Australia. Sydney is the country's largest city in population and a major world port and business center.

R

B MOUNTAIN SPECTACLE A hiker looks toward Mount Cook, New Zealand's highest mountain. Mount Cook lies in the Southern Alps, a mountain range that runs the length of South Island.

Step Into the Time

W **TIME LINE** Choose at least two events from the time line. For each event, write a paragraph describing some of the positive and negative effects that event had on the region. WHST.6-8.2, WHST.6-8.4

c. A.D. 800–1300 Maori arrive in New Zealand from Polynesia

1770 Captain James Cook explores Australian coast

1800

B.C. 48,000 Aboriginal people begin migrating to Australia

1642 Explorer Abel Tasman lands on what is now Tasmania

414 Chapter 14

(t to b) © Blaine Harrington III/Corbis; Scott Markewitz/Taxi/Getty Images; Peter Dennis/Getty Images

---

Project-Based Learning 🖑

Hands-On

Research a Controversial Current Issue

Students will work in groups to research a controversial current issue related to Australia and New Zealand. As a class, decide on which issues to debate and organize the class into groups to debate an issue assigned to them. Each sub-group must research and develop arguments for its position. Have the class hold a classroom debate. The debate will be moderated by the teacher. Have students who are not participating in that specific debate vote on which group best defended its position.

Digital Hands-On

Research Preservation of the Great Barrier Reef

In groups using online resources, students will research preservation efforts to sustain the Great Barrier Reef as a natural resource. Each group will contact an environmental organization as part of their research. Groups will write questions and submit them to the organization. In a classroom discussion, students will talk online with members of the organization to discuss conservation efforts to preserve the Great Barrier Reef.

ANSWERS, p. 414

STEP INTO THE PLACE
1. Canberra
2. Tasman Sea
3. the Great Barrier Reef
4. **CRITICAL THINKING** Most of Australia's large cities are in the south and southeast part of the country, so most people live there.

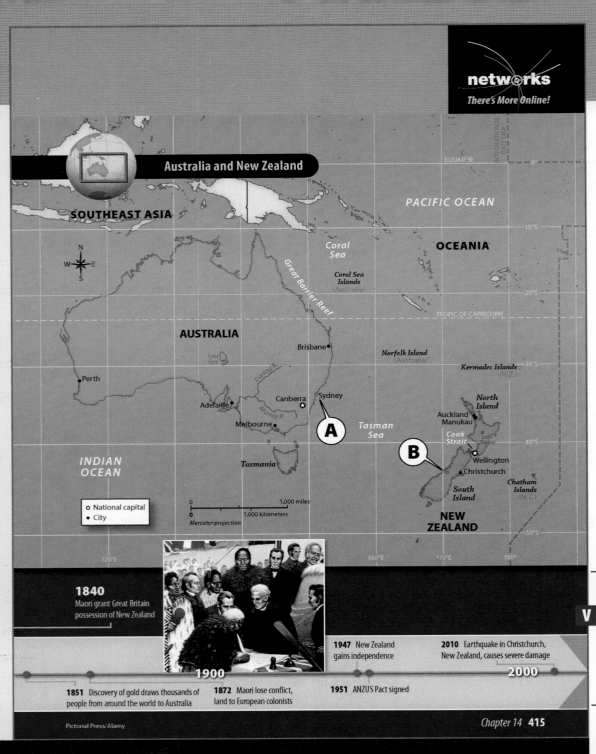

Australia and New Zealand

SOUTHEAST ASIA

PACIFIC OCEAN

Coral Sea

OCEANIA

Coral Sea Islands (Australia)

AUSTRALIA

Great Barrier Reef

Perth

Lake Eyre

Darling R.

Brisbane

Norfolk Island (Australia)

Kermadec Islands (N.Z.)

Adelaide

Canberra

Murray R.

Sydney

Melbourne

Tasman Sea

North Island

Auckland Manukau

Cook Strait

Lake Taupo

INDIAN OCEAN

Tasmania

Wellington

Christchurch

South Island

Chatham Islands (N.Z.)

NEW ZEALAND

o National capital
• City

0   1,000 miles
0   1,000 kilometers
Mercator projection

1840
Maori grant Great Britain possession of New Zealand

1900

1947 New Zealand gains independence

2010 Earthquake in Christchurch, New Zealand, causes severe damage

2000

1851 Discovery of gold draws thousands of people from around the world to Australia

1872 Maori lose conflict, land to European colonists

1951 ANZUS Pact signed

Pictorial Press/Alamy

Chapter 14 **415**

Step Into the Time

V Visual Skills

Reading a Time Line Have students review the time line and images. As a class, discuss its major points of interest. **Ask:**

- **Where does the island of Tasmania get its name?** *(from explorer Abel Tasman who landed on the island in 1642)*
- **When did Great Britain gain possession of New Zealand? (1840) Why?** *(The Maori gave it to Great Britain.)*
- **How many years later did New Zealand gain its independence?** *(107)*
- **What event caused thousands of people from around the world to come to Australia in the 1850s?** *(the discovery of gold in 1851)*
- **What geologic event occurred in 2010?** *(An earthquake hit Christchurch, New Zealand, causing severe damage.)*

Encourage students to create their own time line of significant events as they read the chapter. Suggest that students itemize events into two categories, Australia and New Zealand. Tell students to use their time line as a review tool when studying the chapter. **Visual/Spatial**

W Writing Skills

Informative/Explanatory Read aloud the activity described at the beginning of the time line. Before students write their paragraphs, have them consider the long-term impact of each event. Then review cause-and-effect signal words, such as *due to, because,* and *as a result,* encouraging students to use them in their paragraphs. Provide the following sentence as an example: *As a result* of gold being discovered in Australia, people from around the world came to the country. Have students share their completed paragraphs with the class. **Verbal/ Linguistic, Logical/Mathematical**

CLOSE & REFLECT

Summarizing Have students briefly review the photographs, map, and time line, and think about what they have learned so far about Australia and New Zealand. Have students write one or two sentences summarizing key information they learned about the region.

TIME LINE

Reading a Time Line and Map

Analyzing Maps Display the time line and map on the whiteboard. Ask volunteers to read events on the time line and guide them to make connections between events. For example, guide students to understand that even though the Maori gave Great Britain possession of New Zealand in 1840, New Zealand eventually gained its independence over a hundred years later. **AL**

See page 413B for other online activities.

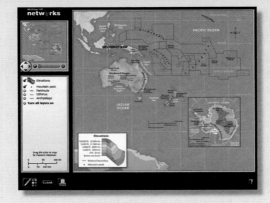

ENGAGE

 Bellringer Before students begin the lesson, have them think about different geographical features near their school or community. Briefly discuss how these features affect the way people live. For example, your region might have certain bodies of water or landforms nearby that people use for recreational purposes. Or some people may use a body of water to earn a living by fishing, and so on. Have students skim through the lesson, noting the photographs.

Display both a physical map and a political map of Australia and New Zealand and read the Essential Question aloud. **Ask: Based on the images and the maps, how might the physical geography of Australia and New Zealand affect the way people live?** *(Students' answers will vary, but might mention that the region is somewhat remote or disconnected from other parts of the world. It appears to have natural beauty and parts appear quite wild and untamed. The images show that people hike in the mountains and also use the land for ranching.)*

Tell students that they will learn about the physical geography and climate of Australia and New Zealand in this lesson.

TEACH & ASSESS

R **Reading Skills**

Specifying Help students understand the difference between an island and continent. Explain that a continent is one of Earth's large, continuous landmasses. An island is smaller than a continent, but is completely surrounded by water. Have a volunteer read aloud the first paragraph and **ask:**

• True or false: Australia is an island. *(False; it is the world's smallest continent.)*

• True or false: New Zealand has two main islands. *(True)*

• Why might New Zealand and Australia have such unique animals and plants? *(The region is completely set off from the rest of the world, and it is south of the Equator.)*

AL **ELL** Verbal/Linguistic, Naturalist

ANSWER, p. 416

Taking Notes Notes should include facts from each section such as, **The Land:** Australia is the smallest, flattest, driest continent; New Zealand is two main islands with diverse landscapes and climates; **Climates:** varied climates; hot, dry deserts in central Australia, more rain along coasts, southeast is fertile farming region; New Zealand's climate varies from subantarctic in the far south to subtropical in the north; mostly mild and slightly warmer on North Island, some snow in Southern Alps and central South Island; **Plants/Animals:** Unique plants and animals in the region evolved separately from other continents over millions of years and adapted to the unique environments of Australia and New Zealand.

---

networks

There's More Online!

☑ **IMAGE** Australia's Outback
☑ **SLIDE SHOW** Views of Australia and New Zealand
☑ **VIDEO**

Reading HELPDESK CCSS

Academic Vocabulary RH.6-8.4
(Tier Two Words)
• overall

Content Vocabulary RH.6-8.4
(Tier Three Words)
• **Outback**
• **monolith**
• **Aboriginal**
• **coral reef**
• **hot spring**
• **geyser**
• **drought**
• **marsupial**
• **eucalyptus**

TAKING NOTES: *Key Ideas and Details* RH.6-8.2, RH.6-8.7

Summarize As you read about the physical geography of Australia and New Zealand, take notes on each section of the lesson using the graphic organizer below.

Heading	Main Idea
The Land	
Climate	
Plants/ Animals	

Lesson 1
Physical Geography

ESSENTIAL QUESTION · *How does geography influence the way people live?*

IT MATTERS BECAUSE
Australia and New Zealand have unique landscapes, plants, and wildlife not found in other parts of the world.

The Land of Australia and New Zealand

GUIDING QUESTION *What physical features make Australia and New Zealand unique?*

R Australia is nicknamed "The Land Down Under" because it is located south of, or "under," the Equator. On a map, Australia looks like a large island, because it is not attached to any other landmasses. Australia, however, is a continent. It is the world's smallest continent, but it is the world's sixth-largest country. New Zealand is made up of two islands with a variety of landscapes, ecosystems, and climate zones. Australia and New Zealand also have some of the world's most unusual plants and animals.

Australia's Landforms

It might not seem that Australia is a flat continent based on images of its huge rock formations and mountain ranges. **Overall**, however, Australia has low elevation. This means that although the land is high in some places, most of its surface is low compared to the land on other continents. Australia generally has a dry climate. One-third of Australia is covered by deserts. Another one-third is semiarid.

Geographers divide Australia into three main geographic regions: the Western Plateau, the Central Lowlands, and the Eastern Highlands. In general, the Western Plateau is rocky

(l to r) ©John Baker/Corbis; Robin Bush/Oxford Scientific/Getty Images; Grant Dixon/Lonely Planet Images/Getty Images; ©Michael Amendolia/In Pictures/Corbis

---

networks   *Online Teaching Options*

VIDEO

World's Best Hot Creatures—Australia

Categorizing Use this video about the physical geography, climate, and wildlife of Australia to introduce the lesson. Have students create flashcards of topics and terms they found interesting or want to learn more about after watching the video. Collect the flashcards and discuss the topics as a class. Distribute the flashcards to students after completing the lesson and have them categorize the terms as follows: *Australia*–Landforms, Waterways, Climate, Natural Resources; *New Zealand*–Landforms, Waterways, Climate, Natural Resources. **Verbal/Linguistic**

See page 413C for other online activities.

BBC Motion Gallery Education

and dry, and the Central Lowlands are flat and rugged. The Eastern Highlands have a variety of high and low areas, forests, and fertile farmlands. In addition, coastal lowlands are found all around the continent, particularly in the north and east.

The Western Plateau makes up the western half of Australia. The plateau is rocky, with few water sources other than small salt lakes. Near the center of the continent are the interior highlands. Here, the Musgrave and Macdonnell mountain ranges rise above a huge expanse of flat plateau.

The Central Lowlands are a rough, dry region. Although a system of rivers runs through the rugged land, much of the region is desert. The most rural and isolated parts of the Central Lowlands are commonly called the **Outback**. Survival is a challenge for humans and animals in the Outback. Strong winds cause harsh dust storms across the desert plains. In many parts of the Outback, water is difficult to find. To get the water they need, ranchers must dig wells deep into the sun-baked earth.

One of Australia's most fascinating landforms is found in the Central Lowlands. A massive, solid stone called a **monolith**, measuring 1,100 feet (335 m) tall and 2.2 miles (3.5 km) long, stands alone on the desolate plain. This amazing monolith has two names. Many Australians know it as Ayers Rock. However, the first humans to live in Australia, the **Aboriginal** people, call it *Uluru*. Uluru is sacred to many Aboriginal people. Small caves along the base of the monolith contain ancient Aboriginal paintings and carvings. Today, Uluru is an official World Heritage site located within a protected national park.

The Eastern Highlands, called the Great Dividing Range, run parallel to Australia's east coast. The mountains and valleys of this range were formed by folding and uplifting movements that occurred in the past within Earth's lithosphere. Today, little movement occurs, and earthquakes are rare.

One of the most spectacular and complex ecosystems on Earth is located in the ocean waters just off Australia's northeastern shore. The Great Barrier Reef is a living **coral reef**, a giant community of marine animals called corals.

Academic Vocabulary

overall as a whole; generally

V

R

Ayers Rock, or Uluru, in central Australia, is all that is left of a large mountain range that slowly eroded over millions of years.
▶ **CRITICAL THINKING**
Describing Why is Ayers Rock (Uluru) called a monolith?

Chapter 14 **417**

SLIDE SHOW

Views of Australia and New Zealand

Comparing and Contrasting Display the slide show about the landforms and waterways of Australia and New Zealand. As a class, discuss the unique geography found in this region. With a partner, have students create a two-column chart labeled *Landforms* and *Waterways* to visually compare and contrast these features in each country. **Visual/Spatial, Naturalist**

See page 413C for other online activities.

Slide Show

V Visual Skills

Creating Charts Have students create a three-column chart like the one below.

Western Plateau	Central Lowlands	Eastern Highlands
_____	_____	_____
_____	_____	_____
_____	_____	_____

As students read this page, have them fill in each column with information from the text about each geographic region. Then, assess students' understanding of each region. **Ask:**

- **How would you describe the Western Plateau?** (*It is rocky and has very little water, other than a few small salt lakes.*)
- **What physical feature is located at the center of Australia?** (*the interior highlands, where the Musgrave and Macdonnell mountain ranges are located*)
- **What is the Outback?** (*the most rural and isolated parts of the Central Lowlands, where water is difficult to find and winds cause harsh dust storms*) **Visual/Spatial, Naturalist**

R Reading Skills

Determining Word Meanings Point to the word *monolith*. Challenge student pairs to create a list of words that have the word part *mono-* in them. (*Sample responses: monotone, monopoly, monorail, monologue*) **Ask:**

- **Based on the words you listed with the prefix *mono-*, what do you think it means?** (*one*)
- **How might the meaning of *mono-* help point to the significance of the monolith?** (*Mono- means "one." The monolith is partly significant because it is the only massive rock in the area. It stands alone.*) **AL ELL Verbal/Linguistic**

ANSWER, p. 417

CRITICAL THINKING Ayers Rock (Uluru) is a massive, solid stone that stands alone on a desolate plain.

Physical Geography

V Visual Skills

Diagramming Have students read the information about the formation of the Great Barrier Reef and analyze the image on this page. Have students work in pairs to create a flow chart or diagram that depicts the information presented in the text. (*Possible series of events: Corals live and grow. Corals die. The dead corals' sekeletons form underwater reefs. Algae and plant and animal matter get stuck in the reefs. This joins the reefs together.*) Encourage students to use a step-by-step visual that shows the sequence of events involved in reef formation. After partners have had time to prepare their visuals, ask volunteers to present their diagrams to the class. **Ask:**

- **How long did it take for the Great Barrier Reef to form?** *(millions of years)*
- **How are the reefs held together?** *(by algae and tiny pieces of plant and animal matter that get stuck in the reefs)* **Visual/Spatial, Interpersonal**

Content Background Knowledge

Share the following information with students about the Great Barrier Reef to help them understand its fragile ecosystem.

A long-term study by the Australian Institute of Marine Science released in 2012 indicates that the Great Barrier Reef remains in decline. The study, which used data collected over a span of 27 years, found that coral cover has declined mostly due to cyclones and breeding of destructive starfish species. Researchers believe that a species known as the crown-of-thorns starfish is responsible for destroying much of the live coral found in the Great Barrier Reef.

After attempting to reduce the invasive species, which increased dramatically in the early 1960s, scientists determined that rapid growth of the starfish's population was part of its natural cycle. Though scientists believe that climate change has caused warmer waters, which cause damaging cyclones, they have been unable to determine what causes this rapid, periodic increase in the starfish population. **Naturalist**

ANSWER, p. 418

Coral reefs form from multiple layers of the hard skeletons of living and dead corals held together by algae and plant and animal matter.

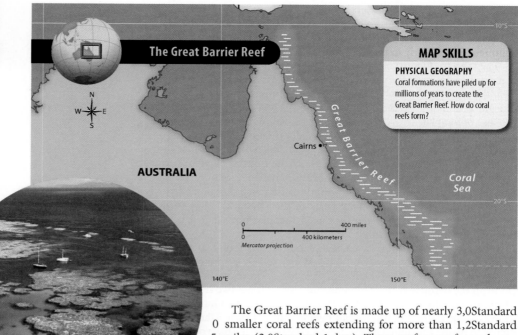

The Great Barrier Reef

AUSTRALIA

Cairns

Coral Sea

0   400 miles
0   400 kilometers
Mercator projection

140°E   150°E

MAP SKILLS

PHYSICAL GEOGRAPHY
Coral formations have piled up for millions of years to create the Great Barrier Reef. How do coral reefs form?

Bait Reef in northeastern Australia

The Great Barrier Reef is made up of nearly 3,0Standard 0 smaller coral reefs extending for more than 1,2Standard 5 miles (2,0Standard 1 km). These reefs were formed over millions of years by natural actions of the biosphere. As corals lived, grew, and died, their hard skeletons built layer upon layer, forming large underwater formations called reefs. Coral reefs are held together by algae and tiny bits of plant and animal matter that become stuck in the reefs.

V

The Great Barrier Reef is teeming with marine life. Brightly colored fish and shellfish search for food and hide among the corals. Sponges, starfish, and anemones cling to the coral reefs, decorating them like living ornaments.

Just south of Australia's southeastern coast is a unique island called Tasmania. Mountains, valleys, and plateaus cover its surface. Some of the world's wildest, unexplored rain forests grow in Tasmania. These are cool temperate rain forests, which differ from the warm tropical rain forests in the northeastern part of Australia. Tasmania's broad Central Plateau is scattered with more than 4,0Standard 0 shallow lakes.

Waterways of Australia
Most of Australia has a dry climate. Lack of rain means few large rivers flow across the land. Australia's largest rivers flow from the eastern mountains. The important Murray-Darling river system flows through a dry basin in southeastern Australia. The many

Gonzalo Azumendi/age fotostock/Getty Images

---

networks *Online Teaching Options*

MAP

The Great Barrier Reef

Discussing Display the map to discuss the Great Barrier Reef with students. Discuss with students the content of the map and any informative facts that are contained in the map. Use the physical layer of the Chapter Opener map to make connections to the landforms near the Great Barrier Reef. Guide a class discussion about the length, size, and environmental issues occurring in the reef. Encourage students who are interested to conduct research on the Internet about how the reef was formed and the wildlife that lives there. **AL Naturalist**

See page 413C for other online activities.

rivers in the Murray-Darling system bring so much water to the area that the land is green and fertile.

Many of Australia's people, plants, and animals depend on underground aquifers for their water. Nearly one-third of all water used in Australia comes from underground sources. In a dry land such as Australia, water is a precious resource.

New Zealand's Landforms and Waterways

New Zealand is made up of two main islands called North Island and South Island plus many small islands. These islands are located in the southeastern Pacific Ocean, far from any other landmasses. Geographers believe that more than Standard 6 million years ago, movements within the lithosphere pushed the land that would become New Zealand up out of the ocean. Over time, processes within the lithosphere and hydrosphere shaped the land. The movement of ice and liquid water has carved out basins and eroded rocks into unusual shapes. Volcanic eruptions and earthquakes created low hills, fertile valleys and plains, and rows of sharp mountain peaks.

R

Today, one-third of New Zealand's lands are protected as national parks and nature reserves. The country is known for its beautiful and unusual landscapes. New Zealand's main islands are similar in that both have many forests, mountains, and waterways. Local climates and other types of landforms, however, show the differences between the two islands.

Many of North Island's landforms were created by volcanic activity. A huge volcanic plateau makes up the center of North Island. Lake Taupo, the largest lake in New Zealand, formed millions of years ago in the massive crater left behind by a devastating volcanic eruption. Lake Taupo is surrounded by fertile plains and

C

Pohutu Geyser in New Zealand's North Island erupts about Standard 2 times each day. The water it releases can reach as high as 1Standard 0 feet (Standard 3 m).

▶ **CRITICAL THINKING**
Describing How has volcanic activity shaped New Zealand's North Island?

valleys. This land is enriched by volcanic soil, which makes good farmland and pasture for grazing. North Island's most productive farm and pasture lands are located in a region called Waikato.

Northeast of Lake Taupo is Rotorua, an area famous for its steaming hot springs, bubbling mud pools, and violent geysers. **Hot springs** are pools of hot water that occur naturally. Hot springs form in rocky areas when rainwater seeps into cracks in Earth's surface. Water is exposed to intense heat, and then bubbles back up to gather in surface

Robin Bush/Oxford Scientific/Getty Images

VIDEO

A Geyser in New Zealand

Determining Cause and Effect After students have watched the video which displays a geyser erupting in New Zealand, discuss geothermal events that occur in the region. Guide students to understand the meaning of the term *geothermal*. Then have students write a cause-effect paragraph to explain why the geyser occurs and what its effects are on the region. Consider using the map from a previous chapter that discusses tectonic plates and the Ring of Fire to make connections to how geysers work. **Naturalist, Logical/Mathematical**

See page 413C for other online activities.

R Reading Skills

Determining Word Meanings Have students find the words *lithosphere* and *hydrosphere*. Tell students that knowing Greek and Latin word parts can help them understand words. Tell students that the Greek word part *lith-* means "related to rock or stone" and *hydro-* and *hydra-* are Greek word parts meaning "water." Tell students that the word *sphere* is derived from the Latin word *sphaera* and the Greek word *sphaira*. Challenge students to list as many words as they can think of with the word parts *lith-* and *hydra-/hydro-*. (Samples: lithograph, monolith, megalith, hydroelectric, hydrogen, dehydrate, hydrant) Then, **ask:**

- **If the word *sphere* relates to Earth, what does *lithosphere* mean?** *(Earth's rock)*
- **What does *hydrosphere* mean?** *(Earth's water and water vapor)*

Making Connections Have students reread the paragraph. Then have them work with a partner to take turns summarizing the information from the text. **Ask:**

- **How do geographers think New Zealand was formed?** *(Movements within the lithosphere pushed the land up out of the ocean.)*
- **How do some rocks get their unusual shapes?** *(from the movement of ice and water that carves out the rock over time)*
  ELL Verbal/Linguistic

C Critical Thinking Skills

Differentiating Before students read the paragraph, ask them to explain what comes to mind when they think of volcanoes. *(Students will likely use terms such as erupt, ash, and lava to describe a volcano's impact.)* Then have students read the information about volcanic activity on New Zealand's North Island. **Ask: How can volcanoes be both good and bad?** *(Sample response: Volcanic activity can be harmful, such as in the devastating eruption that formed Lake Taupo, but the volcanic soil has enriched the lake's surrounding land, which makes for good farmland and pastures for grazing.)* **BL Logical/Mathematical**

ANSWER, p. 419

CRITICAL THINKING Volcanic activity created a large volcanic plateau in the center of the island. A volcanic eruption millions of years ago left behind a massive crater that is now filled by Lake Taupo, the largest lake in New Zealand. Today, North Island's rich volcanic soil makes good farmland and pasture for grazing. In the Rotorua area, heat energy from deep within Earth warms water and mud that comes to the surface as hot springs, mud pools, and geysers.

Physical Geography

W Writing Skills

Informative/Explanatory Have students use what they have learned about New Zealand's two main islands to write a compare and contrast essay. Students should briefly describe the physical features of the islands, noting their similarities and differences. Review compare-contrast signal words, such as *different from, same as, although, but, however,* and *except,* and encourage students to use them in their essays. Tell students to use at least one content vocabulary term in their essay that shows their understanding of the word's meaning. Students may wish to create a visual to accompany their essays that shows how North Island is similar to and/or different from South Island. Ask volunteers to share their essays with the class. **Verbal/Linguistic**

C Critical Thinking Skills

Predicting Consequences Have students locate the Ring of Fire on a map of the region. Discuss what it might be like to live in a region where so many earthquakes occur. **Ask: What might community officials and emergency-preparedness workers do to prepare people for a severe earthquake in the region?** *(Students' answers will vary, but might mention that community officials would likely hold town meetings to discuss strategies people can take to be prepared, such as stocking up on bottled water, batteries, and so on. Emergency-preparedness officials would likely hold drills in various communities, especially those along the coast, to make sure people know where to find exit routes out of buildings and shelters.)* **Logical/Mathematical**

Make Connections Point out that the fjords of South Island are part of a national park in New Zealand. Have students identify some national parks in the United States. **Ask: Why would a country want to create a national park?** *(to protect the land and wildlife so that people can enjoy it for many years to come)*

Have students consider how the two main goals *(preserving the natural state of the area and allowing people to enjoy it)* may not go hand in hand. Encourage students to think of strategies that can help both of these objectives to be accomplished.

ANSWER, p. 420

CRITICAL THINKING The movement of glaciers carved deep valleys in the rocky land. As the glaciers melted, they formed lakes in inland areas. Near the coast, deep valleys left by glaciers were filled with ocean water and became fjords.

The stunning landscape of the Dark Cloud Range stretches across the southern end of New Zealand's South Island.

▶ **CRITICAL THINKING**
Analyzing Why does the southern end of South Island have many deep valleys, fjords, and lakes?

W

Grant Dixon/Lonely Planet Images/Getty Images

pools. **Geysers** are hot springs that sometimes shoot hot water out of the ground. The water in hot springs and geysers is warmed by heat energy from deep within Earth.

New Zealand's South Island is famous for its spectacular Southern Alps. These towering mountains are higher than the mountains on North Island. The Southern Alps cover hundreds of miles along the western side of South Island.

The southern end of South Island is filled with an incredible variety of landforms and environments. Millions of years ago, the movement of glaciers cut deep valleys into the rocky land. As the glaciers melted, clear, cold lakes formed. Some glacier valleys were so deep they were not completely filled until rising sea levels flooded them with ocean water more than 6,0Standard 0 years ago. These water-filled landforms are called *fjords.* The fjords of South Island are such fascinating landforms that many are preserved within a huge national park.

C The Ring of Fire
New Zealand's location in the southeastern Pacific Ocean puts it within the volcano-studded Ring of Fire. Active volcanoes and the frequent movement of tectonic plates along the Ring of Fire often

420 Chapter 14

---

netw⊙rks *Online Teaching Options*

IMAGE

Fjords

Sequencing Use the interactive image about a fjord to discuss this landform. Have students explain why it is unique and how a fjord is formed. Have students work with a partner to create a flow chart depicting the sequence of events that occurs in the formation of fjords. **BL Visual/Spatial**

See page 413C for other online activities.

Interactive Photos

©Pete Atkinson/Getty Images

100 of these yearly earthquakes, however, are large enough to be noticed by humans. Scientists predict that New Zealand will experience at least one severe earthquake each century.

☑ **READING PROGRESS CHECK**

Citing Text Evidence In what ways are the lands of Australia and New Zealand alike, and in what ways are they different?

Climates of the Region

GUIDING QUESTION *What types of climates and climate zones are found in Australia and New Zealand?*

Australia and New Zealand are located in the Southern Hemisphere, so their seasons are at opposite times of the year from seasons in the United States. For example, June, July, and August are winter months in the region. Summer months are December, January, and February.

Australia's Climates

The climate changes dramatically from one part of Australia to another. The northern third is in a tropical climate zone, and most of the other two-thirds are in a subtropical climate zone. Northern Australia, generally, has a warm, tropical climate. Winter months are dry, and summer months are rainy and hot. Seasonal monsoons can bring damaging winds and heavy rainfall.

Climate in most areas of the western, southern, and eastern regions changes with the seasons. Winters in Queensland, the Northern Territory, and Western Australia are warm and dry. Most rainfall in these regions happens during the long, hot spring and summer seasons. Coastal areas tend to be sunny and dry, with seasonal rains. The climate along the east coast is more humid, and the area receives more rainfall than the rest of the continent.

Much of central and western Australia, such as the Outback, has a desert climate with bands of semiarid steppes to the north, east, and south. These dry areas have extremely hot weather during much of the year. Weather in the Outback can change quickly from one extreme to another. Daytime temperatures in the Outback can reach 122°F (50°C), yet temperatures can fall below freezing at night.

Australia is the driest inhabited continent in the world. Only the icy continent of Antarctica receives less precipitation than Australia. A major problem in the dry areas is that long periods of little or no rain can result in **drought**.

Droughts are common in Australia and threaten the survival of wildlife, livestock, and farm crops. Low water reserves can lead to poor-quality drinking water for humans. Geographers can now predict some droughts by monitoring climate changes caused by El Niño. El Niño occurs every few years when global winds and ocean currents shift, affecting global rainfall patterns.

Chapter 14 **421**

MAP

Climates: Australia and New Zealand

Comparing Display the climate layer of the Chapter Opener map and discuss the various climate zones found in Australia and New Zealand. As you discuss each climate zone, help students make connections by asking them to compare the climate zones to other climates in other regions with which they are familiar. **Logical/ Mathematical**

See page 413C for other online activities.

V **Visual Skills**

Creating Maps Have students locate Australia and New Zealand on a map of the world. Ask a volunteer to point out continents in the Southern Hemisphere, and then locate the United States, pointing out that it is in the Northern Hemisphere. Instruct small groups of students to create two outline maps, one of the Southern Hemisphere and one of the Northern Hemisphere. Using information in the text about seasons, have students create icons for their maps (such as snowflakes or sunbursts) that indicate the climate during a certain time of year. For example, students might label their maps "Northern/Southern Hemisphere in January." Check students' maps to be sure the icons have been placed accurately. **AL** **Visual/Spatial**

R **Reading Skills**

Applying As an extended class activity, call out the name of a continent or country and a month of the year. Tell students to respond without words, showing they know the climate. For example, students might shiver with their arms crossed when you say, "Australia in June" or pretend to wipe sweat off their brow when you say "New Zealand in January." **ELL** **Kinesthetic**

T **Technology Skills**

Researching on the Internet Have students consider how droughts affect Australian farmers. Organize students into seven groups and assign each group one of the world's seven continents. Have each group complete the following activity for homework.

Have students conduct online research to find additional information about the impact of El Niño on their assigned continent. Tell groups to interpret the information from their research in visual displays, such as charts or graphs. Students should prepare a short presentation in which they summarize El Niño's impact on their assigned continent using visuals to support their findings. You may wish to direct students to the following Web sites: http://www.elnino.noaa.gov/; http://science.nasa.gov/earth-science/oceanography/ocean-earth-system/el-nino/. **BL** **Visual/Spatial, Logical/ Mathematical**

ANSWER, p. 421

☑ **READING PROGRESS CHECK** **Similarities:** mountain ranges, plains, plateaus, and being surrounded by the ocean; **Differences:** Australia's larger land area and vast central desert area, Australia's land features such as Uluru and the Great Barrier Reef, and New Zealand's smaller size, its great number of lakes, rivers, hot springs, geysers, glaciers, fjords, snow-topped Southern Alps

See page 413C for other online activities.

R Reading Skills

Summarizing Have students read the section titled, "New Zealand's Climates," and take turns summarizing the information. Remind students that summaries should only include the most important information. Then have them compare and contrast New Zealand's two main islands. **Ask:**

- How do temperatures on North Island differ from those on South Island? *(They are higher on North Island.)*
- What is similar about the climate of both islands? *(Both islands receive plenty of rain.)* **Verbal/Linguistic**

Content Background Knowledge

The Southern Alps are the highest mountains in Australia and New Zealand. There are 16 mountains that are above 10,000 feet (3,050 meters). The highest mountain in the Southern Alps is Mount Cook, also known as Aoraki. The name Aoraki is a Maori name and means "cloud piercer." Provide the following list of mountains for comparison.

Mountain	Country	Height
Mt. Everest	Nepal and Tibet	29,035 feet (8,859 meters)
Mt. Aconcagua	Argentina	22,736 feet (6,930 meters)
Mt. McKinley	United States	20,320 feet (6,194 meters)
Mt. Kilimanjaro	Tanzania	19,340 feet (5,895 meters)
Vinson Massif	(continent) Antarctica	16,050 feet (4,892 meters)
Mont Blanc	France and Italy	15,771 feet (4,807 meters)
Mount Cook	New Zealand	12,316 feet (3,754 meters)
Kosciusko	Australia	7,310 feet (2,228 meters)

Naturalist

A cattle driver on a station, or ranch, in Australia's Northern Territory herds Brahman cattle, a breed that is well adapted to the area's climate extremes.
▶ **CRITICAL THINKING**
Analyzing How does climate in inland Australia compare with climate in coastal areas of the country?

©Michael Amendolia/In Pictures/Corbis

predict some droughts by monitoring climate changes caused by El Niño. El Niño occurs every few years when global winds and ocean currents shift, affecting global rainfall patterns.

R New Zealand's Climates

New Zealand's climate is as varied as its land. Climates range from subantarctic in the south to subtropical in the north. Most areas on North Island and South Island have mild, temperate climates, however, with average daily temperatures between 86°F (30°C) and 50°F (10°C). For most of the year, temperatures on North Island are higher than temperatures on South Island. South Island experiences the hottest summers and the coldest winters in New Zealand. Both islands receive plenty of rain, keeping their forests and grasslands healthy.

Although average temperatures are generally mild and extremes of heat and cold are rare, snow does fall in New Zealand. The central region of South Island experiences the coldest winters of any part of the country. Highland zones, such as the Southern Alps, receive the most snowfall.

☑ **READING PROGRESS CHECK**

Describing What problems are caused by drought in Australia? Why are geographers monitoring climate changes there?

Plant and Animal Life

GUIDING QUESTION What plants and animals are unique to Australia and New Zealand?

If you have seen pictures of plants and animals from Australia and

net**w**orks *Online Teaching Options*

VIDEO

Kangaroos in the Grasslands

Categorizing After students have viewed the video about kangaroos in the grasslands, guide a class discussion on the wide variety of animals in the region. Then have students work with a partner to create a chart listing the different animals discussed both in the video and in the text. Students may wish to categorize the animals according to the region they inhabit or by their species classification, size, type of habitat, and so on. **BL** **Visual/Spatial, Naturalist**

©Beren Patterson/Alamy

ANSWERS, p. 422

☑ **READING PROGRESS CHECK** Drought threatens the survival of wildlife, livestock, and farm crops. It can lead to poor-quality drinking water for humans. Geographers are monitoring climate changes there to help predict droughts, so people can prepare for them.

CRITICAL THINKING Climate in inland Australia is dry and often hot, with irregular rainfall at best. Coastal areas, especially in eastern Australia, receive more rainfall and have milder temperatures.

New Zealand, you already know that many of them are unusual. Why are plants and animals in this region so different from living things in other parts of the world?

The landmasses that would become Australia and New Zealand separated from other lands millions of years ago. The animals and plants living on these lands developed in isolation, separated from living things on other landmasses. Over millions of years, the plants and animals in Australia and New Zealand adapted to live in their own unique environments.

Plants and Animals of Australia

Bandicoots, kangaroos, and koalas are 3 of the 1Standard 5 native species of marsupials in Australia. A **marsupial** is a type of mammal that raises its young in a pouch on the mother's body. Marsupials vary in size from tiny kangaroo mice to 6-foot-tall, gray kangaroos.

In the driest regions of Australia, water can be difficult to find. Over time, many native animals learned to get water from plants. The leaves, stems, and roots of desert plants contain water. Koalas adapted to eating only one type of plant—the leaves of the eucalyptus tree. **Eucalyptus** trees are native Australian evergreen trees with stiff, pleasant-smelling leaves.

Plants and Animals of New Zealand

Many of New Zealand's trees, ferns, and flowering plants are unique to New Zealand and cannot be found on other continents. Much of the land is covered in hardwood beech tree forests. Alpine plants such as sundew and edelweiss have adapted to the cold, windy, dry environments of South Island's mountain regions.

Lizards such as geckos are common sights in New Zealand. Other reptiles, such as the chevron skink, have become rare. Long ago, New Zealand was home to two types of flightless birds—the kiwi and the moa. The moa was hunted to extinction, but the kiwi was more fortunate. Today, the kiwi is a common sight on both islands and has become a symbol of New Zealand and its people.

©Paul A. Souders/Corbis

C

Road signs in rural Australia often warn motorists about kangaroo crossing areas.
▶ **CRITICAL THINKING**
Citing Text Evidence Why is the kangaroo found in Australia and nowhere else?

W

FOLDABLES
Study Organizer

Include this lesson's information in your Foldable®.

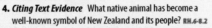
Australia
New Zealand

☑ **READING PROGRESS CHECK**
Determining Central Ideas Explain why animals and plants native to Australia

LESSON 1 REVIEW (CCSS)

Reviewing Vocabulary (Tier Three Words)
1. What kinds of equipment might you need to explore a *coral reef*? RH.6-8.4

Answering the Guiding Questions
2. *Identifying* List three physical features that make Australia unique and three physical features that make New Zealand unique. RH.6-8.2

3. *Identifying* Identify one of the two locations in New Zealand that has a cold, snowy climate in winter. RH.6-8.2

4. *Citing Text Evidence* What native animal has become a well-known symbol of New Zealand and its people? RH.6-8.2

5. *Informative/Explanatory Writing* Write a paragraph explaining why either Australia or New Zealand would be an interesting place to visit. Use information from the lesson to describe landscapes, ecosystems, climates, and other features of either Australia or New Zealand. WHST.6-8.2, WHST.6-8.9

Chapter 14 **423**

LESSON 1 REVIEW ANSWERS

Reviewing Vocabulary

1. Answers should mention underwater equipment such as scuba or snorkeling gear, oxygen tanks, cameras, a boat, and so on.

Answering the Guiding Questions

2. **Identifying** Answers may include: Australia: Coral reefs, Uluru (Ayer's Rock), the Outback, Mount Kosciusko, Great Dividing Range, Lake Eyre, the Murray-Darling River system; New Zealand: Canterbury Plain, the Southern Alps, Lake Taupo, Rotorua, Mount Ruapehu, hot springs, geysers, mud pools

3. **Identifying** Students should identify either the Southern Alps in the southern part of South Island, or the central region of South Island.

4. **Citing Text Evidence** the kiwi

5. **Informative/Explanatory Writing** Students' paragraphs should include information from the lesson describing landscapes, ecosystems, climates, or other features of either Australia or New Zealand. Example: New Zealand would be a fascinating place to visit because it has so many different types of land features within such a small area. Visitors could take advantage of New Zealand's miles of rivers to canoe or kayak through beautiful valleys, canyons, grasslands, and forests. The enormous Southern Alps would be an amazing place to hike or ski. Those who enjoy nature will be amazed at the many types of plants and unusual animals living in New Zealand, especially the flightless kiwi bird, the weta, and the mighty kauri tree.

C Critical Thinking Skills

Making Connections Explain that scientists believe kangaroos did not start out hopping, but over time, when rain forests dried up and water was scarce, they developed long hind legs that allowed them to access water quickly.
Ask: How might other animals of the region adapted? *(Students' answers will vary but should name an animal of the region and how it may have adapted to the environmental changes.)* **Logical/Mathematical**

W Writing Skills

Narrative Tell students they will act as nature tour guides for visitors through a region of either Australia or New Zealand. Students should use the information from the text about plants and animals in Australia and New Zealand to write a narration for their tour. Encourage students to visualize the tour as they write, citing specific flora and fauna along the way. Students may wish to conduct additional research for their tour information. Ask volunteers to share their essays with the class. **Verbal/Linguistic, Intrapersonal**

Content Background Knowledge

Kangaroos have been an important resource of Australia for centuries. Indigenous people have hunted kangaroos for thousands of years. European explorers who came to the continent in the late 1700s also hunted kangaroos.

The Australian government has controlled commercial hunting of kangaroos by imposing strict regulations. Though Australia exports kangaroo meat and skin to other countries, including the United States, it is illegal to transport live kangaroos except in some instances, such as for trade between zoos.

CLOSE & REFLECT

Comparing and Contrasting Guide a whole class discussion to review how the physical geography of Australia and New Zealand are similar and different.

ANSWERS, p. 423

☑ **READING PROGRESS CHECK** The isolation of Australia and New Zealand from other landmasses meant that the plants and animals adapted to their own unique environments.
CRITICAL THINKING Millions of years ago, the landmass that became Australia separated from other landmasses. The animals living in Australia developed in isolation, separated from living things on other landmasses. New species unique to Australia eventually emerged.

ENGAGE

Bellringer Tell students that this lesson discusses the history of Australia and New Zealand. Have students preview the lesson by skimming the headings and Guiding Questions and by looking at the images. Help students make connections to the history of Australia and New Zealand by drawing parallels to what they know about the history of the United States. **Ask: Based on the headings and images in this lesson, what similarities do you notice between the history of Australia and New Zealand and the history of the United States?** *(Students may note that, like Native Americans in the United States, Aboriginal people of Australia and the Maori of New Zealand inhabited the region before settlers arrived. They may also note that, just like in the United States, the English set up colonies in Australia and New Zealand.)*

TEACH & ASSESS

V Visual Skills

Creating Visuals Have pairs visualize the information about early humans in Australia. As one student slowly reads each sentence in the section, "Aboriginals of Australia," have their partner relate the information visually by creating an illustration depicting human migration to Australia. After students have had time to read the paragraph and create their visuals, assess their understanding. **Ask: The continent of Australia is surrounded by water, so how were early humans able to get there from New Guinea?** *(When the first humans came to Australia, the sea levels were much lower, so more land was exposed. This allowed early humans to walk on a land bridge from New Guinea to Australia.)* **Visual/Spatial**

R Reading Skills

Determining Word Meanings Remind students that the word *aboriginal* comes from the Latin word *aborigine*, which means "original inhabitants." **Ask: How did the first Aboriginal people get food?** *(They gathered fruit, roots, and other plant parts and hunted animals. They developed the boomerang to stun their prey.)* **AL** **ELL** **Verbal/Linguistic**

ANSWER, p. 424

Taking Notes Sample notes: **Cause:** Humans migrated from New Guinea to Australia; **Effect:** Aboriginal peoples settled in locations across Australia; **Cause:** The Maori hunted the flightless moa for food. **Effect:** The moa became extinct; **Cause:** Captain James Cook claimed Australia for Great Britain. **Effect:** British colonists and convicts came to Australia and took lands from the native Aboriginal peoples; **Cause:** Colonists brought nonnative species such as rabbits and dogs to Australia and New Zealand. **Effect:** Native animals and plants were killed and introduced species multiplied.

---

networks

There's More Online!

☑ **IMAGES** Aboriginal Rock Paintings
☑ **MAP** History of Australia
☑ **TIME LINE** Australian Gold Rush
☑ **VIDEO**

Reading HELPDESK CCSS

Academic Vocabulary RH.6-8.4
(Tier Two Words)
- **unify**

Content Vocabulary RH.6-8.4
(Tier Three Words)
- **boomerang**
- **dingo**
- **tikanga**
- **kapahaka**
- **station**
- **introduced species**
- **dominion**

TAKING NOTES: Key Ideas and Details RH.6-8.5, RH.6-8.7

Determine Cause and Effect As you read about the histories of Australia and New Zealand, use a graphic organizer like this one to take notes about the causes and effects of human settlement in the region.

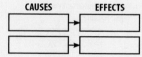

CAUSES		EFFECTS
☐	→	☐
☐	→	☐

424

Lesson 2
History of the Region

ESSENTIAL QUESTION · *Why does conflict develop?*

IT MATTERS BECAUSE
Australia and New Zealand have made many advances in democratic government and have close ties to the United States.

First People

GUIDING QUESTION How and when did the first humans settle in Australia and New Zealand?

Ancient tools, cave paintings, rock art, and fossilized human remains provide clues that humans traveled to this region from other places on Earth. There is still some debate, however, about where the early people came from and when they first arrived in the region. Most scientists agree that the lands of Australia and New Zealand existed for millions of years before the first human settlers arrived.

Aboriginals of Australia

V Fossil evidence shows that humans began migrating to Australia at least 50,000 years ago. At that time, much of Earth's surface water was frozen, and sea levels were hundreds of feet lower than they are today. Areas that are underneath the ocean today were exposed above the surface of the water. This created land bridges and peninsulas over which groups of people left New Guinea and walked across to Australia. Other migrating groups from the Asian mainland may have traveled longer distances by boat. These early people journeyed far and wide across the land, even to the island of Tasmania. In time, humans settled the entire Australian continent.

R The first people of Australia are known as Aboriginal people. They generally lived a hunter-gatherer lifestyle. These early people survived by gathering fruit, roots, and other

(l to r) ©Bill Bachman/Alamy; ©Stapleton Collection/Corbis; Frans Lemmens/The Image Bank/Getty Images; SuperStock/Getty Images; The Print Collector/Alamy

---

networks   *Online Teaching Options*

VIDEO

Ancient Lives—Aborigines

Analyzing Visuals Use this video about the history of the Aborigines in Australia to introduce the lesson. Ask students to share what they learned from the video and if anything surprised them. Have students write one or two sentences describing an interesting fact they learned. Have students consider how colonization by the English might have affected the region. **Verbal/Linguistic**

See page 413D for other online activities.

BBC Motion Gallery Education

plant parts for food and by hunting animals. They developed a flat, bent, wooden weapon called a **boomerang**. Hunters threw the L-shaped boomerang to stun their prey. If the boomerang missed, it curved and sailed back to the hunter.

Early Settlements

Some hunter-gatherers were nomadic, moving from place to place, following animals or searching for water sources. Nomadic people did not practice farming. The only domesticated animals they owned were dingoes. **Dingoes** are a species of domestic dog first brought to Australia from Asia about 4,000 years ago. Today, wild dingoes roam free in the Outback and other parts of Australia. There is controversy regarding the animal's suitability as a pet.

Other Aboriginal people settled permanently in one location. Some settled in the rain forests of the northeast. Some made their homes in the mountains of the Great Dividing Range. Others traveled as far as the humid lands of the southeast and the island of Tasmania. Some even learned to live in the harsh, dry lands of the Outback. Eventually, Aboriginal settlers began farming the land.

Aboriginal Culture

Traditional Aboriginal culture takes many forms. Aboriginal peoples living in different parts of Australia developed their own languages, religions, traditions, and ways of life. It was difficult for separate tribes of native people to communicate with one another, because about 400 different languages were spoken across Australia. Yet, many of Australia's native people share a number of common beliefs and cultural traditions. Aboriginal culture is closely connected to the natural world. Australia's native cultures have traditional beliefs about the creation of Earth and of plants and animals. They use song, dance, poetry, drama, storytelling, and visual arts to retell the creation story known as "the Dreaming" or "the Dreamtime." The creation story tells how the Spirit Ancestors created the world around them, the universe, and the laws of life, death, and society.

The concept of Dreaming is central to many of Australia's native cultures' social structures and belief systems. Music, dance, storytelling, and other art forms remain an important part of Aboriginal culture.

An Anangu woman prepares wood for carving. In addition to wood carving, Australia's aboriginal artists work in media such as painting on leaves, rock carving, fabric printing, and sandpainting. The Anangu people live in an area extending from Uluru in Northern Territory to the Nullarbor Plain in southwestern Australia.

▶ **CRITICAL THINKING**
Determining Central Ideas What do the Aborigines see as the purpose of their art forms?

©Bill Bachman/Alamy

Chapter 14 **425**

IMAGE

360° View: Aboriginal Rock Paintings

Making Connections Use this 360° image of Aboriginal rock paintings to discuss the culture of the Aborigines in this region. Discuss the connection between nature and the beliefs of Aboriginal people. To help students make the connection, draw parallels to Native American beliefs and their strong ties to the natural world. **Naturalist**

See page 413D for other online activities.

©Pete Atkinson/Getty Images

C Critical Thinking Skills

Comparing and Contrasting Have students review the information about Aboriginal people who were nomadic and those who settled in one location. Have partners collaborate to identify how the groups were similar and different. Encourage students to create a visual representation of the information, such as a Venn diagram. Then, use the following questions to help students identify the main ideas about the emergence of Aboriginal cultures. **Ask:**

- **What animal did nomadic people domesticate?** *(dingoes)*
- **Why do you think there is a controversy about dingoes being suitable as pets?** *(Possible answer: Dingoes roam free in the wild so they may still pose a threat to humans.)*
- **Where did some Aboriginal people settle?** *(They settled in the rain forests of the northeast, in the mountains of the Great Dividing Range, in the southeast, on the island of Tasmania, and even in the Outback.)* **Verbal/Linguistic**

W Writing Skills

Informative/Explanatory Have students discuss some of the challenges that would arise in having 400 different spoken languages. *(Challenges include communicating for purposes of commerce, social events or interaction, and negotiating agreements related to each group's rights to the resources in an area.)*

Point out that even with this communication challenge, many of Australia's indigenous people share beliefs and traditions. For homework, have students conduct research to write an informative essay using one of the following ideas from the text as a prompt:

- **Aboriginal culture is closely connected to nature.**
- **The concept of Dreaming is central to many Aboriginal peoples' social structures and belief systems.**
- **Music, dance, storytelling, and other art forms remain important to Aboriginal culture.**

Tell students their essays should include relevant facts and supporting examples to convey important information found in their research. **BL** **Verbal/Linguistic**

ANSWER, p. 425

CRITICAL THINKING The Aborigines use art forms to express their closeness to nature and to retell their creation story known as "the Dreaming."

C Critical Thinking Skills

Making Connections Ask a volunteer to locate New Zealand and the Polynesian islands on a globe or world map. Explain that historians believe that early humans travelled to the North Island of New Zealand in canoes. **Ask: Why do you think the first Maori settlements were on North Island?** *(That was the island geographically closest to Polynesia where early people sailed from in canoes.)* **AL** **Logical/Mathematical**

V Visual Skills

Creating Visuals Have students work in pairs to create a poster that depicts information about the Maori way of life. After students have had time to read the section, "The Maori of New Zealand," and create their visuals, assess their understanding. **Ask:**

- **What did the Maori hunt? Why?** *(They hunted wild animals, including huge birds that did not fly called moa, because they were easy prey.)*
- **Why was boating important to the Maori life?** *(They used boats for transportation and as vehicles for warfare.)* **Visual/Spatial**

R Reading Skills

Summarizing Have students work in pairs to summarize the section titled, "Maori Culture." Then, **ask:**

- **What is at the center of Maori culture?** *(tikanga, traditional Maori customs and traditions that have been passed down through generations)*
- **What is an example of how the Maori belief system is part of everyday life?** *(Possible answer: Maori apply tikanga to their everyday life, including how they build homes, prepare food and medicine, honor social customs, and create art.)*
- **What American artform might be similar to kapahaka? How might it be different?** *(Possible answer: Musicals, in the movies and in live performances, include music, dance, singing, and dramatic expression. Musicals might be different from kapahaka because musicals are not necessarily a traditional form of entertainment in American culture.)* **Verbal/ Linguistic, Auditory/Musical**

The Maori of New Zealand

The first humans to live on the islands of New Zealand were the Maori. The Maori people came to New Zealand much later than the Aboriginal people came to Australia. Historians believe that sometime between A.D. 800 and 1300, humans began traveling in canoes from Polynesian islands such as Tahiti to New Zealand. The Maori built villages and lived in tribal groups led by chiefs. Tribes traded and went to war with other Maori tribes. Nearly all early Maori settlements were located on North Island.

The Maori way of life had minimal impact on the environment. They fished, gathered plants, and hunted wild animals for food. Huge, flightless birds called moa were easy prey and became an important part of the Maori diet. Eventually, the Maori hunted all 10 species of moa to extinction. In time, the Maori introduced food crops such as taro and yams. Boating and diving were important parts of Maori life. Canoes carved from the trunks of massive trees were used for transportation and also as vehicles for warfare.

Maori Culture

The Maori have a spiritual belief system based on the concept that all life in the universe is connected. At the heart of Maori culture is *tikanga*. **Tikanga** are traditional Maori customs and traditions passed down through generations. Maori tradition says that tikanga come from *tika*, the "things that are true," which began with all creation at the dawn of time. According to tikanga, the past is always in front of an individual, there to teach and guide that person. The future is behind the individual, hidden and unknown. Tikanga is part of everyday Maori life, from building homes and preparing food and medicine to social customs and arts, such as *kapahaka*. **Kapahaka** is a traditional Maori art form combining music, dance, singing, and facial expressions.

Maori warriors sail in a war canoe below one of their lookout points on the North Island coast. To get to their battlefields, the Maori built large war canoes called *waka taua*. Each vessel held about 100 people and was up to 130 feet (40 m) in length. Viewed as sacred, the war canoes were elaborately carved with images of deities and ancestors.

▶ **CRITICAL THINKING**
Analyzing Why do you think the early Maori carved sacred images on their war canoes?

©Stapleton Collection/Corbis

network s **Online Teaching Options**

MAP

The Maori of New Zealand

Discussing Display the map to students and discuss the movement of the Maori to New Zealand. Use the map to determine how far the Maori travelled by canoe to reach New Zealand. Guide a class discussion about the Maori people and why boating was an important aspect of their lives. **ELL** **Interpersonal**

See page 413D for other online activities.

One of the most important parts of any culture is language. Before Europeans arrived in New Zealand, the Maori people spoke different dialects of the same language. When New Zealand was colonized by the British, many Maori began speaking English. Over time, fewer and fewer people spoke the traditional Maori language, even in their homes. By the mid-1900s, the language had become so rare it was in danger of dying out. The efforts of Maori leaders and activists brought the Maori language back from the brink of extinction. During the 1970s and 1980s, the Maori language was reborn, as language recovery programs and schools across New Zealand taught younger generations to speak Maori. In 1987 Maori became an official language of New Zealand.

A unique part of Maori culture is the sacred practice of facial tattooing. Maori tattoos are permanent decorations on the body made by cutting designs into the skin, then rubbing black soot into the cuts. Traditionally, Maori boys were tattooed during puberty as a rite of passage into manhood.

Each individual's tattoo was unique, showing his ancestry, status in the tribe, military rank, profession, and family relationships. Maori tattooing is still practiced in New Zealand as an expression of cultural pride and identity. Other Maori art forms such as weaving, painting, and wood carving are also important parts of past and present Maori culture.

☑ **READING PROGRESS CHECK**

Describing How did the early hunter-gatherers live?

Colonial Times

GUIDING QUESTION *What happened when Europeans came to Australia and New Zealand?*

Australia and New Zealand were colonized by the British. However, the British were not the first Europeans to visit the region. Explorers from other European countries had been sailing around Australia and landing on its shores for hundreds of years before the British arrived.

A Maori meeting house in New Zealand's Waitangi area displays detailed wooden carvings, all done by hand. Maori meeting houses have long served as centers for important community events and ceremonies.

▶ **CRITICAL THINKING**
Analyzing How do Maori meeting houses reflect Maori beliefs about their society?

Frans Lemmens/The Image Bank/Getty Images

Chapter 14 **427**

Comparing Aborigines and Maori

Diagramming Display the interactive graphic organizer to students. As a class, review the cultures of the Aborigines and the Maori and use the graphic organizer to compare these two cultures. Then have students work in pairs to create and fill in their own Venn diagrams that compare the two groups. **AL** **Visual/Spatial, Logical/Mathematical**

See page 413D for other online activities.

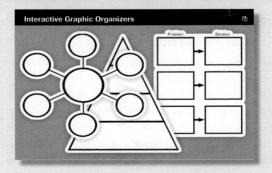

Interactive Graphic Organizers
Problem   Solution

C **Critical Thinking Skills**

Determining Cause and Effect Discuss the evolution of language in New Zealand's history. **Ask:**

- **What happened to the traditional Maori language after British colonists arrived in New Zealand?** *(The Maori began speaking English. Over time, the traditional Maori language nearly died out because fewer and fewer people were speaking it.)*
- **What happened to the Maori language in the 1970s and 1980s? Why?** *(The traditional Maori language was reborn because of language recovery programs. New Zealand schools began teaching younger generations to speak Maori.)*
- **What was the effect of these events?** *(Maori became an official language of New Zealand.)*
- **Why do you think it was important to the Maori leaders to bring back the Maori language?** *(Possible answer: Language is an important part of a culture. They did not want to lose their culture.)* **Verbal/Linguistic**

T **Technology Skills**

Making Presentations Culminate your discussion about Maori culture by assigning each of several student groups a different aspect of Maori culture such as art, music, hunting/fishing, creation traditions, tattooing, and so on. Assign the following activity as homework.

Tell students they will conduct online research to find information for a presentation about their aspect of Maori culture. You may wish to direct students to specific Web sites, such as: http://www.teara.govt.nz/en, reminding students that sites with the suffix ".gov" are often more reliable than many tourism Web sites. As students conduct research, tell them to evaluate the Web sites they used to compare their findings with information presented in the text. Tell students to include visual and audio clips or to create visuals, posters, and even face-painting to enhance their presentations. Students' presentations should include a paragraph summarizing their evaluation of the Web site(s) used in conducting their research. **Auditory/Musical, Interpersonal**

ANSWERS, p. 427

☑ **READING PROGRESS CHECK** They were nomads, moving from place to place, following animals or searching for water.

CRITICAL THINKING The meeting houses reflect the importance of community life. Traditionally, Maori tribal groups lived in villages. Meeting houses were used for community members to gather, celebrate, and make decisions as a group under their chief. Meeting houses also demonstrated the Maori's building and artistic skills.

V Visual Skills

Creating Time Lines To help students understand the sequence of events that occurred regarding colonization of Australia and New Zealand, have them create a time line with key dates and events from the text. Organize students into groups, and assign each group one of the following time periods for each country: 1600s, 1700s, or 1800s.

Provide students with large sheets of newsprint or poster board. As students read this page, have them collaborate to create a visual time line that depicts key historical events that occurred during their assigned century and country. Encourage students to add to their time lines as they read the remainder of this lesson. When students have completed their time lines, have them connect the time lines for a classroom display and use as a visual review tool. **Visual/Spatial**

C Critical Thinking Skills

Making Inferences Help students understand the significance of Australia's use as a prison colony. **Ask:**

- **How do you think Australian people felt about having so many prisoners sent to live there?** (They probably did not like having the prisons built there.)
- **How do you think Britains felt about having prisoners sent all the way to Australia?** (Some people may have been happy because they did not want more prisons near where they lived. Others would have been very unhappy about it because they would never be able to see a prisoner again.)

Tell students that in the early 1800s, British officials offered "tickets of leave" as a reward for prisoners who showed good behavior. This led to reduced sentences for many prisoners, who eventually were able to acquire farm land and become productive members of society. **Ask: How do you think the system using "tickets of leave" affected prisoners?** (Students might infer that the tickets of leave likely served as a better way to motivate prisoners.) **BL Interpersonal**

R Reading Skills

Creating Visuals To help students comprehend the series of events presented on this page and the next, have them work in pairs to read and visualize the information. **Ask: How is the information in these paragraphs presented?** (sequentially, by showing cause and effect of different events) **AL Visual/Spatial**

Europeans Come to the Region

V During the 1600s, 1700s, and 1800s, Dutch, Spanish, French, and Portuguese explorers visited Oceania. Some of them mapped Australia's coastline. Some even went ashore to explore coastal areas and search for supplies. In 1642 the Dutch East India Company sent Abel Tasman on a mission to sail around the Australian continent. During this voyage of discovery, Tasman circled the island of Tasmania and then sighted the coast of New Zealand. More than a century would pass, however, before Europeans started colonizing the region.

British Australia

C Perhaps the most well-known British explorer was the sailor Captain James Cook. He carried out three voyages in the 1760s and 1770s. Following Cook's explorations, the British government prepared to send settlers to the wild, unexplored lands of Australia. Most of the first colonists sent to Australia did not go by choice. In 1788 a group of 11 British ships, known as the First Fleet, landed on Australia's east coast. The crowded ships carried 778 convicted criminals from the British Isles. The First Fleet also included 250 soldiers and government officials. This was the first shipment of about 160,000 convicts sent to Australia during the next 80 years, due to a lack of space in England's prisons. Living conditions were terrible, and punishments were harsh for convicts held in Australia's cruel, filthy prisons. For many years, Australia was known to most of the world as a prison colony.

On April 29, 1770, Captain James Cook made his first landing in Australia at Botany Bay, near present-day Sydney. This imagined view of the landing was painted by E. Phillips Fox, an Australian artist of the early 1900s.

R Beginning in the late 1700s, a settlement began to form in Sydney. Colonists were slow to come to the area, but in time, Sydney grew into a busy center of trade and industry. Settling the inland areas of Australia did not happen for many years. Only a few people other than escaping criminals dared to venture into the rough Outback. By the 1880s, however, most of the continent had been explored by Europeans.

In 1851 an English prospector found gold near Bathurst, New South Wales. Soon after, thousands of people from all over Australia were camped in the area, digging for gold. Gold was discovered in other parts of Australia, and word spread across the globe. People

428 Chapter 14

SuperStock/Getty Images

netw⦾rks — *Online Teaching Options*

MAP

History of Australia

Interpreting Use the map and time line with students to help them understand the significance of events in Australian history. Guide a discussion about the region's early history and how that history may have impacted later events. Discuss with students the impact of the colonization of Australia by the British and its impact on the Aborigines. In small groups, have students write a brief essay about one of the lasting effects of an event that happened in Australia's history. **BL Interpersonal**

See page 413D for other online activities.

from around the world flocked to Australia at a rate of 90,000 per year, all hoping to find a bounty of gold. Prospectors came from as far away as England, Ireland, China, and the United States.

Australia began to grow for other reasons, as well. When resources such as coal, tin, and copper were discovered, workers came for mining jobs. Business owners started and built shops and hotels wherever towns sprang up, and there were people to spend money. Small towns grew into cities. Farmers planted crops in Australia's most fertile areas. Ranchers brought sheep and cattle from overseas, and Australia's ranching industry was born. Vast ranches called **stations** covered millions of acres in the Outback and other areas. Today, millions of sheep and cattle live on ranches all across Australia.

Challenges and Conflict

As humans from other parts of the world moved to Australia, they brought animals with them. Ranchers brought dogs for guarding and herding sheep. Wealthy landowners imported European rabbits to hunt for sport. In an effort to rid sugarcane fields of a destructive beetle, farmers brought in huge, poisonous cane toads. These and other nonnative animal species caused major problems. Rabbits multiplied quickly to a population of 1 billion. They ate so much grass and so many wildflowers that entire areas were left bare. The cane toads also multiplied, crowding out and killing native animal species. Animals that are not native to an area but are brought from other places are called **introduced species**. It is impossible to estimate how much damage has been done to Australia's environment by introduced species. Some introduced species are now under control, but others continue to cause problems for humans and native animals.

British settlers built their homes and farms all over Australia, often forcing native Aboriginal people off their land. Thousands of Aboriginal families and tribes were forced to leave lands where their ancestors had lived for generations.

The Print Collector/Alamy

A gold prospector sits outside a hut he built in the settlement of Gippsland, Australia. During the late 1800s, gold discoveries in southeastern Australia drew many prospectors to the area.
▶ **CRITICAL THINKING**
Describing How did the discovery of gold and other mineral resources contribute to Australia's development?

W Writing Skills

Narrative Direct students' attention to the photograph of the prospector. Have students use the photo as a launch point for a narrative essay about what life was like in southeastern Australia during the 1800s. Encourage students to develop imagined events based on facts presented in the image, caption, and text. Essays should include relevant descriptive details and sensory language to convey events. Ask volunteers to share their essays with the class. **Verbal/Linguistic**

W

C Critical Thinking Skills

Making Connections Help students understand the connection between the fairly quick change from Australia as a prison colony to a nation that changed dramatically after the discovery of gold. Share the following information with students:

• In 1852, roughly 370,000 immigrants came to Australia. **Ask: How do you think this impacted Australia's economy?** *(It probably led to shortages of goods and services which created inflation. It also probably led to the creation of many new businesses.)*

• By 1871, Australia's population had tripled and the number of immigrants now exceeded the number of prisoners. **Ask: How do you think this population change impacted Australian society?** *(Possible answer: The various immigrants would have different skills and would also have come with the intention of making a life for themselves. Their views and ideas would have impacted Australian society.)* **Interpersonal**

R Reading Skills

Determining Central Ideas Have students review the information about the impact of introduced species. **Ask: Why were animals not native to the area brought to Australia?** *(to guard and herd sheep, to hunt for sport, and to prevent destructive bugs from ruining crops)* **AL** **Verbal/Linguistic**

TIME LINE

Australian Gold Rush

Determining Cause and Effect Use the time line about the Australian gold rush to discuss how the desire for gold affected the population of Australia. Have students write a paragraph about how the discovery of gold and other gems in southeastern Australia affected the region. **Logical/Mathematical**

See page 413D for other online activities.

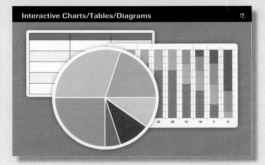
Interactive Charts/Tables/Diagrams

ANSWER, p. 429

CRITICAL THINKING Mineral discoveries brought more settlers to Australia and led to the rise of mining and other industries that boosted Australia's economy and added to the country's wealth.

C1 Critical Thinking Skills

Comparing and Contrasting Have students read the first two paragraphs of the section, "British New Zealand." Guide a brief discussion to begin making connections between the European settlers in the United States and their impact on Native Americans to British settlers and their impact on New Zealand. Remind students that in the 1830s, Native Americans were forced off land in the southeastern part of the United States and had to walk thousands of miles to specially designated areas. This forced relocation is referred to as the Trail of Tears.

Have students consider the impact of foreign settlers on New Zealand's Maori population. **Ask: What similarities can you think of between the way European settlers treated Native Americans in America and the way they treated the Maori in New Zealand?** *(Students' responses may vary but might include that the experiences of Native Americans and the Maori were probably similar because both groups were forced off land and their populations dwindled.)*

Have students consider whether the United States and New Zealand governments should provide restitution, or payment for losses, to Native Americans and the Maori people. *(Students may discuss the fact that it is difficult to determine a dollar value for the losses because of inflation and the various natural resources that might have existed on the land. Students might also say that native people lost more than land—they lost their homes and their way of life. In addition, many of the people died.)*

BL Logical/Mathematical, Interpersonal

C2 Critical Thinking Skills

Suggesting a Solution Read the last paragraph in the section, "British New Zealand," aloud to students. Have volunteers explain the phrases *introduced species* and *survival of entire species*. Invite students to discuss any species they know of that have been introduced to an area and are causing problems with destroying natural habitats or threatening the survival of other species. Then have each student create a list of suggestions that could be used to solve the issue of introduced species that have resulted in more harm than good. **Naturalist**

ANSWER, p. 430

CRITICAL THINKING Participation in the world wars made Australians, who often felt isolated, more aware of the global community, more self-confident, and less dependent on Britain, the homeland of most of their ancestors. As a result, Australia was able to move toward complete independence and develop contacts on their own with other nations.

In both world wars, Australia sent its soldiers to foreign battlefields in support of the British Empire. The heroism and sacrifices of Australian soldiers in these global conflicts attracted the attention of people in other parts of the world.
▶ **CRITICAL THINKING**
Analyzing How did involvement in both world wars change the way Australians viewed themselves and their country?

©Bettmann/Corbis

Academic Vocabulary

unify to unite; to join together; to make into a unit or a whole

European diseases and violence steadily reduced the Aboriginal population. The survivors had no choice but to live on rugged lands that European settlers did not want.

British New Zealand

Captain Cook explored the islands of New Zealand during the early 1770s. Cook reported to the British government that the fertile islands had many valuable natural resources and would be good places to colonize. Soon, British colonists and British, American, and French traders and whalers built settlements on North Island. At first, most relations between the Maori and foreign settlers were peaceful. In 1840 the British government, ruled by Queen Victoria, convinced Maori leaders to sign the Treaty of Waitangi. This treaty gave legal ownership and control of New Zealand to Great Britain, but it guaranteed protection and certain land rights to the Maori.

As Europeans continued to arrive in New Zealand, the Maori saw more and more of their land taken by foreign settlers. Maori society and ways of life weakened when British settlers brought new methods of farming and other features of European culture. Conflict between the Maori and British continued sporadically, until 1872 when many Maori were killed and they lost most of their land to the British.

As was happening in Australia, businesses, industries, farms, and sheep ranches were built across New Zealand. Sheep ranching changed the land, as native scrubland and forests were cleared to make pastures for livestock. Introduced species, such as rabbits, goats, pigs, deer, rodents, and feral cats, began destroying natural habitats. They killed many native animals and threatened the survival of entire species.

Independent Countries

In 1901 the six British colonies set up in Australia took action to **unify** as a federation. This action formed a political alliance between New South Wales, Queensland, Northern Territory, Western Australia, South Australia, and Tasmania. The former colonies set up the Commonwealth of Australia. The new country was a

---

networks *Online Teaching Options*

IMAGE

Australia in World War II

Collaborating Display the interactive image of Australia in World War II and use it to discuss the participation of Australia in this major world event. With a partner, ask students to consider how Australia's involvement in the war affected its relations with New Zealand and the United States, whose soldiers fought alongside Australian soldiers in the war. Have the pairs share their answers with the class. **Interpersonal**

See page 413D for other online activities.

©Pete Atkinson/Getty Images

dominion, a largely self-governing country within the British Empire. Like Canada, Australia had a form of government that blended a U.S.-style federal system with a British-style parliamentary democracy.

Throughout the 1800s, New Zealand residents pushed independence from Great Britain. The 1852 New Zealand Constitution Act recognized local governments in the six provinces, but New Zealand was still a long way from independence. In 1907 the British government named New Zealand an independent dominion with a British-style parliamentary democracy. Even before independence, New Zealand had made a number of political advances. In 1893 it became the first country in the world to legally recognize women's right to vote.

The Region in Contemporary Times

Australia and New Zealand were pulled into World War I and World War II through their ties to Great Britain. During World War II, Australian, New Zealand, and U.S. soldiers fought together in the Pacific region. This alliance created closer ties among the three countries.

After World War II, Australia became completely independent. Australia loosened ties with Britain and established closer ties to the United States and Asia. In 1951 Australia, New Zealand, and the United States signed a mutual security treaty called the ANZUS Pact. The treaty was meant to guarantee protection and cooperation among the three countries in case of military threats in the Pacific region.

In recent years, a huge increase in Asian immigration has led to more diversity in Australia and New Zealand. Today more people of Asian background live in New Zealand than native Maori. The governments of both countries have also continued to address Aboriginal and Maori rights and social concerns. The native people of Australia and New Zealand and their supporters continue to work for justice and equal rights under the law.

☑ READING PROGRESS CHECK

Determining Central Ideas How and when did Australia and New Zealand become independent nations?

 FOLDABLES Study Organizer

Include this lesson's information in your Foldable®.

 Australia / New Zealand

LESSON 2 REVIEW (CCSS)

Reviewing Vocabulary (Tier Three Words)
1. Are *dingoes* native to Australia? RH.6-8.4

Answering the Guiding Questions
2. *Identifying* For whom was the island of Tasmania named? RH.6-8.2

3. *Identifying* Name one native species and one introduced species in Australia. RH.6-8.2

4. *Determining Central Ideas* In what ways were the colonization of Australia and the colonization of New Zealand alike? RH.6-8.2

5. *Narrative Writing* Imagine you are a young Australian Aboriginal or New Zealand Maori living during the time the first Europeans came to your homeland. Write a few paragraphs telling how you feel about the arrival of these foreign settlers. Whenever possible, include details from the lesson in your narrative. WHST.6-8.4, WHST.6-8.9

Chapter 14 **431**

LESSON 2 REVIEW ANSWERS

Reviewing Vocabulary

1. No; dingoes were first brought to Australia from Asia about 4,000 years ago.

Answering the Guiding Questions

2. **Identifying** Abel Tasman

3. **Identifying** Answers should mention one native species, such as koalas, bird-wing butterflies, pygmy possums, alpine grasshoppers, saltwater crocodiles, goanna lizards, tiger snakes, funnel-web spiders, magpies, bandicoots, kangaroos, platypuses, or echidnas; and one introduced species, such as dogs, rabbits, or cane toads.

4. **Determining Central Ideas** Answers should mention similarities such as harvesting resources, land use for farming and ranching, and land conflicts with indigenous people and resulting human rights issues.

5. **Narrative Writing** Students' writing should be written from the perspective of an Aboriginal or Maori. The writing should be based on facts and details from the lesson. Paragraphs should also express clearly the writer's feelings toward the newcomers.

C Critical Thinking Skills

Sequencing Help students organize information about the quest for independence in New Zealand. Remind students to add the information to the visual time lines they created earlier in the lesson. **Ask: What key historical event occurred in New Zealand before the nation gained its independence?** *(It became the first country in the world to legally recognize women's right to vote in 1893.)* **Logical/Mathematical**

T Technology Skills

Researching on the Internet Organize students into groups of five or six, and have them choose either Aboriginal or Maori rights to research online. Assign the following activity as homework.

Tell students their research should focus on what has been done by the Australian and New Zealand governments to address Aboriginal and Maori rights and social issues. In conducting their research, students should be sure to note the accuracy of of Web sites used to gather information. Tell students they will "produce" a talk show titled "Past and Progress" in which a host interviews historians and representatives from the Aboriginal and Maori groups. Student "hosts" should prepare a list of questions relating to each group. Students acting as group representatives should be prepared to discuss their past and how much progress has occurred to improve their rights.

Allow time for groups to prepare and present their talk shows. Following each group's presentation, allow the "studio audience" to ask questions of panelists. **Kinesthetic, Interpersonal**

CLOSE & REFLECT

Organizing Have students work in pairs to create a three-column chart labeled *Native People, Colonial Times,* and *Conflict.* Charts should have two rows labeled *Australia* and *New Zealand.* As a lesson review, have students complete the chart with information from the lesson.

ANSWER, p. 431

☑ **READING PROGRESS CHECK** Australia federated in 1901, but remained tied to the British monarchy and Parliament until after WWII. New Zealand became an independent dominion in 1907, but did not gain full independence from British rule until 1947.

ENGAGE

Bellringer Review with students the geographical location of Australia and New Zealand in relation to the rest of the world. Explain that a flight from New York heading west to Melbourne, Australia, takes about 22 hours. Because of traveling across time zones, if you leave on a Saturday, you would get to Australia on Monday. Returning from Melbourne to New York, however, you might arrive about an hour after you left! Calling might be easier, but the difference is about 17 hours, so if you call from New York at 3 P.M. on a Friday, it will be Saturday afternoon in New Zealand. Have students imagine what it would be like to actually live in Australia or New Zealand. **Ask: If you and your family moved to Australia or New Zealand, what do you think would be some pros and cons of living there?** *(Students' answers will vary but might include pros such as experiencing a new culture and already knowing the language; cons might be missing friends who would be very far away and in a much different time zone.)*

Explain that the cultures and lifestyles of people who live in Australia and New Zealand are similar to those in the United States. Then read aloud the "It Matters Because" section. As students read, tell them to think about the Essential Question: *What makes a culture unique?*

TEACH & ASSESS

Ⅴ Visual Skills

Creating Graphs Have pairs review the information about the populations of New Zealand and Australia. Have them use the percentage figures to create a circle graph to visually display the population makeup of each nation. **Ask: How does each nation's population contribute to its unique culture?** *(Students' answers may vary but might include that in Australia there is more of a European influence because of its high percentage of people of European descent, whereas the cultural makeup of New Zealand is much more diverse.)* **Visual/Spatial, Logical/Mathematical**

ANSWER, p. 432

Taking Notes Natural resources: Australia—coal, iron, silver and gold, natural gas oil; **New Zealand**—geothermal energy, farmland and livestock, minerals, coal, iron ore, natural gas, timber, and limestone. **Economy: Australia**—exporting natural resources, manufacturing, tourism; **New Zealand**—agriculture, manufacturing, exports

---

networks

There's More Online!

☑ **IMAGE** Wool Processing

☑ **SLIDE SHOW** Comparing Football Around the World

☑ **VIDEO**

Reading HELPDESK 〈CCSS〉

Academic Vocabulary RH.6-8.4
- **controversy** (Tier Two Words)

Content Vocabulary RH.6-8.4
(Tier Three Words)
- **bush**
- **didgeridoo**
- **action song**
- **geothermal energy**
- **kiwifruit**
- **lawsuit**

TAKING NOTES: Key Ideas and Details RH.6-8.2, RH.6-8.7

Summarize As you read the lesson, use a graphic organizer like the one below to write a short summary about each of the topics.

Topic	Australia	New Zealand
Natural Resources		
Economy		

432

Lesson 3
Life in Australia and New Zealand

ESSENTIAL QUESTION · *What makes a culture unique?*

IT MATTERS BECAUSE
The people of Australia and New Zealand are working to blend diverse populations successfully.

Life in the Region

GUIDING QUESTION *What is it like to live in Australia and New Zealand?*

European culture exercises the most influence in Australia and New Zealand, but indigenous cultures also play an important role. In recent years, Asian influences have increased in the region.

The People of the Region

Australia and New Zealand are multicultural lands. They have diverse human populations where different cultures, languages, and lifestyles are mixed together. New Zealand has had a diverse population for much of its history. Today, New Zealand's population is about 57 percent European, 12 percent Asian and Pacific Islander, and 8 percent Maori. Other groups account for the rest. Australia's population is much less diverse. About 92 percent of Australians are of European descent, 7 percent are Asian, and 1 percent are Aboriginal and other groups.

Religion and Culture

Christianity is the most common religion in the region. Also practiced in the region are Buddhism, Islam, Hinduism, and native religions. In addition, about 30 percent of the people in the region describe themselves as "nonreligious" or did not state a religious affiliation.

Ⅴ

(l to r) Bradley Kanaris/Getty Images Sport/Getty Images; Bill Bachman/Alamy; Greg Balfour Evans/Alamy; Ian Waldie/Getty Images News/Getty Images; Mark Coote/Bloomberg/Getty Images

---

networks *Online Teaching Options*

VIDEO

Around the World—Eastern Australia

Analyzing Visuals Use the video about the physical geography of Eastern Australia to introduce some of the current issues that are occurring in the region, such as the increase in tourism, the damage to the Great Barrier Reef, and the effects of human-environment interaction. Have students write a paragraph about an aspect of each country in this region that they find intriguing or appealing, or one that they want to know more about. Tell students to think about the images shown in this video as they read the lesson. **AL Verbal/Linguistic**

See page 413E for other online activities.

BBC Motion Gallery Education

English is the official language in Australia. New Zealand has three official languages: English, Maori, and New Zealand sign language. The sign language, the main language used for communicating by members of the deaf community, became an official language in 2006.

The lifestyles in Australia and New Zealand are similar to modern American and British lifestyles. The residents drive cars and use public transportation. In their free time, Australians and New Zealanders shop, go out to eat, watch television, and go to movies. They keep pets such as cats and dogs. Outdoor activities, such as hiking, biking, running, boating, surfing, and swimming, are popular. Watching and playing sports such as football (soccer) and rugby are popular pastimes.

Urban Life

Human populations are unevenly distributed in the region. The vast majority of Australians and New Zealanders live in urban areas. A population map of Australia shows something interesting: The highest populations are concentrated in small land areas, while the smallest populations are scattered throughout the largest land areas. Approximately 89 percent of Australia's people live in cities and suburbs. Most New Zealanders, about 87 percent of the population, live in cities and suburbs.

R

Australia's largest cities are Sydney, Melbourne, Brisbane, and Perth, all with populations of more than 1 million. New Zealand's largest cities are Auckland, Christchurch, and Wellington. Life in these cities is busy. People who live in cities face everyday challenges—noise, traffic, urbanization and crowding, rising housing prices, pollution, and crime. Cities also offer an endless variety of culture, recreation, shops, restaurants, and entertainment. Urban residents must balance the challenges of city life with its many benefits.

V

Rural Life

Life in Australia's rural areas moves at a slower pace. Many individuals and families live alone on huge sheep or cattle stations. These people tend to be isolated, far from towns and other people. Farm life can be hard, with work from sunrise to nighttime. The term **bush** means any large, undeveloped area where few people live. The phrase "in the bush" can refer to any location that is wild, unsettled, and rough, such as the Australian Outback.

W

A player from Australia's Queensland Reds charges forward during a rugby match between the Reds and New Zealand's Canterbury Crusaders at Suncorp Stadium in Brisbane, Australia. Sports like football (soccer) and rugby are popular in Australia and New Zealand.

Chapter 14 **433**

Bradley Kanaris/Getty Images Sport/Getty Images

(l) ©Ocean/Corbis, ©Kryssia Campos/Getty Images, (tr) Erica Simone Leeds, (br) ©JG Photography/Alamy

R Reading Skills

Calculating Have students read the sections, "Urban Life," and, "Rural Life," independently. Review the formula for converting percentages to fractions (write percent divided by 100; simplify). **Ask: If you round out the percentage to an even number, approximately what fraction of Australia's population lives in cities and suburbs?** *(Students should round out 89% to 90%, answering that about 9/10 of the population live in cities and suburbs.)* **Logical/ Mathematical**

V Visual Skills

Creating Maps Have students work in small groups to create a population map of cities in Australia and New Zealand based on information in the text. Students may wish to view examples of population maps online. Have students organize locations or regions and their populations to visually integrate the information from the text. Have students present their maps to the class. **Logical/Mathematical, Visual/Spatial**

W Writing Skills

Narrative Help students understand the sharp contrast between Australia's bustling modern cities and its sparsely populated rural areas. Have them consider which type of place they would prefer to live. Tell students to use what they have learned from the two sections of text to write a short narrative about a day in the life of a person who lives in either area. Students may choose which point of view from which to tell their stories, such as the first-person point of view or third-person narrator. Students may wish to search the Internet for images to help them get ideas for their stories. Have volunteers share their narratives with the class. When students have finished giving presentations, tally the class choices—urban life vs. rural life. Then make a class list of reasons for each of the two choices. Guide a class discussion about the differences between urban and rural life in Australia. **Verbal/Linguistic, Intrapersonal**

SLIDE SHOW

Sports of Australia

Comparing and Contrasting Display the slide show and use each image to discuss and review popular sports that take place in the daily lives of Australians. Have students turn to a partner and discuss the similarities and differences of sports in Australia compared to those in the United States. **Verbal/Linguistic, Interpersonal**

Slide Show

See page 413E for other online activities.

C1 Critical Thinking Skills

Determining Cause and Effect Briefly review cause-and-effect signal words with students, reminding them that words and phrases like *because, due to,* and *as a result* show cause and effect. **Ask:**

- **Why are rural areas in New Zealand not as remote as those in Australia?** *(New Zealand has a smaller land area so farms are closer together and farm families have more contact with their friends and neighbors.)*
- **What has caused a decrease in the populations of New Zealand's small towns?** *(More people have moved from rural areas to cities.)*

As they continue to read this lesson, encourage students to look for other signal words to identify cause-and-effect relationships. **AL** **Verbal/Linguistic**

C2 Critical Thinking Skills

Analyzing Information Briefly discuss some of the nicknames and slangs discussed in the section, "Australian English." **Ask:**

- **What is Australian English?** *(a unique vocabulary made up of Aboriginal words, terms used by settlers, and slang created by modern Australians)*
- **How did New Zealanders get the nickname "Kiwis"?** *(Australian soldiers gave New Zealand soldiers the nickname when they served together during World War I.)*

Have students brainstorm words to describe their town or community based on its features and characteristics as you write them on the board. Then take a class vote as to which nickname best fits. **AL** **Verbal/Linguistic**

T Technology Skills

Researching on the Internet Have students conduct online research to identify specific universities in New Zealand and Australia. Tell students to present a short summary of the schools they find to answer the following questions: **Where is the school located? How big is the school? What do students study at the school?** Have students present their summaries to the class. **Verbal/Linguistic**

ANSWER, p. 434

CRITICAL THINKING In the past, classes were conducted by short wave radio, and students relied on mail service to deliver assignments. Today, the Internet provides quicker and more reliable delivery of assignments. In addition, students are able to see and talk directly with teachers on home computers through a video connection provided by satellite. As a result, students can learn through visual means as well as improve their technology skills.

A student on a remote sheep station in rural Australia takes part in a School of the Air lesson on her home computer. She can see and talk to her teacher by way of a live video cam hookup made possible by a satellite system.
▶ **CRITICAL THINKING**
Analyzing How has electronic technology improved the education of Australian students living in remote areas?

Rural areas in New Zealand are not as remote as those in Australia, because New Zealand has a much smaller land area. Lush pasture lands can feed herds of sheep and cattle on fewer acres than the dry Australian Outback. As a result, New Zealand farms are located closer together, and farm families have more contact with friends and neighbors. Many people in rural areas live near small towns, where they can shop and interact with others. In recent decades, the populations of New Zealand's small towns have been shrinking as more and more rural people move to cities.

Australian English
Australians are famous for their use of nicknames and slang. Australian English, called *Strine,* has a unique vocabulary made up of Aboriginal words, terms used by early settlers, and slang created by modern Australians. Common slang in Australia uses rhymes and word substitutions. For example, "frog and toad" is slang for "road," and "steak and kidney" is a slang nickname for the city of Sydney. The Australian people are nicknamed "Aussies." New Zealanders also have a common nickname. During World War I, New Zealand soldiers and Australian soldiers served together. The Australian soldiers nicknamed the New Zealanders "Kiwis." The nickname is still used today, even by New Zealanders.

Education
The people of Australia and New Zealand take pride in their educational systems. Both countries are home to well-respected universities that rank as some of the best schools in the world.

Bill Bachman/Alamy

434 *Chapter 14*

---

netwⓘrks *Online Teaching Options*

CHART

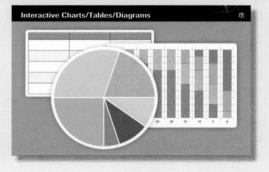

Interactive Charts/Tables/Diagrams

Australian and New Zealand Universities

Analyzing Charts Display the chart and discuss the universities of the region. Have students use the chart to discuss the role of universities in the educational system of Australia and New Zealand. Then have students turn to a person sitting close to them to consider what it might be like to attend a university in Australia or New Zealand. **Verbal/Linguistic, Interpersonal**

See page 413E for other online activities.

Australia is a huge continent with many isolated communities. Many students, especially in the Outback, use modern methods of communication to receive and turn in their lessons. Beginning in the 1950s, classes were conducted via shortwave radio, with students having direct contact with a teacher in town. Previously, students relied on mail service to deliver assignments. Today, the Internet provides quicker and more reliable delivery.

Aboriginal and Maori Culture

Australia and New Zealand have experienced revivals in Aboriginal and Maori cultures. In Australia, some Aboriginal storytellers still use oral tradition to pass down history and myths from one generation to the next. Traditional customs and tools such as the boomerang are still part of daily life. Boomerangs have been used for centuries as tools for hunting, as toys, and as weapons for hand-to-hand combat. Today, boomerangs are used for recreation and contests of skill. Another Aboriginal artifact still used today is a musical instrument called the didgeridoo. The **didgeridoo** is a long wood or bamboo tube that creates an unusual vibrating sound when the player breathes into one end. Aboriginal instruments such as the didgeridoo are part of modern Australian culture, helping to keep traditional music alive.

As part of the modern movement to restore Maori culture in New Zealand, performers created **action songs**. These performances combined body movement with music and singing, often with lyrics that celebrated Maori history and culture.

☑️ **READING PROGRESS CHECK**

Identifying Points of View Based on information in the lesson, decide if the nicknames "Aussie" and "Kiwi" are offensive to Australians and New Zealanders, respectively.

Maori young people in the city of Christchurch, New Zealand, perform an action song. Both men and women perform action songs, using tight arm motions with straight, vibrating hands.
▶ **CRITICAL THINKING**
Determining Central Ideas Why do you think the performance of action songs is important to Maori people today?

Greg Balfour Evans/Alamy

Chapter 14 **435**

IMAGES

360° Views: Sydney Opera House—Outside and Inside

Expressing Use the 360° images to discuss the Sydney Opera House, its location and construction, and its contribution to culture in Australia and New Zealand. Have students write a short paragraph to express why they think the Sydney Opera House is so famous worldwide. Encourage students to visit the Web site for the Sydney Opera House and the current shows that are taking place. **Auditory/Musical**

See page 413E for other online activities.

Interactive Photos

W Writing Skills

Argument Have students recall what they learned about the Outback in Lesson 1. *(rural, isolated, dust storms, etc.)* Then have students review the section, "Education," and consider what it might be like to live and go to school in the Outback. Tell students to write a short argumentative essay supporting or refuting the following statement: **Living in the Outback is isolating for school-aged children and prevents socialization.** Students should logically organize reasons they employ to defend or oppose the statement, supporting their position with evidence from the text. Have volunteers share their essays with the class. **Verbal/Linguistic, Intrapersonal**

R Reading Skills

Determining Word Meanings Point out the word *revivals* in the section, "Aboriginal and Maori Culture." Explain that the word *revive* means "to bring back to life," as in the sentence: *The lifeguard was able to revive the drowning swimmer.* **Ask: How does this definition relate to the meaning of revivals as it is used in the text?** *(Possible answer: This definition relates to the text because Aboriginal and Maori cultures have been "brought back to life.")* **Verbal/Linguistic**

T Technology Skills

Making Presentations Organize students into small groups and assign them an aspect of Aboriginal or Maori culture such as storytelling, traditional customs and tools, clothing, arts, or music. Tell students to prepare an oral report about their assigned cultural aspect based on information found in their research. Students' presentations should include visuals as well as examples of their assigned cultural aspect. For example, students may play an audio clip of music or may perform a traditional song or dance. Students may also wish to compose and perform an "action song" with lyrics that reflect Maori history and culture. **ELL Auditory/Musical, Kinesthetic**

ANSWERS, p. 435

☑️ **READING PROGRESS CHECK** Student responses should note that these nicknames are not considered offensive, as they are used by Australians and New Zealanders to refer to themselves.

CRITICAL THINKING Performing this traditional art form helps keep Maoris in touch with their culture and its values despite widespread modernization and the influence of European-derived ideas and practices.

Visual Skills

Drawing Maps Guide a class discussion about Australia's natural resources. Have students work in small groups to create a visual representation of information about the different natural resources discussed in the text and where they can be found. Tell students to create an outline map of Australia including a key with icons to represent each natural resource. For example, students might draw a sheep to represent wool production, a tree or log to symbolize the timber industry, and so on. Students may wish to conduct additional research to identify specific locations for the natural resources. Display students' maps in a classroom exhibit entitled "Australia's Natural Resources." **Visual/Spatial, Interpersonal**

R1 Reading Skills

Determining Word Meanings Point out the word *exports* in the section, "Australia's Economy." Guide students to understand the difference between imports and exports. Remind students that the prefix *im-* means "into" as in products being shipped into a country. The prefix *ex-* means "out of" or "away from" as in products being shipped out of a country. Remind students that the words *import* and *export* can be used as nouns *(products going into or out of a country)* and verbs *(going into or going out of)*. **Ask: What products does Australia export to other countries?** *(coal, iron ore, gold, meat, wool, wheat, and manufactured goods)* **Verbal/Linguistic**

R2 Reading Skills

Determining Word Meanings Point out the word *geothermal* in the section, "New Zealand's Natural Resources." Explain that the prefix *geo-* means "earth" and the root *therm* means "heat." **Ask: How does knowing these word parts help you understand how geothermal energy works?** *(Sample response: Knowing these word parts helps to explain how heat in the Earth's crust can help produce energy.)* **ELL Verbal/Linguistic**

Natural Resources and Economies

GUIDING QUESTION *What resources are important to the economies of Australia and New Zealand?*

Australia's Natural Resources

Australia is rich in valuable natural resources. Coal mining is a major industry in eastern and northwestern Australia and also in Tasmania. Iron ore is plentiful in the northwest. Gold discovered in Western Australia in the 1850s spurred a gold rush. Precious metals, including gold and silver, are still mined today. Large offshore oil and natural gas reserves are located in northern Australia and also in the Bass Strait between Australia and Tasmania. Australia exports some of its oil and natural gas.

The fertile farmland in southeastern Australia and other areas is one of the country's valuable natural resources. Wool, food crops, and other agricultural products are raised in many different parts of Australia. Timber and other products come from various species of trees growing across Australia. For example, eucalyptus trees are harvested for their wood, oil, resin, and leaves.

Australia's Economy

Australia's economy relies heavily on exports of its many natural resources. Coal, iron ore, and gold are Australia's three leading exports. Australia's economy also depends on its exports of meat, wool, wheat, and manufactured goods to countries all over the world. Australia's chief trading partners are China, Japan, South Korea, and the United States. Australia's manufacturing sector is not as strong as is the manufacturing sector in several East Asian nations, but Australia has enjoyed robust economic growth in recent years. Unemployment is relatively low. Australia ranks twelfth in world gas reserves and eleventh in world gas exports. Tourism continues to be a vital industry. More than 5 million people visit Australia each year, bringing revenue to local businesses and employing thousands of Australians. During the past few decades, Australia's film industry has grown to international status.

New Zealand's Natural Resources

New Zealand enjoys one important benefit of its location along the Ring of Fire: easy access to geothermal energy. **Geothermal energy** is naturally occurring heat energy produced by extremely hot liquid rock in Earth's upper mantle. As magma rises up through cracks or holes in Earth's crust, it heats the rock and water within the crust. Humans reach this heat and hot water by digging and drilling. The heat energy is used to warm homes, to provide hot water,

An Australian worker empties recently shorn wool into a bin for cleaning. Traditionally, Australian wool sold mostly in Europe and North America. Today, Australian wool suppliers rely increasingly on growing markets in China and other countries of Asia.

Identifying What countries are Australia's major trading partners?

Ian Waldie/Getty Images News/Getty Images

436 *Chapter 14*

netw⊘rks *Online Teaching Options*

IMAGE

Wool Processing

Making Connections Use the interactive image of wool processing to begin a discussion of the economies and resources of the region. Using wool processing as an example, guide a discussion to help students make the connection between a country's resources and its economy. **Logical/Mathemetical**

See page 413E for other online activities.

Interactive Photos

©Pete Atkinson/Getty Images

ANSWER, p. 436

Identifying China, Japan, South Korea, and the United States

V and to generate power. Another benefit of geothermal energy is that it is clean and does not pollute the environment. Hydroelectric power, derived from the energy of moving water, and windmills are other kinds of nonpolluting renewable resources.

R1 Farmland is one of New Zealand's most valuable resources. Almost one-half of all land on the islands is used for farming and livestock grazing. The grass growing on steep hillsides tends to dry out as rainwater drains down to lower pastures. Low-lying lands can become too soaked with rain, which is not good for most crops. The most productive farmland in New Zealand is in places where the soil receives enough rain but is well drained. The dark soil of North Island's volcanic plateau also holds ribbons of mineral deposits. New Zealand's other valuable natural resources include coal, iron ore, natural gas, gold, timber, and limestone.

New Zealand's Economy
During the past two decades, New Zealand's economy has gone through a major transformation. What was once a farm-based economy has become an industrialized, free-market economy. New Zealand's government has plans to continue to increase production of wood and paper products, food products, machinery, and textiles. Agriculture is still a key part of the economy, though. Products such as beef, lamb, fish, wool, wheat, flowering plants, vegetables, and fruits are exported and shipped around the world. One notable food export is the **kiwifruit**, a type of gooseberry fruit that originated in East Asia but has become a symbol of New Zealand.

New Zealand is not as wealthy as Australia, but it has a strong economy: It is forty-eighth in the world in per capita gross domestic product (GDP). New Zealand's chief trading partners are Australia, **R2** China, and the United States. Because New Zealand depends on export income, low export demand can badly damage its economy. As in Australia, tourism is a major industry. After the release of the hugely popular *Lord of the Rings* films in the early 2000s, tourists from all over the world flocked to New Zealand. New Zealand's film industry continues to grow, producing top-grossing films that are viewed worldwide.

New Zealand produces specialized food products that are exported around the world. (Top) A fruit grower inspects his kiwifruit grown on supported vines. (Bottom) A factory worker prepares pieces of New Zealand's famous Egmont cheese for wrapping.

☑ **READING PROGRESS CHECK**

Distinguishing Fact From Opinion Is the following statement a fact or an opinion? *Tourism is an important industry in Australia and New Zealand.*

(t) Bloomberg/Getty Images ; (b) Mark Coote/Bloomberg/Getty Images

Chapter 14 **437**

MAP

Resources: Australia and New Zealand

Comparing and Contrasting Use the resources layer of the Chapter Opener map to review the resources of the region and their impact on the economy. Have students work in pairs to create a Venn diagram that compares and contrasts resources found in each country in the region.

AL Logical/Mathematical

See page 413E for other online activities.

V Visual Skills

Diagramming Have students reread the information in the text about geothermal energy. Then have them draw a diagram or flow chart to show the step-by-step process in which the energy is extracted and then used for different purposes. Have students work with a partner to conduct a peer evaluation of their flow charts or diagrams to ensure that each step is adequately depicted. **Ask: What are the benefits of geothermal energy?** *(It can be used to heat homes, to provide hot water, and to generate power, and it does not pollute the environment.)* **Visual/Spatial, Logical/Mathematical**

R1 Reading Skills

Summarizing To help students understand the significance of New Zealand's farmland and other natural resources, have them work with a partner to summarize the information. **Ask:**

- **Approximately how much of New Zealand's land is used for farming and livestock grazing?** *(about one half)*
- **How does rainfall affect land in New Zealand?** *(Steep hillsides can dry out when rainwater drains down to lower pastures, and low-lying lands can become soaked with rain.)*
- **Other than farmland, what are some of New Zealand's most valuable natural resources?** *(mineral deposits found in the North Island's dark, volcanic soil; coal, iron ore, natural gas, timber, and limestone)* **Naturalist**

R2 Reading Skills

Determining Word Meanings Explain that the term *per capita* means "per person." It is a way of looking at some aspect of a country and dividing it by the number of people within the country. Read aloud for students the sentence about New Zealand's gross domestic product in the section, "New Zealand's Economy." **Ask:**

- **What does it mean to be 48th in the world in per capita gross domestic product?** *(There are 47 countries that have a higher per capita GDP.)*
- **Does this tell you how much each worker produces? Why or why not?** *(No because the per capita GDP is determined by using the total population, not the number of workers.)* **Logical/Mathematical**

ANSWER, p. 437

☑ **READING PROGRESS CHECK** It is a fact because it can be proven to be true. There is a high number of people employed in tourism related industries, and the amount of revenue brought into the countries through tourism is also significant.

V Visual Skills

Creating Visuals Help students comprehend the controversy surrounding indigenous rights by staging a mock protest. Have students analyze the photograph and caption on this page and use the information in the section, "Indigenous Rights," to determine the central issues and to create slogans for signs and banners. After students have had time to brainstorm slogans and create their banners, guide a discussion about the controversy over indigenous rights. **Ask:**

- **What do big businesses want to do with the land?** *(They want to use the land to develop its resources.)*
- **Why have Aboriginal lawsuits been filed over the years?** *(Aboriginal activist groups want rights to the land to protect it from development.)*
- **Why do you think that some of the cases are still being decided?** *(Possible answer: It probably takes a long time to determine specifically how the land would be used by big businesses, and how or if it would pose a threat to the environment.)* **BL** **Verbal/Linguistic, Kinesthetic**

T Technology Skills

Researching on the Internet Have students research the issues related to the traditional homelands of the Aboriginal people in Australia. Have students use reliable resources and give a short presentation to share their findings with the class. **Verbal/Linguistic**

C Critical Thinking Skills

Identifying Central Issues Lead a discussion about the native Maori's quest for land rights. Have students recall what they have already learned about the history of the Maori. **Ask:**

- **Why have the Maori petitioned the government to return their lost land?** *(They only own about 5 percent of the land in New Zealand.)*
- **Why did the government not want to return the land?** *(It would hurt the people currently living on the land.)*
- **What compromise did the government reach?** *(They agreed to pay the Maori for lost land and lost fishing rights, but the payments have been slow in coming.)* **Verbal/Linguistic**

ANSWER, p. 438

CRITICAL THINKING drought, limited water supplies, bushfires, and threats to reefs and geothermal hot springs and geysers

Activists protest the development of a gas project in a coastal area of Western Australia that is rich in petroleum and natural gas. The protestors claim the building of a gas plant and a port will damage offshore reefs and the fossil remains of prehistoric animals.
▶ **CRITICAL THINKING**
Citing Text Evidence What other environmental challenges do Australia and New Zealand face?

Academic Vocabulary

controversy a dispute; a discussion involving opposing views

Current Issues

GUIDING QUESTION *What challenges do the people of Australia and New Zealand face?*

Australia and New Zealand face challenges resulting from their locations, populations, climates, and physical geography. Just as the landforms and wildlife of the region are unique, so are the issues and problems facing Australia and New Zealand.

Indigenous Rights

The concern over Aboriginal people's rights has been an ongoing issue in Australia for well over a century. Aboriginal activist groups in Australia have filed several major lawsuits over land rights and environmental issues. A **lawsuit** is a legal case that is brought before a court of law. Many Aboriginal lawsuits have sparked **controversy** over the rights of the Aboriginal people versus the rights of big businesses to use the land and its resources. Some cases are still being decided. Similar human rights issues continue in New Zealand between New Zealanders of European descent and native Maori.

The Maori own only about 5 percent of the land in New Zealand. They petitioned the government to return their lost land. The government could not return land to the Maori without hurting the people who were living on it. The government agreed to pay the Maori for lost land and lost fishing rights. Payments continue, but they have been slow in coming.

438 Chapter 14

©Ingetje Tadros/Demotix/Demotix/Corbis

netw⊙rks   *Online Teaching Options*

IMAGE

Aboriginal and Maori Protests

Identifying Points of View Allow time for students to study the interactive image. Explain the various protests for the rights of indigenous groups in the region. Guide a class discussion about the differing points of view people have about indigenous rights. Have students write a paragraph that explains their own point of view on this issue. **BL** **Intrapersonal**

See page 413E for other online activities.

Interactive Photos

©Pete Atkinson/Getty Images

Protecting Natural Resources

Protecting the environment and natural resources is important to many Australians and New Zealanders. Recent environmental issues in Australia are drought and limited water supplies, bushfires, and threats to the survival of the Great Barrier Reef. All of these are affected by global warming. For example, the Great Barrier Reef is affected as water temperatures in the oceans rise, resulting in the death of organisms that need a cooler climate. The corals are also sensitive to climate change and water pollution. Parts of the Great Barrier Reef have already died. Scientists are concerned that if global warming continues, this entire massive reef system will be lost.

In recent decades, many geothermal hot springs and geysers have disappeared in New Zealand, but many of the remaining hot springs and geysers are located in protected areas. Geographers believe human activities such as drilling for hot water and building power stations have destroyed many natural wonders. Such environmental issues are of great concern to Australians and New Zealanders.

Other Issues

Australia and New Zealand have low birthrates. They also have low death rates. Low birthrates result from families having fewer children. Low death rates result from Australia's and New Zealand's high life expectancies. While such rates are generally beneficial for a country, the combination produces a gradually aging population. It also creates a need for more workers to support the older population. People immigrating to Australia and New Zealand are filling some of these positions, which helps meet the need for care providers. Immigration is also changing the region's ethnic makeup.

Australia and New Zealand face many other issues and challenges. Both countries are affected by the overall health of the planet. Their economies depend upon trade with other countries. Their industries could not survive without strong economic relations with one another and without trade with other countries.

FOLDABLES
Study Organizer

Include this lesson's information in your Foldable®.

☑ **READING PROGRESS CHECK**

Describing In your own words, explain why survival of the Great Barrier Reef is threatened.

LESSON 3 REVIEW CCSS

Reviewing Vocabulary (Tier Three Words)
1. What is the *bush* like? RH.6-8.4

Answering the Guiding Questions
2. ***Identifying*** What type of resource is *geothermal energy*? RH.6-8.2
3. ***Describing*** How is daily life in Australia and New Zealand similar to life in the United States? RH.6-8.5

4. ***Identifying*** Give three examples of resources found in Australia and three examples of resources found in New Zealand. RH.6-8.2
5. ***Argument Writing*** Think about the issues facing Australians and New Zealanders today. Write a paragraph in the form of an argument describing which issue you believe is the most important and why. WHST.6-8.1, WHST.6-8.4

Chapter 14 **439**

LESSON 3 REVIEW ANSWERS

Reviewing Vocabulary

1. The bush refers to any large, undeveloped area where few people live. It is often wild, unsettled, and rough.

Answering the Guiding Questions

2. **Identifying** Geothermal energy is a renewable (also accept inexhaustible) resource because it can never be used up or depleted.

3. **Describing** Responses should mention similarities such as transportation, housing, jobs, foods, language, music, and so on.

4. **Identifying** Answers should include three resources for each country. Sample answers: Australia: Coal, iron ore, gold, silver, oil and natural gas, farmland. New Zealand: Geothermal energy, wind energy, hydroelectric power, farmland, coal, iron ore, natural gas, gold, timber, and limestone.

5. **Argument Writing** Students' paragraphs should include valid reasons to support the selected issue based on evidence in the text.

C Critical Thinking Skills

Determining Cause and Effect Have students consider the environmental issues facing Australians and New Zealanders. As they read the section, "Protecting Natural Resources," have them think about the causes and effects involved in developing natural resources. **Ask:**

- **How does global warming relate to the Great Barrier Reef?** *(Global warming, as well as water pollution, is having a negative impact on the marine life in the reef. As air and water temperatures rise, organisms and corals in the Great Barrier reef struggle for survival. Warmer temperatures also mean more cyclones, which cause damage to the reef.)*
- **What do scientists worry might happen to the Great Barrier Reef if global warming continues?** *(The entire reef system will be lost.)* **Verbal/Linguistic**

R Reading Skills

Explaining To help students comprehend the information about population rates in Australia and New Zealand, have them read the section, "Other Issues," and then explain it to a partner. Then, **ask:**

- **Why do Australia and New Zealand have low birthrates?** *(Families are having fewer children.)*
- **Why do Australia and New Zealand have gradually aging populations?** *(The aging populations are caused by a combination of low birthrates and low death rates; the population is made up of fewer young people, and people are living longer.)* **AL** **Logical/Mathematical**

CLOSE & REFLECT

Identifying Central Issues To close the lesson, have students work in pairs to create a four-column chart labeled with the headings *Environment, Economy, Rights,* and *Resources.* As a lesson review, have students complete the chart with information from the lesson. Then guide a class discussion about the current issues facing people in Australia and New Zealand.

ANSWER, p. 439

☑ **READING PROGRESS CHECK** Responses should paraphrase the information about the threats to the Great Barrier Reef presented in the lesson. Sample response: The Great Barrier Reef is in danger of dying off completely because the corals cannot live in rising ocean temperatures caused by global warming.

ENGAGE

🔔 Bellringer Before students read the Global Connections feature, explain that the feature provides information on different invasive species and their negative impacts on environments. Provide an example of an invasive species in your region, such as the impact of zebra mussels (http://fl.biology.usgs.gov/Nonindigenous_Species/Zebra_mussel_FAQs/zebra_mussel_faqs.html) on aquatic environments, or Japanese Knotweed on terrestrial environments (http://www.invasivespeciesinfo.gov/plants/knotweed.shtm). **Ask:**

- **What is an invasive species?** *(animals, plants, and infectious organisms that take over the natural environment)*
- **What is the impact on native ecosystems when invasive species enter the environment?** *(disruption of ecosystems; they cause harm to the environment)*

Further engage students in the material by directing their attention to the quote that starts with "Wild rabbits are. . ." Have a volunteer read the quote. **Ask: How might rabbits negatively affect the environment to the point of becoming a destructive pest?** *(They eat vegetation other animals depend on for survival.)*

TEACH & ASSESS

R₁ Reading Skills

Determining Word Meanings Write *native, invasive,* and *infectious* on the board. Pronounce each word out loud. **Ask: What is a *native* species?** *(Possible answer: something naturally found within an ecosystem)*

Underline the prefix *in-* in the words *invasive* and *infectious.* **Ask: How are the words *invasive* and *infectious* alike?** *(Both have negative meanings.)* Have students share their knowledge of invasive species and infectious organisms and how they negatively affect native organisms and ecosystems. **ELL** **Verbal/Linguistic**

R₂ Reading Skills

Citing Text Evidence Write *Cane Toads* on the board. Invite a volunteer to read the section about this species. **Ask: What was the purpose of introducing this nonnative species into Australian environments?** *(control beetles that attacked sugarcane crops)*

Draw three arrows away from *Cane Toads* and add a fact at the end of each arrow as students answer the following question. **Ask: What negative environmental effects are directly caused by cane toads?** *(poison native animals, eat large numbers of honeybees reducing pollination, carry diseases that affect other frogs and fish)* Have students speculate on what options the Australian government might have regarding the negative impact of cane toads and how such mitigation efforts might affect an area's ecology. **AL**

UNFRIENDLY Invaders

R₁ *Invasive species are animals, plants, and infectious organisms that take over the natural environment of other species. Invasive species often harm the environment and cause the native species to decline in number. They can also harm the health of humans.*

R₂ **Cane Toads** Cane toads were brought to Australia in 1935 to control beetles that attacked sugarcane crops. But cane toads contain toxins that poison many native animals that eat them. Cane toads also eat large numbers of honeybees that pollinate plants and crops. The toads carry diseases that can be passed on to other frogs and to fish.

Animals That Prey Australia has many wild foxes and feral cats that prey on other animals, and rabbits that devastate vegetation. Their numbers are so great that the government says it cannot eliminate them. The goal is to reduce the damage they cause. **C₂**

" Wild rabbits are considered Australia's most widespread and destructive pest. " **C₁**

A Vast Number Why are cane toads so plentiful? Twice every year, female cane toads produce 8,000 to 35,000 eggs. That's many more eggs than the average frog lays. These eggs quickly hatch and form a school of tiny, black tadpoles. Many of the tadpoles do not survive. Those that survive can live for 10 to 40 years.

$4 Billion Per Year Invasive alien plants present problems for the economy. The cost of the damage and attempts to control the plants amounts to $4 billion per year.

Did You Know ❓

The International Union for Conservation of Nature (IUCN) assesses the risk of extinction for species. The four categories are:
- **Extinct**—Species has died out and no longer exists
- **Critically endangered**—Species faces a high risk of becoming extinct
- **Endangered**—Species faces a risk of extinction
- **Vulnerable**—Species is likely to become endangered unless circumstances improve

A worker weighs a cane toad at a collection point in Cairns , Australia. ▶

(t) ©John Carnemolla/Corbis; (b) Ashley Cooper/Alamy

---

netw✸rks   *Online Teaching Options*

SLIDE SHOW

Invasive Plant Species

Integrating Visual Information Display the slide show and discuss the various types of invasive plant species around the world and the damage done by them. Divide students into small groups and assign each group an invasive species noted in the slide show to research. Have each group create an invasive species poster using art rather than text that carries important information about the invasive species. **ELL** **Visual/Spatial**

Slide Show

(l) ©Ocean/Corbis, ©Kryssia Campos/Getty Images, (tr) Erica Simone Leeds, (br) ©JG Photography/Alamy

Brian Casey/AP Images

THERE'S MORE ONLINE

HEAR cane toads • SEE invasive plant species • WATCH an animation on invasive species

C1 Critical Thinking Skills

Determining Cause and Effect Have students read the text information in the center column. Write *animal* and *plant* on the board. Have students share ideas for reducing populations of invasive animals and plants and list their ideas. **Ask:**

- What are some methods used to reduce overpopulations of invasive animal species? *(hunting, trapping, poisoning, birth control vaccines)*
- What are some ways of reducing the overpopulation of invasive plants? *(burning, spraying, physical removal)*
- What economic benefit is there to a reduction in invasive animal species, such as rabbits and feral cats in Australia? *(improved crop production and sales)*
- Why are decisions about how to reduce populations of invasive animals and plants difficult to make? *(Students might suggest that people may be opposed to hunting or concerned about the health effects of herbicides.)* **Logical/ Mathematical**

V

C2 Critical Thinking Skills

Problem-Solving Direct student attention to the Did You Know? section. Have students read the four risks of extinction categories. As a class, discuss the information, then have students provide possible solutions. **Ask:**

- What potential impact is there to other species when an endangered species becomes extinct? *(Other species that rely on that species for food may become at risk.)*
- Does the discovery of new species make up for the loss or severe reduction in numbers of other species? Why or why not? *(Students may suggest that the loss of any species impacts the environment in some way, even if new species are discovered.)*
- What is important in the management of regional environments? *(Governments must work with scientists and the people of different regions to seek answers to problems to help local economies without harming the region's environment.)* **Verbal/Linguistic**

V Visual Skills

Analyzing Images Have students study the large image. Explain that the woman in the photograph is a scientist studying cane toads. **Ask: Why is the scientist wearing a glove?** *(to prevent transfer of harmful organisms from and to the cane toad)*

Tell students that a scientist studying cane toads would gather more information than just the weight of the toads. **Ask: What else do you think the scientist is observing?** *(Possible answers: physical characteristics, possible diseases or environmental effects, behavior)* **AL Visual/Spatial**

VIDEO

Rabbits

Integrating Visual Information After students have viewed the video, discuss the impact of rabbits on the region. Divide the class into groups of three. Have each group use the information about rabbits from the text and video to create a graphic organizer that shows the impact of rabbits on the environment, why the problems of this invasive species are so difficult to address, and possible management solutions. Have groups share their graphic organizers.
BL Visual/Spatial

V1 Visual Skills

Creating Visuals Write the statistic headlines from this page as column heads on the board. Put students in teams and provide each team with a sheet of chart paper. Assign each team one of the statistics. Using chart paper to create a visual, have each team display its chart showing the highlighted statistic, the impact of that statistic, and its possible effects on the environment. **Ask: Given each of these statistics, which problem do you believe is the most critical for the long-term health of Australia's environment?** *(Allow students to compare and contrast the environmental issues presented.)* **Interpersonal**

C Critical Thinking Skills

Speculating Circle the *3,300 mile fence* listed on the board. **Ask: What might be the effect on an environment when an overpopulation of one species inhabits it?** *(Students may speculate that other species will become endangered or extinct, and that food sources a species depends on may disappear.)*

Have students read the remaining text on the page. **Ask: What can the impact of overpopulation be on a species?** *(conflict, starvation)* **Naturalist, Logical/Mathematical**

V2 Visual Skills

Analyzing Charts In pairs, have students analyze the information provided in the chart at the bottom of the page. Have them discuss other animals that they know of that are close to extinction. **Ask: What information does this chart provide?** *(examples of species found within the four at-risk categories)*

Allow partners time to consider how humans impact the survival of each of the animals shown on the chart. **Ask:**

- **What can humans do to improve the chances for each of these animals to increase in number and survive as a species?** *(Answers will vary: restrict hunting, increase their natural habitats, prosecute poachers, increase government protections)*

- **How might ecotourism, where individuals pay to visit animal reserves and conservation regions in foreign countries, help protect animals?** *(Students might respond that a country may be more prone to protect vulnerable species if there is an economic advantage to do so.)* **BL Logical/Mathematical**

V1 These numbers and statistics can help you learn about the invasive species of Australia.

TWENTY-TWO EXTINCT

There are 22 extinct mammals in Australia. *Extinct* means no more are left. Many other animals are in danger of dying out. Australia has more endangered species than any other continent.

The red fox, the feral cat, and the rabbit are probably responsible for the loss of 20 of the 22 extinct marsupials and rodents in Australia. Other animals that have become major agricultural and environmental problems are wild pigs, goats, and deer.

12 pounds

C In many parts of Australia, all native mammals weighing up to 12 pounds (5.4 kilograms) are extinct. Nine species of mammals exist only on Australian islands that have no cat or fox population.

No. 1 Wild rabbits are considered Australia's most destructive pest. European rabbits were introduced in Australia more than 150 years ago. The rabbit population grew huge because few animals prey on the rabbits. A virus in the 1950s killed many rabbits, but as rabbits built up an immunity to the virus, the rabbit population began to grow again. Today, millions of wild rabbits live in all parts of Australia.

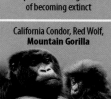

NO. 1 RABBIT PROOF FENCE
THE LONGEST FENCE IN THE WORLD
COMMENCED HERE IN 1901
LENGTH 1837 km (1139 miles)
COMPLETED 1903 AT ESPERANCE ON
THE SOUTH COAST AND 1907 AT
PORT HEDLAND ON THE NORTH COAST

1974 Epidemic

Phytophthora root rot is an invasive disease that threatens many important crops and plant species in Australia. For example, a 1974 root rot epidemic destroyed more than one-half of all the avocado trees in eastern Australia.

3,300-MILE FENCE

The dingo looks like a dog and is the largest carnivorous animal in Australia. More than 100 years ago, Australians built a long fence to keep the dingo away from sheep flocks and other animals. At 3,300 miles (5,311 km) long, the dingo fence is the world's longest fence. Rabbit-proof fences were built to protect Western Australian crops and pasture lands.

27,000 In the 1800s, a weed called the prickly pear overran large areas, forcing many farmers off their land. Today, more than 27,000 invasive alien plants grow in Australia.

V2

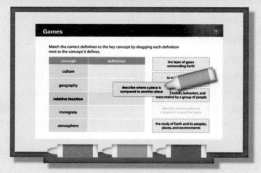

VULNERABLE	ENDANGERED	CRITICALLY ENDANGERED	EXTINCT
Species is likely to become endangered unless circumstances improve	Species faces a risk of extinction in the wild; usually when fewer than 250 mature individuals exist	Species faces a high risk of becoming extinct	Species has died out and no longer exists
African Elephant, Polar Bear, **Great White Shark**	Blue Whale, Giant Panda, **Asian Elephant**	California Condor, Red Wolf, **Mountain Gorilla**	Zanzibar Leopard, Caspian Tiger, **Passenger Pigeon**

---

networks   *Online Teaching Options*

GAME

Battling Invasive Species

Using and Citing Information Have students play the drag-and-drop game to review the ways to battle invasive species. Then provide each student with three index cards. Assign each student one invasive species. The student should write the name of the invasive species on one card, its location and how it was introduced on another card (without naming the species), and ways it is being addressed on another card (without naming the species). Divide students into groups. Collect the cards, mix them up, and redistribute the cards to group members. Students with species names should lay them on a table as column heads. Other students should place the other cards under the correct species. **AL Kinesthetic**

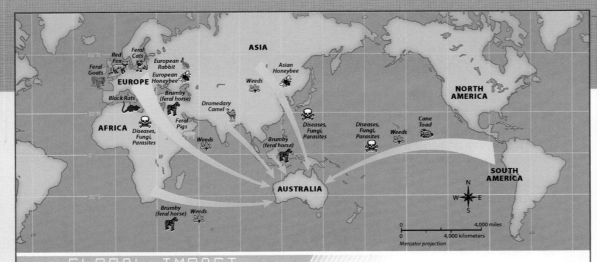

GLOBAL IMPACT

AUSTRALIA'S INVASIVE SPECIES

The map shows the location from where various species were brought to Australia. But why were they brought to Australia? To European settlers, Australia seemed strange. There were no familiar wild animals. In 1859 a rancher brought wild rabbits from England and set them free on his land. As the number of rabbits grew, businesses began to can rabbit meat to sell and used the skins and fur to make clothing and hats. When the rabbit population continued to grow, steps were taken to control them. In the 1950s, a virus was developed that killed most of the rabbits. However, rabbits became resistant to the virus, and the population grew again.

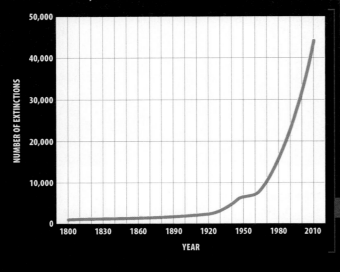

Global Species Extinction

Mass extinctions are time periods in the history of Earth when an extraordinarily large number of species go extinct. Today, many scientists believe the evidence shows a mass extinction is underway.

(Graph: NUMBER OF EXTINCTIONS vs. YEAR, 1800 to 2010, values 0 to 50,000)

Thinking like a Geographer

1. *Physical Geography* Why was the cane toad introduced into Australia? Why did the cane toad population grow so fast?

2. *The Uses of Geography* Find out what invasive species have been introduced into your area. Prepare a poster to show how to protect native plants and animals against invasive species.

3. *Environment and Society* Research to find information about an endangered species. Write about what is being done to protect these animals.

W

Chapter 14 **443**

MAP

How Invasive Species Get to Australia

Comparing Display the map to students. As a class, review how invasive species of Australia and New Zealand arrived at the two locations. Compare the arrival of invasive species in Australia to what occurred with the Columbia Exchange. Have students individually research invasive species common to their locality. Have students share what they learned and compare the problems associated with locally present invasive species with those found in Australia. **BL** **Visual/Spatial**

C Critical Thinking Skills

Drawing Conclusions Using the map at the top of the page, point out that Australia's invasive species came from a variety of places around the world. Allow time for students to track a species and where it came from on the visual, and then guide students in a discussion. **Ask:** How did good ideas go bad regarding the large presence of invasive species in Australia? *(Individuals initially believed they were improving Australia's environment by introducing different species, without understanding how foreign species would impact environments or affect them in negative ways.)* **Verbal/Linguistic**

C

W Writing Skills

Informative/Explanatory Have students research and make a list of animals that have become extinct in the last 100 years. Have individuals select one of the extinct animals from the class list to research. Have them gather research on the animal and on what happened that it became extinct. Then have students write an informative paragraph about the animal and another paragraph on what happened to it. Remind students that these are informative paragraphs and should include facts only. Finally have students write a third paragraph expressing their opinion on whether the animal could have been saved by proper management of the environment. **Verbal/Linguistic**

CLOSE & REFLECT

Have students research and create a list of countries that promote ecotourism. Divide the class into groups of 5 to 7 students. Assign each group a country from the list generated by students. Students should research the animals that are endangered in the country and learn how the country is using ecotourism as a means to support endangered and vulnerable animal populations and protect reserves. Allow time for groups to create a multimedia presentation that includes images, text, and music on their research. Have groups share their presentations with the class. **BL** **Auditory/Musical**

ANSWERS, p. 443

Thinking Like a Geographer
1. *Physical Geography* to control a type of beetle that attacked sugarcane; it lays many more eggs than the typical toad.
2. *The Uses of Geography* Many invasive species have been introduced into the United States, including the Japanese beetle and kudzu. Students may focus on measures such as care when importing items to see that species do not hitch-hike on goods or packaging.
3. *Environment and Society* Student work should provide viable resources. Written work should include detailed information on what is being done to protect the animals.

CHAPTER REVIEW ACTIVITY

To help students review the chapter, have them create a chart like the one below. Have students fill in the appropriate column in the chart with key information from each lesson. *(Students' answers may vary but should include key concepts discussed in each of the three lessons in the chapter.)*

	Australia	New Zealand
Physical Geography	• • •	• • •
History	• • •	• • •
Daily Life	• • •	• • •

REVIEW THE ENDURING UNDERSTANDINGS

Review this chapter's Enduring Understanding with students:

- *People, places, and ideas change over time.*

Now pose the following questions in a class discussion to apply this to this chapter.

- **How would you describe the physical geography of Australia and New Zealand?** *(In addition to its coastal lowlands, Australia is made up of three main geographic regions: the Western Plateau, which is rocky and dry; the Central Lowlands, which are flat and rugged; and the Eastern Highlands, which have high and low areas, forests, and farmland. New Zealand is made up of two main islands called North Island and South Island, which have forests, mountains and waterways. New Zealand also has a number of small surrounding islands.)*

- **How would you describe the first humans who inhabited Australia and New Zealand?** *(Australia's first humans are known as Aboriginal people. They lived a hunter-gatherer lifestyle, and some were nomadic, moving from place to place in search of water sources. New Zealand's first people are the Maori, who built villages and lived in tribal groups led by chiefs.)*

- **What are two similarities of Australian and New Zealand cultures and life today?** *(Sample response: Both nations are proud of their strong educational systems as each is home to well-respected universities and both Aboriginal and Maori cultures have experienced revivals in recent years.)*

Directions: Write your answers on a separate piece of paper.

1 Use your **FOLDABLES** to explore the Essential Question.
INFORMATIVE/EXPLANATORY WRITING Review the physical map and the population map at the beginning of this unit. In two or more paragraphs, explain how Australia's physical geography has affected the country's settlement patterns. WHST.6-8.2, WHST.6-8.4

2 21st Century Skills
INTEGRATING VISUAL INFORMATION Work in small groups to research the physical geography, people, and culture of each of Australia's three main geographic regions, New Zealand's North and South Islands, and Tasmania. Present the information as a slide show or a poster. WHST.6-8.6, WHST.6-8.7

3 Thinking Like a Geographer
IDENTIFYING Create a two-column chart similar to the one shown here. Label one side Australia and the other side New Zealand. Use the chart to list the natural resources of each country. WHST.6-8.9, WHST.6-8.10

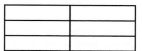

4 **GEOGRAPHY ACTIVITY**

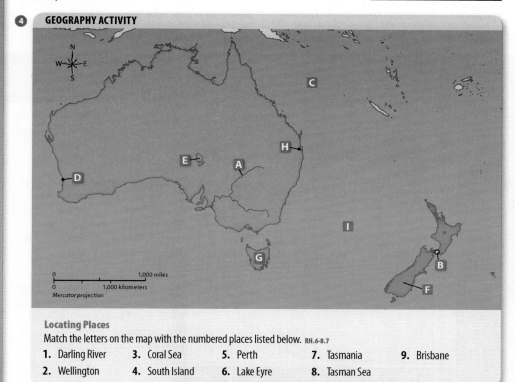

Locating Places
Match the letters on the map with the numbered places listed below. RH.6-8.7

1. Darling River   3. Coral Sea   5. Perth   7. Tasmania   9. Brisbane
2. Wellington   4. South Island   6. Lake Eyre   8. Tasman Sea

ACTIVITIES ANSWERS

Exploring the Essential Question

1 **INFORMATIVE/EXPLANATORY WRITING** Students should describe the impact of Australia's physical geography on the country's settlement patterns. Students' work should offer a solid explanation, be well organized, and display the accepted standards for spelling and grammar.

21st Century Skills

2 **INTEGRATING VISUAL INFORMATION** Students' slideshows or posters should demonstrate an understanding of the physical geography, people, and culture of the regions. They should show evidence of solid research, be accurate, interesting, and well organized.

REVIEW THE GUIDING QUESTIONS

Directions: Choose the best answer for each question.

1 New Zealand can best be described as a land of RH.6-8.2
  A. extremely diverse landscapes, ecosystems, and climate zones.
  B. nomadic people.
  C. harsh, dry deserts.
  D. cold, barren landscapes.

2 How much of Australia is covered by desert? RH.6-8.2
  F. one-half
  G. one-fourth
  H. two-thirds
  I. one-third

3 The first people to live in Australia are called RH.6-8.2
  A. Maori.
  B. Indians.
  C. Aboriginal people.
  D. convicts.

4 The first people to inhabit New Zealand came from RH.6-8.2
  F. Borneo across a land bridge.
  G. Polynesia in canoes.
  H. Australia in sailboats.
  I. Britain in convict ships.

5 What is the basis for New Zealand's economy? RH.6-8.2
  A. coal
  B. geothermal energy
  C. agriculture
  D. fishing and hunting

6 What is the name of the bamboo instrument used by Aboriginal musicians to make traditional music? RH.6-8.4
  F. boomerang
  G. kiwi
  H. marsupial
  I. didgeridoo

Chapter 14 **445**

Thinking Like a Geographer

3 **IDENTIFYING** Students' charts should include the following: Australia—coal, iron ore, gold, silver, oil, natural gas, wool, other agricultural products, and timber. New Zealand—geothermal energy, hydroelectric power, wind power, rich agricultural land, coal, iron ore, natural gas, gold, timber, and limestone.

Geography Activities

4 **LOCATING PLACES**

1. A
2. B
3. C
4. F
5. D
6. E
7. G
8. I
9. H

ASSESSMENT ANSWERS

Review the Guiding Questions

1 **A** Students may be confused initially by choice C, but it describes much of Australia, not New Zealand. Choice B also refers to Australia, as early Aboriginal people were nomadic. Students should recall that New Zealand has a diverse geography and climate. Refer students to Lesson 1 for help.

2 **I** Students may be confused by choice H, as one third of Australia is semi-arid. Students should recall that Australia has a generally dry climate. If students need clarification, direct them to reread Lesson 1.

3 **C** Students should recognize choice A as a distractor, as the Maori were the first people to live in New Zealand, not Australia. They may be confused by choice D, which refers to the country's use as a prison colony. Refer students to Lesson 1 and Lesson 2 for help.

4 **G** To answer this question, students need to recall the section in Lesson 2 ,"The Maori of New Zealand." Choice F may confuse students, as the text mentions a land bridge, but it refers to the Aboriginal people traveling to Australia. Choice H should be an obvious distractor, and choice I refers to Australia not New Zealand.

5 **C** Students should remember that even though New Zealand's economy has gone through a major transformation in the past two decades, agriculture is still a key part of the economy. Students should recognize choices A and B as distractors, as coal and geothermal energy are natural resources, not the basis for the economy. Refer students to the section, "New Zealand's Economy," in Lesson 3 for clarification.

6 **I** Students should recognize choice H as a distractor, as it refers to a type of animal, not an instrument. Students should recognize choice F as a distractor, as it is not used to make music. Refer students to the section, "Aboriginal and Maori Culture," in Lesson 3 for clarification.

DBQ Analyzing Documents

7 D Economic growth in China and India—causing them to have a growing "appetite" for coal and iron—is causing the boom in construction in Australia, which will ship its coal and iron ore to those markets. Have students who answer A reread the last sentence in the passage to see that the demand is the primary factor.

8 G Since the Australian building boom is fueled by the prospect of trade with China and India, it demonstrates global interdependence. Make sure students understand that mining coal and iron ore are not high-technology or service industries.

Short Response

9 "Continuous indigenous occupation" means a Maori tribe would have to show that they had lived in and used an area without break since 1840 in order to win a claim to have "customary title" to the area.

10 Sample answer: The agreement protects Maori rights by recognizing the rights of Maori tribes to certain areas under certain conditions. It recognizes non-Maori rights by limiting the tribes' abilities, for instance by preventing them from barring people from the area.

Extended Response

11 Students should clearly state a preference between the two countries and then support their choice with reasoned judgment that includes references to climate, landforms, recreation, cost of living, and employment opportunities. Essays should be written in a clear and logical manner and meet standards for grammar and spelling.

DBQ ANALYZING DOCUMENTS

7 ANALYZING Read the following passage about new construction taking place in Australia:

"Australia is set for an . . . $115 billion infrastructure boom as the nation adds ports and railways to feed China and India's appetite for coal and iron ore. . . . The demand, coupled with economic slowdowns in the U.S. and Europe, has helped make Australia the developed world's fastest-growing construction market."

—from David Fickling, "China Trade Spurs $115 Billion Australia Building Boom: Freight"

What factor spurred this upcoming building boom in Australia? RH.6-8.1, RH.6-8.10

A. slumping economies in the United States and Europe

B. discovery of new sources of coal and iron in Australia

C. development of new uses for coal and iron ore

D. economic growth in China and India

8 DETERMINING CENTRAL IDEAS What economic trend does the Australian building boom demonstrate? RH.6-8.2, RH.6-8.10

F. increasing productivity

H. growth of high-technology industries

G. global interdependence

I. growth of service industries

SHORT RESPONSE

"In June 2010, the government signed a new agreement with the Maori over contentious [disputed] foreshore and seabed rights, replacing a 2006 deal that had ended Maori rights to claim customary titles in courts of law. Tribes can now claim customary title to areas proven to have been under continuous indigenous occupation since 1840. Maori tribes that secure a customary title will be granted title deeds, but cannot sell the property or bar public access to the area."

—from "New Zealand," FreedomHouse.org

9 DETERMINING WORD MEANINGS What does the term "continuous indigenous occupation" mean in the agreement? RH.6-8.4, RH.6-8.10

10 ANALYZING How does the 2010 agreement protect the rights of Maori and non-Maori? RH.6-8.1, RH.6-8.10

EXTENDED RESPONSE

11 INFORMATIVE/EXPLANATORY WRITING If you had the opportunity to relocate and live for a couple of years in Australia or New Zealand, which country would you choose? Explain your choice in a short essay. Be sure to consider such things as climate, landforms, recreation, cost of living, and employment opportunities in your writing. WHST.6-8.2, WHST.6-8.4

Need Extra Help?

If You've Missed Question	❶	❷	❸	❹	❺	❻	❼	❽	❾	❿	⓫
Review Lesson	1	1	2	2	3	3	3	3	2	2	1

---

netw●rks   *Online Teaching Options*

Practicing 21st Century Skills

Practicing Skills Your students can practice important 21st Century skills such as geography, reading, writing, and critical thinking by using resources found in the Skills Builder tab of the online Student Learning Center. Resources include templates, handbooks, and slide shows. These same resources are also available in the Resource Library of the Teacher Lesson Center.

Oceania Planner

National Geography Standards covered in Chapter 15

Learners will understand:

I. The World in Spatial Terms

Standard 1: How to use maps and other geographic representations, geospatial technologies, and spatial thinking to understand and communicate information

Standard 3: How to analyze the spatial organization of people, places, and environments on Earth's surface

II. Places and Regions

Standard 4: The physical and human characteristics of places

Standard 5: That people create regions to interpret Earth's complexity

Standard 6: How culture and experience influence people's perceptions of places and regions

III. Physical Systems

Standard 7: The physical processes that shape the patterns of Earth's surface.

IV. Human Systems

Standard 9: The characteristics, distribution, and migration of human populations on Earth's surface

Standard 10: The characteristics, distribution, and complexity of Earth's cultural mosaics

Standard 11: The patterns and networks of economic interdependence on Earth's surface

Standard 12: The processes, patterns, and functions of human settlement

Standard 13: How the forces of cooperation and conflict among people influence the division and control of Earth's surface

V. Environment and Society

Standard 14: How human actions modify the physical environment

Standard 15: How physical systems affect human systems

VI. The Uses of Geography

Standard 17: How to apply geography to interpret the past

Standard 18: How to apply geography to interpret the present and plan for the future

---

UNDERSTANDING BY DESIGN®

Enduring Understandings

- *People, places, and ideas change over time.*

Essential Questions

- *How does physical geography influence the way people live?*
- *What makes a culture unique?*
- *Why do people make economic choices?*

Predictable Misunderstandings

- *Oceania's geography is mostly ice.*
- *There are no resources in this region.*
- *There is very little interest to other countries in this region.*

Assessment Evidence

Performance Tasks:

- *Project-Based Learning Digital Hands-On Chapter Project*
- *Project-Based Learning Hands-On Chapter Project*

Other Evidence:

- *Technology Skills Activity*
- *Geography and History Activity*
- *Participation in Interactive Whiteboard Activities*
- *Contribution to small-group activities*
- *Interpretation of slide show images and special purpose maps*
- *Participation in class discussions about cultural and economic topics*
- *Lesson Reviews*
- *Chapter Assessments*

SUGGESTED PACING GUIDE

Introducing the Chapter . . . . 1 Day	Lesson 3 . . . . .2 Days
Lesson 1 . . . . .2 Days	Chapter Wrap-Up and Assessment . . . . . . 1 Day
Lesson 2 . . . . .2 Days	

TOTAL TIME 8 Days

Key for Using the Teacher Edition

SKILL-BASED ACTIVITIES

Types of skill activities found in the Teacher Edition.

* **V Visual Skills** require students to analyze maps, graphs, charts, and photos.

W Writing Skills provide writing opportunities to help students comprehend the text.

R Reading Skills help students practice reading skills and master vocabulary.

C Critical Thinking Skills help students apply and extend what they have learned.

T Technology Skills require students to use digital tools effectively.

*Letters are followed by a number when there is more than one of the same type of skill on the page.

DIFFERENTIATED INSTRUCTION

All activities are written for the on-level student unless otherwise marked with the leveled labels below.

BL Beyond Level
AL Approaching Level
ELL English Language Learners

All students benefit from activities that utilize different learning styles. Many activities are marked as below when a particular learning style is highlighted.

Intrapersonal	Naturalist
Logical/Mathematical	Kinesthetic
Visual/Spatial	Auditory/Musical
Verbal/Linguistic	Interpersonal

CHAPTER OPENER PLANNER

Students will know:

- that there are marine resources in Oceania that interest other countries.
- that Oceania has important shipping routes that make it important to the global economy.

Students will be able to:

- *analyze* a world map to identify countries of Oceania.
- *use* a time line to discuss various events in the history of Oceania.

UNDERSTANDING
BY DESIGN®

☑ *Print Teaching Options*

V Visual Skills

☐ **P. 448** Students analyze the map of Oceania and make generalizations. **AL** **ELL** Visual/Spatial

☐ **P. 448** Students use the map of Oceania to reinforce map skills. Visual/Spatial, Logical/Mathematical

☐ **P. 449** Students read the time line and discuss its major points of interest. Visual/Spatial, Verbal/Linguistic

W Writing Skills

☐ **P. 449** Students choose two events from the time line and write a paragraph about how the region's strategic location makes it an important resource for many countries. Logical/Mathematical, Verbal/Linguistic

☑ *Online Teaching Options*

☐ **MAP** **Reading a Map**—Students identify aspects and locations of the region on a map.

☐ **TIME LINE** **Reading a Time Line and Map**—Students learn about where and when historical events occurred in Oceania using the time line and map.

☐ **MAP** **Interactive World Atlas**—Students use the interactive world atlas to identify the region and describe its terrain.

☑ *Printable Digital Worksheets*

☐ **WORKSHEET** **Technology Skills: Creating a Presentation**—Students use the worksheet and what they have learned to create a presentation.

☐ **WORKSHEET** **Geography and History: How Geographers Divide Oceania**—Students use the worksheet to understand more about the division of Oceania by culture and physical location.

Project-Based Learning

Hands-On

Creating a Style Book

Students will work in small groups to create a "Choose Your Own Adventure" style book about Oceania. Each groups will identify ten to fifteen important ideas to include that capture and describe the physical geography, history, and cultures of Oceania. On each page, students will determine what ideas the reader will be able to connect to next as they progress through the book. Students should look for logical connections between topics when developing the path and options in their books.

Digital Hands-On

Creating an Online Infographic

Students will work independently or in pairs to create an online infographic that will present information about one of the islands, territories, or countries in Oceania. Infographics might include interactive diagrams, videos, and sounds. Students will then present their infographics to the class.

Print Resources

ANCILLARY RESOURCES

These ancillaries are available for every chapter and lesson.

- **Reading Essentials and Study Guide Workbook** **AL** **ELL**
- **Chapter Tests and Lesson Quizzes Blackline Masters**

PRINTABLE DIGITAL WORKSHEETS

These printable digital worksheets are available for every chapter and lesson!

- **Hands-On Chapter Projects**
- **What Do You Know? Activities**
- **Chapter Summaries (English and Spanish)**
- **Vocabulary Builder Activities**
- **Quizzes and Tests**
- **Reading Essentials and Study Guide (English and Spanish)** **AL** **ELL**
- **Guided Reading Activities**

More Media Resources

SUGGESTED VIDEOS

NOTE: Be sure to preview videos to ensure they are age-appropriate.

- **Hidden Hawaii** (50 min.)
- **Lost Mummies of New Guinea** (50 min.)
- **The Alien Deep** (2 discs, 240 min.)

SUGGESTED READING

- *The Mystery in Hawaii: Our 50th State,* by Carole Marsh **AL**
- *Call It Courage,* by Armstrong Perry
- *Shoal of Time: A History of the Hawaiian Islands,* by Gavin Davis **BL**

PHYSICAL GEOGRAPHY OF OCEANIA

Students will know:
- *that there are marine resources in Oceania that interest other countries.*
- *that Oceania has important shipping routes that make it important to the global economy.*

Students will be able to:
- **describe** *the landforms of Oceania.*
- **explain** *the division of Oceania into three sections.*
- **compare and contrast** *high islands and low islands.*
- **describe** *the climates of Oceania.*
- **explore** *the resources of Oceania.*

UNDERSTANDING BY DESIGN®

☑ Print Teaching Options

V Visual Skills

☐ **P. 450** Students create a three-column chart and fill in the island groups for each section of Oceania. **ELL** **ALL**

☐ **P. 454** Students create a map to show New Guinea's climate zones. **BL** Naturalist

W Writing Skills

☐ **P. 453** Students write an essay explaining how the Oceania islands were created. **AL** Verbal/Linguistic

R Reading Skills

☐ **P. 450** Students discuss the word parts and meanings of the names of the three sections of Oceania. **ELL**

☐ **P. 452** Students create a game to compare and contrast the high islands and low islands and identify the characteristics of the islands. **AL** Kinesthetic

☐ **P. 453** Students use text evidence to answer questions about how the low islands in the region formed. Verbal/Linguistic, Intrapersonal

☐ **P. 454** Students use context clues to define *typhoons* and *monsoon winds*. **ELL** **AL** Verbal/Linguistic

C Critical Thinking Skills

☐ **P. 451** Students draw conclusions about why some islands are independent and others are under the jurisdiction of other countries. **AL** Logical

☐ **P. 452** Students make a Venn diagram of the two parts of New Guinea. **ELL**

☐ **P. 454** Students evaluate the economic choice of French Polynesia to rely on the black pearl industry. **AL** Intrapersonal

☐ **P. 455** Students discuss how the smaller islands' locations and climates affect their resources and economies. Verbal/Linguistic, Naturalist

T Technology Skills

☐ **P. 451** Students draw a sketch of an archipelago and research information about the Malay Archipelago. **ELL** Visual/Spatial

☐ **P. 453** Students create presentations to illustrate the process of volcanoes erupting and forming the high islands. **BL** Logical/Mathematical

☑ Online Teaching Options

V Visual Skills

☐ **IMAGE** Lagoons—Use the interactive photo to discuss lagoons and how they are formed and then compare them to atolls.

☐ **MAP** Climates: Oceania—Students make inferences about the climate zones of the islands of Oceania and then use the climate layer of the map to check their inferences. Visual/Spatial

☐ **MAP** Resources: Oceania—Use the resources layer to discuss the resources of the region.

☐ **SLIDE SHOW** Alternative Energy: Solar and Wind Power—Use the slide show to review the uses and development of alternative energy sources.

W Writing Skills

☐ **VIDEO** Captain Cook & Tupaia—Students watch the video about the exploration and discovery of Oceania by Captain Cook and write three questions they have about this region. **ELL**

☐ **SLIDE SHOW** Views of Oceania—Students use the slide show to learn about landforms and waterways of Oceania and write a paragraph describing the one that most interests them. **AL**

R Reading Skills

☐ **GAME** Drag-and-Drop: Different Spheres—Use the drag-and-drop asset about the different spheres of Earth to discuss how these spheres affect the climate of this region.

☐ **LECTURE** The Tropics—Use the lecture slide to describe and understand this climate zone.

☐ **GAME** Drag-and-Drop: Resources—Use the drag-and-drop asset of renewable and nonrenewable resources to help extend content and understanding.

☐ **GAME** Drag-and-Drop: Low and High Islands—Students use the interactive game to review the concepts of low and high islands of Oceania and take turns dragging and dropping the characteristics of each island into the correct category. **AL** Kinesthetic, Verbal/Linguistic

C Critical Thinking Skills

☐ **ANIMATION** How Volcanoes Form Islands—Students use the animation to learn about how volcanoes form islands and sketch pictures with labels and descriptions to show this process. **AL**

☐ **CHART** Comparing Rainfall: Oceania and the United States—Use the chart that compares average rainfall for the region to the United States and discuss the different climate zones.

☐ **MAP** Physical Geography: Oceania—Use the physical geography layer of the Chapter Opener map to discuss the landforms and waterways of the region.

T Technology Skills

☐ **ONLINE SELF-CHECK QUIZ** Lesson 1—Students receive instant feedback on their mastery of lesson content.

☑ Printable Digital Worksheets

W Writing Skills

☐ **WORKSHEET** Technology Skills: Creating a Presentation—Students use the worksheet and what they have learned to create a presentation.

☐ **WORKSHEET** Geography and History: How Geographers Divide Oceania—Students use the worksheet to understand more about the division of Oceania by culture and physical location.

THE HISTORY OF OCEANIA

Students will know:
- that there are marine resources in Oceania that interest other countries.
- that Oceania has important shipping routes that make it important to the global economy.

Students will be able to:
- **explore** the early history of Oceania and the Polynesian migrations.
- **explore** the later history of Oceania and the coming of Europeans.
- **describe** the people of Oceania, their languages, and cultures.

UNDERSTANDING BY DESIGN®

☑ Print Teaching Options

V Visual Skills

☐ **P. 456** Students create a time line and plot events from the text. **Visual/Spatial**

☐ **P. 457** Students add a break to their time lines to show how long the people of Oceania lived without contact from others. **AL**

☐ **P. 458** Students analyze the image and discuss how it illustrates the effects of European colonization and use of an area's resources. **AL** **Visual/Spatial**

☐ **P. 461** Students visualize the description of the *fale* and explain why the people of Samoa use *fales* as homes. **AL** **Visual/Spatial**

W Writing Skills

☐ **P. 460** Students write an informative essay about a cultural aspect of a Polynesian or Micronesian culture. **Verbal/Linguistic**

R Reading Skills

☐ **P. 456** Students discuss wayfinding and navigation before the invention of navigation tools. **ELL** **Kinesthetic**

☐ **P. 459** Students discuss how the people of Oceania must feel about outsiders' views of the islands. **Interpersonal**

☐ **P. 461** Students choose an Oceania culture to represent and perform an activity representative of that culture. **AL** **Kinesthetic, Verbal/Linguistic**

C Critical Thinking Skills

☐ **P. 457** Students give examples why Europeans wanted to colonize Oceania. **ELL**

☐ **P. 458** Students create a Venn diagram or T-chart to compare and contrast trust territories and possessions. **Verbal/Linguistic**

☐ **P. 460** Students discuss population distribution in Papua New Guinea. **Logical/Mathematical**

T Technology Skills

☐ **P. 457** Students use the Internet to find out about early ships that were used to travel between islands in Oceania.

☐ **P. 460** Students research pidgin languages and create a vocabulary list of words. **Verbal/Linguistic**

☑ Online Teaching Options

V Visual Skills

☐ **IMAGE** **Colonizing Oceania**—Students use the interactive photo to discuss the early people who colonized Oceania.

☐ **IMAGE** **Copra**—Students use the interactive photo about copra to discuss how it used and why.

W Writing Skills

☐ **IMAGE** **360° View: Bora Bora in the South Pacific**—Students view the image of Bora Bora and write three sentences describing which resources are the most valuable. **AL** **Intrapersonal**

☐ **VIDEO** **Ancient Mysteries—Mystery of Moai**—Students watch the video about early human life in Oceania and write a summary of what they learned. **AL** **Visual/Spatial, Verbal/Linguistic**

☐ **MAP** **Oceania in World War II**—Students view the map and write a description of Oceania's strategic location to the United States military and how that affected the outcome of World War II. **BL** **Visual/Spatial**

R Reading Skills

☐ **GAME** **Drag-and-Drop: Modern Wayfinding**—Students use the drag-and-drop game to review and make connections to the text.

☐ **LECTURE SLIDE** **Pidgin Language**—Students use the lecture slide to discuss the pidgin language and its uses in Oceania.

C Critical Thinking Skills

☐ **IMAGE** **Colonizing Oceania**—Students discuss the early settlement of Oceania and compare and contrast navigation methods, including GPS, compasses, and maps. **Visual/Spatial, Verbal/Linguistic**

☐ **MAP** **Population: Oceania**—Students use the population layer of the Chapter Opener map to discuss the population distribution and density of the region.

☐ **CHARTS AND GRAPHS** **The Population of Papua New Guinea**—Students use the charts and graphs to discuss the changes in population in Papua New Guinea and summarize the breakdown of the population by age and gender. **AL** **Visual/Spatial, Logical/Mathematical**

T Technology Skills

☐ **ONLINE SELF-CHECK QUIZ** **Lesson 2**—Students receive instant feedback on their mastery of lesson content.

LIFE IN OCEANIA

Students will know:
- *that there are marine resources in Oceania that interest other countries.*
- *that Oceania has important shipping routes that make it important to the global economy.*

Students will be able to:
- *describe the economies of Oceania.*
- *explore the major concerns of migration, economics, and the environment in the region.*

UNDERSTANDING
BY DESIGN®

☑ *Print Teaching Options*

V Visual Skills

☐ **P. 463** Students interpret how the image supports the idea that many people live by subsistence farming in Oceania. **AL** Visual/Spatial

☐ **P. 465** Students create graphs to track an economic activity and analyze graphs made by other groups. **BL**

☐ **P. 466** Students write a rap song or musical lyrics that describes the challenges that "pollute" Oceania. **ELL**

W Writing Skills

☐ **P. 463** Students write a three-paragraph essay arguing for or against the policy some Oceania countries have of selling fishing rights to other countries. **Intrapersonal, Naturalist**

☐ **P. 466** Students write a narrative from the point of view of a child whose family lives abroad to earn more money than they could in Tonga. **BL** Verbal/Linguistic

R Reading Skills

☐ **P. 464** Students define words and address multiple meanings of words. **Verbal/Linguistic**

☐ **P. 465** Students cite text evidence to answer questions about the reliance of Oceania on foreign governments. **AL**

☐ **P. 467** Students practice the difference between paraphrasing and summarizing. **Verbal/Linguistic**

C Critical Thinking Skills

☐ **P. 462** Students review the resources they have learned about that have made Oceania attractive to other countries throughout history. **AL** Interpersonal

☐ **P. 463** Students identify problems and obstacles to economic development facing the countries of Oceania and brainstorm solutions. **BL** Interpersonal

☐ **P. 467** Students identify evidence that the nations of Oceania are not immune to conflicts relating to social, cultural, religious, and political issues. **AL** Verbal/Linguistic

T Technology Skills

☐ **P. 465** Students visit the Web sites of Guam and Wake Island and write an evaluation of each. **AL** Visual/Spatial

☑ *Online Teaching Options*

V Visual Skills

☐ **IMAGE** **A Beach in Polynesia**—Students use the image to discuss tourism in Polynesia and make a travel poster to attract visitors to Polynesia. **ELL** Visual/Spatial

☐ **MAP** **Resources: Oceania**—Students use the resources layer of the Chapter Opener map to review the resources of the region.

☐ **VIDEO** **Tropical Fish and Sharks in Tahiti**—Students use the video of tropical fish and sharks to discuss the wildlife of the region and the environment issues of the region.

W Writing Skills

☐ **VIDEO** **Football Samoa**—Students watch the video about the attitudes and goals of young student-athletes in Samoa and write three questions they would like to ask the students and then answer the questions after they watch the video. **BL**

☐ **GRAPHIC ORGANIZER** **Scarce Resources in Oceania**—Students use the cause and effect interactive graphic organizer to discuss the reasons why resources are scarce to the region.

R Reading Skills

☐ **GRAPHIC ORGANIZER** **Economy of Oceania**—Students use the interactive graphic organizer to compare and contrast the economies of Oceania. **AL** Visual/Spatial

☐ **LECTURE SLIDE** **MIRAB economies**—Use the lecture slide to review this economic concept.

C Critical Thinking Skills

☐ **MAP** **Roads and Accessible Resources in New Guinea**—Students use the interactive map to discuss the roads of New Guinea and challenges in constructing roads to accessible areas of the country. Visual/Spatial, Verbal/Linguistic

☐ **VIDEO** **Farming in Papua New Guinea**—Students use the video of farming in Papua New Guinea to extend the discussion about accessible resources.

☐ **CHART** **Cause-and-Effect: Human Migration**—Students use the chart to identify causes and effects of human migration on Oceania and identify factors that could limit human migration and how these would benefit or cause challenges. Visual/Spatial

T Technology Skills

☐ **ONLINE SELF-CHECK QUIZ** **Lesson 3**—Students receive instant feedback on their mastery of lesson content.

INTERVENTION AND REMEDIATION STRATEGIES

LESSON 1 Physical Geography of Oceania

Reading and Comprehension

Have students scan the lesson and use context clues to define the meaning of each content vocabulary word and the academic vocabulary word. Have students write a sentence using each vocabulary word that demonstrates their understanding of each word's meaning. To assess students' comprehension of lesson concepts, have students write a paragraph that uses at least two of the words. For example, students might use the terms *continental island* and *archipelago* to describe the island of New Guinea. Ask volunteers to read their paragraphs to the class.

Text Evidence

Assign six student groups one of the following topics: Micronesia Climate, Micronesia Resources, Melanesia Climate, Melanesia Resources, Polynesia Climate, and Polynesia Resources. Have groups use information from the text to identify key facts about each topic. Students may wish to conduct online research to find additional facts about their topic. Remind students to cite text evidence when making claims about their topic. When students have had time to gather information, have groups present their findings to the class, listing reasons for and against living in the region and defending each side with evidence from the text.

LESSON 2 History and People of Oceania

Reading and Comprehension

To help students organize and comprehend the concepts discussed in this lesson, have them work in pairs to create an outline using the lesson's main headings and subheadings. As students gather information, have them note key ideas and details under each subheading. Encourage students to note content vocabulary terms in their outlines. Students may wish to use a two-column chart to organize their ideas. Encourage students to illustrate their outlines to develop a coherent understanding of each concept. Ask volunteers to present their outlines and charts to the class.

Text Evidence

Read aloud this lesson's Essential Question: *What makes a culture unique?* Assign student groups a region, island, or group of islands in Oceania discussed in this lesson. Tell students they will create a series of storyboards for a television commercial about their region seeking to boost tourism. Storyboards should use simple sketches and phrases to describe the region's cultural features and a list of reasons tourists might want to visit. Students may wish to conduct additional research about their region to give them ideas for their storyboards. After students present their storyboards, guide a class discussion about what makes each region's culture unique.

LESSON 3 Life in Oceania

Reading and Comprehension

Have students work in mixed-ability pairs to look up the definitions of each of the content vocabulary terms in a print or online dictionary. If a term is not listed, such as *MIRAB economies,* have students use context clues in the text to determine the term's meaning. Have students write sentences using each word, showing a clear understanding of each word's meaning as it is used in the lesson. Then have students work with their partner to brainstorm other ways to use each word in a sentence. Encourage students to use the academic vocabulary word in one of their sentences. Circulate to provide corrective guidance.

Text Evidence

To ensure that students have a firm grasp of lesson content, have them write a summary of a topic or issue discussed in the lesson. You may wish to assign topics to students to avoid duplication. For example, students might describe the economic obstacles faced by small, independent countries in Oceania. Remind students to support claims in their summaries with evidence from the text. Encourage students to use content vocabulary words in their summaries.

Online Resources

Approaching Level Reader

Use this online lower-level text that corresponds directly to the text in the online Student Edition.

Guided Reading Activities

This resource uses graphic organizers and guiding questions to help students with comprehension.

Assessing Background Knowledge

Use these worksheets to pre-assess students' background knowledge before they read the chapter.

Reading Essentials and Study Guide Workbook

This resource offers writing and reading activities for the approaching-level student.

Self-Check Quizzes

This online assessment tool provides instant feedback for students to check their progress.

OCEANIA

ESSENTIAL QUESTIONS · How does geography influence the way people live?
· What makes a culture unique? · Why do people make economic choices?

©Charles & Josette Lenars/Corbis

A man of Papua New Guinea wears an elaborate ceremonial headdress.

Lesson 1
Physical Geography of Oceania

Lesson 2
History and People of Oceania

Lesson 3
Life in Oceania

The Story Matters...

Thousands of islands make up the three sections of Oceania in the Pacific Ocean—Micronesia, Melanesia, and Polynesia. Because of their location, the islands attracted Europeans. Oceania's colonization and occupation during World War II had a tremendous impact on the region. Many countries, including the United States, still have strategic military bases there.

FOLDABLES
Study Organizer

Go to the Foldables® library in the back of your book to make a Foldable® that will help you take notes while reading this chapter.

447

ENGAGE

Bellringer Ask a volunteer to find the Equator on a map or globe and to explain how being close to the Equator might affect an area's climate, people, and culture. Then discuss with students how island nations are isolated from other nations. Point out that there are both positive and negative aspects of living on an island. Invite students to provide a list of examples for you to list on the board. Then have students read "The Story Matters..." about Oceania, a collection of islands in the Pacific Ocean. **Ask:**

- **Why would the European countries want to build military bases on islands in the Pacific Ocean?** *(Possible response: This would give European and American countries the ability to get a military force to Asia much more quickly than if the force had to come from the continental United States.)*
- **What are some other reasons the location of these islands may have attracted Europeans?** *(Possible responses: The islands could provide a way for ships to stop and refuel while traveling long distances in the Pacific Ocean. The islands have warm weather and could provide a vacation spot.)*

Comparing and Contrasting Have students look at the picture and then locate the country of Papua New Guinea on the Chapter Opener map. Explain that according to the United States Embassy, Papua New Guinea is one of the most diverse nations in the world. The Melanesians comprise the largest group in the nation, but they are distinct and unique. The rest of the population is made up of Micronesians, Filipinos, Australians, and Chinese. **Ask:**

- **Why do you think Australians and Filipinos might have been attracted to Papua New Guinea?** *(They also come from Pacific Ocean nations that are similar in many respects to Papua New Guinea.)*
- **Why do you think many Chinese have immigrated to Papua New Guinea?** *(Possible answer: Although China is not an island nation, it is located on the Pacific Ocean. The Chinese may have been attracted to the warm climate or job opportunities.)* **Logical/Mathematical, Visual/Spatial**

FOLDABLES®
Study Organizer

Go to the Foldables® library for a cumulative chapter-based Foldable® activity that your students can use to help take notes and prepare for assessment.

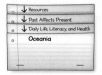

Letter from the Author

Dear Geography Teacher,

Perhaps the most intriguing issue facing the vast region of Oceania is the impact of global warming. Rising sea levels and warming ocean waters will have a noticeable effect on this region of the world. Low islands might disappear beneath the water. Island beaches and shorelines will be altered. Changes in water temperature will affect different types of fish caught. Of greatest concern is that the islands of Oceania will be more susceptible to destruction from typhoons and tsunamis.

Richard G. Boehm

TEACH & ASSESS

Step Into the Place

V1 Visual Skills

Analyzing Maps Have students read the introductory paragraph and look at the map. Explain that the map shows a region in the Pacific Ocean that encompasses groups of islands thousands of miles away from each other. Have students use the map to answer the Step Into the Place questions. **Ask:**

- Why do you think geographers group all of these islands that are far away from each other in the same region? (*Possible answer: They share common characteristics.*)

- What generalizations can you make about the island nations that are possessions or territories of other nations? (*Possible answer: The nations that have authority over some of the island nations may have started colonies on the islands years ago. Some of these nations include New Zealand, the United Kingdom, France, and the United States.*)

- Why are some island nations independent while others are not? Do you notice any patterns? (*Possible answer: Some of the islands that are located in tight clusters are still possessions or territories, but in other places where the island nations are spread out, there are some free nations and others that are not. The island nations that are north and closer to the United States are U.S. possessions. Island nations that are south and closer to New Zealand are possessions of New Zealand.*) **AL** **ELL** Visual/Spatial

V2 Visual Skills

Reading a Map Use the following questions to reinforce students' map skills. **Ask:**

- Which four groups of islands lie closest to the Equator? (*Nauru, Kiribati, Palau, Federated States of Micronesia*)

- Which group of islands has an absolute location of about 20°S, 140°W? (*French Polynesia*)

- Are more of the islands in Oceania north or south of the Equator? (*south*)

- Based on the latitude of this region, what conclusion can you draw about its climate? (*Possible answer: The island nations are close to the Equator, so the region has a warm climate.*) Visual/Spatial, Logical/Mathematical

---

ANSWERS, p. 448

STEP INTO THE PLACE
1. Papua New Guinea
2. Southeast
3. Melekeok
4. **CRITICAL THINKING** None of them are east of the International Date Line because the line is not straight.

Chapter 15
OCEANIA (CCSS)

V1 *Thousands of islands differing in size and extending across millions of square miles of the Pacific Ocean are located in the region called Oceania.*

Step Into the Place

MAP FOCUS Use the map to answer the following questions.

1 **THE GEOGRAPHER'S WORLD** What is Oceania's largest country in land area?

2 **THE GEOGRAPHER'S WORLD** In which direction would you travel to go from the Marshall Islands to the Cook Islands?

3 **PLACES AND REGIONS** What is the capital of Palau?

4 **CRITICAL THINKING** **Describing** Of the Solomon Islands, Tonga, and Samoa, which are located east of the International Date Line?

Map labels: Oceania; NORTHERN MARIANA ISLANDS (U.S.); Saipan; Philippine Sea; Hagåtña GUAM (U.S.); Melekeok; PALAU; FEDERATED STATES OF MICRONESIA; Palikir; SOUTHEAST ASIA; PAPUA NEW GUINEA; Port Moresby; Honiar...; INDIAN OCEAN; Coral Sea; AUSTRALIA; 120°E; 140°E

Step Into the Time

TIME LINE Choose two events from the time line to explain why many countries, including the United States, view the strategic location of Oceania's islands as an important resource. WHST.6-8.2, WHST.6-8.4

W

c. 1500 B.C. First humans come to Oceania

1521 Explorer Ferdinand Magellan lands in Guam

B.C. A.D.

1660 Dutch claim possession of New Guinea

1766 French explore Tahiti, Samoa, and the Solomon Islands

1800

448 Chapter 15

(l) Art Wolfe/Iconica/Getty Images; (r) DeAgostini/SuperStock

---

Project-Based Learning ✋

Hands-On

Creating a Style Book

Students will work in small groups to create a "Choose Your Own Adventure" style book about Oceania. Each group will identify ten to fifteen important ideas to include that capture and describe the physical geography, history, and cultures of Oceania. On each page, students will determine what ideas the reader will be able to connect to next as they progress through the book. Students should look for logical connections between topics when developing the path and options in their books.

Digital Hands-On

Creating an Online Infographic

Students will work independently or in pairs to create an online infographic that will present information about one of the islands, territories, or countries in Oceania. Infographics might include interactive diagrams, videos, and sounds. Students will then present their infographics to the class.

edtechteacher
21st Century Learning

networks
There's More Online!

MIDWAY ISLANDS (U.S.)

TROPIC OF CANCER

HAWAII (U.S.)

WAKE ISLAND (U.S.)

PACIFIC OCEAN

○ National capital
○ Department or territory capital

MARSHALL ISLANDS
○ Majuro

500 miles at Equator
500 kilometers at Equator
Mercator projection

○ Tarawa

Yaren ○
NAURU

EQUATOR

KIRIBATI

TUVALU
SOLOMON ISLANDS
Funafuti ○

TOKELAU (N.Z.)

SAMOA
AMERICAN SAMOA (U.S.)
WALLIS AND FUTUNA ISLANDS (FR.)
Mata-Utu ○ Apia ○ ○ Pago Pago

COOK ISLANDS (N.Z.)

FRENCH POLYNESIA (FR.)

VANUATU
○ Port-Vila
Suva ○
NIUE (N.Z.)
Nouméa ○
NEW CALEDONIA (FR.)
FIJI
Nuku'alofa ○
TONGA

PITCAIRN ISLANDS (U.K.)
○ Adamstown

PACIFIC OCEAN

TROPIC OF CAPRICORN

1946
U.S. conducts atomic bomb tests in Marshall Islands

1830 Christian mission established in Samoa

1900

1860s Conflict and disease kill nearly the entire population of Easter Island

1941–1945 World War II in Pacific and Oceania

2000

2000 U.S. air force base in Guam stores conventional cruise missiles

akg-images/Newscom

Chapter 15 **449**

TIME LINE

Reading a Time Line and Map

Integrating Visual Information Display the interactive time line and map on the whiteboard. Have volunteers read each event as it is revealed on the time line. Ask students to specify the date and the island nation in which the event took place and find its location on the map. **AL ELL** Visual/Spatial

See page 447B for other online activities.

Step Into the Time

V Visual Skills

Reading a Time Line Have students review the time line and as a class, discuss its major points of interest. **Ask:**

- **What generalization can you make about the types of events that have taken place in this region from about 1500 to 2000?** *(Other nations have taken possession of many of the islands or have used them for military purposes.)*

- **How do you think Easter Island's population was nearly wiped out from disease?** *(Possible answer: Outsiders may have brought the disease to the island and introduced it. People did not have immunity to the disease so it spread quickly and devastated the island.)*

- **What event prompted the United States military to conduct atomic bomb tests in the Marshall Islands?** *(World War II)*

- **Why would Guam be a good location to store missiles?** *(Possible answer: Guam is closer to Asia than the United States. The missiles serve as a defense against a potential threat to the United States. The missiles could be launched from Guam in the event of an attack and reach the enemy faster than if they were launched from the United States.)*

Ask students to list some historical events that could be added to the time line. *(Student answers will vary but should include accurate event placement.)* **Visual/Spatial, Verbal/Linguistic**

V

W Writing Skills

Informative/Explanatory Read aloud the activity described at the beginning of the time line. Before writing their paragraphs, have students review the time line events and choose the two they wish to write about. Have students who choose the same events work together to brainstorm ideas about how the region's strategic location makes it an important resource for many countries. Have students share their completed paragraphs with the class. **Logical/Mathematical, Verbal/Linguistic**

CLOSE & REFLECT

Formulating Questions Have students generate a list of questions they have about Oceania based on the chapter introduction. Tell students to look for answers to these questions as they read the chapter.

ENGAGE

🔔 **Bellringer** Point out to students that as the largest ocean in the world, the Pacific Ocean covers 63.8 million square miles, nearly one-third of Earth's surface. Even though Oceania covers only a small part of that area, it is quite a unique region in that it includes many uninhabited areas, and island nations can be spread out over many miles. **Ask: Why is Oceania unique from other regions of the world?** *(Possible answer: Most nations in other regions have neighbors that are relatively close. Nations around the world are inhabited. There really are no other places that have zero population like some islands of Oceania.)*

Have students continue to think about what unique aspects Oceania has and how its unique geography has influenced the way people in the region live. Then make a connection between students' answers and the Essential Question and "It Matters Because" statement.

TEACH & ASSESS

R **Reading Skills**

Determining Word Meanings Discuss with students the names of the three sections of Oceania.

- *Polynesia* comes from Greek words with *poly-* meaning "many" and *nesos* meaning "islands."
- *Melanesia* comes from the Greek words *melas*, which means "black," and *nesos*, which means "islands."
- The Greek words *micros* and *nesos* are the basis for the word Micronesia.

After reviewing these word meanings, **ask: What do you think *Micronesia* means knowing the meanings of the word parts?** *(little or small islands)* **ELL** Verbal/Linguistic

V **Visual Skills**

Creating Charts To reinforce their reading, have students create a three-column chart and label the columns with the three sections that geographers have created in the region: Micronesia, Melanesia, and Polynesia. Have students fill in the islands or island groupings for each section. *(Micronesia: Federated States of Micronesia, Palau, Guam, Marshall Islands; Melanesia: New Guinea, Solomon Islands, Vanuatu, Fiji, Tonga, Samoa; Polynesia: French Polynesia, Kiribati, Niue, Hawaiian Islands, Cook Islands)* **ELL** **AL** Visual/Spatial

---

ANSWER, p. 450

Taking Notes Students' notes should include key facts about the islands, landforms, and climates of Micronesia, Melanesia, and Polynesia.

450

---

networks

There's More Online!

- ☑ **ANIMATION** How Volcanoes Form Islands
- ☑ **SLIDE SHOW** Views of Oceania
- ☑ **VIDEO**

Reading **HELP**DESK (CCSS)

Academic Vocabulary RH.6-8.4
(Tier Two Words)
- capable

Content Vocabulary RH.6-8.4
(Tier Three Words)
- **continental island**
- **archipelago**
- **high island**
- **low island**
- **lagoon**
- **atoll**

TAKING NOTES: *Key Ideas and Details* RH.6-8.2, RH.6-8.7

Organize On a chart like the one below, fill in important facts about the physical geography for each of the areas.

Micronesia	
Melanesia	
Polynesia	

450

Lesson 1
Physical Geography of Oceania

ESSENTIAL QUESTION • *How does geography influence the way people live?*

IT MATTERS BECAUSE
The United States has many interests in Oceania, including marine resources and important shipping routes across the Pacific.

Landforms of Oceania

GUIDING QUESTION *How did thousands of islands appear across the Pacific Ocean?*

Oceania covers 3.3 million square miles (8.5 million sq. km) of the Pacific Ocean between Australia, Indonesia, and the Hawaiian Islands. An estimated 10,000 islands make up Oceania. Most of the islands are small, and many are uninhabited. The smallest inhabited island country is Nauru, which measures a mere 8 square miles (21 sq. km) of land area. Some islands in Oceania are located close together in clusters or island chains. Others stand alone, hundreds of miles from their nearest neighbors.

Islands, Nations, and Territories

R Geographers divide Oceania into three sections, according to culture and physical location. The sections are called Micronesia, Melanesia, and Polynesia. Micronesia is located in the northwest section of Oceania, east of the Philippines. Major islands and island groups in Micronesia are the Federated States of Micronesia, Palau, Guam, and the **V** Marshall Islands. Melanesia is located south of Micronesia and east of Australia. Melanesia's largest island is New Guinea. Other islands and island groups in Melanesia are the Solomon Islands, Vanuatu, Fiji, Tonga, and Samoa. Polynesia is a vast

(l to r) Images & Stories/Alamy; Friedrich Stark/Alamy; Visual&Written/Newscom

---

networks   *Online Teaching Options*

VIDEO

Captain Cook & Tupaia

Formulating Questions Use this video about the exploration and discovery of Oceania by Captain James Cook, and his rival Tupaia, to introduce the lesson. Ask students to write three questions they have about this exploration after watching the video. Lead a class discussion to answer student questions. **ELL** Verbal/Linguistic

See page 447C for other online activities.

BBC Motion Gallery Education

section of Oceania located in the central Pacific Ocean. Major islands and island groups in Polynesia include French Polynesia, Kiribati, Niue, the Hawaiian Islands, and the Cook Islands.

The islands of Oceania range in size from New Guinea, which is 303,381 square miles (785,753 sq. km), to tiny rock outcroppings and patches of sand covering less than 1 square mile (2.6 sq. km). Oceania's islands vary in physical characteristics such as landforms and native plants and animals. The islands also differ in their forms of government. Some islands, such as Fiji and Palau, are independent countries. Other islands, such as American Samoa, Guam, and New Caledonia, are overseas territories that are under the jurisdiction of other countries. Australia, England, France, New Zealand, and the United States have island territories in Oceania. One island, New Guinea, is divided politically.

The Divided Island of New Guinea

New Guinea is the largest island in Oceania. New Guinea is a **continental island**, an island that lies on a continental shelf and was once connected to a larger continental landmass. New Guinea lies on the same continental shelf as Australia and was part of that continent during the past when sea levels were lower. New Guinea is now part of the Malay Archipelago. (An **archipelago** is a group of islands clustered together or closely scattered across an area.)

Traditional homes along the Sepik River in Papua New Guinea are thatched houses on stilts. In this swampy and isolated area, the dugout canoe is the only means of travel.

Chapter 15 **451**

SLIDE SHOW

Views of Oceania

Describing Show students the slide show on the landforms and waterways of Oceania. Have students write a paragraph to describe the landform and waterway that most interests them. Ask students to exchange their paragraphs with a partner to decide if they would like to change their choices based on their partner's descriptions. **AL** Intrapersonal, Naturalist

See page 447C for other online activities.

(l) ©Ocean/Corbis, ©Kryssia Campos/Getty Images, (tr) Erica Simone Leeds, (br) ©IG Photography/Alamy

Images & Stories/Alamy

C Critical Thinking Skills

Drawing Conclusions Review with students how island nations in Oceania are diverse politically. **Ask: Why are some islands independent while others in Oceania are under the jurisdiction of other countries?** *(Possible answer: Some colonizing nations did not want to give up these islands as possessions. They realized the strategic importance of the islands' location.)* **AL** Logical/Mathematical

R Reading Skills

Defining After reading the section, "The Divided Island of New Guinea," ask a volunteer to explain what a continental shelf is *(an underwater plain that forms a border to a continent and often ends at the continental slope)*. Verbal/Linguistic

T Technology Skills

Using and Citing Information Ask students to draw a sketch of an archipelago based on the description in their text. Then ask students to write three details about the Malay Archipelago. Point out useful text and online materials in which students can find details and information about the Malay Archipelago. Ask them to find out what other archipelagos exist around the world and to share their findings with the class. **ELL** Visual/Spatial

Content Background Knowledge

Share these facts about New Guinea with students:

- New Guinea is the second largest island in the world *(Greenland is the largest)*.
- The Fly-Digul shelf and surrounding area boast one of the wettest places around the globe. This area is also one of the places in the world with the fewest inhabitants.
- Kuk Early Agricultural Site, a UNESCO World Heritage site, serves as a rare example of the development of independent farming over thousands of years.
- The island is situated in the Ring of Fire, an area of high earthquake and volcanic activity. Dozens of earthquakes hit the region each year.
- A volcano in Bougainville, Papua New Guinea, is the most active volcano in the area.

Children play in a highland village in the Owen Stanley Range of Papua New Guinea. The rugged mountain range is the southeastern part of a long mountain chain that stretches across New Guinea, the world's second-largest island after Greenland.

C Critical Thinking Skills

Comparing and Contrasting Have students work with a partner to read about New Guinea and then to complete a Venn diagram that compares and contrasts the two parts of the island. Point out that they should include political as well as geographical differences. Ask student pairs to trade diagrams with another pair to check their work, making revisions as needed. **ELL** Verbal/Linguistic

R Reading Skills

Identifying Divide the class into two groups. One group will write characteristics of high islands and the other group will write about low islands. Give students slips of paper on which to write the characteristics. Each slip of paper should have one unique characteristic. After students have completed writing the characteristics, mix up all the slips of paper from both groups. Tape one of the slips of paper to each student's back. Provide about 5 minutes for students to walk around the classroom asking other students *yes* and *no* questions to try to determine if they have a characteristic of a high island or low island. Example: "Am I very green?" "Am I a flat island?" Discuss as a class how this activity helped them learn the differences between high islands and low islands. **AL** Kinesthetic, Visual/Spatial

Content Background Knowledge

Many scientists predict that the low island Tuvalu will be completely covered by water within the next fifty years. In 2005 the population of Tuvalu was about 11,000 people. The land area of this island nation is about 10 square miles. Some Tuvaluans are already seeking refuge in other countries, such as Australia. In fact, Australia has promised to take in all of the Tuvaluans in the event the island should be swallowed by the sea. Have students discuss the challenges facing the Tuvalu people and government. Prompt students with questions such as the following:

- What will happen as people leave the country?
- Should the country try to convince people to stay?
- What happens if the people who have the most education and skills leave?
- How will the government help people if the waters overtake the land very quickly?

Physically, New Guinea is one island; however, the island is divided into two parts. The western part belongs to Indonesia. The eastern part is an independent country called Papua New Guinea. Both parts of the island have the same types of land features, plants, animals, climate, and resources. Only the eastern part of the island, Papua New Guinea, however, is considered part of Oceania. When describing the physical features of the island, we will use the name of the country, Papua New Guinea.

Papua New Guinea has a great many different landforms. A very large mountain range stretches across the island. This chain of rugged mountain peaks and glaciers dominates the inland areas of the island. Low mountains and fertile river valleys roll across northern Papua New Guinea. Papua New Guinea also has a northern coastal plain. In the south, swampy lowlands lead to the Owen Stanley Range, which is considered the "backbone" of Papua New Guinea.

The Smaller Islands

Oceania includes several physically different types of islands. **High islands** have steep slopes rising from the shore, higher landforms, and diverse plant and animal life. High islands are generally the largest and greenest of Oceania's small islands. The soil that covers high islands is fertile, and the climates are generally humid and rainy. Many have freshwater streams, rivers, and waterfalls. These conditions allow dense rain forests to grow. Tahiti and the Hawaiian islands are examples of high islands.

Low islands are smaller, flatter islands with sandy beaches. Low islands tend to have fewer forests and less diverse plant and animal life. Most of the islands scattered across Micronesia and Polynesia are low islands. The typical "desert island" described in books and seen in films could be classified as a low island. Some desert islands in Oceania are so low they just break the water's surface. The island country of Tuvalu is an example of a low island with an extremely low elevation. Tuvalu is gradually being eroded by ocean waters. With each passing decade, Tuvalu loses more surface area, as its land washes away with the tides. If sea levels continue to rise, Tuvalu and Oceania's other lowest islands will disappear below the water.

Friedrich Stark/Alamy

---

netw⊙rks   *Online Teaching Options*

GAME

Drag-and-Drop: Low and High Islands

Identifying Use the interactive game to review the concepts of the low and high islands of Oceania. Have students take turns dragging and dropping the characteristics of each island type into the correct category. After students have practiced, divide the class into two teams and see which team can get the most correct answers. **AL** Kinesthetic, Verbal/Linguistic

See page 447C for other online activities.

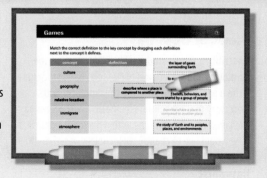

The islands of Oceania were formed by processes involving the lithosphere, the hydrosphere, and the biosphere. Most of Oceania's low islands were formed by a gradual process involving volcanic eruptions (lithosphere), erosion by water movement (hydrosphere), and the growth of coral (biosphere). This process began millions of years ago with the eruption of an undersea volcano. As lava from the volcano cooled, it formed a buildup of volcanic rock below the surface of the water. Corals started growing on the volcano, eventually forming large reefs that circled the volcano. Over time, the volcano crumbled and sank, while the coral reefs continued to grow higher and higher. The coral reefs built up layer upon layer until they grew above the water's surface. Waves crashing against the reefs eventually eroded channels, allowing ocean water to flood the center area of the island and form shallow pools called **lagoons**. As the reef aged, crumbled, and died, ocean waves deposited sediment, such as sand and tiny specks of plant and animal life, on the coral remains. The resulting landform is called an **atoll**, a coral island made up of a reef island surrounding a lagoon. If the center of an island does not fill with water, or if the atoll becomes completely covered with sediment over time, a desert island forms.

R

The majority of the high islands in Oceania were formed by underwater volcanoes. As lava from erupting volcanoes flowed into the ocean waters, it cooled and formed huge mounds of volcanic rock. Eventually the volcanic rock built up above the water's surface, forming high islands.

T

☑ **READING PROGRESS CHECK**

Identifying What are the names of Oceania's sections?

DIAGRAM SKILLS >

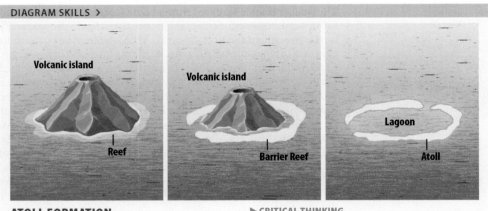

ATOLL FORMATION
South Pacific atolls are known for their beautiful coral reefs and marine life, which draw tourists from around the world. The typical atoll takes about 30 million years to form.

▶ **CRITICAL THINKING**
1. *Describing* What two processes are involved in atoll formation?
2. *Analyzing* How might tectonic plate movements affect the formation of an atoll?

Chapter 15 **453**

R **Reading Skills**

Citing Text Evidence Have students read the text about the detailed process of how the low islands formed in this region. Then have students use text evidence to answer the questions.
Ask:

- **What are the three main parts of the process?** *(volcanic eruptions, erosion and deposition by water movement, the growth of coral)*
- **How did coral reefs grow after the volcano erupted?** *(After the eruption, the volcano crumbled over time and the coral grew higher and higher in a circle around the sinking volcano.)*
- **What happened to the coral reef as waves crashed on them?** *(Waves eroded channels, causing ocean water to flood the center of the island.)*
- **What happens when the center of an island does not fill with water, or if the atoll becomes covered with sediment?** *(A desert island forms.)* **Verbal/Linguistic, Intrapersonal**

T **Technology Skills**

Transferring Knowledge Have a student volunteer explain the process of volcanoes erupting and forming the high islands, as described in the text. Point out to students that this is a process that occurs over a long period of time. Pair students and ask them to create a presentation to illustrate this process. Encourage students to use a software program. Explain that technology such as a software program can speed up a lengthy process so that it appears the process happens quickly. Provide support as needed, including giving students access to additional resources. Have students show their presentations to the class. **BL** **Logical/Mathematical**

W **Writing Skills**

Informative/Explanatory Have students use the text and the diagram to write a five-paragraph essay explaining how the Oceania islands were created. Provide students with this question as a writing prompt: ***How were the islands in Oceania created?*** Remind students that they should use clear and concise writing, strong transitions to illustrate sequence in the process, and an introduction and conclusion. **AL** **Verbal/Linguistic**

ANSWERS, p. 453

☑ **READING PROGRESS CHECK** Micronesia, Melanesia, and Polynesia
CRITICAL THINKING
1. coral reef growth and the gradual sinking of a volcanic island
2. Tectonic plate movements begin the process by creating a volcanic island around which coral reefs later form and build up as the island slowly sinks.

C Critical Thinking Skills

Interpreting Have students read the caption and study the photograph of the diver harvesting black pearls in an oyster farm under the water. **Ask:** Do you think it is a good economic choice for French Polynesia to rely on the black pearl industry for its export economy? Why or why not? *(Students answers will vary but should be explained and supported with economic understanding of relying too heavily on one export.)* **AL** Intrapersonal

V Visual Skills

Creating Maps Have students use the descriptions in the text as a guide to create a sketch of New Guinea's climate zones. Ask them to use colored pencils or markers as well as a map key to illustrate the differences in temperatures and precipitation in the two climate zones of the island. **BL** Naturalist

R Reading Skills

Using Context Clues After students read the section, "Climates of the Smaller Islands," have them scan the paragraph and jot down any words that were unfamiliar to them. Remind students that identifying context clues can often help to reveal the meaning. **Ask:**

- **What context clues help you to determine the meaning of** *typhoons*? *(storms, intense winds, powerful waves, toppling trees and houses and eroding island shores)*
- **How does knowing the meaning of** *typhoon* **help you to understand what a monsoon wind is and how it is different from a typhoon?** *(Sample answer: I know that a typhoon is a storm that can cause high winds, high waves, and heavy rain. Typhoons are part of the island's normal weather patterns during the rainy season. Monsoon winds are brought by different weather patterns and only affect one island in the island group, probably because of its location near the western Pacific and Indian Oceans.)* **ELL** **AL** Verbal/Linguistic

French Polynesia is known for its black pearl industry. Oysters containing the black pearls are raised in underwater farms. Black pearls make up more than half of French Polynesia's exports.
▶ **CRITICAL THINKING**
Analyzing Why are other abundant ocean resources, such as fish and seafood, used by Oceania's people but not exported?

Academic Vocabulary

capable having the ability to cause or accomplish an action or an event

Climates of Oceania

GUIDING QUESTION *What factors affect climate in Oceania?*

Nearly all of Oceania's islands are located within the Tropics. Only a few, such as the Midway and Pitcairn Islands, lie north or south of this climate zone. Thus, most of Oceania's islands have warm, humid, tropical climates. The islands located outside the Tropics have mixed tropical and subtropical climates. Some islands experience local climate variations caused by elevation, winds, and ocean currents.

Papua New Guinea Climates

Papua New Guinea has two climate zones: tropical and highland. The lowland areas have warm to hot temperatures. The highland regions are much cooler. For example, the average daily temperature in the lowland coastal plains is 82°F (28°C). The average daily temperature in the highland mountains is 73°F (23°C). Papua New Guinea's climate is wet, with an average of 45 inches (114 cm) of rain falling on the island annually. February is the month with the most rainfall, and July has the least. Monsoon rains are common. Dense rain forests grow well in the warm, wet conditions, and much of the island is covered in trees and other forest plants. Papua New Guinea does, however, experience occasional droughts caused by the El Niño effect.

Climates of the Smaller Islands

The smaller islands scattered throughout Oceania have tropical and subtropical climates. Temperatures on the islands are generally warm throughout the year. Oceania's islands receive large amounts of rain. Seasonal rainfall patterns determine an island's wet season, which is the time of year when the heaviest rains fall. Islands located north of the Equator, such as the Marshall Islands and Palau, have a wet season from May to November. Islands located south of the Equator, such as Samoa and Tonga, have a wet season from December to April. The rainfall patterns occur under normal conditions. Heavy rains can also be caused by storms, such as typhoons. Typhoons cause intense winds and powerful waves **capable** of toppling trees and houses and eroding island shores. Only the island of Yap is affected by monsoon winds, which are brought by weather patterns of the western Pacific and Indian oceans.

☑ **READING PROGRESS CHECK**

Analyzing The Northern Mariana Islands experience a wet season from May to November. Based on this information, are the Northern Mariana Islands located north or south of the Equator?

Visual&Written/Newscom

netw♦rks   *Online Teaching Options*

MAP

Climates: Oceania

Making Inferences Have students make inferences about the climate zones of the islands in Oceania. Then dislay the climate layer on the Chapter Opener map. Work with students to check to see if their inferences were correct. **Visual/Spatial, Verbal/Linguistic**

See page 447C for other online activities.

ANSWERS, p. 454

CRITICAL THINKING One possible answer is Oceania's distance from major markets in places like the United States and Europe. Another is the fact that Oceania's people fish on a small-scale basis for themselves and their families and do not have enough left over to export.
☑ **READING PROGRESS CHECK** north of the Equator

Resources of Oceania

GUIDING QUESTION *What natural resources do the islands of Oceania possess?*

Most of Oceania's islands are small. Limited land area limits the amount of natural resources, such as minerals, to be found on land. Still, the islands have some valuable resources. Resources that the islanders trade or sell are essential to the islands' economies.

Papua New Guinea's Resources

The independent nation of Papua New Guinea has natural resources such as gold, copper, timber, fish, petroleum, and natural gas. Compared to the island's size, Papua New Guinea's natural gas reserves, discovered fairly recently, are large. They have the potential to benefit the nation's economy.

Resources of the Smaller Islands

Oceania's smaller islands have few valuable natural resources for trading on the international market. Limited land area is one reason for this; another reason is that low islands, based on coral, do not have rock foundations. It is in deep layers of rock that large deposits of metal ores, such as gold, are found. New Caledonia is also developing wind power by building large stands of wind turbines. This technology is beginning to spread to other islands. People living in rural areas of Kiribati and the Solomon Islands have begun using solar-powered lighting in their homes. Wind and solar energy are renewable, nonpolluting resources. Because of the sunny climates and ocean winds, these resources are plentiful throughout Oceania.

Some of Oceania's high islands have large trees that are used for timber, rubber, and other products. Soil quality varies from island to island. Some islands, such as those with rich volcanic soil, have excellent soil for growing farm crops. Other islands have poor-quality soil, making farming difficult. Fish and other seafood are important resources for the people in Oceania. Most islands use fish only for their own food, not for export.

✔ READING PROGRESS CHECK

Identifying What are two types of renewable resources in Oceania?

FOLDABLES
Study Organizer

Include this lesson's information in your Foldable®.

LESSON 1 REVIEW (CCSS)

Reviewing Vocabulary (Tier Three Words)
1. Why is New Guinea called a *continental island*? RH.6-8.4

Answering the Guiding Questions
2. *Identifying* Which countries have territories in Oceania? RH.6-8.2
3. *Describing* What is the difference between New Guinea and Papua New Guinea? RH.6-8.5

4. *Determining Central Ideas* In what ways are low islands and high islands alike and different? RH.6-8.2
5. *Analyzing* What factors affect the climates of Oceania? RH.6-8.1
6. *Analyzing* Why would people living in rural Kiribati and the Solomon Islands use solar-powered lights in their homes? RH.6-8.1
7. *Informative/Explanatory Writing* In your own words, write a paragraph describing how an atoll forms. WHST.6-8.2, WHST.6-8.4

Chapter 15 **455**

T Technology Skills

Collaborating Point out to students that natural gas is a more recent discovery and a resource that is being developed and expanded in Papua New Guinea. Have students work in small groups or pairs to research what natural gas is used for in China, how China ranks in the world's production and consumption of natural gas, and how much natural gas is produced and consumed in Papua New Guinea. Then have students use the information they gathered to create a graph or chart using computer software. Use the charts as a reference for a class discussion on the consumption and production of natural gas and the limits created by reliance on such a nonrenewable resource for energy needs. **BL** Naturalist

C Critical Thinking Skills

Determining Cause and Effect Discuss with students the importance of the smaller islands' locations and climates and how these affect their resources and economies. **Ask:**

- Why have people on the islands developed inexhaustible resources such as sun and wind power? *(Because they do not have many mineral resources such as natural gas, coal, and petroleum, which many other nations often use for energy needs.)*
- How is the climate an asset to the islands? *(The abundant sunshine provides the resource to produce solar energy.)* **Verbal/Linguistic, Naturalist**

Content Background Knowledge

A major gas and oil company initiated the Papua New Guinea liquefied natural gas (PNG LNG) project to develop three large gas deposit regions located in the southern and western highlands of Papua New Guinea. The natural gas discoveries were found in Hides, Angore, and Juha. Estimates of total natural gas reserves in these locations are substantial. A major factor in this initiative was an agreement signed in 2009 with China to import gas from the island nation via a pipeline.

CLOSE & REFLECT

Formatting Questions To close this lesson, have students write questions based on the information presented about landforms and waterways, climates, and natural resources of Oceania. Review these questions as well as the questions the students wrote at the beginning of the lesson. If any questions remain unanswered, ask for a volunteer to research the answer.

> **ANSWER, p. 455**
>
> ✔ **READING PROGRESS CHECK** Answers should include two of the following: solar energy, wind energy, trees, fish, or other seafood.

LESSON 1 REVIEW ANSWERS

Reviewing Vocabulary

1. The island lies on a continental shelf and was once connected to a larger continental landmass, Australia.

Answering the Guiding Questions

2. **Identifying** Australia, England, France, New Zealand, and the United States

3. **Describing** New Guinea is the name of the entire island. Papua New Guinea, an independent nation located on the eastern part of the island, is the only part of the island that is included in Oceania.

4. **Determining Central Ideas** Alike: island types in Oceania; formed by processes involving lithosphere. Different: Low islands—built on coral reefs, sandy and flat, little plant and animal life; high islands—

built on volcanic rock, rocky and steep, dense forests, diverse plant and animal life, often larger

5. **Analyzing** Answers should mention physical location (north or south of the Equator, within the Tropics), elevation, the El Niño effect, weather patterns of western Pacific and Indian Oceans.

6. **Analyzing** Sample answers: Solar energy is plentiful. Homes are not wired for electricity. Energy resources such as oil, coal, and natural gas are scarce.

7. **Informative/Explanatory Writing** Students' paragraphs should describe how atolls form, including volcanic eruptions, coral growth and erosion, deposition of sand, sediment, and plant and animal matter, erosion by waves, and formation of lagoons.

ENGAGE

Bellringer Help students understand that civilization in Oceania began much later than in other areas of the world. Explain that even though 1500 B.C. seems like a long time ago, compared to other civilizations it is young. Ask students to brainstorm ideas about why civilization began much later in Oceania than in other regions of the world. **Ask: From where do you think most of the first inhabitants migrated?** *(Possible response: Asia or Australia)*

TEACH & ASSESS

V Visual Skills

Creating Time Lines After students read about the first humans in Oceania, have them create a time line and plot the events from the text on it. Ask students to keep this time line handy while reading the lesson and to add new events to it as they continue to read. **Visual/Spatial**

R Reading Skills

Calculating After reading, have students describe *wayfinding* and how ancient people used this method of early navigation. Invite volunteers to describe how to get from one place in the school to another by using landmarks and referring to distance by the amount of time it might take. Explain that wayfinding usually uses the sun and stars, and as such is not the same as the physical landmarks students used in the activity. **Ask:**

- Why might using wayfinding be particularly useful when traveling out at sea? *(There are no actual landmarks at sea. Using the relationship to the stars, sun, and patterns of ocean movement would be more helpful.)*
- How would people using wayfinding describe distances? *(how long it would take to get somewhere, such as a day's or week's travel)*
- How does using the method of wayfinding differ from using a compass, sextant, or other measuring tool? *(Using wayfinding does not provide as precise a measurement of distance because the stars are at about the same angle or in the same relative place for a longer distance when traveling on the ground or in the ocean.)* **ELL** Kinesthetic, Logical/Mathematical

---

ANSWER, p. 456

Taking Notes Students' notes should summarize important information from each section of the lesson.

---

networks

There's More Online!

☑ **CHART/GRAPH** The People of Oceania

☑ **IMAGE** Colonizing Oceania

☑ **VIDEO**

Reading **HELP**DESK

Academic Vocabulary RH.6-8.4
(Tier Two Words)
- distinct

Content Vocabulary RH.6-8.4
(Tier Three Words)
- **wayfinding**
- **trust territory**
- **possession**
- **pidgin**
- **fale**

TAKING NOTES: Key Ideas and Details RH.6-8.2, RH.6-8.7

Summarize Using a chart like the one shown here, summarize important information from each section of the lesson.

History of Oceania	People of Oceania

Lesson 2

History and People of Oceania

ESSENTIAL QUESTION · *What makes a culture unique?*

IT MATTERS BECAUSE
Oceania has a unique culture but one that faces challenges.

History of Oceania

GUIDING QUESTION *How were the islands of Oceania populated?*

The first humans began settling in Oceania sometime around 1500 B.C. Historians believe the early settlers came from Southeast Asia, using available resources to build large sailing canoes. They filled their sturdy canoes with people, food, plants, and animals. Traveling from west to east and powered only by sails, the settlers crossed the waters of the Pacific Ocean.

The Polynesian Migrations

Their only way of navigating was to use the ancient practice of wayfinding. **Wayfinding** is a method of navigation that relies on careful observation of the natural world. For many thousands of years, humans have charted courses across the open ocean by watching the sun, the stars, and the movement of ocean currents and swells. Wayfinding was practiced long before the invention of navigation instruments, such as compasses and sextants. Even today, navigators practice wayfinding as a way to stay connected to Earth and to keep cultural traditions alive.

Over many centuries, people from areas such as the Philippines and Indonesia sailed from their homelands and settled the islands across Oceania. Many islands were uninhabited until settlers from other islands migrated farther into unexplored areas of Oceania.

(l to r) Douglas Peebles/Alamy; Mark Harris/The Image Bank/Getty Images; PIF/Alamy; Patrice Coppee/Stockimage/Getty Images

456

---

networks · *Online Teaching Options*

VIDEO

Ancient Mysteries—Mystery of Moai

Summarizing Use this video about the history of the Moai on Easter Island to introduce the lesson. As they watch the video, ask students to jot down notes. Then have them write a summary of what they learned. Invite volunteers to share their summaries with the class. **AL** Visual/Spatial, Verbal/Linguistic

See page 447D for other online activities.

BBC Motion Gallery Education

The Coming of Europeans

European explorers began sailing through Oceania in the 1500s. They began colonizing the islands in the 1600s. Often, violent conflict broke out between colonists and native people. During the 1800s and 1900s, Christian missionaries came to thousands of islands in the region. Native people did not always welcome the missionaries. Many missionaries succeeded, however, in converting local populations to Christianity. Christian faiths are still widely practiced across Oceania.

Europeans had many reasons for wanting to colonize territories in Oceania. For practical reasons, the locations of many islands made them convenient stops for ships crossing the vast Pacific Ocean. Travelers wanted safe, reliable locations to restock their ships with food, drinking water, and other supplies. European powers were also interested in claiming resources.

Some Europeans mined gold and other precious metals from the islands. Some governments also saw the advantage of building military bases in Oceania. In fact, many islands in the region were occupied by Japanese, German, English, and American forces during World War II. Several battles were fought in the region. Unfortunately, some islands in the Pacific also became testing sites for nuclear weapons.

Contemporary Times

After World War II, many island colonies began to demand independence. Some independence movements involved conflict, but many islands were able to negotiate freedom with their former colonial powers. Some islands negotiated independence by "free association" with foreign powers.

A typical South Pacific canoe lies on a beach in Fiji. Early people, originally from the Asian mainland, sailed and settled in Oceania centuries before the arrival of Europeans in the 1500s.

▶ CRITICAL THINKING
Describing How were early people able to sail vast distances to settle Oceania?

Douglas Peebles/Alamy

Anja Fleig/age fotostock

V Visual Skills

Creating Time Lines After students read about the arrival of the Europeans in Oceania, have them draw a break in their time line to indicate a large amount of passing time and add this event after the break. Remind students to keep this time line handy as they will be adding more events to it. **Ask: How many years did the people of Oceania live without contact from Europeans?** *(about 3,000 years)* **AL** Logical/Mathematical

C Critical Thinking Skills

Giving Examples Display a world map or a map showing European exploration and colonization, 1500–1945. After students read about why Europeans wanted to colonize in Oceania, distribute sticky notes to them. Ask pairs of students to write the reasons for the European and United States interest in Oceania on the sticky notes.

Challenge students to think of additional reasons that are not listed in their text. Allow students to take turns posting the reasons on the map. After students have exhausted all examples, discuss them as a class. **ELL** Visual/Spatial, Kinesthetic

T Technology Skills

Researching on the Internet Have students work in pairs or small groups to use the Internet to find out about early ships that were used to travel between islands in Oceania. Here are two Web sites that may be helpful for students:

• www.taimaui.org/polynesia.html
• www.sea.edu/spice233.

Students can choose an island or group of islands and then click on maritime history. Then, have students create a poster or other visual presentation that summarizes the main points of what they learned about the types of ships that were used to travel between the islands hundreds of years ago. **Verbal/Linguistic**

IMAGE

Colonizing Oceania

Comparing and Contrasting Use the interactive image to begin a discussion about the early settlement of Oceania. Have students view the image and discuss the type of vessel used by settlers to navigate the Pacific Ocean. Review the practice of wayfinding. Have students compare and contrast this method of navigation with modern methods like GPS, compasses, and maps. Have students share an experience they have had using any of these methods. **Visual/Spatial, Verbal/Linguistic**

See page 447D for other online activities.

Interactive Photos

ANSWER, p. 457

CRITICAL THINKING Without navigational instruments, the early people charted courses across the open ocean by observing the sun, the stars, and the movement of ocean currents and swells.

V Visual Skills

Integrating Visual Information Use the image to review with students how missionaries introduced Christianity to the people of Oceania. **Ask: How does this image illustrate the effects of European colonization of Oceania?** *(One lasting effect of European colonization is that Christianity became a lasting part of the culture and this mission in particular has some European elements to its architecture.)* **AL** **Visual/Spatial**

C Critical Thinking Skills

Comparing and Contrasting Have students work with partners to create a Venn diagram or T-chart to compare and contrast trust territories and possessions. **Ask:**

- **Could an island nation in Oceania that is a possession ever enjoy independence? If so, how?** *(Yes, it could gain independence from the foreign government that controls it.)*
- **What is the involvement of the United Nations in trust territories?** *(The UN places governing authority of a nation over another country.)*
- **Do you think it is fair for the United States and European countries to have control in this region?** *(Possible answers: No because these countries are very far from the United States and Europe. Yes because Europe and the United States provide support for the local people.)* **Verbal/ Linguistic**

Content Background Knowledge

Share these facts about the island of Palau with students:

- Palau is comprised of about 340 coral or volcanic islands.
- Japan took Palau from Germany during World War I but lost control of it during World War II.
- The Republic of Palau was formerly part of the UN Trust Territory of the Pacific Islands, which was set up in 1947.
- In 1981, the United States set up a government in Palau with a presidential head.
- In 1994, Palau became an independent republic.
- Palau has free association with the United States.
- The United States military provides defense for Palau.
- Palau's population has a literacy rate of nearly 100 percent.

ANSWER, p. 458

✓ READING PROGRESS CHECK The first Europeans came to Oceania to explore the region and later to colonize the islands to exploit their resources and to use them as military bases and supply stations; missionaries came to convert local people to Christianity.

V

The bicycles of worshippers are parked outside a picturesque Catholic church on the Fakarava atoll in the Tuamotu Islands. Built mostly of coral in 1874, the building is the oldest church in Polynesia. Christian faiths are widely practiced in Oceania today.

The island of Palau, for example, is an independent republic, but it has a voluntary free association with the United States. Palau has its own constitution and governs itself. Palau and the United States have an agreement that benefits both: Palau allows the United States to keep military facilities on one of its islands, and in return, the United States provides millions of dollars of aid money to Palau each year.

Other islands in Oceania have agreements of various kinds with foreign governments, including Australia, New Zealand, Great Britain, France, and the United States. The agreements generally involve use of land or other resources in exchange for military protection and economic aid. Relationships between island territories and foreign governments have different levels of political control and responsibility. A **trust territory** is one that has been placed under the governing authority of another country by the Trusteeship Council of the United Nations. The Marshall Islands were a trust territory until they gained independence in 1986. **Possession** is another name for a territory occupied or controlled by a foreign government and its people. French Polynesia can be classified as a possession because it is an overseas territory of France. Trust territories and possessions do not govern themselves but are run by foreign governments.

C

✓ READING PROGRESS CHECK

Describing Why did the first Europeans come to Oceania?

Mark Harris/The Image Bank/Getty Images

netw⌖rks   *Online Teaching Options*

MAP

Oceania in World War II

Describing Have students view the map that shows Oceania's role during World War II. Point out how vital Oceania was to the Allied effort in the Pacific Theatre during the war. Ask students to write a description of Oceania's strategic location to the United States military and how that location affected the outcome of World War II.
BL **Visual/Spatial**

See page 447D for other online activities.

The People of Oceania

GUIDING QUESTION *What is life like in Oceania?*

Many people imagine the South Sea Islands as tropical paradises. There are many wonderful things about living in this beautiful region of the world. On the other hand, life in Oceania has many challenges.

The People of the Region

Oceania has one of the world's most diverse populations. So many different ethnic groups live on Oceania's thousands of islands that it is impossible to classify them all. Groups have their own **distinct** languages, cultures, and ways of life. Many islands are home to a wide range of ethnic groups. The most amazing diversity is found in Papua New Guinea.

Papua New Guinea has a total human population of more than 6 million. This is by far the largest population of any of Oceania's islands. Papua New Guinea's large population is condensed onto an island about the size of California.

The island country's population is made up of people from many different ethnic and native tribal groups. Natives of Papua New Guinea make up about 84 percent of the total population. The native population includes people from hundreds of tribal groups. The other 16 percent come from various backgrounds, including Polynesian, Chinese, and European.

The different groups have their own lifestyles, cultural traditions, beliefs, and languages. Geographers and language experts believe 860 different languages are spoken in Papua New Guinea. In other words, 10 percent of all languages known to exist are used in Papua New Guinea.

Academic Vocabulary

distinct separate; easily recognized as separate or different

The *USS Bonhomme Richard* pulls into Apra Harbor in Guam. The *Bonhomme Richard* is an amphibious assault ship. These ships are able to land and aid forces on shore during armed conflict.

▶ **CRITICAL THINKING**
Describing What are the terms of agreement between foreign governments and the islands of Oceania?

PIF/Alamy

Chapter 15 **459**

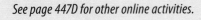
CHARTS

The Population of Papua New Guinea

Analyzing Charts and Graphs Use the charts and graphs about population to discuss with students the changes in population of this region. Have students work with a partner to summarize the breakdown of the population by age and gender. Then have them make predictions about how the population will change in the next fifty years. **AL** Visual/Spatial, Logical/Mathematical

See page 447D for other online activities.

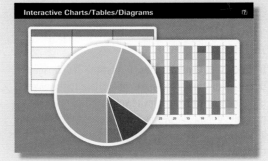

Interactive Charts/Tables/Diagrams

R Reading Skills

Discussing Have students read aloud the introductory paragraph for the section, "The People of Oceania." Then, **ask:** How do you think people of Oceania feel about the fact that others simply imagine the area as a tropical paradise and think nothing more about the islands? *(Possible response: In some ways they may think this is a good thing because tourism is important to the region. If people think of the area as a paradise, then they are more likely to come there for a vacation. In other ways it is not good because this means that people are not thinking about the politics and economy of the region.)* **Interpersonal**

C Critical Thinking Skills

Finding the Main Idea Have the class read aloud the first two paragraphs of the section, "The People of the Region." **Ask:**

- What is the main idea of this section? *(Oceania has one of the world's most diverse populations.)*
- What are some examples of this diversity? *(In Papua New Guinea, over 860 different languages are spoken. There are many different ethnic groups and hundreds of tribal groups.)* **AL** Verbal/Linguistic

V Visual Skills

Creating Graphs Use this activity to help students grasp the significance of the number of languages spoken in Papua New Guinea. Tell students that the world's population is roughly 8 billion. Have students create a circle graph that shows the percentage of the world's population living in Papua New Guinea. *(To find the percentage represented divide 6 million by 8 billion. At 0.75 percent, Papua New Guinea's population is less than 1 percent of the world's population.)* Then have students create another graph that shows the percentage of the world's languages spoken in Papua New Guinea *(10 percent).* Finally, have students compare the graphs. **Ask:** How do the graphs help to illustrate the diversity of the population? *(They show that the percentage of languages is much greater than the percentage of people in relation to the world population. This helps to visually illustrate how diverse the population of New Guinea really is.)* **Logical/Mathematical, Visual/Spatial**

ANSWER, p. 459

CRITICAL THINKING In return for economic aid and military protection, governments in Oceania allow foreign countries, such as the United States, to keep military facilities on certain islands.

This village is located on Viti Levu, the largest and most populous of Fiji's more than 300 islands. About 75 percent of Fiji's 600,000 people live on Viti Levu. The island measures about 65 miles (106 km) from north to south and 90 miles (146 km) east to west.

T Technology Skills

Researching Have pairs who are interested research pidgin languages using reliable sources and create a vocabulary list of words that would most likely be used in a pidgin language. Then have students research a specific pidgin language and find the meaning of several of the words they listed. Have pairs demonstrate using the pidgin language they have created for the class. Challenge students to combine their lists into one chart that shows the meanings of the various words in the pidgin languages that were researched. **Verbal/Linguistic**

C Critical Thinking Skills

Reasoning Discuss with students how much of the population of Papua New Guinea lives in rural areas. **Ask:** Why do you think more people live in rural, versus urban, areas? *(Possible answer: The physical geography of the island makes it more conducive. The region does not have the resources to create urban settings, and cultural influences lean toward rural life.)*

Explain to students that in many places around the world, coastal areas are often more populated than the highlands. **Ask:** Why do you think Papua New Guinea has the opposite population distribution? *(Possible answer: because the area is near the Equator the lowlands may be too hot or perhaps bug-infested. The highland areas would offer cooler temperatures. Also a factor are earthquakes and tsunamis which make highland areas safer and therefore better places to build a community.)* **Logical/Mathematical**

W Writing Skills

Informative/Explanatory After students read the section on the culture of the region, have them choose a topic to write about related to Polynesian or Micronesian culture, such as storytelling, dancing, celebrations, art, or food. Explain to students that they should write an informative essay in which they inform, or explain, how a particular Oceania group practices the tradition, where the group lives, a brief history, and any other information that would be relevant to the topic. **Verbal/Linguistic**

In spite of speaking many different languages, the people of Papua New Guinea are still able to speak to one another. Many of the people speak their own language, as well as a pidgin language. A **pidgin** is a simplified language that is used for communication between people who speak different languages.

Such a wide diversity has both positive and negative effects. For instance, Papua New Guinea's many different ethnic groups create a rich and varied culture on the island. An endless variety of music, foods, clothing, and artwork can be enjoyed. At the same time, serious problems, such as crime, ethnic discrimination, and violent conflicts among tribal groups, are common.

Papua New Guinea's population is denser in some parts of the main island than in others. In general, highland areas have higher population densities than do the lowlands and coastal plains. Only about 12 percent of the population live in urban areas. Isolated towns are hidden in rugged mountain areas. Thousands of distinct tribal groups live in small villages in the islands' many remote locations. A traditional folk saying in Papua New Guinea is, "For every village, a different culture."

The Culture of the Region

Life in the villages of Oceania is based on tradition. Many traditions involve fishing, diving, and celebrating battle victories. Another tradition is an important event in the lives of young people called coming-of-age ceremonies. In Polynesian cultures, ceremonies and celebrations include feasts and dancing. Like their ancestors, Polynesian people practice artistic wood carving and use the carvings to decorate their homes. Many traditional Polynesian and Micronesian cultures practice tatooing. Micronesian people use storytelling to retell history and to keep track of family heritage. The Melanesian people were the only traditional culture of Oceania known to use bows and arrows in hunting.

Patrice Coppee/StockImage/Getty Images

netw⊙rks   *Online Teaching Options*

IMAGE

Interactive Photos

360° View: Bora Bora in the South Pacific

Determining Central Ideas Display the 360° image of Bora Bora to students to make connections to the physical geography of the region. Invite volunteers to point out examples of how the people of the area use the land and location as resources. Ask students to write three sentences describing which resources are the most valuable. **AL** **Intrapersonal, Verbal/Linguistic**

See page 447D for other online activities.

©Pete Atkinson/Getty Images

In the island nation of Samoa, traditional homes called **fales** are common. *Fales* are open structures made of wood poles with thatched roofs. Local trees are used to make the poles, and palm leaves are used for roof thatch. The dwellings have no walls and are used mainly for shade and shelter from frequent rainfall.

Today, Oceania's many island cultures are mixtures of traditional and modern practices, beliefs, and lifestyles. Although they have adopted many Western attitudes, people see the value in continuing some of the traditional ways.

For example, Christianity is widely practiced in island communities, along with elements of traditional religions, such as songs, dances, and ceremonial costumes. Many island people wear Western-style clothing and hairstyles. Cell phones and laptop computers are common. Elements of local traditional cultures, including tribal tattoos, jewelry, and art forms such as wood carving, are common on many islands, as well.

Traditional celebrations are practiced throughout Oceania. Some traditional events, such as the Hawaiian luau, have become more modern in recent decades. Luaus were traditionally ritual ceremonies and feasts celebrating important events, such as victories in battle. Centuries ago, men and women ate in separate areas during luaus, and only chiefs ate certain foods. Some luaus were attended only by men. Today, luaus are banquets of traditional and modern foods eaten on a low table.

Maintaining elements of traditional cultures in their lives is important to the people of Oceania. Respecting and continuing certain traditions keeps cultures alive. Celebrating the traditional culture of their ancestors gives young people a sense of pride and identity. Making the past part of the present keeps people of all ages connected to their cultural heritage.

FOLDABLES
Study Organizer

Include this lesson's information in your Foldable®.

☑ **READING PROGRESS CHECK**

Analyzing Why might using a pidgin language be useful to the population of Papua New Guinea?

LESSON 2 REVIEW (CCSS)

Reviewing Vocabulary (Tier Three Words)
1. For what purpose did the early people of Oceania use *wayfinding*? RH.6–8.4

Answering the Guiding Questions
2. *Identifying* For approximately how long have humans been living on the islands of Oceania? RH.6–8.2

3. *Identifying* List three of the many groups of people who came to Oceania from other parts of the world. RH.6–8.2

4. *Determining Word Meanings* Would a *fale* be an appropriate home for the climate where you live? Why or why not? RH.6–8.4

5. *Distinguishing Fact From Opinion* Is the following statement about the culture of Oceania a fact or an opinion?

   With more than 860 different spoken languages, Papua New Guinea has one of the most culturally diverse populations in the world. RH.6–8.8

6. *Narrative Writing* Write a short story from the perspective of a young person living a traditional lifestyle in a small village on one of the islands of Oceania. Include details about your daily life. Describe your home, your family and friends, the foods you eat, the work you do, and what you do for fun. WHST.6–8.4, WHST.6–8.10

Chapter 15 **461**

LESSON 2 REVIEW ANSWERS

Reviewing Vocabulary

1. to navigate at sea

Answering the Guiding Questions

2. **Identifying** since about 1500 B.C.; approximately 3,500 years

3. **Identifying** Students should list three of the following: Southeast Asians, Australians, Taiwanese, Indonesians, Europeans, and Americans.

4. **Determining Word Meanings** Possible response: No because I need walls to keep out strangers and wild animals.

5. **Distinguishing Fact from Opinion** This statement is a fact. The number of languages spoken can be counted and proved. The cultral diversity can also be determined by counting the various groups.

6. **Narrative Writing** Students' narratives should describe the life of a young person living a traditional lifestyle on one of the islands of Oceania, including details of daily life such as housing, family, work, and so on. Narratives should be well-organized and meet standards for spelling and grammar.

V **Visual Skills**

Visualizing Invite a volunteer to read the paragraph describing a *fale*. **Ask: Why do you think the people of Samoa make this kind of structure to serve as a home?** *(Possible answer: They use the resources in their environment, which include palm trees. They need protection from the sun and rain, but do not need walls for warmth.)* **ELL** **Visual/Spatial**

R **Reading Skills**

Expressing Explain to students that even though many people in Oceania live in rural areas and practice traditional cultures, Western culture also exists. Ask students to choose an Oceania culture to represent. You may allow them to choose on their own or provide them with one to achieve a good mixture. Remind them that both Western and non-Western cultures need to be represented. Inform them that they will be walking around the classroom performing an activity that is representative of a culture in Oceania.

Allow time for students to gather or make props. Set aside time for students to walk around the classroom with their props, performing and observing. After students have completed the exercise, give them the following writing prompt to summarize what they learned. **Ask: How did this activity help you to better understand the cultural diversity in Oceania? What did you learn?** *(Students' summaries will vary but should include that Oceania is mostly rural and its cultural diversity is high.)* **AL** **Kinesthetic, Verbal/Linguistic**

CLOSE & REFLECT

Drawing Conclusions To close this lesson, have students use the time lines that they made at the beginning of the lesson as a snapshot of the history of Oceania. Ask them to add any events that they missed and to look for connections between events and the people and cultures that represent Oceania today. Then have students write about 2–3 events that helped shape the history and culture of the region.

ANSWER, p. 461

☑ **READING PROGRESS CHECK** The peoples of Papua New Guinea speak more than 800 different languages, so using a pidgin language would help them communicate with one another during daily life.

ENGAGE

Bellringer Lead students in a discussion about different types of economic challenges. Begin by having students list the types of economic challenges that a nation might face and those that individuals and families might face. A sample T-chart is shown below. Then ask students to read the Essential Question and "It Matters Because" statement. Invite volunteers to reflect upon the connection between them and discuss the challenges people face in caring for others.

Economic Challenges	
National	**Individual or Family**
high unemployment	personally not working or having trouble finding a better-paying job
lack of natural resources	housing costs are too high
unskilled workforce	personal skills have become obsolete
inflation or recession	difficulty paying for food or clothes
shortage of goods	

TEACH & ASSESS

C Critical Thinking Skills

Making Comparisons Review with students the resources they have learned about that have made Oceania attractive to other nations throughout history *(location and mineral resources)*. **Ask:**

• What other resources are important to Oceania? *(the region's people and its agricultural products)*

• How are people, the human resource, the most important to the future of Oceania? *(The people are the ones who do the work, who make the decisions about how to use resources, and who enable the economy to grow.)*

AL Interpersonal

ANSWER, p. 462

Taking Notes Responses should demonstrate understanding of the main causes and effects of issues in modern Oceania, such as economic challenges, migration issues, and current issues and events.

---

networks

There's More Online!

☑ **IMAGES** Tropical Fish and Sharks in Tahiti

☑ **SLIDE SHOW** A Beach in Polynesia

☑ **VIDEO**

Reading HELPDESK (CCSS)

Academic Vocabulary RH.6-8.4
(Tier Two Words)
• collapse

Content Vocabulary RH.6-8.4
(Tier Three Words)
• cash crop
• resort
• remittance
• MIRAB economy

TAKING NOTES: *Key Ideas and Details* RH.6-8.5, RH.6-8.7

Determine Cause and Effect As you read, use a graphic organizer like the one shown here to identify two important issues and describe the effects of the issue.

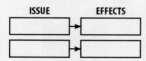

ISSUE	EFFECTS

462

Lesson 3
Life in Oceania

ESSENTIAL QUESTION • *Why do people make economic choices?*

IT MATTERS BECAUSE
The people of Oceania face economic challenges that affect the United States and other countries.

The Economies of Oceania

GUIDING QUESTION *How do the people of Oceania earn their living?*

The islanders of Oceania face difficult economic challenges. With small land areas, few valuable resources, and vast distances between islands, earning a living in Oceania can be difficult. The people of Oceania, however, have found ways to support their families. They also take great care in using the natural resources available to them. Despite challenges, Oceania's island communities have the potential for a bright economic future.

Papua New Guinea's Economy

Papua New Guinea has the most valuable natural resources in Oceania, other than Australia and New Zealand. The challenge is to locate, harvest, and transport the resources through Papua New Guinea's wild and rough terrain.

Gold and copper are Papua New Guinea's most profitable resources. Sales of gold and copper account for about 60 percent of the country's total export income. Other major exports are silver, timber, and agricultural products. **Cash crops** are crops grown or gathered to sell for profit. Papua New Guinea's cash crops include coffee, cacao, coconuts, rubber, and tea.

Mining and farming provide jobs for many people in Papua New Guinea. Industries such as timber processing, palm oil refining, and petroleum refining employ many

(l to r) Peter Solness/Lonely Planet Images; AARON HUEY/National Geographic Stock; ©George Steinmetz/Corbis

---

networks *Online Teaching Options*

VIDEO

Football—Samoa

Formulating Questions Use this video about the attitudes and goals of young student athletes living on the island of American Samoa to introduce the lesson. Ask students to write three questions they would most like to ask students who live on this island nation. After students watch the video, ask them to write the answers to these questions based on the information they learned watching the video.

BL Interpersonal, Verbal/Linguistic

See page 447E for other online activities.

BBC Motion Gallery Education

others. The tourist industry also provides many jobs. The vast majority of Papua New Guinea's people, however, live by subsistence farming. Most families raise their own food crops, such as yams, taro, bananas, and sweet potatoes. Some raise pigs or chickens for meat and eggs. Although the unemployment rate in Papua New Guinea is low, most people earn low incomes. The government of Papua New Guinea plans to increase exports of minerals and petroleum to strengthen the country's economy.

Economies of Small, Independent Countries

Smaller independent island countries throughout Oceania face many obstacles to economic development. With limited land, poor soil quality, and large populations, many islands must import much of their food, fuel, finished goods, and raw materials. Most islands import far more than they export—many import five or six times more goods and materials than they export. On the tiny island country of Tuvalu, for example, import values exceed export values by 200 to 1. People on the smaller islands raise what food they can by subsistence farming.

Some islands in Oceania raise limited cash crops, such as fruits, vegetables, sugar, nuts, coffee, tea, cocoa, and palm and coconut oils. The farms and plantations that produce cash crops employ some island residents. This type of agricultural work can be physically exhausting and usually pays very little.

Fish and other seafood are available across Oceania. Fishing operations on the smaller islands are usually small; fishers catch only enough to feed their families or to sell to local markets. Most island countries do not have the equipment or processing facilities for operating large fishing industries. Some island countries earn revenue by selling fishing rights to other countries. Japan, Taiwan, South Korea, and the United States are some of the foreign lands that pay for access to Oceania's marine resources.

On islands that have minerals and other marketable resources, many people work for industries such as mining, fishing, clothing, and farming. Some people make a living by using local materials, such as shells, wood, and fibers, to create art and to craft tools and artifacts.

Farmers in Oceania often grow taro, a root vegetable, brought from Southeast Asia centuries ago. The leaves and the root of the taro plant are widely used in South Pacific cooking.

▶ **CRITICAL THINKING**
Describing Why is subsistence farming widely practiced in Oceania?

Peter Solness/Lonely Planet Images/Getty Images

MAP

Roads and Accessible Resources in New Guinea

Comparing and Contrasting Display the map for students and then use it to discuss the roads of New Guinea. Click on the vegetation layer and ask students what challenges they think the people of New Guinea face in constructing roads to accessible areas of the country. Ask volunteers to point out where these areas are and what solutions they can offer. **Visual/Spatial, Verbal/Linguistic**

See page 447E for other online activities.

C Critical Thinking Skills

Identifying Problems Have students name the obstacles to economic development that are described in the section, "Economies of Small, Independent Countries," *(limited land, poor soil quality, large populations)*. Divide the class into groups and have each group discuss one of the three problems. Challenge groups to brainstorm reasons that this problem is particularly difficult in the region. If students are able to think of solutions, they should share these as well. Have group representatives summarize the discussion for the class.
BL **Interpersonal**

W Writing Skills

Argument Read aloud the sentences about some island countries in Oceania that sell fishing rights to other countries. Discuss with students the positive and negative effects on resources and the environment of this economic policy. Then ask students to write a three-paragraph essay arguing for or against this policy. Remind students that they should write a topic sentence that clearly states their argument and then to include specific details that support their argument in the main body of their essay. Provide an opportunity for students to do additional research to gather information for their essays. Invite students to present their essays to the class. **Intrapersonal, Naturalist**

V Visual Skills

Integrating Visual Information Provide time for students to read the caption and study the image. **Ask:** How does this image of a local man farming in Oceania support the statement, *"Many people live by subsistence farming in the region"*? *(Possible answer: The plot of land for this farm is small and is near what appears to be the man's home. The crop looks to be sufficient to feed a small group of people. The farmer may have enough left after feeding his family to sell a little bit in the marketplace. But this is not the same as raising a crop that is mainly intended for sale in the marketplace or for use as an export.)* **AL** **Visual/Spatial**

ANSWER, p. 463

CRITICAL THINKING Limited land and poor quality soil prevent widespread commercial farming. People raise what they can to provide food for their families.

V Visual Skills

Visualizing Have students read the caption and study the image. Discuss with them how this image could be used by the tourist industry to attract tourists to French Polynesia. **Ask: What words could you use to describe what you observe in this image?** *(Possible answers: breathtaking view, clear water, amazing fish, paradise, island getaway)* Have students use the information from the text to create a tourism advertisement for the region. **AL** **Verbal/Linguistic**

R Reading Skills

Defining Read aloud the sentence with the word *remittances* in it. Ask volunteers to share the definition of the word. *(wages that are earned in a foreign country and sent back to the home country)* **Ask: What does it mean when you are asked to *remit* a payment?** *(to pay or to make a payment)* Point out that remit has multiple meanings, but in this usage it refers to sending money back to family members, not making a required payment. **Verbal/Linguistic**

C Critical Thinking Skills

Predicting Consequences After students have finished reading the paragraph on MIRAB economies, discuss with them how Oceania is not the only region of the world with such economies. Explain that this economic model has worked in the region because of Oceania's unique situation—its physical geography and resources. **Ask: Do you think that many of Oceania's nations will continue to use the MIRAB model? Why or why not?** *(Possible answer: Yes, I think that many nations of the region will continue to use this model because such a large percentage of the population relies on the money earned by people who live and work far away.)* **BL** **Logical/Mathematical**

Content Background Knowledge

Studies have shown that the majority of remittances in Oceania are used for food. In the small island of Ware, New Guinea, nearly 90 percent of remittances are spent on food. Other basic necessities such as clothing are also purchased with remittances. Little money is left over from these earnings for savings or education because many people are working to meet basic needs.

Tourists go snorkeling at a beach resort in French Polynesia. Tourism is now the major industry in Oceania, creating jobs and bringing in money for many people of the region. Most of Oceania's tourists come from Australia, New Zealand, Japan, and other countries of the Pacific area.

Academic Vocabulary

collapse a sudden failure, breakdown, or ruin

Tourism is important to the economies of many small, independent countries in Oceania. Tourists come from all over the world to enjoy the sunshine, warm ocean waters, and panoramic views. **Resorts** provide comfortable lodging, food, recreation, and entertainment. Most resorts are located in beautiful natural areas, such as tropical beaches, mountains, and forests. Tourist businesses employ thousands of people. Without the revenue from tourism, many small island countries would be at risk of economic **collapse**.

Many people on the islands that have less-developed economies depend on income earned by family members living overseas. Thousands of young people have left Oceania in search of jobs in other countries. Most have settled in Australia, New Zealand, and the United States. Young workers support their families in Oceania by sending them the money they earn. Foreign-earned wages, called **remittances**, are vital sources of income for families. Workers employed overseas also send remittances to pay for community projects, such as schools. Workers contribute to their home countries' tourist industries when they return for visits.

Many of the islands of Oceania with less-developed economies are known as **MIRAB economies**. MIRAB is an acronym for *migration, remittances, aid,* and *bureaucracy*. Island countries with MIRAB economies are not able to fully support the needs of their people through their own resources and labor. These countries depend on outside aid and remittances from workers who have migrated to overseas areas. One example of a MIRAB economy is the Polynesian island nation of Tonga. Tonga raises a few export crops, such as squash, vanilla beans, and root vegetables. The tourist industry also brings in some revenue. Still, the most important source of income for most Tongans is remittances. Seventy-five percent of all Tongan families receive money from family members who live and work elsewhere.

464 Chapter 15

AARON HUEY/National Geographic Stock

net**w**rks *Online Teaching Options*

IMAGE

360° View: A Beach in Polynesia

Analyzing Images Make use of the 360° image to illustrate the tourism industry in Polynesia. Have students take turns pointing out details and examples of the industry. Invite students to share stories of people they know who have visited Polynesia or another islands around the world. Have small groups of students make a travel poster to attract visitors to Polynesia. **ELL** **Visual/Spatial**

See page 447E for other online activities.

Interactive Photos

©Pete Atkinson/Getty Images

Tonga and many other small island countries also depend on aid from foreign governments. The governments of Australia, Great Britain, Japan, New Zealand, and the United States have created international trust funds for many islands in Oceania. Foreign governments also give money directly to various island countries. Governments of MIRAB economies use some of the foreign aid for food, schools, water and sanitation, and other basic needs. Foreign aid also funds economic development by expanding local industries and exports. **R**

Economies of America's Pacific Islands

American Samoa is a territory of the United States. Nearly all of American Samoa's economic activity involves the United States. The island group's chief industry is tuna fishing and processing, which employs 80 percent of its people. American Samoa produces a few cash crops, such as bananas, coconuts, taro, papayas, breadfruit, and yams.

The unemployment rate is high at nearly 30 percent. One cause of unemployment in American Samoa is the lasting impact of a 2009 earthquake and tsunami. The disasters caused terrible damage to the islands and their transportation systems, electrical systems, and businesses. Some industries were completely ruined, causing loss of jobs. Other industries, such as tourism, are starting to regain strength and show promise for future development. **V**

Other U.S. territories in Oceania include Guam and Wake Island. Both islands are home to U.S. military bases. Local people are employed in transportation, housing, maintenance, food service, and other industries that serve the needs of military personnel. Guam also has a well-developed tourist industry. **T**

☑ **READING PROGRESS CHECK**

Describing In your own words, briefly explain MIRAB economies.

Issues Facing the Region

GUIDING QUESTION *What challenges do the people of Oceania face?*

Despite signs of progress, the future is uncertain for the islands of Oceania. Three major areas of concern in the region are migration, economics, and the environment.

Human Migration

The movement of people from the islands of Oceania to other parts of the world is a major issue. So many young people have left Oceania to seek employment overseas that the populations of some islands have changed dramatically. The island of Tonga is an extreme example: Population estimates show that 50 percent of all Tongan people live abroad in foreign countries.

R Reading Skills

Citing Text Evidence Have students use text evidence to answer the following questions about the reliance of Oceania nations on foreign governments. **Ask:**

- **Which foreign countries provide the bulk of financial support to the nations of Oceania?** *(Australia, New Zealand, Great Britain, Japan, and the United States)*
- **How is some of the foreign aid used?** *(food, schools, water and sanitation, other basic needs, economic development)*
  AL **Verbal/Linguistic**

V Visual Skills

Creating Graphs Discuss with students the economic challenges that American Samoa faces. Then assign small groups of 2–3 students to create graphs to track an economic activity such as tuna fishing, cash crop production (bananas, coconuts, taro, papayas, yams), and tourism in American Samoa, over the last 5–10 years. Depending on class size and the number of groups you have, you may want to assign one or two cash crops to a group. Explain that students may create line graphs or bar graphs and that they must list their sources below their graphs.

After students have completed their graphs, post them in the classroom for all to study. Have students identify any trends they notice about the economy of American Samoa. Then have the class note any changes that might indicate the impact of the 2009 earthquake and tsunami. **BL** **Logical/Mathematical**

T Technology Skills

Evaluating a Web Site Point out to students that even though the nations of the Pacific Islands are small, many do have Web sites. Explain that Guam and Wake Island are both home to United States military bases. Have students work with a partner to evaluate the Web sites of these two Pacific Island nations. Then have students work independently to write an evaluation of the Web sites. They should compare the type of information that both sites provide and to rate the "user experience." Invite volunteers to share their evaluations with the class. **AL** **Visual/Spatial**

Economy of Oceania

Comparing and Contrasting Use the interactive graphic organizer to review with students the elements of the economies of Oceania. Encourage volunteers to compare and contrast the economies. Then have students complete their own graphic organizer to compare and contrast two Oceania economies of their choice.
AL **Visual/Spatial, Logical/Mathematical**

See page 447E for other online activities.

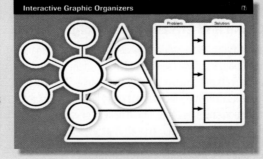

Interactive Graphic Organizers

ANSWER, p. 465

☑ **READING PROGRESS CHECK** Students should paraphrase the text about MIRAB economies, including information about remittances and the need for foreign aid.

W Writing Skills

Narrative Explain to students that narrative writing involves writing a story describing something that happens. Ask students to write a narrative from the point of view of a child whose family lives abroad so that his or her parents can earn more money than they could back in Tonga. Narratives can be about a day in the life of the child, what it is like to go to school in a new country, or some other aspect of daily living. Students can address issues such as missing family or friends who are still living in Tonga, differences in culture, and/or leisure activities. Tell students to be sure their narratives contain dialogue and have a logical flow. Encourage students to share their narratives either in small groups or with the class. **BL Verbal/Linguistic**

C Critical Thinking Skills

Speculating Have students discuss the challenges (cultural, social, economic, and political) that sending workers to other countries to earn a living has caused for these Pacific Island nations. **Ask: How will sending workers to other countries affect Oceania in the future?** *(Possible answer: If emigration is not controlled or immigration is not encouraged, the islands of Oceania will serve primarily as military bases and tourist destinations. Some cultures may lose their influence in this region.)* **Interpersonal**

V Visual Skills

Simulating Ask students to read the caption and examine the image of trash covering the beach on the island of Kiribati. **Ask: How does this image represent the challenges facing many of the island nations of Oceania?** *(It shows one problem created by growing urban populations. It also shows how the population growth is leading to other problems, such as environmental problems.)*

Have students work with a partner to write a rap song or musical lyrics that describe the challenges facing Oceania, such as pollution. Encourage students to perform their completed work for the class. **ELL Auditory/Musical, Verbal/Linguistic**

The major population shift has had negative effects. A large percentage of the people remaining in Tonga are children or older people who are unable to work. Migration has left many young and elderly Tongans without caregivers. The income that migrating workers send home helps.

Most Tongan workers who live abroad maintain strong ties to their homeland. With half of all Tongans now living overseas, however, more and more Tongan children are born in other countries. These children will grow up as natives of their adopted lands, not as native Tongans. Within the next few years, the majority of Tongan people will be born and raised overseas. This situation can weaken cultural ties to the homeland, as more foreign-born Tongans adapt to the cultures where they live.

Economics and Society

Another major issue in Oceania is the need for economic development. Many islands have slow economic development because of lack of resources. New industries cannot be planned and built without money to invest in growth and development. The need is urgent on islands where large numbers of people are migrating from farms and rural villages to cities to try to find work. With fewer people living in rural areas, fewer people are growing their own food. There is a continuing need across Oceania to buy food, energy resources, and raw materials from other countries. Many countries of Oceania import more goods and services than they export. When a less-developed country imports more than it exports, the entire economy is affected. Countries like to export more than they import because this creates jobs and demand for their goods and services.

Trash covers an otherwise-attractive beach on the island nation of Kiribati. Oceania, like other parts of the world, faces serious problems with waste pollution caused by an increasing population, rapid economic development, and the concentration of people in urban centers.

©George Steinmetz/Corbis

466 Chapter 15

networks   *Online Teaching Options*

CHART

Cause and Effect: Human Migration

Identifying Have students review the chart of human migration. Randomly select students to identify causes and effects of human migration on Oceania. Then ask students to identify factors that could limit human migration and how these would benefit or cause challenges for Oceania. **Visual/Spatial**

See page 447E for other online activities.

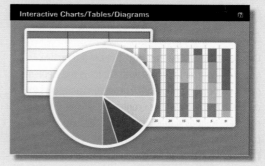

Interactive Charts/Tables/Diagrams

Tensions and Conflict

Although most island nations in Oceania are free of conflict, some unrest occurs. Crime and human rights abuses are problems on some of the islands. In Fiji, tensions between native Fijians and immigrants from India led to conflicts. The Solomon Islands have also seen conflict on issues. Disagreement on the issue of land rights led to conflict between the native people of Guadalcanal and people from the neighboring island of Malaita. Peace was restored with help from the United Nations.

C

Environmental Issues

The islands of Oceania face serious environmental issues, including climate change, deforestation, pollution, natural disasters, and declining fish populations. Many scientists and island residents view climate change as one of the most urgent and serious issues in the region. With continued global warming, sea levels are already rising. If this continues, many of Oceania's low islands could be completely covered by water. Some of the lowest islands are already experiencing surface flooding from rising oceans and eroding beaches.

R

Natural disasters such as earthquakes, tsunamis, typhoons, and resulting floods continue to threaten the islands. These events have the potential to destroy homes and claim lives, and they can also damage farmland and natural habitats.

Survival of Marine Animals

Commercial fishing companies have harvested so many fish from some areas that almost no fish remain for local people to catch and eat. When huge numbers of fish are caught at one time, the remaining fish are unable to reproduce quickly enough to restore populations. In time, entire populations of fish will be gone. Ocean pollution also threatens the survival of fish and other marine animals.

FOLDABLES
Study Organizer

Include this lesson's information in your Foldable®.

✓ **READING PROGRESS CHECK**

Citing Text Evidence Why is climate change a serious concern for the islands of Oceania?

LESSON 3 REVIEW

Reviewing Vocabulary (Tier Three Words)
1. What is the major difference between *cash crops* and subsistence crops? RH.6-8.4

Answering the Guiding Questions
2. *Identifying* List three ways the people of Oceania earn a living. RH.6-8.2
3. *Describing* How does aid from foreign countries benefit islands with MIRAB economies? RH.6-8.5
4. *Citing Text Evidence* The birthrate in Tonga has increased, but the island's population has decreased. Explain. RH.6-8.1

5. *Citing Text Evidence* What do you think is the most serious issue or challenge in Oceania today? Use information from the lesson in your explanation. RH.6-8.1, WHST.6-8.9
6. *Argument Writing* Using information from the lesson, write an argument either in favor of or against remittances. Explain why you believe remittances benefit or harm the cultures and economies of Oceania. WHST.6-8.1, WHST.6-8.4

Chapter 15 **467**

LESSON 3 REVIEW ANSWERS

Reviewing Vocabulary

1. Cash crops are grown to sell for profit; subsistence crops are grown by families and individuals for their own use as food.

Answering the Guiding Questions

2. **Identifying** Students should identify any three of the following: fishing, cash crop farming, mining, fish and timber processing, clothing manufacturing, making crafts, and working in the tourist industry.

3. **Describing** Foreign aid pays for people's basic needs, such as food, water and sanitation, schools, and so on; foreign aid also funds economic development by expanding local industries and increasing exports.

4. **Citing Text Evidence** Although the birthrate is

high, more people migrate away from Tonga than are born in the nation. Therefore, the overall population is decreasing.

5. **Citing Text Evidence** Responses should identify the problem the student thinks is the most serious, and provide supporting details from the text. *Sample response: I feel that deforestation is the most serious issue in Oceania, because lack of trees will harm the environment, threaten the survival of other species, deprive humans of building materials and timber resources, and add to existing soil erosion problems by removing supportive root systems from the soil.*

6. **Argument Writing** Students' arguments should be in the form of a clear argument, including facts from the lesson and students' personal opinions.

C Critical Thinking Skills

Identifying Evidence Tell students that conflicts are common problems in various regions of the world and can relate to social, cultural, religious, or political issues. Help them understand that civil wars do not need to break out in order for there to be conflict between groups of people. **Ask: What evidence does the text give that the nations of Oceania are not immune to such conflicts and tensions?** *(In Fiji, tensions between native Fijians and immigrants from India have led to conflicts. The native people of the Solomon Islands have argued over land rights with the people of Malaita.)*

Ask students to make a list of possible solutions to these tensions, and then use them as a starting point for small-group discussions. **AL** **Verbal/Linguistic**

R Reading Skills

Paraphrasing Tell students that a paraphrase is a restatement of text that captures all of the ideas. This is different from a summary because a summary includes only the most important ideas or details. Have half of the class write paraphrases of the section, "Environmental Issues." Have the other half of the class write summaries of the section. Then have volunteers read aloud their paraphrases and summaries. Help students identify whether or not the person wrote a summary or a paraphrase. **Verbal/Linguistic**

CLOSE & REFLECT

Summarizing To close this lesson, have students discuss ways in which the nations of Oceania are trying to handle the many challenges that the region faces. Help them understand that Oceania is unlike other regions of the world that face tensions and conflicts because of cultural differences. Instead, Oceania's issues are more economic and environmental. Discuss the measures that the governments of Oceania have taken to diversify their economies. Point out that the many environmental problems that Oceania is dealing with are also unique to this world region. Ask students to revisit the Essential Question and "It Matters Because" statement to make connections by discussing how the governments of Oceania will care for their people in the wake of these challenges.

ANSWER, p. 467

✓ **READING PROGRESS CHECK** Climate change is leading to rising sea levels and declining fish populations. These create serious problems for the islands of Oceania.

CHAPTER REVIEW ACTIVITY

Have students review the chapter and create a T-chart listing the resources of Oceania and the challenges that the region currently faces. Tell students to list their examples in the appropriate column of the chart for each type. *(Possible answers: **Resources**—climate, location, fish, petroleum, natural gas, agricultural products: palm oil, coconut, bananas, rubber, copra, papaya, tea, coffee, cocoa; **Challenges**—severe weather conditions such as tsunami, flooding, and typhoons; earthquakes, land disputes, emigration, pollution caused by population growth and urban sprawl, unemployment)* **Visual/Spatial, Logical/Mathematical**

Resources	Challenges

REVIEW THE ENDURING UNDERSTANDINGS

Review this chapter's Enduring Understanding with students:

- *People, places, and ideas change over time.*

Now pose the following questions in a class discussion to apply this to this chapter.

- **How are the island nations of Oceania making use of their resources?** *(Possible answer: The region's location is a resource and some islands allow other countries to establish military bases there. Their climate is a resource, which attracts tourists to the islands, so some islands cater to this source of income by building hotels and restaurants. The islands are also preparing for the future by looking into the use of renewable resources like solar energy and wind.)*

- **How did European colonization affect Oceania?** *(Possible answer: Some island nations have gained their independence, while others have remained or have become possessions or trust territories.)*

- **How have the island nations of Oceania avoided serious tensions and conflicts among the many diverse groups of people?** *(Possible answers: The islands are separate and distinct. Their borders were not drawn by outsiders, such as Europeans during the colonization period.)*

Chapter 15 ACTIVITIES CCSS

Directions: Write your answers on a separate piece of paper.

❶ Use your FOLDABLES to explore the Essential Question.
INFORMATIVE/EXPLANATORY WRITING It is generally believed that inhabitants of Southeast Asia began to populate the islands of Oceania more than 2,500 years ago. Describe their method of navigation known as *wayfinding*. RH.6-8.4, WHST.6-8.2

❷ 21st Century Skills
DETERMINING CENTRAL IDEAS Work in a group to learn more about one of the island countries of Oceania. Put together a travel brochure to appeal to people who are interested in traveling there. Annotate your brochure with information from the text and from online sources. RH.6-8.2, WHST.6-8.9

❸ Thinking Like a Geographer
ANALYZING How did the South Pacific's physical geography contribute to Oceania's cultural diversity? RH.6-8.1

❹ GEOGRAPHY ACTIVITY

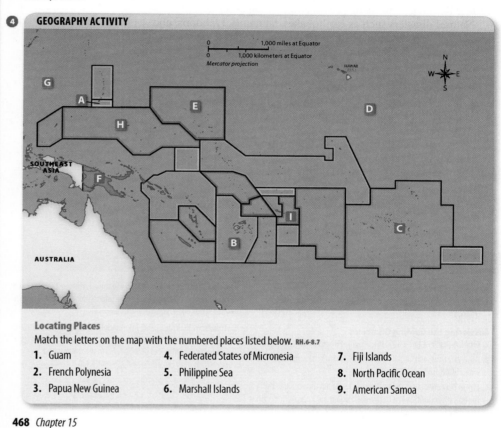

Locating Places
Match the letters on the map with the numbered places listed below. RH.6-8.7

1. Guam
2. French Polynesia
3. Papua New Guinea
4. Federated States of Micronesia
5. Philippine Sea
6. Marshall Islands
7. Fiji Islands
8. North Pacific Ocean
9. American Samoa

ACTIVITIES ANSWERS

Exploring the Essential Question

❶ **INFORMATIVE/EXPLANATORY WRITING** The navigational method known as *wayfinding* is based on careful observation of the natural world. As the early travelers to Oceania made their way eastward across the Pacific, they relied on the sun, the stars, and ocean currents to guide them. Wayfinding was used before instruments such as the compass and the sextant were developed, and is still practiced by some as a means to keep their ancient cultures alive.

21st Century Skills

❷ **DETERMINING CENTRAL IDEAS** The students' travel brochures should identify points of interest for visitors to the islands of Oceania based on information from the text and from research they have done on the region. Suggest that students include activities that they would enjoy on a trip to the region and have them create art for their brochures or find photographs of fun activites and the natural beauty of the islands to include.

REVIEW THE GUIDING QUESTIONS

Directions: Choose the best answer for each question.

1 What is the smallest inhabited island in Oceania? RH.6-8.2
- A. Micronesia
- B. Nauru
- C. Guam
- D. Papua New Guinea

2 New Guinea is a continental island, which means that RH.6-8.4
- F. like Australia, it is also a continent.
- G. it is part of an archipelago.
- H. it was at one time connected to a continent.
- I. its people are highly educated.

3 From what region did the original settlers of the islands of Oceania come? RH.6-8.2
- A. New Zealand
- B. East Africa
- C. Southeast Asia
- D. the Bering Strait

4 Apart from Australia and New Zealand, which island of Oceania has the largest population? RH.6-8.2
- F. American Samoa
- G. Solomon Islands
- H. Papua New Guinea
- I. Tahiti

5 Why, despite abundant fish and seafood, do the islands of Oceania not export more of these resources? RH.6-8.1
- A. Oceania does not have enough workers.
- B. The nations do not have enough equipment or processing facilities.
- C. Other countries steal the fish from Oceania's waters.
- D. Mercury poisoning is a major threat.

6 Guam and Wake Island are territories of the United States that are maintained to support RH.6-8.2
- F. movie filming.
- G. forestry.
- H. military bases.
- I. the MIRAB program.

Chapter 15 **469**

Thinking Like a Geographer

3 **ANALYZING** Vast distances between the various islands of the region and the isolation created by the difficulty of traveling these vast distances contributed to the different island groups developing their own unique cultures. After these different cultures developed, the people maintained their individuality.

Geography Activities

4 **LOCATING PLACES**

1. A
2. C
3. F
4. H
5. G
6. E
7. B
8. D
9. I

ASSESSMENT ANSWERS
Review the Guiding Questions

1 **B** To answer this question, students might need to refer to the Chapter Opener map and identify the locations of all of the answer choices. This resource will help them to eliminate answers A, C and D. This leaves answer choice B, Naura, as the only correct answer. Refer students to the section, "Landforms of Oceania," in Lesson 1 for help.

2 **H** Remind students that Australia is a continent but that the island of New Guinea is not; it is just an island and is self-contained (it is not an archipelago, or group of islands). This will eliminate answer choices F and G. Point out that even though answer choice I is true, it does not have anything to do with the island's physical geography, thus eliminating it as an option. Refer students to reread, "The Divided Island of New Guinea," section in Lesson 1 for additional help.

3 **C** Refer students to the Chapter Opener map and ask them to identify the locations of East Africa and the Bering Strait. Based on their locations, students should be able to eliminate answer choices B and D. Remind them that the people who migrated to Oceania used wayfinding and came from Southeast Asia. Direct students to read the introductory paragraph of the "History of Oceania," in lesson 2 for help.

4 **H** Students may recall the description of the diversity of culture and langauges in Papua New Guinea from lesson 2. This lesson also points out that this island nation has a population of about 6 million, which is the largest population of the region. As an additional resource, have students read, "The People of the Region," in lesson 2.

5 **B** Since some island nations have sold fishing rights to other nations, answer choices A and C must be wrong. Review with students how in many ways the region is still developing and cannot handle the technical demand for processing this important resource. Refer students to the section, "Economies of Small, Independent Countries."

6 **H** The United States maintains the islands of Guam amd Wake Island to support military bases. Refer students to "Economies of America's Pacific Islands" in lesson 3 for additional help.

DBQ Analyzing Documents

7 C The best explanation for people leaving Tonga to find work is that there are not enough available jobs on the island.

8 F Equipment for a village health clinic is a practical community project because it can be used by the entire community. All the other examples apply only to the migrant's family.

Short Response

9 Sample answer: The phrase "for each village a different culture" refers to the great diversity in population and the huge number of languages spoken in Papua New Guinea. The cultures of each village were distinct because the island's mountainous geography kept individual population groups isolated from one another.

10 Sample answer: Environments that can have a similar effect on groups of people are islands and city neighborhoods, which can foster the development of unique cultures because they often isolate groups from one another. In a city where many people live in apartment buildings, it is not unusual for residents to barely know their neighbors in the same building, let alone in nearby buildings.

Extended Response

11 Possible response: The major flaw in the system of MIRAB is that the less developed nations of Oceania are drained of their young people. While the youth move to other countries *(migration)* to get jobs and to send the largest part of their pay back to their families and communities *(remittances)*, only the very young and the elderly are left in the native land. This leaves an unbalanced population, with still-high levels of unemployment. In addition, the youth who leave do not usually return, except as visitors. When they have children, the children become citizens of their new country. As the children grow up in a new country, they are much less likely to hold the same regard for their parents' native land, and thus less likely to continue the remittances.

DBQ ANALYZING DOCUMENTS

7 DETERMINING CENTRAL IDEAS Read the following passage about Tonga's economy:

"*The remittances of cash and goods from migrants who live and work overseas . . . [keep] the Tongan economy afloat. . . . Remittances . . . accounted in [2002] for about 50 percent of [gross domestic product]. . . . Although individuals and families are the main benefactors, . . . overseas Tongans [also] regularly send back money to their villages and local institutions, . . . funding practical community projects.*"

—from Cathy A. Small and David L. Dixon, "Tonga: Migration and the Homeland"

What best explains why Tongans leave the island to find work? RH.6-8.2, RH.6-8.10

A.   Tongans traditionally have loved to travel.

B.   Tonga's climate makes farming difficult.

C.   Tonga's economy does not offer enough jobs.

D.   Wages in Tonga are higher than elsewhere.

8 IDENTIFYING What is an example of a "practical community project"? RH.6-8.4, RH.6-8.10

F.   equipment for a village health clinic   H.   the education of a cousin

G.   better housing for a migrant's family   I.   wedding presents to a sister

SHORT RESPONSE

"*The isolation created by the mountainous [landscape] is so great that some groups, until recently, were unaware of the existence of neighboring groups only a few kilometers away. The diversity, reflected in a folk saying, 'For each village, a different culture,' is perhaps best shown in the local languages. . . . Over 850 of these languages have been identified; of these, only 350–450 are related.*"

—from "Papua New Guinea," State Department Background Notes

9 DETERMINING CENTRAL IDEAS Explain the meaning of the folk saying quoted in the passage. RH.6-8.2, RH.6-8.10

10 ANALYZING What other kinds of environments have a similar effect on groups of people? RH.6-8.1, RH.6-8.10

EXTENDED RESPONSE

11 INFORMATIVE/EXPLANATORY WRITING The MIRAB system (migration, remittances, aid, bureaucracy) has helped the economies of some of the islands of Oceania. What are the disadvantages of the MIRAB system? In an essay, identify some of its flaws, and predict their future impact on the region. WHST.6-8.2, WHST.6-8.4

Need Extra Help?

If You've Missed Question	❶	❷	❸	❹	❺	❻	❼	❽	❾	❿	⓫
Review Lesson	1	1	2	2	3	3	3	3	2	2	3

Originally published on the Migration Information Source, the online journal of the Migration Policy Institute, an independent, nonpartisan think tank in Washington D.C., dedicated to the study of the movement of people worldwide. (www.migrationinformation.org)

---

netw⊙rks   *Online Teaching Options*

Evaluation and Assessment

Assessing Use eAssessment to create your own tests from hundreds of available questions. eAssessment helps you design assessments that meet the needs of different types of learners.

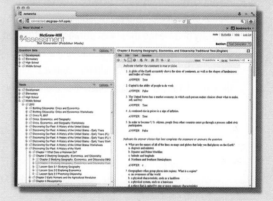

CHAPTER 16
Antarctica Planner

National Geography Standards covered in Chapter 16

Learners will understand:

I. The World in Spatial Terms
Standard 1: How to use maps and other geographic representations, geospatial technologies, and spatial thinking to understand and communicate information

Standard 3: How to analyze the spatial organization of people, places, and environments on Earth's surface

II. Places and Regions
Standard 4: The physical and human characteristics of places

Standard 5: That people create regions to interpret Earth's complexity

Standard 6: How culture and experience influence people's perceptions of places and regions

III. Places and Regions
Standard 7: The physical processes that shape the patterns of Earth's surface.

IV. Human Systems
Standard 11: The patterns and networks of economic interdependence on Earth's surface

Standard 12: The processes, patterns, and functions of human settlement

Standard 13: How the forces of cooperation and conflict among people influence the division and control of Earth's surface

V. Environment and Society
Standard 14: How human actions modify the physical environment

Standard 15: How physical systems affect human systems

VI. The Uses of Geography
Standard 17: How to apply geography to interpret the past

Standard 18: How to apply geography to interpret the present and plan for the future

UNDERSTANDING BY DESIGN®

Enduring Understandings
- *People, places, and ideas change over time.*

Essential Questions
- *How does physical geography influence the way people live?*

Predictable Misunderstandings
- *Antarctica's physical geography is unimpressive because it is mostly ice.*
- *There are no resources in this region.*
- *There is very little interest to other countries in this region.*

Assessment Evidence

Performance Tasks:
- *Project-Based Learning Digital Hands-On Chapter Project*
- *Project-Based Learning Hands-On Chapter Project*

Other Evidence:
- *Critical Thinking Skills Activity*
- *Geography and Economics Activity*
- *Technology Skills Activity*
- *Participation in Interactive Whiteboard Activities*
- *Contribution to small-group activities*
- *Interpretation of slide show images and special purpose maps*
- *Participation in class discussions about cultural and economic topics*
- *Lesson Reviews*
- *Chapter Assessments*

SUGGESTED PACING GUIDE

Introducing the Chapter . . . . 1 Day	What Do You Think? . . . . .3 Days
Lesson 1 . . . . .2 Days	Chapter Wrap-Up and Assessment . . . . . . 1 Day
Lesson 2 . . . . .2 Days	

TOTAL TIME   9 Days

Key for Using the Teacher Edition

SKILL-BASED ACTIVITIES

Types of skill activities found in the Teacher Edition.

* **V Visual Skills** require students to analyze maps, graphs, charts, and photos.

W Writing Skills provide writing opportunities to help students comprehend the text.

R Reading Skills help students practice reading skills and master vocabulary.

C Critical Thinking Skills help students apply and extend what they have learned.

T Technology Skills require students to use digital tools effectively.

*Letters are followed by a number when there is more than one of the same type of skill on the page.

DIFFERENTIATED INSTRUCTION

All activities are written for the on-level student unless otherwise marked with the leveled labels below.

BL Beyond Level
AL Approaching Level
ELL English Language Learners

All students benefit from activities that utilize different learning styles. Many activities are marked as below when a particular learning style is highlighted.

Intrapersonal	Naturalist
Logical/Mathematical	Kinesthetic
Visual/Spatial	Auditory/Musical
Verbal/Linguistic	Interpersonal

CHAPTER OPENER PLANNER

Students will know:
- that there are unique aspects to Antarctica's physical geography including its size and the ice that covers it.
- how the climate of Antarctica is unlike any other region.
- that Antarctica does have some resources, but it is hard to access them.
- how Antarctica plays a role in the climate of the Earth.
- how Antarctica plays a role in the global issues of today.

Students will be able to:
- **analyze** a world map to identify Antarctica.
- **use** a time line to discuss various events in the history of Antarctica.

UNDERSTANDING
BY DESIGN®

☑ *Print Teaching Options*

V Visual Skills

☐ **P. 472** Students analyze the map of Antarctica and practice map skills. **Visual/Spatial**

☐ **P. 473** Students use the time line to explore the history of Antarctica. **AL** **Visual/Spatial**

W Writing Skills

☐ **P. 473** Students write an informative paragraph about an event on the time line. **BL** **Verbal/Linguistic**

R Reading Skills

☐ **P. 472** Students identify the Queen Maud mountain range, find it on a map or globe, and trace it from Antarctica to the Andes in South America.

T Technology Skills

☐ **P. 472** Students conduct Internet research on travel to Antarctica and discuss what they learn. **Verbal/Linguistic**

☑ *Online Teaching Options*

☐ **MAP** **Reading a Map**—Students identify aspects and locations of the region on a map.

☐ **TIME LINE** **Reading a Time Line and Map**—Students learn about where and when historical events occurred in Antarctica using the time line and map.

☐ **MAP** **Interactive World Atlas**—Students use the interactive world atlas to identify the region and describe its terrain.

☑ *Printable Digital Worksheets*

☐ **WORKSHEET** **Technology Skills: Creating a Multimedia Presentation**—Students use the worksheet and what they have learned to create a multimedia presentation.

☐ **WORKSHEET** **Critical Thinking Skills: Drawing Conclusions**—Students use the worksheet to draw conclusions about mapping and exploring Antarctica.

☐ **WORKSHEET** **Geography and Economics: The Antarctic Treaty**—Students use the worksheet to learn more about this treaty.

Project-Based Learning

Hands-On

Creating a Graphic Organizer

Students will work in small groups to create a visually-appealing graphic organizer that compares and contrasts life in their community with life in Antarctica. The graphic organizers might be similar to Venn diagrams and be created on poster board. They should contain photos, text excerpts, or words that illustrate key similarities and differences between the two regions. Then, have groups present their graphic organizers to the class.

Digital Hands-On

Creating an Online Interactive Map

Students will work in small groups to create an online interactive map of Antarctica. The online map will be embedded with interesting and fun geographic facts in the forms of photos, sounds, and videos. Have groups present their maps to the class. Discuss the different types of information that groups found.

Print Resources

ANCILLARY RESOURCES

These ancillaries are available for every chapter and lesson.

- **Reading Essentials and Study Guide Workbook** **AL** **ELL**
- **Chapter Tests and Lesson Quizzes Blackline Masters**

PRINTABLE DIGITAL WORKSHEETS

These printable digital worksheets are available for every chapter and lesson!

- **Hands-On Chapter Projects**
- **What Do You Know? Activities**
- **Chapter Summaries (English and Spanish)**
- **Vocabulary Builder Activities**
- **Quizzes and Tests**
- **Reading Essentials and Study Guide (English and Spanish)** **AL** **ELL**
- **Guided Reading Activities**

More Media Resources

SUGGESTED VIDEOS

NOTE: Be sure to preview videos to ensure they are age-appropriate.

- **March of the Penguins** (documentary; 85 min.)
- **Encounters at the End of the World** (101 min.)

SUGGESTED READING

- ***Antarctica: Journey to the Pole,*** by Peter Lerangis **BL**
- ***Poles Apart: Why Penguins and Polar Bears Will Never Be Neighbors,*** by Elaine Scott **AL**
- ***The Race to the South Pole,*** by Jim Pipe **AL**
- ***Life Under Ice,*** by Mary M. Cerullo **AL**
- ***After the Last Dog Died: The True-Life, Hair-Raising Adventure of Douglas Mawson and His 1911-1914 Antarctic Expedition,*** by Carmen Bredeson

PHYSICAL GEOGRAPHY OF ANTARCTICA

Students will know:

- that there are unique aspects to Antarctica's physical geography including its size and the ice that covers it.
- how the climate of Antarctica is unlike any other region.
- that Antarctica does have some resources, but it is hard to access them.
- how Antarctica plays a role in the climate of the Earth.

Students will be able to:

- **describe** the landforms and waters of Antarctica.
- **describe** the ice of Antarctica.
- **discuss** the climate and resources of Antarctica.
- **describe** the plants and animals of Antarctica.

UNDERSTANDING BY DESIGN®

☑ *Print Teaching Options*

V Visual Skills

☐ **P. 475** Students create a two-column chart to list unusual statistics about Antarctica. **Visual/Spatial**

☐ **P. 475** Students interpret a photograph and make inferences.

☐ **P. 476** Students create diagrams of the formation of ice shelves and the calving of icebergs. **Visual/Spatial**

☐ **P. 477** Students analyze an image and make a list of concerns about living in Antarctica.

☐ **P. 478** Students make a cause-effect chart to illustrate Antarctica's effect on the global climate. **Visual/Spatial**

☐ **P. 479** Students draw a diagram showing an Antarctic food chain. **Visual/Spatial, Naturalist**

W Writing Skills

☐ **P. 477** Students write a brief biography of an explorer or scientist for which one of the seas surrounding Antarctica was named. **Verbal/Linguistic**

R Reading Skills

☐ **P. 474** Students discuss the geography of Antarctica and determine central ideas. **Verbal/Linguistic**

☐ **P. 478** Students make a two-column chart to list all the land plants and animals of Antarctica. **ELL AL Verbal/Linguistic, Visual/Spatial**

☐ **P. 479** Students identify main ideas about Antarctica's resources. **Verbal/Linguistic**

C Critical Thinking Skills

☐ **P. 477** Students discuss the causes of the continent's extremely cold weather. **Visual/Spatial**

T Technology Skills

☐ **P. 476** Students use the Internet to research the Bentley Subglacial Trench. **BL Logical/Mathematical**

☐ **P. 478** Students research and give an oral report on a plant or animal of Antarctica. **Verbal/Linguistic, Naturalist**

☑ *Online Teaching Options*

V Visual Skills

VIDEO **Scenes of Antarctica**—Students watch the video about various aspects of life in Antarctica and discuss the landscape and climate.

IMAGE **Hot Springs**—Students use the interactive image of hot springs to discuss how this geothermal event can occur in a place of extreme cold.

VIDEO **Penguins' Adaptation to Climate**—Students watch the video and discuss how the wildlife of Antarctica survives in an extreme environment.

ANIMATION **How Icebergs Form**—Students use the animation to analyze the mechanisms involved in the formation of icebergs.

IMAGE **360° View: Antarctica**—Students use the 360° view of Antarctica to show a visual representation of the extreme cold of the region.

C Critical Thinking Skills

CHART **Comparing Continent Sizes**—Students use the chart to compare and contrast Antarctica with the other continents.

MAP **Physical Geography: Antarctica**—Students use the physical geography layer of the Chapter Opener map to discuss the landforms of the region.

ANIMATION **Earth's Layers**—Students use the animation of Earth's layers to review how this aspect of Earth creates the various geothermal events in the region.

MAP **Resources: Antarctica**—Students use the resources layer of the Chapter Opener map to discuss the lack of resources in the region and the reasons why.

VIDEO **Planet Wild: Antarctica**—Students watch the video about the physical geography of Antarctica and contrast it with the geography of North America. **AL Visual/Spatial**

IMAGE **Icebergs**—Students use the interactive image to learn more about how icebergs are formed and the dangers they can cause, along with why they are increasing.

SLIDE SHOW **Life in Antarctica**—Students use the slide show to speculate how various species may have adapted to Antarctica's climate over time.

MAP **Climates: Antarctica**—Students use the climate layer of the Chapter Opener map to discuss the climate of the region and how it creates the extreme environment therein.

T Technology Skills

ONLINE SELF-CHECK QUIZ **Lesson 1**—Students receive instant feedback on their mastery of lesson content.

☑ *Printable Digital Worksheets*

W Writing Skills

WORKSHEET **Technology Skills: Creating a Multimedia Presentation**—Students use the worksheet and what they have learned to create a multimedia presentation.

WORKSHEET **Critical Thinking Skills: Drawing Conclusions**—Students use the worksheet to draw conclusions about mapping and exploring Antarctica.

LIFE IN ANTARCTICA

Students will know:
- that Antarctica does have some resources, but it is hard to access them.
- how Antarctica plays a role in the climate of the Earth.
- how Antarctica plays a role in the global issues of today.

Students will be able to:
- **discuss** the Antarctic Treaty.
- **describe** life on Antarctica.
- **discuss** scientific research on Antarctica.
- **explore** climate change as it is related to Antarctica.

UNDERSTANDING
BY DESIGN®

☑ *Print Teaching Options*

V Visual Skills

☐ **P. 483** Students discuss what ozone is and its important role in protecting life on Earth. **Visual/Spatial, Logical/Mathematical**

W Writing Skills

☐ **P. 481** Students write a fictional email from one of the research scientists on Antarctica. **Verbal/Linguistic**

☐ **P. 483** Students write a summary of the section "Studying Earth from Above." **Verbal/Linguistic**

☐ **P. 485** Students write a script for a tour as if they were tour guides in Antarctica. **Verbal/Linguistic**

R Reading Skills

☐ **P. 481** Students discuss the way Antarctica is governed. **AL Verbal/Linguistic**

☐ **P. 484** Students identify the effects of global warming on Antarctica. **ELL AL Logical/Mathematical, Naturalist**

C Critical Thinking Skills

☐ **P. 481** Students make inferences about why some nations still claim large sections of Antarctica despite the Antarctic Treaty. **Logical/Mathematical**

☐ **P. 482** Students summarize key ideas about living in Antarctica. **Verbal/Linguistic**

T Technology Skills

☐ **P. 480** Students research more about Amundsen's and Scott's expeditions. **BL Verbal/Linguistic**

☐ **P. 482** Students explore web sites on the different research stations to learn more about living in Antarctica. **Verbal/Linguistic, Visual/Spatial**

☐ **P. 484** Students find a recording of a humpback whale song and use the song and the photograph to discuss the link between people and other mammals. **Auditory/Musical, Naturalist**

☑ *Online Teaching Options*

V Visual Skills

☐ **MAP Antarctica Explored**—Students use the animated map to discuss the exploration of Antarctica. **Visual/Spatial, Interpersonal**

☐ **IMAGE Earth's Ozone Layer**—Students explore changes in the ozone layer over time. **Kinesthetic, Visual/Spatial**

☐ **IMAGE Snow Soccer**—Students use the video of the researchers playing snow soccer to show that the people who are there try to incorporate activity into their daily life. **AL Intrapersonal**

☐ **IMAGE Tourism in Antarctica**—Students can use the interactive images to discuss tourism in Antarctica and extreme vacationing.

W Writing Skills

☐ **VIDEO Antarctica's Dry Valley**—Students watch the video about Antarctica's dry valley and write a paragraph about what they learned. **Visual/Spatial**

C Critical Thinking Skills

☐ **GRAPHIC ORGANIZER Research Stations**—Students use the interactive graphic organizer to discuss how a researcher would prepare for a long stay in Antarctica. **Logical/Mathematical**

☐ **GRAPHIC ORGANIZER Antarctic Food Chain**—Students use the interactive flow chart to discuss an Antarctic food chain and the effect climate change might have on it. **Visual/Spatial**

☐ **GAME Drag-and-Drop: When to Stay on Antarctica**—Students use the drag-and-drop game to discuss the reasons why summer is the best time to stay in this region and why winter is not a good time to visit the region.

T Technology Skills

☐ **ONLINE SELF-CHECK QUIZ Lesson 2**—Students receive instant feedback on their mastery of lesson content.

☑ *Printable Digital Worksheets*

W Writing Skills

☐ **WORKSHEET Geography and Economics: The Antarctic Treaty**—Students use the worksheet to learn more about this treaty.

INTERVENTION AND REMEDIATION STRATEGIES

LESSON 1 Physical Geography of Antarctica

Reading and Comprehension

Have students skim the lesson to look for unfamiliar or confusing words. Assist them in pronouncing difficult words correctly, such as *archipelago,* and clarify pronunciation of content vocabulary words *katabatic wind* and *lichen.* When students have compiled a list of words they find confusing, have them write down what they think each word might mean based on context clues in the text. Then have students look up each word in the dictionary to find the definition of each word. Have students count how many definitions they guessed correctly. Finally, tell students to work in pairs to practice using their list of words and the content vocabulary words to explain a concept in this lesson.

Text Evidence

Have students work in small groups to review the text under the subheading *Rock, Ice, and Water.* Tell students to choose one of these elements and write a paragraph describing how it relates to the climate and resources of Antarctica. Tell students their paragraphs should cite specific textual evidence to support their statements. After groups have presented their paragraphs, have them play a game of "Rock, Paper, Scissors," but replace Paper with Ice using the same hand motion, and Scissors with Water using a hand motion to indicate waves. As you call out a term or concept that relates to one of the three elements, instruct students to make the appropriate hand signal.

LESSON 2 Life in Antarctica

Reading and Comprehension

Have students work in pairs to play a guessing game in which one person gives clues about a content vocabulary term, and the other student tries to guess it. Then write the following words on the board, and have students write the significance of each term or phrase based on information in the text: *Roald Amundsen, Robert Scott, Antarctic Treaty, ozone layer, Gondwana, plate tectonics,* and *climate change.* To ensure that students understand the concepts presented in the lesson, have them work together to summarize how each term relates to the continent of Antarctica. Encourage students to use content vocabulary terms in their summaries.

Text Evidence

Have students work in small groups to write and perform a short skit about life in Antarctica. Aside from using information in the text, students may conduct research using reliable online sources to find additional facts about the region. Tell students to use the information from their research to write a script for their skits, including characters (such as researchers and tourists) and dialogue. Tell students that their skits should answer a self-generated question in addition to the following questions: *What is daily life like in Antarctica? Do people live or visit there? If so, why? What do they eat? What do they wear? What is the climate like? What is the plant and animal life like? How has climate change affected life in the region?* Allow students time to write and practice their skits before they present them to the class.

Online Resources

Approaching Level Reader

Use this online lower-level text that corresponds directly to the text in the online Student Edition.

Guided Reading Activities

This resource uses graphic organizers and guiding questions to help students with comprehension.

Assessing Background Knowledge

Use these worksheets to pre-assess students' background knowledge before they read the chapter.

Reading Essentials and Study Guide Workbook

This resource offers writing and reading activities for the approaching-level student.

Self-Check Quizzes

This online assessment tool provides instant feedback for students to check their progress.

How do I use the

btw: Stuff You Should Know

Current Events Web Site?

Connecting with your digital natives in the classroom and beyond can take many forms. Using social media in the classroom sounds like a great idea. Teachers are always looking for fresh strategies to enhance the way information is presented or to facilitate student interaction. But where do you start? You can use web-based products to improve student learning.

The articles on btw offer engaging, student-centric coverage of current events. These articles can be used in your classroom in a number of ways. Visit the site at http://blog.glencoe.com to familiarize yourself with the Web site and the different types of articles offered.

Option 1 As a Bellringer ENGAGE activity

- Start your class with an article. Then, launch a class discussion by having students respond to the questions that accompany each of the articles.

- Or, post the article on your classroom blog or discussion board and have the students respond to the questions over the weekend before you teach the content.

Option 2 Activate Critical Thinking

- You might choose to assign an article and the questions to get your students to think critically about the topic at hand.

- Some of the accompanying activities may also be appropriate for group work during class time.

ANTARCTICA

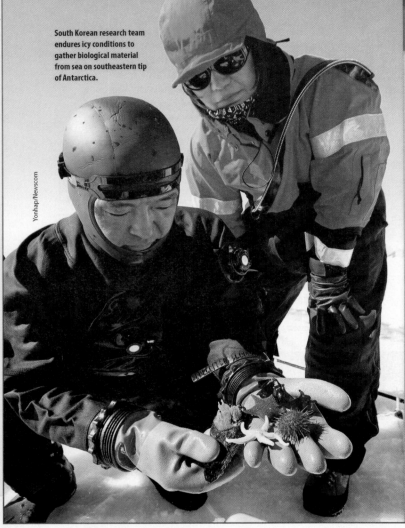

South Korean research team endures icy conditions to gather biological material from sea on southeastern tip of Antarctica.

Yonhap/Newscom

networks

There's More Online about Antarctica.

CHAPTER 16

Lesson 1
The Physical Geography of Antarctica

Lesson 2
Life in Antarctica

The Story Matters...

For centuries, explorers from many countries set out on dangerous expeditions, competing to be the first to reach the frozen continent of Antarctica. Antarctica, which means "opposite to the Arctic," is shared today by many nations whose scientists are researching its vital role in maintaining the world's climate balance.

FOLDABLES
Study Organizer

Go to the Foldables® library in the back of your book to make a Foldable® that will help you take notes while reading this chapter.

471

ENGAGE

Think-Pair-Share Tell students that they are about to study a continent that is unlike any other. To help students appreciate the uniqueness of Antarctica, read aloud the information in the Content Background Knowledge box below and "The Story Matters...." Then have students create their own K-W-L charts like the one shown below. Ask them to think about what they know about Antarctica and list these ideas in the first column and to write what they would like to learn about the continent in the second column. Have pairs share what they have written and add ideas from partners to their indivudal charts. Explain that students will complete the third column of their charts after they finish the chapter.

Antarctica

K What I Know	W What I Want to Know	L What I Learned

Content Background Knowledge

Antarctica is unique among the world's continents in many ways.

- It is the coldest continent on Earth. A temperature of −128.56°F (−89.2°C)—the world's record low—was measured there.
- Antarctica is the windiest place on Earth. Wind gusts of 0.06 miles (90 meters) *per second* have occurred there. That is more than 200 miles (322 kilometers) per hour!
- The continent is the driest one on Earth. The interior of Antarctica is a frozen desert where the precipitation averages under 5 centimeters (2 inches) a year. Even though is it the world's driest continent, it contains 70 percent of all the fresh water on Earth. This water is frozen in the ice sheet that covers the continent.
- For all of the above reasons and more, Antarctica is the only continent that has no native people.

Letter from the Author

Dear Geography Teacher,

Some government leaders in the United States whose communities need fresh water have discussed acquiring water from the Antarctic Ice Sheet. It has been suggested that engineers capture giant icebergs from the ice sheet and have them pulled north where they would melt and provide a dry, heavily populated area with an abundance of water. Is this a viable solution to end water shortages in dry regions of the United States? Challenge your students to analyze this intriguing possibility.

Richard G. Boehm

FOLDABLES
Study Organizer

Go to the Foldables® library for a cumulative chapter-based Foldable® activity that your students can use to help take notes and prepare for assessment.

TEACH & ASSESS

Step Into the Place

V Visual Skills

Analyzing Maps Have students read the introductory paragraph and study the map of Antarctica. **Ask:**

- **Within what circle of latitude does most of Antarctica lie?** *(within the Antarctic Circle)*
- **What countries claim territory on the continent?** *(Chile, Great Britain, Argentina, Norway, Australia, France, New Zealand)*
- **What is unusual about the shapes of the territories claimed by different countries?** *(All the territories are shaped like pieces of pie, with the South Pole at the center.)*

Have students look at a world map. **Ask: What do the countries of Australia, New Zealand, Chile, and Argentina have in common in relation to Antarctica?** *(They are the closest countries to Antarctica.)* Then have students answer the Step Into the Place questions. **Visual/Spatial**

R Reading Skills

Identifying Have students read the caption for photo A and use a physical world map or globe to locate the Queen Maud mountain range and trace it from Antarctica to the Andes in South America. **Ask: Why do you think this mountain range has two different names?** *(It was probably named by explorers who encountered it on land. One explorer would have named it in South America and another explorer would have named it in Antarctica. The explorers did not realize this was the same mountain range.)* **Verbal/Linguistic**

T Technology Skills

Researching on the Internet Note that the two photographs show a climber and kayakers in Antarctica. Have students work in pairs or small groups to conduct Internet research on travel to Antarctica. Suggest that students find out what they would need to know to take a trip there: the cost, what clothes to pack, what time of year to go, and what activities to expect. After students finish their research, hold a class discussion for students to share what they have learned.

ANSWERS, p. 472

STEP INTO THE PLACE
1. Australian
2. Amundsen Sea
3. New Zealand's
4. **CRITICAL THINKING** A remote location increases the expenses of bringing in needed equipment, shipping goods to other regions, and attracting skilled workers.

Chapter 16
ANTARCTICA

V *The continent of Antarctica lies at the southern extreme of Earth, with its land lying beneath a massive ice cap. It is larger in size than either Europe or Australia.*

Step Into the Place

MAP FOCUS Use the map to answer the following questions.

1 THE GEOGRAPHER'S WORLD Which country's claim in Antarctica is larger: the Australian, the Argentine, or the French?

2 THE GEOGRAPHER'S WORLD What sea is located between longitudes 100°W and 120°W?

3 PLACES AND REGIONS Which country's claim is adjacent to the Ross Sea?

4 CRITICAL THINKING **Analyzing** Think about the location of Antarctica in relation to other parts of the world. How might its location affect the development of natural resources?

R

ICY SUMMIT A climber approaches the summit of Mount Vaughn in the Queen Maud Mountain range. The range runs from Antarctica along the ocean floor and continues into South America as the Andes Mountains.

T

ANTARCTIC ISLAND Kayakers paddle near the rugged cliffs of Petermann Island off the west side of the Antarctic Peninsula. The island is home to large numbers of penguin colonies.

Step Into the Time

TIME LINE Based on events on the time line, write a paragraph explaining the international importance of Antarctica.
WHST.6-8.2, WHST.6-8.4

W

1760s Several nations hunt the seals of the Antarctic seas

1700

1800

Project-Based Learning ✋

Hands-On

Creating a Graphic Organizer

Students will work in small groups to create a visually-appealing graphic organizer that compares and contrasts life in their community with life in Antarctica. The graphic organizers might be similar to Venn diagrams and be created on poster board. They should contain photos, text excerpts, or words that illustrate key similarities and differences between the two regions. Then have groups present their graphic organizers to the class.

Digital Hands-On

Creating an Interactive Map

Students will work in small groups to create an online interactive map of Antarctica. The online map will be embedded with interesting and fun geographic facts in the forms of photos, sounds, and videos. Have groups present their maps to the class. Discuss the different types of information that groups found.

edtechteacher
21st Century Learning

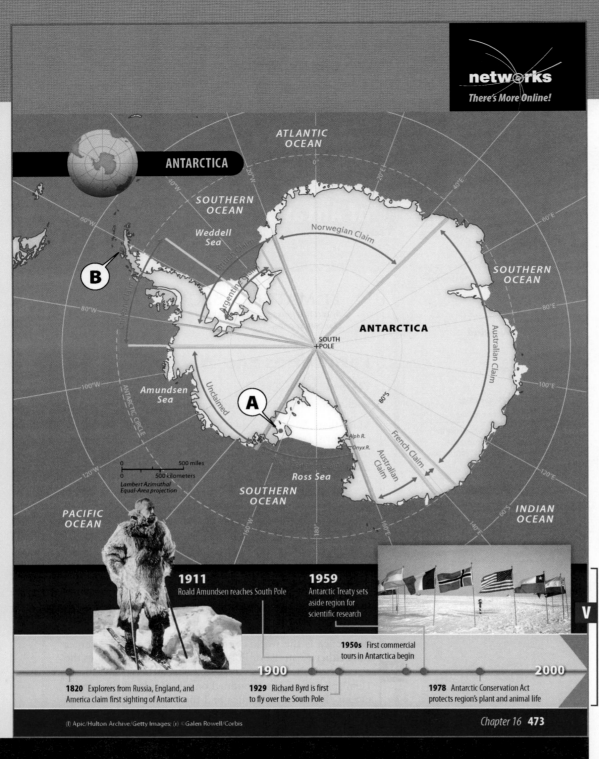

ANTARCTICA

ATLANTIC OCEAN

SOUTHERN OCEAN

Weddell Sea

Norwegian Claim

SOUTHERN OCEAN

ANTARCTICA

SOUTH +POLE

Amundsen Sea

Australian Claim

Undaimed

80°S

Alph R.

Onyx R.

French Claim

Australian Claim

0   500 miles

0   500 kilometers

Lambert Azimuthal Equal-Area projection

Ross Sea

SOUTHERN OCEAN

PACIFIC OCEAN

INDIAN OCEAN

1911 Roald Amundsen reaches South Pole

1959 Antarctic Treaty sets aside region for scientific research

1950s First commercial tours in Antarctica begin

1900

2000

1820 Explorers from Russia, England, and America claim first sighting of Antarctica

1929 Richard Byrd is first to fly over the South Pole

1978 Antarctic Conservation Act protects region's plant and animal life

(l) Apic/Hulton Archive/Getty Images; (r) ©Galen Rowell/Corbis

Chapter 16 **473**

Step Into the Time

V Visual Skills

Interpreting Draw students' attention to the time line and note the short period of time covered, from the 1760s to 2000. Explain that no one knows who was the first person to set foot on Antarctica. Historians believe it was probably whale or seal hunters. **Ask:**

- **When did the first recorded sighting of Antarctica take place?** *(1820)*
- **When did the first explorer reach the South Pole?** *(in 1911)*
- **Why do you think Antarctica was not explored until the 1900s?** *(Students should cite its extreme climate and the difficulty in even reaching the continent.)*

Have students add other events they know of to the time line of Antarctica. **AL Visual/Spatial**

W Writing Skills

Informative/Explanatory Have students choose one event on the time line or another they know of in the history of Antarctica to research further. Have them write a few informative paragraphs detailing their research and report their findings back to the class. **BL Verbal/Linguistic**

Content Background Knowledge

Share with students the following information about the individuals named on the time line:

- Roald Amundsen was a Norwegian explorer who raced against the English explorer Robert Scott to be the first person to reach the South Pole. Amundsen's team reached the South Pole 34 days before Scott's team. Scott's team not only lost the race but lost their lives when they encountered a raging blizzard on the return trip.
- Richard Byrd was an American aviator and explorer who headed several Antarctic expeditions besides the one in which he flew over the South Pole.

CLOSE & REFLECT

Summarizing Call on students to summarize what they have learned so far about Antarctica and direct them to add this information to the last column of their K-W-L charts.

TIME LINE

Reading a Time Line and Map

Analyzing Visuals Display the time line and map on the whiteboard. Have volunteers read each event as it is revealed on the time line. Ask students to speculate on the possible effects of human activities on the environment of Antarctica. **Visual/Spatial, Logical/Mathematical**

See page 471B for other online activities.

ENGAGE

Bellringer To introduce the lesson, divide students into small groups and tell them to imagine that they are a research team headed to Antarctica for a month-long expedition. Direct each group to compile a list of the most important survival items each person will want to pack for the trip. Give the groups about five minutes to create their lists. Then ask a member of each group to identify their items and explain the reason each item would be useful in Antarctica. Then tell students that they will learn more about conditions in Antarctica in this lesson.

TEACH & ASSESS

R Reading Skills

Determining Central Ideas Conduct a question and answer activity to discuss the geography of Antarctica. Divide students into small groups, and have the students in each group number off. When you ask a question, give the groups a minute to "put their heads together" and agree on an answer, using their textbooks as needed. Then call out a number and have the student with that number give the group's answer. **Ask:**

- Why is Antarctica called "the last continent"? *(because it was the last continent to be discovered)*
- Why is Antarctica called "the bottom of the world"? *(because it is at the bottom of the Southern Hemisphere)*
- Why didn't people know that Antarctica existed before 1820? *(because the severe weather surrounding the continent made exploration extremely difficult and dangerous)* **Verbal/ Linguistic**

V Visual Skills

Creating Visuals Have students use a globe and tracing paper to trace Antarctica and physically place the tracing over the other continents to compare them in size. **Ask: How does Antarctica compare in size to other continents and to the United States?** *(It is the fifth-largest continent and is larger than either Australia or Europe. It is about 1.5 times larger than the United States.)* **AL ELL Visual/Spatial**

ANSWER, p. 474

Taking Notes Students' notes will vary but should include the main ideas from each section of the lesson.

---

networks

There's More Online!

☑ **IMAGES** Antarctica

☑ **ANIMATION** How Icebergs Form

☑ **VIDEO**

Reading HELPDESK CCSS

Academic Vocabulary RH.6-8.4
(Tier Two Words)
- **visible**

Content Vocabulary RH.6-8.4
(Tier Three Words)
- **ice sheet**
- **ice shelf**
- **calving**
- **iceberg**
- **katabatic wind**
- **lichen**
- **krill**
- **plankton**

TAKING NOTES: *Key Ideas and Details* RH.6-8.2, RH.6-8.7

Summarize Using a chart like the one shown here, summarize the information presented in each section of the lesson.

Landforms and Water
Climate and Resources

474

Lesson 1
The Physical Geography of Antarctica

ESSENTIAL QUESTION · *How does physical geography influence the way people live?*

IT MATTERS BECAUSE
Antarctica plays an important role in maintaining world climate balance.

Landforms and Waters of Antarctica

GUIDING QUESTION *Is Antarctica the last unknown land region on Earth?*

R More than 2,500 miles (4,023 km) south of the Tropic of Capricorn, far from the warm, sunny islands of Oceania, is the coldest, cruelest, darkest land on Earth. Nicknamed "the last continent" and "the bottom of the world," this frozen continent is Antarctica. Throughout most of history, humans did not know that this bitterly cold, windy, barren land even existed. Scholars and scientists had theories and ideas that a large "southern land" might be at the bottom of Earth. There was no proof that Antarctica was real, however, until explorers first sighted its icy shores in 1820. Exploration was, and still is, extremely difficult in this harsh land. It was not until 20 years after the first sighting that geographers confirmed that Antarctica is, in fact, a continent, not a mass of floating ice as some early explorers believed.

Size of Antarctica
V Antarctica is the world's fifth-largest continent. It is larger than either Australia or Europe, and it is about 1.5 times the size of the United States. Antarctica is located in the Southern Hemisphere and is surrounded on all sides by the Southern Ocean. Together, Antarctica and the Southern Ocean cover

(l to r) Geoff Renner/Newscom; ©David Ball/Corbis; ©George Steinmetz/Corbis; ©Momatiuk - Eastcott/Corbis

---

networks *Online Teaching Options*

VIDEO

Planet Wild—Antarctica

Contrasting Use this video about the physical geography, climate, and wildlife of Antarctica to preview and introduce the lesson content. Have students create a short presentation, contrasting the geography, climate, and wildlife of Antarctica with the geography of a region from a previous chapter. Encourge students to use visuals for their presentation. **AL Visual/Spatial, Logical/ Mathematical**

See page 471C for other online activities.

BBC Motion Gallery Education

about 7 percent of Earth's surface. However, very few people reside, even for a short time, within these millions of square miles. The South Pole is located near the center of the continent.

Rock, Ice, and Water

Antarctica is called the highest continent because it has the highest overall elevation of any continent. Antarctica's surface is an average of 7,000 feet (2,134 m) above sea level. This figure measures the height of the **visible** surface of the continent, which is mostly solidly packed ice. While some of Antarctica's mountains rise above the ice, most of the land that makes up the foundation of the continent is much lower than the dense ice layer that covers it. In fact, the weight of so much ice has forced some of Antarctica's surface land far below sea level. Entire mountains are completely buried under layers of ice.

It might be difficult to believe, but the ice sheet covering most of Antarctica is 2 miles (3.2 km) thick in some places. An **ice sheet** is a thick layer of ice and compressed snow that forms a solid crust over an area of land. This vast ice sheet covers about 98 percent of Antarctica's surface. Scientists estimate that two-thirds of all freshwater on Earth is frozen in the Antarctic ice sheet. But it is important to remember that land lies beneath this ice sheet. By using high-resolution satellites and other specialized equipment, geographers have learned that Antarctica is one large landmass that also has an archipelago of rocky islands.

Many extremes of high and low elevation can be found across this frozen land. The highest point on the continent is Vinson Massif, which measures an incredible 16,066 feet (4,897 m) high. The Transantarctic Mountains stretch for 2,200 miles (3,541 km) across Antarctica. This enormous mountain range divides the continent into two regions: East Antarctica and West Antarctica.

R

Academic Vocabulary

visible able to be seen

V₁

Tourists bathe in a thermal pool, which is actually an inactive volcanic crater on Deception Island, Antarctica. Volcanic activity creates the thermal pools by heating underground water that comes to the surface.

Geoff Renner/Newscom

Chapter 16 **475**

R Reading Skills

Defining Suggest that students create flash cards of the lesson's vocabulary words, writing each vocabulary word on one side of an index card and its definition on the other side. Direct students to form pairs and test each other on the words. Encourage students to use each word in a sentence. **ELL** **AL** Verbal/Linguistic, Kinesthetic

V₁ Visual Skills

Creating Charts Note that Antarctica is a land of many extremes. Direct students to create a two-column chart like the one below listing some of the unusual statistics about Antarctica. Have students add to the chart as they progress through the lesson. Visual/Spatial

V₂

Antarctica Statistics

Category	Statistic
Average elevation (highest of any continent)	7,000 feet (2,134 m)
Thickness of ice sheet	2 miles (3.2 km) in some places
Portion of Earth's fresh water frozen in Antarctic ice sheet	two-thirds
Highest point on continent	Vinson Mountain, 16,066 feet (4,897 m)

V₂ Visual Skills

Interpreting Direct students' attention to the photograph at the bottom of the page and **ask:**

- **How did the tourists get to this thermal pool?** *(The guides brought them by boat.)*
- **How does this location appear different from typical tourist attractions along shorelines?** *(Sample answer: There are no buildings, such as hotels or restaurants, along the shoreline.)*
- **Why is it important for the tour guides to remain dressed for the cold?** *(The guides need to be able to help the tourists so they need to be dressed warmly. Also, it is very cold there; the only place it is warm is in the water itself.)* Visual/Spatial

VIDEOS

Scenes of Antarctica

Analyzing Use the videos that show various aspects of life in Antarctica to illustrate the physical geography and climate of the region. Connect the content of the videos to the map of Antarctica in the Chapter Opener. In a class discussion, prompt students to identify details about the landscape and climate. **Verbal/Linguistic**

See page 471C for other online activities.

T Technology Skills

Using Digital Tools Have students create video or slide show presentations showing different pictures of the Bentley Subglacial Trench. Tell students to write captions for the pictures and to include some interesting facts about the trench. Direct students to choose background music for the presentation, specifically music that creates similar feelings of the majesty and grandeur of the spectacular views.
BL Auditory/Musical, Visual/Spatial

R Reading Skills

Summarizing After students read the rest of the page, pose the following questions to help students summarize the main ideas about the icy conditions in Antarctica. **Ask:**

- What are ice shelves, and how are they related to the ice sheet that covers most of Antarctica? *(Ice shelves are thick slabs of ice attached to a coastline but floating on the ocean. Ice shelves are seaward extensions of the ice sheet that covers most of Antarctica.)*

- Why does Antarctica appear to double in size in winter? *(because so much coastal water freezes into the ice shelves that surround Antarctica)*

- What happens to the frozen coastal water during the spring and summer months? *(Large chunks of the ice break off and form icebergs.)*

- Why do icebergs pose a danger to ships? *(Most of their mass is hidden below the water's surface, and ships sometimes crash into the icebergs' enormous, unseen bulk under water.)*

- How much of an iceberg's mass remains underwater? *(as much as 90 percent)* **Verbal/Linguistic**

V Visual Skills

Diagramming Suggest that students with artistic skill create diagrams of the formation of ice shelves and the calving of icebergs. Display these diagrams in the classroom and encourage other students to study them. **Visual/Spatial**

ANSWER, p. 476

CRITICAL THINKING Icebergs form as weather warms during Antarctica's spring and summer months and parts of ice shelves far from land break up into large chunks of floating ice.

T The lowest point on the continent is deep within the Bentley Subglacial Trench. This low area is also the lowest place on the surface of Earth that is not under seawater.

R Ice not only covers the land in ice sheets but also extends out into the ocean in what are called ice shelves. An **ice shelf** is a thick slab of ice that is attached to a coastline but floats on the ocean. It is a seaward extension of the ice sheet that forms a thick, hard plain of ice. During the dark winter months, temperatures fall to unbelievable lows in Antarctica. The air and water get so cold that the seawater next to the ice shelves freezes. This increases the size of the ice shelf. So much coastal water freezes into the ice shelves that Antarctica appears to double in size every winter. As the weather warms during the spring and summer months, parts of the ice shelves farthest away from the land break up into huge, floating islands of ice.

V The process of ice breaking free from an ice shelf or glacier is called **calving**. The large chunk of ice that breaks off is called an **iceberg**. Icebergs are made of freshwater, not salt water. These massive bodies of ice slowly drift through frigid ocean waters with only their top portions showing. As much as 90 percent of an iceberg remains underwater. Because most of their mass is hidden below the water's surface, icebergs appear much smaller than they really are. This has led to accidents when ships have come close to what appeared to be small chunks of ice floating on the surface but then crashed into the icebergs' enormous, unseen bulk under the water. Icebergs are classified as chunks of ice larger than 16 feet (5 m) across. While many icebergs are the size of houses and mountains, some are the size of small islands. Satellite images show a huge crack in an Antarctic glacier that could produce an iceberg of 350 square miles (906 sq. km), the size of New York City.

In the middle of summer, a special-purpose ship called an icebreaker moves through an ice pack in the Ross Sea along the coast of Antarctica. The Ross Sea region has permanent year-round icy conditions, and a powerful icebreaker is the best vessel suited for its exploration.
▶ **CRITICAL THINKING**
Describing How do icebergs form?

©David Ball/Corbis

476 *Chapter 16*

netw⊚rks *Online Teaching Options*

ANIMATION

How Icebergs Form

Analyzing Use the animation to help students analyze the mechanisms involved in the formation of icebergs. Call on volunteers to describe the process in their own words. Encourage students to use the animation to consider the causes behind why icebergs break. Discuss with students the environmental factors that cause icebergs and glaciers to melt and break. **Verbal/Linguistic**

See page 471C for other online activities.

Antarctica is surrounded by stormy seas. These include the Weddell Sea, the Scotia Sea, the Amundsen Sea, the Ross Sea, and the Davis Sea. These icy waters were named by and for explorers and scientists who have mapped and studied the region. In recent years, hundreds of new species of marine animals have been discovered in the mysterious depths of these cold seas.

Researchers battle powerful winds as they carry out their research in the interior of Antarctica.

W

✓ **READING PROGRESS CHECK**

Determining Central Ideas Does the continent of Antarctica increase in size during the winter?

Climate and Resources

GUIDING QUESTION *Does any life exist on such a forbidding continent?*

How would you like to live in a place where summer brings a high temperature of only a few degrees above freezing?

A Dry, Frigid Climate

Because of its high latitude, Antarctica never receives direct rays from the sun, even when the Southern Hemisphere is tilted toward the sun. Thus, the sun's energy is spread out over a wider surface area than at lower-latitude places such as the Equator. The result is that very little heat energy reaches the surface of the land. In addition, being south of the Antarctic Circle, most of Antarctica receives no sunlight at all and is completely dark for at least three months of the year.

C

The high elevation across Antarctica affects its climate, as well. Strong, fast winds blow colder air down from high interior lands toward the coasts. These powerful gusts, called **katabatic winds**, are driven by the force of Earth's gravity.

©George Steinmetz/Corbis

Chapter 16 **477**

SLIDE SHOW

Life in Antarctica

Speculating Use the slide show to help students gain an appreciation for the variety of life that exists in Antarctica. Ask students to speculate on how the various species may have adapted to the continent's extreme climate over time. Encourage students to research a particular plant or animal that exists in the region to learn more about their adaptations to the environment. **Naturalist**

See page 471C for other online activities.

Slide Show

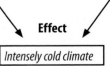

V

V Visual Skills

Analyzing Images Direct students to examine the photograph of researchers in the interior of Antarctica. Ask students to think about the living conditions shown in the photograph. Then give the class five minutes to make a list of the concerns they might have if they had to live under these conditions. After five minutes, call on volunteers to share their lists. *(Students might list the following concerns: having warm enough clothes, being able to work when bundled up, type of toilet facilities, what to do with wastes, how to keep drinking water from freezing, how to keep food from freezing, how to keep warm at night, how to find your way to and from places.)* **Visual/ Spatial, Logical/Mathematical**

W Writing Skills

Informative/Explanatory Write the names of the seas surrounding Antarctica on the board: Weddell Sea, Scotia Sea, Amundsen Sea, Ross Sea, and Davis Sea. Direct students to choose one of the seas and research the explorer or scientist after which it was named. Have students write a brief biography of the person. As an alternative, some students might research the new species of marine animals that have been discovered in the depths of these seas and write a short report on the subject. **Verbal/Linguistic**

C Critical Thinking Skills

Determining Cause and Effect As the class discusses Antarctica's climate, reproduce the chart below to highlight the two main causes of the continent's extremely cold climate. Then remind students that when the Southern Hemisphere is tilted toward the sun, it is summer in the Southern Hemisphere. **Ask:**

- **What season is it when Antarctica receives no sunlight at all and is completely dark?** *(winter)*
- **How is the Southern Hemisphere tilted then?** *(away from the sun)* **Visual/Spatial**

Causes

Due to its high latitude, Antarctica never receives the sun's direct rays.	*Katabatic winds blow cold air from high interior lands toward the coast.*

Effect

Intensely cold climate

ANSWER, p. 477

✓ **READING PROGRESS CHECK** No, because the land area does not increase. The continent seems to grow in size only because of the growth of ice shelves.

V Visual Skills

Creating Charts As you continue the discussion of Antarctica's climate, ask students to make a cause-and-effect chart to highlight the causes of the continent's extremely dry climate. (**Causes:** *Extremely cold temperatures limit amount of air moisture;* **Effect:** *Low precipitation of only 2-4 inches a year, Driest climate in world*)

Then have students make another cause-and-effect chart to illustrate Antarctica's effect on the global climate. (**Cause:** *White, smooth surface of ice sheet and shelf reflects solar radiation back into upper atmosphere;* **Effect:** *Lowers temperature of entire planet*)

To help students make connections with the reflective quality of snow and ice, ask if they have ever been bothered by the glare reflected off a field of snow on a sunny day. **Visual/Spatial**

R Reading Skills

Listing As students read the section "Plants and Wildlife," suggest that they make a two-column chart to create a list of all the land plants and animals of Antarctica mentioned in this lesson. (**Plants:** *mosses, algae, lichens, Antarctic hair grass, Antarctic pearlwort;* **Animals:** *insects, mites, Weddell seals, albatross, cormorants, gulls, emperor penguin, gentoo penguin*)
AL Verbal/Linguistic, Visual/Spatial

Life in Antarctica

Plants	Animals

T Technology Skills

Researching on the Internet Suggest that each student become an "expert" on one of the plants and animals of Antarctica by conducting Internet research. Have students give a brief oral report on his or her plant or animal and share a photograph with the class. **Verbal/Linguistic, Naturalist**

A gentoo penguin leaps onto an iceberg to join its companion near Antarctica's Gerlache Strait. The gentoo is one of six penguin species that populate the Antarctic Peninsula and the many islands around the frozen continent. An orange beak, white head marking, and longer tail distinguish the gentoo from the other penguin species.

All of these factors combined produce an intensely cold climate. Temperatures are coldest in the interior highlands and warmest near the coasts.

Antarctica also has an extremely dry climate. The continent receives only 2 inches to 4 inches (5 cm to 10 cm) of precipitation each year. The extreme cold makes the climate even drier by limiting the amount of moisture the air can hold. This effect combined with lack of precipitation makes Antarctica the world's driest continent.

Antarctica plays a vital role in maintaining the global climate balance. The millions of square miles of ice covering Antarctica act like a giant reflector. The white, smooth surface of the ice shelf reflects sunlight. An estimated 80 percent of the solar radiation that reaches Antarctica is reflected back into the upper atmosphere. So, this continent-sized reflector reduces the amount of solar energy that is absorbed by Earth. On such a large scale, this effect lowers the overall temperature of the entire planet.

Plants and Wildlife

Antarctica's harsh climate limits the types of plants and animals that can live on its surface. Only 1 percent of Antarctica's land area is suitable for plant life. Plants found in Antarctica include mosses, algae, and **lichens**, which are organisms that usually grow on solid, rocky surfaces and are made up of algae and fungi. Only two species of flowering plants grow in the region: Antarctic hair grass and Antarctic pearlwort. Most plants are found on the Antarctic Peninsula and its surrounding islands. These are the warmest, wettest areas in the region. However, a few plants have been discovered in intensely cold inland areas. Scientists have found hardy species of mosses, lichens, and algae growing in the tiny cracks and pores of rocks in Victoria Land.

©Momatiuk · Eastcott/Corbis

netw⊚rks   *Online Teaching Options*

VIDEO

Zee Evans/National Science Foundation

Penguins' Adaptation to Climate

Integrating Visual Information Have students watch the video about penguins and their adaptations to the harsh environment of Antarctica. Then discuss with students how the wildlife of Antarctica survives in an extreme environment. Challenge students to think about and discuss what humans can learn from the adaptive methods they observe in nature. **Naturalist**

See page 471C for other online activities.

Most of Antarctica's land animals are tiny insects and spiderlike mites. Most other land animals are only part-time visitors to the region. Weddell seals are water animals, but they only come to Antarctica's shores during summer months to raise their pups. Many species of seabirds, such as albatross, cormorants, and gulls, visit Antarctica in the summer to breed. Only the emperor penguin stays in the region year-round. These giant penguins are adapted to extremely cold temperatures and cannot survive outside of Antarctica's frozen climate.

Although the land of Antarctica is not home to many living things, the Antarctic seas are filled with life. Many kinds of seals, dolphins, fish, and other marine animals live in waters surrounding Antarctica. Whales come to the Southern Ocean to feed during the summer. Sea mammals and seabirds eat **krill**, tiny crustaceans similar to shrimp. Krill thrive in the waters of the Southern Ocean, feeding on even smaller life-forms called plankton.

Plankton are tiny organisms floating near the water's surface. Some types of plankton are single-celled bacteria; others are plants such as algae. Plankton, krill, fish, sea mammals, seabirds, and land animals are part of Antarctica's ecosystem. These creatures are essential parts of the food chain that supports life on the continent.

Resources of Antarctica

Several factors make it difficult or impossible to explore Antarctica for natural resources. The harsh climate creates dangerous conditions for human workers. The land that could hold mineral resources is buried by the thick ice sheet. Even reaching the interior of the continent with heavy mining equipment could prove impossible. As a result, mineral and energy resources that might exist have not been exploited. Some species of fish are plentiful in the Southern Ocean, and commercial fishing operations harvest fish from Antarctica's waters.

☑ **READING PROGRESS CHECK**

Describing Where in Antarctica would you find the most living things? Explain why this is so.

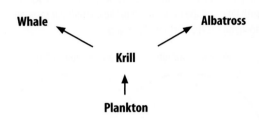

FOLDABLES
Study Organizer

Include this lesson's information in your Foldable®.

Reviewing Vocabulary (Tier Three Words)
1. How are *krill* important to the survival of Antarctica's seabirds and sea mammals? RH.6-8.4

Answering the Guiding Questions
2. *Analyzing* Why do you think Antarctica was nicknamed "The Last Continent"? RH.6-8.1

3. *Determining Central Ideas* How are ice sheets and ice shelves alike and different? RH.6-8.2

4. *Identifying* What types of life-forms are found on the Antarctic Peninsula? RH.6-8.2

5. *Describing* Explain why Antarctica's mineral and energy resources are not commercially mined or harvested. RH.6-8.5

6. *Informative/Explanatory Writing* In your own words, explain why Antarctica's climate is so cold and dry. Use facts and details from the lesson in your writing. WHST.6-8.2, WHST.6-8.9

Chapter 16 **479**

LESSON 1 REVIEW ANSWERS

Reviewing Vocabulary

1. Seabirds and sea mammals feed on krill.

Answering the Guiding Questions

2. **Analyzing** Accept all reasonable responses; students may infer that Antarctica was the last continent to be seen or "discovered" by humans.

3. **Determining Central Ideas** Alike: Both are made of frozen water and form in the Antarctic region. Different: An ice sheet is a huge mass of ice that forms a solid crust over the land; an ice shelf is a hard layer of ice that forms around Antarctica's coasts during the winter, extending outward and doubling the appearance of the continent before melting in the spring; an ice sheet is more permanent than an ice shelf.

4. **Identifying** mosses, algae, lichens, flowering plants called Antarctic hair grass and Antarctic pearlwort; Students may correctly surmise that birds and other animals can be found living on the Antarctic Peninsula during the summer season.

5. **Describing** because accessing and removing them is too difficult in the harsh climate and remote location of Antarctica

6. **Informative/Explanatory Writing** Students' explanatory writings will vary but should mention such facts and details as latitude, the sun, lack of precipitation, and katabatic winds.

Diagramming Have students draw a diagram showing an Antarctic food chain. Students might create their food chain based on information in the text, or they might research for a more elaborate and detailed Antarctic food chain. Display completed diagrams in the classroom. A sample food chain is shown below. **Visual/Spatial, Naturalist**

Antarctic Food Chain

Whale ← → Albatross

Krill

↑

Plankton

Determining Central Ideas Use the following questions to help students identify the main ideas about Antarctica's resources. **Ask:**

• What are the main reasons that any mineral and energy resources of Antarctica have not been exploited? *(The harsh climate creates dangerous working conditions. A thick ice sheet covers the land, making it difficult to reach any underlying deposits. Bringing heavy mining equipment to the interior might be impossible.)*

• What resource of the region has been exploited? *(fish)* **Verbal/Linguistic**

CLOSE & REFLECT

Direct students to take out the K-W-L charts that they made at the beginning of the chapter and have them add to the "What I Learned" column of the chart. Then suggest that they also look at the list of survival items they made at the beginning of this lesson and note any changes they would make based on what they have learned.

ANSWER, p. 479

☑ **READING PROGRESS CHECK** Most living things on the continent live in the seas around Antarctica. The small organisms that live in the waters are essential parts of the food chain for the sea mammals and land animals that are part of Antarctica's ecosystem. The harsh climate of Antarctica's interior limits the plants and animals that can live there.

ENGAGE

Bellringer Create a Venn diagram on the board and ask students to think about the similarities and differences between polar exploration and space exploration. Write students' responses in the appropriate sections of the diagram. Prompt students to draw conclusions from the completed diagram. For example, students might note that both polar exploration and space exploration challenge people's ability to survive in extreme environments. Then read aloud the first two paragraphs about Amundsen's and Scott's race to reach the South Pole and the information in the Content Background Knowledge at the bottom of this page.

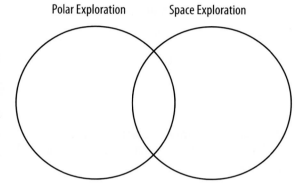

Polar Exploration   Space Exploration

TEACH & ASSESS

T **Technology Skills**

Researching on the Internet Many people have been intrigued by the story of Amundsen's and Scott's race to the South Pole. Suggest that interested students conduct Internet research to find out more about the two men's expeditions and the conditions they faced. Ask students to share highlights of the story with the rest of the class. **BL** **Verbal/Linguistic**

Content Background Knowledge

Robert Scott not only lost the race to be the first person to reach the South Pole, he also lost his life in the pursuit of his dream. Scott and four members of his team arrived at the South Pole on foot on January 18, 1912, only to see Amundsen's flag already there and realize they had lost the race. Their return trip was plagued by severe weather, and two team members soon died. With only 11 miles to go to the base camp, Scott and the other two became trapped in their tent by a blizzard. Their frozen bodies were found months later.

ANSWER, p. 480

Taking Notes Students' notes will vary but should include the main idea and supporting details from each section of the lesson.

---

networks

There's More Online!

- ☑ **IMAGES** Earth's Ozone Layers
- ☑ **MAP** Antarctica Explored
- ☑ **SLIDE SHOW** Life in Antarctica
- ☑ **VIDEO**

Reading HELPDESK CCSS

Academic Vocabulary RH.6-8.4
- **acknowledge** (Tier Two Words)

Content Vocabulary RH.6-8.4
(Tier Three Words)
- **treaty**
- **research station**
- **ozone**
- **remote sensing**

TAKING NOTES: *Key Ideas and Details* RH.6-8.2, RH.6-8.7

Determining Central Ideas Using a chart like this one, take notes on the central idea from each section of the lesson.

Section	Central Idea
Sharing the Land	
The Scientific Continent	

480

Lesson 2
Life in Antarctica

ESSENTIAL QUESTION · *How do people adapt to their environment?*

IT MATTERS BECAUSE
Antarctica is a region shared by many nations. It is important to scientific research.

Sharing the Land

GUIDING QUESTION *How do people share common resources and protect unique lands?*

In 1911, two explorers, Roald Amundsen and Robert Scott, were in a race to be the first to reach the South Pole. Amundsen was a Norwegian explorer who had experience dealing with cold and snow. Scott was an English explorer who had commanded one previous expedition to Antarctica but had little experience traveling in the cold. Both men were driven to compete by a combination of curiosity and national pride. The two explorers and their teams made incredible journeys across the brutal land, losing men, ponies, and sled dogs to cold and starvation along the way. In the end, it was Amundsen's team that reached the South Pole first. Scott and his team arrived 34 days later.

The remarkable feats of Amundsen and Scott gave the world an insider's view of Antarctica for the first time. Their experiences and discoveries helped the scientists and explorers that came after them. Memorials to both men have been built in Antarctica.

The Antarctic Treaty
Antarctica is the only continent with no native population. Therefore, when the first humans visited the continent, there were no previous claims to the land. Several countries made territorial claims to sections of Antarctica's land, but these

(l to r) ©Deborah Zabarenko/Reuters/Corbis; ©YONHAP/epa/Corbis; Hugh Rose/Danita Delimont/Alamy

---

networks   *Online Teaching Options*

VIDEO

Antarctica's Dry Valley

Comparing and Contrasting Use this video about Antarctica's active volcano and dry valley to preview the lesson content. Ask students to write a paragraph describing what they learned by watching this video. Discuss with students how Antarctica's unique geography might encourage scientists to want to research and spend time in this harsh environment. **Visual/Spatial**

See page 471D for other online activities.

BBC Motion Gallery Education

claims were set aside by the Antarctic Treaty. A **treaty** is an agreement or a contract between two or more nations, governments, or other political groups. Signed by 12 countries in 1959, the Antarctic Treaty states that the continent of Antarctica should be used only for scientific research and other peaceful purposes. In later years, 33 additional countries signed the Antarctic Treaty. The treaty also sets rules for the management of the land and its resources. The Antarctic Treaty is an effort to protect Antarctica's environment and to prevent weapons testing and other military actions from being carried out on the continent. Other agreements such as the Antarctic Conservation Act relate to protecting the region's wildlife.

R

Regulating Relations

Nations including Argentina, Australia, Great Britain, New Zealand, and Norway still claim large sections of the continent as territories, but not all governments **acknowledge** these claims. Because Antarctica is not considered a nation or a country and it has no government, issues relating to the continent's use and protection are decided by the Antarctic Treaty System. This is a group of representatives from 48 countries that have interests in Antarctica. Important decisions affecting Antarctica's environment, wildlife, and resident scientists are made by annual meetings of the Antarctic Treaty System.

☑ **READING PROGRESS CHECK**

Citing Text Evidence What is the purpose of the Antarctic Treaty?

Academic Vocabulary

acknowledge to recognize the rights, status, or authority of a person, a thing, or an event

C

The Amundsen-Scott station is a U.S. scientific research center at the South Pole. The original station was built in 1956 for the International Geophysical Year—a special period of international scientific investigations in Antarctica during 1957 and 1958. The rebuilt station today houses as many as 200 people in summer and about 50 in winter.

©Deborah Zabarenko/Reuters/Corbis

THE UNITED STATES OF AMERICA
WELCOMES YOU TO
AMUNDSEN - SCOTT SOUTH POLE STATION

Chapter 16 **481**

Antarctica Explored

Analyzing Maps Display the map to students and discuss the exploration of Antarctica by various groups of researchers and countries. Have students identify the territories claimed by various countries based on the nations' flags. Discuss with students some of the difficulties that could arise with so many nations trying to claim various regions of Antarctica. **Visual/Spatial, Interpersonal**

See page 471D for other online activities.

Identifying Pose the following questions to focus students' attention on the way that Antarctica is governed. **Ask:**

• **What is the Antarctic Treaty?** *(an agreement signed by more than 40 countries to regulate the use of Antarctica)*

• **What does the Antarctic Treaty state?** *(It states that Antarctica should only be used for scientific research and other peaceful purposes, and it sets rules for the management of the land and its resources.)*

• **Why do you think that only 12 countries signed the treaty in 1959?** *(These may have been the only countries who had explored the area. Or they may have been the most powerful countries in the world at the time.)*

• **Why would it be important for additional countries to sign the treaty in later years?** *(The treaty is only meaningful if the world's nations agree to honor it.)* **AL** **Verbal/ Linguistic, Interpersonal**

W

Making Inferences Remind students to use their background knowledge and other information in the text to make inferences when information is not given in the text. **Ask:**

• **Why do you think some nations still claim large sections of Antarctica as territories despite the Antarctic Treaty?** *(Sample answer: Nations may want to maintain their claims in case the situation in Antarctica changes in the future.)*

• **Do you think that it is better to have many nations laying claim to the land or to have no nations claiming the land? Explain.** *(Sample answers: It is better when many nations claim the land because this means they will be more likely to cooperate with one another. I do not think any nation should claim the land because it is mainly a natural resource and not a place for people to live.)* **Logical/Mathematical, Interpersonal**

Narrative Have students do research to learn more about this scientific research center in Antarctica. Then have them write a fictional email from one of the research scientists living there. Encourage students to include descriptive details and factual information about the life or work being done there. **Verbal/ Linguistic**

ANSWER, p. 481

☑ **READING PROGRESS CHECK** The treaty ensures the land is used for peaceful purposes, such as research, and sets rules for managing the environment and wildlife.

Life in Antarctica

C Critical Thinking Skills

Summarizing Pose the following questions to help students summarize the key ideas about living in Antarctica. **Ask:**

- **How does Antarctica's population vary from summer to winter?** *(It drops by three-fourths, from about 4,400 people in summer to about 1,100 people in winter.)*

- **What are weather conditions like in the summer?** *(The temperatures usually stay below freezing, but the sun shines 24 hours a day.)*

- **What are the conditions like in the winter?** *(The winds create blizzard-like conditions. Temperatures are so low that people can freeze to death within minutes without protective clothing. It is dark for 24 hours a day, and ice shelves along the coasts prevent ships from coming near the land.)* **Verbal/ Linguistic**

Making Connections Ask students to think about the kinds of accommodations they would want in a research station in Antarctica if they had to live there for several months or even a year. Have volunteers describe what they would want to the rest of the class. Then, tell students that the Amundsen-Scott South Pole Station, which was built by the United States, includes the following accommodations:

- small private bedrooms for the staff, who work in three shifts around the clock
- a cafeteria with chefs to prepare the meals
- a greenhouse that provides some fresh vegetables to eat as well as a place to sit and enjoy being around green plants, something the outside environment does not provide
- a workout station and a full basketball court
- an activity room with a variety of musical instruments
- a sauna

T Technology Skills

Researching on the Internet Encourage students to check out websites on the different research stations in Antarctica. Suggest that they find out more about the living conditions and the types of research being conducted. Ask volunteers to share some of the interesting information they discover. **Verbal/ Linguistic, Visual/Spatial**

ANSWER, p. 482

CRITICAL THINKING Scientists come to the isolated continent to study climate change, oceanography, geology, and other sciences involving Antarctic landforms, weather, climate, animals, plants, and the ancient rocks that form the continental shelf below the land.

The Scientific Continent

GUIDING QUESTION *How and why do scientists study Antarctica?*

Because of its harsh climate, Antarctica is the only continent that has no permanent human settlement. Its largely unspoiled environment has made it a favorable place for scientific research.

Living in Antarctica

No one lives in Antarctica full time, but many people stay in this harsh world for months or even years at a time. During the summer, when the sun shines brightly and temperatures are cold but not deadly, about 4,400 people reside in Antarctica. When the temperatures fall and the constant darkness of winter sets in, this temporary population shrinks to about 1,100 people. Most of these people are scientists and support teams living in shelters on land, but some stay aboard ships near the coasts. People from all over the world come to the frozen continent to study climate change, oceanography, geology, and countless other sciences involving Antarctica's landforms, weather, plants, animals, and the ancient rocks that form the continental shelf below the land.

Why do most research scientists stay in Antarctica only during the summer season? Weather conditions during summer months are still cold and windy, but they are not nearly as severe as those in winter. Summer temperatures usually remain below freezing, but the sun shines 24 hours a day. In winter, powerful winds tear across the land from the mountains, creating blizzard-like conditions. Temperatures are so low that without protective clothing, humans can freeze to death in a matter of minutes. The ice shelves that form along the coasts prevent ships from coming anywhere near the land. For these reasons, summer is the best time for scientists to work in Antarctica. Only a small number of brave, patient researchers continue their work through the long winters, staying sheltered indoors as much as possible.

Governments with scientific interests in Antarctica have built research stations in different locations across the continent. A **research station** is a base where scientists live and work. These stations usually consist of a few

A scientist from South Korea collects meteorites on an ice field in the Ross Sea region of Antarctica. Meteorites are rocks from space that have fallen on earth. They provide clues about the history of our solar system. Antarctica is the best place in the world to collect meteorites. There, meteorites fall into ice rather than hard rock and so are damaged less. Also, Antarctica's icy environment makes them more visible and easier to collect.

▶ **CRITICAL THINKING**
Analyzing Why do scientists come to Antarctica despite its climatic conditions?

482 *Chapter 16*

©YONHAP/epa/Corbis

---

net**w**@rks   *Online Teaching Options*

GRAPHIC ORGANIZER

Research Stations

Analyzing Use the interactive graphic organizer to discuss how a researcher would prepare for a long stay in the extreme environment of Antarctica and the reasons to conduct research there. Discuss the supplies they might need and how they might differ from supplies needed in other parts of the world. Have student volunteers discuss whether or not they would want to visit, research, or stay in Antarctica for an extended period of time and why. **Logical/Mathematical**

See page 471D for other online activities.

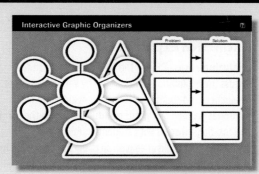

Interactive Graphic Organizers

DIAGRAM SKILLS >

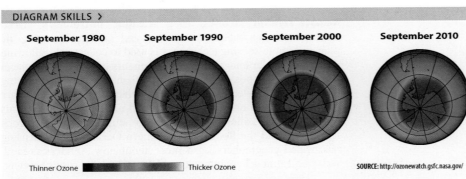

September 1980   September 1990   September 2000   September 2010

Thinner Ozone [gradient bar] Thicker Ozone   SOURCE: http://ozonewatch.gsfc.nasa.gov/

OZONE HOLE
Images show changes in the size of the ozone hole over Antarctica during a 30-year period.

▶ **CRITICAL THINKING**
Analyzing How has the size of the ozone hole changed over time? What do these changes reveal?

buildings set close together, each built with special insulation against the brutally cold and windy weather. Currently, Antarctica has about 50 research stations. Each station has living quarters for the scientists and other staff, such as medical doctors, cooks, and mechanics. Stations also have laboratories, other types of research facilities, and large storage areas filled with fuel, food, and equipment. Research stations need to have enough food stored away to feed teams of scientists for a year or more. Having extra food is important because violent storms can happen at any time, making it impossible for planes or ships to bring in fresh food and other supplies.

The Ozone Layer
One important area of study focuses on the ozone layer that is high in Earth's atmosphere. **Ozone** is a gas in the atmosphere that absorbs harmful ultraviolet radiation from the sun. Through decades of research and study, scientists discovered that the layer of ozone in our planet's atmosphere had thinned and decreased. This means that less ozone exists to protect Earth and life on Earth from damaging solar radiation.

The two locations on Earth where levels of ozone are the lowest are over the Arctic Circle and over Antarctica and the Southern Ocean. Loss of ozone affects all life on the planet. Scientists in Antarctica and other parts of the world are working to find a way to protect and preserve the ozone layer.

V

Studying Earth From Above
Have you ever wondered how scientists are able to figure out what lies below the surface of Earth? For example, how do scientists know what landforms lie under the thick Antarctic ice sheet? Scientists are able to study what they cannot see, such as layers of rock under the ice, by using an amazing kind of technology called remote sensing.

W

Chapter 16 **483**

Anja Fleig/age fotostock

IMAGE

Earth's Ozone Layer

Contrasting Display the interactive image of the ozone layer and use the slider to show the changes over time, illustrating its depletion. Explain that since the late 1980s nations have agreed to phase out the use of chemicals that have contributed to the depletion of the ozone layer. Discuss with students the growing concern over the rising temperatures and extreme weather conditions.
Encourage students to conduct research on ways that countries are trying to protect the environment. **Kinesthetic, Visual/Spatial**

See page 471D for other online activities.

Interactive Photos

V Visual Skills

Analyzing Maps Have students read the section, "The Ozone Layer," and discuss what ozone is and the important role that the atmosphere's ozone layer plays in protecting life on Earth from damaging solar radiation. Read the Content Background Knowledge to students. Then, direct students' attention to the images at the top of the page. **Ask:**

- **How did the ozone hole change between 1980 and 1990?** *(It grew considerably larger and thinner.)*
- **How did it change between 1990 and 2000?** *(It grew larger and thinner.)*
- **How did it change between 2000 and 2010?** *(It grew smaller and thicker.)*
- **Would you interpret the most recent change as encouraging or discouraging? Why?** *(It would be interpreted as encouraging. If the ozone hole grows smaller and the ozone thickens, then it appears the ozone layer is healing, which means it will provide more protection from damaging solar radiation.)* **Visual/Spatial, Logical/Mathematical**

W Writing Skills

Informative Have students read the section, "Studying Earth from Above," on this page and the next and write a summary of the section. Then have students choose one of the scientific instruments to research and report their findings back to the class. **Verbal/Linguistic**

Content Background Knowledge

Researchers have recorded ozone depletion at the South Pole with instruments on the ground, on balloons, and on satellites. Scientists attribute the formation of the ozone hole over Antarctica at least partially to people's former use of ozone-depleting chemicals as solvents and in refrigeration and in aerosol spray cans. These chemicals persist in the atmosphere for a long time. The 1987 Montreal Protocol, an international treaty designed to protect the ozone layer, phased out the use of such chemicals and has been successful in bringing about their decline in the atmosphere. However, other factors, such as natural fluctuations in temperatures, also affect the ozone layer. For this reason, researchers do not expect to see an even, continual decline in the ozone hole, though they hope for an eventual recovery.

ANSWER, p. 483

CRITICAL THINKING From 1980 to 2000 the ozone hole over Antarctica grew rapidly and the ozone layer thinned, but by 2010 recovery seemed to be taking place; the hole became smaller and the ozone layer thickened. This would indicate that regulations to reduce emissions and laws against the use of chemicals known to destroy the ozone layer are working.

Life in Antarctica

R Reading Skills

Identifying Effects Direct students' attention to the section titled, "Climate Change." **Ask:**

- **What is happening to the Antarctic ice sheet?** *(It is shrinking.)*
- **What do many scientists believe is causing this?** *(global warming)*
- **What are some other effects of climate change and global warming on Antarctica?** *(Massive chunks of ice are breaking away from glaciers, producing more icebergs in the waters. Traveling by ship is becoming more dangerous because of the increased number of icebergs. As these icebergs melt, global sea levels may rise. The populations of plankton and krill are declining. Without enough plankton and krill, fish may die off or leave, and then seals and penguins will not have enough fish to eat.)*
- **What might make Antarctica a "global barometer?"** *(It is the only continent that does not have people inhabiting it. This means that it is not being destroyed or affected by everyday human activity. This may mean that changes that take place there are things that are happening globally--they are easier to observe on a pristine land.)* **ELL** **AL** **Logical/ Mathematical, Naturalist**

T Technology Skills

Using Digital Tools Use the Internet to find a recording of the song of a humpback whale and play the song for the class. Then ask another student to read aloud the caption to the photograph of a humpback whale at the bottom of the page. Use the song and the photograph to spark a discussion of the link between people and other mammals. **Ask:**

- **Why do you think humpback whales attract tourists?** *(They are an unusual animal that people cannot see every day.)*
- **After examining the photograph, do you think it would be interesting to see a rare species like the humpback whale up close?** *(Students' answers may vary but should suggest that the opportunity to study rare species would be important and interesting.)*
- **Why is it important to protect rare or endangered species?** *(Students' answers should suggest that other species play a vital role in the environment of Earth, that they work within the food chain and without these species, there could be future environmental impact.)* **Auditory/Musical, Naturalist**

ANSWER, p. 484

CRITICAL THINKING Scientists believe that global warming and changing water currents are lowering the amount of plankton and krill on which fish and larger sea animals depend for food.

Remote sensing involves using scientific instruments placed onboard weather balloons, airplanes, and satellites to study the planet. Remote-sensing technology is used to collect data, allowing scientists to take images and measurements of objects and places that would be impossible to reach in person. Some remote-sensing equipment emits electromagnetic waves that create detailed images of landforms and bodies of water buried under miles of ice. This technology has allowed scientists to study Antarctica's rock foundation and the floor of the Southern Ocean. Remote sensing has helped geographers learn more about how Antarctica's land, water, and atmosphere interact and affect the global climate system.

Research Yields Clues

The research work done in Antarctica has resulted in many amazing discoveries. Scientists have learned about our planet's birth and evolution over time, and they have found clues about the origins of the universe. By comparing rocks and fossils found in Antarctica to those found on other continents, scientists have determined that the Antarctic continent was once part of a huge landmass called Gondwana. Antarctica, Asia, Africa, and other continents broke away from this supercontinent millions of years ago and drifted across Earth's surface as a result of plate tectonics.

Climate Change

Another major area of research in Antarctica is climate change. Through satellite imagery and local measurements, geographers have learned that the Antarctic ice sheet is shrinking. Many people are concerned that this shrinkage might be caused by global warming. This concern is twofold: First, scientists fear that the impact of climate change will permanently damage Antarctica's environment and ecosystems. Second, Antarctica is seen as a "global barometer," or an indicator of what is happening to the climate of the entire planet. Signs such as melting ice and shrinking icebergs tell geographers and scientists that global temperatures are rising quickly. As massive chunks of ice calve, or break away, from

Tourists enjoy close-up views of a female humpback whale and her calf. Humpback whales receive their name because they raise and bend their backs to begin diving. They gather in groups along the Antarctic coast, where they feed and breed. Because humpback whales are slow swimmers, tourist boats can easily approach them.
▶ **CRITICAL THINKING**
Describing How is climate change affecting the life of Antarctica's sea animals?

R

Hugh Rose/Danita Delimont/Alamy

484 *Chapter 16*

---

networks *Online Teaching Options*

CHART

Antarctic Food Chain

Analyzing Charts Use the flow chart to discuss the relationships in the Antarctic food chain and to point out how climate change might affect those relationships. Emphasize that a disruption at a low level in the food chain affects many other levels. **Logical/ Mathematical**

See page 471D for other online activities.

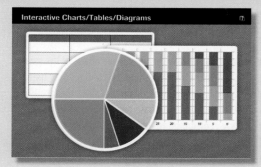
Interactive Charts/Tables/Diagrams

Antarctica's glaciers, more icebergs clutter the surrounding waters. This makes traveling by ship in these areas more difficult and dangerous. Even more serious is the possibility that as these icebergs melt, global sea levels will rise. Rising sea levels would make survival impossible in many parts of the world.

C Climate change is also affecting the food supplies of Antarctic land and sea animals. Scientists believe that global warming and changing water currents are affecting the amount of plankton and krill in the region. Recent studies have found low populations of these tiny water organisms in the waters around Antarctica. Without enough plankton and krill to eat, fish will die off or leave the area. This leaves seals and penguins without enough fish to eat. This disruption in the local food chain could have terrible consequences for Antarctica's animal life.

Taking a Tour

The bitterly cold, icy shores of Antarctica might not seem like a great place to spend a vacation. Still, about 6,000 tourists visit Antarctica each year. Most visitors are interested in seeing the incredible natural beauty of the area, taking photographs of wildlife, and visiting the research stations. Some are excited by the idea of visiting a harsh, dangerous place that few humans will ever see firsthand. Most tourists choose Antarctica because they want an adventure more than a vacation.

W Thanks to the work of the scientists who have studied Antarctica, humans have come a long way in understanding this mysterious continent. However, there is still much to learn. Geographers and other scientists living and working in Antarctica are dedicated to their research. With each passing year, they discover more clues about our planet's past. They also use what they learn to make predictions about our planet's future. Antarctica's secrets are slowly being uncovered, but much remains unknown about this frozen land at the bottom of the world.

☑ **READING PROGRESS CHECK**

Determining Central Ideas Why do scientists think Antarctica was part of a larger landmass that included continents such as Africa and Asia?

Thinking Like a Geographer

Lake Vostok

After spending years drilling through more than two miles (3 km) of solid ice in Antarctica, Russian scientists reached the surface of a gigantic freshwater lake in February 2012. Named Lake Vostok, it is the largest of the hundreds of the continent's subglacial lakes—roughly the size of Lake Ontario in North America. Scientists are taking samples of the water hoping to find living organisms that could provide clues about the unusual environment.

FOLDABLES
Study Organizer

Include this lesson's information in your Foldable®.

LESSON 2 REVIEW CCSS

Reviewing Vocabulary (Tier Three Words)
1. Why is *ozone* high in the atmosphere important? RH.6-8.4

Answering the Guiding Questions
2. ***Describing*** Describe the 1911 race to the South Pole in your own words. RH.6-8.5

3. ***Analyzing*** What are some of the advantages of using remote sensing to study Earth? RH.6-8.1

4. ***Identifying*** What are the possible causes and effects of Antarctica's shrinking ice sheet? RH.6-8.2

5. ***Narrative Writing*** Imagine that you are a young scientist who has just arrived in Antarctica for the summer. Write a fictional journal entry describing your research and daily life at a research station. Whenever possible, use facts, details, and vocabulary terms from the lesson in your narrative. WHST.6-8.4, WHST.6-8.9

Chapter 16 **485**

LESSON 2 REVIEW ANSWERS

Reviewing Vocabulary

1. Ozone is a gas in the atmosphere that protects Earth from the sun's harmful ultraviolet radiation.

Answering the Guiding Questions

2. **Describing** Sample response: Roald Amundsen and Robert Scott competed to see who would be the first human being to reach the South Pole. Roald Amundsen and his team got there first. Robert Scott's team arrived a little over a month later.

3. **Analyzing** Remote sensing enables scientists to learn about Earth using more than the observation of what people can see. For example, it allows scientists to figure out how deep beneath the ice and snow the land is.

4. **Identifying** Scientists believe global warming may be causing the ice sheet to melt. Effects include large numbers of icebergs breaking off into the water, harm to local ecosystems, and rising global sea levels.

5. **Narrative Writing** Student responses will vary, but narratives should demonstrate an appreciation for life at a research station.

CHAPTER 16, Lesson 2
Life in Antarctica

C Critical Thinking Skills

Making Inferences Have students make connections between this content and what they read in the chapter on the islands of Oceania. Then have them make connections to other coastal areas around the world as well. **Ask:**

- **How would rising sea levels make it difficult to live in other parts of the world?** *(Areas that are now near the shoreline would be underwater. As people moved from these areas to other places, some regions would experience overcrowding and would not be able to provide for all of the needs of the people living there.)*
- **What can you infer about the type of water that plankton and krill need to survive?** *(They need cooler water and are accustomed to certain water currents.)* **Logical/Mathematical**

W Writing Skills

Informative/Explanatory Tell students to imagine that they are tour guides, leading a group of Americans on a visit to Antarctica. Ask them to choose the sites that the group will visit and then write a script for the tour. Encourage students to incorporate as much information about Antarctica as they can, based on what they have learned in this chapter. If there is enough time, ask volunteers to share their scripts with the class. **Verbal/Linguistic**

Making Connections Point out that even though Antarctica has never had a native human population, has been declared off-limits to development, and is sometimes called the last pristine region on Earth, it has not been immune to the effects of human activities elsewhere. The consequences of pollution have even reached "the last continent," the most isolated region on Earth. Emphasize that Antarctica serves as a prime example of the interconnectedness of all life on Earth.

CLOSE & REFLECT

To close the lesson, ask students to think back to the Venn diagram that they created comparing space exploration to exploration of Antarctica. Have students discuss the importance of maintaining science bases in Antarctica that can be used for research. Students should describe the types of things that they learned about the continent from this lesson.

ANSWER, p. 485

☑ **READING PROGRESS CHECK** Scientists have found rocks and fossils on Antarctica, Africa, Asia, and other continents that indicate they were once all part of one huge landmass.

ENGAGE

Bellringer Before students read, draw a concept web and ask students what they know about global warming, its causes, and its effects. Write their responses in the web. Tell them that they will analyze two viewpoints on the cause of global warming. Remind students that when analyzing an opinion, they should consider the background of the person and ask themselves:

- **Does this author have the credentials to offer a knowledgeable opinion?**
- **Does this author have a reason to be biased?**

Advise students to check the background of an author and not just assume that he or she is an expert. Then share the information in the Content Background Knowledge and have students read the introductory paragraph and the *No!* viewpoint. Then, **ask:**

- **Do these authors potentially have a bias that would affect their position? If so, what is the bias?** *(Yes, the authors work for the Heartland Institute which promotes "free-market solutions," which would generally oppose government regulation of industry.)*

TEACH & ASSESS

C Critical Thinking Skills

Analyzing Primary Sources Pose the following questions to help students analyze the *No!* viewpoint. **Ask:**

- **What is the source of the *No!* viewpoint?** *(two authors who are not scientists, one of whom is a lawyer)*
- **What position on global warming do these authors promote?** *(They say that scientists indicate it is impossible to tell if recent warming is natural or the result of human actions.)*
- **What evidence do the authors cite to support their position?** *(They say that thousands of peer-reviewed articles point to natural sources of climate variability.)*
- **Is this evidence convincing?** *(Answers will vary. Some may note that the evidence is convincing. Others may say that the question remains whether the current change is due to natural causes or to human activities.)* **Logical/Mathematical**

Content Background Knowledge

- The authors of the *No!* opinion are not scientists. James M. Taylor has a law degree. Both authors work for the Heartland Institute, a research organization that promotes "free-market solutions to social and economic problems."
- The source of the *Yes!* opinion is a report by a group of the world's leading climate change scientists and experts. The report represents the work of more than 150 authors from more than 30 countries.

What Do You Think?

Is Global Warming a Result of Human Activity?

Scientists agree that Earth's climate is changing. They do not agree on what is causing the change. Is it just another natural warming cycle like so many cycles that have occurred in the past? Scientists who support this position cite thousands of years' worth of natural climatic change as evidence. Or is climate change anthropogenic—caused by human activity? Scientists who support this position cite the warming effect of rapidly increasing amounts of greenhouse gases in the atmosphere. Greenhouse gases occur naturally, but they also result from the burning of fossil fuels. Which side's evidence is more convincing?

No!

PRIMARY SOURCE

❝ The Intergovernmental Panel on Climate Change (IPCC), an agency of the United Nations, claims the warming that has occurred since the mid-twentieth century "is *very likely* due to the observed increase in anthropogenic greenhouse gas concentrations." Many climate scientists disagree with the IPCC on this key issue.

Scientists who study the issue say it is impossible to tell if the recent small warming trend is natural, a continuation of the planet's recovery from the more recent "Little Ice Age," or unnatural, the result of human greenhouse gas emissions. Thousands of peer-reviewed articles point to natural sources of climate variability that could explain some or even all of the warming in the second half of the twentieth century. S. Fred Singer and Dennis Avery documented natural climate cycles of approximately 1,500 years going back hundreds of thousands of years. ❞

—Joseph Bast and James M. Taylor, "Global Warming: Not a Crisis," The Heartland Institute

A scientist weighs an ice core sample on a glacier in Antarctica. Ice cores provide detailed information about changes in Earth's climate over many centuries.

---

net**works** *Online Teaching Options*

WORKSHEET

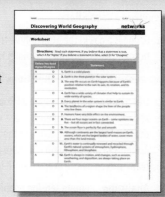

Fact Vs. Opinion

Distinguishing Fact from Opinion Divide the class into small groups, and have each group follow the steps in the worksheet to practice distinguishing fact from opinion using the arguments in this feature. Have the groups share their analyses with the class. **Logical/Mathematical**

Afternoon traffic flows along the streets of Beijing, China, on a smog-filled day. Despite efforts to improve air quality, the Chinese capital remains one of the world's most polluted cities.

TEXT: Climate Change (2007): The Physical Science Basis: Working Group I Contribution to the Fourth Assessment Report of the Intergovernmental Panel on Climate Change Fig. V2, p. 702. Cambridge University Press.

Yes!
PRIMARY SOURCE

" It is very unlikely that the 20th-century warming can be explained by natural causes.... Palaeoclimatic reconstructions show that the second half of the 20th century was likely the warmest 50-year period in the Northern Hemisphere in the last 1300 years. This rapid warming is consistent with the scientific understanding of how the climate should respond to a rapid increase in greenhouse gases like that which has occurred over the past century, and the warming is inconsistent with the scientific understanding of how the climate should respond to natural external factors such as variability in solar output and volcanic activity. Climate models provide a suitable tool to study the various influences on the Earth's climate. When the effects of increasing levels of greenhouse gases are included in the models, as well as natural external factors, the models produce good simulations of the warming that has occurred over the past century. The models fail to reproduce the observed warming when run using only natural factors. "

— Contribution of Working Group I: The Physical Science Basis to the Fourth Assessment Report of the Intergovernmental Panel on Climate Change, 2007

What Do You Think? DBQ

1 *Analyzing* What specific evidence is offered to support the position that warming is caused by human activity? RH.6-8.1, RH.6-8.10

2 *Identifying Point of View* What specific evidence is offered to support the position that warming results from natural causes? RH.6-8.6, WHST.6-8.9

Critical Thinking
3 *Analyzing* What effect could belief in one viewpoint or the other have on people or governments? RH.6-8.1, RH.6-8.5

Chapter 16 **487**

C Critical Thinking Skills

Analyzing Primary Sources Use the following questions to help students analyze the *Yes!* viewpoint. **Ask:**

- **What is the source of the *Yes!* viewpoint?** *(a report from a group of climate change scientists from around the world)*
- **Do the authors potentially have a bias that would affect their position? If so, what is the bias?** *(Students' answers will vary but could suggest a bias towards the idea that climate change is the result of human activity.)*
- **What position on global warming does this group promote?** *(The present global warming is due to a rapid increase in greenhouse gases over the past century.)*
- **What evidence does the group provide to support their position?** *(Climate models only reproduce the observed global warming when the effects of increasing levels of greenhouse gases are included in the models.)*
- **Is this evidence convincing?** *(Answers will vary. Most will probably have a difficult time assessing the validity of scientific models and base their opinion on the credibility of the source, which is what most adults do.)* **Logical/Mathematical**

T Technology Skills

Analyzing Data Have interested students do further research and analyze the data they find. Have them check the background of the authors of the sources they use and share their findings with the class. **BL** **Logical/Mathematical**

CLOSE & REFLECT

To close this lesson, ask students to summarize what they have learned about judging the validity of an argument. Emphasize that it is important to consider the background and potential bias of a source when you do not have expertise on a subject, which is the case with most people on the subject of global warming.

ANSWERS, p. 487

DBQ What Do You Think?

1. The source cites "climate models" based on "scientific understanding" of how climate would respond to a rapid rise in greenhouse gases, such as has occurred during the 20th and 21st centuries.
2. The source cites studies of "natural sources of climate variability" and says that it is "impossible to tell" what is causing global warming.
3. Answers will vary. Sample response: People who believe that human activity causes global warming may take steps to reduce their use of energy. Governments might encourage energy-reducing or energy-saving efforts by individuals or corporations. People who believe that global warming is a natural cycle will see no reason to change their lifestyle or to use resources differently.

WORKSHEET

Formulating a Main Idea

Argument Distribute the writing skills worksheet for formulating a main idea and have students write a paragraph presenting their own views on the issue of global warming. If time allows, ask volunteers to share their paragraphs with the class. **Verbal/Linguistic**

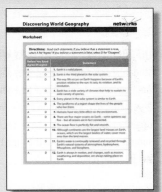

CHAPTER REVIEW ACTIVITY

To summarize the chapter, divide the class into five groups and direct each group to complete a concept web on one of the following subjects: Landforms and Waters of Antarctica, Climate and Resources of Antarctica, The Antarctic Treaty, Living in Antarctica, and Research in Antarctica. Tell groups to identify at least five main ideas for each topic. Have groups share their concept webs and summaries of their assigned topic with the rest of the class.

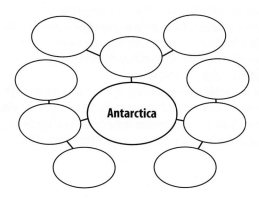

REVIEW THE ENDURING UNDERSTANDINGS

Review this chapter's Enduring Understanding with students:

• *People, places, and ideas change over time.*

Pose the following questions in a class discussion to apply this to this chapter.

• **How did scientists determine that Antarctica was formerly part of one huge landmass along with all the other continents?** *(by comparing the rocks and fossils found in Antarctica with those found on other continents)*

• **How has the human presence in Antarctica changed over time?** *(Sample answer: Before the 1820s, no people had even seen Antarctica, and at first people only explored the continent. Now there are a number of research stations where people live temporarily. But even now, no one lives in Antarctica permanently.)*

• **How has global warming changed Antarctica's environment?** *(Sample answer: The Antarctic ice sheet is shrinking, more icebergs are cluttering the surrounding waters, and the populations of plankton and krill are declining.)*

Chapter 16 **ACTIVITIES** CCSS

Directions: Write your answers on a separate piece of paper.

❶ **Exploring the Essential Question**
INFORMATIVE/EXPLANATORY WRITING In two or more paragraphs, explain why Antarctica can be described as a polar desert. WHST.6-8.2, WHST.6-8.4

❷ **21st Century Skills**
PEER REVIEW Work with a partner. Each partner will write a paragraph to answer the question: What do you think it's like to live in a cold climate like Antarctica? Check your partner's paper for meaning, grammar, and complete sentences. Discuss the review of your paragraph with your partner. Revise as needed. WHST.6-8.5, WHST.6-8.10

❸ **Thinking Like a Geographer**
LISTING Create a Venn diagram like the one shown here. Label one side West Antarctica and the other side East Antarctica. List some physical geography features that can be found in each. In the center of the diagram, list features found in both. RH.6-8.7, WHST.6-8.10

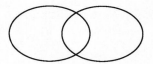

❹ **GEOGRAPHY ACTIVITY**

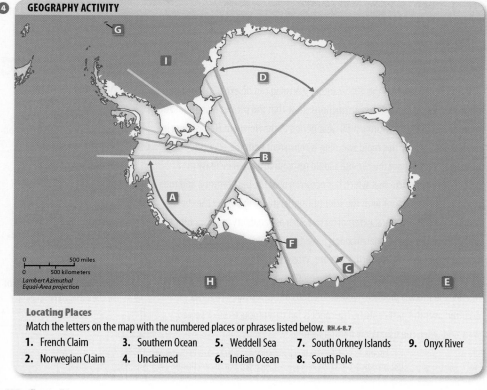

Locating Places
Match the letters on the map with the numbered places or phrases listed below. RH.6-8.7

1. French Claim   3. Southern Ocean   5. Weddell Sea   7. South Orkney Islands   9. Onyx River
2. Norwegian Claim   4. Unclaimed   6. Indian Ocean   8. South Pole

---

ACTIVITIES ANSWERS

Exploring the Essential Question

❶ **INFORMATIVE/EXPLANATORY WRITING** While students' writings will vary, they should note that Antarctica has a dry climate and generally receives only 2–4 inches of precipitation a year. While temperatures occasionally rise slightly above freezing during the summer months, most of the time they are well below the freezing point.

21st Century Skills

❷ **PEER REVIEW** Paragraphs should describe how everyday life would be affected by the cold climate of Antarctica. This includes being able to go outside on a daily or regular basis, traveling to see other people, finding and preparing food, the type of clothing and shelter they would need, and so on. Paragraphs should use correct spelling and follow the rules of grammar.

REVIEW THE GUIDING QUESTIONS
Directions: Choose the best answer for each question.

1 How much of Earth's freshwater is frozen in Antarctic ice? RH.6-8.2
- A. one-half
- B. one-third
- C. one-fourth
- D. two-thirds

2 Who was the first explorer to reach the South Pole? RH.6-8.2
- F. Ernest Shackleton
- G. Roald Amundsen
- H. Robert Scott
- I. Richard Byrd

3 It gets so cold in Antarctica during the winter that salt water from the surrounding seas freezes into RH.6-8.5
- A. huge ice sculptures.
- B. ice shelves.
- C. ice cliffs.
- D. icebergs.

4 During the summer, birds, whales, and other sea mammals come to the Southern Ocean around Antarctica to feed on tiny crustaceans called RH.6-8.4
- F. plankton.
- G. shrimp.
- H. krill.
- I. lichens.

5 How does the Antarctic Treaty protect the continent's environment? RH.6-8.1
- A. It prohibits drilling for oil in the Southern Ocean.
- B. It restricts the number of people who can be there at any one time.
- C. It prohibits tourism.
- D. It reserves the continent for peaceful scientific research.

6 In which months of the year do researchers in Antarctica have to tolerate months of total darkness, frigid temperatures, and howling winds? RH.6-8.2
- F. July, August, September
- G. only December
- H. all 12 months
- I. April, May, June

Chapter 16 **489**

Thinking Like a Geographer

3 **LISTING** Answers may include: West Antarctica: Antarctic Peninsula, Ross Ice Shelf, Ronne Ice Shelf, Vinson Massif, Bentley Subglacial Trench; East Antarctica: South Pole, Avery Ice Shelf, Davis Sea; Both: Transantarctic Mountains, volcanoes, glaciers, lakes under the ice layer

Geography Activities

4 **LOCATING PLACES**

1. C
2. D
3. H
4. A
5. I
6. E
7. G
8. B
9. F

ASSESSMENT ANSWERS
Review the Guiding Questions

1 **D** In Lesson 1, the text states that two-thirds of Earth's freshwater is frozen in the Antarctic ice sheet. If students answer incorrectly, have them review, "Landforms and Waters of Antarctica," in Lesson 1.

2 **G** The text in Lesson 2 identifies Roald Amundsen as the first explorer to reach the South Pole, beating Robert Scott. Ernest Shackleton is not mentioned in the chapter, and Robert Byrd is identified in the chapter opener time line as the first person to fly over the South Pole. If students answer incorrectly, have them review the opening paragraphs of Lesson 2.

3 **B** In Lesson 1, the text states that the coastal waters around the continent freeze into ice shelves during the winter. Ice cliffs and ice sculptures are not mentioned in the chapter. Icebergs are floating chunks of ice that break from the ice shelves in the summer. If students answer incorrectly, have them review, "Landforms and Waters of Antarctica," in Lesson 1.

4 **H** In Lesson 1, the text states that sea mammals and seabirds eat krill in the Southern Ocean. Krill are crustaceans and are similar to shrimp. Lichens are plants, not crustaceans, and plankton are food for krill. If students answer incorrectly, have them review, "Plants and Wildlife," in Lesson 1.

5 **D** The text in Lesson 2 states that the Antarctic Treaty reserves the continent for peaceful scientific research. Remind students that the ice sheet prevents people from accessing any mineral resources and the climate limits the number of people who can live there. If students answer incorrectly, have them review, "The Antarctic Treaty," in Lesson 2.

6 **F** In Lesson 1, the text states that the continent is completely dark for at least three months of the year, which would be in the winter of the Southern Hemisphere which is July, August, and September.

Analyzing Documents

7 **A** The sea ice of the two regions is different because of the differences in their geography. Arctic sea ice is in water surrounded by land, so it cannot move far. Antarctic sea ice is in water rimming land, so it can float northward.

8 **H** Since the passage says that Antarctic sea ice is free to float northward into warmer waters, it is more likely to melt, not pile up in ice jams or get tightly packed with other ice.

Short Response

9 Sample answer: Lindblad thought that people who had first-hand experience of a place like Antarctica would have more understanding of its place in the world's environment and be more committed to protecting it.

10 Sample answers: I agree with Lindblad's idea, although I believe it is also possible for people to become committed to preserving a unique resource on the basis of reading about it, seeing a movie or documentary about it, or learning about it on the Internet or in some other way. Lindblad took the risk that the travelers would have an unpleasant trip from the extreme cold and dangerous climate and not care to preserve the region. I disagree with Linblad's idea because too much tourism can have a destructive effect on an area's geography. People may love the area more because they have seen and experienced it.

Extended Response

11 Students' writings will vary, but should reflect serious research using reliable resources of what it is like to live and work on a research station in Antarctica and what it was like to build these research stations. Their papers should be clearly organized and meet your standards for spelling and grammar.

DBQ ANALYZING DOCUMENTS

7 **DETERMINING CENTRAL IDEAS** Read the following passage about sea ice in the Arctic and Antarctic regions:

"*Sea ice differs between the Arctic and Antarctic, primarily because of their different geography. The Arctic is . . . almost completely surrounded by land. As a result, the sea ice that forms in the Arctic is not [very] mobile. . . . Antarctica is a land mass surrounded by an ocean. . . . Sea ice is free to float northward into warmer waters.*"

—from "Arctic vs. Antarctic," National Snow & Ice Data Center

What causes the differences between the two kinds of sea ice? RH.6-8.2, RH.6-8.10

A. the different geographies of the two regions
B. the colder temperatures of Antarctica
C. different impacts of global warming
D. coldness of Arctic waters

8 **ANALYZING** Which of these events is more likely to occur to Antarctic sea ice than Arctic sea ice? RH.6-8.1, RH.6-8.10

F. growing larger over time
G. piling up in high ice jams
H. slowly melting over time
I. being packed tightly with other ice

SHORT RESPONSE

"*Lars-Eric Lindblad led the first traveler's expedition to Antarctica in 1966. Lindblad once said, "You can't protect what you don't know." He believed that by providing a first-hand experience to tourists you would . . . promote a greater understanding of the earth's resources and the important role of Antarctica in the global environment.*"

—from "Tourism Overview," International Association of Antarctic Tour Operators

9 **CITING TEXT EVIDENCE** According to Lindblad, how is experience connected to environmental preservation? RH.6-8.1, WHST.6-8.9

10 **IDENTIFYING POINT OF VIEW** Do you agree with Lindblad? Why or why not? RH.6-8.6, RH.6-8.10

EXTENDED RESPONSE

11 **INFORMATIVE/EXPLANATORY WRITING** Conduct research and then write a paper on what it is like to live and work on a research station in Antarctica. To find out what it was like to build these research stations under such harsh conditions and how the stations are equipped to handle the weather and protect their inhabitants from the coldest weather on Earth. RH.6-8.7, RH.6-8.8

Need Extra Help?

If You've Missed Question	1	2	3	4	5	6	7	8	9	10	11
Review Lesson	1	2	1	1	2	2	1	1	2	2	2

National Snow & Ice Data Center. "All About Sea Ice: Arctic vs. Antarctic." http://nsidc.org/cryosphere/seaice/characteristics/difference.html. Accessed August 8, 2012; Courtesy of International Association of Antarctic Tour Operators (IAATO)

---

network's *Online Teaching Options*

Remediation and Assessment

Evaluating The *Assess* tab in the online Teacher Lesson Center includes resources to help students improve their test-taking skills. It also contains many project-based rubrics to help you assess students' work.

Using **FOLDABLES®** is a great way to organize notes, remember information, and prepare for tests. Follow these easy directions to create a Foldable® for the chapter you are studying.

CHAPTER 1: STUDYING EARTH'S LAND, PEOPLE, AND ENVIRONMENTS

Describing Make this Foldable and label the top *Geographer's View* and the bottom *Geographer's Tools*. Under the top fold, describe three ways you experience geography every day. Under the bottom fold, list and describe the tools of geography and explain how a map is a tool. In your mind, form an image of a map of the world. Sketch and label what you visualize on the back of your shutter fold.

Step 1
Bend a sheet of paper in half to find the midpoint.

Step 2
Fold the outer edges of the paper to meet at the midpoint.

CHAPTER 2: THE PHYSICAL WORLD

Identifying Make this Foldable and label the four tabs *Processes*, *Forces*, *Land*, and *Water*. Under *Processes*, identify and describe the processes that operate above and below Earth's surface. Include specific examples. Under *Forces*, give examples of how forces are changing Earth's surface where you live. Finally, under *Land* and *Water*, identify land and water features within 100 miles (161 km) of your community and explain how they influence your life.

Step 1
Fold the outer edges of the paper to meet at the midpoint. Crease well.

Step 2
Fold the paper in half from side to side.

Step 3
Open and cut along the inside fold lines to form four tabs.

Step 4
Label the tabs as shown.

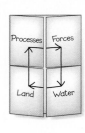

Foldables® Library

CHAPTER 3: THE HUMAN WORLD

Analyzing Create this Foldable, and then label the tabs *Adaptations*, *Cultural Views*, and *Basic Needs*. Under *Adaptations*, describe how humans have adapted to life in two different geographic regions and describe population trends in each. Under *Cultural Views*, analyze what makes two different cultures unique. Finally, under *Basic Needs*, describe how your basic needs might be met in two different economic systems.

Step 1
Fold a sheet of paper in half, leaving a ½-inch tab along one edge.

Step 2
Then fold the paper into three equal sections.

Step 3
Cut along the folds on the top sheet of paper to create three tabs.

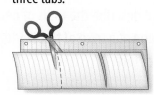

Step 4
Label your Foldable as shown.

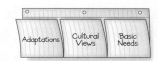

CHAPTER 4: EAST ASIA

Analyzing Create the Foldable below. Write the chapter title on the front and label the tabs *Mainland and Islands*, *Cultural Influences*, and *Economic Growth*. Under *Mainland and Islands*, describe the physical environment of the mainland and the islands. Under *Cultural Influences*, draw a three-circle Venn diagram and label the circles *China, Japan,* and *Korea*. Use the diagram to analyze similarities and differences in the history of these countries. Under *Economic Growth*, summarize the present economy of the region.

Step 1
Stack two sheets of paper so that the back sheet is 1 inch higher than the front sheet.

Step 2
Fold the paper to form four equal tabs.

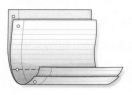

Step 3
When all tabs are an equal distance apart, fold the papers and crease well.

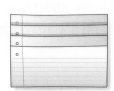

Step 4
Open the papers, and then glue or staple them along the fold.

CHAPTER 5: SOUTHEAST ASIA

Identifying Sketch a map of Southeast Asia on the back of the Foldable and label the 11 countries discussed in the text. Label the top of each of the three columns: *Geography*, *History*, and *Cultural Diversity*. Use the sections to identify three geographic features that make Southeast Asia unique, make a time line of events that occurred during the history of the spice trade, and explain why Southeast Asia is such a culturally diverse region.

Step 1
Fold a sheet of paper into thirds to form three equal columns.

Step 2
Label your Foldable as shown.

CHAPTER 6: SOUTH ASIA

Organizing Make the Foldable below. Cut notebook paper into eighths to make small note cards that fit in the pockets. Label the pockets *Geography*, *History*, and *Economy*. Use small note cards to record information on major geographic features in this region, to record important historical events, and to document economic and political events that have affected the region over the last century.

Step 1
Fold the bottom edge of a piece of paper up 2 inches to create a flap.

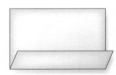

Step 2
Fold the paper into thirds.

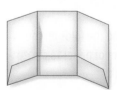

Step 3
Glue the flap on both edges and at both fold lines to form pockets. Label as shown.

Foldables® Library

CHAPTER 7: CENTRAL ASIA, THE CAUCASUS, AND SIBERIAN RUSSIA

Identifying Sketch an outline of Central Asia, the Caucasus, and Siberian Russia on the back of the Foldable and label the physical features. Label the top two tabs *Waterways—Landforms,* and list examples of each that form borders between countries within this region. Label the two middle tabs *Conquest—Independence,* and list examples of empires from the region and countries that are currently independent. Label the bottom two tabs *Rural—Urban*. Then describe and differentiate between rural and urban life in the region.

Step 1
Fold the outer edges of the paper to meet at the midpoint. Crease well.

Step 2
Open and cut three equal tabs from the outer edge to the crease on each side.

Step 3
Label the tabs as shown.

CHAPTER 8: SOUTHWEST ASIA

Describing On your Foldable, label the three tabs *Water, Civilization and Religion*, and *Oil and Water*. Under *Water*, describe the role of freshwater and salt water in the development of Southwest Asia. Under *Civilization and Religion*, explain why this region in called the "cradle of civilization." Under *Oil and Water*, describe and compare the importance of oil and water to the economy of the region.

Step 1
Fold a sheet of paper in half, leaving a ½-inch tab along one edge.

Step 2
Then fold the paper into three equal sections.

Step 3
Cut along the folds on the top sheet of paper to create three tabs.

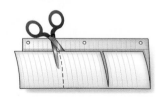

Step 4
Label your Foldable as shown.

CHAPTER 9: NORTH AFRICA

Organizing Label the rows *Geography*, *History*, and *Economy*. Label the columns *Know* and *Learned*. Use the table to record what you know and what you learn about the geography, history, and economy of North Africa.

Step 1
Fold the paper into three equal columns. Crease well.

Step 2
Open the paper and then fold it into four equal rows. Crease well. Unfold and label as shown.

CHAPTER 10: EAST AFRICA

Analyzing Write the chapter title on the cover and label the tabs *"Great" Things*; *Past Affects Present*; and *Daily Life, Literacy, and Health*. Under the first tab, describe the Great Rift Valley and the Great Migration and their impact on the economy of the region. Under the second tab, give examples of historical events that affect the region's current economy and politics. Under the third tab, compare two countries in East Africa using literacy rates and life expectancy.

Step 1
Stack two sheets of paper so that the back sheet is 1 inch higher than the front sheet.

Step 2
Fold the paper to form four equal tabs.

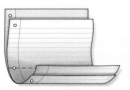

Step 3
When all tabs are an equal distance apart, fold the papers and crease well.

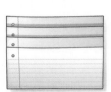

Step 4
Open the papers and then glue them along the fold.

Foldables® Library

CHAPTER 11: CENTRAL AFRICA

Describing Label the four tabs *Rain Forests*, *Savannas*, *Triangular Trade*, and *Rural vs. Urban*. Under the *Rain Forests* and *Savannas* tabs, differentiate between the climate and vegetation of rain forests and savannas. Under *Triangular Trade*, describe the three stages of the triangular trade route and explain why each was profitable for merchants. Under *Rural vs. Urban,* explain why you think the capital cities of many of the countries within this region are becoming huge metropolises.

Step 1
Fold the outer edges of the paper to meet at the midpoint. Crease well.

Step 2
Fold the paper in half from side to side.

Step 3
Open and cut along the inside fold lines to form four tabs.

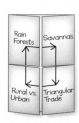

Step 4
Label the tabs as shown.

CHAPTER 12: WEST AFRICA

Analyzing Label the first tab *Natural Resources,* and identify which resources you think should be protected and which should be developed. Label the second tab *Trade*. Summarize the importance of trade to the region and list three valuable trade goods. Finally, label the third tab *Population Growth*. Describe how and why rapid population growth is negatively affecting the economy of the region.

Step 1
Fold a sheet of paper in half, leaving a ½-inch tab along one edge.

Step 2
Then fold the paper into three equal sections.

Step 3
Cut along the folds on the top sheet of paper to create three tabs.

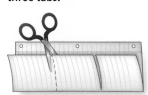

Step 4
Label your Foldable as shown.

CHAPTER 13: **SOUTHERN AFRICA**

Organizing Cut notebook paper into eighths to make small note cards that fit in the pockets. Sketch an outline of Southern Africa on the back of the Foldable and label geographic features of the region. On the front, label the pockets *Geography*, *History*, and *Economy*. On the note cards, record information about major geographic features, important historical events, and economic and political events that occurred in the region.

Step 1
Fold the bottom edge of a piece of paper up 2 inches to create a flap.

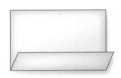

Step 2
Fold the paper into thirds.

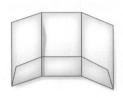

Step 3
Glue the flap on both edges and at both fold lines to form pockets. Label as shown.

CHAPTER 14: **AUSTRALIA AND NEW ZEALAND**

Describing Label the top section *Australia* and the bottom section *New Zealand*. Under the top-left tab, describe three geographic features of Australia. Under the bottom-left tab, describe the geography of New Zealand. Under the middle tabs, describe the ethnic groups in the regions. Under the top- and bottom-right tabs, describe issues facing Australia and New Zealand.

Step 1
Fold the outer edges of the paper to meet at the midpoint. Crease well.

Step 2
Label the tabs as shown.

Step 3
Open and cut three equal tabs from the outer edge to the crease on each side.

Foldables® Library

CHAPTER 15: OCEANIA

Identifying Write the chapter title on the cover tab, and label the three small tabs *Resources; Past Affects Present;* and *Daily Life, Literacy, and Health*. Under *Resources*, explain the impact of limited resources on Oceania's economy. Under *Past Affects Present*, explain how past colonization affects the economy and government of two countries in Oceania. Under *Daily Life, Literacy, and Health*, explain how the migration of young adults from Oceania to other countries is affecting the region.

Step 1
Stack two sheets of paper so that the back sheet is 1 inch higher than the front sheet.

Step 2
Fold the paper to form four equal tabs.

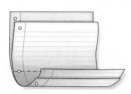
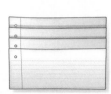

Step 3
When all tabs are an equal distance apart, fold the papers and crease well.

Step 4
Open the papers, and then glue or staple them along the fold.

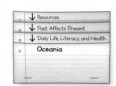

CHAPTER 16: ANTARCTICA

Describing Label the top three columns of your Foldable *Extremes*, *The Antarctic Treaty*, and *Global Importance*. Under *Extremes*, describe the geographic and climate extremes that make this continent unique. Under *The Antarctic Treaty* and *Global Importance*, summarize the history of Antarctica and the Antarctic Treaty, and explain the global importance of this protected continent.

Step 1
Fold a sheet of paper into thirds to form three equal columns.

Step 2
Label your Foldable as shown.

Gazetteer

A gazetteer (ga•zuh•TIHR) is a geographic index or diction-ary. It shows latitude and longitude for cities and certain other places. Latitude and longitude are shown in this way: 48°N 2°E, or 48 degrees north latitude and two degrees east longitude. This Gazetteer lists many important geographic features and most of the world's largest independent countries and their capitals. The page numbers tell where each entry can be found on a map in this book. As an aid to pronunciation, most entries are spelled phonetically.

A

Abidjan [AH•BEE•JAHN] Capital of Côte d'Ivoire. 5°N 4°W (p. RA22)

Abu Dhabi [AH•BOO DAH•bee] Capital of the United Arab Emirates. 24°N 54°E (p. RA24)

Abuja [ah•BOO•jah] Capital of Nigeria. 8°N 9°E (p. RA22)

Accra [ah•KRUH] Capital of Ghana. 6°N 0° longitude (p. RA22)

Addis Ababa [AHD•dihs AH•bah•BAH] Capital of Ethiopia. 9°N 39°E (p. RA22)

Adriatic [AY•dree•A•tihk] **Sea** Arm of the Mediterranean Sea between the Balkan Peninsula and Italy. (p. RA20)

Afghanistan [af•GA•nuh•STAN] Central Asian country west of Pakistan. (p. RA25)

Albania [al•BAY•nee•uh] Country on the Adriatic Sea, south of Serbia. (p. RA18)

Algeria [al•JIHR•ee•uh] North African country east of Morocco. (p. RA22)

Algiers [al•JIHRZ] Capital of Algeria. 37°N 3°E (p. RA22)

Alps [ALPS] Mountain ranges extending through cen-tral Europe. (p. RA20)

Amazon [A•muh•ZAHN] **River** Largest river in the world by volume and second-largest in length. (p. RA17)

Amman [a•MAHN] Capital of Jordan. 32°N 36°E (p. RA24)

Amsterdam [AHM•stuhr•DAHM] Capital of the Netherlands. 52°N 5°E (p. RA18)

Andes [AN•DEEZ] Mountain system extending north and south along the western side of South America. (p. RA17)

Andorra [an•DAWR•uh] Small country in southern Europe between France and Spain. 43°N 2°E (p. RA18)

Angola [ang•GOH•luh] Southern African country north of Namibia. (p. RA22)

Ankara [AHNG•kuh•ruh] Capital of Turkey. 40°N 33°E (p. RA24)

Antananarivo [AHN•tah•NAH•nah•REE•voh] Capital of Madagascar. 19°S 48°E (p. RA22)

Arabian [uh•RAY•bee•uhn] **Peninsula** Large peninsula extending into the Arabian Sea. (p. RA25)

Argentina [AHR•juhn•TEE•nuh] South American country east of Chile. (p. RA16)

Armenia [ahr•MEE•nee•uh] European-Asian coun-try between the Black and Caspian Seas. 40°N 45°E (p. RA26)

Ashkhabad [AHSH•gah•BAHD] Capital of Turkmenistan. 38°N 58°E (p. RA25)

Asmara [az•MAHR•uh] Capital of Eritrea. 16°N 39°E (p. RA22)

Astana Capital of Kazakhstan. 51°N 72°E (p. RA26)

Asunción [ah•SOON•see•OHN] Capital of Paraguay. 25°S 58°W (p. RA16)

Athens Capital of Greece. 38°N 24°E (p. RA19)

Atlas [AT•luhs] **Mountains** Mountain range on the northern edge of the Sahara. (p. RA23)

Australia [aw•STRAYL•yuh] Country and continent in Southern Hemisphere. (p. RA30)

Austria [AWS•tree•uh] Western European country east of Switzerland and south of Germany and the Czech Republic. (p. RA18)

Azerbaijan [A•zuhr•BY•JAHN] European-Asian coun-try on the Caspian Sea. (p. RA25)

B

Baghdad Capital of Iraq. 33°N 44°E (p. RA25)

Bahamas [buh•HAH•muhz] Country made up of many islands between Cuba and the United States. (p. RA15)

Bahrain [bah•RAYN] Country located on the Persian Gulf. 26°N 51°E (p. RA25)

Baku [bah•KOO] Capital of Azerbaijan. 40°N 50°E (p. RA25)

Balkan [BAWL•kuhn] **Peninsula** Peninsula in south-eastern Europe. (p. RA21)

Baltic [BAWL•tihk] **Sea** Sea in northern Europe that is connected to the North Sea. (p. RA20)

Bamako [BAH•mah•KOH] Capital of Mali. 13°N 8°W (p. RA22)

Bangkok [BANG•KAHK] Capital of Thailand. 14°N 100°E (p. RA27)

Bangladesh [BAHNG•gluh•DEHSH] South Asian country bordered by India and Myanmar. (p. RA27)

Bangui [BAHNG•GEE] Capital of the Central African Republic. 4°N 19°E (p. RA22)

Banjul [BAHN•JOOL] Capital of Gambia. 13°N 17°W (p. RA22)

Barbados [bahr•BAY•duhs] Island country between the Atlantic Ocean and the Caribbean Sea. 14°N 59°W (p. RA15)

Beijing [BAY•JIHNG] Capital of China. 40°N 116°E (p. RA27)

Beirut [bay•ROOT] Capital of Lebanon. 34°N 36°E (p. RA24)

Belarus [BEE•luh•ROOS] Eastern European country west of Russia. 54°N 28°E (p. RA19)

Belgium [BEHL•juhm] Western European country south of the Netherlands. (p. RA18)

Belgrade [BEHL•GRAYD] Capital of Serbia. 45°N 21°E (p. RA19)

Belize [buh•LEEZ] Central American country east of Guatemala. (p. RA14)

Belmopan [BEHL•moh•PAHN] Capital of Belize. 17°N 89°W (p. RA14)

Benin [buh•NEEN] West African country west of Nigeria. (p. RA22)

Berlin [behr•LEEN] Capital of Germany. 53°N 13°E (p. RA18)

Bern Capital of Switzerland. 47°N 7°E (p. RA18)

Bhutan [boo•TAHN] South Asian country northeast of India. (p. RA27)

Bishkek [bihsh•KEHK] Capital of Kyrgyzstan. 43°N 75°E (p. RA26)

Bissau [bihs•SOW] Capital of Guinea-Bissau. 12°N 16°W (p. RA22)

Black Sea Large sea between Europe and Asia. (p. RA21)

Bloemfontein [BLOOM•FAHN•TAYN] Judicial capital of South Africa. 26°E 29°S (p. RA22)

Bogotá [BOH•GOH•TAH] Capital of Colombia. 5°N 74°W (p. RA16)

Bolivia [buh•LIHV•ee•uh] Country in the central part of South America, north of Argentina. (p. RA16)

Bosnia and Herzegovina [BAHZ•nee•uh HEHRT•seh•GAW•vee•nuh] Southeastern European country bordered by Croatia, Serbia, and Montenegro. (p. RA18)

Botswana [bawt•SWAH•nah] Southern African country north of the Republic of South Africa. (p. RA22)

Brasília [brah•ZEEL•yuh] Capital of Brazil. 16°S 48°W (p. RA16)

Bratislava [BRAH•tih•SLAH•vuh] Capital of Slovakia. 48°N 17°E (p. RA18)

Brazil [bruh•ZIHL] Largest country in South America. (p. RA16)

Brazzaville [BRAH•zuh•VEEL] Capital of Congo. 4°S 15°E (p. RA22)

Brunei [bru•NY] Southeast Asian country on northern coast of the island of Borneo. (p. RA27)

Brussels [BRUH•suhlz] Capital of Belgium. 51°N 4°E (p. RA18)

Bucharest [BOO•kuh•REHST] Capital of Romania. 44°N 26°E (p. RA19)

Budapest [BOO•duh•PEHST] Capital of Hungary. 48°N 19°E (p. RA18)

Buenos Aires [BWAY•nuhs AR•eez] Capital of Argentina. 34°S 58°W (p. RA16)

Bujumbura [BOO•juhm•BUR•uh] Capital of Burundi. 3°S 29°E (p. RA22)

Bulgaria [BUHL•GAR•ee•uh] Southeastern European country south of Romania. (p. RA19)

Burkina Faso [bur•KEE•nuh FAH•soh] West African country south of Mali. (p. RA22)

Burundi [bu•ROON•dee] East African country at the northern end of Lake Tanganyika. 3°S 30°E (p. RA22)

C

Cairo [KY•roh] Capital of Egypt. 31°N 32°E (p. RA24)

Cambodia [kam•BOH•dee•uh] Southeast Asian country south of Thailand and Laos. (p. RA27)

Cameroon [KA•muh•ROON] Central African country on the northeast shore of the Gulf of Guinea. (p. RA22)

Canada [KA•nuh•duh] Northernmost country in North America. (p. RA6)

Canberra [KAN•BEHR•uh] Capital of Australia. 35°S 149°E (p. RA30)

Cape Town Legislative capital of the Republic of South Africa. 34°S 18°E (p. RA22)

Cape Verde [VUHRD] Island country off the coast of western Africa in the Atlantic Ocean. 15°N 24°W (p. RA22)

Caracas [kah•RAH•kahs] Capital of Venezuela. 11°N 67°W (p. RA16)

Caribbean [KAR•uh•BEE•uhn] **Islands** Islands in the Caribbean Sea between North America and South America, also known as West Indies. (p. RA15)

Caribbean Sea Part of the Atlantic Ocean bordered by the West Indies, South America, and Central America. (p. RA15)

Caspian [KAS•pee•uhn] **Sea** Salt lake between Europe and Asia that is the world's largest inland body of water. (p. RA21)

Caucasus [KAW•kuh•suhs] **Mountains** Mountain range between the Black and Caspian Seas. (p. RA21)

Central African Republic Central African country south of Chad. (p. RA22)

Chad [CHAD] Country west of Sudan in the African Sahel. (p. RA22)

Chang Jiang [CHAHNG jee•AHNG] Principal river of China that begins in Tibet and flows into the East China Sea near Shanghai; also known as the Yangtze River. (p. RA29)

Chile [CHEE•lay] South American country west of Argentina. (p. RA16)

China [CHY•nuh] Country in eastern and central Asia, known officially as the People's Republic of China. (p. RA27)

Chişinău [KEE•shee•NOW] Capital of Moldova. 47°N 29°E (p. RA19)

Colombia [kuh•LUHM•bee•uh] South American country west of Venezuela. (p. RA16)

Colombo [kuh•LUHM•boh] Capital of Sri Lanka. 7°N 80°E (p. RA26)

Comoros [KAH•muh•ROHZ] Small island country in Indian Ocean between the island of Madagascar and the southeast African mainland. 13°S 43°E (p. RA22)

Conakry [KAH•nuh•kree] Capital of Guinea. 10°N 14°W (p. RA22)

Congo [KAHNG•goh] Central African country east of the Democratic Republic of the Congo. 3°S 14°E (p. RA22)

Congo, Democratic Republic of the Central African country north of Zambia and Angola. 1°S 22°E (p. RA22)

Copenhagen [KOH•puhn•HAY•guhn] Capital of Denmark. 56°N 12°E (p. RA18)

Costa Rica [KAWS•tah REE•kah] Central American country south of Nicaragua. (p. RA15)

Côte d'Ivoire [KOHT dee•VWAHR] West African country south of Mali. (p. RA22)

Croatia [kroh•AY•shuh] Southeastern European country on the Adriatic Sea. (p. RA18)

Cuba [KYOO•buh] Island country in the Caribbean Sea. (p. RA15)

Cyprus [SY•pruhs] Island country in the eastern Mediterranean Sea, south of Turkey. (p. RA19)

Czech [CHEHK] **Republic** Eastern European country north of Austria. (p. RA18)

D

Dakar [dah•KAHR] Capital of Senegal. 15°N 17°W (p. RA22)

Damascus [duh•MAS•kuhs] Capital of Syria. 34°N 36°E (p. RA24)

Dar es Salaam [DAHR EHS sah•LAHM] Commercial capital of Tanzania. 7°S 39°E (p. RA22)

Denmark Northern European country between the Baltic and North Seas. (p. RA18)

Dhaka [DA•kuh] Capital of Bangladesh. 24°N 90°E (p. RA27)

Djibouti [jih•BOO•tee] East African country on the Gulf of Aden. 12°N 43°E (p. RA22)

Dodoma [doh•DOH•mah] Political capital of Tanzania. 6°S 36°E (p. RA22)

Doha [DOH•huh] Capital of Qatar. 25°N 51°E (p. RA25)

Dominican [duh•MIH•nih•kuhn] **Republic** Country in the Caribbean Sea on the eastern part of the island of Hispaniola. (p. RA15)

Dublin [DUH•blihn] Capital of Ireland. 53°N 6°W (p. RA18)

Dushanbe [doo•SHAM•buh] Capital of Tajikistan. 39°N 69°E (p. RA25)

E

East Timor [TEE•MOHR] Previous province of Indonesia, now under UN administration. 10°S 127°E (p. RA27)

Ecuador [EH•kwuh•dawr] South American country southwest of Colombia. (p. RA16)

Egypt [EE•jihpt] North African country on the Mediterranean Sea. (p. RA24)

El Salvador [ehl SAL•vuh•dawr] Central American country southwest of Honduras. (p. RA14)

Equatorial Guinea [EE•kwuh•TOHR•ee•uhl GIH•nee] Central African country south of Cameroon. (p. RA22)

Eritrea [EHR•uh•TREE•uh] East African country north of Ethiopia. (p. RA22)

Estonia [eh•STOH•nee•uh] Eastern European country on the Baltic Sea. (p. RA19)

Ethiopia [EE•thee•OH•pee•uh] East African country north of Somalia and Kenya. (p. RA22)

Euphrates [yu•FRAY•teez] **River** River in southwestern Asia that flows through Syria and Iraq and joins the Tigris River. (p. RA25)

F

Fiji [FEE•jee] **Islands** Country comprised of an island group in the southwest Pacific Ocean. 19°S 175°E (p. RA30)

Finland [FIHN•luhnd] Northern European country east of Sweden. (p. RA19)

France [FRANS] Western European country south of the United Kingdom. (p. RA18)

Freetown Capital of Sierra Leone. (p. RA22)

French Guiana [gee•A•nuh] French-owned territory in northern South America. (p. RA16)

G

Gabon [ga•BOHN] Central African country on the Atlantic Ocean. (p. RA22)

Gaborone [GAH•boh•ROH•nay] Capital of Botswana. (p. RA22)

Gambia [GAM•bee•uh] West African country along the Gambia River. (p. RA22)

Georgetown [JAWRJ•town] Capital of Guyana. 8°N 58°W (p. RA16)

Georgia [JAWR•juh] European-Asian country bordering the Black Sea south of Russia. (p. RA26)

Germany [JUHR•muh•nee] Western European country south of Denmark, officially called the Federal Republic of Germany. (p. RA18)

Ghana [GAH•nuh] West African country on the Gulf of Guinea. (p. RA22)

Great Plains The continental slope extending through the United States and Canada. (p. RA7)

Greece [GREES] Southern European country on the Balkan Peninsula. (p. RA19)

Greenland [GREEN•luhnd] Island in northwestern Atlantic Ocean and the largest island in the world. (p. RA6)

Guatemala [GWAH•tay•MAH•lah] Central American country south of Mexico. (p. RA14)

Guatemala Capital of Guatemala. 15°N 91°W (p. RA14)

Guinea [GIH•nee] West African country on the Atlantic coast. (p. RA22)

Guinea-Bissau [GIH•nee bih•SOW] West African country on the Atlantic coast. (p. RA22)

Gulf of Mexico Gulf on part of the southern coast of North America. (p. RA7)

Guyana [gy•AH•nuh] South American country between Venezuela and Suriname. (p. RA16)

H

Haiti [HAY•tee] Country in the Caribbean Sea on the western part of the island of Hispaniola. (p. RA15)

Hanoi [ha•NOY] Capital of Vietnam. 21°N 106°E (p. RA27)

Harare [hah•RAH•ray] Capital of Zimbabwe. 18°S 31°E (p. RA22)

Havana [huh•VA•nuh] Capital of Cuba. 23°N 82°W (p. RA15)

Helsinki [HEHL•SIHNG•kee] Capital of Finland. 60°N 24°E (p. RA19)

Himalaya [HI•muh•LAY•uh] Mountain ranges in southern Asia, bordering the Indian subcontinent on the north. (p. RA28)

Honduras [hahn•DUR•uhs] Central American country on the Caribbean Sea. (p. RA14)

Hong Kong Port and industrial center in southern China. 22°N 115°E (p. RA27)

Huang He [HWAHNG HUH] River in northern and eastern China, also known as the Yellow River. (p. RA29)

Hungary [HUHNG•guh•ree] Eastern European country south of Slovakia. (p. RA18)

I

Iberian [eye•BIHR•ee•uhn] **Peninsula** Peninsula in southwest Europe, occupied by Spain and Portugal. (p. RA20)

Iceland Island country between the North Atlantic and Arctic Oceans. (p. RA18)

India [IHN•dee•uh] South Asian country south of China and Nepal. (p. RA26)

Indonesia [IHN•duh•NEE•zhuh] Southeast Asian island country known as the Republic of Indonesia. (p. RA27)

Indus [IHN•duhs] **River** River in Asia that begins in Tibet and flows through Pakistan to the Arabian Sea. (p. RA28)

Iran [ih•RAN] Southwest Asian country that was formerly named Persia. (p. RA25)

Iraq [ih•RAHK] Southwest Asian country west of Iran. (p. RA25)

Ireland [EYER•luhnd] Island west of Great Britain occupied by the Republic of Ireland and Northern Ireland. (p. RA18)

Islamabad [ihs•LAH•muh•BAHD] Capital of Pakistan. 34°N 73°E (p. RA26)

Israel [IHZ•ree•uhl] Southwest Asian country south of Lebanon. (p. RA24)

Italy [IHT•uhl•ee] Southern European country south of Switzerland and east of France. (p. RA18)

J

Jakarta [juh•KAHR•tuh] Capital of Indonesia. 6°S 107°E (p. RA27)

Jamaica [juh•MAY•kuh] Island country in the Caribbean Sea. (p. RA15)

Japan [juh•PAN] East Asian country consisting of the four large islands of Hokkaido, Honshu, Shikoku, and Kyushu, plus thousands of small islands. (p. RA27)

Jerusalem [juh•ROO•suh•luhm] Capital of Israel and a holy city for Christians, Jews, and Muslims. 32°N 35°E (p. RA24)

Jordan [JAWRD•uhn] Southwest Asian country south of Syria. (p. RA24)

Juba [JU•buh] Capital of South Sudan. 5°N 31°E (p. RA22)

K

Kabul [KAH•buhl] Capital of Afghanistan. 35°N 69°E (p. RA25)

Kampala [kahm•PAH•lah] Capital of Uganda. 0° latitude 32°E (p. RA22)

Kathmandu [KAT•MAN•DOO] Capital of Nepal. 28°N 85°E (p. RA26)

Kazakhstan [kuh•ZAHK•STAHN] Large Asian country south of Russia and bordering the Caspian Sea. (p. RA26)

Kenya [KEHN•yuh] East African country south of Ethiopia. (p. RA22)

Khartoum [kahr•TOOM] Capital of Sudan. 16°N 33°E (p. RA22)

Kigali [kee•GAH•lee] Capital of Rwanda. 2°S 30°E (p. RA22)

Kingston [KIHNG•stuhn] Capital of Jamaica. 18°N 77°W (p. RA15)

Kinshasa [kihn•SHAH•suh] Capital of the Democratic Republic of the Congo. 4°S 15°E (p. RA22)

Kuala Lumpur [KWAH•luh LUM•PUR] Capital of Malaysia. 3°N 102°E (p. RA27)

Kuwait [ku•WAYT] Country on the Persian Gulf between Saudi Arabia and Iraq. (p. RA25)

Kyiv (Kiev) [KEE•ihf] Capital of Ukraine. 50°N 31°E (p. RA19)

Kyrgyzstan [s•gih•STAN] Central Asian country on China's western border. (p. RA26)

L

Laos [LOWS] Southeast Asian country south of China and west of Vietnam. (p. RA27)

La Paz [lah PAHS] Administrative capital of Bolivia, and the highest capital in the world. 17°S 68°W (p. RA16)

Latvia [LAT•vee•uh] Eastern European country west of Russia on the Baltic Sea. (p. RA19)

Lebanon [LEH•buh•nuhn] Country south of Syria on the Mediterranean Sea. (p. RA24)

Lesotho [luh•SOH•TOH] Southern African country within the borders of the Republic of South Africa. (p. RA22)

Liberia [ly•BIHR•ee•uh] West African country south of Guinea. (p. RA22)

Libreville [LEE•bruh•VIHL] Capital of Gabon. 1°N 9°E (p. RA22)

Libya [LIH•bee•uh] North African country west of Egypt on the Mediterranean Sea. (p. RA22)

Liechtenstein [LIHKT•uhn•SHTYN] Small country in central Europe between Switzerland and Austria. 47°N 10°E (p. RA18)

Lilongwe [lih•LAWNG•GWAY] Capital of Malawi. 14°S 34°E (p. RA22)

Lima [LEE•mah] Capital of Peru. 12°S 77°W (p. RA16)

Lisbon [LIHZ•buhn] Capital of Portugal. 39°N 9°W (p. RA18)

Lithuania [LIH•thuh•WAY•nee•uh] Eastern European country northwest of Belarus on the Baltic Sea. (p. RA21)

Ljubljana [lee•oo•blee•AH•nuh] Capital of Slovenia. 46°N 14°E (p. RA18)

Lomé [loh•MAY] Capital of Togo. 6°N 1°E (p. RA22)

London Capital of the United Kingdom, on the Thames River. 52°N 0° longitude (p. RA18)

Luanda [lu•AHN•duh] Capital of Angola. 9°S 13°E (p. RA22)

Lusaka [loo•SAH•kah] Capital of Zambia. 15°S 28°E (p. RA22)

Luxembourg [LUHK•suhm•BUHRG] Small European country bordered by France, Belgium, and Germany. 50°N 7°E (p. RA18)

M

Macao [muh•KOW] Port in southern China. 22°N 113°E (p. RA27)

Macedonia [ma•suh•DOH•nee•uh] Southeastern European country north of Greece. (p. RA19). Macedonia also refers to a geographic region covering northern Greece, the country Macedonia, and part of Bulgaria.

Madagascar [MA•duh•GAS•kuhr] Island in the Indian Ocean off the southeastern coast of Africa. (p. RA22)

Madrid Capital of Spain. 41°N 4°W (p. RA18)

Malabo [mah•LAH•boh] Capital of Equatorial Guinea. 4°N 9°E (p. RA22)

Malawi [mah•LAH•wee] Southern African country south of Tanzania and east of Zambia. (p. RA22)

Malaysia [muh•LAY•zhuh] Southeast Asian country with land on the Malay Peninsula and on the island of Borneo. (p. RA27)

Maldives [MAWL•DEEVZ] Island country southwest of India in the Indian Ocean. (p. RA26)

Mali [MAH•lee] West African country east of Mauritania. (p. RA22)

Managua [mah•NAH•gwah] Capital of Nicaragua. (p. RA15)

Manila [muh•NIH•luh] Capital of the Philippines. 15°N 121°E (p. RA27)

Maputo [mah•POO•toh] Capital of Mozambique. 26°S 33°E (p. RA22)

Maseru [MA•zuh•ROO] Capital of Lesotho. 29°S 27°E (p. RA22)

Masqat [MUHS•KAHT] Capital of Oman. 23°N 59°E (p. RA25)

Mauritania [MAWR•uh•TAY•nee•uh] West African country north of Senegal. (p. RA22)

Mauritius [maw•RIH•shuhs] Island country in the Indian Ocean east of Madagascar. 21°S 58°E (p. RA3)

Mbabane [uhm•bah•BAH•nay] Capital of Swaziland. 26°S 31°E (p. RA22)

Mediterranean [MEH•duh•tuh•RAY•nee•uhn] **Sea** Large inland sea surrounded by Europe, Asia, and Africa. (p. RA20)

Mekong [MAY•KAWNG] **River** River in southeastern Asia that begins in Tibet and empties into the South China Sea. (p. RA29)

Mexico [MEHK•sih•KOH] North American country south of the United States. (p. RA14)

Mexico City Capital of Mexico. 19°N 99°W (p. RA14)

Minsk [MIHNSK] Capital of Belarus. 54°N 28°E (p. RA19)

Mississippi [MIH•suh•SIH•pee] **River** Large river system in the central United States that flows southward into the Gulf of Mexico. (p. RA11)

Mogadishu [MOH•guh•DEE•shoo] Capital of Somalia. 2°N 45°E (p. RA22)

Moldova [mawl•DAW•vuh] Small European country between Ukraine and Romania. (p. RA19)

Monaco [MAH•nuh•KOH] Small country in southern Europe on the French Mediterranean coast. 44°N 8°E (p. RA18)

Mongolia [mahn•GOHL•yuh] Country in Asia between Russia and China. (p. RA23)

Monrovia [muhn•ROH•vee•uh] Capital of Liberia. 6°N 11°W (p. RA22)

Montenegro [MAHN•tuh•NEE•groh] Eastern European country. (p. RA18)

Montevideo [MAHN•tuh•vuh•DAY•oh] Capital of Uruguay. 35°S 56°W (p. RA16)

Morocco [muh•RAH•KOH] North African country on the Mediterranean Sea and the Atlantic Ocean. (p. RA22)

Moscow [MAHS•KOW] Capital of Russia. 56°N 38°E (p. RA19)

Mount Everest [EHV•ruhst] Highest mountain in the world, in the Himalaya between Nepal and Tibet. (p. RA28)

Mozambique [MOH•zahm•BEEK] Southern African country south of Tanzania. (p. RA22)

Myanmar [MYAHN•MAHR] Southeast Asian country south of China and India, formerly called Burma. (p. RA27)

N

Nairobi [ny•ROH•bee] Capital of Kenya. 1°S 37°E (p. RA22)

Namibia [nuh•MIH•bee•uh] Southern African country south of Angola on the Atlantic Ocean. 20°S 16°E (p. RA22)

Nassau [NA•saw] Capital of the Bahamas. 25°N 77°W (p. RA15)

N'Djamena [uhn•jah•MAY•nah] Capital of Chad. 12°N 15°E (p. RA22)

Nepal [NAY•PAHL] Mountain country between India and China. (p. RA26)

Netherlands [NEH•thuhr•lundz] Western European country north of Belgium. (p. RA18)

New Delhi [NOO DEH•lee] Capital of India. 29°N 77°E (p. RA26)

New Zealand [NOO ZEE•luhnd] Major island country southeast of Australia in the South Pacific. (p. RA30)

Niamey [nee•AHM•ay] Capital of Niger. 14°N 2°E (p. RA22)

Nicaragua [NIH•kuh•RAH•gwuh] Central American country south of Honduras. (p. RA15)

Nicosia [NIH•kuh•SEE•uh] Capital of Cyprus. 35°N 33°E (p. RA19)

Niger [NY•juhr] West African country north of Nigeria. (p. RA22)

Nigeria [ny•JIHR•ee•uh] West African country along the Gulf of Guinea. (p. RA22)

Nile [NYL] **River** Longest river in the world, flowing north through eastern Africa. (p. RA23)

North Korea [kuh•REE•uh] East Asian country in the northernmost part of the Korean Peninsula. (p. RA27)

Norway [NAWR•way] Northern European country on the Scandinavian peninsula. (p. RA18)

Nouakchott [nu•AHK•SHAHT] Capital of Mauritania. 18°N 16°W (p. RA22)

O

Oman [oh•MAHN] Country on the Arabian Sea and the Gulf of Oman. (p. RA25)

Oslo [AHZ•loh] Capital of Norway. 60°N 11°E (p. RA18)

Ottawa [AH•tuh•wuh] Capital of Canada. 45°N 76°W (p. RA13)

Ouagadougou [WAH•gah•DOO•goo] Capital of Burkina Faso. 12°N 2°W (p. RA22)

P

Pakistan [PA•kih•STAN] South Asian country northwest of India on the Arabian Sea. (p. RA26)

Palau [puh•LOW) Island country in the Pacific Ocean. 7°N 135°E (p. RA30)

Panama [PA•nuh•MAH] Central American country on the Isthmus of Panama. (p. RA15)

Panama Capital of Panama. 9°N 79°W (p. RA15)

Papua New Guinea [PA•pyu•wuh NOO GIH•nee] Island country in the Pacific Ocean north of Australia. 7°S 142°E (p. RA30)

Paraguay [PAR•uh•GWY] South American country northeast of Argentina. (p. RA16)

Paramaribo [PAH•rah•MAH•ree•boh] Capital of Suriname. 6°N 55°W (p. RA16)

Paris Capital of France. 49°N 2°E (p. RA18)

Persian [PUHR•zhuhn] **Gulf** Arm of the Arabian Sea between Iran and Saudi Arabia. (p. RA25)

Peru [puh•ROO] South American country south of Ecuador and Colombia. (p. RA16)

Philippines [FIH•luh•PEENZ] Island country in the Pacific Ocean southeast of China. (p. RA27)

Phnom Penh [puh•NAWM PEHN] Capital of Cambodia. 12°N 106°E (p. RA27)

Poland [POH•luhnd] Eastern European country on the Baltic Sea. (p. RA18)

Port-au-Prince [POHRT•oh•PRIHNS] Capital of Haiti. 19°N 72°W (p. RA15)

Port Moresby [MOHRZ•bee] Capital of Papua New Guinea. 10°S 147°E (p. RA30)

Port-of-Spain [SPAYN] Capital of Trinidad and Tobago. 11°N 62°W (p. RA15)

Porto-Novo [POHR•toh•NOH•voh] Capital of Benin. 7°N 3°E (p. RA22)

Portugal [POHR•chih•guhl] Country west of Spain on the Iberian Peninsula. (p. RA18)

Prague [PRAHG] Capital of the Czech Republic. 51°N 15°E (p. RA18)

Puerto Rico [PWEHR•toh REE•koh] Island in the Caribbean Sea; U.S. Commonwealth. (p. RA15)

P'yŏngyang [pee•AWNG•YAHNG] Capital of North Korea. 39°N 126°E (p. RA27)

Q

Qatar [KAH•tuhr] Country on the southwestern shore of the Persian Gulf. (p. RA25)

Quito [KEE•toh] Capital of Ecuador. 0° latitude 79°W (p. RA16)

R

Rabat [ruh•BAHT] Capital of Morocco. 34°N 7°W (p. RA22)

Reykjavík [RAY•kyah•VEEK] Capital of Iceland. 64°N 22°W (p. RA18)

Rhine [RYN] **River** River in western Europe that flows into the North Sea. (p. RA20)

Riga [REE•guh] Capital of Latvia. 57°N 24°E (p. RA19)

Rio Grande [REE•oh GRAND] River that forms part of the boundary between the United States and Mexico. (p. RA10)

Riyadh [ree•YAHD] Capital of Saudi Arabia. 25°N 47°E (p. RA25)

Rocky Mountains Mountain system in western North America. (p. RA7)

Romania [ru•MAY•nee•uh] Eastern European country east of Hungary. (p. RA19)

Rome Capital of Italy. 42°N 13°E (p. RA18)

Russia [RUH•shuh] Largest country in the world, covering parts of Europe and Asia. (pp. RA19, RA27)

Rwanda [ruh•WAHN•duh] East African country south of Uganda. 2°S 30°E (p. RA22)

S

Sahara [suh•HAR•uh] Desert region in northern Africa that is the largest hot desert in the world. (p. RA23)

Saint Lawrence [LAWR•uhns] River River that flows from Lake Ontario to the Atlantic Ocean and forms part of the boundary between the United States and Canada. (p. RA13)

Sanaa [sahn•AH] Capital of Yemen. 15°N 44°E (p. RA25)

San José [SAN hoh•ZAY] Capital of Costa Rica. 10°N 84°W (p. RA15)

San Marino [SAN muh•REE•noh] Small European country located on the Italian Peninsula. 44°N 13°E (p. RA18)

San Salvador [SAN SAL•vuh•DAWR] Capital of El Salvador. 14°N 89°W (p. RA14)

Santiago [SAN•tee•AH•goh] Capital of Chile. 33°S 71°W (p. RA16)

Santo Domingo [SAN•toh duh•MIHNG•goh] Capital of the Dominican Republic. 19°N 70°W (p. RA15)

São Tomé and Príncipe [sow too•MAY PREEN•see•pee] Small island country in the Gulf of Guinea off the coast of central Africa. 1°N 7°E (p. RA22)

Sarajevo [SAR•uh•YAY•voh] Capital of Bosnia and Herzegovina. 43°N 18°E (p. RA18)

Saudi Arabia [SOW•dee uh•RAY•bee•uh] Country on the Arabian Peninsula. (p. RA25)

Senegal [SEH•nih•GAWL] West African country on the Atlantic coast. (p. RA22)

Seoul [SOHL] Capital of South Korea. 38°N 127°E (p. RA27)

Serbia [SUHR•bee•uh] Eastern European country south of Hungary. (p. RA18)

Seychelles [say•SHEHL] Small island country in the Indian Ocean off eastern Africa. 6°S 56°E (p. RA22)

Sierra Leone [see•EHR•uh lee•OHN] West African country south of Guinea. (p. RA22)

Singapore [SIHNG•uh•POHR] Southeast Asian island country near tip of the Malay Peninsula. (p. RA27)

Skopje [SKAW•PYAY] Capital of the country of Macedonia. 42°N 21°E (p. RA19)

Slovakia [sloh•VAH•kee•uh] Eastern European country south of Poland. (p. RA18)

Slovenia [sloh•VEE•nee•uh] Southeastern European country south of Austria on the Adriatic Sea. (p. RA18)

Sofia [SOH•fee•uh] Capital of Bulgaria. 43°N 23°E (p. RA19)

Solomon [SAH•luh•muhn] Islands Island country in the Pacific Ocean northeast of Australia. (p. RA30)

Somalia [soh•MAH•lee•uh] East African country on the Gulf of Aden and the Indian Ocean. (p. RA22)

South Africa [A•frih•kuh] Country at the southern tip of Africa, officially the Republic of South Africa. (p. RA22)

South Korea [kuh•REE•uh] East Asian country on the Korean Peninsula between the Yellow Sea and the Sea of Japan. (p. RA27)

South Sudan [soo•DAN] East African country south of Sudan. (p. RA22)

Spain [SPAYN] Southern European country on the Iberian Peninsula. (p. RA18)

Sri Lanka [SREE LAHNG•kuh] Country in the Indian Ocean south of India, formerly called Ceylon. (p. RA26)

Stockholm [STAHK•HOHLM] Capital of Sweden. 59°N 18°E (p. RA18)

Sucre [SOO•kray] Constitutional capital of Bolivia. 19°S 65°W (p. RA16)

Sudan [soo•DAN] East African country south of Egypt. (p. RA22)

Suriname [SUR•uh•NAH•muh] South American country between Guyana and French Guiana. (p. RA16)

Suva [SOO•vah] Capital of the Fiji Islands. 18°S 177°E (p. RA30)

Swaziland [SWAH•zee•land] Southern African country west of Mozambique, almost entirely within the Republic of South Africa. (p. RA22)

Sweden Northern European country on the eastern side of the Scandinavian Peninsula. (p. RA18)

Switzerland [SWIHT•suhr•luhnd] European country in the Alps south of Germany. (p. RA18)

Syria [SIHR•ee•uh] Southwest Asian country on the east side of the Mediterranean Sea. (p. RA24)

T

Taipei [TY•PAY] Capital of Taiwan. 25°N 122°E (p. RA27)

Taiwan [TY•WAHN] Island country off the southeast coast of China; the seat of the Chinese Nationalist government. (p. RA27)

Tajikistan [tah•JIH•kih•STAN] Central Asian country east of Turkmenistan. (p. RA26)

Tallinn [TA•luhn] Capital of Estonia. 59°N 25°E (p. RA19)

Tanzania [TAN•zuh•NEE•uh] East African country south of Kenya. (p. RA22)

Tashkent [tash•KEHNT] Capital of Uzbekistan. 41°N 69°E (p. RA26)

Tbilisi [tuh•bih•LEE•see] Capital of the Republic of Georgia. 42°N 45°E (p. RA26)

Tegucigalpa [tay•GOO•see•GAHL•pah] Capital of Honduras. 14°N 87°W (p. RA14)

Tehran [TAY•uh•RAN] Capital of Iran. 36°N 52°E (p. RA25)

Thailand [TY•LAND] Southeast Asian country east of Myanmar. 17°N 101°E (p. RA27)

Thimphu [thihm•POO] Capital of Bhutan. 28°N 90°E (p. RA27)

Tigris [TY•gruhs] **River** River in southeastern Turkey and Iraq that merges with the Euphrates River. (p. RA25)

Tiranë [tih•RAH•nuh] Capital of Albania. 42°N 20°E (p. RA18)

Togo [TOH•goh] West African country between Benin and Ghana on the Gulf of Guinea. (p. RA22)

Tokyo [TOH•kee•OH] Capital of Japan. 36°N 140°E (p. RA27)

Trinidad and Tobago [TRIH•nuh•DAD tuh•BAY•goh] Island country near Venezuela between the Atlantic Ocean and the Caribbean Sea. (p. RA15)

Tripoli [TRIH•puh•lee] Capital of Libya. 33°N 13°E (p. RA22)

Tshwane [ch•WAH•nay] Executive capital of South Africa. 26°S 28°E (p. RA22)

Tunis [TOO•nuhs] Capital of Tunisia. 37°N 10°E (p. RA22)

Tunisia [too•NEE•zhuh] North African country on the Mediterranean Sea between Libya and Algeria. (p. RA22)

Turkey [TUHR•kee] Country in southeastern Europe and western Asia. (p. RA24)

Turkmenistan [tuhrk•MEH•nuh•STAN] Central Asian country on the Caspian Sea. (p. RA25)

U

Uganda [yoo•GAHN•dah] East African country south of Sudan. (p. RA22)

Ukraine [yoo•KRAYN] Eastern European country west of Russia on the Black Sea. (p. RA25)

Ulaanbaatar [oo•LAHN•BAH•TAWR] Capital of Mongolia. 48°N 107°E (p. RA27)

United Arab Emirates [EH•muh•ruhts] Country made up of seven states on the eastern side of the Arabian Peninsula. (p. RA25)

United Kingdom Western European island country made up of England, Scotland, Wales, and Northern Ireland. (p. RA18)

United States of America Country in North America made up of 50 states, mostly between Canada and Mexico. (p. RA8)

Uruguay [YUR•uh•GWAY] South American country south of Brazil on the Atlantic Ocean. (p. RA16)

Uzbekistan [uz•BEH•kih•STAN] Central Asian country south of Kazakhstan. (p. RA25)

V

Vanuatu [VAN•WAH•TOO] Country made up of islands in the Pacific Ocean east of Australia. (p. RA30)

Vatican [VA•tih•kuhn] City Headquarters of the Roman Catholic Church, located in the city of Rome in Italy. 42°N 13°E (p. RA18)

Venezuela [VEH•nuh•ZWAY•luh] South American country on the Caribbean Sea between Colombia and Guyana. (p. RA16)

Vienna [vee•EH•nuh] Capital of Austria. 48°N 16°E (p. RA18)

Vientiane [vyehn•TYAHN] Capital of Laos. 18°N 103°E (p. RA27)

Vietnam [vee•EHT•NAHM] Southeast Asian country east of Laos and Cambodia. (p. RA27)

Vilnius [VIL•nee•uhs] Capital of Lithuania. 55°N 25°E (p. RA19)

W

Warsaw Capital of Poland. 52°N 21°E (p. RA19)

Washington, D.C. Capital of the United States, in the District of Columbia. 39°N 77°W (p. RA8)

Wellington [WEH•lihng•tuhn] Capital of New Zealand. 41°S 175°E (p. RA30)

West Indies Caribbean islands between North America and South America. (p. RA15)

Windhoek [VIHNT•HUK] Capital of Namibia. 22°S 17°E (p. RA22)

Y

Yamoussoukro [YAH•MOO•SOO•kroh] Second capital of Côte d'Ivoire. 7°N 6°W (p. RA22)

Yangon [YAHNG•GOHN] City in Myanmar; formerly called Rangoon. 17°N 96°E (p. RA27)

Yaoundé [yown•DAY] Capital of Cameroon. 4°N 12°E (p. RA22)

Yemen [YEH•muhn] Country south of Saudi Arabia on the Arabian Peninsula. (p. RA25)

Yerevan [YEHR•uh•VAHN] Capital of Armenia. 40°N 44°E (p. RA25)

Z

Zagreb [ZAH•GREHB] Capital of Croatia. 46°N 16°E (p. RA18)

Zambia [ZAM•bee•uh] Southern African country north of Zimbabwe. (p. RA22)

Zimbabwe [zihm•BAH•bway] Southern African country northeast of Botswana. (p. RA22)

GLOSSARY/GLOSARIO

- Content vocabulary words are words that relate to geography content.
- Words that have an asterisk (*) are academic vocabulary. They help you understand your school subjects.
- All vocabulary words are **boldfaced** or **highlighted in yellow** in your textbook.

Aboriginal • **axis**

A

ENGLISH

Aboriginal the first people to live in Australia (p. 417)

absolute location the exact location of something (p. 21)

absolute monarchy a system of government in which the ruler has complete control (p.161)

*accurate without mistakes or errors (p. 44)

acid rain rain that contains harmful amounts of poisons due to pollution (p. 65)

*acknowledge to recognize the rights, status, or authority of a person, thing, or event (p. 481)

action song a song that combines singing and dancing to celebrate Maori history and culture in order to instill pride among Maori people (p. 435)

alluvial plain an area built up by rich fertile soil left by river floods (pp. 177; 228)

animist a person who believes in spirits that can exist apart from bodies (p. 370)

*annual yearly or each year (p. 178)

apartheid the system of laws in South Africa aimed at separating the races (p. 393)

aquifer an underground layer of rock through which water flows (p. 271)

archipelago a group of islands (pp. 118; 451)

atmosphere the layer of gases surrounding Earth (p. 44)

atoll a circular-shaped island made of coral (pp. 177; 453)

axis an imaginary line that runs through Earth's center from the North Pole to the South Pole (p. 42)

ESPAÑOL

Aborigen el primer pueblo que habitó en Australia (pág.417)

localización absoluta ubicación exacta de algo (pág. 21)

monarquía absoluta sistema de gobierno en el cual el gobernante detenta el control absoluto (pág. 161)

*exacto sin faltas o errores (pág. 44)

lluvia ácida lluvia que contiene cantidades nocivas de venenos debido a la polución (pág. 65)

*admitir reconocer los derechos, el estatus o la autoridad de una persona, cosa o suceso (pág. 481)

canción de acción canción que combina el canto y la danza para honrar la historia y cultura maoríes e inculcar orgullo entre el pueblo maorí (pág. 435)

llanura aluvial área formada por los sedimentos fértiles que dejan las inundaciones fluviales (págs. 177; 228)

animista persona que cree en espíritus que viven por fuera del cuerpo (pág. 370)

*annual cada año (pág. 178)

apartheid sistema jurídico de Sudáfrica que establecía la segregación racial (pág. 393)

acuífero estrato rocoso subterráneo por donde corre el agua (pág. 271)

archipiélago grupo de islas (págs. 118; 451)

atmósfera capa de gases que rodea la Tierra (pág. 44)

atolón isla coralina de forma anular (págs. 177; 453)

eje línea imaginaria que atraviesa el centro de la Tierra desde el Polo Norte hasta el Polo Sur (pág. 42)

B

basin an area of land that is drained by a river and its tributaries (p. 355)

*behalf in the interest of (p. 87)

biodiversity the wide variety of life on Earth (p. 332)

birthrate the number of babies born compared to the total number of people in a population at a given time (p. 72)

blood diamonds diamonds that are sold on the black market, with the proceeds going to provide guns and ammunition for violent conflicts (p. 387)

boomerang the flat, bent wooden tool of the Australian Aborigines that is thrown to stun prey when it strikes them and that sails back to the hunter if it misses its target (p.425)

boycott to refuse to buy items from a particular country or company (p. 186)

bush a rural area in Australia (p. 433)

cuenca area de terreno drenada por un río y sus afluentes (pág. 355)

*a favor de en beneficio de (pág. 87)

biodiversidad la amplia variedad de vida terrestre (pág. 332)

tasa de natalidad número de nacimientos comparado con el número total de habitantes de una población en un tiempo determinado (pág. 72)

diamantes sangrientos diamantes que se venden en el mercado negro y cuyas ganancias se utilizan para adquirir armas y municiones en conflictos violentos (pág. 387)

búmeran utensilio de madera curvo y plano de los aborígenes australianos, que se lanza para aturdir a las presas cuando las golpea y regresa al cazador en caso de fallar el blanco (pág. 425)

boicotear rehusarse a comprar los artículos de un país o compañía en particular (pág. 186)

brezal área rural de Australia (pág. 433)

C

caliph the successor to Muhammad (p. 276)

calving the process in which a section of ice breaks off the edge of a glacier (p. 476)

*capable having the ability to cause or accomplish an action or an event (p. 454)

cash crops a farm product grown for sale (p. 462)

cassava a tuberous plant that has edible roots (p. 336)

caste the social class a person is born into and cannot change (p. 183)

*channel a course for a river to flow through (p. 266)

*characteristic a quality or an aspect (p. 343)

civil disobedience the use of nonviolent protests to challenge a government or its laws (pp. 187; 393)

civil war a fight between opposing groups for control of a country's government (p. 279)

califa sucesor de Mahoma (pág. 276)

ablación proceso en el que un bloque de hielo se desprende del borde de un glaciar (pág. 476)

*capaz que tiene habilidad para provocar o llevar a cabo una acción o un suceso (pág. 454)

cultivo comercial producto agrícola que se cultiva para la venta (pág. 462)

yuca planta tuberosa de raíces comestibles (pág. 336)

casta clase social en la que nace una persona y no puede cambiar (pág. 183)

*canal curso artificial por donde fluye un río (pág. 266)

*característica cualidad o aspecto (pág. 343)

desobediencia civil rebatir un gobierno o sus leyes mediante protestas no violentas (págs. 187; 393)

guerra civil lucha entre grupos opositores por el control del gobierno de un país (pág. 279)

clan a large group of people who have a common ancestor in the far past (p. 311)

climate the average weather in an area over a long period of time (pp. 23; 48)

*collapse a sudden failure, breakdown, or ruin (pp. 235; 464)

collective a farm that is owned by the government but run by a group of farmers who work together (p. 208)

colonialism a policy based on control of one country by another (p. 337)

command economy an economy in which the means of production are publicly owned (p. 96)

*commodity a material, resource, or product that is bought and sold (p. 152)

communism a system of government in which the government controls the ways of producing goods (p. 129)

compass rose the feature on a map that shows direction (p. 28)

*complex highly developed (p. 210)

*component a part of something (p. 23)

condensation the result of water vapor changing to a liquid or a solid state (p. 64)

*consist to be made up of (p. 294–95)

constitution a document setting forth the structure and powers of a government and the rights of people in a country (p. 286)

constitutional monarchy a form of government in which a monarch is the head of state but elected officials run the government (p. 163)

*contact communication or interaction with someone (p. 396–97)

continent a large, unbroken mass of land (p. 52)

continental island an island formed centuries ago by the rising and folding of the ocean floor due to tectonic activity (p. 451)

continental shelf the part of a continent that extends into the ocean in a plateau, then drops sharply to the ocean floor (p. 60)

*controversy a dispute; a discussion involving opposing views (p. 438)

*convert to change from one thing to another (pp. 27; 276)

clan agrupación extensa de personas que tienen un ancestro común en el pasado remoto (pág. 311)

clima tiempo atmosférico promedio en una zona durante un periodo largo (págs. 23; 48)

*colapso bancarrota, caída o ruina súbita (págs. 235; 464)

colectiva granja de propiedad del gobierno que administra una cooperativa de granjeros (pág. 208)

colonialism política que se basa en el control o dominio de un país sobre otro (pág. 337)

economía planificada sistema económico en el que los medios de producción son de propiedad pública (pág. 96)

*mercancía materia prima, bien o producto que se compra y se vende (pág. 152)

comunismo forma de gobierno en la que el gobierno controla los modos de producción de los bienes (pág. 129)

rosa de los vientos convención de un mapa que señala la dirección (pág. 28)

*complejo muy desarrollado (pág. 210)

*componente parte de algo (pág. 23)

condensación cambio del vapor de agua a un estado líquido o sólido (pág. 64)

*consistir estar hecho de (pág. 294–95)

constitución documento que establece la estructura y los poderes de un gobierno así como los derechos de las personas en un país (pág. 286)

monarquía constitucional sistema de gobierno en el que un monarca ostenta la jefatura del Estado pero el gobierno lo administran funcionarios elegidos (pág. 163)

*contacto comunicación o interacción (pág. 396–97)

continente extensión de tierra grande e ininterrumpida (pág. 52)

isla continental isla formada siglos atrás por el levantamiento y plegamiento del fondo oceánico resultantes de la actividad tectónica (pág. 451)

plataforma continental parte de un continente que se adentra en el océano en forma de meseta y luego desciende abruptamente hasta el fondo oceánico (pág. 60)

*controversia disputa; discusión que involucra puntos de vista opuestos (pág. 438)

*convertir cambiar de una cosa a otra (págs. 27; 276)

Glossary/Glosario

coral reef a long, undersea structure formed by the tiny skeletons of coral, a kind of sea life (p. 417)

arrecife coralino extensa estructura submarina formada por los diminutos esqueletos de los corales, una especie de vida marina (pág. 417)

cottage industry a home- or village-based industry in which people make simple goods using their own equipment (p. 192)

industria artesanal industria doméstica o aldeana en la cual las personas elaboran bienes sencillos utilizando sus propios equipos (pág. 192)

coup an action in which a group of individuals seize control of a government (p. 339)

golpe (de Estado) acción mediante la cual un grupo de individuos se apodera del control de un gobierno (pág. 339)

couscous a small, round grain used in North African and Southwest Asian cooking (p. 282)

cuscús cereal pequeño y redondo que se utiliza en la cocina de África del Norte y el Sudeste Asiático (pág. 282)

Creole two or more languages that blend and become the language of the region (p. 369)

criollo dos o más lenguas que se mezclan y convierten en la lengua de una región (pág. 369)

cultural region a geographic area in which people have certain traits in common (p. 86)

región cultural área geográfica donde las personas tienen ciertos rasgos comunes (pág. 86)

culture the set of beliefs, behaviors, and traits shared by a group of people (p. 82)

cultura conjunto de creencias, comportamientos y rasgos compartidos por un grupo de personas (pág. 82)

***currency** the paper money and coins in circulation (p. 101)

***moneda** dinero en billetes y monedas en circulación (pág. 101)

cyclone a storm with high winds and heavy rains (p. 178)

ciclón tormenta con vientos huracanados y lluvias torrenciales (pág. 178)

D

dalit the lowest caste of Indian society; also called the "untouchables" (p. 193)

paria casta más baja de la sociedad india; también se le denomina "los intocables" (pág. 193)

de facto actually; in reality (p. 116)

de facto de hecho; en la realidad (pág. 116)

death rate the number of deaths compared to the total number of people in a population at a given time (p. 72)

tasa de mortalidad número de defunciones comparado con el número total de habitantes de una población en un tiempo determinado (pág. 72)

deciduous describing trees that shed their leaves in the autumn (p. 205)

caducifolios árboles que pierden sus hojas en el otoño (pág. 205)

***define** to describe the nature or extent of something (p. 201)

***definir** describir la naturaleza o el alcance de algo (pág. 201)

delta an area where sand, silt, clay, or gravel is dropped at the mouth of a river (pp. 62; 177; 266)

delta área donde se deposita arena, sedimento, lodo o gravilla en la desembocadura de un río (págs. 62; 177; 266)

democracy a type of government run by the people (p. 86)

democracia tipo de gobierno dirigido por el pueblo (pág. 86)

***demonstrate** to show (p. 274)

***demostrar** probar (pág. 274)

***depict** to describe or show (p. 344)

***representar** describir o mostrar (pág. 344)

desalinization a process that makes salt water safe to drink (p. 61)

desalinización proceso que elimina la sal del agua para hacerla potable (pág. 61)

desertification the process by which an area turns into a desert (p. 299)

desertización proceso por el cual un área se transforma en un desierto (pág. 299)

dialect a regional variety of a language with unique features, such as vocabulary, grammar, or pronunciation (p. 83)

dialecto variedad regional de una lengua con características únicas, como vocabulario, gramática o pronunciación (pág. 83)

dictatorship a form of government in which one person has absolute power to rule and control the government, the people, and the economy (p. 87)

dictadura forma de gobierno en la que una persona detenta el poder absoluto para mandar y controlar al gobierno, el pueblo y la economía (pág. 87)

didgeridoo a large, bamboo musical instrument of the Australian aboriginal people (p. 435)

diyiridú instrumento musical de bambú, de gran tamaño, de los aborígenes australianos (pág. 435)

dingoes wild dogs of Australia (p. 425)

dingos perros salvajes de Australia (pág. 425)

***displace** to take over a place or position of others (p. 361)

***desplazar** tomar el lugar o la posición de otros (pág. 361)

***distinct** separate; easily recognized as separate or different (p. 459)

***distinto** separado; fácilmente reconocible como separado o diferente (pág. 459)

***distort** to change something so it is no longer accurate (p. 27)

***distorsionar** cambiar algo de modo que ya no es correcto (pág. 27)

***diverse** composed of many distinct and different parts (pp. 311; 368–69)

***diverso** compuesto de muchas partes distintivas y diferentes (págs. 311; 368–69)

diversified increased variety to achieve a balance (p. 284)

diversificado variedad incrementada para lograr un equilibrio (pág. 284)

***dominate** to have the greatest importance (p. 117)

***dominar** tener la mayor importancia (pág. 117)

dominion a largely self-governing country within the British Empire (p. 431)

dominio país autónomo dentro del Imperio británico (pág. 431)

doubling time the number of years it takes a population to double in size based on its current growth rate (p. 73)

tiempo de duplicación número de años que le toma a una población doblar su tamaño con base en la tasa de crecimiento actual (pág. 73)

drought long period of time without rainfall (p. 421)

sequía periodo largo sin lluvias (pág. 421)

***dynamic** always changing (p. 20)

***dinámico** en permanente cambio (pág. 20)

dynasty a line of rulers from a single family that holds power for a long time (p. 124)

dinastía serie de gobernantes de una sola familia que detentan el poder por mucho tiempo (pág. 124)

E

earthquake an event in which the ground shakes or trembles, brought about by the collision of tectonic plates (p. 54)

terremoto suceso en el cual el suelo se agita o tiembla como consecuencia de la colisión de placas tectónicas (pág. 54)

economic system how a society decides on the ownership and distribution of its economic resources (p. 96)

sistema económico la forma en que una sociedad decide la propiedad y distribución de sus recursos económicos (pág. 96)

ecotourism a type of tourism in which people visit a country to enjoy its natural wonders (p. 168)

ecoturismo tipo de turismo en el cual las personas visitan un país para disfrutar de sus maravillas naturales (pág. 168)

***element** an important part or characteristic (p. 361)

***elemento** parte o característica importante (pág. 361)

elevation the measurement of how much above or below sea level a place is (p. 29)

elevación medida de cuánto más alto o más bajo está un lugar respecto del nivel del mar (pág. 29)

embargo a ban on trade with a particular country (p. 393)

embargo prohibición de comerciar con un país específico (pág. 393)

emigrate to leave one's home to live in another place (p. 78)

emigrar abandonar el hogar propio para vivir en otro lugar (pág. 78)

*emphasis an expression that shows the importance of something (p. 283)

*énfasis expresión que muestra la importancia de algo (pág. 283)

endemic specific to a particular place or people (p. 155)

endémico específico de un lugar o una persona en particular (pág. 155)

environment the natural surroundings of a place (p. 23)

medioambiente entorno natural de un lugar (pág. 23)

Equator a line of latitude that runs around the middle of Earth (p. 21)

ecuador línea de latitud que atraviesa la mitad de la Tierra (pág. 21)

equinox one of two days each year when the sun is directly overhead at the Equator (p. 46)

equinoccio uno de dos días al año cuando el sol se halla situado directamente sobre el ecuador (pág. 46)

erg a large area of sand (p. 268)

erg zona extensa de arena (pág. 268)

erosion the process by which weathered bits of rock are moved elsewhere by water, wind, or ice (p. 55)

erosión proceso por el cual fragmentos desgastados de rocas son llevados a otra parte por acción del agua, el viento o el hielo (pág. 55)

escarpment a steep cliff at the edge of a plateau with a lowland area below (p. 381)

escarpado acantilado pendiente, al borde de una meseta, que tiene debajo un área de tierras bajas (pág. 381)

*establish to start (p. 190)

*establecer comenzar (pág. 190)

estuary an area where river currents and the ocean tide meet (p. 329)

estuario área donde convergen corrientes fluviales y la marea oceánica (pág. 329)

ethnic group a group of people with a common racial, national, tribal, religious, or cultural background (p. 83)

grupo étnico grupo de personas con un antecedente racial, nacional, tribal, religioso o cultural común (pág. 83)

eucalyptus a tree found only in Australia and nearby islands that is well suited to dry conditions with leathery leaves, deep roots, and the ability to survive when rivers flood (p. 423)

eucalipto árbol de hojas carnosas y raíces profundas que solo se encuentra en Australia e islas adyacentes. Se adapta bien a las condiciones de sequía y puede sobrevivir a las inundaciones fluviales (pág. 423)

evaporation the change of liquid water to water vapor (p. 63)

evaporación cambio del agua en estado líquido a vapor (pág. 63)

*expand to spread out; to grow larger (p. 234)

*expandir extender; agrandar (pág. 234)

*exploit to use a person, resource, or situation unfairly and selfishly (pp. 169; 390)

*explotar utilizar a una persona, un recurso o una situación de manera injusta y egoísta (págs. 169; 390)

export to send a product produced in one country to another country (p. 99)

exportar enviar un bien producido en un país a otro país (pág. 99)

extended family a unit of related people made up of several generations, including grandparents, parents, and children (p. 370)

familia extensa unidad de personas emparentadas conformada por varias generaciones, incluidos abuelos, padres e hijos (pág. 370)

F

*factor a cause (p. 285)

fale a traditional Samoan home that has no walls, leaving the inside open to cooling ocean breezes (p. 461)

fault a place where two tectonic plates grind against each other (p. 54)

fauna the animal life in a particular environment (p. 155)

fellaheen the peasant farmers of Egypt who rent small plots of land (p. 281)

flora the plant life in a particular environment (p. 155)

fossil water water that fell as rain thousands of years ago and is now trapped deep below ground (p. 247)

foundation the basis of something (p. 335)

free trade arrangement whereby a group of countries decides to set little or no tariffs on quotas (p. 100)

fundamentalist a person who believes in the strict interpretation of religious laws (p. 279)

*factor causa (pág. 285)

fale casa tradicional de Samoa que carece de paredes, de manera que el interior queda abierto a las frescas brisas del océano (pág. 461)

falla lugar donde dos placas tectónicas chocan entre sí (pág. 54)

fauna vida animal en un medioambiente específico (pág. 155)

fellaheen campesinos de Egipto que arriendan pequeñas parcelas (pág. 281)

flora vida vegetal en un medioambiente específico (pág. 155)

agua fósil agua que cayó en forma de lluvia hace miles de años y ahora se encuentra atrapada en las profundidades del subsuelo (pág. 247)

fundamento la base de algo (pág. 335)

libre comercio acuerdo por el cual un grupo de países decide imponer aranceles bajos a las cuotas o no fija ningún arancel (pág. 100)

fundamentalista persona que cree en la interpretación estricta de las leyes religiosas (pág. 279)

G

genocide the mass murder of people from a particular ethnic group (p. 308)

geography the study of Earth and its peoples, places, and environments (p. 18)

geothermal energy the electricity produced by natural, underground sources of steam (pp. 301; 436)

geyser a spring of water heated by molten rock inside Earth that, from time to time, shoots hot water into the air (p. 419)

glacier a large body of ice that moves slowly across land (p. 56)

globalization the process by which nations, cultures, and economies become mixed (p. 89)

*grant to allow as a right, privilege, or favor (p. 391)

genocidio asesinato masivo de personas de un grupo étnico específico (pág. 308)

geografía estudio de la Tierra y de sus gentes, lugares y entornos (pág. 18)

energía geotérmica electricidad producida por fuentes naturales de vapor subterráneas (págs. 301; 436)

géiser fuente de agua calentada por rocas fundidas en el interior de la Tierra que, de vez en cuando, expulsa agua caliente al aire (pág. 419)

glaciar masa de hielo enorme que se mueve lentamente sobre la tierra (pág. 56)

globalización proceso mediante el cual naciones, culturas y economías se integran (pág. 89)

*conceder permitir como un derecho, privilegio o favor (pág. 391)

Glossary/Glosario

green revolution the effort to use modern techniques and science to increase food production in poorer countries (p. 192)

revolución verde esfuerzo por utilizar técnicas modernas y la ciencia para aumentar la producción de alimentos en los países más pobres (pág. 192)

gross domestic product (GDP) the total dollar value of all final goods and services produced in a country during a single year (p. 98)

producto interno bruto (PIB) valor total en dólares de todos los bienes y servicios finales producidos en un país durante un año (pág. 98)

groundwater the water contained inside Earth's crust (p. 61)

agua subterránea agua contenida en el interior de la corteza terrestre (pág. 61)

H

harmattan a wind off the Atlantic coast of Africa that blows from the northeast to the south, carrying large amounts of dust (p. 357)

harmattan viento de la costa atlántica de África que sopla del nordeste al sur, arrastrando consigo grandes cantidades de polvo (pág. 357)

hemisphere each half of Earth (p. 26)

hemisferio cada mitad de la Tierra (pág. 26)

hieroglyphics the system of writing that uses small pictures to represent sounds or words (p. 274)

jeroglífico sistema de escritura que representa sonidos o palabras con dibujos pequeños (pág. 274)

high island a type of island in the Pacific Ocean formed many centuries ago by volcanoes and still having mountainous areas (p. 452)

isla alta tipo de isla del océano Pacífico formada hace muchos siglos por volcanes y que aún tiene zonas montañosas (pág. 452)

homogeneous made up of many things that are the same (p. 216)

homogéneo compuesto por muchas cosas iguales (pág. 216)

hot springs places where naturally heated water rises out of the ground (p. 419)

fuentes termales lugares donde agua calentada por medios naturales brota del suelo (pág. 419)

human rights the rights belonging to all individuals (p. 87)

derechos humanos los derechos que tienen todos los individuos (pág. 87)

hydroelectric power the electricity that is created by flowing water (p. 300)

energía hidroeléctrica electricidad producida por agua en movimiento (pág. 300)

hydropolitics the politics surrounding water access and usage rights (p. 247)

hidropolítica política relativa al acceso al agua y los derechos de su uso (pág. 247)

I

ice sheet a large, thick area of ice that covers a region (p. 475)

manto de hielo área extensa y gruesa de hielo que cubre una región (pág. 475)

ice shelf a thick layer of ice that extends above the water (p. 476)

plataforma de hielo capa gruesa de hielo que se extiende sobre la superficie del agua (pág. 476)

iceberg a huge piece of floating ice that broke off from an ice shelf or glacier and fell into the sea (p. 476)

iceberg témpano gigante de hielo flotante que se desprendió de una plataforma de hielo o glaciar y cayó al mar (pág. 476)

immigrate to enter and live in a new country (p. 78)

inmigrar entrar a un nuevo país y vivir allí (pág. 78)

impact an effect or influence (p. 305)

imperialism a policy by which a country increases its power by gaining control over other areas of the world (pp. 305; 365)

import when a country brings in a product from another country (p. 99)

infrastructure a system of roads and railroads that allow the transport of materials (p. 372)

*inhibit to limit (p. 207)

insular separate from other countries (p. 150)

*intense strong (p. 54)

*intertwine to become closely connected or involved (p. 127)

introduced species a nonnative species that is brought to a new environment (p. 429)

irrigate to supply land with water through ditches or pipes (p. 209)

isthmus a narrow strip of land that connects two larger land areas (p. 59)

impacto efecto o influencia (pág. 305)

imperialismo política mediante la cual un país aumenta su poder ejerciendo control sobre otras áreas del mundo (págs. 305; 365)

importación cuando un país ingresa un producto de otro país (pág. 99)

infraestructura sistema de carreteras y ferrocarriles que permite el transporte de materiales (pág. 372)

*inhibir limitar (pág. 207)

insular separado de otros países (pág. 150)

*intenso poderoso (pág. 54)

*entretejer unirse o envolverse estrechamente (pág. 127)

especie introducida especie foránea que se lleva a un medioambiente nuevo (pág. 429)

irrigar suministrar agua a un terreno por medio de zanjas o ductos (pág. 209)

istmo franja estrecha de tierra que conecta dos áreas de tierra más grandes (pág. 59)

K

kapahaka a traditional art form of the Maori people that combines music, dance, singing, and facial expressions (p. 426)

katabatic winds the strong, fast, cold winds that blow down from the interior of Antarctica (p. 477)

kente the colorful, handwoven cloth produced in Ghana (p. 371)

key the feature on a map that explains the symbols, colors, and lines used on the map (p. 28)

kiwifruit a small, fuzzy, brownish-colored fruit with bright green flesh (p. 437)

krill the tiny, shrimplike sea creatures that are eaten by whales and many other sea creatures (p. 479)

kapahaka manifestación artística tradicional del pueblo maorí que combina música, danza, canto y expresiones faciales (pág. 426)

vientos catabáticos vientos fuertes, rápidos y fríos que soplan desde el interior de la Antártida (pág. 477)

kente tela tejida de vivos colores que se fabrica en Ghana (pág. 371)

clave elemento de un mapa que explica los símbolos, colores y líneas usados en este (pág. 28)

kiwi fruta pequeña y vellosa de tono marrón cuya carne es verde brillante (pág. 437)

krill crustáceo diminuto, similar al camarón, que comen las ballenas y otras criaturas marinas (pág. 479)

L

lagoon a shallow pond near a larger body of water (p. 453)

laguna pozo poco profundo cercano a una masa de agua mayor (pág. 453)

Glossary/Glosario

landform a natural feature found on land (p. 23)

accidente geográfico formación natural que se encuentra sobre la tierra (pág. 23)

landlocked having no border with an ocean or a sea (p. 382)

sin salida al mar que no limita con un océano o un mar (pág. 382)

landscape the portions of Earth's surface that can be viewed at one time from a location (p. 19)

paisaje partes de la superficie terrestre que se pueden observar a un mismo tiempo desde una ubicación (pág. 19)

latitude the lines on a map that run east to west (p. 21)

latitud líneas sobre un mapa que van de este a oeste (pág. 21)

lawsuit a legal action in which people ask for relief from some damage done to them by someone else (p. 438)

demanda acción legal en la que las personas exigen una indemnización por algún daño que les causó un tercero (pág. 438)

lichen tiny, sturdy plants that grow in rocky areas (p. 478)

líquenes plantas pequeñas y resistentes que crecen en las zonas rocosas (pág. 478)

loess a fine-grained, fertile soil deposited by the wind (p. 119)

loes suelo fértil y de granos finos depositado por el viento (pág. 119)

longitude the lines on a map that run north to south (p. 21)

longitud líneas sobre un mapa que van de norte a sur (pág. 21)

low island a type of island in the Pacific Ocean formed by the buildup of coral (p. 452)

isla baja tipo de isla del océano Pacífico formada por acumulaciones de coral (pág. 452)

M

map projection one of several systems used to represent the round Earth on a flat map (p. 28)

proyección cartográfica uno de los varios sistemas que se usan para representar la esfera terrestre en un mapa plano (pág. 28)

*margin an edge (p. 265)

*margen borde (pág. 265)

market economy an economy in which most of the means of production are privately owned (p. 96)

economía de mercado economía en la cual la mayoría de los medios de producción son de propiedad privada (pág. 96)

marsupial a type of mammal that carries its young in a pouch (p. 423)

marsupial tipo de mamífero que carga a su cría en una bolsa (pág. 423)

*mature fully grown and developed as an adult; also refers to older adults (p. 73)

*maduro adulto plenamente crecido y desarrollado; también se refiere a los adultos mayores (pág. 73)

megalopolis a huge city or cluster of cities with an extremely large population (pp. 80; 133)

megalópolis ciudad enorme o cúmulo de ciudades que tienen una población extremadamente grande (págs. 80; 133)

millennium a period of a thousand years (p. 233)

milenio period de mil años (pág. 233)

millet a grass that produces edible seeds (p. 335)

mijo especie de pasto que produce semillas comestibles (pág. 335)

minority a group of people that is different from most of the population (p. 166)

minoría grupo de personas diferente a la mayoría de la población (pág. 166)

MIRAB economy a lesser-developed economy that depends on aid from foreign countries and remittances from former residents working elsewhere (p. 464)

economía MIRAB economía menos desarrollada que depende de la ayuda de países extranjeros y de las remesas de antiguos residentes que trabajan en otro lugar (pág. 464)

missionary someone who tries to convert others to a certain religion (p. 338)

misionario persona que trata de convertir a otras a una religión específica (pág. 338)

mixed economy an economy in which parts of the economy are privately owned and parts are owned by the government (p. 96)

economía mixta economía en la cual unos sectores son de propiedad privada y otros son de propiedad del gobierno (pág. 96)

monarchy the system of government in which a country is ruled by a king or queen (p. 87)

monarquía sistema de gobierno en el que un rey o una reina gobiernan un país (pág. 87)

monolith a single standing stone (p. 417)

monolito piedra erguida de una sola pieza (pág. 417)

monotheism the belief in one god (pp. 233; 276)

monoteísmo creencia en un solo dios (págs. 233; 276)

monsoon a seasonal wind that blows steadily from the same direction for several months at a time but changes directions at other times of the year (p. 178)

monzón viento estacional que sopla regularmente desde la misma dirección durante varios meses pero cambia de dirección en otras épocas del año (pág. 178)

myrrh a sweet perfume used as medicine in ancient times (p. 273)

mirra perfume dulce que antiguamente se empleaba como medicamento (pág. 273)

N

*network a complex, interconnected chain or system of things such as roads, canals, or computers (p. 383)

*red cadena o sistema complejo e interconectado de carreteras, canales o computadoras, entre otros (pág. 383)

nomad a person who lives by moving from place to place to follow and hunt herds of migrating animals or to lead herds of grazing animals to fresh pasture (p. 269)

nómada persona que vive trasladándose de un lugar a otro para seguir y cazar manadas de animales migratorios o para conducir rebaños de animales de pastoreo hacia pastos frescos (pág. 269)

nonrenewable resources the resources that cannot be totally replaced (p. 95)

recursos no renovables recursos que no se pueden reponer por completo (pág. 95)

nuclear family the family group that includes only parents and their children (p. 371)

familia nuclear grupo familiar que solo incluye a padres e hijos (pág. 371)

nuclear proliferation the spread of control of nuclear power, particularly the knowledge of how to construct nuclear weapons (p. 187)

proliferación nuclear expansión del dominio de la energía nuclear, en particular el conocimiento para construir armas nucleares (pág. 187)

O

oasis a fertile area that rises in a desert wherever water is regularly available (p. 213)

oasis área fértil que se desarrolla en un desierto cuando hay una fuente regular de agua (pág. 213)

oral tradition the process of passing stories by word of mouth from generation to generation (p. 314)

tradición oral forma de transmitir historias de generación en generación, mediante la palabra hablada (pág. 314)

orbit to circle around something (p. 42)

orbitar moverse en círculo alrededor de algo (pág. 42)

Outback the inland areas of Australia west of the Great Dividing Range (p. 417)

Outback zonas del interior de Australia ubicadas al oeste de la Gran Cordillera Divisoria (pág. 417)

Glossary/Glosario

outsourcing hiring workers in other countries to do a set of jobs (p. 192)

subcontratar contratar trabajadores en otros países para que hagan una serie de trabajos (pág. 192)

*overall as a whole; generally (p. 416–17)

*global como un todo; generalizado (pág. 416–17)

ozone the certain kind of oxygen that forms a layer around Earth in the atmosphere; it blocks out many of the most harmful rays from the sun (p. 483)

ozono tipo de oxígeno que forma una capa alrededor de la Tierra en la atmósfera; bloquea el paso de los rayos más dañinos del sol (pág. 483)

P

Pacific Rim the countries bordering the Pacific Ocean, particularly Asian countries (p. 167)

Cuenca del Pacífico países que bordean el océano Pacífico, en particular los países asiáticos (pág. 167)

palm oil an oil that is used in cooking (p. 335)

aceite de palma un aceite que se usa para cocinar (pág. 335)

pastoral describing a society based on herding animals (p. 206)

pastoril sociedad que vive del pastoreo de animales (pág. 206)

periodic market an open-air trading market that spring ups at a crossroads or in larger towns (p. 399)

mercado ambulante mercado al aire libre que se instala en una aldea o en pueblos más grandes (pág. 399)

permafrost the permanently frozen, lower layers of soil found in the tundra and subarctic climate zones (p. 202)

permacongelamiento capas bajas del suelo, permanentemente congeladas, que se encuentran en la tundra y las zonas de clima subártico (pág. 202)

pharaoh the name for a powerful ruler in ancient Egypt (p. 272)

faraón nombre dado a un poderoso gobernante en el Antiguo Egipto (pág. 272)

phosphate a chemical salt used to make fertilizer (p. 271)

fosfato sal química utilizada para producir fertilizantes (pág. 271)

pidgin a language formed by combining parts of several different languages (pp. 369, 460)

pidgin lengua formada por la combinación de partes de varias lenguas distintas (págs. 369, 460)

plain a large expanse of land that can be flat or have a gentle roll (p. 58)

llanura gran extensión de tierra plana o con ligeras ondulaciones (pág. 58)

plankton plants or animals that ride along with water currents (p. 479)

plancton plantas o animales que se desplazan con las corrientes de agua (pág. 479)

plantation a large farm (p. 161)

plantación granja grande (pág. 161)

plateau a flat area that rises above the surrounding land (p. 58)

meseta área plana que se eleva por encima del terreno circundante (pág. 58)

poaching illegal fishing or hunting (pp. 317, 387)

caza furtiva pesca o caza ilegal (págs. 317, 387)

*policy a plan or course of action (p. 187)

*política plan o curso de acción (pág. 187)

polytheism the belief in more than one god (p. 233)

politeísmo creencia en más de un dios (pág. 233)

population density the average number of people living within a square mile or a square kilometer (pp. 76; 310)

densidad de población número promedio de personas que habitan en una milla cuadrada o un kilómetro cuadrado (págs. 76; 310)

population distribution the geographic pattern of where people live (p. 76)

distribución de la población patrón geográfico que muestra dónde habita la gente (pág. 76)

possession an area or a region that is controlled by another country (p. 458)

posesión zona o región controlada por otro país (pág. 458)

*potential the possibility (p. 333)

*potencial posibilidad (pág. 333)

precipitation the water that falls on the ground as rain, snow, sleet, hail, or mist (p. 48)

precipitación agua que cae al suelo en forma de lluvia, nieve, aguanieve, granizo o rocío (pág. 48)

primate city a country's main city that is so large and influential that it dominates the rest of the country (p. 165)

ciudad principal la ciudad más importante de un país, tan grande e influyente que domina el resto del país (pág. 165)

Prime Meridian the starting point for measuring longitude (p. 21)

primer meridiano punto de partida para medir la longitud (pág. 21)

productivity the measurement of what is produced and what is required to produce it (p. 98)

productividad medición de lo que se produce y lo que se requiere para producirlo (pág. 98)

*project a planned activity (pp. 272–73)

*proyecto actividad planificada (págs. 272–73)

R

rain shadow an area that receives reduced rainfall because it is on the side of a mountain facing away from the ocean (p. 49)

sombra pluviométrica zona que recibe pocas precipitaciones porque se halla en la ladera de una montaña que está en el lado contrario al océano (pág. 49)

Raj the period of time in which Great Britain controlled India as a part of the British Empire (p. 186)

Raj periodo durante el cual Gran Bretaña controló India como parte del Imperio británico (pág. 186)

refugee a person who flees a country because of violence, war, persecution, or disaster (pp. 78; 309; 341)

refugiado persona que huye de un país por la violencia, una guerra, una persecución o un desastre (págs. 78; 309; 341)

regime a government (p. 279)

régimen gobierno (pág. 279)

region a group of places that are close to one another and that share some characteristics (p. 22)

región agrupación de lugares cercanos que comparten algunas características (pág. 22)

reincarnation the belief in Hinduism that after a person dies, his or her soul is reborn into another body (p. 184)

reencarnación creencia del hinduismo según la cual el espíritu de una persona muerta renace en otro cuerpo (pág. 184)

relative location the location of one place compared to another place (p. 20)

localización relativa la ubicación de un lugar comparada con la de otro (pág. 20)

relief the difference between the elevation of one feature and the elevation of another feature near it (p. 29)

relieve diferencia entre la elevación de una formación y la de otra formación cercana (pág. 29)

remittance the money sent back to the homeland by people who have gone somewhere else to work (p. 464)

remesa dinero enviado al país de origen por personas que se han ido a trabajar a otro lugar (pág. 464)

remote sensing the method of getting information from far away, such as deep below the ground (pp. 32, 484)

detección remota método para obtener información muy lejana, como de las profundidades del subsuelo (págs. 32; 484)

renewable resources a resource that can be totally replaced or is always available naturally (p. 95)

recursos renovables recursos que pueden reponerse totalmente o siempre se encuentran disponibles en la naturaleza (pág. 95)

Glossary/Glosario

Glossary/Glosario

representative democracy a form of democracy in which citizens elect government leaders to represent the people (p. 87)

democracia representativa forma de democracia en la que los ciudadanos eligen líderes de gobierno para que representen al pueblo (pág. 87)

research station a base for scientific research and observation, often in a remote location (p. 482)

estación de investigación base para la investigación y observación científicas , por lo general ubicada en un sitio remoto (pág. 482)

reservoir an artificial lake created by a dam (p. 283)

embalse lago artificial creado por una presa (pág. 283)

resort a vacation place where people go to relax (p. 464)

centro vacacional lugar de vacaciones donde las personas van a descansar (pág. 464)

resource a material that can be used to produce crops or other products (p. 23)

recurso materia prima que se puede utilizar para obtener cultivos u otros productos (pág. 23)

*revenue the income generated by a business (p. 364)

*renta ingresos generados por un negocio (pág. 364)

revolution a complete trip of Earth around the sun (p. 42)

revolución recorrido completo de la Tierra alrededor del Sol (pág. 42)

rift to separate two pieces from one another (p. 294)

escindir separar dos partes entre sí (pág. 294)

Ring of Fire a long, narrow band of volcanoes surrounding the Pacific Ocean (p. 54)

Cinturón de Fuego banda larga y estrecha de volcanes que rodean el océano Pacífico (pág. 54)

rural describes an area that is lightly populated (p. 77)

rural área poco poblada (pág. 77)

S

samurai a powerful, land-owning warrior in Japan (p. 128)

samurái poderoso guerrero japónes dueño de tierras (pág. 128)

scale the relationship between distances on the map and on Earth (p. 29)

escala relación entre distancias en un mapa y en la Tierra (pág. 29)

scale bar the feature on a map that tells how a measured space on the map relates to the actual distance on Earth (p. 28)

escala numérica elemento cartográfico que muestra la relación entre un espacio medido sobre el mapa y la distancia real sobre la Tierra (pág. 28)

secede to withdraw from a group or a country (p. 367)

separarse retirarse de un grupo o un país (pág. 367)

semiarid having lower temperatures and cooler nights than hot, dry deserts (p. 230)

semiárido que tiene temperaturas más bajas y noches más frías que los desiertos cálidos y secos (pág. 230)

shogun a military leader who ruled Japan in early times (p. 128)

sogún líder militar que gobernaba Japón antiguamente (pág. 128)

*significant important (p. 214)

*significativo importante (pág. 214)

silt small particles of rich soil (p. 266)

limo pequeñas partículas de suelo fértil (pág. 266)

sitar a long-necked instrument with 7 strings on the outside and 10 inside the neck that provides Indian music with a distinctive sound (p. 191)

cítara instrumento de cuello largo con 7 cuerdas en la parte exterior y 10 dentro del cuello, que da a la música india un sonido distintivo (pág. 191)

slash-and-burn agriculture a method of farming that involves cutting down trees and underbrush and burning the area to create a field for crops (p. 331)

agricultura de tala y quema método agrícola que consiste en talar árboles y rastrojos y quemar el área despejada para crear un campo de cultivo (pág. 331)

solstice one of two days of the year when the sun reaches its northernmost or southernmost point (p. 45)

solsticio uno de dos días al año cuando el sol alcanza su máxima declinación norte o sur (pág. 45)

souk a large, open-air market in North African and Southwest Asian countries (p. 281)

zoco mercado grande al aire libre propio de África del Norte y los países del Sudoeste Asiático (pág. 281)

spatial Earth's features in terms of their places, shapes, and relationships to one another (p. 18)

espaciales características de la Tierra en cuanto a sus lugares, formas y relaciones entre sí (pág. 18)

*sphere a round shape like a ball (p. 26–27)

*esfera figura redonda como una pelota (pág. 26–27)

sphere of influence an area of a country where a single foreign power has been granted exclusive trading rights (p. 128)

esfera de influencia área de un país donde se le ha concedido a una sola potencia extranjera derechos comerciales exclusivos (pág. 128)

standard of living the level at which a person, group, or nation lives as measured by the extent to which it meets its needs (p. 98)

estándar de vida nivel en que vive una persona, grupo o nación, medido según la capacidad de satisfacer sus necesidades (pág. 98)

station a cattle or sheep ranch in rural Australia (p. 429)

estación rancho de ganado vacuno o lanar del área rural de Australia (pág.429)

steppe a partly dry grassland often found on the edge of a desert (p. 202)

estepa pradera parcialmente seca que se encuentra con frecuencia al borde de un desierto (pág. 202)

*structure an arrangement of parts (p. 135)

*estructura organización de las partes (pág. 135)

subcontinent a large landmass that is part of a continent (p. 176)

subcontinente gran masa de tierra que forma parte de un continente (pág. 176)

subsistence farming a type of farming in which the farmer produces only enough to feed his or her family (pp. 168; 313)

agricultura de subsistencia tipo de agricultura en el que los granjeros producen apenas lo suficiente para alimentar a su familia (págs. 168; 313)

sultan the ruler of a Muslim country (p. 159)

sultán gobernante de un país musulmán (pág. 159)

sustainability the economic principle by which a country works to create conditions where all the natural resources for meeting the needs of society are available (p. 101)

sostenibilidad principio económico según el cual un país crea condiciones para que estén disponibles todos los recursos naturales que satisfacen las necesidades de la sociedad (pág. 101)

T

taiga a large coniferous forest (p. 202)

taiga gran bosque de coníferas (pág. 202)

technology any way that scientific discoveries are applied to practical use (p. 30)

tecnología cualquier forma en que los descubrimientos científicos se aplican para un uso práctico (pág. 30)

tectonic plate one of the 16 pieces of Earth's crust (p. 53)

placa tectónica uno de las 16 partes de la corteza terrestre (pág. 53)

Glossary/Glosario

thatch a bundle of twigs, grass, and bark (p. 399)

techo de paja armazón de ramas, pasto y corteza (pág. 399)

thematic map a map that shows specialized information (p. 30)

mapa temático mapa que muestra información especializada (pág. 30)

tikanga Maori customs and traditions passed down through generations (p. 426)

tikanga costumbres y tradiciones maoríes transmitidas de generación en generación (pág. 426)

trade deficit a situation that occurs when the value of a country's imports is higher than the value of its exports (p. 138)

déficit comercial situación que ocurre cuando el valor de las importaciones de un país es superior al valor de sus exportaciones (pág. 138)

trade language a common language that emerges when countries trade with each other (p. 342)

lenguaje comercial lenguaje común que surge cuando los países comercian entre sí (pág. 342)

trade surplus a situation that occurs when the value of a country's exports is higher than the value of its imports (p. 138)

superávit comercial situación que ocurre cuando el valor de las exportaciones de un país es superior al valor de sus importaciones (pág. 138)

traditional economy an economy where resources are distributed mainly through families (p. 96)

economía tradicional economía en la que los recursos se distribuyen principalmente entre las familias (pág. 96)

*transform to change something completely (p. 64)

*transformar cambiar algo por completo (pág. 64)

treaty an official agreement, negotiated and signed by each party (p. 481)

tratado acuerdo oficial, negociado y firmado por las partes (pág. 481)

trench a long, narrow, steep-sided cut on the ocean floor (p. 60)

fosa depresión larga, estrecha y profunda del fondo oceánico (pág. 60)

*trend a general tendency or preference (p. 399)

*tendencia inclinación o preferencia general (pág. 399)

tribute money paid by one country to another in surrender or for protection (p. 305)

tributo dinero que un país paga a otro por sometimiento o para obtener protección (pág. 305)

trust territory an area temporarily placed under control of another country (p. 458)

territorio en fideicomiso área puesta transitoriamente bajo el control de otro país (pág. 458)

tsunami a giant ocean wave caused by volcanic eruptions or movement of the earth under the ocean floor (pp. 54; 118)

tsunami gigantesca ola oceánica provocada por erupciones volcánicas o movimientos de la tierra bajo el lecho oceánico (págs. 54; 118)

tundra a flat, treeless plain with permanently frozen ground (p. 202)

tundra llanura plana y sin vegetación cuyo suelo permanece helado (pág. 202)

U

*ultimate most extreme or greatest (p. 161)

*supremo extreme o mayor (pág. 161)

*unify to unite; to join together; to make into a unit or a whole (p. 430)

*unificar unir; juntar; integrar en una unidad o totalidad (pág. 430)

urban describes an area that is densely populated (p. 77)

urbana área densamente poblada (pág. 77)

urbanization when a city grows larger and spreads into nearby areas (pp. 80; 133)

utilities the infrastructure provided by companies or governments such as electricity, water, and trash removal (p. 398)

urbanización cuando una ciudad crece y se expande hacia las áreas adyacentes (págs. 80; 133)

servicios públicos infraestructura que proveen algunas compañías o gobiernos, como electricidad, agua y recolección de basuras (pág. 398)

V

*vary to show differences between things (p. 230)

*visible able to be seen (p. 475)

*volume an amount (p. 355)

*variar mostrar diferencias entre cosas (pág. 230)

*visible que se puede ver (pág. 475)

*volumen antidad (pág. 355)

W

wadi a dry riverbed that fills with water when rare rains fall in a desert (pp. 230; 268)

water cycle the process in which water is used and reused on Earth, including precipitation, collection, evaporation, and condensation (p. 63)

watershed land drained by a river and its tributaries (p. 328)

wayfinding the system of navigating a foreign place through observation of natural phenomena, such as the movement of the sun and stars (p. 456)

weathering the process by which Earth's surface is worn away by natural forces (p. 55)

*widespread commonly occurring (p. 242)

vado lecho seco de un río que se llena de agua cuando ocasionalmente llueve en un desierto (págs. 230; 268)

ciclo del agua proceso en el cual el agua se usa y reutiliza en la Tierra; incluye la precipitación, recolección, evaporación y condensación (pág. 63)

cuenca territorio cuyas aguas afluyen a un mismo río y sus afluentes (pág. 328)

orientación sistema que consiste en navegar por un lugar desconocido con la ayuda de la observación de fenómenos naturales, como el movimiento del sol y las estrellas (pág. 456)

meteorización proceso mediante el cual la superficie terrestre se deteriora por la acción de fuerzas naturales (pág. 55)

*extendido que ocurre con frecuencia (pág. 242)

Y

yurt a large, circular structure made of animal skins that can be packed up and moved from place to place (p. 216)

yurta estructura grande y circular, hecha de pieles de animales, que se puede empacar y trasladar de un lugar a otro (pág. 216)

Glossary/Glosario

The following abbreviations are used in the index: *m=map, c=chart, p=photograph or picture, g=graph, crt=cartoon, ptg=painting, q=quote, i=infographic, d=diagram*

Abkhaz Republic, 216
Aboriginal: in Australia, 424–25, 432; British settlers vs., 429; culture of, 85; defined, 417; rights of, 438. *See also* Native Americans
absolute location, 21
absolute monarchy, 161
Abu Dhabi, 241
Abuja, Nigeria, 370
Achebe, Chinua, 372
acid rain, 65
action songs, 435
active layer, *d203*
Addis Ababa, Ethiopia, 310
Adebajo, Adekeye, *q346*
Adulis, 303
Aegean coast, climate of, 230
Afghani people, 243
Afghanistan, *m225*; civil wars in, 238; climate of, 230; Hindu Kush mountain range, 226, 230; Khyber Pass and, 176; Kunduz, outdoor market in, *p97*; languages of, 243; as poor country, 245; Taliban and, 239; where people live in, 241. *See also* Southwest Asia
Africa, *m30*; as continent, 52; emigration from, 78; forests in, 51; Gondwana land mass, 484; Islam religion and, 234; population growth in, 73, 75; slaves from, 390; urbanization in, 81. *See also* Central Africa; East Africa; North Africa; Southern Africa; West Africa.
African National Congress (ANC), 393
Africans, The (Lamb), *q350*
African enslaved people. *See slave trade*
Afrikaners, in South Africa, 393, 398
Afrikaans language, 393
Age of Discovery, Southeast Asia and, 159
Agra, India, *p185*
agricultural revolution, 334
agriculture: development of, in Central Africa, 332, 334–35; farming methods, 233; India, 189; industry, 97; Mesopotamia, 232–33; prehistoric societies, 156–57; slash-and-burn, *p74*, 331–32; Tanzania, 316. *See also* farming
Ahmad, Muhammad, 306
AIDS-related deaths: in Southern Africa, 400–1; in West Africa, 373. *See also* HIV/AIDS
Aimak people, 243
Air Massif, 354

Akbar the Great, 185
Akosombo Dam, 356
Aksum, 302–3
Al-Azhar University, 285
Alexander the Great, 208
Alexandria, Egypt, 269, 303
Algeria, *m262*; aquifer in, 271; cooking in, 282; economic issues in, 283–84; film industry in, 282–83; independence of, 278; location of, 264; mountains in, 265; Muslim fundamentalists and, 286; natural gas in, 270; North Africa and, 277; rock formations in, *p55. See also* North Africa
Algiers, Algeria, 281
Allah, 234
alluvial plain, 177, 228
Alma-Ata, 213
al-Mawahib, Abu, 304
Almoravids, 362
al-Qaddafi, Muammar, *p263*, 278–79, *p278*, 283
al-Qaeda, 239
Amazon rain forest. *See* **rain forest; tropical rain forest**
Ambo peoples, 396
American Pacific islands, economies of, 465
American Somoa, 451, 465
Amin, Idi, 308
Amman, Jordan, 81
Amnok River, 120
Amu Dar'ya River, 204, 209, 213, 219
Amundsen, Roald, 480
Amundsen Sea, 477
Amur River, 204
Anabon, 329
Anatolian Peninsula, 235, 236
Anatolian Plateau, 227
ANC. *See* **African National Congress (ANC)**
ancient Egypt, 272–75, *m273*; expansion of Egypt, 273; influence of, 274–75; religion and culture in, 273–74; rise of, 272. *See also* Egypt
Andaman Sea, 153
Angkor Thom, 158
Angkor Wat, 158; Hindu temple at, *p157*
Angola, *m379*; colonialism in, 391; escarpment in, 381; ethnic and culture groups, 396; hard times in, 346; independence for, 392; infant death in, 400; as oil producer, 386, 401; population of, 394–95; Portuguese language in, 397; progress and growth in, 401; in Southern Africa, 380. *See also* Southern Africa
animals. *See* **wildlife**

anime characters, *p136*
animism, 166, 370
Annamese Cordillera, 151
Antarctica, 471–90; climate of, 477–78; as continent, 52; freshwater in ice caps of, 61; in Gondwana land mass, 484; ice sheets covering, 56; living in, 482–83; ozone levels over, 484; physical geography of, 474–79; plants and wildlife, 478–79; researcher in, *p471*; resources of, 479; results of research, 484–85; rock, ice, and water on, 475–77; as scientific continent, 482–85; size of, 474–75; surrounded by water, 59; timeline, *c472*–73; tourism to, 485
Antarctic Circle, 477
Antarctic Conservation Act, 481
Antarctic Treaty, 480–81
ANZUS Pact, 431
apartheid, 393, 401. *See also* human rights violation
aquifer, 271, 419
Arabian Desert, 228, 229
Arabian Peninsula, 227, 294; Arabian Desert and, 228; as arid region, 229; birth of Islam and, 276; religion of, 234, 243
Arabian Sea, 177, 180, 227, 294
Arabic language, 242, 283, 303, 312
Arab-Israeli conflict, 237–38, 246
Arabs, 243, 280; language of, 242; settlement of East African coast of Indian Ocean, 303
Arab Spring, 246, 279, 284, 286
Arab traders, 396
Aral Sea, 204; shrinking, 218–19, *p218*
Ararat Plain, Armenia, 215
Ararat volcano, Turkey, 227
archipelago, 118, 451–52
Arctic Circle, 202; ozone levels over, 484
Arctic climate, 203. *See also* polar climate
Arctic Ocean: freshwater in ice caps of, 61; *Rossiya* breaks ice in, *p204*; as smallest ocean, 62
Argentina: Antarctica and, 481
arid climate: in Central Asia, 203; in North Africa, 268; in Southwest Asia, 229–31; of West Africa, 356–57
Armenia, *p215*; in the Caucasus region, 201; climate of, 203; ethnic unrest in, 216; as independent state, 210, 211; language and religion of, 215; people of, 214. *See also* Caucasus region
Armenian Apostolic Church, *p215*
Armstrong, Neil, *c17*
arts/culture, 85; Central Africa, 344; East Africa, 314–15; East Asia, 134–37; Maori people,

427, 435, p435; North Africa, 282–283; South Asia, 191; Southeast Asia, 166; Southwest Asia, 243–44; West Africa, 371–72. *See also* culture

Aryan civilization, 183, 184

Ascension, 354

ASEAN. *See* **Association of Southeast Asian Nations (ASEAN)**

Ashoka, 185

Asia: as continent, 52; emigration from, 78; forests in, 51; immigration from, 396; as part of Gondwana land mass, 484; population growth in, 73, 75. *See also* Central Asia; East Asia; South Asia; South East Asia; Southwest Asia

Association of Southeast Asian Nations (ASEAN), 101, 168

astronomy, 274

Aswam High Dam, 267

Atatürk ("Father of the Turks"), 236

Atlantic Ocean: Central African coast on, 329; relative size of, 62; Southern African coast on, 380

Atlas Mountains, 265, 268, 270, p265

atmosphere, 44; pollution of Earth's, 74

atoll, 177, 453, p178; formation of, d453

Auckland, New Zealand, 433

Aussies, 434, 435. *See also* Australia

Australia, 413–46, m415; Aboriginals of, 424–25; agreements with Oceania, 458; Antarctica and, 481; ANZUS Pact, 431; climates of, 421; as continent, 52; culture in, 435; economy of, 436; humans migrating to, 424; international trust funds for islands in Oceania, 465; landforms, 416–18; life in, 432–39; migration from Oceania to, 464; natural resources, 436, 438; people of, 432; plants and animals of, 423; rural areas of, 433; surrounded by water, 59; territories in Oceania, 451; timeline, c414–15; trading partner with New Zealand, 437; waterways of, 418–19

Australian Outback, 417, 421, 433

axis, 42

Ayers Rock, 417, p417

Azerbaijan, m198; in the Caucasus region, 201; climate of, 203; ethnic unrest in, 216; as independent state, 211; as oil and gas producer, 205; people of, 214; religion in, 215; Soviet legacy in, 218; territorial issues in, 219

Azeris people, 214

Babylonians, 232–33

Baghdad, Iraq, 241; woman after voting, p223

Bahrain: Arab Spring and, 246; border of Persian Gulf, 228; democracy movements in, 239

Baloch people, 243

Bamako, Mali, 370

Bambuti people, 341

Bamileke people, 342

bananas, 361

Banda Aceh tsunami, p153

Bangalore, India, 189

Bangladesh, 190, m175; British rule of, 186; population, 188. *See also* South Asia

Bangla language, 190

Bangui, Central African Republic, 344

Bani Wadi Khalid riverbed, p229

Bantu language, 303, 341, 342, 361

barracoons, 336

basin, 355

Bass Strait, 436

Bast, Joseph, q486

Bathurst, New South Wales, 428

Battle of Adwa, 306

Battle of Omduman (Sudan), p305

Battuta, Ibn, 304

bay, 62

Bay of Bengal, 177, 178

Bedouin peoples, 229, 241

Beijing, China, 121

Belgium: as colonizing country, 338, 339; in West Africa, 365

Bengali language, 190

Bengaluru, India, 189

benga **music,** 314

Benghazi, Libya, young people protest Qaddafi in, p286

Benguela ("Skeleton Coast"), 385

Benin, 359, 365, m353. *See also* West Africa

Benue River, 355

Berber people, 276, 282, 361; language of, 283

Berlin Conference of 1884–1885, 365, 391

Bhutan, m175. *See also* South Asia

Biafra, 367

biodiversity, 332

Bioko, 329

biome, 50

biosphere, 44, 74; Australia, 439; New Zealand, 439; Oceania island formation, 453

Black Sea: in Caucasus region, 201, 203; connected to Atlantic Ocean, 228; Turkey on, 227

Black Volta River, 356

blood diamonds, 387

Blue Nile, 266, 296, p296

Boers (Dutch) peoples, 390

Boer War (1899), 390, p391

Bokassa, Jean-Bédel, 339

"Bollywood," 191

Bombay, 191

boomerang, 435

Borneo, 151, 156

Botswana, m379; British control of, 391; climate in, 384; democratic governments in, 401; energy resources in, 386; ethnic and culture groups, 396; HIV/AIDS, 400; infant death in, 400; Kalahari desert covering, 381; population of, 394; in Southern Africa, 380. *See also* Southern Africa

boycott, 186

Brahman, 183

Brahmaputra River, 176–78

Brazzaville, Republic of the Congo, 341

Brisbane, Australia, 433

Britain. *See* **Great Britain; United Kingdom**

British rule: in Australia, 427–30; in New Zealand, 430; in Southern Africa, 390

British territory: in modern South Asia, 186–87, m186. *See also* colonial history

Brunei, 151, m149. *See also* Southeast Asia

Bryce Canyon National Park, 55

Buddha, 184, p184

Buddhism, c84, 184–185; in Australia, 432; in China, 126, 135; in Korea, 127; in New Zealand, 432; in South Asia, 191; in Southeast Asia, 166; spread of, 157

Buddhist monastery: Thimphu, Bhutan, p174

Buddhist monk: in Cambodia, p161

Burkina Faso, m353; in Empire of Mali, 363; as French colony, 366; rivers in, 356; in West Africa, 354; young girl from, p69. *See also* West Africa

Burma. *See* **Myanmar**

Burundi, 307, 308, 347

bush, 433

cacao tree, 366

CAFTA-DR. *See* **Dominican Republic-Central America Free Trade Agreement**

Cairo, Egypt, 276, 281; craftsperson in, p283; as primate city, 81; spices sold at souk in, p281

Calcutta, India, 189, 191

caliph, 234, 276

calligraphy, 135

call to prayer, 280

calving, 476

Cambodia, 150, m149; Buddhist monk in, p161; economy of, 163; independence of, 162; literacy rate in, 167; Mekong River through, 153; as poor country, 168; shadow-puppet theater in, 166; Tonle Sap in, 158; Vietnamese forces invade, 163. *See also* Southeast Asia

Cameroon: ethnic groups in, 341; German rule of, 338; as independent nation, 339, m338; Lake Chad in, 356; mineral resources in, 333; urban population in, 342

Canaan, 233

Canada: farmland in rural, p77; population doubling time in, 73

canals, 57

Cantonese cuisine, 136

Cantonese language, 134

canyons, 383

Cape Colony, 390

Cape of Good Hope, 380, 390

Cape Ranges, 381

Cape Town, South Africa, 23, 397, p378

Cape Verde, 354

capital: as factor of production, 97

Index

carbon dioxide, 181
Carthage, 275
cartographer, 29
cartography, p30
Casablanca, Morocco, 281
cash crops, 462–63
Caspian Sea: in Caucasus, 201; desert land near, 209; Kazakhstan along, 202; as landlocked, 228; oil fields and, 205; territorial issues, 219
cassava, 336
Catholic Church. *See* **Christianity; Roman Catholic Church**
Caucasus Mountains, 201, 203
Caucasus region, 197–222, *m198*; climates in, 203; countries of, 201; early history of, 210; electricity production in, 205; energy and mineral resources, 205; ethnic unrest in, 216; forests in, 205; history of, 210–11; Islam and, 210; language and religion of, 215; musicians performing in, *p201*; natural resources, 204–5; people and places of, 214–15; population of, *m214*; Russian and Soviet rule, 210–11; Soviet legacy in, 217–18; Soviet Union annex of, 211; waterways in, 204
Central Africa, 325–50, *m327*; agriculture, development of, 334–35; city and country, 341–42; climate zones, 330; colonialism, 337–39; crops, adoption of new, 336–37; culture and arts, 344; daily life, 343–44; early settlement, 334–35; European contact and afterward, 335–38; growth and environment, 345; history, 334–39; how people live, 343–44; independence of, *m338*; independent nations, 339; landforms, 328–29; language, 342–43; life in, 340–45; mineral resources, 335; people of, 340–43; population, 340–41; rain forest, 330–31; religion, 343; resources, 332–33; savannas, 331–32; slave trade, 335–36; timeline, *c326–27*; waterways, 329–30; woman carrying produce on head, *p335*
Central African Republic: city-dwellers in, 342; French rule over, 338; as independent nation, 339; as landlocked, 329, 333; life expectancy in, 340; modernization and, 344
Central Asia, 197–222, *m198–99*; climates in, 203; countries of, 200–1; energy and mineral resources, 205; ethnic unrest, 216; forests in, 205; history of, 208–10; Islam religion and, 208–9, 234; landforms in, 201–2; mountains areas of, 203; natural resources in, 204–5; oil and gas resources in, 205; people and places, 212–14; plains and deserts in, 202; population, 213–14, *m214*; public health in, 218; regions of, 200–1; Russian rule and after, 209–10; Soviet legacy in, 217–18; territorial issues in, 219; timeline, *c198–99*; waterways in, 204. *See also entries for individual countries*
central Australia, 422

central highlands, South Asia, 177
Central Lowlands, 416–17
Central Rift, 311
Central Siberian Plateau, 205
Chad, 354–58, *m353. See also* West Africa
Chaggas peoples, 314
Chandragupta, 185
Chang Jiang River, 119, 123
Chao Phraya River, 153
Chennai, India, 189
cherry trees, Mount Fuji and, *p118*
Chewa ethnic group, 396
Chiang Kai-shek, 128
China, 200–1, 204, *m115*; as Australia trading partner, 436; climate of southeastern, 121; coal deposits in, 123; conquest of Red River delta, 157; Cultural Revolution, 130; dynasties of, 125, *c126*; early, 124–25; on East Asia mainland, 117; human rights in, 139; modern, 129–30; as New Zealand trading partner, 437; "one-child" policy in, 132; population concentration along, 76; population of, 188; Qinzang rail system in, *p117*; religions in, 135; Republic of (see Taiwan); rivers in, 119; Siberia and, 208; Sichuan Province, 136; as Southern Africa trading partner, 388; Three Gorges Dam in, *p56*; "two Chinas," 129; U.S. trade deficit with, 138, *g139. See also* East Asia
Chinese New Year, 79
Chinese peoples, 206, 208
cholera, 400
Choson dynasty, 127
Christchurch, New Zealand, 433
Christian Armenians, 210–11
Christian Bible, 244
Christianity, *c84*; Age of Discovery and, 159; Aksum kings adoption of, 303; in Armenia, 210, *p215*; in Australia and New Zealand, 432; birth of, 233; in East Africa, 313; in Georgia, 210; in Kazakhstan, 215; in Kenya, 313; in Lebanon, 243; in North Africa, 276; in Oceania, 457, 461; palm procession in Jerusalem, *p234*; in Siberia, 215; in Siberian Russia, Central Asia, and Caucasus, 215; in South Asia, 191; in Southern Africa, 396; in Syria, 243; in Tanzania, 313; in West Africa, 367, 369, 370. *See also* Christian missionaries
Christian missionaries: in Africa, 338; in Japan, 129; in Oceania, 457. *See also* missionaries
Church of St. George: Lalibela, Ethiopia, *p312*
CIA World Factbook: on Libya, *q290*
civil disobedience, 187, 393
civil war: defined, 279; Somalia, 308–9; in Southwest Asia, 238–39; in West Africa, 367
clan, 311
climate: Australia, 416, 421; Central Africa, 330; Central Asia, Siberia, and Caucasus, 203; changes to, 51; climate zones, 49–51, *p49*; defined, 23,

48; East Africa, 298–99; East Asia, 120–121; elements affecting, 46–49; elevation and, 47; landforms and, 48–49; Mediterranean, 230; New Zealand, 422; North Africa, 267–70; Oceania, 454; South Asia, 178–79; Southern Africa, 383–85; Southwest Asia, 229–30; weather vs., 48; wind and ocean currents and, 47–48. *See also entries for specific countries*
climate change: Antarctica and, 484–85; worldwide, 51. *See also* global warming
Clinton, Hillary, 284
coal mining: in Australia, 429; in Russian Siberia, 207; in Southwest Asia, 231
coastal area, 62
coastal plain, 56
cocoa, 366
Cold Temperate climate, 49–50
collectives, 208
colonial history, 191
colonialism: in Central Africa, 337–39; in Southeast Asia, 159–61; in Southern Africa, 390–91
colonization. *See* **European colonization**
command economy, 96
commercial fishing. *See* **fish and fishing**
communication system, 192
communism, 129
Communist government: in Myanmar, 163; in North Vietnam, 162; People's Republic of China, 129
Comoros, 380, 391
compass rose, 28
component, 23
condensation, 64
Confucianism, 126, 127, 135
Confucius, 125
Congo. *See* **Democratic Republic of the Congo; Republic of the Congo**
Congo Free State, 337, 338
Congo River, 328, 329, 341
coniferous tree, 205
constitution, 286
constitutional monarchy, 163
continent, 52
continental island, 451
continental shelf, 60
continents, 59, *m16–17*
converted, 276
Cook, James, 428, *p428*, 430
Cook Islands, 451
Coptic Christian church, 280, 287
coral, growth of, 453
coral reef, 418
core, Earth's, 43, *d43*
Côte d'Ivoire, *m353*, 365, 366. *See also* West Africa

cottage industry, 192
cotton cloth trade, *m365*
countries, boundaries of, 29
coup, 339
couscous, 282
***Couscous and Other Good Food from Morocco* (Wolfert),** 290
craftsperson: in Cairo Egypt, *p283*
creole language, 369
Crusades, 235
crust, Earth's, 43, *d43*
Cuba: command economy in, 96
cultural blending, 79, 89
cultural region, 86
Cultural Revolution, in China, 130
culture, 82–86; Central Africa, 344; cultural changes, 88–89; cultural regions, 86; customs and, 84–85; defined, 82; East Africa, 314–15; East Asia, 134–37; economy and, 86; elements of, 82–86; ethnic groups and, 83; global, 89; government and, 85–89; history and, 85; language and, 83; Oceania, 460–61; population growth and, 75. *See also* arts/culture
culture groups: Aboriginal, 435; Australia, 435; Maori, 435; New Zealand, 435; North Africa, 280–83; Oceania, 460–61; Southern Africa, 396. *See also* ethnic groups *and entries for individual groups*
cuneiform, 233
currency, 101; Indian, *p190*
customs, cultural, 84–85
cyclone, 155, 178
daily life: Central Africa, 343–44; East Africa, 313–14; East Asia, 136–37; Kazakhstan, 216; North Africa, 281–82; Southeast Asia, 166–67; Southwest Asia, 244–45; Tajikistan, 217; Uzbekistan, 216–17; West Africa, 371–72
dalits, 193
dam: Akosombo Dam, 356; Aswām High, 267; in Central Africa, 330; Kariba Gorge, 386; Sayano-Shushenskaya, *p209*; in South Asia, 180
Damascus, 241
Danakil Plain, 295
dance: in Maori, 427, 435, *p435*; in South Asia, 191; in West Africa, 372. *See also* arts/culture
Daoism, 125, 126, 135
Dar es Salaam, Tanzania, 310
Darfur, 318, 320
Davis Sea, 477
Dead Sea, 61, 228, 295, *p224*
death rate, 72–73
de Blij, H.J., *q38*
debt relief, 373
Deccan Plateau, 177, 178, 179
deciduous trees, 205
de facto state, 116
deforestation, 193, 333, 386
Dehejia, Vidya, *q196*

Delhi, India, 80
delta, 62, 177, 178
democracy, 86–87; Arab Spring and, 246; in Australia, 430–31; in Ghana, 366; in North Africa, 285; in Southern Africa, 401; in Southwest Asia, 239
Democratic Republic of the Congo (DRC), 296, 332, 333; population of, 340; religion in, 343; Savoia glacier on border of, *p298*; subsistence farming in, 341
Denakil plain, 295
Denver, Colorado: as "mile High City", 22
desalinization, 61, 247
desert: as biome, 50; in Central Asia, 202–3; formation of, 43; in North Africa, 268; in Siberia, 202–3; in Southern Africa, 385; of Southwest Asia, 228–31. *See also* dry zone *and entries for individual desert regions*
desert climate, 49–50
desertification, 299, 360, 376
"desert island," 452
developed countries, 98
dialect, 83
diamonds: industrial, from DRC, 332; in South Africa, 364, 386, 387
dictatorship, 87
didgeridoo, 435
Dien, Albert, *q222*
dingoes, 425
disease: population growth and, 74–75; in Southern Africa, 400, *p400*
Disney World, *p22*
diverse, 311–12, 368. *See also* ethnic groups
diversified economy, 284
Dixon, David L, *q470*
Djibouti, 294, 296; Arabic and French languages spoken in, 312; drought in, 299; *futa* garments, 314; geothermal energy and, 301; mineral resources of, 300; population, 310; temperature of, 298
Dominican Republic-Central America Free Trade Agreement (CAFTA-DR), 101
dominion, 430–31
Dong Son, 157
Douala, Cameroon, 342
doubling time, 73
Drakensberg Mountains, 381
DRC. *See* **Democratic Republic of the Congo**
"Dreaming, the," 425
drought: Australia, 421; Ethiopia, 308–9; health issues and, 317; land abuse during, 376; northwestern India, *p180*; Papua New Guinea, 454; Somalia, 299; South Asia, 183; Southern Africa, 384
drugs: pharmaceutical, making new, *i95*
drumming, 344

dry zone: South Asia, 178; West Africa, 357–58
Dubai, 241
Durban, South Africa, 397
Dutch East India Company, 428
Dutch settlement, in South Africa, 364
dynamic, 20
dynasty, 124. *See also* China, dynasties of
dysentery, 400
Earth, 42–51, *p44*; atmosphere of, 51; climate on, 46–51 (*See also* climate); crust of, 53; deepest location on, 60; effects of human actions on, 56; erosion and, 55; forces of change, 52–57; inside, 43; landforms on, 56, 58–60; layers of, 43–44, *d43*; orbit of, 42, 45–46; physical systems of, 44; plate movements on, 53–54; population growth on, 72–75; saltwater vs. freshwater on, *i60*; seasons and tilt of, *d45*; seasons on, 45–46; sun and, 42–43; surface of, 52; tilt of, 45, *d45*; water on, 60–65; weathering of, 55
earthquake: American Samoa, 465; Caucasus region, 201; defined, 54; Japan, 118, 142; New Zealand, 419, 421; Oceania, 467; Philippines, *p54*; plate movement and, 54; South Asia, 183; Turkey (1999), *p227*
East Africa, 291–324, *m36*, *m293*; Aksum, 303; Ancient Nubia, 302; anthropology and ecology, 315; Bantu people in, 361; bodies of water, 296–97; climates of, 298–99; colonization of, 304–7; daily life, 313–14; economic development in, 315–16; environmental issues, 316–17; health issues, 317; history of, 302–9; independence, 307–9; land and wildlife, 301; landforms, 294–96; life in, 310–17; national park system, 315; people of, 310–13; physical geography of, 294–301; regions, 294 (*See also entries for individual regions*); religion in, 312–13; resources of, 300–1; Sahel in, 357; timeline, *c292–93*; trade cities, 303–4
East African Rift, Kenya, *p295*
East African Rift Valley, 294–95
East Antarctica, 475
East Asia, 113–46, *m115*; art forms in, 135; bodies of water, 119–20; challenges facing, 138–39; in change, 128–29; climate of, 120–21; culture in, 134–37; daily life in, 136–37; economies and environments, 137–38; education in, 136; energy resources, 122–23; forests in, 123; history of, 124–31; landforms of, 116–19; mainland of, 117; minerals in, 122; modern, 129–31; natural resources of, 121–23; physical geography of, 116–23; population of, 132–33; regional overview, 116–17; Silk Road, *m127*; timeline, *c114–15*; trade with, 138; urbanization in, 133
East China Sea, 119
Eastern Ghats, 177, 179, 181
Eastern Hemisphere, 26, *c27*
Eastern Highlands, 417

East Jerusalem, 238
East Sea, 118
East Timor: independence of, 162; literacy rate in, 167; religion in, 166
economic systems, 96
economy: American Pacific islands, 465; Australia, 436; basic economic question, 94–96; culture and, 86; East Asia, 137–38; economic activities, 97; economic organizations, 100–1; economic performance, 98; economic systems, 96–98; factors of production, 97, *d98*; global, 99–101; Japanese, 131; Oceania, 462–65; Papua New Guinea, 462–63; Southeast Asia, 168–69; three economic questions, *i95*; types of national economies, 98–99; West Africa, 372–73
ecotourism, 168, 192, 317
Edo peoples, 366
Egypt, *m263;* Ancient (see Ancient Egypt); break with Muslim nations, 287; farms in, 281; independence of, 278; location of, 264; natural gas in, 271; new constitution in, 286; Nile River in, 264, 266, 271, 296; population concentration in, 76; population growth in, 284; rainfall in, 269; Rome's defeat of, 275; water in, 271. *See also* North Africa
Eid al-Fitr (Festival of Breaking Fast), 245
Ekurhuleni, South Africa, 397
electricity: in Caucasus, 205; in Southern Africa, 386
elephant, 383
elevation, 58; climate and, 47; on maps, 29
El Niño, 421, 454
embargo, 393
emigrate, 78
Emi Koussi, 355
Empire of Mali, *m362,* 363
endemic, 155
Energy Information Administration: *Saudi Arabia, q252*
energy resources, 74; South Asia, 180–81; Southern Africa, 386; West Africa, 359
engineering, 274
England. *See* **Great Britain; United Kingdom**
English language: in Australia, 433; in East Africa, 312; by Maori peoples, 427; in New Zealand, 433; in North Africa, 283; in South Asia, 190; in West Africa, 369
English South Africans, 393, 398
Ennedi, 355
environment, the: Australia and New Zealand, 438–39; Central Africa, 345; climate zone and, 50; defined, 23; East Africa, 316–17; East Asia, 137–38; Oceania, 467; population growth's effects on, 74; society and, *c24;* in South Africa, 23; Southeast Asia, 169

environmental disaster, Aral Sea, 218–19
environmental hazards, 23
Environmental Protection Agency, "Smart Growth and Schools," *q104*
Epic of Gilgamesh, 233
Equator, 21, *c21,* 26; Central Africa on, 330; climate around, 46; warm air masses near, 47; water currents and, 48
Equatorial Guinea, 329, 333, 338–40, 344
equinoxes, 46
ergs, 268, 269
Eritrea, 294, 306
erosion, 55, 452; in West Africa, 354
escarpment, 381. *See also* Great Escarpment
estuary, 329
Ethiopia, 294; Blue Nile in, 266; Danakil Plain in, 295; drought/famine in (1980s), *p41;* drought in, 299; earliest known humans from, 315; ethnic groups in, 311; HIV/AIDS, 317; independent, 306–7, 309; manufacturing in, 316; Menelik II, *p306;* mineral resources of, 300; population of, 310–11; religion in, 312; tsunami in, 140. *See also* East Africa
Ethiopian Orthodox Church, 312
ethnic groups: Caucasus, 216; Central Africa, 340–41; defined, 83; East Africa, 310–12; East Asia, 134; Oceania, 459–60; South Asia, 190; Southeast Asia, 166; Southern Africa, 396; Southwest Asia, 242–43; West Africa, 368–69
Etosha National Park, 383
Etosha Pan, 383
EU. *See* **European Union**
eucalyptus tree, 423, 436
Euphrates River, 228, 232, 247
Eurasia, 235
Eurasian Plate, 152
Europe, *m30;* as continent, 52; emigration from, 78; urbanization in, 81
European colonization: in Africa, 305–6; in Australia and New Zealand, 427–28; in East Africa, 304–6; in Southern Africa, 390–91. *See also* colonialism
European Union (EU), 101
evaporation, 63
experience, perspective of, 20
exports, 99
extended families, 370
factors of production, 97, *d98*
fales, 461
family: in Southern Africa, 399. *See also* daily life
famine, 317
Fang people, 341
farming, *p246;* Australia, 429, 434; Egypt, 281; Libya, 282; Morocco, 282; New Zealand, 434, 437; Nile River and, *p266;* Papua New Guinea, 463; Southeast Asia, 168; Tanzania, 314. *See also* agriculture

Farsi language, 242
Fatamids, 276
fault, 54
fauna, 155
Federated States of Micronesia, 450
felafel, 282
fellaheen, 281
Festival of Breaking Fast (Eid al-Fitr), 245
feudalism: in Japan, 128
Fickling, David, *q446*
Fiji, 451, *p457,* 467
film industry: in Algeria, 282–83; in New Zealand, 437
First Fleet, 428
fish and fishing: American Samoa, 465; Antarctica, 479; Central Africa, 333; Lake Victoria, *p297;* Oceania, 463; overfishing, 467; Papua New Guinea, 455; South Asia, 192; Southeast Asia, 168
fishing grounds, 271
fjords, 420
floods and flooding, 178; of Niger River (West Africa), 355; Oceania, 467
flora, 155
food: East Asia, 136; in North Africa, 282; in West Africa, 361
foreign rule, of North Africa, 277–78
forests: cutting and burning, *p74,* 331–32; in Siberia, 204–5; in South Asia, 181
fossil fuels: effects on water supply, 65
fossil water, 247
Four Noble Truths, 184
Fouta Djallon, 355, 356
France: agreements with Oceania, 458; colonies in Southern Africa, 391; as colonizing country, 338, 339, 364–65; Morocco and, 278; North Africa and, 277, 278; possession of Madagascar, 389; territories in Oceania, 451; trading in West Africa and, 364; West Africa and, 365–66
Freetown, 364
free trade, 100
French language, 283, 369; in Djibouti, 312
French Polynesia, 451, 458
French Sudan, 366
freshwater, 61; in Antarctic ice sheet, 475; salt water vs., *i60*
Fukushima Daiichi nuclear power plant, 142
Fulani people, 342, 344
fundamentalist, 279
futa, 314
Gabon: city-dwellers in, 342; independence of, *m338;* as independent nation, 339; minerals in, 332; slave trade in, 336
Gambia, 365, 366
Gandhi, Indira, 193, *p175*

Gandhi, Mohandas, *p175*, 186, *p187*; on Indian currency, *p190*

Gandhi, Rajiv, 193

Ganges Delta, 180

Ganges River, 176–78, *p177*

gas. *See* **natural gas**

Gautama, Siddhãrtha, 184

Gaza Strip, 238, 246

GDP. *See* **gross domestic product (GDP)**

Gebel Katherina, 265

gems. *See* **mineral resources**

genocide, 308, 346

geographer's tools, 26–33; geospatial technologies, 30–33; globes, 26; maps, 27–30

geographic information system (GIS), 31–32

geography: defined, 18; five themes of, 20–24; human, 70–104; physical, 39–68; six essential elements of, 24, *c24*; skill building, 25; uses of, *c24*

Geography (de Blij and Muller), *q38*

Geography Activity: Antarctica, *m488*; Australia and New Zealand, *m444*; Central Africa, *m348*; Central Asia and Siberian Russia, *m220*; continents, *m66*; East Africa, 322; East Asia, *m144*; India, *m102*; Kenya, *m36*; North Africa, *m288*; Oceania, *m468*; South Africa, *m402*; South Asia, *m194*; Southeast Asia, *m170*; Southwest Asia, *m250*; West Africa, *m374*

Georgia (Caucasus region), 201; climate of, 203; ethnic unrest in, 216; independence of, 210–11, *p210*; population of, 214; religion in, 215; Soviet legacy in, 218

geospatial technologies, 30–33; geographic information system (GIS), 31–32; Global Positioning System (GPS), 31; limits of, 33; satellites and sensors, 32–33

geothermal energy, 301, 436–37, 439

Germany, 211; Cameroon and, 338, 339; invasion of Caucasus, 211; invasion of Russia, World War II, 208; occupation of islands in Oceania during World War II, 457; West Africa and, 365

geysers, 419, 439

Ghana, *m353*; economic challenges for, 373; energy resources in, 358–59; people of, 376; rivers in, 356. *See also* West Africa

Ghana Empire, 362–63, *m362*

Gio people, 367

GIS. *See* **geographic information system (GIS)**

glacier, 56, 61, 420

global economy, 99–101; trade, 99–100. *See also* globalization

globalization: defined, 89; and indigenous cultures, 34–35. *See also* global economy

Global Positioning System (GPS), 31; satellites, *p32*

global warming, 439; debate over, 486–87; defined, 51; Oceania and, 467; ozone, 483, *d483*, 484

globes, 26, 27

Gobi Desert, 121

Golan Heights, 238

gold and gold trade: Afghanistan, 231; Ancient Egypt, 273; Australia, 428–29, 436; Kazakhstan, 205; New Caledonia, 455; Papua New Guinea, 455, 462; Russia, 205; salt and, 361, *p361*, 363; Southern Africa, 387, 388, 390; Uzbekistan, 205; West Africa, 359, 361, 366, 372

Gold Coast, 359, 366

Gold-for-salt trade, 361, *p361*, 363

Gondwana, 484

gorges, 382–83

government: Caucasus and Central Asia, 217–18; China, 135; forms of, 86–87; Myanmar, 169; Southern Africa, 401; Southwest Asia, 246; West Africa, 372–73

GPS. *See* **Global Positioning System (GPS)**

Grand Canyon, 55

Grand Mosque, *p234*

graphite, 180

graph skills, GDP comparison, *g99*

grassland, 50

Great Barrier Reef, 418, 439, *p418*

Great Britain: agreements with Oceania, 458; Antarctica and, 481; Australia and, 430–31; control of New Zealand, 430; control of Sudan, 306; international trust funds for islands in Oceania, 465; North Africa and, 278; occupation of islands in Oceania during World War II, 457; territories in Oceania, 451; trade in West Africa, 364; trading in West Africa, 366. *See also* United Kingdom

Great Dividing Range, 417, 425

Great Escarpment, 381, 382

Great Karoo, 381

Great Leap Forward, 130

Great Migration, 301

Great Rift System, 328

Great Rift Valley, 294–95, 301, 328, 383

Great Salt Lake, 61

Great Trek, 390

Great Wall of China, 125, *p125*

Great Zimbabwe, 388–89. *See also* Zimbabwe

Greek Empire, 210

Greenland, 52; ice sheets covering, 56

green revolution, 192

Greenwich, England, 21, 213, *m213*

griot, 371

gross domestic product (GDP), 98; comparing, *g99*

groundwater, 61, 419

Guam, 450, 451, *p459*, 465

Guangdong Province, 136

Guinea Highlands, 355

Guinea: bodies of water in, 355–56; Empire of Mali in, *m362*, 363; as French possession, 366; tropical rain forest in, 358

Guinea-Bissau, *m352*

Gujarati language, 190

gulf, 62

Gulf of Mexico: surrounded by landmasses, 62

Guptas, 185

haiku, 135

Hainan, China, rubbish-covered beach in, *p138*

hamadas, 269

Han, People of, 126

Han Chinese, 83

Han dynasty, 125, 126, *c126*, 157

Han ethnic group, 134

Hanoi, Vietnam, tourism in, *p168*

Han River, 120

Harappa, 182

Harare, Zimbabwe, 397

harmattan winds, 357

Hausa people, 367, 368

Hawaiian Islands, 451, 452; luau, 461

Hazari people, 243

health issues: in East Africa, 317; in Southern Africa, 399–401

heat energy, 436–37

Hebrew Bible, 244, *p234*

Hebrew language, 242

hemisphere, 26

hieroglyphics, 274

high islands, of Oceania, 452

highland countries, 308

High Mountain climate, 49–50

Hillary, Edmund, *p17*

hills, as landforms, 23

Himalaya Mountains: high altitudes in, *p181*; Kashmir region in, 187; Plateau of Tibet and, 117, 121; temperate zone and, 179

Hinduism, *c84*; in Australia, 432; birthplace of, 184; Ganges River and, 180, *p177*; growth of, 184; in India, 185; Islam and, 187; man in traditional clothes, *p173*; in New Zealand, 432; Sanskrit as language of, 183; in South Asia, 191; in Southeast Asia, 166; spread of, 157

Hindu Kush mountain range, 176, 226, 230

Hindu temple, *p184*; at Angkor Wat, *p157*

history: Australia and New Zealand, 424–31; Central Asia and Siberian Russia, 206–11; culture and, 85; East Africa, 302–9; East Asia, 124–31; New Zealand, 424–31; North Africa, 272–79; Oceania, 456–61; South Asia, 182–87; Southeast Asia, 156–63; Southern Africa,

388–93; Southwest Asia, 232–39; West Africa, 272–79

HIV/AIDS, 317; in Southern Africa, 400, 401; in West Africa, 373

holidays, in East Asia, 137

Holland, spice trade and, 160

Holocaust, 237

homelands, 393

homogenous, 216

Hong Kong: anime characters on billboards in, *p136*; China, Temple Street Night Market in, *p114*; high-rise buildings in, *p133*; languages in, 134; population of, 133

Honshū Island, Japan, 117, *p118*

Horn of Africa, 308–9

hot springs, 419, *p52*

Hot Springs, in Mount Hakone, Japan, *p53*

Huang He River, 119, 120, *p120. See also* Yellow River

human actions: damage to water supply, 65; effects on Earth's surface, 57

human-environment interaction, 23

human geography, 70–104; culture, 82–89; population growth, 72–75; population movement, 77–81; population patterns, 76–77; timeline, *c70–71*

human migration, from Oceania, 464, 465–66

human rights, 87

human rights violation, 393; Holocaust, 237; Liberia, 367; in New Zealand, 438; Oceania, 467; Rwanda, 308; Sudan, 318–21; Uganda, 308; United Nations and, 346–347

human systems, *c24*

Humid Temperate climate, 49–50

Huns, 206, 208

hunter-gatherers, 156; Aboriginals as, 424–25; in Central Africa, 334; in Siberia, 206

hurricanes: defined, 155

Hussein, Saddam, 239

Hyderabad, India, 189

hydroelectric power: Central Africa, 330, 333; East Africa, 300–1; Mekong River, 169; Togo and Nigeria, 359; West Africa, 356

hydropolitics, 247

hydrosphere, 44, 419, 453

Ice Age, 56

iceberg, 476

ice caps, 56, 61

ice sheet, 56, 61, 475

ice shelf, 476

Igbo peoples, 367

IMF. *See* **International Monetary Fund (IMF)**

immigrate, 78

immigration: to Australia and New Zealand, 439; to Zambia, 397

imperialism, 305, 365

import, 99

inactive volcano, *p292*

India, 80, *m175*; British rule of, 186, 187; climates in, 178, *m179*; conflicts with Pakistan, 193; drought in, *p180*; influence on early Southeast Asia, 157; man in traditional clothes for Hindu festival, *p173*; population of, *m102,*188; slaves from, in South Africa, 390; trading with Southern Africa, 388; tsunami in, 140; water in streets after rain in, *p46. See also* South Asia

Indian currency note, *p190*

Indian National Congress, 186–87

Indian Ocean: Arabian Sea as part of, 227; East African cities on, 310; East Asia and, 119; moisture from, 121, 178; relative size of, 62; Southeast Asia, 153; Southern Africa and, 380–82; tsunami in, 140, 142

Indian Plate, 152

indigenous peoples, *q34–q35. See also entries for individual indigenous groups*

indigenous rights, in New Zealand and Australia, 438

Indo-Australian Plate, 152

Indonesia, *m149*; Banda Aceh tsunami, *p153*; climate in, 23, 155; fishing in, 168; independence of, 162; invasion of Timor-Leste, 162; languages in, 166; latex plantation, *p154*; manufacturing in, 163; Mount Lokon volcano, *p53*; natural resources in, 152; plantations in, 168; shadow-puppet theater in, 166; Sunda Isles, 153; tin mining in, 169; tsunamis in, 140, 142, 152; volcanoes in, 152. *See also* Southeast Asia

Indus River, 176–77, 182, 193

industrialized countries, 98

Industrial Revolution, 81

industry: cottage, 192; defined, 97. *See also entries for individual industries*

Indus Valley, 182–83

Indus Valley civilization, 182–83

infant death, in Southern Africa, 400–1

infrastructure, 372

inland delta, 355

insular, 150

Intergovernmental Panel on Climate Change (IPCC), 486, *q487*

International Association of Antarctic Tour Operators, "Tourism Overview," *q490*

International Date Line, 26, 213, *m213*

International Forum on Globalization (IFG), *q35*

International Monetary Fund (IMF), 101, 373

international trade, *p88*, 99–101, *p100*

introduced species, 429, 440–43

Inya Lake, Myanmar, floating market in, *p148*

IPCC. *See* **Intergovernmental Panel on Climate Change (IPCC)**

Iran, *m225*; border of Persian Gulf, 228; carpets from, 244; civil wars in, 238–39; coal deposits in, 231; command economy in, 96; ethnic groups, 242; oil in, 231; plateau and mountain ranges in, 227; population of, 240–41; Shias of, 243; temperatures in mountainous areas of, 230; territorial issues in, 219. *See also* Southwest Asia

Iranian peoples, 206

Iraq, *m225*; civil wars, 238–39; ethnic groups, 242; oil in, 231; oil well fires in Kuwait, *p245*; Persian Gulf, 228; population of, 241; Tigris-Euphrates River system in, 247; tribal identity in, 242–43. *See also* Southwest Asia

Ireland, 429

iron artifact, *p326*

iron ore, 333, 350; in Australia, 436

iron-smelting technology, 361

iron tools, 335

Irrawaddy delta, 158

Irrawaddy River, 153

irrigation, 209; methods, 232–33; in Saudi Arabia, 247

Irtysh River, 204

Islam, *c84*; Africa, 86; Australia, 432; Central Asia, 208; daily life in, 244; modern, 287; monotheistic religion, 276; Mozambique, 396–97; in New Zealand, 432; North Africa, 369; prophet Muhammad, 233; Quran, 244; rise of, 276; South Asia, 191; Southeast Asia, 158–59, 166; Southwest Asia, 86; Soviet leaders and, 209; spread of, 234–35, *m235*, 243; Sunnis and Shia, 243; Tanzania, 313; Uzbekistan mosque, *p208*; West Africa, 363, 370. *See also* Islamic expansion; Muslims; North Africa, culture of

Islamic expansion, 234–36, *m235*

Islamic fundamentalism, 286

Islamic republic, 239

Island: formation of, 53; as landmass, 59; in Southeast Asia, 150–51

Israel, *m237*; area, 233; coast of, 227; Dead Sea and, 228; ethnic groups, 242; Muslim peace treaty with, 287; population of, 240–41. *See also* Arab-Israeli conflict

Israelites, 233

Istanbul, Turkey, 241

isthmus, 59

Italy: Carthage rule in, 275; Eritrea colony, 306; Libya and, 277

ivory, 387; trade, 388

Jaffa, Israel, *p224*

Jainism, 184, 185, 191

Jakarta, Indonesia, 165; climate in, 23; skyscrapers, *p148*; urbanization, 169

Japan, *m115*; access to Oceania's marine resources, 463; birthrate in, 133; climate of, 121; cultured

pearls harvested offshore, 122; economic growth of, 131; feudal system in, 128; forests in, 123; history of, 127–28; Honshu Island, Mt. Fuji on, *p118*; international trust funds for islands in Oceania, 465; Kuril Islands dispute with Russia, 139, 219; mineral resources in, 122; modern, 131; Mount Hakone in, *p53*; occupation of islands in Oceania during World War II, 457; religion in, 135; rise of, 129; rivers in, 120; Sea of Japan and, 119; trading partner with Australia, 436; tsunami in (2011), 142; World War II and, 131. *See also* East Asia

Japanese folding screen, *p128*

Java, 151, 152, 156

Javanese people, 166

Jerusalem: as holy city, 233; three religions in, *p234*

Jesus of Nazareth, 233

Jews, 242. *See also* Judaism

Jingxi, 135

Johannesburg, South Africa, 23, 398

Johor, Malaysia, *p88*

Jonglei Canal, 297

Jordan, *m225*; Arab Spring and, 246; coast of, 227; Dead Sea and, 228; ethnic groups, 242; Great Rift in, 295. *See also* Southwest Asia

Jordan River, 295

Jos Plateau, 355

Judaism, 233, 243, *c84*; Hebrew Bible scroll, *p234*

Kaaba, *p234*

Kabul, 227

Kalahari, 381, 385, 404

Kamba people, 311

Kamchatka, 219

Kannada language, 190

Kanuri people, 342

kapahaka, 426

Kaplan, Gordon, *q248*

Karakoram, 176, 187

Kara-Kum, 202

Kara-Kum Canal, 209

Kariba Gorge dam, 386

karma, 184

Karnow, Stanley, *q172*

Kashmir, 193

katabatic winds, 477

Kazakhstan, *m198*; in Central Asia, 200; coal in, 205; daily life in, 216; language and religion of, 215; mineral resources in, 205; mountain range in, *p202*; oil and gas resources in, 205; plains and deserts in, 202; population of, 213; Russian rule of, 209; territorial issues in, 219; USAID for, 222. *See also* Central Asia

Keen, Cecil, *q404*

Kemal, Mustapha (General), *p236*

kente, 371

Kenya, East Africa, 294; benga music, 314; climate of, 298; drought in, 299; earliest known humans in, 315; East African Rift in, 295, *p295*; energy resources in, 300–1; ethnic groups in, 311; geothermal energy and, 301; HIV/AIDS, 317; independence of, 307; as independent trading state, 303; Lake Victoria and, 297; languages spoken in, 312; life expectancy, 317; map of, *m36*, *m293*; Masai Mara National Reserve in, 301, 315; Masai nomadic lifestyle, 314; mineral resources of, 300; Mombasa, *p313*; Nairobi (capital), 310, *p311*, 313; oral tradition in, 314; rainfall in, 298; refugees from Somalia in, 309; religion in, 313; Samburu National Reserve, 315; temperatures in, 298; wildlife reserves in, 301

Kenya National Assembly, 312

Kenya National Museum, *p315*

Kenyatta, Jomo, 307, *p307*

key, map, 28

Khalkha Mongolian language, 134

Khan, Azmat, *q196*

Khan, Genghis, 235

Khan el-Khalili, spices sold at, *p281*

Khartoum, Sudan, *p296*, 302, 306, 309

Khmer Empire, 158

Khmer Rouge, 163

Khyber Pass, 176, 227, *p174*

Kikuyu people, 307, 311

Kilamanjaro, farming in plains around, 314

Kilwa trade city, 304

Kimbanguist Church, 343

Kingdom of Madagascar, 389. *See also* Madagascar

Kinshasa, Democratic Republic of the Congo, 341, 344

Kirghiz people, 216

Kiribati Island, 451, 455

kiwifruit, 437

Kiwis, 434, 435. *See also* New Zealand

knowledge, advances in, 274–75

Kolkata, India, 189, 191

Kongo people, 344

Köppen, Wladimir, 49

Korea, *m130*; divided, 130–31; history of, 126–27; Japanese control of, 129; religion in, 135; rivers in, 120. *See also* Korean Peninsula; North Korea; South Korea

Korean language, 134

Korean Peninsula, 118; forests in, 123; rivers on, 120; Yellow Sea and, 119

Korean War, 131

Koryo dynasty, 127

Kpong, 359

K-pop, 135

kraal, 314

Krahn people, 367

Krakatoa volcano, 152

krill, 479, 485

Kunduz, outdoor market in, *p97*

Kunlun Shan mountain range, 117

Kurdish families, traveling by cart, *p238*

Kurdish language, 242

Kurds, 238, 242, 243

Kuril Islands, 139, 219

Kurtz, Lester, *q404*

Kush, 302; pyramids of ancient, *p303*

Kushites, 302

Kuwait, *m225*; border of Persian Gulf, 228; civil wars in, 239; Iraq's invasion of, 245, *p245*; oil in, 231; oil wells on fire in, *p245*; population of, 240–41; as wealthy country, 245

Kyrgyzstan, *m198*; climate in, 203; in Central Asia, 200, 201; mineral resources in, 205; people of, 213, *m214*. *See also* Central Asia

Kyzyl Kum, 202

labor, as factor of production, 97

laborers and peasants, in South Asia, 183

lagoon, 453

Lagos, Nigeria, 370

Lake Albert, 295, 296

Lake Assal, 300; workers collect salt at, *p300*

Lake Baikal, 204

Lake Chad, 356, *p356*

Lake Malawi, 295, 297, 329, 383

Lake Nyasa, 329

lakes, 61; freshwater, *i60*, 61, 62; pollution of, *p65*

Lake Tanganyika, 295, 297, 329

Lake Taupo, 411

Lake Victoria: fishers in, *p297*; as largest lake in Africa, 297; Luhya people and, 311; Nile River begins at, 266, 296; Sukuma people and, 314

Lake Volta, 356

Lake Vostok, 485

Lalibela, Ethiopia: Church of St. George, *p312*

Lamb, David, *q350*

Lamu, 303

land: on Earth's surface, 44; as factor of production, 97, *d98*; surface features on, 58–59

landforms: bodies of water and, 59–60; Central Africa, 328–29; changing, 52–54; classification of, 58–59; climate and, 48–51; creation of, 53–57; defined, 23; East Africa, 294–96; ocean floor, 59–60; Southern Africa, 381–82; types of, 44; weathering of, 55; West Africa, 354–55

landlocked, 382

landmasses, shifting, 52–54

landscapes, 19; formation of, 43

languages and language groups: Arabic, 276; Australia, 433; Bantu, 361; Berber, 283; Caucasus, 215; Central Africa, 342–43; Central Asia, 215; culture and, 83; East Africa, 312; East Asia, 134; English, 283; French, 283; Maori, 427; New Zealand, 433; North Africa, 283; Oceania, 459–60; Papua New Guinea,

Index

460; Siberia, 215; slang, in Australia, 434; South Asia, 190; Southeast Asia, 166; Southern Africa, 396–97; Southwest Asia, 242–43; trade, 342; West Africa, 369. *See also entries for individual languages*

Laos, *m149*; collapse of government in, 163; independence of, 162; literacy rate in, 167; Mekong River through, 153; outdoor market in, *p78*; as poor country, 168; on Southeast Asia peninsula, 150. *See also* Southeast Asia

Laozi, 125

La Perouse, Jean-Francois, 457

Latex plantation, Indonesia, *p154*

Latin America. *See* **Mexico; South America**

latitude, 21, *c21, c27*

lawsuit, 438

leap year, 43

Lebanon, *m225*; in Canaan, 233; Christians in, 243; civil wars in, 238; coast of, 227. *See also* Southwest Asia

Lena River, 204, 205, 212

Leopold II (King of Belgium), 337, 338, *p337*

Leptis Magna, *p275*

Lesotho, *m379*; British control of, 390; climate of, 384; HIV/AIDS, 400; independence of, 391; Orange River in, 382; population in, 394; religion in, 396; subsistence farming in, 387; Taiwan's textile industry in, 401. *See also* Southern Africa

Liberia, 358, 364, 367

libraries, earliest, 275

Libya, *m263*; aquifers and, 271; Arab Spring and, 279; economic issues in, 283; farms in, 282; Italy seizure of, 277; Muammar al-Qaddafi in, 278, *p278*; in North Africa, 264; oil in, 270; population growth in, 284; poverty in, 283; rainfall in, 269; self-rule, 286; urbanization, 280. *See also* North Africa

Libyan Desert, 302, *p268*

Libyan refugees, *p79*

lichens, 202, 478, *p202*

life expectancy: in East Africa, 317; in West Africa, 373

Limpopo River, 382, 389

lions, 383

literacy: among North African women, 284–85; in East Africa, 316; in Libya, 284–85

lithosphere, 44, 54, 419, 453

Little Karoo, 381

Little League teams, in East Asia, 137, *p137*

Lituya Bay, Alaska, tsunami in, 140

Livingstone, David, 304–5

location, types of, 20–21

loess, 119

London, England: port security worker in, *p248–49*

longitude, 21, *c21, c27*

***Lord of the Rings* (Tolkein),** 437

low islands, of Oceania, 452

Lowland, of North Africa, 265

Luanda, Angola, 397, 398

luau, 461

Luhya people, 311

Luo people, 311; benga music and, 314

Lusaka, Zambia, 397

Luzon, 151

Macau, China, religious shrines in, *p134*

MacDonnell mountain range, 417

Madagascar, *m379*; early kingdoms of, 389; French-controlled, 391; land area, 380; language of, 396; tsunami in, 140. *See also* Southern Africa

Madras, India, 189

Magellan, Ferdinand, 160

magma, 43, 53

Mahabharata, 191

Mahatma, 186. *See also* Gandhi, Mohandas

Mahfouz, Naguib, 283

maize (corn), 336–37

Makkah (Mecca), Saudi Arabia, 233, 234, *p234*, 363

Malabo, Equatorial Guinea, 344

Malacca, Malaysia, 159; mosque on stilts near, *p158*; Portuguese conquest of, 160

Malagasy language, 396

malaria, 400

Malawi, *m379*; democratic governments in, 401; independence for, 391–92; infant death in, 400; Lake Malawi in, 297, 383; Malawian income, 395; Muslim population in, 396; population of, 395. *See also* Southern Africa

Malay Archipelago, 151, 158, 451

Malay Peninsula, 151, 153; climate in, 154–55; Malacca on, 159; religion in, 166

Malaysia, 150, 151, *m149*; fishing in, 168; independence of, 162; international trade, *p88*; manufacturing in, 163; natural resources in, 152; plantations in, 168; shadow-puppet theater in, 166; tin mining in, 152, 168, 169. *See also* Southeast Asia

Maldives, 176, 177. *See also* South Asia

Mali, *m353*; climate of, 356–57; Empire of, 363; as French colony, 366; mineral resources in, 359; Niger River in, 355–56; North African culture and, 371. *See also* Empire of Mali; West Africa

Malindi, 303

malnutrition, 400; in East Africa, 317

Manchuria, China, 206

Mandarin Chinese, 134

Mandela, Nelson, 393, *p393*, 404

Manila, Philippines: slum areas near, *p165*; urbanization in, 165, 169

Mano people, 367

Mansa Musa, 363, *p363*

mantle, Earth's, 43, *d43*

manufacturing: in Ethiopia, 316; in South Africa, 398. *See also* industry

Maori language, 427

Maori tattoo, 427

Maori tribe, 83, 426–27; population of, 432; rights of, 438, 446

Mao Zedong, 129, 130

map projections, 28–29

maps, 27–30; cartography as science of making, *p30*; distortion of, 27; information on, 27; large- vs. small-scale, *p28*, 29; map projections, 28–29; map scale, 29; parts of, 28; physical, 29–30; political, 29; relief on, 29, 30; types of, 29–30

Maputo, Mozambique, 397

Marathi language, 190

Margherita Peak, 328

Mariana Trench, 60

market economy, 96

Marshall Islands, 450, 454, 458

Masai Mara National Reserve, 301, 315

Masai people, 311; mother and son with mud home, *p313*; as nomads, 314

Massif, 354

Matadi, 329

mathematics, 274

Matmata, Tunisia: family meal in, *p282*

mature, 73

Mauritania: climate of, 356–57; Empire of Mali in, *m362*, 363; as French colony, 366; independence of, 366; North African culture and, 371; Sahara desert in, 354

Mauritius, 380, 389, 391

Mauryas, 185

Maya people: cassava cultivated by, 336; organized team sports and, 85

Mbundu peoples, 396

Mbuti people, 341

McDougall, Leanne, *q222*

Mecca. *See* **Makkah (Mecca), Saudi Arabia**

Mediterranean Sea: description of "sea" fits, 228; as link to North Africa, 266; Nile River empties to, 296; in Southwest Asia, 227; Suez Canal and, 267, 364

megalopolis, 80, 133, 165

Mekong Delta, Vietnam War and, *p162*

Mekong River, 153; hydroelectric power from, 169

Mekong River Commission, 169

Melanesia, 447, 450–51, *m448–49*. *See also* Oceania

Melbourne, Australia, 433

Menelik II (Ethiopian King), 306–7, *p306*

Mercado Camon del Sur, 101

merchant class, in South Asia, 183

MERCOSUR, 101

meridians, 21

Meru people, 311

Mesopotamia: early history in, 232–33; as "land between the rivers", 228; location of, 232; population density in, 241; social advances in, 232–33; Ziggurat of Ur in, *p233*

Mexico, population concentration along, 76

Mexico City, as megalopolis, 81

Micronesia, 447, *m448–49;* culture of, 460–61; location of, 450; low islands of, 452. *See also* Oceania

Mid-Atlantic Ridge, 60

Middle Ages, 275–76

Middle East, 239. *See also* Southwest Asia

migration: causes of, 78–79; to cities, 80; effects of, 79; human, from Oceania, 465–66

millet, 335

Mindanao, 151

mineral resources: Central Africa, 332–33, 335; Central Asia and Siberian Russia, 205; East Africa, 300; East Asia, 121–22; New Zealand, 437; North Africa, *p284;* Oceania, 455; South Asia, 180–81; Southeast Asia, 152; Southern Africa, 386, 387, 390; Southwest Asia, 231; West Africa, 359

Ming dynasty, 125, *C126*

mining, Papua New Guinea, 462; South Africa, 398. *See also* mineral resources

Min language, 134

minorities, 166

Minott, Geoff, *q222*

MIRAB economies (migration, remittances, aid, and bureaucracy), 464–65

missionaries, 338. *See also* Christian missionaries

mixed economy, 96

Mogadishu, Somalia, 303, 310; war-torn buildings in, *p292*

Mohenjo-Daro, 182, *p183. See also* Pakistan

Mombasa, 303, 310

monarchy, 87

Mongolia, *m115,* 202; on East Asia mainland, 117; population density in, 133. *See also* East Asia

Mongols: Central Asia conquest, 208, 212; invasion of China, 127; Persian conquest, 235; as Siberian invaders, 206

monolith, 417

monotheism, 191, 233, 276

monsoon, 178, 384, 454

Mopti, 355

Moroccans, 363

Morocco, *m262;* economic issues in, 284; farms in, 282; fishing grounds of, 271; food from, 290; freedom from France, 278; French influence of, 280; location of, 264; mountains in, 265, *p265;*

Muslim fundamentalists and, 286; rainfall in, 269

Moscow, Russia, 200

Mosi-oa-Tunya **("The Smoke That Thunders"),** 382

mosque, 281; in Samarkand, Uzbekistan, *p208*

mountains: Central Asia, 203; elevation of, 58–59; formation of, 43, 53; as landforms, 23; South Asia, 176–77, 180; tunnels through, 57; underwater, 60. *See also entries for specific mountains*

mountain spring, *p229*

Mount Everest, 31, 117, 176

Mount Fuji, *p118*

Mount Hakone, *p53*

Mount Kenya, 295, 329

Mount Kilimanjaro, *p292,* 295, 298, 329

Mount Lokon, *p53*

Mount Mayon, *p152*

Mount Toubkal, 265

movies, 191, 282, 436, 437

Mozambique, *m379;* aluminum in, 401; climate, 383, 384; escarpment, 382; ethnic groups in, 396; Great Rift Valley, 295; infant death in, 400; mineral resources in, 387; Muslim population in, 396; population of, 395; Portuguese language in, 397; Portuguese rule, 391, 392; size of, 380; tourism in, 401. *See also* Southern Africa

Mugabe, Robert, 392

Mughals and Mughal Empire, 185, 186

Muhammad, 233, 276

Muller, Peter O, *q38*

Mumbai, India, *p93,* 181, 189, 191

Murray-Darling River system, 418

Musgrave mountain range, 417

Music: Caucasus region, musicians in, *p201;* Central Africa, *p326,* 344, *p344;* East African, 314; Maori, 426, 435; North Africa, 281, 372; South Asia, 191; West African, 371–72. *See also* arts/culture

Muslim Brotherhood, 286

Muslims, 86; Central Africa, 342; daily life of, 244–45; East Africa, 312–13; Georgia, 215; Grand Mosque in Makkah, Saudi Arabia, *p234;* Hindus and, 187; Kashmir territory, 193; Kazakhstan, 215; Mughal rules as, 185; North Africa, 280, 367; Pakistan, 190; rulers of North Africa, 276; Siberia, 215; South Asia, 191; Sudan, 309; Sunni *vs.* Shia, 243; West Africa, 363, 369. *See also* Islam

Mutapa Empire, 389

Myanmar, 151, 158, *m149;* communist government in, 163; independence of, 162; Inya Lake in, *p148;* Mekong River through, 153; political challenges in, 169; as poor country, 168. *See also* Southeast Asia

NAFTA. *See* **North American Free Trade Agreement (NAFTA)**

Nagorno-Karabakh, ethnic unrest in, 216

Nagoya, Japan, 133

Nairobi, Kenya, *p311;* Kenya National Museum, *p315;* population of, 313

Nejd, Saudi Arabia, *p246*

Namib Desert, 381, 385

Namibia, *m379;* climate of, 384; democratic governments in, 401; desert region in, 385; escarpment in, 381; ethnic and, 396; natural resources in, 386–87; population of, 394, 395; relative land area of, 380; religion in, 396. *See also* Southern Africa

Narmada River project, 180

national identity, 243

Nationalists, Taiwanese, 129

National Map-Hazards and Disasters, The **(U.S. Geological Service),** *q38*

National Snow & Ice Data Center, "Arctic *vs.* Antarctic," *q490*

Native Americans: as ethnic group, 83. *See also entries for individual groups*

natural disaster: emigration after, 78; in Indus Valley, 183; in South Asia, 183. *See also entries for individual natural disasters*

natural gas: Australia, 436; North Africa, 270–71; Oceania, 455; Papua New Guinea, 455; South Asia, 181; Southern Africa, 386; Southwest Asia, 231

natural resources: mineral resources: Australia, 436, 438, 539; Caucasus, 204–5; Central Asia, 204–5; New Zealand, 436–39; Oceania, 455; Papua New Guinea, 462–63; Siberia, 204–5; South Asia, 179–81; Southwest Asia, 231. *See also entries for specific resources, countries, or areas*

Nauru, 450

navigable, 329

Nazi Germany, 237

Nehru, Jawaharlal, 187, *p187,* 193

nenets peoples, *p202*

Nepal, 31, *m175,* 180, *p181,* 193. *See also* South Asia

Netherlands, the. *See* **Holland**

New Caledonia, 451, 455

New Delhi, India, 81, 189

New Guinea, 151, 451–52

newly industrialized countries (NICs), 98–99

New Orleans, Louisiana: as "the Crescent City", 22

New South Wales, 430

New York City: Spanish Harlem in, 86

New Zealand, 413–46, *m415;* agreements with Oceania, 458; Antarctica and, 481; ANZUS Pact, 431; British in, 430; climates of, 422; culture in, 432–34, 435; economy of, 436–37; international trust funds for islands in Oceania,

Index

465; landforms and waterways, 419–21; life in, 432–39; Maori of, 83, 426–27, 435, 438; migration from Oceania to, 464; natural resources in, 436–39; people of, 432–33; plants and animals of, 423; rural areas of, 434; territories in Oceania, 450–51; timeline, c414–15; trading partners, 437

"New Zealand" (FreedomHouse.org), q446

New Zealand Constitution Act (1852), 431

Nguema, Francisco Macías, 339

NICs. See newly industrialized countries

Niger, m353; Air Massif in, 354; delta region, 359; in Empire of Mali, m362, 363; as French colony, 366; independence of, 366; North African influence in, 371. See also West Africa

Nigeria, m353; climate of, 357; debt relief for, 373; eastern region secedes from, 367; ethnic groups in, 368–69; Jos Plateau in, 355; kingdom of Benin in, 364; as new country, 366–67; Niger River in, 355; Songhai Empire in, m362, 363. See also West Africa

Niger River, 355

Nile Basin, 296

Nile River: Ancient Nubia and, 302; deep gorge formed by, 265; delta at mouth of, 266; in East Africa, 296; farmland along, p266; importance to Egypt, 264, 266, 271; population concentration along, 76; rise of Egypt and, 272

Nile River valley, 261, 302

Niue Island, 451

Nkrumah, Kwame, 366, p366

nomadic peoples, p202, 269; Australia, 425; Bedouins, 229, 241; Central Asia, 208; desertification and, 376; East Africa, 314; Siberia, 206

nonrenewable resources, 95

Norgay, Tenzing, p17

Norlisk, Russia, 23

North Africa, 261–90, m262–63; art, 282–83; climate in, 267–70; coastal plains and mountains, 265, p265, p269; countries of, 264–65; culture of, 280–83; daily life, 281–82; early trading kingdom, 362; economic issues in, 283–84; food, 282; future of, 285–87; history of, 272–79; independence of, m277; languages and literature, 283; life in, 280–87; lowland of, 265; in Middle East vs. Southwest Asia, 239; natural resources, 270–71; people of, 280; physical geography of, 264–71; religion in, 276, 280, 369; Rome's control of, 275–76; size of, 265; society in, 280–87; timeline, c262–63; water pump in, p270; waterways, 266–67

North America: as continent, 52. See also Canada; Mexico; United States

North American Free Trade Agreement (NAFTA), 101

North China Plain, 119, 125

Northern Angola, 383

Northern Hemisphere, 26, c27; seasons in, 45, d45

Northern Territory (Australia), 421, p422, 430

North Island, 419, 420, 423, 430

North Korea, m115; Korean Peninsula; command economy in, 96; as communist nation, 130–31; on Korean Peninsula, 118, 120. See also East Asia

North Pole, 21; climate in, 46; Earth's axis and, 42; region around, 52; seasons and, 45

North Vietnam, 162

Northwestern Mozambique, 382

Norway, Antarctica and, 481

Nubia, 302

nuclear family, 371

nuclear proliferation, 187

nuclear weapon, 187

Nyika people, 311

oasis, 213, 229, 271

Obama, Barack (U.S. President), q376

Ob River, 204, 205

ocean currents: climate and, 47–48; effect of, 56

ocean floor: landforms on, 59–60; mining of, 63; plate movements and, 53

Oceania, 447–70, m448–49; climates of, 454; conflicts with colonists, 457; countries paying for marine resources of, 463; culture of, 460–61; economics and society, 466; economies of, 462–65; European explorers in, 457–58; first humans settling in, 456; formation of island, 453, d453; history of, 456–58; human migration from, 464, 465–66; landforms of, 450–53; life in, 462–67; location of, 450; MIRAB economies, 464–65; modern times, 457–58; natural resources of, 455; people of, 459–61; physical geography of, 450–55; Polynesian migrations, 456; population growth, 465–66; resources of, 455; smaller islands of, 452–53; timeline, c448–49

oceans, 61–63

oil, 180–81; Angola, 401; Australia, 436; dependency on, Southwest Asia and, 245, 246; North Africa, 270–1; Oceania, 455; Southern Africa, 386; Southwest Asia, 231; West Africa, 358

oil consumption, i230

oil tanker, in Strait of Hormuz, p228

Okavango Delta, 404

Olduvai Gorge, 315

Oman, m225; in Arabian Peninsula, 227; Arab Spring and, 246; border of Persian Gulf, 228. See also Southwest Asia

Omotic language, 312

oral tradition, 314

Orange River, 382, 390

orbit, 42

Organization for the Development of the Senegal River, 359

Oriya language, 190

Orlando, Florida, Disney World in, p22

Osaka, Japan, 133

Ottoman Empire: decline of, 236; North Africa in, 277; Southwest Asia in, 235; World War I and, 211

Ottoman Turks, 210

Outback, 417, 421, 433, 435

outer space, 44

outsourcing, 192

overfishing, 467

Ovimbundu peoples, 396

Owens Stanley Range, 452

oxygen, 181

ozone, 484; hole in, 483, d483

Pacific Islander, 432

Pacific Islands, Aboriginal peoples of, 85

Pacific Ocean: East Asia, 119; Magellan exploration crosses, 160; Mariana Trench, 60; New Zealand, 419; Oceania, 450; relative size of, 62; Ring of Fire in (see Ring of Fire); Siberian Russia, 200; Southeast Asia, 153; typhoons over, 155

Pacific Plate, 152

Pacific Rim, 167

Padaung woman, in Myanmar, p166

Pagan kingdom, 158

Pakistan, 201, m175, p183, m198; British rule of, 186, 187; conflicts with India, 193; Hindu Kush mountain range, 226; Khyber Pass in, 176, 227; language in, 190; population, 188; religion in, 190; Thar Desert in, 178. See also South Asia

Pakistanis, 190

Palau Island, 450, 451, 454, 458

Palestine, 237, m237. See also Arab-Israeli conflict; Palestinian territory

Palestinian territory, 233

palm oil, 335

palm oil trade, 364, 463

Pamirs, 201

Panama: as isthmus, 59

Panama Canal, 59

Pana people, 343

pans, 383

Papua New Guinea: drought in, 454; economy of, 462–63; in Oceania, 450–52; population of, 459–60; resources of, 455

Paris, France, as primate city, 81

Paschal, G. Zachary, q324

Pashto people, 243

Pashtun peoples, 243

Index

pastoral, 206
Paul, Ron, *q249*
PBC (Peacebuilding Commission), 347
Peking opera, 135
peninsula(s), 59, 118, *p119*; in Southeast Asia, 150–51
People's Republic of China, 129
periodic market, 399
permafrost, 202, *d203*
Perry, Matthew C, 129, *p129*
Persia: trade with Southern Africa, 388. *See also* Iran
Persian Empire, 210
Persian Gulf: oil spill on fire in, *p245*; petroleum in, 231; Strait of Hormuz and, 228
Persian Gulf War, 239, *p245*
Persian people, 208, 243
Perth, Australia, 433
Peshawar, Pakistan, 227
Peter the Great (Russian Czar), 209
petroleum, 245; in Papua New Guinea, 455, 463; in Southwest Asia, 231, 239; in West Africa, 358, 372. *See also* oil
pharaohs, 272, 273, *p273*
Philippines, 151, *m149*; bridge collapse after earthquake in, *p54*; climate in, 155; fishing in, 168; independence of, 161–62; manufacturing in, 163; Mount Mayon volcano in, *p152*; religion in, 166. *See also* Southeast Asia
Philippine Sea, 153
phosphate mine, in Tunisia, *p284*
physical geography, 39–68; changing Earth, 52–57; land, 58–60; planet Earth, 42–51; water, 60–65. *See also entries for individual regions*
physical map, 29
physical systems, *c24*; Earth's, 44
pidgin language, 369, 460
Pillars of Islam, 234
pine tree, 205
pita bread, 282
place, *c24*; as geography theme, 22; perspective of, 19–20
plains, 58; Central Asia, 202; creation of, 56; Siberia, 202–3
plankton, 479, 485
plantation agriculture, 161
plant life, in salt water, 61
plateau: in Arabian Desert, 228; Deccan, 177; defined, 58; in Southern Africa, 381–83; in Southwest Asia, 226–27
Plateau of Tibet, 117, 119, 121, 153
plate movements, 53–54
poaching, 317, 387; burning elephant tusks in Kenya, *p316*
polar climate, 49–50
polar ice caps, 61

policy, 187
political map, 29
pollution: effects on Earth, 57; of lakes and rivers, *p65*; population growth and, 74–75
Polynesia, 447, 450, *m448–49*; culture of, 460–61; islands of, 451; low islands of, 452. *See also* Oceania
Polynesian migrations, 456
polytheism, 233, 271
population: Aboriginals in Australia, 429–30; aging, in Australia and New Zealand, 439; America, 188; Australia, 432; Central Africa, 340–41; East Africa, 310–12; Maoris in New Zealand, 432; Nairobi, Kenya, 313; New Zealand, 432–33; North Africa, 280; Oceania, 459–60, 465–67; Papua New Guinea, 460; South Africa's four cities, 397; South Asia, 188, 189, 193; Southern Africa, 394–95; Southwest Asia, 240; West Africa, 370, 373. *See also entries for specific regions*
population density, 76–77; defined, 190, 310; Southern Africa, *m395*
population distribution, 76
population growth, 72–75; causes of, 72–73; challenges of, 74; as East Asian challenge, 138; effects on environment, 74; rates of, 73, 75
population movement, 77–81
population patterns, 76–77
population pyramid, *g73*
Portugal: colonization of East Africa, 305; in Ghana, 359; Islam religion, 234; North Africa and, 277; rule of Timor-Leste, 162; slave trade, 335; Southern Africa and, 390, 392; trading in West Africa, 366; West African kingdoms and, 365
Portuguese explorers, in Southeast Asia, 160
Portuguese language, 369
Portuguese peoples, 389
possession, 458
poverty: population growth and, 74–75
precipitation: defined, 48; evaporation and, 64, *d64*
primate city, 81, 165
Prime Meridian, 21, *c21*, 26, *c27*, 213, *m213*
Principe, 329, 338–40
prison colony (Australia), 428
productivity, 98
Ptolemy, *p16*
Puncak Jaya, 154
Punjabi language, 190
Push-pull factors for migration, 78–79
pyramids: ancient Egypt, 274; ancient Kush (Sudan), *p303*; making of, *i274*
Qaddafi. *See* al-Qaddafi, Muammar
Qatar: Persian Gulf border, 228; population of, 240; as wealthy country, 245

Qattara Depression, 265
Qing dynasty, 125, *c126*
Qinzang rail system, *p117*
Queen Elizabeth National Park, 315
Queensland, 421, 430
Queen Victoria, 430
Quran, 244, *p283*
railroad: Qinzang rail system in China, *p117*; Trans-Siberian, 207, *m207*, 208, 212
rainfall: Australia, 421; Central Africa, 330; East Africa, 298–99; Georgia, 203; North Africa, 264, 269–70; Oceania, 452, 454; Sierra Leone and Liberia, 358; South Asia, *m179*; Southern Africa, 384; Southwest Asia desert, 230; West Africa, 358. *See also* monsoon
rain forest, Amazon, 33, 90; as biome, 50; in Central Africa, 330–31; climate and, 51; GIS and, 33; loss of, 57; resources and, 90–93. *See also* tropical rain forest
rain forest research, *p93*
rain shadow, 49, *g48*
rainwater, 64
Raj, 186
Ramadan, 234, *p244*, 245
Ramayana, 191
Rangoon. *See* Yangon
recycling, of water supply, 63–64
Red River, 153
Red River delta, 157, 158
Red Sea: Adulis on, 303; Ancient Egyptian control along, 273; Ancient Nubia and, 302; Eritrea, 306; Great Rift Valley and, 295; mountains on shores of (Egypt), 265; in Southwest Asia, 227–28; Suez Canal and, 267
refugees, 318–21, *g321*; in Central Africa, 341; defined, 78; Somolian, 309; Sudanese, 318, *p319*, 320, 321
regime, 279
region, 22, *c24*
reincarnation, 184
relative location, 20–21
relief, on physical maps, 29
religion: ancient Egypt, 273–74; Australia, 432; birthplace of, 233; Central Africa, 343; culture and, 84; East Asia, 135; major world, *c84*; New Zealand, 432; population growth and, 75; rivalry in West Africa, 367; Siberia, Central Asian, and Caucasus, 215; South Asia, 182–85, 191; Southeast Asia, 166; Southern Africa, 396–97; Southwest Asia, 243–44. *See also entries for individual religions*
remittance, 464, 470
remote sensing, 32, 483–84
renewable resources, 95
representative democracy, 87
Republic of China, 129
Republic of Ghana, 366

Republic of Mali, 366
Republic of South Africa, 386. *See also* Southern Africa
Republic of the Congo, 338; as independent nation, 339; State Department Background Notes about, *q350*
research station, 482–83
reservoir, 383
resort, 464
resources: defined, 23; nonrenewable, 95; renewable, 95; wants and, 94–95. *See also* energy resources; mineral resources; natural resources
revolution: of Earth around the sun, 42–43
Rig Veda, 184
Rhodesia, 392. *See also* Zimbabwe
rice: agricultural societies in Southeast Asia and, 158; Asian cultures and, 120; crop in Philippines, *p152*; in prehistoric Southeast Asia, 156; in Southeast Asia, 168
Richter scale, 140
rifted, 294–95
Ring of Fire: defined, 54; Japanese islands in, 118; New Zealand in, 436; Southeast Asian islands in, 151; tsunamis and, 140
rivers: freshwater, 62; liquid water in, 61; mouth of, 62; in South Asia, 176–77. *See also* entries for *individual rivers*
Riyadh, 241
Roman bath, *p275*
Roman Catholic Church, in Southeast Asia, 166
Roman Empire, 210, 275–76
Rossiya, *p204*
Ross Sea, 477
Rotorua, 421
Roughing It (Twain), *q68*
Rowan, Chris *q146*
Royal Thai guard, *p147*
Rozwi kingdom, 389
Rub' al-Khali (Empty Quarter), 229
rubber, *p154*, 168, 337, 455
rural areas, 77
Russia: Amur River and, 204; borders with Siberia and Mongolia, 202; climate in, 23; Kuril Islands dispute with Japan, 139; territorial issues in, 219. *See also* Siberian Russia
Russian Empire, 207, 211; German invasion of, 208
Russian Republic, 207
Russian Siberia, 206–7. *See also* Siberia
Ruwenzori Mountains, 296, 298, 329
Rwanda: ethnic tensions in, 308; genocide in, 346; independence of, 307; as landlocked country, 296; life expectancy, 317; mineral resources of, 300; population density of, 310; Volcanoes National Park, 315

Sahara desert, *p355*, harmattan winds in, 356–57; landscapes in, *p268*; the Sahel and, 299; size of, 268; temperatures in, 269; trade across, 361; in West Africa, 354–55, 360
Sahel, 299, 357
salt and salt trade, *p361*; in Central Africa, 335; gold-for-salt (Mali), 363; in Lake Assal, 300; in Southern Africa, 383
salt water, 61; freshwater *vs.*, *i60*
salt water sea, 228
Salween River, 153
Samarkand, Uzbekistan, 208, *p208*
Samburu National Reserve, 315
Samburu people, 311
Samoa, 450
samurai, 128
sand dunes, 268, *p268*. *See also* desert
San people, 396
Sanskrit language, 183, 190
Sao people, 342
Sao Tomé: independence of, 339; life expectancy in, 340; location of, 329; Portuguese colony on, 335, 338
Satellites: remote sensing, 32
Saudi Arabia, *m225*; in Arabian Peninsula, 227; border of Persian Gulf, 228; command economy in, 96; ethnic groups, 242; irrigation in Nejd region, *p246*; Makkah (Mecca), 233; oil in, 231; population of, 240–41. *See also* Southwest Asia
savanna, 354–57; in Central Africa, 331–32
Sayano-Shushenskaya Dam, *p209*
scale, map, 29
scale bar, on map, 28
Schlein, Lisa, *q324*
Scotia Sea, 477
Scott, Robert, 480
Sea of Japan, 118, 119, 212
seas, characteristics of, 228
seasons: Earth's orbit and, 45–46; tilt of Earth and, *d45*
seceded, 367
Second Continental Congress, *p86*
Second Persian Gulf War, 239
semiarid, 121, 230, 357
Seminomadic peoples, 311, 360
Senegal, 357, 366
Senegal River, 356, 359
Senghor, Léopold, 372
Seoul, South Korea, 120; population density in, *p76*
sepaktakraw, 167
Serengeti National Park, 301, 315
Serengeti Plain, 301
service industries, 97
settlement patterns, in West Africa, 370
Seychelles, 380, 391
Shang dynasty, 125, *c126*

Shanghai, China, 119, 133
Shankar, Ravi, 191
Shia Muslims, 243
Shinto, 128, 135
shogun, 128
Shona peoples, 389
Siam, absolute monarchy in, 161
Siberia: below ground in, *d203*; climates in, 203; energy and mineral resources, 205; history of, 206–8; language and religion of, 215; nomadic and nenets people of, *p202*; plains and deserts in, 202; revolution and development, 207–8; Russian, 206–7; settlement, invasion and conquest, 206; waterways, 204; woman of northwestern, *p197*. *See also* Siberian Russia
Siberian Russia, 197–222, *m198–99*; climates in, 203; landforms in, 201–2; people and places of, 212; population of, 212; timeline, *c198–99*; waterways in, 204. *See also* Siberia
Sichuan Province, 136
Sidney, Australia, 433, 434
Sierra Leone: British colony in, 364, 365; civil war in, 367; Peacebuilding Commission (PBC) and, 347; tropical rain forests in, 358
Sikhism, *c84*; in South Asia, 191
Silk Road, 126, *m127*, 208, 222
Silla, the, 126
silt, 266
silver: in Australia, 436; in Namibia, 387
Sinai Peninsula, 238, 264, 265
Singapore: cargo containers in port of, *p249*; Chinatown district in, *p165*; economy of, 163; independence of, 162; off Malay Peninsula, 151
Sinhalese, 190
sitar, 191
Skaka, 389
"Skeleton Coast" (Benguela), 385
skill building, interpreting visuals, 25
slash-and-burn agriculture, *p74*, 331–32
slavery, in Southern Africa, 390
slave trade, 364, *m365*; in Central Africa, 335–36
slums, 75
Small, Cathy A, *q470*
soccer, *p85*
Sogdians, 222
solar panels, *p75*
solar-powered lighting, 455
Solomon Islands, 450, 455, 457, 467
solstice, 45
Somalia, 82; civil war, 308–9; clan, attachment to, 312; drought in, 299; in East Africa, 294; independence of, 307; as independent trading state, 303; Somali language spoken in, 82, 312; temperature of, 298; United Nations and, 346, *p346*; where people live, 310
Somali language, 82, 312
Song dynasty, *c126*

Songhai, *m362*, 363
souk, 281
South Africa, *m379. See also* Southern Africa
South America: birthrates in, 75; as continent, 52
South Asia, 173–96; British in, 186; climates, 178–79; cultures, 191; daily life in, 191; history of, 182–87; homes in, 188–89; Independence, achieving, 186–87; Indian empires, 185; Islam religion and, 234–35; islands of, 177; issues in, 187, 192–93; modern, 185–87; natural resources, 179–81; northern mountains and plains, 176–77; people, 190; physical geography of, 176–81; population, 188, 189, 190; rainfall, *m179*; religion and arts, 191; timeline, *c174–75*
South Australia, 430
South China Sea, 119, 123, 153; rubbish-covered beach along, *p138*
Southeast Asia, 147–72, *m149*; arts in, 166; Association of Southeast Asian Nations (ASEAN), 168; bodies of water in, 152–53; climate in, 154–55; colonies/independence, *m160*, 161–63; daily life in, 166–67; early societies in, 156–59; earning a living in, 168; economic and environmental challenges for, 169; ethnic and language groups, 166; European traders in, 159–60; four plates meet in, 152; green islands in, *p151*; history of, 156–63; independent nations in, 161–63; Islam and, 158–59, 234; landforms in, 150–52; modern, 163; mountains and volcanoes in, 151–52; natural resources of, 152; peninsulas and islands in, 150–51; people and cultures, 165–67; plants and animals, 155; population in, 164–65; prehistoric cultures in, 156–57; religion in, 166; slaves from, in South Africa, 390; spices in, 159, *p159*; sports in, 167; timeline, *c148–49*; in transition, 167; Western colonization of, 159–61
Southern Africa, 377–404, *m379*; Bantu people in, 361; bodies of water, 382–83; clashes in, 390; climate, 383–85; desert regions, 384–85; Dutch settling in, 364; energy resources in, 386; environmental characteristics in, 23; equal rights in, 392–93; ethnic and, 396; European colonies, 390–91; family and traditional life in, 399; health issues today, 399–401; history of, 388–93; independence, 391–92; landforms, 381–82; languages of, 396–97; life in, 394–401; physical geography of, 380–87; population density, *m395*; population patterns, 394–95; progress and growth, 401; region of, 380; religion and languages, 396–97; resources, 385–87; rise of kingdoms, 388–89; timeline, *c378–79*; urban life in, 397–98; wildlife, 387. *See also* Union of South Africa
Southern Alps, 420, 422

Southern Hemisphere, 26, *c27*; seasons in, 45, *d45*; tropics in, 154–55
Southern Ocean, 62, 483, 484
South Island, 419, 420, 422
South Korea, *m115*; access to Oceania's marine resources, 463; climate of, 121; K-pop in, 135; as peninsula, 118; urbanization of, 133; U.S. support of, 130–31. *See also* East Asia; Korean Peninsula
South Ossetia, 216
South Pole, 21, 480; climate in, 46; Earth's axis and, 42
South Sudan, *m293*, *m321*; in East Africa, 294; energy resources in, 300; independence of, 309, 318; villagers in, *p308*
Southwest Asia, 223–52, *m225*; bodies of water in, 227–28; civil wars in, 238–39; climates, 229–30; as cradle of religions, 233; daily life, 244–45; early, 232–35; ethnic and language groups, 242–43; Islamic expansion, 234–35; issues in, 245–47; life in, 240–47; Mesopotamia, 232–33; modern, 236–39; natural resources, 231; oil reserves and consumption, *i230*; physical features, 226–29; physical geography of, 226–29; population profile, 240; religion and art, 243–44; timeline, *c224–25*; water scarcity in, 247; where people live, 241
Soviet legacy: in Caucasus and Central Asia, 217–18
Soviet Union, *m198*; Caucasus and, 210–11; collapse of, 210. *See also* Union of Soviet Socialist Republics (USSR)
Sovoia glacier, *p298*
space, perspective of, 18–20
***Space, Time, Infinity* (Trefil),** *q68*
Spain: Islam religion and, 234; North Africa and, 277; trade with West African kingdoms, 364
Spanish-American War, 161
Spanish explorers, in Oceania, 457
Spanish Harlem, 86
spatial, 18
sphere of influence, 128
spheres, 26, 27
spices: at souk in Cario, Egypt, *p281*; from Southeast Asia, 159, *p159*
sports: culture and, 85; first organized team, 85
Sri Lanka: civil war in, 193; climate of, 178; language in, 190; location of, 177; mineral resources in, 180; in South Asia, 176; timber resources in, 181. *See also* South Asia
Srivijaya empire, 157–58
St. Helena, 354, 365
Stalin, Joseph, 211
standard of living, 98
Stanley, Henry Morton, 304–5
stations, 429

steppe, 202
Strait of Hormuz, 228, *p228*
Strait of Malacca, 153, 157, 159, 160
streams, freshwater, 62
subcontinent, 176
subsistence agriculture, 168, 313, 341, 343
Sudan, *m293*, *m321*; Ancient Nubia in, 302; Battle of Omduman, *p305*; as British colony, 306; in East Africa, 294; independence, 309; landforms in, 295–96; life expectancy, 317; president's palace, *p296*; refugees and displacement, 318–21; statistics about people of, 320; temperature of, 298
Sudd, 296–97
Suez Canal: building of, 277, 365; completion of, 236; container ship in, *p267*; importance of, 267, 278; in Southwest Asia, 227
Sukuma farm, 314
Sulawesi, 151
sultans, 159
Sumatra: earthquake in, 142, 152; Islamic kingdoms in, 158; prehistoric, 156; in Southeast Asia, 151; Srivijaya kingdom, 157–58
Sumerians, 232–33
sun, Earth and, 42–43
Sunda Isles, 153
Sunni Muslims, 243
sustainability, 101
Swahili language, 303, 312
Swaziland, *m379*; British control of, 390; climate of, 384; HIV/AIDS in, 400; independence for, 391; as landlocked, 382; Muslim population in, 396; political unrest in, 401; population of, 394; resources of, 387. *See also* Southern Africa
Syr Dar'ya River, 204, 219
Syria, *m225*; alluvial plain, 228; Arab Spring and, 246; Christians in, 243; coast of, 227; democracy movements in, 239; ethnic groups, 242; on Mediterranean Sea, 227; religion in, 243; Tigris-Euphrates River system through, 247. *See also* Southwest Asia
Szechuan Province, 136
Tagalog people, 166
Tahiti, 452
taiga, 202, 205
Taiwan, *m115*, 118, 119; access to Oceania's marine resources, 463; China's view of, 139; climate of, 121; forests in, 123; Japanese control of, 129; language in, 134; limited mineral reserves in, 122; population of, 132–33; textile industry in Lesotho, South Africa, 401. *See also* East Asia
Tajikistan, *m198*, 200, 201; civil war in, 216; coal in, 205; culture and daily life, 217; people of, 214; Soviet legacy in, 218. *See also* Central Asia
Tajik people, 243
Taj Mahal, *p19*, *p185*
Taklimakan Desert, 121, 123

Index

Taliban, 239
Tamil language, 190
Tamil Nadu, 190
Tanganyika, 308
Tang dynasty, 126, *p126*
Tanzania, East Africa, *m293*, 294; agriculture in, 316; Denakil Plain in, 295; energy resources in, 300; ethnic groups in, 311; farming in, 313; HIV/AIDS, 317; independence of, 307–8; as independent trading state, 303, 304; Lake Victoria in, 297; language of, 312; Masai nomadic lifestyle and, 314; mineral resources of, 300; rainfall in, 298–99; religion in, 313; Serengeti National Park in, 301, 315; *tarab* music, 314; wildlife reserves in, 301. *See also* East Africa
tarab **orchestra,** *p314*
taro, 361
Tartars, 206
Tashkent, Uzbekistan, 213
Tasman, Abel, 428
Tasmania, *m415*, 418; early people in, 425; European explorers in, 428; as independent nation, 430–31; natural resources in, 436
Taylor, Charles, 367
technology, 30–31; globalization and, 89; widespread use of, *p89*
tectonic plates, 53; boundaries, *m40–41*
Tehran, 241
Telugu language, 190
textiles, 314
Thailand, *m149*, 151; absolute monarchy in, 161; as constitutional monarchy, 163; fishing in, 168; manufacturing in, 163; Mekong River through, 153; natural resources in, 152; plantations in, 168; rice exports, 168; tin mining in, 152, 168, 169
Thar Desert, 178. *See also* Southeast Asia
thatch, 399, 461
thematic maps, 30
thermal image, *p51*
Thimphu, Bhutan: Buddhist monastery in, *p174*
Things Fall Apart **(Achebe),** 372
thinking spatially, 18–19
Thiong'o, Ngugi wa, 314
Thousand and One Nights, The, 244
Three Gorges Dam, *p56*, 123
Through the Dark Continent **(Stanley),** 304–5
Tian Shan, 201
Tibesti Mountains, 354–55
Tibet: China's treatment of, 139; nomadic shepherd in, *p114*
Tigris River, 228, 232, 247
Tikanga, 426
Tikar people, 342

Timbuktu, 355, 363
timelines: Antarctica, *c472–73*; Australia, *c414–15*; Caucasus, *c198–99*; Central Africa, *c326–27*; Central Asia, *c198–99*; Earth's land, people, environment, *c16–17*; East Africa, *c292–93*; East Asia, *c114–15*; human geography, *c70–71*; New Zealand, *c414–15*; North Africa, *c262–63*; Oceania, *c448–49*; physical world, *c40–41*; Siberian Russia, *c198–99*; South Asia, *c174–75*; Southeast Asia, *c148–49*; Southern Africa, *c378–79*; Southwest Asia, *c224–25*; West Africa, *c352–53*
time zones, 213, *m213*
Timor, 151
Timor-Leste, 162
Timur, 208
Togo, *m353*, 359, 365. *See also* West Africa
Tokyo, Japan, 133
tombs, in ancient Egypt, 274, *i274*
Tonga: aid from foreign governments, 465; European explorers in, 457; migration from, 465–66; MIRAB economy in, 465; in Oceania, 450; remittances to, 464, 470
Tonle Sap, 158
tourism: Antarctica, 485; Australia, 436; Oceania, 464; Vietnam, *p168*
townships, in South Africa, 398
trade deficit, 138
trade languages, 342
trade restrictions, 248–49
trade surplus, 138
trading market, *p398*, 399
traditional economy, 96
traditional music: of Central Africa, *p326*; in East Africa, 314, *p314*
Transantarctic Mountains, 475
Trans-Siberian Railroad, 207, *m207*, 208, 212
treaty, 481
Treaty of Waitangi, 430
Trefil, James S, *q68*
trench, 60
"triangular trade," 336
tribal identity, 243
tribute, 305
Tripoli, Libya, *p278*
Tristan da Cunha, 354
tropical climate, 49–50; South Asia, 178; Southeast Asia as, 154–55; Southern Africa, 383–84
tropical rain forest: in Central Africa, 330–31. *See also* rain forest
Tropic of Cancer, 45, 46
Tropic of Capricorn, 45, 46, 383, 474
Trusteeship Council of the United Nations, 458
trust territory, 458

Tsaatan people, *p121*
Tsonga peoples, 396
tsunami, 54, 140–43; America Samoa, 465; Banda Aceh, *p153*; Krakatoa eruption triggered, 152; statistics about 2011, 142
Tswana population, 396
Tuareg people, 354; with livestock, *p355*
tuberculosis, 400
tundra: in biome, 50; defined, 202; Siberian, 203, 205
Tunis, Tunisia, 281
Tunisia, 239, *m263*; aquifer in, 271; Arab Spring and, 279; cooking in, 282; freedom from France, 277, 278; French influence of, 280; iron ore and phosphates in, 271, *p284*; location of, 264; mountains in, 265; Muslim Brotherhood and, 286; women's rights and, 287. *See also* Carthage
Turkana people, 311
Turkey, *m225*; Ararat volcano, 227; birth of, 236; civil wars in, 238; coal deposits in, 231; coasts of, 227; earthquake in (1999), *p227*; ethnic groups, 242; ethnic unrest in, 216; Islam religion spreading in, 234; Kurdish families in, 238, *p238*; Mediterranean climate, 230; population of, 240–41; reforms in, 239; temperatures in mountainous areas of, 230; Tigris-Euphrates River system and, 228, 247. *See also* Southwest Asia
Turkic people, 206, 212
Turkish language, 242
Turkish people, 210
Turkish republic, creation of, *p236*
Turkmenistan, *m198*; in Central Asia, 200; Kara-Kum desert in, 202; oil and gas resources in, 205; population of, 213; relative size of, 201; Soviet legacy in, 218; territorial issues in, 219. *See also* Central Asia
Turkmen people, 243
Turkomans, ethnic, 213
Turks, 243
Tutankhamen, *p273*
Tuvalu, 452, 463
Twain, Mark, *q68*
typhoon, 155, 454, 467
UAE. *See* **United Arab Emirates**
Uganda: in East Africa, 294; energy resources in, 300; independence for, 308; Lake Victoria in, 266; mineral resources of, 300; Queen Elizabeth National Park in, 315; Ruwenzori Mountains in, 296; Savoia glacier on border of, *p298*; temperatures in, 298
Uluru, 417
UN. *See* **United Nations**
underwater volcano, 453
unfrozen soil, *d203*
Union of South Africa, 390

Index

Union of Soviet Socialist Republics (USSR): formation of, 207. *See also* Soviet Union

United Arab Emirates (UAE), *m225*; border of Persian Gulf, 228; oil in, 231. *See also* Southwest Asia

United Kingdom: monarchy in, 87, *p87*; Second Persian Gulf War and, 239

United Nations (UN): Arab-Israeli conflict and, 237; Darfur estimates, 320; Department of Economic and Social Affairs, on population growth, 73; effectiveness regarding Africa, 346–47; Korean War and, 131; land rights in Solomon Islands and, 467; Security Council, 346, 347, *q347*; World Refugee Day, 318

United Nations Development Programme (UNDP), *q34*

United States: access to Oceania's marine resourcs, 463; agreements with Oceania, 458; al-Qaddafi, Muammar and, 279; al-Qaeda and, 239; Declaration of Independence approval, *p86*; early immigrants to, 78; economic activity of American Samoa and, 465; gold prospectors to Australia from, 429; international trust funds for islands in Oceania, 465; life expectancy, 317; migration from Oceania to, 464; Muslim fundamentalists and, 287; Myanmar and, 169; occupation of islands in Oceania during World War II, 458; Persian Gulf Wars, 239, *p245*; representative democracy, 87; territories in Oceania, 451; trade deficit with China, 138, *g139*; trade with Australia, 436; trade with New Zealand, 437; voluntary free association with Palau Island, 458. *See also entries for individual American territories*

United States Geological Survey: "Desertification," *q376*

"untouchables," 193

Ural Mountains: as Siberian Russia border, 200, 202

uranium, 181, 387

urban areas, 77

urbanization, 80–81, 133, 165, 169

Urdu language, 190

U.S. Geological Service, *The National Map-Hazards and Disasters, q38*

U.S. State Department: Background Notes: "Israel," *q252*; "Singapore: History," *q172*

USSR. *See* **Russian Empire; Union of Soviet Socialist Republics (USSR)**

utilities, 398

Uzbekistan, *m198*, 200–2, *p208*, 209; coal in, 205; daily life in, 216–17; mineral resources in, 205; oil and gas resources in, 205; population of, 213–14; village women weaving in, *p216*. *See also* Central Asia

Uzbek people, 243; in Tajikistan, 214

valleys, 56, 58–59

Vanautu, 450

Van Sant, Shannon, *q146*

Varanasi, India, *p177*

varna, 183

Vedas, 183, 184

vegetation, 178

Victoria Land, 478

Vietnam, *m149*, 151; Communist forces in, 162; Dong Son culture in, 157; independence of, 162; literacy rate in, 167; manufacturing in, 163; Mekong River through, 153; as poor country, 168; rice exports, 168; tourist, 168; Vietnam War, 162–63, 162. *See also* Southeast Asia

Vietnam: A History **(Karnow),** *q172*

Vietnam War, 162–63; Mekong Delta during, *p162*

Vinson Massif, 475

visuals, interpreting, 25

Vladivostok, 212

volcanoes, *p178*; Ararat, in Turkey, 227; Caucasus region, 201; Emi Koussi (West Africa), 355; eruption of, 43, 453; inactive, *p292*; lava from, *p295*; Mount Kilamanjaro, *p292*; New Zealand, 419; Oceania, 453; plate movement and, 54; Southeast Asia, 152; underwater, 60, 453

Volcanoes National Park, 315

wadis, 230, 268

Waikato, 419

Wake Island, 465

wants, resources and, 94–95

warriors, in South Asia, 183

Washington, D.C: absolute location of, 21

water: earning a living on, *p62*; Earth's surface, 44; freshwater *vs.* salt, *i60*, 61; locating, 61–63; North Africa, 271; recreational activities on, *p62*; resources for, in North Africa, 271; three states of matter, 61; use to humans, *p62*, 63. *See also* rainfall *and entries for specific bodies of water*

water, scarcity of: Australia, 423; North Africa, 270, 271; population growth and, 271; Southwest Asia, 231

water cycle, 63–65, *d64*

watershed, 328

waterways: Australia, 418–19; Central Africa, 329–30; Central Asia, Caucasus, and Siberia, 204; New Zealand, 419–21; North Africa, 266–67; Southwest Asia, 227–28; Suez Canal, 236, 365

wattle-and-daub houses, 343

waves, ocean, 56

wayfinding, 456

weather, 23; climate *vs.,* 48

weathering, 55

Weddell Sea, 477

Weep Not, Child **(Ngugi),** 314

Wellington, New Zealand, 433

West Africa, 351–76, *m352–53*; ancient herders, 360; arts, 371–72; bodies of water, 355–56;

challenges, 372–73; civil war, 367; climate of, 356–58; coastal kingdoms, 363; daily life in, 371; energy in, 358–59; *i358*; ethnic groups, 368–69; first trading kingdom, 362; health and education, 373; history of, 360–67; kingdoms of, 363; landforms, 354–55; languages, 369; life in, 368–73; new countries, 365–67; people, movement of, 361; physical geography of, 354–59; religions in, 369–70; resources in, 358–59, 372; settlement patterns, 370; timeline, *c352–53;* wet zones, 357

West Antarctica, 476

West Bank, 238, 246

Western Australia, 422, 430

Western Ghats, 177–79

Western Hemisphere, 26, *c27*

Western Plateau, 416–17

Western Sahara, *m262*, 264

Western Wall, in Jerusalem, *p234*

west Siberian plain, 203

wetland ecosystems, 56

wet zones, in West Africa, 357–58

White Nile, 296, *p296*, 297

White Volta River, 356

wildlife, *p315*; East Africa, 301, 317; reserve, 301; South Asia, 50, 181; Southern Africa, 383, 387

wind: climate and, 47–48. *See also* typhoon

wind patterns, *m47*

wind power, 455

Wolfert, Paula, *q290*

women: in male roles, in Southern Africa, 399; rights of, in North Africa, 285, *p285*, 287

woodblock printing, 126

world: changing, 20; interconnected, 24; in spatial terms, *c24*

World Bank, 100–1, 373

World Heritage site, 417

World Refugee Day, 318

World Trade Organization, 100

World War I: Ottoman Empire and, 236

World War II: Australia post-, 431; Holocaust and, 237; Japan controls Southeast Asia during, 161–62; Japan's defeat in, 131

written record, in early South Asia, 182

Xhosa people, 396

Yaka people, 344

Yalu River, 120

yams, 361

Yangon, Padaung woman in car near, *p166*

Yaoundé, Cameroon, 342

Yap Island, 454

Yellow River, 119, 120, *p120. See also* Huang He River

Yellow Sea, 118, 119

Yemen, *m225*; in Arabian Peninsula, 227; Arab Spring and, 246; civil wars in, 238; democracy movements in, 239; Eritrea military conflict, 309; population of, 240, 241. *See also* Southwest Asia

Index

Yenisey River, 202, 204, 205, 212
Yerevan, Armenia, 215
Yokohama, Japan, 133; Matthew Perry in, 129, *p129*
Yoritomo, Minamoto, 128
Yoruba, 367, 369
Yuan dynasty, 127
Yucatán Peninsula, 336
yurt, 216, *p216*
Zambezi River, 382, 386, 389

Zambia, 380, 382, *m379*; British control of, 391; democratic governments in, 401; electricity source for, 386; independence for, 392; languages of, 397; mineral resources in, 387; Muslim population in, 396; population of, 395. *See also* Southern Africa
Zanzibar: Tanganyika merged with, 308; tarab orchestra in, *p314*; trade city of Kilwa near, 304
Zheng He, 125
Zhou dynasty, 125
Ziggurat of Ur, *p233*

Zimbabwe, *m379*; birth of, 392; coastal plain of, 382; colonialism in, 391; energy resources in, 386; ethnic and, 396; infant death in, 400; mineral resources in, 387; political unrest in, 401
zinc, in Southern Africa, 387. *See also* Great Zimbabwe; Southern Africa
zones, climate, 49–51, *p49*
Zoroastrianism, 222
Zulu Empire, 389
Zulu peoples, 396
Zulu War of 1879, 389

Index

McGraw-Hill Networks™ meets you anywhere—takes you everywhere.
Go online at connected.mcgraw-hill.com.

Circle the globe, travel across time. How do you access networks?

1. Log on to the internet and go to connected.mcgraw-hill.com
2. Get your User Name and Password from your teacher and enter them.
3. Click on your networks book.
4. Select your chapter and lesson. Start networking.

CONSULTANTS AND REVIEWERS

ACADEMIC CONSULTANTS

William H. Berentsen, Ph.D.
Professor of Geography and European Studies
University of Connecticut
Storrs, Connecticut

David Berger, Ph.D.
Ruth and I. Lewis Gordon Professor of Jewish History
Dean, Bernard Revel Graduate School
Yeshiva University
New York, New York

R. Denise Blanchard, Ph.D.
Professor of Geography
Texas State University–San Marcos
San Marcos, Texas

Brian W. Blouet, Ph.D.
Huby Professor of Geography and International Education
The College of William and Mary
Williamsburg, Virginia

Olwyn M. Blouet, Ph.D.
Professor of History
Virginia State University
Petersburg, Virginia

Maria A. Caffrey, Ph.D.
Lecturer, Department of Geography
University of Tennessee
Knoxville, Tennessee

So-Min Cheong, Ph.D.
Associate Professor of Geography
University of Kansas
Lawrence, Kansas

Alasdair Drysdale, Ph.D.
Professor of Geography
University of New Hampshire
Durham, New Hampshire

Rosana Ferreira, Ph.D.
Assistant Professor of Geography and Atmospheric Science
East Carolina University
Greenville, North Carolina

Eric J. Fournier, Ph.D.
Associate Professor of Geography
Samford University,
Birmingham, Alabama

Matthew Fry, Ph.D.
Assistant Professor of Geography
University of North Texas
Denton, Texas

Douglas W. Gamble, Ph.D.
Professor of Geography
University of North Carolina
Wilmington, North Carolina

Gregory Gaston, Ph.D.
Professor of Geography
University of North Alabama
Florence, Alabama

Jeffrey J. Gordon, Ph.D.
Associate Professor of Geography
Bowling Green State University
Bowling Green, Ohio

Alyson L. Greiner, Ph.D.
Associate Professor of Geography
Oklahoma State University
Stillwater, Oklahoma

William J. Gribb, Ph.D.
Associate Professor of Geography
University of Wyoming
Laramie, Wyoming

Joseph J. Hobbs, Ph.D.
Professor of Geography
University of Missouri
Columbia, Missouri

Ezekiel Kalipeni, Ph.D.
Professor of Geography and Geography Information Science
University of Illinois
Urbana, Illinois

Pradyumna P. Karan, Ph.D.
Research Professor of Geography
University of Kentucky
Lexington, Kentucky

Christopher Laingen, Ph.D.
Assistant Professor of Geography
Eastern Illinois University
Charleston, Illinois

Jeffrey Lash, Ph.D.
Associate Professor of Geography
University of Houston–Clear Lake
Houston, Texas

Jerry T. Mitchell, Ph.D.
Research Professor of Geography
University of South Carolina
Columbia, South Carolina

Thomas R. Paradise, Ph.D.
Professor, Department of Geosciences and the King Fahd Center for Middle East Studies
University of Arkansas
Fayetteville, Arkansas

David Rutherford, Ph.D.
Assistant Professor of Public Policy and Geography
Executive Director, Mississippi Geographic Alliance
University of Mississippi
University, Mississippi

Dmitrii Sidorov, Ph.D.
Professor of Geography
California State University
Long Beach, California

Amanda G. Smith, Ph.D.
Professor of Education
University of North Alabama
Florence, Alabama

Jeffrey S. Ueland, Ph.D.
Associate Professor of Geography
Bemidji State University
Bemidji, Minnesota

Fahui Wang, Ph.D.
Professor of Geography
Louisiana State University
Baton Rouge, Louisiana

TEACHER REVIEWERS

Precious Steele Boyle, Ph.D.
Cypress Middle School
Memphis, TN

Jason E. Albrecht
Moscow Middle School
Moscow, ID

Jim Hauf
Berkeley Middle School
Berkeley, MO

Elaine M. Schuttinger
Trinity Catholic School
Columbus, OH

Mark Stahl
Longfellow Middle School
Norman, OK

Mollie Shanahan MacAdams
Southern Middle School
Lothian, MD

Sara Burkemper
Parkway West Middle Schools
Chesterfield, MO

Alicia Lewis
Mountain Brook Junior High School
Birmingham, AL

Steven E. Douglas
Northwest Jackson Middle School
Ridgeland, MS

LaShonda Grier
Richmond County Public Schools
Martinez, GA

Samuel Doughty
Spirit of Knowledge Charter School
Worcester, MA

AUTHORS

SENIOR AUTHOR

Richard G. Boehm, Ph.D., was one of the original authors of *Geography for Life: National Geography Standards,* which outlined what students should know and be able to do in geography. He was also one of the authors of the *Guidelines for Geographic Education*, in which the Five Themes of Geography were first articulated. Dr. Boehm has received many honors, including "Distinguished Geography Educator" by the National Geographic Society (1990), the "George J. Miller Award" from the National Council for Geographic Education (NCGE) for distinguished service to geographic education (1991), "Gilbert Grosvenor Honors" in geographic education from the Association of American Geographers (2002), and the NCGE's "Distinguished Mentor Award" (2010). He served as president of the NCGE, has twice won the Journal of Geography award for best article, and also received the NCGE's "Distinguished Teaching Achievement." Presently, Dr. Boehm holds the Jesse H. Jones Distinguished Chair in Geographic Education at Texas State University in San Marcos, Texas, where he serves as director of The Gilbert M. Grosvenor Center for Geographic Education. His most current project includes the production of the video-based professional development series, *Geography: Teaching With the Stars*. Available programs may be viewed at www.geoteach.org.

CONTRIBUTING AUTHORS

Jay McTighe has published articles in a number of leading educational journals and has coauthored 10 books, including the best-selling *Understanding by Design* series with Grant Wiggins. McTighe also has an extensive background in professional development and is a featured speaker at national, state, and district conferences and workshops. He received his undergraduate degree from the College of William and Mary, earned a master's degree from the University of Maryland, and completed post-graduate studies at the Johns Hopkins University.

Dinah Zike, M.Ed., is an award-winning author, educator, and inventor recognized for designing three-dimensional, hands-on manipulatives and graphic organizers known as Foldables®. Foldables are used nationally and internationally by parents, teachers, and other professionals in the education field. Zike has developed more than 150 supplemental educational books and materials. Her two latest books, *Notebook Foldables®* and *Foldables®, Notebook Foldables®, & VKVs® for Spelling and Vocabulary 4th–12th* were each awarded *Learning Magazine's* Teachers' Choice Award for 2011. In 2004 Zike was honored with the CESI Science Advocacy Award. She received her M.Ed. from Texas A&M, College Station, Texas.

About the Cover: Young warrior of Samburu people wearing traditional bracelets and headdress; Tiras Mountain landscape in country of Namibia in Africa

Front cover: (tl)©Image Source/Getty Images, (tc)©Pete Atkinson/Getty Images, (tcr)Erica Simone Leeds, (tr)Lissa Harrison, (c)Roy Toft/National Geographic Stock, (bkgd)Christian Heinrich/Getty Images.

Back cover: (l to r, t to b)Anja Fleig/age fotostock, Adam Crowley/Getty Images, George Clerk/Getty Images, Fancy Collection/SuperStock, D. Normark/PhotoLink/Getty Images, Christian Heinrich/Getty Images.

Common Core State Standards© Copyright 2010. National Governors Association Center for Best Practices and Council of Chief State School Officers. All rights reserved.

Understanding By Design® is a registered trademark of the Association for Supervision and Curriculum Development ("ASCD").

National Council for the Social Studies (NCSS), National Curriculum Standards for Social Studies: A Framework for Teaching, Learning, and Assessment (Silver Spring, MD: NCSS, 2010). See www.socialstudies.org/standards

Heffron, Susan Gallagher and Roger M. Downs, eds. Geography for Life: National Geography Standards, Second Edition, Copyright 2012. National Council for Geographic Education, 1145 17th Street NW, Rm. 7620, Washington, D.C., 20036.

www.mheonline.com/networks

Send all inquiries to:
McGraw-Hill Education
8787 Orion Place
Columbus, OH 43240

Teacher Edition
ISBN: 978-0-07-663610-5
MHID: 0-07-663610-0

Student Edition
ISBN: 978-0-07-663609-9
MHID: 0-07-663609-7

Printed in the United States of America.

2 3 4 5 6 7 8 9 10 11 12 RJC 19 18 17 16 15 14 13

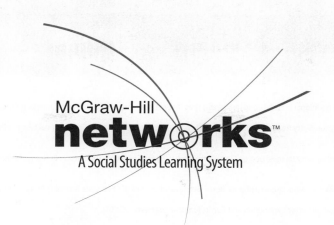

McGraw-Hill networks™

A Social Studies Learning System

Teacher Edition

DISCOVERING
WORLD
GEOGRAPHY

Eastern Hemisphere

Richard G. Boehm, Ph. D.

Mc Graw Hill Education

Bothell, WA • Chicago, IL • Columbus, OH • New York, NY

McGraw-Hill
netw⊙rks™

**MEETS YOU ANYWHERE—
TAKES YOU EVERYWHERE**

CONNECT with colleagues, students, experts, and content

1. Log on to the Internet and go to *connected.mcgraw-hill.com*.
2. Enter User Name and Password.
3. Click on your **Networks** book.
4. Select your chapter and lesson.

start **netw⊙rk**ing

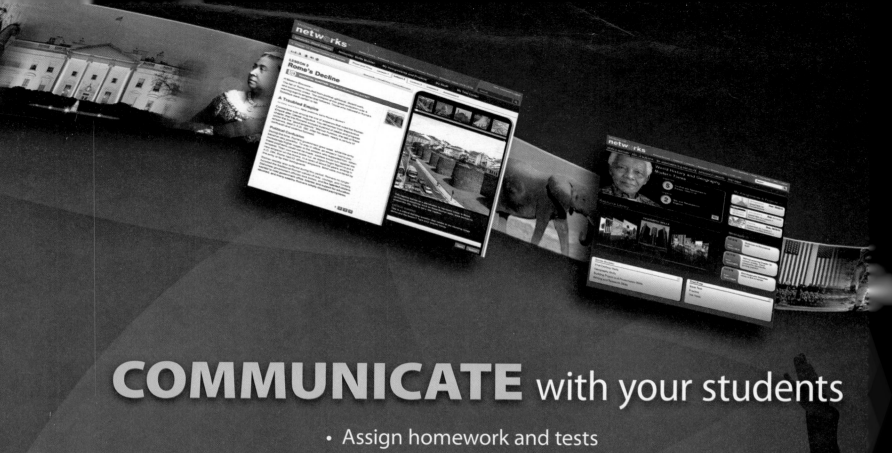

COMMUNICATE with your students

- Assign homework and tests
- Send messages
- Track and print student results

start **netw rk**ing

McGraw-Hill networks™

MEETS YOU ANYWHERE — TAKES YOU EVERYWHERE

ENGAGE your students for the way they want to learn

- Hands-on projects
- Interactive maps, presentations, and primary sources
- Streaming video and games

DIFFERENTIATE instruction to meet the needs of all your students

- Assign different reading levels
- Access full audio
- Use PDFs or modify worksheets
- Print or assign online

start **network**ing

Chapter 5
Lesson 1 Wildlife of Southeast Asia

Chapter 6
Lesson 3 Culture Groups in Southeast Asia

Chapter 9
Lesson 2 Egyptian Artifacts
Lesson 3 Artisans of North Africa

Chapter 10
Lesson 1 The Nile's River Source
Lesson 2 Ancient Africa
Global Connections: Effects of Climate on Refugee Camps

Chapter 11
Lesson 1 Rain Forest and Savanna
Lesson 3 Types of Housing in Central Africa

Chapter 12
Lesson 1 West Africa's Variety of Land
Lesson 2 The Salt Trade

Chapter 13
Lesson 1 Diamonds
Lesson 3 Cities in Southern Africa

Chapter 14
Lesson 1 Views of Australia and New Zealand

Chapter 15
Lesson 2 Life in Antarctica
Global Connections: Invasive Plant Species

Chapter 6
Lesson 1 Monsoons
Lesson 2 The British in India

Chapter 7
Lesson 2 Trans-Siberian Railroad
Lesson 2 The Soviet Union

Chapter 8
Lesson 1 Bodies of Water in Southwest Asia
Lesson 2 Islamic Expansion

Chapter 9
Lesson 2 360° View: Ancient Egypt
Lesson 2 The Punic Wars

Chapter 10
Lesson 1 Desertification of the Sahel; Resources in East Africa
Lesson 2 African Trade Routes and Goods
Global Connections: Crisis in Darfur

Chapter 12
Lesson 2 The First Trading Kingdoms

Chapter 13
Lesson 3 Population: Southern Africa

Chapter 14
Lesson 1 The Great Barrier Reef
Lesson 2 The History of Australia

Chapter 15
Global Connections: How Invasive Species Get to Australia

⌄ Interactive Maps

Chapter 4
Lesson 2 The Silk Road and Trade

Chapter 5
Lesson 1 Volcanoes in Southeast Asia
Lesson 2 History of Southeast Asian Civilizations

⌄ Interactive Images

Chapter 1
Lesson 1 360° View: Times Square, New York City

Chapter 2
Lesson 3 Ocean Floor; Garbage

Chapter 3
Lesson 1 Refugee Camps
Lesson 2 Cultural Change

Chapter 4
Lesson 1 Mount Fuji in Art
Lesson 2 360° View: China's Great Wall; Samurai
Lesson 3 Baseball in Japan

Chapter 5
Lesson 1 Indonesian Tsunami
Lesson 3 Minority Groups in Southeast Asia

netw⊙rks STUDENT ONLINE RESOURCES

Videos

Every lesson has a video to help you learn more about your world!

Infographics

Chapter 2
Lesson 3 Fresh and Salt Water in the World

Chapter 5
Lesson 2 The Spice Islands

Chapter 6
Lesson 3 Population of India

Interactive Charts/Graphs

Chapter 2
Lesson 1 Rain Shadow; Climate Zones

Chapter 3
Lesson 1 Understanding Population
Lesson 3 Economic Questions

Chapter 6
Lesson 1 Water Wells

Chapter 7
Lesson 3 Living in a Yurt

Chapter 8
Lesson 1 Oases
Lesson 2 Ziggurats

Chapter 11
Lesson 3 Social Issues in Central Africa

Chapter 14
Lesson 2 Australian Gold Rush

Animations

Chapter 1
Lesson 1 The Earth; Regions of Earth
Lesson 2 Elements of a Globe

Chapter 2
Lesson 1 Earth's Daily Rotation; Earth's Layers; Seasons on Earth
Lesson 3 How the Water Cycle Works

Chapter 3
Global Connections: Social Media

Chapter 4
Global Connections: How Tsunamis Form

Chapter 6
Lesson 1 Rivers in South Asia

Chapter 8
Lesson 1 Why Much of the World's Oil Supply Is in Southwest Asia

Chapter 9
Lesson 2 How the Pyramids Were Built

Chapter 10
Lesson 2 East African Independence
Global Connections: Refugees in Sudan

Chapter 14
Global Connections: Aussie Invasive Species

Chapter 15
Lesson 1 How Volcanoes Form Islands

Chapter 16
Lesson 1 How Icebergs Form

Slide Shows

Chapter 1
Lesson 1 Spatial Effect; Places Change Over Time
Lesson 2 Special Purpose Maps; History of Mapmaking

Chapter 2
Lesson 1 Effects of Climate Change
Lesson 2 Human Impact on Earth

Chapter 3
Lesson 1 Different Places in the World

Chapter 4
Lesson 1 Chinese Mountain Ranges
Lesson 3 Influence of Japanese Anime

Jochen Schlenker/Getty Images

CHARTS, GRAPHS, DIAGRAMS, AND INFOGRAPHICS

UNIT 1: OUR WORLD: THE EASTERN HEMISPHERE

Diagram: Latitude and Longitude **21**
Chart: The Six Essential Elements **24**
Diagram: Earth's Hemispheres **27**
Diagram: Earth's Layers **43**
Diagram: Seasons **45**
Diagram: Rain Shadow **48**
Infographic: Salt Water vs. Freshwater **60**
Graph: Population Pyramid **73**
Chart: Major World Religions **84**
Infographic: Making a New Drug **95**
Diagram: Factors of Production **98**
Graph: GDP Comparison **99**

UNIT 2: ASIA

Chart: Dynasties of China **126**
Graph: U.S. Trade Deficit With China, 2001–2011 . . . . **139**
Diagram: Below Ground in Siberia **203**
Infographic: Oil: Reserves and Consumption **230**

UNIT 3: AFRICA

Infographic: Pyramids of Egypt **274**
Infographic: West African Energy **358**

UNIT 4: OCEANIA, AUSTRALIA, NEW ZEALAND, AND ANTARCTICA

Diagram: Atoll Formation **453**
Diagram: Ozone Hole **483**

UNIT 4: OCEANIA, AUSTRALIA, NEW ZEALAND, AND ANTARCTICA

The Region: Physical **408**

The Region: Political **409**

The Region: Population Density. **410**

The Region: Economic Resources. **411**

The Region: Climate **412**

Australia and New Zealand. **415**

Global Impact: Australia's Invasive Species. **443**

Oceania. **448**

Antarctica **473**

MAPS

REFERENCE ATLAS MAPS

World: Political **RA2**
World: Physical **RA4**
North America: Political **RA6**
North America: Physical **RA7**
United States: Political **RA8**
United States: Physical **RA10**
Canada: Physical/Political **RA12**
Middle America: Physical/Political **RA14**
South America: Political **RA16**
South America: Physical **RA17**
Europe: Political **RA18**
Europe: Physical **RA20**
Africa: Political **RA22**
Africa: Physical **RA23**
Middle East: Physical/Political **RA24**
Asia: Political **RA26**
Asia: Physical **RA28**
Oceania: Physical/Political **RA30**
World Time Zones **RA32**
Polar Regions: Physical **RA34**
A World of Extremes **RA35**
Geographic Dictionary **RA36**

UNIT 1: OUR WORLD: THE EASTERN HEMISPHERE

The World: Physical **4**
The World: Political **6**
The World: Population Density **8**
The World: Economic **10**
The World: Climate **12**
The World **16**
Tectonic Plate Boundaries **40**
Earth's Wind Patterns **47**
Human Geography **70**
Global Impact: The World's Rain Forests **93**

UNIT 2: ASIA

Asia: Physical **108**
Asia: Political **109**
Asia: Population Density **110**
Asia: Economic Resources **111**
Asia: Climate **112**
East Asia **115**
The Silk Road **127**
Korean War, 1950–1953 .... **130**
Southeast Asia **149**
Independence of Southeast Asian Countries **160**
South Asia **175**
South Asia: Seasonal Rains **179**
Central Asia, the Caucasus, and Siberian Russia **198**
Trans-Siberian Railroad **207**
World Time Zones **213**
Population Density **214**
Southwest Asia **225**
The Spread of Islam **235**
Territorial Changes **237**
Language Groups of Southwest Asia **242**

UNIT 3: AFRICA

Africa: Physical **256**
Africa: Political **257**
Africa: Population Density **258**
Africa: Economic Resources **259**
Africa: Climate **260**
North Africa **262**
Ancient Egypt **273**
North African Independence **277**
East Africa **293**
Desertification in the Sahel **299**
Trade in East Africa **304**
Sudan and South Sudan **321**
Central Africa **327**
Independence for Central African Countries **338**
West Africa **352**
Trading Kingdoms of West Africa **362**
Triangular Trade Routes **365**
Southern Africa **379**
Population of Southern Africa **395**

Think Again?

The Height of Mount Everest 31
Immigration 78
Command Economy 96
The Great Wall of China 125
Hurricanes, Typhoons, and Cyclones 155
The Middle East and Southwest Asia 239
The Sahara 269
Great Migration 301
Madagascar 396

EXPLORE the CONTINENT

Explore the World 2
Asia 106
Africa 254
Oceania, Australia, New Zealand, and Antarctica 406

Thinking Like a Geographer

Relief 29
Rice 120
Place Names 191
World Time Zones 213
Seas 229
Religious Rivalry 367
Pans 383
Lake Vostok 485

GLOBAL CONNECTIONS

Rain Forest Resources 90
The Fury of a Tsunami 140
Sudan: Refugees and Displacement 318
Unfriendly Invaders 440

What Do You Think?

Is Globalization Destroying Indigenous Cultures? 34
Are Trade Restrictions Effective at Changing a
    Government's Policies? 248
Has the UN Been Effective at Reducing Conflict in Africa? 346
Is Global Warming a Result of Human Activity? 486

CONTENTS

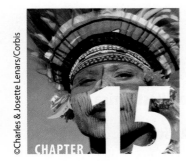

©Charles & Josette Lenars/Corbis

CHAPTER 15

Chapter and Lesson Planner Pages 447A

Intervention and Remediation Strategies 447F

Oceania 447

ESSENTIAL QUESTIONS

How does geography influence the way people live? • What makes a culture unique? • Why do people make economic choices?

LESSON 1 **Physical Geography of Oceania** 450

LESSON 2 **History and People of Oceania** 456

LESSON 3 **Life in Oceania** 462

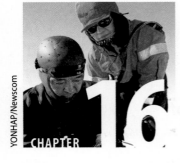

YONHAP/Newscom

CHAPTER 16

Chapter and Lesson Planner Pages 471A

Intervention and Remediation Strategies 471E

Antarctica 471

ESSENTIAL QUESTIONS

How does geography influence the way people live? • How do people adapt to their environment?

LESSON 1 **Physical Geography of Antarctica** 474

LESSON 2 **Life in Antarctica** 480
Thinking Like a Geographer Lake Vostok 485
What Do You Think? Is Global Warming a Result of
    Human Activity? 486

FOLDABLES® LIBRARY 491

GAZETTEER 499

ENGLISH-SPANISH GLOSSARY 507

INDEX 524

CCSS This icon indicates where reading skills and writing skills from the *Common Core State Standards for English Language Arts & Literacy in History/Social Studies, Science, and Technical Subjects* are practiced and reinforced.

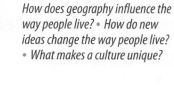

Chapter and Lesson Planner Pages 351A
Intervention and Remediation Strategies 351F

West Africa 351

ESSENTIAL QUESTIONS
How does geography influence the way people live? • How do new ideas change the way people live? • What makes a culture unique?

LESSON 1 **Physical Geography of West Africa** 354

LESSON 2 **The History of West Africa** 360
Thinking Like a Geographer Religion 367

LESSON 3 **Life in West Africa** 368

Chapter and Lesson Planner Pages 377A
Intervention and Remediation Strategies 377F

Southern Africa 377

ESSENTIAL QUESTIONS
How does geography influence the way people live? • How do new ideas change the way people live?

LESSON 1 **Physical Geography of Southern Africa** 380

LESSON 2 **History of Southern Africa** 388

LESSON 3 **Life in Southern Africa** 394
Think Again Madagascar 396

UNIT FOUR

Unit Planner Pages 405A

Oceania, Australia, New Zealand, and Antarctica 405

Chapter and Lesson Planner Pages 413A
Intervention and Remediation Strategies 413F

Australia and New Zealand 413

ESSENTIAL QUESTIONS
How does geography influence the way people live? • Why does conflict develop? • What makes a culture unique?

LESSON 1 **Physical Geography** 416

LESSON 2 **History of the Region** 424

LESSON 3 **Life in Australia and New Zealand** 432
Global Connections Unfriendly Invaders 440

CONTENTS

UNIT THREE

Tips Images/SuperStock

CHAPTER 9

Unit Planner Pages 253A

Africa   253

Chapter and Lesson Planner Pages 261A

Intervention and Remediation Strategies 261F

North Africa   261

ESSENTIAL QUESTIONS

How do people adapt to their environment? • How does religion shape society? • Why do conflicts develop?

LESSON 1 **The Physical Geography of North Africa** **264**
Think Again The Sahara Desert 269

LESSON 2 **The History of North Africa** **272**

LESSON 3 **Life in North Africa** **280**

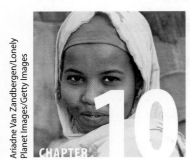

Ariadne Van Zandbergen/Lonely Planet Images/Getty Images

CHAPTER 10

Chapter and Lesson Planner Pages 291A

Intervention and Remediation Strategies 291F

East Africa   291

ESSENTIAL QUESTIONS

How does geography influence the way people live? • Why do people trade? • Why does conflict develop?

LESSON 1 **Physical Geography of East Africa** **294**
Think Again Great Migration 301

LESSON 2 **History of East Africa** **302**

LESSON 3 **Life in East Africa** **310**
Global Connections Sudan Refugees and Displacement 318

Andrew McConnell/Robert Harding World Imagery/Getty Images

CHAPTER 11

Chapter and Lesson Planner Pages 325A

Intervention and Remediation Strategies 325F

Central Africa   325

ESSENTIAL QUESTIONS

How do people adapt to their environment? • How does technology change the way people live? • Why do people make economic choices?

LESSON 1 **Physical Geography of Central Africa** **328**

LESSON 2 **History of Central Africa** **334**

LESSON 3 **Life in Central Africa** **340**
What Do You Think? Has the United Nations Been Effective at Reducing Conflict in Africa? 346

©Amit Bhargava/Corbis

CHAPTER 6

Chapter and Lesson Planner Pages **173A**

Intervention and Remediation Strategies **173F**

South Asia **173**

ESSENTIAL QUESTIONS
How does geography influence the way people live? • How do governments change? • What makes a culture unique?

LESSON 1 Physical Geography of South Asia **176**

LESSON 2 History of South Asia **182**

LESSON 3 Life in South Asia **188**
Thinking Like a Geographer   Place Names 191

©Strunin Anatoly/ITAR-TASS Photo/Corbis

CHAPTER 7

Chapter and Lesson Planner Pages **197A**

Intervention and Remediation Strategies **197F**

Central Asia, the Caucasus, and Siberian Russia **197**

ESSENTIAL QUESTIONS
How does geography influence the way people live? • How do governments change?

LESSON 1 Physical Geography of the Regions **200**

LESSON 2 History of the Regions **206**

LESSON 3 Life in the Regions **212**
Thinking Like a Geographer   World Time Zones 213

Wathiq Khuzaie/Getty Images News Collection/Getty Images

CHAPTER 8

Chapter and Lesson Planner Pages **223A**

Intervention and Remediation Strategies **223F**

Southwest Asia **223**

ESSENTIAL QUESTIONS
How does geography influence the way people live? • Why do civilizations rise and fall? • How does religion shape society?

LESSON 1 Physical Geography of Southwest Asia **226**
Thinking Like a Geographer   Seas 228

LESSON 2 History of Southwest Asia **232**
Think Again   The Middle East and Southwest Asia 239

LESSON 3 Life in Southwest Asia **240**
What Do You Think?   Are Trade Restrictions Effective at Changing a Government's Policies? 248

CONTENTS

Aurora Photos/Alamy

Chapter and Lesson Planner Pages **69A**

Intervention and Remediation Strategies **69F**

The Human World **69**

ESSENTIAL QUESTIONS

How do people adapt to their environment? • What makes a culture unique? • Why do people make economic choices?

LESSON 1 Earth's Population **72**
Think Again Immigration 78

LESSON 2 The World's Cultures **82**
Global Connections Rain Forest Resources 90

LESSON 3 Economies of the World **94**
Think Again Command Economy 96

UNIT TWO

Unit Planner Pages **105A**

Asia **105**

Chapter and Lesson Planner Pages **113A**

Intervention and Remediation Strategies **113F**

Jon Arnold/Alamy

East Asia **113**

ESSENTIAL QUESTIONS

How does geography influence the way people live? • What makes a culture unique? • How do cultures spread? • Why do people trade? • How does technology change the way people live?

LESSON 1 Physical Geography of East Asia **116**
Thinking Like a Geographer Rice 120

LESSON 2 History of East Asia **124**
Think Again The Great Wall of China .125

LESSON 3 Life in East Asia **132**
Global Connections The Fury of a Tsunami 140

©ADREES LATIF/X90022/Reuters/ Corbis

Chapter and Lesson Planner Pages **147A**

Intervention and Remediation Strategies **147F**

Southeast Asia **147**

ESSENTIAL QUESTIONS

How does geography influence the way people live? • What makes a culture unique? • Why does conflict develop?

LESSON 1 Physical Geography of Southeast Asia **150**
Think Again Hurricanes, Typhoons, and Cyclones 155

LESSON 2 History of Southeast Asia **156**

LESSON 3 Life in Southeast Asia **164**

CONTENTS

Student Online Resources T15

Teacher Online Resources T19

How to Use the Teacher Edition T25

Correlation to the Revised National Council for the
    Social Studies Thematic Strands T36

Correlation to the National Geography Standards T41

Correlation to the Common Core State Standards T44

Using Foldables® in the Classroom T56

Using BTW T57

Understanding By Design® T58

Why Teach With Technology? T62

Background Knowledge: The Key to Understanding T64

College and Career Readiness T66

Meeting the Diverse Needs of Our Students T68

Academic Vocabulary T72

ePals® Global Community T74

Reference Atlas Maps RA1

World: Political RA2
World: Physical RA4
North America: Political RA6
North America: Physical RA7
United States: Political RA8
United States: Physical RA10
Canada: Physical/Political RA12
Middle America: Physical/Political RA14
South America: Political RA16
South America: Physical RA17
Europe: Political RA18

Europe: Physical RA20
Africa: Political RA22
Africa: Physical RA23
Middle East: Physical/Political RA24
Asia: Political RA26
Asia: Physical RA28
Oceania: Physical/Political RA30
World Time Zones RA32
Polar Regions RA34
A World of Extremes RA35
Geographic Dictionary RA36

Scavenger Hunt RA38

UNIT ONE

Prisma/SuperStock

Carsten Peter/National Geographic/Getty Images

Unit Planner Pages 1A

Our World: The Eastern Hemisphere 1

Chapter and Lesson Planner Pages 15A

Intervention and Remediation Strategies 15E

Earth's Land, People, and Environments 15

ESSENTIAL QUESTION
*How does geography influence the
way people live?*

LESSON 1 **How Geographers Think** 18

LESSON 2 **Geographers and Their Tools** 26
    Thinking Like a Geographer Relief 29
    Think Again The Height of Mount Everest 31
    What Do You Think? Is Globalization Destroying
        Indigenous Cultures? 34

Chapter and Lesson Planner Pages 39A

Intervention and Remediation Strategies 39F

The Physical World 39

ESSENTIAL QUESTION
*How does geography influence the
way people live?*

LESSON 1 **The Earth-Sun Relationship** 42

LESSON 2 **Forces Shaping Earth** 52

LESSON 3 **Earth's Land and Water** 58

networks STUDENT ONLINE RESOURCES

⌄ Games

Chapter 12
Lesson 1 Fill in the Blank
Lesson 2 Columns
Lesson 3 Flashcard

Chapter 13
Lesson 1 Tic-Tac-Toe
Lesson 2 Flashcard
Lesson 3 Concentration

Chapter 14
Lesson 1 Crossword
Lesson 2 True or False
Lesson 3 Fill in the Blank

Chapter 15
Lesson 1 Crossword
Lesson 2 Identification
Lesson 3 Columns

Chapter 16
Lesson 1 Flashcard
Lesson 2 Tic-Tac-Toe

networks STUDENT ONLINE RESOURCES

Chapter 7
Lesson 1 Taiga Trees
Lesson 2 360° View: Samarkand, Uzbekistan
Lesson 3 The Aral Sea

Chapter 8
Lesson 3 360° View: Khalifa, Dubai, United Arab Emirates; Foods of Ramadan

Chapter 9
Lesson 1 360° View: Berber Homes; 360° View: Cairo on the Nile; The Suez
         Canal; Mediterranean Climate and Agriculture
Lesson 2 Islam

Chapter 10
Lesson 1 360° View: Lake Bogoria in the Great Rift Valley; Glaciers in East
         Africa
Lesson 2 British at Omdurman; Ethiopian Freedom and the Battle of Adwa
Lesson 3 360° View: Masai and Kenya; Animal Poaching

Chapter 11
Lesson 1 Congo River; Slash-and-Burn Agriculture; Mining for Gold
Lesson 2 Triangular Trade
Lesson 3 Brazzaville

Chapter 12
Lesson 1 Lake Chad
Lesson 2 Kwame Nkrumah
Lesson 3 360° View: Lagos, Nigeria; West African Art

Chapter 13
Lesson 1 Drakensberg Mountains; 360° View: Etosha Pan; Kalahari Dunes
Lesson 2 Boer War

Chapter 14
Lesson 1 Fjords; 360° View: Australia's Outback
Lesson 2 Australia in World War II
Lesson 3 Wool Processing

Chapter 15
Lesson 2 Colonizing Oceania; 360° View: Bora Bora in the South Pacific
Lesson 3 360° View: A Beach in Polynesia

Chapter 16
Lesson 1 360° View: Antarctica
Lesson 2 Earth's Ozone Layer

∨ Games

Chapter 1
Lesson 1 True or False
Lesson 2 Concentration

Chapter 2
Lesson 1 Fill in the Blank
Lesson 2 Tic-Tac-Toe
Lesson 3 Columns

Chapter 3
Lesson 1 Crossword
Lesson 2 Identification
Lesson 3 Flashcard

Chapter 4
Lesson 1 Identification
Lesson 2 Flashcard
Lesson 3 Columns

Chapter 5
Lesson 1 Crossword
Lesson 2 Tic-Tac-Toe
Lesson 3 Concentration

Chapter 6
Lesson 1 Fill in the Blank
Lesson 2 True or False
Lesson 3 Columns

Chapter 7
Lesson 1 Columns
Lesson 2 Concentration
Lesson 3 Identification

Chapter 8
Lesson 1 True or False
Lesson 2 Flashcard
Lesson 3 Fill in the Blank

Chapter 9
Lesson 1 Tic-Tac-Toe
Lesson 2 Crossword
Lesson 3 Identification

Chapter 10
Lesson 1 True or False
Lesson 2 Columns
Lesson 3 Fill in the Blank

Chapter 11
Lesson 1 Concentration
Lesson 2 Crossword
Lesson 3 Identification

Chapter 7   Time Line and Map of Central Asia and Siberian Russia
  Lesson 1   Country Names Lecture Slide
              Drag-and-Drop Siberia, Central Asia, and the Caucasus Game
              Climates of Central Asia Map
              Breaking Ice Interactive Image
              Russian Forests Interactive Image
              Resources of Central Asia Map
              World Record Waterways in Central Asia Map
  Lesson 2   Settling Siberia Graphic Organizer
              Influences on Central Asia Map
              History of the Caucasus Graphic Organizer
              Gulag Interactive Image
  Lesson 3   Challenges in Central Asia Graphic Organizer
              Defining Nomad Lecture Slide
              The Armenian Apostolic Church Interactive Image
              The Soviet Union Map
              Understanding Time Zones Map
              Population of Central Asia Map
              Religions of the Region Graph

Chapter 8   Time Line and Map of Southwest Asia
  Lesson 1   Southwest Asia as a Region Graphic Organizer
              Physical Geography of Southwest Asia Map
              Resources of Southwest Asia Map
              Climates of Southwest Asia Map
              Oil Reserves in the World Graph
  Lesson 2   Israel and Palestine Map
              The Kurds Interactive Image
              Conflicts in Southwest Asia Map
              Three Major Religions of Southwest Asia Chart
              Independence of Southwest Asia Time Line
  Lesson 3   Population of Southwest Asia Map
              Chart of English Words with Roots in Languages of Southwest Asia
              Resources of Southwest Asia Map

Unit 3
  Africa Video Montage
  Political Boundaries: Africa Game
  Interactive Maps of Africa

Chapter 9   Time Line and Map of North Africa
  Lesson 1   Climate Map of North Africa
              Resource Map of North Africa
              Physical Geography Map of North Africa
              Animated Map of the Nile River
              Suez Canal Image
              Mediterranean Climate Map
  Lesson 2   Roman and Islamic Empires in North Africa Graphic Organizer
              Europeans in North Africa Graphic Organizer
              Map Comparing Independence Movements in North Africa
              Islam Interactive Image
              Drag-and-Drop Game: Governments and Dictatorships
  Lesson 3   Population Map of North Africa
              Population Pyramid Chart of North Africa
              Economies of North Africa Graphic Organizer
              Literacy Rates Around the World Chart
              Arab Spring Image

Chapter 10   Time Line and Map of East Africa
  Lesson 1   Resource Map of East Africa
              The Nile River's Source Image
              Diverse Physical Features of East Africa Graphic Organizer
              The Great Rift Valley Viewed From Space Image
              Lake Victoria Image
              Map of the Nile River
              Map of the Desertification of the Sahel
              Alternative Energy Sources in Africa Graphic Organizer
  Lesson 2   Vasco de Gama Image
              Reviewing East African Independence Graphic Organizer
              Ancient Africa Slideshow
              Battle at Omdurman Image
              East African Colonization Map
              African Trade Routes and Goods Map
              East African Independence Map
              Refugee Camps Slide Show
              Resource Map of East Africa
  Lesson 3   Islam in Africa Map
              Population Map of East Africa
              Map of Kenya's Regional Museums
              Language in East Africa Chart
              Issues in East Africa Today Graphic Organizer
              Urban and Rural Life in East Africa Graphic Organizer
              Literacy Rates Across Africa Chart
              Life Expectancy Across Africa Chart

Chapter 11   Time Line and Map of Central Africa
  Lesson 1   Physical Geography Map of Central Africa
              Climate Map of Central Africa
              Resource Map of Central Africa
              Rain Forest and Savanna Slide Show
              Resources of Central Africa Graphic Organizer
              The Route of the Congo Map
              Rain Forest of Gabon Image
  Lesson 2   Drag-And-Drop Game: Historical Changes in Central Africa
              Triangular Trade Map
              Resistance to Colonization Map
              Impact of the African Slave Trade Chart
  Lesson 3   Population Map of Central Africa
              Trade Languages Lecture Slide
              Subsistence Farming in Central Africa Graphic Organizer
              Rural and City Life in Central Africa Image
              Population of Central Africa Graph
              Cultural Influences on Central Africa Map
              Social Issues in Central Africa Chart

INTERACTIVE WHITEBOARD ACTIVITIES

Unit 1
The World Video Montage
Drag-and-Drop Physical Geography Game of the World
Interactive World Maps

Chapter 1 Time Line and Map of the World
Lesson 1 Drag-and-Drop Vocabulary Game
Chart of the Six Essential Elements
Animation of Relative Location
Spatial Effect
Lesson 2 Forms of Technology Graphic Organizer
Map Legends

Chapter 2
Lesson 1 World Climates Map
Chart of How Temperature and Precipitation Affect Biomes
Lesson 2 Architecture for Earthquakes Slide Show
Lesson 3 Physical Geography of Earth Map
Population of Earth Map
Uses of Water for Recreation vs. Livelihood Graphic Organizer

Chapter 3
Lesson 1 Population Changes Slide Show
Population Density Map
Why Do People Move? Graphic Organizer
Lesson 2 Elements of Culture Graphic Organizer
Chart of the Major World Religions
Chart of Different Types of Government
Lesson 3 Drag-and-Drop Economic Systems Game
Types of Economic Activities and Sectors Interactive Image
GDP Around the World Graph
Bartering and Trade Game

Unit 2
Asia Video Montage
Drag-and-Drop Physical Geography Game of Asia
Interactive Maps of Asia

Chapter 4 Time Line and Map of East Asia
Lesson 1 Landforms and bodies of Water in East Asia Graphic Organizer
Defining Archipelago Lecture Slide
Defining Tsunamis Lecture Slide
Drag-and-Drop Resources in East Asia Game
Physical Geography of East Asia Map
Climates of East Asia Map
Resources of East Asia Map
Lesson 2 Drag-and-Drop Chinese Dynasties Game
History of Korea Lecture Slide
Types of Government Lecture Slide
The Korean War Map
Japan and the West Image
Governments in East Asia Map

Lesson 3 Personal Buddhist Shrines Interactive Image
Population of East Asia Map
Writing in East Asia Slide Show
Population Pyramids of East Asia Graphic Organizer
Religion in East Asia Graphs
Chart Comparing U.S. and East Asia Resources
Population Concerns in East Asia Map

Chapter 5 Time Line and Map of Southeast Asia
Lesson 1 Drag-and-Drop Mainland or Island Country in Southeast Asia Game
Drag-and-Drop Geographic Terms for Southeast Asia Game
Defining Archipelago Lecture Slide
Types of Landforms in Southeast Asia Lecture Slide
Landforms in Southeast Asia Graphic Organizer
Seas and Rivers of Southeast Asia Graphic Organizer
Malaysia/Indonesian Islands Map
Physical Geography of Southeast Asia Map
Volcanic Islands Map
Tectonic Plates Map
How a Tsunami Forms Animation
Lesson 2 France's Role in Southeast Asia Lecture Slide
Trade in Southeast Asia Map
Resources of Southeast Asia Map
Early Civilizations of Southeast Asia Map
Islam in Southeast Asia Video
Lesson 3 Religion in Southeast Asia Graphic Organizer
Challenges in Southeast Asia Graphic Organizer
Ecotourism Image
Population of Southeast Asia Map
Rice Farming Slide Show
Urban Southeast Asia Map

Chapter 6 Time Line and Map of South Asia
Lesson 1 Weather Extremes in South Asia Lecture Slide
Hurricanes, Cyclones, and Typhoons Lecture Slide
Mount Everest Interactive Image
Physical Geography of South Asia Map
Climates of South Asia Map
Salt Water vs. Fresh Water Infographic
Resources of South Asia Map
Teak Wood Interactive Image
Geographic Features of South Asia Slide Show
Drag-and-Drop Adapting to Climate Game
Lesson 2 Caste System Organization Lecture Slide
Nuclear Threat Lecture Slide
Three Indian Empires Graphic Organizer
Major Religions of South Asia Graphic Organizer
Buddhist Eightfold Path Chart
Lesson 3 Languages and Cultures of South Asia Graphic Organizer
Issues in South Asia Today Graphic Organizer
Population of South Asia Map
Outsourcing in India Interactive Image
Chart Comparing Urban Population in India and the United States

McGraw-Hill
netw⊕rks™

**MEETS YOU ANYWHERE —
TAKES YOU EVERYWHERE**

MANAGE your classroom anytime

- Use prepared model lessons
- Clear pathway through critical content
- Quick, targeted instruction

From anywhere

- Plan instruction
- Create presentations
- Differentiate instruction